ROYAL AIR FORCE

SQUADRON LOSSES

1st January 1921 - 31st December 1930

W R Chorley and P J McMillan

Commanding Officers, Short Service Commission Officers,
RAF College Cranwell Graduates

and

Rolls of Honour

MENTION
THE WAR
PUBLICATIONS

www.bombercommandbooks.com

First published in the United Kingdom in 2022 by:
Mention the War Limited
25 Cromwell Street
Merthyr Tydfil
CF47 8RY

Cover design: Topics – The Creative Partnership www.topicdesign.co.uk

Cover photograph – Greg Harrison.

RAF crest from war grave headstone (Sgt. Peter Gosnold); the Gosnold family.

A CIP catalogue reference for this book is available from the British Library.

ISBN 9781911255581

BOOKS by W R CHORLEY

Squadron Histories

In Brave Company - 158 Squadron [with R N Benwell]
To See The Dawn Breaking 76 Squadron Operations
In Brave Company - 158 Squadron Operations

Royal Air Force Bomber Command Losses of the Second World War

Volume 1 1939-1940
Volume 2 1941
Volume 3 1942
Volume 4 1943
Volume 5 1944
Volume 6 1945
Volume 7 Operational Training Units 1940-1947
Volume 8 Heavy Conversion Units and Miscellaneous Units 1939-1947
Volume 9 Roll of Honour 1939-1947
Volume 1 1939-1940 2nd Edition Including Prewar Losses July 1936-September 1939

Royal Air Force & Australian Flying Corps Squadron Losses 1st April-30th June 1918
Royal Air Force & Australian Flying Corps Squadron Losses 1st July-11th November 1918

WITH P J McMILLAN

Royal Air Force & Australian Flying Corps Squadron Losses 12th November 1918-31st December 1920

PUBLISHED ARTICLES by W R CHORLEY

AVIATION NEWS

Vixen Victims - Volume 7 Number 22
Lost over France - Volume 10 Number 26
From 'The Menace' to 'Maori Chief' - Volume 11 Number 11
Norfolk and Suffolk Aeronautical Museum - Volume 12 Number 23
No 76 Squadron and the Battle over the Ruhr - Volume 13 Number 5
What Happened on 6 November 1944 - Volume 15 Number 4
The Raid on Mailly-le-Camp 3-4 May 1944 - Volume 15 Number 10

THE DOWNSMAN
SIXPENNY HANDLEY COMMUNITY MAGAZINE

Sixpenny Handley War Memorial
Biographies of the twenty-six servicemen named on the Memorial
Dorset at War

TABLE of CONTENTS

GLOSSARY of TERMS

AACU	Anti Aircraft Co-operation Unit
AAF	Auxiliary Air Force
AC	Aircraftman
ACM	Air Chief Marshal
ADC	Aide De Camp
AFC	Air Force Cross
AFL	Air Force List
AM	Air Marshal, Air Ministry and Albert Medal
AONS	Air Observer Navigation School
ASN	Aviation Safety Network
ATA	Air Transport Auxiliary
A/Cmdr	Air Commodore
AV-M	Air Vice-Marshal
A&AEE	Aeroplane and Armament Experimental Establishment
A&GS	Armament and Gunnery School
BBC	British Broadcasting Corporation
BCATP	British Commonwealth Air Training Plan
BGS	Bombing and Gunnery School
BSM	Bronze Star Medal [USA]
BOAC	British Overseas Airways Corporation
CB	Companion of the Order of the Bath
CBE	Companion of the Most Excellent Order of the British Empire
CCS	Casualty Clearing Station
CFE	Central Flying School
CFS	Central Flying School/Civil Flying School
CGS	Central Gunnery School
CMG	Companion [of the Order of] St. Michael and St. George
Cpl	Corporal
CVO	Companion of the Royal Victorian Order
CWGC	Commonwealth War Graves Commission
DC	Dual Control
DFC	Distinguished Flying Cross
DSC	Distinguished Service Cross
DCM	Distinguished Conduct Medal
DNCO	Duty Not Carried Out
DSO	Distinguished Service Order
EFTS	Elementary Flying Training School
EG	Edinburgh Gazette
E&RFTS	Elementary & Reserve Flying Training School
FAA	Fleet Air Arm
FCU	Fighter Control Unit
FTS	Flying Training School
F/Cdt	Flight Cadet
F/Lt	Flight Lieutenant
F/O	Flying Officer
F/Sgt	Flight Sergeant
GAL	General Aircraft Limited
GC	George Cross
GCB	Grand Commander of the Bath
GOO	Group Operations Order
G/Capt	Group Captain
HAD	Home Aircraft Depot [Henlow]
HMHS	His Majesty's Hospital Ship
HMS	His Majesty's Ship
HMT	His Majesty's Transport
HQ	Headquarters
HS	Hospital Ship
IAF	Indian Air Force
IGSM	Imperial General Service Medal
IRA	Irish Republican Army
JP	Justice of the Peace
KBE	Knight Commander of the Most Excellent Order of the British Empire
KC	King's Councillor
KCB	Knight Commander of the Bath
KCMG	Knight Commander of the Order of St. Michael and St. George
KCVO	Knight Commander of the Royal Victorian Order
Kt	Knight
LAC	Leading Aircraftman
LG	Landing Ground and London Gazette
LRCP	Licentiate of the Royal College of Physicians
Lt	Lieutenant
Lt-Cdr	Lieutenant-Commander
MAEE	Marine Aircraft Experimental Establishment
MBE	Member of the Most Excellent Order of the British Empire
MC	Military Cross
MCS	Metropolitan Communications Squadron
MGC	Machine Gun Corps
MI	Military Intelligence
MM	Military Medal
MP	Member of Parliament
MRAF	Marshal of the Royal Air Force
NATO	North Atlantic Treaty Organisation
NEI	Netherlands East Indies
NFS	National Flying Services [Hanworth]
NWF	North West Frontier
OADU	Overseas Aircraft Delivery Unit
OATS	Officers' Advanced Training School [Cranwell]
OBE	Order of the Most Excellent Order of the British Empire
OC	Officer Commanding
OM	Order of Merit
OTC	Officer Training Corps
O/O	Observer Officer
PAF	Polish Air Force
PC	Privy Councillor
PFF	Path Finder Force

PHU	Personnel Holding Unit
PR	Photographic Reconnaissance
PRU	Photographic Reconnaissance Unit
P/O	Pilot Officer
P & O	Peninsular & Orient
QFI	Qualified Flying Instructor
RA	Royal Artillery
RAAF	Royal Australian Air Force
RAE	Royal Aircraft Establishment
RAFBCL	Royal Air Force Bomber Command Losses
RAFC	Royal Air Force College
RAFM	Royal Air Force Museum Hendon
RAFO	Reserve of Air Force Officers
RAFVR	Royal Air Force Volunteer Reserve
RAMC	Royal Army Medical Corps
RFC	Royal Flying Corps
RFS	Refresher Flying School
RM	Royal Marines
RMA	Royal Military Academy
RN	Royal Navy
RNAS	Royal Naval Air Service
RNLI	Royal National Lifeboat Institution
RNR	Royal Navy Reserve
RNZAF	Royal New Zealand Air Force
SAC	School of Army Co-operation
SF	Station Flight
Sgt	Sergeant
SHAPE	Supreme Headquarters Allied Powers Europe
SR	Special Reserve
SRO	Supplementary Reserve of Officers
SS	Steam Ship
S/Ldr	Squadron Leader
TA	Territorial Army
TAG	Telegraphist Air Gunner
TD	Territorial Decoration
TDS	Training Depot Station
TF	Territorial Forces
TNA	The National Archives [Kew]
UK	United Kingdom
USA	United States of America
USAAF	United States Army Air Force
USAF	United States Air Force
VC	Victoria Cross
VIP	Very Important Person
WOC	Written off Charge
WO1	Warrant Officer 1st Class
W/Cdr	Wing Commander

BIBLIOGRAPHY
and
SOURCES

THE NATIONAL ARCHIVES, KEW

AIR 2/9621
AIR 10/1441 Report on Flying Accidents January to June 1926
AIR 20/2336 The Royal Air Force and Commonwealth Air Forces Prisoner of War File
AIR 27/203 XV Squadron Operations Record Book, AIR 27/655 77 Squadron Operations Record Book, AIR 27/681 82 Squadron Operations Record Book, AIR 27/807 102 Squadron Operations Record Book
AIR 76/25/8, AIR 76/109, AIR 76/132/10, AIR 76/137, AIR 76/409/90, AIR 76/411/107, AIR 76/530/98, AIR 76/566/150
AIR 81/99, 81/3017, AIR 81/3763, AIR 81/5289, AIR 81/5700, AIR 81/6194, AIR 81/6914

ROYAL AIR FORCE MUSEUM HENDON

Officer's Casualty Forms Of the Royal Flying Corps & Royal Air Force - Casualty Forms Home and Story Vault

PUBLICATIONS

After the Battle	
After the Battle - Then and Now Six Nations Locked in Aerial Combat September 1939 to June 1940	Peter D Cornwell, 2007
Air-Britain [Historians]	
Always Prepared - The Story of 207 Squadron Royal Air Force	John Hamlin, 1999
Broken Wings - Post-War Royal Air Force Accidents	James J Halley, 1999
Flat Out - The story of 30 Squadron Royal Air Force	John Hamlin, 1999
Fleet Air Arm Aircraft 1939 to 1945	Ray Sturtivant & Mick Burrows, 1995
Impressment Log - Volume III	Peter W Moss, 1964
Royal Air Force Aircraft J1-J9999 and WW1 Survivors	Dennis Thompson & Ray Sturtivant, 1987
Royal Air Force Aircraft L1000-N9999 - Revised	James J Halley, 1993
Royal Air Force Aircraft P1000-R9999 - Revised	James J Halley, 1996
Royal Air Force Aircraft T1000-V9999 - Revised	James J Halley, 1997
Royal Air Force Aircraft V1000-V9999 W1000-W9999	James J Halley, 1983
Royal Air Force Aircraft X1200-X9999 Z1000-Z9999	James J Halley, 1984
Royal Air Force Aircraft EA100-EZ999	James J Halley, 1988
Royal Air Force Aircraft FA100-FZ999	James J Halley, 1989
Royal Air Force Aircraft HA100-HZ999	James J Halley, 1989
Royal Air Force Aircraft JA100-JZ999	James J Halley, 1990
Royal Air Force Aircraft KA100-KZ999	James J Halley, 1990
Royal Air Force Aircraft NA100-NZ999	James J Halley, 1992
Royal Air Force Aircraft PA100-RZ999	James J Halley, 1992
Royal Air Force Aircraft SA100-VZ999	James J Halley, 1985
Royal Air Force Aircraft XA100 to XZ999	James J Halley, 2001
Royal Air Force Flying Training and Support Units	Ray Sturtivant, John Hamlin James J Halley, 1997
Squadrons of the Royal Air Force & Commonwealth 1918-1988	James J Halley, 1988
The DH.4/DH.9 File	Ray Sturtivant & Gordon Page, 1999
The K File - The Royal Air Force of the 1930s	James J Halley, 1995
The Stirling File [Revised Edition]	Bryce B Gomersall, 1987
Air-Britain [Historians] in Association with Cross & Cockade International	
Bristol Fighter - Frank Barnwell's Ubiquitous Multirole Masterpiece	Ray Sturtivant, Gordon Page, James J Halley & Philip Jarrett, 2021
Airdata Publications [Revised edition]	
We Landed by Moonlight - Secret RAF Landings in France 1940-1944	Hugh Verity, 1995
Alison Hodge	
Winged Shell Oil Company Aviators 1927-87	Hugh Scanlan, 1987

Amberley Publishing
Flying To The Edge - The Groundbreaking Career Of Test Pilot Duncan Menzies Matthew Willis, 2017
School of Aces : The RAF Training School That Won The Battle of Britain Alastair Goodrum, 2019

Classic Publications an imprint of Ian Allan Publishing
2nd Tactical Air Force - Volume One Spartan to Normandy June 1943 to June 1944 Christophers Shores and Christopher Thomas, 2004
2nd Tactical Air Force - Volume Two Breakout to Bodenplatte July 1944 to January 1945 Christopher Shores and Christopher Thomas, 2005

Collins
Reach For The Sky Paul Brickhill, 1954

Faber and Faber
Mosquito C Martin Sharp and Michael J F Bower,, 1967
2 Group RAF - A Complete History 1936-1945 Michael J F Bowyer, 1974

Fetubi Books
The Sky Their Battlefield II - Expanded Updated Trevor Henshaw, 2014

General Store Publishing House
Bless You, Brother Irvin - The Caterpillar Club Story John Neal, 2005

Grub Street
Footsteps On The Sands Of Time - RAF Bomber Command Prisoners of War In Germany 1939-45 Oliver Clutton-Brock, 2003
Buffaloes over Singapore Brian Cull with Paul Sortenhaug and Mark Haselden, 2003
Hurricanes over Singapore Brian Cull with Paul Sortenhaug, 2004
My Golden Flying Years David D'Arcy Alexander Greig, edited by Norman Franks & Simon Muggleton, 2010
RAF Evaders Oliver Clutton-Brock, 2009

Hodder & Stoughton
Nine Lives Group Captain Alan C Deere, 1959

Horsburgh Publishing
Nottinghamshire Aviation Diary - Aviation Incidents 1930-1945 A P and R M Glover, 2010

Hutchinson
The Narrow Margin Derek Wood & Derek Dempster, 1961

Ian Allan Publishing
Royal Air Force Bomber Command Losses of the Second World War Volume 1 1939-1940 2nd Edition - Including prewar losses July 1936 - September 1939 W R Chorley, 2013
The Seafire David Brown, 1973

Little, Brown and Company
Breakdown - The Crisis of Shell Shock on The Somme 1916 Taylor Downing, 2016

Macdonald
Fighter Squadrons of the RAF and their Aircraft John Rawlings, 1969
Sent Flying - The Autobiography of Bill Pegg Bill Pegg, 1959
The Gloster Meteor Edward Shacklady, 1962

Mention The War Publications
Royal Air Force & Australian Flying Corps Squadron Losses 1st April - 30th June 1918 W.R. Chorley, 2018
Royal Air Force & Australian Flying Corps Squadron Losses 1st July - 11th November 1918 W.R. Chorley, 2019
Royal Air Force & Australian Flying Corps Squadron Losses 12th November 1918 - 31st December 1920 W R Chorley and P J McMillan, 2021

Michael Joseph
Bomber Command — Max Hastings, 1979
Enemy Coast Ahead — Guy Gibson VC, 1946
They Called it Passchendaele — Lyn Macdonald, 1978

Midland Counties Publications
Fallen Eagles - A Guide to Aircraft Crashes in North-East & Mid-Wales — Edward Doylerush, 1990

Midland Publishing Limited
Avro Manchester - The Legend behind the Lancaster — Robert Kirby, 1995
Royal Air Force Bomber Losses in the Middle East and Mediterranean Volume 1: 1939-1942 — David Gunby & Pelham Temple, 2006
Royal Air Force Bomber Command Losses of the Second World War - Volume 2 — W R Chorley, 1993
Royal Air Force Bomber Command Losses of the Second World War - Volume 3 — W R Chorley, 1994
Royal Air Force Bomber Command Losses of the *Second World War - Volume 4* — W R Chorley, 1996
Royal Air Force Bomber Command Losses of the Second World War - Volume 5 — W R Chorley, 1997
Royal Air Force Bomber Command Losses of the Second World War - Volume 6 — W R Chorley, 1998
Royal Air Force Bomber Command Losses - Volume 7 Operational Training Units 1940-1947 — W R Chorley, 2002
Royal Air Force Coastal Command Losses of the Second World War Volume 1 Aircraft and Crew Losses 1939-1941 — Ross McNeill, 2003
Royal Air Force Fighter Command Losses of the Second World War Volume 1 Operational Losses : Aircraft and Crews 1939-194 Revised Edition — Norman L R Franks, 2008
Royal Air Force Fighter Command Losses of the Second World War Volume 2 Operational Losses : Aircraft and Crews 1942-1943 — Norman L R Franks, 1998

Patrick Stephens Limited
Action Stations - 1. Military airfields of East Anglia — Michael J F Bowyer, 1979

Penguin Books
Hundred Days - The End of the Great War — Nick Lloyd, 2014
Pop Goes the Weasel - The Secret Meanings of Nursery Rhymes — Albert Jack, 2010

Putnam
Blackburn Aircraft since 1909 — A J Jackson, 1968
De Havilland Aircraft — A J Jackson, 1962
Fairey Aircraft Since 1915 — H A Taylor, 1974
Hawker Aircraft Since 1920 — Francis K Mason, 1961

The Pentland Press
Sweeping The Skies - A History of No. 40 Squadron RFC and RAF 1916-56 — David Gunby, 1995

Thomas Allen Publishers, Inc
Behind the Glory : Canada's Role in the Allied Air Way — Ted Barris, 2010

Viking
The Bomber Command War Diaries - An Operational Reference Book 1939-1945 — Martin Middlebrook and Chris Everitt, 1985

Volplane Press, New Zealand
By Such Deeds - Honours and Awards in the Royal New Zealand Air Force 1923-1999 — C M Hanson, 2001
For Your Tomorrow - Volume Two : Fates 1943 - 1998 — Errol W Martyn, 1999
For Your Tomorrow - Volume Three : Biographies & Appendices — Errol W Martyn, 2008

Weidenfeld & Nicholson
Cambrai 1917 - The Myth of the First Great Tank Battle — Bryn Hammond, 2008
The War Behind The Wire - The Life, Death and Glory of British Prisoner of War, 1914-18 — John Lewis-Stempel, 2014

William Kimber
For Valour - The Air VCs — Chaz Bowyer, 1978

RAF Operations 1918-1938 — Chaz Bowyer, 1988
The Wellington Bomber — Chaz Bowyer, 1986

PRIVATE PUBLICATIONS

Aircraft Accidents in Lincolnshire During the Second World War — Compiled by Graham J Platt
In conjunction with Bomber County Aviation Resource Crash Project Team
Funded by the Heritage Lottery Fund, supported by The National Lottery

Broken Wings - A Century of Malta's Aviation Accidents, Incidents And Other Stories 1915 - 2015 — Colonel Mark Said, 2015
Handley Page O/400 Night Bomber Pilot "A Brave Aviator and a Gentleman" A Short History of One Pilot's Service in No. 215 Squadron RAF in World War I — C G & P V Hunt, 2018
In Brave Company - 158 Squadron Operations — W R Chorley, 1990
Leads the field: The history of No. 12 Squadron, Royal Air Force — Timothy Mason, 1960
The Flying Camels - The History of No 45 Sqn RAF — Wg Cdr C G Jefford MBE BA, 1995
The Stained Glass of St. Andrew's Church, Taunton - Updated — Alison Perry and Lesley Gold, 2018

UNPUBLISHED

List of Graduates - The Royal Air Force College Cranwell February 5th, 1920 - December 18th, 1962 — RAFC Cranwell

FORUMS

Bomber Command Forum Group
Royal Air Force Forum
Sussex History Forum
The Wings over New Zealand Forum

MAGAZINES

Aeroplane
Flight and Aircraft Engineer, Volume 65
Flight and Aircraft Engineer, Volume 66
Flight and Flight Engineer, Volume 69
Flight and Flight Engineer, Volume 70
Flight and Flight Engineer, Volume 71
Flight and Flight Engineer, Volume 75
Wingspan

THE BRITISH LIBRARY LIBRARY BOARD NEWSPAPERS AND JOURNALS

The Edinburgh Gazette
The London Gazette

Aberdeen Press and Journal
Belfast News Letter
Birmingham Daily Gazette
Blythe News, Ashington Post
Bradford Observer
Bucks Herald
Central Somerset Gazette
Cheltenham Chronicle and Gloucestershire Graphic
Coventry Evening Telegraph
Dundee Courier
Eastbourne Chronicle
Evening News [Gosport]
Evening Standard
Exeter and Plymouth Gazette
Forfar Despatch
Grantham Journal
Hampshire Telegraph and Post
Hastings and St. Leonards Observer
Leeds Mercury
Acton Gazette
Belfast Telegraph
Birmingham Gazette
Bognor Regis Observer
Bristol Post
Burnley Express and Burnley News
Chelmsford Chronicle
Chester Chronicle
Dover Express
Dundee Evening Telegraph
Essex Chronicle
Evening Sentinel
Evening Telegraph and Post [Dundee]
Folkestone, Hythe, Sandgate & Cheriton Herald
Gloucestershire Echo
Hampshire Telegraph
Hartlepool Northern Daily Mail
Hendon & Finchley Times
New South Wales Police Gazette

New Zealand Police Gazette
Nottingham Journal
Nottingham Post
Portsmouth Evening News
Salisbury & Winchester Journal
Sheffield Daily Telegraph
Somerset Guardian and Radstock Observer
Surrey Mirror
Surrey Mirror and County Post
The Advertiser and Gazette
The Bedfordshire Chronicle and Bedfordshire Gazette
The Belfast Gazette
The Chronicle and Courier
The Cornishman
The Courier [Somerset]
The Daily Mail
The Daily News
The Diss Express and Norfolk and Suffolk Journal
The Glasgow Herald
The Grantham Journal
The Halifax Courier and Guardian
The Haverhill Echo
The Herald
The Herald [Melbourne, Australia]
The Lancashire Daily Post
The Londonderry Sentinel
The North Devon Journal - Herald
The Observer and West Sussex Recorder
The Post [New Zealand]
The Shepton Mallet Journal

The South Australia Police Gazette
The Sydney Morning Herald
The Times of India
The Yorkshire Evening Post
Warwick & Warwickshire & Leamington Gazette
Western Daily Press
Western Morning News
Westminster & Pimlico News

Northern Daily Mail
Nottingham Evening Post
Otago Daily Times
Reading Standard
Sheerness Times
St. Andrews Citizen
South of England Advertiser: Sussex, Surrey, Hampshire and Kent
Taunton Courier and Western Advertiser
The Argus [Melbourne]
The Bedfordshire Times and Independent
The Chester Observer
The Citizen
The Cornishman and Cornish Telegraph
The Courier and Advertiser
The Daily Mirror
The Daily Telegraph
The Edinburgh Evening News
The Gosport Journal
The Guardian from London
The Hampshire Advertiser and Independent
The Hendon, Finchley, Edgware and Mill Hill Times and Golders Green Guardian
The Illustrated Police News
The Lincoln, Rutland and Stamford Mercury
The Manchester Guardian
The Northern Whig and Belfast Post
The Portadown News
The Scotsman
The Singapore Free Press and Mercantile Advertiser
The Sun [Sydney, Australia]
The Times
The Western Morning News and Mercury
Uxbridge & West Drayton Gazette
Wells Journal
Western Mail [Perth, Australia]
Westminster Gazette
Yorkshire Post

Addendum

Derby Daily Telegraph
The Biggleswade Chronicle and Bedfordshire Gazette

WEBSITES

A Fleeting Place - Golden Age Aviation in the British Empire
Retitled
The Ferry Pilots of the Air Transport Auxiliary 1939-1945
*A List of Fatal Accidents to British Aircraft Overseas 12 Nov 1918-1929**
*A List of Fatal Accidents to British Aircraft Overseas 1930- 2 Sep 1939**
*Fatal Air Accidents in Britain 1786-1939**
The Orders and Medals Research Society

* Compiled by R Cawsey, to whom the authors are deeply indebted.

*Air of Authority - A History of RAF Organisation**

* Compiled by Malcolm Barrass , to whom the authors are deeply indebted.

Air History
All Spitfire Pilots
Australian War Memorial
Aviation Brussels
Bangor Cemetery Project
Battle of Britain London Monument

Airport of Croydon
Archive Search - Bryant Thomas Shelley collection
Aviation Safety Network
BAE Systems
Billion Graves

British Modern Military History Society
Bureau of Aircraft Accidents Archive
Charterhouse
Commonwealth War Graves Commission
Find A Grave
Graces Guide to British Industrial History
Hibbitt & Barnes Family History - Quetta Earthquake 1935- The RAFs Account
Highgate RSL
History of Manston Airfield
Hobsonville Point
Holme Pierrepont and Gamston
Hong Kong Escape
Imperial War Museum London
Kenley Revival
Lancing College War Memorial
Lincolnshire Aviation
Maplandia
Military Images
Military Wikja Org
Pacific Wrecks
Pahiatu Herland
Puke Ariki
Radcliffe on Trent and the First World War
Royal Air Force Historical Society
Strange Company
Teynham - The Sons of Colonel James Frederick Honeyball
The Aerodrome
The Auxiliaries
The Battle of Britain London Monument
The Cheltonian
Traces of War
Uboat Net
UK Register of Habitual Criminals
Wikipedia
Wrecksite - Hesperian
Yorkshire Aircraft
4th Canadian Mounted Rifles
35 Squadron
39 Squadron
75NZ Squadron

ATLASES

AA Largest Scale Britain
Grosser Auto Atlas Deutschland Europa

INTRODUCTION and ACKNOWLEDGEMENTS

"The Best Flying Club in the World," is an expression frequently expressed to describe the Royal Air Force between the two world wars, an age when the frontline squadron throughout the 1920a were equipped exclusively with biplanes, many of their designs having had a tried and tested history of participation in the *Great War* whose embers were still fresh in the mind of many of the serving personnel.

It is a very sad fact that between January 1921 and December 1930, three hundred and fifty-five members of "The Best Flying Club in the World" attached to squadrons paid the ultimate price for their membership. Many others, as is evident by entries in the appendices died during their training or in circumstances not connected to frontline service.

Although the work that follows is primarily concerned with the huge number of flying accidents effecting the squadrons at home and abroad, it is also by way of the appendices a reasonably comprehensive account of the officers who were attached to the squadrons and whose duties encompassed the defence of the British Isles and "policing" the far-flung regions of the Briths Empire from the Middle East to "The Jewel in the Crown," British India.

Numerous books of quality have been penned in telling the myriad of stories of the Royal Air Force maintaining "peace" in these lands where the British presence was often challenged, and, therefore, only passing references to historical events may appear from time to time as the unremitting toll of losses were repeated year on year. However, an example of maintaining the "status quo" as far as British interests were concerned has been kindly submitted by Christopher Dean and has been extracted from the diary of No. 8 Squadron stationed in Iraq where insurrection flared from time to time: *"In November and December 1923, most of the RAF Squadron, including 8, went south again for operations against some marsh tribes in the area between the Tigris and Euphrates rivers. It was here that Pilot Officer Vincent won the first Cranwell DFC. The way in which it was won is typical of the carefree spirit of those days. The Squadron was living in a train not more than ten minutes from the target area, yet Vincent, with Flight Lieutenant Jones as gunner, ran out of fuel and landed within a mile of the target! Taffy Jones was a famous WW1 fighter ace with the DSO, MC, DFC and MM. He also played rugby for Wales. The desert was quite flat so a second aircraft landed along side and the pilot suggested that Vincent and Jones should climb in and return to base. This offer was declined and the second aircraft was sent for more fuel. When they were alone again some Arabs, not unnaturally, arrived from the target area and started shooting at them. At first, Jones managed to keep them at bay by replying with his Lewis gun from the back seat. Soon the Arabs realised that the gun could not fire forwards, so they started approaching from the nose. Vincent, who was no weakling, picked up the aircraft tail by himself [normally it took two or three men to do this] and swung the aeroplane round so Jones could continue to fire at the Arabs. This was successful for a while, but eventually they were forced into a position where Vincent had to stand in front of the nose with a revolver to keep the attackers at a distance while both flanks and the tail were covered by the Lewis gun. The situation was beginning to look black when a Sopwith Snipe arrived and drove off the attackers. The petrol arrived shortly after this and no time was wasted in re-fuelling and taking off."*

The appendices attached at the end of each year are self explanatory and the authors hope readers with an interest in ancestry and whose forebear may have held a commission in the Royal Air Force will find the appendices devoted to short service commission officers and graduates from the Royal Air Force [Cadet] College at Cranwell, subsequently retitled on the 1st of February 1929, Royal Air Force College Cranwell and elevated to Command status [though all previous commandants were air commodore ranked], of particular interest.

In addition to short service commissioned officers and graduates from Cranwell, *The London Gazette* contains details of numerous officers granted commissions in the Reserve of Air Force Officers, Special Reserve, Auxiliary Air Force commissions, and attached officers from other services granted temporary commissions whilst attached. With regret it has not been possible to include all this data in this volume. But with a fifth volume in the planning this myriad of information will be included to complete coverage of the huge expansion of officer manpower commencing in the late '20s and continuing throughout the '30s as Germany's "sabre rattling" became more pronounced.

Appendix F provides summaries of Royal Navy and Royal Marine officers who were killed in flying accidents during their attachment, while information concerning more than a few Royal Air Force officers who lost their lives whilst attached to the Fleet Air Arm flights may be found against their names in appendices C and D.

Throughout readers will come across numerous entries pertaining to non-commissioned officers and the authors have in cases of fatalities included the airman's service number, usually with supporting notes. For the data thus appended the authors are indebted to The Orders and Medals Research Society. The most common number blocks appearing in this volume are:

2691 - 17400	RFC General 1915
155001 - 160000	RFC and RAF and Boys October 1917 to December 1918
185001 - 200000	RAF, Civilians and transfers May and June 1918
225061 - 244710	Transfers from RNAS 1917 entrants
244711 - 260000	Transfers from RNAS 1918 entrants
275001 - 307973	Civilians and transfer July to October 1918
326001 - 329000	Boys December 1918 to March 1919
329001 - 335000	Civilians March to August 1919
335001 - 336000	Boys August 1919 to January 1921

336001 - 338000 Civilians August to September 1919
340001 - 360000 Civilians September 1919 to June 1925
361601 - 370000 Boys July 1922 to January 1924
370001 - 370986 Civilians June to September 1925
505001 - 549999 Civilians October 1925
560001 - 579999 Aircraft Apprentices commencing January 1926

Information regarding service number blocks set aside for short service commission and flight cadets graduating with permanent commissions are reported in appendices C and D for 1921. The former appendix also contains information on the flying training schools to which both officers and selected non-commissioned officers were sent.

By way of acknowledgment, the authors express their gratitude for the far-sighted undertaking, decades ago, to preserve for the nation copies of the myriad of national and local newspapers, reports from which enhance many of the summaries reporting accidents [principally fatal] that befell aircraft within the British Isles. Where reports are used, full credit to the appropriate newspaper has been recorded.

The authors are also indebted to the myriad of official organisations that through the medium of websites provide invaluable information and in this context *The London Gazette* and *The Commonwealth War Graves Commissions* spring immediately to mind, while other important websites are credited in the Biography and Sources section and are acknowledged in the text when referenced.

To Christopher Dean, Greg Harrison and Dave Gilbert, "champions" of No. 8 Squadron, No. 100 Squadron and the International Bomber Command Centre respectively, our grateful thanks for sharing their extensive knowledge; Christopher and Greg searching out photographs relevant to the period, while Dave has provided official records extracted from Squadron Operations Books in respect of a number of officers whose commissioning is recorded in this volume and who were killed, or taken prisoner of war while flying bomber operations in the Second World War.

To conclude this introduction to the fourth volume the authors express their appreciation to the continuing support and encouragement from Simon Hepworth, publisher of the series.

Bill Chorley and Paul McMillan,
April 2022

SQUADRON LOSSES
1921

Throughout the year the Royal Air Force continued to be equipped with aeroplanes of *Great War* design, more than handful having seen operational service during the conflict itself. This speaks volumes for the ground crews whose skill in maintaining airframes and engines now well past their best, thereby ensuring that the active squadrons were able to carry out their allotted tasks.

With the bulk of operational squadrons deployed overseas, the defence of the United Kingdom rested with the Sopwith Snipes of 25 Squadron, based at Hawkinge in Kent.

JANUARY

Thursday 13 January 1921
30 Squadron *Not reported*
DH.9A H80
Merely reported as *"crashed."* From the block H1-H200 [H176-H200 cancelled] built by the Aircraft Manufacturing Company at Hendon, H80 was sent to the Packing Depot at Ascot where it was prepared for shipment to the Middle East. Here it was reconstructed at the Baghdad Aircraft Park and was in use with 30 Squadron by mid-1920.

Monday 17 January 1921
238 Squadron *Not reported*
Felixstowe F.21 N4460
T/o Cattewater and owing to engine failure came down in the sea some fifteen miles from its base; no further details,

Wednesday 19 January 1921
20 Squadron F/O L H I Bell Interned
Bristol F.2b H1658 F/O C R Smythe Interned
T/o Tank carrying mail and wireless stores to Wada column operating in the NWF but strayed across the border and forced-landed in Afghanistan. The crew, though not their aircraft, were later repatriated.

Flying Officer Laurence Herbert Irving Bell changed his name by deed poll, the following entry being *Gazetted* 10th March 1922, issue 32635, pages 2098 and 2099: *"Notice is herby given that Laurence Herbert Irving Irving Bell [formerly known as Laurence Herbert Irving Bell], of Leadhall Grange, Harrogate, in the county of York, a Flying Officer of the Royal Air Force, being a natural born British Subject, has by deed poll, dated the 21st day of February, 1922, duly enrolled in the Central Office of the Supreme Court of Judicature, on the 8th day of March, 1922, assumed and taken from the said21st day of February, 1922, and declared his intention to use the surname of "Irving," so that henceforth he should be known under the surname of "Irving Bell" as his last and principal surname, and has thereby declared that he should at all times thereafter in all deeds and writings and in all dealings and transactions and all occasions whatsoever use the surname of "Irving Bell" in lieu of his former surname "Bell," and he has thereby expressly authorised and desired every person whatsoever to describe him of of such surname accordingly. - Dated the 8th day of March, 1922." "Collyer-Bristow and Co., 4 Bedford-row, W.C.1. Agent for:- Titley and Paver-Crow, 28 James-street, Harrogate, Solicitors for the said Laurence Herbert Irving Irving Bell."*

Flying Officer Cyril Richard Smythe rose to the rank of wing commander and retired from the service on 26th August 1946.

FEBRUARY

Friday 4 February 1921
84 Squadron *Not reported*
DH.9A H117
T/o Shaibah and on arrival at Nasiriyeh crashed; damaged beyond repair. Its service prior to issue to the squadron mirrors that of H80, reported on 13th January 1921

Tuesday 8 February 1921
6 Squadron *Not reported*
Bristol F.2b D7833
T/o Baghdad West and wrecked soon after in a crash-landing with engine failure. The Bristol had been shipped from the UK in February 1920, destined for the Aeroplane Supply Deport at Aboukir from where it was issued to the squadron by September 1920.

Wednesday 9 February 1921
30 Squadron F/O G C Bladon Safe
DH.9A E821
T/o Baghdad West in company with Flying Officer William Bentley to transit to Kasvin where Flight Lieutenant Raymond Collishaw DSO* OBE DSC AFC, B Flight commander had been detached the previous November to establish a forward operating base. On arrival, Flying Officer Bladon landed on a snow-covered landing strip and swung into deep snow causing his DH to turn over.

An account of this incident is recorded on pages 76 and 77 of *Flat Out - The story of 30 Squadron Royal Air Force*. Flying Officer Graham Clarke Bladon subsequently rose to the rank of air commodore, retiring from the Air Force on the 22nd of February 1959; his death was announced on Saturday, 11th of October 1967.

A profile on the Air of Authority website, admirably administered and kept up to date by Malcolm Barrass, notes that while attached to 208 Squadron at San Stephano he was seriously injured when his Bristol F.2B H1678 overturned on landing. Consulting several sources, notably *Bristol Fighter,* the movements for H1678 are ambiguous in that it is annotated *"wrecked 10.7.23 ... when undercarriage collapsed on landing,"* followed by *"Repaired"* after which there are no further entries.

Thursday 10 February 1921
2 Squadron F/O N V Moreton Safe
Bristol F.2b H1487 F/O E P Mackay pow
T/o Fermoy tasked for delivery of mail during which the engine overheated, forcing the crew to make an emergency landing. On the ground members of the Irish Republican Army apprehended Flying Mackay but released him four days later.; meanwhile, the rebels had set light to the aircraft.

Flying Officer Noel Vivian Moreton served until retirement as a group captain on the 1st of July 1950. His colleague attained the same rank and retired on 16th January 1948.

Friday 18 February 1921
30 Squadron F/O G Kidd Safe
DH.9A H40 General W E Ironside* Injured See 8 April 1921
T/o Kasvin with mail destined for the squadron's base at Baghdad but near Kermanshah the DH forced-landed in deep snow. The impact was severe enough to fracture one of General Ironside's legs and this injury prevented him from taking up the post of commanding British troops in Iraq [at the time he was commanding British forces in Persia].

Bringing him and his pilot to safety proved extremely difficult and for the General a painful evacuation. Flying Officer Geldart Kidd is mentioned on page 231 of my third volume; an addition to his entry appears in Appendix G.

* Field Marshal William Edmund Ironside, 1st Baron Ironside GCB CMG DSO, born in Edinburgh on 6th May 1880, and died at the age of 79, in Queen Alexandria Military Hospital, London, on Tuesday, 22nd September 1959. A relatively short biography for William Ironside is published on the *Wikipedia* website.

Sunday 20 February 1921
30 Squadron F/O F J Barrett Safe
DH.9A E9691
T/o Baghdad and wrecked after forced-landing with a failing engine in a river at Karradesh. There are numerous websites reporting this, but it is not mentioned in John Hamlin's history of the squadron.

Thursday 24 February 1921
4 Squadron F/O W L G Spinney + Wembley [St. John] Churchyard
Avro 504K F8751 O/O A Hesketh Injured See 8 February 1922
T/o Farnborough and spun in at Cove on the NW side of the airfield. Observer Officer William Leslie Gordon Spinney was a short service commissioned officer, his details being recorded in my third volume on page 284.

The accident was reported the following day in Dundee's *Evening Telegraph and Post* beneath the headline *'Pilot Killed in Aeroplane Crash - Officer's Agonised Appeal - "Help Me to Pull My Pal Out"'*

"An aeroplane crashed, in which one officer was killed and another escaped uninjured, occurred at Farnborough.

"Flying Officer Spinney was piloting an Avro machine, and carrying with him Observer Officer Hesketh. About noon it was discovered that engine trouble had developed. The machine then made a sudden nose dive, and crashed to earth.

"Residents rushed to the spot, and met Mr. Hesketh staggering towards them. He was seen to rise from the ruins of the machine, stumble, fall, and then rise again. He then shouted in an agonised voice:- "For God's sake come and help me to pull my pal out. He is under the wreckage."

"Mr Spinney was found to be already dead, and was lying in a mass of wreckage. He was an experienced pilot and had flown in France. He was married, and recently lived at Wembley, London."

On Saturday, 26th February 1921, at Ramleh, a Bristol F.2b H1534 belonging to 14 Squadron, stalled at a height of twelve feet as it arrived over the landing area. Its crew, Flying Officer Alan Jerrard, attached from 56 Squadron, and Aircraftman G Reeves were shaken, but otherwise unharmed.

However, the subsequent inquiry, forwarded by Paul McMillan, makes for interesting reading;

'Finding of Court of Inquiry'

"Caused by stalling at a height of 12 feet. The stalling was due to an error of judgement on the part of the pilot. [A] Inexperienced of landing on this aerodrome which is very undulating. [B] Small number of hours flown by pilot on this type of machine.

"O.C. 14 Squadron does not concur with [A] as the pilot had been attached to 14 Squadron long enough to know the aerodrome. "B" is very unlikely as the pilot has had considerable air experience. Consider the incidence was caused by careless flying on the part of the pilot.

"O.C. Palestine Group concurs with O.C. 14 Squadron& recommends stoppage of 14 days pay towards cost of repair."

MARCH

Monday 21 March 1921
55 Squadron *Not reported*
DH.9A E790
T/o Mosul and wrecked on landing, turning over in the process, a flat tyre being a contributory factor. This was the squadron's first accident since arriving from Baghdad West the day before.

Thursday 31 March 1921
On this day the Royal Australian Air Force was formed with an establishment of 151 aircraft, 124 of these having been received through the Imperial Gift, a subject expanded upon by Sebastian Cox, Head of the Air Historical Branch, in a lecture given at the RAF Museum, Hendon, on 7th April 2010, and reported in Journal 49 which the authors have pleasure in acknowledging.

APRIL

Friday 1 April 1921
2 Squadron F/O J McBain Safe
Bristol F.2b F4797
T/o Oranmore and forced-landed with engine trouble between Banteer and Kanturk two villages in Co. Cork. The wreckage of F4797 was returned the next day to Oranmore by rail. Historically, the former village featured in the bitter Irish Confederate Wars and according to *Wikipedia* was the site of the *Battle of Knocknaclashy* fought in July 1651 between the Parliamentarian forces led by Roger Boyle, Lord Broghill [later the1st Earl of Orrery] and the Confederates led by Donagh MacCarthy [Viscount Muskerry]. This was the last pitched battle in the war and was an overwhelming success for Cromwell's well trained army.

216 Squadron F/O H N Hampton DFC Injured
DH.10 E9073 AC1 T H Cressy Safe
T/o Aboukir for delivery to the squadron either at Qantara or Abu Sueir but crashed out of control before completion of the flight. Co-author, Paul McMillan reports that the DH ran into thick vegetation which caused the tail plane to be thrown up. A second attempt to take off resulted in the DH crashing into a hill on becoming airborne. Flying Officer Herbert Nind Hampton was short service commissioned [see page 230 of my third volume] but, subsequently, received a permanent commission and retired as a group captain on 25th June 1946. His DFC was promulgated in the Edinburgh edition of the *Gazette* on August 7th, 1918, issue 13300, page 2814: *"He recently carried out a night reconnaissance lasting three hours; at times he descended to within 500 feet of the ground, following down his Michelin flares to this height in the face of intense machine-gun fire. By this means he and his observer were able to obtain valuable information. During the past five months he has taken part in forty-one bombing raids, many of which were long distance over the enemy's lines."*

Friday 8 April 1921
30 Squadron F/O H W Baggs Safe See 29 July 1921
DH.9A H81 General W E Ironside Injured See 18 February 1921
T/o Basra bound for Baghdad and forced down by a sandstorm. In much reduced visibility the DH trundled into an irrigation ditch near Khidive and turned over. This incident [and that of 18th February] are reported by John Hamlin on page 77 of his history of the squadron, noting that the squadron despatched another DH with a medical officer as passenger to aid the General whom, I suspect, had been undergoing treatment in Basra for his injuries received on 18th February. In this accident, poor General Ironside suffered a fracture to his right thigh.

Thursday 14 April 1921
14 Squadron F/O P J Cox + Jerusalem Protestant Cemetery
Bristol F.2b H1533 F/O C Pilkington AFC Injured
T/o Ramleh and crashed after stalling. Flying Officer Pierse Joseph Cox was born on the 17th of April 1890, enlisting in the RFC on the 27th of February 1917, and commissioned to the General List [LG 8 March 1917, supplement 29975, page 2354]. He arrived in France of the 7th of October 1917, and was initially attached to 2 Aircraft Depot before proceeding to Proven on the 17th where he joined 9 Squadron to fly RE.8s on Corps reconnaissance duties. For reasons not explained, he was posted back to England on 6th November, this being the last entry on his service record. Then, on the 5th of December 1919, he was granted a short service commission in the rank of flying officer [LG 5 December 1919, issue 31674, page 15061]. At the time of his death he was the squadron's adjutant.

Flying Officer Christopher Pilkington was granted his short service commission on the 24th of October 1919 [LG 24 October 1919, issue 31616, page 13033]. Although I cannot be certain, I believe he served in the war with 7 Squadron [BE.2s], his first operational tour lasting from 16th April to 30th November 1916. On the 28th of April 1917, he returned to France and was posted to 9 Squadron on the 2nd of May, but four days later he rejoined 7 Squadron. The reverse of his Record of Service form has not been copied, so I am not able to report his subsequent movements. However, following the crash in which he was injured, two *Gazette* entries show, first that he was transferred to the Reserve Class A on 24th October 1926, in the rank of flight ieutenant and second, within the Reserve of Air Force Officers he was transferred to class C on the 24th of October 1931, the relevant entries being made on 26th October 1926, issue 33215, page 6823 and 27th October 1931, issue 33766, page 6879.

208 Squadron F/O W A Armstrong + Ismailia War Memorial Cemetery
Bristol F.2b D7831 F/O E B Jones + Ismailia War Memorial Cemetery
T/o Ismailia and destroyed in a crash near Bilbeis following a midair collision with the Bristol reported below. Army Form B.103 in respect of Flying Officer William Ash Armstrong shows he sailed from Marseilles on 14th June 1919, and arrived at Alexandria on the 19th, joining RAF Base Aboukir the same day. While attached to a training brigade he sustained accidental contusions to his legs and face on 22nd November and was admitted to a hospital in Cairo

On his discharge he was posted to 206 Squadron [DH.9] at Helwan but within days went to 'Z' Unit on the 18th of December but returned two days later and embarked on HMS *Ark Royal* which was preparing to sail with aircraft, stores and equipment to Berbera for operations in Somalia, described in the third chapter of Chaz Bowyer's *RAF Operations 1918-1938* under the heading 'Z' Force and the Mad Mullah. The outcome was a success and helped to cement Trenchard's vision that the Royal Air Force could be effective in helping to police vast tracts of the Empire at a relatively reasonable cost - a most attractive proposition that found favour with politicians and in particular Winston Churchill wearing his dual hats of Secretary of State for War and Air.

The second Army Form B.103 raised for Flying Officer Armstrong commences on January 6th, 1921, indicating an attachment to 208 Squadron to which he was permanently posted on the 24th. Of note is the penultimate entry on the form which reads *"26.2.21 Qualified to wear wings under AMWO 655 of 1920 Category "E" [Auth. AM letter 77116/21/T.1 of 11.1.21].* The final entry starkly announces *16.4.21 Killed in Aeroplane Accident & Struck off Strength 14.4.21."*

Information regarding Flying Officer Edward Blake Jones is confined to a single *Gazette* entry published in issue 31656, page 14317, of 25 November 1919, indicating an entry made in respect of this officer in its issue of 4th November 1919, is cancelled.

208 Squadron F/Lt G M Clarke AFC + Ismailia War Memorial Cemetery
Bristol F.2b E2298 O/O F J Smith MC MM + Ismailia War Memorial Cemetery
T/o Ismailia and lost in the manner described above. Flight Lieutenant George Malcolm Clarke formerly served with the Leinster Regiment and in 1916, is known to have been attached to 12 Squadron. His observer, Observer Officer Frank James Smith MM was *Gazetted* with the MC in supplement 30780, page 7924, of 5th July 1918, for his actions with the Royal Berkshire Regiment; *"For conspicuous gallantry and devotion to duty. He led two platoons to their objective, captured thirty prisoners and a machine gun, shooting the man who was firing the gun. He established touch with the troops on his flanks and took command of men of other companies whom he found near his post."*

Friday 15 April 1921
47 Squadron F/Lt E B Grenfell Injured
DH.9A E8598 F/O C A Horn Safe
T/o Helwan and while in flight a smoke bomb ignited and with his DH on fire Flight Lieutenant Grenfell forced-landed near Orbendofa [sic]. He escaped with minor burns. Of the 2nd/5th Battalion, Duke of Cornwall's Light Infantry, Lieutenant Eric Blake Grenfell was seconded for duty with the RFC on 15th August 1916 [LG 16 September 1916, supplement 29753, page 9099]. On 20th October 1916, he arrived in France [St. Omer] with 46 Squadron equipped with 2-seater Nieuports for artillery and photographic duties, moving to Droglandt on the 26th. Promoted captain on 16th February 1917, he was posted to 42 Squadron [RE.8] at Bailleul on 14th April as a flight commander.

On 1st August 1919, he was included in the list of captains appointed to a permanent commission, serving until retirement as an air commodore on 22nd October 1944. His death occurred during September 1972.

His observer, Flying Officer Charles Austin Horn, born on 30th May 1894, late of a Trench Mortar Company, Royal Artillery, was accepted in the RFC on 9th January 1918, joining 2 Squadron [FK.8] at Hesdigneul on 19th April, serving with the squadron until 10th October 1918, when he returned to the UK. He, too, was a permanent officer, rising to group captain rank before retiring on 27th September 1945.

Monday 18 April 1921
14 Squadron P/O P W T Hare Safe
Bristol F.2b E2288 O/O J C Buteel Safe
T/o Ramleh to make an aerial delivery of mail. Owing, so the report indicates, to poor flying and *"gross carelessness"* the petrol tube fractured and the throttle jammed. Forced landed on the airfield and damaged beyond repair. The indications are that Observer Officer Buteel was flying the aircraft. Pilot Officer Bertram William Trelawney Hare was in the Naval Entry to RAF [Cadet] College, Cranwell, in February 1920; please refer to Volume 3 and page 270 for details of his service.

Friday 22 April 1921
55 Squadron *Not reported*
DH.9A H57 *Not reported*
T/o Mosul and following a forced-landing in the desert was very effectively looted by a band of Arabs which left the DH as little more than scrap wood.

Friday 29 April 1921
2 Squadron F/O R G Mullette Injured
Bristol F.2b E2546 AC2 L H Hall Injured
T/o Fermoy only to stall and crash out of control. Presumably the crew were intending to return to Oranmore.

56 Squadron F/O F W Deane DFC + Alexandria [Chatby] Military and War Memorial Cemetery
7F.1 Snipe E7647
T/o Aboukir and came down in the sea. Subsequently, Flying Officer Frederick William Deane's body was recovered; he was from Knock in Co Down. The citation for his award was published in the Edinburgh edition of the *Gazette,* December 5th, 1918, issue 13363, page 4472: *"An exceptionally able officer, who has taken part in numerous hostile air raids by day and night. On the night of 19/20th May, when at 10,000 feet altitude, his machine took fire; with rare presence of mind and cool courage Captain Deane brought it down safely, thereby saving the life of his observer."*

MAY

By Sunday the 1st, No. 1 Squadron appears to have completed its transfer from RAF Bangalore in British India to RAF Hinaidi, Mesopotamia.

Wednesday 4 May 1921
12 Squadron F/O G B Pershouse + Cologne Southern Cemetery
Bristol F.2b F4895 LAC R Roberts + Cologne Southern Cemetery
T/o Bickendorf and destroyed following a collision with telephone wires in Köln's Lindenthal district on the west bank of the Rhine. Flying Officer Geoffrey Bradney Pershouse, an army officer with the North Staffordshire Regiment, had been seconded for duty with the Royal Air Force for two years, effective from 12th June 1920 [LG 18 June 1920, issue 31946, page 6704].

A file for this officer, born 2nd May 1898, is held by TNA Kew under AIR 76/400/90.

The deaths of these two airmen were the last to be reported from an operational squadron carrying out duties in the Rhineland, though it would not be until the 22nd of July 1922, before the squadron was stood down and disbanded.

Leading Aircraftman Robert Roberts 244301, aged 20, and from South Willesborough in Kent is commemorated by the inscription on his headstone *"In The Path Of Duty He Found An Early Grave."* He was a transferee from the 1917 RNAS entry.

Thursday 5 May 1921
55 Squadron F/Lt R S Maxwell DFC Safe See 16 April 1926 - 47 Squadron
DH.9A E918 *Not reported* Safe
T/o Mosul for an operational patrol during which the DH was hit by rebel fire and forced to land in hostile territory. 'Dame Fortune' smiled upon them for their plight was seen by the crew of F2775 [see 4th June 1921] who landed and took Flight Lieutenant Maxwell, a permanent officer appointed on 1st August 1919, and his observer to safety.

See Appendix B for 1923, when appointed Commanding Officer of 24 and 32 Squadron, and the citation of a First Bar to his DFC.

55 Squadron *Not reported*
DH.9A H46
T/o Baghdad West and crashed whilst landing at Mosul.

Saturday 14 May 1921
30 Squadron *Not reported*
DH.9A F2785
T/o Baghdad and damaged beyond repair following a forced-landing on uneven ground. Ten months previously it had been slightly damaged by rebel gunfire.

John Hamlin in his excellent history of 30 Squadron records that around the time of the accident shown above the squadron had been tasked along with 47 Squadron to survey and prove an air route from Cairo to Baghdad for both commercial and military air traffic with the ultimate aim of ensuring safe passage of aircraft to India and thence to Singapore and on to Australia. Although the accident which wrote off F2785 is not mentioned, I suggest there is little doubt it occurred while assisting with this survey.

Thursday 19 May 1921
30 Squadron *Not reported*
DH.9A H109
T/o Baghdad and wrecked while landing at Shaibah where the DH ran into soft sand and lost its undercarriage.

Friday 20 May 1921
210 Squadron F/O J H T Carr + Southwold [St. Edmund] Churchyard
Panther N7433 Mechanic J Armstrong + Beverley [St. Nicholas] Churchyard
T/o Gosport but stalled and crashed almost immediately at Fort Romer. A biography of Flying Officer John Henry Talbot Carr can be read on the Lancing College War Memorial website, which the authors acknowledge. Born on 10th March 1899, Flying Officer Carr gained his Royal Aero Club Aviators' Certificate 3613 on 21st September 1916, and following further instruction joined 12 Squadron RNAS at Dunkirk on 17th January 1918. Within eight days he was shot down and taken prisoner of war. Repatriated on 14th December 1918, he was placed on the Unemployed List on 9th July 1919. On 22nd November 1920, he was granted a short service commission for three years on the active list [LG 28th January 1921, issue 32209, page 781]. At the time of his death he had recently completed a deck landing

course on HMS *Argus*. Mechanic Jack Armstrong's funeral was arranged by his parents; his headstone is inscribed *"Loved And Remembered Always."*

His service number 157422 shows he joined the service as a boy twixt October 1917 and December 1918, the block of numbers being 155001 - 160000. Paul McMillan adds that he was known to family and friends as 'Jack' and that he was a cinema operator.

Tuesday 24 May 1921
100 Squadron F/O C Chambers Injured
Avro 504K F2574
T/o Howden and on arrival at York Racecourse stalled and crashed; probably damaged beyond repair.

JUNE

Wednesday 1 June 1921
8 Squadron S/Ldr D L Allen AFC Safe
DH.9A H110
T/o Baghdad but got into difficulties and crashed out of control. Born, so Paul McMillan reports, on 12th July 1890 in Calcutta, Dermot Lang Allen passed through RMA Sandhurst and in 1912 undertook flying lessons at Hendon and CFS Upavon. Following Staff College Andover in 1922, he held appointments in the Middle East, including Turkey, and in India. The announcement of his AFC was published by the Air Ministry on 3rd June 1919, in recognition of distinguished service rendered during the *Great War.* His service number was 0112.

An extensive collection of his private papers which includes his inter-war flying log books et al are held by the Imperial War Museum, the collection taking up two boxes. The IWM description notes that during the *Great War* he was attached at various times to 3, 7 and 8 Squadrons.

Saturday 4 June 1921
55 Squadron F/O H W Westaway Safe See 23 April 1923
DH.9A F2775
T/o Mosul and damaged beyond repair when a tyre burst on landing. It will be recalled this was the DH that rescued Flight Lieutenant Maxwell and his observer during operations as recently as the 5th of May.

A General List officer, Flying Officer Horace William Westaway's Army Form B.103 shows he was attached to 53 Squadron [RE.8] at Bailleul on 28th August 1917, and two weeks later on 14th September, he was wounded during an early morning reconnaissance, his RE A3238 hit by anti-aircraft fire which killed his observer, 2nd Lieutenant Leonard Hodkinson. Landing in Allied held territory, 2nd Lieutenant Westaway was admitted to 20 General Hospital for treatment to facial injuries before being sent to the UK by way of HS *Ville de Liege.* Flying Officer Westaway relinquished his commission on 27th August 1931 [LG 1 December 1931, issue 33776, page 7742]. Subsequently, he joined the Royal Canadian Air Force and was awarded an AFC *Gazetted* 1 December 1944, supplement 36820, page 5515.

Formerly of the 15th Battalion, Royal Welsh Fusiliers, Leonard Hodkinson is buried in the extension to Bailleul Communal Cemetery. For additional information, please refer to page 116 of Trevor Henshaw's indispensable *The Sky Their Battlefield - Expanded Edition*

Wednesday 8 June 1921
216 Squadron F/O H M Coombs DFC + Cairo War Memorial Cemetery
DH.10 E9061
T/o Heliopolis and while over the rifle ranges at Abbassia, and practically within sight of the airfield, entered a flat-spin from which it was impossible to correct and recover. Under the heading Territorial Forces, Herbert Milbourne Coombs was commissioned as a 2nd Lieutenant to the Wessex [Howitzer] Brigade, Royal Field Artillery, on the 4th of September 1915 [LG 17 September 1915, supplement 29302, page 9307]. On the 5th of June 1916, he was accepted in the RFC and on qualifying as a pilot arrived in France on 16th March 1917, and reported three days later to 20 Squadron [FE.2d] at Ste Marie Cappel. On the last day of April he was admitted to 12 CCS suffering from concussion of the brain and following examination was taken to 14 General Hospital and thence to the UK on 6th May aboard HS *Pieter de Coninck.* Herbert's recovery was quick and he was back on French soil by the 20th and two days later arrived at Treizennes to fly FE.2ds with 100 Squadron. His operational tour lasted well into 1918 [between the 12th and 18th June he was treated in 8 Canadian Stationary Hospital for influenza], but, unfortunately, the reverse of the form which would have shown he return to Home Establishment has not survived.

His DFC was *Gazetted* in the Edinburgh edition, less citation, on 6 January 1919, issue 13378, page 76, where his second Christian name is shown as Melbourne. From Newport on the Isle of Wight, his epitaph reads: *"Amor Omnia Vincit"* [Love Conquers All].

Thursday 9 June 1921
30 Squadron F/O H G W Lock DFC Safe
DH.9A H90
T/o Baghdad and damaged beyond repair following a forced-landing in a raging sandstorm. Flying Officer Henry George Watts Lock's name appears in Volume 3, Appendix E listing officers granted a short service commission with effect from 24th October 1919. Subsequently, he saw service in the Second World War and retired owing to medical

unfitness for Air Force service on 25th April 1946, retaining his rank of group captain [LG 7 May 1946, supplement 37556, page 2169].

It is possible the DH was operating out of Ramadi, a former German airfield abandoned at the end of the *Great War* or from either of four landing grounds, simply identified as LG1, LG2, LG3 and LG4 which provided safe landing areas, LGs 1 and 2 which were west of Ramadi being of natural bitumen. Page 78 of John Hamlin's history of the squadron explains the nature of the sites and the dates that they were in use.

Friday 10 June 1921
20 Squadron *Not reported*
Bristol F.2b C996
T/o Parachinar and forced-landed at an undisclosed location, smashing the undercarriage to the extent that the Bristol was deemed beyond repair. A war veteran, C996 saw extensive service on the Italian front after issue to 139 Squadron.

Wednesday 15 June 1921
55 Squadron F/O F Carpenter Safe
DH.9A F2833
T/o Mosul and wrecked here in a landing accident. Initially on charge with 30 Squadron at Baghdad, F2833 was badly damaged in a forced-landing at Shora circa mid-August 1920, repairs being carried out by the squadron before its despatch to the Aircraft Park at Baghdad on 18th September 1920, from whence it was taken over by 55 Squadron.

Thursday 16 June 1921
100 Squadron F/O H C Black Safe
Bristol F.2b J6690 Cpl J E Brown Injured
T/o Oranmore and headed for Baldonnel and following engine failure forced-landed near Ballinasloe, near Galway Bay, overturning in the process. Salvaged, the Bristol was later deposited at No. 1 School of Technical Training at Halton for use as a ground instruction airframe.

Friday 24 June 1921
25 Squadron F/O H M Struben + Hawkinge [St. Michael] Churchyard
7F.1 Snipe E6156
T/o Hawkinge and while engaged in practicing landings near Caesar's Camp near Folkestone, lost control and crashed. Flying Officer Harry Marinus Struben was born on 13th August 1899, and on 19th July 1918, was attached to 32 Squadron [SE.5a] at Le Touquin and within less than a week he was a prisoner of war [see page 82 of the second volume in this series]. He was repatriated on 13th December. On 12th September 1919, Harry was granted a short service commission [LG 12 September 1919, issue 35148, page 11469].

The report in *The Lancashire Daily Post* of Monday, June 27th, 1921, reads as follows: *"When at an altitude of 1,400 feet Flying Officer Struben attempted a half-roll. The machine came spinning down, and his neck was broken." This statement was made by Flight-Commander Williamson at the inquest at Shorncliffe on Saturday on Flying Officer Harry Marinus Struben of the 25th Squadron RAF, stationed at Hawkinge Aerodrome. The jury found that death was due to misadventure."*

The Times, meanwhile, carried the following in their *Births, Marriages, Deaths* column: *"STRUBEN- On the 24th June, whilst flying on duty at Hawkinge, near Folkestone. FLYING OFFICER HARRY MARINUS STRUBEN, eldest son of Major and Mrs. Arthur Struben, "Bronwydd," Beaconsfield, Bucks., aged 22 years. [South African papers, please copy.]"*

Saturday 25 June 1921
30 Squadron F/Lt L Maclean MC Safe
DH.9A H3504/C *Not reported* Safe
T/o Baghdad and wrecked when the undercarriage collapsed whilst landing at LG2. Paul McMillan suggests this may be Flight Lieutenant Lourdon James MacLean MC who at one time was attached to Central Air Communication Section at Shaibah.

Monday 27 June 1921
100 Squadron F/Lt B M Fleming Injured
Bristol F.2b J6707 Cpl R F Bond Injured
T/o Oranmore for a rigging test and ditched in Galway Bay following engine failure. Both airmen were picked up by HMS *Urchin*, an Admiralty R-class destroyer that was part of the Grand Fleet and saw action in the *Second Battle of the Heligoland Bight* [November 1917].

Greg Harrison adds [on his spreadsheet] that having climbed to 3,000 feet, Flight Lieutenant Fleming indulged in aerobatics but having come down to a thousand feet he was somewhat alarmed to see petrol flowing from the relief valve. Shutting off the petrol pressure-taps caused the engine to stop and this was followed by the ditching described in the opening paragraph.

JULY

Friday 1 July 1921
100 Squadron F/O V Croome Injured
Bristol F.2b J6709 LAC C Grant Safe
T/o Baldonnel presumably to return to Oranmore but wrecked after flying into a tree near Mullingar in County Westmeath, Ireland. Weather conditions at the time were poor with fog forming.

Historian, Greg Harrison, adds that the crew had been tasked for train escort duty but within ten minutes of becoming airborne they encountered thick fog and in trying to find a suitable place to land struck the tree. The force of the impact in the ensuing crash broke Flying Officer Victor Croome's jaw.

Included on the spreadsheet: *"... Victor Croombe was born in Westminster in late September 1899, the son of Gloucestershire cricketer Arthur Croombe. Between 1928 and 1930, he* [Victor] *played first class cricket for the RAF. He made his debut against the army in 1928, and played his final first class game for the RAF in 1930, again against the army. He went on to play for Straights Settlement cricket team against Malay Straits [in 1932 and 1933] and for Malaya against Hong Kong and Shanghai in 1933. He died in Essex in September 1973, just a few days short of his 74th birthday."*

Saturday 2 July 1921
1 Squadron *Not reported*
7F.1 Snipe H4884
T/o Hinaidi and reported as being written off in a landing mishap, thus becoming the squadron's first Snipe to be consigned to the scrap yard since arriving from British India on the 1st of May 1921.

Tuesday 12 July 1921
25 Squadron *Not reported*
7F.1 Snipe E6266
T/o Hawkinge but on becoming airborne the engine 'cut' and in the emergency landing that followed the Snipe flipped over onto its back; believed damaged beyond repair.

Tuesday 26 July 1921
4 Squadron F/O G V Wheatley Safe See 8 December 1926
Bristol F.2b J6608 AC1 R P Thompson Safe
T/o Farnborough where on landing the undercarriage buckled owing to a heavy touch down. On inspection the damage was deemed beyond economical repair.

Friday 29 July 1921
30 Squadron F/O H W Baggs Safe
DH.9A H161
T/o Baghdad but as the DH gathered speed the wind speed suddenly increased sending a shower of sand into the cockpit and temporarily blinding Flying Officer Baggs. Damaged beyond repair in the ensuing crash. For the majority of officers, RAFM Hendon holds only a single Casualty Form charting his history; for Humphrey William Baggs, late of the Army Service Corps, no less that three Army Form B.103s have survived, the earliest entry showing he was admitted to hospital in Alexandria on 2nd August 1915, for treatment to a septic foot, his discharge being recorded as 6th September. The first card ends with an entry made on 1st October 1917, *"Posted to No. 21 Reserve Squadron 14.9.17."* Air-Britain's *Royal Air Force Flying Training and Support Units* show this to be at Abbassia with an establishment of eighteen Maurice Farman.

At this stage Humphrey Baggs was still a humble soldier but on 1st October 1917, he was *Gazetted* as a temporary 2nd Lieutenant on the General List for duty with the RFC and attached that same day to 23 Training Squadron at Aboukir. Another spell in hospital disrupted his training which was still continuing at the end of December, but he was granted flying officer rank, subject to War Office approval on 9th December. His 1918 service is a 'blank' but the first entry [18th July] on the third card indicates he had been in India, while a plethora of movements in July shows him being sent to Aboukir, Heliopolis, back to Aboukir and thence to Suez and Cairo from where on the 30th, he was ordered to report to the 31st Wing at Baghdad for duties in Mesopotamia.

The second Form B.103 shows his date of birth as 11th January 1895, and next of kin, father, residing in 83 Ebury Buildings, Ebury Square, London, this detail being repeated on the third form; however, a second entry on this card for next of kin states Mrs P Champion, 121 Fowlers Walk, Wrentham, North Ealing, Middlesex.

Turning to *The London Gazette* supplement 31974, page 7423, issued on 12th July 1920, shows he was mentioned in despatches for his work in Kurdistan with 63 Squadron, while the paper for 22nd April 1924, issue 32929, page 3302, shows his appointment to a permanent commission with effect from 23rd April in the rank of flight lieutenant.

Very sadly, he never lived to see retirement for on Thursday, 16th June 1927, while serving as a flying instructor at CFS Wittering and giving instruction to Flying Officer Sydney Fleetwood Bell in a 7F.1 Snipe DC something amiss happened and both officers died in the crash at Wothorpe to the SW of Stamford, Lincolnshire. A partial report, taken from the *Portsmouth Evening News* and appended to ASN Wikibase Occurrence 212231 reads; *"the aeroplane was flying at a tremendous height when suddenly its engine stopped. It re-started and then the machine fell into a spin, and dropping at a terrific rate, crashed into the ground."*

Flying Officer Baggs was 32, Pilot Officer Bell 26, the latter receiving a short service commission in the summer of 1924 [LG 15 July 1924, issue 32956, page 5406].

Saturday 30 July 1921
30 Squadron F/O W Bentley DFC Safe See summary 9 February 1921
DH.9A H119
T/o Baghdad and wrecked in a landing accident on reaching LG4. Flying Officer William Bentley, born 25th February 1899, and joining the RFC on 5th August 1917, served with 218 Squadron [DH.9] between 13th June and 14th October 1918. During the night 17th-18th October, while raiding Melle his aircraft, DH.9 D2921 was hit by shrapnel from anti-aircraft fire which wounded him in his right hand. Landing at St. Pol, he subsequently returned to England on 25th October, aboard the HS *Ville de Liege.* His aircraft was not seriously damaged but was written off before the month was out - see Appendix G to this volume for details. His DFC was *Gazetted,* less citation, on New Year's Day 1919.

AUGUST

Tuesday 9 August 1921
12 Squadron Lt J W Baker Safe See 12 December 1921
Bristol F.2b F4661/B6
T/o Bickendorf and wrecked following an uncontrolled sideslip over, or near the airfield. The Bristol had been on squadron charge for the better part of two years.

55 Squadron F/O J Silvester Safe
DH.9A H79 *Not reported*
T/o Mosul for a reconnaissance of Iraq's Nisibin region during which the petrol tank burst. Forced-landing, it was abandoned to its fate.

Sunday 14 August 1921
1 Squadron *Not reported*
7F.1 Snipe F2345
T/o Hinaidi and believed to have been damaged beyond repair here in a landing accident.

47 Squadron F/O S H Potter + Cairo War Memorial Cemetery
DH.9A E9900 Cpl H M Lake + Cairo War Memorial Cemetery
T/o Helwan and on arrival at Heliopolis control was lost and the DH spun in with fatal consequences for the crew. Flying Officer Sydney Hugh Potter's headstone has a very formal inscription *"Formerly Of St, Hugh's Clapham Park Faithful Unto Death R I P."* It is noted he was the adopted son of Norman Franklin Potter of Chalet Genise, Arveyes-sur-Bex, Switzerland. His short service commission was *Gazetted* on 5th December 1919, issue 31674, page 15062. He was mentioned in despatches [along with many others] on 31st March 1920, for his service in Somalia [LG 12 July 1920, supplement 31974, page 7423].

Corporal Horace Merilion Lake is commemorated by the words *"The Lord's Will Be Done."* He joined the service between May and June 1918, this being established by his service number 195212.

Monday 15 August 1921
208 Squadron F/O I C Slater + Ismailia War Memorial Cemetery
Bristol F.2b F4926 General C R Newman Injured
T/o Ismailia and on arrival at Heliopolis stalled off a turn and spun to the ground. Flying Officer Ian Cecil Slater was granted a short service commission on 24th October 1919 [LG 24 October 1919, issue 31616, page 13034]. His esteemed passenger was Chief of the General Staff in Egypt. In retirement Major-General Charles Richard Newman CB CMG DSO was appointed as a Deputy Lieutenant for the County of Devon, serving as such until resigning this commission on 3rd October 1953 [LG 9 October 1953, issue 39983, page 5368]. With the squadron by March 1921, F4926 had already been involved in a minor accident at Suez on the 1st of June.

216 Squadron F/O G W Wilson AFC Injured See 12 December 1921
DH.10 E9085 F/O A R Jones Safe See 6 February 1923
LAC A Balfour Safe
T/o Heliopolis and owing to failing engines forced-landed in the desert to the east of Beni-Sola in PalestineFlying Officer. Ran into soft sand and tipped forward; possibly damaged beyond repair as no further trace of movements recorded. Grenville Wainwright Wilson's short service commission details are reported in my third volume on page 241; he received his award for distinguished services while serving with the squadron in Palestine [LG 12 July 1920, supplement 31974, page 7422]. Arthur Reginald Jones is also reported in my third volume on page 239, having received his short service commission at the same time as his skipper. His fate in a flying accident on the 5th of August 1931 is noted, and will be recorded again in the next volume.

Saturday 20 August 1921
30 Squadron S/Ldr M Thomas Safe
DH.9A H3500
T/o Mosul and damaged beyond repair when the port tyre burst during landing. Squadron Leader Meredith Thomas commanded the squadron's A Flight which had been detached to Mosul [page 73 of *Flat Out*]. As recently as 1st August he had flown from Baghdad to Cairo *"in eight hours ten minutes."*

Born on 6th July 1892, he was serving as a private soldier with The Queen's Westminster Rifles when war was declared in August 1914. On being commissioned in December 1915, he was attached to The Welsh Regiment, transferring to the RFC in October 1916.

On completion of his flying training he joined 41 Squadron [DH.5] at Abeele on 6th May 1917, and by the time of returning to the UK in December, he had carried out the duties of flight commander. Postwar, he was posted to Eil in Germany where 43 Squadron [7F.1 Snipe] was employed as part of the Allied occupation force until returning to Spittlegate where it was reduced to a cadre. However, prior to disbandment, he was granted a short service commission*continuing to serve until retirement on 18th April 1946, by which time he had been promoted air vice marshal. His final appointment in the Royal Air Force commenced in March 1944, when he went out to India as Air Officer Commanding, Air Headquarters India. His death was reported on Sunday, 20th May 1984.

* Later converted to a permanent commission. See Appendix 2E and pages 227 and 228 of Volume 3 for details of his honours and death. Oddly, for the time of his service and having attained squadron leader rank, he never commanded a squadron. In the *Great War* he was a flight commander with 41 Squadron and prior to his appointment on 30 Squadron commanded a flight with 6 Squadron.

Monday 23 August 1921
On this day the British authorities installed Faisal as the King of Mesopotamia and with his installation the name of country was changed to Iraq.

Friday 26 August 1921
14 Squadron *Not reported*
Bristol F.2b H1672
T/o Ramleh only to be overtaken by the all too familiar engine failure, this leading to a crash-landing on LG 1 at Jerusalem.

Tuesday 30 August 1921
27 Squadron F/Lt J L Vachell Safe
DH.9A H51 F/O C C Jackson Safe
T/o Risalpur and on return swung badly and lost its undercarriage; wrecked. H51 reached the squadron by the usual route; manufacturer, Packing Depot Ascot, shipment and re-erected at Aircraft Depot Drigh Road.

Note. On this day *The London Gazette* promulgated the following announcement from the Air Ministry: "*All officers who are on the unemployed list of the Royal Air Force on the 31st of August 1921, are released from further liability to serve as officers of the Royal Air Force. They will relinquish their commissions with effect from the 1st of September, 1921, with permission to retain the rank which was notified to them in the Air Ministry letter intimating that they were transferred to the unemployed list.*"

Wednesday 31 August 1921
55 Squadron F/O C D Spiers Safe
DH.9A H77
T/o Mosul and wrecked here in a crash-landing. I strongly suspect the pilot to be Flying Officer Cyril Douglas Spiers, formerly of the Gloucestershire Regiment. Having served his time on the Reserve, Flight Lieutenant Spiers relinquished his commission on completion of service on 13th September 1931 [LG 1 December 1931, issue 33776, page 7742].

SEPTEMBER

Friday 2 September 1921
25 Squadron F/O E F Mattock Safe
7F.1 Snipe E7501
T/o Hawkinge and written off near the airfield while trying to reach the landing area with a failing engine.

100 Squadron F/O F F Tattam Injured
Bristol F.2b J6725 Cpl H S Roadnight Injured Maidenhead Cemetery
T/o Baldonnel and climbed to 1,500 feet over the airfield whereupon it went into a spin which was eventually partially corrected at 150 feet, and, then, dived into the ground and wrecked. Corporal Harold Stanley Roadnight's military service started as a boy [his service number, 158676, falls within the block 155001 - 160000 used between October 1917 and December 1918]. He was born in Maidenhead, Berkshire, on 13th January 1901, and enlisted in the Royal Flying Corps on 18th December 1917, going on to serve in France at No. 1 Aircraft Depot.

A recent arrival on the squadron, he was taken to the King George V Hospital in Dublin where he died from his injuries at around 1730 in the evening.

The Court of Inquiry into the loss of J6725, came to the conclusion that Flying Officer Francis Frederick Tattam, having recovered from the spin, lapsed into unconsciousness, and was insufficiently fit for flying duties on the day of the accident.

Monday 12 September 1921
55 Squadron F/O C H Teagle Injured Baghdad [North Gare] War Cemetery
DH.9A H153 AC1 S S S Cox Injured
T/o Mosul briefed for a contact patrol in support of a force of levies tracking Arab insurgents. Flying low over the Catas settlement the DH came under rifle fire and Flying Officer Cyril Hollis Teagle was mortally wounded. Despite near fainting he forced-landed near Desht-i-Harir some 20 miles SW of Rowanduz, Iraq.

To prevent their aircraft from being looted, aided by his observer/air gunner, he set his aircraft on fire. Flying Officer Teagle served as a private soldier with the Wiltshire Regiment and was commissioned to the 4th Battalion, The Duke of Edinburgh's [Wiltshire Regiment] on 17th August 1915 [LG 16 August 1915, supplement 29265, page 8148].

On 5th December 1919, he was granted a short service commission as a flying officer [LG 5th December 1919, issue 31674, page 15062]. Evidence presented on his Casualty Form suggests he trained as a pilot in the Middle East and with effect from 23rd September 1918, he was attached to the RAF Base in Salonica before returned to the UK from Alexandria on 15th October 1918, aboard the *Kaisar-I-Hind* [Empress of India of the P & O Steam Navigation Company].

Four days after the forced-landing, he succumbed to his wounds. A file held by the CWGC contains correspondence by way of a telephone conversation between the Commission and his mother regarding the exhuming of her son's body from its original place of burial at Mosul and re-internment at Baghdad [North Gate] War Cemetery in 1923. In addition, the file contains letters from his sister and other parties that continued, with the former, up to December 1932.

Thursday 22 September 1921
12 Squadron P/O Brookham Safe
Bristol F.2b F4855/B4
T/o Bickendorf and wrecked while forced-landing with engine failure near Lehman [sic] near Koblenz in Rhineland-Pfalz. The Bristol had been on the squadron's establishment for just over two years.

Friday 30 September 1921
14 Squadron F/O W W Elliot Safe
Bristol F.2b H1504
T/o from Landing Ground 1 Jerusalem only for the engine to 'cut' and in the ensuing crash the Bristol was wrecked.

14 Squadron F/O E R Stafford Safe
Bristol F.2b H1661
T/o from Landing Ground 1 Jerusalem but failed to gain altitude and as a consequence failed to clear the bank at the western end of the landing ground; wrecked.

84 Squadron F/O B E Hobart DCM Injured
DH.9A E9919 LAC A W Graham Injured
While awaiting clearance to take off at Nasiriyeh the bomb that fell from the DH summarised below exploded wrecking E9919 and severely injuring Flying Officer Hobart [sic], while Leading Aircraftman Graham was less badly hurt. This entry, reported in *The DH.4/DH.9 File* differs in content from that filed by the Basra correspondent of *The Times* which I reproduce in the summary that follows.

84 Squadron F/O M Hyslop +
DH.9A H66 AC2 E Plummer +
T/o Nasiriyeh armed with bombs one of which exploded as the DH climbed away. This was reported in *The Times* on October 8th, 1921; *"A remarkable flying accident is reported from Nasiriyeh resulting in the death of Flying Officer Maitland Hyslop and Second Air Craftsman Plummer. Mr Hyslop's aeroplane, which was carrying bombs, attained a height of 40ft when one of the bombs exploded. The machine immediately burst into flames and crashed, killing both men instantaneously. Three minutes later the second bomb-carrying aeroplane rose from the same aerodrome and a bomb exploded at an altitude of 100ft, causing a second crash. Flying Officer B E Herbert escaped with a severe concussion and other injuries, while his mechanic got a black eye.*

I [the paper's Basra correspondent whose report was filed to his editor on 5th October] *am informed that the second explosion was not caused by the first. An exhaustive inquiry is now in progress."*

The Casualty Card for Aircraftman Edward Plummer shows his service number as 158676 [block 155001-160000 allocated to RFC/RAF Boys October 1917-December 1918] and his trade as Air Mechanic 2nd Class.

OCTOBER

Saturday 8 October 1921
3 Squadron F/O R M Trevethan MC Safe
DH.9A H3533 O/O WA Thompson Safe
AC1 F R Thornton Safe
T/o Leuchars and on approach to Delny the tail skid struck the top wing of H3515, which was parked [repaired and ended its days in Iraq]. Seconds later the DH was on the ground where its undercarriage collapsed. Flying Officer Richard Michael Trevethan was born on 24th January 1896, and joined the RFC on the last day of March 1917. I suspect he was already a qualified pilot for he reported to Ste Marie Capel on 27th May where he was attached to 20 Squadron [FE.2d], winning the MC [LG 17 September 1917, supplement 30287, page 9585]: *"For conspicuous*

gallantry and devotion to duty when on offensive patrols. He has continuously displayed the greatest dash and determination in attacking enemy formations, regardless of their superiority in numbers, and has shot down at least four, driving others down out of control." At the time of his award, the squadron had been equipped with Bristol F.2b, the first arriving during the previous month and which would stand '20' in good stead until March 1932!

A permanent officer, appointed on the 1st of August 1919, he achieved a total of twelve aerial victories [a table of these combats can be accessed on the Aerodrome website]. A file held at the Imperial War Museum, catalogue No. Document 22390, contains a selection of his private papers spanning the years 1914 through to 1960. Additional details to his very full life can be read on the Military Wikja Organisation website, which the authors acknowledge, showing he was born in Utah on 24th January 1895 [though he always described himself as 'English'] and died in Cornwall on Thursday, 30th December 1971.

Saturday 15 October 1921
31 Squadron F/O R A Vosper Safe
Bristol F.2b E2334
T/o Cawnpore and set a course for Peshawar but *en route* written off in a crash-landing at Agra.

Monday 17 October 1921
1 Squadron *Not reported*
7F.1 Snipe H4883
T/o Hinaidi where it was wrecked whilst landing. Surviving records indicate H4883 was on 3 Squadron's establishment ahead of being issued to 1 Squadron.

Wednesday 26 October 1921
8 Squadron F/O R E Keys DFC Safe
DH.9A F2826 *Not reported* Safe
T/o Baghdad West and crashed out of control while attempting an emergency landing close to the airfield. Within a fortnight of his accident, Flying Officer Ralph Edmund Keys, a permanent officer, resigned his commission, this being reported in *The London Gazette* on 22nd November 1921.

An investigation by Paul McMillan indicates Ralph joined the de Havilland Aircraft Company and died while testing DH.16 G-EALM on the 10th of January 1923. An account of the accident, which happened over Stanmore Common, appeared in the *Hendon & Finchley Times* two days later, part of the newspaper's account reading as follows: *"Mr. Harding, landlord of the Abercorn Arms, Stanmore Hill, where Major Keys had been staying since October last, stated that the pilot was in the hotel less than two hours previous to the accident, leaving there at 2.30 in the afternoon to take up the* [aeroplane] *for experimental purposes. "He was one of the nicest fellows I have known," said Mr. Harding. One informant told the Hendon and Finchley Times that Major Keys had promised to hover over* [a] *friend who was fishing in the Stanmore ponds. Major Keys home is stated near Yarmouth, but his mother is at present siding at Clapham, from whence* [she] *came* [from] *Edgware yesterday morning to identify the body. He was a well-known flying officer, and one of his greatest feats was the bringing down of a Zeppelin off Scarborough at night during the war. He held the DSO [with bar] and the Distinguished Flying Cross. Air Mechanic Arnell, who was identified late on Wednesday night, was the eldest child of Mrs. Arnell, 5 Ingleway, Woodhouse road, North Finchley, a widow, whose husband, Charles Arnell, was killed in France during Armistice week. Arnell, who had lived with this mother in Finchley about six years was 20 years of age. At* [?] *Years of age he joined the Army, but after he had served for three years his mother claimed his discharge. He then obtained position mechanic with the De Havilland Aircraft Works, Kingsbury."*

According to Putnam's *De Havilland Aircraft* compiled by A J Jackson and published in 1962, a total of ten DH.16s were built using DH.9A airframes modified to carry four passengers in the widened central fuselage aft of the pilot's cockpit. A photograph of DH.16 G-EALM may be viewed on the website BAE Systems.

Note. Although not coming within the parameters of this volume as Ralph Edmund Keys died after leaving the service, and was not, as far as I am aware, in any form of military reserve, the newspaper account raises several interesting points. The assertion that he held the DSO and First Bar is incorrect, but he had been *Gazetted* with the DFC, this being reported in supplement 30913, page 11256, of 21st September 1918: *"Capt. [T./Maj.] Egbert Cadbury, DSC, [Pilot], Lieut. [T./Capt.] Robert Leckie, DSO DSC [Observer], Lieut. Ralph Edmund Keys [Pilot] [Sea Patrol]. These officers attacked and destroyed a large enemy airship which recently attempted a raid on the North-East Coast, and also succeeded in damaging a second airship. The services rendered on this occasion were of the greatest value, and the personal risk was very considerable for aeroplanes a long way from land."*

It is mentioned that the mechanic, Leslie Lihou Arnell, killed had once been a boy soldier. An excellent account of these 'boy soldiers' is told by the historian and author Richard van Emden in his book *Boy Soldiers of the Great War - Their Own Stories For The First Time* [Headline, 2005], a copy of which graces the shelves in my library. The paper also reports that Leslie's father was killed during the week of the signing of the Armistice in 1918. A search on the CWGC website quickly identifies him as Lance Corporal Charles George Arnell, aged 38, of the 13th Battalion, Middlesex Regiment, who died on 4th November 1918, and is buried in Villers-Pol Communal Cemetery extension where his headstone is inscribed with the words: *"God Be With You Till We Meet Again."* Thus, the loss of her son, Leslie, must have been a heartbreaking blow for Annie Theresa Arnell of Finchley.

In conclusion, it is a certainty that Ralph Keys did fly over to see his friend fishing on Stanmore ponds and while banking he stalled and spun in, injuring his friend and two others who were with him, their names being reported by the paper as Edward Burnett, Samuel Hawkes and Harry Picken, all being taken to Bushey Heath Cottage Hospital.

NOVEMBER

Monday 14 November 1921

8 Squadron F/O H B Pett MC Safe
DH.9A H116 *Not reported* Safe

T/o Baghdad West and damaged beyond repair during landing at Mosul. The airframe was handed over to 55 Squadron as a source for spares. Flying Officer Henry Basil Pett, a General List officer, was born on 14th February 1888, and came to the RFC on 22nd December 1916. His training completed, he arrived in France on 1st September 1917, and following attachment to No. 2 Aircraft Supply Depot reported on the 17th of the month to 15 Squadron [RE.8] at Longavesnes. From 30th January to 3rd February 1918, he was attached to 11 Squadron [Bristol F.2b] at La Bellevue for temporary duty before returning to 15 Squadron where in April he was made a flight commander and recommended for the MC.

The citation for the award duly appeared in *The London Gazette* on 22nd June 1918, supplement 30761, page 7420: *"For conspicuous gallantry and devotion to duty. He showed great courage and skill while engaged on reconnaissances and contact patrols during operations, flying at very low altitudes under heavy rifle and machine-gun fire. On many occasions he located the enemy's line by deliberately drawing their fire from the ground. On one occasion he made a reconnaissance of a whole corps front in very bad weather, which made it necessary for him to fly at a height of 350 feet. He was continuously under very heavy fire, but completed his reconnaissance and obtained valuable information."*

A short service commission officer, he was transferred to the Reserve on 4th October 1923 [LG 2 October 1923, issue 32867, page 6586] and while in the Reserve he resigned his commission on transfer to the Auxiliary Air Force with an appointment as a flight lieutenant to No. 601[County of London] Bombing Squadron on 6th April 1926 [LG 6 April 1926, issue 33148, page 2436]. Subsequently, he resigned his commission on 8th December 1927, this being promulgated in the *Gazette* on 10th January 1928, issue 33346, page 228.

DECEMBER

Monday 12 December 1921

12 Squadron Lt J W Baker Safe
Bristol F.2b H1568/C6

T/o Bickendorf and merely reported as *"crashed."* For the unfortunate Lieutenant Baker this was his second serious mishap in less than six months, his previous crash being summarised on 9th August 1921.

216 Squadron F/O G W Wilson Injured
DH.10 E9084

T/o Baghdad West presumably to return to Heliopolis but swung and crashed out of control, the accident undoubtedly brought about when Flying Officer Wainwright [see my summary for 15th August 1921] was waving to bystanders while taxying and the tip of one his fingers was caught by one of the propellers.

Saturday 17 December 1921

6 Squadron F/Lt E R Tempest MC DFC + Baghdad [North Gate] War Cemetery
DH.10 E9084 F/O D D'A A Greig DFC Injured See 24 February 1927 - 23 Squadron

T/o Baghdad West for an air test prior to making a mail run to Cairo but swung out of control and crashed. The cause of the accident was the inability of the pilot to connect with the aircraft's rudder bars. A biography of Flight Lieutenant Edmund Roger Tempest can be read on *Wikipedia* which notes his appointment to a permanent commission on 1st August 1919. A table of his 17 combat victories [four shared] while attached to 64 Squadron is also presented. Turning to the *Gazette* and supplement 30989, page 12974, of 2nd November 1918, the citation for his DFC reads: *"Since March last this officer has destroyed nine enemy machines. A daring and most capable officer, who never hesitates to engage the enemy. By brilliant leader-ship he achieves success with minimum loss."* An addendum shows his MC was *Gazetted* on 13th May 1918.

55 Squadron F/O H S P Walmsley MC Safe
DH.9A H163

T/o from the Desht-i-Harir strip and crashed; wrecked. Flying Officer Hugh Sidney Porter Walmsley was granted a permanent commission on the 1st of August 1919 [see Appendix D in Volume 3], his military service having commenced as a private soldier in the Royal North Lancashire Regiment. Following secondment to the RFC and flying training he joined 55 Squadron [DH.4] at Boisdinghem on 17th September 1917, and on 7th June 1918, was appointed a flight commander.

Postwar, and becoming a permanent officer, he spent time as an instructor at No. 1 School of Technical Training for Boys at Halton, before re-joining 55 Squadron, now equipped with DH.9As, at Baghdad West on 11th February 1921.

His service followed very much the pattern for permanent officers with promotion coming at regular intervals and at the time of his retirement as Air Officer Commanding in Chief Flying Trining Command on 1st August 1952, he had received a knighthood.

Air Vice Marshal Sir Hugh Walmsley died on Monday, 2nd September 1895, the citation for his MC being *Gazetted* in supplement 30901, page 11030, of the paper issued on 18th September 1918: *"For conspicuous gallantry and devotion to duty on long-distant bomb raids. In four of these he acted as leader, and displayed great skill and tenacity in getter the better of the enemy. He has carried out twelve raids into the enemy's country, and his work throughout has been consistently of a high order."*

The Air of Authority website shows he received a DFC on 10th October 1922, and was five times mentioned in despatches.

Wednesday 21 December 1921

39 Squadron	F/O C G Halliday	Injured
DH.9A E974	AC2 H R Warry	Safe

T/o Spittlegate and while landing was caught in a severe downdraft and crashed on to the roof a bungalow at Digby. Flying Officer Christopher George Halliday's injuries were not serious. Born on the 6th of April 1899, he joined the RFC on 27th November 1916, and on completion of his training eventually joined 19 Squadron [5F.1 Dolphin] at Ste Marie Capel on 11th February 1918, remaining attached until 29th May 1918, when he returned to the UK.

Note. According to contemporary documents, 39 Squadron at this time was a cadre at Kenley and remained as such until moving to Spittlegate in February 1923, where it received DH.9As. Nevertheless, *The DH.4/DH.9 File* records the loss of E974 as occurring on 21st December 1921, and various websites support his. Furthermore, according to notes on *Wikipedia* Avro 504s were received in May 1921, the decision to bring the squadron up to operational standards having being decided in the April. Consulting the squadron's official website, here it states that DH.9As were received in 1921.

216 Squadron	F/O R S Martin	Safe
DH.10 E7847	F/O J A Rudd	Safe
	AC1 G W Pheby	Safe

T/o Heliopolis and crashed near the airfield after control was lost in a very low altitude turn. Aircraftman Pheby's service number 284343 identifies him as joining the service between July and October 1918, his number coming within the block 275001 - 307973 allocated to civilians joining and transferees from other of the service arms.

APPENDICES
1921

Appendix A - Squadron Losses and Losses by Aircraft Type

Column 1 - Squadron

Column 2 - Aircraft type

Column 3 - Written off

Column 4 - Fatalities

1 Squadron	Sopwith 7.F1 Snipe	3	
2 Squadron	Bristol F.2b	3	
3 Squadron	Airco DH.9A	1	
4 Squadron	Avro 504K	1	1
	Bristol F.2b	1	
6 Squadron	Airco DH.10	1	
	Bristol F.2b 1	1	
	Airco DH.10	1	
8 Squadron	Airco DH.9A	3	
12 Squadron	Bristol F.2b	5	2
14 Squadron	Bristol F.2b	5	1
20 Squadron	Bristol F.2b	2	
25 Squadron	Sopwith 7.F1 Snipe	3	1
27 Squadron	Airco DH.9A	1	
30 Squadron	Airco DH.9A	12	
31 Squadron	Bristol F.2b	1	
39 Squadron	Airco DH.9A	1	
47 Squadron	Airco DH.9A	2	2
55 Squadron	Airco DH.9A	8	
56 Squadron	Sopwith 7.F1 Snipe	1	1
84 Squadron	Airco DH.9A	3	2
100 Squadron	Avro 504K	1	
	Bristol F.2b	4	1
208 Squadron	Bristol F.2b	3	5
210 Squadron	Parnall Panther	1	2
216 Squadron	Airco DH.10	4	2
238 Squadron	Felixstowe F.2A	1	
Totals		73	20

	Airco DH.9A	31	4
	Airco DH.10	6	2
	Avro 504K	2	1
	Bristol F.2b	25	9
	Felixstowe F.2A	1	
	Parnall Panther	1	2
	Sopwith 7.F1 Snipe	7	2
Totals		73	20

Note. Although designed by Geoffrey de Havilland, production of the DH.9A was placed in the hands of the Aircraft Manufacturing Company Limited, Hendon, commonly referred to as "Airco." The same applies to the DH.10.

Appendix B - Squadron Locations and Commanding Officers

As in all previous volumes the table of locations has been compiled from *Squadrons of the Royal Air Force & Commonwealth 1918-1988.* With the situation little changed from December 1920, the Royal Air Force may be described as *"treading water"* while at the same time being tasked to 'policing' huge areas of the Middle East and British India where in the case of British India squadrons were frequently called upon for operations over the North West Frontier.

In respect of air force activities in the Rhineland, only 12 Squadron [Bristol F.2b] at Bickendorf remained with the army of occupation.

The basis for the list of squadron commanding officers comes from the website Air of Authority - A History of RAF Organisation, hosted by Malcolm Barrass whom the authors have great pleasure in acknowledging.

Squadron	Aircraft	Location	Dates	Remarks
1 Squadron	7F.1 Snipe	Hinaidi	01.01.21-31.12.21	Iraq
2 Squadron	Bristol F.1b	Oranmore	01.01.21-31.12.21	Ireland army co-operation duties
3 Squadron	7F.1 Snipe	Bangalore	01.01.21-01.04.21	British India
		Ambala	01.04.21-30.09.21	Disbanded
	DH.9A	Leuchars	01.10.21-31.12.21	Reformed - Fleet Cooperation duties
4 Squadron	Bristol F.2b	Aldergrove & Baldonnel	01.01.21- 01.21	Ireland - A Flight for security duties
		Farnborough	01.01.21-31.12.21	UK army co-operation squadron
5 Squadron	Bristol F.2b	Quetta	01.01.21-31.12.21	British India
6 Squadron	Bristol F.2b	Baghdad West	01.01.21-31.12.21	Iraq
8 Squadron	DH.9A	Suez	01.01.21-23.02.21	Egypt
		Basra	23.02.21-04.03.21	Iraq
		Baghdad West	04.03.21-29.12.21	Iraq
		Hinaidi	29.12.21-31.12.21	Iraq
12 Squadron	Bristol F.2b	Bickendorf	01.01.21-31.12.21	Germany
14 Squadron	Bristol F.2b	Ramleh & Amman	01.01.21-31.12.21	Palestine & Transjordan patrol duties
20 Squadron	Bristol F.2b	Tank	01.01.21-11.04.21	British India
		Parachinar	11.04.21-17.10.21	British India
		Ambala	17.10.21-31.12.21	British India
24 Squadron	Bristol F.2b	Kenley	01.01.21-31.12.21	UK communications & training
25 Squadron	7F.1 Snipe	Hawkinge	01.01.21-31.12.21	UK fighter squadron
27 Squadron	DH.9A	Risalpur	01.01.21-31.12.21	British India
28 Squadron	Bristol F.2b	Ambala	01.01.21-15.10.21	British India
		Kohat	15.10.21-31.12.21	British India
30 Squadron	DH.9A	Baghdad	01.01.21-31.12.21	Iraq
31 Squadron	Bristol F.2b	Cawnpore	01.01.21-19.10.21	British India
		Peshawar	19.10.21-31.12.21	British India
39 Squadron		Kenley	01.01.21-31.12.21	UK remaining as a cadre
45 Squadron	Vimy	Helwan	01,04.21-31.12.21	Egypt reformed
47 Squadron	DH.9/DH.9A	Helwan	01.01.21-31.12.21	Egypt army co-operation duties
55 Squadron	DH.9A	Baghdad West	01.01.21-20.03.21	Iraq
		Mosul	20.03.21-31.12.21	Iraq
56 Squadron	7F.1 Snipe	Aboukir	01.01.21-31.01.21	Egypt fighter squadron
60 Squadron	DH.10A	Risalpur	01.01.21-31.12.21	British India
70 Squadron	Vimy	Heliopolis	01.01.21-31.12.21	Egypt bomber transport squadron
84 Squadron	DH.9A	Shaibah	01.01.21-31.12.21	Iraq
100 Squadron	Bristol F.2b	Baldonnel	01.01.21-31.12.21	Ireland army co-operation duties
202 Squadron	Short 184	Alexandria	01.01.21-16.05.21	Egypt naval co-operation - disbanded
203 Squadron	F.1 Camel	Leuchars	01.01.21-31.12.21	UK Fleet fighter squadron
205 Squadron	Panther	Leuchars	01.01.21-31.12.21	UK Fleet reconnaissance squadron
207 Squadron	DH.9A	Bircham Newton	01.01.21-31.12.21	UK day bomber squadron
208 Squadron	Bristol F.2b	Ismailia	01.01.21-31.12.21	Egypt army co-operation duties
210 Squadron	T.1 Cuckoo	Gosport	01.01.21-31.12.21	UK torpedo bomber duties
216 Squadron	HP O/400 & DH.10	Abu Sueir	01.02.21-15.04.21	Egypt bomber transport duties
		Helipolis	15.04.21-31.12.21	Egypt
238 Squadron	Felixstowe F.21	Cattewater	01.01.21-31.12.21	Great Britain
267 Squadron	Short 184/F.2a/F.3/Fairey IIIC & D	Calafrana	01.01.21-31.12.21	Malta

Squadron	Commanding Officer	Date	Subsequent career
1 Squadron	Squadron Leader J B Graham MC AFC	In situ	G/Capt retirement 01.07.39 Recalled G/Capt retirement 08.12.44
2 Squadron	Squadron Leader A J Butler MC	In situ	W/Cdr retirement 28.10.37 Recalled W/Cdr retirement 23.05.46
3 Squadron	Squadron Leader G G A Williams	In situ	S/Ldr retirement 10.08.33
	Squadron Leader D G Donald	01.10.21	AM retirement 24.05.47
4 Squadron	Squadron Leader C H B Blount	In situ	AV-M killed in air crash 23.10.40
5 Squadron	Squadron Leader P C Maltby	In situ	AV-M retirement 02.10.46
6 Squadron	Squadron Leader E A B Rice MC	In situ	AV-M retirement 01.03.461
8 Squadron	Squadron Leader D L Allen AFC	In situ	W/Cdr retirement 26.09.33
12 Squadron	Squadron Leader R E Saul DFC	In situ	AV-M retirement 29.06.44
	Squadron Leader H J F Hunter MC	01.03.21	A/Cmdr retirement 15.06.39
14 Squadron	Squadron Leader W L Welsh DSC AFC mid	In situ	AM retirement 01.12.44
	Squadron Leader J S T Bradley OBE	01.12.21	AM retirement 27.10.45
20 Squadron	Squadron Leader J H S Tyssen MC	In situ	AV-M retirement 21.02.42
24 Squadron	Squadron Leader E H Johnston OBE	In situ	W/Cdr retirement 01.10.32
25 Squadron	Squadron Leader Sir N A R D Leslie CBE	In situ	W/Cdr retirement 25.07.29
27 Squadron	Squadron Leader R J Mounsey OBE	In situ	G/Capt died 18.06.39 natural causes
28 Squadron	Squadron Leader R J F Barton OBE	In situ	G/Capt retirement 01.01.31
30 Squadron	Squadron Leader R Collishaw DSO* OBE DSC DFC three times mid	In situ	AV-M retirement 29.10.43

31 Squadron	Squadron Leader A L Neale MC	In situ	F/Lt resigned 25.03.25
	Squadron Leader A T Harris AFC	26.01.21	MRAF retirement 15.09.45
39 Squadron	Squadron Leader T S Impey	01.04.21	S/Ldr relinquished 11.11.26
45 Squadron	Squadron Leader E M Murray DSO MC	02.04.21	G/Capt retirement 31.07.33
47 Squadron	Squadron Leader K C Buss	In situ	A/Cmdr retirement 03.11.40 Recalled A/Cmdr retirement 21.01.46
55 Squadron	Squadron Leader C H Nicholas AFC	In situ	A/Cmdr retirement 12.11.44
	Squadron Leader V Gaskell-Blackburn DSO AFC	26.01.21	G/Capt retirement 21.08.41
56 Squadron	Squadron Leader P Babington MC AFC twice mid	In situ	AM retirement 01.12.45
	Squadron Leader G C A William	01.11.21	S/Ldr retirement 10.08.33
60 Squadron	Squadron Leader P C Sherren MC Canada	In situ	W/Cdr killed 10.09.37 See Volume 3 page 188 for details
70 Squadron	Squadron Leader S W Smith OBE	In situ	A/Cmdr retirement 21.09.41
84 Squadron	Squadron Leader B L Huskisson DSC	In situ	W/Cdr relinquished 01.09.38
	Squadron Leader W Sowery AFC	01.10.21	A/Cmdr retirement 21.09.42
100 Squadron	Squadron Leader J V Steel	In situ	W/Cdr retirement 03.03.39
	Squadron Leader F Sowery DSO MC AFC	19.02.21	G/Capt retirement 26.05.40
202 Squadron	Squadron Leader P A Shepherd	In situ	W/Cdr retirement 24.02.39
203 Squadron	Flight Lieutenant J S T Fall DSC AFC	15.03.21	G/Capt retirement 11.03.45
	Flight Lieutenant L H Slatter OBE DSC* DFC	01.10.21	AM retirement 01.02.49
205 Squadron	Squadron Leader R M Bayley DFC	In situ	G/Capt died 11.09.32 natural causes
207 Squadron	Squadron Leader A W Tedder	In situ	MRAF retirement 30.05.51
208 Squadron	Squadron Leader W J Y Guilfoyle OBE MC	In situ	A/Cmdr retirement 21.09.41
210 Squadron	Wing Commander N J Gill OBE MC	In situ	A/Cmdr retirement 01.01.37
216 Squadron	Squadron Leader M Henderson DSO	In situ	AV-M retirement 29.04.45
238 Squadron	Squadron Leader G F Breese DSC mid	In situ	S/Ldr retirement 18.02.31
267 Squadron	Squadron Leader W G Sitwell*DSC	In situ	W/Cdr retired list 25.05.27
	Squadron P A Shepherd	16.05.21	See 202 Squadron

* Paul McMillan reports that when placed on the Retired List on account of ill health, Wing Commander William George Sitwell DSC was a very sick gentleman and within two months of leaving the service he died at RAF Halton Hospital in Buckinghamshire on Thursday, 21st July 1927.

During the morning of 22nd November 2011, Bonham's of New Bond Street, London, sold an extensive collection of Wing Commander Sitwell's papers, including his 'Pilot's Flying Log Book' covering the period 13th May 1913, when he commenced flight training, and 26th March 1919, plus a photograph album and a large collection of negatives. The pre-sale catalogue makes reference to the types of aircraft that he flew and quite extensive notes on his numerous operational flights, included a night search in May 1915 over London for a Zeppelin. By February 1916, he was stationed at Ismailia, briefly, before more operational flying from Mudros.

Back in the UK by the spring of 1917, he spent the rest of the *Great War* engaged in anti-submarine patrols over the North Sea and test flying.

Annex

Captain Edward Arthur Beckton Rice was *Gazetted* with the MC on 18th July 1917 [DH.4] for his services whilst attached to 55 Squadron as a flight commander. In the early afternoon of 10th May 1917 along with his observer 2nd Lieutenant A Clarke and flying DH.4 A2145 they engaged and sent down an enemy scout machine out of control in the vicinity of Le Cateau [Nord] some 26km ESE of Cambrai.

Major Richard Ernest Saul was *Gazetted* with the DFC, less citation, on 1st January 1919, supplement 31098, page 96. At the time of his award he had recently ceased to command 93 Squadron [Sopwith 7F.1 Dolphin] which disbanded at Port Meadow on 21st November 1918 without becoming operational. I suspect, therefore, his honour was in recognition of his services on the Western Front where he had served with 16 Squadron as an observer, later as a flight commander with 10 Squadron and from 2nd December 1917 to at least March 1918 commanding 4 Squadron; briefly, he had been attached from 24th April to 4th May 1918 as a supernumerary attached to 92 Squadron.

Captain Henry John Francis Hunter attached to 34 Squadron [BE.2c] a corps reconnaissance squadron based at Allonville was *Gazetted* with the MC on 20th October 1916, supplement 29793, page 10183: *"For conspicuous gallantry and skill. He has done fine work for the artillery, and has accounted for many enemy guns. On one occasion, when a heavy storm drove all other machines back to their aerodromes, and the enemy guns took the opportunity to become active, he remained up and did fine work."* Shortly before the official publication of his award, he had been appointed Flight Commander within the squadron.

Flight Commander William Lawrie Welsh RNAS was mentioned in despatches on 12th May 1917, supplement 30066, page 4627. This may have been in recognition of his work either as a seaplane pilot based at Dover, or while a flight commander at the Dunkirk Seaplane Station. His DSC, as yet untraced, was promulgated in the *Gazette* on 26th April 1918. His AFC, gained with 216 Squadron [HP O/400 and DH.10], was *Gazetted* in the Edinburg edition on July 16th, issue 13615, page 1666.

Captain [Acting Lieutenant-Colonel] John Stanley Travers Bradley [MGC] was appointed OBE in The King's Birthday Honours list, 3rd June 1919, and promulgated in the Edinburgh edition on 3rd June 1919, issue 13458, page 2043.

Lieutenant [temporary Captain] John Hugh Samuel Tyssen's MC was *Gazetted* 14th November 1916, supplement 29824, page 11069: *"For conspicuous skill and gallantry. He has done fine work in photography, often fighting against odds to get his work done. On one occasion, when five enemy machines interfered with our patrol, he, with another officer, dived at one and brought it down."* At the time he was serving with 22 Squadron engaged on reconnaissance work and equipped with FE.2b.

Flight Lieutenant Raymond Collishaw serving with 10 Squadron RNAS was *Gazetted* with the DSC on 20th July 1917, supplement 30194, page 7426: *"In recognition of his services on various occasions, especially the following:*

"One June 1st, 1917, this officer shot down an Albatross scout in flames.

"On 3rd June 1917, he shot down an Albatross scout in flames.

"On 5th June 1917, he shot down a two-seater Albatross in flames.

"On the 6th June 1917, he shot down two Albatross scouts in flames and killed the pilot in a third.

"He has displayed great gallantry and skill in all his combats.

The citation for his DSSO, *Gazetted* 11th August 1917, supplement 30227, page 8206 reads: *"For conspicuous bravery and skill in successfully leading attacks against hostile aircraft. Since the 10th June 1917, Flt. Lieut. Collishaw has himself brought down four machines completely out of control and driven down two others with their planes shot away.*

"Whilst on an offensive patrol on the morning of 15th June 1917, he forced down a hostile scout in a nose dive. Later, on the same day, he drove down one hostile two-seater machine completely out of control, one hostile scout in a spin, and a third machine with two of its planes shot away.

"On 24th June1917, he engaged four enemy scouts, driving one down in a spin and another with two of its planes shot away; the latter machine was seen to crash."

In a supplement to the Edinburgh edition of August 7th, 1918, issue 13300, page 2813, his DFC was promulgated: *"This officer is an exceptionally capable and efficient squadron commander, under whose leadership the squadron has maintained a high place in the ArmyWing. He has carried out numerous solo patrols and led many offensive patrols, on all occasions engaging the enemy with great bravery and fearlessness. Up to date he has accounted for forty-seven enemy machines, twenty-two in the last twelve months."*

The First Bar to his DSO was *Gazetted* on 21st September 1918, supplement 30913, page 11247: *A brilliant squadron leader of exceptional daring, who has destroyed fifty-one enemy machines. Early one morning he, with another pilot, attacked an enemy aerodrome. Seeing three machines brought out of a burning hangar he dived five times, firing bursts at these from a very low altitude, and dropped bombs on the living quarters. He then saw an enemy aeroplane descending over the aerodrome; he attacked it and drove it down in flames. Later, when returning from a reconnaissance of the damaged hangars, he was attacked by three Albatross scouts, who pursued him to our lines, when he turned and attacked one, which fell out of control and crashed."*

The Edinburgh paper also notified his appointment of the OBE for his service in South Russia, 16th July 1920, issue 13615, page 1665. After leaving 10 Squadron RNAS in July 1917, Raymond went back to Canada for three months leave. On his return and prior to the merger of the two air services he commanded 13 Squadron RNAS [briefly] followed by 3 Squadron RNAS which on 1st April 1918 became 203 Squadron which he commanded until returning to the UK on 21st October 1918.

For a table listing his sixty combat success, I direction your attention to the excellent Aerodrome website. During his tenure of command of 203 Squadron his personal aircraft was F.1 Camel D3417 in which he accounted for twenty-one enemy aircraft between 11th June and 26th September 1918 and which was still on establishment with '203' in January 1919.

Squadron Leader Arthur Travers Harris was *Gazetted* with the Air Force Cross on 2nd November 1918, supplement 30989, page 12958. In February 1942, he arrived at High Wycombe, Headquarters of Bomber Command, to assume the duties of Air Officer Commanding-in-Chief, Bomber Command, a post that he would hold for the remainder of the war.

Temporary Major Philip Babbington took over 46 Squadron [Nieuport 12] at Wyton on the 1st of June 1916 by which time he had already been mentioned twice in despatches for his work on the Western Front and was honoured with the MC on the 3rd [LG 3 June 1916, supplement 29608, page 5571].

Flight Lieutenant Leonard Horatio Slatter was *Gazetted* with the DSC on November 20th, 1917, issue 13168, page 2378 of the Edinburgh edition. The citation reads as follows: *"For conspicuous gallantry and skill on many occasions both as observer and pilot. He has taken part in numerous night bombing raids, and on one occasion he ascended at night for the purpose of attacking hostile machines, notwithstanding the fact that he had only returned a few hours previously from a successful action with hostile aircraft in superior numbers.*

"On the 4th September 1917, he attacked an enemy Torpedo Boat Destroyer with machine gun fire."

A First Bar to his DSC was *Gazetted* in the London paper, supplement 30687, page 5856: *"For distinguished service rendered during a bombing attack on Ostende Seaplane Station on 26th March 1918, when, in spite of intense anti-aircraft fire and the glare of numerous searchlights, he descended to 400 feet over his objective to drop bombs.*

"Flt. Cdr. Slatter is a leader of unqualified keenness and dash and possessed of exceptional courage and judgement."

The award of a Distinguished Flying Cross, less citation, was promulgated in the Edinburgh paper on January 6th, 1919, issue 13378, page 76.

As Captain William James Yule Guilfoyle he was *Gazetted* with the MC on 3rd March 1917, supplement 29968, page 2193: *"For conspicuous gallantry in action. He carried out a daring bombing raid and made a valuable reconnaissance under heavy fire during the same flight. He has at all times set a fine example."* I strongly suspect at the time he was attached to the Australian Flying Corps with which he served from 27th October 1916 to 11th August 1917. During this time, he was a flight commander with 1 Squadron and from January 1917, 3 Squadron.

Wing Commander Napier John Gill's MC was promulgated in the New Year's Honours List for 1917 and appeared in the Edinburgh edition, issue 13033 page 34 of January 1st, 1917.

Squadron Leader Malcolm Henderson won his DSO under the most hazardous circumstances when he was Temporary Lieutenant attached to the Royal Flying Corps, the citation published in the *Edinburgh Gazette* April 3rd, 1916, issue 12923, page 642: *"For conspicuous gallantry when, on photographic reconnaissance, his machine was struck by a shell from an enemy anti-aircraft gun. The shell passed through the nacelle of the machine, and took off his left leg just below the knee. In spite of this he succeeded in coming down from 7,000 feet, and landing 3,000 yards behind our lines, thus saving his aeroplane and the life of the Observer."*

Referring to Trevor Henshaw's *The Sky Their Battlefield* the author records, on page 32, that this dramatic incident occurred on 20th February 1916, when Lieutenant Henderson and 2nd Lieutenant O J F Scholte were airborne in 18 Squadron Vickers FB.5 5476. After forced-landing *"Scholte got Henderson clear, needing to sever trapped leg with knife."*

Admitted to 1 Field Ambulance, Malcolm Henderson remained in their care until he was considered fit enough to be transferred for further treatment in the UK, this being effected on 15th March 1916, by way of HMHS *Brighton*.. According to his biography on the Air of Authority website, he was back with 18 Squadron by April 1st, 1916, for duties as flight commander.

Paul McMillan reports the following concerning Squadron Leader George Fred Breese: *"... born 5th September 1886, and entered the RNAS, qualifying as a pilot, Royal Aero Club's pilots certificate 1003, on 19th December 1914. During the war he saw service in Dunkirk, long distance patrols and submarine searching. He was promoted flight commander in December 1916, squadron commander in December 1917, and, on the foundation of the Royal Air Force in April 1918, Squadron Leader Breese commanded 238 Squadron at Cattewater. Retired on 18th February 1931, having seen service with the Iraq Command based at Basrah from 30th October 1923.*

"On the formation of the Observer Corps he joined it, and in 1938, he was the Observer Group Officer of No. 36 Group, Scottish Area. For his services with the Royal Observer Corp [George Fred] *Breese was recommended for the MBE, but it came to nothing. The recommendation states" "this officer was the original Observer Group Officer in the Scottish Area. He has always shown exceptional devotion to duty. His tact, enthusiasm and attention to detail has brought the standard of No. 36 Group up to a very high level. The whole spirit and efficiency of the Group is of a very high order."*

His DSC was *Gazetted* on the 1st October 1917, for his work in the Orkney Islands area: *"For services on patrol duties and submarine searching in home waters."* A mention in despatches, *Gazetted* on New Year's Day, 1919, amplified this: *"For distinguished service in the Orkneys war area."*

Appendix C - Officers Granted Short Service Commissions

The majority of the officers reported in this appendix had served in the *Great War* and, therefore, were experienced in flying duties. The remarks in the final column are, in the main, self-explanatory. Perhaps the most intriguing is the term "Removed" which is often followed by *"... from the RAF, His Majesty having no further use for his services."* I believe there were a number of reasons for such an humiliating termination of an officers' service; conviction by the civil powers for a very serious misdemeanour being one

It will be noted there are numerous references to commissions being relinquished on 10th February 1954. Such entries refer to the Navy, Army and Air Force Reserves Act of this date.

Names recorded without a central heading may be regarded as pilot officers under probation [the ten probationary officers *Gazetted* on 28th January 1921 may have been the first to join the Royal Air Force without any previous military service]. An attempt has been made by the authors to establish the officers service numbers, though as will be evident there are many omissions. Referring to issues made in 1920, the sequence of issues appear not to be in any logical order though by the start of 1921 a semblance of pattern appears to have established within the 091.. block. There are, however, numerous examples of duplication between the service numbers issued to Royal Air Force personnel and other arms of the military, the 15000 block [issues commencing circa April 1921] being a particularly good example where a *Gazette* search will frequently identify army officers issued with the same number as their Royal Air Force counterpart, an example being 15013 issued to Edgar Morrison Milling, short service commissioned on 12th April 1921, and Gerald Arthur Eastwood of the Regular Army promoted lieutenant-colonel on 29th September 1944. The same number was also issued to Private D McClure of the King's Own Scottish Borders, his name appearing in the *Gazette* during 1917.

Information attached to many of the entries has been gleaned from various sources, all of which are acknowledged in the 'Sources' section; *The London Gazette* being a primary example. The Officer's Casualty Forms Of the Royal Flying Corps & Royal Air Force have also provided much useful information, as has numerous press reports of fatal flying accidents [of which there were many throughout the 1920s]; I have copied many of these in full as they make not only fascinating reading but illustrate the gulf in the depth of reporting of yesteryear compared with today.

In parallel with press reporting, the Aviation Safety Network website has provided additional detail thus helping to explain the reason behind many of the flying accidents.

Deaths on squadrons post 31st December 1930 will be summarised in Volume 5, the exception being those that occurred on active service of which there were four in the Second World War where a description of the circumstances has been noted.

To facilitate the flying training of pilots entering the service a small number of flying training schools were set up, and by 1921, the following had been established. Formerly known as the Netheravon Flying School, No. 1 Flying Training School formed on 23rd December 1919, and was equipped, mainly, with variants of the Avro 504, though more advanced types were also employed as the pupil became more proficient in his flying skills.

On 26th April 1920, four more schools were added; in Cambridgeshire, No. 2 Flying Training School formed at Duxford; at Scopwick [subsequently re-named Digby to avoid confusion with Shotwick], Lincolnshire No. 3 Flying Training School came into being and at Shotwick in Flintshire No. 5 Fling Training School opened. Lastly, 6 Flying Training School formed at Spittlegate, near Grantham, the latter transferring to Manston in Kent on 21st September 1920.

During the year No. 4 Flying Training School opened in Egypt at Abu Sueir equipped with Bristol F.2b, DH.9A and Avro 504K, all three types assigned to A Flight, while B Flight was exclusively Avro 504K.

Apart from the school at Scopwick which appears to have received Bristol F.2b types, it was variants of the ubiquitous Avro 504 that would stand them in good stead throughout the decade and beyond, though all schools were issued with more advanced types as the trainee pilot became more proficient in his flying abilities.

Returning to the subject of service numbers, here it will be useful to show the blocks issued to officers granted short service commissions between 1920 and 1930:

09181 - 09259	January 1921 - March 1921
15001 - 15250	April 1921 - June 1922
17001 - 17250	July 1922 - July 1923
18001 - 18259	July 1923 - July 1924
19001 - 19250	July 1924 - July 1925
22001 - 22250	July 1925 - July 1926
24001 - 24256	July 1926 - March 1928
27001 - 27261	March 1928 - March 1929
28001 - 29197	March 1929 - December 1930

LG 7 January 1921, issue 32185, page 185 - Various dates of seniority

FLYIMG OFFICERS
6

09181 de FONTENAY Phillipe André F/Lt 23.12.26 Cashiered

By sentence of General Court Martial [LG 4 January 1927, issue 33236, page 44]. Formerly a flight cadet, Phillipe André de Fontenay was commissioned to the General List as a temporary 2nd Lieutenant on 1st February 1917 [LG 23rd February 1917, issue 29958, page 1887]. It appears that he was transferred to class C of the reserve on 18th December 1924, and ceased to be employed with the regular air force on 7th September 1926. Paul McMillan, co-author, reports that the *Westminster Gazette* published on Thursday, 11th November 1926, reported on the proceedings of the Court Martial held at RAF Duxford concerning charges brought against five officers charged with irregularities over their mess bills and in the case of Flight

Lieutenant de Fontenay he faced three serious charges for fraudulently misapplying three sums, albeit small, belonging to the officers' mess. A document for the aforesaid officer is held by TNA Kew under AIR 76/130/58.

It is further established that de Fontenay, who was born in Mauritius on 30th November 1897 joined the RFC on 10th January 1917 and between June and September he was attached to two squadrons, initially with 40 Squadron [Nieuport 17] and next 29 Squadron, also equipped with Nieuport 17. He spent two spells in hospital undergoing treatment for scabies, the first in 25 General Hospital and the second in 50 Casualty Clearing Station. He served during the Second World War in a flying capacity, possibly with the Free French Air Force.

	HARRINGTON	Hubert Bernard Delma	F/O	+	06.01.22	60 Squadron

Formerly of the 19th London Regiment, Hubert Bernard Delma Harrington, born 25th August 1896 was accepted by the RFC on 22nd September 1916. His early service, presumably on the Western Front, appears devoid of any squadron service and he returned to the UK on 6th August 1917, I suspect to train as a pilot. Returning to France on the 7th of January 1918, he joined 65 Squadron [F.1 Camel] at Bailleul.

07146	HEWITT	Edward Norman	F/O		12.12.26	Relinquished

Formerly a 2nd Lieutenant with the 20th Battalion, Lancashire Fusiliers, Edward Norman Hewitt transferred to the RFC on 23rd January 1915 but it was 21st December 1917 before he joined 9 Squadron [RE.8] at Proven. His date of birth is given as 1st October 1894.

09184	SAWARD	Norman Cuthbert	G/Capt		26.05.46	Retirement

Prior to his transfer to the RFC, Norman Cuthbert Saward had served with the Royal Field Artillery. Joining 70 Squadron [Sopwith 1½ Strutter] on 25th March 1917 at Vert Galand he was shot down and made a prisoner of war on 9th September 1917. Consulting *The Sky Their Battlefield* Trevor Henshaw records on page 115 that he took off [Poperinghe] at 1645 for an operational patrol with three fellow pilots and circa 1800 the patrol came under attack from ten hostile aircraft, one of which shot through Saward's carburettor and fuel tank causing the engine of his F.1 Camel B3928 [the squadron had converted to Camels in July 1917] to 'cut' out at 11,500 feet. Gliding down he forced-landed behind the lines at Roulers. It is believed Lieutenant Saward was wounded. Turning to Air-Britain's *The Camel File* this shows the Camel was delivered to 70 Squadron on 24th August 1917 and in the action that led to it being shot down accounted for an enemy two-seater, shared with Captain Clive Franklyn Collett MC flying B2341, at 1705, while Gheluvelt-Houthulst is given as the crash location at 1800, his assailant being *Leutnant* K Hammes of *Jasta 35*.

During his incarceration Lieutenant Saward frequently disrupted the routine of his captors, so much so that on 16th December 1919 *The London Gazette* in its Sixth Supplement, 31691, page 15613, published the following: *"His Majesty the KING has been pleased to approve of recognition being accorded, as indicated, below, to Officers and other ranks of the Royal Air Force, for gallantry whilst Prisoners of War in escaping, or attempting to escape from captivity, or for valuable services rendered in the Prison Camps of the Enemy."* Lieutenant Saward's name appearing on page 15614. Two websites of interest refer to his time as a prisoner. First, the Holme Pierrepont and Gamston website, which the authors acknowledge, contains the following: *"The eldest of three children of Rev William Thomas and Violet Georgina Saward, Norman Cuthbert Saward was born 14th July 1898 in London and baptised in St. Lawrence, Kent on 4th August 1898.*

"An article in the Nottingham Post dated 27th September 1917 states that Lieut. Norman Cuthbert Saward was reported missing. The young officer was educated at Nottingham High School and trained for his commission under Capt. Trotman with the University College OTC. Gazetted to the RFA he subsequently transferred to the RFC and had been fighting in France for the last 5 months.

"In 1918 Reverend W T Saward made a request for an enquiry into the welfare of his son following an attempt to escape from Schweidnitz POW camp in Eastern Germany. He was subsequently repatriated on 6th January 1919.

"In 1924 he flew one of two aeroplanes purchased by the Afghan government to Kabul and was accorded an audience with his Majesty the Amir where he was decorated with the Order of Izzatt first class. It was reported that although only 24 years old he had had remarkable experiences in connection with flying with the RAF in particular during the war and had been on the Indian North-West frontier for sometime.

"In June 1928 he sailed from Bombay to Plymouth aboard the Macedonia. He continued service through the 2nd World War and was mentioned in the Gazette several times. He married Valeria and their son George Alexandra Douglas was christened at St. Edmund's Church on 25th September 1935. Norman Cuthbert Saward died in December 1970in Maidstone in Kent." Two photographs are attached; one captioned 'Officers and Cadets of the OTC Nottingham' and the other 'The British Orchestra Schweidnitz POW Camp.'

The second website in which he is mentioned, along with photographs, is the Radcliffe on Trent and the First World War which expands on Norman's escape attempt from Schweidnitz, though it is not certain if he actually got out of the camp, or remained behind. According to a letter written by Tarn Hacker: *"... the tunnel was made by excavating with metal spoons, putting soil into mugs - tied with string which was shuttled back and forth. Only one man could work in the tunnel at one time."* It seems twenty-four officers got away; three were killed were killed on recapture after crossing into Austria with neutral Switzerland as there aim and the nineteen survivors were all faced court martial on their return to Schweidnitz. They had eluded capture for three weeks.

In conclusion, a note on New Zealander, Captain Clive Franklyn Collett MC. Wounded in action on 9th September 1917, and returned to the UK, he was attached to 73 Squadron at Lilbourne in Warwickshire working up F.1 Camels in readiness for operations on the Western Front. For reasons I am unable to explain Captain Collett MC* was test-flying a captured German Albatross fighter over the First of Forth when it suddenly dived and crashed in the water. hIs body was recovered and buried in Edinburgh [Comely Bank] Cemetery, his headstone being inscribed *The Lord Hath Called Him To Peace."* I strongly suspect at the time of his death he was no longer on the strength of 73 Squadron ass no unit detail has been appended.

01985	STEPHENSON DFC	Richard	F/O		12.11.21	Cashiered

By sentence of General Court Martial. Formerly of the Cheshire Regiment his DFC was *Gazetted* for his services in France with 5 Squadron [RE.8], December 5th, 1918, issue 13363, page 4477 of the Edinburgh paper: *"During recent operations this officer has been conspicuous for courage, skill and perseverance, markedly on 4th September, when he carried out a special reconnaissance to ascertain the exact locality of the enemy's position, which information was urgently required; flying at two hundred feet, was subjected to heavy fire, but with fine courage and determination he completed the reconnaissance, rendering a most valuable and accurate report of the situation."*

	TATTAM	Francis Frederick	Lieutenant		06.12.22	Relinquished

On account of ill-health contracted on active service [LG 5 December 1922, issue 32774, page 8616]. I am reasonably certain that he returned to service and received a commission as a pilot officer in the Administrative and Special Duties Branch on 11th October 1939 [LG 27 October 1939, issue 34718, page 7184]] his new identity being 75318. S/Ldr 10.02.54 Relinquished

	LUSH	Eric Raven	P/O	+	19.08.21	2 FTS Duxford

Pilot Officer Eric Raven Lush and Pilot Officer Edward Arthur Rush died when their Bristol F.2b H1419 lost engine power and following loss of control spun and crashed at Croxton on the north side of Thetford, Norfolk. The Bristol had departed Duxford for a cross-country to Bircham Newton and return. *Flight* in its issue of August 25th, 1921, reported that the exercise should have only taken around thirty minutes, whereas they were in the air for over three hours and an examination of the wreckage revealed they had used up all their petrol. It is believed the Bristol was flying downwind when the engine failed and in attempting to turn into wind for a forced landing it stalled. A verdict of "Accidental death" was returned. This accident is also noted on page 287 of my third volume and the entry for Pilot Officer Rush whom, I suspect, was one of the earliest officers to be granted a commission without any previous military service. Pilot Officer Rush had seen a few weeks of war service and had been accepted on 18th October 1918 for training as an observer while attached to the 2nd Army Signals School RE. He returned to Home Establishment four days later.

LG 14 January 1921, issue 32193, page 376 - Various dates of seniority

FLIGHT LIEUTENANT [from SQUADRON LEADER]

09186	WYNNE-EYTON DSO	Charles Sandford	W/Cdr	+	14.11.44	144 Maintenance Unit

Charles Sandford Wynne-Eyton transferred from the Royal Artillery to the RFC circa July 1915 and by the 9th of November of that year was at Chocques flying BE.2s with 10 Squadron. Then, on 31st December 1915 he was posted to 2 Squadron [BE.2] at Hesdigneu for flight commander duties which for eight days in April 1916 was elevated to command of the squadron. Returning to the UK on 10th May 1916, he received his first mentioned in despatches, *Gazetted* on 15th June 1916.

A broad 'brush-stroke' account of his life, which shows hie was born at Mold in Flintshire on 22nd October 1889, may be read on the British Modern Military History Society website with the title'The Wynne-Eytons & The Letcombe Lion' [which the authors are delighted to acknowledge], this noting that while attached to 127 Battery, Royal Field Artillery, he was badly gassed near Ypres on 24th May 1915 which resulted in a recovery period lasting for three months.

Leaving the service in 1927 he went out to Rhodesia to become a tobacco planter, a profession he shared by becoming a flying instructor with the newly formed Salisbury Light Plain Club. A spell with Wilson Airways in Nairobi followed before his attempt to emulate Charles Lindberg's east to west solo crossing of the Atlantic, an attempt that came close to ending his life when the DH Puss Moth in which he hoped to make the crossing crashed on take off from St. John's [Newfoundland] and burst into flames.

On recovering from his severe injuries he returned to Kenya from where in 1940 he rejoined the service and by late 1940 he was at Heliopolis attached to 267 Squadron [reformed here on 19th August 1940] which, eventually, he commanded. In July 1942 he proceeded to Asmara in Eritrea to command 163 Squadron [Hudson] but soon returned to '267' before being posted in February 1943 to HQ RAF Middle East.

Wing Commander Charles Sandford 'Sandy' Wynne-Eyton DSO AFC four times mentioned in despatches, was killed during a flight from Algiers to Paris in Liberator II AL584 coming down near Atun [Saône-et-Loire], France. He is buried along with other Royal Air Force members of the crew and passengers in Choloy War Cemetery.

There are many other details of interest, principally concerning his marriage, on the website which has been compiled from an article kindly supplied by Trevor Hancock, a local historian at Letcombe Regis near Wantage in Oxfordshire.

FLYING OFFICERS
2

09188 GOGARTY Alfred James F/O 06.07.21 Resigned

Two Army Form B.103 have 'survived' for Alfred James Gogarty, the first showing he was attached to 9 Squadron [BE.2e] at Morlandcourt on 26th January 1917. Much involved in operational flying, he was wounded in the foot during an early morning patrol with his observer, Lieutenant E Thornton, on 28th April 1917 when their BE.2e A2916 was hit by ground fire near Bois Lateau, Trevor Henshaw noting on page 84 of *The Sky Their Battlefield*: *"2Lt Gogarty had led six BE.2s of 9 Squadron on a bombing raid on Busigny Station four days earlier, on the 24th, from which only three aircraft had returned. He may have been dropping a message over the lines when he was wounded, enquiring about the fate of the three crews the unit had lost in that raid."* Using the same source, page 82 indicates BE.2e 7195, A2937 and A2941 flown respectively by Lieutenant G E Hicks taken prisoner, while 2nd Lieutenant F A Matthews and Lieutenant C L Graves were killed.

On the 1st of May 1917 he returned to duty only to be wounded for a second time [details not known] and this time he was evacuated to England aboard HMHS *Panama*.

The second form opens on 14th June 1919 when he embarked at Marseilles on HMT *Valdivia* and stepping ashore at Alexandria five days later. Assigned for flying training duties he was demobilised at Kantana on 25th March 1920, embarking on 5th April 1920 at Alexandria on the SS *Kursk*.

09189 MARTIN Reginald Stanhope F/Lt 03.01.31 Relinquished

Granted a commission in class C of the Reserve of Air Force Officers 1st June 1937 [LG 15 June 1937, issue 34408, page 3861]. Served throughout the Second World War until: S/Ldr 10.02.54 Relinquished

FLYING OFFICER [from PILOT OFFICER]

09187 CARR-HALFEY John Albert Bernard F/O + 15.05.21 5 Squadron

My co-author, Paul McMillan, reports that Flying Officer John Albert Bernard Carr-Halfey died through a self-inflicted gunshot wound; a tragic end to a young officer who as a flight cadet was *Gazetted* temporary 2nd Lieutenant on 28th July 1918 [LG 9 August 1918, issue 30836, page 9384]. He is commemorated on the Delhi Memorial [India Gate].

LG 28 January 1921, issue 32209, page 781 - Various dates of seniority

FLIGHT LIEUTENANT

LOWE MC DFC Cyril Nelson G/Capt 07.10.44 Retirement

His MC was *Gazetted* on 16th September 1918, supplement 30901, page 10980: *"For conspicuous gallantry and devotion to duty. This officer and another pilot were escorting a formation of machines engaged on a bombing raid when seven enemy scouts attacked the bombers. They both attacked these scouts, but at the outset this officer's machine was set on fire, and the other pilot's right hand top plane broke. During the fight that ensued each came to the rescue of the other. The other pilot first caused Capt. Lowe's pursuer to break off his attack, and then Capt. Lowe shot down the scout attacking his comrade. The action of both these officers, in practically un-manoeuvrable machines in coming to the rescue of each other in turn, showed courage and self-sacrifice of a very high order."* Through a quirk of administration the citation for his DFC preceded that of his MC though acknowledging that he was a recipient of such an honour: *"This officer has destroyed five enemy machines and driven down two others out of control. On one occasion he attacked two enemy triplanes, although at the time only one of his guns was serviceable; he shot down one of the machines in flames. On another occasion, while leading a formation of eight scouts he engaged a hostile formation of twenty-six machines. Having shot down a Fokker biplane he went to the assistances of one of our scouts and drove the enemy machine down to 500 feet; at this low altitude half of a blade of his propeller was shot off by fire from the ground."* Prior to these awards his arrival on the Western Front can be traced back to 2nd October 1916 on which date he was attached to 11 Squadron [FE.2b] at Izel-le-Hameau. Appointed flight c*f*ommander on 11th February 1917 he was wounded in action on 24th March when his FE.2b A5442 was forced down near Croisilles his observer 2nd Lieutenant Masters escaping unhurt [see page 73 of Trevor Henshoaw's *The Sky Their Battlefield*]. Treated at 6 Stationary Hospital he was invalided home aboard HMHS *Grantually Castle* on 19th April 1917. Group Captain Cyril Nelson 'Kit' Lowe was an outstanding sportsman with particular emphasis in regard to his prowess at rugby football. His achievements are recorded on *Wikipedia* which notes that his career total of eighteen tries at international level was still a record at the time of his death at the age of 91 on 6th February 1983. Rather appropriately his record was eventually broken by Rory Underwood who like 'Kit' Lowe was a Royal Air Force pilot and whose international career spanned the years 1984 to 1996. Of his fifty appearances he was on the winning side forty-four times.

FLYING OFFICER [from FLIGHT LIEUTENANT]

09214 MOULTON-BARRETT Edward Selwyn G/Capt 29.01.46 Retirement

FLYING OFFICERS
8

09194 BRIGHT Raymond Eric F/O 07.05.24 Relinquished

On account of ill health. Returned to the service and granted a commission in the rank of pilot officer for the duration of hostilities 6th November 1939, as 75738, within the Administrative and Special Duties Branch [LG 28 November 1939, issue 34742, page 7966]. Continued to serve post war until: F/Lt 10.02.54 Relinquished

09195 CARR John Henry Talbot F/O + 20.05.21 210 Squadron

09196 CUMMING William Neville S/Ldr 14.10.54 Relinquished

On account of medical unfitness for Air Force service. As temporary Group Captain William Neville Cumming OBE DFC was conferred by Her Majesty The Queen of the Netherlands with Commander of the Order of Orange Nassau [LG 6 July 1945, supplement 37164, page 3515].

09198 JAY Noel Hamilton W/Cdr 10.02.54 Relinquished

09199 McGREGOR Malcolm Kenneth F/O 16.05.28 Resigned

Malcolm Kenneth McGregor, born on 10th March 1896, had been commissioned to the 2nd Battalion, Scots Guards, before joining the RFC for training as an observer having past the qualification test on 25th May 1917. Returning to France he joined 18 Squadron [DH.4] at Baizieux on 28th

June 1917, his tour of operations ending on 8th December 1917 when he returned to the UK. I believe he completed a second operational tour as appended is a note *"27.7.18 To Home Establishment 20.7.18 B213 82 Sqdn"* [82 Squadron being a corps reconnaissance squadron equipped with Armstrong Whitworth FK.8 and at the time of his return to England operating out of Haussimont].

09200 TIPPER Sidney Thomas W/Cdr 10.02.54 Relinquished

Sidney Thomas Tipper, born on 16th August 1899, joined the RFC on 15th August 1917 and on completion of his training reported to Bertangles to fly SE.5as with 84 Squadron. However, a mere five days after his arrival he was admitted to 24 General Hospital Etaples with an undisclosed illness and on discharge on 7th July 1918 he was ordered to report to 2 Aeroplane Supply Depot at Hesdin.

WALLAGE MC Stanley Harry F/Lt + 17.04.26 14 Squadron

Stanley Harry Wallage arrived in the world on 24th July 1895 and was *Gazetted* to the General List of the RFC on 9th February 1917. Qualifying as a fighter pilot he went to 22 Squadron [Bristol F.2b] at Boisdinghem on 9th September 1917 moving the next day to Estrée Blanche where on 2nd October he was struck down with tonsillitis. Returning to duty on the 18th he was back in hospital on 4th November 1917 with a septic throat, this being treated at 7 General Hospital. His much interrupted tour of duty recommenced on 13th December. There are no further entries on his Casualty Form. However, supplement 30901, page 11030 of the *Gazette* 16th September 1918 records the following citation: *"For conspicuous gallantry and devotion to duty during recent operations. He personally destroyed seven enemy machines. He showed a fine spirit of dash and tenacity, and his skill and success as a fighting pilot was a fine example to others in his squadron."* That these were achieved while on establishment of 22 Squadron is confirmed by The Aerodrome website which shows he achieved ten combat victories between 18th February and 4th November 1918.

09190 WEBSTER DFC Eric John F/Lt 11.01.33 Relinquished

His DFC was *Gazetted* on 21st September 1918, supplement 30913, page 11256: *"Has carried out several long-distance reconnaissances and engaged enemy aircraft who were in superior numbers on many occasions. A few months ago he was engaged in a fight, and the return journey home he had three forced landings. When he reached his base one engine had practically stopped."*

FLYING OFFICERS [from PILOT OFFICERS]
2

09191 CURTIS Philip Frank Axford F/0 + 23.02.23 216 Squadron

09193 WHITE Robert Vivian Douglas F/O 18.01.30 Relinquished

Robert Vivian Douglas just qualified for operational service in the *Great War* when he joined 7 Squadron [RE.8] at Proven on 5th October 1918. Eleven months later he was posted to 12 Squadron [Bristol F.2b] at Heumar in the Rhineland but four months later he was earmarked for demobilisation which became effective on 28th December 1919.

09204 ADAMS John Simon Leslie W/Cdr 31.10.46 Retirement

09205 BAHIN Geoffrey John Tress P/O 01.10.21 Relinquished

09206 BROWN George Stanley S/Ldr 2o.03.46 Relinquished

09207 ELY Maurice Hibbert G/Capt 10.11.46 Retirement

During his service Flight Lieutenant Maurice Hibbert Ely was involved in the loss of Blackburn Iris III N238 attached to 209 Squadron which crashed in Batten Bay, Plymouth on 4th February 1931. A full account of the accident will be published in the fifth volume. Previously, during his time with 207 Squadron, he survived a ditching in a DH.9A on 22nd February 1923, which is summarised in full.

09208 GEESON Denis Harold F/O 15.01.30 Relinquished

09209 HOPKINS George P/O + 07.04.22 2 FTS Duxford

Pilot Officer George Hopkins crashed during the course of a cross-country training flight when his Bristol F.2b F4420 crashed at Chettisham Hill, a mile or so NNE of Ely in Cambridgeshire. Prior to being relegated for flying training duties, F4420 had seen service with 4 and 24 Squadrons. *The Times* in its issue of Saturday, April 8th, 1922, reported beneath the banner:

'Fatal Air Crash - London Pilot Officer Killed Near Ely'

"George HOPKINS, pilot officer, from Duxford Aerodrome, Cambridgeshire, was fatally injured in an aeroplane crash at Chettisham Hill, two miles north of Ely, yesterday.

"The officer, whose home address is Springbank-road, Hither Green, London, was alone in the machine, and, while flying low from the east, the aeroplane suddenly nose-dived and crashed to the ground. He was removed from the wreckage in an unconscious condition and was attended by local doctors. Both thighs were found to be badly fractured, and the pilot died while being removed to hospital at Cambridge. The body was taken to the mortuary at Ely. An inquest will be held to-day."

As a dark reminder of the hazards of air operations of the time, on the same day that Pilot Officer George Hopkins lost his life, six civilians perished when a Daimler Line DH.18 G-EAWO collided with a Goliath F-GEAD operated by Grand Express Aériens over the village of Thieuloy St. Antoine to the south of Granvilliers. The DH was *en route* from Croydon to Paris-Le Bourget while the Goliath had departed Le Bourget and was heading for Croydon. Both machines were flying at a low altitude [600 feet] owing to cloud and mist. There was one survivor, a boy steward aboard the DH which was carrying newspapers but no passengers. He was terribly injured and according to the report in *The Times* he was not expected to live. *The Daily Telegraph* also reported the midair collision and the loss of the Bristol Fighter, adding to that of *The Times* that *"... name found in a glove in the machine is R L Ragg, but there was no address."*

09210 PRESTON John de la Poer Beresford F/O 28.11.29 Removed from the Service

On 16th October 1940, he returned to the service and was granted a commission in the rank of pilot officer, on probation. He served until ill-health enforced retirement on 3rd October 1944, by which time he had been promoted flight lieutenant, a rank he was permitted to retain. A document for this officer is held by TNA Kew under AIR 76/411/107.

09211 RAGG Robert Linton AV-M 29.04.55 Retirement

Air Vice-Marshal Robert Linton Ragg CB CBE AFC twice mentioned in despatches, died on Wednesday, 19th December 1973. Following a brief attachment to 4 Squadron, Pilot Officer Ragg went out to Iraq where on 13th December 1922, he joined 45 Squadron and as was common throughout the '20s and '30s, pilots often were called upon to fill the role of observer and as such young Robert Ragg found himself acting as a bomb aimer for Squadron Leader Arthur Harris who in the Second World War would be Bomber Command's commander-in-chief from February 1942 through to September 1945. A photograph of Flying Officer Ragg is published on page 87 of *The Flying Camels* where the caption indicates that Squadron Leader Harris nicknamed him *"Bones."* During his service, *"Bones"* Ragg would serve two tours of duty as Navigation Officer at Bomber Command headquarters, but I suspect his second tour ended before the arrival of Sir Arthur Harris. After leaving the service, Air-Vice Marshal Ragg was Bursar to Gordonstoun School and from 1958 to 1962, was County Commissioner for Scouts in the County of Cornwall.

09212 SMITH Gilbert Harcourt AV-M 01.11.55 Retirement

Air Vice-Marshal Gilbert Harcourt-Smith CB CBE MVO mentioned in despatches, died on Monday, 16th December 1968. He adopted his second Christian name into his surname at some time after 1928.

09213 SOUTH Burns Alan Campbell P/O + 25.02.22 2 FTS Duxford

During the late stage of his training, Pilot Officer Burns Alan Campbell South lost control of Bristol F.2b F4807 shortly after taking off and while banking near the airfield spun and crashed; he was 21 years of age.

I strongly suspect all ten probationary Pilot Officers [commencing with 09204 Philip Frank Axford Adams] were trained at No. 2 Flying Training School, Duxford.

LG 15 February 1921, issue 32227, page 1283 - Various dates of seniority

FLYING OFFICER [from FLIGHT LIEUTENANT]

ADAMS* Stanley Edward F/O 14.11.22 Permanent
On account of ill-health [LG 16 March 1926, issue 33142, page 1923] S/Ldr 16.03.26 Retired list
A gunnery instructor, Stanley Edward Adams, born 13th October 1895, joined the RFC in October 1915. His early service remains a 'mystery' but on 25th October 1917 he sailed from Southampton for the Middle East disembarking at Alexandria on 10th November following a brief stop at Taranto. By the December of that year he was fulfilling gunnery instructor duties at Heliopolis from where on 23 April 1918 he travelled to Suez for attachment to 58 Training Squadron which was equipped with a mixture of BE.2 and Martinsyde. He was still on establishment on 1st August 1918, the date of his discharge to duty from hospital where he had been treated for a mild dose of fever.

* His commission, with seniority 31st January 1921, appeared in the *Gazette* on 3rd May 1921, issue 32311, page 3542. To avoid duplication I have excluded him from the short service commissions notified on this date.

FLYING OFFICERS
2

09216 LEETE Bernard More Troughton Shute F/O 26.01.30 Relinquished
The Casualty Form for Bernard More Troughton Shute Leete is spartan in content. Annotated 83 Squadron [FE.2b] it merely records *"Leave 1.7.18 to 14.7.18 B213 83 Sqd"* followed by *"To England per A.T. Pieter de Coninek 7.9.18 W3083 14 Gen."*
SOLE John William F/O 12.03.24 Resigned
John William Sole, born 10th March 1899 and to the RFC 9th May 1917 joined 70 Squadron [F.1 Camel] at Boisdinghem on 10th July 1918. A month later he was posted to 22 Wing for attachment to 209 Squadron, likewise equipped with F.1 Camel - see my summaries on pages 140 and 375 of my second volume *Royal Air Force & Australian Flying Corps Squadron Losses 1st July - 11th November 1918* and the losses of E4389 and F5923. A photograph of E4389 standing on its nose at Villers-lès-Roye and being inspected by a couple of French soldiers features on page 153 of Air-Britain's *The Camel File.*

FLYING OFFICER [from PILOT OFFICER]

09218 STEWART Cecil Rhodes W/Cdr 10.02.54 Relinquished

LG 1 March 1921, issue 32243, page 1700 - Various dates of seniority

FLYING OFFICERS
3

09219 BURGE Glynguard Robert F/O 10.02.30 Relinquished
09220 LOCKE-WATERS Evelyn Archer F/O + 06.10.22 30 Squadron
South Africa Of Sea Point, a suburb of Cape Town, Evelyn Archer Locke-Waters was born on 26th January 1898 joining the RFC on 10th October 1917. Posted to 5 Squadron [RE.8] at Ascq on 26th April 1918 he was wounded on 1st September 1918 with a gunshot wound to one of his thighs [Trevor Henshaw has only been able to enter *"... shot up un action"* without being able to identity the serial of his RE.8]. He was returned to the UK for treatment on HMHS *Cambria.*

09221 O'NEILL AFC Henry Dunboyne A/Cmdr 19.12.45 Retirement
Air Commodore Henry Duboyne O'Neill CBE AFC, died on Thursday, 9th January 1975. His long service began in April 1915 as an officer commissioned to the 3rd Battalion, Royal Dublin Fusiliers and ended as the first appointee as Director of Accident Prevention.

LG 8 March 1921, issue 32250, pages 1899 and 1900 - Various dates of seniority

FLYING OFFICER [from FLIGHT LIEUTENANT]
2

09226 FITZ-GIBBON DSC Desmond Fitz-Gerald F/Lt 28.02.29 Relinquished
The Aerodrome website identifies him as Desmond Fitzgerald Fitzgibbon and giving his date of birth as 1st November 1890. Joining the RNAS on 28th May 1960 he was awarded his Royal Aero Club Aviator's Certificate [3529] at RNAS Cranwell on 14th August 1916 having mastered the intricacies pf the Maurice Farman biplane. Gaining further flying experience he was posted to 10 Squadron RNAS and made his mark by scoring eight combat victories, five at the controls of Sopwith Triplanes and three flying F.1 Camel B6202. The Edinburgh edition of the *Gazette* published on November 5th, 1917, issue 13162 page 2293 carried the citation for his DSC: *"For exceptional courage and determination for leading offensive patrols against enemy formations, although often outnumbered by them. On the 14th September 1917, he and his patrol of seven machines attacked a hostile formation of eight enemy scouts. In the combat that ensued three hostile machines were brought down completely out of control, one of these by Flt.-Lieut. Fitzgibbon, while the patrol suffered no casualties.*
"On the 26th September 1917, he attacked with his patrol of eight machines fifteen hostile scouts. He himself engaged four different machines, one after the other, finally driving one down completely out of control." Both these successes were at the controls of F.1 Camel B6202 and the enemy scouts were Albatros D.V.
On the 1st of September 1939 he obtained a commission in the Administrative and Special Duties Branch, his rank being described as 'Captain' and with the service number 75421 [LG 7 November 1939, issue 34727, page 7503]. S/Ldr 01.01.45
RIDDLE Cecil Brimble S/Ldr 17.03.36 Retired list
At his own request [LG 17 March 1936, issue 34265, page 1743]. This strongly suggests his Short Service Commission had been converted to a Permanent Commission. On 2nd June 1937, he was granted a commission in class C of the Reserve of Air Force Officers in the rank of flight lieutenant [honorary squadron leader] [LG 3 August 1937, issue 34423, page 4957] but on completion of service this was relinquished on 23rd August 1937 [LG 9 November 1937, issue 34452, page 6970]. Then, on 11th May 1939, he was *Gazetted* with the Honorary rank of wing commander [LG 4 July 1939, issue 34642, page 4581].
Consulting his Casaulty Form - Officers, this shows he was born on 28th September 1894 transferring from the Durham Light Infantry to the RFC on 2nd June 1916. His first operational posting was to 42 Squadron [BE.2] at Bailleul on 7th December 1916, returning to the UK for temporary duty towards the end of March 1917. Returning to France, he rejoined his squadron, serving until 20th July 1917 when he was ordered to Abeele for attachment to 6 Squadron [RE.8] as a flight commander.

FLYING OFFI CERS
3

HARRICKS Frank Simon F/O + 24.10.22 1 Squadron
Frank Simon Harricks, born on 8th September 1896, was accepted by the RFC on 22nd April 1917 and is known to have performed observer duties with 2 Squadron [FK.8] from 11th June 1917 to 16th December 1917 when he bade farewell to his colleagues and departed Hesdigneul for England.
09230 RIDLEY Leslie Howard S/Ldr 10.02.54 Relinquished
WALSH William John F/O 26.02.30 Relinquished
William John Walsh born, probably in London on 2nd February 1894, was first served with the Connaught Rangers before gaining a commission on the General List RFC for observer training on 19th June 1917. On 14th August 1917 he was attached to 45 Squadron [F.1. Camel] at Ste. Marie

Cappel but 24-hours later was sent to 10 Wing [headquarters at Chocques] from where he was instructed to report on 16th August to 43 Squadron, another F.1 Camel scout squadron, at Auchel. Then, on 13th September 1917 he, at last, joined a squadron where his observer qualification would be put to good use, when he was cross-posted to 25 Squadron [DH.4]. He receives one entry in *The DH.4/DH.9 File* when on 11th October 1917 and flying with Canada born Lieutenant John Edwardes Pugh their DH.4 A7470 developed a radiator leak obliging them to forced-land, the location not being recorded.

FLYING OFFICERS [from PILOT OFFICERS]

5

09224 ARTHUR Cyril Ernest Frederick S/Ldr 14.06.47 Class A

Granted an extension of service for five years [LG 9 August 1949, supplement 38684, page 3854]. A further five year extension, effective from 31st July 1952, was *Gazetted* 23rd December 1952, supplement 39724, page 6728. W/Cdr 31.07.57 Relinquished

BROWN Esmond Chodwick F/O 04.04.23 Resigned

McDONOUGH William John F/O 22.02.29 Relinquished

William John McDonough was attached to 1 Aeroplane Supply Depot, Marquise, between 29th September 1918 and 16th March 1919 at which time he was undergoing treatment at 14 General Hospital from where he was evacuated to the UK by way of HMHS *St. Andrew.*

SYKES Benjamin F/O + 20.11.32

Born in Lancashire on 18th January 1900, Benjamin Sykes joined the RFC on 28th October 1917 and on completion of his flying training went out to Italy where he joined 28 Squadron [F.1 Camel] at Grossa on 28th June 1918. His health, however, was far from being robust and he underwent several spells in 62 General Hospital until being sent back to England on HMS *Grantually Castle* on 2nd January 1919. He was placed on the Unemployed List on 21st August 1919 [LG 5 September 1919, issue 31539, page 11247]. Sadly, having returned to the service he died from a self-administered overdose of morphia while staying in the Hotel de Londres, Constantinople. He rests in Haidar Pasha Cemetery.

09232 THORNTON-NORRIS George F/O 22.02.29 Relinquished

George Thornton-Norris arrived at Boisdinghem on 28th August 1918 and joined 48 Squadron [Bristol F.2b]. Following the Armistice he continued to serve on the Continent, joining 88 Squadron, also equipped with Bristol F.2b, at Nivelles in Belgium on 19th May 1919.

LG 15 March 1921, issue 32257, pages 2095 and 2096 - Various dates of seniority

FLYING OFFICER [from SQUADRON LEADER]

FULLER Charles Drury S/Ldr 07.03.26 Relinquished

On account of ill-health [LG 23 March 1926, issue 33144, page 2111]. It is known that Charles Drury Fuller served with 27 Squadron [Martinsyde G.100] at St. Omer from 1st March 1916 until he was wounded on the 24th March 1916, the squadron having moved to Treizennes. Admitted to 3 General Hospital where it was discovered he had sustained rib fractures, he was sent back to England on the last day of March as patient aboard HMHS *Dieppe.*

FLYING OFFICER [from FLIGHT LIEUTENANT]

BRYANT Edgar Henfrey F/Lt 01.03.32 Relinquished

Lance Corporal Edgar Henfrey Bryant was commissioned to the Essex Regiment on 19th December 1915 [LG 28 December 1915, issue 29418, page 12928]. Subsequently, he went on to serve with the 5th Battalion before transferring to the RFC on 14th August 1916. His first operational deployment was to 12 Squadron [BE.2e] at Avesnes-le-Comte on 11th March 1917 and thence to Bailleul and 42 Squadron [RE.8] on 26th April 1917. He was born on 3rd May 1891 and was married.

FLYING OFFICERS

CHRISTIE Henry Lawrence F/O 01.03.34 Relinquished

A General List officer, he joined the RFC on 13th April 1917 and appears to have flown Bristol F.2bs with 22 Squadron from 26th January 1918 until returning home on 23rd August 1918. From the Ealing district of London, he was born on 16th January 1893.

LG 29 March 1921, issue 32271, page 2472 - Seniority 29th March 1921 - Block 09243 to 09259

FLYING OFFICER

LUARD Robert Blaine F/O + 17.08.22 27 Squadron

Flying Officer Robert Blaine Luard's details are outlined in Appendix G of this volume.

09243 ATKINSON* Henry Anthony Charles F/O 28.03.28 Relinquished

On account of ill-health [LG 27 March 1928, issue 33370, page 2244].

09244 BOOTHMAN John Nelson ACM 03.05.56 Retirement

Air Chief Marshal Sir John Boothman KCB KBE DFC AFC mentioned in despatches *Croix de Guerre* [France] DFC [USA], died on 29th December 1957. His death was a result from the illness first contracted during his tour as Air Officer Commanding Air Headquarters, Iraq [8th November 1948 to 4th September 1950]. His final appointment, commencing 15th November 1953, was Air Officer Commanding in Chief, Coastal Command and Commander in Chief [Air] Eastern Atlantic Area which he held until his retirement. Prior to the outbreak of the Second World War, Flight Lieutenant Boothman was a Member of the RAF High Speed Flight from May through to October 1931 during which he secured the Schneider Trophy when he flew Supermarine S6B at the speed of 340 m.p.h. and in doing so won the Trophy out right for the United Kingdom. His illustrious service career is reported both on *Wikipedia* and on the Air of Authority - A History of RAF Organisation website.

09245 BROWN Thomas William Stephen W/Cdr 11.11.46 Relinquished

Subsequently he was commissioned on 7th July 1952 as a flight lieutenant in class J of the Reserve of Air Force Officers [LG 5 August 1952, supplement 39615, page 4194]. F/Lt 07.06.55 Relinquished

09246 CAMPBELL Patrick Kellie W/Cdr 10.02.54 Relinquished

09247 COLES Douglas Mark Newbery F/O 29.03.29 Relinquished

09248 CREE Angus Broke F/O 29.03.30 Relinquished

During his service with 31 Squadron, Flying Officer Angus Broke Cree was injured when his Bristol F.2b crash-landed at Quetta; for additional details see my summary for 10th August 1923.

09249 DAWSON John P/O 19.04.22 Relinquished

On account of ill-health.

09250 DINGLE* Frederick Morley P/O 02.11.21 Terminated

Born on 21st February 1900 at St. Austell in Cornwall, my co-author has discovered he sailed for America in 1923, arriving in New York City on 5th April. Subsequently settling in Michigan he became an American citizen circa 1931.

09251 EDWARDES Edwin Stapleton F/O 29.03.38 Relinquished

See my summary for 207 Squadron on Monday 4 June 1923, for details of a serious crash in which he was seriously injured.

09252 EMBRY Basil Edward ACM 26.02.56 Retirement

Air Chief Marshal Sir Basil Embry GCB KBE DSO*** DFC AFC four times mentioned in despatches Commander Legion of Honour [USA] *Croix de Guerre* [France], died on Thursday, 8th December 1977. Sir Basil Embry was one of the most decorated airmen from the Second World and whose operational exploits are legion, particularly in regard to his long service attached to units in No. 2 Group which following a tour of duty in the Middle East he commanded from 1st June 1943 for the remainder of the European War. At the outbreak of hostilities in September 1939, he was commanding 107 Squadron, equipped with Blenheim IVs, and was while leading '107' [he was appointed to command the squadron on 15th September 1939] during the desperate air fighting over France that followed the *Blitzkrieg* he was shot down on 27th May 1940 [see my RAFBCL Revision 1939-1940, page 139]. Briefly held as a prisoner of war he slipped away from his guards and evaded capture by way of the Pyrenees and down to Gibraltar and arriving back in Plymouth aboard HMS *Vidette* on 2nd August 1940. His final service appointment, commencing 16th July 1953, was Commander in Chief Allied Air Forces Central Europe. In 1957 he wrote *Mission Completed* which was published by Methuen & Company, copies of which are still available.

09253 FINDLEY* Arthur F/O + 20.05.25 31 Squadron

09254 FOSTER* Arthur Derrick Huthersoll G/Capt 27.04.46 Retirement

09255 GARDNER* Cyril W/Cdr 09.08.47 Relinquished

On account of medical unfitness for Air Force service [LG 19 August 1947, supplement 38049, page 3899].

09256 GODBY* Robert George Rhodes F/O 29.03.29 Relinquished

09257 MOON* Ernest Cecil F/O 17.2.26 Relinquished

On account of ill-health [LG 16 February 1926, issue 33133, page 1164].

09258 NIVEN Oswald Lewis P/O 02.11.21 Terminated

My co-author has through the *Central Somerset Gazette* unearthed a little gem that Oswald Lewis Niven, second cousin to the film star David Niven, and in the employment of Bristol Hydrological Corporation and living at Little Court, Blagdon, won £17,866 in a football pool. This being reported in the paper's Friday, 13th May 1949, edition.

09259 RAYNER George James F/O 12.12.23 Relinquished

On account of ill-health [LG 11 December 1923, issue 32887, page 8642].

Note. I believe the sequence 15000 [or 15001] commenced in either late March or early April 1921. The asterisk indicates from the Unemployed List.

LG 8 April 1921, issue 32284, pages 2798 and 2799 - Various dates of seniority

FLYING OFFICERS
2

FREEMAN Oswald Denzil F/O 22.03.29 Relinquished

15003 OLIVER AFC John A/Cmdr 26.03.46 Retirement

FLYING OFFICER [from PILOT OFFICER]

ATKINSON Gerald Arthur F/O 28.10.25 Relinquished

On account of ill-health [LG 27 October 1925, issue 33096, page 6924].

DROMGOLE Cecil Gordon P/O 05.07.21 Terminated

LOCH Desmond Reginald F/O + 07.04.23 20 Squadron

ROBERTS John Vaughan F/O 29.03.29 Relinquished

But with effect from 18th April 1929, he was granted a commission in the Special Reserve, retaining his rank of flying officer [LG 4 June 1929, issue 33503, page 3694]. F/O 27.10.31 Class C

Commissioned to the Administrative and Special Duties Branch on 26th July 1939, retaining his rank [LG 21 November 1939, issue 34738, page 7805], his service number now reported as 15600.

SELBY-LOWNDES George William P/O 24.05.22 Resigned

Gazetted in supplement 29682, page 7418 of *The London Gazette* under the Special Reserve of Officers as a 2nd Lieutenant attached to the Grenadier Guards.

STANSFIELD Jack Wolryche P/O 09.10.21 Terminated

LG 12 April 1921, issue 32288, page 2899 - Various dates of seniority

FLYING OFFICERS
4

BREAKELL Thomas Knowles F/O 01.08.22 Resigned

From Derbyshire and born on 27th June 1894 Thomas Knowles Breakell enlisted with the RFC during July 1916, his service number being 40348. Commissioned from the rank of sergeant while attached to 9 Squadron he was posted on 12th April 1917 to 8 Squadron [BE.2e] at Soncamp where it was employed as a corpss reconnaissance unit.

HUTCHINSON Ralph de Heppele F/O 28.01.25 Dismissed

By sentence of General Court Martial [LG 17 February 1925, issue 33021, page 1172].

KENT Edmund Alfred Wise F/O 14.06.23 Resigned

2nd Lieutenant Edmund Alfred Wise Kent joined 29 Squadron [SE.5a] at St. Omer on 29th April 1918 and a month later on 30th May he was wounded whilst flying SE.5a 3915. First treated at 13 Casaulty Clearing Station he was transferred to 30 General Hospital before being returned to England on 13th June 1918 aboard HMHS *Brighton.*

15013 MILLING Edgar Morrison F/O 24.03.29 Relinquished

Edgar Morrison Milling, born on 24th April 1895, joined the RFC on 4th June 1916 and on completion of his training appears to have spent the next few years in England before embarking for the Western Front on the overnight sailing 4th May 1918. Disembarking the next morning he spent the next couple of weeks at No. 1 Aeroplane Supply Depot at Marquise before travelling to Ascq on 17th May 1918 for duty with 5 Squadron [RE.8]. On 26th September 1918 he was admitted to 14 General Hospital with an undisclosed illness and 48-hours later he was placed aboard HMHS *St. David* and returned to England. Following the granting of a short service commission and leaving the service, He returned to the service and retaining his rank was granted a commission in the Royal Air Force Volunteer Reserve, Equipment Branch, with effect from 17th May 1938 [LG 17 May 1938, issue 34511, page 3200], his service number now being 72223. F/Lt 08.12.43 Relinquished

On account of ill-health [LG 21 December 1943, supplement 36294, page 5537] by which time he had reverted to his original service number.

FLYING OFFICERS [from PILOT OFFICERS]
2

15012 MATTOCK Edwin Frank F/O 23.11.41 Resigned

Edwin Fran Mattock was born on 15th December 1899 and joined the RFC on 1st October 1917. His war was spent in Italy flying F.1 Camels out of Grossa and other Italian bases with 28 Squadron before leaving for home on 25th March 1919. During his time with the squadron he was involved in two landing accidents, the first on 1st July 1918 when B7383 overturned at Grossa; repaired, it later served with 66 Squadron, while the second on 28th November 1918 at Sarcedo is summarised on page 36 of my third volume, complied in conjunction with Paul McMillan - see also his entry on page 101 for another landing accident at Sarcedo on 17th January 1919 involving , by coincidence, B7823!

SMITH Victor Dudley F/O 08.10.23 Resigned

GREENBERRY Harry Edward F/O 29.03.31 Relinquished

Returned to service in the Royal Air Force Volunteer Reserve. S/Ldr 10.02.54 Relinquished

LG 26 April 1921, issue 32303, page 3292 Various dates of seniority

FLYING OFFICER [from FLIGHT LIEUTENANT]

	SOAR DSO	Reginald Rhys	F/O	16.01.24	Resigned

Flying Officer Reginald Rhys Soar, formerly a flight lieutenant with the RNAS, was *Gazetted* with the DSO on 11th August 1917, supplement 30227, page 8207: *"For courage and skill as a scout pilot. On 23rd May 1917, he attacked a two-seater artillery machine, and as the result of a well thought out attack brought the machine down out of control.*

"On 12th June 1917, he brought down to enemy machines out of control.

"On 29th June 1917, in company with Flt. Lieut. Little, he attacked and brought down an Albatross Scout.

"On 3rd July 1917, whilst leading an offensive patrol, a formation of seven Albatross Scouts was engaged, and he brought down one, out of control.

"On 13th July 1917, in company with Flt. Lieut. Little, he attacked and drove down out of control one two-seater machine, following it down to within 1,000 feet of the ground."

The Aerodrome website, which the authors acknowledge, indicates that during his service with 8[Naval] Squadron RNAS he achieved a dozen victories between 20th December 1916 and 22nd July 1917. His aircraft in the actions referred to above were in descending order Sopwith Triplane N6292, Sopwith Triplane - airframe serial not identified, Sopwith Triplane N6292 and Sopwith F.1 Camel N6376. His biography on *Wikipedia* shows that prior to joining 8[Naval] Squadron RNAS he saw service in the Dardanelles with No. 3 Wing RNAS and later with No. 5 Wing RNAS flying operations from Dunkirk.

FLYING OFFICERS

3

15016	ANDERSON	David Forgham	G/Capt	26.04.46	Retirement
	BURT	Percy Harry	S/Ldr	19.06.43	Retired list

A General List officer who was commissioned to the RFC on or by 9th April 1917 was born, probably in Birmingham, on 10th April 1897. Posted to 24 Squadron [SE.5a] at Teteghem on 27th September 1917 he was posted home a a fortnight later on 5th October and it was not until 6th February 1918 that he returned to France where, four days later, at Couucelles-le-Comte he joined 59 Squadron a corp reconnaissance squadron equipped with RE.8. It would seem he was found unsuited as a scout pilot. Almost immediately he was ordered to attend a course of instruction under the aegis of 3rd Army's artillery section, returning to to his squadron on 20th February. On 11th March 191 he was wounded, though the circumstances are, as yet, unknown. On 24th June 1919 he was placed on the Unemployed List [LG 11 July 1919, issue 31449, page 8855].

On his return to the service, and initially serving in the General Duties Branch, he transferred to the Stores Branch, his service number being amended to 21001.

07023	CLINTON	Arnold Cadman	F/O	10.02.54	Relinquished

A General List officer from the start, Arnold Cadman Clinton, born on 21st September 1896, joined the RFC in February 1917 and was serving with 10 Squadron at Droglandt when he was wounded on 30th May 1918, the circumstances being summarised on page 197 of my first volume.

FLYING OFFICERS [from PILOT OFFICERS]

3

15018	HILL	Reginald William	W/Cdr	16.01.61	Relinquished

Squadron Leader Reginald William Hill appointed to command No. 3617 [County of Hampshire] FCU.

15019	LAMB	Arthur Charles	F/O	13.04.35	Relinquished

Returned to the service and granted a commission in class C of the General Duties Branch, Reserve of Air Force Officers, with effect from 28th October 1938 [LG 28 February 1939, issue 34603, page 1395. S/Ldr 10.02.54 Relinquished

15021	MOLLARD	Rene George	F/O	04.04.34	Relinquished
	MAYBURN	Albert	P/O	01.01.24	Resigned

From the Unemployed List. Returned to the service and served throughout the Second World War and beyond. F/Lt 10.02.54 Relinquished

LG 3 May 1921, issue 32311, page 3542 - Various dates of seniority

FLYING OFFICERS

	STAFFORD	George Robert	F/O	02.09.28	Relinquished

FLYING OFFICER [from PILOT OFFICER]

15023	PEARCE	Alfred Leslie	F/O	15.04.30	Relinquished

Alfred Leslie Pearce was granted a commission as a probationary Pilot Officer for the duration of hostilities in the Administrative and Special Duties Branch on 25th August 1940 and with a new service number 85085 [LG 8 October 1940, issue 34964, page 5909]. However, when *Gazetted* [8th August 1941, issue 35241, page 4581] Flying Officer war substantive on 7th April 1941, he had reverted to his original service number 15023. He continued to serve until: S/Ldr 10.02.54 Relinquished

15025	ROGENHAGEN	Arthur Erik	W/Cdr	16.10.46	Retired list

Paul McMillan reports Arthur Erik Rogenhagen was born in Epsom, Surrey on 24th February 1901 and died in Worthing, Norfolk in February 1985.

	GODBY	Robert George Rhodes	F/O	29.03.29	Relinquished

[Substituted for the notification in the *Gazette* of 29th March 1921]

LG 10 May 1921, issue 32319, page 3752 - Seniority 28th April 1921

	BOLDERO	Stephen Richard	F/O	15.04.25	Relinquished

On account of ill-health.

09254	FOSTER*	Arthur Derrick Huthersoll	G/Capt	27.04.46	Retirement
	GAYES	William James	F/O +	29.11.22	A&GS Eastchurch

Flying Officer William James Gayes had been briefed, along with Flying Officer John Harold Vickers to practice camera gun tactics and it was whilst so engaged that Flying Officer Gayes who was flying Bristol F.2b F4340 came into a very minor collision with Sopwith 7F.1 Snipe E6479 flown by Flying Officer Vickers, the incident occurring at around 1150. For some inexplicable reason Flying Officer Gayes crashed, sustaining fatal injuries. The findings of the Court of Inquiry reported in the following terms:

"Primarily due to the collision which resulted from F/O Gayes diving slightly when the Snipe was passing beneath him. It is not considered that that the machines were in too close proximity during the exercise. It is considered that owing to nerve strain resulting from the collision F/O Gayes crashed through an error judgement when attempting to land, as his machine does not appear to have been damaged by the impact. We do not consider that F/O Vickers was in any way to blame.

"O.C. A & G School reports:-

"I am of the opinion the collision was caused by the Bristol Fighter being dipped at the moment when the Snipe was rising from beneath. It is not apparent that the Bristol Fighter sustained damage by the collision other than to the propeller and it therefore seems likely that F/O Gayes crashed through an error judgement, his machine being under control during the greater part of the glide. I concur in the finding of the Court."

The accident card raised for the Snipe indicates it crash-landed with Flying Officer Vickers being slightly injured with minor abrasions to both legs and, unsurprisingly, slight shock.

Meanwhile, *The Daily Mail* picked up on the death of Flying Officer Gayes and in its edition of Saturday, 2nd December 1922, reported as follows:

'Shock on Tail'

'Airman's Story of Flying Tragedy'

"Eastchurch, Sunday - An inquest was held here to-day relative to the death of Flight Officer William James Gayes, following an aeroplane collision over Warden.

"Flying Officer Vickers stated he was flying a Sopwith Snipe machine, while deceased was in a Bristol Fighter. They were engaged in manoeuvres and at a height of 2,000 feet deceased signalled him to come on as he wanted more camera gun pictures.

"Witness estimated he would pass 50 feet under the Bristol Fighter. He suddenly felt a shock on the tail of his machine and found it badly damaged. Witness had not started to rise when he felt the bump, and his impressions was that deceased must have depressed his machine to map him with his ring sight.

"A verdict of "Accidental death" was returned.

	SCOTT-ATKINSON	Arthur Edward Lennox	P/O		07.06.22	Resigned
	HUGH-JONES*	David Jasper	F/O	+	29.01.24	27 Squadron
21036	SLATER*	Edward Albert	W/Cdr		06.03.44	Relinquished

On account of ill-health [LG 21 March 1944, supplement 36432, page 1320].

	THOMAS*	Kenneth Rhys	F/O	28.04.30	Relinquished

Paul McMillan reports Kenneth Rhyrs Thomas died in January 1979, at Brent in Greater London.

* Denotes previous Royal Air Force service.

LG 24 May 1921, issue 32332, pages 4099 and 4100 - Various dates of seniority

FLYING OFFICER [from FLIGHT LIEUTENANT]

	HORSEY	John Frederick	F/O	10.04.29	Relinquished

FLYING OFFICERS

3

	BLACKBURN	Graeme Fleming	F/O	23.04.30	Relinquished

I am reasonably confident that Graeme Fleming Blackburn was a South African. His officers casualty form shows G F Blackburn of the RFC Special Reserve embarking at Durban on HMHT *Magdalena* and disembarking at Suez 19th-20th April 1918. The entries then continue:-

27.418	*Joined RAF Base Depot from 25 SA Sqd*	*21.4.18*	*B213 B.Depot*
22.4.18	*Adm. Mil. Hos. Ras el Tin duodenal ulcer*	*22.4.18*	*W3034*
27.4.18	*Adm. Hospital*	*22.4.18*	*B213 B. Depot*
16.5.18	*Duodenal Ulcer. Trans. To UK for further treatment & possible operation. Embarked 14.5.18 per HS Durban Castle : Med. Br. Mil. Hos. Ras el Tin MFC/33080/A*		

15035	HARRISON	George Frederick Embrey	F/O	04.02.29	Relinquished

Flying Officer George Frederick Embry Harrison returned to the service and on 21st June 1939 was granted Squadron Leader rank in the Royal Ai Force Reserve of Officers, class CC, attached to the General Duties Branch [LG 8 September 1939, supplement 34674, page 6134. Unfortunately, his service ended under a cloud: S/Ldr 10.03.42 Cashiered

By sentence of General Court Martial [LG 31 March 1942, issue 35508, page 1466]. His officers casualty form shows he was born on 30th September 1898 and was commissioned to the General List RFC on or by 11th April 1917. Interestingly, he received his flying instruction at the British Flying School at Vendôme [Loir-et-Cher] in France where he was injured in a flying accident on 21st July 1917. Admitted to a hospital in Vendôme he was discharged to resume his flying instruction on the last day of August 1917. Following a spell of sick leave and the completion of his training he returned to England on 4th October 1917.

Returning to France in February 1918 it seems he spent most of the year - at least until until the end of June - at No. 2 Aeroplane Supply Deport at Fienvillers and from May 1918 at Hesdin. There are no indications that he served with a squadron, merely a note to the effect that he was attached to 8th Brigade for temporary duty, presumably returning to Hesdin on completion.

	HEWSON	Henry Willis	F/O	15.05.24	Resigned

A General List officer Henry Willis Hewson joined the RFC on 1st May 1917 and between 3rd March until at least late July 1918 he flew DH.4 and DH.9s with 27 Squadron from various aerodromes on the Western Front. On 26th March 1918 he took off from Beauvois in DH.4 B2104 with Sergeant V Cummins as his observer, but was forced to land at Villers-Bretonneux with a burst radiator. This was the opening day of the German spring offensive, the *Kaiserschlacht,* and with the aerodrome in danger of being overrun Henry ordered a detachment of the Royal Field Artillery to ensure that the DH was torched before they withdrew.

Earlier, 1st March 1918, with 2nd Lieutenant J D Parker as his observer, Henry took off from Serny in B2123/S [see page 247 of my first volume] and at around 1050 while east of Valenciennes engaged an Albatros D which was last seen going down in a spin. Flying Officer Hewson features in this volume on 1st November 1922 at which time he was serving with 84 Squadron.

FLYING OFFICER [from PILOT OFFICER]

	MATTHEWS	Donald Marmaduke	F/O	19.07.22	Resigned

LG 28 June 1921, issue 32372, page 5139 - Various dates of seniority

FLYING OFFICERS

3

15083	HALL	John Thomas	F/O	13.02.33	Resigned

On appointment to a commission in the South African Air Force Reserve of Officers. Reinstated as a flying officer in the Reserve Class A with effect from 19th April 1934. S/Ldr 10.02.54 Relinquished

	WARNER	William Francis	F/O	20.06.30	Relinquished

Believed to have flown SE.5as with 24 Squadron until he was wounded on 23rd March 1918 while flying B167; he was evacuated to England five days later aboard HMHS *Cambria.*

15085	WINGATE	John Leslie	G/Capt	04.01.47	Retirement

Born 30th April 1899 and commissioned to the General List RFC 2nd May 1917 John Leslie Wingate served, briefly, with 65 Squadron [F.1 Camel] from 5th April to 1st June 1918 when he was detached for temporary duty with Headquarters 30 Division. He returned to Bertangles on the 13th and was posted home on 26th June 1918.

LG 5 July 1921, issue 32380, page 5359 - Various dates of seniority

FLYING OFFICERS
6

BAKER Philip Douglas F/Lt 13.07.27 Relinquished

Owing to ill-health. On 28 August 1939, his health restored, he returned to the service for duties in the General Duties Branch and served throughout the Second World War until: S/Ldr 07.08.54 Relinquished

Paul McMillan adds: *"Philip Douglas Baker, born 19th July 1894, Brasted, Kent, enlisted with the Royal Kent Mounted Rifles in 1914, and transferred to the 3rd Home Counties [Cinque Fort] Brigade, RFA. He was appointed 2nd Lieutenant in August 1915and transferred to the RFC, stationed at No. 4 Flight Training School, Egypt. He was discharged while serving with 110 Irish Group in 1919, but rejoined. Whilst serving with 216 Squadron, RAF, he was slightly injured in an air accident on 5th November 1923, in Heliopolis which was due to a control column failure. He married on 6th February 1917, and died in Huntingdon 27th April 1963."* Paul adds: *"Worthy of more research."*

CARROLL AFC Reginald Sheridan F/Lt 27.06.30 Relinquished

FITZMAURICE James Christopher Lt 10.11.21 Resigned

A reasonable biography of James Christopher Fitzmaurice may be read on *Wikipedia.*

15050 KELLY Charles Edmund S/Ldr 08.01.47 Resigned

THRES DFC Leslie Walter F/O 11.03.38 Relinquished

Returned to the service and granted a commission as a pilot officer, on probation, in the General Duties Branch on 3rd July 1940, but appears to have left the service at sometime between January and March 1941.

WHEATLEY Gilbert Vernon F/O + 07.12.26 A&AEE Martlesham

Flying Officer Gilbert Vernon Wheatley had been restored to the active list, for temporary duty, on 15th April 1921 [LG 3 May 1921, issue 32311, page 3545]. On the day of his death he had been briefed to carry out a test flight in a Gloster Gamecock I J7891 to investigate a recurrent problem of aileron flutter. With the aforesaid ailerons rebalanced he took off but within eight to ten minutes of becoming airborne structural failure of the wings occurred and the fuselage plunged to the ground near woods bordering Kesgrave on the eastern side of Ipswich.

Note. For a detailed insight into the work of testing at Martlesham Heath, I thoroughly recommend the autobiography of Bill Pegg who penned *Sent Flying* and was published by Macdonald in 1959.

LG 12 July 1921, issue 32387, page 5561 - Various dates of seniority

FLYING OFFICERS [from FLIGHT LIEUTENANTS]
3

15055 DE ST. LEDGER Rene John Max G/Capt 25.04.50 Retirement

15060 REEVE Francis Henry Ernest A/Cmdr 27.12.45 Retirement

Air Commodore Francis Henry Ernest Reeve CBE mentioned in despatches, died in Swindon circa July 1975. His final appointment, which commenced on 9th October 1942, was as Senior Air Staff Officer in No. 60 [Signals] Group Headquarters.

SLOAN AFC Lawrence Hay Thomson F/O 21.12.21 Relinquished

On account of physical unfitness for flying duties. Flying Officer Lawrence Hay Thomson Sloan AFC died in Edinburgh on Wednesday, 22d August 1956.

FLYING OFFICERS
6

DAVENPORT William Frost F/O 04.07.30 Relinquished

15056 DOVE Cecil Beck W/Cdr 10.02.54 Relinquished

15057 GREENLAW Robert Ritchie G/Capt + 18.01.43 Air Attache Teheran

Group Captain Robert Ritchie Greenlaw OBE is buried in Tehran War Cemetery where his headstone is inscribed *"To My Dear Husband."* His fate is described in some detail by a senior member, Col Bruggy [whom the authors gratefully acknowledge], on the RAF Commands website who following up on the information that the Group Captain was a passenger in Hudson VI EW969 of the Iraq Communications Flight captained by Squadron Leader George Ewart Milnes who took off from Tehran to transit to Habbaniya writes: *"The Hudson;s wreckage was located six days later by members of the Persian Cavalry in the Karaqhan mountains near Nowbaran, 50km west of Saveh. All on board died, the five crew being buried at Teheran, as is at least one of the six non-Air Force passengers."* He then quotes details of Squadron Leader Milne's service from information reported by Errol Martyn on page 53 of his *For Your Tomorrow - Volume Two : Fates 1943 - 1998* before adding the names of the non-Air Force passengers: *"General Ibrahim Arfaa, Colonel Qahramani, Colonel Shaibami, Colnel Afkhami, Mr. Stephen Childs, Director of Public Relations Bureau in Teheran and Captain Yale of British GHQ in Baghdad."* Also posted on the Forum page [submitted by Alex Smart, again acknowledged] was the fact that although Group Captain Greenlaw's parents lived in the UK, his now widow was domicile in France and the point raised was who would notify her of his death - the Red Cross or the *Luftwaffe.* Unanswered, so perhaps we will never know. Finally in respect of the crash, the three other airmen who perished were all Leading Aircraftman in rank; Stanley Ellis Gatley, Herbert Pilling Gilchrist and Rae Medina.

Formerly of the 3rd Battalion, Argyll and Sutherland Highlanders, Robert Ritchie Greenlaw [born 15th March 1897] joined the RFC on 20th August 1917 and by the summer of 1918 was attached to 149 Squadron [FE.2d] at Alquines. Laid low with influenza in the autumn he underwent two spells in hospital before being discharged to duty on 18th October; then, three days before the armistice was signed he joined 38 Squadron [FE.2b] at Harlebeke.

HASLEGRAVE Charles Frederic Pridden F/O 03.05.22 Relinquished

On account of physical unfitness for full flying duties. Flying Officer Charles Frederic Pridden died on Wednesday, 21st May 1975.

15061 SHEPHERD Ronald Thomas F/O

On leaving the service, Flying Officer Ronald Thomas Shepherd became a flying instructor, but in 1931 he joined Rolls-Royce and in 1935 was appointed as the Company's Chief Test Pilot. In the New Year's Honour List for 1946 he was appointed OBE but in 1951 a serious illness curtailed his work as a test pilot, though he continued to work as a flying consultant and on 3rd July 1953 he wrote his name into aviations history when he made the first free flight of the Rolls-Royce Thrust Measuring Rig [dubbed the "Flying Bedstead"]. Sadly, his health continued to fail and he died at the comparatively early age of 59 on Tuesday, 1st March 1955.

Born in London on 21st January 1896 he was commissioned to the General List RFC on 15th July 1917 and between 19th September of that year and 10th February 1918 when he was posted to Home Establishment, he flew FE.2ds on the Western Front with 102 Squadron.

SHIIPWRIGHT Alan Thomas Kingston S/Ldr 12.08.39 Retired list

On account of ill-health. However, my co-author reports that on leaving the service Squadron Leader Alan Thomas Kingston Shipwright DFC became a coal miner working in the Kent coal fields. Subsequently, he was commissioned as a 2nd Lieutenant in the Special List for service with the Army Cadet Force effective 25th April 1947 in the county of Kent [LG 31 October 1947, supplement 38112, page 5137]. See my summary for 25th October 1926 for additional information regarding this officer.

FLYING OFFICERS [from PILOT OFFICERS]
2

BRUNTON Frederick James F/O 30.06.33 Relinquished

MAITLAND EDWARDS Richard Sheridan F/O 04.10.22 Relinquished

On account of ill-health. Subsequently Flying Officer Richard Sheridan Maintland Edwards emigrated, arriving in Quebec on 15th August 1923.

ADAMS* Philip Walter F/O 29.10.24 Relinquished
On account of ill-health [LG 28 October 1924, issue 32986, page 7749].
15064 ADDISON* Edward Barker AV-M 29.04.55 Retirement
Air Vice-Marshal Edward Barker Addison CB CBE mentioned in despatches, died on Saturday, 4th July 1987. A signals specialist he transferred to the Technical Branch in April 1940 and was given the task of overseeing the counter measures to the German radio beams employed by the *Luftwaffe* in their bombing campaign against the British Isles. Subsequently, this led to the formation at Radlett of No. 80 Wing on 14th October 1940 with Group Captain Addison being appointed its first commanding officer. For the remainder of the Second World War he was employed in one capacity or another in the development of radio counter measures and from 3rd December 1943 he commanded No. 100 Group whose squadrons played a vital role in helping to reduce the enemy's effectiveness in countering Bomber Command's bombing campaign.
ANDERSON* Ian Patrick F/O + 28.07.24 28 Squadron
During his flying training at 5 FTS Shotwick, Pilot Officer Ian Patrick Anderson was injured on 2nd May 1922, when his Bristol F.2b D7804 spun and crashed near the airfield, killing 19-year old Aircraftman Samuel Thompson.
DASHWOOD Edward John F/O + 21.03.25 27 Squadron
DRYSDALE Arthur Douglas F/O 27.06.30 Relinquished
GLOVER Alfred Meyrick F/O 12.07.27 Resigned
On appointment to a commission in the Auxiliary Air Force [LG 26 July 1927, issue 33297, page 4841]. [See Appendix H for 1927].
HARRIS* Arthur Leslie F/O 28.06.29 Relinquished
Granted a commission in the Reserve of Air Force Officers, General Duties Branch, class C 29th March 1937 [LG 18 May 1937, issue 34399, page 3251]. S/Ldr 10.02.54 Relinquished
HILLS Geoffrey Paulet French F/O + 25.06.34 Bristol Aeroplane Company
While still in the Reserve Flying Officer Geoffrey Paulet French Hills was killed along with two fellow Reserve of Air Force Officers in a midair collision involving DH.82 Tiger Moths G-ACBB and G-ACBE registered to the Bristol Aeroplane Company [Filton Reserve School] and operated under Air Ministry contract. The tragedy occurred between Westerleigh and Nibley, villages south and northwest of Yate in Gloucestershire. From the sole survivor, Flying Officer Hamish McKenzie Kerr who was instructing Flying Officer Hills in G-ACBB stated that they were in inverted flight but lost height and struck G-ACBE which was in the process of turning. Flying Officer Hamish Kerr owes his survival to the fact that he fell into a quarry where his descent was cushioned by water in the bottom of the quarry. The two officers who died in G-ACBE were Flying Officers John Macphee Darroch and Cyril Raymond Lawrence Shaw.
15076 JEFFRIES* Edward Charles Norman F/Lt + 23.10.40 24 Squadron
Flight Lieutenant Edward Charles Norman Jeffries is buried in Putney Vale Cemetery.
15077 KIRCHNER* Leo George Alexander F/Lt 09.10.55 Relinquished
MOLLARD Roger Pierre F/O 28.06.26 Class A
According to Graces Guide to British Industrial History and its section Who's Who in British Aviation, Flying Officer Roger Pierre Mollard was born in France and educated in the United Kingdom. Following his commission he received his flying instruction at 5 FTS, subsequently serving in India before joining the European Division of Imperial Airways [while serving his time in the Reserve]. Consulting the list of Fatal Accidents to British Aircraft Overseas 1930 - 2 September 1939 [as recorded on the website rcawsey which I have pleasure inn acknowledging] Captain Mollard was involved in a a very serious crash on 5th December 1937 when the Short S.23 Empire G-ADUZ *Cygnus* of Imperial Airways of which he was the pilot crashed while taking off from Brindisi in Italy. The cause of the accident was traced to an incorrect flap setting. A steward and a passenger were killed and nine others injured, including Air Marshal Sir John Maitland Salmond. On 3rd January 1945 Captain Roger Pierre Mollard of British Overseas Airways Corporation was Commended for valuable services in the air [LG 3 January 1945, supplement 36869, page 138]. Then, in the New Year's Honours list for 1958 [LG 1 January 1958, supplement 41268, page 25] he was appointed MBE for his services ass Managing Director, Malayan Airways Ltd., Singapore.
SCLATER Gerald Clifton F/O 28.06.29 Relinquished
Returned to the service and granted a commission in the Administrative Special Duties Branch as Flight Lieutenant on 14th September 1939 [LG 26th December 1939, issue 34760, page 8552]. S/Ldr 10.02.54 Relinquished
STEVENSON James Arthur Radford P/O 27.12.22 Resigned
WRIGHT* Frank Kenneth F/O 16.07.23 Relinquished
On account of ill health [LG 17 July 1923, issue 32845, page 4926].

COLES Stanley Frederick F/O 13.08.24 Resigned
15068 COOPER* Stanley Herbert F/O 07.06.33 Relinquished
On account of ill-health [LG 6 June 1933, issue 33947, page 3828]. Returned to the service and was commissioned for the duration of hostilities in the Administrative and Special Duties Branch with effect from 29th April 1940 [LG 28 May 1940, issue 34859, page 3193] initially as 79023 but reverted to his original service number. S/Ldr 10.02.54 Relinquished
DOUGLAS Charles F/O Relinquished
On account of ill-health.
HANSTOCK Brendan John O'Connor F/O + 26.06.35 Anglo American Oil Co.
While still in the Reserve Flying Officer Brendan John O'Connor Hanstock was appointed General Manager of Anglo-American Oil Company and it was while on a flight in DH 89A Dragon Rapide G-ADCL that he was killed when the Rapide overturned on landing at Redhill Aerodrome. The Aviation Safety Network report reports two persons were on board, but Brendan Hanstock was the only fatality. The Rapide was rebuilt and later found its way to Spain for use by General Franco's Nationalist Air Force. The ferry pilot for its flight out of Heston on 1st August 1936 was Lord Malcolm Douglas-Hamilton [see my summary for 3 Squadron on 12th June 1930].
STUART-MURRAY Frank Harley P/O 22.11.21 Resigned

The seniority dates for probationary Pilot Officer Adams to Pilot Officer Wright was 28th June 1921 and for Pilot Officers Coles to Pilot Officer Stuart-Murray 4th July 1921. The asterisk indicates previous Royal Air Force service.

LG 19 July 1921, issue 32394, page 5733 - Various dates of seniority

FLYING OFFICERS
10

15086 ARGLES John Greville F/O 07.07.29 Relinquished
Born on 21st September 1892 and joining the RFC on 2nd October 1917, the following is an extract, copied from his officers casualty form:

1.6.18	*Posted to 14 Sqd*	*26.5.18*	*B213 14 Sqd*
7.7.18	*Posted to Training Bde*	*1.7.18*	*B213 14 Sqd*
8.7.18	*Fit for duties of instructor, test pilot or ferry pilot for two months*	*8.7.18*	Unreadable
27.7.18	*Posted to S A G [Asst Inst]*	*18.7.18*	*S.45*
10.8.18	*Adm hospital*	*5.8.18*	*B213 S A G*
11.9.18	*Disc. Sirdariels Hospital - Malaria*	*11.9.18*	*W3034*
21.9.18	*Posted to Fighter School for duty*	*14.9.18*	*B213 F S*
5.8.18	*Adm Nasrah Hosp. Temp. N Y D*	*5.8.18*	*W3034*

21.9.18 *Discharged fro Sirdariels hosp.* *11.9.18* *B213 5 F Sch*

The term S A G is probably the abbreviation for School of Air Gunnery while N Y D probably translates as Not Yet Diagnosed.

ARNOLD DFC Edward Enos F/Lt 01.03.34 Retired list

Born 1st March 1894 and to the RFC in May 1917, having previously served with 2/22 Battalion, The London Regiment, Edward Enos Arnold rates two forms, the second being mainly typed which shows he embarked Southampton 17th August 1916 disembarking Le Havre 18th August 1916 while Serving with the London Regiment. On 8th October he was wounded in action, rejoining his battalion on the 19th. The next entry shows he embarked Marseilles 15th December 1916, disembarking Salonica on 21st December 1916. On 14th May 1917 he reported to the Base Depot in Salonica in readiness to go Egypt having being accepted for the RFC. He arrived at Port Said aboard the *Chargres* on 23rd May travelling to Aboukir the same day from where he was posted the next day to No. 3 School at Abbassia.

On 27th June 1917 he joined 57 Reserve Squadron at Ismailia after which a handwritten note records his posting back to Aboukir on 9th August 1917 and attachment to the School of Aerial Gunnery. His DFC, less citation, was *Gazetted* on 1st January 1919, supplement 31098, page 96.

BEAL mid Leslie Wallis F/O + 03.10.21 6 FTS Manston

Flying Officer Leslie Wallis Beal was piloting Vickers Vimy F9157 and while making a turn in turbulent air at low altitude lost control and spun into the ground where on impact the bomber turned over and burst into flames. In addition to the death of Flying Officer Beal, four Aircraftman also perished; Terence Curtiss, Robert John Reeves, Albert Arthur Revell and Walter Edward Thrupp. Born on 21st February 1899, Leslie Wallis Beal joined the RFC on 5th August 1916 and on completion of his training reported to Chipilly where he was attached to 22 Squadron [FE.2b]. During the next three months he would survive twice being wounded; on 11th March 1917 with Air Mechanic F G Davin and flying in FE.2b 7685 their machine as shot about and with the controls damaged, and both wounded, they forced landed near Combles [page 71 of Trevor Henshaw's *The Sky Their* Battlefield]. Treated locally, he was back on duty the same day. Six weeks later he on 26th April 1917 he sustained wounds to his fact [the identity of his FE.2b is not known; Henshaw on page 83 merely noting he was on a photographic sortie] for which he he was taken to 13 Casualty Clearing Station. This time it would be a wekk before he returned to his squadron. No doubt assessed has requiring a rest from operations he was posted back to the UK on 9th May 1917.

Omitted from the Casualty Form is the fact that he later joined 36 Squadron [various detached Flights in the northeast of England], though an undated note reads *Mentioned in Despatches* and this was for his work with the Squadron [FE.2b/Bristol F.2b] on Sea Patrols [LG 21 September 1918, supplement 30913, page 11258].

Prior to rejoined the service Flying Officer Beal had been employed by Handley Page Transport on its London to Paris route.

CAWDELL Peter Raymond F/O 14.07.26 Resigned

Of the Army Service Corps he was attached to 7 Squadron [BE.2c] at Warloy Baillon on 7th August 1916 where he was graded as a qualified observer on 10th October 1916. Presumably he remained attached until returning to England on 13th April 1917.

	HOPE	Lawrence Walter	F/O		11.09.22	Resigned
15091	MORRIS	Ira Mortimer	W/Cdr		10.02.54	Relinquished
15092	REID	Harry Redvers McLaren	G/Capt		21.02.48	Retirement
	SAYERS	Herbert Robert	Captain		28.08.23	Resigned

Glaswegian, Herbert Robert Sayers was born on 17th May 1897 and was commissioned to the General List RFC on 4th May 1917. Arriving at Longavesnes on the 3rd of July 1917 he reported to 59 Squadron [RE.8], the squadron's principal role being working with the artillery and carrying out tactical reconnaissances. Transferring to 13 Squadron, similarly equipped and tasked, at at Etrun on 12th February 1918 for flight commander duties with the rank of captain, it is presumed he completed his tour of operations with the squadron.

STUART Charles Edwin F/O 16.03.27 Relinquished

On account of ill-health [LG 15 March 1927, issue 33257, page 1700]. His *Great War* service was brief; attached to 70 Squadron at Poperinghe on 22nd August 1917 he was shot down on 26th September 1917, his fate being described on page 121 of *The Sky Their Battlefield.* Briefed to carry out a low patrol over the Ypres Salient where fierce ground fighting was still in progress, Charles took off in F.1 Camel B5151 at around 1105 and was seen, probably by fellow pilots from the squadron, in the vicinity of Passchendaele in combat with three enemy scouts. This appeared to be inconclusive but soon after from out of the clouds appeared more hostile aircraft, the time now being around 1215 with 2nd Lieutenant Stuart heading in the direction of the British lines. He never made them, crashing in the general area of Ypres.

For a description of the near unimaginable horrors facing the soldiers involved in the *Third Battle of Ypres* I have no hesitation in recommended Lyn Macdonald's *They Called it Passschendaele* published by Michael Joseph in 1978.

WHITE AFC Archer Statham F/O + 29.07.29

Born on the 3rd of October 1891 Archer Statham White joined the RFC on 5th September 1916. Between 8th and 30th May 1917 he was attached to 56 Squadron [SE.5A] at Vert Galand where he was cross-posted to 66 Squadron [Sopwith Pup]. His time with '66' was brief and he returned to Home Establishment on 8th June 1917.

Notification of the death of Flying Officer Archer Statham White of Finchley, Middlesex, was published in *The London Gazette* 25th October 1929, issue 33546, 6818, the insertion made by Moon, Gilks and Moon,Solicitors of 24 Bloomsbury Square, London WC.1.

GRANT*	Walter Irving Newby	P/O	18.03.22	Terminated
MAHON	Raymond Henry	F/O	16.08.30	Relinquished
SHAW*	Thompson James	F/O	05.07.29	Relinquished
SHARMAN MC	Donald Risborough	F/O	28.10.28	Class C

Formerly of the Surrey Regiment and as a temporary 2nd Lieutenant, he was *Gazetted* with the MC on 10th January 1917, issue 29898, page 462: *"For conspicuous gallantry in action. He displayed great courage and determination in holding an isolated trench under very heavy fire, and was indefatigable in collecting and sending down several wounded men."*

At the time of Flying Officer Donald Risboroiugh Sharman's transfer to class C he was attached to the Special Reserve. Later, on 22nd April 1937, he was granted a commission in class C of the Reserve of Air Force Officers, General Duties Branch in the rank of flight lieutenant [LG 8 June 1937, issue 34405, page 3670]. On 1st September 1939, he transferred to the Administrative and Special Duties Branch where his rank is shown as Captain and his service number as 75216. S/Ldr 10.02.54 Relinquished

15100 WANSBROUGH* Robert Cecil A/Cmdr 29.07.49 Retirement

Air Commodore Robert Cecil Wansbrough died on Thursday, 5th June 1975. His very distinguished service began early in the *Great War* when he was commissioned in December 1914 to the Staffordshire Regiment. For most of his Royal Air Force service he specialised in signals and technical research during which he served tours of duty at Farnborough and from April 1946 to February 1948 he was Chief Signals Officer at Headquarters RAF Mediterranean and Middle East. Shortly before the end of the Second World War he received the news that his only son, Flying Officer Peter Tarlington Wansbrough attached to 69 Squadron [Wellington XIII]*had failed to return from an operational sortie over NW Germany on 26th April 1945. Peter Wansbrough, 20 years of age, is buried in Kiel War Cemetery, his headstone inscribed with the words *"Well Done, Thou Good And Faithful Servant."* * Possibly Wellington XIII NC539 which according to Air-Britain's NA100-NZ999 register failed to return on 27th April 1945 from a reconnaissance between the Schleswig-Holstein towns of Itzehoe and Pinneberg northwest of Hamburg.

WHITMORE Fielding Griffith F/O + 21.08.23 28 Squadron

* Denotes previous Royal Air Force service.

LG 2 August 1921, issue 32409, page 6102 - Various dates of seniority

FLYING OFFICERS [from FLIGHT LIEUTENANTS]
4

	NARES AFC	Malcolm Dent	F/Lt	26.07.29	Relinquished
	SHERLOCK	Walter Nugent	F/O	09.04.27	Class C

Formerly of the 1st Battalion, Seaforth Highlanders, Walter Nugent Sherlock saw action in Mesopotamia where he was wounded on 22nd April 1916. Taken to Basra he was invalided to India by way of HMHS *Cleopatra* disembarking at Bombay on 10th May 1916. Declared fit, he left Karachi on 13th October 1916 and arrived at Basra on HMT *Balmoral Castle* on the 17th, rejoining his battalion in the field on the 29th.

Twelve months later, 2nd November 1917 to be precise, he was detached to 63 Squadron [BE.2e] at Basra for employment as an observer, qualifying as such on the 11th, a year to the date before an armistice would be signed.

72933 Administrative and Special Duties Branch. Granted a commission in the rank of pilot officer on probation 4th April 1939 [LG 14 April 1939, issue 34616, page 2489]. F/O 16.06.42 Resigned

	WORSLEY	Oswald Ewart	F/O	25.02.25	Permanent

Oswald Ewart Worsley was born on 20th April 1898 and joined the RFC as early as 14th November 1914. However, his service record shows him disembarking at Alexandria on 28th April 1918 and attachment to the Seaplane Base on the 28th. On 14th February 1919 he was posted to the demobilisation camp at Kantara from where on 16th March 1919 he bordered HMT *Canberra* at Port Said, sailing for home. On the 2nd of April 1919 he was placed on the Unemployed List [LG 18 April 1919, issue 31302, page 5046]. A document for Oswald Ewart Worsley may be accessed at TNA Kew under ADM 188/565/1508.

LG 9 August 1921, issue 32416, page 6284 - Various dates of seniority

FLYING OFFICERS
2

	FEENY DSO	Francis Joseph Edward	S/Ldr	29.07.33	Relinquished
	McALERY	John Mecredy	F/Lt +	04.01.24	1 Squadron

Late of the 6th Battalion, Royal Irish Rifles, John Mecredy McAlery joined 27 Squadron [Martinsyde G.100] at Fienvillers on 29th July 1916 and by the end of the year he had been appointed acting flight commander. He had also spent a little over a fortnight, 5th to 23rd August, in 25 Stationary Hospital undergoing treatment for chicken pox.

	BARLOW	Arthur John	F/O	14.02.23	Relinquished

On account of ill-health [LG 13 February 1923, issue 32795, page 1075].

15116	HAYLOCK	Edward Fowles	G/Capt	25.04.43	Retired list
	PAGE MM	Alec Dudley	F/O	10.06.33	Class C

LG 23 August 1921, issue 32432, page 6674 - Various dates of seniority

FLYING OFFICER [from FLIGHT LIEUTENANT]

15121	MELLERSH AFC	Francis John Williamson	AV-M	28.09.54	Retirement

Air Vice-Marshal Sir Francis Mellersh KBE AFC twice mentioned in despatches, died on Wednesday, 25th May 1955 in a bizarre accident at Itchenor Yacht Club. It is known that he survived one serious air accident, in which he was injured, when on 8th January 1922 his 84 Squadron DH.9A spun in at Shaibah. My summary for this date provides additional in formation.

FLYIN G OFFICERS
4

15119	AIREY DFC	James Lionel	G/Capt	01.08.50	Retirement
	ANNESLEY	William Robert Bathurst	F/Lt +	16.08.27	Training Base Leuchars

[Substituted for the notification in the *Gazette* of 2nd August 1921]. Appointed to a permanent commission on 26th August 1925 [LG 26th August 1925, issue 33078, page 5633] Flight Lieutenant William Robert Bathurst Annesley was in Canada when suddenly he was taken ill and died within a few days. My co-author reports notification of Flight Lieutenant Annesley's death appeared in the *St. Andrews Citizen* newspaper on 20th August 1927. He was the son of Major W R N Annesley of the Royal West Kent Regiment.

Further investigation reports he died from a cerebral haemorrhage and his body, at the request of mother, was brought back to Scotland by way of The White Star liner *Doric* which docked at Liverpool on Sunday 28th August 1927, this being reported in the *Dundee Courier* the next day.

The same source published a brief account of Flight Lieutenant Annesley's funeral in their edition on Wednesday 31st August stating that he was buried with full military honours in the Western Cemetery and St. Andrews. A detachment of airmen under the command of Squadron Leader Dunn from Leuchars accompanied the funeral cortege and that many civilians lined the streets leading to the cemetery.

Apparently, as Geoffrey Negus of Air-Britain in correspondence with my co-author explains, Flight Lieutenant Annesley was in Canada to attend the enquiry into the crash of a Curtiss HS-2L G-CAOM a government aircraft pilot by William Lyons and operated by the Forestry Branch - Department of Lands and Forests at Shebandowan Lake, Ontario north of Toronto. A description of the Curtiss HS series may be read on *Wikipedia.*

15120	BRUCE MC	Talbot Baines	G/Capt	16.09.46	Retirement

Talbot Baines Bruce may accurately be described ass having a rather action packed *Great War* which had its beginnings when he was posted to Lavieville on 3rd March 1917 and attachment to 3 Squadron, at the tine equipped with Moraine Parasols and engaged on artillery spotting duties. During September of that year its role changed when the Parasols were exchanged for F.1 Camels and the squadron became a scout unit.

Thus, on 6th November 1917 at around 0735 a patrol of four Camels took off from Warloy Baillion for a standard offensive patrol during which the wind increased to a strong westerly and in failing visibility all four machines were blown over the lines and into hostile territory. Uncertain of their position the four pilots forced-landed, more of less in company, between Namur and Liège. Having made enquiries from locals as to their position, thee managed to take off but unable to make headway eventually ran out of fuel and forced-landed a second time, this time in the Sedan/Rheims area where they were taken prisoner [B5160/2nd Lieutenant R C Taylor, B6355/2nd Lieutenant A G Cribb and B6382/2nd Lieutenant E P Wilmot MC, an Australian].

Bruce, however, was unable to get off the ground owing to engine problems s, setting light to his machine he went 'on the run' but was eventually picked up and despatched 'beyond the wire'.

This drama is explained by Trevor Henshaw on page 129 of his *The Sky Their Battlefield* where he heads the main activities for 6th November as *"... day saw the final push by the Canadians into Passchendaele which they took after bitter fighting."* Four days later the *Third Battle of Ypres* was wound down. Photographic images of the battlefield show a landscape torn up by the constant shelling which in the winter rain was turned into a quagmire in which thousands, including numerous horses, perished as they were sucked down into the glutinous mud and filth.

Meanwhile Talbot Baines Bruce made good an escape from his prison camp, the final entry on his casualty form reading *"11.2.18 Reported as having escaped from Germany & being sent to England."* His MC awarded in recognition of his escape was *Gazetted* in the Edinburgh edition on December 19th, 1919, issue 13541, page 4106.

15122	NIXON	Leslie Gordon	G/Capt	30.08.45	Retirement

At his own request [LG 29 January 1946, supplement 37447, page 712]. By sheer co-incidence Leslie Gordon Nixon arrived with 3 Squadron on the day following the episode reported above and within a month he, too, was a prisoner of the enemy when on 5th December 1917 his F.1 Camel B6234 coded A fell victim to an enemy scout. His fuel tank shot through, he forced-landed near Cambrai where local troops quickly seized the fighter [see page 137 of the aforementioned publication]. 2nd Lieutenat Nixon arrived at Hull on 14th December 1918.

PILOT OFFICER [from FLYING OFFICER]

	THORNTON	Henry Norman	A/VM		19.01.47	Retirement

Air Vice-Marshal Henry Norman Thornton CBE mentioned in despatches, died on Wednesday, 6th January 1971. A little known item of Royal Air Force history is revealed on the Air of Authority website which reports that in *"in late 1939 he led the mission to Italy to investigate the purchase of Italian aircraft for the RAF."*

LG 6 September 1921, issue 32447, page 7055 - Seniority 29th August 1921 - Block 15131 to 15137

15131 BAYNE Hugh Alexander F/O 29.08.30 Relinquished
15132 FFRENCH* Nigel Meredyth F/O 29.08.30 Relinquished
Returned to the service and granted a commission in the Administrative and Special Duties Branch effective 18th March 1941, in the rank of pilot officer [LG 11 April 1941, issue 35134, page 2121]. F/Lt 04.03.44 Resigned

15133 GARDNER Herbert Patrick Legge F/O + 11.08.29
Flying Officer Herbert Patrick Legge Gardner transferred from class A to class C of the Reserve on 23rd October 1926 [LG 26 October 1926, issue 33215, page 6824] and as Paul McMillan has discovered he was *en route,* presumably, to the Federated Malay States when he was taken ill at Marseilles. His death occurred following admission to the British Hospital in Marseilles, a report on his passing being published in *The Singapore Free Press and Mercantile Advertiser* on 25th September 1929.
15134 GOLDS Arthur Edwin F/O 19.05.28 Resigned
15135 HUDSON Francis Llewellyn F/O 29.08.29 Relinquished
15136 NIMMO Benjamin John James F/O 29.08.28 Relinquished
On account of ill-health [LG 7 September 1928, issue 33419, page 5898].
15137 WINDSOR* Robert Howard S/Ldr 10.02.54 Relinquished

* Denotes previous Royal Air Force service.

LG 27 September 1921, issue 32468, page 7569 - Various dates of seniority

FLYING OFFICERS [from PILOT OFFICERS]
2

15138 BRUCE Ronald Reid Hardcastle F/O + 17.01.25 14 Squadron
Born 22nd January 1899, Ronald Reid Hardcastle Bruce arrived with 40 Squadron [SE.5a] at Bryas on 7th July 1918 but less than three weeks later he was returned to the UK. Unsurprisingly, he is not mentioned in David Gunby's history of the squadron.
15139 LONG Francis William AV-M 02.11.53 Retirement
Born on 10th October 1899 the son of the Revered F P Long of 5 Winchester Road, Oxford, Francis joined the RFC on his eighteenth birthday. Four days prior to the signing of the armistice, he arrived at Bissighem to fly F.1 Camels with 65 Squadron. In 1931 he was a member of the Royal Air Force High Speed Flight having spent the previous two years at Martlesham Heath as a test pilot. Promoted wing commander on New Year's Day 1939 his war service was principally concerned with Staff Duties.
Air Vice-Marshal Francis William Long CB DL, died on Friday, 25th March 1983.

15140 SHACKLETON John Gailey F/O 07.01.25 Relinquished
On account of ill-health [LG 5 January 1925, issue 33009, page 142].

LG 30 September 1921, issue 32473, page 7679 - Various dates of seniority

FLYING OFFICER [from FLIGHT LIEUTENANT]

15141 MARSDEN Marmaduke Scott Major 05.07.22 Resigned

FLYING OFFICER

15142 FORD DFC Hedley F/Lt 10.03.26 Relinquished
South Africa On account of ill-health [LG 9 March 1926, issue 33140, page 1744]. Born on 28th October 1899 he was quite seriously injured on 2nd June 1918 when his 49 Squadron DH.9 C6183 crashed into a wheat field [see page 208 of my first volume]. His casualty form shows he was admitted to 55 Casualty Clearing Station with injuries to his back and chest, and most painfully he had bitten through his tongue. Postwar, he was sidelined for eight days with influenza and within three days of returning to duty, and still, obviously, far from well, he was admitted to 14th General Hospital with an undiagnosed illness.
15143 WINCH Christopher Edward Bluett F/O 07.09.34 Relinquished

LG 4 October 1921, issue 32476, page 7766 - Various dates of seniority

FLYING OFFICERS
3

15144 EMBLETON Clifford Frederick F/O + 23.02.23 216 Squadron
15145 SMITH Sydney William F/O + 03.03.24 Night Flying Flight
During the course of making an official Air Ministry film which would feature a mock dogfight, Flying Officer Sydney William Smith accompanied by Sergeants Frederick Lister and Hedley Sydney Horace Meech in Vimy F9181 of the Night Flying Flight, Biggin Hill, failed to recover in time from a dive, collided with some trees, crashed and caught fire. Flying Officer Smith and Sergeant Lister perished but, amazingly, Sergeant Meech escaped though no doubt very badly shocked.
15146 STACK Thomas Neville F/O 21.09.29 Relinquished
His son of the same name entered RAFC Cranwell with the September 1937 term of Flight Cadets retiring on 11th February 1978 having achieved the rank of air chief marshal. Additional information will be reported in Volume 5.

LG 11 October 1921, issue 32483, page 7984 - Seniority 4th October 1921

FLYING OFFICERS [from FLIGHT LIEUTENANT]
2

DEAN AFC Ronald Eric Captain 18.05.22 Resigned

	RODNEY MC	Hon. James Henry Barty	F/Lt	14.10.28	Retired list

At own request [LG 30 October 1928, issue 33434, page 7019].

LG 18 October 1921, issue 32490, page 8205 - Various dates of seniority.

FLYING OFFICERS
2

15147	BUCHANAN DFC	Wilfred James	F/O	05.10.29	Relinquished

Born 8th October 1896 the entries on his casualty form are of interest:

18.1.18	*Per HMT San Rita*	*Embarked Port Said 9.1.18*	
	Ex HMS San Rita	*Disembarked Salonica 17.1.18*	
19.1.18	*Taken on strength of RFC Base Depot from Egypt*	*17.1.18*	*B213 from RFC*
" " "	*Struck off strength of RFC Base Depot : Posted to 17 Sqdn 17.1.18*		" " "
" " "	*Taken on strength of 17 Sqdn as Flying Offr*	*17.1.18*	" " "
12.2.18	*To be temporary lieutenant*	*12.9.17*	*4/Supp to LG of 8/2/18*
21.9.18	*Missing*	*19.9.18*	*Aero Svc*
" " "	*Missing - Failed to return from Special Mission*	" " "	

Trevor Henshaw not only covered losses on the Western Front but examined documents for every theatre of war in which the RFC and RAF operated and on page 282 of *The Sky Their Battlefield* where he reports losses from Macedonia and the Aegean he records for 17 Squadron [aircraft type and serial not known] *Spy Drop ldg PETRIC dropped passenger but forced to take off again by enemy troops, shot up engine ftl crashed RUPEL PASS MIA [Lt W J Buchanan POW/unnamed Sgt POW ?] Left 5 pm."* In case the reader is unfamiliar with the two abbreviations, ldg = landing and ftl = forced to land.

15148	CUDEMORE MC DFC	Charles William	S/Ldr	10.02.54	Relinquished

A General List officer, and as temporary 2nd Lieutenant, Charles William Cudemore was *Gazetted* with the MC on 7th March 1918, supplement 30561, page 2911: *"For conspicuous gallantry and devotion to duty in attacking enemy aircraft and kite balloons. He has brought down at least three enemy machines and three kite balloons, and has taken part in numerous other engagements. He has consistently set a very fine example of pluck and determination in all his attacks."* His DFC was promulgated, less citation, on 3rd June 1919, supplement 31378, page 7031. RAFM Hendon holds a single Casualty Form - Officers in respect of Charles William Cudemore his military service commenced with the Kings Shropshire Light Infantry. Born on 19th November 1897 he joined the RFC on 20th December 1916 and on 28th April 1917 he was attached to 40 Squadron [Nieuport 17] and Auchel. On 21st July 1917 he was posted to 29 Squadron [Nieuport 17] at Poperinghe. The final entry is dated 13th October 1917 on which date he returned to Home Establishment. He is mentioned twice in David Gunby's history of 40 Squadron pages 24 and 84.

FLYING OFFICER [from PILOT OFFICER]

	HOWARD	Robert Douglas Vernon	F/O	05.10.36	Class A

Subsequently killed during his employment with Imperial Airways whilst still on the reserve - see summary for 14 Squadron on 25th May 1927. During the *Great War* he served, briefly, with 110 Squadron [DH.9/DH.9A] operating from Bettoncourt, his date of joining being recorded as 8th September 1918. Between 11th October and 4th November he was in hospital with tonsillitis and a month after his discharge he was posted back to the UK on 3rd December 1918.

LG 1 November 1921, issue 32504, page 8634 - Seniority 18th October 1921

FLYING OFFICER

15155	HARDMAN DFC	James Donald Innes	ACM	29.01.58	Retirement

Air Chief Marshal Sir Donald Hardman GBE KCB DFC mentioned in despatches, died on Tuesday, 2nd March 1982. Born on 21st February 1899 James Douglas Innes Hardman joined the RFC on the 8th of March 1917 and with his trainingg completed he reported to Bailleul on 19th March 1918 where he was attached to 19 Squadron equipped with Sopwith 7F.1 Dolphin. He remained on establishment until at least 18th November 1918 on which date he was admitted to 14 General Hospital with an undiagnosed illness.

It was on 30th October 1918 that he came to the notice of his commanding officer when he was briefed to lead the squadron on an escort to DH.9s from 98 Squadron raiding rail communications at Mons. Returning from their mission the bombers were ferociously attacked by a strong force of Fokker DVIIs [in the confusion of the aerial fighting that followed it was estimated the enemy scouts numbered between thirty and forty]. The outcome of the engagements are recorded in my second volume between pages 363 and 368. Here it is only necessary to remark that from the escort only Acting Captain Hardman and two other pilots from the squadron's B Flight returned to Abscon, A Flight, headed by Captain John Wilbur Crane, an American, who had transferred to the RFC from the Canadian Infantry, were lost in entirety.

LG 8 November 1921, issue 32511, page 8844 - Various dates of seniority

FLYING OFFICERS [from FLIGHT LIEUTENANT]
2

	BOBY	Robert Sydney Pearce	F/Lt	28.10.34	Relinquished

Formerly of the 6th Battalion, Lancashire Fusiliers, Flight Lieutenant Robert Sydney Pearce Boby's *Great War* service appears to have been confined to 22 Squadron [Bristol F.2b] which he joined at Boisdinghem on 16th August 1917, serving until 8th April 1918 when he returned to England. In between these dates he enjoyed two spells of leave and two brief spells attached for temporary duty; he was promoted temporary captain on 7th December 1917 upon assuming the duties of flight commander.

	ROBERTSON AFC	Brian Kyte David	S/Ldr	24.10.36	Retired list

On account of ill-health [LG 27 October 1936, issue 34335, page 6840]. Late of the 2nd/6th Battalion, The Gloucestershire Regiment, Brian Kyte David Robertson was accepted for permanent duty with the RFC in early August 1916 at which time he was serving as an observer with 9 Squadron [BE.2 variants] at Morlancourt.

FLYING OFFICERS
2

	TULLY AFC	Terence Bernard	F/O	20.04.26	Relinquished
	WINDLE DFC	Beresford Cooper Webb	F/O	27.10.25	Relinquished

On account of ill health [LG 27 October 1925, issue 33096, page 6923]. Beresford Cooper Webb Windle was born on 11th July 1899 and joined the RFC as a General List officer on 1st February 1917. Attached to 102 Squadron [FE.2b] he forced-landed behind the lines on 21st February 1918 when his FE.2b B451 developed a radiator leak followed by engine failure. Both members of crew were captured but his observer, 2nd Lieutenant S G Williams later escaped from captivity and, subsequently, was honoured with the Military Cross. Beresford, meanwhile, sat out the war, eventually being repatriated and arriving at Hull on 14th December 1918. The loss of B451 is recorded on page 145 of *The Sky Their Battlefield.*

BLOXHAM	Cecil Cazalet Keeling	P/O	31.05.22	Resigned
BOULTON	Kenneth Roy	F/O	06.05.35	Relinquished
COMERFORD*	John Joseph	F/O	08.11.29	Relinquished

21042	HORSFIELD	Cecil Bamfleur	W/Cdr		01.10.51	Retirement

Flying Officer Cecil Bamfleur Horsfield transferred from the General Duties Branch to the Stores Branch and was appointed to a permanent commission [LG 26 January 1926, issue 33127, page 622]. His retirement was at his own request [LG 30 October 1951, supplement 39371, page 5653].

15165	KIRSTEN	Siegfried Stanley	F/O		27.07.30	Relinquished
15166	REID	Claude McLaren	F/O		01.11.34	Relinquished
15167	WARD	Maurice Vavasour	F/Lt		03.11.34	Retired list

At his own request [LG 13 November 1934, issue 34104, page 7273].

* Previous service with the Royal Air Force

LG 15 November 1921, issue 32518, page 9058 - Various dates of seniority

FLYING OFFICER

15168	PAGE	John Herbert	F/Lt		08.11.30	Relinquished

Subsequently, Flight Lieutenant John Herbert Page was granted a commission in class C of the Reserve, General Duties Branch, which was later relinquished on being commissioned in the Royal Air Force Volunteer Reserve with the service number 75183. He later transferred to the Secretarial Branch and served until: G/Capt 10.02.54 Relinquished

15169	BECK	Henry Wolferstan	F/O		08.11.29	Relinquished
15170	BEESLEY	Frank	F/O		02.11.30	Relinquished
15171	BUMSTEAD MC	Leslie Bernard James	P/O		07.06.22	Resigned
15172	BYTHELL	John Francis	F/O		02.11.30	Relinquished
15173	DODD	Thomas Courtenay	F/O		14.01.25	Relinquished

On account of ill-health [LG 13 January 1925, issue 33011, page 302.

15174	MARSHALL	George Henry	P/O		24.05.22	Resigned
15175	PRITCHARD MM	Wilson	P/O		29.03.22	Resigned
15176	WINDHAM	William Thelluson Doughty	F/Lt	+	05.07.41	

Flight Lieutenant William Thelluson Doughty Windham was a passenger aboard SS *Anselm* [a troop transport vessel] torpedoed some 300 miles off the Azores by U-96*[*Kapitänleutnant* Heinrich Lehmann-Willenbrock]. Flight Lieutenant Windhma is commemorated on panel 29 of the Runnymede Memorial. He is also remembered on the Canadian Virtual War Memorial. His service number is recorded as 76519 thus suggesting he left the service prior to the Second World War but returned on the outbreak of hostilities. He was 43 years of age.

* The German war correspondent, Lothar-Günther Buchheim was permitted to join U-96 during the autumn of 1941, and it was his experiences whilst aboard that led to him writing the best selling novel *Das Boot* which, subsequently, was adapted for film and television. The book is still available from Amazon and other booksellers.

LG 29 November 1921, issue 32533, page 9674 - Various dates of seniority

FLYING OFFICERS
3

15177	ADAMS	Francis Philip	F/O		18.11.37	Relinquished
15178	LANE	Sydney Archibald	F/O		10.07.29	Relinquished

On account of ill-health [LG 9 July 1929, issue 33515, page 4545].

15179	NICHOLLS	William Graham	W/Cdr		10.02.54	Relinquished
15180	BRAIN	Anthony Romer Maximilian	F/O		15.11.33	Relinquished

LG 6 December 1921, issue 32540, page 9891 - Seniority 28th November 1921

15181	BARLOW	Ernest Cecil	W/Cdr		15.05.40	40 Squadron

Wing Commander Ernest Cecil Barlow, commanding 40 Squadron, died when his Blenheim IV N6217 was shot down by fighters during operations to Dinant. His death, along with his crew, is summarised in my RAFBCL 139-1940 revised edition on page 126, and on page 133 of David Gunby's history of 40 Squadron. A few months prior to be granted a short service commission, he had been granted a commission as a 2nd Lieutenant in the 4th Battalion, Dunke of Cornwall's Light Infantry, TA, *Gazetted* 11th October 1921, supplement 32484, page 8044, where it is noted he was formerly a Cadet Corporal in the Rugby School Contingent, Junior Division, OTC.

15892	GOATCHER*	Charles Alexander	S/Ldr		02.07.58	Relinquished
	HARRISON*	Robert Cuthbert	F/O	+	04.01.24	84 Squadron
	WATERFIELD	Harry Kenneth	F/O		31.12.28	Relinquished

* Indicates previous service with the Royal Air Force.

LG 20 December 1921, issue 32554, page 10373 - Various dates of seniority

FLYING OFFICER
5

15186	DAVY	Brian Augustus	W/Cdr		10.02.54	Relinquished
	MACKAY	George Frederick	F/O		12.12.30	Relinquished
15187	DU BOULAY	Guy George Hussemayne	G/Capt		05.04.46	Retirement

The entries on his casualty form are herewith reported in full:-

24.7.18	*100241 3/AM G G H Du Boulay RAF granted temp. commission as 2/Lieut. [A & S]*		*HQ ME*
	Royal Air Force on graduating B	*19.6.18*	*List No. 7*
26.8.18	*Entitle to wear wings on graduation C*	*15.8.18*	*List No. 8*
4.9.18	*Assumes duties as asst. instructor*	*28.8.18*	*B213 58 T Sqn*
14.9.18	*Adm. General Hosp. Suez*	*10.9.18*	*B213 58 T Sqn*
30.8.18	*Granted temp. comm. as 2/Lieut. [A & S]*	*19.6.18*	*London Gaz.*
28.9.18	*Discharged from hospital*	*19.9.18*	*B213 58 T Sqn*
9.9.18	*Adm. Gen. Hospital Suez Boil of Face*	*9.9.18*	*W3034*
19.9.18	*Discharged Gen. Hosp. Carbuncle cheek*	*19.9.18*	*" " "*

15189	MARSDEN	John	A/Cmdr		16.06.48	Retirement
	WILLIAMS	Sydney George	F/O		09.12.29	Relinquished

ROLL OF HONOUR
FOR
1921 SHORT SERVICE COMMISSION
OFFICERS

F/O	ANDERSON	Ian Patrick	28 July 1924	28 Squadron
F/Lt	ANNESLEY	William Robert Bathurst	16 August 1927	Training Base Leuchars
F/O	BEAL mid	Leslie Wallis	3 October 1921	6 FTS Manston
F/O	BRUCE	Ronald Reid Hardcastle	17 January 1925	14 Squadron
F/O	CARR	John Henry Talbot	20 May 1921	210 Squadron
F/O	CARR-HALFEY	John Alexander Bernard	15 May 1921	5 Squadron
F/O	CURTIS	Philip Frank Axford	23 February 1923	216 Squadron
F/O	DASHWOOD	Edward John	21 March 1925	27 Squadron
F/O	EMBLETON	Clifford Frederick	23 February 1923	216 Squadron
F/O	FINDLEY	Arthur	20 May 1925	31 Squadron
F/O	GARDNER	Herbert Patrick Legge	11 August 1929	
F/O	GAYES	William James	29 November 1922	A & GS Eastchurch
G/Capt	GREENLAW	Robert Ritchie	18 January 1943	Air Attaché Teheran
F/O	HANSTOCK	Brendan John O'Connor	26 June 1935	
F/O	HARRICKS	Frank Simon	24 October 1922	1 Squadron
F/O	HARRINGTON	Hubert Bernard Delma	6 January 1922	60 Squadron
F/O	HARRISON	Robert Cuthbert	4 January 1924	84 Squadron
F/O	HILLS	Geoffrey Paulet French	25 June 1934	Bristol Aeroplane Company
P/O	HOPKINS	George	7 April 1922	2 FTS Duxford
F/Lt	JEFFERIES	Edward Charles Norman	23 October 1940	24 Squadron
F/O	LOCH	Desmond Reginald	7 April 1923	20 Squadron
F/O	LOCKE-WATERS	Evelyn Archer	6 October 1922	30 Squadron
F/O	LUARD	Robert Blaine	17 August 1922	27 Squadron
P/O	LUSH	Eric Raven	19 August 1921	2 FTS Duxford
F/Lt	McALERY	John Mecredy	4 April 1924	1 Squadron
F/O	SMITH	Sydney William	3 March 1924	Night Flying Flight
P/O	SOUTH	Burns Alan Campbell	25 February 1922	2 FTS Duxford
F/O	SYKES	Benjamin	20 November 1932	
F/Lt	WALLAGE MC	Stanley Harry	17 April 1926	14 Squadron
F/O	WHITE AFC	Archer Statham	29 July 1929	
F/O	WHITMORE	Fielding Griffith	21 August 1923	28 Squadron
F/Lt	WINDHAM	William Thelluson Doughty	5 July 1941	
W/Cdr	WYNNE-EYTON	Charles Sandford	14 November 1944	144 Maintenance Unit
	DSO AFC four times mentioned in despatches			

Appendix D - RAF [Cadet] College Cranwell

Commandant
Air Commodore Charles Alexander Holcombe Longcroft DSO

The September 1921, intake of Flight Cadets included the first cadets from the Siam with the arrival of Mont Sinhaseni and Vishta Syastirake. And here the authors are indebted to Jagan Pilarisetti [PVS Jagan Mohan] who hosts the website RAF Commands and is an acknowledged expert on matters concerning the Indian Air Force.

As a writer one of his outstanding contributions to aviation in India is his meticulously researched *The Westland Wapiti in the Indian Air Force : A Complete History [1933-1943]* published in 2014.

Service numbers issued to the graduates on commissioning for the intakes February 1921 to September 1930 are as follows:

16068 - 16259
26001 - 26260
33001 - 33016

February 1921 entry : 20

16068 APTHORPE* Dudley Frederick Arthur P/O 31.10.23 Retired list
On account of ill-health. Despite poor health being given for the reason of his placement on the Retired list, Dudley Frederick Arthur Apthorpe lived a very full life until his passing on Tuesday, 20th September 1988.
16069 BERRIDGE* Thomas Donald F/O + 30.03.25 28 Squadron
16070 CARTER* North A/Cmdr 26.11.54 Retirement
Air Commodore North Carter CB DFC mentioned in despatches, died on Saturday, 13th October 1984. In retirement he took up a post in Nigeria as a temporary administration officer for the northern region; subsequently in 1963, he settled in Australia.
16071 CARTER* Ronald Hartley G/Capt 29.11.49 Retirement
Group Captain Ronald Hartley Carter DSO OBE DFC twice mentioned in despatches, died on Sunday, 17th January 1971. His DFC was *Gazetted* 21st December 1937, issue 34465, page 8001: *"... for gallant and distinguished services rendered in connection with the operations in Waziristan during the period 17th January to 15th September 1937."* As Commanding Officer of 240 Squadron, Coastal Command, he was awarded the DSO [LG 24 December 1940, issue 35022, page 7214]. Formerly of the Royal Naval Colleges at Osborne and Dartmouth, his Service medals were sold at an auction held between the 5th to the 8th of April 2005, by Noble Numismatics at the Hotel Intercontinental, Sydney, Australia. The estimate for a Group of 8 was $11,000 Australian and the bidding closed at $15,500 Australian.
16072 CATOR* Francis Gerald G/Capt 26.04.51 Retirement
Group Captain Francis Gerald Cator CBE three times mentioned in despatches, died on Saturday, 30th December 1995, a shade under six years short of his 100th birthday. Prior to his arrival at Cranwell, he was a Cadet at the Britannia Royal Naval College, Dartmouth.
16073 FITZMAURICE* Maurice James P/O + 14.07.23 56 Squadron
16094 FRESSANGES Francis Joseph AM 17.10.57 Retirement
Air Marshal Sir Francis Fressanges KBE CB mentioned in despatches Legion of Merit USA, died on Friday, 17th October 1975 in Kenya.
16074 GILLMORE Vyvian Osborne F/Cdt + 07.07.22 RAF [Cadet] College
Flight Cadet Vyvian Osborne Gillmore, aged 19, died in a midair collision when his Avro 504K F8747 came into collision over, or near the airfield, with H2364 flown by Flight Cadet Francis Gerald Cator who was injured, but managed to land safely.
16074 GOLDSMID* Francis Frederic Rowsell P/O + 08.04.24 SAC Old Sarum
Pilot Officer Francis Frederick Rowsell Goldsmid and Leading Aircraftman Harold Samuel Nicholls died when their Bristol F.2b F4606 of the School of Army Co-operation at Old Sarum stalled while turning near the airfield. This accident was reported in a number of newspapers, the *Hampshire Telegraph* published on the 14th April, carried the following: *"Two airmen were killed in a flying accident at Old Sarum, on Tuesday afternoon, Pilot Officer Francis Frederick Rousell* [sic] *Goldsmid [21], of Havant, went up in a Bristol fighter plane with Leading Airccraftsman Harold Samuel Nichols* [sic] *[20], of Devonport, for the purpose of demonstration. The machine had just passed over the heads of some cavalry officers, who were watching the flight in the vicinity of the aerodrome, when it was observed to nose-dive, and crashed to earth from 200 feet. The two airmen, who were unconscious and suffering from severe head injuries, were taken by ambulance to Salisbury Infirmary. Nichols died on arrival and Goldsmid succumbed shortly afterwards."* In a following edition a full report of the funeral service was reported under the banner 'Havant Airman's Funeral - A Brilliant Young Pilot': *"The funeral took place at Salisbury Cemetery on Friday of Lieut. Francis Frederic Rowsell Goldsmid, the 21-year old Pilot Officer who met with his death in a flying accident on April 7th. The young officer was demonstrating with a Bristol fighter over the Plain at an elevation of 200 feet for photographic purposes, and was accompanied by LAC Nicholls, of Devonport. The machine was seen to suddenly crumple and nose-dive to the aerodrome grounds and Lieut. Goldsmith* [sic] *died forty-five minutes after being extricated from the debris. He was educated at Stratheden College, Blackheath, and the Imperial Service College, Windsor, and was trained for the RAF at Cranwell. He was the only son of Major G S Goldsmith, retired Indian Staff Corps, and Mrs Goldsmith of "Connaught" House, Denville, Havant, and grandson of Major-General Sir Frederic J Goldsmith KCSI CB, and also grandson of Mr. Francis William Rowsell CB CMG Chevalier de la Legion d'Honneur. Interested in all branches of sport, Lt Goldsmith became deservedly popular at Old Sarum Depot, and was loved and respected by officers and men alike. His Commanding Officer, Wing Commander O Boyd paid his tribute when he said "The lad was a promising officer and a brilliant pilot," whilst his schoolmaster's sentiments are "he left behind a wonderful and an inspiring record of blameless school life." The funeral was impressive in the extreme, and with full military honours being accorded, the entire station turned out to do homage to their dead colleague, and the body was placed on a gun carriage, and covered with the Union Jack. Deceased's colleagues followed the cortege to St. Mark's Church, where a service was held prior to the interment, whilst at the graveside the "Last Post' was sounded, and a volley fired. The only music in the service was the hymn "On the Resurrection Morning" and Chopin's "Funeral March." The Rev. Waddy C F was the officiating clergy. The mourners at the graveside were Major and Mrs G S Goldsmith [parents], Dr. Whitestone, Maidstone [uncle], Mrs Dewar Durie [aunt], Mr A and Miss V Cotton [London], Colonel Penne, Wing Commander O Boyd, Flight Officers Murgatroyd, Askerman and Gore, and Mr. Veness [Farnham]. There was an extraordinary number of floral tributes laid upon the grave, and the included wreaths from his parents, Miss Rowsell, Ronie [aunt], Miss Goldsmith [aunt], His Commanding Officer, his brother officers, NCOs and men of Old Sarum."* The authors are indebted to Di Ablewhite, photoshoot location owner and amateur historical researcher for graciously sharing the newspaper reports covering the death of Pilot Officer Golddsmid.
16075 HARRIS* Frederic Samuel P/O + 24.04.23 39 Squadron
16076 JORDAN* Richard Bowen AM 02.06.58 Retirement
Air Marshal Sir Richard Jordan KCB DFC ADC four times mentioned in despatches, died at Royal Tunbridge Wells on Sunday, 24th April 1994. He is mentioned on page 61 of RAFBCL 1941 when his 214 Squadron Wellington II W5450 crashed near Bury St. Edmunds on return from operations to Berlin. His biography can be read on *Wikipedia.* Air Marshal Jordan was also a recipient of the Commander of Order of Polonia Restituta [Poland].
16077 LEWES* Richard F/O + 29.01.25 403 Flight HMS *Eagle*
Graduating on 20th December 1922 [LG 23 January, issue 32789, page 532], Pilot Officer Richard Lewes underwent carrier training and was subsequently posted to 442 Flight aboard HMS *Argus*. On Tuesday 11th March 1924, he crashed while taking off from the carrier in Parnall Panther N7461, falling into the sea off Mallorca. His observer, Flight Lieutenant Kenneth Cromar Tilman was killed, but Richard was picked up with non-life

threatening injuries. Then, on Thursday, 29th January 1925, and now aboard HMS *Eagle* and attached to 403 Flight he crashed at RAF Hal Far on Malta in Flycatcher N9666, overturning with fatal results.

16078 LYWOOD* Ralph Woodcock Gifford G/Capt 21.04.46 Retirement

Group Captain Ralph Woodcock Gifford Lywood died on Monday, 29th December 1958.

16079 NEWALL* John Sydney F/O 11.02.28 Resigned

In company with Neville Vintcent DFC [see page 272 of Volume 3], with the intention, as discovered by my co-author, of making a long-distance flight in DH.9s G-EBUM and G-EBUN from Stag Lane, Edgware to India, an account appearing in the Australian newspaper, *The Advertiser Adelaide* on Saturday, February 11th, 1928. Subsequently, John Sydney was granted a commission in class C of the Reserve of Air Force Officers and later to Class A on 30th April 1931, his service number now being 70496. S/Ldr 06.07.47 Resigned

By 1959, Squadron Leader John Sydney Newall, formerly of the Britannia Royal Naval College, Dartmouth, appears to have alternating between Eire and Bermuda, eventually, it seems, settling in Switzerland where he died in Lausanne at the age of 91 on Friday, 26th March 1993.

16080 NICHOLETTS* Gilbert Edward AM 01.07.59 Retirement

Air Marshal Sir Gilbert Nicholetts KBE CB AFC* twice mentioned in despatches, died on Wednesday, 7th September 1983. Arriving in the Far East having commanded RAF Shaluffa, he was taken prisoner in the Dutch East Indies by the Japanese. There are a number of websites devoted to this officer who prior to arrival at Cranwell was at the Britannia Royal Naval College, Dartmouth, *Wikipedia* reporting a brief resume of his Royal Air Force service.

16081 NUTTALL* Frank Edward F/Lt 30.06.37 Retired list

At his own requesst [LG 29 June 1937, issue 34413, page 4181]. Returned to service [LG 20 September 1940, issue 34949, page 5580] as a wing commander [temporary]. He reverted to the Retired List on 17th November 1946, retaining the rank of group captain. He was appointed CBE in the New Year's Honours List for 1946. Three times mentioned in despatches, his death was announced on Sunday, 23rd February 1992.

16082 OPIE* William Alfred AV-M 01.06.59 Retirement

Air Vice-Marshal William Alfred Opie CB CBE twice mentioned in despatches, died on Friday, 14th October 1977. On the 14th of March 1935, he assumed command of a flight with 5 Squadron at Kohat, moving the next day to Quetta and it was here on 31st May 1935, that he was one of thousands injured in the earthquake that struck the region with a magnitude of 7.7 on the Richter scale. Death and destruction was widespread and it is estimated that between 30,000 and 60,000 persons perished including 54 Royal Air Force personnel. A detailed account of this awful tragedy is reported on the Hibbitt & Barnes Family History [Quetta Earthquake 1935 - The RAFs Account] which the authors dutifully acknowledge. On 20th July 1935, Flight Lieutenant Opie was invalided to Home Establishment. Subsequently, he commanded 2 Squadron at Hawkinge where he oversaw the squadron's conversion from biplanes to Lysanders, while from May 1939 to April 1940, he commanded 18 Squadron [Blenheims] before transferring from the General Duties Branch to the Technical Branch.

16083 RANDLE* George Hirst A/Cmdr 12.02.57 Retirement

Air Commodore George Hirst Randle Legion of Merit USA, died on Sunday, 24th March 1974.

16119 SLOAN William John Patrick F/Lt 20.11.31 Retirement

Returned to service and granted a commission as a probationary Pilot Officer in the Administrative and Special Duties Branch, effective from 30th December 1939 [LG 23 January 1940, supplement 34778, page 466]. Subsequently, he was granted a commission as Flight Lieutenant retaining the rank of squadron leader in the Secretarial Branch on 12th March 1947 [LG 8 April 1947, supplement 37924, page 1589]. Reverting to Flying Officer and as 91285 served for eighteen months in Royal Auxiliary Air Force before resigning his commission on 23rd February 1950. Born in India in January 1904, he died in Co, Antrim during 1972.

Flight Cadets with an asterisk appended against their surname graduated from the College with permanent commissions, with effect from 20th December 1922 [LG 23 January 1923, issue 32789, pages 532 and 533].

SWORD OF HONOUR
Flight Cadet North Carter

ROLL OF HONOUR
FEBRUARY 1921 ENTRY

F/Lt	BERRIDGE	Thomas Donald	30 March 1935	28 Squadron
P/O	FITZMAURICE	Maurice James	14 July 1923	56 Squadron
F/Cdt	GILLMORE	Vyvian Osborne	7 July 1922	RAF [Cadet] College
P/O	GOLDSMID	Francis Frederic Rowsell	8 April 1924	SAC Old Sarum
P/O	HARRIS	Frederic Samuel	24 April 1923	39 Squadron
F/O	LEWES	Richard	29 January 1925	403 Flight HMS *Eagle*

September 1921 entry : 22

16105 BAXTER Henry Richard Frederick F/Lt + 17.02.31 13 Squadron

Flight Lieutenant Henry Richard Frederick Baxter died from heart failure while undergoing treatment in RAF Hospital Hillingdon, Middlesex. At the time he was Armaments Officer for the squadron which was equipped with Armstrong Whitworth Atlas and based at Netheravon in Wiltshire.

16089 BEAMISH* Francis Victor F/Lt 18.10.33 Relinquished

On account of ill-health [LG 17 October 1933, issue 33987, page 6694]. Reinstated 23rd March 1937 [LG 9 February 1937, issue 34369, page 895]. G/Capt + 28.03.42 RAF Kenley

Group Captain Francis Victor Beamish DSO* DFC AFC died while commanding RAF Kenley. On the day of his death, and flying in his personal Spitfire Vb W3649 FV-B attached to 485 Squadron RNZAF he was shot down over the English Channel while taking part in a *Rodeo* operations. His body was never recovered and he is commemorated on the Runnymede Memorial, panel 64. From Castle Rock in Co. Derry he was the eldest of the Beamish boys, two Charles Eric and George Robert following in his footsteps to Cranwell in 1926 and 1923 respectively. An account of Francis's life is recorded on *Wikipedia.* Turning to *The Gazettes* the Edinburgh issue 15455, page 31, of January 7th, 1938, reports his award of the AFC with his DSO being published in the London paper on 23rd July 1940, issue 34903, pages 4529 and 4530: *"Wing Command Beamish took over command of a Royal Air Force station after two squadrons there had been intensively engaged in successful fighting operations over France for thirteen days and personally led them on many patrols against the enemy. In June 1940, during an offensive mission over France, six Messerschmitt 109's were destroyed, two of them by Wing Commander Beamish himself, and twelve driven off. One day recently he assisted in the destruction of a Messerschmitt 110, whilst leading the escort to a convoy, and three days later he shot down a Dornier 17. This officer's outstanding leadership and high courage have inspired all those under his command with great energy and dash."* A DFC was *Gazetted* on 8th November 1940, issue 34987, page 6440: *"The work of this station commander has been outstanding. He has displayed exceptional keenness in his engagements against the enemy and has recently destroyed one and possibly a further seven enemy aircraft. His coolness and courage have proved an inspiration to all."* A First Bar to his DSO appeared in issue 35263, page 5103, of the London edition on 2nd September 1941: *"Group Captain Beamish Commanded a Royal Air Force Station from October 1940, to March 1941, and during that period carried out 71 operational sorties in which he destroyed an enemy fighter, probably destroyed three other hostile aircraft and damaged others. Since his appointment to Group headquarters he has taken part in further sorties and has probably destroyed two more enemy aircraft. The courage and devotion to duty displayed by Group Captain Beamish are of the highest order and he has set a magnificent example."* Shortly before his death and during a general reconnaissance sortie over the Channel with Wing Commander R F Boyd on the morning of 12th February 1942, they caught sight of elements of the German Fleet steaming at high speed towards the Dover Strait in what has been imprinted on history as the *Channel Dash*. This audacious break out from the French ports by the *Scharnhorst, Gneisenau* and *Prinz Eugen* had been reported earlier by pilots from 91 Squadron, but it was only when Victor Beamish alerted the authorities to what was happening were operations set in train to try and destroy the enemy battleships and their escort [operations that won a posthumous VC for Lieutenant-Commander Eugene Esmonde of 825 Squadron [Swordfish]], but ultimately were unsuccessful and were deemed a humiliating episode in our military history.

16106 BEAUMONT Francis William Lionel Collings F/Lt 03.10.38 Resigned

As a Flight Cadet he wrote off Bristol F.2b E2431 in a landing accident at the College on Tuesday 31st July 1923. Early in the Second World War he returned to the service and was granted a commission in the Administrative and Special Duties Branch [LG 3 October 1939, issue 34700, page 6662], effective 26th September 1939, his service number now being 74420. F/Lt + 06.05.41 RAF Film Unit

Although shown as belonging to the Royal Air Force Film Unit, this is not confirmed. However, an investigation into his death by Paul McMillan reveals that he died at the Carnegie First Aid Post in Cambridge Street, Liverpool. At the time Liverpool was undergoing sustained bombing by the *Luftwaffe,* the period between the 1st and 7th of May 1941, often referred as the 'Liverpool Blitz' though the city had been subjected to heavy raids since the previous August. A report in *The Times* on Saturday, May 10th, reports that Miss Mary Lawson, the stage and film actress, was killed along with her husband *"Mr F W L C Beaumont, the film producer."* Flight Lieutenant Francis William Lionel Collings Beaumont is buried in Liverpool [Kirkdale] Cemetery.

16090 BROADWAY* Basil Douglas John F/O + 14.05.26 32 Squadron

16091 CLIFFORD* George Richard Melville G/Capt 14.03.53 Retirement

Group Captain George Richard Melville Clifford died on Wednesday, 31st March 1971.

16092 COGGLE* Cyril Kenneth Joseph G/Capt 12.07.53 Retirement

Group Captain Cyril Kenneth Joseph Coggle who in the Second World War had been taken prisoner of war in Java by the Japanese died on Saturday, 16th January 1960. He had been honoured with thE Spanish Cross, 1st Class, Order of Military Merit.

16093 DAVIES* Adolphus Dan A/Cmdr 25.08.54 Retirement

Air Commodore Adolphus Dan Davies CB, CBE, died on Thursday, 5th January 1984.

16108 DICKENS Louis Walter A/Cmdr 22.08.47 Retirement

Air Commodore Sir Louis Walter Dickens Kt DFC AFC three times mentioned in despatches, died on Tuesday, 30th August 1988. He is buried in Wokingham [St. Sebastians] Cemetery. As a wing commander commanding 139 Squadron at the time of the *Blitzkrieg* he won an immediate DFC, *Gazetted* 31st May 1940, supplement 34860, page 3252: *"This officer led nine Blenheim aircraft in an exceedingly determined and gallant attack which he succeeded in pressing home with success in the face of extremely heavy enemy opposition. While no exact estimate can be given ass to the number of enemy fighters in contact, a formation of nine Messerschmitt 109's and four Messerschmitt 110's attacking the leading formation were identified, and the remaining two sections were simultaneously heavily engaged by a superior number of Messerschmitt 110's. The attack was of great moment and courage and leadership displayed by this officer inspired the squadron in an operation which otherwise might have completely failed."*

I am reasonably confident that the action referred to in the citation took place on the 12th of May 1940, when the squadron was based in France at Plivot. Seven of the Blenheims were shot down, their fates of their crews being summarised in my RAFBCL 1939-1940, pages 52 and 53. Other actions in which his squadron sustained losses before returning to West Raynham on 30th May 1940, included Sedan on the 14th and Montherme on the 16th.

16110 FULLER-GOOD James Lawrence Fuller AV-M 29.03.59 Retirement

Air Vice-Marshal James Lawrence Fuller Fuller-Good CB CVO CBE BSM mentioned in despatches, died on Wednesday, 11th May 1983.

16095 HALL* Francis Frederick Walby G/Capt 16.04.47 Retirement

Group Captain Francis Frederick Walby Hall retired to South Africa. He had been mentioned in despatches.

16112 HUTCHINSON John Harvey W/Cdr + 08.10.40 RAF Pembrey

Wing Commander John Harvey Hutchinson mentioned in despatches is buried in Pembrey [St. Illtyd] Churchyard. He died along with Flying Officer Cyril Clifford Hicks when their Magister I P6347 of PRU Heston collided with a barrage balloon cable and crashed near Langley in Buckinghamshire. Interestingly, the service movements of the Magister shows it was a 'squadron hack' with 229 Squadron and 46 Squadron and prior to transfer to PRU was attached to the Station Flight at RAF Pembrey. My suspicion is that Wing Commander Hutchinson was returning to Pembrey either following an appointment in London, or possible leave, as his address is shown as Finchampstead, a village in the Wokingham Borough of Royal Berkshire. Flying Officer Hicks rests in Kingston Cemetery, his headstone inscribed: *"Sacred To The Memory Of Cyril."*

16096 JONES* Philip A/Cmdr 01.04.58 Retirement

Air Commodore Philip Jones CB five times mentioned in despatches, died on Monday, 12th November 1979. For most of his active service he specialised in signals, his final appointment being a five year post as Air Officer - Signals at HQ Middle East Air Force.

16097 MELLOR* Harry Manners W/Cdr + 26.05.40 22 Squadron

Wing Commander Harry Manners Mellor and his crew disappeared off Heligoland while on a minelaying sortie from North Coates in Beaufort I L4450 OA-F; he is commemorated on the Runnymede Memorial panel 3. He was the senior Flight Cadet to be killed on operational duty during the Second World War.

16116 MOSS Charles William P/O + 09.04.24 4 Squadron

16098 PRICKMAN* Thomas Bain A/Cmdr 04.10.54 Retirement

Air Commodore Thomas Bain Prickman CB CBE, died on Saturday 1st February 1992.

16099 PRITCHETT* Norman Anthony Pelynt A/Cmdr 03.10.51 Retirement

Air Commodore Norman Anthony Pritchett Pelynt twice mentioned in despatches, died on Friday15th March 1963.

16100 ROBERTS* Reginald Austen Poyntz F/Lt 25.08.35 Retirement

Flight Lieutenant Reginald Austen Poyntz Roberts died in Totnes, Devon, on Monday, 25th October 1965.

16101 SCOTT-TAYLOR* Ronald F/O 05.09.28 Resigned

My co-author suggests that Flying Ronald Scott-Taylor, who was attached to the Armament and Gunnery School, Eastchurch, and lately residing at the Central Flying School at Upavon, filed for Bankruptcy through the Salisbury Court on 29th October 1926, and was subsequently declared bankrupt owing to the high cost of messing. He was released from the bankruptcy order on 8th July 1929. On Saturday, 11th July 1942, the *Chester Chronicle* reported that Ronald Scott-Taylor of Lache Lane, Chester had been fined a total £3 for being in possession of a rifle and revolver ammunition without a firearms certificate. Born 8th November 1902, in Alverstoke, Hampshire, he died on Friday, 2nd June 1967, in Chester.

SINHASENI Mont

Siam AIR 76/464/111 held by TNA Kew contains a Record Card upon which the following information has been recorded:

"Christian Names [in full] Mont *Surname Sinhaseni*

Permanent Home Address: Add for communication, The Supt.
Siamese Legation, 21 Ashdown Place, SW.,
General in the Siamese Army
Phya, Bharata, Siamese Legation

Name of Person to be Informed of Casualties *Father Phya Amyito* *Registered Papers No. 236119/21 Above add. Per File 6/2/24*

Post to Fulford It is indicated this Cadet is to complete 2 years service at the RAF [Cadet] College, but is ineligible to compete for any prizes. At the end of his training he will return to Siam as [unreadable] *with the Siamese Air Force.*
93313/21 RAF Cadet College Sept. 1921."

A second Record Card may be accessed on AIR 76/491/142 which suggests he remained at the College for just three days, arriving on 3rd December and departing 6th December 1921. It is suspected that in 1924, he received flying instruction under the tutelage of the United States Army Air Corps at San Antonio in Texas, returning to the United Kingdom by 19267.

	SVASTIRAKSE Siam	Vishta			
16102	THOMSON*	Donald Leslie	A/Cmdr	29.09.55	Retirement

Air Commodore Donald Leslie Thomson DSO DFC twice mentioned in despatches, died on Friday 5th January 1973.

16103	WORTHINGTON*	Geoffrey Luis	P/O	22.10.24	Resigned

21028 Returned to the service and appointed to a permanent commission in the Stores Branch [LG 6 April 1926, issue 33150, page 2554].

AV-M	12.04.61	Retirement

Air Vice-Marshal Sir Geoffrey Worthington KBE CB mentioned in despatches, died on Tuesday, 28th April 1992.

Flight Cadets with an asterisk appended against their surname graduated from the College with a permanent commission on 15th August 1923 [LG 18th September 1923, issue 32863, page 6279]. Flight Cadet Francis Joseph Franges from the February 1921, also graduated.

SWORD OF HONOUR
Flight Cadet Geoffrey Luis Worthington

ROLL OF HONOUR
SEPTEMBER 1921 ENTRY

F/Lt	BAXTER	Henry Richard Frederick	17 February 1931	13 Squadron
G/Capt	BEAMISH DSO* DFC AFC	Francis Victor	28 March 1942	RAF Kenley
F/Lt	BEAUMONT	Francis William Lionel Collings	6 May 1941	RAF Film Unit
F/O	BROADWAY	Basil Douglas John	14 May 1926	32 Squadron
W/Cdr	HUTCHINSON	John Harvey	8 October 1940	RAF Pembrey
W/Cdr	MELLOR	Harry Manners	26 May 1940	22 Squadron
P/O	MOSS	Charles William	9 April 1924	4 Squadron

FLYING ACCIDENTS

Monday 12 December 1921
Avro 504K E3446 F/Cdt C B B Maturin Injured
T/o Sleaford and became lost whilst on a cross-country exercise and while attempting a forced-landing stalled and crashed. Possibly repaired, but no further entries recorded for the aircraft after this date.

A.M. Form 470 indicates the flight started from the Flying Wing Sleaford and the mishap occurred at 1045 hours. Flight Cadet [Corporal] Charles Baggart Beaumont Maturin [see Volume 3 page 272 for his service history] was not seriously hurt, but he was admitted to the College's hospital for treatment. The Court of Inquiry duly observed *"Due to the pilot stalling the aeroplane when quite close to the ground while attempting to land after losing his way due to inexperience in forced landing."*

Note. No location reported on the Form, but I very much suspect it was at Potter Hanworth, 6 miles SE from Lincoln, which Air-Britain's *J File* records against H2446 and for which no Form A.N. 470 has been raised. Thus, it appears a certainty that only one Avro from the College was lost on the 12th December.

Avro 504K H2446 *Not reported*
T/o Cran for a cross-country flight; became lost and in making a forced-landing stalled and crashed at Potterhanworth, 6 miles SE from Lincoln. The duplication of the last three digits of the airframe serial hints only one accident took place on this day, though this may be a coincidence.

Appendix E - Roll of Honour

The Roll of Honour for 1921 has been constructed from a number of sources, not least from the Commonwealth War Graves Commission data base.

Notes have been added in respect of non-commissioned officers whose deaths are not attributed to flying accidents.

ROYAL AIR FORCE

Mechanic ARMSTRONG Jack 20 May 1921 210 Squadron
F/O ARMSTRONG William Ash 14 April 1921 208 Squadron
Mechanic ASHCROFT Frederick Charles 6 July 1921 4 Squadron
Propeller accident at Farnborough during starting a Bristol F.2b. His service number 328219 comes within the block 326001 - 329000 allocated for Boys enlisting between December 1918 and March 1919.
P/O BREWE Cyril 22 June 1921 84 Squadron
Pilot Officer Cyril Brewe died in No. 3 British General Hospital, Basra where he was undergoing treatment for acute alcoholism; he is buried in Basra War Cemetery, his age being recorded as 35 and that he had served for eighteen years. I believe much of this service had been with the RNAS for his name was amongst the extensive list *"mentioned in despatches by the Vice-Admiral Commanding the Eastern Mediterranean Squadron for the good services in action during the period above referred to."* [the Gallipoli campaign waged between April and December 1915, and extending to January 1916] *Gazetted* 15th May 1916, supplement 29581, page 4832. His rank at the time was that of a petty officer.
AC2 BROWNING Alfred Walter 26 March 1921 100 Squadron
Aircraftman Alfred Walter Browning had been taken to the King George V Hospital, Dublin, with gun shot wounds sustained in an action with the IRA. Repatriated and buried in Lambeth [Tooting] Cemetery. Joining as a civilian, he was attested as 34790 [block 340001 - 360000 commencing September 1919 and used until June 1925].
F/O CARR John Henry Talbot 20 May 1921 210 Squadron
F/O CARR-HALFEY John Albert Bernard 15 May 1921 5 Squadron
F/Lt CLARKE AFC George Malcolm 14 April 1921 208 Squadron
AC2 COMPORT Thomas George Henry 26 January 1921 3 Squadron
Aircraftman Thomas George Henry Comport died in the Station Hospital at Bangalore while being treated for typhoid and was laid to rest in Bangalore [Hosur Road] Cemetery. At the time of his death 3 Squadron was based at Bangalore and equipped with Sopwith 7F.1 Snipe. Aircraftman Comport entered the service between March and August 1919, his service number 331540 coming from the block 329001 - 33500.
F/O COOMBS DFC Herbert Milbourne 8 June 1921 216 Squadron
F/O COX Pierse Joseph 14 April 1921 14 Squadron
F/O DEANE DFC Frederick William 29 April 1921 56 Squadron
F/O HALFEY John Albert Bernard 15 May 1921 5 Squadron
Flying Officer John Albert Bernard Halfey is believed to have died from natural causes; he is buried in Delhi.
F/O HILL Hepworth Ambrose Vyvian 25 February 1921 100 Squadron
Flying Officer Hepworth Ambrose Vyvian Hill was accidentally shot by a sentry. He is buried in Belfast City Cemetery. His entry on the CWGC data base indicates he was attached to the detachment of 4 Squadron [Aldergrove and Baldonnel] but contemporary records show these detachments returned to Farnborough during the January.
F/O HYSLOP Maitland 30 September 1921 84 Squadron
AC2 JOHNSTON Simon 12 March 1921 202 Squadron
Aircraftman Simon Johnston died in Ras-el-Tin Military Hospital where he had been admitted with pneumonia. He is buried in Alexandria [Chatby] Military and War Memorial Cemetery, his headstone bearing the words *"To Memory Ever Dear The Lord Is My Shepherd."* It is certain that his enlistment was either August or September 1919, for his service number 336305 comes in the block allocated for these two months, 336001 - 338000.
F/O JONES Edward Blake 14 April 1921 208 Squadron
Cpl LAKE Horace Merilion 14 August 1921 47 Squadron
Corporal Lake was a late entrant to the *Great War,* joining at some time between May and June 1918, from civilian life, though the possibility of transfer from the army cannot be ruled out as his service number, 195212, falls within the block 185001 - 200000 set aside for such entrants.
O/O NIXON John Walpole 1 June 1921 6 Squadron
Observer Officer John Walpole Nixon had been invalided to the UK for treatment in the RAF Central Hospital, Finchley. Here he was operated on for tonsilectomy and while under anaesthetic he suffered a cardiac arrest and died. He is commemorated on panel 6 at the Brookwood 1914-1918 Memorial.
AC2 PLUMMER Edward 30 September 1921 84 Squadron
A former boy entrant, Aircraft Edward Plummer's service number was 158676 [Block 155001 - 160000 issues between October 1917 and December 1918].
F/O POTTER mid Sydney Hugh 14 August 1921 47 Squadron
Cpl ROADKNIGHT S H 2 September 1921 100 Squadron
LAC ROBERTS Robert 4 May 1921 12 Squadron
Leading Aircraft Robert Roberts started his military service with the Royal Naval Air Service in 1917, transferring automatically to the Royal Air Force on April 1st, 1918. This is confirmed by his service number 244301 which comes with the block 225061 -244710.
F/O SLATER Ian Cecil 15 August 1921 208 Squadron

O/O	SMITH MC MM	Frank James	14 April 1921	208 Squadron
F/O	SPINNEY	William Leslie Gordon	24 February 1921	4 Squadron
F/O	STRUBEN	Harry Marinus	24 June 1921	25 Squadron
F/O	TEAGLE	Cyril Hollis	12 September 1921	55 Squadron
F/Lt	TEMPEST MC DFC	Edmund Roger	17 December 1921	216 Squadron
AC2	WATSON	William	28 February 1921	216 Squadron

Aircraftman William Watson, aged 18, had been detached from 216 Squadron to the Aircraft Depot at Aboukir and while on escort duty on a train died following an accidental discharge of a rifle. He is buried in Alexandria [Chatby] Military and War Memorial Cemetery where his headstone is engraved *"What Words Could Paint His Parents Grief."*

He joined as a civilian and was attested as 341323 [Block 340001 - 360000].

F/O	YOUNG DFC* mid	Horace Norman	13 July 1921	12 Squadron

Flying Officer Horace Norman Young's death was caused by drowning in the River Nene, at Polebrook, whilst on leave in the UK; he is buried in Prees [St. Chad] Churchyard, Shropshire. His commissioning details are recorded on page 233 of my third volume to which I now add the citation for the award of his DFC as recorded in *The London Gazette* 3rd August 1918, supplement 30827, page 9205. It was awarded jointly with his observer, Lieutenant Harry Bowen Davies: *"Whilst engaged during the past month on a bombing raid they observed a large amount of rolling stock in a railway siding. The pilot, Lt. Young, brought his machine down to within 2,000 feet from the ground after releasing his bombs, and Lt. Davies then made an exhaustive reconnaissance of the area, notwithstanding an intense concentration of anti-aircraft and machine-gun fire which the enemy brought to bear upon the machine.*

"Whilst engaged on this reconnaissance numerous groups of enemy troops engaged on the railway trucks were scattered in all directions by fire from the aeroplane.

"On completion of this duty these two officers located a very active enemy anti-aircraft battery, and immediately directed the attention of our artillery thereto, consequent on an explosion which followed a salvo.

"Courage, determination, and ability are the marked qualities of these officers."

Lieutenant Young's First Bar was *Gazetted* on 2nd November 1918, supplement 30989, page 12961: *"In a recent engagement this officer displayed marked courage and determination. He bombed and silenced an anti-tank battery, and then attacked some motor transport, destroying four lorries. Later on he engaged with machine guns enemy troops and transport, causing a stampede, returning to our lines with a most valuable report as to the position of our troops. Unfortunately, on the following day he was seriously wounded."*

Royal Air Force deaths recorded on the CWGC website in respect of airmen whose squadrons had been disbanded.

2nd Lt	SMITH	Royden Morehouse	8 January 1921	34 Squadron

Canada Royden Morehouse Smith is buried in Canada at the family plot in Kilburn Community Cemetery. At the time of his death 34 Squadron had long since disbanded at Old Sarum on 25th September 1919.

Sgt	TOURLAMAIN	Henry James	8 January 1921	217 Squadron

217 Squadron disbanded at Driffield on 18th October 1919; I suggest Sergeant Tourlamain had served with the squadron. He is commemorated on the screen wall at Tottenham Cemetery. His service number 51768 indicates he joined the Royal Flying Corps in 1915.

ARMY

F/O	PERSHOUSE	Geoffrey Bradley	4 May 1921	12 Squadron

North Staffordshire Regiment

SQUADRON LOSSES
1922

Another year when the Royal Air Force had to make do with aircraft of *Great War* vintage. For the aircraft industry as a whole, money from the government was in short supply and for the better part of the year a much reduced work force was employed in completing contracts that had survived the cull of orders post-November 1918.

Nevertheless, despite these severe restrictions a number of prototype aircraft were produced, the majority finding their way to Martlesham Heath for service trials.

Here, one example will suffice, namely the Gloster Nightjar of which three prototypes [J6925-J6927] were produced and flown by the autumn of 1922. Eventually, all were shipped to the Middle East for service trials where they were issued to 8 Squadron at Hinaidi. It is known that J6925, following further tests with 1 and 55 Squadrons and a rebuild at Hinaidi as JR6925, went to 208 Squadron at Ismailia where it was written off, date not known, in a landing accident.

Meanwhile, a production order for a dozen Nightjars had been approved, the first example J6930 being written off on its delivery flight [18th December 1922] from Brockworth when the engine failed at 200 feet. Attempting to regain the airfield the Nightjar stalled and crashed.

Despite this disappointing start, the order was completed with at least five seeing service with 203 Squadron at Leuchars before being disbanded on 1st April 1923, and its aircraft disposed of, in the main, to 401 Flight.

JANUARY

Friday 6 January 1922

60 Squadron F/O H B D Harrington +
DH.10 E5450 F/O J C Belford Safe
LAC W A Woodall +

T/o Risalpur and destroyed here while trying to land. Flying Officer Hubert Bernard Delma Harrington had been granted a short service commission on the 7th of January 1921, as reported in the *Gazette* issue 32185, page 185. His observer, Flying Officer James Charles Belford 'walked away' without injury. He was commissioned as a temporary 2nd Lieutenant to The Prince of Wale's Own [West Yorkshire Regiment], 13th Battalion on 7th August 1915 [LG 14 August 1915, supplement 29263, page 8111].

He was promoted flight lieutenant on 1st January 1928 [LG 2 January 1928, supplement 33343, page 8] and is believed to have faced a General Court Martial in 1931: *"Flight Lt. James Charles Belford takes rank and precedence as if his appointment as Flight Lt. bore date 1st Jan. 1930; immediately following Flight Lt. J L F Fuller-Good on the gradation list. Reduction takes effect from 28th Mar. 1931."* [LG 9 June 1931, issue 33724, page 3765].

On 13th May 1932, he was placed on the retired list at his own request [LG 31 May 1932, issue 33830, page 3503].

L:Eading Aircraftman William Albert Woodall began his military service with RNAS, his service number 246146 coming within the block 244711 - 260000 with numbers being allocated during April 1918.

Note. I am reasonably confident that James Charles Belford was born on 31st May 1894, and transferred to the RFC on 14th July 1917, his unit prior to transfer being recorded as King's Liverpool Regiment. Army Form B.103C shows he was attached to No. 2 Aeroplane Supply Depot on 24th June 1918, from where he was attached to 58 Squadron [FE.2b] at Fauquembergues on 6th July 1918. Apart from a spell in hospital and leave, he appears to have served with '58' until returning to England on HMHS *Brighton* on 26th May 1919.

60 Squadron *Not reported*
DH.10 E6040

T/o Risalpur possibly for continuation training as E6040 had been modified as a dual control aircraft. Reported as crashed, but no location given.

Tuesday 10 January 1922

25 Squadron F/Lt E B Mason Injured
Avro 504K H2978

T/o Hawkinge and wrecked whilst trying to land at Manston, Flight Lieutenant Eric Barnes Mason sustaining a compound fracture of the right tibia.

Army Ministry Form 470 under the heading Nature and Cause of Accident shows: *"Attempting to land put aero into a steep left-hand bank. Not allowing enough room he crashed."* The findings of the Court Inquiry added: *"An error of judgement on the part of the pilot in that he partially stalled his machine too near the ground to recover control. The Court is of the opinion that the stick and attaché case should have been firmly secured before the flight."*

The Court of Inquiry findings appear to be at odds with the information on the reverse of the card. The reference to *"the stick"* I suggest was a walking stick [or cane] which was a common accessory for officers of that period.

Friday 13 January 1922

8 Squadron F/Lt A G Peace AFC +
DH.9A E8474 AC2 W W S Bown +

T/o Hinaidi for formation flying practice. On return to the airfield the DHs broke formation in readiness to land and it was during this phase of the exercise that two of the machines collided and crashed out of control. Flight Lieutenant Albert Grounds Peace, a sapper with the Canadian Divisional Signals Company was commissioned to the General List on 16th June 1916 [LG 18 July 1916, issue 29671, page 7102]. The website 4th Canadian Mounted Rifles, which the authors have pleasure in acknowledging, shows he was born in Leicester on the 16th of January 1894, his parents emigrating to Canada in December 1911, aboard the SS *Hesperian**which by coincidence was the vessel which brought Albert and his fellow troops of the 4th Canadian Mounted Rifles to England in 1915.

During the *Great War* he flew RE.8s with 9 Squadron. At the time of his death he was the squadron's adjutant. His commanding officer, Wing Commander Dermott Allen wrote to Albert's wife, Dorothy, part of his letter being quoted on the website: *"You will want to know how the accident occurred. We were doing a practice formation with eight machines. The exercise was completed and I fired the signal light for the formation to break up. As the machines dispersed your husband, who was piloting one machine, collided in the air with his next ahead. The wing tip of the latter struck the tailplane of your husband's machine, breaking it. The machines were at a height of about 2,000 feet. Both machines struck the ground out of control. The pilot of the other machine died within half an hour, his passenger had a miraculous escape and got away with a few minor cuts and bruises. Your husband and his mechanic were dead when the ambulance got to them."*

Aircraftman Walter William Stephen Bown's service number 157806 shows he had at least eight years of service to his credit for it is almost a certainty that he enlisted with the RFC in 1915.

* The SS *Hesperian* was sunk by a German U-boat commanded by *Kapitänleutnant* Walther Schweiger as she returned to Canada on the 4th of September 1915. For additional information, please refer to the website Wrecksite - Hesperian. It is further noted that Walther Schweiger was responsible for the sinking of the RMS *Lusitania* on 7th May 1915. He was killed in action north of Terschelling on 5th September 1917, when U-88 was sunk with all hands by the British Q-Ship HMS *Stonecrop.*

Note. Christopher Dean has kindly advised that Flight Lieutenant Albert Grounds Peace was known in the squadron, and to his friends, as "Pax."

8 Squadron F/O F H Barton +
DH.9A H102 AC2 E Pattison Injured

T/o Hinaidi similarly instructed and destroyed in the circumstances described above. Aircraftman Eric Pattison was freed from the wreckage, injured, but very much alive. Flying Officer Frank Henry Barton was one of hundred of young 2nd Lieutenants commissioned to the General List in 1917, in Henry's case the 16th of August, as reported in *The London Gazette* 11th September 1917, supplement 30279, page 9425. He was granted a short service commission on 1st October 1920 [LG 1 October 1920, issue 32071, page 9623].

Wednesday 18 January 1922

25 Squadron F/O D M I MacArthur Injured
7F.1 Snipe E7423

T/o Hawkinge and wrecked following engine failure and a forced-landing in a snow covered field that had been put to the plough. As the fighter touched down the wheels sank through the snow and immediately caught the sharp frozen ridges of earth that had been turned by the plough, its forward speed sufficient to catapult the Snipe onto its back.

Flying Donald Michael Ian MacArthur's injuries are recorded as *"slight."* On 21st September 1923, and now in the Reserve of Air Force Officers, he was transferred from class C to class A [LG 6 May 1924, issue 32933, page 3636].

Sunday 29 January 1922

100 Squadron F/O A Knox Safe
Bristol F.2b J6706 AC2 C S Scott Injured

T/o Baldonnel with the intention of transferring the Bristol to 5 FTS at Shotwick but having reached North Wales ran out of petrol and in forced-landing at Dysert, 3 miles SE of Rhyl, Flintshire, the machine was wrecked. Aircraftman Scott's injuries were not serious.

The Court of Inquiry reported as follows: *[1] Due to lack of petrol pressure. [2] Might have been avoided by the pilot turning off all pressure taps except the pressure taps leading from the hand pump v to the front tank. [3] The damage on landing cannot be attributed to any error of judgement on part of the pilot.*

"AOC Inland Area issued instructions that disciplinary action is to be taken against the pilot & that he is immediately to make himself thoroughly acquainted with the petrol pressure exchange on Bristol Fighter machines."

Tuesday 31 January 1922

60 Squadron F/O P J Gardiner +
DH.10 E7839 Australia
AC2 G F Stewart Injured

T/o Risalpur and spun in, owing to engine failure, possibly near the airfield. Australian born, Flying Officer Percy Justice Gardiner was appointed 2nd Lieutenant in the Special Reserve of Officers attached to the Military Wing of the RFC, on probation, from an Officer Cadet Unit, on 17th March 1917 [LG 11 April 1917, supplement 30014, page 3467]. George Fletcher Steward died from his injuries the next day. He was 19 years of age and would have joined the Royal Air Force after the cessation of the recent war.

FEBRUARY

Friday 3 February 1922
14 Squadron *Not reported*
Bristol F.2b H1653
T/o Ramleh and on arrival at LG 1 Jerusalem executed a heavy landing, bounced and overturned.

Wednesday 8 February 1922
4 Squadron F/Lt R C Jenkins MBE MC +
Avro 504K H9829 O/O A Hesketh DFC Injured
T/o Farnborough and flew into tree. A year ago Observer Officer Hesketh had survived a similar crash in which the pilot was killed; now history repeated itself for when help arrived, Flight Lieutenant Robert Charles Jenkins was beyond aid.

Formerly of the Duke of Cornwall's Light Infantry he had been invested with the Order of the Nile, 4th Class [LG 18th November 1919, supplement 31647, page 14002]. He is commemorated on the Charterhouse website, which the authors have pleasure in acknowledging, in regard to a silver model of an Avro 504 which is awarded as a music prize. Various commemorations are reported and in order a selection these read: *"Robert Jenkins' mother, Mrs Jeudwine, presented the model aeroplane in his memory as a music prize for the annual 'House Glee Competition' [still continuing today as the House Music Competition]. Glee Clubs were a particularly popular form of choir in the late 19th and early 20th centuries, specialising in short-part songs. Robert had been Mrs Jeudwine's last surviving child - his elder brother, Captain Edgar Kynnersley Jenkins [not an OC] was killed in action at the Somme. She also left the School Robert's medals, papers and flying log-book."*

Obituary from *The Carthusian*, April 1922: *"JENKINS - On the 8th Feb., at South Farnborough, owing to an accident while flying, Robert Charles Jenkins MBE MC RAF, dearly beloved and only surviving child of the late E F Jenkins and of Mrs E J W Jeudwine, of Bicton Croft, Godalming, aged 26. The deceased came to Charterhouse in Long Quarter, 1910 [Lockites] and left in 1913. He first joined the Duke of Cornwall's Light Infantry; and later was attached to the RAF. He was twice wounded."*

Extract from *The Times* of March 9th: *"A correspondent writes. Although Flight-Lieutenant R C Jenkins had scarcely attained the age of 26 when he was accidentally killed when on duty at Farnborough, his short career had been full of adventure and his reputation as a master of the art of flying throughout Egypt, Palestine and Mesopotamia well established. But he was looked up to and admired also for the whole-hearted way in which he spent himself for the good of the Service and of his particular unit. He repeatedly refused advancement, or even promotion on the Staff, that he might do full justice to the instruction of his subordinates. To this unselfishness were added a personal charm of sympathy, good humour, and gaiety. He was know as 'Bobbie' to his immediate friends, and as 'Jenks' to the Royal Flying Corps in general in the East, and although quite unknown in England when he joined at Farnborough last August, he is deeply regretted. Many at the Bar will remember his father, Edgar Jenkins, of Doctors' Common."*

Friday 10 February 1922
100 Squadron F/O P J Parry Injured Llanllyfin [St. Rhedyw] Churchyard
Bristol F.2b D7856 AC2 J E Harris Injured
T/o Baldonnell intending to transit to Spittlegate but crashed soon after becoming airborne. Aircraftman James Ernest Harris died shortly after being admitted to hospital, his pilot, Flying Officer Palmer John Parry dying 24-hours later.

On the 21st February, as reported in ASN Wikibase Occurrence 210658, one of the local papers published in North Wales reported: *"On Friday the sad news was received by Mr and Mrs T G Parry, Miners, Snowdon Street, Penygroes that their son Mr Palmer J Parry had met with a fatal accident in an aeroplane at Blandonnel* [sic], *Dublin when he and a colleague were about to fly over to England. After rising some hundreds of feet the machine fell to earth and they were seriously injured, both dying later in hospital on Tuesday. His body was brought to Pengroes under military escort on Thursday. A large congregation met to bury him at St. Rhedyw, Llanllyfin. A number of Air Force Officers were present, There was a volley of shots over his grave and the last post was sounded."*

Returning to Aircraft Harris, his service number 341857 suggests fairly recent enlistment for it comes within the block 340001 - 360000 set aside for civilians entering military service between September 1919 and extending to June 1925.

On the spreadsheet, generously supplied to the authors by Greg Harrison, the following is annotated: *"In November 1921, whilst serving with 207 Squadron, Flying Officer Parry had been involved in a motorcycle accident, causing "contused wound of face, left upper jaw, nose and lips. Abrasions to left knee, and shock." The cause of the accident to his motorcycle is not recorded, although the report does indicate he wasn't on duty at the time. Previous to that, whilst serving with 221 Squadron in Russia to aid Russian forces fighting the Bolsheviks, he had fractured his right radius, although the circumstances of how he did this are not revealed on his casualty card."*

MARCH

Friday 3 March 1922
20 Squadron F/Lt J B Fox MC +
Bristol F.2b E2442 F/Sgt A B Hemmings +
T/o Ambala and destroyed in a midair collision near Amritsar with the Bristol summarised below. Flight Lieutenant John Bertram Fox, born 24th July 1893, was a General List officer who came to the RFC on 18th January 1917, and won the MC whilst flying DH.4s with 55 Squadron. His first tour with '55' was from 29th July 1917 to 1st May 1918, during which he was appointed flight commander, while his second tour commenced 11th September 1918.

He is mentioned on three occasions in *The DH.4/DH.9 File*, the first on 5th September 1917, when with Mechanic S L Leyland as his observer/air gunner and while flying DH.4 A7418, they despatched an Albatros in the early afternoon in the vicinity of Thielt. In the same DH, and on 10th March 1928, Captain Fox crash-landed following an in-flight fire, sustaining slight burns while Lieutenant S S Jones MC escaped unharmed. The fire was quickly extinguished and A7418 was sent to No. 2 Air Salvage Depot for repair and eventual return to service.

Then, during his second tour with the squadron, and flying DH.4 A7427 with Lieutenant J Parke DFC in the rear cockpit, two hostile Fokker DVIIs attacked their aircraft shortly after they bombed Saarbrücken. Sustained and accurate return fire totally destroyed one of their aggressors while the second was driven down out of control.

The citation for his MC, *Gazetted* 13th May 1918, supplement 30681, page 5699, reads: *"For conspicuous gallantry and devotion to duty. During a period of two months he has led his formation on six long-distant bombing raids into enemy territory. On the last occasion, though engaged by three separate hostile formations, he dropped his bombs with excellent effect over his objective and brought the whole formation back to the aerodrome intact. His formation accounted for three enemy aeroplanes destroyed and four driven down out of control. He has carried out upwards of 40 successful operations, his skill and leadership being of the highest order."*

His observer, Flight Sergeant Allen Benjamin Hemmings may be accurately described as an *"old sweat"* for his service number 466 identifies him as having joined the RFC in 1912, when a block of numbers 1 - 515 were issued, 516 not being allocated until 1913.

20 Squadron F/O J Buckley +
Bristol F.2b H1548 AC2 C R Richardson +
T/o Ambala and lost in the circumstances described above. Flying Officer Joseph Buckley's details are reported in the previous volume, while Aircraftman Charles Reginald Richardson attested between March and August 1919, his service number 332609 falling within the block 329001 - 335000 issued to civilian entrants.

Wednesday 8 March 1922
55 Squadron F/O P W Lingwood Safe See 5 February 1923
DH.9A H3638
T/o Mosul where, on return, the engine lost power resulting in a forced-landing which damaged the aircraft beyond economical repair. Flying Officer Percy William Lingwood, born on the last day of July 1896, served with 56 Squadron [SE.5a] in the recent war and, according to his Casualty Form - Active Service he was injured in an accident on 15th October 1918. I have checked for details in my second volume, and in Trevor Henshaw's *The Sky Their Battlefield* but can find no reference to the accident; it seems, however, that he was taken to 21 CCS for treatment to bruises to his face and hands and was then admitted to 20 General Hospital before being evacuated to England aboard HMHS *Princess Elizabeth.*

In the spring of 1919, he arrived in Belgium and was attached on 23rd April, to 84 Squadron [SE.5a] and Thuilles, subsequently going with the squadron to Germany as support for the Allied occupation. On 8th August, four days prior to the squadron's return ton Tangmere, he was posted to 70 Squadron which was inactive as a cadre at Spittlegate.

Flying Officer Lingwood was granted a short service commission [LG 14 September 1920, issue 32050, page 9223] and, sadly, died in the crash of Vickers Vimy, which he was piloting, on 18th June 1923, having survived a second crash with 55 Squadron.

Thursday 9 March 1922
27 Squadron F/O S B Harris Safe
DH.9A F1643 F/O R B Luard Injured See 17 August 1922
T/o Risalpur for formation flying practice. On return Flying Officer Harris landed rather heavily, breaking a shock absorber which sent the DH ballooning into the air and on arriving on *terra firma* for the second time it turned over. Flying Officer Robert Blaine Luard, late of the Royal Field Artillery, was born on 14th June 1898, and transferred to the RFC on 20th July 1917. On completion of his training he joined 64 Squadron [DH.5] at Izel-le-Hameau on 20th January 1918, subsequently converting to SE.5a and becoming a prisoner of war after being shot down on 30th August 1918. Omitted from my second volume, details of this loss are reported in Appendix G attached to the 1921 appendices.

Friday 24 March 1922
30 Squadron *Not reported*
DH.9A H45
T/o Baghdad and believed damaged beyond repair in a forced-landing.

Tuesday 28 March 1922
39 Squadron F/O C W Bragg +
DH.9A E967 LAC W Warne +
T/o Spittlegate only to enter a spin and crash to the ground from a height estimated at around 300 feet. Eyewitnesses state the DH was in a steep turn, downwind, when the loss of control occurred. A brief account of the crash is recorded on the Aviation Safety Network [ASN] website under Occurrence Report 210683, where the passenger's name is reported as Leading Aircraftman Walter Wren, service number 345790 [see Aircraft Harris summarised on 10th February 1922, for details].

Note. See my footnote for DH.9A E974 written off on 21st December 1921.

APRIL

Saturday 8 April 1922
6 Squadron F/O A E Beilby Safe
Bristol F.2b F4937
T/o Baghdad West and reported to have run onto a sharp ridge which damaged the Bristol beyond repair. It is not clear if this was during take off, or on landing. Flying Officer Arthur Edward Beilby had been granted a short service commission on 10th August 1920 [see page 281 of my third volume for details] and in 1929 was a flight commander attached to 35 Squadron [DH.9A], by which time he was a permanent officer as promulgated in *The London Gazette* 4th December 1923, issue 32885, page 8451. He died on 9th May 1937 while being treated in Guy's Hospital, London.

Tuesday 11 April 1922
27 Squadron F/Lt R T B Houghton Injured
DH.9A H28/A F/O R J M de St. Ledger Injured
T/o Risalpur and while flying at 7,000 feet the Liberty engine suddenly failed leaving the crew with little option but to seek an emergency landing. This was duly carried out on a nullah*near the landing ground at Walla. In order to prevent their aircraft becoming a target for looters and the remote chance that it might be salvaged, the crew, who were not serious hurt, set the DH on fire.

* A nullah is described as a water course or a steep ravine and I suspect the latter in respect of the above summary.

Wednesday 12 April 1922
31 Squadron F/Lt T F Wailes Injured
Bristol F.2b H1659 AC1 A Allison Injured
T/o Peshawar and reported to have been damaged beyond repair after an uncontrolled sideslip, possibly at Quetta, at 1445. The Casualty Card AM Form 470 [a red line has crossed through the Form number and *"India"* has been inserted] reads: *"Error of judgement. Crash. Sideslipping into land, met bump on under outer wing at moment of flattening out. Unable to take off bank on account of bump. Machine crashed and turned over."*
Both airmen were injured, though only slightly, and were admitted to *"B S H Tank"*. The Remarks section contains the following notes: *"Test Flight* [thus suggests the Bristol took off from Quetta] *Forms 551in file 35/652/22. No C of I held. D of P decides this is a case of "casual flying"."*

84 Squadron P/O C E Kelly Safe
DH.9A F1644
T/o Shaibah where it crashed on landing.

Friday 14 April 1922
30 Squadron *Not reported*
DH.9A H86
T/o Baghdad and written off in an accident at Quizil-Ribat, Iraq.

Sunday 23 April 1922
30 Squadron F/O G A Atkinson Safe See 1 September 1922
DH.9A H78
T/o Baghdad and wrecked while forced-landing in a sandstorm, the DH striking a very sharp ridge.

MAY

Monday 1 May 1922
6 Squadron *Not reported*
Bristol F.2b D8037
T/o Baghdad West and destroyed in a midair collision, near the airfield, with the Bristol summarised below.

6 Squadron F/O J G Argles Safe
Bristol F.2b H1453
T/o Baghdad West and written off in the circumstances described above. Although conjecture, I suspect the Bristols were flying in formation at the time, although a landing mishap cannot be ruled out.
For details regarding Flying Officer John Greville Argles, please refer to Appendix D for 1921, and LG 19 July 1921.

Tuesday 16 May 1922
6 Squadron F/Lt L C Hooton MC* +
Bristol F.2b D7845 AC2 G W Butler +
T/o Baghdad West but within seconds of becoming airborne the engine 'cut' and in the ensuing crash the Bristol went up in flames. Flight Lieutenant Lionel Conrad Hooton received his commission on 30th May 1917 [LG 26 June 1917, supplement 30151, page 6355]. Lionel was born on 21st May 1890, and with his flying training completed he reported to Mons-en-Chaussée on 4th December 1917, where he joined 8 Squadron [FK.8]. He immediately demonstrated his prowess as a fighter pilot and in April 1918, gained an MC quickly followed by a First Bar. On 27th May, during operations over the Aisne where the German's had that day launched a surprise attack on the French front, he was

wounded in the neck - his FK.8's serial not being noted [page 176 of *The Sky Their Battlefield*] and following treatment in a CCS and later at 20 General Hospital went back to the UK aboard HMHS *Brighton* on June 3rd.

Referring back to the *Gazette*, the citations for his awards appeared in supplement 30761, page 7413, published on 22nd June 1918, and supplement 30813, page 8759, of 26th July1918.

"For conspicuous gallantry and devotion to duty. On one occasion, during a very thick mist, he and his pilot by flying very low, despite very heavy machine gun fire, succeeded in locating the enemy's position. Though their machine was hit in all the vital parts, it was flown back to the aerodrome in safety. On a later occasion, when on contact patrol in failing light, they succeeded in locating accurately the position of the enemy. They have shown the utmost gallantry and skill during recent operations, and have carried out their duties with the greatest courage and determination."

For reasons that are unclear, what is obviously meant to be a joint citation, the name of the 'pilot' has not been appended. The second citation clearly identifies him as the pilot of his machine: *"For conspicuous gallantry and devotion to duty. While flying at 1,000ft his petrol tank was shot through and immediately afterwards his left aileron control shot away. He tried to turn his machine without success, and it was side-slipping down out of control into the enemy's lines. Realising the danger, his observer climbed out on the right wing, enabling him to turn and land just within our lines. It was owing to his extraordinary coolness that he was able to land the machine in safety. He has also done fine work on reconnaissance and in attacking enemy infantry."*

Flight Lieutenant Hooton was mentioned in despatches for his work in North Russia [LG 22 December 1919, supplement 31703, page 15841].

Aircraftman George William Butler, 328510, was a former boy airman who enlisted twixt December 1918 and March 1919.

Wednesday 24 May 1922

2 Squadron F/O E G Green MC + Jesmond Old Cemetery
Bristol F.2b J6673 Sgt W J Stivey +

T/o Digby but stalled out of a tight turn and dived to the ground near the airfield. Flying Officer Ernest George Green was awarded the MC whilst flying as an observer [LG 26 May 1917, supplement 30095, page 5181]: *"For conspicuous gallantry and devotion to duty as an observer. He has on several occasions brought down hostile machines, and has carried out many successful photographic reconnaissances. He has at all times set a fine example of courage and initiative."*

A former territorial with the Royal Engineers, Ernest was born in Dunstan, Gateshead-on-Tyne on 2nd February 1892, and transferred to the RFC on 14th November 1916. He joined 25 Squadron [DH.4] at Boisdinghem on 8th December 1917, but was posted as "missing" on 3rd February 1918, Trevor Henshaw writing on page 142: *"B MELLE Rlwy Sdgs, followed by 6 Dr1s who attacked rear crew near GRAND ST BIGARD 15,000' shot up, cut off, then 3 Albatros Ds hit engine at 3,000', tank on fire ftl near GHENT MIA [Lt E G Green MC WIA POW/Lt PC Campbell-Martin WIA POW] left 7-40am, pilot WIA severe stomach and hip, observer WIA neck and leg but escaped. RPS's vary, e.g. got behind by engine problems? ['DH' claim combat MARIAKERKE, GHENT 9-40am Ltn O Löffler JaB]."*

Page 142 identifies their DH.4 as A7873, which *The DH.4/DH.9 File* shows was delivered to the squadron on 6th January 1918, and given the letter 'M', and adding: *"A/c captured by Germans."*

Sergeant Walter John Stivey joined the RNAS in 1914, his service number being 200158, which comes within the block 200001 - 202902 for transferees on formation of the RAF in April 1918.

Wednesday 31 May 1922

6 Squadron F/Lt F N Hudson MC Injured Ma'asker A; Raschid RAF Cemetery
Bristol F.2b D7844 F/Lt E Drudge MBE Injured

T/o Suleimaniyeh only for the engine to fail and in the ensuring crash Flight Lieutenant Frank Neville Hudson and his passenger, Flight Lieutenant Ernest Drudge, were seriously injured. Despite receiving the best care available, Flight Lieutenant Hudson died on Tuesday of the following week.

A permanent officer, his military service began as a Sandhurst Cadet and on graduating he was commissioned to the Buffs [East Kent] Regiment but immediately seconded to the RFC and was soon on active duty with 15 Squadron [BE.2c] operating from Droglandt. However, his service with the squadron was brief for on 21st February 1916 [the day that the German unleashed their attack on the French at Verdun], he was reconnoitring the Linselles area when an anti-aircraft shell burst near his aircraft and a piece of shrapnel struck him in the head. In severe pain he continued with his task and when satisfied he had the information required he landed at Bailleul [see page 33 of Trevor Henshaw's *The Sky Their Battlefield*]. With so much loss of blood he passed out within minutes of landing and was rushed to 7 Stationary Hospital for immediate aid. Subsequently, he was sent back to England aboard HMHS *St. Denis* to continue his recovery. Such devotion to duty was recognised by an immediate award of the MC: *:For conspicuous gallantry and skill on serral occasions, notably when, although severely wounded in the head, he successful completed his aerial reconnaissance. After crossing the lines and landing at an aerodrome, he at once lost consciousness. This young officer is only 18 years of age, but has many times driven off enemy machines and twice forced them to the ground."* [LG 30 March 1916, supplement 29528, page 3429].

Recovered, he returned to the Western Front, this time as a scout pilot flying Sopwith Pups with 54 Squadron and in March 1917, he was made a flight commander. Once again, however, he became a victim of enemy fire and was shot down on 13th July 1917, during an evening patrol over the Bruges to Oostende area [Trevor Henshaw writes on page 102: *"... heavy AA on return, engine cut then attacked by 5 EAs, Flt ZEEBRUGGE"* adding: *1-Str' claim de Haan 7-30 pm Ltn Flecken Ja20."*

It was September before his father learnt that his son was being held at Karlsruhe and as with so many Allied prisoners of war it was several weeks after signing of the Armistice that he returned home. That he had not been a model captive was recognised by a mention in despatches *"for valuable services whilst in captivity."* [LG 12 December 1919, supplement 31691, page 15614].

Flight Lieutenant Frank Neville Hudson MC and mentioned in a despatch joined 6 Squadron on 24th February 1922.

JUNE

Friday 2 June 1922
8 Squadron F/Lt J Leacroft MC Safe
DH.9A H54
T/o Hinaidi and written off whilst landing at Sulaimania. Flight Lieutenant John Leacroft, born on 4th November 1888, was a General List officer who joined the RFC on 15th August 1916. He served two tours of duty with 19 Squadron, the first from 9th May to 25th October 1917, during which he was appointed as a flight commander. He returned to France in February 1918, and was re-attached to 19 Squadron at Bailleul on the 27th. Award the MC during his first tour, in April 1918, he earned a First Bar.

His *Wikipedia* entry credits him with 22 combat victories and also publishes the citations for his MC and First Bar: *"For conspicuous gallantry and devotion to duty. On one occasion he flew at very low altitude in extremely bad weather and successfully engaged enemy troops with machine-gun fire, and on another occasion carried out a most valuable reconnaissance and engaged enemy troops from a height of 100 feet. He destroyed two hostile machines, and has proved himself a courageous and determined pilot."* [LG 27 October 1917, supplement 30355, page 11109].

The citation to the First Bar was published on 22nd June 1918, supplement 30761, page 7399: *"For conspicuous gallantry and devotion to duty. During a period of six months he has destroyed four and brought down completely out of control six hostile machines. In all he has destroyed eight enemy machines and driven down thirteen out of control. On one occasion, when leading an offensive patrol, his formation destroyed six enemy planes and drove another down out of control without suffering any damage itself. He has displayed exceptional qualities as a leader, and his patrols have always been characterised by vigour and dash."*

On 1st May 1924, now ranked squadron, he assumed command of 17 Squadron on its re-formation at Hawkinge. Granted a permanent commission he retired in the rank of group captain on 1st December 1937, but returned to the service, in an administrative capacity, for the Second World War before leaving the service for a second time on 19th April 1945. Group Captain John Leacroft MC* died aged 82 at Bexhill, Sussex, on Thursday, 26th August 1971.

Thursday 8 June 1922
84 Squadron F/O F J W Mellersh Injured
DH.9A E786 F/O C E Kelly Injured
T/o Shaibah only to stall and spin into the ground. It is thought the injuries to the crew were not serious. Flying Officer Francis John Williamson Mellersh, formerly of the RNAS, served in the *Great War* with 209 Squadron [F.1 Camel] and postwar was granted a short service commission on 24th October 1919, only to be transferred to the Unemployed list on Christmas Eve of that year. However, on 9th April 1921, he was restored to the Active list for temporary duty and, subsequently, was granted a short service commission on the 11th of August [LG 23 August 1921, issue 32432, page 6674].

On completion of his attachment to 84 Squadron, Flying Officer Mellersh became a qualified flying instructor at 4 FTS Abu Sueir and on his return to the UK at 2 FTS Duxford where on the 1st of June 1926, he was appointed to a permanent commission. His subsequent service was principally engaged with Staff Duties having attended the RAF Staff College at Andover from January 1933 to February 1934 [prior to Staff College he was a flying instructor with the Oxford University Air Squadron]. The bizarre circumstances of his death in May 1955, are reported in my third volume.

Wednesday 14 June 1922
30 Squadron F/O F J H Ayscough Safe
DH.9A E773
T/o Baghdad and damaged beyond repair following a forced-landing.

Thursday 15 June 1922
100 Squadron F/O L J V Bates Safe
Avro 504K J734 AC1 Pridmore Safe
T/o 1515 Spittlegate for an engine and rigging test but while climbing away the engine 'cut'. With what he considered sufficient height in hand the pilot attempted to regain the airfield but stalled and crashed into a stone wall which damaged the Avro beyond repair.

The following remarks appear on Form AM 470: *"Obscure. Pilot states due to controls jamming. "Casual Flying."* On the reverse of the Form the Court of Inquiry observed: *"Was due to the pilot attempting to regain the aerodrome after his engine had failed. O.C. No. 11 Wing considers that the accident was due to an error of judgement on the part of the pilot, brought on by the sudden chocking of engine, and not to any mechanical defect in the machine."*

Flying Officer Leslie John Vernon Bates first entered military service in the spring of 1915, joining the Royal Naval Air Service as an air mechanic. In February 1918, he commenced flying training and was commissioned in the Air Branch on 25th August 1918.

As with so many of his contemporaries he was transferred to the Unemployed List [11th October 1919] before returning with a short service commission in 1920. Following the accident, here reported, he continued to be attached to

100 Squadron until 2nd May 1923, on which date he transferred from the General Duties Branch to the Stores Branch in which he was to serve until retirement on 2nd October 1955, with the rank of air vice-marshal. Knighted in the New Year's Honours List, Air Vice-Marshal Sir Leslie Bates died on Friday, 18th November 1966.

Tuesday 20 June 1922
4 Squadron F/O A A Ward Safe
Bristol F.2b J6666 Captain D F Ward Safe
T/o Farnborough and while over the Chobham Ridges near Pirbright Camp the Bristol's engine failed. Believed damaged beyond repair following an emergency landing on the Ridges. Captain Ward is described as being attached to the Bombay University Cadet Corps [possibly brother of the pilot].

30 Squadron F/Lt S M Kinkead Safe
DH.9A H104 South Africa DSO DSC* DFC* mentioned in despatches
T/o Baghdad and damaged beyond repair while landing at nearby Baghdad West. Flight Lieutenant Samuel Marcus Kinkead, born in Johannesburg on 25th February 1897, was a notable fighter pilot during and after the *Great War* making his mark initially with the 2nd Wing RNAS during the ill-planned Gallipoli Campaign of 1915, and subsequently continuing his aerial successes on the Western Front with the 1st Wing RNAS.

In the immediate postwar era he served with 47 Squadron, active in the fighting in Southern Russia, where he added to his already impressive tally of victories.

Citations for his awards were *Gazetted* on 22nd February 1918, supplement 30536, pages 2304 and 2305 for his DSO: *"In recognition of the gallantry and skill displayed by him in the face of the enemy in aerial combats, notably on the following occasions:- On the 24th October 1917, he brought down an enemy machine, and immediately afterwards encountered and drove off a group of seven hostile aeroplanes. On the 4th December 1917, he brought down an enemy two-seater machine completely out of control. By his skill and determination in attacking enemy machines he has always shown a fine example to other pilots."*

The supplement, 30654, to the *Gazette* published on 26th April 1918, page 5060, carries the citation for a First Bar to his DSC: *"For the skill and courage displayed by him as a pilot. On the 22nd March 1918, he attacked and drove down out of control an Albatross scout which was attacking a French machine. He has brought down many other enemy machines. He is an exceptionally good pilot, and a clever and plucky fighter, and has performed very fine work, both on offensive patrols and on low flying missions."*

That for his DFC appeared in supplement 30827, page 9201, on 3rd August 1918: *"A skilful and gallant leader, who has attacked enemy formations superior in numbers with marked success. In a recent engagement his patrol flew to the assistance of some of our machines which were greatly outnumbered by the enemy, and succeeded in accounting for three enemy machines and scattered the remainder."* A First Bar was *Gazetted* on 2nd November 1918, supplement 30989, page 12960: *"On a recent date this officer engaged a large party of troops in a wood. The engagement lasted for an hour, but so persistent was his attack that the enemy finally broke and dispersed. During this attack he was harassed by six hostile scouts. Later on he shot down an enemy two-seater in our lines. A bold and daring airman."*

On 28th October 1919, he was appointed to a permanent commission [LG 28 October 1919, issue 31620, page 13139]. His mentioned in a despatch for services in South Russia was published on 12th July 1920, supplement 31974, page 7423.

By 1928, Samuel was commanding the High Speed Flight and it was while at its helm that on the 12th of March 1928, he lost his life during a test flight in the Supermarine S.5 when flying low and fast in the vicinity of the Calshot Lightship that his aircraft suddenly dived into deep water. His body and the wreckage were recovered and this very gallant airman rests in Fawley Churchyard.

JULY

Monday 3 July 1922
30 Squadron F/O C G F Arthur Safe
DH.9A E758
T/o Baghdad and wrecked in a forced-landing having become completely lost, and occurrence common while flying over near featureless deserts and with instruments that were far from accurate.

Thursday 13 July 1922
1 Squadron *Not reported*
7F.1 Snipe H4896
T/o Hinaidi and on arrival at Baghdad the pilot misjudged his approach and crashed.

Monday 17 July 1922
205 Squadron F/O A T J Anderson Injured
Panther N7509 F/O R D Lambert Injured
T/o Donibristle to return to Leuchars but the engine 'cut' at sixty feet and the Panther side-slipped into the ground. Flying Officer Alex Thomas James Anderson died the same day from his injuries in the Cottage Hospital at Dunfirmline, but Flying Officer Robert Dyet Lambert, formerly of The Queen's Own Cameron Highlanders and now a stores officer, recovered. However, his health failed and he was placed on the retired list on 3rd March 1926 [LG 2 March 1926, issue 33138, page 1570].

On 4th April 1940, he returned to the service, rejoining as a stores officer - now termed Equipment Branch - as a flight lieutenant for the duration of hostilities [LG 30 April 1940, issue 34840, page 2561], subsequently attaining the rank of wing commander, temporary, which was relinquished on 1st November 1947 [LG 18 November 1947, supplement 38124, page 5437].

Saturday 22 July 1922
At Bickendorf in Germany, No. 12 Squadron [Bristol F.2b] which had been based here since 17th November 1920, as part of the Royal Air Force's role in providing assistance to the Allied occupation of the Rhineland was disbanded, thus ending air operations by the Royal Air Force on the Continent of Europe which had begun with the despatch of two squadrons to Amiens on 13th August 1914, nine days after Great Britain declared war on Germany.

Monday 24 July 1922
25 Squadron F/O H E Walker MC DFC Injured
7F.1 Snipe E6600 AC1 F Kershaw +
T/o Hawkinge and while over Sugar Loaf Hill near Folkstone when into a spin from which Flying Officer Henry Edward Walker was unable to recover. Born on 23rd April 1897, Henry was granted a permanent commission on 28th October 1919, by which time he held the two honours shown above. His MC was *Gazetted* on 16th September 1918, supplement 30901, page 11029: *"For conspicuous gallantry and devotion to duty during many flights and encounters in the air, often single-handed, he was most successful in bringing down enemy machines, and invariably displayed the utmost skill and resolution. He has been engaged in fourteen combats, which have either been decisive or have resulted in enemy aircraft being driven down to a low height, and he has on occasions gone up as many as five times in a day."*

On 8th February 1919, the citation for his DFC, gained in Egypt, was published: *"A gallant and courageous officer who has served continuously on the front for twelve months, during which period he has shot down several enemy machines. Throughout recent operations his bombing has been exceptionally accurate, a large percentage of direct hits on transport, etc., being obtained."* [LG 8 February 1919, issue 31170, page 2048].

In the wake of his flying accident, he was posted as a supernumerary, non-effective sick at the RAF Depot, and on recovering his fitness he was posted on 4th April 1923, to 32 Squadron [which had re-formed at Kenley with Sopwith Snipes four days previously] for flight commander duties. With flying duties and ground tours his rise through the ranks was steady, his final active flying appointment being to command 99 Squadron at Mildenhall during which he oversaw the squadron's conversion from Heyfords to Wellingtons.

Henry Edward Walker MC DFC retired as an air commodore on 1st March 1951.

Aircraftman Frank Kershaw's service number 327181 indicates he joined as a boy airman a few weeks [or months] before Aircraftman Butler who lost his life on 16th May 1922.

AUGUST

Tuesday 1 August 1922
207 Squadron F/Lt A D Pryor Safe
DH.9A J559 S/Ldr A W Tedder Safe
T/o Gosport in the company of other squadron aircraft for a bombing trial involving the radio controlled HMS *Agamemnon* and it was while over the sea, and at an altitude of 8,000 feet that the engine failed leaving Flight Lieutenant Pryor with no alternative to ditch. This 'incident' receives full coverage on page 25 of John Hamlin's history of 207 Squadron, where the author writes that the impact propelled the pilot from the cockpit but *"Tedder, however, remained in the aircraft, and the pilot soon joined him. They were quickly rescued unhurt by a destroyer before the aircraft sank, but Tedder was blamed for the loss of the precious bomb-sight."*

Squadron Leader Arthur William Tedder, first commissioned to the Special Reserve and attached in 1913 to the Dorsetshire Regiment, was destined to become one of that band of significant commanders that charted the Allied victory in the Second World War. Following a succession of key posts in the Middle East and Mediterranean theatre between November 1940 and early 1944, during which he was closely involved with planning the invasions of Sicily and Italy, Air Chief Marshal Tedder was appointed Air Commander-in-Chief and Deputy Supreme Commander to General Dwight D Eisenhower at Supreme Headquarters Allied Expeditionary Force. With the unconditional surrender of German forces in May 1945, he was present for the official ceremony - a photograph on *Wikipedia* shows him seated next to Soviet Marshal Zhukov who is standing and reading the act of the surrender.

Postwar, and now Chief of the Air Staff, he threw all his energy into ensuring the Royal Air Force remained a force with sufficient air power to counter any threat from the emerging hostility towards the West from the Soviet Union and in this he was successful in redressing the reductions in fighter squadrons so that by the time of handing over to Sir John Slessor in January 1950, Fighter Command had doubled in squadron strength.

While still serving, he had been granted a peerage as Baron Tedder of Glenguin in the County of Stirling, and on leaving the service at the end of May 1951, he was honoured with a number of academic and commercial posts. In conclusion, page 184 of my third volume has additional comments regarding this outstanding gentleman.

Tuesday 8 August 1922
6 Squadron F/O V C Cordingly Safe
Bristol F.2b D7838
T/o Baghdad West for night flying practice and came to grief during landing; wrecked.

Thursday 10 August 1922
8 Squadron F/O G L Carter Safe
DH.9A F2844
T/o Hinaidi and on reaching the landing ground at Kirkuk the sun was low on the horizon and this resulted in Flying Officer Carter failing to see a very sharp ridge in the ground which upon striking damaged his aircraft beyond repair.

Monday 14 August 1922
24 Squadron F/O W J Cooke Injured
DH.9A E883
T/o Kenley and immediately came to grief after flying into a tree. Flying Officer Cooke was fortunate to escape with only a few bumps and bruises.

Wednesday 16 August 1922
5 Squadron *Not reported*
Bristol F.2b F4611/D
T/o Pislim but crashed out of control. At the time the squadron's main base was at Quetta.

Thursday 17 August 1922
27 Squadron F/O D C Duncan +
DH.9A H70 F/O R B Luard +
T/o Dardoni for bombing operations but banked far too steeply, stalled and now out of control crashed to the ground bursting into a ball of fire as it impacted. For an appreciation of Flying Officer Robert Luard's service, please refer to his entry on 9th March 1922. Flying Officer David Chalmers Duncan was granted a short service commission on 12th December 1919, issue 31685, page 15484]. He was formerly of the RNAS, serving as a probationary flight officer.

Wednesday 23 August 1922
8 Squadron F/O R L Hartley AFC +
DH.9A E9913 AC1 A Glasby +
T/o Hinaidi for an air test but at a height estimated by eyewitnesses as about 1,000 feet the DH appeared to stall and dive, uncontrolled, to the ground and burst into flames. Flying Officer Robert Lionel Hartley's AFC was *Gazetted* on 3rd June 1919, supplement 31378, page 7033.

Aircraftman Alfred Glasby was a recent enlistment from civilian life, his service number 336172 coming with the block 336001 - 338000, and issued during August and September 1919.

SEPTEMBER

Friday 1 September 1922
30 Squadron F/O G A Atkinson Safe
DH.9A E9908
T/o Mosul but the engine 'cut' and in the crash that followed the DH was wrecked. It will be recalled that Flying Officer Atkinson had walked away, unscathed, from a forced-landing on 23rd April 1922.

Tuesday 5 September 1922
30 Squadron F/O D Maclaren Safe
DH.9A H1
T/o Baghdad and on landing at Sulaimania the undercarriage axle was bent out of alignment. On evacuation of the landing ground the DH was burnt to prevent it from falling into the hands of looters. Flying Officer Duncan Maclaren, a General List, officer, joined the RFC precisely one year to the date before the establishment of the Royal Air Force and although he arrived in France in November 1917, it was almost a year before he was attached to an operational squadron, reporting to Vert Galand and 57 Squadron [DH.4]. From Brockenhurst in Hampshire, Duncan was born on 7th March 1898.

A short service commissioned officer, he resigned his commission on 5th March 1924 [LG 4 March 1924, issue 32915, page 1931].

30 Squadron F/O C W Attwood Safe
DH.9A H114
T/o Baghdad in the company of Flying Officer Maclaren and crash-landed with a failing engine at Sulaumania. Subsequently H114 joined Duncan Maclaren's DH on the bonfire.

Wednesday 6 September 1922
3 Squadron F/O C P Brown DFC Injured
DH.9A H3530 O/O L H Stewart Safe
O/O A B Ball Safe
T/o Novar and over the Moray Firth at 4,000 feet the engine 'cut' and soon after the DH was ditched.

8 Squadron S/Ldr G H Bowman Safe
DH.9A F1640 DSO MC* DFC
T/o Hinaidi and on arrival at Halebja*crashed whilst landing. Before the DH could be recovered rebel tribesman set it on fire. Formerly of the 3rd Battalion, Royal Warwickshire Regiment, Squadron Leader Geoffrey Hilton Bowman had been appointed to a permanent commission on the 1st of August 1919. He transferred to the RFC circa April 1916, becoming a fighter pilot first with 29 Squadron [DH.2] in July 1916, and later, in the spring of 1917, with 56 Squadron [SE.5a] for flight commander duties. At the time of the armistice his combat successes stood at thirty-two.

As can be seen, his honours were extensive with his MC *Gazetted* on 17th September 1917, supplement 30287, page 9564: *"For conspicuous gallantry and devotion to duty. He has taken part in many offensive patrols, which he led on twenty occasions, in the course of which four enemy aircraft were destroyed and twelve others driven down out of control. Although out numbered by five to one on one occasion he handled his patrol of four machines with such skill and gallantry that after a very severe fight he was able to withdraw them without loss, having destroyed at least two enemy machines and driven down one out of control. His fearlessness and fine offensive spirit have been a splendid example to others."*

A First Bar appeared on 18th March 1918, supplement 30583, page 3418: *"For conspicuous gallantry and devotion to duty in leading twenty-five offensive patrols in two months, shooting down five enemy aircraft and showing marked skill as a leader."*

The award of a DSO preceded that of his DFC and was published on 24th August 1918, supplement 30682, page 9902: *"For conspicuous gallantry and devotion to duty. He has recently destroyed six enemy aeroplanes and driven down others out of control. He has at all times shown splendid courage and determination, and by his leadership and good example has contributed largely to the success of his squadron."*

His DFC, less citation, was *Gazetted* on 3rd June 1919, supplement 31378, page 7031.

Born on 2nd May 1891, Group CaptainGeoffrey Hilton Bowman died on Wednesday, 25th March 1970. A useful biography of his service may be read on *Wikipedia.*

* I am reasonably confident that 'Halebja' is now known as 'Halabja' and which in a spring morning on Wednesday, 16th March 1988, in the closing phases of the bloody Iran-Iraq War was subjected to a chemical attack which left between 3,000 and 5,000 Iraqi Kurds dead and in excess 7,000 suffering the most terrible after effects of the raid. The vast majority of those that suffered were civilians and the images of children suffering the most horrible chemical burns shocked the world. Subsequently, in the aftermath of the two wars that have followed, and which led to the overthrow of Saddam Hussein the Supreme Iraqi Criminal Tribunal has defined the attack at Halabja as a crime of genocidal massacre.

Monday 11 September 1922
5 Squadron *Not reported*
Bristol F.2b H1523
T/o Quetta to make a test climb to an altitude of 16,000 feet; reported as *"crashed."*

Wednesday 13 September 1922
84 Squadron F/O J S Harrison Safe
DH.9A E9909
T/o Shaibah and wrecked here following a heavy landing.

Saturday 16 September 1922
84 Squadron F/O J L Airey DFC Injured
DH.9A E899 AC1 B Hayes +
T/o Shaibah where in a night landing it crashed with some force. Flying Officer James Lionel Airey had been granted a short service commission thirteen months previously [LG 23 August 1921, issue 32432, page 6674]. He recovered well from his injuries and, subsequently, was appointed to a permanent commission [LG 12 May 1925, issue 33046, page 3224]. His award, *Gazetted* on 22nd December 1919, supplement 31703, page 15840, was for his services in South Russia.

Promoted group captain on 11th March 1941 [LG 11 March 1941, issue 35102, page 1448], he retired on the 1st of August 1950. An extremely useful and comprehensive set of documents, including his flying log books and service records, are held by the Imperial War Museum.

Aircraftman Bernard Hayes, 334346, was conscripted from civilian life [though he may have volunteered] between March and August 1919, when numbers in the block 329001 - 33500 were issued.

Monday 18 September 1922
25 Squadron F/O S G Williams Injured
7F.1 Snipe E7558
T/o Hawkinge to transit to Dymchurch, and it was during the return flight to Hawkinge that he went into the English Channel off Folkestone after its engine had 'cut'.

A Court of Inquiry followed, the findings of which read: *"Engine failure through engine siezingthrough some reason not yet known & no suitable landing ground being available."*

However, the AOC Inland Area took a rather dim view of the events that may well have resulted in Flying Officer William's early demise, adding: *"... is of the opinion that Flying Officer Williams was gravely to blame under AMWO*

608/21, & and that he should made to some extent financially responsible for this accident; recommended that he be called upon to show cause why he should not pay £5 towards making good the damage which has been caused by his recklessness & negligence of orders."

Appended in red ink on the reverse: *"Decided not to impose financial penalty, but to record a 'statahead' entry - casual flying 127811/21."*

25 Squadron *Not reported*
7F.1 Snipe E7758
T/o Hawkinge and damaged beyond repair following a forced-landing, with its engine failing, on a beach near the port of Folkestone.

Note. I believe this to be the machine mentioned in newspaper report appended to Flying Officer Davy's summary which includes the accident involving Flying Officer Williams, though erroneous recording in the *J File* should not be ruled out.

Tuesday 19 September 1922
25 Squadron F/O B A Davy Injured See 15 December 1922
7F.1 Snipe F2437
T/o Hawkinge and wrecked near the airfield during a forced-landing in adverse weather conditions. A report on Flying Officer Brain Augustus Davy's crash, and that for Flying Officer Sydney George Williams, appeared in the *Folkestone, Hythe, Sandgate and Cheriton Herald* in their edition of September 23rd, 1922, under the headline *Aeroplane Crashes - Pilots Lucky Escape*

"In the early part of the week two machines of the 25th Squadron of the Royal Air Force, stationed at Hawkinge, have met with accidents. Fortunately there has been no loss of life, the pilots on each occasion having wonderful escapes.

"On Monday evening Flying Officer Sydney George Williams was flying a single seater Sopwith Snipe machine back from Dymchurch, where he had been to assist another pilot who had made a forced-landing when his engine "seized" over the sea.. At the time he was flying about 300 feet up. His machine crashed into the water about 100 yards from the beach along the Riviera, Sandgate. The pilot was taken down under the water with his half submerged 'plane. He managed, however, while under the water, to undo the belt holding him in his seat, and once released he rose to the surface. In his full flying kit he then swam to the beach, a distance of some fifty yards or 100 yards. He was kindly given a hot bath, a change of clothing and a cup of tea at the house of Mr. Henry Brookes, of Radner-cliff, and later was present to superintend the efforts to salvage the machine.

"The escape of Flying Officer Williams was little short of miraculous. The fall of his machine into the sea was witnessed by Mrs. Booke and her daughter. They thought there was little hope of the pilot surviving, but after watching for half a minute or more they saw a head appear above water. When the pilot swam ashore Miss Brooke went to his assistance, one foot was bootless and a shin was "barked." His foot had been entangled in the machine and he had to wrench it out, leaving his boot behind. In conversation with his hostess he said he seemed to be a long time under the water, and he thought he was never coming up again. Fortunately his belt was fitted with a contrivance whereby the fastening could be released by a good tug.

"All efforts to get the 'plane to the beach failed, but on Tuesday afternoon the wreckage was washed ashore by the heavy sea, and it was later removed to Hawkinge on one of the RAF lorries.

"F/O B A Davies [sic] *also of the 25th Squadron RAF, crashed at Swingfield on Tuesday about midday whilst flying a single seater Sopwith Snipe. A heavy wind, accompanied by a rain storm, was blowing at the time, and the poor visibility caused the pilot to lose his bearings. After narrowly missing a house and some trees, he crashed into a field, not very far from the main Folkestone to Canterbury road. The machine was totally wrecked, but the pilot got off with a severe shaking and a sprained wrist. He was removed to the squadron's hospital at Hawkinge."*

The Court of Inquiry reported: *"Unfavourable climatic conditions did not enable the pilot to get sufficient height to ascertain whether his engine had completely failed or only temporarily failed for some reason unknown.*

'AOC Inland Area considers that the cause of the accident is obscure & that the pilot not in anyway to blame."

Thursday 28 September 1922
Following several days of intense activity 25 Squadron departed Hawkinge for Turkey where it was to provide fighter support for Allied forces involved in the Chanak crisis.

OCTOBER

Tuesday 3 October 1922
3 Squadron F/O C G Hancock Safe
DH.9A H3511 F/Lt J A Macnab Safe
O/O A B Ball
T/o Leuchars to reconnoitre and carry out a practice attack on an RN destroyer operating in the Moray Firth. Landing at Novar the DH ran onto a ridge and is believed to have been damaged beyond repair. H3511 was one of several 9As converted to a three-seater configuration.

By the spring of 1924, Flying Officer Hancock was attached, as an instructor, to the Central Flying School at Upavon on Salisbury Plain. Here, on 21st May 1924, he was providing flying instruction to Aircraftman T Gomersall in Avro 504K '3567' and as the subsequent Court of Inquiry reported, the Avro was damaged *"Through an error of judgement on the part of the pilot who did not realise his hit* [on telegraph wires] *in relation to the wires until it was too late to avoid the accident."*

The Avro was repaired; Flying Officer Hancock is shown as having 260 flying hours to his credit, though I suspect this was an under-estimate, though, possibly, may refer to hours on Avro 504s. Aircraftman Gomersall's service number is recorded as 347710.

Wednesday 4 October 1922

45 Squadron F/Lt A L Messenger AFC Injured
Vernon J6865 AC1 A A Milne Injured
F/Lt R C L Holme MC +

T/o Kirkuk possibly intending to return to the squadron's base at Hinaidi but crashed almost immediately and burst into flames. Aircraftman Albert Annott Milne died within hours of the accident, but poor Flight Lieutenant Alfred Lewis Messenger lingered in agony for the next ten days before succumbing to his terrible burns. Flight Lieutenant Robert Charles Lyon Holme was a passenger; he was attached to 1 Squadron [Snipe], also stationed at Hinaidi.

Both officers were 'veterans' of the *Great War.* Flight Lieutenant Holme, I suspect, trained in the Middle East following his transfer from the Somerset Light Infantry, and on reaching the Western Front, following three years in the United Kingdom, he was attached to 29 Squadron [Nieuport] at St. Omer on 3rd May 1918 and in the absence of Major C H Dixon assumed command of '29' from 29th August to 12th September 1918. His MC, less citation, was *Gazetted* in supplement 29916, page 927, of the paper published on 24th January 1917.

Flight Lieutenant Messenger was born in the Bournville district of Birmingham on 2nd November 1895, and was a General List officer in the RFC from 5th August 1916, serving initially with 59 Squadron [RE.8] at La Bellevue from 26th April 1917, and from 23rd November 1917, with 15 Squadron [RE.8] at Lechelle. Twixt the two he was temporarily attached between 30th May and 10th June to Etrun for duty with 13 Squadron [RE.8]. He was granted a short service commission on 12th September 1919 [LG 12 September 1919, issue 31548, page 11468].

Aircraftman Albert Annott Milne joined as a boy airman, his service number 326172, coming within the block 326001 - 329000 issued between December 1918 and March 1919.

6 October 1922

30 Squadron F/O E A Locke-Waters +
DH.9A H155

T/o Baghdad loaded with spares destined for Kirkuk but when some six miles short of its destination the DH crashed, caused, it is reported, by rebel action. Flying Officer Evelyn Archer Locke-Waters received a short service commission on 1st March 1921 [LG 1 March 1921, issue 32243, page 1700].

Monday 9 October 1922

2 Squadron F/O D Craik Injured
Bristol F.2b J6705 W/Cdr A V Bettington Injured

T/o Aldergrove*and ditched in Loch Neagh some three miles from the Loch's eastern shore and six miles from Aldergrove.

* The main body of the squadron left Aldergrove for Farnborough on 27th September 1922, but maintained a detachment at Aldergrove.

Tuesday 24 October 1922

1 Squadron F/O F S Harricks +
7F.1 Snipe H4866

T/o Hinaidi armed with bombs for operations well to the east of Mosul and while making a low-level attack on his target flew into the roof of a house at Rania. Flying Officer Frank Simon Harricks was appointed a General List officer following previous service with the Army Service Corps. For the last six months of 1917, he flew FK.8s with 2 Squadron.

His Army Form B.103, shows he was born in Rochdale, Lancashire on 8th September 1896. He left the service, briefly, before being granted a short service commission on 8th March 1921 [LG 8 March 1921, issue 32250, page 1900].

24 Squadron P/O M C Hayter + Whyteleafe [St. Luke's] Churchyard
Bristol F.2b F4831

T/o 1600 Kenley and had climbed to around 2,000 feet when Pilot Officer Matthew Charles Hayter lost control and spun into the ground. Matthew had graduated from the Cadet College at Cranwell as recently as 16th August.

A detailed description of the crash is recorded on the Kenley Revival website, which the authors gratefully acknowledge. The report goes on to state: *"Prior to Hayter's fatal flight, the aircraft had been flown 6 times that day without incident. The inquiry was held in the Medical Hut at RAF Kenley by Mr F J Nightingale, East Surrey Coroner. Dr. Elijah Brown, the Station Medical Officer, stated that Hayter had been killed by a fracture to the base of the skull. In addition, both his legs and left arm were broken in the crash. The Coroner was satisfied that normal precautions had been taken in preparation of the aircraft for the flight, and recorded a verdict of accidental death."*

The report also notes that Pilot Officer Hayter was expecting to be posted in the very near future to Egypt. He rests in the Airmen's Corner of St. Luke's churchyard. Credit is extended to the *Surrey Mirror and County Post* and to Linda Duffield. The crash is also recorded by the Sussex History Forum group.

Tuesday 31 October 1922
8 Squadron F/O H R Sayes Safe
DH.9A E9921
T/o Amaida landing ground, stalled and crashed.

NOVEMBER

Wednesday 1 November 1922
84 Squadron F/O H W Hewson Safe
DH.9A H108 Canada
Not reported Safe
T/o Shaibah for bombing operations and wrecked here on completion of the sortie. Flying Officer Henry Willis Hewson, born 2nd January 1898, and enlisting with the RFC on 1st May 1917, served during the *Great War* with 27 Squadron [DH.4/DH.9]. Postwar he was granted a short service commission, but handed in his papers on 15th March 1924 [LG 11th March 1924, issue 32917, page 2136].

Tuesday 7 November 1922
100 Squadron F/O W E Windover Safe
Avro 504K J739
T/o Spittlegate during which a collision occurred with Avro 504K H5252 which was parked outside No. 3 hangar. H5252 was repaired and subsequently went on to serve with 9 Squadron at Manston. See my summary for Thursday 9th October 1924.

Please refer to Volume 2 of this series and page 334 [summary for 110 Squadron DH.9A F1005] for mention of then Captain W E Windover.

Tuesday 21 November 1922
24 Squadron F/Lt The Hon. H J B Rodney Safe
Bristol F.2J H1408 P/O D Macfadyn Safe
T/o Kenley and while indulging in low flying stalled and crash-landed at Addington on the SE outskirts of Croydon.

Friday 24 November 1922
208 Squadron *Not reported*
Bristol F.2b FR4582
T/o Ismailia and while over Egypt's Ismid*Peninsular the engine failed. Forced-landing near Shile [sic] the Bristol ran into soft sand and turned over. When the salvage party reached the scene it was obvious that recovery of the wreck was not viable and, consequently, it was burnt in situ.

* Believed to be in the Sinai region.

DECEMBER

Thursday 14 December 1922
4 Squadron *Not reported*
Bristol F.2b J6720
T/o Kilid el Bahr and failed to return. Subsequently, the Bristol was found at Chan-Bazar Kevi, some 34 miles east of Chanak, Turkey. The names of the crew are not reported but, presumably, both were safe for it is reported they became lost after flying into cloud.

Friday 15 December 1922
25 Squadron F/O F E C Benstead Safe
7F.1 Snipe E6623
T/o San Stephano and on return landed in an area where the mud was particularly soft thereby causing the Snipe's wheels to sink into the morass. It is believed the airframe was damaged to an extent that it was abandoned in situ.

Note. F.S. Form 559 has been scored through in red and 'Constantinople' inserted in its place.

56 Squadron F/Lt J S T Fall Safe
7F.1 Snipe E6484 F/O D A Davy Safe See 19 September 1922
T/o 1230 Manston with the intention of returning to Hawkinge but before becoming airborne collided with a Hucks starter which probably wrecked the starter as well as the Snipe.

A typed copy of the Court of Inquiry reads: *"That the primary cause of the accident was lack of co-operation between the Pilot* {Flight Lieutenant Joseph Stewart Temple Fall] *and ground staff as to the direction in which the machine would take off. At the same time it is considered that before opening up his engine the Pilot should have ascertained more definitely that the aerodrome was clear. It is also considered that the warning given to the Pilot might have been more definite as he does not appear to have understood it.*

"OC S of TT considers that the Pilot was to blame.

"AOC Inland Area recommends that F/Lieut. Fall be made to pay £20 towards the damage for gross carelessness."
Flying Officer Brian Augustus Davy had attended Manston for a medical examination.

Thursday 28 December 1922
27 Squadron F/O E E Turner DFC +
DH.9A E8468 AC1 J F Sly +
T/o Dardoni for bombing operations in the tribal area of the NWF and while in the target area a bomb from the DH above smashed through the top port 'plane sending E8468 crashing out of control near Palose*in Waziristan. Flying Officer Edward Eric Turner's award was *Gazetted* on 11th June 1918, in supplement 30742, page 6991: *"Whilst piloting his machine during a hostile air raid he displayed great determination and skill in manoeuvring at a height of 11,000 feet under heavy enemy fire, which enabled his Observer to bring effective fire on an enemy aeroplane, resulting in its being driven to the ground."* He had been granted a short service commission on 24th October 1919, *Gazetted* in issue 31616, page 13034.
Aircraftman James Frederick Sly's service number 246141 [block 244711 - 260000] identifies him as a 1918 entrant to the RNAS, prior to April 1918.

* The website Maplandia illustrates the mountainous area in which the DHs were operating. I very much doubt if the bodies were recovered.

During the month, the precise date not being established, the following aircraft was written off:

24 Squadron P/O L K Barnes Safe
Bristol F.2b J6692
T/o Kenley and owing to a shortage of petrol made an emergency landing on golf links near Walsall in Staffordshire. Replenished, Pilot Officer Barnes attempted to resume his flight but before becoming airborne crashed into a hedge, wrecking his aircraft.

APPENDICES
1922

Appendix A - Squadron Losses Table and Losses by Aircraft Type

Column 1 - Squadron

Column 2 - Aircraft type

Column 3 - Written off

Column 4 - Fatalities

1 Squadron	Sopwith 7F.1 Snipe	2	1
2 Squadron	Bristol F.2b	2	2
3 Squadron	Airco DH.9A	2	
4 Squadron	Avro 504K	1	1
	Bristol F.2b	2	
5 Squadron	Bristol F.2b	2	
6 Squadron	Bristol F.2b	6	3
8 Squadron	Airco DH.9A	7	6
14 Squadron	Bristol F.2b	1	
20 Squadron	Bristol F.2b	2	4
24 Squadron	Bristol F.2b	3	1
	Airco DH.9A	1	
25 Squadron	Avro 504K	1	
	Sopwith 7F.1 Snipe	4	1
27 Squadron	Airco DH.9A	6	4
30 Squadron	Airco DH.9A	10	1
31 Squadron	Bristol F.2b	1	
39 Squadron	Airco DH.9A	1	2
45 Squadron	Vickers Vernon	1	3
55 Squadron	DH.9A	1	
56 Squadron	Sopwith 7F.1 Snipe	1	
60 Squadron	Airco DH.10	3	4
84 Squadron	Airco DH.9A	5	1
100 Squadron	Avro 504K	2	
	Bristol F.2b	2	2
205 Squadron	Parnall Panther	1	1
207 Squadron	Airco DH.9A	1	
208 Squadron	Bristol F.2b	1	
Totals		72	37

	Airco DH.9A	34	14
	Airco DH.10	3	4
	Avro 504K	4	1
	Bristol F.2b	22	12
	Parnall Panther	1	1
	Sopwith 7F.1 Snipe	7	2
	Vickers Vernon	1	3
Totals		72	37

The year 1922, witnessed a reduction by one in major air accidents but a significant increase in aircrew deaths, and for the second year running, 30 Squadron, based in Iraq, reported the loss of ten of their DH.9As. Unsurprisingly, the majority of accidents where the aircraft was deemed to be a total write-off it was the Bristol F.2b and DH.9A equipped squadrons that recorded the highest losses both in material and manpower.

Appendix B - Squadron Locations and Commanding Officers

Yet another lean year for the Royal Air Force with the number of squadrons reduced by one from 1921 and by the end of the year the 'number plate' for 12 Squadron had been laid up following disbandment in Germany. One minor ray of light was the increase of Home Defence squadrons from one to two with 56 Squadron joining 25 Squadron at Hawkinge both equipped with Sopwith 7F.1 Snipe of *Great War* vintage. The role of the overseas squadrons remained the same as that recorded in the appendix for 1921.

Squadron	Aircraft	Location	Dates	Remarks
1 Squadron	7F.1 Snipe	Hinaidi	01.01.22-31.12.22	Iraq desert policing duties
2 Squadron	Bristol F.2b	Oranmore	01.01.22-13.02.22	
		Digby	13.02.22-31.05.22	
		Aldergrove	31.05.22-27.09.22	
		Farnborough	27.09.22-31.12.22	
3 Squadron	DH.9A/Walrus	Leuchars	01.01.22-08.11.22	
	Walrus	Gosport	08.11.22-31.12.22	
4 Squadron	Bristol F.2b	Farnborough	01.01.22-22.08.22	Detached to Turkey - Chanak crisis
		Kilid el Bahr	28.09.22-11.10.22	
		Kilia	11.10.22-31.12.22	
5 Squadron	Bristol F.2b	Quetta	01.01.22-26.10.22	
		Ambala	26.10.22-31.12.22	
6 Squadron	Bristol F.2b	Baghdad West	01.01.22-09.10.22	
		Hinaidi	09.10.22-31.12.22	
8 Squadron	DH.9A	Hinaidi	01.01.22-31.12.22	
12 Squadron	Bristol F.2b	Bickendorf	01.01.22-27.07.22	Germany - Disbanded
14 Squadron	Bristol F.2b	Ramleh & Amman	01.01.22-31.12.22	
20 Squadron	Bristol F.2b	Ambala	01.01.22-24.10.22	
		Quetta	24.10.22-31.12.22	
24 Squadron	*Various*	Kenley	01.01.22-31.12.22	UK communications & training
25 Squadron	7F.1 Snipe	Hawkinge	01.01.22-28.09.22	Detached to Turkey - Chanak crisis
		Stan Stephano	11.10.22-31.12.22	
27 Squadron	DH.9A	Risalpur	01.01.22-14.12.22	
		Dardoni	14.12.22-31.12.22	
28 Squadron	Bristol F.2b	Kohat	01.01.22-15.04.22	
		Parachinar	15.04.22-10.10.22	
		Kohat	10.10.22-12.12.22	
		Dardoni	12.12.22-31.12.22	
30 Squadron	DH.9A	Baghdad	01.01.22-03.12.22	
		Hinaidi	03.12.22-31.12.22	
31 Squadron	Bristol F.2b	Peshawar	01.01.22-31.12.22	
39 Squadron		Kenley	01.01.22-31.12.22	Please refer to my note 21.12.21
45 Squadron	Vimy/Vernon	Almaza	01.01.22-14.03.22	
		Basra	14.03.22-16.05.22	
		Hinaidi	16.05.22-31.12.22	
47 Squadron	DH.9A	Helwan	01.01.22-31.12.22	
55 Squadron	DH.9A	Mosul	01.01.22-31.12.22	
56 Squadron*	7F.1 Snipe	Aboukir	01.01.22-23.09.22	Egypt - Disbanded
	7F.1 Snipe	Hawkinge	01.11.22-31.12.22	Reformed for Home Defence duties
60 Squadron	DH.10A	Risalpur	01.01.22-31.12.22	
70 Squadron	Vimy/Vernon	Heliopolis	01.01.22-31.05.22	
		Hinaidi	31.05.22-31.12.22	
84 Squadron	DH.9A	Shaibah	01.01.22-31.12.22	
100 Squadron	Bristol F.2b	Baldonnel	01.01.22-04.02.22	
	DH.9A/Vimy	Spittlegate	04.02.22-31.12.22	
203 Squadron	F.1 Camel	Leuchars	01.01.22-18.09.22	UK Fleet fighter squadron
	Nightjar	HMS *Argus*	18.09.22-27.09.22	
		Kilya Bay	27.09.22-19.12.22	
		HMS *Argus*	19.12.22-31.12.22	
205 Squadron	Panther	Leuchars	01.01.22-31.12.22	UK Fleet reconnaissance squadron
207 Squadron	DH.9A	Bircham Newton	01.01.22-29.12.22	Detached to Turkey - Chanak crisis
		San Stephano	11.10.22-31.12.22	
208 Squadron	Bristol F.2b	Ismailia	01.01.22-28.09.22	Egypt
		San Stephano	28.09.22-31.12.22	Turkey
210 Squadron	T.1 Cuckoo	Gosport	01.01.22-31.12.22	
216 Squadron	DH.10/Vimy	Heliopolis	01.01.22-31.12.22	Egypt
267 Squadron	F.2a/Fairey IIIC & D	Calafrana	01.01.22-31.12.22	Malta - Fairey IIID to Turke

* On 23rd September 1922, a detachment of the squadron was attached to 208 Squadron at San Stephano and continued to use '56' as its identity until August 1923, despite the fact that the squadron had re-formed at Hawkinge on 1st November 1922.

Squadron	Commanding Officer	Date	Remarks
1 Squadron	Squadron Leader J B Graham MC AFC	In situ	See Appendix B 1921
	Squadron Leader G G A Williams	10.11.22	See 3 Squadron 1921
2 Squadron	Squadron Leader A J Butler MC	In situ	See Appendix B 1921
	Squadron Leader L F Forbes	15.05.22	G/Capt retirement 30.04.45
3 Squadron	Squadron Leader D G Donald	In situ	See Appendix B 1921
4 Squadron	Squadron Leader C H B Blount	In situ	See Appendix B 1921
5 Squadron	Squadron Leader P C Maltby	In situ	See Appendix B 1921
6 Squadron	Squadron Leader E A B Rice MC	In situ	See Appendix B 1921
	Squadron Leader E R Manning DSO MC Australia	21.04.22	A/Cmdr retirement 10.08.35

8 Squadron	Squadron Leader D L Allen AFC	In situ	See Appendix B 1921
	Squadron Leader G H Bowman DSO MC* DFC	24.02.22	G/Capt retirement 20.01.37
12 Squadron	Squadron Leader H J F Hunter MC	In situ	See Appendix B 1921
	Flight Lieutenant P F Fullard DSO MC AFC	……..22	A/Cmdr retirement 20.11.46
14 Squadron	Squadron Leader J S T Bradley	In situ	See Appendix B 1921
20 Squadron	Squadron Leader J H S Tyssen MC	In situ	See Appendix B 1921
24 Squadron	Squadron Leader E H Johnston OBE	In situ	See Appendix B 1921
	Squadron Leader O T Boyd MC	23.10.22	AV-M died 05.08.44
25 Squadron	Squadron Leader Sir N A R D Leslie CBE	In situ	See Appendix B 1921
27 Squadron	Squadron Leader R J Mounsey OBE	In situ	See Appendix B 1921
28 Squadron	Squadron Leader R J F Barton OBE	In situ	See Appendix B 1921
	Squadron Leader J T Whittaker MC	07.03.22	S/Ldr died India 12.12.27
	Squadron Leader A W F Glenny MC DFC	01.08.22	A/Cmdr retirement 01.07.40
30 Squadron	Squadron Leader R Collishaw DSO* OBE DSC DFC three times mentioned in despatches	In situ	See Appendix B 1921
	Squadron Leader E H Johnston OBE	13.12.22	See 24 Squadron 1922
31 Squadron	Squadron Leader A T Harris AFC	In situ	See Appendix B 1921
	Squadron Leader A C Maund CBE DSO	06.05.22	AV-M died 13.12.42
39 Squadron	Squadron Leader T S Impey	In situ	See Appendix B 1921
	Squadron Leader A A B Thomson MC* AFC	18.01.22	A/Cmdr killed 28.08.39
45 Squadron	Squadron Leader E M Murray DSO MC	In situ	See Appendix B 1921
	Squadron Leader A T Harris AFC	20.11.22	See 31 Squadron 1922
47 Squadron	Squadron Leader K C Buss	In situ	See Appendix B 1921
	Squadron Leader M Henderson DSO	13.03.22	See 216 Squadron 1921
55 Squadron	Squadron Leader V Gaskell-Blackburn DSO AFC	In situ	See Appendix B 1921
56 Squadron	Squadron Leader G C A William	In situ	See Appendix B 1921
	Squadron Leader I T Lloyd	25.11.22	G/Capt retirement 31.07.39
60 Squadron	Squadron Leader P C Sherren MC Canada	In situ	See Appendix B 1921
	Squadron Leader H V Champion de Crepigny MC DFC	27.03.22	AV-M retirement 06.11.45
70 Squadron	Squadron Leader S W Smith OBE	In situ	See Appendix B 1921
84 Squadron	Squadron Leader W Sowery AFC	In situ	See Appendix B 1921
100 Squadron	Squadron Leader F Sowery DSO MC AFC	In situ	See Appendix B 1921
	Squadron Leader N M Martin CBE	10.08.22	S/Ldr retired list 10.09.24
203 Squadron	Flight Lieutenant L H Slatter OBE DSC* DFC	In situ	See Appendix B 1921
205 Squadron	Squadron Leader R M Bayley DFC	In situ	See Appendix B 1921
207 Squadron	Squadron Leader A W Tedder	In situ	See Appendix B 1921
208 Squadron	Squadron Leader W J Y Guilfoyle OBE MC	In situ	See Appendix B 1921
	Squadron Leader A ap Ellis	17.02.22	G/Capt retirement 28.08.41
	Re-employed		G/Capt retirement 20.04.45
210 Squadron	Wing Commander N J Gill OBE MC	In situ	See Appendix B 1921
216 Squadron	Squadron Leader M Henderson DSO	In situ	See Appendix B 1921
	Squadron Leader C O F Modin DSC mid	17.02.22	A/Cmdr retirement 25.01.42
267 Squadron	Squadron Leader P A Shepherd	In situ	See Appendix B 1921

Annex

Squadron Leader Edye Rolleston Manning was commissioned to the 15th Hussars on 9th September 1914, previously having served as a trooper with the Lothians and Border Horse which he joined on the outbreak of the *Great War* when he was studying medicine at Edinburgh University. During his tenure of command of 6 Squadron he oversaw the evacuation of the British High Commissioner, his wife and staff from Suliemanieh in Kurdistan for which he was *Gazetted* with the DSO, adding to the MC which he gained, having now transferred to the RFC, on 18th July 1917, supplement 30188, page 7237: *"For conspicuous gallantry and devotion to duty when conducting photographic reconnaissances. On one occasion he obtained successful photographs though attacked by eight hostile machines, and he has on all occasions displayed the utmost pluck and gallantry."*

Following retirement, at his own request, he returned to Australia, joining the Sydney Stock Exchange. Recalled to service with the Royal Air Force he served throughout the Second World War, initially as Senior Air Force Officer, Ceylon, and subsequently in various staff appointments in India before reverting to the Retired List on 20th May 1945. Additional information concerning Air Commodore Manning may be accessed on the Air of Authority website.

Group Captain Geoffrey Hilton Bowman, formerly commissioned to the 3rd Battalion, Royal Warwickshire Regiment, and was seconded for duty with the RFC on 20th March 1916, and gaining the Royal Aero Club's Aviator's Certificate No. 7977 on 27th June of that year. An incomplete record of his service shows he was born on 2nd May 1891, and was officially accepted by the RFC on 2nd July 1916, with orders to proceed four days later to 29 Squadron [DH.2] at Abeele. His first tour of duty ended on 18th December 1916, when he returned to the UK, remaining on Home Establishment until 11th May 1917, on which date he crossed the Channel, joining 56 Squadron [SE.5a] at Estrée Blanche. The last recorded movement on his Casualty Form shows *"Leave 25/8/17 to 8/9/17"* by which time he had been recommended for a Military Cross. This was duly *Gazetted* on 17th September 1917, supplement 30287, page 9564: *"For conspicuous gallantry and devotion to duty. He has taken part in many offensive patrols, which he led on twenty occasions, in the course of which four enemy aircraft were destroyed and twelve others driven down out of control. Although outnumbered by five to one on one occasion he handled his patrol of four machines with such skill and gallantry that after a very severe fight he was able to withdraw them without loss, having destroyed at least two enemy machines and driven down one out of control. His fearlessness and fine offensive spirit have been a splendid example to others."*

A First Bar was promulgated in *The London Gazette,* 18th March 1918, supplement 30583, page 3418: *"For conspicuous gallantry and devotion to duty in leading twenty-five offensive patrols in two months, shooting down five enemy aircraft, and showing marked skill as a leader."*

This, and subsequent, honours are in recognition as Commanding Officer of 41 Squadron [SE.5a] from January 1918 to February 1919.

A DSO was later added, this being *Gazetted* on 24th August 1918, supplement 30682, page 9902: *"For conspicuous gallantry and devotion to duty. He has recently destroyed six enemy aeroplanes and driven down others out of control. He has at all times shown splendid courage and determination, and by his leadership and good example has contributed largely to the success of his squadron."*

His DFC, less citation, appeared in *The Edinburgh Gazette,* June 5th, 1919, issue 13458, page 2047. Recalled to the service on 1st September 1939, he reverted to the retired list on 15th December 1941. His death was reported on Wednesday, 25th March 1970, and his body was cremated at the Southwest Middlesex Crematorium on 2nd April, followed by a memorial service at the Royal Air Force central church of St. Clement Danes, Aldwych, two weeks later.

An excellent biography in respect of Flight Lieutenant Philip Fletcher Fullard, born 27th May 1898, may be read on the Air of Authority website, and which authors repeat their grateful acknowledgement. This notes that Flight Lieutenant Fullard was one of the outstanding fighter pilots of the *Great War* achieving a remarkable score of forty-six hostile machines destroyed in a six month period between May and November 1917, when just three days before the opening of the *Battle of Cambrai* he broke his ankle playing football.

His MC and First Bar to the award were published on 10th January 1918 in *The Edinburgh Gazette* issue 13192, page 266 and 233 respectively: *"For conspicuous gallantry and devotion to duty when engaged in aerial combat. He has on four occasions attacked and destroyed enemy aircraft, and has in addition engaged in 25 indecisive combats, in which he has shown fine leadership, great dash and determination to close with the enemy."*

The First Bar citation reads: *"for conspicuous gallantry and devotion to duty. He has on many occasions displayed the utmost dash and fearlessness in attacking enemy aircraft at close range and destroying at least eight hostile machines during a period of about ten days. His determination and fine offensive spirit have in almost every instance resulted in disaster to the enemy."*

On 6th April 1918, *The London Gazette,* supplement 30614, page 4197, published his DSO: *"For conspicuous gallantry and devotion to duty. As a patrol leader and scout pilot he is without equal. The moral effect of his presence in a patrol is most marked. He has now accounted for fourteen machines destroyed and eighteen driven down out of control in a little over four months."*

An incomplete Casualty Form shows he joined the RFC on 4th August 1916, and during the period referred to above was attached to 1 Squadron [Nieuport 17] which he joined at Bailleul on the last day of April 1917. It is recorded that between the 7th and 11th of September 1917, he was treated in 83 General Hospital for temporary blindness caused when he damaged a blood vessel while recovering from a violent spin.

Air Commodore Fullard lived to a good age, his death being reported on Tuesday, 24th April 1984.

Squadron Leader Owen Tudor Boyd's MC was *Gazetted* in the Edinburgh paper on August 22nd, 1916, issue 12974, page 1449: *"For conspicuous gallantry when on a bombing raid in unfavourable weather. He descended to less than 1,000 feet and bombed a train, which he afterwards attacked with his machine gun, though heavily attacked by rifle and machine gun fire."*

A Sandhurst cadet, Owen Tudor Boyd was appointed to a commission on the Unattached List of the Indian Army as early as January 1909, subsequently serving with the 5th Cavalry. By 1916, he had been attached to the RFC and the action referred to in the above citation places him with Martynside G100 Elephant equipped 27 Squadron.

Rising to air rank prior to the outbreak of the Second World War he was appointed designate Air Officer Commanding in Chief HQ RAF Middle East and was *en route* to take up this appointment when the 214 Squadron Wellington IC T2873 in which he was a passenger ran out of fuel before reaching Malta and landed in Sicily. The details of this very unfortunate affair are reported in full by David Gunby and Pelham Temple on page 31 of their first volume of *Royal Air Force Bomber Losses in the Middle East and Mediterranean.*

A prisoner of war for the next three years and three months, he returned to the UK following a successful escape and took up the post as Air Officer Commanding No. 93 Group which came under the aegis of Bomber Command. It seems his personal life took a turn for the worse when his wife divorced him on the grounds of adultery in July 1944, and just days later he died on Sunday, 5th August 1944. Aged 54, he is buried in Mill Hill Cemetery.

Initially serving as an observer before re-mustering to pilot, Arthur Willoughby Falls Glenny was primarily employed on reconnaissance duties as the citations for his award confirm. The citation for his MC, promulgated in *The Edinburgh Gazette,* issue 13143, page 1983, reads: *"For conspicuous gallantry and devotion to duty when in co-operation with our artillery. By dint of great perseverance, skill and very gallant flying he has accomplished splendid work under very difficult circumstances. On one occasion, during a gale of wind, he successfully ranged three of our heavy batteries upon an enemy battery which was completely obliterated. He has consistently set a very fine example to his squadron."*

The citation for a First Bar appeared in the *Edinburgh* edition of July 29th, 1918, issue 13296, page 2630: *"For conspicuous gallantry and devotion to duty, both in reconnaissance and as an artillery observer. On one occasion, although shot down, he brought in valuable information. On several occasions he conducted successful knock-out shoots with various batteries, obtaining excellent photographs, and did work of a very high standard."*

A richly deserved DFC was published postwar for his work in France in *The London Gazette* 3 December 1918, supplement 31046, page 14321: *"This officer has rendered valuable and gallant service on many occasions when on photographic and other reconnaissances. On 16th May, when directing fire on a hostile battery, he was attacked by twelve hostile scouts; his observer's gun jammed, and he was driven down to 2,000 feet, but handling his machine with great skill, he avoided serious damage; after the scouts had been driven off he returned and carried on the shoot with successful results. In this flight, which lasted four hours, he succeeded in taking fifteen photographs over corps' counter-battery area."*

His operational service in the *Great War* had spanned three years from October 1915 to October 1918, a period when the RFC and from April 1918, the RAF, had experienced numerous difficult challenges in carrying out its operational work, the ultimate success of which lies solely with the likes of Arthur Willoughby Falls Glenny. In the three years in which he was actively engaged, he was attached to 5 Squadron, 52 Squadron, 9 Squadron, 4 Squadron and 7 Squadron, with last three carrying out the duties of flight commander.

Air Commodore Glenny died on Wednesday, 29th January 1947, a few months before his 50th birthday.

Squadron Leader Arthur Clinton Maund happened to be in Canada when the *Great War* broke out and he immediately enlisted as a private, initially with the 32nd Canadian InfantryBattalion subsequently transferring to the 8th in which he was commissioned.

By March 1916, his 'marching days' were over and he was on the Western Front as an observer with 8 Squadron at Bellevue and equipped with BE.2c. When the Armistice came into effect in November 1918, he was Officer Command-ing Archangel, remaining in North Russia as head of the training mission until sometime in 1919. His overseas excursions continued with postings to Turkey, India [following a spell at Martlesham Heath] and at the outbreak of the Second World War he was fulfilling a staff appointment in Iraq, and later in 1939, transferring to Headquarters RAF Middle East before returning home by December 1941, to take the duties of Air Officer Administration at Technical Training Command headquarters at Shinfield Park, Reading, and it was while so employed that he succumbed to infective endocarditis on 13th December 1942. Air Vice Marshal Maund CB CBE DSO mentioned in despatches and conferred with the *Croix de Guerre* with Palms [France] is buried in Brookwood Military Cemetery where his head-stone carries the inscription *"Only The Actions Of The Just Smell Sweet And Blossom In Their Dust"* [James Shirley, *The Contention of Ajax and Ulysses*].

Squadron Leader Arthur Ashford Benjamin Thomson was *Gazetted* with the MC on 2nd October 1915, supplement 29313, page 9721: *"For conspicuous gallantry and determination on 29th August 1915, near Neuve Chapelle. When ranging a heavy gun on the German trenches he stayed up over two hours in heavy rain, with clouds at about 500 feet. At one time he found himself in cloud on the far side of the German trenches; but, after coming back under heavy fire, he continued to observe with the greatest bravery and skill, only returning when too dark for more work. His gallant conduct resulted in 10 direct hits on the enemy's parapet."*

Gained while attached to 16 Squadron [BE.2c] at Merville, and whilst carrying out the duties of a flight commander.

On June 1st, 1916, the *Edinburgh Gazette,* issue 12945, page 956, promulgated the following: *"For conspicuous gallantry and good work during Zeppelin raids."* Although the indication is for the first award of a MC, it was, in fact, a First Bar, as amended by *The London Gazette* on 9th September 1916.

Air Commodore Thomson died shortly before the outbreak of the Second World War when as Air Officer Command-ing No. 3 Group, Bomber Command, he accompanied the crew of a 115 Squadron Wellington which took off from Marham and landed at Boscombe Down. Alighting, Air Commodore Thomson inspected the aircraft's bomb bay and then turned and walked into a still revolving propeller. Critically injured, he died in the ambulance conveying him to hospital.

Squadron Leader Ivor Thomas Lloyd retired from the service at his own request on the last day of July 1939, but was recalled to active duty a week before the Second World War was declared. During the second conflict he was promoted acting air commodore, a rank he retained on reverting to the Retired List on 29th March 1946. Appointed CB CBE and four times mentioned in despatches, he died on Monday, 28th October 1966.

Squadron Leader Hugh Vivian Champion de Crespigny, formerly commissioned to the Suffolk Regiment, was honoured with the MC on 16th May 1916, promulgated in *The London Gazette* supplement 29584, page 4929: *"For conspicuous gallantry and skill, notably when he attacked five enemy machines over the enemy's lines.He drove away one, and brought another to the ground badly hit. His own machine was then crippled by the fire of the remaining three, but, after emptying one more drum at them, he brought his machine down safely in our lines."*

The Edinburgh Gazette, December 5th, 1918, issue 13363, page 4471, published his DFC [France]: *"A brilliant and gallant officer who displays high initiative in night flying, in which service his example has been invaluable to those under his command. On the night of 23rd-24th September, Major Champion de Crispigny carried out a long-distance bombing raid. Flying a machine unsuitable for night duty, and in the face of adverse weather conditions, he reached, and successfully bombed, his objective. A fine performance, calling for cool courage and determination."*

These two awards reflect on his service with 11 Squadron [Vickers FB.5] and 65 Squadron [Sopwith F.1 Camel] respectively.

Squadron Leader Charles Oscar Frithiof Modin commenced his military service in October 1909, when he was commissioned as a Sub-Lieutenant in the Royal Naval Volunteer Reserve. Subsequently, he received a commission in the Royal Marines and by January 1917, he had transferred to the Army, but in the same year was accepted by the RFC.

Transferred to the Unemployed List on 11th February 1919, he returned to the Royal Air Force with a short service commission on 10th October 1919 [LG 10 October 1919, issue 31593, page 12554]. Posted to Felixstowe and attached to 230 Squadron, he came close to losing his life when the Felixstowe F.5 N4044 crashed during an instructional flight [see page 256 of Volume 3 for details].

According to the Air of Authority website, Air Commodore Modin was taken prisoner of war while in the Fac East attached to Headquarters RAF Far East as Air Officer Administration. For his actions during captivity, he was mentioned in despatches. His DSC, untraced, was promulgated in the New Year's Honours List for 1915, in recognition of his part in operations around Antwerp the previous October.

Appendix C - Officers Granted Short Service Commissions

The year 1922 witnessed a continuation of officers with previous Royal Air Force service being granted short service commissions; where available their previous records have been checked. The observations heading the 1921 appendix continue to apply.

On the 1st of April 1922, No. 3 Flying Training School at Digby disbanded, as did Manston based No. 6 Flying Training School where it was planned to open No. 7 Flying Training School but this was cancelled.

LG 13 January 1922, issue 32576, page 375 - Various dates of seniority - Block 15191 to 15198

15191 ALDER* Herbert Victor F/O 11.10.26 Dismissed

By sentence of General Court Martial [LG 26 October 1926, issue 33215, page 6824].

15192 CROWTHER Arthur Kennith P/O 01.04.22 Cancelled

15193 GRACE Charles Frederick Hallyburton G/Capt 15.02.46 Retirement

At his own request [LG 8 March 1946, supplement 37497, page 1335]. Group Captain Charles Frederick Hallyburton Grace had been conferred by the King of Norway with the Order of St. Olav[Grand Cross], *Gazetted* 18th December 1942, supplement 35827, page 5506. His death was announced on Sunday, 30th March 1975.

15194 MARLER Eric F/O 29.12.29 Relinquished

Returned to the service and within the Royal Air Force Volunteer Reserve was granted a commission in the rank of pilot officer attached to the Administrative and General Duties Branch, with effect from 19th September 1939 [LG 26 September 1939, issue 34694, page 6506], his service No. 74183 S/Ldr 10.02.54 Relinquished

15195 PALMER* Robert Lester W/Cdr 10.02.54 Relinquished

As a squadron leader, Robert Lester Palmer was *Gazetted* with the AFC in the King's Birthday Honours List on 2nd June 1943, supplement 36033, page 2452.

15196 PHILLIPS John Sever W/Cdr 09.10.42 Retired list

On account of ill-health [LG 5 January 1943, supplement 35849, page 164].

15197 WYKES Horace John F/Lt 06.06.39 Relinquished

Flight Lieutenant Horace John Wykes was granted a commission in class CC, in the Reserve of Air Force Officers and in the General Duties Branch 26th July 1939 [LG 14 November 1939, issue 34733, page 7644]. F/Lt 25.08.41 Relinquished

15198 YEARSLEY William Arthur Charles Allison F/O 29.09.26 Relinquished

On account of ill-health [LG 1 October 1926, issue 33207, page 6297].

* Denotes former Royal Air Force service.

LG 17 January 1922, issue 32579, page 469 - Various dates of seniority.

FLYING OFFICERS
3

15199 HYSON John Edward Reginald F/O 02.01.24 Relinquished

On account of ill-health. John Edward Reginald Hyson was born on 30th September 1899, possibly at 256 Kings Road in Chelsea. Joining the RFC on 26th January 1917 his first operational posting was to 8 Squadron [FK.8] at Mons-en-Chaussée on 22nd February 1918. However, a month later on 19th March he was admitted to 24 General Hospital with an undisclosed illness on discharge was attached to 2 Aeroplane Supply Depot Fienvillers from where he was sent to 35 Squadron [FK.8] at Poulainville o 27th April 1918 and less than a week later he was wounded while flying an operational patrol - see page 117 of my first volume for details. First treated as 61 Casualty Clearing Station he was returned to the UK on 6th May 1918 as a patient aboard the HS *Ville de Liège*.

15200 JONES Basil Potier F/O 20.02.40 Relinquished

On account of ill-health [LG 12 March 1940, issue 34810, page 1475].

15201 SIEVEKING DSC Lancelot de Giberne Captain 14.03.23 Relinquished

On account of ill-health. As Flight Lieutenant Lancelot de Giberne Sieveking DSC he had been restored to the active list for temporary duty with effect from 9th April 1921 [LG 3 May 1921, issue 32311, page 3544].

FIRMIN Leslie Arthur Lewis F/O 11.02.26 Dismissed

By sentence of General Court Martial [LG 23 February 1926, issue 33135, page 1343]. As Lieutenant Leslie Arthur Lewis Firmin he had received a commission in the 4th Battalion, The Buffs, TA.

LG 28 February 1922, issue 32624, page 1725 - Seniority 16th February 1922

15204 MEALING Rupert Henry Steinbach F/O 16.02.31 Relinquished

Returned to the service and granted a commission in the Administrative and Special Duties Branch, 1st September 1939 [LG 31 October 1939, issue 34721, page 7276] with 73819 as his service number. W/Cdr 10.02.54 Relinquished

LG 7 March 1922, issue 32631, page 1953. Various dates of seniority.

FLYING OFFICERS
2

HAMILTON Wallace Ferrier F/O 04.06.29 Relinquished

On account of ill-health [LG 4 June 1929, issue 33503, page 3694]

MASON Cyril Arthur F/O 09.05.29 Relinquished

LG 21 March 1922, issue 32645, page 2329. Seniority 7 March 1922..

FLYING OFFICERS
2

BUCKNALL Claude Vernon Aristides F/Lt + 05.09.23 RAF Flowerdown

Formerly Lieutenant, The Inniskilling Dragoons

Army Form B.103 shows 2nd Lieutenant Bucknall being attached to No. 1 Aeroplane Supply Depot at Marquise [Pilots Pool] on 4th August 1918, ahead of his posting to 41 Squadron [SE.5a] at Conteville on the 13th August. Two months later and he was a prisoner of war, the details of this being reported on page 291 of my Second Volume and at which time the squadron had mover by way of St. Omer to Droglandt.

His death by suicide occurred in the most awful circumstances, a full report being published in the *Westminster Gazette* on 11the September 1923, beneath the headline *'Love Drama in a Flat - Inquest of Young Airman - Girl Artist's Story'*

"The story of the shooting of Flight Lieutenant Claude Vernon Aristides Bucknall in the presence of Miss Grace Chapman, an Australian artist, who had rejected his proposal of marriage, was told at the Hammersmith Coroner's Court yesterday.

"The tragedy took place in the flat of Miss Chapman's father at Iverne-gardens, Kensington, on Wednesday evening of last week.

"The first witness was Mr. Sylvis Paul Bucknall, who stated that his brother was 31 years of age, and was stationed with the Royal Air Force at Flowerdown Camp, Winchester.

"The last he saw of Lieutenant Bucknall was at Ventnor Railway Station on 2 September, when he was alright in health except for a touch of neuritis. He also told him that the neurasthenia from which he suffered two years ago in India was coming back.

"He complained of sleeplessness owing to this trouble, and also of the fact that he was very worried about his wireless course.

"flight-Lieut. Soden identified a small pistol produced as belonging to him, and said he had lent it to Mr. Bucknall on the afternoon of his death, for practice.

"Mr. Thomas John Francis Chapman, retired merchant, described how Lieut. Bucknall had called out and said, "I am ordered to Mesopotamia. I have just come to say good-bye." "While I was dressing for dinner I heard a shot," said Mr. Chapman. "I rushed back to the room immediately and found him collapsing on a settee.

"Miss Grace Evelyn Chapman was then called. She was dressed in deep mourning, and was heavily veiled.

"She said that while she was staying in the Isle of Wight she had a proposal of marriage from Lieut. Bucknall, but declined him, telling him she had not known him long enough. "He seemed very depressed," she said, "but he did not tell me why."When Lieut. Bucknall came to London in the first week of August he made another proposal and she made the same reply again.

"Speaking of the visit of 5 September, Miss Chapman said she did not notice anything unusual about him, he seemed quite cheerful.

"He told her when they were alone that he was not going to Mesopotamia, but he was going away himself, and wished to say good-bye.She did not reply, but went to light the fire. The next moment she heard a shot. She saw Lieutenant Bucknall stagger, and she rushed towards him, assisting him until her father came.

"The Coroner read extracts from a letter written by Flight-Lieutenant Bucknall to his mother, in which he said: "I have decided I can bear this world no longer, I am going to the next whatever that may be. The war killed me really; I have never been happy since. I feel happy at the prospect of release from the hellish torture from which I am suffering. I can't sleep, and my nights are one long agony. It is no one's fault but mine."

"The Coroner tendered his sympathy to Miss Chapman, and to the relatives, and returned a verdict of "Suicide while temporarily insane."

The previous Saturday, September 8th, 1923, *The Daily Mirror* published a studio photograph of Flight Lieutenant Bucknall, resplendent in his uniform with side cap and wearing gauntlets and a 'Sam Browne' belt; although not quite sharp enough for clarity, his 'flying bade' appears to be of RFC pattern. What is obvious, he was a strikingly handsome young officer.

The two medical terms reported by Mr. Sylvis Paul Bucknall, deceased's brother, concern in the case of neuritis inflammation of a nerve while neurasthenia relates to a number of conditions and may be associated with emotional disorder.

Paul McMillan, who traced the newspaper reports, also notes that Miss Chapman, born in New South Wales on 25th October 1888, married George Thomas Thalben-Ball, a fellow Australian and an organist of great merit. Their marriage resulted in a daughter, Evelyn Pamela who like her mother followed an artistic career, and a son, John Michael. With the death of his wife on 13th July 1961, George later married for a second time.

15207 CHASE Wilfred Arthur F/O 07.03.31 Relinquished

Returned to service and granted a commission in the Administrative and Special Duties Branch as a pilot officer on probation, with effect from 4th March 1941 [LG 16 May 1941, issue 35165, page 2817, and allocated 64343 but subsequently reverted to 15207, serving until:-

S/Ldr 18.08.49 Resigned

LG 28 March 1922, issue 32653, page 2517. Various dates of seniority.

FLYING OFFICERS

2

SAINT DSC Howard John Thomas F/O 01.02.31 Relinquished

Flying Officer Howard John Thomas Saint was *Gazetted* with the DSC on 2nd November 1917, supplement 30363, page 11320: *"For conspicuous bravery in attacking superior hostile formations of enemy aircraft. On the 21st September 1917, he, with three other machines, attacked five hostile scouts. After getting to close quarters with one of them, he fired three bursts from his machine-gun and drove it down completely out of control. On the 23rd September 1917, while leading a patrol of eight scouts, he attacked a hostile formation of ten machines. One of these drove down, diving vertically, out of control. He has forced won other machines completely out of control, one of them in flames; and has also shown great courage in attacking enemy troops and aerodromes with machine-gun fire from very low altitudes."* In total he scored seven confirmed combat victories between the afternoon of 9th August and the early afternoon of 20th October 1917, all with No. 5 Squadron RNAS, the first four at the controls of Sopwith Triplanes and the last three flying Camels. `his brief biography can be read on *Wikipedia* which shows his birth as being in Ruabon, Denbeighshire on 20th January 1893, and his death in his early 80s at Hove, Sussex, on Tuesday, 10th August 1976.

TALLENTIRE Miles F/O + 11.10.23 31 Squadron

As a 2nd Lieutenant, Miles Tallentire served with 82 Squadron [FK.8] between 17th September 1918 and 25th March 1919 on which date he was posted to Home Establishment.

LG 4 April 1922, supplement 32661, page 2728 - Seniority 1st April 1922

15213 GREET Cyril Bennet G/Capt 22.01.46 Retirement

On account of medical unfitness for Air Force service [LG 5 February 1946, supplement 37456, page 812].

LG 18 April 1922, issue 32673, page 3090 - Seniority 1st April 1922 apart from James Barclay Rose 3rd April 1922 - Block 15214 to 15232

15214 BASSETT Horace Sydney Claude F/O 30.06.26 Relinquished

On account of ill-health [LG 17 August 1926, issue 33192, page 5447].

15215 BATEMAN Anthony Edward Barthrop S/Ldr 10.02.54 Relinquished

15216 DANIELL Robert Frederic P/O 28.02.23 Terminated

During the Second World War he was granted a commission as a 2nd Lieutenant in the Royal Corps of Signals [LG 30 January 1940, supplement 34781, page 598].

15217 DAWSON Dennis Rodgers F/O 09.10.25 Resigned

15218 DUKE Bernard Cecil F/O 01.04.26 Relinquished

On account of ill-health [LG 30 March 1926, issue 33146, page 2278].

15219 FLEMING Robert Bruce G/Capt 11.02.55 Retirement

Transferred from the General Duties Branch to the Stores Branch and was issued with a new service number 21137. Prior to this, and whilst attached to 7 Squadron at Worthy Down he escaped injury, along with two other members of crew, when Vickers Vimy F9187 overturned landing at night on Tuesday, 16th October 1923. Sadly, the fourth member, Aircraftman Ronald Sinclair was killed. The Vimy, although badly damaged, was repaired and was extant on 25th January 1925, undergoing repairs at Vickers following a forced-landing at the hands of 58 Squadron on 9th Sept- ember 1924.

21137 Transferred to the Stores Branch [LG 25 January 1929, issue 33460, page 619]. G/Capt 01.07.47

15220 HEAVEN Eustace Joseph P/O 28.02.23 Terminated

15221 HIRSH Lawrence Pilkington F/O 01.04.33 Class C
Whilst still on the Reserve, my co-author reports that Flying Officer Lawrence Pilkington Hirsch, now the manager of Gravesend Airport, died in a road traffic accident on 3rd September 1935 when his car clipped a kerb and overturned near Meopham some 7 miles south of Gravesend.
15222 HUME-WRIGHT Patrick John Antony G/Capt 04.08.48 Retirement
15223 LINDSAY MC John Clyde P/O 01.11.22 Terminated
Formerly a 2nd Lieutenant with the Middlesex Regiment, Special Reserve, John Clyde Lindsay was *Gazetted* with the MC on 7th November 1918, supplement 30977, page 13160: *"For conspicuous gallantry and good work on patrol. Under heavy fire he led his patrol through the enemy wire and located a strong enemy post, which he attacked. Later, although his company had been relieved in the front line, he volunteered to take out a strong patrol, with which he lay out all day in "No Man's Land," and obtained valuable information."*
15224 PIERCE Harry West F/O 01.04.31 Relinquished
15225 ROSE James Barclay P/O + 14.06.23 RAF Gosport
Took off from the Westlands airfield near Yeovil in Westland Walrus II N9510 on Thursday, 14th June 1923, James Barclay Rose last control while making a climbing turn and crashed at Bunford on the eastern edge of the airfield. Then open land, Bunford has since been absorbed in Yeovil's development and is now referred to as Bunford Heights. A very brief report of the accident was published the next day [a Friday] in *The Western Morning News and Mercury* beneath the heading *'Airman Killed - Machines Fatal Nose-Dive Near Yeovil'*

"Yesterday afternoon Flight-Lieut. Rose, RAF, was killed just outside Yeovil. He had come from Gosport to deliver a machine built at the Westland Aircraft Works. He got off from the aerodrome safely, but a few minutes afterwards the machine nose-dived, and got into a vertical spin, and did not have sufficient altitude to recover. It crashed in the ground, and the pilot was killed instantly."
15226 TROWER Stephen Herbert Gerard F/O 01.04.30 Relinquished
Subsequently, it would seem, he obtained a commission in the Royal Navy but had retired in the rank of Lieutenant when granted a commission in the Reserve of Air Force Officers, Class A on 27th March 1934. Then, as my co-author has discovered, he was killed in Belgium on 17th July 1935 when the Fairey Fantôme G-ADIF registered to the Company crashed during a demonstration at Evère Airport, Brussels. It is believed Flying Officer Trower may have 'blacked-out' while pulling a high-speed turn, losing control and diving into the ground. An excellent description of the Fantôme is reported between pages 260 and 263 of H A Taylor's *Fairey Aircraft since 1915*, the author writing in his opening remarks *"... might fairly be described as a splendid but still-born fighting aeroplane. It was probably the cleanest and certainly the most handsome biplane ever produced."*
15227 VAUGHAN MC Edwin Stephen Campion F/Lt 17.12.29 Retired list
On account of ill-health [LG 17 December 1929, issue 33561, page 8210]. As Lieutenant Edwin Stephen Campion Vaughan of the 1/8th Battalion, Royal Warwickshire Regiment, Territorial Force, he was *Gazetted* with the MC on 10th December 1919, supplement 31680, page 15373: *"During the attack on Landrecies on 4th November 1918, he displayed great courage and determination. In face of strong opposition he led his men forward to their objective, resulting in the capture of the bridge across the canal before the enemy could destroy it. Later, during the advance towards Maroilles on 5th/6th November he again did good work."*
15228 WAKE Guy P/O + 11.07.23 422 Flight Gosport
While flying near Lee-on-Solent on Wednesday, 11th July 1923, in Blackburn N9583 entered a nose dive from which he failed to recover. His demise was reported by *The Evening News* on Thursday, July 12th, 1923, under the headline *'The Lee-on-Solent Crash - Inquest on the Dead Flying Officer'*

"The story of the fatal aeroplane crash which occurred at Lee-on-the-Solent yesterday morning was told to Mr. Leonard Warner [Coroner for South Hants] this afternoon, at an inquiry held at RN Hospital Haslar. The victim of the crash was Pilot Officer Guy Wake [24], attached to Fort Grange, Gosport.

"The first witness was Pilot Officer John S Charlton, stationed at Fort Grange, who said the deceased officer, under orders from his flight commander, took up a Blackburn Fleet-spotter about 10.30 on Wednesday morning. It was a new type of machine, capable of carrying three other passengers in addition to the pilot. Wake rose from the ground quite normally, and flew for seven or eight minutes, having risen about 1,500 feet, before anything happened. Flying conditions were good. Wake started to turn to the right, and the machine spun three or four times in that direction, with the engine running. The pilot shut the engine off and pulled the machine round to natural flying position. The machine was then about 200 feet up, and the engine started again. The plane appeared to be travelling alright, and was gathering speed with the nose slightly inclined downwards. After about twenty seconds the deceased again started a right-hand turn and witness noticed the nose drop. The machine appeared to go down in a steep skid behind the trees. Witness found the machine nose downwards in a field near the golf links. The deceased officer had been removed from the machine, but there were no signs of life. The nose of the machine was bashed in, and the engine forced out at the back.

"Flight-Lieut. J H Musgrave, Medical Officer, arrived on the scene immediately after the crash, and found Wake dead. His main injuries were a fracture and dislocation of the lower part of the spine, while the fifth to the tenth ribs were fractured; the nose and one ankle were also fractured, and there were incised wounds on both legs. Death was due to shock from the injuries described. Witness added that he did not think the extreme prejudicial to flying.

"Flight-Lieut. Richard Barnard Munday, the officer in charge of 422 Flight, Fort Grange, said the deceased officer had had about 50 hours flying as a pilot and about 200 as an observer since 1917. His first experience was on kite balloons. He saw service in Russia after the Armistice. His pilot duties commenced in 1921. Wake had been up in a similar type of machine before. In witnesses's opinion, they were perfectly normal machines. A Court of Inquiry was being held. An Air Ministry official had since examined the machine, and found nothing wrong.

"Flight-Lieut. Busey added that there must have been either something imperfect in the machine or its engine, or an error of judgement on the part of the pilot in flying the machine, to cause it to fall. The machine had not been flown for three weeks. The witness was the last to fly it, and was then in the air for two hours.

"The Coroner expressed his sympathy in regard to the death of the young officer, remarking that there was always an element of risk, and everyone admired the risks these men took now, as in the war, to perfect the flying service. He returned a verdict of "Accidental Death.""
15229 WALKER Archie William Beesse P/O 03.10.23 Resigned
15230 WIBLIN Maurice W/Cdr 13.07.48 Retirement
15231 WILSON John Borthwick F/Lt 19.06.39 Relinquished
On appointed to the Air Branch of the Royal Navy [LG 8 September 1939, supplement 34674, page 6134].
15232 YOUNG Leonard W/Cdr 08.12.46 Retirement

LG 16 May 1922, issue 32701, page 3796 - Seniority 4th May 1922 and 1st May 1922

FLYING OFFICER

HUNTER Henry John F/Lt 01.04.38 Retired list
At own request [LG 5 April 1938, issue 34499, page 2251]. Formerly of the 4th Battalion, Seaforth Highlanders, Henry John Hunter was born on 8th June 1895 and was accepted by the RFC on 20th April 1917 to be trained as an observer. Qualified, he joined 34 Squadron [RE.8] at Bray Dunes on 30th October 1917 to discover that the squadron was to move the next day to Candas from where it would prepare to leave with an Anglo-French force to the Italian front. His service in Italy was interrupted with two spells in 24 General Hospital while between 3rd and 5th March 1918 he was attached to 42 Squadron [RE.8] at San Luca. The final entry on his casualty form shows he was granted leave from 22nd March to 5th April 1918. On his return to the service he served at first in the General Duties Branch but by the time he left, at his own request, he had transferred to the Stores Branch.

PILOT OFFICERS
4

DEAN Godfrey Webster F/O 01.05.30 Relinquished
HOLMAN John Vivian F/O 01.05.39 Relinquished

15237 REYNOLDS Bryan Vernon AM 13.07.59 Retirement
Air Marshal Sir Bryan Reynolds KCB CBE twice mentioned in despatches, died on Monday, 6th December 1965.
VERNEY-CAVE Thomas Adrian F/O 25.06.24 Resigned

LG 6 June 1922, issue 32717, page 4335 - Various dates of seniority

FLYING OFFICERS
3

15240 CREES Archibald William F/O 25.05.39 Relinquished
Returned to the service and commissioned in the Administrative and Special Duties Branch, effective from 1st September 1939 [LG 31 October 1939, issue 34721, page 7276]. S/Ldr 10.02.54 Relinquished
TAYLOR MC Rowallan Masson W/Cdr 07.05.47 Retirement
By February 1926 he had transferred from the General Duties Branch to the Stores Branch, his service number being amended to 21041. On 5th September 1940 he was placed on the Retirement List but was re-employed [LG 7 December 1943, supplement 36276, page 5441]. As Acting Captain Rowallan Masson Taylor of the 5th Battalion, Seaforth Highlanders TF he was *Gazetted* in the Edinburgh edition, issue 13510, page 3312 with the MC on October 8th, 1919: *"At Avesnes le Sec, during operations on 13th Oct. 1918, he performed very gallant service. He was in command of a support company. When the units on his left were held up, and finally had to withdraw, he at once formed a defensive flank and prevented the enemy from advancing to counter attack. He also enabled the forward companies of his battalion to hold on in their advanced positions. Though wounded, he remained on duty."*
15239 YOUNG Frank Boniface S/Ldr 10.02.54 Relinquished

LG 27 June 1922, issue 32723, page 4834 - Seniority 10th June 1922

COLLINS Robert F/O + 28.02.26 480 Flight Calshot
Flying Robert Collins was critically injured when the Fairey IIID in which he was a passenger stalled while turning having taken off from Calshot on the 26th. Flight Lieutenant Geoffrey Hemming DSC, the pilot, was killed in the crash. He had been granted a short service commission on 12th September 1919, full details of his tragic accident being reported in my third volume on page 219.
COOPE Brownlow Richard Christopher F/O 10.06.30 Relinquished
DENISON Christopher F/O + 30.04.25 440 Flight HMS *Eagle*
Flying Officer Christpher Denison crashed at Mellieha on the northern side of the Island of Malta, his Fairey IIID N9780 being destroyed by fire. His observer, Lieutenant Henry Thew Rust RN survived, though badly injured, while the telegraphist, Carl Llewellyn Dewhurst Oliver died a week later on the 6th of May while being treated for his horrific burns in Mtarfa Hospital.

This accident is recorded on pages 39 and 40 of Colonel Mark Said's *Broken Wings - A Century of Malta's Aviation Accidents, Incidents and Other Stories 1915 2015* which the authors are most pleased to acknowledge. It seems Flying Officer Denison, his age is shown as 20, had taken off from Hal Far to take part in a military exercise and was witnessed overflying the nearby bay before coming down in a field overlooked by Mellieha Church, the time being at around 6.30 a.m. Some local farmerss rushed to the scene, but poor Christopher Denison was trapped un his seat. Heroically, the rescuers managed to pull clear the observer and the telegraphist, but in the case of the latter they were unable to release his flying helmet which had caught fire.

Both Flying Officer Denison, a Londoner from Elm Park Gardens, and Telegraphist Oliver were buried with full military honours in Capuccini Naval Cemetery at Kalkara.

It is believed the deaths of these two airmen were the first fatalities incurred by HMS *Eagle* which had commissioned in February 1924.
DOWNER Frederick Wilmot Middlemist F/Lt 19.02.37 Relinquished
On appointment to a commission in the South African Air Force Special Reserve of flying officers [LG 18 May 1937, issue 34399, page 3251].
FISHER Richard
15248 FLINT MC Maxwell Charles William Craig G/Capt 06.05.46 Retirement
MORPHY Douglas McGillycuddy F/O + 04.08.24 28 Squadron
PINNELL Leonard Gaster F/O 10.06.30 Relinquished
REEVES Guy Francis F/O + 12.09.24 404 Flight Leuchars
Flying Officer Guy Francis Reeves died when his Nieuport Nightjar J6932 spun out of control at 60 feet and crashed near the airfield. The Court of Inquiry's findings, attached to A.M. Form 470 read: *"The cause of the accident was in our opinion an error of judgement on the part of the pilot, who attempted to turn to the left with insufficient flying speed. A spin followed, from which the machine only just failed to recover, as is shown by the horizontal position of the fuselage after the crash, and the undamaged wings. The evidence of the second witness, Flying Officer Fleming, does not agree with this finding, but that of other eye-witnesses leads us to suppose that Flying Officer Fleming is mistaken when he says that the machine had regained flying speed. Our examination of the controls shows that all of them to have been in good working order, and we do not consider that anything went wrong with the machine in the air." 'AOC concurs."*

The following appeared in th *Aberdeen Press and Journal* the day after the crash: *"Leuchars Aerodrome was the scene yesterday of an aeroplane tragedy, as the result of which Flying-Officer Reeves lost his life.*

"Reeves was engaged in flying what is known as a "fly-catcher"and had been in the air for an hour or so in the vicinity of the aerodrome. He was observed to be negotiating a landing. Just when the machine was some 50 feet from the ground it suddenly nose-dived into the ground and smashed.

"A rush was at once made by the aerodrome staff to the scene of the accident, but the machine was found badly smashed up and the officer killed, one of his legs being severed.

"Flying Officer Reeves had been stationed at the Leuchars Aerodrome for some time, and had only returned from leave on Monday morning. He was about 23 years of age, and belonged to London."
RICHARDS Alfred Coombe Wall F/O 10.06.35 Relinquished
THOMSON Alan F/O 10.06.30 Relinquished
WATSON Myles Birket Foster F/O + 21.07.24 1 Squadron

LG 4 July 1922, issue 32726, page 5039 - Seniority 22 June 1922

FLYING OFFICER

17005 BANTING Harold William Russell F/O 22.06.39 Relinquished

LG 11 July 1922, issue 32728, page 5208 - Seniority 1st July 1922

FLYING OFFICER

17006 JEFFREY MC James Cairns F/O 16.04.31 Ceased employment
Temporary 2nd Lieutenant James Cairns Jeffery of the South Lancashire Regiment and attached to the 29th Battalion, Durham Light Infantry was *Gazetted* with the MC, less citation, on 8th March 1919, supplement 31219, page 3242. On 13th March 1933, Flying Officer Jeffrey MC relinquished his commission on appointment to a commission in the Regular Army Reserve of Officers and was permitted to retain his rank [LG 25 April 1939, issue 33934, page 2768].

LG 18 July 1922, issue 32730, page 5364 - Seniority 10th July 1922

FLYING OFFICER

17007	CLIFFORD	Edmond King	F/O		27.06.29	Relinquished

LG 28 July 1922, issue 32733, page 5612 - Seniority 14th July 1922

	CHAPELL	Richard Graham	F/O		18.08.26	Resigned

Temporary 2nd Lieutenant Richard Graham Chapell was commissioned to The Gordon Highlanders on 1st October 1915 [LG 7 October 1915, supplement 29319, page 9875]. During a solo practice cross-country flight in Avro 504K H2458 belonging to the Inland Area Communication Flight the engine failed through lack of petrol and he forced-landed, the Avro colliding with trees in Southwark Park in Rotherhithe in Central Southeast London. Although shaken, otherwise he was unhurt.

LG 15 August 1922, issue 32738, page 6022 - Seniority 1st August 1922

FLYING OFFICER

17009	CULVERWELL	Eric Vincent	F/O		01.08.31	Relinquished

LG 22 August 1922, issue 32740, issue 6163 - Seniority 11th August 1922

FLYING OFFICER

17010	BUTLIN	Harry	F/O	+	28.08.25	111 Squadron

LG 5 September 1922, issue 32744, page 6445 - Seniority 21st August 1922 - Block 17011 to 17018

17011	BARNES	John Owen	P/O	+	14.12.23	55 Squadron
17012	COLE	Cecil Archibald	P/O		25.04.23	Terminated
17013	GUEST	Charles Edward Neville	AM		29.08.56	Retirement

Air Marshal Sir Charles Guest KBE CB twice mentioned in despatches, died on Thursday, 23rd June 1977. During his time as Assistant Chief of the Air Staff [Operations] he was the Royal Air Force representative at the funeral of King George VI at St. George's Chapel, Windsor on Friday, 15th February 1952. His final service appointment was Inspector General of the Royal Air Force during which he instigated a review aimed at improving the Accident Investigation Organisation. This was at a time when major flying accidents were rife within the service; on the day that he took up his appointment, 19th April 1954 three Harvard T.2s from 1340 Flight Eastleight, Kenya, were written off in the Aberdare Mountains when a severe downdraft prevented them from climbing out of the valley into which they had flown. Fortunately there were no fatalities, but by year's end the overall number of aircrew deaths for 1954 totalled 280 [151 had been killed since AM Guest arrived at his desk] from a quite staggering 452 accidents where the aircraft was declared 'written off charge.' The most serious crash had occurred in a blizzard on 6th January 1954 when in failing light the pilot of a Valetta T.3 WJ474 took off from Bovingdon intending to return to Thorney Island where the Valetta was based with 2 Air Navigation School. On board were a crew of four and thirteen passengers, all members of the station's rugby team that had been visiting RAF Halton. Four minutes into the flight the Valetta flew into trees on rising ground north of the airfield near the village of Alburg, a couple of miles ENE of Tring, Hertfordshire. There was one survivor, Pilot Officer P D Cliff.*The names of the crew and passengers who perished were reported in *Flight* on page 83 of their issue of 15th January 1954.

* Probably Patrick Dewhirst Cliff, a trainee navigator, who was *Gazetted* with a cadetship on 17th June 1953 [but effective from 11th February 1953] [LG 1 September 1953, supplement 39951, page 4698]. He retired as a wing commander OBE at his own request on 17th July 1982 [LG 28 September 1982, supplement 49122, page 12548].

17014	HOPKINS	Geoffrey Gethin	P/O		02.10.23	Removed

Pilot Officer Geoffrey Gethin Hopkins *"is removed from the RAF. His Majesty having no further use for his services."* [LG 9 October 1923, issue 32869, page 6757].

17015	MALONE	Anthony	F/O		23.09.25	Resigned

Posted to 7 Squadron at Bircham Newton, Anthony Malone escaped injury, along with two other members of crew, when Vickers Vimy F9187 turned over on landing at night on 16th October 1923. Please refer to Pilot Officer Robert Bruce Fleming's [LG 18 April 1922] entry for further details.

17016	PINNELL	Denis Geoffrey	F/O		21.08.30	Relinquished
17017	ROWE	Alexander Meredith	F/O	+	10.12.27	Class A

Flying Officer Alexander Meredith Rowe died from an undisclosed illness while being treated in the National Hospital, Holburn. At the time he was still on the Reserve.

17018	SWAIN	Francis Ronald Downs	A/Cmdr		14.07.54	Retirement

Air Commodore Francis Ronald Downs Swain CB CBE AFC mentioned in despatches, died on Thursday, 28th September 1989. Fifty-three years earlier to the date, and while attached to RAE Farnborough, he set a new high altitude record when he attained a height of 49,967 feet in a Bristol 138A K4879.

LG 19 September 1922, issue 32748, page 6715 - Seniority 2nd September 1922 - Block 17019 to 17044

17019	BROOKE-HUNT	Robert Cecil	P/O	+	26.03.23	5 FTS Shotwick

Robert Cecil Brooke-Hunt was in the advanced stage of his flying training when during a solo flight in DH.9A E8628 on Monday, 26th March 1923, he attempted to carry out a loop. While doing so structural failure occurred and the DH plunged into the ground near Heswall on the right bank of the River Dee in the Wirral. AM Form 70 [Royal Air Force Casualty Card] gives the cause as *"Obscure"* adding *"Necessary to remove crash to present - immersion at high tide. Machine believed to have broken in air."*

17020	DALRYMPLE	Henry Charles Emanuel Cyril Ponsonby	F/O		02.09.30	Relinquished
17021	FRANCIS	John	P/O		11.09.23	Resigned
17022	FRANKLIN	John Hayward Godfrey	F/O	+	11.10.24	84 Squadron
17023	HATTON	Victor John	F/O		01.04.28	Resigned

During his flying training at 5 FTS Shotwick, Victor John Hatton survived a serious crash on Monday, 9th October 1922, when the Avro 504K H2482 in which he was being instructed spun in while performing a loop. His instructor, Flying Officer Hubert Everitt Ranson was killed. AM 470 records the time of the crash as 1450 and that Pilot Officer Hatton was admitted to Chester Infirmary with serious injuries.

On 6th December 1924, and now attached to 99 Squadron, he was at the controls of Avro Aldershot III J6955 when it struck a fence while landing at Bircham Newton. On this occasion he was uninjured and the Aldershot continued in service , probably ending its days at HAD Henlow where it was reported in April 1926.

17024 KENYON Harry Melvin P/O Not in AFL 1926

It seems Pilot Officer Harry Melvin Kenyon, whom my co-author has discovered trained at 2 FTS Duxford, left the service and by the autumn of 1928 was on the Supplementary Reserve of Officers Royal Army Service Corps. He died in the King Edward Hospital at Ealing on 17th April 1930 from injuries received in a motorcycle accident.

17025 LABATT Wilfrid Henry Ernest P/O 08.11.22 Terminated

17026 MAYNARD Leslie Edward F/O 02.09.31 Relinquished

On Friday 17th February 19278, Flying Officer Leslie Edward Maynard was obliged to abandon Grebe II J7412 of 25 Squadron following a midair collision, the other aircraft involved has, as yet, not been identified.

17027 MELLOR Nick Peter Christian P/O 07.05.24 Relinquished

On account of ill-health.

17028 MICHELL Harold Victor F/O 02.09.30 Relinquished

17029 MURGATROYD Benjamin Norman F/O 02.09.35 Relinquished

During his service, Flying Officer Benjamin Norman Murgatroyd served in Iraq where he was attached to 55 Squadron at Hinaidi and it was here on 11th January 1927, that he was involved in a landing accident which wrote off his aircraft, and another that was parked nearby.

17030 ODBERT Reginald Vere Massey G/Capt + 18.07.43

On Sunday, 18th July 1943, Reginald Vere Massey Odbert and three fellow senior officers on his course joined the crew of Wellington III BK275 of 1485 Flight captained by Warrant Officer J W Heard for a gunnery and fighter affiliation demonstration and it was during the second phase of the exercise that structural failure of the mainplanes occurred. Out of control, the Wellington crashed with total loss of life just over a mile SE of Appleby in Lincolnshire. For further information, please refer to page 205 of my 8th Volume of Royal Air Force Bomber Command losses. Group Captain Reginald Vere Massey Odbert is buried in Newark-upon-Trent Cemetery. His headstone is inscribed with the words: *"His Life A Fragrant MemoryHis Absence A Silent Grief."*

17031 PEACEY Arthur John F/O + 09.03.29 Nottingham Aero Club

While serving his time in the Reserve of Air Force Officers, Flying Officer Arthur John Peacey went down in the sea some 90 miles ESE of the fishing port of Hull whilst flying DH.60X Moth G-AABA. This most unusual incident, as recorded on the Aviation Safety Network website, which the authors acknowledge, quotes from a report in *Flight* published March 14th, 1929: *"We learn from the Nottingham Aero Club of an accident to one of their members last Saturday afternoon, namely Mr. A J Peacey of Derby. After having 30 minutes dual with Mr. Brown, Mr. Peacey was told to go up and carry out landing practice for 20 minutes during which time he was told not to leave the immediate vicinity of the aerodrome. He was observed to carry out two landings and then at 1140 he disappeared, nothing further being heard of the machine until 14* [00] *hours on Sunday when a message was received from the Air Ministry to say that a DH Moth had been found by a German steamer* [the *Margot*] *90 miles ESE of Hull. The machine was wrecked and there was no trace of the pilot. Mr. Peacey was a Flying Officer on the Reserve of Air Force Officers and had done just over 800 hours."* It is assumed that following his two circuits and landings, he entered low cloud and became disorientated. The German steamer reported finding the wreckage 60 miles west of Terschelling. The report also notes that G-ABAA, a replacement for G-EBSK was taken on charge by Nottingham Aero Club on 8th September 1928.

17032 PHILLIPS William Henry F/O 10.02.54 Relinquished

17033 POOLEY Cecil James S/Ldr 10.02.54 Relinquished

By 1925, Flying Officer Cecil James was in India and serving with 60 Squadron. On Monday, 14th September 1925, he had the misfortune to write off DH.9A E728 - please refer to the summary for details.

17034 RODWELL William John Ellerton F/O 02.09.30 Relinquished

17025 SHAW Bryan Hirst F/O 02.09.30 Relinquished

17036 STEPHEN Donald Caird Dyer P/O 30.06.23 Terminated

17037 STEWART Albert Edward F/O 02.09.30 Relinquished

17038 SWAIN Oswald Bertie W/Cdr + 22.09.40

Wing Commander Oswald Bertie Swain, aged 41, is commemorated on panel at Golders Green Crematorium. His entry on the CWGC website indicates his wife, Irene Edith Clarissa Jane Swain, of Hendon, was killed in the same incident which leads me to suspect that both were victims of the London Blitz which opened on the 7th September 1940. The entry notes she was of British Guiana.

17039 TAYLOR Arthur William P/O 08.11.22 Terminated

17040 TRENDELL Archibald Charles P/O 23.05.23 Resigned

17041 VENMORE William Charles W/Cdr 17.07.50 Retirement

On account of medical unfitness for Air Force service [LG 18 July 1950, supplement 38970, page 3694].

17042 WALTERS Samuel Roy P/O 20.06.23 Terminated

17043 WILTSHIRE William Percy F/O 02.09.30 Relinquished

17044 WOODS Thomas Joseph F/O 12.01.26 Relinquished

On account of ill-health [LG 12 January 1926, issue 33123, page 301.

17045 WRIDE Leonard Basil William Blake P/O + 20.03.23 5 FTS Shotwick

Leonard Basil William Blake Wride, aged 19, died on Tuesday, 20th March 1923, when his Bristol F.2b F4761 stalled as he approached the airfield to land. Alive when help arrived at the scene, Leonard was critically injured and he died in Chester Infirmary. The cause of the crash was attributed to an *"Error of Judgement."*

According to notes on A.M. Form 470, the accident happened at 1205 hours, with the cause attributed as outlined above. It is also noted *"Under Instruction for Aviation."* Subsequently, the Court of Inquiry reported *"An error of judgement on the part of the pilot and was not, in the opinion of the Court, due to any defect in either aeroplane or engine."*

A press report concerning the inquest, which returned a verdict of "Accidental Death" appeared in the *Nottingham Journal* published on Friday, 23rd September 1923. The article notes Pilot Officer Wride lost control of the Bristol when turning at a height of 150 feet.

LG 29 September 1922, issue 32751, page 6910 - Seniority 6th September 1922

FLYING OFFICER

17051 OFFORD Francis Revel S/Ldr 10.02.54 Relinquished

Formerly of the 3rd Battalion, Munster Fusiliers, Lieutenant Francis Revel Offord sailed from Southampton on 27th April 1917, landing at Alexandria a month later on 23rd May and reported to 20th Reserve Wing HQ at Aboukir the next day. His 'Casualty Form - Active Service' then shows:-

26.5.17	*School of Military Aeronautics - Attached for instruction Abbaesia*		*24.5.17*	*B213*
7.7.17	*21 Res. Sqd.*	*" from S.M.A. Abbaesia*	*30.6.17*	*B213*
15.7.17	*22 Res. Sqd.*	*" from 21 Res. Sqd. Aboukir*	*9.7.17*	*B213*
22.7.17	*23 Res. Sqd.*	*" from 22 Res. Sqd "*	*197.7.17*	*B213*
29.7.17	*" " "*	*Admitted to hospital*	*23.7.17*	*B213*
24.7.17	*19th Gen. Hospital*	*Discharged [slight] Alexandria*	*26.7.17*	*B213*
12.8.17	*23 Reserve Squadron*	*Discharged from hospital*	*9.8.17*	*B213*
19.8.17	*S.A.Gunnery*	*Attached from 23 Res. Squadron*	*18.8.17*	*B213*
2.9.17	*23 Res. Sqd.*	*Attached from S.A.Gunnery*	*31.8.17*	*B213*
9.9.17	*" " "*	*Graded as Flying Officer subject to W. Office approval*		

The second 'Casualty Form - Active Service' reads:-

22.4.19	*H.T. Caledonia*	*Embarked for Constantinople*	*18.4.19*	*W/R*

from Alexandria

29.4.19 27 CCS Batoum Admitted - Sprained knee 4 Batoum. 29.4.19 W3034

Letter received from 27th C.C.Station Batoum - Invalided U.K. per HMT "Egypt" S. Russia 20.8.19 - G G Touling, Capt. For O I/c RAF Base Records

His commission to The Royal Munster Fusiliers was *Gazetted* 11th May 1915, supplement 29159, page 4540.

17052	ROARK	Edmund Charles	S/Ldr		10.02.54	Relinquished
	RYDER	Walter Harry	P/O	+	17.03.24	45 Squadron

LG 3 October 1922, issue 32752, page 1922 - Seniority various dates

FLYING OFFICERS

3

	CARR	Charles Roderick	AM		01.02.47	Retirement

Air Marshal Sir Roderick Carr KBE CB DFC AFC mentioned in despatches, died on Wednesday, 15th December 1971. His DFC was promulgated in the Edinburgh edition of the *Gazette* on November 21st, 1919: *"On the 17th June 1919, this officer flew a scout machine over the enemy aerodrome at Puchega, at an average height of only 500 feet, for thirty minutes. During this time he succeeded in setting fire to a Nieuport enemy machine, to a hangar which contained three aeroplane [all of which were destroyed], drove all the personnel off the aerodrome, and killed some of the mechanics."* At the time he was commanding No. 2 Squadron Slavo-British Aviation Corps, North Russian Expedition.

Transferred to the Unemployed List on 21st October 1919 he was appointed Chief of the Lithuania Air Staff in 1920 and followed this in 1921 by joining Sir Edward Shackleton's Antarctic Expedition.

For the better part of the Second World War he was Air Officer Commanding No. 4 Group Bomber Command with his headquarters at Heslington Hall in North Yorkshire. During his tenure of command he oversaw the Group convert from Whitley/Wellington to the Halifax and participate in every major part of the 'Bombing Campaign.'

His final service appointment was Air Officer Commanding in Chief, Air Headquarters India. On retirement he was appointed King of Arms to the Most Excellent Order of the British Empire [LG 14 February 1947, supplement 37881, page 757].

	GLYN-ROBERTS	Idris	F/O		22.09.30	Relinquished
17050	STILES	William Henry	S/Ldr		24.07.45	Resigned

FLIGHT LIEUTENANT

	BALFOUR	Donald Creighton	F/Lt		01.10.29	Relinquished

FLYING OFFICER

	KYSH	George Anthony	F/O		0B1.10.31	Relinquished

LG 7 November 1922, issue 32764, page 7874 - Seniority various dates

FLIGHT LIEUTENANT

	HUTTON	Robert	S/Ldr		16.05.28	Relinquished

FLYING OFFICERS

6

17059	BAKER	Frederick Charles	F/O			Not in AFL 1926
21032	BEDFORD MC MM	Frank Henry	G/Capt		26.09.50	Retirement

Formerly of the Northumberland Fusiliers and as a temporary 2nd Lieutenant Frank Henry Bedford was *Gazetted* with the MC on 23rd April 1918, supplement 30645, page 4860: *"For conspicuous gallantry and devotion to duty. While he was engaged in road construction an intense enemy barrage caused several casualties among his men. He put the remaining men under cover and himself remained assisting the wounded and carrying some of them away, one on his back. He was knocked down twice and partially buried, but continued his efforts and saved many lives."* During the Second World War he was *Gazetted* with the CBE [LG 24 September 1941, supplement 35284, page 5568].

	HINE	Alexander Claude	F/O	+	22.05.23	CFS Upavon

Flying Officer Alexander Claude Hine was killed and Aircraftman Baden Powell injured when their Avro 504K E9213 lost power and crashed in the vicinity of Tidworth Garrison. Born on 25th January 1896 he joined the RFC on 10th February 1917 and on completion of his training reported to Clairmarais on the last day of January 1918 to fly FE.2ds with 101 Squadron. His operational tour came to an abrupt halt on 20th April 1918 when he was wounded and following treatment in 2 Stationary Hospital he was sent back to the UK on 2nd May 1918 by way of HMHS *St. Andrew.*

	LESLIE-MOORE	Arthur	F/O		30.10.26	Relinquished

On account of ill-health [LG 21 December 1926, issue 33231, page 8344]. It is noted on his Casualty Form that he was taken prisoner of war on 21st October 1918 though in what circumstances has not been recorded. He returned to England on 17th January 1919.

	PARKER	Hugh Wilson	F/O		01.10.29	Relinquished
	WATSON	Charles James	F/O		01.10.29	Relinquished

LG 14 November 1922, issue 32767, page 8038 - Seniority 3rd, 2nd and 1st November respectively

FLYING OFFICERS

2

17066	ANSON	Henry Adelbert	W/Cdr		10.02.54	Relinquished
	OVERBURY	Richard Fox	F/O		02.11.31	Relinquished
	LINES	Francis Richard	G/Capt		08/03.50	Retirement

LG 21 November 1922, issue 32769, page 8218 - Seniority various dates - Block 17069 to 17073

FLYING OFFICERS

5

17069	HORNIMAN	Robert Henry	G/Capt		28.05.45	Retired list
17070	SCOTT	Stuart Douglas	F/Lt		08.11.33	Relinquished
17071	STRINGER	Hugh Mansfield	F/O	+	07.04.23	20 Squadron
17072	SWOFFER MBE	Frank Arthur	W/Cdr		10.02.54	Relinquished

From the 7th Battalion, Middlesex Regiment TF, 2nd Lieutenant Frank Arthur Swoffer, born 17th March 1892 transferred to the RFC on 29th July 1916 and between 22nd September 1917 and the end of February 1918 [at least] was a scout pilot flying SE.5As with 84 Squadron.

17073	WRIGHT	Ernest James Henry	F/Lt		13.11.35	Relinquished

LG 28 November 1922, issue 32771, page 8416 - Seniority 13th November 1922

17074 BAIN Richard Erskine G/Capt 01.07.50 Retirement
17075 BROWN Keith Kendle F/O 30.11.31 Relinquished
Flying Officer Keith Kendle Brown was granted a commission in class C of the Royal Air Force Reserve, effective from 7th September 1937 [LG 17th September 1937, issue 34436, page 5838].
17076 BUCKMASTER Cuthbert Harold Septimus P/O 20.12.23 Resigned
17077 BYRNE Cyril William Anthony F/O + 28.11.24 29 Squadron
17078 DAWSON David Lancelot P/O 13.06.23 Terminate
17079 FRASER Malcolm P/O + 08.08.23 1 FTS Netheravon
Pilot Officer Malcolm Fraser died in the Salisbury Infirmary from injuries received when he walked into the path of an oncoming motorcycle.
17080 GRACE Alfred Herbert S/Ldr 10.02.54 Relinquished
GRATTE Alfred Edward St. George P/O 18.03.25 Resigned
Subsequently Alfred Edward St. George Gratte was granted a commission as 2nd Lieutenant to the 1st Battalion Monmouthshire Regiment, Territorial Army, on 19th June 1925 [LG 10 July 1925, issue 33065, page 4626]. In the winter of 1939 he returned to the Royal Air Force and for the duration of hostilities he was granted a commission in the Administrative and Special Duties Branch with effect from 29th December 1939 [LG 4 June 1940, issue 34864, page 3357] his new service number being 79257
HUTTON Aymer Stritch P/O 04.04.25 Resigned
17085 JARVIS Edward Vesey Hill F/O 25.03.34 Relinquished
MARESCAUX Laurence Mortimer Tracton P/O 10.09.24 Terminated
My co-author has found two entries for Pilot Officer Laurence Mortimer Tracton Marescaux both in reference to flying accidents. The first occurred on 28th March 1924 when he forced-landed Bristol F.2b F4718 while undergoing instruction at 1 FTS Netheravon. The second is recorded on 31st July 1924 by which time he was attached to 24 Squadron at Kenley. Again, it was a forced-landing, this time in Bristol F.2b F4716 which overturned.
17088 MORRIS Harold Pilgrim F/O 13.11.30 Relinquished
RAWLINSON Gerald Henry F/O 13.11.30 Relinquished
STOREY Harlie James F/O 13.07.25 Dismissed
By sentence of General Court Martial [LG 28 July 1925, issue 33070, page 5051].
17093 UNWIN Noel Hamilton Forbes S/Ldr 16.05.54 Relinquished

LG 5 December 1922, issue 32774, page 8615 - Seniority various dates

FLYING OFFICERS
2

LUGG George Charles F/O 13.08.30 Relinquished
On account of ill-health [LG 15 August 1930, issue 33634, page 5095].
VERNON-KNIBBS William Douglas F/O 25.07.24 Removed
Flying Officer William Douglas Vernon-Knibbs *'is removed from the Royal Air Force, His Majesty having no further use for his services."* The following, which has been found by my co-author, probably had a bearing on his removal from the service. He had been charged of obtaining *"by fake pretence"* the sum of £8 12 shillings and 6 pence on or about 16th July 1921 from Mr. Percy Edwin Henry Lewis. At the time Vernon-Knibbs who appeared before the Chichester City Bench before Mr. T S Adcock, was described by the *Bognor Regis Observer* on Wednesday, 14th September 1921 as an ex-Air Force captain. To the charge he pleaded guilty and was sentenced to two years imprisonment, this being reported in the same paper in their edition of 12th October 1921. It would seem that his previous misdeeds had eluded the authorities until the summer of 1924 when his past caught up with him and his ignominious departure from the service. Although he had been sentenced to two years it appears he was released early or perhaps had his sentence reduced.

GRAY Ian Bury P/O 04.02.25 Resigned
HENDERSON Frank Stuart F/O 27.11.30 Relinquished
RICKMAN Richard George P/O 27.08.24 Relinquished
On account of ill-health [LG 26 August 1924, issue 32968, page 6425].
17091 TERRELL George F/O 27.11.30 Relinquished
Flying Officer George Terrell was granted a commission in Class A of the Reserve of Air Force Officers, General Duties Branch, with effect from 14th September 1937 [LG 28 September 1937, issue 34439, page 6021]. S/Ldr 10.02.54 Relinquished

LG 12 December 1922, issue 32776, page 8799 - Seniority various dates

FLYING OFFICER

17095 KINGSTON-McCLOUGHRY DSO DFC* Australia Edgar James AV-M 06.05.53 Retirement
Air Vice-Marshal Edgar James Kingston-McCloughry CB CBE DSO DFC* three times mentioned in despatches, died on Monday, 13th November 1972. This much decorated Australian who during the *Great War* for a time was a flight commander attached to 4 Squadron Australian Flying Corps commanded by his brother Major Kingston Wilfred Ashton McCloughry and it was during this tour of operations that he was wounded on 24th September 1918 when his F.1 Camel E7160 was shot about by a gaggle of Fokker DVIIs. The citations for his awards were published in *The London Gazette* during September and December 1918, and in order read: *"Early one morning this officer left the ground, and, meeting an enemy two-seater ten miles over the lines, he engaged and destroyed it. He was immediately by five scouts; these he out-manoeuvred, destroying one and driving the remainder down. He is a determined and successful scout leader, who in recent operations has accounted for nine enemy machines, in addition to three others and one balloon while serving with another squadron."* Possibly 23 Squadron [Spad S.7]. The first Bar to his DFC continues in similar vein" *"In the short space of one month this officer has destroyed ten enemy aeroplanes and balloons. He has organised and carried out numerous raids on the enemy, frequently at very low altitudes. Altogether he has destroyed fifteen aeroplanes and four balloons. Early one morning he crossed our lines to attack a balloon which he had previously located. As soon as daylight allowed he dived and opened fire on the balloon, which was on the ground, descending to within fifty feet of it. He then attacked some horse transport, dropping bombs and firing some 300 rounds at 1,500 feet altitude."* That for his DSO reads: *"A bold and fearless officer who has performed many gallant deeds of daring, notably on 24th September when, attacking a train at 250 feet altitude, he obtained a direct hit, cutting it in two, the rear portion being derailed. He then fired a number of rounds at the fore portion, which was pulled up. Sighting a hostile two-seater he engaged it and drove it down. Proceeding home he observed seven Fokker biplanes; although he had expended the greater part of his ammunition, Captain McCloughry never hesitated, but engaged the leader. During the combat that ensued he was very severely wounded by fire from a scout that attacked him from behind; turning, he drove this machine off badly damaged. His ammunition being now expended he endeavoured to drive off two hostile scouts by firing Very lights at them. Exhausted by his exhertions he temporarily lost consciousness, but recovered sufficiently to land his machine safely. This officer has destroyed fourteen* [sic] *machines and four balloons and has repeatedly displayed an utter disregard for danger in attacking ground targets."* According to the website Aerodrome which the authors acknowledge, he accounted for four balloons and seventeen enemy aircraft. Postwar he wrote two books, both published by Frederick A Praegar, New York, *Direction of War* [1958] and *Defence Policy and Strategy* [1960].

CAPTAIN

REED OBE George Stanley S/Ldr 01.10.33 Relinquished

Formerly on the Indian Army Reserve of Officers. My co-author believed Squadron Leader George Stanley Reed who was attached to a Department of the Foreign Office may have been an MI.6 Officer and is known to have been active in Palestine early in 1938.

LG 19 December 1922, issue 32778, page 8958 - Seniority various dates

FLYING OFFICERS

3

DAVIDSON Harold Scott F/O 22.12.26 Dismissed

By sentence of General Court Martial. His dismissal is linked to the Court Martial held at RAF Duxford in the November when five officers faced charges, mainly concerned with offences regarding mess bills. In the case of Flying Officer Davidson, he was found guilty of making false statements to hiss Commanding Officer whilst performing the duties of Mess Secretary.

17098 LYNCH John Brayne G/Capt 14.09.46 Retirement

17100 VERNON Frederick Edward A/Cmdr 14.03.50 Retirement

Air Commodore Frederick Edward Vernon CB OBE mentioned in despatches, died in Launceston Hospital, Cornwall, on Monday, 15th July 1963. He had trained as a pilot in the closing months of the *Great War* and was granted a commission in the Aeroplane and Seaplane Branch but with the end of hostilities he was placed on the Unemployed List where he remained for the better part of three years before returning to the service. He had one very narrow escape when on 11th December 1923 he was approaching to land at Gosport where the airfield was shrouded in fog he realised he was going to collide with a hangar. Banking sharply the starboard wing of his Blackburn Dart N9548 struck the jib of a crane leading to a crash on the airfield. At the time he was serving with 461 Flight.

PILOT OFFICER

STEWART Donald Ramsay F/O + 24.07.24 84 Squadron

LG 26 December 1922, issue 32780, pages 9119 and 9120 - Seniority various dates

FLYING OFFICERS

3

07052 DICKSON AFC Clift Neil Charles F/Lt + 22.01.39 RAF Reception Depot

Flight Lieutenant Clift Neil Charles Dickson was granted a commission, in his rank, in class CC of the Reserve of Air Force Officers on 9th November 1936 [LG 15 November 1938, issue 34570, page 7196]. His death occurred in Uxbridge Cottage Hospital where he was being treated for pneumonia; at the time he was Adjutant and Trade and Testing Officer at the RAF Reception Depot at West Drayton.

WHITLOCK Douglas Kelly F/O 20.01.24 Cashiered

By sentence of General Court Martial [LG 9 May 1924, issue 32934, page 3741].

17124 WINCOTT Cyril Beresford A/Cmdr 14.09.48 Retirement

Air Commodore Cyril Beresford Wincott CBE, died on Friday, 21st July 1972.

ALMS Edward Langley Wilson Hill F/O + 01.03.26 5 Squadron

Flying Officer Edward Langley Wilson Hill Alms died in an accidental bombing incident at Risalpur. Subsequently, his parents commissioned for the placement of a stained glass window in his memory at St. Andrew's Church, Taunton, the County town of Somerset and is described on page 2 of the excellent booklet describing the stained glass - see Sources - Private Publications. A report of the accident appeared in the *Taunton Courier and Western Advertiser* on Wednesday, 10th March 1926: *"Sympathy's are extended to Mr. And Mrs. Edward T. Alms of Windsor Lodge, Taunton. The loss they have sustained in the death of their second son, Flying Officer E L W H Alms [Bob] RAF aged 26 years, on March 1st, Risalpur, India. Mr. Alms was, at the time, acting range officer when he was accidentally hit by a bomb from an aeroplane."*

17102 BLUCKE Robert Stewart AV-M 01.07.52 Retirement

Air Vice-Marshal Robert Stewart Blucke CB CBE DSO AFC* twice mentioned in despatches, died on Sunday, 2nd October 1988. As a squadron leader, Robert Stewart Blucke was *Gazetted* with the AFC on 11th May 1937, supplement 34396, page 3105. By the autumn of 1943 he was ranked Group Captain and commanding RAF Ludford Magna. On 5th October 1943 he was *Gazetted* with the DSO, promulgated in the third supplement to the *Gazette* supplement 36196, page 4407: *"One night in September 1943, Group Captain Blucke was the captain of a Lancaster aircraft detailed to attack a target at Mannheim. During the outward flight the rear turret became unserviceable and, owing to icing, the elevator trimming gear jammed and rendered the bomber almost uncontrollable. Assisted by another member of the crew Group Captain Blucke skilfully maintained control and proceeded to the target, which was bombed and photographed. The aircraft was then flown safely back to base. Group Captain Blucke has participated in a number of sorties in recent months and, by his personal example and magnificent leadership, has produced a high standard of efficiency in the personnel at the station he commands."* This was undoubtedly a 101 Squadron Lancaster. Throughout 1944 and until 5th February 1945 he was Base Commander No. 14 Base followed by the prestigious appointment as Air Officer Command No. 1 Group, Bomber Command. For much of postwar service he was overseas before his final appointment on New Year's Day 1952 as Air Officer Commanding in Chief Transport Command. The Air of Authority website, which has two photographs of Air-Vice Marshal Blucke, notes that when Watson Watt carried out his experiment in developing what would become known as radar it was Squadron Leader Blucke who flew the Heyford bomber on that historic day on 26th February 1935.

BRIGGS Frederick Albert F/O 27.10.27 Resigned

BRINSMEAD Eric Sydney F/O 09.12.30 Relinquished

17105 DALY Alison Wenley F/O 09.12.30 Relinquished

Flying Officer Alison Wenley Daly was granted a commission in Class A of the Reserve of Air Force Officers, General Duties Branch on 14th November 1939 [LG 28 November 1939, issue 34742, page 7964]. S/Ldr 10.02.54 Relinquished

FINN Basil John F/O 29.09.30 Relinquished

FORDE Arthur Michael Alexander P/O 13.03.23 Terminated

HARDSTAFF Jack Wilkinson P/O + 16.02.23 2 FTS Duxford

On Friday, 16th February 1923, just two months into his service, Jack Wilkinson Hardstaff was killed during a solo flight in Avro 504K H2613, his trainer coming down at Stanmore Hill Farm, Whittlesford on the NNW side of the airfield. He was 20-years of age.

The tragedy occurred circa 1500 hours and the following notes have been appended to F.S. Form 559 *"Practice solo flight. C of I in file 411694/23. Findings of C of I Entirely obscure. AOC Inland Area it appears most probable that the accident was caused owing to the failure of P/O Hardstaff to fasten his safety belt."*

17109 LARMAN Francis F/O 09.12.30 Relinquished

17110 LUMSDEN Carlos Gerald Hugh Edward S/Ldr + 29.10.42

Squadron Leader Carlos Gerald Hugh Edward is commemorated on column 411 of the Singapore Memorial but, it seems, he died many thousands of miles away from the Burma and Pacific theatres. According to the website Uboat Net, which the authors acknowledge, he was a passenger aboard the MS *Abosso* which was sunk by U-575 [*Leutnant* Günther Heydemann] in the hour before midnight after being struck by torpedoes some 700 miles NW of the Azores while on passage from Cape Town to Liverpool with a cargo of wool and mail. From a complement of 393 crew and passengers,

362 perished, the survivors being picked up on 2nd November 1942 by HMS *Bideford* under the command of Lieutenant-Commander W J Moore RNR. *Leutnant* Günter Heydemann survived the war and lived until his death at the age of 72 on 2nd January 1986 in Hamburg.

	MARSH	Francis Caldwell	F/Lt	+	26.12.28	RAF Risalpur

Flight Lieutenant Francis Caldwell Marsh was killed in a motorcycle accident whilst serving at Risalpur in the State of Bengal. The son of Canon S F March, vicar of St. Ives in Cornwall, his death was published in *The Cornishman* on Wednesday, 23rd January 1929.

17112	MASON	Barrington Calver	W/Cdr		10.02.54	Relinquished
17113	MOORES	Charles Lawrence	P/O		30.09.24	Removed

Pilot Officer Charles Lawrence Moores *"is removed from the RAF, His Majesty having no further use for his services."* [LG 7 October 1924, issue 32980, page 7255].

17114	MOSS	Albert James Robert	F/Lt		09.12.37	Relinquished
17115	NEWBIGGING	Eric Robert	F/O		16.01.27	Relinquished

On account of ill-health.

17116	O'DOHERTY	Francis Joseph	F/Lt	+	12.01.32	208 Squadron
17117	PIGOTT	Owen Rupert	W/Cdr		01.09.46	Retirement

On account of medical unfitness for Air Force service [LG 17 September 1946, supplement 37724, page 4619].

17118	ROBINSON	Frank Bailey	F/O		08.12.39	Relinquished

On account of ill-health [LG 12 December 1939, issue 34752, page 8255].

	SAVORY	John Charles	P/O	+	15.02.24	56 Squadron
	SCOTT	Charles William Anderson	F/O		09.12.30	Relinquished

The London Gazette of 30th June 1931, issue 33731, page 4250 carried the following announcement: *"The KING has been graciously pleased to approve of the award of the Air Force Cross to Mr Charles William Anderson SCOTT in recognition of the distinguished services rendered to aviation by his recent flights between England and Australia."* A biography of Charles Scott is published on *Wikipedia* which reports he was born on Friday the 13th of February 1903 and died by his own hand on 15th April 1946 at Bad Arolsen in Germany while suffering from depression. During his long career in aviation his crowning moment of success was in winning the MacRobertson Air Race from London to Melbourne in 1934 in a time of 71 hours. For this epic flight he teamed with Tom Campbell Black to fly DH.88 Comet G-ACSS *Grosvenor House*. This iconic and historic aircraft is now in the Shuttleworth Collection at Old Warden where it is maintained in flying condition.

	UNDERHILL	George Townley	P/0		20.06.23	Resigned
	WOODYATT	Arthur Reinagle	P/O	+	22.05.25	32 Squadron

ROLL OF HONOUR
FOR
1922 SHORT SERVICE COMMISSIONED
OFFICERS

F/O	ALMS	Edward Langley Wilson Hill	1 March 1926	5 Squadron
F/O	BARNES	John Owen	14 December 1923	55 Squadron
P/O	BROOKE-HUNT	Robert Cecil	26 March 1923	5 FTS Shotwick
F/Lt	BUCKNALL	Claude Vernon Aristides	5 September 1923	RAF Flowerdown
F/O	BUTLIN	Harry	28 August 1925	111 Squadron
F/O	BYRNE	Cyril William Anthony	28 November 1924	29 Squadron
F/O	COLLINS	Robert	28 February 1926	480 Flight Calshot
F/O	DENISON	Christopher	20 April 1925	HMS *Eagle*
F/Lt	DICKINSON AFC	Clift Neil Charles	22 January 1939	RAF Reception Depot
F/O	FRANKLIN	John Hayward Godfrey	11 October 1924	84 Squadron
P/O	FRASER	Malcolm	8 August 1923	1 FTS Netheravon
P/O	HARDSTAFF	Jack Wilkinson	16 February 1923	2 FTS Duxford
F/O	HINE	Alexander Claude	22 May 1923	CFS Upavon
S/Ldr	LUMSDEN	Carlos Gerald Hugh Edward	29 October 1942	
F/Lt	MARSH	Francis Caldwell	26 December 1928	RAF Risalpur
F/O	MORPHY	Douglas McGillycuddy	4 August 1924	28 Squadron
G/Capt	ODBERT	Reginald Vere Massey	18 July 1943	
F/Lt	O'DOHERTY	Francis Joseph	12 January 1932	208 Squadron
F/O	PEACEY	Arthur John	9 March 1929	Nottingham Aero Club
F/O	REEVES	Guy Francis	12 September 1924	404 Flight Leuchars
P/O	ROSE	James Barclay	14 June 1923	RAF Gosport
F/O	ROWE	Alexander Meredith	10 December 1927	Class A of the RAFO
P/O	RYDER	Walter Harry	17 March 1924	45 Squadron
P/O	SAVORY	John Charles	15 February 1924	56 Squadron
F/O	STEWART	Donald Ramsay	24 July 1924	84 Squadron
F/O	STRINGER	Hugh Mansfield	7 April 1923	20 Squadron
W/Cdr	SWAIN	Oswald Bertie	22 September 1940	
F/O	TALLENTIRE	Miles	11 October 1923	3 Squadron
P/O	WAKE	Guy	11 July 1923	422 Flight Gosport
F/O	WATSON	Myles Birket Fraser	21 July 1924	1 Squadron
P/O	WOODYATT	Arthur Reinagle	22 May 1925	32 Squadron
P/O	WRIDE	Leonard Basil William Blake	30 March 1923	5 FTS Shotwick

Appendix D - RAF [Cadet] College Cranwell

COMMANDANT
Air Commodore Charles Alexander Holcombe Longcroft DSO

February 1922 entry : 15

16106 ARMSTRONG* Gerald Christopher Alan F/Lt + 30.09.30 17 Squadron
16107 DAVIS* Edward Simeon Colbeck W/Cdr + 21.07.40 204 Squadron
On the 21st of July 1940, a Sunday, Wing Commander Edward Simeon Colbeck Davis OBE AFC, commanding 204 Squadron took off from Sullum Voe in Sunderland I N9028 KG-A and set a course for a reconnaissance of the Trondheim area of Norway, now firmly under the control of German forces. The outcome of his mission is recorded by Ross McNeill on page 49 of *Royal Air Force Coastal Command Losses of the Second World War.* From the crew of twelve there was not a single survivor and all are commemorated on the Runnymede Memorial.
16109 EDWARDS* Christopher Caswell F/Lt 05.10.32 Retired list
On account off ill-health [LG 4 October 1932, issue 33870, page 6252]. According to the *List of Graduates* he was active from 1st September 1939, until: F/Lt 31.12.41 Relinquished
Flight Lieutenant Christopher Caswell Edwards died on Tuesday, 8th October 1985.
16111 GROVES* Hugh Marsland G/Capt 01.06.52 Retirement
Group Captain Hugh Marsland Groves died in Sarasota in Sarasota County, Florida on Thursday, 21st March 1974.
16113 JACKSON* Rolf Booth Hilton F/Lt + 20.02.28 55 Squadron
16142 LOUGHNAN Gerald Hamilton W/Cdr + 11.02.44 25 AACU Eastleigh
Wing Commander Gerald Hamilton Loughnan was killed when the Defiant TT.III DS154 in which he was flying crashed near the airfield; he is buried in Kenya in Nairobi War Cemetery, Educated at Clongowes Wood College in Co. Kildare, Ireland. As a Flight Cadet he was assigned to A Squadron and being noted for his performances as an athlete and footballer.
16114 MASON* Neville Walter Frederick G/Capt 05.09.50 Retirement
As a young Pilot Officer, and attached to 60 Squadron, he wrote off a DH.9A on 20th July 1925, the details for this being summarised in the 1925 reports of accidents. Group Captain Neville Walter Frederick Mason died on Saturday, 22nd October 1994.
16115 MATTHEWS Francis William Macdonald F/O 18.04.28 Resigned
Subsequent to his resignation, he was granted a commission in Class A of the Reserve of Air Force Officers [LG 24 April 1928, issue 33378, page 2905] but on 24th April 1929, he relinquished his commission on account of ill-health [LG 26 April 1929, issue 33489, page 2766]. Flying Officer Francis William Macdonald Matthews died on Wednesday, 5th February 1964.
16116 McKINLEY-HAY* Edgar Archibald F/Lt 06.05.34 Retirement
Flight Lieutenant Edgar Archibald McKinley-Hay was privately educated. Flying Officer Edgar Archibald McKinley-Hay died on Thursday, 1st August 1974.
16117 OMMANNEY* Montagu Douglas A/Cmdr 01.07.54 Retirement
Air Commodore Montagu Douglas Ommanney CBE mentioned in a despatch, died on Wednesday, 7th October 1959. Shortly after graduating he was injured in a motorcycle accident in London on 26th April 1924.
16119 REEDMAN* Reginald Richard F/O + 10.09.26 2 Squadron
16132 REYNOLDS Joseph Herbert McCarthy G/Capt 20.01.54 Retirement
Group Captain Joseph Herbert McCarthy Reynolds CBE Silver Star USA, died on Friday, 6th January 1989. Common to the Cranwell cadets, he had a motorcycle and also common to his ilk he fell off and was injured when the front tyre came off in Leadenham.
16120 THOMAS* John Edward Gray-Hill G/Capt 19.01.54 Retirement
Group Captain John Edward Gray-Hill Thomas DFC mentioned in a despatch, died on Friday, 8th August 1986. A document for his time as a probationary Midshipman at HMS *Conway* is held at TNA Kew under ADM 240/60/191 which shows he was born on 19th January 1904.
16121 WARD* William Charles F/Lt 06.04.27 Retired list
80972 Allocated on his return to service [LG 9 July 1940, issue 34892, page 4185]. F/Lt + 15.09.41 305 Squadron PAF
Posted as an air gunner to 305 Squadron PAF, William Charles Ward was killed during operations to Le Havre on 15-16 September 1941, when his Wellington II W5526 SM-J captained by the squadron's Commanding Officer, Wing Commander J K M Drysdale DSO crashed in the target area. Apart from the aircraft's rear gunner, Flying Officer I D Jeremy DFC, all are buried in Le Havre's Ste. Marie Cemetery. For additional details, please consult my RAFBCL 1941, page 147. My co-author adds that William was born on 11th May 1901, that he was married and prior to returning to active duty was employed as assistant secretary to the London District Federation of British Industries.
16122 YOUNG* Norman W/Cdr 12.09.50 Retirement
Prior to his entry to Cranwell, Norman Young had attended the Britannia Royal Navy College, Dartmouth. Wing Commander Norman Young died suddenly in September 1967; he was 64 years of age.

* Permanent commissions on graduation from the College on 19th December 1923 [LG 22 January 1924, issue 32900, page 688]. Noteworthy is that only one cadet from the February 1922, entry achieved air rank and just short of 50 per cent died while on active service. Interestingly, the *List of Graduates* shows Montagu Douglas Ommanney as retiring with the rank of group captain. Additional to those with an asterisk appended, Flight Cadet William John Patrick Sloan from the February 1921 entry, and Flight Cadets Henry Richard Frederick Baxter, Francis William Lionel Collings Beaumont, Louis Walter Dickens, John Harvey Hutchinson and Charles William Moss from the September 1921 entry, also graduated as did Flight Cadet James Laurence Fuller Fuller-Good also of the September 1921, entry, but his seniority was backdated to 15th August 1923.

SWORD OF HONOUR
Flight Cadet Gerald Christopher Alan Armstrong

ROLL OF HONOUR
FEBRUARY 1922 ENTRY

F/Lt	ARMSTRONG	Gerald Christopher AlN	30 September 1930	17 Squadron
W/Cdr	DAVIS	Edward Simeon Colbeck	21 July 1940	204 Squadron
F/Lt	JACKSON	Rolf Booth Hilton	20 February 1928	55 Squadron
W/Cdr	LOUGHNAN	Geral Hamilton	11 February 1944	25 AACU Eastleigh
F/O	REEDMAN	Reginald Richard	10 September 1926	2 Squadron
F/O	WARD	William Charles	15 September 1941	305 Squadron PAF

September 1922 entry : 18

16140 ATCHERLEY* Richard Llewellyn Roger AM 04.04.59 Retirement
Air Marshal Sir Richard Atcherley KBE CB AFC* three times mentioned in despatches, died on Saturday, 18th April 1970. As recorded on the Air of Authority website, Sir Richard was known universally as 'Batchy' and throughout his long service he displayed many traits of eccentricity, not least while serving in Palestine being the acquisition of a lion cub which he often took with him into the air. And it was around this time that he fell foul of

Sir Cyril Newell, Air Officer Commanding, RAF Middle East, and in the Court Martial than resulted, Flight Lieutenant 'Batchy' Atcherley was demoted fifty places in the list of seniority and his selection for RAF Staff College delayed until January 1937. What led to this 'hiccup' in his career was a tennis party where Sir Cyril was one of the guests and over which 'Batchy' gave a rather spirited display of aerobatics that perhaps was appreciated by the younger element but created ire amongst the more staid members of the party. The website contains a raft of interesting comment on this talented office, but here I will conclude by remarking that he was the first ex-Flight Cadet to be appointed Commandant of Royal Air Force College, Cranwell, a post that he took up in January 1946, and held for the next three years. The fact that he would inspect the entire College staff, including cadets, by flying his personal Meteor in inverted flight demonstrates that his eccentricity still lingered. Additional to these notes, in March 1930, while attached to 23 Squadron at Kenley he was involved in a serious crash at Farnborough, details of which are reported in my summary for 17th March 1930.

During his time as a Flight Cadet he received a painful burn on 15th April 1923, when ironing his kit.

16141 BARLOW*Sir Richard Hugh F/Lt 31.07.35 Retired list

At his own request [LG 30 July 1935, issue 34185, page 4913]. Returned to the service and was promoted squadron leader [LG 20 September 1940, issue 34949, page 5581]. W/Cdr 06.03.46 Retired list

Nine months after reverting to the retired list, Wing Commander Sir Richard Hugh Barlow, 6th Baronet, lost his life on 3rd December 1946, when the aeroplane in which he was a passenger crashed in the Andes mountains near Quito in Ecuador. At the time of his death he was Airwork's South American Manager. Contemporary newspaper report he was on a flight from Shell Mera to Quito. Research by my co-author reveals the aircraft was a Grumman Goose HC-SBL belonging to Shell's Ecuador operations and was piloted by their chief pilot, Captain Gene Gates. An account of the tragedy appears in Hugh Scanlan's book *Winged Shell Oil Company Aviators 1927-87* which I have pleasure in acknowledging: *"Just prior to the transfer of management from Shell one of Airwork's top men, Sir Richard Barlow, came out to make a survey of the operation. His task complete, Sir Richard left Shell Mera for Quito, the capital in a Grumman Goose flown by Gene Gates, the Chief Pilot, with two sick men accompanied by a male nurse. Visibility was poor. After gaining height over the Oriente the Goose turned back for its run westward through the Banos Pass, up which rain-clouds perpetually funnelled towards the Altplano. Evidently while still on instruments it struck a mountain bordering the pass, a couple of hundred feet from the summit. After three days of searches the wreckage was spotted from the air on a small ridge 14,000 feet up in the Llanganate, one of the bleakest and most forbidding ranges in the world."*

See also my summary for 21st March 1927, when he ditched his 9 Squadron Virginia VIII J7425 in the Thames Estuary.

16139 BOWLES* John Edward Wymer G/Capt 21.11.47 Retirement

Group Captain John Edward Wymer Bowles DFC mentioned in despatches, died in Chichester between October and December 1963.

16138 BOYLE* Dermot Alexander MRAF 01.01.60 Retirement

Marshal of the Royal Air Force Sir Dermot Boyle GCB KCVO KBE AFC three times mentioned in despatches, died on Wednesday, 5th May 1993. Sir Dermot Boyle was the first ex-Cranwell Flight Cadet to achieve the position of Chief of the Air Staff, an appointment that he held from 1st January 1956 until his retirement and during which he undertook a tour of bases in the Middle East and Far East. *Flight* carried two brief reports of Sir Dermot's tour, the first on page 150 of its issue on 3rd February 1956: *"Flying his own Canberra recently, Air Chief Marshal Sir Dermot Boyle, the new Chief of the Air Staff, set up a record time of 3 hr 40 min for the flight from Hong Kong to Kuala Lumpur, Malaya. Sir Dermot Boyle, who piloted a Canberra across the South Atlantic in 1952, is the first pilot to fly a twin-jet over this far-eastern route. He was making a familiarization tour of RAF bases in the Far East."* The following week, *Flight* continued on the theme of Sir Dermot's flight: *"After his 20,000 mile tour of establishments in the Mediterranean and the Middle and Far East, Air Chief Marshal Sir Dermot Boyle, Chief of the Air Staff, landed his Canberra B.6 at London Airport, five minutes ahead of schedule, on February 8th. He had taken off from Malta 2 hr 55 min earlier. During most of his tour Sir Dermot piloted the aircraft. By using this means of travel he had saved several working days and had had to spend less than 48 hours in the air. The new C.A.S. has considerable experience of jet flying, even before this tour he had made several notable long-distance flights in Canberras."* Previous to that appointment, he was Air Officer Commanding-in-Chief Fighter Command.

16137 BROOKES* Hugh Hamilton AV-M 10.11.58 Retirement

Air Vice-Marshal Hugh Hamilton Brookes CB CBE DFC twice mentioned in despatches, died on Wednesday, 16th March 1988.

16130 DENNY* Frank Maynard G/Capt 21.12.46 Retirement

Group Captain Frank Maynard Denny, died on Saturday, 7th July 1984. Like many Flight Cadets at the time, Frank Maynard Denny had a motorcycle and on 8th April 1923, he was slightly injured when he came off his machine.

DON* John Colquhoun P/O 30.09.25 Resigned

Following his resignation, John Colquhoun Don initially, it seems, entered the burgeoning market of providing 'pleasure-flights' and in an exchange of messages with my co-author, Keith Palmer reports: *"John Colquhoun Don gets a brief mention in the A-B* [Air-Britain] *book those 'Fabulous Flying Years' by Colin Cruddas. In Appendix II under Dominion Aircraft Ltd he is listed with a 'F S Miles' [probably a misprint for F G Miles] as operating in summer 1928. It was registered ass a Company on 26 November 1928. The registered address is initially the Hand & Sceptre Hotel, Southborough, Tunbridge Wells. The first aircraft was Avro 504K G-EAJU obtained from F G Mile's company Gnat Aero Co and registered to Don on 7 August 1928. It is believed to have been used for joy-riding along the South Coast and to have been based in a field near Gatwick Racecourse [this was before Gatwick Aerodrome came into being]. A further two Avro 504Ks were ordered from Gnat Aero Co, to be built from spares, which were registered G-AACW & X. G-AACX was registered on 19 November 1928 and received its C of A [No 1706] on the next day. Don departed for South Africa at about this time. Flight in its issue dated 21 March 1929 carried the following notice: "Deaths - John Colquhoun Don [Ian], who died on March 2, at Willowmore, South Africa, as the result of a flying accident, was the youngest son of John Birrell Don, of Maulesden, Brechin. He was in his 25th year." According to G-INFO* [a website] *G-AACX was cancelled on 2 April 1929 with the date in the 'Destruction or Permanent With-drawal Use of Aircraft' column. G-EAJU and G-AACW both were used [if only briefly] in the UK subsequent to these events. I suggest G-AACX is a good candidate for the aircraft involved."* Additional to this, Michael Haslam, also of Air-Britain, in a message to my co-author, expands on the crash itself and an extract from the *Forfar Despatch* published on 7th March 1929, reads: *"Mr Don was taking up two passengers for joy-rides at Willow-more, Cape Province, on Saturday afternoon, and accompanied by Mr and Mrs Veermaak on one of these trips. He was on the point of landing when the machine suddenly nose-dived to earth. He went to South Africa at the end of last year, his purpose being to develop commercial flying. He took with him two pilots and one or two aeroplanes."* The tragic deaths of the Veermaak's left two children as orphans. The authors wish to express their appreciation to Michael Haslam and Keith Palmer for their generous input into post-military service of Pilot Officer Don.

An additional item regarding Flight Cadet Don, while at Cranwell he fell off his bed on 29th February 1924, and injured himself to a degree that warranted an entry in his service records.

DU PORT* William Osmond F/O + 01.09.26 55 Squadron

ELIAS* Aubrey William F/Lt + 23.09.36 27 Squadron

Flight Lieutenant Aubrey William Elias died from an undisclosed illness while serving in India.

EVE* Jack Terence P/O + 25.05.25 100 Squadron

KAY* Alexander Bruce F/O + 04.07.28 6 Squadron

16124 RYDE* John Alexander Thomson G/Capt 17.11.45 Retirement

Group Captain John Alexander Thomson Ryde AFC Officer of Legion of Merit USA, died on Sunday, 24th April 1966.

16136 STANLEY-TURNER* Guy Neil Jacobson G/Capt 02.03.53 Retirement

Group Captain Guy Neil Jacobson Stanley-Turner CBE mentioned in a despatch, died on Friday, 7th August 1964, whilst being treated in RAF Hospital Halton.

TERRY Paul McKenna F/Lt 18.07.33 Cashiered

By sentence of General Court Martial [LG 25 July 1933, issue 33963, page 4966]. Prior to his fall from grace, as a flying officer he had been awarded the AFC *"in recognition of gallant and distinguished services rendered in connection with operations in Southern Kurdistan, during the period October 1930 - May 1931."* [LG 6 May 1932, issue 33823, page 2961]. At the time of his Court Martial, Flight Lieutenant Paul McKenna Terry was attached to RAF Bircham Newton. His life after departing the service remains something of a mystery and what little has been reported is unsubstantiated, particularly one source that states he served in the Second World War as a squadron leader and attaining a DFC and First Bar.

	TILLARD*	Leslie Robert Watson	F/Lt		07.05.36	Retired list

On account of ill-health [LG 12 May 1936, issue 34283, page 3088]. Flight Lieutenant Leslie Robert Watson Tillard is reported to have died in July 1991, whilst residing at Wesstwood, a few miles WNW from Trowbridge, Wiltshire. As a Flight Cadet he was subject to a non-flying accident report when he reported to sick quarters on 26th April 1923, with a badly pinched finger, and on 8th May 1924, whilst running, he sprained an ankle.

	WAGHORN*	Henry Richard Danvers	F/Lt	+	07.05.31	RAE Farnborough

On Tuesday, 5th May 1931, Flight Lieutenant Henry Richard Danvers Waghorn AFC, accompanied by a civilian Flight Observer, Mr E R Alexander, took off from Farnborough in Horsley J8932 for a test flight during which Henry lost control in unseasonably high winds. Both managed to bale out with Mr Alexander being slightly injured after falling onto to the roof of a factory, but Flight Lieutenant Waghorn was critically injured and died two days later. At the time the Horsley was being used to carry out radiator testing and its Condor engine had been replaced with a prototype Rolls-Royce Buzzard. As a member of the British team contesting the Schneider Trophy, Henry piloted the winning aircraft, a Supermarine S.6, in the 1929 race, for which he was *Gazetted* with the AFC [issue 33536, page 6035]. It is noted that included in the 1929, was a fellow Cranwellian, Richard Llewellyn Roger 'Batchy' Atcherley who was in the same entry ass Henry. Subsequently, his younger brother, David John Waghorn would enter Cranwell in January 1926, and in 1945, having attained the rank of Air Commodore, lose his life on 1st April 1945, in a flying accident at Boscombe Down.

16134	WARBURTON*	James	A/Cmdr		06.09.53	Retirement

Air Commodore James Warburton died on Saturday, 16th February 1980.

	WOODE*	Cecil Stanley Marshal	P/O	+	27.02.25	99 Squadron

While at Cranwell, and on the 19th of February 1924, Flight Cadet Woode sought additional excitement by persuading a fellow cadet, not named, to ride his motorcycle to which he, the intrepid Woode, would attach a towrope to his tricycle; the 'adventure' came to an abrupt end when Flight Cadet Woode parted company with his mount, his injuries requiring treatment in the station's medical centre.

* Permanent commissions on graduation, 31st July 1924 [LG 26 August 1924, issue 32968, page 6424]. Also graduating were Flight Cadets Francis William Macdonald Matthews and Joseph Herbert McCarthy Reynolds, back-classed from the February 1922 intake. Either arriving with the February or the September entries, Flight Cadet Harry Howarth Aspinall, aged 20, was killed on Tuesday, 29th July 1924, when his Bristol F.2b F4552 spun in from 500 feet on the approach to Spittlegate, coming down near Cold Harbour on the eastern side of the airfield

SWORD OF HONOUR
Flight Cadet Henry Richard Danvers Waghorn

ROLL OF HONOUR
SEPTEMBER 1922 ENTRY

F/O	DU PORT	William Osmond	1 September 1926	55 Squadron
F/Lt	ELIAS	Aubrey William	23 September 1936	27 Squadron
P/O	EVE	Jack Terence	25 May 1925	100 Squadron
F/O	KAY	Alexander Bruce	4 July 1298	6 Squadron
F/Lt	WAGHORN	Henry Richard Danvers	7 May 1931	RAE Farnbrough
F/Cdt	ASPINALL	Harry Howarth	29 July 1924	RAF [Cadet] College

FLYING ACCIDENTS

Friday 7 July 1922
Avro 504K F8747/3 F/Cdt V O Gilmore +
T/o Cranwell and on return from his exercise was involved in a collision with the Avro summarised below. Flight Cadet Vyvian Osborne Gilmore was fatally injured in the crash that followed.

Avro 504K H2364 F/Cdt F G Cator Injured
T/o Cranwell and wrecked in the circumstances described above. Flight Cadet Francis Gerald Cator was on approach to the landing area and despite the damage to his machine he managed to crash-land, sustaining injuries. Both aircraft were wrecked.

Flight Cadet Cator entered the College in February 1921, and I suspect flight Cadet Gilmore arrived at the same time, but as he was killed before graduating, his name is omitted from the *List of Graduates.*

A report of the Inquest appeared in *The Grantham Journal* of Saturday, July 15th, 1923, *'Young Flying Cadet Killed At Cranwell - Fatal Turn In Close Formation'*

"An Inquest was held at Cranwell on Saturday touching the death of a cadet, Vyvian Osborne Gilmore, 19 of Highworth, Wiltshire, whose machine came into collision with another, also piloted by a cadet, over Cranwell Camp the previous morning. Gilmore was killed instantaneously, but there are hopes of the recovery of the other pilot.

"Flying Officer R E M B Milne said deceased was a pupil of his, and a competent soloist. He had completed 14 solo flights.

"Squadron Leader Wm R Read said that about 11.45 on Friday morning said he saw two Avros coming from east to west, close together. One was about two lengths ahead of the other, and they were about 300 feet uo. The leading machine made a turn to the left, but the rear machine continued on its course, and they collided. The rear machine spun to the ground at once, and the machine that made the turn also spun to the ground three or four seconds later. Warning was at once given to the hospital by the alarm bell, and the ambulance arrived within three minutes of the accident,

"The man in the first machine might not have known they were so close, but he thought he did, and they were practising formation flying, when it was customary to fly as close as this.

"Replying to questions put by the Coroner, said it was usual to give warning of a turn by dipping the wing on the side they were turning, but he was not sure that the pilot of the leading machine did do this. He noticed the port wing dip slightly, but this might have been caused by a bump.

"Dr. J Daly Leahy, Medical Service, RAF Cranwell, said he was on the spot two minutes after the machines came down. Death was instantaneous, and was caused by laceration of the brain. The other pilot was considerably injured, but they were not without hopes of his recovery, though they could hardly say what the extent of his injuries was.

"Evidence was given that the machines, which had been previously flown, were in good order. The verdict was "Accidental death" due to collision when flying in the execution of his duty."

Thursday 9 November 1922
Avro 504K D7191 F/Cdt C K J Coggle Injured
T/o Cranwell and damaged beyond repair following avoidance with another aircraft. The circumstances of the mishap are recorded on F.S. Form 559, that for Flight Cadet Cyril Kenneth Joseph Coggle reading: *"At about 1205 I was approaching the Aerodrome with a view to land. I noticed another aeroplane taking off in front of me. Judging that it would foul me if I glided straight in, I attempted to turn. Seeing that the ground was very near, I attempted to flatten out & stalled about 12' up."*

Flight Cadet Coggle was treated for a slight abrasion to his forehead. The Avro 504K in the process of taking off was E3320 with Flight Cadet Ellis Reid at the controls. From the September 1920, entry to the College, Flight Cadet Reid would survive two crashes, the accident on 26th March 1923,* while attached to 2 Squadron at Farnborough, coming close to claiming his life, before on 12th November 1924, and now serving with 1 Squadron at Hinaidi, he was fatally injured in the crash of a Sopwith 7F.1 Snipe, my summary for that date reporting the circumstances.

Flight Cadet Coggle was the subject of an injury report on 11th April 1923, on which date he needed treatment for an abrasion to one of his legs while taking part in an obstacle race at the College.

* According to A.M. Form 470, he came down on the airfield at Farnborough in Bristol F.2b J6593 and was dangerously injured. However, according to Air Britain's 2021 publication regarding the Bristol Fighter, J6593 did not see any service in the United Kingdom, being sent ex-works to the packing depot at Ascot for onward despatch to Egypt where it was reassembled at Aboukir and issued to 14 Squadron at Amman. Surviving a crash on 9th September 1923, it was still on the squadron's establishment during January 1926.

Appendix E - Roll of Honour

ROYAL AIR FORCE

F/O	ANDERSON	Alex Thomas James	17 July 1922	205 Squadron
F/O	BARTON	Frank Henry	13 January 1922	8 Squadron
AC2	BOWN	Walter William Stephen	13 January 1922	8 Squadron
F/O	BRAGG	Charles Willie	28 March 1922	100 Squadron
F/O	BUCKLEY	Joseph	3 March 1922	20 Squadron
AC2	BUTLER	George William	16 May 1922	6 Squadron
F/O	DUNCAN	David Chalmers	17 August 1922	27 Squadron
F/Lt	FOX MC	John Bertram	3 March 1922	20 Squadron
F/O	GARDINER	Percy Justice	31 January 1922	60 Squadron
	Australia			
AC1	GLASBY	Alfred	23 August 1922	8 Squadron
F/O	GREEN MC	Ernest George	24 May 1922	2 Squadron
	Formerly of the Royal Engineers			
F/O	HARRINGTON	Hubert Bernard Delma	6 January 1922	60 Squadron
F/O	HARRICKS	Frank Simon	24 October 1922	1 Squadron
	Formerly of the Army Service Corps			
AC2	HARRIS	James Ernest	10 February 1922	100 Squadron
F/O	HARTLEY AFC	Robert Lionel	23 August 1922	8 Squadron
AC1	HAYES	Bernard	16 September 1922	84 Squadron
P/O	HAYTER	Matthew Charles	24 October 1922	24 Squadron
F/Sgt	HEMMINGS	Allen Benjamin	3 March 1922	20 Squadron
F/Lt	HOLME MC	Robert Charles Lyon	4 October 1922	1 Squadron
	Formerly of the Somerset Light Infantry			
F/O	HOOTON MC*	Lionel Conrad	16 May 1922	6 Squadron
	Mentioned in a despatch			
F/Lt	HUDSON MC	Frank Neville	6 June 1922	6 Squadron
	Mentioned in a despatch			
F/Lt	JENKINS MBE MC	Robert Charles	8 February 1922	4 Squadron
	Formerly of the Duke of Cornwall's Light Infantry			
AC1	KERSHAW	Frank	24 July 1922	25 Squadron
F/O	LOCKE-WATERS	Evelyn Archer	6 October 1922	30 Squadron
F/O	LUARD	Robert Blaine	17 August 1922	27 Squadron
F/Lt	MESSENGER AFC	Alfred Lewis	16 October 1922	45 Squadron
AC1	MILNE	Albert Annott	4 October 1922	45 Squadron
F/O	PARRY	Palmer John	11 February 1922	100 Squadron
F/Lt	PEACE	Albert Grounds	13 January 1922	8 Squadron
AC2	RICHARDSON	Charles Reginald	3 March 1922	20 Squadron
AC1	SLY	James Frederick	28 December 1922	27 Squadron
AC2	STEWART	George Fletcher	1 February 1922	60 Squadron
Sgt	STIVEY	Walter John	24 May 1922	2 Squadron
F/O	TURNER DFC	Edward Eric	28 December 1922	27 Squadron
LAC	WOODALL	William Albert	6 January 1922	60 Squadron
LAC	WREN	Walter	28 March 1922	100 Squadron

SQUADRON LOSSES
1923

Throughout this fifth year since the cessation of hostilities Royal Air Force squadrons continued to carry out their duties with aircraft of *Great War* design. On the horizon, however, was the promise of the first 'new' fighter aircraft, namely the Gloster Grebe II, the prototype flying for the first time in May 1923, and following service trials at Martlesham Heath sufficient airframes were ready by the autumn for a flight of 111 Squadron which had reformed at Duxford in Cambridgeshire on October 1st, 1923, to equip a single flight.

In comparison with the Sopwith 7F.1 Snipe, which it would replace, the Grebe had a significant improvement in maximum speed and service ceiling, but in other respects it remained very much a design of 'yesteryear' - a biplane of wood and fabric construction and a fixed undercarriage. Nevertheless, it had all the attributes of an air fighting machine in that it was quick to respond to the controls and for the experienced pilot a delight to fly, though problems with 'wing flutter' led to a number of crashes until an additional Vee-strut was fitted to support the outer upper wing.

A total of 133 Grebes were built and would remain in service for the remainder of the decade, by which time it would be joined by the marginally improved Gloster Gamecock and Armstrong Whitworth's Siskin,*when all would be over-shadowed by the Bristol Bulldog.

For the squadrons employed on policing the British Empire, the tried and trusted Bristol F.2b and DH.9A would have to suffice, though in the case of the latter a replacement in the form of the Westland Wapiti was introduced in 1928, though with finances still a major issue, the Wapiti would incorporate a high proportion of DH.9A components.

By a quirk of coincidence, when copying the report of an inquest held into the deaths of two officers at Spittlegate in April 1923, as reported by *The Grantham Journal,* the following item pertaining to Air Estimates appeared alongside:

'Air Estimates - Charge of Extravagance - Cranwell Items' [little doubt it was the latter that prompted publication].

"The second report of the Select Committee on Estimates, issued on Tuesday, dealt with Air Estimates, and covers a wide range of the administrative work of the Air Ministry. Criticism of the Ministry is a feature of the report, which concludes with the comment that "the Committee are of the opinion that while the flying Branch of the Air Service is well managed, there is a great tendency to extravagance and lack of proper financial control or efficient organisation in the Ministry itself."

"Reviewing the subject of officers' allowances, the Committee state that: "It would appear that a Group Captain and Chaplin, after eighteen years' service have two batmen, i.e., personal servants. No information was forthcoming as to why a clergyman in the Air Force after eighteen years' service should have two personal servants, beyond the fact that as officers advance in rank there is a certain dignity to be kept up which is recognised in all walks of life. An Air Marshal has three batmen. Entertainment allowance is also given to officers. The Air Attaché at Washington received £5 a day, or £1,800 a year, for entertaining, in addition to his salary, and he is not required to make any return showing what amount has been spent in entertaining. An Air Marshal get £385 [difficult to read print] *a year entertainment allowance. Before the war no allowance was given to a regiment in the army for entertaining, but an allowance was made to the General Officer Commanding a district. The Air Ministry considered it better to distribute the entertainment grant in small quantities over a small number of stations rather than to centralise it. The amount allotted to the year's estimates for entertaining is £9,200 of which £5,000 is for the Air Attachés and £4,200 for the senior ranks of the Air Service. When men of the Air Force are serving abroad, and the exchange is against them the Government makes up the difference; if the exchange, however, is in their favour they make no corresponding return to the Government."*

"An interesting analysis of pay increases which very from 50 per cent, up to 200 per cent, shows that the pay of an Air Commodore - a rank corresponding to a Colonel Commandant or Brigadier-General - is now £4. 8s. a day; that of an Air Vice-Marshal £5. 2s.; and of an Air Marshal £7. 7s. 6d., increases from £2. 14s. 9d., £4. 2s. 2d., and £4. 9s. 7d., respectively in 1919; whereas the pilot officer's pay has only been increased from £1. 3s. 7d., a day to £1. 5s. 10d., or £1. 6s. 8d., if married. On the other had, a sergeant-major [first class] has had his pay rates increased from a range of 9s., to 12s., to 18s., and a flight-sergeant from 7s., to 9s., to 11s. 6d., to 12s. 6d.

'The School at Halton'

"The Committee priases highly the management, discipline, training at the School of Technical Training for Boys at Halton, and was much struck by the arrangement by which boys were efficiently taught a trade which, when they left the Service, would enable them to earn a living. The boys, in addition to being fed, clothed, and housed, received 10s 6d a week payment, and the Committee takes the view that as the lads are in the position of apprentices such a payment is unnecessary, and that if any payment has to be made it should be made by the parents of the boys and not by the State. There is strong criticism of a proposed expenditure of £182,000 of a permanent hospital of 178 beds and subsidiary buildings, and the Committee considers the whole scheme should be completely revised

'At Cranwell'

"Complaint is made that the total cost of at Cranwell cannot be readily ascertained from the studying the Estimates, and the Committee say that a paper put in showed the cost per head for the eighty-five cadets now there, exclusive of flying training costs, is £650, and that with an expansion to 120 cadets the gross cost would be £480 per head, or deducting the parents contributions, £415.

"It would appear from another paper put," the Committee continues, "that in the cadet wing there is a chef at £266 a year, a second chef at £199 year, each, an assistant chef at £152 a year, two vegetable cooks at £152 a year each, three kitchen porters and scullery hands at £122 a year each, three stewards at £104 a year each, two carvers at £145 a year each, an accountant at £420 a year, four silver men at £120 a year each, and thirty-one gatemen, storemen, house porters, and servants - these latter costing in the aggregate £3,500 a year. It would hardly appear necessary to have a kitchen staff of this description.

"The Committee, after remarking on the incomprehensible accounts of a farm of three hundred acres at Cranwell, the existence of which was justified on the grounds that the cadets should have pure milk, express the opinion that the farming operation should be shut down, and the farm let, while the grass on the Aerodrome of two thousand acres should be sold by auction as a growing crop and not turned into hay under the arrangement of the Air Officer Commanding."

* A prototype Siskin flew on 24th March 1923, but production Siskins did not arrive on squadrons until 1924.

JANUARY

Thursday 4 January 1923
24 Squadron F/O I Glyn-Roberts Safe
DH.9A E8510
T/o Kenley and whilst banking at 150 feet stalled and side-slipped to the ground; wrecked. The cause was attributed to an error judgement on the part of the pilot. Flying Officer Idris Glyn-Roberts was a short service commissioned officer whose details are recorded in Appendix D for 1922, and the *Gazette* entry for 3rd October 1922.

Friday 5 January 1923
4 Squadron F/O A C Lamb Safe
Bristol F.2b J6764 Lt Cooper RA Safe
While in the process of taxying at Kilid el Bahr ran onto soft ground and sunk up to its axle. In attempting to turn round the Bristol overturned; deemed beyond economical repair. F.S. Form 559, marked in red, Constantinople, notes that Flying Officer Arthur Charles Lamb was attached to A Flight. His short service commission, *Gazetted* 26th April 1921, details may be read in Appendix D for 1921.

Saturday 20 January 1923
24 Squadron P/O C H A Stevens Injured
Bristol F.2b H1426
T/o Kenley and damaged beyond repair after forced-landing on Lewisham's Ladywell Recreation Ground. A Cranwell graduate from the September 1920 entry, Pilot Officer Charles Herbert Algernon Stevens served until his retirement on 12th January 1948 by which time he had attained group captain rank and invested with the OBE and three times mentioned in despatches. He died in November 1986 in the South Devonshire resort of Torbay.

Thursday 25 January 1923
25 Squadron F/O A E T Bruce Safe See 24 October 1924
7F.1 Snipe E7429
T/o San Stephano tasked for patrol duties and crash-landed at Haidi Pasha with an engine that was 'cutting' in and out. So that it would serve no useful purpose with hostile forces the Flying Officer Alan E T Bruce set his machine on fire. It is noted that Flying Officer Bruce was on the squadron's C Flight strength.

FEBRUARY

Friday 2 February 1923
39 Squadron F/O J E L Drabble Injured
Avro 504K J732 F/O C Chambers +
T/o Spittlegate and while indulging in aerobatics over, or near, the airfield lost control at 500 feet and crashed. Flying Officer Cyril Chambers had been granted a short service commission on 10th August 1920, his details appearing on page 8278 of the *Gazette* issue 32012 of the same date. It is believed Flying Officer John Edmund Layard Drabble may have lost his right foot and ankle and at the subsequent Court of Inquiry it was considered the crash occurred owing to an error of judgement on the part of the pilot.

As a former midshipman he had the distinction of being in the first entry to the Cadet College at Cranwell in February 1920. Formerly of the Naval college at Dartmouth he is listed among the naval entry and during his time at Cranwell distinguished himself as an athlete and in the College's cricket and rugby teams. He graduated with a permanent commission on 21st December 1920 [LG 28 January 1921, issue 32209, page 781] and served until retiring at his own request on 14th December 1932, at which time he was a flight lieutenant [LG 13 December 1932, issue 33891, page 7932].

In his last months of service, as traced by my co-author, and now promoted, Flight Lieutenant Drabble was attached to 40 Squadron [Hind] at Upper Heyford where he was flight commander of A Flight. During this time the vigilant eye of Police Sergeant Snelling spotted Flight Lieutenant Drabble's car, parked at Waddesdon on Tuesday, 26th April 1932, was displaying an out of date Road Fund licence for which he was summoned to appear before the magistrates at a sitting in the June. However, he telephoned the Court to explain that he was on service duties; as to failing to have a current Road Fund licence he had told Sergeant Snelling *"I forgot all about it."*

On 27th February 1941, he joined the Air Transport Auxiliary but his contract was terminated on 10th April 1942, for *"Disciplinary Reasons."* Prior to this rather inglorious end his log book had been endorsed *"A pilot of considerable experience" ... "a capable pilot who is working hard and well."*

By the winter of 1943-'44, he was serving with the RNVR, his name appearing in *The London Gazette* 26th May 1944, issue 36532, page 2441: *"Proby. Tempy. Lt [A] J E L Drabble to be Temp. Lt [A] with orig, seny, of 3rd Jan. 1944."* No further traces.

Coverage of the crash was published in *The Yorkshire Post* in its edition of February 7th, 1923, *'Grantham Flying Accident - Pilot's Error of Judgement'*

"There has been a Military Court of Inquiry into the circumstances of last Friday's aeroplane smash at the Spittlegate Aerodrome, Grantham in which Flying Officer C Chambers lost his life, and the pilot of the machine, Flying Officer J E L Drable, was very seriously injured. The whole of the evidence taken has been submitted to Mr. T Norton, the Grantham district Coroner, and he has come to the conclusion that the finding of the Court - that the accident was due to an error of judgement on the part of Mr. Drabble - was correct. He has therefore issued a certificate to the effect, decreeing a Coroner's inquiry unnecessary.

"On Monday the body of the deceased officer was conveyed to Hastings for burial. Mr. Drabble is still an inmate at the RAF Hospital at Cranwell Aerodrome."

The official Court of Inquiry findings are very detailed and record the crash as occurring around noon. The first part of the report is in type: *"1. The accident was caused by the fact that the pilot was unable to recover from spin resulting from the manoeuvre of a half-roll.*

"2. Taking into consideration our own examination of the wreckage, the evidence of the 6th witness and the evidence of the7th witness, the Court can only assume the following to arrive at the cause of the accident.

"[a] If the elevator king post did not give way in the air, the disconcerting effect on the pilot may have had a direct bearing on his inability to recover from the spin.

"[b] If the king post did not break until the machine crashed it must be assumed that the pilot did not apply the best methods necessary to bring the machine out of the spin. As however we are unable to put the necessary questions to the pilot at the time this point cannot be definitely established."

To this transcript a handwritten note has been added *'Further C of I'*

"1. The Aeroplane was being flown without the authority of the Flt. Commander.

"2. Neither of the pilots strapped themselves in the machine.

"3. The height of the machine when the final half roll was executed was not more than 500 ft above the aerodrome.

"4. Blame is attributable to both the pilots in contravening AMWO relating to flying."

An obituary to Flying Officer Chambers was published on Saturday, 10th February 1923, in the *Hastings and St. Leonards Observer* - *"The many friends of Mr. and Mrs. A E Chambers, 28 Githa-road, Hastings, learnt with sincere regret that their son, Flying Officer Cyril Chambers, was killed in a flying accident at Spittlegate Aerodrome, Grantham, last Friday. The young officer, who was 24 years of age, was well known in the town. When a boy he entered the Clive ValeSchool, of which his father is the popular headmaster, and while there won a scholarship and proceeded to the Hastings Grammar School. After leaving school he was for some time in the Account's Department of the Hastings Gas Company. At the age of 18 years he joined up and after a few months in the infantry was given a commission in the Royal Air Force. He saw active service in France during the latter months of the War and went with the British Army to Germany. Later he was sent to Ireland, leaving there when the Peace Treaty was signed. He then became Sports Officer of his squadron, taking great interest in Rugby football, cross-country running, and swimming. At the time of his death he was serving Staff Officer to his CO. When on home leave he frequently played the Hastings Golf Links, being very fond of the game. The funeral took place at the Hastings Borough Cemetery on Wednesday amid manifestations of great sympathy."*

Monday 5 February 1923

55 Squadron F/O P W Lingwood Safe See 18 June 1923 - 216 Squadron
DH.9A E9885

T/o Mosul and while patrolling over the desert attracted fire from a band of insurgents, a well aimed bullet piercing the petrol tank. *En route* for base the last of his fuel drained away and he was obliged to forced-land near Agra. On doing so the DH ran onto soft sand and turned over. On 11th January 1922, he had crashed while landing at the Zakho landing ground, but on that occasion the damage was slight and his aircraft [E9912] was repaired.

207 Squadron F/O W E Knowlden Safe
DH.9A J557 F/O H J Payne Safe

T/o San Stephano where following a fast approach, and landing, the DH ran onto very soft ground and sustained structural damage that was deemed uneconomical to repair.

Formerly a lieutenant with the Border Regiment, Flying Officer William Eyles Knowlden, now promoted flight lieutenant, was appointed to a permanent commission on 14th July 1925, *Gazetted* in issue 33066, page 4704. The next day he resigned his commission with the Border Regiment [LG 21 July 1925, issue 33068, page 4867].

At some point he left the service before the outbreak of the Second World War but rejoined and was promoted squadron leader on 1st June 1942, still within the General Duties Branch [LG 3 July 1942, issue 35618, page 2925].

At his own request he reverted to the Retired List on 1st March 1945, retaining the rank of wing commander, as *Gazetted* 3rd April 1945, supplement 37011, page 1775.

Tuesday 6 February 1923

216 Squadron	F/O P F A Curtis	+
Vimy F9150	F/O C F Embleton	+
	LAC W P Plows	+
	AC1 F Moss	Injured

T/o Heliopolis intending to transit to El Ras but crashed in the northwest part of the Mokattam Hills to the southeast of Cairo and was burnt out. Flying Officers Philip Frank Axford Curtis and Clifford Frederick Embleton were short service commission officers, *Gazetted* 28th January 1921, issue 32209, page 781 and 4th October 1921, issue 32476 page 7766 respectively.

Leading Aircraftman William Percival Plows had served his country since early 1918, his service number 251126 indicating he joined the RNAS prior to its merger with the RFC to form the RAF on April 1st, 1918.

216 Squadron	F/O A R Jones	Injured See 15 August 1921
Vimy F9165	F/O H J Bradley	+
	AC2 P L Leavesley	Injured

T/o Heliopolis and when in the area of Ziza, some 20 miles south of Amman lost engine power and a forced-landing was made, down wind, and upon running into soft sand the Vimy went up on to its nose and was damaged beyond repair.

Flying Officer Arthur Reginald Jones is mentioned on page 239 of Volume 3 [short service commission officers], and features in a 216 Squadron summary for 15th August 1921, when the DH.10 in which he was the 2nd pilot came to grief. Sadly, his name will appear in the next volume where his death in a flying accident on 5th August 1931, will be summarised.

Flying Officer Harold Joseph Bradley, formerly of the RNAS, was granted a commission as a temporary 2nd Lieutenant, qualified on aircraft and seaplanes, on 8th August 1918 [LG 6 September 1918, issue 30887, page 10554].

Monday 19 February 1923

25 Squadron	F/O W R K Atkinson	Safe
7F.1 Snipe E7456		

T/o San Stephano and as appended to F.S. Form 559 *"At a height of about 50' & in a vertical climbing turn the engine suddenly cut out & the machine side-slipped & struck a telegraph post on the side of the railway line damaging the port bottom plane. Cause of engine failure is unknown.*

Thursday 22 February 1923

207 Squadron	Lt L E Storrer	Safe
DH.9A J556	F/O M H Ely	Safe

T/o San Stephano for bombing practice during which the crew had cause to alight in the sea some 16 miles south of the airfield, their rescue being effected by HMS *Iron Duke* a dreadnaught battleship that had taken part in the *Battle of Jutland* in May 1916. At the time *Iron Duke* came to where the DH had ditched, she was serving as the flag-ship of the *Mediterranean Fleet.*

Subsequently, Lieutenant Sydney Ernest Storer reported; *"Whilst carrying out Bombing practice with the Navy in Formation about 16 miles south of San Stephano, I noticed smoke coming up into the cockpit. A moment or two later the Observer* [Flying Officer Maurice Hibbert Ely] *coming up through Bomb-Sight aperture. I left the formation and turned towards the aerodrome, but had not proceeded more than about 1/4 mile when the engine seized and the propeller stopped. Both temperature and oil pressure OK up to the time of seizure. I landed in the Sea near HMS Iron Duke, and we were picked up by them 5 minutes later. The machine was also salved by "Iron Duke.""*

Flying Officer Maurice Hibbert Ely was granted a short service commission on 28th January 1921 [see Appendix D for that year for details of his service]; promoted flying officer he was appointed to a permanent commission on 30th June 1925, issue 33062, page 4370.

The crew were attached to the squadron's C Flight.

MARCH

Thursday 8 March 1923

6 Squadron	F/O H J Bradley	Injured
Bristol F.2b D7832	Sgt R A Long	Safe

T/o Hinaidi and crashed while landing at Kirkuk. This was the Bristol's second mishap with the squadron for on 26th August 1920 it bounced on landing at Hillah and turned over; however, the damage on this occasion was relatively slight and repairs were immediately sanctioned.

Wednesday 14 March 1923

27 Squadron	F/Lt P G Scott	Injured
DH.9A E8595	Sgt A B Lewis	Safe

T/o Dardoni for bombing operations and on return stalled, hit the ground, bounced and on its second arrival turned over.

Saturday 24 March 1923 and the first flight of the Armstrong Whitworth Siskin III J6981 construction number AW19. The order for three production aircraft had been placed on 13th October 1922; subsequently 485 examples would be built and in Royal Air Force service the type would remain in service until 1932 when the last examples were withdrawn in favour of the Bristol Bulldog. Of all metal construction, it proved to be popular with squadron pilots. In addition to the fighter version, two-seat dual controlled Siskins were ordered as advanced trainers.

Friday 16 March 1923
28 Squadron F/O P A de Fontenay Injured
Bristol F.2b J6779/D AC2 C N Tippen Injured
T/o Dardoni for an air test and during the flight the Bristol collided with a vulture, the impact causing significant damage to an interplane strut. Attempting to land the Bristol crashed near the airfield.

F.S. Form 559 describes the injuries sustained by Flying Officer Philippe Auguste de Fontenay as *"Contusion right knee, lacerated wound chin, multiple abrasions of a temporary nature."* [I suspect the vulture had made his final flight].

On the reverse of the Form are the findings of the Court of Inquiry:

1. That B/F 2b No. J6779 was crashed whilst on a test flight& that the cause of the accident was that a vulture struck the front outer interplane strut planes breaking it in half.

2. .....

3. That no blame can be attached to the pilot."

Aircraftman Cleon Norval Tippen's birth and death have been traced by Paul McMillan as 12th April 1902, and October 1984 respectively at Kidderminster in Worcestershire.

The next day 28 Squadron departed for Tank where it would stay for the next four weeks before settling at Pershawar.

Saturday 31 March 1923
11 Squadron F/O A A Ward Injured
Avro 504K H1929 AC1 C N Tippen* Safe
T/o Andover but with seconds of becoming airborne the engine 'cut' and the trainer crashed either on or near the airfield. At the time of the accident, it was being used by officers attending the Staff College course at Andover.

Flying Officer Andrew Augustus Ward at the time appears to have been waiting for confirmation of his short service commission was eventually *Gazetted* on 19th May 1923, issue 32824, page 3533; however, referring to his entry in the Short Service Commission appendix suggests previous air force service.

In respect of Aircraftman Tippen, Paul McMillan reports that an incorrect service number has been appended to his name.

This was the squadron's first serious mishap since reforming at Andover on 13th January 1923.

* I suspect this may well be an error in reporting, unless by coincidence two airmen with the surname 'Tippen' and initials 'C N' were serving at the same time.

APRIL

Wednesday 4 April 1923
56 Squadron F/O G R C Spencer Safe See 17 October 1923
7F.1 Snipe E6791
T/o Hawkinge for a practice flight and on landing at around noon the Snipe bounced and before action could be taken to cushion its second arrival it hit the ground and turned over; wrecked. Flying Officer Geoffrey Roger Cole Spencer was a Cranwell graduate from the February 1920 [Naval entry], and is named on page 270 of the third volume,

Saturday 7 April 1923
20 Squadron F/O D R Loch +
Bristol F.2b J6594 F/O H M Stringer +
T/o Quetta for local flying practice and it was while making a low turn some distance from the airfield that control was lost and the Bristol spun to the ground. During its brief service with the squadron it had crashed on no less than three previous occasions, each time being sent to the Aircraft Deport at Drigh Road for repair. Its first 'mishap' occurred on 21st November 1922, when it was damaged at Kach on the NWF, and this was followed by two take off accidents, both at Drigh Road, on 7th March and 2nd April. Flying officers Desmond Reginald Loch and Hugh Mansfield Stringer were short service commission officers, their details being promulgated in *The London Gazette* on 8th April 1921, issue 32284 page 2798 and 21st November 1922, issue 32769 page 8218, respectively.

Wednesday 18 April 1923
56 Squadron F/O M V Ward Safe See 8 November 1923
7F.1 Snipe E6819
T/o Hawkinge and on return at 1200 ran up against a ridge and turned over; wrecked. Maurice Vavasour Ward had been granted a short service commission on 8th November 1921 - see the 1921 Short Service Commission appendix for details.

Monday 23 April 1923
55 Squadron F/O H W Westaway Safe See 4 June 1921
DH.9A E8640
T/o Mosul and damaged beyond repair while forced-landing in the desert, in the process becoming inverted. Posted to 27 Squadron, Flying Officer Horace William Westaway crashed during a test flight in DH.9A E8723 on Friday, 21st March 1924. Along with his passenger, Aircraftman Caldicott, he escaped injury and E8723 was sent for repair at the

Aircraft Depot at Drigh Road. For an appreciation of Flying Officer Westaway's service, please refer to my summary of 4th June 1921.

Tuesday 24 April 1923

39 Squadron F/O M C Trench +
DH.9A E8489 P/O F S Harris +

T/o Spittlegate and at a height estimated by eyewitnesses as about 100 feet stalled off a low turn and crashed to the ground where it caught fire and was burnt out. Flying Officer Maurice Crosbie Trench was aged 26 and Pilot Officer Frederic Samuel Harris 20. Maurice had first seen military service with the Royal Engineers where he was attached to the 1st Army Signal Company. Accepted for training as an observer in March 1918, and, subsequently, served for the last few weeks of the war with 110 Squadron [DH.9A]. In February 1919, he was struck down by the influenza pandemic. Seriously ill, he
was evacuated from 20 General Hospital to England aboard the *Jan Breydel.* He returned to his squadron early in April 1919, and later re-mustered as a pilot.

Pilot Officer Harris had graduated as a permanent officer from the Cadet College at Cranwell as recently as 20th December 1922 [LG 23 January 1923, issue 32789, page 533]. Educated at King William's College on the Isle of Man he was assigned to B Squadron.

It was not until Saturday, July 28th, 1923, that *The Grantham Journal* published the Inquest's conclusion, the verdict reached that it was "Accidental Death," the full article reading: *"Mr. T Norton, District Coroner, on Monday concluded his enquiry into the deaths of Flying Officer Maurice Crosby Trench, aged 26, Watford, and Pilot Officer Frederic Samuel Harris, aged 20, of Union Mills, Isle of Man, who were killed in a crash at the Spittlegate Aerodrome, on April 24th. Mr. Norton opened the Inquest on April 25th, when evidence was given that the aeroplane was an entirely new one, and that Trench was the pilot, Harris acting as his observer. It was also reported to the Coroner that a Court of enquiry had found that the aeroplane stalled out of a flat turn at a low altitude, but the Court were unable to express as to whether the flat turn was a manoeuvre on the part of the pilot, but was caused by some unknown structural defect.*

"At the resumed inquest on Monday, Flying Officer Roberts represented the RAF, Spittlegate.

"The Coroner said the inquest had been adjourned from April 25th in order that further enquiries could be made, if possible, to ascertain nothing further had transpired, and there did not appear to him to be any reason why the matter should remain open longer. At the opening of the inquest, evidence was given by Squadron-Leader J T Whittaker and Dr. J A Perdrau. The evidence taken by the Court of Enquiry was also produced. He had since had the opportunity of carefully going through and testing that evidence, which confirmed the statement made by Squadron-Leader Whittaker that both the deceased officers were experienced men in flying, that the machine was a new one and in perfect order, and there was nothing, so far as one could tell, to account for the accident, except an error of judgement. He did not, therefore, think it was necessary to call any further evidence, as he wished to avoid duplicating an enquiry of that sort, and to spare the feelings of the relatives as much as possible, so that, on the evidence which had been submitted to him, he found in the case of each officer that the cause of death was accidental.

"Subsequently, Mr. Norton read a letter he had received from the late Mr. Tench's father, in which he said: "My son was a very cool and skilful pilot, and would not have turned back as he did unless there had been some serious defect in his 'plane or engine.' Major Harris, father of the other officer, also wrote and said he was quite satisfied that his son's death was due to an accident, and he was glad to hear the Coroner was also of the same opinion."

Consulting Air-Britains *DH.4/DH.9 File* DH.9A E8489 was one of 400 aircraft ordered on 21st March 1918, and built at Hendon by the Aircraft Manufacturing Company, the block commencing E8407. Records show E8489 was delivered to RAF Turnhouse during the week ending 24th October 1918, and was disposed during January 1919 - presumably to long term storage, though the date of its issue to 39 Squadron has not been recorded, but from the evidence given by Squadron Leader Whittaker it seems feasible that it arrived at Spittlegate just before its fatal crash.

Alongside the paper's report on the inquest is a most interesting article, titled *'Air Estimates - Charge of Extravagance - Cranwell Items.'* A full copy has been entered with my opening notes for 1923.

56 Squadron F/O G H D Gossip +
7F.1 Snipe F2487 Australia

T/o San Stefano where it was destroyed following an uncorrected spin. Although Flying Officer George Hatfield Dingley Gossip's name is 'absent' from the *Gazette,* The Aerodrome website, which the authors acknowledge, shows George as being born in Sydney on the 6th of January 1897, and during the *Great War* he served with distinction with the RNAS, gaining his Aviator's Certificate at RNAS Chinford on 21st April 1917. Subsequently, he was attached to 4 Squadron RNAS which on the merger of the two air arms on April 1st, 1918, became 204 Squadron.

Flying Sopwith Camels he opened his scoring on the 1st of October 1917, with victory over an Albatros D.V sent down out of control near Zeebrugge and ending with the destruction of a Fokker D.VII southeast of Ostend on the 30th of July 1918. He is mentioned by Norman Franks in his book *Sopwith Camel Aces of World War I* published by Osprey in 2003.

At the time of his death he was commanding the squadron's detachment at San Stephano having arrived here in September 1922 where it was attached to 208 Squadron.

By one of those odd quirks of co-incidence his Christian names and surname match those of who is described on *Wikipedia* as *"a minor American-English chess master and writer"* who lived between 6th December 1841 and 11th May 1907, and who gained the sobriquet *"The King of the Wooden Spoonists"* from another writer on chess, G H Dingle - apparently, in major chess tournament, George Gossip was usually placed last.

Saturday 28 April 1923
45 Squadron F/Lt I M Matheson Safe
Vernon I J6882
Golden Gain
T/o Kirkuk and while flying to Serkhuma was obliged to forced-land. A photograph of the Vernon appears on page 76 of *The Flying Camels* and although damage appears mainly confined to the undercarriage the terrain in which it had come down was totally unsuitable for recovery. Subsequently, Flight Lieutenant Matheson salvaged the squadron's badge and nameplate after which the airframe was burnt on site.

MAY

During the month the prototype Gloster Grebe J6969 took to the air for the first time; it was initially referred to as the 'Thick Wing Nighthawk.' And, it seems, the month was free of major aircraft accidents.

JUNE

Monday 4 June 1923
25 Squadron F/Lt E B Mason Safe
7F.1 Snipe E6339
T/o San Stephano and on return, and landing, the port wheel sheered from the axle and now out of balance the Snipe turned over.

207 Squadron F/O E S Edwardes Injured
DH.9A H19 AC1 A Smith Safe
T/o San Stephano but soon after taking to the air Aircraft Smith caught his foot between the dual control column in his cockpit and the camera fittings and before he could free his foot the DH went into a spin and crashed, the impact being heavy and resulting in Flying Officer Edwin Stapleton Edwardes being serious injured. Young Smith, however, apart from bumps and bruises was not badly hurt. This incident is recorded on page 28 of John Hamlin's excellent history of 207 Squadron.

Flying Officer Stapleton's short service commission is recorded in Appendix D for 1921, under the entry for officers granted commissions on 29th March 1921. As will be seen, he recovered from his injuries

Monday 18 June 1923
216 Squadron F/O P W Lingwood +
Vimy FR3173 F/Lt N B Ward +
AM1 W Jarvis +
AM2 F W Skuse +
T/o Heliopolis and reported down in Mokattam Hills southeast of Cairo and in the same area where the squadron lost a Vimy on Tuesday, 6th February 1923, with the deaths of three of its crew. For an appreciation of Flying Officer Percy William Lingwood's service, please refer to my summary for 55 Squadron on 8th March 1922.

Despite the severity of the loss, a Reuters report, published the same day in the *Hartlepool Northern Daily Mail*, gave scant information, confining the remarks to the deaths of two officers and two mechanics.

The service numbers for Aircraftman William Jarvis and Mechanic Frederick William Skuse are 342745 and 348074 respectively. Both enlisted as civilians, probably in the early '20s as their numbers are in the block 340001 - 360000 issued between September 1919 and June 1925.

Thursday 28 June 1923
11 Squadron F/O C Ayling Injured
Avro 504K H2366
T/o Northolt to practice aerobatics in connection with the forthcoming fourth RAF Pageant to be held at Hendon on Saturday, 30th June. Whilst over the airfield a collision occurred with Avro 504K F8752 belonging to the Electrical and Wireless School at Flowerdown near Winchester.

The subsequent of Court of Inquiry reported: *"The cause of the accident was in our opinion due to both pilots of both Avro H2366 and Avro 8752 failing to see each others machine in time to avoid collision owing to the fact that one machine was diving & the other climbing at a steep angle at the finish of the roll.*

"The Court recommends that in future aeroplane races steps should be taken to prevent machines from climbing & descending steeply and of their positions, particularly when passing the finishing line."

Thought to be Christopher Ayling who was granted a short service commission on 5th December 1919 as recorded on page 238 of my third volume and possibly the same Christopher Ayling who was injured in a motorcycle accident on 4th June 1922 while serving with 4 Squadron. In the incident here summarised he was dangerously injured with concussion.

JULY

Friday 6 July 1923
2 Squadron F/Lt D Gilley Injured
Bristol F.2b J6693 F/O L L Hudson Injured
T/o Farnborough and wrecked in a forced-landing near Crowthorne in Berkshire, the Bristol unable to avoid a tree as it approached the field selected by the pilot. It is not thought that Flight Lieutenant Denys Gilley's injuries were of a serious nature, or those sustained by his observer.

According to A.M. Form 470, the crash happened at around 1945 in the evening near Wellington College after the Bristol experienced failure in the petrol feed system. No Court of Inquiry held.

56 Squadron P/O M J Fitzmaurice Injured
7F.1 Snipe E8259
T/o Biggin Hill but stalled and crashed heavily, Pilot Officer Maurice James Fitzmaurice dying on the 14th July from his injuries. Maurice graduated from Cadet College at Cranwell on 20th December 1922 [LG 23 January 1923, issue 32789, page 532].

The first newspaper report to hand concerning the crash is that published by *The Yorkshire Evening Post* on Monday, July 16th, 1923, with the heading *'Young Airman's Fate - Wrong Method of Averting a Crash.'*

"A verdict of "Accidental Death" was recorded at the inquest, at Lewisham today, on Maurice James Fitzmaurice, a wing officer in the Royal Air Force, who died after an air crash at Biggin Hill on Friday.

"Squadron Leader Lloyd said Fitzmaurice had instructions to carry out flights on a Sopwith machine with a view to co-operating with the Anti-Aircraft Defence School.

"Witness saw the engine running satisfactorily, but when Fitzmaurice got a few feet up his engine seemed to lose power. He turned round, apparently with a view to saving his machine, which lost its flying speed, stalled, and crashed. Efforts to save the machine in that way had caused hundreds of accidents.

"Another witness expressed the view that the accident was probably due to air getting into the petrol pipes of the engine.

"Medical evidence ascribed death to shock from injuries."

Beneath the headline *'Airman's Fatal Accident'* Saturday, July 21st, 1923, of *The Westerham Herald* read:

"On Friday morning of last week, Pilot Officer M J Fitzmaurice, of the Biggin Hill Aerodrome, met with an accident, his injuries being so serious that he succumbed after admission to hospital at Woolwich. He only passed out of Cranwell College in December last, and his early death is a great loss to his brother officers with whom he was very popular.

"The funeral took place at Keston on Wednesday, The mourners included Rear Admiral Fitzmaurice and Mrs. Fitz-maurice [father and mother], Capt. Fitzmaurice [uncle], and other near relatives.

"Others present to pay their last tribute of respect were: Foreign Naval Attachés, Sqdn. Leader I T Lloyd and the entire squadron 56, Colonel Simon CBE, and other officers representative of the Anti-Aircraft School, Capt. E L Gerrard, CMG, DSO,, Air Commodore commanding No. 1 Group.

"A firing party was present from the Aerodrome, and at the close of the service three buglers sounded the Last Post. There were many beautiful floral tokens."

100 Squadron F/O M W J Boxall Injured
Avro 504K E3507
T/o Spittlegate and thought to have been damaged beyond repair and failing to recover from a stall near the airfield. Flying Maurice William James Boxall, whose commission was granted earlier in the year on 17th April 1923, sadly, departed the service in June 1928, in disgrace following a General Court Martial.

Entries on A.M. Form 470 read: *"Category "D" Test, No. 2 Solo,"* and on reverse a handwritten note recording the Court of Inquiry's findings: *"The cause of the accident was in our opinion an error judgement in stalling the machine whilst turning in a glide, due to inexperience of the pilot."*

In respect of his dismissal, Paul McMillan reports that although uncertain as to the reason for his Court Martial, it is known that his personal life was in turmoil for in the autumn of 1927, as reported in the *Sheffield Daily Telegraph* on Thursday, 20th October 1927, *"Mrs Margaret Mary Boxall, of Rectory, Emley, near Wakefield, petitioned yesterday in the Divorce Court for the dissolution of her marriage with Maurice William James Boxall, and officer in the Royal Air Force, on the grounds of misconduct, which was not denied, and gave Mrs. Boxall the custody of the child."*

His name next appears in the press when *The Daily Mirror* in its issue of Saturday, 1st September 1928, reported: *"Removed from Army Captain William James Boxall, I.A.[retired], is removed from the Indian Army, on conviction by a General Court Martial whilst serving with the Royal Air Force, announces the London Gazette."*

Saturday 7 July 1923
24 Squadron F/O M G L Trepagna-Leroy AFC +
DH.9A H3431
F/O E W Logsdail + Whyteleafe [St. Luke's] Churchyard
T/o Kenley and while recovering from a steep dive over the aerodrome structural failure occurred and the tailplane detached from the rear fuselage. Eyewitnesses to the tragedy estimate the tail section came off at around 1,500 feet and seconds later the DH crashed into a house and burst into flames.

The Kenley Revival website, which the authors respectfully acknowledge, states that Flying Officer Marcel Trapagna-Leroy was very experienced and he had been tasked to give instruction to Flying Officer Edward William Logsdail who had been with the squadron but for just a few days. The website continues with a *Western Daily Press* report published in their edition of Monday, 9th July 1923: *"Two flying officers were killed in an aeroplane crash at Kenley, Surrey on Saturday, and a house on which the aeroplane fell was almost totally burned. The victims of the accident were Flying Officers Marcel Gustavo Louis Trapagna Leroy [pilot] and Flying Officer E W Logsdail [passenger]. The machine was a DH.9a from Squadron 24, Kenley, and the flight was an instructional one. Flying Officer Leroy, a distinguished and experienced airman, had been at Kenley about three years, but Flying Officer Logsdail had only been at the aerodrome a few days and was receiving instruction in flying. The aeroplane, which went up from Kenley Aerodrome shortly before 10 o'clock, was noticed in difficulties, when the tail appeared to crumple up. In its fall the machine collided with some trees and telegraph wires, and finally crashed in flames on to the centre of the roof of a house named Colescroft, in the occupation of Mr and Mrs Collinson. Immediately the machine struck the roof flames shot up and the whole house was quickly alight. Mr Collinson and his daughter, with servants, managed to get out of the house in time. Mrs Collinson was out shopping. A staff of men from Kenley Aerodrome arrived soon afterwards and removed fragments of the machine, among which were found the two bodies charred beyond recognition."*

The website contains additional details, compiled from various sources, which states the tree was an oak flanking Firs Road and on hitting the roof plunged into the second floor nursery. Mr. Collinson was in the hallway at the time and he escaped through a side porch. Meanwhile, neighbours had called the Coulsdon and Purley Fire Brigade fire brigade which arrived on the scene at 1011 a.m. with Chief Officer Carter in command. As mentioned in the newspaper account, airmen from Kenley were already present and were bravely trying to reach the crew but were being driven back by the intense heat from the fire, one airman, it is said, fainting. It took the brigade an hour to bring the fire under control, during which time some of the furniture and smaller items were saved from destruction.

Colescroft was certainly a large residence; seven rooms on the upper floor being completely gutted. With the fire out the remains of the two officers were recovered, Edward Logsdail being buried with full military honours a few days later. He had been born in Venice where his father, William,*was a successful painter and in 1896, the young Edward became the subject of one of William's best known portraits, namely *"The Bluecoat Boy"* painted when his son was a scholar at Christ's Hospital School.

A useful thumbnail sketch of Edward's teenage years as a merchant seaman which may well have influenced his decision to join the RNAS in June 1917. Postwar, and now serving in the fledgling Royal Air Force, he saw service aboard the carrier HMS *Furious*. At the time of his death his parents were living in Oxfordshire.

At the subsequent Court of Inquiry their deaths were attributed to a *"failure of the tail unit in the air resulting from excessive strain imposed on it when pulling out of the steep dive."*

* William Logsdail, [25th May 1859-3rd September 1944] is described by *Wikipedia* as *"a prolific English landscape, portrait, and genre painter."* His paintings which from time to time are offered for sale fetch high prices, the record to date being £420,000 achieved by Duke's when selling 'The Bank and the Royal Exchange'. A Blue Plaque to his memory is fixed to the family home at Noke in Oxfordshire.

Friday 27 July 1923
2 Squadron F/O H P L Gardner Injured
Bristol F.2b H1603 Lt J C Holmes Injured
T/o Farnborough and on arrival at Old Sarum the engine 'cut' in those crucial moments before touch down. Unable to effect a safe landing the Bristol stalled and crashed heavily. Lieutenant Holmes was attached to the Royal Sussex Regiment.

Referring to A.M. Form 470, is appears the accident occurred around noon during Army co-operation exercises, the Court of Inquiry reporting: *"The cause of the acc. was in our opinion an error of judgement on the part of the pilot in attempting to turn into aerodrome when engine cut out [cause unknown] when flying down wind at low altitude and stalling the a/c in a turn."*

Flying Officer Gardner's injuries were slight, but it is reported Lieutenant Holmes was *"dangerously injured."*

AUGUST

Wednesday 8 August 1923
100 Squadron F/O R Jaques +
Avro 504K H2002
T/o Spittlegate and wrecked following a side-slip while banking. Flying Officer Robin Jaques had been granted a short service commission as recently as 3rd April 1923, and was still undergoing flying instruction, his previous service being with the Army Education Corps [LG 17 April 1923, issue 32815, page 2816]. His terms of engagement were for seven years on the active list.

'Crashed to Death - Aeroplane Goes Wrong at Thousand Feet Altitude' was the headline in *The Lincoln, Rutland and Stamford Mercury* on Friday, August 10th, 1923. *"Mr. T. Norton, the Grantham District Coroner, held an inquest on Wednesday evening on the body of Robin Jaques, aged 25 years, a flying officer in the 100th Squadron of the Royal Air Force, stationed at Spittlegate Aerodrome, Grantham, who was killed that morning in an aeroplane in which he was piloting.*

"Flight-Lieut. J F P Gallagher, senior medical officer at Spittlegate Aerodrome, identified the body of the deceased, who, he said had been undergoing instruction at Spittlegate since April 2nd. On hearing of the crash at 11.30 that morning he proceeded to the scene of the accident in a field between Cold Harbour and the Bridge End road, and there saw an aeroplane completely smashed up. Deceased's head was smashed in, and witness detailed other serious injuries to neck, trunk, legs and feet. He gave it as his opinion that death must have been instantaneous. Deceased must have struck the ground with tremendous force. He was a married man, with two children, and lived at Newton near Falkingham.

"Flying Officer A E G Forrest said he twice flew the machine, an Avro, altogether for an hour on Wednesday morning. When he got out of it the second time deceased got in and flew straight away. Witness was certain the machine was perfectly right for flying. Witness saw deceased take off, and ten minutes later he looked up into the air and saw the machine about 1,000 feet up. It appeared to diving and side-slipping straight to the ground, and witness thought the engine was still running. The machine obviously struck the ground, and he proceeded to the spot and found Jaques dead, and the machine smashed to splinters.

"Chief Flying Instructor A P Ritchie said he saw deceased in the air about 800 feet up. The machine appeared to be coming down in what seemed to be a very steep side-slip. Witness at once flew to the scene of the accident, and arrived in about three minutes. The machine was smashed to pieces, and deceased was lying dead just clear of it. Deceased had had between 29 and 30 hours' flying, and was quite capable of taking a solo flight in a machine of that type. He was quite up to average in flying capabilities and was a promising officer.

"Flying Officer A N Marreal said he was on the Aerodrome when he noticed a machine about 1,000 feet up in the direction of Old Somerby. It appeared as if the pilot was executing a left-hand turn. The bank on the machine increased until the bank became vertical, and the result was that the machine went into a very fast vertical dive. When about 300 feet from the ground the machine appeared for one moment to come out of the dive, but it went back into it again, and dived sideways to the ground. Deceased had not been "stunting" and witness thought he was taking an ordinary turn.

"Flying Officer Ritchie, re-called, said he was expressing an opinion as it was extremely difficult to say with any precision what deceased was trying to do. He might have intended to spin, but over-banked and forced the nose of the machine down with the bottom rudder, and then he must have lost his head, as he was at a sufficient height to have ... of it; or he might have been trying a side-slip and stalled.

"The Coroner returned a verdict of "accidental death" and sympathised with the widow and the squadron."

Additional information recorded by Greg Harrison makes interesting reading: *"Robin Jaques was born in the Heaton area of Newcastle, the son of a local billiard hall manager. He was the eldest of eight children. In his teens he developed a keen interest in sports, particularly football, and became semi-professional, playing for Clapton Orient and later Fulham FC. Serving in the Middlesex Regiment during World War 1 as a private, he joined the Royal Air Force shortly after its formation. Postwar he stayed in the service, eventually arriving at 100 Squadron for pilot training."*

"In 1920, Robin had married a 20-year old nurse, Mary Adelaide Thorn. They had two children, Robin and Josephine, who were three years old and eighteen months respectively when their father was killed. Josephine showed much promise as a child at dancing and acting, and after working as a hairdresser, changed her surnames to "Jacques" to make it sound more French. Her nickname was Hattie, and as Hattie Jacques she became one of Britain's most famous and loved actresses."

Friday 10 August 1923
31 Squadron F/O A B Cree Injured
Bristol F.2b J6626
T/o Dardoni and reported as being wrecked following an attempted forced-landing with engine failure. As recently as July 1923, it had been on 28 Squadron establishment.

The accident report shows the location as Quetta; the extent of Flying Officer Angus Broke Cree's injuries are not stated. He was granted a short servicer commission on 19th March 1921, details being recorded in Appendix D for that year.

Monday 13 August 1923
2 Squadron F/O A Maybaum Safe
Bristol F.2b J6717 AC2 F G Richardson Injured
T/o Farnborough tasked for a photographic detail and wrecked at 1500 after running out of fuel and thus forced to make an emergency landing near Elsted, some 5 miles SW of Midhurst, Sussex.

Flying Officer Albert Maybaum escaped unharmed, although no doubt rather shaken by the experience, but his observer, Aircraftman Richardson was admitted to the Cottage Hospital at Petersfield suffering from concussion.

The Court of Inquiry found: *"The cause of the accident was in our opinion due to petrol pressure failure& the pilot endeavoured to locate faults but had to effect a forced landing before the fault was cleared."*

Tuesday 21 August 1923
28 Squadron F/O F G Whitmore +
Bristol F.2b J6769 LAC G A Taylor +
T/o Peshawar for an exercise in camera gun techniques during which the Bristol entered a spin and crashed. Flying Officer Fielding Griffith Whitmore's short service commission was *Gazetted* 19th July 1921, issue 32394, page 5733.

Leading Aircraftman Gerald Arthur Taylor enlisted early in the '20s [see Aircraftman Jarvis and Mechanic Skuse, summarised on 18th June 1923, for details], his service number being 341512.

Friday 31 August 1923
41 Squadron P/O R G Chapell Injured
Avro 504K H5245
T/o Northolt with the intention of visiting Kenley but despite the relatively short distance became hopelessly lost and eventually a precautionary landing was made near Orpington in Kent. Having ascertained his position the pilot took off only to lose control and dive back to the ground.

Pilot Officer Richard Graham Chapell's short service commission was granted on 28th July 1922, details being recorded in Appendix D for that year. He had the unenviable distinction of writing off the squadron's first machine since reforming on the 1st if April 1923.

Appended to the reverse of A.M. Form 470 is the findings of the Court of Inquiry: *"The cause of the accident was in our opinion an error of judgement on the part of the pilot, who, in taking off from a confined area, climbed the a/c at too low a speed & stalled."*

It is noted that Pilot Officer Chapell's injuries were severe and he was admitted to the Queen's Hospital at Sidcup. Recovered, and fifteen months later, he was attached to E Flight on the Inland Area's Communication Flight and it was during a flight over London on Monday 8th December 1924, that he experienced his second serious flying accident: *"When the aircraft* [Avro 504K H2458] *was passing over southwest London at about 3,000 feet the engine ceased to fire. The pilot attempted to land in Southwark Park but the aircraft crashed into some trees. The pilot escaped injury. Opinion. That the accident was due to the pilot exhausting the main supply of petrol and failing to make use of the emergency tank and misjudging his glide to the only ground within ready reach on which a landing was possible."*

SEPTEMBER

Monday 3 September 1923
5 Squadron *Not reported*
Bristol F.2b H1515
T/o Ambala and moments later was in a very second-hand state after forced-landing in nearby Rajpur Road with a failing engine.

14 Squadron P/O R W Pontifex Injured See 18 April 1925 - 6 Squadron
Bristol F.2 F4459
T/o Ramleh and crashed at Aboukir*while banking, possibly while preparing to land. Pilot Officer Rupert William Pontifex reported to the Cadet College at Cranwell with the Schools' Entry, February 1920.

* The accident report shows Abu Sueir.

Friday 7 September 1923
24 Squadron F/O A F Wynne Injured
Avro 504K H3008
T/o Kenley and whilst flying locally in the vicinity of Shirley the engine failed and the Avro came down in a meadow bordering Wickham Road. The Court of Inquiry reported: *"The pilot had not found the correct setting of the fine adjustment & not having a suitable place to land into wind, turned back to the aerodrome & stalled. No one to blame.*

Friday 21 September 1923
56 Squadron F/O A Jerrard VC Injured
7F.1 Snipe E8359
T/o Biggin Hill for night flying practice and came to grief in a heavy landing. As recently as 13th July it had been damaged while taking off when the pilot lost control and turned over; however, the damage on this occasion was fairly minimal and the Snipe was soon repaired.

Flying Officer Alan Jerrard, initially commissioned to the 5th Battalion, South Staffordshire Regiment, Territorial Forces, won his country's highest award for valour in the face of the enemy while attached to 66 Squadron [F.1 Camel] forty-eight hours before the formation of the Royal Air Force. Published in the Third Supplement to *The London Gazette* on 1st May 1918, issue 30663, page 5287, the citation reads as follows: *"When on an offensive patrol with two other officers he attacked five enemy aeroplanes and shot one down in flames, following it down to within one hundred feet of the ground.*

"He then attacked an enemy aerodrome from a height of only fifty feet from the ground, and, engaging single-handed some nineteen machines, which were either landing or attempting to take off, succeeded in destroying one of them, which crashed on the aerodrome. A large number of machines then attacked him, and whilst thus fully occupied he observed that one of the pilots of his patrol was in difficulties. He went immediately to his assistance, regardless of his own personal safety, and destroyed a third enemy machine.

"Fresh enemy aeroplanes continued to rise from the aerodrome, which he attacked one after another, and only retreated, still engaged with five enemy machines, when ordered to do so by his patrol leader. Although apparently wounded, this very gallant officer turned repeatedly, and attacked single-handed the pursuing machines, until he was eventually overwhelmed by numbers and driven to the ground.

"Lt. Jerrard has greatly distinguished himself on four previous occasions, within a period twenty-three days, in destroying enemy machines, displaying bravery and ability of the very highest order."

The first entry on his Army Form B103c reads *"To be Flying Officer & to be seconded,"* the entry being dated 14th June 1917. On 24th July 1917, he was posted to 19 Squadron [Spad S.13] at Lièttres and within a fortnight he was being treated, initially by the doctors at No. 2 Australian Field Hospital, for wounds sustained on 5th August [though details are omitted from *The Sky Their Battlefield'*]. Transferred to 20 General Hospital, he was evacuated to England on the 10th aboard HMHS *Ville de Liège.*

Recovered, he was sent out to Italy where at Treviso on 22nd February 1918, he was attached to 66 Squadron and a little over a month later he was shot down in the action recorded above, at which time the squadron was operating out of San Pietro.

Born on 3rd December 1898, Alan Jerrard remained in the postwar Royal Air Force and was mentioned in despatches for his services with the 14th Wing, Royal Air Force [Italy], 9th July 1920, supplement 31974, page 7423. He was placed on the retired list on account of ill-health on 24th August 1933 [LG 29 August 1933, issue 33973, page 5668].

His death occurred on 14th May 1968, at the age of 70, and his body was cremated at the Exeter & Devon Crematorium; his ashes being interred in the family grave at Hillingdon Churchyard, Middlesex, where his name has been added to the headstone.

He is mentioned by the historian and author Norman Frank in his *Sopwith Camel Aces of World War I* [Osprey, 2003] noteworthy in the fact that he was the only Camel pilot to be honoured with the Victoria Cross. His medals are displayed on rotation at the Imperial War Museum.

A second air VC was *Gazetted* in the same issue, this being awarded to Canadian born 2nd Lieutenant Alan Arnett McLeod attached to 2 Squadron [FK.8]. Sadly, whilst recuperating from his wounds in Canada he fell ill with the influenza pandemic now sweeping the world and died on 6th November 1918; he was just 19 years of age. He is buried in Winnipeg [Old Kildonan] Presbyterian Cemetery.

Saturday 29 September 1923
39 Squadron P/O E B Coventry +
DH.9A E8695 Cpl W Wardle +
T/o Spittlegate and crashed almost immediately. Burnt out. Pilot Officer Edward Bernard Coventry was educated at Haileybury near Hertford and was successful in his application for entry to Cranwell where he arrived with the September 1920 entry. Placed with A Squadron he excelled in field sports. He graduated just over a year previously on 16th August 1922 [LG 29 September 1922, issue 32751, page 6910].

This was the fifth serious crash involving Spittlegate aircraft since January, a point not lost on the press with *The Boston Guardian* October 6th, headlining its account *'Two Airmen Killed - Another Crash at Spittlegate Aerodrome'*

"An air tragedy occurred at Spittlegate Aerodrome, Grantham, on Saturday, when two men were killed:- Flight-Lieutenant [sic] *Edward B Coventry, of Fovant Rectory, Hants., Corporal William Wardle, of Tenth Street, Trafford Park, Manchester.*

"No information as to the probable cause of the accident is available at the moment, but a Coroner's inquiry is set for Monday.

"A number of Grantham people saw the aeroplane descend in flames.

"Another messages says that it appears that the machine, which was a DH.9a, had just taken off, when, at a height of about 50ft, it nose-dived and crashed. On striking the ground the aeroplane was wrecked, the petrol tank burst, and the escaping liquid caught fire. When the flames were extinguished and the aviators were removed, they were both dead, their bodies being badly burnt. Apparently they were killed before the machine caught fire.

"The inquest on the bodies of Pilot Officer Edward Bernard Coventry, 21, and Corpl. William Wardle, 21, both of the 39th Squadron, RAF, the victims of Saturday's aeroplane crash at Spittlegate Aerodrome, was held at the Aerodrome on Monday by Dr. C H D Robbs, the Grantham District Deputy Coroner.

"Flight-Lieut. J A Perdeau, the medical officer at the Aerodrome, said he saw the aeroplane crash. The machine at the time was about 50ft up, and it nose-dived and burst into flames on crashing. Witness was on the spot in a few seconds. It took about 20 minutes to put the fire out, and the bodies of the deceased were then extricated. There was considerable charring of the head, trunk, and extremities, and in the case of Mr. Coventry there was a fracture of the left forearm. Death in both cases was due, first to concussion, and secondly to severe burns. Neither of the men would suffer, for death took place almost instantaneously.

"Flight-Lieut. P J Barnett said on Saturday last he was the officer in temporary command of 39 Squadronand he flew the machine, a DH.9a, immediately before Mr. Coventry took off with it. There was nothing wrong with it when he flew it. He saw the machine crash. When Mr. Coventry took off he pulled the machine up to about 50ft, and before getting full flying speed attempted to turn vertically to the left, at the same time over-ruddering. He lost flying speed and crashed to the ground.

"A few seconds after crashing, the machine burst into flames. There was no movement on the part of either of the deceased before it fired, and therefore they must have been either dead or unconscious when the machine burst into flames. Witness though the whole thing was an error of judgement.

"Squadron Leader J Tudor Whittaker, of the 39th Squadron, gave the opinion that the cause of the crash was over-confidence on the part of Mr. Coventry. He tried to turn before he had got sufficient height and speed. Mr. Coventry was a very experienced pilot.

"The Deputy Coroner returned a verdict of accidental death."

Corporal William Wardle must have impressed the authorities for his service number 344993 indicates the earliest he could joined the Royal Air Force would be September 1919, as his number is within the block issued to civilians joining in September 1919, and valid until June 1925. It is possible, of course, that he had served in the *Great War* and had been demobilised, but finding civilian life not to his liking re-enlisted.

OCTOBER

Wednesday 3 October 1923
14 Squadron F/O R R H Bruce Safe See 17 January 1925
Bristol F.2b J6619
T/o Ramleh and believed damaged beyond repair following a forced landing between the airfield and the Palestinian settlement at Ludd. Flying Officer Ronald Reid Hardcastle Bruce was a short service commission officer whose details are recorded in Appendix D for 1921, and the entries for officers *Gazetted* on 27th September 1921.

Thursday 11 October 1923
31 Squadron F/O M Tallentire Injured
DH.9A E8678 AC1 A L Young Injured
T/o Dardoni and crashed following an uncontrollable spin. Critically injured, both airmen died on 14th and 12th October respectively. Flying Officer Miles Tallentire had emerged unscathed from a crash on Monday 24th September

1923, when Flying Officer W N Cumming of 60 Squadron lost power while taking off from Risalpur in DH.9A E8729 [see 20th July 1925]. Miles had been granted a short service commission, *Gazetted* 28th March 1922, issue 32653, page 2517.

There is some confusion as to whether he was attached to 31 Squadron or 60 Squadron. *The DH.4/DH.9 File* indicates 31 Squadron, while the compilation of overseas fatal air accidents shows 60 Squadron.

Aircraftman Arthur Leonard Young joined between March and August 1919, his service number 330260 coming within the block for the period, 329001 - 335000.

Monday 15 October 1923
60 Squadron F/O L G Nixon Injured
DH.9A H3651 F/O W J T Gomm Safe
T/o Risalpur and flying at 8,500 feet the engine failed. Crash-landed near Duncan's Picquet, Razmak.

Wednesday 17 October 1923
56 Squadron F/O G R C Spencer Injured See 4 April 1923
7F.1 Snipe E7559
T/o Hawkinge for an exercise in squadron formation flying during which the pilot became detached from the formation. Uncertain of his bearings he decided to land and ascertain his position but while attempting to land in the field that he had selected stalled and crashed at Brittons Farm near Sevenoaks in Kent. Slightly injured he was taken to Sevenoaks Hospital for treatment for facial abrasions.

This was Flying Officer Geoffrey Roger Cole Spencer's second serious accident, his previous crash being summarised on 4th April 1923.

NOVEMBER

Thursday 8 November 1923
56 Squadron F/O M V Ward Safe
7F.1 Snipe F2465
T/o Biggin Hill and wrecked following a misjudged landing during practice night flying. According to A.M. Form 470 the engine 'back-fired' into the carburettor and Flying Officer Ward was obliged to forced-land [his second of the year] by the aid of a Holt Flare. Subsequently, the Court of Inquiry reported: *"The Court having duly considered the evidence laid before them & having examined the faulty cylinder head are of the opinion that:-*
"1. The accident was due to a forced landing at night on bad ground; this landing being made necessary by failure of the valve gear on No. 6 cylinder.
"2. No blame can be attached to the pilot.
"O.C. 56 Sqdn concurs."

In Germany on the 8th of November, just three days before the fifth anniversary of the signing of the Armistice, now regarded by many Germans, including the infamous Austrian born Adolf Hitler, as a 'stab in the back,' occurred an event now referred to as the *Beer Hall Putsch* or, commonly called, the *Munich Putsch* where throughout the day and into the 9th, members of the *Nationalsozialistische Deutsche Arbeiterpartie* [Nazi Party] clashed with the police in what would be a failed *coup-d'état.* Hitler, who was wounded, managed to escape immediate arrest but was soon brought to book and sentenced to five years imprisonment for treason. He would be released after only nine months, but it was during his incarceration in Landsberg Prison that he put 'pen to paper' and produced *Mein Kampf.*

This event may be regarded as the start of the lighting the touchpaper which by 1945, and the end of the Second World War, would result in millions of deaths across Europe and by a concerted bombing campaign by the Allies reduce Germany's towns and cities to a desolate wasteland of fire-blackened rubble.

Thursday 22 November 1923
2 Squadron *Not reported*
Bristol F.2b J6763
T/o Andover and came to grief near Camberley, Surrey.

DECEMBER

Tuesday 4 December 1923
55 Squadron F/O A Ledger +
DH.9A H173 *Not reported* Injured
T/o Mosul but while banking at a fairly low altitude went into a flat spin and crashed. Flying Officer Aubrey Ledger was killed by the impact, but his unnamed Indian Army officer passenger was assisted from the wreckage with only minor injuries.

Flying Officer Ledger had been commissioned from Sergeant-Major rank on 10th September 1917, his appointment to 2nd Lieutenant being *Gazetted* on 5th October 1917, supplement 30323, page 10270.

Wednesday 12 December 1923
31 Squadron F/O A J Pearce Safe
Bristol F.2b J6652
T/o Dardoni but failed to clear a line of telegraph wires; wrecked in the ensuing crash.

Friday 14 December 1923

55 Squadron P/O J O Barnes +
DH.9A F1642 LAC G R Sainsbury +

T/o Mosul and crashed following a spin that developed at 1,500 feet from which Pilot Officer John Owen Barnes was unable to recover. Relatively inexperienced, he had been granted a short service commission on 5th September 1922, his details appearing in the *Gazette* published that same date, issue 32744, page 6445.

Leading Aircraftman George Redvers Sainsbury service number 250084 immediately identifies him as a 1918, RNAS serviceman conscripted prior to the April of that year.

Tuesday 18 December 1923

32 Squadron P/O C W A Scott Safe
7F.1 Snipe F2434

T/o Kenley and believed to have been damaged beyond repair following a misjudged landing. Should this be the case, then Pilot Officer Charles William Anderson Scott had written off the squadron's first aircraft since reforming at Kenley on the fifth anniversary of the formation of the Royal Air Force.

He had been short service commissioned for a year and his details are reported in Appendix D for 1922, and the officers *Gazetted* on 26th December 1922.

APPENDICES
1923

Appendix A - Squadron Losses Table and Losses by Aircraft Type

Column 1 - Squadron

Column 2 - Aircraft type

Column 3 - Written off

Column 4 - Fatalities

2 Squadron	Bristol F.2b	4	
4 Squadron	Bristol F.2b	1	
5 Squadron	Bristol F.2b	1	
6 Squadron	Bristol F.2b	1	
11 Squadron	Avro 504K	2	
14 Squadron	Bristol F.2b	2	
20 Squadron	Bristol F.2b	1	2
24 Squadron	Avro 504K	1	
	Bristol F.2b	1	
	Airco DH.9A	2	2
25 Squadron	Sopwith 7F.1 Snipe	3	
27 Squadron	Airco DH.9A	1	
28 Squadron	Bristol F.2b	2	2
31 Squadron	Bristol F.2b	3	2
32 Squadron	Sopwith 7F.1 Snipe	1	
39 Squadron	Avro 504K	1	1
	Airco DH.9A	2	4
41 Squadron	Avro 504K	1	
45 Squadron	Vickers Vernon	1	
55 Squadron	Airco DH.9A	4	3
56 Squadron	Sopwith 7F.1 Snipe	7	2
60 Squadron	Airco DH.10	1	
100 Squadron	Avro 504K	2	1
207 Squadron	Airco DH.9A	3	
216 Squadron	Vickers Vimy	3	8
Totals		51	27

	Airco DH.9A	12	9
	Airco DH.10	1	
	Avro 504K	7	2
	Bristol F.2b	16	6
	Sopwith 7F.1 Snipe	11	2
	Vickers Vernon	1	
	Vickers Vimy	3	8
Totals		51	27

This was a welcome reduction in accidents resulting in the total loss of an aircraft, and but for three crashes reported from 216 Squadron at Heliopolis in which eight aircrew perished, and six deaths at Spittlegate, 1923 fatalities overall would have been markedly down. Also of note, 30 Squadron which in 1921 and 1922 reported ten of their DH.9As being written off in each year, appears to have operated throughout the twelve months with no major incidents.

Appendix B - Squadron Locations and Commanding Officers

The year 1923, witnessed the first green shoots of recovery in squadron expansion. For two years fighter cover for the UK had been in the doldrums but at year's end seven squadrons existed, though four consisted on a single flight. Six were equipped with 7F.1 Snipe whose lineage can be traced back to the *Great War* while Gloster Grebe IIs, the first postwar fighter, had been issued to Duxford for use with 111 Squadron. A total of 133 aircraft, including four prototypes, would emerge from the production line, 108 built as single-seat and 21 twin-seat fitted with dual controls. Superior in performance to the 7F.1 Snipe, the Grebe was deemed to be extremely agile and in general was well liked by those who flew this fighter.

Also to be noted was the resurrection of three home based squadrons, two as day bomber units and one for night bombing. On the negative side, three coastal squadrons were down-graded to Flight status and 210 Squadron at Gosport 'hung up its number plate' which would lie dormant for the next eight years.

1 Squadron	7F.1 Snipe	Hinaidi	01.01.23-31.12.23	
2 Squadron	Bristol F.2b	Farnborough	01.01.23-17.09.23	
		Andover	17.09.23-31.12.23	
3 Squadron	Walrus	Gosport	01.01.23-01.04.23	Disbanded
4 Squadron	Bristol F.2b	Kilia	01.01.23-18.09.23	
		Farnborough	18.09.23-31.12.23	
5 Squadron	Bristol F.2b	Ambala	01.01.23-31.12.23	
6 Squadron	Bristol F.2b	Hinaidi	01.01.23-31.12.23	
7 Squadron	Vimy	Bircham Newron	01.06.23-31.12.23	Reformed for bomber duties
8 Squadron	DH.9A	Hinaidi	01.01.23-31.12.23	
11 Squadron	DH.9A	Andover	13.01.23-16.09.23	Reformed day bomber squadron
		Bircham Newton	16.09.23-31.12.23	
12 Squadron	DH.9A	Northolt	01.04.23-31.12.23	Reformed day bomber squadron
14 Squadron	Bristol F.2b	Ramleh & Amman	01.01.23-31.12.23	
19 Squadron	7F.1 Snipe	Duxford	01.04.23-31.12.23	Reformed as part of No. 2 FTS
20 Squadron	Bristol F.2b	Quetta	01.01.23-31.12.23	
22 Squadron	*Various*	Martlesham Heath	24.07.23-31.12.23	Within A&AEE
24 Squadron	*Various*	Kenley	01.01.23-31.12.23	
25 Squadron	7F.1 Snipe	San Stephano	01.01.23-22.09.23	*En route* UK
		Hawkinge	03.10.23-31.12.23	UK fighter squadron
27 Squadron	DH.9A	Dardoni	01.01.23-20.04.23	
		Risalpur	20.04.23-31.12.23	
28 Squadron	Bristol F.2b	Dardoni	01.01.23-17.03.23	
		Tank	17.03.23-19.04.23	
		Peshawar	19.04.23-31.12.23	
29 Squadron	7F.1 Snipe	Duxford	01.04.23-31.12.23	Reformed Home Defence squadron
30 Squadron	DH.9A	Hinaidi	01.01.23-31.12.23	
31 Squadron	Bristol F.2b	Peshawar	01.01.23-17.04.23	
		Dardoni	17.04.23-31.12.23	
32 Squadron	7F.1 Snipe	Kenley	01.04.23-31.12.23	Reformed Home Defence squadron
39 Squadron	Cadre	Kenley	01.01.23-08.02.23	
	DH.9A	Spittlegate	08.02.23-31.12.23	
41 Squadron	7F.1 Snipe	Northolt	01.04.23-31.12.23	Reformed Home Defence squadron
43 Squadron	7F.1 Snipe	Henlow	01.07.23-31.12.23	Reformed Home Defence squadron
45 Squadron	Vernon	Hinaidi	01.01.23-31.12.23	
47 Squadron	DH.9A	Helwan	01.01.23-31.12.23	
55 Squadron	DH.9A	Mosul	01.01.23-31.12.23	
56 Squadron*	7F.1 Snipe	Hawkinge	01.01.23-07.05.23	UK fighter squadron
		Biggin Hill	07.05.23-31.12.23	
60 Squadron	DH.10A/DH.9A	Risalpur	01.01.23-31.12.23	
70 Squadron	Vernon	Hinaidi	01.01.23-31.12.23	
84 Squadron	DH.9A	Shaibah	01.01.23-31.12.23	
100 Squadron	DH.9A/Vimy	Spittlegate	01.01.23-31.12.23	
111 Squadron	Grebe II	Duxford	01.10.23-31.12.23	Reformed Home Defence squadron
203 Squadron	Nightjar	HMS *Argus*	01.01.23-04.01.23	
		Leuchars	04.01.23-01.04.23	Re-designated 402 Flight
205 Squadron	Panther	Leuchars	01.01.23-01.04.23	Re-designated 441 Flight
207 Squadron	DH.9A	San Stephano	01.01.23-03.10.23	
		Eastchurch	03.10.23-31.12.23	
208 Squadron	Bristol F.2b	San Stephano	01.01.23-26.09.23	
		Ismailia	26.09.23-31.12.23	
210 Squadron	T.1 Cuckoo	Gosport	01.01.23-01.04.23	Disbanded
216 Squadron	Vimy	Heliopolis	01.01.23-31.12.23	
267 Squadron	F.2A/Fairey IIIC&D	Calafrana	01.01.23-01.08.23	Re-designated 481 Flight

1 Squadron	Squadron Leader G G A Williams	In situ	See 3 Squadron 1921
	Squadron Leader E O Grenfell MC DFC AFC mid	8 October 1923	G/Capt retired list 17.02.42
2 Squadron	Squadron Leader L F Forbes	In situ	See Appendix B 1922
3 Squadron	Squadron Leader D G Donald	In situ	See Appendix B 1921
	Squadron Leader C C Miles MC	February 1923	W/Cdr retired list 06.06.37
4 Squadron	Squadron Leader C H B Blount	In situ	See Appendix B 1921
5 Squadron	Squadron Leader P C Maltby	In situ	See Appendix B 1921
	Squadron Leader A J Capel	23 November 1923	AV-M retirement 03.11.45
6 Squadron	Squadron Leader E R Manning DSO MC	In situ	See Appendix B 1922

	Australia		
	Squadron Leader D S K Crosbie OBE	23 November 1923	W/Cdr retired list 08.12.28
7 Squadron	Flight Lieutenant D A Stewart MC* DFC AFC	1 June 1923	Relinquished 30.08.24
	Squadron Leader C H Hayward	5 July 1923	S/Ldr retired list 22.07.25
8 Squadron	Squadron Leader G H Bowman DSO MC* DFC	In situ	See Apendix B 1922
11 Squadron	Squadron Leader E A B Rice MC	15 January 1923	See 6 Squadron 1921
12 Squadron	Flight Lieutenant F P Fullard DSO MC AFC	In situ	See Appendix B 1922
	Flight Lieutenant J R Howett	4 April 1923	S/Ldr relinquished 24.10.30
	Squadron Leader A Gray MC	19 November 1923	AV-M retirement 27.03.49
14 Squadron	Squadron Leader J S T Bradley	In situ	See Appendix B 1921
	Squadron Leader W H Dolphin	21 September 1923	G/Capt retired list 05.08.41
20 Squadron	Squadron Leader J H S Tyssen MC	In situ	See Appendix B 1921
	Squadron Leader R T Leather AFC	1 May 1923	G/Capt retired list 26.05.41
24 Squadron	Squadron Leader O T Boyd MC	In situ	See Appendix B 1922
	Squadron Leader R S Maxwell MC DFC* AFC	22 October 1923	G/Capt retired list 01.04.41
25 Squadron	Squadron Leader Sir N A R D Leslie CBE	In situ	See Appendix B 1921
	Squadron Leader A H Peck DSO MC*	16 February 1923	G/Capt retired list 08.09.44
27 Squadron	Squadron Leader R J Mounsey OBE	In situ	See Appendix B 1921
	Squadron Leader R T Whitehead	15 March 1923	S/Ldr retired list 21.01.25
28 Squadron	Squadron Leader A W F Glenny MC DFC	In situ	See Appendix B 1922
	Squadron Leader H S Powell MC	14 September 1923	W/Cdr retired list 15.07.38
29 Squadron	Wing Commander The Hon. L J E Twistleton-Wykehan-Fiennes	1 April 1923	G/Capt retirement 1939
	Squadron Leader R H G Neville MC	12 August 1923	G/Capt retirement 15.03.46
30 Squadron	Squadron Leader E H Johnston OBE	In situ	See 24 Squadron 1922
31 Squadron	Squadron Leader A C Maund CBE DSO	In situ	See Appendix B 1922
32 Squadron	Flight Lieutenant H E Walker MC DFC	4 April 1923	See summary 24 July 1922
	Flight Lieutenant T E B Howe AFC	1 May 1923	See 22 October 1923
	Squadron Leader R S Maxwell MC DFC* AFC	2 July 1923	See 24 Squadron 1923
	Squadron Leader T E B Howe AFC	22 October 1923	A/Cmdr retirement 19.08.41
39 Squadron	Squadron Leader A A B Thomson MC* DFC	In situ	See Appendix B 1922
	Squadron Leader T Whittaker MC	8 February 1923	See 28 Squadron 1922
41 Squadron	Squadron Leader B E Smythies DFC	1 April 1923	W/Cdr killed 17 June 1930
	Squadron Leader R Collishaw DSO* DSC DFC three times mid	1 October 1923	See Appendix B 1921
45 Squadron	Squadron Leader A T Harris AFC	In situ	See Appendix B 1922
47 Squadron	Squadron Leader M Henderson DSO	In situ	See 216 Squadron 1921
55 Squadron	Squadron Leader V Gaskell-Blackburn DSO AFC	In situ	See Appendix B 1921
	Squadron Leader T F Hazell DSO MC* DFC	15 January 1923	See summary 4 April 1925
	Squadron Leader A Coningham DSO MC DFC Autralia	12 July 1923	AM retirement 07.11.47
56 Squadron	Squadron Leader I T Lloyd	In situ	See Appendix B 1922
	Squadron Leader Sir C J Q Brand KBE DSO MC DFC South Africa	24 September 1923	AV-M retirement 06.11.43
60 Squadron	Squadron Leader H V Champion de Crespigny MC DFC	In situ	See Appendix B 1922
70 Squadron	Squadron Leader S W Smith OBE	In situ	See Appendix B 1921
84 Squadron	Squadron Leader W Sowery AFC	In situ	See Appendix B 1921
	Squadron Leader V S Brown	6 May 1923	A/Cmdr resigned 30.11.37
100 Squadron	Squadron Leader N M Martin CBE	In situ	See Appendix B 1922
111 Squadron	Squadron Leader T F Hazell DSO MC DFC	1 December 1923	See summary 4 April 1925
203 Squadron	Flight Lieutenant A H Slatter OBE DSC* DFC	In situ	See Appendix B 1921
205 Squadron	Squadron Leader D M Bayley DFC	In situ	See Appendix B 1921
207 Squadron	Squadron Leader A W Tedder	In situ	See Appendix B 1921
	Squadron Leader V Gaskell-Blackburn DSO AFC	6 August 1923	See 55 Squadron
208 Squadron	Squadron Leader A ap Ellis	In situ	See Appendix B 1922
	Wing Commander A C Winter	October 1923	G/Capt retired list 01.06.37
210 Squadron	Wing Commander N J Gill OBE MC	In situ	See Appendix B 1921
216 Squadron	Squadron Leader C O F Modin DSC mid	In situ	See Appendix B 1922
267 Squadron	Squadron Leader P A Shepherd	In situ	See Appendix B 1921

Annex

Eustace Osborne Grenfell was commissioned to the 5th Battalion, The Dunke of Cornwall's Light Infantry. Territorial Army, as a 2nd Lieutenant on 2nd June 1913 [LG 5 September 1913, issue 28753, page 6330], subsequently transferring to the Royal Garrison Artillery before joining the Royal Flying Corps on 8th October 1914. The citation for his MC, promulgated in *The Edinburgh Gazette* on March 16th, 1916, issue 12916, page 541 was relatively brief: *"For conspicuous gallantry and skill. He attacked single-handed and brought down three Fokker aeroplanes.*

"Captain Grenfell has shown great bravery and initiative at all times."

The London Gazette published on 2nd November 1918, supplement 30989, page 12958, records his name in the list of officers granted the Air Force Cross, while his DFC was announced as follows: *"His Majesty the KING has been graciously pleased to approve of the undermentioned rewards in recognition of distinguished services rendered with the Waziristan Force between January 1922, and April 1923."* [LG 30 May 1924, issue 32940, page 4313].

The Aerodrome Website, which the authors are pleased to acknowledge, show that he attained a total of eight aerial combat victories between 13th September 1915 and 11th December 1916, six with 1 Squadron flying Morane Parasol Ns and two with 60 Squadron [Nieuport 16]. His appointment to command No. 1 Squadron in 1923, nust have given him great pleasure.

Born in the Essex resort of Southend-on-Sea on 26th August 1890, his death was reported from Chichester, Sussex, on the 7th of March 1964.

As a 2nd Lieutenant [temporary Captain] Charles Cleaver Miles gained his MC, the citation appearing on page 1895 of issue 13001 of *The Edinburgh Gazette* of October 23rd, 1916: *"For conspicuous gallantry and skill. He has shown great dash in contact patrol work. On one occasion he reconnoitred an enemy trench at 500 feet altitude, under heavy fire, which severely damaged his machine, Five days later, while working at 600 feet, he was severely wounded."*

Born in Shirehampton in Gloucestershire on 6th June 1887, he joined the RFC on 9th April 1915, and a year later was operational on the Western Front, initially with 1 Squadron [Morane Parasol] at Bailleul before transferring on 13th April 1916, to 3 Squadron [Morane BB] at La Houssoye where on 20th August 1916, he won his Military Cross. Then, on the 25th, as indicated in the citation, he was wounded from rifle fire over the trenches, the identity of his Morane has not been recorded in *The Sky Their Battlefield,* though Trevor Henshaw writes in his heading for the day on page 49; *"Delville*Wood was finally cleared of the enemy."*

For Captain Miles he was *hors de combat* having sustained a gunshot wound to his back and was evacuated to England on 1 September 1916, as a patient aboard HMHS *Lafranc* [subsequently sunk by *SM UB-40* north of Le Havre during the evening of 17th April 1917]. By the late autumn of 1917, he was deemed fit to resume active service and he returned to France on 20th November 1917, joining 43 Squadron [F.1 Camel] at Auchel the next day.

On leaving the service, and now ranked wing commander, he settled in Suffolk where he became an apple farmer, presumably remaining so until his death on 15th May 1949.

* The clearing of Delville Wood was one of the bloodiest actions during the *Battle of the Somme,* a personal account by Private Archibald McAllister Burgoyne, Lancashire born but having emigrated in 1893, to South Africa, was now serving with the South African Brigade, being the opening observations in the prologue of Taylor Downing's excellent book *Breakdown - The Crisis of Shell Shock on The Somme 1916* [Little, Brown and Company, 2016].

Flight Lieutenant D A Stewart's awards were gained while attached to 18 Squadron [DH.4] in whose service as a bomber pilot he scored fourteen of sixteen confirmed aerial victories, a remarkable achievement and one which was rewarded by an MC and First Bar, followed by a DFC, all *Gazetted* between April and November 1918, the first being promulgated on 22nd April, supplement 30643, page 4832: *"For conspicuous gallantry and devotion to duty. On one occasion, when returning from bombing an enemy dump, he was intercepted by a formation of thirty hostile machines. He attacked the leader and shot his machine down out of control, whilst his observer shot down another enemy scout. He then fired a burst at another large scout, which dived down vertically out of control. On his observer being hit whilst engaged with another four machines, he spun down 4,000 feet and dived for our lines. Later, when on photographic duty, he was attacked by five enemy scouts, three of which were accounted for by his observer and himself. In the face of heavy odds, his courage, skill and fine fighting spirit have been most conspicuous."*

Supplement 30761, page 7400, of the *Gazette* published on 22nd June 1918, reported the First Bar: *"For conspicuous gallantry and devotion to duty. During the past month, when engaged with superior numbers of enemy aircraft, he has destroyed four hostile machines, all of which were seen to crash by other observers. He has in addition carried out nine successful reconnaissances, as a result of which he had returned with information of the greatest value. He has displayed the greatest courage and determination at all times on his many low flying and bombing attacks on hostile troops and transports."*

A richly deserved DFC was *Gazetted* on 2nd November 1918, supplement 30989, page 12973: *"An able leader, conspicuous for his initiative and dash. He has destroyed three enemy machines, and has, in addition, taken part in many bombing raids, reconnaissances and photographic flights. In the majority of these he has been leader, and frequently in order to obtain accurate information he has led his flight at very low altitudes."*

Consulting Air-Britain's *DH.4/DH.9 File,* Captain Stewart's association with the DH.4 is noted with eight separate airframe serials. In chronological order his name is appended to:-

A7501 *"Damaged by AA in cloud, landed to examine m/c but crashed 23.11.27 [2/Lt DA Stewart & Lt HWM Mackay OK].* A7501 was sent for repairs and was extant in April 1918.

A7594 *"In combat with 2-str SE Béthune, observer in German machine shot 13.10 26.11.17 [2Lt DA Stewart & Lt HWM Mackay]; Albatros C OOC Valenciennes 10.30 6.12.17 [2Lt DA Stewart & Lt HWM Mackay].*

A7653 *"Albatros D OOC Valenciennes 1205 6.1.8 [2Lt DA Stewart & Lt HWM Mckay]*

A7707 *"Returning from raid on dump nr Carvin intercepted by 3 formations of EA mainly Pfalz and in total about 30 a/c, pilot two Pfalz OOC, observer* [Mackay] *Pfalz then wounded in chest but continued to fire and sent another EA OOC, m/c badly shot up, 11.05 6.3.18 [2Lt DA Stewart OK Lt HWM Mackay*DoW on way to hospital].* A7797 was sent for repair, but was struck off charge 14th April 1918.

A7799 *"Pfalz OOC Neuve Chapelle-Fromelles 1245 [2Lt DA Stewart & Sgt C Beardmore].*

A7800 *"Fokker Dr1 crashed Albert 11.30 27.3.18 [2Lt DA Stewart MC & Capt LI Collins].* See Volume 1 page 59 for details of its last flight.

A8101 *"On reconnaissance with A7799, attacked by six Pfalz DIIIs at Hulluch, one of which broke up 20.45 17.6.18 [Capt DA Stewart MC & Capt LI Collins].*

A8038 *"Pfalz crashed 1255 15.3.18 [2Lt DA Stewart & Sgt AOA Pollard]; Aviatik C crashed Loupart Wood S of Bapaume 17.15 25.3.18 [2Lt DA Stewart MC & Capt LI Collins]; Albatros D crashed W of Douai 11.40 28.5.18 [Capt DA Stewart MC & Capt LI Collins MC]; Scout DD smoking, Pfalz BU, Scout OOC Neuve Chapelle-Richebourg St Vaast 13.00 30.5.18 [Capt DA Stewart MC & Lt W Miller].*See Volume 2 and page 24 for its demise.

After leaving the Royal Air Force he was employed by Imperial Airways only to lose his life within four months of employment. The tragedy occurred on Christmas Eve 1924, when he took off from Croydon in DH.34 G-ABBX on a scheduled flight to Paris-Le Bourget with seven passengers named as Mrs. Annie Chaffey Bailey, 64, Dr. Plinio Barbosa Lima, 32, a Brazilian national, Mr. Maurice Edward Luxemburg, 18, Mr. Archibald John Sproston, 39 and his father Mr. George Sproston, 76 and Miss Marie Sproston, 21, and Cedric Trudgett, 21, listed as a Chilean national.

The flight was in difficulties almost from the start. Eyewitnesses observed the DH flying low over Purley before it suddenly nosedived and crashed on Castle Hill. On impact, it turned over and burst into flames and in the opinion of those in the area all eight persons on board must have died instantaneously, such was the force of the crash and the all consuming fire that followed. For Imperial Airways it was their first fatal accident and the inquiry which followed was the first investigation into a civil aviation crash.

* Previously of the 9th Battalion, Gordon Highlanders, Territorial Forces, Lieutenant Harry William Mackintosh Mackay was accepted for training as an observer, on probation, on 29th July 1917, and was sent back to the UK for training, re-embarking 24th October of that year. He reported to Auchel the next day and joined 18 Squadron. He enjoyed a spell of leave between 14th and 28th January 1918, and from n23rd February to 5th March 1918, he was detached to England for temporary duty. He was buried in Aire Communal Cemetery within a few days of being mortally wounded, the burial service conducted by the Reverend W H Stubbs, attached Stationary Hospital. Just 20 years of age, his headstone has been cheerfully inscribed *"Tell Them At Home It Is All Right."*

Formerly commissioned to the Argyll & Sutherland Highlanders, Temporary Captain Alexander Gray's MC was *Gazetted* on 18th March 1918: *"For conspicuous gallantry and devotion to duty. He took part in many successful operations over the enemy's lines, in over twenty of which he acted as leader. On one one occasion, when leading a bombing raid, his formation was heavily attacked by enemy aeroplanes. He shot one of them down, and brought back the whole of his formation safely. He also led a successful raid on an enemy aerodrome, and on several occasions obtained valuable photographs. He has accounted for two enemy aeroplanes with his front gun, and always showed great coolness, ability, and resource."*

The successful clashes with enemy scouts took place when he was attached to 55 Squadron [DH.4] , though I can find no reference to these combats in Air-Britain's *DH.4/DH.9 File.*

To date, only the First Bar to the DFC in respect of Squadron Leader Reginald Stuart Maxwell has been traced, this being *Gazetted* on 28th October 1921, issue 32501, page 8495, for services in Mesopotamia: *"For gallantry and devotion to duty. This officer has recently carried out 14 raids over hostile country and 60 hours flying. He has at all times shown constant courage and a very high sense of devotion to duty. On one occasion when forced to descend in hostile territory owing to engine failure he displayed great coolness in endeavouring to remedy it under fire, and only when this was found to be impossible did he take advantage of the landing of another machine, and by lying flat on its lower plane was carried away to safety. He has always set a fine example to the rest of his flight by keenness and hard work in the air and on the ground."*

Arthur Hicks Peck, born on 25th April 1889, at Darjeeling in India's tea producing region, appears to have been a direct entrant to the RFC, his acceptance date being recorded as 4th August 1916, though an entry in the *Gazette* published on 8th December 1914, issue 29000, page 10452, list an

Arthur Hicks Peck being *Gazetted* Temporary 2nd Lieutenant on 7th December 1914, having previously been a cadet with the Officer Training Corps. His MC was promulgated, less citation,*in *The London Gazette* of 18th January 1918, supplement 30482, page 957.

A DSO, again no citation,*followed soon after on 4th March 1918, supplement 30555, page 2728, where it is indicated he was a General List officer and holding the rank of Temporary Captain. Then, on 26th July 1918, supplement 30813, page 8763, was the announcement of a First Bar to his MC and with it the following citation: *"For conspicuous gallantry and devotion to duty. While patrolling at a height of 14,000 ft., he observed a formation of five enemy aircraft attempting a reconnaissance. He attacked the top machine, a scout, and drove it down out of control. He then attacked the second scout, which he also drove down out of control. He finally attacked a two-seater, and so quickly that he got to close quarters and opened fire with both guns. That, too, he sent down out of control. His performance was a splendid one, besides being costly for the enemy."*

His entry on the Aerodrome website, which the authors acknowledge, show he achieved eight combat victories while serving with 111 Squadron, three at the controls of Bristol F.2b A7194 with Captain John Lloyd-Williams as his observer, and the remainder flying the potent SE.5a. All were achieved between 30th October 1917 and 23rd March 1918, in the Palestine theatre when 111 Squadron was operating from Deir-el-Bahleh and Julis.

Group Captain Arthur Hicks Peck DSO MC and First Bar died on St. Valentine's Day 1975.

* This was published on 25th April 1918, supplement 30651, page 5011: *"For conspicuous gallantry and devotion to duty. He engaged singlehanded three enemy aeroplanes, though they had superior height. He drove them back over their lines and prevented them from carrying out their reconnaissances."* The citation for his DSO subsequently appeared in supplement 30845, page 9564, of the *Gazette,* 16th August 1918: *"For conspicuous gallantry and devotion to duty. Whilst on patrol he engaged nine Albatross scouts, five of these being driven down, two of which he accounted for. On another occasions, whilst leading his flight on an offensive patrol, he dived on a formation of six enemy scouts, driving one down out of control. During the course of his patrol work he has brought down ten* [sic] *enemy machines, and his work on all occasions has been magnificent. He is a dashing patrol leader, and inspires all with the greatest keenness."*

Squadron Leader Henry Stewart Powell, formerly of the Ceylon Rifles, was *Gazetted* with the Military Cross [no citation appended] on 24th January 1917, supplement 29116, page 927.

Squadron Leader Arthur Coningham whose name is synonymous with the successful fighter campaign in the Western Desert when he was Air Officer Commanding Air Headquarters Western Desert, was appointed to the Special Reserve of the Royal Flying Corps on 8th August 1916, and by the winter of 1916-1917 was in France flying DH.5s with 32 Squadron. On 30th July 1917, eve of the *Third Battle of Ypres,* as recorded by Trevor Henshaw on page 106 of *The Sky Their Battlefield* he received a wound to his head while on patrol in DH.5 9179.

Sent back to the UK to recuperate, he returned to France at the end of March 1918, commanding 92 Squadron [SE.5a] for the remainder of hostilities, eventually handing over 'the chair' to Major Arthur John Capel in February 1919 [see 5 Squadron above].

His MC, gained with 32 Squadron, was *Gazetted* 17th September 1917, supplement 30287, page 8566: *"For conspicuous gallantry and devotion to duty in attacking enemy aircraft. On numerous occasions he has displayed great dash and a fine offensive spirit in engaging the enemy at close range, and driving them down completely out of control."*

The citation for his DSO picks up on the engagement during which he was wounded on 30th July 1917: *"For conspicuous gallantry and devotion to duty. With three other pilots he attacked an enemy machine which was protected by ten others, shot it down, and destroyed another one the same evening. Shortly afterwards he and two others attacked five of the enemy, and although wounded and rendered unconscious for the moment, he succeeded in driving down two of the enemy. In spite of being much exhausted by loss of blood he continued his patrol until he was sure no more enemy machines were in the vicinity, setting a splendid example of pluck and determination."*

His work with 92 Squadron was recognised with a DFC *Gazetted,* less citation, on 3rd June 1919, supplement 31378, page 7031.

It has to be said that post-1945, at which time from October of that year he was Air Officer Commanding in Chief Flying Training Command, he was not appointed to a post commensurate with his great knowledge of inter-service cooperation and the position of Air Officer Commanding in Chief 2nd Tactical Air Force, which he had commanded from January 1944, saw him replaced by Sir Sholto Douglas. This, in my opinion, rightly, he viewed as a snub and on 7th November 1947, he retired at his own request.

Entering the world of commerce, he was a passenger on the British South American Airways Tudor IV G-AHNP *Star Tiger* which departed the Azores for Bermuda on 30th January 1948, and disappeared without trace. For a full account of its ill-fatal flight, the authors recommend a reading of the many on-line websites featuring the aircraft.

An incomplete Army Form B.103 for Christopher Joseph Quinton Brand reads as follows:-

			Embarked	*8.6.18*	*SL 1882*
10.6.18	*1 Sqdn*	*Posted to 1 Sqdn*	*Field*	*9.6.18*	*B.213*
16.7.16	*GOC - RFC*	*Wounded*	*Field*	*14.7.18*	*summy 60*
15.7.16	*1 Can. CCS*	*Admitted [Shpl. wound, back]*	*Field*	*14.7.16*	*E D 399*
22.7.16	*- " -*	*Discharged to duty*	*Field*	*18.7.16*	*E D 762*
2.9.16	*1 Sqdn*	*Leave 27.8.16 to 3.9.16*	*Field*		*B 213*
1.11.16	*- " -*	*To Paris on Tempy Duty*	*Field*	*4.11.16*	*- " 1*
11.11.16	*- " -*	*Returned*	*Field*	*8.11.16*	*- " -*
30.12.16	*- " -*	*Leave 23.12.16 to 6.1.17*	*Field*		*- " -*
27.1.17	*- " -*	*To School of Aerial Gunnery*	*Field*	*21.1.17*	*- " -*
3.2.1y	*- " -*	*Ret. from School of Aerial Gunnery*	*Field*	*27.1.17*	*- " -*

The citations for his MC and DFC, as recorded on the Air of Authority website, read: *"For conspicuous gallantry and devotion to duty while on patrol with one other machine. He attacked a formation of five hostile machines and shot one of them down in flames. On another occasion he brought down two hostile machines. He has at all times shown great courage and initiative."*

The above was awarded for his work with 1 Squadron, while the DFC that follows reflects his command of 151 Squadron [F.1 Camel] the only night-fighter squadron to operate over the Western Front: *"On the night of 15th/16th September* [1918] *this officer attacked and enemy aeroplane at 8,000 feet. In the combat that ensued his tracers burst the sump of one of the aeroplane's engines and the oil from it covered his machine in a black spray. Almost blinded by this he still continued the engagement and eventually drove the enemy machine down to 200 feet, when, owing to intense hostile machine-gun fire rom the ground, he was compelled to break off the combat. There is every reason to believe that this machine crashed. The foregoing is only one of many gallant deeds performed by this officer, who by his indomitable spirit and example has raised the efficiency of his squadron to a very high level."*

Appendix C - Officers Granted Short Service Commissions

Throughout the year short service commissions were granted to officers with previous military experience, some going back to the early years of the *Great War.* Where available I have made observations of their previous service, in some cases quoting in full the entries of their Army Form B.103c commonly titled Casualty Form - Officers.

I have also found the RAF Museum Story Vault cards a useful source for information regarding air accidents, in particular mishaps at the Flying Training Schools.

The sequence of allocation of Service Numbers continues to raise as many questions as answers though I believe it is reasonably safe to say that the block for the four probationary Pilots Officers granted short service commissions with seniority 1st January 1923 commenced 17125. By the end of the year allocations in the 18001 block were being issued.

LG 16 January 1923, issue 32787, page 382 - Seniority 2nd January 1923 and for the four Pilot Officers 1st January 1923

FLYING OFFICER

	WINGFIELD	Cecil Percy	F/O	31.03.26	

And transferred from the General Duties Branch to the Stores Branch and appointed to a permanent commission [LG 30 March 1926, issue 33146, page 2278] his service number now being 21037. G/Capt 22.05.48 Retirement

Formerly commissioned as a probationary 2nd Lieutenant to the 4th Battalion, Royal Irish Fusiliers [LG 7 April 1915, supplement 29120, page 3422], he was attached to 2 Aeroplane Supply Depot at Fienvillers for just over two weeks between 30th October and 14th November 1917.

17125	CALLEN	Vaughan Morgan	P/O	01.06.24	Terminated
17126	COFFIN	Geoffrey	P/O	29.07.24	Removed

Pilot Officer Geoffrey Coffin *"is removed from the Royal Air Force, His Majesty having no further use for his service."*[LG 12 August 1924, issue 32964, page 6054].

17127	HALLIWELL	Reginald Thomas	S/Ldr	10.02.54	Relinquished
17128	ROUPELL	Charles Frederick	F/O	01.01.32	Relinquished

My co-author reports that Flying Officer Charles Frederick Roupell was born into a military family, his elder brother George Rowland Patrick Roupell, who attained the rank of Brigadier, distinguished himself during the *Great War* during which his bravery under fire won him the nation's highest honour, the Victoria Cross. *Gazetted* in the Edinburgh edition on June 25th, 1915, issue 12882, page 910, the citation reads: *"For most conspicuous gallantry and devotion to duty on April 20th, 1915, when he was commanding a company of his battalion* [1st Battalion, The East Surry Regiment] *in a front trench on "Hill 60" which was subjected to a most severe bombardment throughout the day. Though wounded in several places, he remained at his post and led his company in repelling a strong German assault. During a lull in the bombardment he had his wounds hurriedly dressed, and then insisted in returning to his trench, which was again being subjected to severe bombardment. Towards evening, his company being dangerously weakened, he went back to his battalion headquarters, represented the situation to his Commanding Officer, and brought up reinforcements, passing backwards and forwards over ground swept by heavy fire. With these reinforcements he held his position throughout the night, and until his battalion was relieved. This young Officer was one of the few survivors of his company, and showed a magnificent example of courage, devotion and tenacity, which undoubtedly inspired his men to hold out till the end."* Subsequently, he served his country with distinction until retirement in 1946. His death was announced on 4th March 1974,

LG 30 January 1923, issue 32791, page 712 - Seniority 17th and 18th January 1923 respectively

FLIGHT LIEUTENANTS
2

17131	BRILL	Charles Harold	G/Capt	01.03.48	Retirement
	STYRAN MC AFC	Arthur John Graham	F/Lt	18.01.31	Relinquished

Formerly of the Royal Artillery, as a 2nd Lieutenant and now serving with the RFC he was *Gazetted* with the MC on 14th November 1916, supplement 29824, page 11068: *"For conspicuous skill and gallantry. He has done fine work with artillery for a long time, often in bad weather and under heavy fire. On one occasion he directed the fire of nine batteries on the enemy's trenches, and obtained a large number of direct hits."*

I am reasonably confident that Albert John Graham Styran MC is the officer named in *The London Gazette.* Two Army Form B.103s have been raised against his name, each indicating the award of an MC. The first card shows the following:-

		Embarked Bombay HT Karajola	
		Disembarked Suez 9.6.18	
15.6.18	*Joined RAF Base Depot from Mesopotamia*	*11.6.18*	
1.7.18	*Fit for graduated flying - class B for seven days*	*1.7.18*	*B.213 B.Depot RAF Med. Bd.*
20.7.18	*Posted to 21 Trg. Sqd.*	*15.7.18*	*B.213 21 T.Sq.*
28.11.18	*Lt. Flying [A] to T/Capt. Whilst empl. As Capt. {Obs][A]*	*18.10.18*	*HQ ME List A*
4.4.19	*Posted to 18 TDS*	*9.2.19*	*T.B.087*
14.2.19	*Reposted to 142 Sqdn for duty*	*11.2.19*	*5 WRD 33*
20.5.19	*To retain acting rank [Act. Captain] pending Air Ministry approval. Auth. A.M. telegram 9490 P.3d 26.4.19*		*List 31 M.E.R.O.d/203*
18.6.19	*Assumes command of 142 Squadron*	*12.6.19*	*P.B.R.O. 97*
9.7.19	*Leave of Absence from 6.7.19 to 8.7.19*	*6.7.19*	*P.B.R.O 111*

The second card commences:-

1.1.21	*Embarked at Port Said for UK per HT Zeppelin*	*31.12.20*	*NR.47*
6.1.21	*Posted from 47 Sqdn to H.E.*	*31.12.20*	*M.E.R.O.1*

LG 20 February 1923, issue 32797, page 1234 - Seniority 12th and 7th February respectively

FLYING OFFICERS
2

BELL	Edward	F/O	+	28.07.24	28 Squadron
BURD MC	John Marsh	F/O	+	12.10.30	30 Squadron

John Marsh Burd, born 10th September 1896 and formerly of the Royal Artillery ahead of joining the RFC on 25th October 1915, was appointed to a temporary commission of flight lieutenant for two years service with effect from 1st August 1919 [LG 27 April 1920, issue 31879, page 4850], this being relinquished on his return to Army duty on 1st August 1921 [LG 16th August 1921, issue 32424, page 6492]. His MC was *Gazetted* on page 4862, supplement 30645 of the paper published on 23rd April 1918: *"For conspicuous gallantry and devotion to duty as a leader of long-distance bomb raids, When returning from a raid he attacked ten enemy aeroplanes which were engaged with another of our formations. He shot down two and his observer another, and he then brought his formation back without loss. In six raids he only lost one machine. He has been leader in seventeen operations and deputy leader in eleven."* Consulting *The DH.4/DH.9 File,* establishes that John Marsh Burd was attached to 55 Squadron and on 16th August 1917, along with his observer 2nd Lieutenant F Singleton they escaped unharmed when their DH.4 A7441 lost power taking off from Boisdingham and finished up, inverted, in a cornfield.

On 1st November 1927, he was appointed to a permanent commission and with effect same date resigned his commission with the Royal Regiment of Artillery [LG 10 October 1930, issue 33651, page 6177] - the wheels of administration turning rather slowly!

Attached to 30 Squadron, he was admitted to the British General Hospital at Hinaidi suffering from abdominal pains and while being treated for such he suddenly collapsed and died. Flying Officer Burd MC is buried in Ma'asker Al Raschid RAF Cemetery. His death was reported on 20th October 1930 in the *Exeter and Plymouth Gazette.*

His father, also John Marsha Burd of Okehampton in Devon, is frequently mentioned in the *Gazette* in a legal capacity.

LG 30 March 1923, issue 32810, page 2420 - Seniority 15th March 1923 for both the Flying Officers and Pilot Officers

Block 17138 to 17152 and Block 17153 to 17168

FLYING OFFICERS
15

17138 ANDERSON James Noel Douglas G/Capt 10.02.46 Retirement
17139 BARKLEY Frederick William F/O 12.01.26 Resigned
17140 BRODIE Ian Eustace A/Cmdr 31.03.51 Retirement
Air Commodore Ian Eustace Brodie OBE mentioned in despatches, died on Thursday, 22nd July 1993. Born on 17th September 1898 he had seen extensive *Great War* serve in the Royal Navy. He was placed on the Navy's Retired List on the same day that he was granted a short service commission in the Royal Air Force.His flying training was carried out at 5 FTS Shotwick. His final appointment following attachment to the Italian Air Force [20th April 1945 to 14th April 1947] was as Deputy Director of Intelligence [Organisation and Security].
17141 BROOKE Lionel Hugh S/Ldr 10.02.54 Relinquished
17142 COCKS John James Crofts F/O + 26.05.27 60 Squadron
Flying Officer John James Crofts Cocks and his observer, Leading Aircraftman Jack Rowston, disappeared while transiting between Konia and Constantinople in a civilian registered DH.9 G-IAAB. Referring to the *DH.9/DH.9A File,* this DH was registered to Flying Officer Cocks attached to 60 Squadron at Lahore and, allegedly, built up from two Imperial Gift aircraft purchased from the Maharajah of Nabha [though the File suggests its previous identity was D3180 and registered to Flying Officer Cocks in April 1927]. On the 11th of May the two airmen had departed Lahore bound for Lympne in Kent, presumably either for leave or on posting to Home Establishment. Konai [Konja] is a major city in south-central, Turkey, while Constantinople is more commonly referred to Istanbul.
17143 DAVIES Hugh Clement F/O 26.08.25 Resigned
17144 DE BURGH Ulric Campbell F/O 20.03.30 Relinquished
17145 KIRKMAN Harry Gayton F/Lt 15.03.30 Relinquished
17146 NOEL Owen Cyril F/O 01.12.24 Resigned
17147 PRENDERGAST Archer Robert F/Lt 15.03.30 Relinquished
While serving with 27 Squadron in India, Archer Robert Prendergast crashed while dropping mail to troops operating in the Lowari Pass on the NWF. See my summary for 21st September 1928, for details.
17148 RIGGS MC Arthur Francis McCausland F/O 05.08.25 Resigned
The military service for Arthur Francis McCausland Riggs began when as a former cadet he was commissioned as a temporary 2nd Lieutenant to the infantry on 19th November 1914 [LG 20 November 1914, issuue 28981, page 9546]. As a temporary Lieutenant he was attached to The King's Own [Yorkshire Light Infantry], promulgated in supplement 29525, page 3398 of the *Gazette* published on 29th March 1916.

During the Second World War he rejoined the army and by October 1943 was Acting Lieutenant Colonel in his old regiment and was *Gazetted* with the DSO, less citation, on 26th October 1943 [LG 26 October 1943, supplement 36222, page 4713].
17149 SOMERSET-THOMAS Vyvyan John F/Lt 15.03.30 Relinquished
17150 STAINFORTH George Hedley
17151 STIVEN Robert F/Lt 15.03.30 Relinquished
17152 WINDHAM John Bayntun Russell F/O 14.11.23 Resigned

The above were retired officers from the Royal Navy, the Army, some having been attached to the Indian Army. All were commissioned to serve for seven years on the active list.

17153 BATH Ronald Edgar P/O 25.06.24 Resigned
17154 BAXTER William Duncan F/O 16.03.38 Relinquished
17155 BROOKES Donald Scott F/O 18.09.26 Permanent
Please refer to Appendix C and LG 5 October 1926, issue 33208, page 6374, for continuation of his service.
17156 BUCKLEY Jack P/O 13.06.23 Resigned
17157 CATTELL Terence William Goodricke F/O 03.06.27 Class C
And on the same day sailed from the UK for Malaya to take up a position as a rubber planter though, subsequently, he switched to tea planting. The website The Auxiliaries, which I have pleasure in acknowledging, shows his birth as 25th July 1900 in Norfolk. While in Malay he contracted Malaria and, it seems, he returned to England in order to recuperate. While at home he met and fell in love with Kathleen Mathilde and together they returned to Malaya where they married in in January 1935. Tragically, Terence Cattell, now acting manager of the Gordon Estate at Kedah, was taken ill and died in the General Hospital [at Kuala Lumpur] on 5th July 1935. His widow returned to England where later in the year she gave birth to a son. The website carried a studio-style photograph of Flying Officer Cattell in his RAF uniform.
17158 COLE Robert Arthur Alexander G/Capt 15.03.48 Retirement
17159 DELANY Cyril Joseph Augustine F/O 21.05.41 Relinquished
On account of ill-health [LG 23 May 1941, page 2948].
17160 DORAN-WEBB James Edward F/O 21.05.30 Relinquished
On account of ill-health [LG 20 May 1930, issue 33607, page 3157]. However, his health recovered sufficiently for him to return to the service and a commission in the Equipment Branch as a pilot officer for hostilities only with effect from 21st November 1939 [LG 5 December 1939, issue 34747, page 8110]. At first he was allocated a new service number 75935 but later reverted to his original identity. He served throughout the Second World War and beyond but seems not to have advanced in rank. P/O 13.02.54 Relinquished
17161 KERCKHOVE MC Herbert Vincent P/O + 02.07.24 19 Squadron
17162 RYPER James Aubrey P/O 17.11.23 Terminated
17163 TOMES James Eric F/O + 15.04.26 84 Squadron
17164 TRIMMER John Kenneth P/O 27.08.24 Resigned
17165 TUKE Athol George Stratford F/O 07.09.25
Flying Officer Athol George Stratford Tuke was transferred from the General Duties Branch to the Stores Branch, his service number being amended to 21047. By April 1940 his surname was STRATFORD-TUKE. G/Capt 29.10.54 Retirement
On account of medical unfitness for Air Force service [LG 2 November 1954, supplement 40315, page 6194].
17166 WHINNEY Edward Gerald S/Ldr 01.03.42 Still in AFL 1945
17167 YOUNG Basil Lambton F/O 15.03.39 Relinquished

17168 YOUNG Stuart Adolphus P/O + 14 May 1926 1 Squadron

LG 6 April 1923, issue 32812, page 2568 - Seniority 26th March 1923

FLYING OFFICER

17169 HAUGHTON Edward Perceval Osburne F/O + 01.05.23 401 Flight Leuchars
While flying Nightjar J6938 of 401 Flight, Flying Officer Edward Perceval Osburne Haughton, who returned to the service as recently as March, spun in while making a steep turn near the airfield. Rushed to Station Sick Quarters he died soon after being admitted. His Casualty Form - Officers reads:-

26.11.18	*Released prisoner of war [captured 20.9.18 Anatolia]*		*N/R*
24.11.18	*Adm. 19 G. Hosp. Influenza - slight*	*24.11.18*	*W3034*
9.12.18	*Discharged 19 Gen. Hosp.*	*9.12.18*	*W3034*
26.12.18	*Embarked Port Said for UK per S/S Canberra*	*26.12.18*	*D29179*

Referring to Trevor Henshaw's indispensable *The Sky Their Battlefield,* page 282 identifies Lieutenant E P O Haughton and his observer/air gunner Gunner A Weller of No. 62 Wing being taken prisoner whilst returning to base - probably Mudros - in DH.9 D2889. The crew had been briefed for a bombing raid but turned back before completing their mission. Air-Britain's *DH.4/DH.9 File* shows D2889 as being at the West India Docks in London by 11th July 1918 arriving at Mudros by the 18th [for the time this seems a pretty quick passage].

LG 17 April 1923, issue 32815, page 2816 - Seniority 3rd April 1923 apart from Lieutenant [Retired] Rowley Kennedy, 4th April 1923

FLYING OFFICERS
9

BOXALL Maurice William James F/O 25.06.28 Dismissed
By sentence of General Court Martial [LG 19 July 1928, issue 33402, page 4662]. See my summary for 6th July 1923, and 100 Squadron for details of an accident involving Flying Officer Boxall at Spittlegate.
FERGUSON Dudley Charles Haden F/O 11.12.26 Resigned
FORREST Albert Edmund George F/Lt 14.03.29 Resigned
Returned to the service and was commissioned to the Administrative and Special Duties Branch in the rank of pilot officer 5th September 1939 [LG 19th September 1939, issue 34687, page 6355] and was issued with the service number 73840. S/Ldr 10.02.54 Relinquished
GOUGH William Frederick Rippen F/L 11.04.30 Relinquished
HERRING Herbert Thrower F/L 03.04.30 Relinquished
JAQUES Robin F/O + 08.08.23 100 Squadron
KENNEDY Rowley F/L 07.07.26 Resigned
MacNEAL Alastair Neal F/L + 29.12.26 28 Squadron
STEWART PETER Robert Hugh F/Lt 01.03.27 Resigned

Of the above, five had served with the Royal Navy and four in the Army. Their terms for service was for seven years on the active list.

LG 24 April 1923, issue 32817, page 2970 - Seniority 25th April 1923

FLIGHT LIEUTENANT

WOMBWELL Albert F/Lt 25.04.26 Relinquished
Appointed MBE [LG 6 July 1926, issue 14246, page 763 of the Edinburgh paper].

FLYING OFFICERS
3

17180 CORDES James Brome Lucas Hope F/O 01.04.36 Relinquished
Born on 6th July 1897 and transferring to the RFC on 27th November 1916 from the 2nd Battalion, Gloucester Regiment, Lieutenant James Brome Lucas Hope Cordes reported to 48 Squadron [Bristol F.2b] at Leffrinckhoucke on 29th September 1917. His tour of duty was relatively brief for he was admitted to 24 General Hospital on 12th December 1917 and ten days later sailed for England as a patient aboard HMS *Brighton.*
RIGG* Robert Owen F/Lt + 12.03.27 60 Squadron
17182 SULLOCK AFC Edward Albert W/Cdr 10.02.54 Relinquished
Edward Albert Sullock, born 10th June 1894, a 2nd Lieutenant with the 7th Battalion, King's Liverpool Regiment, joined the RFC on 17th September 1917 and on completion of his training flew SE.5As from various airfields on the Western Front occupied by 60 Squadron from 17th March 1918 until the armistice, and beyond, probably returning to the UK circa February 1919 and joining the unemployed list on 11th April 1919.

* Formerly a Lieutenant [Retired] in the Royal Navy. His term of engagement was for seven years on the active list, commencing 10th April 1923.

LG 1 May 1923, issue 32819, page 3150 - Seniority various dates; terms of engagement five years on the active list

FLYING OFFICERS
3

DAVIS Francis Edward Williams F/O 18.04.32 Relinquished
HIGGS George William F/O 16.04.28 Relinquished
2nd Lieutenant George William Higgs is summarised on page 85 of my first volume when he was injured in the crash of 83 Squadron FE.2b A5605. To this summary I can now add that George was born on 22nd January 1895, possibly in Canada, joining the RFC on 11th October 1916. He joined 83 Squadron prior to the squadron\s deployment to France, crossing the Channel to St. Omer by air on 6th March 1918.

Paul McMillan, my co-author, reports that TNA Kew hold a file on Flying Officer Higgs under AIR 76/226/132 which records his date of birth as 22nd January 1895. Furthermore, Paul is of the opinion that he may have relinquished his commission 'quietly' as, apparently, he was in financial difficulties, this being supported by the following entry in *The London Gazette* 24th April 1928, issue 33378, page 2955:-

ADJUDICATION ANNULLED

HIGGS G W the Aerodrome, Duxford, in the County of Cambridge, an OFFICER in H.M. ROYAL AIR FORCE, and lately residing at 22, Chesterton Hall-crescent, Cambridge.
Court - CAMBRIDGE
No. of Matter_23 of 1927
Date of Adjudication_Jan. 21, 1928
Date of Annulment_April 18, 1928
Grounds of Annulment_That a sufficient sum of money is in the Hands of the Official Receiver to pay 20s in the pound on all claims by the creditors.

PENTLAND MC DFC Alexander Augustus Norman Dudley F/Lt 21.07.30 Relinquished
Born on the 5th of August 1895 Alexander Augustus Norman Dudley Pentland's father was a Major in the Australian Imperial Forces. Joining the RFC 21st February 1916, Alexander's service record shows attachment to three squadrons between 2nd June 1916 [joining 16 Squadron [variants of

the BE.2] at La Gorgue] and 30th July 1917 [19 Squadron [Spad S.13] then at Liëttres]. In between he was attached to 29 Squadron [DH.2/FE.8] from 23rd to 30th June when he was admitted to 7 Stationary Hospital and thence back to England by way of the HS *Jan Breydel.*

Returning to the Western Front and joining 19 Squadron, Alexander was wounded on 26th September 1917 when an artillery shell exploded close to his aircraft, Spad VII B3620 which Trevor Henshaw believes Alexander had scored around seven of his twenty-three combat successes and for which he had been *Gazetted* with the Military Cross, the citation being recorded on the Aerodrome website, which the authors acknowledge. It was initially published in *The London Gazette* on 9th January 1918, supplement 30466, page 635: *"For conspicuous gallantry and devotion to duty. On a recent occasion he flew to and aerodrome fifteen miles behind the enemy lines, descended to within twenty feet of the ground, and fired into eight hostile machines. On his return journey he attacked a train with considerable effect from a low altitude. He has in addition brought down several enemy machines, and has always set a splendid example of fearlessness and devotion to duty in attacking enemy balloons and troops on the ground."*

His nine combat victories with 19 Squadron were encompassed between 20th July and 23rd September 1917 all in the vicinity of the Ypres Salient. I have little doubt that he was hospitalised to the UK following his wounds, he returned to France and between 7th May and 25th August 1918 he scored an additional thirteen victories flying Sopwith 5F.1 Dolphins with 87 Squadron, gaining a DFC which was *Gazetted* on 3rd August 1918, supplement 30827, page 9202: *"A gallant flight commander, who in the last three months has destroyed to enemy machines and driven down four out of control. Recently, whilist on special patrol, he, single-handed, attacked four enemy aeroplanes; having driven down one out of control, he engaged the leader, damaged his engine, and compelled him to glide to his lines. One of the remaining machines followed the leader, but he attacked the other and drove it down in a steep dive."* Referring to his table of victories, I suspect this action took place during the early morning of 18th June 1918 in the vicinity of Arras, his Dolphin on that occasion being C3827 and his two victims Rumpler C two-seater reconnaissance machines.

In its preamble, the compiler of Captain Pentland's aerial service records that his war service began in March 1915 as a machine-gunner with the 12th Light Horse Regiment in Gallipoli where in the September he contracted enteric fever and was shipped to England for treatment.

LG 8 May 1923, issue 32821, page 3316 - Seniority 1st May and 28th April 1923 respectively and terms of service five years on the active list

FLYING OFFICERS
2

17187 HARSTON John W/Cdr 10.02.54 Relinquished

I am reasonably confident that as a 2nd Lieutenant, John Harston flew F.1 Camels with 73 Squadron between 24th July 1918 and the squadron's return to the UK [Yatesbury] in February 1919.

17188 MURRAY John Gordon F/Lt 21.04.37 Relinquished

On account of ill-health [LG 20 April 1937, issue 34390, page 2558]. John Gordon Murray was born on 15th February 1899 and joined the RFC on 23rd March 1917. It seems most of his flying during the *Great War* was confined to collecting and delivering aircraft from 2 Aeroplane Supply Depot at Fienvillers and later from Hesdin.

LG 19 May 1923, issue 32824, page 3533 - Seniority 4th and 16th May 1923 respectively, their terms of service being five and seven years.

FLYING OFFICERS
2

17189 PUMPHREY Frederic Alan F/O 03.07.29 Relinquished

On account of ill-health. Returned to the service and commissioned to the Administrative and Special Duties Branch in the rank of flying officer with effect from 1st September 1939 and with seniority backdated to 1st November 1936 [LG 20 October 1939, issue 34713, page 7043]. His new service number being 75085. W/Cdr 10.02.54 Relinquished

17190 WARD Andrew Augustus F/Lt 10.12.26 Resigned

Born on 2nd February 1896 and joining the RFC on 19th July 1917 little is known of his service but a near unreadable entry on 11th October 1917 suggests he may have been involved with experimental flying.

17191 EAGLE William John F/Lt 07.04.36 Relinquished

LG 22 May 1923, issue 32825, page 3616 - Seniority 9th and 14th May 1923 respectively

FLYING OFFICER

17192 SATTIN Arthur F/O + 27.01.27 405 Flight HMS *Furious*

While attempting to land aboard HMS *Furious*, operating off the Portuguese coast, Flying Officer Arthur Sattin misjudged his landing and went over the side in his Fairey Flycatcher N9916 and, sadly, drowned before help could arrive. Flying Officer Sattin had been attached to 405 Flight for the last three years and on 24th June 1924 when the Fligght was shore based at Leuchars he was slightly injured when his Parnall Panther N7477 crash-landed owing to its engine 'cutting' out. The findings of the Court of Inquiry read as follows: *"The cause of the accident was in our opinion due to engine failure through stoppage of the petrol supply. OC considers that stoppage in petrol flow was caused by pilot making mistake in manipulation of the ..wrance cocks. AOC concurs in opinion of O.Commanding."*

It seems he was a keen rugby football player and during a game on 26th January 1924 he sustained a painful blow to his right leg which required medical treatment.

Although most likely born in England on 8th July 1893, Arthur Sattin emigrated to Canada and on the outbreak of the *Great War* enlisted with, it is believed, the 10th Battalion, Canadian Infantry. Transferring to the RFC of 25th June 1917 he gave his bank details as the Bank of Montreal. On 14th August 1917 he was attached to 55 Squadron [DH.4] at Boisdinghem for observer duties and with his pilot 2nd Lieutenant J H Hedding succeeded in driving down an Albatros D out of control near Thielt in West Vlaanderen on 5th September 1917, their DH being A7579 which was subsequently lost during a bombing raid to Freiburg on 13th March 1918, 2nd Lieutenant T S Wilson captured in a wounded state while 2nd Lieutenant L Cann, his observer, being killed.

17193 GILES Richard Howard F/O 14.05.32 Relinquished

LG 29 May 1923, issue 32828, page 3753 - Seniority 14th May 1923 and terms of engagement seven years on the active list; the seniority of the Pilot Officers was also effective from 14th May 1923. The single asterisk denotes previous RN service and the double asterisk against Flying Officer Knocker indicates he was attached as Lieutenant to the Indian Army.

Block 17194 to 17202 and Block 17203 to 1712

FLYING OFFICERS
9

17194	BERTHON*	Henri Jacques Maurice	F/O		17.02.26	Resigned
17195	GEORGE	Sandys Parker	F/Lt		14.05.30	Relinquished
17196	HOWELL*	Herbert Roy Bond	F/Lt		10.04.37	Relinquished
17197	KNOCKER**	John Bedingfield	F/O		19.04.27	Resigned
17198	McCLINTOCK*	Geoffrey	F/O		05.11.24	Resigned
17199	PHILLIPS*	Leonard William Hennell	F/O	+	12.07.27	403 Flight HMS *Hermes*

Flying Officer Leonard William Hennell Phillips was killed when his Fairey Flycatcher N9910 crashed into the water off Chang Chan Island in Hong Kong harbour.

17200 SMITH DCM Harold Victor F/O 14.05.30 Relinquished
17201 SMYTHIES* Francis Palmer W/Cdr 29.07.46 Retirement
17202 STIRLING WEBB Oswald Kempson F/O + 26.07.26 45 Squadron

17203 BOSTON Frank F/Lt 08.08.34 Relinquished
On account of ill-health but resumed his service with effect from 6th July 1938 and continued to serve throughout the Second World War.
17204 BUCHANAN Angus Ross F/O 30.09.25 Resigned
17205 COZENS Henry Iliffe A/Cmdr 12.09.56 Retirement
Air Commodore Henry Iliffe Cozens CB AFC mentioned in despatches, died on Friday, 21st June 1995. As a squadron leader he took over command of 19 Squadron at Duxford on 18th December 1937. At the time '41' was equipped with Gauntlet as was 66 Squadron, also based at Duxford. Through the grapevine Squadron Leader Cozens heard that their rivals were earmarked to received the first examples of Supermarine's brilliant new fighter, the Spitfire. Determined to be the first, Henry Cozens pulled enough strings in the Air Ministry to ensure that '19' would be the first and this duly materialised on 4th August 1938 with the acceptance of K9789 and K9790 WZ-N. Subsequently, 66 Squadron commanded by Squadron Leader J L F Fuller-Good received their first Spitfires on 31st October 1938 with the arrival of K9802 and K9810 RB-S. On 3rd May 1943 and now a group captain, Henry Cozens arrived at RAF Hemswell to take command of the station and it was during his tenure that he made the only colour film of Lancasters on night operation - appropriately it was titled *'Night Bombers'* and is currently available on video. In conclusion, when ranked Flight Lieutenant he was attached from 2nd July 1930 to 2nd November 1931 to the British Arctic Air Route Expedition for which he was *Gazetted* with the Polar Medal on 1st November 1932. For further information regarding this officer, please consult the Air of Authority - A History of RAF Organisation website from which I have been able to extract some of the detail here reported.
17206 HOOKE Douglas Thomas Howard P/O 09.12.25 Relinquished
On account of ill-health [LG 8 December 1925, issue 33112, page 8131]. However, his general well being improved and he returned to the service and on 9th November 1939 he was commissioned within the Equipment Branch as a pilot officer for the duration of hostilities and issued with the service number 75785 [LG 28 November 1939, issue 34742, page 7967]. S/Ldr 10.02.54 Relinquished
17207 LEWIS Alfred Spencer F/O 09.11.28 Relinquished
On transfer to the Indian Army [LG 13 November 1928, issue 33438, page 7390].
17208 PLEDGER Jack Hamilton P/O + 04.04.24 1 FTS Netheravon
Pilot Officer Jack Hamilton Pledger was killed in the final stages of his flying training when, flying solo, his Bristol F.2b D7816 caught fire and dived to the ground near West Kennett, 5 miles W of Marlborough, Wiltshire, the time being noted as around 1530 hours. The Court of Inquiry reported:
"Some unknown mechanical defect which caused the machine to catch fire in the air."
17209 POCOCK James Reginald F/O 14.04.33 Relinquished
Returned to the service, transferring from the General Duties Branch to the Equipment Branch, his service number amended to 72163.
17210 SCHOFIELD Harry Methuen F/Lt 14.05.37 Class C
At the time of Flight Lieutenant Harry Methuen Schofield's transfer to class C of the Reserve he was employed by General Aircraft Limited as their Chief Test Pilot. His biography may be accessed on *Wikipedia* where it is noted he was a member of the 1927 Schneider Trophy Team while in July 1934 and now employed by GAL he won the King's Cup Race in a GAL Monospar ST-10 registered was G-ACTS. During his flying career he suffered a number of head injuries which, subsequently, ended his days as a test pilot. Turning to farming he to suffer a massive stroke from which left him incapacitated. He died in December 1955 and was cremated at Putney Vale Crematorium.
17211 TAAFFE Rudolph Trevor G/Capt 21.09.51 Retirement
17212 WILTSHIRE Norman James F/O 17.06.36 Relinquished
Flying Officer Norman James Wiltshire was commissioned in his rank to the Royal Air Force Volunteer Reserve, General Duties Branch, on 28th November 1940 and issued with the service number 88401 [LG 31 December 1940, issue 35028, page 7299]. He served throughout the Second World War and beyond. F/Lt 10.02.54 Relinquished

LG 5 June 1923, issue 32831, page 3978 - Seniority 22nd May 1923

FLYING OFFICER

17213 McKINNON James Urquhart F/O 01.09.25 Resigned
Returned to the service and was granted a commission in the Administrative and Special Duties Branch as a probationary Pilot Officer on 3rd March 1940 [LG 26 March 1940, issue 34827, page 1782]. S/Ldr 10.02.54 Relinquished

LG 12 June 1923, issue 32833, page 4142 - Seniority 1st June 1923

FLYING OFFICER

17214 WEEDON Lionel Hanks F/O 18.05.28 Resigned

LG 19 June 1923, issue 32835, page 4279 - Seniority various dates

Block 17214 to 17220

FLYING OFFICERS

6

17215 BUTLER Leonard F/O + 18.05.29 The Irving Air Chute Co
Flying Officer Leonard Butler while in the Reserve of Air Force Officers and whilst in the employment of The Irving Air Chute Company was flying with the registered owner, Hilbert Gustave Hamer, in DH.60X Moth G-EBUW and according to eyewitnesses Flying Officer Butler performed a couple of aerobatic loops when the engine "shut off" and the Moth spiralled nose first into the ground. The accident happened at Odsey a Cambridgeshire village roughly mid-distance between Baldock and Royston. The Aviation Safety Network website, which the authors dutifully acknowledge, states that Mr. Hamer was the son of the Chief Constable of Barnsley and that the DH was a replacement for G-EBNX. A fortnight before his death, Flying Officer Butler was *Gazetted* in the June 4th, Edinburgh edition of the paper with the Air Force Cross, issue 14553, page 580.
17216 CUMMINGS AFC Eric Douglas W/Cdr 10.02.54 Relinquished
17217 DAVID Howell Vernon F/O 07.06.29 Relinquished
On account of ill-health [LG 11 June 1929, issue 33505, page 3864].
17218 LEE Owen Vincent F/O 12.06.32 Relinquished
Held the ranl of Captai commissioned to the Royal Fusiliers, Reserve of Royal Army Officers.
17219 PENNY Claud Edmund Clayton F/Lt 06.06.32 Relinquished
17220 POOL Bernard George
Flying Officer Bernard George Pool transferred from the General Duties Branch to the Stores Branch on 28th April 1928 [LG 8 May 1928, issue 33382, page 3251] and was issued with the service number 21129. W/Cdr 29.03.55 Retirement
I believe Bernard George Pool to be 'F/O B G Pool' of 207 Squadron who was seriously injured in the crash of DH.9A J7112 [see my summary for 25th April 1925 for details]. During the *Great War* he was attached to 49 Squadron and was wounded during operations on 2nd October 1918, his observer 2nd Lieutenant W A Greig escaping unharmed. Their DH.9 F6125 [C6195 rebuilt] landed safely and was later exchanged for a DH.9A.

Meanwhile, 2nd Lieutenant Pool following treatment at 12 Stationary Hospital and later at 3 General Hospital was sent back to England aboard HMHS *Grantley* Castle. I very much suspect the injuries sustained on 25th April 1925 was the precursor for his transfer to the Stores Branch..

LG 26 June 1923, issue 32837, page 4436 - Seniority 14th June 1923

FLYING OFFICERS
2

17221 MONEY Robert Raymond F/O 14.06.32 Relinquished
From the Royal Air Force Reserve though his relinquishment entry [LG 14 June 1932, issue 33835, page 3876] notes that he was a Lieutenant in the East Yorkshire Regiment, Reserve of Army Officers, as, indeed, he was. Posted to 12 Squadron at Avesnes-le-Comte on 17th August 1916 he was taken prisoner of war the following month when on 17th September his BE.2c 2741 received a direct hit from anti-aircraft fire which, as Trevor Henshaw reports, took away the lower part of the engine. In the ensuring forced-landing he was slightly injured.

17222 PUDNEY Walter Godfrey F/O 31.05.28 Resigned
Posted to 22 Squadron [Bristol F.2b] at Estrée Blanche on 4th November 1917 his tour of duty appears to have ended on the 3rd of March 1918 when he was taken to 24 General Hospital. Eight days later he was sent back to England as a patient aboard HMHS *Newhaven.*

LG 17 July 1923, issue 32845, page 4925 - Seniority 4th July 1923

FLYING OFFICER

COWAN Willard Edwin F/O 29.11.27 Removed from the Service
Canada As promulgated in *The London Gazette* 6th December 1927, issue 33335, page 7825. Born on 8th January 1898 Willard Edwin Cowan joined the RAF on the merger of the RNAS, where he had been flying F.1 Camels with 8 Squadron RNAS, and the RFC. He is summarised in my first volume on page 153 at which time 8 Squadron RNAS had become 208 Squadron of the Royal Air Force.

LG 24 July 1923, issue 32847, page 5074 - Seniority various dates

This issue reported a variety of short service commissions including retired RN and Indian Army personnel, these officers being granted commissions for seven years of the active list and I will list their names first with an asterisk indicating former RN officers. All were ranked as Flying Officer.

ANDERSON George
BATES* Albert Wentworth F/Lt 14.07.30 Relinquished
BURROWS* Henry Montagu F/Lt 28.09.25 Resigned
CAVIS-BROWN* Geoffrey Ashton F/Lt + 04.09.25 RAF Gosport
Honorary Flight Lieutenant Geoffrey Ashton Cavis-Brown was killed when his Blackburn N9827 went out of control and spun in at Lee-on-Solent. The previous year on 13th October 1924 he escaped unhurt after failing to flatten out whilst landing in Avro Bison N9599. His death was reported on Thursday, September 10th, 1925, in the *South of England Advertiser: Sussex, Surrey, Hampshire and Kent* under Gosport news:

"The Coroner for South Hants., Mr. Leonard Warner, sitting without a jury, held an inquest at the Royal Naval Hospital on Monday concerning the death of Hon. Flight-Lieut. Geoffrey Ashton Cavis-Brown, who succumbed to injuries received while flying near the Lee Golf Links on Friday. Flight-Lieut. John Henry Alexander McNab, RAF, stationed at Fort Grange, said that while on the Lee Golf Links he noticed that the machine in question was flying on an even keel at a height of about 2,o000ft; a moment later he noticed that the machine was in a slow left-hand flat spin, which was checked by the pilot at about 70ft from the ground. The machine was then head on, and continued to nose dive until it disappeared from view behind some trees and crashed. He could only imagine that the spin started through loss of flying speed, which might have been caused by the stalling of the machine possibly on the turn. Lieut. George Francis Bradford, RN, stationed at Fort Grange, said that on Friday afternoon he took the machine out immediately before deceased went up. It was a Blacburn Fleet Spotter. Before witness took the machine out it was thoroughly tested. He took it for a trial at the request of the deceased officer, who had not much experience on this type machine, although he had been out with the aeroplane in question in the morning. Witness carried passengers, but deceased was not allowed to do so, and the machine was ballasted. In reply to the Coroner, witness stated that this particular machine was easy to fly in some respects, but it required "knowing." It was a heavy machine, and, therefore, more difficult get out of a spin than a fighter type. He imagined it would be difficult to get out of a spin at a height of 600ft. William Henry Taylor, …… rigger RAF, Fort Grange, who examined the machine before the flight in questions, said it was in good order, and deceased signed the document agreeing that it was alright. Lieut. James MacCammell Kilpatrick, Medical Services of the RAF, said he was on the spot immediately after the accident. Deceased, who had been removed from the machine, was dying from shock due to multiple injuries, the chief of which was fracture of the skull. The Coroner, in recording a verdict of "Accidental death," said it was more than two years since he had had to inquire into a similar accident. He felt grieved that a young officer should lose his life in this way, and he offered sincere sympathy to the relatives."

CROXFORD* DSC Charles Wilfred F/Lt 14.07.30 Relinquished
FLEMING Robert Stevenson Tristram F/Lt 28.10.25 Relinquished
On account of ill-health [LG 27 October 1925, issue 33096, page 6923].

GARVIE Kenneth Clephan F/O 19.07.30 Relinquished
During his service he was attached to 30 Squadron and while taking off from Hinaidi in DH.9A E8513 collieded with Bristol F.2b J7622 which was parked on the airfield [see my summary for the date in question].

18004 JOHNSON* John Charles Eric Arnott W/Cdr 24.03.43 Retired list
Wing Commander John Charles Eric Arnott Johnson died on Sunday, 18th December 1983.

LAWRIE* Frederick Bernard F/Lt 30.09.26 Resigned
18013 RIPPON Percy Ivor Vincent F/Lt 18.07.30 Relinquished
He returned to the service during the Second World War and was commissioned as a pilot officer, his new service number being 78777. However, he relinquished his commission owing to ill-health on 5th August 1940. According to Amazon, Percy Ivor Vincent Rippon wrote and had published in 1933 a book titled *Air Force Law in a Nutshell.*

ROSE* Richard Edgar Bryant F/Lt 09.07.30 Relinquished

Three Flying Officers were granted commissions, one being noted as on probation, followed by thirty-one Pilot Officers, all on probation and, I suspect, apart from one, fresh to military service - Seniority various dates

FLYING OFFICERS
3

BUCHANAN Donald Seafield F/O 28.05.24 Relinquished
On account of ill-health [LG 27 May 1924, issue 32939, page 4204]. Believed to be ex-Indian Army Reserve of Officers and 23 Squadron [Spad S.7] twixt 2nd June and 7th July 1917 when he was wounded and returned to the UK aboard HMHS *St. David.*

OULD John Vander F/O 09.04.24 Relinquished
On account of ill-health [LG 8 April 1924, issue 32925, page 2924].

WILLIAMS William Cay F/O + 16.09.25 2 FTS Digby

Flying Officer William Cay Williams and his pupil, Pilot Officer Frederick Martin Kellaway,*who was at the controls, perished when their Bristol F.2b F4485 spun and crashed near Branston, Lincolnshire. Reports from the subsequent in quest were reported by *The Courier* On Friday, September 18th, 1925: *'Officers' Deaths in 'Plane Smash - Inquest Stories'*

"At the inquest yesterday at Cranwell Hospital, Lincs., on Flying Officer William Cay Williams, [32], and Pilot Officer Frederick Martin Kellaway, [29], who were killed in a flying accident near Digby on Wednesday, Flight-Lieut. Anderson, adjutant of No. 2 Flying School, Digby, said the machine, a Bristol Fighter, was inspected on the morning of the accident and found to be in perfect order. It made a flight before being taken up by the deceased officers. The latter were flying for thirty minutes before they crashed.

"A horseman employed on a farm said the machine was about 2,000 feet up when in making a turn it got into a spin and fell, rebounding after hitting the ground. Witness found one of the occupants dead by the machine and the other near it still alive.

"Medical evidences showed Kellawy died instantly from a fractured skull and other injuries. Williams succumbed an hour later. The last named was instructing Kellaway.

"Impossible to say what caused the accident, the Coroner recorded a verdict of accidental death."

* Please refer to Appendix D 1925, and the names of officers commissioned on 27th January 1925, for details regarding Pilot Officer Kellaway.

ADDAMS Anthony Clifford F/O + 16.06.26 41 Squadron
BAILLIE Arthur Douglas P/O + 15.09.24 17 Squadron
17231 BARRETT Ralph F/O 28.03.32 Relinquished

On his return to the service in the Second World War he received a commission in the Royal Air Force Volunteer Reserve, though retaining his original service number. S/Ldr + 31.12.53

Squadron Leader Ralph Radcliffe died in the Radcliffe Infirmary, Radcliffe, Oxfordshire three weeks and a day after his 54th birthday. Paul McMillan, co-author, suspects that at the time he was still a serving officer.

BIBBY Richard Henry F/O 15.04.32 Relinquished
BURNETT Yvon William F/O + 18.03.29 47 Squadron
CATZ Joseph P/O + 17.12.23 4 FTS Abu Sueir

Spun into the ground during a solo flight in Avro 504K E1772 on Monday 17th December 1923. Although not the first fatality since the formation of No. 4 FTS Abu Sueir on the 1st of April 1921, I believe Pilot Officer Joseph Catz was first probationary officer to lose his life in a flying accident at this flying school. He was 25 years of age.

17241 CHICHESTER Patrick George G/Capt 15.09.47 Retirement
17242 COLQUHOUN James Woods G/Capt 01.12.52 Retirement

At own request [LG 1 January 1953, supplement 39739, page 57].

17243 DAVIES Hugh Norman F/Lt 09.10.32 Relinquished

On appointment to a commission in the South African Air Force [LG 6 June 1933, issue 33947, page 3828].

17244 DAWE Henry Stuart F/Lt 06.05.37 Relinquished
17245 DICK John Stewart F/Lt 07.03.47 Resigned
EVERETT Arthur George P/O 21.05.24 Terminated
GAIN Douglas Elphinstone P/O + 04.12.24 CFS Upavon

Spun into the ground while making a gliding turn 1145 near the airfield in Avro 504K E6671, Douglas Elphingstone Gain died from his injuries 24-hours following the crash. His passenger, Aircraftman Denham Brown Waight was found with only slight injuries. The findings of the Court of Inquiry read: *"The cause of the accident was in our opinion that the pilot in making a gliding turn lost flying speed thereby stalling the a/c and spinning into the ground before he could regain control. It is considered that the accident was due to lack of experience on the part of the pilot.*

"O/C CFS .. Group concurs in finding of Court except second part. AOC concurs."

At this point in his flying, Pilot Officer Gain's total solo experience was noted as seventy-seven and a half hours, of which forty five hours were on Avro 504 variants.

A brief report beneath the heading *'RAF Officer Killed - Fatal Smash at Flying School'* was published in *The Edinburgh Evening News* in its edition of Friday, December 5th, 1924: *"Pilot Officer Douglas Elphinstone Gain died yesterday from injuries received in an air accident at Upavon on the previous day.*

"The announcement is made by the Air Ministry, which states that the machine involved was of the Avro type, and belonged to the RAF Central Flying School. Aircraftman instructor [sic] *Denholm Brown Waight was slightly injured."*

GAYNOR George James

Flying Officer George James Gaynor was transferred, in his rank, from the General Duties Branch to the Stores Branch on 21st May 1927 [LG 31st May 1927, issue 33279, page 3535]. His new service number was 21022. W/Cdr 21.08.47 Retirement

GODWIN Dudley Ernest F/O 04.08.26 Relinquished

On account of ill-health [LG 3 August 1926, issue 33188, page 5131].

GOUGH Henry Leslie Raymond F/O 14.07.32 Relinquished
18003 JENNINGS Frederick Godfrey Lt-Cdr + 02.07.41 768 Squadron FAA

Flight Lieutenant Frederick Godfrey Jennings was transferred to the Reserve Class A on 15th July 1933 [LG 18 July 1933, issue 33961, page 4805]. My co-author reports that with effect from 15th July 1937 his Class A reserve was extended by four years and it would appear it was during this time he transferred to the Fleet Air Arm for at the time of his death he was a Lieutenant-Commander attached to 768 Squadron based at RNAS Arbroath [HMS *Condor*]. On the day of his death he had taken off in Grumman Martlet I BJ558 for an air test only for the fighter's engine to fail which resulted in the Martlet diving into the sea some 220 yards east of Cuthlie Station, Abirlot a village 2 miles to the west of Arbroath; he is buried in Arbroath Western Cemetery.

MACKENZIE- Campbell F/O + 09.11.27 RAE Farnborough

RICHARD Flying Officer Campbell MacKenzie-Richard lost his life during a night experimental flight testing a navigational device in Bristol F.2b C810. Accompanying him was Professor Harry Norman Green, the test commencing from Croydon. Subsequently, the crew became uncertain of their position and with the Bristol's fuel running low both took to their parachutes. Professor Green landed safely, but Flying Officer Mackenzie-Richard was found, dead, in a field at Tilkhurst on the outskirts of East Grinstead, Surrey. For a detailed explanation of the accident and the life of Flying Officer Mackenzie-Richard who during the *Great War* served with distinction in the Merchant Navy, please refer to his biography reported by *Wikipedia*.

MARTIN MC Eric P/O + 02.05.24 2 FTS Duxford

As 2nd Lieutenant Eric Martin, attached to the London Regiment, he was *Gazetted* with the MC on 25th August 1917, supplement 30251, page 8813: *"For conspicuous gallantry and devotion to duty. With great gallantry he repeatedly led bombing attacks agains the enemy, only desisting when all his party had been either killed or wounded. He was wounded himself, but brought back information of great value, having set a magnificent example to his men."* Sadly, Eric Martin died while undergoing pilot training at Duxford when his Bristol F.2b F4485 in which he was accompanied by Pilot Officer John Frederick Young [who was unhurt] came into collision with Avro 504K F8945, details of which have not been reported. Pilot Officer Young was short service commissioned early in 1924 [LG 29 January 1924, issue 32902, page 875].

The accident that took his life occurred at around 1535, the Findings of the Court of Inquiry being recorded as: *"The cause of the accident was in our opinion due to the inattention of both pilots with regard to the 'blind spots' of their respective aircraft, & in the case of the Bristol Fighter possibly the fact that the Avro was in line with the sun. The onus in giving way lay with the Bristol Fighter [vide KR. Appdx 1, para* [possibly 28*].*

"AOC concurs & does not consider that blame can be attributed to either of the pilot."

	MOLLISON	James Allan	F/O	08.06.28	Removed

Flying Officer James Allan Mollison was removed from the service, three months after being transferred to the Reserve class C, the removal notice being *Gazetted* 12th June 1928, issue 33393, page 4023.

18009	MOON	Arthur Graham	F/O	01.06.32	Relinquished
18010	NEW	John William	W/Cdr	10.02.54	Relinquished
	PERRY	Arthur Raymond	F/O	06.07.27	Relinquished

On account of ill-health [LG 15 October 1929, issue 33543, page 6551].

18015	SELBY-LOWNDES	Geoffrey Howard William	S/Ldr	08.09.53	Relinquished

On appointment to a short service commission in the RAF [LG 20 October 1953, supplement 39990, page 5574].

18016	STROUD	Patrick Roberts			
18017	SUNNUCKS	Stephen Reginald	F/Lt	27.11.40	Relinquished

At his own request and to be transferred from the Administrative and Special Duties Branch to the General Duties Branch in the rank of flying officer [LG 21 October 1940, issue 35319, page 6121]. S/Ldr 01.02.45 Relinquished

On ceasing to be employed and transfer to the RCAF [LG 6 February 1945, supplement 36923, page 749].

18018	SYKES	Joseph Talbot	P/O	10.01.24	Resigned
18019	TROUP	Charles Roy	F/O	07.05.32	Relinquished

Paul McMillan has discovered some fascinating information regarding Flying Officer Charles Roy Troup [he was born in West Ham on the last day of July 1903]. After leaving the service he emigrated to Canada, but prior to this, and while still serving, his name crops up in *The London Gazette* 13th March 1925:-

No. 1,039 TROUP, Charles Roy, RAF Depot, Uxbridge, in the County of Middlesex
Court_WINDSOR
Date of Filing Petition_Feb. 14, 1925
No. of Matter_4 of 1925
Date of Receiving Order_March 10, 1925
No. of Receiving Order_5
Whether Debtor's or Creditor's Petition_Creditor's
Act of Bankruptcy proved in Creditor's Petition_Section1-1 [G], Bankruptcy Act, 1914

This is followed over the next two years with seven entries, all pertaining to the above, before *The London Gazette* 11th November 1927, issue 33328, page 7258 reports:-

TROUP, Charles Roy, RAF Depot, Uxbridge, in the County of Middlesex
Court_WINDSOR
No. of Matter_4 of 1925
Trustee's Name, Address and Description_Gourlay, Thomas, 29 Russell-square, London, WC.1, Official Receiver
Date of Release_Nov. 3, 1927

Now in Canada his name crops up in Ted Barris's *Behind the Glory : Canada's Role in the Allied Air War* published by Thomas Allen, 2010:

"Calls went out to a couple of commercial pilots flying in Quebec - Charles Roy Troup and Walter Woollett. "Pter" Troup had served in the RAF's peacetime No. 39 Bomber Squadron but had resigned his commission, emigrated to Canada, and pursued a career in Quebec's bush country with Fairchild Aviation. Not long thereafter, "Babe" Woollett did the same, leaving No. 29 RAF Fighter Squadron to seek his fortune at Fairchild in Canada.

"Between them, Troup and Woollett did every conceivable kind of flying in the 1920s and 1930s. Troup raced seaplanes at the Canadian National Exhibition and led the Trans Canada Air Tour of eight Bellanca aircraft as part of a sales promotion. Woollett flew some of the first survey crews into northern Quebec and Labrador, flew an international mail route, and led countless rescue missions, including one to locate and retrieve his friend "Peter" Troup. But the greatest of their collaberations cast Troup and Woollett as co-designers of the BCATP Air Observer Schools, right after war was declared.

"By New Year's Day 1941, the Troup/Woollett-managed Dominion Skyways Training School [and three others up and running in Edmonton, Regina and London] had graduated 115 air observers, who, unlike Woollett on his first solo, could guide an aircraft home."

In recognition of his part in setting up these Observer Schools, Walter Woollett was included in the long list of names whom *"The KING has been graciously pleased on the occasion of Dominion Day in Canada, and on the advice of His Majesty's Canadian Ministers, to give orders for the following appointments to the Most Distinguished Order of Saint Michael and Saint George."* And within the section *"To be additional Officers of the Civil Division of the said Most Excellent Order:- Walter Woollett, Esq. , No. 9 Air Observer's School, St. John's, Quebec."* [LG 1 July 1946, supplement 37633, page 3343].

Although it has to be conjecture on my part, was his previous bankruptcy a factor that prevented Charles Roy Troup from being similarly honoured?

18020	WHEATLEY	Terence Richard	S/Ldr	10.02.54	Relinquished
18021	WING	Eric Charles Allen	F/O	04.02.36	Relinquished

Returned to the service and granted a commission in the Administrative and Special Duties Branch [LG 5 November 1940, issue 34986, page 6401] with effect from 11th October 1940 as a pilot officer. W/Cdr 10.02.54 Relinquished

18022	WRIGHT	Harold Marshall Stanley	G/Capt	29.10.50	Retirement

At his own request [LG 21 November 1950, supplement 39071, page 5815].

LG 31 July 1923. Issue 32849, page 5244 - Seniority 18th July 1923

18023	MITCHELMORE	Henry Douglas	S/Ldr	17.02.47	Resigned

LG 7 August 1923, issue 32851, page 5431 - Seniority 23rd July 1923

	LANGDON	William Frederick	A/Cmdr	14.02.55	Retirement

William Frederick Langdon was formerly a flying officer. Although commissioned to the General Duties Branch by 1st April 1932 he had been transferred to the Stores Branch and promoted flight lieutenant [LG 5 April 1932, issue 33814, page 2218]. His amended service number was now 21049 and he was promoted wing commander on 11th March 1940 [LG 16 April 1940, issue 34831, page 2248].

The Air of Authority website shows his birth as 11th February 1898 and his military service starting in September 1915 as a Seaman in the 1st Battalion, Royal Naval Division, subsequently transferring to the 6th Battalion ahead of war service during which he received a commission on 29th August 1917 in the RNVR for service with the 63rd Division. A qualified machine gunner he was wounded in action on 29th September 1918, being admitted to No. 2 Stationary Hospital at Abbeville with a gunshot wound to the pelvis and hand. Sent back to England the *Great War* was over before he was passed fit to resume duty on 27th November 1918.

Following his short service commission he trained at 5 FTS Shotwick, joining 14 Squadron [Bristol F.2b] at Amman on 4th April 1925, this being his one and only flying appointment before the above mentioned transfer.

Air Commodore William Frederick Langdon CBE, died on Thursday, 22nd July 1976.

LG 14 August 1923, issue 32853, page 5559 - Seniority 4th and 3rd August respectively

FLYING OFFICERS
2

18026 BROWN DFC John Renwick S/Ldr 10.02.54 Relinquished
Born 24th August 1897 as 2nd Lieutenant John Renwick Brown he was attached to 9 Squadron [RE.8/Bristol F.2b] from 16th July 1918 until 19th March 1919 when he was admitted to 14 General Hospital with an undisclosed illness which resulted in his return to England on 26th March 1919 as a patient on HMS *St. Andrew.* Meanwhile, his DFC, less citation, had been *Gazetted* on 7th February 1919, issue 31170, page 2036.

CONNOLLY Albert Edward W/Cdr 16.07.53 Retirement
Subsequently transferred from the General Duties Branch to the Stores Branch, his new service number being 21099. His retirement was at his own request [LG 14 August 1953, supplement 39940, page 4478].

LG 24 August 1923, issue 32856, page 5768 - Seniority 8th and 5th August; terms of engagement seven and five years respectively

FLYING OFFICER

18027 CAIRNES Douglas Stein F/Lt 08.07.32 Relinquished
Formerly a Captain in the Rifle Brigade. As Captain Douglas Stein of the Regular Army Reserve of Officers he was commissioned in the Admin-Istrative and Special Duties Branch with effect from 1st September 1939 [LG 20 October 1939, issue 34713, page 7045], his service number now being 75087 but by the time of his leaving the service he had reverted to 18027; S/Ldr 10.02.54 Relinquished

LIVOCK Arthur Henry Denzil F/O 20.05.27 Relinquished
On account of ill-health [LG 17 May 1927, issue 33275, page 3210]. With an overall improvement in his well being, he returned to the service and was granted a commission as a probationary Pilot Officer in the Administrative and Special Duties Branch on 16th January 1940, his amended service number now being 77243 [LG 6 February 1940, issue 34786, page 722]. W/Cdr 10.02.54 Relinquished

LG 28 August 1928, issue 32857, page 5844 - Seniority 20th and 15th August 1923 respectively

FLYING OFFICERS
2

18092 FARRINGTON MC Frank Cecil S/Ldr 10.02.54 Relinquished
Lieutenant in the Regular Army Reserve of Officers though in the Great War he had transferred from the Royal Artillery to the Royal Air Force*and it was with the latter that he was honoured with the MC: *"For conspicuous gallantry and devotion to duty. On several occasions during heavy hostile attacks he has sent down calls to the artillery to engage hostile infantry forming up for attack. Thanks to his skill in discovering enemy formations, and to his speed in communicating the requisite information to the artillery, the most severe casualties were inflicted on the enemy, the failure of their attacks being largely due to his splendid work. On numerous other occasions his work has proved of exceptional value, and he has at all times set a magnificent example to all ranks of his squadron."* [LG 26 July 1918, supplement 30813, page 8798].

* Born 10th September 1891 Frank Cecil Farrington was serving with the 291st Brigade RFA when he was accepted for training as an observer. The date of his acceptance by the RFC is shown as 23rd August 1917 and his excellent work was carried while attached to 13 Squadron [RE.8] between 24th October 1917 and 7th April 1918 when he was posted to 'Home Establishment.'

18030 WOOLLIAMS Frank Hawker F/O 16.01.64 Relinquished
By which time he was serving in the Training Branch of the Royal Air Force Volunteer Reserve.

LG 4 September 1923, issue 32859, page 5993 - Seniority 22nd August 1923

FLYING OFFICERS
2

18031 FARNAN Charless Henry Alcroft S/Ldr 26.05.47 Resigned
18032 STOCKS Stanley John F/Lt + 17.07.51

The London Gazette London of 24th December 1937, issue 34466 page 8071 carried the following notice in respect of Stanley John Stocks RAFO

Whitehall, December 24, 1937.

The KING has been pleased to give and grant the undermentioned gentlemen His Majesty's Royal licence to wear Decorations conferred upon them by His Majesty the King of Egypt, in recognition of valuable services rendered by them in the employment of the Egyptian Government:-

ORDER OF THE NILE

Insignia of Officer

Flight Lieutenant Stanley John Stocks RAFO

Although his death occurred in the Australian State of Victoria, Paul McMillan believe he was still in the Reserve of Air Force Officers. My co-author also reports that AIR 76/486/63 records his date of birth as 14th November 1891 and by 1939 was residing in Stockport, Lancashire and employed as an Aeronautical Engineer.

His name and service number appear in the post Second World War Air Force Lists, and following his death *The Herald* [a Melbourne newspaper] published on Saturday, 28th July 1951 that Major Stanley John Stocks, Director General of Civil Aviation for Pakistan will, following a service, be cremated in the Springvale Crematorium.

In the year before his death, and in his capacity of Inspector of Accidents, he attended the Court at Burnham in Berkshire where Fairflight Limited of Deepwood House, Farnham, Royal Berkshire was being prosecuted in connection with the loss on 12th March 1950 of Avro Tudor 5 G-AKBY *Star Girl* which had been chartered by rugby fans to take them to Dublin for the Five Nations Championship match between Ireland and Wales. On the return flight to RAF Llandow the Tudor was approaching runway 28 and had descended to approximately 150 feet when eyewitnesses describe hearing an increase in the engine noise followed by the airliner climbing at a steep angle of attack to around 300 feet whereupon it stalled, veered to the right and moments later it struck the ground, the starboard wing taking the impact. It was down in a field near Park Farm in the hamlet of Sigingstone. All five members of crew perished but of the seventy-eight passengers three who were seated at the rear of the fuselage escaped almost without injury.

The prosecution of Fairflight, as reported in *The Courier and Advertiser* on November 2nd, 1950, had been brought by the Ministry of Civil Aviation for contravening the conditions under which a certificate of airworthiness was issued for a Tudor aircraft. The key factor hinged on the loading of the passengers luggage when the aircraft was on the ground at Dublin and its alleged incorrect stowage which shifted the Tudor's centre of gravity by as much as thirteen inches out of the accepted norm.

I am not able to be 100 percent certain, but I believe Stanley John Stocks served with 40 Squadron [Nieuport 17] during the *Great War.* His Casualty Form - Officers indicates he was first commissioned to the South Lancashire Regiment - Special Reserve [this would be in line with the report that in 1939 he was residing in Stockport] and that following his transfer to the RFC and training as a pilot, he joined '40' at Treizennes on 15th March 1917.

A week later on the 22nd he was wounded in action while flying Nieuport 17 A6679, this being reported on page 17 of David Gunby's excellent history of the squadron, where he writes *"... was shot in the stomach during a clash with enemy scouts. Besides his wound he had to cope with a holed petrol tank and a dead engine, but the Nieuport did not catch fire and Stocks was able to forced-land safely."*

Following emergency treatment in 13 General Field Hospital he was evacuated to England aboard the HS *Stad Antwerpen* on 8th April 1917.

LG 11 September 1923, issue 32861, page 6137 - Seniority 31st, 29th and 30th August respectively

FLYING OFFICERS
3

18033 DUNCANSON Robert F/O 31.08.23 Resigned

The London Gazette 16th July 1929, issue 33517, page 4705 shows promotion to Flight Lieutenant with effect from 17th July 1929. Thence serving until: F/Lt 31.08.37 Relinquished

Returned to the service and commissioned as a pilot officer in the Royal Air Force Volunteer Reserve, General Duties Branch, 15th August 1942 [LG 6th October 1942, supplement 35731, page 4343]. F/O 15.06.46 Resigned

Born on 20th May 1896 and joining the RFC on 18th June 1917 his *Great War* flying appears to have been restricted to six weeks work on the myriad of tasks carried out by the RE.8s of 52 Squadron between 1st March and 18th April 1918 when he accidentally fractured the frac radius bone in his right wrist. First treated in 2 Stationary Hospital he was despatched to the UK on 23rd April 1918 aboard HS *Pieter de Coninck*.

18034 HADOW MC Douglas Patrick F/O 21.09.25 Dismissed

By sentence of General Court Martial [LG 6 October 1925, issue 33090, page 6421]. Before this fall from grace it should be noted that of the 1st Battalion, Northumberland Fusiliers, attached to 3rd Division, Douglas Patrick Hadow [born 28th February 1896] transferred to the RFC on 12th March 1917 and as an observer flew with 42 Squadron [RE.8] from various Western Front aerodromes between 18th July 1917 to 18th April 1918 when he was posted to 'Home Establishment.'

His MC was gained whilst serving with the Fusiliers and was *Gazetted* on 25th November 1916, supplement 29837, page 11536: *"For conspicuous gallantry in action. He led a raid against the enemy with great courage and determination. He set a splendid example to his men."*

18035 WILSON Laurance Farrell F/O + 07.11.23 CFS Upavon

Just two months after his return to the service, and probably while undergoing refresher flying at the Central Flying School, Flying Officer Laurance Farrell Wilson was killed when during an aerobatics exercise the wings of his 7F.1 Snipe F2492 collapsed. A comprehensive account of Flying Officer Wilson's funeral was published by the *Surrey Mirror and County Post* on Friday, November 16th, 1923. *'Flying Officer Killed - Impressive Reigate Funeral'*

"Amid many manifestations of grief and sympathy the remains of Flying Officer Laurance Farrell Wilson, the only son of Mr. and Mrs. C H Wilson, 4, The Grange, Redhill, who met his death in a flying accident at Upavon, Wiltshire, on November 7th, were laid to rest in the Reigate Cemetery on Mondayafternoon.

"The deceased officer qualified as a pilot in the Royal Naval Air Force during the war, and was demobilised early in 1919. He had recently been granted a commission as a flying officer in the Royal Air Force, and in the final stage of his "refresher" course he was on, what was believed to be, his last obligatory flight, when coming out of a loop, the wings of the machine, a "Snipe"bi-plane, and which had recently been reconditioned, suddenly collapsed for some unexplained reason, crashing him to the ground, from a height of 2,500 feet.Experts have been investigating the cause of the disaster, and the result will be made known in the ordinary course, but meanwhile it may be a sad consolation to the brave officer's many sorrowing friends to know that, apart from what has been described as, "his exceeding popularity with all ranks," he was looked upon as a keen and capable officer, and the accident is stated at been one for which he could not in any way be held accountable. To the bereaved parents much sympathy has been shown in their sad loss.

"An impressive service, which was largely attended, was conducted at the Reigate Parish Church, by the Rev. H F S Adams, Vicar of Holy Trinity Church, Redhill. Officers and men from the aerodrome at Kenley, under the command of Group Commander Holt, attended and acted as pall bearers. The coffin was draped with a Union Jack, and was covered with wreaths. At the church a surpliced choir was in attendance, and special muusic was feeling played by the organist.

"The anthem, "I heard a voice from Heaven," was sympathetically rendered by the choir, and the hymns, "The king of Love," and "Peace, Perfect Peace," were also sung. At the conclusion of the service in the Church, the coffin was borne by the pall bearers to the cemetery, where the last rites were said. A firing party, also supplied from the RAF, Kenley Aerodrome, fired a salute at the graveside, and buglers sounded the "Last Post," and "Reveille." The coffin bore the inscription "Laurance Farrell Wilson. Died November 7th, 1923, aged 24 years."

"Floral tributes were sent by the following:- Father and Mother; Iris and Roy; Grandfather; Helen and Van; Mrs. Butler; Garrit Butler; Nole; the Commandant, Central Flying School, Upavon; Air Officer Command and OfficersInland Area, headquarters; Staff of the Hong King and Shanghai Bank; Old Friends in Hong Kong and Shanghai Bank tennis team; Mrs. H D C Jones; Herbert, George, and Foster, 'To the proud memory of our dear old friend Laurance," Mr. and Mrs. R C Griffith; Geoffrey Griffith and Raymond Cox; Mrs. Strong; Walter and Harry Strong; Mrs. Robert Scott and Mr. Hubert Scott; Mrs. C M Clark and Peggy; Mr. and Mrs. Gurney Ayre and John; Col. And Mrs. Liveing; Mrs. Teigner; Mr. and Mrs. Leonard Healing and daughter; Dr. And Mrs. Douglas White and George; Mrs. Orme; Gwynyth and Ruth; Mr. W Adams Oram; the Misses Oram; Mrs. Cooper' Miss Weller and friends at No. 1, The Grange; Mr. and Mrs. Mellhuish, Comfort and Betty; Mr. and Mrs. Stenning; Miss Johnson; Mr. and Mrs Williamson; all at "Enmore"; and Hannah and May.

"Messers J Stoneman and Sons, Station-road, Redhill, carried out the funeral arrangements."

LG 18 September 1923, issue 32863, page 6279 - Seniority 1st, 10th and 7th September respectively

FLIGHT LIEUTENANT

KENNY-LEVEK MBE Vivian Mortimer F/Lt 01.09.28 Relinquished

On account of ill-health. Subsequently, he returned to the service [see Appendix D and the entry for 15th October 1929.

FLYING OFFICERS
2

BAMBER Alexander Kelway F/O 10.09.32 Relinquished

HOLLICK-KENYON Herbert F/O 02.10.33 Relinquished.

LG 25 September 1923, issue 32865, page 6429 - Seniority various dates - the twenty-nine probationary Pilot Officers from 15th September 1923

FLYING OFFICERS
6

CARROLL* George Noad F/Lt + 23.04.36

18047 COPE William Norman Lazenby S/Ldr 10.02.54 Relinquished

Born 5th September 1896 2nd Lieutenant William Norman Lazenby Cope reached 23 Squadron [5F.1 Dolphin] at Bertangles on 7th August 1918, the *Great War* now about to enter its final stages - see my second volume and page 113 for a description of the opening day of the triumphant [for the Allies] *Battle of Amiens* which saw 23 Squadron heavily involved [page 116 summaries their seven losses on this day]. It is unlikely that William was in action on this day and following a spell in hospital he was posted on 9th October 1918 to 79 Squadron, also equipped with 5F.1 Dolphin, at Sste. Marie Cappel. The last entry on his Casualty Form indicates he was wounded on the 26th October and admitted to 17 Casualty Clearing Station, but I can find no record of this in *The Sky Their Battlefield* and I have no entries for 79 Squadron in my second volume for the day in question.

	LEEDS*	Reginald Arthur St. John	F/O		12.08.25	Relinquished

On account of ill-health. An investigation by my co-author reveals that Flying Officer Reginald Arthur St. John Leeds was born on 13th May 1899. His parents were William Henry Arther St. John Leeds and Edith Mabel Muspratt-Williams. Reginald, who was destined to be the 6th Baronet, was educated at the Royal Naval Colleges at Osborne on the Isle of Wight and at Britannia Royal Naval College, Dartmouth, subsequently seeing active service in the *Great War.* He succeeded to the 6th baronetcy on 31st May 1924 and two years later on 22nd November 1926 he married Winneretta Singer. During the Second World War he was the Naval Liaison Officer at Fighter Command and in 1952 was High Sheriff of the County of Devon. His death was announced on Sunday, 18th January 1970.

	MUNDY-COX*	Robert	F/O		16.09.30	Relinquished
	SAUNDERS*	William Eric Pentland	F/O		08.08.24	Resigned
	WILSON	Charles Bernard	F/Lt		18.09.32	Relinquished

* Retired officers appointed for seven years on the active list; remainder to serve for five years.

18039	ANDERSON	Cuthbert Geoffrey Munro	F/Lt		03.12.58	Relinquished
18040	BATSON-JAMES	Edward Lionel	P/O		04.07.25	Dismissed

By sentence of General Court Martial [LG 14 July 1925, issue 33066, page 4704].

18041	BOLDERO	Cyril Henry William	G/Capt		15.09.53	Retirement

Flying Officer Cyril Henry William Boldero transferred from the General Duties Branch to the Stores Branch and was promoted flight lieutenant on 10th January 1935 [LG 19 February 1935, issue 34134, page 1174]. His service number was amended to 21138. His retirement was at his own request [LG 13 October 1953, supplement 39985, page 5433].

18042	BRANCH	John Stroyan	P/O	+	16.10.25	SAC Old Sarum

Along with a fellow officer, Pilot Officer John Alexander Ballantyne, John Stroyan Branch died when their Bristol F.2b crashed near Wilton on the WNW side of the Cathedral City of Salisbury and and roughly 3 miles SW from the airfield. Visibility was poor at the time. A detailed account of the accident was published in the *Salisbury & Winchester Journal* on Friday 23rd October 1925: *"A shocking accident, involving the deaths of Pilot Officer John Stroyan Branch and John Alexander Ballantyne, both aged 20, and both attached to the School of Army Co-operation, Old Sarum, occurred soon after midday on Friday. At a quarter-past ten that morning Pilot Officer Branch was ordered to carry out a reconnaissance in a Bristol Fighter Aeroplane, with Pilot Officer Ballantyne as observer. The Bristol Fighter was one of five machines ordered on flights about that time, when weather conditions were favourable, with a light westerly breeze. The flight was to last about an hour and a-half, but before the machines were due to return to the Aerodrome the wind and weather changed. From west, the wind swung round to the north-east, bringing with it mist, rain and low clouds, and under these circumstances unfavourable to flying, four of the five machines returned to the Aerodrome with the tasks assigned to them uncompleted. The fifth, piloted by Branch, apparently lost direction in the mist, which later developed to rain. About noon it was observed flying at low altitude over Salisbury, apparently in an endeavour to get its bearings, but instead of heading for Old Sarum Aerodrome made off in the direction of Wilton. Meantime every endeavour was made at the Aerodrome to assist the pilot. A noise similar to that of a Bristol Fighter was heard from the direction of Salisbury and, surmising that it came from the machine piloted by Branch, the Officer Commanding at the Aerodrome gave instructions for Verey lights to be fired in the hope of attracting the attention of the pilot. When the hum of the aeroplane died away in a northerly direction a warning was sent to Netheravon Aerodrome that a machine was heading towards them. Later a message was received that the machine had crashed near Wilton.*

"After passing over Salisbury, the Bristol Fighter was seen circling over the water meadows between Netherhampton and Quidhampton, the pilot apparently searching for a suitable landing place. Fog obscured the ground at the time. At one moment it appeared that the pilot was making for Salisbury Raceplace, where it is possible he would have landed without mishap, but he turned, and barely clearing the trees, again appeared over the water meadows. Suddenly the tail of the machine was seen to rise in the air, and the aeroplane nosedived to earth with such force that the engine was practically buried in the ground. The body of the machine was completely wrecked. Mr. J Luffman, of Quidhampton, and Mr. J Wilson, of Wilton, were the first on the spot, and with others who quickly arrived did all that was possible under the circumstances. A messenger was sent for brandy and another for a doctor, but both officers were beyond human aid. They were shockingly injured. Pilot Officer Branch was just breathing when civilians reached the machine, but died before he was taken from the cockpit. Ballantyne was removed from the wreckage unconscious and died shortly before one o'clock, Both bodies were placed on an ambulance and removed to the mortuary at Salisbury.

"The inquest on the bodies of both officers was conducted by Mr. A M Wilson, the Salisbury City Coroner at the Council Chamber on Saturday evening. Superintendent Townsend was present on behalf of the Wilts police. William Alexander Beck of the Royal Air Force, stationed at Old Sarum, said he attended the City Mortuary on Friday afternoon, and identified the bodies of both the deceased, who were attached to the School of Army Co-operation, Old Sarum. He described the injuries to Pilot Officer Branch, who, in addition to other wounds, sustained a compound fracture of the base of the skull, and severe crushing of the right side of the neck.

"Flight Lieutenant Arthur Hyde Flower, Officer Commanding the Training Squadron at the School of Army Co-operation, Old Sarum, disposed that on Friday morning he detailed Pilot Officer Branch to take up a Bristol Fighter, with Pilot Officer Ballantyne as observer, and carry out a practice reconnaissance. They were ordered to leave the ground at 10,15 and to land again at 11.45. They actually left the ground at 10.20 a.m. At that time the weather conditions were good; the sky was partially clear, and there was a light breeze blowing from the west. This particular machine had been flown by Pilot Officer Branch some four or five days previously. At the conclusion of every day's flying, the machines were inspected and filled up with petrol, oil and water; and at the beginning of the day's work a rigger and fitter attached to each machine carried out an inspection and certified on an aeroplane inspection board. This procedure was carried out in respect of the machine taken up by Pilot Officer Branch on Friday. The pilot who was carrying out a flight satisfied himself that the machine had been inspected; tested his engine on the ground, and if he was satisfied that it was running perfectly he initialled the aeroplane inspection board. This was done on Friday morning. There were four other machines which left the ground at about the same time as the Bristol Fighter piloted by Branch. Witness made it a practice of watching all the pilots test their engines and leave the ground. All the pilots on Friday morning had definite jobs assigned to them, Branch being instructed to make a reconnaissance in the vicinity of Christ Church. About eleven o'clock the wind changed and swung round to the north east, bringing mist and rain and low clouds. As a result of this change four of the machines returned, none of them having completed their instructions. The last of these four returned about ten minutes past eleven. Witness remained at the aerodrome, and at about 12 o'clock heard an aeroplane in the vicinity of Salisbury. He could not actually see the machine, but from the noise could tell it was their type of machine. When he heard the noise he concluded that the pilot was looking for the Aerodrome, and instructed one of his officers to fire some Verey lights into the air in the hope of attracting the pilot's attention. This was continued until the noise of the engine became inaudible. He judged from the noise that the machine was heading north. He immediately instructed the Officer of the Watch to warn Netheravon Aerodrome that a machine was out and heading towards that place. About 12.45 he received a message that an aeroplane had crashed near Wilton. He despatched a party to the scene of the crash. Pilot Officer Branch had been at Old Sarum Aerodrome between six and seven weeks and had done about 12 ½ pilot hours.

"Arthur James Godfrey, aero engine fitter, stationed at Old Sarum Aerodrome, said he had had charge of this particular engine. He was on duty on Friday morning, when he carried out the usual inspection, and signed the inspection board to the effect that everything was as it should be. He afterwards saw the pilot "run" the engine and sign the board. The machine left the ground perfectly in order.

"Joesph Henry Luffman, labourer, of Nadder-road, Quidhampton, deposed that on Friday morning he working in Nethampton meadows, and at about 12 o'clock saw an aeroplane coming from the direction of Salisbury flying rather low. It twice circled round near him, and it appeared that the pilot was looking for a landing ground. It was very foggy, and at times witness lost sight of the machine. The engine appeared to be running perfectly. It was shut off twice, and when it started again ran perfectly. As the engine was shut off the last time witness saw the machine coming through the fog

just over the tree tops. Witness turned away his head for a moment, thinking the pilot was going to re-start the engine again; and then he heard a crash. The machine crashed about 200 yards from where witness was working. He went up to the machine and found both officers in it. The pilot was lying on his right side with his face across the tank in front of him. He was just breathing when witness reached the machine. Witness, with the help of Mr. J Wilson and others, removed the pilot from the machine. Branch was then dead. The observer, Ballantyne, appeared to be lying on his back with his right arm under the arm of the pilot. He was alive when witness got to the machine, and died about 12.55. A doctor was sent for, and was soon on the spot. The nose of the aeroplane was buried several feet in the ground.

"The Coroner:- When you saw the 'plane coming out of the clouds over the trees just before it crashed, do you think it touched a tree?

"Witness:- No, sir, I am sure it didn't.

"Joseph William Wilson, agent for an insurance company, living at Riverside, Wilton, stated that on Friday about midday he was cycling with a companion on the Netherhampton-road towards Wilton. They had stopped under some trees to shelter from the rain, when witness saw an aeroplane at a low altitude overhead. It appeared to be looking for a place to land. He saw it circle two or three times between Netherampton and the Wilton-road; it came down with the engine shut off; then started up again, and appeared to be going towards the Raceplain. It then circled to the left and then travelled over Netherhampton to the water meadows. It was about 150 to 200 feet up. At the end of the water meadows the machine turned when it was over the tops of the trees, and appeared to be about to land. The engine stopped, and in about two seconds witness noticed the tail of the machine go straight in the air, and the machine nosedived straight to the ground. He went to the scene of the crash, and found the previous witness there. At his request Luffman went to the nearest public-house for brandy and for any assistance he could get. As far as he could, witness released the observer, who was alive, but unconscious. Further assistance arrived, and Ballantyne was removed from the machine. The pilot was just breathing when witness arrived, and died before he could be got out of the machine. A doctor arrived and attended to Ballantyne, who, however, died at 12.55 p.m. The ambulance arrived at 1.15 p.m. and conveyed the bodies away. When witness arrived on the scene of the accident he noticed that the belts, by which the pilot and observer were fastened in, were both undone and the observer was clutching the right arm of the pilot. The machine was completely wrecked. Witness was quite sure that the machine did not touch the trees as it passed over them.

"Pilot Officer George Dare Blakely Russell, attached to the Training Squadron, Old Sarum, deposed that about 1.10 p.m. he received orders to proceed to the scene of the accident, and arrived about 2.15 p.m. He found the engine of the machine was completely buried in the earth at a very steep angle. The fore longerons were broken. The rear portion of the fuselage was leaning to the right. Both engine switches were in contact, and the magneto control was advanced. The back tank was broken, and petrol was issuing in a steady stream. Witness could not see it the front tank was also broken. The front cockpit was extensively damaged and the observer's cockpit was also damaged, though not so severely. The machine had crashed in a field bordered by several trees. Witness examined the machine, but found no marks or indications that it had fouled the trees. The machine as whole was completely wrecked.

"The Coroner:- From the evidence that you have heard, can you form any opinion as to what actually happened?

"Witness:- I can form an opinion, but I can't state it as a fact. I am of the opinion that Pilot Officer Branch may have switched off his engine to converse with his observer. While turning round he may have held up the nose of the machine, stalling it, and it came spinning to the ground, and owing to the low altitude it would not have time to recover from the spin.

"The Coroner said he was quite satisfied from the expert evidence that had been given that the machine was in order when the flight started. It was impossible to say exactly how the crash occurred, but he thought it was quite probable that the opinion given by the last witness might be, as a matter of fact, what did actually happen. He brought in a verdict that these two officers died from injuries received owing to the accidental fall of an aero-plane, of which Branch was the pilot, near the Netherhampton-road on Friday."

"The funeral of Pilot Officer Branch took place at Eastbourne on Monday, and that of Pilot Officer Ballantyne at Streatham on Tuesday. The bodies were taken from the city mortuary by RAF escorts from Old Sarum to the Southern Railway Station and conveyed thence by raid."

18043 BURNLEY Darrell Clinton F/O 15.09.36 Relinquished

Commissioned in class C of the Reserve of Air Force Officers on 9th May 1939 [LG 9 May 1939, issue 34624, page 3114]. Served throughout the Second World War and beyond, S/Ldr 10.02.54 Relinquished

BUSHBY Francis Walter Dudley P/O 24.12.24 Terminated

18048 DEARTH Eric Charles G/Capt 30.07.47 Retirement

On account of medical unfitness for Air Force service [LG 19 August 1947, supplement 38049, page 3897].

GIBSON Geoffrey Daniel F/O 25.11.25 Relinquished

On account of ill-health [LG 24 November 1925, issue 33107, page 7706].

KEELY Reginald Philipps P/O 01.12.24 Resigned

LAWSON Robert Dixon P/O 11.06.24 Terminated

Subsequently, Robert Dixon Lawson obtained a commission as a Lieutenant with the Dorset Regiment.

LEWIS Leonard Code F/O 18.11.25 Resigned

18056 MACONOCHIE Kenneth F/O 15.09.32 Relinquished

Flying Officer Kenneth Maconochie granted a commission in Class A of the Reserve of Air Force Officers, 19th July 1935 [LG 6 August 1935, issue 34187, page 5055]. F/Lt + 19.11.35 9 BGS Penrhos

Flight Lieutenant Kenneth Maconochie and Pilot Officer Douglas Roy James Paterson died shortly after taking off from Penrhos in Harrow K6939 with the elevator control locks still in place. As a consequence it stalled and crashed, bursting into flames on impact. Flight Lieutenant Maconochie is buried in Somerset at Camerton [St. Peter] Churchyard.

McMILLAN Douglas James Frederick F/O + 05.06/28 3 Squadron

McDEIVITTE Charles Douglas Staples Irwin P/O 13.08.24 Resigned

MORGAN Charles Henry Purday P/O 01.04.25 Relinquished

On account of ill-health [LG 7 April 1925, issue 33036, page 2376].

01858 MUMBY Charles Nicolas Alexander Bernard F/O 15.09.32 Relinquished

NEILL Terence de Lancey P/O 24.12.24 Resigned

18061 READ Roderick Fearon de Rede S/Ldr 20.01.45 Relinquished

On ceasing to be employed [LG 18 September 1945, supplement 37269, page 4629].

ROSS Leslie Harold F/O 29.07.37 Relinquished

01865 SHAW Hampden Charlton Mason P/O + 12.08.24 5 FTS Sealand

Pilot Officer Hampden Charlton Mason Shaw lost his life in the final stages of his flying training when his Bristol F.2b C806 spun and crashed near the airfield; see also Pilot Officer Christopher Ernest Hillier whose details are reported for short service commissioned officers, 25th March 1924. A report of the accident was published in *The Nottingham Evening Post* with the dramatic headline *'Leap From Falling 'Plane - Two Officers Killed On Eve of Leave'*

"Two officers of the air force - Flying Officers Hillier and Shaw were killed at the Shotwick Aerodrome, Flintshire, yesterday.

"They were making a trial flight in a Bristol Fighter, Flying Officer Shaw occupying the pilot's sea. The flying conditions were in every way favourable, and the 'plane had been up about half an hour when it began a spiral dive. Eye witnesses state that the 'plane did not come out of the spin properly and nosedived.

"It is stated that Officer Hillier, realising a crash was inevitable jumped from the falling machine. Officer Shaw came to earth with the 'plane. Both officers were killed instantaneously. Shaw being buried beneath the wreckage.

"The aeroplane, which lies near the edge of a turnip field, is smashed to pieces, and the engine, which is twisted and smashed, buried itself between two and three feet in the ground. The spot where officer Hillier fell is about six feet away from the wrecked 'plane.

"It is understood that both officers had completed their training and were about to go on leave."

01858 SHAW Leslie Raymond F/O 11.07.26 Resigned

New Zealand

SLACKE Randal Earl F/O + 24.06.27 31 Squadron
SOUTHAM George Justice F/Lt + 19.12.31 SF Boscombe Down
Flight Lieutenant George Justice Southam and Flying Officer George Walter Lawsson died when their DH.60M Moth K1854 came down between Beacon Hill and Bulford Camp just to the north of the airfield.
STRACHAN George Cathcart Irvine P/O 16.02.25 Dismissed
By sentence of General Court Martial.
THOMAS Sydney Martin F/O 15.09.36 Relinquished
TOWNEND John Beverly F/O 22.06.27 Relinquished
On account of ill-health. Subsequently served in the RNZAF and rose to the rank of squadron leader. He also turned his hand to penmanship and writing under the pseudonym John Templer published *Jaggers Air Detective, Jaggers Swoops Again* and *Jaggers at Bay* published respectively by Oxford University Press in 1936, 1937 and 1938, copies of which are still available on the second-hand book market.
TUSSAUD Francis William Curtius George F/O 12.05.26 Relinquished
On account of ill-health [LG 11 May 1926, issue 33161, page 3146]. Regaining his fitness to serve, he was commissioned to the Administrative and Special Duties Branch on 18th July 1940 [LG 14 January 1941, issue 35042, page 287] and issued with the service number 77248. He served throughout the Second World War. S/Ldr 20.05.46 Resigned
18073 WOODIN John Horton G/Capt 13.11.45 Retirement
At his own request [LG 18 December 1945, supplement 37393, page 6150].
YEARSLEY James Alexander Powys Allison F/O 29.09.26 Relinquished
On account of ill-health [LG 1 October 1926, issue 33207, page 6297].

LG 23 October 1923, issue 32873, page 7118 - Seniority 9th and 12 October 1923 respectively

FLYING OFFICER
2

18077 STOCKEN Reginald Herbert F/O 15.10.23 Resigned
A General List officer, 2nd Lieutenant Reginald Herbert Stocken reported to Bertangles on 8th October 1916 for duty with 21 Squadron [BE.12]. Theoretically a fighter squadron, the single-seater BE.12 was found to be ineffective in this role and was used for bombing operations until re-equipping with RE.8s in February 1917 and reverting to its original task as a corps reconnaissance unit. However, 2nd Lieutenant Stocken bade farewell to '21' on 6th March 1917 and joined 23 Squadron [Spad S.7] at Baizieux but appears to have done little operational work with the squadron and while on leave in the UK in June 1917 was struck off strength on the orders of a medical board. There are no further entries on his Casualty Form.
Although resigning his commission, ass shown above, Flying Officer Stocken obviously returned to the service and on 1st June 1941 was promoted squadron leader by which time he had transferred from the General Duties Branch to the Technical Branch [LG 9 September 1941, issue 35270, page 5223]. W/Cdr 10.02.54 Relinquished
TODD Gourley F/O 02.01.24 Relinquished
On account of ill-health [LG 15 January 1924, issue 32898, page 472]. Born on 2nd January 1900, 2nd Lieutenant Gourley Todd flew 7F.1 Snipes with 43 Squadron from 6th September 1918 until 18th April 1919 when he was posted to Home Establishment. At the time of his departure '43' was part of the Allied Occupation Force in Germany and based at Bickendorf.

18076 PAISH Atholl Ernest G/Capt 23.10.53 Retirement
On account of medical unfitness for Air Force service [LG 27 October 1953, supplement 39996, page 5710].

LG 9 November 1923, issue 32878, page 7662 - Seniority 1st August 1923, 25th October 1923 and 4th October 1923 respectively

FLIGHT LIEUTENANT

QUINLAN Arthur Francis F/L + 01.11.24 5 Squadron

FLYING OFFICER

LINGARD Asa Foster F/Lt 25.10.37 Relinquished
His Casualty Form - Officers shows he was born on 22nd February 1899 and was accepted by the RFC in July 1917. On 29th December 1917 he was attached to 66 Squadron [F.1 Camel] at Grossa in Italy where he was cross-posted to 45 Squadron [F.1 Camel] on 11th February 1918. On page 56 of *The Flying Camels* a table of pilots serving as at 1st August 1918 indicates he was in B Flight while on page 61 a table of pilots still attached as the squadron was being reduced to a cadre indicates he was the regular pilot for F.1 Camel D8211 [extant 19th January 1919 with 151 Squadron]. On the page opposite [60] a formal photograph of the squadron's A Flight shows him seated 6th from the left and looked directly into the camera. During the Second World War Flight Lieutenant Asa Foster Lingard joined the Air Transport Auxiliary and served from 22nd January 1940 to November 1945. He was appointed MBE in the New Year's Honours List 1943 when he was Flight Captain at No. 3 Ferry Pool Hawarden in Cheshire. His death was announced on 1st January 1971 at which time he was living in the New Forest, Hampshire.

WEBLIN* Howard Ernest Evens F/Lt 04.11.33 Resigned

* Formerly RN retired and appointed for seven years on the active list.

LG 20 November 1923, issue 32881, page 7952 - Seniority 6th November 1923

FLYING OFFICER

18081 THOMPSON Chester William McKinley S/Ldr + 16.09.40 19 OTU Kinloss
Squadron Leader Chester William McKinley Thompson died shortly after taking off from Kinloss in Magister I T9814 with the intention of flying to RAF Manby in Lincolnshire. Encountering marginal flying conditions and without the air of a full 'blind flying' panel he crashed into high ground some 6 miles south of Dalwhinnie which would place him in the general area of Cregan Mor. His body was recovered and taken back to Kinloss where he now rests in Kinloss Abbey Burial Ground. Squadron Leader Thompson, born 11th April 1899, joined 22 Squadron at at Serny on 22nd April 1918 and with his observer Lieutenant L R James was taken prisoner of war after their Bristol F.2b E2517 was shot down on 29th September 1918 [see page 270 of my Second Volume]. He arrived back in England by way of HMHS *Cambria* on 30th December 1918.
His death and its circumstances are also reported on page 28 of Volume 7 of my RAFBCL series, the seventh book reporting the Command's losses from the OTUs that came under its control.

LG 4 December 1923, issue 32885, page 8452 - Seniority 10th November 1923

FLYING OFFICERS
7

AXTELL Leslie Harry Westwood F/O 17.09.24 Resigned
Returned to India circa 1941 where in 1947 he was employed by *The Times* newspaper.

DANN MC Charles Walter F/O 27.01.28 Relinquished
On account of ill-health [LG 26 January 1926, issue 33127, page 622]. He was a retired Indian Army captain.
DULEY MM Bertie Williams F/Lt 09.04.29 Resigned
FOX Walter Basil Orlando F/Lt 04.05.28 Resigned
18087 MAJOR Eric Victor F/Lt 15.09.39 Relinquished
MULLALY Hugh Alexander F/O 08.01.25 Cashiered
By sentence of General Court Martial [LG 20 January 1925, issue 33013, page 454]. He was formerly a Lieutenant in the Indian Army.
WOLEDGE Frank Leonard F/Lt 31.12.29 Resigned
Holding a commission in class CC of the General Duties Branch, this was relinquished on 1st September 1939 on appointment to a commission in the Royal Air Force Volunteer Reserve [LG 20 October 1939, issue 34713, page 7041]. On page 7044 of the same issue he is shown as Captain Frank Leonard Woledge [late Indian Army] within the Administrative and Special Duties Branch from 16th January 1939 with the service number 74870.
On 21st November 1946, in the rank of flight lieutenant, he was granted a commission in class CC to the Administrative and Special Duties Branch [LG 31 December 1946, supplement 37833, page 6324]. S/Ldr 10.02.54 Relinquished

The above were appointed for seven years on the active list; apart from Flying Officer Major, formerly of the Royal Navy, the remainder were retired Indian Army officers.

BRAMLEY Jack Alexander P/O 08.07.25 Relinquished
On account of ill-health [LG 7 July 1925, issue 33064, page 4534]
BUSHELL Eric Alfred Claude F/O 20.10.26 Relinquished
On account of ill-health [LG 19 October 1926, issue 33212, page 6691]
CAULFIELD Jack Harley F/O + 30.07.29 National Flying Services
Flying Officer Jack Harley Caulfield was flying a Simmonds Spartan G-AAMC on 28th July 1929 in the vicinity of Hanworth aerodrome and indulging in low-level aerobatics when he lost control and spun into some trees. It appears he survived the crash, but before he could free himself, or be helped from the cockpit, the Spartan caught fire and he was critically burned, dying from his injuries two days later while undergoing treatment in Hounslow Hospital. A detailed report of the accident is held at TNA Kew under AVIA 5/11/C143.
CAUNTER Cyril Francis F/O 28.03.28 Relinquished
On account of ill-health [LG 27 March 1928, issue 33370, page 2243].
DENNY Charles Herbert Anthony P/O 21.09.24 Relinquished
On account of ill-health [LG 26 September 1924, issue 32977, page 7043].
DOREY Donald John P/O 27.08.24 Resigned
DRACOTT Henry St. Elmo P/O 14.01.25 Resigned
FEVEZ Cecil Victor P/O 22.08.25 Resigned
While undergoing flying training at Netheravon on 20th June 1924, under the tutelage of 11 Squadron, he wrote off Avro 504K E9381 when on landing he collided with a bank, the impact being sufficient to cause him injuries.
18099 HALE-MONRO Thomas Adrian S/Ldr 10.02.54 Relinquished
See my summary for Thursday, 18 December 1924, for information regarding a flying accident in which he was involved.
18100 HAMILTON George Douglas P/O 14.01.25 Resigned
18101 HEMSLEY Bernard William G/Capt 07.03.45 Retirement
Transferred from the General Duties Branch to the Stores Branch and appointed to a permanent commission [LG 26 January 1926, issue 33127, page 622], his service number becoming 21043. His retirement was on account of medical unfitness for Air Force service [LG 20 March 1945, supplement 36989, page 1491.
18102 HILL James Cecil S/Ldr 10.02.54 Relinquished
Flying Officer James Cecil transferred from the General Duties Branch to the Medical Branch and was promoted flight lieutenant on 27th February 1941 [LG 2 May 1941, issue 35151, page 2521]. Promotion to Squadron Leader, temporary, on 1st January 1944 was promulgated in LG 21st January 1944, supplement 36340, page 418. His commission was relinquished under the terms of the Navy, Army and Air Force Reserves Act of 1954.
18103 LE FEUVER Henry Albert P/O 21.05.24 Terminated
18104 MASON Antony Cecil Carbery P/O + 08.04.25 A&GS Eastchurch
Tasked for a practice target shoot, Pilot Officer Antony Cecil Carbery Mason flying solo in a Bristol F.2b misjudged his dive and flew into the sea off Leysdown-on-Sea on the eastern end of the Isle of Sheppey.
18105 MILN Malcolm Murree F/O 09.10.28 Relinquished
On account of ill-health [LG 9 October 1928, issue 33428, page 6498].
18106 PEARSON Wilfred Joshua F/Lt 01.08.40 Relinquished
On account of ill-health [LG 13 August 1940, issue 34920, page 4944].
18107 PIGOTT Ian Bertram P/O 17.02.25 Relinquished
On account of ill-health [LG 17 February 1925, issue 33021, page 1172].
18108 ROSS Victor Andrè Corsane F/O 23.09.38 Resigned
18109 SLOCOMBE Philip A/Cmdr 15.09.52 Retirement
On account of medical unfitness for Air Force service [LG 16 September 1952, supplement 39645, page 4913]. Air Commodore Philip Slocombe mentioned in despatches, died three years later on Friday, 9th December 1955. His final service appointment was as Senior Air Staff Officer at Headquarters 24[Training] Group.
18110 STAINER Peter F/Lt 10.11.32 Relinquished
18111 SULLIVAN Cyril George Charles F/O 10.11.28 Class A
18112 ST. GEORGE-TAYLOR Harold P/O + 09.10.24 41 Squadron
18113 TRISTRAM Cecil Uvedale George
18114 WALL John Arnold P/O 24.12.24 Terminated
18115 WINTOUR St. John Fitzgerald F/O 16.06.26 Relinquished
On account of ill-health [LG 15 June 1926, issue 33172, page 3901]. At the time he had transferred from the General Duties Branch to the Stores Branch and, it is noted, permission to retain his rank has not been appended. This may have a bearing on the bankruptcy notice being issued against him as *Gazetted* on 20th July 1926, issue 33184, page 4840.

LG 11 December 1923, issue 32887, page 8642 - Seniority 3rd December 1923

FLYING OFFICER

18116 ALLEN Henry Woodward S/Ldr 13.03.41 Dismissed
By sentence of General Court Martial [LG 28 March 1941, issue 35119, page 1813]. At the time of his dismissal he was serving with the Equipment Branch.

LG 28 December 1923, issue 32892, page 9112 - Seniority 13 December 1923

FLYING OFFICER

18117 HILL Arthur Gerald F/O 12.12.32 Relinquished

Subsequently, he was granted a commission in Class A of the Reserve of Air Force Officers, General Duties Branch [LG 11 May 1937, issue 34397, page 3114]. S/Ldr 10.02.54 Relinquished

ROLL OF HONOUR
FOR
1923 SHORT SERVICE COMMISSIONED
OFFICERS

F/O	ADDAMS	Anthony Clifford	16 June 1926	41 Squadron
P/O	BAILLIE	Arthur Douglas	15 September 1924	17 Squadron
S/Ldr	BARRETT	Ralph	31 December 1953	
F/O	BELL	Edward	28 July 1924	28 Squadron
P/O	BRANCH	John Stroyan	16 October 1925	CFS Upavon
F/O	BURD MC	John March	12 October 1930	30 Squadron
F/O	BURNETT	Yvon Williams	18 March 1929	47 Squadron
F/O	BUTLER	Leonard	18 May 1929	The Irving Air Chute Co
F/Lt	CARROLL	George Noad	23 April 1936	
P/O	CATZ	Joseph	17 December 1924	CFS Upavon
F/O	CAULFIELD	Jack Harley	30 July 1929	National Flying Services
F/Lt	CAVIS-BROWN	Geoffrey Ashton	4 September 1925	RAF Gosport
F/O	COCKS	John James Crofts	26 May 1927	60 Squadron
P/O	GAIN	Douglas Elphinstone	4 December 1924	CFS Upavon
F/O	HAUGHTON	Edward Perceval Osburne	1 May 1923	401 Flight Leuchars
F/O	JAQUES	Robin	8 August 1923	100 Squadron
F/Lt-Lt. Cdr	JENNINGS	Frederick Godfrey	2 July 1941	768 Squadron FAA
P/O	KERCKHOVE MC	Herbert Vincent	2 July 1924	19 Squadron
F/O	MACKENZIE-	Campbell	9 November 1927	RAE Farnborough
F/Lt	MacNEAL	Alastair Neal	29 December 1926	28 Squadron
F/Lt	MACONOCHIE	Kenneth	19 November 1935	9 BGS Penrhos
P/O	MARTIN MC	Eric	2 May 1924	2 FTS Duxford
P/O	MASON	Antony Cecil Carbery	8 April 1925	A&GS Eastchurch
F/O	McMILLAN	Douglas James Frederick	5 June 1928	3 Squadron
F/O	PHILLIPS	Leonard William Hennell	12 July 1927	403 Flight HMS *Hermes*
P/O	PLEDGER	Jack Hamilton	4 April 1924	1 FTS Netheravon
F/Lt	QUINLAN	Arthur Francis	1 November 1924	5 Squadron
F/Lt	RIGG	Robert Owen	12 March 1927	60 Squadron
F/O	SATTIN	Arthur	27 January 1927	405 Flight HMS *Furious*
P/O	SHAW	Hampden Charlton Mason	12 August 1924	5 FTS Shotwick
F/O	SLACKE	Randal Earl	24 June 1927	31 Squadron
F/Lt	SOUTHAM	George Justice	19 December 1931	SF Boscombe Down
F/O	STIRLING WEBB	Oswald Kempson	26 July 1926	45 Squadron
F/Lt	STOCKS	Stanley John	17 July 1951	
P/O	St. GEORGE TAYLOR	Harold	9 October 1924	41 Squadron
S/Ldr	THOMPSON	Chester William McKinley	16 September 1940	19 OTU Kinloss
F/O	TOMES	James Eric	15 April 1926	84 Squadron
F/O	WILLIAMS	William Cay	16 September 1925	2 FTS Digby
F/O	WILSON	Laurance Farrell	7 November 1923	CFS Upavon
P/O	YOUNG	Stuart Adolphus	14 May 1926	1 Squadron

Appendix D - RAF [Cadet] College Cranwell

COMMANDANT

Air Commodore Charles Alexander Holcombe Longcroft DSO
Air Commodore Amyas Eden Borton CB CMG DSO AFC mentioned in despatches

The change in command took place on on 15th August 1923. As a Captain attached to 8 Squadron [BE.2c] Amyas Eden Borton had been dangerously wounded when his BE.2c 1783 was forced down over Staden at midday on 7th June 1915, Trevor Henshaw recording on page 14 of *The Sky Their Battlefield* that the engagement took place at 6,700 feet and while on the ground was *"shot up enemy rifle fire and shelled."* Captain Borton, as noted, was dangerously wounded while his observer, Captain A Marshall escaped unhurt.

Consulting Captain Borton's 'Casualty Form', the relevant entry reads: *"Transferred to England per Hosp. Ship 25/6/15 To be a Companion of the "Distinguished Service Order.""* This was duly *Gazetted* on 3rd July 1915, in supplement 29215, page 6533, as a dual citation with Captain Anthony Marshall: *"When on flying reconnaissance over the neighbourhood of Staden on 7th June 1915, Captain Borton was wounded in the head and neck by a bullet fired from a hostile aeroplane, and although suffering severely from loss of blood he continued with the assistance of the observer, Captain Marshall, to bandage his wounds and complete the reconnaissance on the prescribed course. His injuries are such that he is not yet out of danger. Captain Marshall continued his observations after rendering all possible aid to the Pilot, who was gradually losing consciousness, notwithstanding that the German aeroplane was persistently attacking. The valuable report supplied by this Officer is as detailed and complete for the last as it is for the first part of the reconnaissance."*

At this point, and purely for interest sake, may I suggest - if you have not already done so - a reading of the lead-in to 1923 and in particular the 'At Cranwell' section at the end of the 'Air Estimates' article.

February 1923 entry : 23

16143 ADDAMS* James Ramage G/Capt 03.07.46 Retirement
Group Captain James Ramage Addams AFC, died on Sunday, 16th September 1990, in Village, Richmond, Virginia. During his time as a pilot he survived a number of aeroplane accidents, three of which are reported when he was attached to 43 Squadron.
16144 ALLINSON* Norman Stuart AV-M 17.09.56 Retirement
Air Vice-Marshal Norman Stuart Allinson CB twice mentioned in despatches, died on Thursday, 8th October 1984. When at the College he was the subject of a non-flying accident report when when on 18th April 1923, he injured himself during training for an inter-squadron cross-country race.
16164 ARMOUR John George Denholme S/Ldr 27.05.33 Retired list
Returned to service 25th August 1940. S/Ldr 18.10.45 Retired list
At own request [LG 24 June 1947, supplement 37993, page 2842].
16145 BANDON* The Earl of Percy Ronald Gardner ACM 06.02.64 Retirement
Air Chief Marshal Percy Ronald Gardner The Earl of Bandon GBE CB CVO DSO three timed mentioned in despatches, died on Thursday, 8th February 1979. At the outbreak of the Second World War, Wing Commander The Earl of Bandon was commanding 82 Squadron which during the desperate air fighting by No. 2 Group Blenheims following the *Blitzkrieg* suffered the most appalling losses on 17th May 1940, when from a force of twelve aircraft despatched to attack enemy columns in the Gembloux area eleven were shot down by Me109s while the twelfth machine, captained by Sergeant T Morrison, returned ton Watton so badly shot about that it was deemed beyond repair [see my RAFBCL 1939-1940 pages 60 and 61]. Initially, it was decided to disband 82 Squadron, but The Earl put forward such a strong case for continuation that twelve Blenheims and crews were delivered that same evening and 24-hours later 'Paddy' Bandon led six crews on a night raid into Germany for which he was *Gazetted* with the DSO.
16146 BEAMISH* George Robert AM 07.02.58 Retirement
Air Marshal Sir George Beamish KCB CBE twice mentioned in despatches, died on Monday, 13th November 1967. Details regarding his brother, Francis Victor Beamish, can be read on the September 1921 entry.
16147 BEARDSWORTH* George Braithwaite AV-M ....57 Retirement
Air Vice-Marshal George Braithwaite Beardsworth CB mentioned in despatches, died on Wednesday, 5th August 1959.
16148 CAMPBELL* John Hunter McNeill S/Ldr 16.04.40 Retired list
On account of ill-health [LG 26 April 1940, issue 34838, page 2475]. On the 1st of November 1946, John Hunter McNeill Campbell joined the Imperial War Graves Commission [retitled Commonwealth War Graves Commission on 28th March 1960] as an Enquiries Officer, serving until 30th September 1968, by which time he held the post of Acting Senior Clerk. His death was announced on Saturday, 3rd August 1974.
16149 COCKS* Adrian Harry William James G/Capt 07.11.56 Retirement
Group Captain Adrian Harry William James Cocks died on Sunday, 21st December 1986.
COX* George Frederick Gardner P/O 03.12.26 Dismissed
By sentence of General Court Martial [LG 21 December 1926, issue 33231, page 8344].
16151 FORD* Richard James Alexander G/Capt 03.07.54 Retirement
Group Captain Richard James Alexander Ford CBE, died on Wednesday, 11th December 1996.
16152 FRANKS* John Gerald AV-M 04.04.60 Retirement
Air Vice-Marshal John Gerald Franks CB CBE mentioned in despatches, died on Saturday, 23rd September 1995.
16153 HARDY* Stephen Haistwell A/Cmdr + 08.04.45 OATS Cranwell
Air Commodore Stephen Haistwell Hardy CBE mentioned in despatches, had been appointed Commandant of the Officers' Advanced Training School which opened at Cranwell on the 1st of March 1944. While serving in this appointment he fell ill and having been admitted to RAF Hospital Rauceby died on Sunday, 8th April 1945.
16154 HARRIS* Sydney Herbert Verder G/Capt 01.07.55 Retirement
Group Captain Sydney Herbert Verder Harris CBE mentioned in despatches, died on Sunday, 16th January 1983.
16155 HAYES* Guy Wingfield A/Cmdr 02.04.57 Retirement
Air Commodore Guy Wingfield Hayes OBE mentioned in despatches, died in October 1996.
16156 HAYES* Montague Ernest De Lannoy P/O 12.05.26 Resigned
Promoted flying officer within the Reserve of Air Force Officers [LG 8 March 1927, issue 33255, page 1526] and on becoming active promoted to flight lieutenant 3rd September 1939 [LG 9 April 1940, issue 34826, page 2073]. S/Ldr 15.10.47 Resigned
16180 LYWOOD Geoffrey Edward Gifford G/Capt 14.10.45 Retired list
At his own request [LG 30 October 1945, supplement 37327, page 5273]. Group Captain Geoffrey Edward Gifford Lywood died on Thursday, 15th January 1970.

16157 MONTGOMERY* Alexander Hutchinson A/Cmdr 16.02.46 Retirement
Air Commodore Alexander Hutchison Montgomery CBE mentioned in despatches, died on Sunday, 12th January 1986. Details pertaining to a flying accident in which he was the pilot is summarised on Wednesday, 4th March 1925.

16160 NOWELL Henry Edward A/Cmdr 15.08.55 Retirement
Air Commodore Henry Edward Nowell CB OBE, died on Wednesday, 1st February 1967.

O'HANLON Francis Stafford F/Lt + 13.06.33 RAE Farnborough
Flight Lieutenant Francis Stafford O'Hanlon met his death while attached to RAE Farnborough, the circumstances being reported on ASN Wikibase Occurrence 211079, in which has been appended the article that appeared in the *Western Daily Press,* Wednesday 145h June 1933, under the headline: *"RAF 'PLANE FALLS ON ARMY WORKSHOP - Doomed Pilot's Frantic Warning to Soldier. Tank towed to Safety. Three hours after the accident, the ruins of a "Vildebeest"* [G-ABJK] *were still smouldering at Farnborough yesterday, when it crashed on to an Army workshop and burnt out, causing the death of Flight-Lieut. Francis Stafford O'Hanlon.*

Shortly after three o'clock the pilot took off from Farnborough aerodrome to take the machine back to Messrs Vickers' works at Gosport. He had just got to the edge of the aerodrome when the machine was seen to be in difficulties over the Mechanical Warfare Experimental Establishment workshop adjoining the RAF establishment. The machine stalled and fell, a wing striking the shed, causing the 'plane to slew round and crash head on into the building in which about 20 men were at work.

Directly the 'plane hit the shed it burst into flames and in a few minutes there was nothing left but a mass of broken and charred debris. The RAF fire brigade were soon on the scene followed by the Aldershot fire brigade, when the flames were got under control. Those who extracted the pilot's body said that he was probably dead before the flames enveloped him, as his head showed signs of serious injury. Apart from that of those men in the workshop, the narrowest escape was experienced by Lance-Bombardier Wigley, of the Royal Artillery Mechanical Warfare Experimental Establishment, who missed death by inches. He was repairing a motor-cycle outside the shed when the 'plane grazed him as it struck a wall. As it caught fire it scorched his neck.

Valuable material was damaged by the fire which ignited the shed, but an armoured car and tank were towed into safety. An eyewitness said that the pilot made desperate effort to land the machine on boggy ground close to the workshop. Seeing that he could not do so he waved frantically from the cockpit for Wigley to get out of the way. If the 'plane had landed in the bog it is probable that it would not have caught fire. This accident makes the total number of fatalities in the RAF this year 29."

The registration G-ABJK had been cancelled on 7th April 1931, and it is suspected that at the time it was being flown with Class B marks O-1.

Whilst at Cranwell he was injured in a road traffic accident at Sleaford on 20th September 1924, when the car in which he was travelling collided with another vehicle coming in the opposite direction.

16175 RHYS-JONES John A/Cmdr 01.10.51 Retirement
Air Commodore Johnl Rhys-Jones twice mentioned in despatches, died on Monday, 25th August 1975.

SCOTT* Ian Malcolm P/O + 25.03.25 32 Squadron
WALKER Neil Coull P/O + 07.04.25 9 Squadron
Pilot Officer Neil Coull Walker was attached to 9 Squadron following graduation from the College as recently as 17th March [LG 7 April 1925, issue 33036, page 2375] and on the day of his death he was flying as second pilot to Pilot Officer Eric Alfred Claude Bushell, captain of Vickers Virginia Mk V J7439. Taking off from Manston, the Virginia was over the Thames Estuary when fog was encountered and Pilot Officer Bushell decided to put his aircraft down in the water. This was accomplished but tragically two members of his crew, including Pilot Officer Walker, were reported missing, presumed drowned. Pilot Officer Bushell escaped with minor injuries, but Aircraftman Horace Eustace Grellis was seriously hurt. Despite the gravity of the accident, the Virginia was recovered by a trawler and was despatched to Vickers Aircraft, Brooklands, where it was rebuilt as the prototype Virginia VI. Subsequently, J7439 went on to serve with a number of squadrons, ending its days in 1937 with 215 Squadron.

16163 WILLETTS Alfred Henry G/Capt 24.01.46 Retirement
Group Captain Alfred Henry Willetts DSO, twice mentioned in despatches, retired to Malloca, Spain, and died there on Wednesday, 21st July 1971.

Officers whose surnames have an asterisk appended graduated on 17th December 1924, as did Pilot Officer Paul McKenna Terry from the September 1922, entry [LG 20 January 1925, issue 33013, page 453].

SWORD OF HONOUR
Flight Cadet George Robert Beamish

ROLL OF HONOUR
FEBRUARY 1923 ENTRY

A/Cmdr	HARDY	Stephen Haistwell	8 April 1945	OATS Cranwell
F/Lt	O'HANLON	Francis Stafford	13 June 1933	RAE Farnborough
P/O	SCOTT	Ian Malcolm	25 March 1925	32 Squadron
P/O	WALKER	Neil Coull	7 April 1925	9 Squadron

September 1923 entry : 24

ANNESS Lionel Hubert F/O AFC 09.01.31
Transferred to the Stores Branch [LG 20 January 1931, issue 33682, page 464]. S/Ldr + 14.05.53

BREMRIDGE* Charles Henry Goodwin F/O 19.09.29 Resigned

16166 CANNON* Leslie William AV-M 04.11.58 Retirement
Air Vice-Marshal Leslie William Cannon CB CBE four times mentioned in despatches, died on Monday, 27 January 1986. On the 14th June 1946, he was *Gazetted* with the Silver Star [supplement 37610, page 3007] conferred by the President of the United States of America.

16167 CARR* Terence Howard G/Capt 07.01.49 Retirement
Group Captain Terence Howard Carr DFC AFC, died on Sunday, 6th July 1986.

16168 CHAMBERLAIN* George Philip AV-M 25.07.60 Retirement
Air Vice-Marshal George Philip Chamberlain CB OBE mentioned in despatches, died Thursday, 2nd November 1995.

16189 COATS Roland A/Cmdr 25.07.56 Retirement
Air Commodore Roland Coats CB mentioned in despatches, died on Sunday, 3rd March 1974.

DANBURY* Basil Augustine Checkland F/O 03.10.30 Dismissed
By sentence of General Court Martial [LG 24 October 1930, issue 33655, page 6480].

EATON* James P/O +

16171 GILLMORE* Alan David AV-M 29.04.59 Retirement
Air Vice-Marshal Alan David Gillmore CB CBE, died on Monday, 27th May 1996.

16172 HAMMOND* Alfred Vavasour G/Capt 21.07.55 Retirement
Group Captain Alfred Vavasour Hammond OBE, died on Friday, 25th September 1992.

16173 HARRISON* Joseph Arthur Patrick G/Capt 02.12.47 Retirement
Group Captain Joseph Arthur Patrick Harrison mentioned in despatches, died on Saturday, 9th December 1967.

HORDEN* Edmund Gwyn F/O 15.01.30 Resigned

On Monday, 30th May 1927, Flying Officer Edmund Gwyn Horden was flying with Flying Officer Horace Miller in an Avro 504N belonging to CFS Wittering with the objective of practising forced-landings and it was while attempting to forced-land in a field near Easston on the NW side of the airfield that control was lost, and the trainer dived into the ground. Flying Officer Miller was killed and Flying Officer Horden badly injured.

16176	KEARY*	John D'Arcy	G/Capt		01.02.48	Retirement

Group Captain John D'Arcy Keary retired to South Africa where he died in 1977. My co-author reports Group Captain Keary is buried in Durban, eThekwini Metropolitan Municipality, KwaZulu-Natal.

16177	KELLETT*	Richard	A/Cmdr		10.04.47	Retirement

Air Commodore Richard Kellett CBE DFC AFC mentioned in despatches, died on Wednesday, 3rd January 1990. On the 6th of November 1939, Richard Kellett, then a wing commander, assumed command of 149 Squadron at Mildenhall and on 18th December 1939, he was the formation leader for a force of 24 Wellington bombers drawn from 9, 37 and 149 Squadrons tasked to attack the German Naval Base at Wilhelmshaven. The outcome of this attack is described in great detail by the writer and historian, Max Hastings, in the prologue of his book *Bomber Command* in which he which he includes on page 27 a brief extract from Wing Commander Kellett's post-raid report; *"The enemy pressed home their attacks in splendid manner."* This, no doubt, in these early stages of the Second World War was a sentiment shared by senior officers, many of whom had flown as pilots in the previous conflict when the concept of chivalrous conduct existed between opponents was sometimes expressed. Subsequently, he was awarded the DFC [LG 16 January 1940, issue 34773, page 301]; *"This officer displayed courage, coolness and determination, in leading his squadron and a combined formation of aircraft in operations over and enemy naval base in December 1939, which resulted in the infliction of heavy casualties on enemy aircraft. In spite of the formidable opposition by aircraft and ground defences, he so controlled the formation for which he was personally responsible that casualties were slight and by his personal example and cool leadership he won the confidence of all pilots under him."* Although in no way detracting from his personal courage, the suggestion that *"casualties were slight"* could not be further from the truth. As shown on pages 94 to 96 of my revision of Royal Air Force Bomber Command losses of the Second World War, from the 24 aircraft that set out from their East Anglia bases, twelve were lost, including two from Richard Kellett's own squadron. Fifty-six aircrew perished, most now commemorated on the Runnymede Memorial, with five surviving to spend the remaining years of the war in captivity.

By the summer of 1942, and now promoted group captain, he was in the Middle East serving as Senior Air Staff Officer in No. 205 Group. On the night of 13th-14th September 1942, he joined the crew of a 70 Squadron Wellington Ic BB462 captained by Pilot Officer M V Hodge operating to Tobruk. Over the target the Wellington lost power on one engine and forced-landed in the desert. For nearly a week the crew evaded capture, but eventually all ended up 'behind the wire'. For details of this, please refer to page 182 of David Gunby and Pelham Temple's *Royal Air Force Bomber Losses in the Middle East and Mediterranean Volume 1: 1939-1942* published by Midland Publishing, 2006.

Group Captain Richard Kellett finished up in Stalag Luft III where he may well have been reconciled with Flight Lieutenant P A Wimberley from 37 Squadron, the sole officer survivor from the twelve aircraft shot down during the attack on Wilhelmshaven on 18th December 1939.

16178	KENNEDY*	William Maxwell Cassilis	G/Capt		27.08.55	Retirement

Group Captain William Maxwell Cassilis CBE mentioned in despatches, died on Friday, 1st March 1957.

16179	KNOX*	Brian Wright	S/Ldr		01.08.46	Retired list

At his own request [LG 13 August 1946], he died on Tuesday, 20th August 1968. During his service he was involved in one serious air accident, this being summarised on Monday 19th April 1926, when he was flying DH.9As with 8 Squadron at Hinaidi.

16182	MAY*	Faulkner Michael Vine	G/Capt	+	22.05.42	

Group Captain Faulkner Michael Vine May died in a prisoner of war camp. He is buried in Benghazi War Cemetery, where his headstone is inscribed: *"They Freely Gave The Fairest Offering It Was In Their Power To Give""Pericles."* Married, his next of kin is shown as Muriel Nora May of Oudtshoorn, Cape Province, South Africa. The circumstances leading up to his death are given on page 142 of David Gunby and Pelham Temple's first volume of Bomber Losses in the Middle East and Mediterranean theatres in the summary for 3rd-4th May 1942, 108 Squadron Liberator II AL511 captained by Flight Lieutenant D H McArthur DFC, shot down over Libya during a raid on Tobruk.

16181	McEVOY*	Theodore Newman	ACM		19.11.62	Retirement

Air Chief Marshal Sir Theodore McEvoy KCB CBE twice mentioned in despatches, died on Thursday, 19th September 1991. During the *Battle of Britain* he was Officer Commanding RAF Northolt and although not listed as flying operationally during the Battle, he is mentioned by Norman Franks on page 112 of his revised Fighter Command losses as being wounded on 16th April 1941, when he joined 601 Squadron AAF tasked for escort duties. Tangling with Me109s from JG51, three of their Hurricanes were shot down and all three pilots wounded, Group Captain McEvoy crash-landing his Hurricane IIa Z2492 at Lydd in Kent.

During his days as a Flight Cadet he had a spill riding his motorcycle through Sleaford on 26th April 1924. By coincidence, a former cadet, Montague Douglas Ommanney fell from his motorcycle in London.

16183	PATCH*	Hubert Leonard	ACM		29.05.61	Retirement

Air Chief Marshal Sir Hubert Patch KCB CBE four times mentioned in despatches, died on Wednesday, 18th November 1987.

	PRIESTMAN	Frederick	P/O	+	19.03.27	11 Squadron

Like so many of his fellow cadets, Frederick Priestman was the proud owner of a motorcycle, and, again, like many of his contemporaries, he fell off while riding in the local area on 25th October 1924. His injuries, however, were of a minor nature.

	RICKS	Arnold William Alexander	F/O	+	26.12.28	47 Squadron
	TRISTEM*	Harry Hugh Vivian	F/Lt	+	26.02.36	8 Squadron

The circumstances of Flight Lieutenant Harry Hugh Vivian Tristem's death will be reported in a future volume.

16185	WILSON*	Ronald Christopher	G/Capt		15.05.52	Retirement

Group Captain Ronald Christopher Wilson died on Thursday, 4th October 1956. Paul McMillan adds: *"Living in Richmond, Surrey in 1939, his wife Gladys M Wilson was a Plotter WAAF."*

	WORSLEY*	Thomas Eric	F/O		24.09.30	Cashiered

By sentence of General Court Martial [LG 6 January 1931, issue 33677, page 148].

John George Denholm Armour, John Rhys Jones, Geoffrey Edwyn Gifford Lywood, all back-classed from the February 1923 entry and those officers with an asterisk appended against their names, graduated on 31st July 1925 [LG 1 September 1925, issue 33080, page 5770].

SWORD OF HONOUR
Flight Cadet Theodore Newman McEvoy

ROLL OF HONOUR
SEPTEMBER 1923 ENTRY

S/Ldr	ANNESS	Lionel Hubert	14 May 1953	
P/O	EATON	James		
G/Capt	MAY	Faulkner Michael Vine	22 May 1942	
P/O	PRIESTMAN	Frederick	19 March 1927	11 Squadron
F/O	RICKS	Arnold William Alexander	26 December 1928	47 Squadron
F/Lt	TRISTEM	Harry Hugh Vivian	26 February 1936	8 Squadron

FLYING ACCIDENTS

Wednesday 18 July 1923
Avro 504K D8843 F/Cdt C W Moss Injured
T/o Cranwell for a navigation detail; became lost and attempting a forced-landing stalled and crashed near the village of Harwick, some 7 miles NW of Lincoln. Flight Cadet Charles William Moss was helped from the cockpit suffered from a painful abrasion to his lower lip and on medical examination it was discovered he had sustained contusions to his chest and both shoulders.

From the September 1921 entry, he would, sadly, be killed on 9th April 1924, while attached to 4 Squadron at Farnborough; my summary for that date has the details.

Tuesday 31 July 1923
Bristol F.2B E243 F/Cdt F W L C Beaumont Injured
Flight Cadet T/o Cranwell allowed his airspeed to drop to a critical level as he approached the College's landing area and as a consequence he stalled and crashed. Please refer to the September 1921 entry for additional information regarding Flight Cadet Beaumont who was only slightly hurt.

Friday 12 October 1923
Avro 504K D8845 *Not reported*
T/o Cranwell for an exercise during which the engine failed; crashed into a tree whilst forced landing near the Colleg

Appendix E - Roll of Honour

ROYAL AIR FORCE

P/O	BARNES	John Owen	14 December 1923	55 Squadron
Sgt	BEAUMONT	Herbert Baden	26 June 1923	100 Squadron

His service number 140367 indicates a transfer from another arm of the services, or conscription, between March and April 1918, the block of numbers for the period being 138001 - 149000

F/O	BRADLEY	Harold Joseph	6 February 1923	216 Squadron
F/O	CHAMBERS	Cyril	2 February 1923	39 Squadron
P/O	COVENTRY	Edward Bernard	29 September 1923	39 Squadron
F/O	CURTIS	Philip Frank Axford	23 February 1923	216 Squadron
F/O	EMBLETON	Clifford Frederick	23 February 1923	216 Squadron
P/O	FITZMAURICE	Maurice James	14 July 1923	56 Squadron
F/O	GOSSIP Australia	George Hatfield Dingley	24 April 1923	56 Squadron
P/O	HARRIS	Frederic Samuel	24 April 1923	39 Squadron
F/O	JAQUES	Robin	8 August 1923	100 Squadron
Mechanic	JARVIS	William	18 June 1923	216 Squadron
F/O	LEDGER	Aubrey	4 December 1923	55 Squadron
F/O	LINGWOOD	Percy William	18 June 1923	216 Squadron
F/O	LOCH	Desmond Reginald	7 April 1923	20 Squadron
F/O	LOGSDAIL	Edward William	7 July 1923	24 Squadron
LAC	PLOWS	William Percival	23 February 1923	216 Squadron
LAC	SAINSBURY	George Redvers	14 December 1923	55 Squadron
Mechanic	SKUSE	Frederick William	18 June 1923	216 Squadron
F/O	STRINGER	Hugh Mansfield	7 April 1923	20 Squadron
F/O	TALLENTIRE	Miles	14 October 1923	60 Squadron
LAC	TAYLOR	Gerald Arthur	21 August 1923	28 Squadron
F/O	TRAPAGNA-LEROY AFC	Marcel Gustave Louis	7 July 1923	24 Squadron
F/O	TRENCH	Murice Crosbie	24 April 1923	39 Squadron
F/Lt	WARD	Neville Byron	18 June 1923	216 Squadron
Cpl	WARDLE	William	29 September 1923	39 Squadron
AC1	WATSON	Ronald Sinclair	16 October 1923	7 Squadron

His service number 353348 identifies him as joining as a civilian, the block of numbers allocated being 340001 - 360000 issued between September 1919 and June 1925.

F/O	WHITMORE	Fielding Griffith	21 August 1923	28 Squadron
AC1	YOUNG	Arthur Leonard	12 October 1923	60 Squadron

SQUADRON LOSSES
1924

The year 1924, witnessed the first serious air accidents of 'new types' being introduced, though as the summaries show the vast majority of crashes involved the machines of yesteryear. And of a concerning nature, reports of serious 'mishaps' in which the airframe was written off rose significantly with over ninety squadron losses reported in the twelve months. Fatalities, too, increased and, it appears, non-commissioned airmen in the form of Sergeant-pilots were arriving on the squadrons in some numbers.

JANUARY

Thursday 3 January 1924
32 Squadron F/O F A Pumpfrey Injured
7F.1 Snipe F2442
T/o Kenley for a cross-country flight only to become lost when a mist descended. Then, through a fleeting break in the conditions a recreation field came into view and a forced-landing was immediately made and ali may have been well but before coming to a stop the Snipe ran into a stout fence and was damaged beyond repair. Making enquiries, the pilot was told he was down at Lewisham in SE London.

Flying Officer Frederic Alan Pumpfrey had returned to the service the previous year [see Appendix D and his entry on 23rd May 1923]. His original commission as a 2nd Lieutenant to the General List of the Royal Flying Corps, effective from 30th May 1917, was promulgated in *The London Gazette* of 26th June 1917, supplement 30151, page 6355. Some *Gazette* entries show an award of a Distinguished Conduct Medal, an example being his transfer to the Reserve Class A on 4th May 1928, which appeared on 8th May 1928, issue 33382, page 3251.

Friday 4 January 1924
1 Squadron F/Lt J M McAlery +
7F.1 Snipe H4906
T/o Hinaidi and 'crashed' it is thought Flight Lieutenant John Mecredy McAlery fainted while in flight. He had been granted a short service commission, effective from 27th July 1921 [LG 9 August 1921, issue 32416, page 6284] in the rank of flying officer, though his service on the General List had commenced during the *Great War,* his details appearing in *The London Gazette* on 26th May 1917, supplement 30096, page 5201.

84 Squadron F/O R C Harrison +
DH.9A D9854 LAC H W Key +
T/o Shaibah and destroyed in a crash to the south of Nasiriyah, eyewitnesses reporting that the DH went out of control and fell in an uncontrolled spin. Flying Officer Robert Cuthbert Harrison was granted a short service commission on 28th November 1921 [LG 6 December 1921, issue 32540, page 9891].

Leading Aircraftman Harold Walter Key whose service number 330927 falls within the block 329001 - 335000 enlisted, or was conscripted, between March and August 1919.

Friday 25 January 1924
20 Squadron F/O J N Jaques Injured
Bristol F.2b D8039 LAC A V Stevens +
T/o Quetta and while attempting to forced-land on the Baleli road some 3 miles distant from the airfield collided with telegraph wires and crashed.

Joining as boy airman between October 1917 and December 1918, Leading Aircraftman Albert Victor Stevens' service number was 158977 which comes a little over halfway through the block of numbers 155001 - 1600000.

Saturday 26 January 1924
5 Squadron P/O C H Ratcliffe Injured
Bristol F.2b D7830
T/o Ambala and on arrival at the landing ground at Kutwa stalled on approach and crashed; wrecked, Pilot Officer Charles Hartington Ratcliffe requiring medical assistance for his injuries. Entering the Cadet College at Cranwell with the September 1920 entry, he graduated with a permanent commission, seniority 16th August 1922 [LG 29 September 1922, issue 32751, page 6910]. He resigned his commission on the 26th of September 1928, by which time he had attained flying officer rank.

Monday 28 January 1924
24 Squadron P/O A W Daly Injured
DH.9A J578
T/o Kenley and wrecked after flying into trees on Taunton Farm near the airfield. Pilot Officer Alison Wenley Daly had received his short service commission on Boxing Day 1922, his details being recorded in Appendix D for the year.

Evidence recorded on the accident card reads: *"The pilot lost control of the aeroplane at a height of about 900 feet and failed to recover normal flight before the machine struck the ground and was wrecked. Error of judgement, mishandling the controls."*

Tuesday 29 January 1924
5 Squadron F/O R A R Mangles Injured
Bristol F.2b F4630 F/O G V Wheatley Injured
T/o Ambala and crashed with a force sufficient to damage the airframe beyond repair while trying to land at the Sangor Maia landing ground. Flying Officers Roland Arthur Ross Mangles and Gilbert Vernon Wheatley both requiring medical attention. The former reported to Cranwell with the Schools' entry in February 1920. He rose to the rank of group captain, retiring on 27th September 1948. His death occurred on 15th March 1976.

Flying Officer Wheatley, born 17th March 1899, was commissioned to the General List, his date of joining the RFC is shown as 13th August 1917. He arrived at Serny on 24th April 1918, where he was attached to 22 Squadron [Bristol F.2b] and appears to have enjoyed a trouble free tour of duty before returning to England on 26th October 1918.

Postwar he joined the mass exodus of officers to the Unemployed List but was recalled for temporary duty until re-transferring to the List on 5th June 1921 [LG 24 June 1921, issue 32368, page 5016]. However, he was accepted back into the service with a short service commission, effective 23rd June 1921 [LG 5 July 1921, issue 32380, page 5359] and on New Year's Day 1926, was appointed to a permanent commission [LG 23 February 1926, issue 33135, page 1342]. Sadly, on the 7th of December of that year while serving as a test pilot at Martlesham Heath he was killed while testing a Gloster Gamecock [see his entry in Appendix D 1921 and the six officers granted short service commissions on 5th July 1921.

27 Squadron F/O D J Hugh-Jones +
DH.9A E8629 Cpl T H Hall Injured
T/o Risalpur but within seconds of leaving the ground collided with a tree, crashed and burst into flames. Flying Officer David Jasper Hugh-Jones perished immediately, but poor Thomas Henry Hall, 22 years of age, lingered until the 11th of February before succumbing to his burns. He joined as a boy and on attesting was given the service number 326962 which identifies his service as beginning twixt December 1918 and March 1919.

Flying Officer Hugh-Jones was commissioned to the Special Reserve of Officers as a 2nd Lieutenant [former cadet] on 26th April 1917, Royal Welsh Fusiliers [LG 17 May 1917, supplement 30074, page 4789].

Accepted by the RFC on 26th October 1917, for training as an observer, he joined 102 Squadron [FE.2b] at Izel-le-Hameau on 6th March 1918, remaining on their establishment until posted back the UK on the last day of August 1918. His short service commission was promulgated on 10th May 1921, issue 32319, page 3752, while Army Form B.103c shows his date of birth as 9th April 1897.

FEBRUARY

Sunday 3 February 1924
2 Squadron P/O R V M Odbert Injured
Bristol F.2b J6703
T/o Manston and damaged beyond repair in the wake of a forced landing, occasioned by engine failure brought about by disruption to the flow of petrol, near the station at Battle, Sussex. Pilot Officer Reginald Vere Massey Odbert's details are recorded in Appendix D under the entries for officers commissioned on 19th September 1922.

Thursday 7 February 1924
32 Squadron P/O A R Woodyatt Safe See 22 May 1925
7F.1 Snipe E7556
T/o Kenley for night flying practice. From one approach the pilot misjudged his flare and hit the ground with a force sufficient to damage the fighter beyond repair. Pilot Officer Arthur Reinagle Woodyatt escaped with no more than a bad shaking.

Friday 15 February 1924
25 Squadron F/Lt G H H Scutt MC + St. Mary's Churchyard, New Ross
7F.1 Snipe E7601
T/o Hawkinge and while engaged in a formation dive failed to recover before flying into the ground. Flight Lieutenant George Howard Homer Scutt, born on the 5th of May 1895, in New Ross, Co. Wexford, and formerly of the 1st Battalion, King's Liverpool Regiment, was accepted by the RFC to train as an observer on 25th August 1917, and between 23rd October 1917, and 12th May 1918, was attached to 48 Squadron [Bristol F.2b]. His award of the MC was approved on 14th April 1918, and *Gazetted* in supplement 30761, page 7422, of the paper issued on 22nd June 1918:
"For conspicuous gallantry and devotion to duty. He has destroyed one hostile machine and driven down three others out of control. He carried out an important single-machine reconnaissance, frequently descending to a height of 100 feet under heavy rifle fire and machine-gun fire, and obtained valuable information. While returning, he attacked 5 enemy machines, and ably assisted his pilot in driving them back over their lines.

He has carried out many successful photographic reconnaissances, and has at all times proved himself to be a keen and daring officer."

At the time of his death he was the squadron's adjutant. He is commemorated by a family memorial in St. Mary's Churchyard, New Ross, Co. Wexford, Ireland.

56 Squadron P/O J C Savory +
7F.1 Snipe F2472
T/o Biggin Hill where on his approach to land Pilot Officer John Charles Savory lost control and in an uncontrolled spin crashed. He had received a short service commission, *Gazetted* on Boxing Day 1922, issue 32780, page 9120. The Court of Inquiry was of the opinion it was an error of judgement on the part of the pilot.

216 Squadron F/Lt B D S Tuke Safe
Vimy F9185 F/O G Archer Injured
T/o Heliopolis and reported damaged beyond repair following a flying accident. Flight Lieutenant Brian Donille Stratford Tuke 'walked away' unharmed, but his co-pilot, Flying Officer Gordon Archer was not quite so fortunate, though his injuries were not of too serious a nature.

Monday 18 February 1924
20 Squadron F/O R V D White Safe
Bristol F.2b J6644 F/O A L Harris Safe
T/o Quetta and while making a turn over the airfield at low altitude stalled and crashed out of control. It had been on squadron charge since the beginning of the year and had required attention after being damaged early in February. The loss of J6644 was, in the opinion of the Court of Inquiry, due to an error of judgement on the part of the pilot.

Flying Officer Robert Vivian Douglas White and Flying Officer Arthur Leslie Harris were both short service commissioned, their details being *Gazetted* on 28th January and 12th July 1921, respectively.

Monday 25 February 1924
60 Squadron P/O G H Rawlinson Safe
DH.9A H3620
T/o Risalpur but within moments of climbing away the engine failed and in the crash-landing that followed the airframe was damaged beyond repair. Pilot Officer Gerald Henry Rawlinson received a short service commission, *Gazetted* 28th November 1922, issue 32771, page 8416.

MARCH

Monday 3 March 1924
111 Squadron F/Lt V A Albrecht Injured
7F.1 Snipe E6617 F/O J G Peck + Warmwell [Holy Trinity] Churchyard
T/o Duxford and on return, and making ready to land, came into collision with an Avro 504K H3071 of the locally based 2 FTS. Flying instructor, Sergeant George Thomas Bond was killed in the Avro but Pilot Officer William Alfred Tattersall, granted a short service commission as recently as 14th January 1924, and *Gazetted* in issue 32902, page 875, his pupil survived.

Flying Officer Jasper Godfrey Peck was a graduate from the naval entry to the Cadet College at Cranwell [see my third volume, page 270]. His passenger, Flight Lieutenant Vaudrey Adolph Albrecht had been granted a temporary commission for four years duty with the Royal Air Force on 25th September 1922 [LG 10 October 1922, issue 32754, page 7135]. His entry in the paper shows he was at the time a captain with the Manchester Regiment and a holder of the OBE and MC. However, he relinquished his temporary commission with effect from 14th October 1924, having been placed on the half-pay list by the Army on account of ill-health [no doubt as a result of injuries sustained in the crash] [LG 13 October 1925, issue 33092, page 6617].

Initially, the following report was filed: *"Just beyond the eastern corner of the aerodrome the Avro aircraft were seen to turn simultaneously to the left and glide down into wind as if about to land. The Avro being below and ahead of the Snipe. During the glide the Snipe closed in on the Avro and at a height of about 150 feet a collision occurred. Both aircraft fell to the ground out of control and were completely wrecked.*

"Opinion: That the collision in the air was due to the non-observance of several Rules of the Air [King's Regulations Appendix IX para [24] by the pilot of the Snipe aircraft."

The findings of the AOC No. 3 Group reads as follows: *"I do not consider that the pilot of the Avro H3071 can be held responsible.*

"There is no evidence to show whether the presence of Snipe E6617 was or was not known to either of the occupants of the Avro during their approach to the Aerodrome.

"The pilot of the Snipe was aware of the presence of the Avro in his vicinity. He is, in my opinion partly responsible for the accident since the machine was the overtaking machine; since he did in part endeavour to avoid the Avro by turning to port - thereby assuming responsibility for its avoidance; and since he failed subsequently to ascertain the other machine.

"It is possible that no collision would have occurred had not the Avro "zoomed" immediately prior to the collision. I do not therefore consider Flight Lieutenant Albrecht, the pilot of the Snipe [in view of the incompleteness of the evidence] be held to blame

"To guard against the repetition of a similar accident when the aerodrome is constricted, OC 2 FTS has been instructed to amplify the Flying Standing Orders so as to prevent machines turning into wind preparatory to landing at Duxford within a radius of 500 yards of the Aerodrome boundaries."

*"[Sd] L. Charlton**
A/C Commanding No. 3 Group, RAF"

* Air Commodore Lionel Evelyn Oswald Charlton whose appointment as Air Officer Commanding No. 3 Group was promulgated on 7th March 1924. Thus, the accident here summarised must have been one of the first that he was called

upon to adjudicate. He is mentioned in my third volume in the appendix for permanent officers, page 179, beneath the heading 'Colonels.'

Monday 17 March 1924
5 Squadron *Not reported*
Bristol F.2b J6628/D
T/o Dardoni and wrecked up on the North West Frontier when engine failure resulted in a crash-landing near Razani.

45 Squadron P/O W H Ryder +
Bristol F.2b D8099 LAC K Turner +
T/o Hinaidi where, it is reported, the Bristol stalled, went into a spin and crashed. Pilot Officer Walter Harry Ryder was granted a short service commission, promulgated in *The London Gazette* 19th September 1922, issue 32748, page 6715.

Leading Aircraftman Kenneth Turner was dangerously injured; his skull was fractured at the base and despite prompt medical help he died within hours of the crash.

A Court of Inquiry was held, the Court subsequently reporting: *"The cause of the accident was probably due to an error of judgement on the part of the pilot. It is thought that he may have attempted to change from front to rear petrol tank and that either he failed to turn the 3 way cock correctly or that the pressure tap to the rear tank was off and that when the engine failed in consequence he put his head inside the cockpit to look at the taps and stalled the machine and just failed to recover from the resulting spin."*

"AOC concurs."

News of the tragedy found its way into the British papers with *The Western Morning News and Mercury* reporting on Thursday, March 20th, 1934, under the heading *'Flying Accident in Iraq - Newton Officer Killed'*

"News of the tragic death of Flight-Lieut.[sic] *Walter Harry Ryder, son of Mr. and Mrs. C T Ryder, of Torquay-road, Newton Abbot, was received yesterday.*

"Lieut. Ryder was on service at Baghdad, where he was piloting a machine for the conveyance of mails, and from the brief communications made by Lord Thomson, Secretary of State for Air, it appears that the young officer met his death in an accident at Hinaidi, last Monday, when piloting a Bristol Fighter which crashed.

"In a letter to his father a few days since the young officer said he longed for the chance of flying the model he was accustomed to during the war instead of the obsolete type his squadron was now provided, the flying of which was martyrdom to any pilot.

"Lieut. Ryder was an exceptionally clever pilot, and had made great progress in the service. He was only 23 years of age, and was well known and highly popular at Newton Abbot, where he had a large circle of friends.

'The greatest sympathy will be extended to the family in their tragic bereavement.

"Lieut. Ryder became a pilot officer in September 1922, and was appointed to 45 Squadron, at Hinaidi, in the Iraq Command last November, following a year's instruction at No. 5 Flying Training School, Shotwick."

The issue of Bristol F.2b D8099 to 45 Squadron must have been a 'one off' as it is not mentioned in Annex L of *The Flying Camels - The History of No. 45 Sqn RAF.* It is recorded in Air-Britain's recent history of the Bristol Fighter, but here their appears to have been some misreporting of its movements. Quoting from page 310: *"D8099 PD Ascot. To Iraq. AD Hinaidi. 45 Sqn by 7.23. AD Hinaidi by 8.23. To Egypt. AD Aboukir. 208 Sqn by 10.24."*

Another oddity is the reference by Pilot Officer Ryder [he was not a flight lieutenant], whose age, if correctly reported by the paper, was 23, makes reference to his wartime flying. In 1918, when hostilities ceased, he could not have been more than 17; there is, however, an Army Form B.103 for a 'W H Ryder' [it is devoid of Christian names, date of birth and next of kin] which shows prior to joining the RFC he was commissioned to Yorks Hussars [Territorials], thus making it highly improbable that they are one and the same person.

His observer, or air gunner, Leading Aircraftman Turner most likely started his service in March 1919, as his number 329084 is one of the early allocations from the block 329001 - 335000 set aside for civilian entrants.

Thursday 20 March 1924
99 Squadron *Not reported*
DH.9A J8460/3
T/o Netheravon and set out for Upper Heyford in Oxfordshire where on arrival it collided with the watch office building and was damaged beyond repair. From the final production run of DH.9As, all built with dual controls, J8460 was one of 23 airframes [J8460-J8482] built by Westland Aircraft at Yeovil, while Parnall & Company of Bristol built the remaining dozen, block J8483-J8494].

Apart from the single issue to 99 Squadron only five are recorded as seeing squadron service; J8469 used by 600 Squadron AAF; J8471 which was passed from 1 FTS Netheravon to 207 Squadron in May 1927, and thence to 39 Squadron before being returned to '207' and by October 1929, in service with 33 Squadron. J8472 direct to 207 Squadron and later given up to 600, 603 and 604 Squadrons of the AAF; J8482 601 Squadron AAF and 35 Squadron who was involved with palisade trials aboard HMS *Glorious* and was lost overboard during 1930. J8491 to 600 Squadron and wrecked after being transferred to 501 Squadron AAF.

APRIL

Tuesday 1 April 1924
24 Squadron P/O R G Rickman Safe
Avro 504K F8936
T/o Kenley but moments later the machine stalled and crashed; wrecked. Pilot Officer Richard George Rickman's short service commission is reported in Appendix D for officers so granted on 5th December 1922. He reported to Kenley for service with 24 Squadron on 1st February 1924.
The report from the Court of Inquiry reads: *"Through an error of judgement on the part of the pilot when taking off the aeroplane stalled and fell to the ground. The machine was wrecked but the pilot who was the only occupant escaped injury."* On 27th August 1924, he left the service, relinquishing his commission on account of ill-health.

Wednesday 9 April 1924
4 Squadron P/O C W Moss +
Bristol F.2b J6784
T/o Farnborough and crashed soon after following an uncontrolled spin. Pilot Officer Charles William Moss graduated from the Cadet College at Cranwell on 19th December 1923 [LG 22 January 1924, issue 32900, page 688]. During his time at the College he had use of a motorcycle and while riding in the vicinity of Golders Green, London, on 2nd February 1923, he had a spill which required medical attention.
His injuries proved slight and he was back at the College where on 16th February 1923, he reported to sick quarters with a cut sustained when the mainspring of the gramophone he was mending suddenly slipped.
His misfortunes continued for on 18th July 1923, in the late stages of his flying instruction he was involved in a serious crash which wrote off his aircraft, the details for this being reported in Appendix E and the College's flying accidents for 1923.
On Friday, April 11th, 1924, the *Birmingham Gazette* beneath the heading *'Airman's Dive to Death'* reported:
"A Farnborough jury yesterday reported a verdict of "Accidental Death" in connection with an aeroplane accident to Flying Officer [sic] *Charles William Moss, RAF, who died from his injuries on Wednesday afternoon after his Bristol Fighter had crashed on Farnborough Common on a practice flight.*
"He taxied off from the flying sheds at Farnborough Aerodrome and had risen 300 feet when his propeller and engine stopped and he nose-dived to earth, being killed instantly.
"The machine was said to have been in perfect flying condition."

20 Squadron F/O H L P Lester Safe
Bristol F.2b J6731
T/o Quetta and wrecked when, on landing at Fort Sandeman, the starboard wheel detached from the axle. Granted a short service commission as a flying officer on 19th December 1919, Hugh Lewis Pingo Lester [see page 244 of the third volume] retired from the service with the rank of wing commander on 22nd December 1943.
The previous October, the 17th to be precise, and while on establishment of the Armament and Gunnery School, Eastchurch, he sprained an ankle while playing football.
On 26th March 2009, his medals were auctioned by Dix Noonan Webb of London, the collection including the Indian General Service Medal Waziristan 1925 with clasp awarded for his service in India with 20 Squadron. Estimated at between £40 and £50, the gavel came down at £90.

Friday 11 April 1924
84 Squadron F/Lt W H E Kemp AFC +
DH.9A J552 AC2 A L Adams +
T/o Jalibah but while banking stalled and crashed. Born on the last day of January 1897, Flight Lieutenant William Horace Ernest Kemp transferred from the army to the RFC in April 1916, and between 4th April and 12th December 1917, was attached to 100 Squadron [FE.2b], I suspect in an observer capacity. His short service commission was *Gazetted* 12th September 1919, issue 31548, page 11468.
Aircraftman Arthur Lee Adams joined from a civilian occupation probably in the autumn of 1919 as his service number 341319 is towards the commencement of the block 340001 which continued to 360000, ending in June 1925.

Thursday 24 April 1924
During a 'trawl' of the numerous incidents reported in the year 1924, many not related to flying accidents, came across the following concerning Flying Officer Charles Frederick Hallyburton Grace of 60 Squadron who was returning to Lahore in DH.9A E8641 and on landing had the misfortune to run into a calf. George was not hurt, but the accident card fails to mention the outcome for the unfortunate calf.
The cow in India is for the Hindu population who form the majority of India's population is a sacred animal, a brief description on *Wikipedia* states for the Hindus *"Its horns symbolise the gods, its four legs, the ancient Hindu scriptures of the "Vedas" and its udder, the four objectives of life, including material wealth, desire, righteousness and salvation."*
The DH was little inconvenienced and its final mention in records shows a forced-landing with engine failure on 27th October 1926, while on establishment 27 Squadron. Damage was of a minor nature and it was sent for repair, after which its fate has not been recorded.
Flying Officer Grace, meanwhile [see Appendix D and the officers granted short service commissions on 13th January 1922] went on to serve throughout the Second World War before retiring at his own request on 15th February 1946. He had risen to the rank of group captain.

Monday 28 April 1924
28 Squadron F/O I P Anderson +
Bristol F.2b F4286 AC1 K R Taylor +
T/o Peshawar armed with bombs and flying in fog smashed into the side of a hill near Razmak; exploded on impact. Flying Officer Ian Patrick Anderson was three years into his short service commission which was published in issue 32387, page 5561, of the *Gazette* published on 12th July 1921. During his flying training at 5 FTS Shotwick, he was seriously injured on 2nd May 1922, when he lost control of Bristol F.2b D7804, crashing close to the airfield. His passenger, 19-year old Aircraftman Samuel Thompson was killed.

Leading Aircraftman Kenneth Robert Taylor was one of the many former boy airmen mentioned in this volume; his number 335262 is within the block 335001 - 336000 with issues commencing August 1919 and finishing during January 1921.

Tuesday 29 April 1924
60 Squadron F/Lt J W Baker MC Safe See 14 October 1924
DH.9A E8473/5 AC1 S Cooper Safe
T/o Risalpur but climbed too steeply and stalled into the ground; damaged beyond repair. Formerly commissioned to the Royal Garrison Artillery and attached to the 12th Heavy Battery, John Wakeling Baker, born 23rd October 1897, transferred to the Royal Flying Corps in 1917, training as an observer and was officially accepted for service on 25th October 1917. He served on the Western Front with 4 Squadron [BE.2c] from that date until 14th May 1918, when he was returned to 'Home Establishment.'

He was *Gazetted* with the Military Cross on 26th July 1918, supplement 30813, page 8773: *"for conspicuous gallantry and devotion to duty in carrying out low-flying reconnaissances and contact patrols under heavy machine-gun, rifle and anti-aircraft fire, when he remained in the air for long hours, often under abnormally bad weather conditions and often in darkness or thick mist. On one occasion he fired into enemy troops and transport, causing great confusion, and remained over their lines taking notes until quite dark, when he returned with his machine riddled with bullets. On every flight he obtained important information, which was dropped at headquarters, and throughout the period of his work has been magnificent."*

Commencing in August 1918, he re-mustered to pilot and trained at Yatesbury in Wiltshire with No. 37 Training Depot Station, returning to France in February 1919, to fly Bristol F.2b with 8 Squadron, transferring to 12 Squadron for duties on the Rhineland in October on the same year. By now he was a permanent officer, having been appointed on the 1st of August 1919.

Remaining in the service, he received a Distinguished Flying Cross on 20th November 1925, supplement 33104, 7601: *"The KING has been graciously pleased to approve of the undermentioned rewards in recognition of gallant and distinguished service in connection with the operations carried out by the Royal Air Force in Waziristan, 9th March 1925, to 1st May 1925."*

His British India service ended in the early spring of 1928, after which service life followed a familiar pattern of Staff Duties mixed with flying appointments. In January 1935, he commanded 35 Squadron [Hart], deploying to Sudan in October 1935, where he fell ill in the December and was evacuated to Egypt for treatment in the military hospital in Cairo. This, was his last flying appointment and for the remainder of his service he filled a variety of Staff Posts at home and abroad, eventually completing his long and distinguished military life as Controller of Aircraft at the Ministry of Supply.

Knight Grand Commander of the Bath, Air Marshal Sir John Baker retired on 17th December 1956; his death was reported from the London Borough of Bromley on 10th March 1978, at the age of 80.

Wednesday 30 April 1924
20 Squadron F/O J A Hollis Safe
Bristol F.2b J6655
T/o Quetta and on arrival at the Chaman landing ground a wheel came off as the Bristol touched down and in the next few moments Flying Officer John Augustus Hollis found his head was closer to *terra firma* than his feet. He was, however, uninjured.

Note. On the same day, and at the same location, 20 Squadron Bristol F.2b J6660 struck a water channel on touch down and overturned; again, no injuries to the pilot, named as Flight Lieutenant Paul Chamberlayne AFC. Indications are that the Bristol was salvaged and following repair was in the hands of 5 Squadron by November 1924.

MAY

Monday 5 May 1924
14 Squadron *Not reported*
Bristol F.2b CR4651
T/o Ramleh and wrecked here in a landing accident. Prior to being accepted by the squadron the Bristol had been rebuilt at the Aircraft Depot at Aboukir.

56 Squadron F/O F H Ronksley MC Injured
7F.1 Snipe E8243
T/o Biggin Hill for night flying practice; wrecked in a heavy landing. Flying Officer Francis Hugh Ronksley was deemed to have made an error of judgement on his approach. His military service started as a cadet in the Officer

Training Corps in which he attained the rank of cadet colour-sergeant at the Repton School Contingent, Junior Division and was *Gazetted* 2nd Lieutenant on 12th September 1914 [LG 29 September 1914, issue 28918, page 7701].

During his service with the Royal Engineers he gained a MC [EG January 1, 1917, issue 13033, page 40]. By the following year he had transferred to the RFC and served, briefly, from 20th February to 30th May 1918, flying Sopwith F.1 Camels with 80 Squadron on the Western Front.

He was placed on the retired list, ranked flight lieutenant, on 26th August 1934 [LG 28 August 1934, issue 34082, page 5463].

Wednesday 7 May 1924

19 Squadron Sgt C C Bird Safe
7F.1 Snipe E7605

T/o Duxford but swung badly and collided with a parked Avro 504K. The accident was attributed to the failure of Sergeant Bird failing to get the tail up; as he had just one hour of flying on type, inexperience obvious played its part. It is possible that Sergeant Bird's niche in Royal Air Force history is that he was the first sergeant-pilot in squadron service to write off his aircraft.

Friday 16 May 1924

20 Squadron F/O E C Usher-Somers + Quetta Christian and Cantonment Cemetery
Bristol F.2b D7821 Lt E C Mackenzie + Quetta Christian and Cantonment Cemetery

T/o Quetta but climbed too steeply, stalled and crashed. Flying Officer Edmund Cronin Usher-Somers was a recipient of various medals, including the India General Service Medal 1 Clasp Waziristan 1919-21. Sold by London auctioneers Dix Doonan Webb, the later sold for £330 on 30th March 2011.

Edward Charrington Mackenzie graduated from RMA Sandhurst on 17th October 1915, and was *Gazetted* as a 2nd Lieutenant to the Royal Garrison Artillery [LG 26 October 1915, issue 29340, page 10518].

JUNE

Thursday 5 June 1924

39 Squadron F/O R H Daly DSC DFC +
DH.9A E8654 Sgt W H Brewer +

T/o Spittlegate and completely destroyed at 1445 following a midair collision with the aircraft summarised below. The biography on *Wikipedia* for Flying Officer Rowan Heywood Daly shows he was born in Trieste, at the time part of the Austrian Empire, on 30th March 1898. On the outbreak of the *Great War* he convinced the recruiting authorities that he was old enough to serve and was accepted as a private soldier in the 14th Battalion London Regiment, one of the many 'New Army' battalions raised in the patriotic fever of the time.

Two years later he was commissioned to the RNAS and the following year while serving with a Home Defence unit he was one of many pilots who were in action on 7th July 1917, when a large force of Gotha heavy bombers arrived over London causing considerable damage and deaths [*Wikipedia* indicates 57 were killed and 193 injured]. Flying a Sopwith Triplane, Rowan chased one of the bombers and succeeded in shooting it down into the sea off Ostend, an action that gained him a mentioned in despatches. However, it seems a DSC would also be appropriate and this was duly *Gazetted* on 11th August 1917, supplement 30227, page 8207: *"For skill and gallantry in attacking enemy aircraft returning from a raid on England. After a long chase he engaged and brought down one machine in flames. Afterwards he engaged a second machine, but his gun jammed, and though he continued the pursuit to the enemy coast, he failed to clear the jamb, and was obliged to return to his aerodrome."*

Postwar, he was involved in supporting the White Russians fighting the Bolsheviks in the south of the country during which he accounted for four of the Bolsheviks' aircraft, this being recognised with the award of a DFC [LG 12 July 1920, supplement 31974, page 7422]. A few weeks later the *Gazette* [10 August 1920, issue 32012, page 8278] reported his granting of a short service commission.

Prior to joining 39 Squadron on 14th May 1923, he had been attached to 100 Squadron, also Spittlegate based, and with '100' he was victorious in a landing competition at Hendon's aerial pageant.

Sergeant William Henry Brewer saw active service pre-April 1918, with the RNAS. His service number is recorded as 244928 and falls within the block 244711 - 260000.

39 Squadron F/O L G Lucas +
DH.9A J7087 AC1 T Copleston +

T/o Spittlegate and destroyed as reported above, both machines being burnt out. Leslie Gordon Lucas had been restored to the active list on 13th April 1921 [LG 3 May 1921, issue 32311, page 3544]. On 4th June 1921, along with a host of other officers that had been re-engaged, he was again transferred to the unemployed list [LG 24 June 1921, issue 32368, page 5016]. Details of his re-employment are as yet not traced.

Aircraftman Leslie Copleston joined as a boy airman in the late autumn or winter of 1917, his service number 155709 falling within the block reserved for boy entrants [155001 - 160000] between October 1917 and December 1918.

41 Squadron F/Lt R H C Usher MC AFC +
DH.42A Dingo J7006

T/o Northolt for a test flight which, tragically, ended near the airfield when the Dingo broke up in the air. At the time of his death Flight Lieutenant Robert Howell Craster Usher*was on the establishment of Headquarters of the Superintendent of Reserves at Northolt, and it is not known why he became involved in the testing of the aircraft which had been sent to the squadron from Martlesham Heath. Consulting A J Jackson's *De Havilland Aircraft* this shows J7006 flew for the first time on 12th March 1924, and crashed at Martlesham Heath, the wreckage being returned to De Havilland's at Stag Lane. However, his entry in *Wikipedia* confirms the accident as occurring at Northolt and further noting that he was a keen Rugby Union player who played for London Scottish and Leicester and had captained Netheravon's team which included another very noted Royal Air Force officer, Basil Embrey. Earlier in 1924, he had captained the Royal Air Force team in matches against the Army and Royal Navy.

According to Air-Britain's *J File* two machines were produced with J7006 flying for the first time on 25th July 1923, and prior to going to 41 Squadron for service trials spent part of April and May 1924, at Martlesham Heath. The second aircraft, J7007 first flew in September 1924, with a slightly more powerful Jupiter engine and was of all-metal construction. Tested in July 1925 at Martlesham Heath, it returned to DH in the October from where it was issued on 16th November 1926, to RAE Farnborough but appears not to have been flown at this establishment.

As will be seen in the press report, the journalist refers to the aircraft as the 'Dormouse.' This was the forerunner of the 'Dingo' and in A J Jackson's excellent *De Havilland Aircraft* a full description of all three aircraft [J7005, J7006 and J7007] is given between pages 154 and 156, three excellent photographs accompanying the text. Had the the Dingo gone into production, it would have been issued to army co-operation squadrons.

The deaths of the above were reported the next day in the *Aberdeen Press and Journal* under the headline *'Two British Air Disasters -Five Airmen Killed.'*

"Two aeroplane were flying over the aerodrome ground at Spittlegate, Grantham, yesterday afternoon when they collided, caught fire, and fell to the ground. All the found occupants were killed. They were named as:-

"Flying-Officer Leslie Gordon Lucas
"Flying-Officer Rowan Hayward Daly
"Sergeant William Henry Brewer
"Aircraftman Leslie Coppleston [sic]

"Inquires at the Air Ministry show that the dead airmen belonged to the 39th Squadron, Spittlegate. Several machines were in the air when the collision occurred, the squadron being engaged in formation flying.

"Air Ministry officials left for Spittlegate Aerodrome on request of the above, and the state of the machines will be fully investigated. The inquest will be held to-day.

'Another Crash'

'Royal Air Force Rugby Player Killed'

"Flight-Lieut. Robert H C Usher, MC, AFC, of the Royal Air Force, crashed at Northolt flying station yesterday. He was flying a DH.42 machine of a type known as the Dormouse.This is a new machine of the fighting type, and has not yet been introduced into the RAF on an extensive scale.

"How the accident occurred is a mystery. Flight-Lieut. Usher's home was at Farrant [sic] *in Wiltshire. He joined the Air Force during the war, and had a distinguished flying career. He was attached to the Department of the Superintendent of the RAF Reserve at Northolt. He achieved considerable fame in sporting circles ass a Rugby forward of more than ordinary ability. He played for the RAF in the inter-service ...... during the last two seasons, and when not needed for the services he ...... Leicester. He was a good hooker, and in the line-outs and the ...... had few equals in either the Army, 5he Navy, or the RAF."*

Turning to the Court of Inquiry into the deaths of the four 39 Squadron airmen, both report read: *"The cause of the accident was in our opinion due to an error of judgement on the part of the pilots concerned. The Court would like to point out that had the machines involved been equipped with safety petrol tanks and parachutes, it is possible two lives would have been saved."*

"AOC concurs."

Ironically, immediately beneath the *Aberdeen Press and Journal's* report on the three crashes is the following headline

'US Planes Collide -Airman Escapes by Parachute'

'San Antonio [Texas], Thursday'

"Coming together in mid air to-day, two army aeroplanes fell 1,300 feet, burying a Mexican peasant boy who was working in a cotton field. One of the pilots was killed, but the other made a sensational descent by a parachute. With his pack on his back he stepped off into space and shot down from the spinning wreckage of the machines, and floated safely to the ground." "Reuter."

Being of special interest to co-author, Paul McMillan, the two machines, out from Kelly Field, were DH.4Bs 22-364 flown by 1st Lieutenant Will Walter White who parachuted to safety, and AS-68113 piloted by trainee 2nd Lieutenant Stuart Leon Thompson who, sadly, was killed. The poor little Mexican boy, aged 11, was Jose Maria Ramos.

* See Appendix C 1922 for additional notes regarding Flight Lieutenant Usher.

Saturday 14 June 1924

60 Squadron F/O E L W Aitken Safe
DH.9A E977/1
T/o Risalpur and wrecked following a collision with a pylon, the outcome of which is in a photograph on page 198 of *The DH.4/DH.9 File* the mainplanes appearing to be totally smashed.

Monday 16 June 1924
31 Squadron F/O R Pyne Injured
Bristol F.2b J6642
T/o Ambala having been authorised for night flying practice, an exercise that resulted in a heavy landing which damaged the Bristol beyond repair. Flying Officer Reginald Pyne was one of three officers *Gazetted* with the DFC on 20th November 1925, for his work with the squadron during operations in Waziristan between 9th March 1925, and 1st May 1925 [see my summary for Flight Lieutenant Baker, Tuesday 29th April 1924].

56 Squadron F/Lt G Martyn Safe
7F.1 Snipe E8247
T/o Biggin Hill and believed to have been damaged beyond repair following a forced-landing with a failing engine [a piston had broken] in a field where the grass was sufficiently high and thick to send the fighter onto its back. The location is reported as Farningham a village 3 miles SE from Swanley in Kent.

Flight Lieutenant Gilbert Martyn had been granted a short service commission on 12th December 1919 [see page 242 of the third volume], this commission being cancelled on 30th January 1923, when he was appointed as a permanent officer [LG 30 January 1923, issue 32791, page 712].

'Flying a desk' at the Air Ministry, Squadron Leader Martyn fell ill and was admitted to Princess Mary Hospital at Halton where he died on 28th October 1936.

Tuesday 17 June 1924
4 Squadron P/O F J O'Doherty Injured
Bristol F.2b J6712
T/o Farnborough authorised to carry out a practice reconnaissance and damaged beyond repair while making a forced-landing near Guildford, Surrey, in bad visibility. Pilot Officer Francis Joseph O'Doherty received a short service commission on Boxing Day 1922 [see Appendix D]; his death on 12th January 1932, whilst attached to 208 Squadron will be reported in the next volume.

Friday 20 June 1924
11 Squadron P/O C V Fevez Injured
Avro 504K E9381
T/o Netheravon and damaged beyond repair after running onto a raised bank, or ridge. According to the accident report, Pilot Officer Cecil Victor Fevez took off for a practice solo flight but 'choked' the engine; landing, he was unable to arrest his progress before running onto a raised bank. He received his short service commission as recently as 4th December 1923 [see Appendix D for 1923]; he resigned his commission on 22nd August 1925.

At the time of his accident he had achieved 7.50 hours flying on type and was under instruction by 11 Squadron.

Monday 23 June 1924
12 Squadron Sgt C Osmond Safe
Fawn II J7199
T/o Andover and on arrival at Upavon overshot the landing area, crashed and turned over. Its active service since first taking to the air on 13th March 1924, had lasted for just three months and now was the first machine of it s type to be written off in squadron service.

Wednesday 25 June 1924
60 Squadron F/O H A Boniface Safe
DH.9A E973
T/o Risalpur and crashed at Tank. Flying Officer Henry Andrew Boniface, born at 18th May 1897, qualified as an observer on 20th July 1918, and was *Gazetted* 2nd Lieutenant on that date [LG 2 August 1918, issue 30825, page 9119]. Earmarked for service on the Western Front he arrived at Azelot on 6th August 1918, and was attached to 99 Squadron [DH.9/DH.9A] of the Independent Force which was commanded by Major-General Sir Hugh Trenchard.

Post armistice, 2nd Lieutenant Boniface was posted to 22 Squadron [Bristol F.2b] at Nivelles, Belgium, on 22nd December 1918, and served until returning to the UK on 14th March 1919.

Still ranked flying officer, he relinquished his commission [though permitted to retain his rank] on completion of his reserve service on 12th September 1934. During the Second World War he was granted a commission in the Royal Air Force Volunteer Reserve, eventually relinquishing his commission as a squadron leader under the provisions of the Navy, Army and Air Force Reserves Act, 1954, and, as before, was permitted to retain his rank.

Thursday 26 June 1924
5 Squadron F/O S McKeever Injured
Bristol F.2b J6599
T/o Dardoni and while flying in turbulent conditions crashed at Razmak in North Waziristan. On 4th June 1918, Flight Cadet Stephen McKeever, born 16th December 1896, was granted a commission as a 2nd Lieutenant [A & S] [LG 12 July 1918, issue 30793, page 8205] and like 2nd Lieutenant Boniface, summarised, above joined the Independent Force at Azelot attached to 99 Squadron.

On Thursday, 26th September 1918, as reported in Volume 2, page 250, *"... the day the Independent Air Force was in continuous action ..."* during which 2nd Lieutenant McKeever and his observer, none other 2nd Lieutenant Henry

Arthur Boniface, was obliged to forced-land their badly shot about DH.9 B9366/Y near Pont-à-Mousson, the details of this being recorded on pages 252 and 253 of the second volume in this series.

My summary indicates both were 'safe' but it transpire that Stephen McKeever was wounded and following treatment at 8 General Hospital was evacuated to England aboard HMHS *Carisbrook Castle* on 19th October 1918; he was out of the war for good.

Granted a short service commission on 28th November 1919 [pages 237 and 238 of the third volume] Flying Officer McKeever rose to the rank of wing commander but while serving in Turkey he died on 8th October 1940, and is buried in Haida Pasha Cemetery.

14 Squadron F/O R C Creamer DFC +
DH.9A H151 LAC F C Perrin +
T/o Ramleh and crashed at LG D where it burst into flames, as reported on page 225 in *The DH.4/DH.9 File* whereas the website reported fatal air accidents overseas shows: *"Spun into ground on take off and burst into flames, Amman, Transjordan."* Flying Officer Reginald Cyril Creamer began his service as a flight cadet and was *Gazetted* temporary 2nd Lieutenant on 17th November 1917 [LG 23 November 1917, supplement 30395, page 12125]. Additional information regarding this officer appears on page 229 of my third volume.

Either conscripted, or a volunteer, Leading Aircraftman Frank Charles Perrin became an airman between March and August 1919, his service number being 327384.

Saturday 28 June 1924
27 Squadron Sgt C D Strickland Injured
DH.9A E846 AC1 C E Upton Injured
T/o Risalpur after being briefed to carry out a height test and carrying a full war load. On return Sergeant Strickland misjudged his approach and flew into the roof of a bungalow. Neither airman was seriously hurt in the ensuing crash.

60 Squadron F/O H E Greenberry Safe
DH.9A E8659 *Not reported* Safe
T/o Risalpur after being briefed for a photographic survey of the Wazai area. Overtaken by engine failure the crew forced-landed in the Khaisora River in a mountainous region of Waziristan. Flying Officer Harry Edward Greenberry had been granted a short service commission on 12th April 1921 [see Appendix D for details]. During the Second World War he served with the Royal Air Force Volunteer Reserve until relinquishing his commission as a squadron leader under the same terms as reported in my summary on 25th June 1924, for Henry Andrew Boniface.

Sunday 29 June 1924
32 Squadron P/O R B H Jackson Injured See 20 February 1928 - 55 Squadron
7F.1 Snipe E6839
T/o Kenley and headed for Bircham Newton where the main body of the squadron was due to arrive the next day. On arrival the wind was gusting strongly and on touch down the Snipe was blown onto its back and wrecked. Pilot Officer Rolf Booth Hilton Jackson had graduated from the Cadet College at Cranwell with the February 1922 entry.

JULY

Tuesday 1 July 1924
24 Squadron DH.9A J7079 Damaged, possibly beyond repair, while being started at Kenley. No further movements recorded.

31 Squadron F/O G W Gay Injured
Bristol F.2b J6657/P
T/o Ambala and wrecked here after flying into a small tree on the border of the landing area. Of the February 1920 Schools' Entry to the Cadet College at Cranwell, Flying Officer George William Gay left the service, owing to ill-health, on 26th September 1946. At the time he was ranked squadron leader.

Thursday 3 July 1924
5 Squadron *Not reported*
Bristol F.2J F4568
T/o Dardoni briefed for a photographic sortie; flying at 500 feet control was lost and the Bristol crashed.

Thursday 10 July 1924
41 Squadron F/O H A Mullaly Safe
Avro 504K H7520
T/o Northolt and thought to have been damaged beyond repair when it overturned in a forced-landing in a field of standing corn near Ashford in Middlesex. Flying Officer Hugh Alexander Mullaly was one of seven officers granted a short service commission on 4th December 1923. Formerly a lieutenant in the Indian Army, he was cashiered by sentence of General Court Martial and departed the service on 8th January 1925; Appendix D for short service commission officers refers.

Friday 11 July 1924
1 Squadron Sgt E P Wells Safe
7F.1 Snipe H4867
T/o Hinaidi and damaged beyond repair in the manner outlined below. All three were in the process of taking off when Flying Officer Rogenhagen [H8692] swung and in a swirl of dust and sand ran into H4867 and moments later Flight Lieutenant James Anderson Slater [H4885] ploughed into the wreckage. All three fighters were damaged beyond repair.

1 Squadron F/Lt J A Slater MC* DFC Injured
7F.1 Snipe H4885
T/o Hinaidi and was involved in a collision with the Snipe summarised below. Flight Lieutenant James Anderson Slater, born 29th November 1896, late of the Sussex Regiment, was accepted by the RFC on 26th September 1915. An incomplete record of his service, taken from the Casualty Form - Officers reads:

		Embarked [18 Sqdn] 10.11.15	
		Disembarked 11.11.15	
1.1.16	*Admitted [Influenza]*	*27.12.15*	*A36 ED 5113 22 CCS*
8.1.16	*Discharged to duty*	*7.1.16*	*A36 ED 5343 "*
22.1.16	*Graded Qualified Observer*	*17.1.16*	*B213/95 18 Sqdn*
5.2.16	*Leave 4.2.16 to 10.2.16*	*4.3.16*	*B213/197 "*
25.3.16	*To Home Est.*	*18.3.16*	*B213/579 "*
	Re-embarked	*2.8.16*	*T Sheet 2087*
12.8.16	*Posted to No. 60 Sqdn*	*9.8.16*	*B213 1 AD*
19.8.16	*Posted to No. 1 Sqdn*	*18.8.16*	*" 60 Sqdn*
4.9.16	*To Machine Gun School*	*13.101.16*	*" 1 Sqdn*

Captain 26.7.17

Appended beneath his surname *DFC, MC.* His entry on *Wikipedia* [which the authors acknowledge] show his prowess as a Scout pilot gaining two victories with 1 Squadron [Nieuport 17] and twenty-two with 64 Squadron [DH.5.SE.5a]. Little surprise, then, that he was honoured with an MC and First Bar and a DFC, the citations for these awards being published in *The London Gazette* the first appearing on 5th July 1918, supplement 30780, page 7924: *"For conspicuous gallantry and devotion to duty. When returning from a patrol he attacked enemy infantry, silenced a field gun and fired on transport. On another occasion he silenced a battery in very difficult weather conditions, fired on ammunition wagons and enemy infantry, and brought back his patrol safely. He also led a patrol of twelves machines in very bad weather to attack a wood held by the enemy. His patrol dropped over thirty bombs, fired 3,000 rounds and drove the enemy from the wood with heavy casualties. In the course of this flight six enemy scouts were engaged and driven off. Later, he led a similar patrol with great success. He showed splendid courage and determination."*

The First Bar was promulgated on 22nd June 1918, supplement 30761, page 7400: *"For conspicuous gallantry and devotion to duty. On one occasion during the recent operations he attacked a large formation of enemy scouts, one of which he drove down in flames. Later, during the same flight, he took part in a general engagement, in which he drove down another enemy machine completely out of control. Two days later he attacked two enemy scouts, causing one of them to crash to earth. In eighteen days he has engaged in twenty-five combats at close quarters, shooting down eight hostile machines. His great gallantry and fine offensive spirit have inspired all ranks to a very high degree."*

Richly deserved, a DFC was added in supplement 30827 of the paper, 3rd August 1918, page 9204: *"This officer has led numerous offensive patrols with the utmost skill and determination, and it is entirely due to his fine leadership that many enemy aircraft have been destroyed with the minimum of casualties to his formation."*

It is noted that his first victory with 64 Squadron occurred on 30th November 1917, when flying DH.5 A9458 he drove down a DFW C over Bourlon Wood. This success came during the final hours of the *Battle of Cambrai,* an account of which has been superbly described by Bryn Hammond in his book *Cambrai 1917 - The Myth of the First Great Tank Battle.* His text includes a number of contributions from RFC pilots who participated in this action, pages 270 and 305 to 307 describing vivid accounts of the air support given to this sector of the battlefield.

Appointed to a permanent commission on 1st August 1919, Flight Lieutenant Slater returned to England soon after and on the 1st of April 1925, reported to Upavon where he was attached to 3 Squadron [7F.1 Snipe] and it was while on their establishment that he was killed in a flying accident on 26th November of that year, which I have summarised.

1 Squadron F/O A E Rogenhagen Safe
7F.1 Snipe H8692
T/o Hinaidi and swung out of control and into the path of the two aircraft shown above. Unhurt, Flying Officer Arthur Eric Rogenhagen was injured in a local motoring accident on 27th July 1924.

Tuesday 15 July 1924
27 Squadron F/O C A Mason Safe
DH.9A E953 LAC W H Fearn Safe
T/o Risalpur with the intention of transiting to Nowshera but the engine was throttled back prematurely and the DH immediately sank back and struck the ground damaging the aircraft beyond repair. Apart from his embarrassment Flying Officer Cyril Arthur Mason was unhurt. His short service commission was *Gazetted* on 7th March 1922, issue 32631, page 1953. On completion of his reserve service he relinquished his commission on 9th May 1929.

Monday 21 July 1924
1 Squadron F/O M B F Watson +
7F.1 Snipe E7638
T/o Kirkuk but stalled and crashed out of control. Flying Officer Myles Birket Foster Watson was *Gazetted* with a short service commission on 27th June 1922, issue 32723, page 4834.

47 Squadron F/O M B Mackay Injured
DH.9A F2762 Cpl H J Bath Injured
T/o Helwan with the intention of ferrying the DH to the Aircraft Depot at Aboukir but stalled off what has been described as a *"gliding turn at 20 ft"* and crashed.

Tuesday 22 July 1924
55 Squadron Sgt C A Dicks +
DH.9A E9911 Mohamed Agha Crag +
T/o Hinaidi carrying mail but on becoming airborne banked without sufficient speed, stalled and crashed. On striking the ground the DH caught fire. Sergeant Charles Albert Dicks passenger is described as a *"Deputy of Lacchi."*

To the best of the authors knowledge, Sergeant Dicks was the first sergeant-pilot to be killed in squadron service in 1924. He joined as a boy airman between October 1917 and December 1918, his service number being 157075.

Thursday 24 July 1924
84 Squadron F/Lt W C Day MC +
DH.9A H147 F/O D R Stewart +
T/o Shaibah for an armed patrol and seeking to locate an Arab raiding party. While in the vicinity of Jaibah in Southern Iraq the crew, it seems, forced-landed. There is some confusion as to the fate of the two airmen; page 225 of *The DH.4/ DH.9 File* states that they were killed and their aircraft declared Cat. W indicating it was a write off. However, the website concerned with overseas aircraft losses uses the term *"died"* and not the customary *"killed"* and this is supported by the website Strange Company which carries a report suggesting that the two airmen were either unhurt, or possibly only slightly injured, and walked off to seek help only to perish in the desert. The article goes on to say that bones, identified as those of Flight Lieutenant William Day were found in February [presumably 1925] and those of flying Officer Donald Stewart soon afterwards, and that both sets of remains were taken to Basra for burial with full military honours. It is also suggested that the DH was undamaged, or only slightly damaged, and that it was flown back to Shaibah.

Flight Lieutenant Day won his MC while serving as a 2nd Lieutenant with the Middlesex Regiment, the citation being reported in *The London Gazette* on 6th April 1918, supplement 30614, page 4211: *"For conspicuous gallantry and devotion to duty in leading his company through two heavy barrages to a postion where he beat off several counter-attacks. Later, when in command of the battalion, after all the senior officers had become casualties, his reports, which were sent back regularly, were of the greatest value to the higher command."*

Granted a short service commission on 19th October 1919 [see page 235 of my third volume], this was cancelled on his commission becoming permanent, as announced by the Air Ministry on 20th February 1923 [LG 20 February 1923, issue 32797, page 1234]. His observer, Donald Ramsay Stewart was granted a short service commission on 4th December 1922 [LG 19 December 1922, issue 32778, page 8958].

Friday 25 July 1924
32 Squadron P/O B D J Broadway Safe See 19 September 1924
7F.1 Snipe F2433
T/o Bircham Newton and wrecked in a crash at Edgefield some 7 miles SSW from the coastal town of Sheringham in Norfolk after running out of petrol. There are two locations in Norfolk with the name 'Edgefield' though one is qualified with the addition of 'Green'; however, they are in such close proximity to each other that the accuracy of the summary is not compromised. The report states the Snipe came down in a rough surfaced field and overturned.

28 Squadron F/O E Bell +
Bristol F.2b J6646 AC1 P Slack Injured
T/o Peshawar similarly loaded and crashed in circumstances similar to those reported above, the location being reported as Duncans Picquet near Razmak. Edward Bell was granted a short service commission on 20th February 1923, issue 32797, page 1234. His passenger, Aircraftman Percy Slack died from his injuries 48-hours later. Joining from civilian life, his service number 345137 falls within the block 340001 - 360000 which was in use from September 1919 until June 1925.

Thursday 31 July 1924
11 Squadron Sgt W F Grey Injured
Fawn II J6990 LAC G W Maskell +
T/o Netheravon and while turning steeply to avoid a midair collision near the airfield stalled and spun in from 200 feet. This was the first fatal accident suffered by the squadron since re-forming from the Air Pilotage School at Andover on 13th January 1923, since when the squadron had moved to Bircham Newton before arriving at Netheravon on the last day of May 1924, and equipping with Fairey Fawn. It was also the first fatal crash involving a Fawn day-bomber.

Developed from the Fairey Pintail amphibian, the Fawn was the first postwar type of a day bomber to enter Royal Air Force service, J6990 being one of two development aircraft ahead of production commencing with J7182.

Leading Aircraftman George William Maskell, service number 157009, joined the service more or less at the same time as Sergeant Charles Albert Dicks who lost his life just over a week ago and is summarised on the previous page.

AUGUST

Monday 4 August 1924
28 Squadron F/O D McG Morphy +
Bristol F.2b D8057
T/o Peshawar and reported to have crashed following engine failure. Flying Officer Douglas McGillycuddy Morphy received a short service commission, effective 10th June 1922 [LG 27 June 1922, issue 32723, page 4834]. The background to the crash as to why the engine failed remains obscure.

28 Squadron F/O E C N Jefferies Safe
Bristol F.2b H1536
T/o Peshawar and while in the vicinity of Rawalpindi on the NWF the weather closed in and while making a precautionary landing the engine 'cut' and the Bristol was wrecked in the ensuing crash.

Flying Officer Edward Charles Norman Jefferies was granted a short service commission on 12th July 1921, issue 32387, page 5561. He died early in the Second World War on 23rd October 1940, when serving with 24 Squadron and was buried in Putney Vale Cemetery.

Wednesday 6 August 1924
2 Squadron F/O F J C Rybot Injured
Bristol F.2J F4484/A
T/o Manston and wrecked here following a landing mishap, the Bristol having stalled while banking. Flying Officer Francis John Chancellor Rybot graduated from Sandhurst as a Gentleman Cadet and was commissioned as 2nd Lieutenant to the Royal Garrison Artillery with effect from 23rd January 1919 [LG 22 January 1919, supplement 31137, page 1142]. He had been seconded for service with the Royal Air Force, and on completion of his attachment returned to army duties.

His final entry in *The London Gazette* 12th August 1949, supplement 38688, page 3908 reads beneath the heading *'Royal Regiment of Artillery' "Maj. [Hon. Lt-Col.] F J C Rybot [6077] having attained the age limit of liability to recall, ceases to belong to the Res. of Offrs., 19th July 1949."*

Tuesday 26 August 1924
13 Squadron F/O J W C Harcourt-Vernon. +
Bristol F.2b F4955 AC1 C Carpenter +
T/o Tangmere tasked for a photographic sortie and it was when near the Lavant's on the northern outskirts of Chichester in West Sussex that John William Carl Harcourt-Vernon allowed his speed to drop as he banked. Losing control, his Bristol dived from a quite low altitude and crashed.

The tragedy happened in the morning, round about 11 o'clock, and the Court of Inquiry gave its findings as follows:

"The cause of the accident was in our opinion that the pilot stalled the machine in a steep left hand turn with the result that the machine hit the ground before the pilot could regain control.

"AOC concurs generally into finding of Court."

A press report, accompanied by a photograph showing the collapsed top mainplanes, appeared in the *Hampshire Telegraph and Post* on Friday, August 29th, 1924, with the headline *'Aeroplane Crash at Lavant - Pilot and Craftsman Killed - Tragic Incident of the Manoeuvres'*

"A shocking aeroplane fatality occurred on Tuesday about 11 a.m. near the factory building at Lavant, near Chichester, when a military machine was making a flight for the purpose of taking photographs for the Fourth Brigade of Guards, at present in camp at Goodwood for the brigade training.

"The plane nose dived into a field of cut corn on Mr. U Mortimer's farm, to the east of the Midhurst railway line. It was badly wrecked, but did not take fire. The two occupants - Flying Officer Harcourt-Vernon and Air Craftman Carpenter - were apparently killed instantly, both being dead when the fallen 'plane was reached. They belonged to No. 13 Squadron, RAF, which is stationed at Andover, Hants.

"The 'plane was a Bristol Fighter, F4955, and was connected with a detachment of the squadron, which is temporarily stationed at Tangmere Aerodrome for the purpose of taking part in the Guards' training. The 'plane left the aerodrome about 10.20on its ill-fated flight.

"In the field were men of the 2nd Grenadier Guards, engaged in field training, and after the crash several NCOs and men hastened to the 'plane. It was at once apparent that both pilot and craftsman were dead, and that they had sustained very bad injuries. A large hole in the hillside denoted where the 'plane had first pitched, and it had rebounded several yards from this spot. The Guardsmen undertook the task of extracting the bodies from the wreckage, and they were removed to the factory building to await the inquest. PC Mason, the Lavant constable, and other police officers were speedily on the spot, and officers from Tangmere Aerodrome also hurried to the scene as soon as the news reached them. A guard of Grenadiers was placed over the machine, and also the buildings, and many people visited the sport during the day.

'The Inquest Story'

'Machine in Perfect Order When it Left'

"The inquest on the victims of the disaster was held at the Lavant factory, on Wednesday afternoon, by Mr. F B Tompkins [the Deputy Coroner]. The full description of the deceased were:- John William Carl Harcourt-Vernon, aged 23, flying officer, of Alexandra Road, Andover, Hants., and Charles Carpenter, aged 23, first class air craftman, of 12 Durfield Road, Brockley, London.

"Christopher Pilkington, a Flight-Lieut., of the RAF, stationed at Tangmere Aerodrome, stated he was the commanding officer of the detachment now at Tangmere, and gave evidence of identification. Both the deceased left the aerodrome about 10.20 a.m., on Tuesday, in a Bristol Fighter 'plane, their instructions being to fly at 500 feet and to take oblique photographs of the railway and river crossings from Mid-Lavant to Preston Farm, B.....ton. The Machine was in perfect order when it left. Flying Officer Harcourt-Vernon was an experienced and capable pilot, and was used to the type of machine. Witness had seen the 'plane, and as far as his examination went, he could find no mechanical fault with the machine. It was completely wrecked. He could say almost definitely that the pilot was flying low, and lost speed during a turn, which caused the machine to dive into the ground. If he had been up 500 feet he would have been able to recover, and the crash would not have occurred. Carpenter was a photographic mechanic, and would have been operating cameras at the time. Bristol fighters seldom took fire in a crash.

'Fractured Skulls'

"Frank Holmes, captain of the RAMC, attached to the Grenadier Guards, said he had examined the deceased men, and found that the flying officer sustained a depressed fracture of the skull, which would cause instantaneous death. The mechanic had fractured his skull, broken his neck, and had a fractured right leg.

"Corpl. A Fellingham, 2nd Grenadier Guards, said that about 11 a.m., he was out on field training in a field to the east of the Lavant factory. He saw the aeroplane flying overhead for about half-an-hour before the accident, and judged the height at about 100 feet. The 'plane came along on his left, made a sharp turn to the right, and crashed to the ground. He went to the fallen 'plane, and found the officer pinned in his seat with a bad gash in his head, and the mechanic was sitting in the cockpit, both being apparently dead. - In answer to Flight-Lieut., Pilkington, witness said he was of the opinion that the engine was running at the time of the crash.

"Mrs. Clara Hamer, who resides at Lavant factory, aid she was watching the aeroplane for about half-an-hour. It was flying very low, at times following the railway line, and also circled round. Ultimately it passed over the railway line and flew over a grass field into the corn field, where it suddenly turned very quickly and came straight down. She noticed the engine stop three times when the 'plane was circling round, but not the last time. As soon as it turned to fall the engine stopped.

"Corpl. Albert Camplough, of the 2nd Grenadier Guards, corroborated the other corporal's evidence except with regard to the question of the engine, which he said was running until the 'plane was within a few feet of the ground.

"The Deputy Coroner recorded a verdict of "Accidental Death" in both cases.

'The Police Thanked'

"Flight-Lieut., Pilkington said he should like to thank the police for the great assistance they had given, more particularly PC Mason.

"Supt., Brett said the police were glad to render what assistance they could on all occasions. They only regretted it should have been necessary on such a sad occasion as this, and were very sorry the accident should have happened.

'Bodies of The Two Victims Entrained'

"There were impressive scenes at Chichester station about mid-day yesterday, when the bodies of Flying Officer Harcourt-Vernon and Aircraftsman Carpenter were brought there, the former for conveyance to Andovrr, and the latter for London.

"The two coffins, covered with Union Jacks, were conveyed on a military motor vehicle, each being escorted by six bearers from the detachment of the RAF at Tangmere Aerodrome, to which they belonged.

"Flight-Lieut., Pilkington was in charge, and Flying Officer Lee and O'Brien Saint were also present. Many people were assembled, and inside the station a guard of honour from the 4th Guards Brigade was drawn up, under Captain Whittaker.

"The guard presented arms, and buglers sounded the "Last Post" as the coffins were entrained. There also chanced to be at the station a draft of 47 men from the Depot, Royal Sussex Regiment, under Captain Clayton, who stood to attention and saluted.

"There were three wreaths on each coffin, one from Major-General Lord Huthven [director of operations in connection with the Guards' training at Goodwood], one from the RAF detachment at Tangmere, and one from the Grenadier Guards."

Aircraftman Charles Carpenter was formerly of the RNAS, joining in 1917, this being reflected by his service number 241173 [block 225061 - 244710].

Thursday 28 August 1924

19 Squadron F/O S J Mason +

7F.1 Snipe F2444

T/o Duxford and crashed, inverted, into a coppice near the airfield injuring three children, named as Ada and Emily Miller and their friend Elsie Riches. Stanley James Mason's details are recorded in my third volume on page 244.

The Court of Inquiry reported thus: *"The cause of the accident was in our opinion an error of judgement on the part of the pilot, in that he did not allow sufficient height for recovery from a stall after a half roll on his back.*

"AOC concurs."

On September 4th, 1924, *The Illustrated Police News* informed its readers beneath a headline that read *'Alarming Aeroplane Crash in Coppice - Two Children Badly Hurt - Pilot Killed'*

"Children playing in a coppice at Duxford, near Cambridge, were badly injured in an aeroplane crash in which Flying-Officer Stanley James Mason, Royal Air Force, a native of Ebbw Vale, Mon., lost his life. Two of the children, Elsie Riches, 5, and Emily Miller, 3 ½, were unconscious when picked up, and were taken to Addenbrooke's Hospital, Cambridge, where both of them were operated on. The scene of the tragedy was a belt of trees which runs along the road between Duxford and Royston at Duxford Grange. The two little girls, with Ada Miller, 11, were playing "house" under a tree nearest the road and away from the aerodrome. With aid of some low branches and sacking they had erected a shelter over their heads, and they sat on stools in front of an imaginary fire. They had found an old fender and some pots and pans with which to play, while hanging on the tree was a looking-glass. The accident occurred about noon, and Flying-Officer Mason was up in a single-seater Snipe machine, apparently stunting. People working in the vicinity declare that the pilot was looping the loop, but this may have been the result of his efforts to extricate himself from a difficulty while flying. In an upside-down position he crashed through the thick coppice, which is about twenty yards deep. The wings of the 'plane were stripped off and fell in the coppice, but the engine and body were found 15 yards or so further on, on the opposite side of the road. The body of Flying-Officer Mason was found fifteen yards away. Ada Miller had a wonderful escape, being only bruised and cut about the head, but the other two, as stated, were taken to hospital unconscious. The engine appeared to be running at full speed at the time, and the wreckage was scarcely recognisable as that of an aeroplane. The grandfather of the Miller children, who saw the machine strike the wood, and Mrs. Riches were among the first on the scene, and the latter ran out into the road in her night clothes and succeeded in pulling the children out from under the wing. Elsie had not regained conscious when taken to the hospital at Cambridge. Emily came round and was found to be suffering from a broken thigh. In the evening both were operated on at the hospital, and afterwards were reported to be as well as could be expected. The theory of the accident put forward by those who were near-by was that the airman got into difficulties very low down, and was trying to right himself when he crashed into the trees. This would account for the fact that he was running his engine at full speed. - At the inquest Flight-Lieutenant Theodore J West stated that Mason was a skilled pilot, having done over 550 hours flying. He had been at Duxford nearly three months. The machine was a single-seater Sopwith "Snipe" and was in good condition, having been overhauled within the last month. Mason had been flying about twenty minutes when the accident happened. - Flight-Officer Sidney T B Cripps, who was flying at the same time, that it was a very good morning and quite fit for flying. - Arthur Miller, farm foreman, and Charles Howe, a farm labourer, declared they saw the machine flying low, with the wheels upside down. - The coroner found that the deceased crashed while flying in the execution of his duties, his death being accidental.

32 Squadron Sgt A H F Murphy Injured
7F.1 Snipe E6834
T/o Hawkinge Air Storage Section for delivery to 32 Squadron at Kenley. The weather was far from ideal and on reaching the vicinity of Upper Warlingham, about 3 miles SE of its destination, the mist and rain was such that Sergeant Alfred Hubert Frederick Murphy attempted a precautionary landing but, unfortunately, crashed.

On the 12th of June 1940, and now ranked warrant officer and serving in the Technical Branch, he was commissioned, for the durations of hostilities, as a flying officer [LG 2 July 1940, issue 34887, page 4018].

Subsequently, he was appointed to a permanent commission on 1st July 1946 [LG 6 May 1947, supplement 37947, page 2009] and retired from the Royal Air Force as a wing commander on 10th July 1954. He had been appointed OBE in the Birthday Honours List for 1950 [LG 8 June 1950, supplement 38929, page 2783].

SEPTEMBER

Sunday 14 September 1924
6 Squadron F/O T J Desmond Injured
Bristol F2b F4877
T/o Mosul and written off following a crash at the Zakho landing ground.

Monday 15 September 1924
17 Squadron P/O A D Baillie +
7F.1 Snipe F2484
T/o Eastchurch to return to Hawkinge but climbing and banking steeply Pilot Officer Arthur Douglas Baillie lost control and crashed. He had been granted a short service commission [LG 24 July 1923, issue 32847, page 5074].

Subsequently, the Court of Inquiry reported: *"The cause of the accident was in our opinion due to an error of judgement on the part of the pilot in that he stalled his machine on a climbing turn at low altitude contrary to flying regulations.*

"AOC concurs."

His death found its way into *The Northern Whig and Belfast Post* of Thursday, September 18th, 1924.

'Airman's Fatal Error'

'Too Steep a Climb Causes Crash'

"At the inquest yesterday on Pilot Officer Arthur Douglas Baille, No. 17 Squadron, RAF, who was killed at East-hurch Aerodrome, Kent, the evidence showed that deceased took off slightly across wind, and after flying 100 yards level with the ground pulled his machine up in a steep climbing turn.

"When at the top of the turn 75 feet up the machine appeared to stall and nose dived, bursting into flames as it struck the ground. Death was due to a fractured skull.

"Wing Commander Smyth Pygott, commanding Eastchurch Armament and Gunnery School, stated that an inquiry had been held, and it was considered that the pilot made too sttep a climb. The engine and controls were in good order.
"A verdict of "Accidental Death" was returned."

Friday 19 September 1924
32 Squadron P/O B D J Broadway Safe See 1 October 1924
7F.1 Snipe F2456
T/o Northolt tasked for an aerobatic display beneath the lights at the Wembley Tattoo and it was while so engaged that the engine 'cut' and the Snipe was wrecked in the emergency landing that followed. This was Pilot Officer Basil Douglas John Broadway's second serious mishap in two months, his previous being summarised on 25th July 1924.

Wednesday 24 September 1924
6 Squadron F/O H P Morris Injured
Bristol F.2b E2662 LAC H C Newman Injured
T/o Mosul for an operational patrol during which the crew came under ground fire from a machine gun; crash-landed at Shirani, Iraq, both being in a wounded state. Flying Officer Harold Pilgrim Morris, short service commissioned on 28th January 1922, issue 32771, page 8416, relinquished his commission on 13th November 1930.

Saturday 27 September 1924
20 Squadron *Not reported*
Bristol F.2b J6623
T/o Quetta and crashed at the Khanai landing ground. Prior to its arrival in India the Bristol had seen service between 1921 and 1922 with 25 Squadron at Hawkinge, thence to 2 Squadron at Oranmore before going to the Packing Depot at Ascot for shipment in 1923 to Drigh Road. On 29th October 1923, whilst in the care of 31 Squadron, it crashed at Sararogba in the North West Frontier. Salvaged, and repaired, it was reported in the hands of 20 Squadron by March 1924.

OCTOBER

Wednesday 1 October 1924
32 Squadron P/O B D J Broadway Safe See 14 May 1926
7F.1 Snipe E6629
T/o Kenley for a formation exercise which involved the pilots landing at Lympne in Kent. Departing Lympne the engine on E6629 'cut' and moments later its flying days were over when it crashed into a telegraph pole, while for third time Pilot Officer Broadway's guardian angel had protected him from injury.

Thursday 2 October 1924
13 Squadron F/O A H Stirling +
Bristol F.2b F4572 AC1 W J A Turton +
T/o Andover for a routine training sortie which ended at Penton Mewsey a couple of miles north of the airfield. Flying Officer Archibald Hay Stirling was one of a number of army officers seconded to the Royal Air Force for four years active duty with effect from 16th October 1922 [LG 24 October 1922, issue 32758, page 7466]. His parent unit was the Royal Scots.

His passenger, Aircraftman William James Arthur Turton, joined as a boy between December 1918 and March 1919, his service number being 326333.

News of the accident was published in *The Courier* [Somerset] on Wednesday, October 8th, 1924.

'Two Airmen Killed'
'Mishap to "Bristol" Fighter at Andover'

"Flying Officer Archibald Hay Stirling and Leading Aircraftman [sic] *William James Arthur Turton have been killed by crashing in a field near Andover.*

"Both experienced airmen, they went up in a "Bristol" fighter, which had been up twice previously. At a height of 2,000 feet the pilot commenced a spiral, and witnesses at the inquest on Friday suggested that he either became giddy or misjudged his distance, and could not right himself before crashing. A verdict of "Accidental Death" was returned."

14 Squadron F/O C Bousfield +
Bristol F.2b J6606
T/o Ramleh and crashed from an uncontrolled spin which commenced at 300 feet over Heliopolis.

Monday 6 October 1924
31 Squadron F/O A Findlay Safe
Bristol F.2b F4593
T/o Ambala and on preparing to land at Lahore the rudder controls jammed and the Bristol crashed out of control.

Thursday 9 October 1924
9 Squadron P/O I B Gray Safe
Avro 504K H5252

T/o Manston and crashed heavily while practicing aerobatics. Two years previous, while on the establishment of 100 Squadron at Spittlegate, it was damaged while landing with a failing engine and in the process colliding with another Avro which was written off; my summary for 7th November 1922 refers.

Granted a short service commission on 5th December 1922, issue 32774, page 8615, Pilot Officer Ian Bury Gray resigned his commission on 4th February 1925.

41 Squadron P/O H St. George-Taylor +
Siskin III J7147
T/o Netheravon in squadron formation upon which Pilot Officer Harold St. George-Taylor decided to perform a loop. Tragically this proved to be a fatal decision for on recovery he banked hard to the right, lost control and crashed in the northern area of the airfield. His short service commission was published in *The London Gazette* on 4th December 1923, issue 32885, page 8452; he had survived for less than a year in service life of which seven had been spent in training. This was the first serious accident involving a Siskin in squadron service. It had been taken on squadron establishment earlier in the year on 7th May

Saturday 11 October 1924
84 Squadron F/O J H G Franklin +
DH.9A J7253 AC2 T Williams Injured
T/o Shaibah where it flew into the ground, turned over and caught fire. Both crew members were trapped beneath the wreckage and though rescuers were quickly on the scene Flying Officer John Hayward Godfrey Franklin was beyond aid, but his passenger, Thomas Williams was pulled free, albeit badly injured.

Aged 20, Flying Officer Franklin had served for a shade over two years having been short service commissioned [LG 19 September 1922, issue 32748, page 6715].

Tuesday 14 October 1924
60 Squadron F/Lt J W Baker MC DFC Safe
DH.9A E8726/3
T/o Risalpur where it was damaged beyond repair in a landing mishap. This was Flight Lieutenant Baker's second accident, the previous being on 29th April when he stalled taking off from the aerodrome.

Thursday 16 October 1924
84 Squadron *Not reported*
DH.9A J7100/N
T/o Shaibah and crashed at Mosul. This DH had followed the similar patter of factory to the Packing Depot Ascot and thence shipment to Hinaidi where it was reassembled.

Friday 24 October 1924
25 Squadron F/O A E T Bruce Safe See 25 January 1923
Grebe II J7411
T/o Hawkinge where it overturned on the airfield following a crash-landing brought about by 'wing flutter.' The first Grebes had arrived at Hawkinge for the squadron during the month and it is believed the loss of J7411 [from the third production batch J7406-J7417] was the first of its type since its introduction in 1923 when 111 Squadron received sufficient aircraft to equip a single flight. Glosster's Grebe was the first post-*Great War* conflict to enter service with the Royal Air Force and in general it was well received by those who flew it; subsequently, the 'wing flutter' problem which led to the crash here summarised was overcome by the fitting of Vee-struts to support the outer upper wing.

32 Squadron P/O R T Taaffe Safe
7F.1 Snipe E6308
T/o Kenley for night flying practice; wrecked when it crashed on landing. Apart, understandably, from rather a bad fright, Pilot Officer Rudolph Trevor Taaffe was unhurt. Short service commissioned on 29th May 1923, issue 32828, page 3753, he was destined to serve for the next twenty-eight years, eventually retiring as a group captain on 21st September 1951. Along the way, he received a permanent commission on 12th June 1928, issue 33393, page 4022.

During the Second World War and while on the Staff at No. 5 Group headquarters at Morton Hall, Swinderby, he was posted to command RAF East Kirby [callsign *Silksheen*], home to 57 Squadron and 630 Squadron both equipped with Lancaster heavy bombers.

Born 21st June 1901, in Ardee, County Louth, and Christened Rudolph Trevor Aloysius Patrick Taafee, his death was announced on 15th February 1985, from Dublin.

Monday 27 October 1924
25 Squadron *Not reported*
7F.1 Snipe E7411
T/o Hawkinge and in banking steeply overstressed the wing spars. On inspection it was deemed that the damage was beyond economical repair.

NOVEMBER

Saturday 1 November 1924
5 Squadron F/Lt A F Quinlan +
Bristol F.2b F4566 LAC F G Jones Injured
T/o Dardoni where in the course of making a turn at low altitude Flight Lieutenant Arthur Francis Quinlan lost control, spun and crashed. His short service commission, granted on 1st August 1923, was *Gazetted* on 9th November 1923, issue 32878, page 7662 where it is noted he had retired from the army in the rank of lieutenant.

Monday 3 November 1924
24 Squadron F/O T B R Meadmore Safe
Bristol F.2J F4748
T/o Kenley where is was wrecked in a landing accident. Pilot Officer Thomas Bennett Robert Meadmore received a short service commission on 8th January 1923, issue 32896, page 269, but 'handed in his papers' on 4th February 1925.

Monday 10 November 1924
11 Squadron Sgt F G Morfett +
Fawn II J7202 Sgt G Taylor +
T/o Netheravon and destroyed close to airfield following a midair collision with 7F.1 Snipe E6968 flown by Flying Officer John Maurice Chandler, aged 24, who had been seconded from the Navy for flying instruction [LG 22 July 1924, issue 32958, page 5553].

A press report appeared in the *Gloucestershire Echo* on Thursday, November 13th, 1924, *'Aeroplane Collision - Coroner's Inquiry'*

"The collision between two aeroplanes at Netheravon last Monday, which resulted in three deaths, was the subject of an inquest there on Wednesday by the Wilts. Coroner. The men killed were Lieutenant John Morrison Chandler, RN, aged 30, of Witley, Surrey; Sergeant George Taylor, aged 42, of No. 1 Flying Training School, Netheravon, whose home address was 23, Walker-street, Glasgow; and Sergeant George Morfett, aged 22, No. 11 Bombing Squadron, Netheravon, who came from Axeholme-road, Goole.

"Evidence given by Flying Officer-Instructor Franklyn and Flying Officer Spiers was to the effect that Chandler was making a flight in a Snipe machine, and Morfett at the same time was piloting a Fairey Lawn [sic] *aeroplane, with Taylor as passenger. Chandler was seen gliding towards the ground, with his engine shut off, and when he was 300 feet up Morfett's machine appeared about 200 yards to starboard, apparently with the object of landing in the same part of the ground. The witnesses thought Morfett did not see the Snipe machine at all, and that Chandler, when it was too late, saw the Fairey 'Lawn' aeroplane and dipped, as if he were trying to avoid a collision. The machines collided 200 feet from the ground, and then crashed. All three men were killed on the spot.*

"A verdict of accidental death was recorded."

It is believed that the deaths of Sergeants Frederick George Morfett and George Taylor may have been the first all non-commissioned crew to perish while in squadron service. Their service numbers were 157406 and 140854 respectively. Thus, Sergeant Morfett joined as a boy airman between October 1917 and December 1918, with his colleague transferred either from another arm of the service, or enlisted as a civilian, circa March - April 1918.

Wednesday 12 November 1924
1 Squadron F/O E Reid +
7F.1 Snipe DC F2499 Lt W H E Cotter Injured
T/o Hinaidi and wrecked here after spinning out of control. A Cranwell graduate, please refer to page 272 of my third volume for details of his service. His Snipe had been converted to a two-seater configuration.

Saturday 15 November 1924
5 Squadron F/O S P George Injured
Bristol F.2b J6770/L
T/o Dardoni and on return landed with some force, bounced and turned over; wrecked. Extricated from the ruins of his cockpit, Flying Officer Sandy Parker George was given medical treatment for his injuries.

Friday 21 November 1924
12 Squadron F/O F H Bugge Injured
Fawn II J7201
T/o Andover and during the flight an oil leak was noticed; forced-landing, the Fawn stalled in the turn towards the selected field and crashed with some force less than a mile west of Basingstoke Station. Its first flight is noted as occurring on 13th March 1924.

Thursday 27 November 1924
27 Squadron Sgt G E Campbell Injured
DH.9A E845 LAC C T Cave Injured
T/o Risalpur and crashed at Thall following an in-flight fire. It is believed both airmen recovered from their injuries.

Friday 28 November 1924
29 Squadron F/O C W A Byrne +
7F.1 Snipe E6839
T/o Duxford and while practicing aerobatics got into a spin which he was unable to recover before hitting the ground at Melbourn, 6 miles WSW from the airfield. Flying Officer Cyril William Anthony Byrne was one of fifteen probationary Pilot Officers granted a short service commission on 13th November 1922, and published in the *Gazette* on 28th November 1922, issue 32771, page 8416.

DECEMBER

Monday 1 December 1924
60 Squadron F/O B P Jones Safe
DH.9A H3396 LAC C J Walsh Safe
T/o Arawauli for a demonstration flight over the Waziristan district of the NWF but was obliged to make an emergency landing near Behrang Khel where it ran onto rough ground and smashed its undercarriage. A fairly late production DH, H3396 came within the block H3396-3545 for 150 airframes produced by the Westland Aircraft Works, Yeovil.

Friday 5 December 1924
20 Squadron F/Lt P R T J M I C Chamberlayne
Bristol F.2b J6796
T/o Quetta though Pad Idan is a strong possibility, a tyre bursting at the moment of becoming airborne. Landing at Pad Idan the undercarriage collapsed and the machine was damaged beyond repair.
See my note for 30th April 1924, for details of his service.

Tuesday 9 December 1924
6 Squadron F/O C Chapman Injured
Bristol F.2J F4731
T/o Mosul and while flying at one hundred feet Flying Officer Cyril Chapman had the alarming experience of realising their aircraft was on fire. Fortunately, it seems, he escaped relatively unscathed but the Bristol was burnt out.

Thursday 18 December 1924
41 Squadron P/O T A Hale-Monroe Safe
Avro 504K H2401
T/o Northolt and wrecked as follows: *"Owing to an error of judgement on the part of the pilot when attempting to land the aeroplane, stalled and fell to the ground. The pilot, who was the only occupant of the machine, escaped injury."*
Pilot Officer Thomas Adrian Hale-Monroe was granted a short service commission [LG 4 December 1922, issue 32885, page 8452]; having served in the Second World War he relinquished his commission under the provisions of the Navy, Army and Air Force Reserves Act, February 1954. At the time he held the rank of squadron leader.

Monday 22 December 1924
4 Squadron P/O H M Groves Injured
Bristol F.2B F4935
T/o Farnborough where it crash-landed with engine failure; damaged beyond worthwhile repair.

Tuesday 30 December 1924
14 Squadron F/O F C T Rowe Injured
DH.9A HR85 LAC G Harding Safe
T/o Ramleh where on return and undershot approach resulted in the DH coming into contact with a railway line. Moments later a slightly injured pilot and his mechanic were walking away from the inverted wreck of their aircraft which as recently as June had undergone a rebuild at Aboukir.
Flying Officer Francis Charles Thorn Rowe entered the Cadet College at Cranwell with the schools entry in February 1920. He retired in the rank of flight lieutenant on 14th August 1933, but in April 1940, he returned to the service and was attached to the Technical Branch. Francis Rowe, now promoted wing command, retired for the second time on 14th November 1945 [see page 271 of my third volume].

APPENDICES
1924

Appendix A - Squadron Losses Table and Losses by Aircraft Type

Column 1 - Squadron

Column 2 - Aircraft type

Column 3 - Written off

Column 4 - Fatalities

1 Squadron	Sopwith 7F.1 Snipe	5	2
	Sopwith 7F.1 Snipe DC	1	1
2 Squadron	Bristol F.2b	1	
	Bristol F.2J	1	
4 Squadron	Bristol F.2b	3	1
5 Squadron	Bristol F.2b	6	1
6 Squadron	Bristol F.2b	2	
	Bristol F.2J	1	
9 Squadron	Avro 504K	1	
11 Squadron	Avro 504K	1	
	Fairey Fawn II	2	3
12 Squadron	Fairey Fawn II	2	
13 Squadron	Bristol F.2b	2	4
14 Squadron	Bristol F.2b	2	1
	Airco DH.9A	2	2
17 Squadron	Sopwith 7F.1 Snipe	1	1
19 Squadron	Sopwith 7F.1 Snipe	2	1
20 Squadron	Bristol F.2b	7	2
24 Squadron	Avro 504K	1	
	Bristol F.2J	1	
	Airco DH.9A	2	
25 Squadron	Sopwith 7F.1 Snipe	2	1
	Gloster Grebe II	1	
27 Squadron	Airco DH.9A	4	2
28 Squadron	Bristol F.2b	4	5
29 Squadron	Sopwith 7F.1 Snipe	1	1
31 Squadron	Bristol F.2b	3	
32 Squadron	Sopwith 7F.1 Snipe	8*	
39 Squadron	Airco DH.9A	2	4
41 Squadron	Armstong Whitworth Siskin III	1	1
	Avro 504K	2	
	DH.42A Dingo	1	1
45 Squadron	Bristol F.2b	1	2
47 Squadron	Airco DH.9A	1	
55 Squadron	Airco DH.9A	1	2
56 Squadron	Sopwith 7F.1 Snipe	3	1
60 Squadron	Airco DH.9A	7	
84 Squadron	Airco DH.9A	5	7
99 Squadron	Airco DH.9A	1	
111 Squadron	Sopwith 7F.1 Snipe	1	1
216 Squadron	Vickers Vimy	1	
Totals		96	47

	Airco DH.9A	25	17
	Armstong Whitworth Siskin III	1	1
	Avro 504K	5	
	Bristol F.2b	31	16
	Bristol F.2J	3	
	DH.42A Dingo	1	1
	Fairey Fawn II	4	3
	Gloster Grebe II	1	
	Sopwith 7F.1 Snipe	24	9
	Vickers Vimy	1	
Totals		96	47

Of the forty-four established squadron, thirteen appear to have operated throughout 1924 free of accidents of a nature serious enough for the aircraft to be written off. However, it has to be borne in mind that not every accident return has survived and, therefore, the statistics here displayed may well be an underestimate.

Nevertheless, the increase compared to 1923 no doubt gave cause to concern, though I suggest the acceptance of death caused by flying accidents were probably an accepted risk taken by all who entered the flying services - both military and civil - not only in the United Kingdom but across the world.

As events would prove, 1924 was the worst year of the decade for accidents resulting in the aircraft being destroyed.

* Pilot Officer Basil Douglas John Broadway, a graduate from the Cadet College at Cranwell, had the misfortune to wreck three of 32 Squadron's establishment of Sopwith 7F.1 Snipes.

Appendix B - Squadron Locations and Commanding Officers

During the year the gradual expansion noted in 1923 continued with seven squadrons reforming in celebration of the Royal Air Force's sixth anniversary on the 1st of April - an eighth squadron, namely XV Squadron having 'returned to the fold' a few days earlier.

Impressive though this may have been for the time initial equipment for the reformed squadrons was of *Great War* vintage though as the year progressed new designs were coming into service, the home based day-bomber squadrons converting from DH.9As to Fairey Fawns whose performance was only marginally better than the aircraft it was replacing and was unpopular with pilots owing to the bulk of its Lion engine restricting their forward vision. The night bomber force was increased from one to four squadrons, all equipped with Vickers Vimy a type that entered service in the last few months of hostilities.

Initial issues of the Gloster Grebe, the first post-war fighter, arrived with 111 Squadron at Duxford in October 1923 a single flight being equipped followed in April and June 1924 respectively by 7F.1 Snipe and Armstrong Whitworth all-metal Siskin, though the honour of being the first squadron to equip with the Siskin fell to 41 Squadron.

Although elevated to squadron status, a handful were also tasked with providing flying instruction to newly commissioned short service officers and non-commissioned officers.

1 Squadron	7F.1 Snipe	Hinaidi	01.01.24-31.12.24	
2 Squadron	Bristol F.2b	Andover	01.01.24-31.03.24	
		Manston	31.03.24-31.12.24	
3 Squadron	7F.1 Snipe	Manston	01.04.24-30.04.24	Reformed Home Defence squadron
		Upavon	30.04.24-31.12.24	
4 Squadron	Bristol F.2b	Farnborough	01.01.24-31.12.24	
5 Squadron	Bristol F.2b	Ambala	01.01.24-10.03.24	
		Dardoni	10.03.24-31.12.24	
6 Squadron	Bristol F.2b	Hinaidi	01.01.24-19.05.24	
		Mosul	19.05.24-31.12.24	
7 Squadron	Vimy	Bircham Newton	01.01.24-31.12.24	
8 Squadron	DH.9A	Hinaidi	01.01.24-31.12.24	
9 Squadron	Vimy	Upavon	01.04.24-30.04.24	Reformed Night Bomber squadron
		Manston	30.04.24-31.12.24	
11 Squadron	DH.9A/Fawn III	Bircham Newton	01.01.24-31.05.24	DH.9A withdrawn
		Netheravon	31.05.24-31.12.24	
12 Squadron	DH.9A/Fawn II/III	Northolt	01.01.24-23.03.24	DH.9A withdrawn during April
		Andover	23.03.24-31.12.24	
13 Squadron	Bristol F.2b	Kenley	01.04.24-30.06.24	Reformed
		Andover	30.06.24-31.12.24	
14 Squadron	Bristol F.2b	Ramleh & Amman	01.01.24-31.12.24	
XV Squadron	*Various*	Martlesham Heath	20.03.24-31.12.24	Reformed Armament testing duties
16 Squadron	Bristol F.2b	Old Sarum	01.04.24-31.12.24	Reformed Army Cooperation duties
17 Squadron	7F.1 Snipe	Hawkinge	01.04.24-31.12.24	Reformed Home Defence squadron
19 Squadron	7F.1 Snipe/Grebe II	Duxford	01.01.24-31.12.24	7F.1 Snipe withdrawn in December
20 Squadron	Bristol F.2b	Quetta	01.01.24-31.12.24	
22 Squadron	*Various*	Martlesham Heath	01.01.24-31.12.24	
24 Squadron	*Various*	Kenley	01.01.24-31.12.24	
25 Squadron	7.F1 Snipe/Grebe II	Hawkinge	01.01.24-31.12.24	7F.1 Snipe withdrawn in November
27 Squadron	DH.9A	Risalpur	01.01.24-31.12.24	
28 Squadron	Bristol F.2b	Peshawar	01.01.24-31.12.24	
29 Squadron	7F.1 Snipe	Duxford	01.01.24-31.12.24	
30 Squadron	DH.9A	Hinaidi	01.01.24-19.05.24	
		Kirkuk	19.05.24-31.12.24	
31 Squadron	Bristol F.2b	Dardoni	01.01.24-13.03.24	
		Ambala	13.03.24-31.12.24	
32 Squadron	7F.1 Snipe/Grebe II	Kenley	01.01.24-30.06.24	
		Bircham Newton	30.06.24-05.08.24	
		Kenley	05.08.24-31.12.24	7F.1 Snipe withdrawn in December
39 Squadron	DH.9A	Spittlegate	01.01.24-31.12.24	
41 Squadron	7F.1 Snipe/Siskin III	Northolt	01.01.24-31.12.24	7F.1 Snipe withdrawn during May
45 Squadron	Vernon	Hinaidi	01.01.24-31.12.24	
47 Squadron	DH.9A	Helwan	01.01.24-31.12.24	
55 Squadron	DH.9A	Mosul	01.01.24-19.05.24	
		Hinaidi	19.05.24-31.12.24	
56 Squadron	7F.1 Snipe/Grebe II	Biggin Hill	01.01.24-31.12.24	7F.1 Snipe withdrawn in November
58 Squadron	Vimy/Virginia	Worthy Down	01.04.24-31.12.24	Reformed Night Bomber squadron
60 Squadron	DH.9A	Risalpur	01.01.24-31.12.24	
70 Squadron	Vernon	Hinaidi	01.01.24-31.12.24	
84 Squadron	DH.9A	Shaibah	01.01.24-31.12.24	
99 Squadron	Vimy/Aldershot	Netheravon	01.04.24-31.05.24	Reformed Night Bomber Squadron
		Bircham Newton	31.05.24-31.12.24	Vimy withdrawn during December
100 Squadron	DH.9A/Vimy/Fawn II	Spittlegate	01.01.24-....05.24	DH.9A/Vimy withdrawn during May
		Eastchurch	....05.24-.....07.24	
		Spittlegate	.....07.24-31.12.24	
111 Squadron	Grebe II/7F.1 Snipe/Siskin III	Duxford	01.01.24-31.12.24	
207 Squadron	DH.9A	Eastchurch	01.01.24-31.12.24	
208 Squadron	Bristol F.2b	Ismailia	01.01.24-31.12.24	
216 Squadron	Vimy	Heliopolis	01.01.24-31.12.24	

1 Squadron	Squadron Leader E O Grenfell MC DFC AFC mid	In situ	See Appendix B 1923
	Squadron Leader E D Atkinson DFC AFC	25 May 1924	S/Ldr 18.01.32 retirement
2 Squadron	Squadron Leader L F Forbes	In situ	See Appendix B 1922
3 Squadron	Squadron Leader J C Russell DSO mid *Croix de Guerre* [Belgium]	23 April 1924	A/Cmdr retirement 6 January 1943
4 Squadron	Squadron Leader C H B Blount	In situ	See Appendix B 1921
5 Squadron	Squadron Leader A J Capel	In situ	See Appendix B 1923
6 Squadron	Squadron Leader D S K Crosbie OBE	In situ	See Appendix B 1923
7 Squadron	Squadron Leader C H Hayward	In situ	See Appendix B 1923
	Squadron Leader E O Grenfell MC DFC AFC mid	20 October 1924	See 1 Squadron 1923
8 Squadron	Squadron Leader G H Bowman DSO MC* DFC	In situ	See Appendix B 1922
	Squadron Leader F Sowrey DSO MC AFC	5 February 1924	G/Capt retirement 26 May 1940
	Squadron Leader W A McClaughry DSO MC DFC three times mid Australia	27 October 1924	AVM died 4 January 1943
9 Squadron	Flight Lieutenant V R Gibbs DSC	1 April 1924	W/Cdr retired list 26 October 1945
	Squadron Leader J C Quinnell DFC	23 April 1924	A/Cmdr retirement 11 December 1944
	Squadron Leader A P V Daly	August 1924	G/Capt retired list 7 April 1945
11 Squadron	Squadron Leader E A B Rice MC	In situ	See 6 Squadron 1921
12 Squadron	Squadron Leader A Gray MC	In situ	See Appendix B 1923
13 Squadron	Squadron Leader C C Durston*	23 May 1924	W/Cdr killed 12 January 1933
14 Squadron	Squadron Leader W H Dolphin	In situ	See Appendix B 1923
	Squadron Leader A N Gallehawk AFC	6 June 1924	A/Cmdr retirement 11 March 1942
XV Squadron	Squadron Leader P C Sherren MC Canada	20 March 1924	See 60 Squadron 1921
16 Squadron	Squadron Leader J O Archer CBE	1 April 1924	G/Capt relinquished 1 May 1946
17 Squadron	Squadron Leader J Leacroft MC*	1 May 1924	G/Capt retired list 18 April 1945
19 Squadron	Flight Lieutenant T J West	1 June 1924	See summary 26 May 1926
	Squadron Leader P Babington MC AFC	26 July 1924	See 56 Squadron 1921
20 Squadron	Squadron Leader R T Leather AFC	In situ	See Appendix B 1923
	Squadron Leader C B Cooke mid	25 January 1924	AM retirement 12 November 1949
22 Squadron	*Not reported*		
24 Squadron	Squadron Leader R S Maxwell MC DFC* AFC	In situ	See Appendix B 1923
25 Squadron	Squadron Leader A H Peck DSO MC*	In situ	See Appendix B 1923
27 Squadron	Squadron Leader R T Whitehead	In situ	See Appendix B 1923
	Squadron Leader L M Bailey AFC	27 November 1924	W/Cdr retired list 1 May 1936
28 Squadron	Squadron Leader H S Powell MC	In situ	See Appendix B 1923
	Squadron Leader C S Wynne-Eyton DSO	23 September 1924	W/Cdr killed 14 November 1944
29 Squadron	Squadron Leader R H G Neville MC	In situ	See Appendix B 1923
	Squadron Leader M L Taylor AFC	12 August 1924	AV-M retirement 19 May 1946
30 Squadron	Squadron Leader E H Johnson	In situ	See 24 Squadron 1922
	Squadron Leader J M Robb DFC	19 January 1924	ACM retirement 26 November 1951
31 Squadron	Squadron Leader A C Maund CBE DSO	In situ	See Appendix B 1922
	Squadron Leader A A Walser MC DFC twice mid *Croix de Guerre*	May 1924	A/Cmdr retirement 21 September 1941
	Squadron Leader H S Powell MC	20 June 1924	See Appendix B 1923
32 Squadron	Squadron Leader T E B Howe AFC	In situ	See Appendix B 1923
	Squadron Leader H P Lale DFC mid	15 April 1924	G/Capt retirement 8 April 1941
39 Squadron	Squadron Leader T Whittaker MC	In situ	See 28 Squadron 1922
41 Squadron	Squadron Leader R Collishaw DSO DSC DFC three times mid	In situ	See Appendix B 1921
	Squadron Leader G W Murlis-Green DSO* MC** three times mid *Croix de Guerre* [France] *Croix de Chevalier Croix de Guerre* [Belgium]	15 April 1924	G/Capt retirement 24 March 1942
45 Squadron	Squadron Leader A T Harris AFC	In situ	See Appendix B 1921
	Squadron Leader R M Hill MC AFC mid	14 October 1924	ACM retirement 1 July 1948
47 Squadron	Squadron Leader M Henderson DSO	In situ	See 216 Squadron 1921
55 Squadron	Squadron Leader A Coningham DSO MC DFC Australia	In situ	See Appendix B 1923
	Squadron Leader E R L Corballis DSO	18 January 1924	W/Cdr retired list 8 February 1932
56 Squadron	Squadron Leader Sir C J Q Brand KBE DSO MC DFC South Africa	In situ	See Appendix B 1923
58 Squadron	Flight Lieutenant E G Hilton*	April 1924	W/Cdr killed 19 September 1937
	Squadron Leader W H Longton DFC AFC	15 July 1924	Killed 6 June 1927
60 Squadron	Squadron Leader H V Champion de Crepigny MC DFC	In situ	See Appendix B 1922
	Squadron Leader A W H James MC	14 September 1924	W/Cdr retired list 21 May 1925
70 Squadron	Squadron Leader S W Smith OBE	In situ	See Annex B 1921
	Squadron Leader T Q Studd DFC	1 September 1924	G/Capt retirement 23 May 1945
84 Squadron	Squadron Leader V S Brown	In situ	See Appendix B 1923
	Squadron Leader E D Atkinson DFC AFC	18 February 1924	See 1 Squadron 1924
	Squadron Leader R H Peck OBE mid	10 May 1924	AM retirement 2 April 1946
	Squadron Leader D E Stodart DSO DFC mid Australia	18 September 1924	S/Ldr retired list 1 March 1931
99 Squadron	Squadron Leader G R M Reid DSO MC*	23 April 1924	AV-M retirement 20 January 1946
100 Squadron	Squadron Leader H F A Gordon	In situ	See Appendix B 1923
111 Squadron	Squadron Leader T F Haazell DSO MC DFC	In situ	See summary 4 April 1925
207 Squadron	Squadron Leader V Gaskell-Blackburn DSO AFC	In situ	See 55 Squadron 1923
208 Squadron	Wing Commander A C Winter	In situ	See Appendix B 1923
	Squadron Leader H M Probyn DSO mid	January 1924	A/Cmdr retirement 29 April 1924
216 Squadron	Squadron Leader C O Modin DSC mid	In situ	See Appendix B 1922
	Wing Commander L D D McKean OBE mid	1 October 1924	AV-M retirement 21 May 1945

Annex

Born in Calcutta on 10th November 1891, Squadron Leader Edward Dawson 'Spider' Atkinson saw active service with three scout squadrons on the Western Front, namely 1, 56 and 64 Squadrons, achieving a total of ten combat successes, some of these being shared with other pilots. *Gazetted* in the Edinburgh edition, issue 13300, page 2812, with the DFC, the citation reads: *"A brilliant fighting pilot whose flight has proved very successful under his leadership, often in combats where the enemy formation was numerically superior. Capt. Atkinson destroyed single-handed five machines during May, and previously, while serving with another squadron, he brought down two enemy aeroplanes and one balloon."*

An award of the AFC was published by *The London Gazette* in the New Year's Honours listing, 1st January 1919, supplement 31098, page 97. Subsequently, his health failed him and he left the service [as indicated above] after which very little is known of this life.

Squadron Leader John Cannan Russell, formerly of the Royal Engineers, was *Gazetted* with the DSO, less citation, on 3rd June 1919. His *Great War* service included flight commander duties with 54 Squadron and command of 32 Squadron [DH.5/SE.5a] from 11th September 1917 to 18th July 1918, followed in the spring of 1919 by a brief attachment in command of 20 Squadron [Bristol F.2b] on the North West Frontier of British India.

It was during the *Battle of Loos* [25th September to 8 October 1915] that Frederick Sowrey, a 2nd Lieutenant commissioned as an infantry officer with the Royal Fusiliers, was seriously wounded and, subsequently, invalided from the army. However, he was accepted by the RFC for pilot training and it was just before midnight on 23rd September 1916, and now attached to 39 Squadron, that he took off from Sutton Farm in a BE.2c with orders to patrol in the direction of Joyce Green. Slowly, 2nd Lieutenant Sowrey managed to climb to 13,000 feet and shortly after 1 o'clock in the morning of the 24th that he caught sight of a German airship; this transpired to be a Zeppelin LZ74. Closing from below he emptied three drums of incendiary bullets into the airship which tumbled burning furiously to crash near Billericay in Essex where in daylight hundreds of local people were drawn to view the skeletal remains of L32.

For this feat, his first aerial success, Frederick Sowrey was honoured with the Distinguished Service Order: *"His majesty the KING has been graciously pleased to appoint the undermentioned Officers, Companions of the Distinguished Service Order, in recognition of their gallantry and distinguished service in connection with the successful attack on Enemy Airships:-*

2nd Lt. Frederick Sowrey, R. Fus., attd. RFC

2nd Lt. Alfred de Bath Brandon MC, RFC, Spec. Res.

The London Gazette, Wednesday 4th October 1916, supplement 29773, page 9635.

In 1917, he went to France on liaison duty during which time he joined 19 Squadron [Spad variants] with whom he scored over a dozen combat victories, some of these being shared with his fellow compatriots. These operations gained him an MC *Gazetted* 6 April 1918, supplement 30614, page 4228: *"For conspicuous gallantry and devotion to duty in shooting down in less than two months two Albatross scouts and a Rumpler two-seaters and a Fokker scout, and in two engagements flying very low and engaging and scattering the hostile infantry."*

An AFC was added in the New Year's Honours List of 1919 [LG 1 January 1919, supplement 31098, page 98].

Squadron Leader Sowrey was succeeded by an equally distinguished Commanding Officer, namely Australian born Squadron Leader Wilfred Ashton McClaughry whose *Great War* service was, in the main, spent with the Australian Flying Corps. His MC was published in the *Edinburgh* paper, issue 13116, page 1427: *"For conspicuous gallantry and devotion. On many occasions he has displayed the highest courage and skill in successfully bombing stations and trains, often at very low altitudes, and has always given a fine example of energy and determination."*

The citation for his DFC appeared in *The London Gazette* 2nd November 1918, supplement 30989, page 12969: *"The squadron commanded by this officer has been remarkably active and successful in attacks at low altitudes on trains, transports, billet and low-flying machines; this success is largely due to his inspiring personality, fine leadership, and the boldness in attack he invariably displays. One evening he bombed a train, which was compelled to stop; he then attacked it with machine-gun fire at 200ft. altitude. Afterwards he engaged a two-seater machine, which unfortunately escaped owing to failures in both his machine guns. Having remedied these, he attacked a party of infantry, which he dispersed, several casualties being noted."*

In both citations his surname is recorded as *'McCloughry.'* On 8th February 1919, he was honoured with the DSO [citation not traced]. Rising to air rank, Air Vice-Marshal Wilfred Ashton McClaughry DSO MC DFC was killed on 4th January 1943, when the aircraft in which he was a passenger crashed as it prepared to land at Cairo; he is buried in Heliopolis War Cemetery. Also killed in this tragic accident was Lady Tedder, wife of Air Chief Marshal Arthur William Tedder who at the time was Air Officer Commanding RAF Middle East Command. It is reported that along with a welcoming party he was at the airfield and witnessed the crash. Air Vice-Marshal McClaughry was Air Officer Commanding Egypt.

Squadron Leader John Charles 'Paddy' Quinnell was *Gazetted* with the DFC in the New Year's Honours List for 1919 [LG 1 January 1919, supplement 31098, page 96]; no citation appended. During the *Great War* he was attached at various time to 10, 7, 6, 83, 63 and 104 Squadrons and, I suspect, his award reflects his service with the latter which he commanded from 1st January 1918 to 3rd February 1919. On 10th July 1916, during the *Battle of the Somme* his 7 Squadron BE.2d 5754 came into land with a bomb still attached and on touch down it fell off and exploded severely wounding Captain Quinnell in the legs [see page 44 of *The Sky Their Battlefield*]. Taken to 7 Stationary Hospital for initial treatment, he was evacuated to the UK on 14th July 1916, aboard HMHS *St. Denis.*

From the Army Service Corps to the Royal Flying Corps in which, initially, he flew as an observer, Squadron Leader John Leacroft served with great distinction with 19 Squadron, first with Spad VIIs and then during his second tour with the squadron, Sopwith 5F.1 Dolphins. Credited with twenty-two aerial combat successes he received the MC [EG March 21, 1918, issue 13226, page 1077]: *"For conspicuous gallantry and devotion to duty. On one occasion he flew at a very low altitude in extremely bad weather and successfully engaged enemy troops with machine-gun fire, and on another occasion carried out a most valuable reconnaissance and engaged enemy troops from a height of 100 feet. He destroyed two hostile machines, and has proved himself a courageous and determined pilot."*

In supplement 30781, page 7399, of the London edition, dated 22nd June 1918, the citation for a First Bar was promulgated: *"For conspicuous gallantry and devotion to duty. During a period of six months he has destroyed four and brought down completely out of control six hostile machines. In all he has destroyed eight enemy machines and driven down thirteen out of control. On one occasion, when leading an offensive patrol, his formation destroyed six enemy planes and drove another down out of control without suffering any damage itself. He has displayed exceptional qualities as a leader, and his patrols have always been characterised by vigour and dash."*

James Milne Robb did not quite emulate Field Marshal Sir William Robertson, affectionately known as *'Wuffy,'* in rising to the pinnacle of his service from the humble rank of private soldier, but he came a very close second for starting out with *"the humble rank of private soldier"* his service ended one rank below Marshal of the Royal Air Force when he retired on 26th November 1951, as Air Chief Marshal Sir James Robb GCB KBE DSO DFC AFC and three times mentioned in despatches. His commission from private to 2nd Lieutenant and attachment to the 4th Battalion, The Northumberland Fusiliers was *Gazetted* on 9th November 1914, supplement 28968, page 9121. Transferring to the RFC he was a qualified pilot by August 1916, and as a flight commander in the service of 32 Squadron [DH.2] he received a painful wound to his right thigh on 11th March 1917, when his DH.2 A2535 was shot about and crashed near Bapaume on the Somme, an event recorded on page 71 of Trevor Henshaw's invaluable *The Sky Their Battlefield.* Following treatment in 8 General Hospital he returned to England as a patient in HMHS *Gloucester Castle.*

Fully recovered, he returned to France and with 92 Squadron [SE.5a] he won the DFC [LG 8 February 1919, issue 31170, page 2045]: *"This officer has destroyed seven enemy aircraft, and under his brilliant leadership his patrols have accounted for numerous others. On 13th October he attacked and silenced three hostile howitzers which were in action."*

As with so many of his generation, Squadron Leader Adolph Andre Walser began his military service as an army officer and was serving in the ill-fated Gallipoli campaign when in late May 1915, he was seconded to the RFC for observer work. By the spring of 1916, he was back in the UK and trained as a pilot, embarking for France for duties as a reconnaissance pilot with 4 Squadron [BE.2c]. In early 1917, and now promoted temporary major, he was appointed to command 52 Squadron [RE.8]. His excellence as a reconnaissance pilots was recognised with awards of the MC and DFC, the two citations being published as follows: LG 14 November 1916, supplement 29824, page 11070: *"For conspicuous gallantry in action. He carried out a most valuable artillery reconnaissance under very heavy fire, displaying great courage and determination. He has, on many previous occasions done fine work,"* and that for his DFC: *"A brilliant and exceptionally able squadron commander who, by his unsparing efforts and his fine personal example, has raised the morale of his squadron to a very high level. The comprehensive and detailed information obtained by Major Walser in the large number of low reconnaissances he has conducted has proved of the greatest value to his corps."*

Supplement 30638, page 4717, of the *Gazette* 18th April 1918, promulgated his *Croix de Guerre.* On 10th February 1956, he changed by deed poll his Christian names to 'Andre Adolphus.'

Squadron Leader Horace Percy Lale's DFC, for service in France, was *Gazetted* on 3rd December 1918, supplement 31046, page 14323: *"A bold and courageous officer, who leads his patrol with marked skill and judgement. He has accounted for twelve enemy aeroplanes - five crashed, four shot down in flames, and three driven down out of control. On 6th September he led his patrol of nine machines to the assistance of some formations that were attacked by thrty or forty enemy aircraft, in the engagement he and his Observer accounted for two Fokkers; eventually the enemy was driven off, five of their machines being destroyed and three shot down out of control.:*

According to the Aerodrome website, which the authors are delighted to acknowledge, his prowess as a fighting scout pilot began with 48 Squadron [24th June 1917 to 14th September 1917] and ended with 20 Squadron [30th June to 30th October 1918] during which time he notched up twenty-three victories. The action on 6th September 1918, and referred to in the citation, took place over St. Quentin when he was flying Bristol F.2b E2181 which according to Air-Britain's file on the Bristol Fighter was deleted on 28th September 1918, as not worth repairing following serious damage four days previously as summarised on page 244 of my second volume. It had accumulated fifty-five hours and twelve minutes flying.

See also Appendix D and page 198 of the third volume.

It is difficult to find a more decorated officer than Squadron Leader Gilbert Ware Murlis-Green whose remarkable courage, determination and energy gained him three mentioned in despatches, a Military Cross and Two Bars, a DSO and First Bar, plus awards conferred upon him by foreign governments, all between 6th December 1916 and 15th July 1919. Through courtesy of the Aerodrome website and *Wikipedia*, which the authors acknowledge, the following citations come to light. In a supplement to *The Edinburgh Gazette* of February 14th, 1917, issue 13051, page 321, appears the citation for the First Bar to his Military Cross: *"For conspicuous gallantry in action. He brought down two enemy machines on successive days under adverse circumstances. He has displayed great dash and courage at every opportunity."* The Second Bar was also published in the *Edinburgh* issue of January 11th, 1918, issue 13193, page 330: *"Whilst flying at night on patrol duty he encountered an enemy aeroplane, which he attacked with great determination and skill, and although there was very little light he succeeded in hitting one of the engines of the machine, which by reason of the damage, was forced to come down in the sea off a South Coast port, where two of the occupants of the machine were made prisoners."*

Via *Wikipedia* the citations for his DSO and First Bar, promulgated in *The London Gazette,* read: *"For conspicuous gallantry and devotion to duty. He has set a magnificent example by his gallant conduct in attacking the enemy's aeroplanes when in superior numbers. He brought down three enemy machines in twenty-four hours,"* and *"In recognition of gallantry and distinguished service in connection with Anti-Aircraft services in the United Kingdom."*

The award of the *Croix de Guerre,* conferred by the King of the Belgians, published in *The London Gazette* 15th July 1919, supplement 31457, page 8987, identifies his attachment to 70 Squadron; the *Croix de Chevalier of the Legion of Honour,* conferred by the Government of the French Republic was *Gazetted* on 21st September 1918, supplement 30913, page 11259.

The Serbian Government honoured him with the Order of the White Eagle, 4th Class with Swords on 3rd October 1917., this in recognition of his operational service in the Balkans.

Born in London on 24th January 1895, his death was reported at the relatively early age of 63 on 26th August 1958.

Squadron Leader Roderic Maxwell Hill was *Gazetted* with a MC on 14th November 1916, supplement 29824, page 11055: *"For conspicuous skill and gallantry. Under very heavy fire he dived at an enemy balloon, and brought it down in flames. On the day before he had dived at a balloon under heavy fire at a low altitude, but had just missed his mark."* Prior to the armistice, and while attached to the Experimental Flight [Orfordness] his work was recognised by the award of the Air Force Cross [EG August 7, 1918, issue 13300, page 2819].

Referring to his MC, at the time he was flying Nieuport 16s with 60 Squadron. Attacking observation balloons was considered by just about every scout pilot on the Western Front as one of the most hazardous tasks that they might be called up to accomplish. Invariably, observation balloons were heavily defended and once a pilot had committed himself to the attack his machine came under a deadly hail of fire from the ground to which was added the possibility of having to fly through the burning remains of the target, still pursued by ground fire. For the enemy artillery observers, parachute equipped, they too ran the risk of their 'chutes being set on fire before reaching the ground.

A Second World War parallel to these operations were the strikes on the V-1 flying bomb sites that had mushroomed in the Pas de Calais and other parts of the Occupied Countries by the Typhoon squadrons of the 2nd Tactical Air Force and to no lesser degree Coastal Command's anti-shipping strikes on enemy merchant vessels protected by *Flak* ships.

As with his contemporary, Squadron Leader James Milne Robb [30 Squadron] who had his 'personal aircraft' [a Spitfire XVI] Squadron Leader Hill in 1946, had a Tempest V which sported his initials 'RH.' Both, at the time, were of air rank.

Edward Roux Littledale Corballis, a Gentleman Cadet, graduated from the Royal Military College and was *Gazetted* 2nd Lieutenant on 20th April 1910 [LG April, 19, issue 28358, page 2682] on augmentation to The Royal Dublin Fusiliers. He was conferred with the *Legion d'Honneur, Croix de Chevalier* [LG 14 July 1917, supplement 30184, page 7094], this being followed by the DSO in the New Year's Honours List for 1918 [LG 1st January 1918, supplement 30450, page 19].

Squadron Leader Walter Hunt Longton achieved the rare distinction of adding two Bars to the DFC which was *Gazetted* 2nd November 1918, supplement 30989, page 12968 and 12969: *"On 22nd August this officer led his formation of six machines to attack an equal number of enemy scouts. All the latter were accounted for, four being crashed and the remaining two being driven down out of control. A brilliant performance, reflecting the greatest credit on this officer as leader, and all who took part in this engagement. During the last seven weeks Lieutenant Longton has destroyed seven enemy machines."* On 8th February 1919, issue 31170, page 2033, a First Bar was published: *"between 29th September and 9th October this officer carried out twelve tactical reconnaissances, bringing back most valuable information; he also displayed great gallantry in attacking enemy troops on the ground. On 9th October, when on a low patrol, a observed a machine-gun nest which appeared to be the sole object to our cavalry advance. Having informed the cavalry and field artillery of the situation, he co-operated with the former in their attack, and, pursued them with machine-gun fire as they retreated."*

The Second Bar, less citation, was *Gazetted* on 3rd June 1919, supplement 31378, page 7030. His AFC had been promulgated on 3rd June 1918. His life was taken from him during an air race at Bournemouth on 6th June 1927; he is buried in Upavon cemetery beneath a headstone supplied by his grieving widow. A detailed description of the accident is reported in Appendix D of the third volume, page 200.

Squadron Leader Archibald William Henry James is probably better known for his parliamentary service than his *Great War* exploits during which he won the Military Cross. *Gazetted* as a 2nd Lieutenant, having successfully applied for a commission from his university [trinity College, Cambridge], he was attached to the 3rd [King's Own] Hussars with effect from 26th August 1914 [LG 25 August 1914, issue 28879, page 6694]. Following acceptance in the RFC, he gained his MC, *Gazetted* June 26, 1916, issue 12955, page 1155, in the *Edinburgh* edition: *"For conspicuous gallantry when making a special reconnaissance. Owing to clouds, he crossed the lines at 1,500ft, and, seeing signs of movement in a particular locality, he came down to 800ft in order to get a better view. He re-crossed the lines at 500ft with very valuable information under heavy fire from rifles, machine-guns, anti-aircraft guns and field guns. His engine and machine were badly damaged by the enemy's fire."*

His first attempt to win a seat in parliament was in the 1929 General Election when stood as a Unionist candidate for Wellingborough in Northamptonshire, but lost to the Labour candidate, George Dallas. Undeterred he contested the same seat in the '31 election, and this time was successful. In 1935, he defended the seat, narrowly winning against his old adversity, George Dallas, holding Wellingborough until the 1945, when he was ousted by Labour's George Lindgren.

For several years he resided in Southern Rhodesia but at the time of his death at the age of 86 on 5th May 1980, he was residing in Worthing, West Sussex. Politics was in the genes of his son, David, and with Conservative colours 'nailed to his mast' he held Brighton Kemptown from 1959 to 1964 and North Dorset from 1970 to 1979.

Squadron Leader Theodore Quintus Studd was awarded the DFC for his gallantry when flying sea patrols. *Gazetted* 21st September 1918, supplement 30913, page, 11255, the citation reads: *"As pilot he has been engaged in more than 60 bombing raids many miles behind the enemy's lines. Captan Studd is a most skilful pilot who can always be relied upon to carry out any task that he may be called upon to perform, no matter what adverse conditions may prevail."*

On 17th October 1933, he had a narrow escape from death when the Southampton boat S1121 crashed while alighting in Southampton Water [see Appendix C for 1930 and the entry for Flying Officer John Charles Francis Peacock].

After leaving the Royal Air Force, Group Captain Studd DFC mid volunteered his service to the Air Training Corps and was commissioned as a flying officer in the training branch of the Royal Air Force Volunteer Reserve serving for seven years before relinquishing his commission on 1st December 1959 [LG 19 January 1960, supplement 41932, page 549]. Although conjecture on my part, I suspect he may have been employed on flying duties at an air experience flight [these flights were established country-wide to provide air cadets the opportunity to fly in Chipmunk T.10 two-seat tandem basic trainers during which they would receive very basic handling of the aircraft's controls]. I base my assumption in that on two occasions his service was extended for periods of two and one year respectively which may have been granted on passing an aircrew medical examination.

Born on 2nd January 1893, he lived to the good age of 96, before dying on 10th September 1989.

Squadron Leader David Edmund Stodart was commission in the Special Reserve of Officers as a probationary 2nd Lieutenant to the Military Wing of the Royal Flying Corps as early as 17th May 1913 [LG 16 May 1913, issue 28719, page 3515]. Held at the Royal Air Force Museum, Hendon, are three Army Form B.103s charting the early part of his *Great War* service and post-armistice movements.

			Embarked 28.8.14	
		To RFC in England	*7.1.15*	*B213 No. 180*
			Re-embarked 9.8.15	*To deliver a machine*
		Left Boulogne	*11.8.15*	
		Posted to No. 1 Squadron	*2.9.15*	
18.9.15	*3 CCS*	*Admitted hosp.*	*11.9.15*	*A 36 SD 1895*
23.9.15	*20 Gen H*	*Discharged hosp.*	*23.9.15*	*W 3034*
		Left Boulogne	*23.9.15*	*Telg*
			Re-embarked 3.10.15	*T ...*
23.2.16	*2 AD*	*Leave 24.2.16 - 2.3.16*	*24.2.16*	*B 213/319*
		Second Army Form B.103		
28.4.17	*3 Sqdn*	*To Home Est.*	*22.4.17*	*B 213*
3.1.18	*London Gazette*	*To Special Appointment [Graded as Squadron Commander] & to be temp. Major*	*12.12.17*	*L G*
		Third Army Form B.103		
			Embarked Australia	
22.5.20			*Disembarked Port Said 20.5.20*	*MERO 75*
22.5.20		*Posted from un-posted leave Australia to Gal. Gro. Hqs. for duty as Sq. Leader Air*	*21.5.20*	- " -
31.5.20		*Assumed the duties of Sq. Ldr. S.Q. Air Staff*	*26.5.20*	*PGRO 11*
29.6.20		*Granted permanent commission as Sq Ldr*	*21.5.20*	*MERO 97/L G 1.6.20*
6.7.20		*Posted to Hqts Palestine Group temporarily filling vacancy as Wing Commander*	*2.6.20*	*MERO 101*
8.11.20		*Attd. to 208 Sq for rations from HQ Pal. Group*	*8.11.20*	*PGRO 248*
18.11.20		*Granted 2 days leave and proceeded to Cairo from Hqts Palestine Group*	*12.11.20*	*PGRO 253*

The single entry for an award, that for his DSO, appeared in *The London Gazette* 21 September 1918, supplement 30913, page 11247 and 11248: *"Whilst commanding a flight of the Royal Air Force the whole of the flying officers had become incapacitated through sickness or wounds, and their duties were then performed by himself, in addition o his administrative work as commanding officer, Major Sttodart dropped 115 bombs on the enemy's positions, exposed 326 negatives over enemy territory, and acted as observer for 163 rounds of our heavy artillery. In a period of twenty-one days this officer was thirty-seven hours in the air, performing all the duties of an entire flight, a record which it would be difficult to surpass."*

His biography appears on The Geelong College website, which the authors acknowledge with pleasure, this showing that he was born on 31st July 1882, and named after his father, a practicing doctor. On matriculation, David proceeded to the United Kingdom, entering Edinburgh University where he studied medicine, graduating as a doctor on 1st September 1910.

Three years after retiring from the service, and now 52 years of age, he teamed up with a Sergeant K Stodart and flying an Airspeed AS.5 Courier G-ACJL in the famous London to Melbourne air race in which they were placed sixth in an elapsed time of 9 days and 18 hours.

Dr. David Edmund Stodart DSO DFC died in London on 28th February 1938.

Gazetted to the 4th Battalion, Argyll and Sutherland Highlanders as a 2nd Lieutenant [LG 16 February 1915, issue 29070, page 1565, George Ranald Macfarlane Reid was awarded the Military Cross on 24th June 1916, to which a First Bar was published in *The Edinburgh Gazette* November 27th, 1916, issue 13017, page 2214: *"For conspicuous gallantry in action. He with his observer pursued a hostile aeroplane for six miles into the enemy's territory, and there shot it down. He has on previous occasions done very fine work."*

Squadron Leader Harold Melsome Probyn is credited on the website All Spitfire Pilots, which the authors acknowledge with gratitude, with visiting Northolt where he carried out some dusk and night flying in Spitfire I N3287 which at the time was on 92 Squadron's establishment. Ironically, this Spitfire, still with 92 Squadron, was abandoned during a night patrol on 27th July 1940, and left to crash near the Devonshire village of Chudleigh some 9 to 10 miles SSW from Exeter.

Just over two decades earlier he performed an action which won his the Distinguished Service Order [LG 17 September 1917, supplement 30287, page 9557]: *"For conspicuous gallantry and devotion to duty. At a critical time when hostile infantry had penetrated our trenches, he went up in unfavourable weather and under heavy machine-gun and anti-aircraft fire from guns of heavy calibre, and managed to locate and report with complete accuracy the position and progress of the enemy. To do this he had to fly at a very low altitude, during which his machine was seriously damaged by enemy fire. The following day he carried out another daring and successful reconnaissance of the enemy's line, bringing back information of the greatest value. He has already experienced a whole year's strenuous flying, a fact which speaks for his gallantry and endurance on both of these particular occasions."*

I strongly suspect he won the DSO whilst attached to 52 Squadron [RE.8] though his service records show he went out to France with 32 Squadron [DH.2] and was shot in the back on 23rd August 1916, his wounds being treated at 39 Casuualty Clearing Station. Fortunately, the wound was minor and he returned to duty two days later. On 14th April 1917, he was posted to 52 Squadron, but on 4th July 1917, he returned to 32 Squadron, now flying DH.5, for flight commander duties.

* While serving as a Staff Officer at Headquarters RAF India, Wing Commander Cecil Campbell Durston was invited to join a shooting party during which he was killed when unable to get out of the way of a Buffalo. His untimely death was reported in *The Central Somerset Gazette* on Friday, January 20th, 1933, beneath the headline *'Game Hunt Death - Bridgwater Man Killed by a Buffalo'* *"Wing Commander Cecil Campbell Durston, Royal Air Force, who was killed by a buffalo during a shooting expedition near Rajputans, was born at Bridgwater 49 years ago. He was educated at Weston-super-Mare and Exmouth, and joined the Honourable Artillery Company in 1908. In 1916, he went to the Central Flying School, and from March to November 1917, he served with the Royal Flying Corps in France. He had been engaged on air staff duties with Air Marshal Sir John Steel in India for the last two years."*

Flight Lieutenant Edward Goodwill Hilton died during the King's Cup Air Race [19th September 1937] when his Miles M3A Falcon Major G-AENG registered to Phillips & Powis Aircraft, Woodley, flew into turbulence at low altitude near Castle Hill Scarborough. At the time he had been promoted wing commander and was filling a staff post at the Air Ministry. An obituary [as forwarded from Paul McMillan] reads: *"Wing Commander Hilton was considered one of the most brilliant of the RAF pilots at Martlesham, where the newest aeroplanes are tested. He had had 6,000 hours' flying experience. Recently he was appointed to the Air Ministry for service on the department of the Air Member for research and development. He had never flown in a King's Cup air race. A few days ago he told a friend he had entered out of curiosity. "I want to get experience and the general impression of what this round-the-country race is like," he said. He recently flew and Airspeed Envoy to Cape Town "for fun" and brought it back in almost record time. "It was just by accident that we flew back so quickly," he said when he returned. Last year delay at Athens robbed him of the chance to break Amy Johnson's Cape record."*

Wing Commander Hilton was 41, his Canadian born passenger, Wing Commander Percy Clark Sherren MC and First Bar was 44, and also perished. A local press report convey the news to its readers thus: *"Wing Commander P C Sherren and Wing Commander E G Hilton, competitors in the King's Cup air race, were killed here today before a crowd of about 1,000 people, who had gathered to watch the aeroplanes fly low over the Castle Hill turning point.*

"The pilots had to fly low so that their machines could be identified, and all of them seemed to be troubled by the currents which were caused by a stiff northerly wind. The aeroplane which crashed took a different course from the others. Flying very close to the cliff-edge, the machine was travelling steadily when it was suddenly flung up about 50ft upwards and one of the occupants [Wing Commander Sherren] *was catapulted through the air to disappear from sight over the edge of the cliff. The aeroplane then crashed to the ground and was smashed to pieces, killing the other occupant.*

"The Coroner's report and results of the inquest into the accident provided further details. The machine piloted by Wing Commander Hilton came down to about 150ft at great speed, and then seemed to get into an air pocket and drop slightly and nose dive to the ground. At 9 o'clock on the morning of the race the wind was blowing at 25 mph, and later it increased to 35 mph. It was also very gusty. Other machines bumped in making the turn at the Castle Hill. Wing Commander Hilton was thrown out of the machine, struck the edge of the cliff, and dropped 200ft down the cliff. Hilton was picked up 20 yards from the wrecked machine, and a mackintosh was found on the telephone wires."

During a two day auction [28th February-1st March 2018] by Dix Noonan Webb , Wing Commander Hilton's medals were sold for £5,500.

Appendix C - Officers Granted Short Service Commissions

On 26th June 1924, No 5 Flying Training School's airfield at Shotwick was re-named Sealand.

LG 8 January 1924, issue 32896, page 269 - Seniority 3rd January 1924; the probationary Pilots Officers were commissioned for five years

FLYING OFFICERS
12

18118 BRETHERTON* Norris Carden F/O + 21.06.25 60 Squadron
18119 EMERSON* Robert Kennedy F/Lt 03.01.31 Relinquished
18120 FOX* Hedley William Avery F/Lt 03.01.31 Relinquished
18121 HALL* Russell Wykeham Morgan F/Lt 14.11.30 Resigned
18122 KELLY* John Vincent F/Lt 04.05.32 Retired list
On account of ill-health [LG 3 May 1932, issue 33822, page 2891].
18123 MEADMORE* Thomas Bennett Robert F/O 04.02.25 Resigned
18124 PECKOVER* Richard Gurney F/O + 17.10.24 4 FTS Abu Sueir
While flying DH.9A F2807 spun from 800 feet and crashed 2 miles NW of the airfield, bursting into flames on hitting the ground. The time of the crash is shown on AM Form 470 as occurring at 0520 hours. Th Findings of the Court read:

"The caused of the accident was in our opinion an error of judgement on the part of the pilot in that he got into an accidental spin and failed to recover.

"The Court is of the further opinion that: 1. The quality of instruction was all that it should be. 2. That the pilot had been properly taught to recognise the tendency of how to check a spin. 3. That there was not a shortage of instruction in this particular flight.

"AOC concurs."

A graduate from the Cadet College at Wellintgon, he was commissioned at a 2nd Lieutenant on the last day of January 1918 [LG 5 November 1918, issue 30992, page 13011]. Within a weekk [5th February 1918] HM The KING had approved his admission to the Indian Army [LG 17 January 1919, issue 31131, page 916].

18125 PILLING* Reginald Westby F/O 21.01.30 Resigned
18126 RADCLIFF* Henry Garnett F/O 17.09.24 Resigned
18127 SPENCE* Edgar Henry Douglas F/Lt 03.01.31 Relinquished
18128 WINTERS* Leo Patrick F/Lt 13.02.30 Relinquished
On account of ill-health [LG 25 February 1930, issue 33583, page 1224].
18129 WISEMAN-CLARKE* Freke William F/Lt 03.01.31 Relinquished

* Denotes retired officers from either the Royal Navy or Indian Army, and appointed for seven years on the active list.

Block 18130 - 18152

18130 ADAMS William Crombie F/O 24.03.26 Relinquished
On account of ill-health [LG 23 March 1926, issue 33144, page 2111]. Returned to the service and granted a commission in the Administrative and Special Duties Branch on 28th February 1940 [LG 26 March 1940, issue 34817, page 1781]. F/O 09.10.43 Resigned
18131 BARNSLEY William Charles P/O 26.08.25 Terminated
18132 BRETT William James F/Lt + 30.03.40
Flight Lieutenant William James Brett, 42 years of age, is buried in Hendon Cemetery. His headstone is inscribed *In Loving Remembrance Of A Darling Husband And Father, Wife Rosamond And Son David."*
18133 BULL Lionel Alfred P/O 25.07.24 Terminated
18134 DIXON MC Frederick Ernest Reginald G/Capt 23.12.47 Retirement
Transferred in from the General Duties Branch to the Equipment Branch, Frederick Ernest Reginald Dixon was promoted squadron leader on 1st June 1938 [LG 31 May 1938, issue 34515, page 3504]. His service number was amended to 21103. Formerly of the Royal Engineers and as a Temporary Lieutenant he was *Gazetted* with the MC on 17th September 1917, supplement 30287, page 9568: *"For conspicuous gallantry and devotion to duty in leading a wiring party to consolidate the front of a captured village. He displayed the greatest courage and determination under heavy shell fire, so inspiring his men by his disregard of danger that the work was successfully accomplished under most trying and dangerous conditions."*
18135 FitzGERALD John Jellett P/O + 12.08.25 84 Squadron
18136 HALL Stanley Edward P/O + 22.09.24 4 FTS Abu Sueir
Pilot Officer Stanley Edward Hall died while flying solo in Avro 504K E9379 after losing control and spinning into the ground near the airfield. The findings of the Court of Inquiry read: *"The cause of the accident was in our opinion that the pilot spun the machine unintentionally and on coming out of the spin probably fainted, fell forward on the control column thus keeping the machine in vertical dive."*
18137 HARDING Basil Frederic Hamilton F/O 01.04.27 Relinquished
On account of ill-health [LG 29 March 1927, issue 33261, page 2053].
18138 HOLDEN Robert Wynne F/O 03.01.33 Relinquished
18139 JONES Robert Owen AM 31.10.56 Retirement
Air Marshal Sir Robert Jones KBE CB AFC, died on Friday, 13th October 1972. His final service appointment was Controller of Engineering and Equipment [he had transferred from the General Duties Branch to the Technical Branch on 24th April 1940 while ranked Wing Commander].
18140 MESSENGER Harry Trimble F/O 03.01.33 Relinquished
18141 NORTH Frank Emmerson F/O 03.01.33 Relinquished
Returned to the service with effect from 1st September 1939 and granted a commission in the Administrative and Special Duties Branch [LG 7th November 1939, issue 34727, page 7503]. S/Ldr 10.02.54 Relinquished
18142 PAVIA Charles John P/O 05.05.26 Resigned
18143 PITTS-TUCKER George Maxwell S/Ldr 10.02.54 Relinquished
18144 PRESTON James Edward F/O 03.01.33 Relinquished
18145 RAEBURN Harold Wyllie W/Cdr 10.02.54 Relinquished
18146 RUSSELL Michael P/O 31.12.24 Terminatec
18147 SIMONS George Albert G/Capt 10.02.54 Relinquished
18148 SLATER Herbert Gerald F/O + 10.08.26 47 Squadron
18149 STACEY Francis Thomas W/Cdr 10.02.54 Relinquished
18150 THOMAS Harold F/O 03.01.38 Relinquished
Returned to service and granted a commission in class C of the Reserve of Air Force Officers. W/Cdr 05.03.45 Resigned
18151 TREVOR Alan Doyle Braddon P/O 06.08.24 Resigned
18152 WYNTER-MORGAN MC Wilfred A/Cmdr 21.08.51 Retirement
Air Commodore Wilfred Wynter-Morgan CB CBE MC, died at Woking, Surrey, on Wednesday, 27th March 1968.

18153 FOWLER Hugh Raymond Vaughan F/O 29.12.32 Relinquished
Lieutenant Hugh Raymond Vaughan Fowler's Casualty Form - Officers contains the following information:

25.5.18	*Attached to No. 4 ASD*		*23.5.18*	*B213 4 ASD*
8.6.18	*To Dover on tempy. duty*		*31.5.18*	" "
15.11.18	*Admitted [Flying sickness]*		*14.11.18*	*W3034 14 Gen.*
17.11.18	*Dis. to Duty*	*[4 ASD]*	*16.11.18*	*W3034 14 Gen.*
16.11.18	*Post to No. 4 ASD*		*13.11.18*	*B213 4 ASD*
18.1.19	*Posted to 1 AD*		*15.1.19*	" "
18.1.19	*Leave 15-30.1.19*			" "
2.2.19	*Posted to No. 2 ASD*		*4.2.19*	" "
15.2.19	" " *6 Irs Sec*		*11.2.19*	" "

Note. No. 4 Aeroplane Supply Depot headquarters was at Guines; 1 Aircraft Depot was at Petite Synthe while No. 2 Aeroplane Supply Depot was probably at Hesdin. A record for Flying Officer Fowler may be obtained from TNA Kew quoting AIR 87/168/72

LG 15 January 1924, issue 32898, page 472 - Seniority 9th January 1924

FLYING OFFICER

18154 BRETT Edward Tillotson St. Maur F/O 17.06.29 Removed
Flying Officer Edward Tillotson St. Maur Brett was formerly of the Indian Army [Retired] and was granted a short service commission in the General Duties Branch for seven years on the active list. His removal from the service carries no explanation; it was promulgated on 25th June 1929, issue 33509, page 4195.

LG 22 January 1924, supplement 32900, page 688 - Seniority 9th January 1924

FLYING OFFICER

18155 HOWLETT Australia Alexander Harold James F/Lt + 25.11.30 100 Squadron
Flying Officer Alexander Harold James Howlett was involved in a number of serious flying accidents during his service, the first traced occurring on 1st February 1927, which is detailed in Appendix C [1924] against Flying Officer [Lieutenant RN] John Yarnton Mills. A second accident, in which a member of his crew was killed, is summarised in 1929, on 28th October, when, as a flight lieutenant, he was attached to 36 Squadron.

LG 29 January 1924, issue 32902, page 875 - Seniority 14th January 1924; the two Flying Officers, formerly Captains in the India Army, were employed for seven years and the probationary Pilot Officers for five years on the Active list

FLYING OFFICERS
2

18156 HAMILTON Leslie Steuart F/Lt 29.08.28 Resigned
18157 SMITH MC Arthur Beaumont F/O 14.01.37 Relinquished
Flying Officer Arthur Beaumont Smith MC was granted a class C commission in the Reserve of Air Force Officers, General Duties Branch, and in the rank of flight lieutenant on 29th May 1937 [LG 18 May 1937, issue 34399, page 3251]. His service number was amended to 75188. His MC, less citation, was *Gazetted* on 3rd June 1818, supplement 31371, page 6929 at which time he was serving with the 42nd Deoli Rifles, Indian Army, attached to 2/124th Baluchistain Infantry, Indian Army.

Block 18158 - 18191

18158 ANNABLE Lionel Will Coupé P/O 12.08.25 Resigned
18159 BOUCHER Eric Comyn W/Cdr 10.02.54 Relinquished
18160 BRYANT Reginald William Edward F/Lt 06.08.44 Relinquished
On account of ill-health.
18161 BULLOCH Stuart Edmund F/O 14.01.37 Relinquished
18162 CLAYTON John Edward W/Cdr 10.02.54 Relinquished
18163 COUPLAND Robert Knyvett F/Lt + 21.02.42 Flying Control Staff Hurn
Flight Lieutenant Robert Knyvett Coupland is buried in Buckland Monachorum Cemetery in the County of Devon. At the time of his death, caused through natural causes, he was on attachment to Harrowbeer Airfield near Yelverton in Devonshire.
18164 CRANSWICK MC Philip F/O + 05.06.28 3 Squadron
His MC, less citation, was *Gazetted* on 3rd June 1918, supplement 30716, page 6464. At the time of his award he was an Acting Captain serving with the Royal Engineers.
18165 CRIPPS Henry Theodore Rivers F/O 29.12.27 Relinquished
On account of ill-health. However, he was granted a commission as a flight lieutenant in class C of the Reserve of Air Force Officers, General Duties Branch, on 23rd March 1936 [LG 28th April 1936, issue 34278, page 2700] but this was relinquished on completion of service on 19th November 1936. Then on 14th September 1939 he was commissioned in the Royal Air Force Volunteer Reserve in the rank of pilot officer, his service number amended to 74040. P/O 10.11.40 Terminated
Unusually, this was not promulgated until 20th February 1945, supplement 36945, page 989. Further research reveals that while undergoing flying training at 2 FTS Duxford he was injured [simple fracture of the third rib] while playing lawn tennis on 1st May 1924.
18166 FIELDEN Edward Hedley AV-M 01.01.62 Retirement
Air Vice-Marshal Sir Edward Fielden GCVO CB DFC AFC twice mentioned in despatches, died on Monday, 8th November 1976. As Wing Commander Fielden he took command of 161 Squadron on its formation on 15th February 1942 from the King's Flight and a nucleus of personnel from 138 Squadron. Operating initially from Newmarket '161' moved to Tempsford on 11th April 1942 where, in October of that year, he assumed the duties of Station Commander. His exploits receive excellent coverage in Hugh Verity's classic *We Landed by Moonlight - Secret RAF Landings in France 1940-1944.* Known to his many friends as 'Mouse', Group Captain Fielden was *Gazetted* with the DFC on 6th April 1943, supplement 35966, page 1751: *"This officer has flown on various operational missions, some of a most hazardous nature. He has displayed a high standard of operational efficiency, setting an example which has contributed materially to the high moral of the air crews under his command. His great organising ability has proved a valuable asset."* Hugh Verity on page 13 of his book notes that 'Mouse' had been personal pilot to the Prince of Wales [hence the honour of the MVO] and had commanded the King's Flight.
18167 FINNEY Terence Holingdale F/O 14.01.33 Relinquished
18168 GLADWIN-ERRINGTON Launcelot Richard P/O 04.02.25 Terminated
18169 GREEN George Douglas G/Capt 26.04.47 Retirement
On account of medical unfitness for Air Force service. On 15th July 1936 while serving with the Station Flight Half Far on the Island of Malta he was involved in a serious accident when his Avro Tutor I K3402 went into the sea off Marfa Point overlooking the Bay of the same name between the

north of the Island and the tiny island of Comino. Flight Lieutenant Green was picked up with serious injuries but his passenger, Flying Officer James Kininmonth Leslie Carstairs was killed. A Cranwell graduate, his details will be published in the next volume in the series.

18170 GREY Phillips Patrick F/O 14.01.33 Relinquished

Returned to service and granted a commission in the Administrative and Special Duties Branch as a probationary Pilot Officer employed for the duration of hostilities, effective 29th April 1940 [LG 4 May 1940, issue 34849, page 2899]. S/Ldr 10.02.54 Relinquished

18171 HALL Geoffrey Shewell P/O + 06.08.24 2 FTS Duxford

Pilot Officer Geoffrey Shewell Hall died when his Bristol F.2b stalled and crashed near the airfield. Prior to this he had been injured on 12th June 1924 when as a passenger he was thrown from the back of the car in which he was travelling, the accident happening at Trumpington, a few miles to the south of Cambridge.

The Times in their Friday edition of August 8, 1924, reported the following: *"At an inquest held at Scopwick, Lincoln, yesterday, on the body of Geoffrey Shewell HALL, 22, pilot officer, of Digby RAF Aerodrome, it was stated that while flying at an altitude of 200ft. he was changing the petrol cock from the front tank to the rear tank when he erroneously pushed the cock over to the off position, cutting off the petrol. The machine stalled as he turned, and fell to the right. The machine turned over and crashed, Mr. Hall dying immediately from fracture of the skull.It was stated that had he kept straight on instead of attempting to turn he could have planed down safely. A verdict of "Death by Misadventure" was returned."*

18172 HUTTON Arthur Francis AV-M 08.12.58 Retirement

Air Vice-Marshall Arthur Francis Hutton CB CBE DFC mentioned in despatches, died on Friday, 16th February 1979. An engineering specialist his final appointment was as Director General Engineering.

18173 IRWIN Gwyther William Powell F/O 14.01.33 Relinquished
18174 JENNINGS-BRAMLY Guy Harrie F/O 08.12.26 Relinquished
18175 MARCY Jack Courtney F/O 14.01.33 Relinquished

During his service Flying Officer Jack Courtney Marcy had survived one very serious crash while serving in India with 31 Squadron. For details, please refer to my summary for 1st August 1926.

18176 McKELLAR Arthur Jackson P/O 10.01.25 Terminated
18177 MEAGHER Dennis William Jeffries P/O 04.02.25 Terminated
18178 MOXHAM Frederick William W/Cdr 10.02.54 Relinquished
18179 NICHOLAS John Francis F/O 14.01.37 Relinquished
18180 NICHOLL Patrick Edward F/O 14.01.33 Relinquished
18181 PELLEW Edward Humphrey Longford P/O + 29.03.24 2 FTS Duxford

Pilot Officer Edward Humphrey Longford Pellew was seriously injured on 27th March 1924 when his motorcycle came into collision with a car. Admitted to Addenbrooke Hospital, Cambridge he died from shock following an operation.

18182 ROBINSON Dennis F/O 12.09.28 Relinquished

On account of ill-health [LG 11 September 1928, issue 33420, page 5977]. During his service with 5 Squadron in India, he was injured when his Bristol F.2b came down in the River Indus, the details of this accident being summarised on 22nd September 1926.

18183 RUSSELL Gerald William Richardson F/O 18.02.29 Class A

While in the Reserve of Air Force Officers and employed as an instructor with York County Aviation Club based at Sherburn he was struck down by a form of paralysis and admitted to Leeds General Infirmary where he died on Tuesday, 16th June 1936. He is buried in Leeds [Harehills] Cemetery.

18184 SMITH Archibald Edward Protheroe
18185 SOLTAU Vincent William W/Cdr 16.07.46 Resigned
18186 STEVENTON Charles Frederick F/Lt 14.01.34 Relinquished

On account of ill-health [LG 16 January 1934, issue 34015, page 393].

18187 SUMMERS Joseph F/O 10.02.29 Class A

Joseph 'Mutt' Summers ranked among the most influential test pilots of his day. On completion of his flying training he was posted to 29 Squadron at Duxford where he flew Sopwith Snipes and Gloster Grebes, but he was to find his niche when he was attached to Martlesham Heath where overt the next five years he assisted in test-flying various single-engined fighters. On leaving the service he joined Vickers Aviation where he wrote himself into aviations history by test-flying no less than 54 prototype aircraft, including the Supermarine Spitfire K5054 on 5th March 1936, and on 18th May 1951, the Vickers Valiant V-bomber WB210. Born on 10th March 1904, 'Mutt' Summers died at the early age of 50 on Tuesday, 16th March 1954. In his long, and at times near heart-stopping' career he logged over 5,600 flying hours. One of his most noteworthy flights was a test carried out in a Wellington off Chesil Beach near Weymouth carrying a mock-up of Barnes Wallis's 'bouncing bomb' for the first aerial test of the weapon.

18188 TATTERSALL William Alfred W/Cdr 08.03.45 Retirement

At his own request [LG 3 April 1945, supplement 37011, page 1775]. William Alfred Tattersall's service came close to being ended before it had hardly begun. Posted to 2 FTS Duxford and while being instructed by Sergeant George Thomas Bond, their Avro 504K H3071 was involved in a midair collision near the airfield on Monday, 3rd March 1924, which left William seriously injured and his instructor dead [see my summary for this date and 111 Squadron and the report submitted by the AOC No. 3 Group].

18189 VENABLES Gilbert David P/O 24.02.26 Relinquished

On account of ill-health [LG 23 February 1926, issue 33135, page 1343].

18190 WILKINSON Francis Frederick S/Ldr 31.05.44 Resigned
18191 YOUNG John Frederick F/O 01.11.32 Relinquished

John Frederick Young had a narrow escape from death, or very serious injury, when on 2nd May 1924, the Bristol F.2B in which he was flying with Pilot Officer Eric Martin MC came into collision near Duxford with an Avro 504K. Pilot Officer Martin was killed but John Young, it is reported, escaped unharmed. For additional detail, please refer to Pilot Officer Martin's entry in Appendix D 1923, and the table of short service commissioned officers reported in *The London Gazette* 24th July 1923, issue 32847, page 5074.

LG 5 February 1924, issue 32904, page 1066 - Seniority 23rd January 1924

FLYING OFFICER

18192 DuCRAY Michael Joseph F/Lt 14.01.45 Resigned

2nd Lieutenant Michael Joseph DuCray is summarised in my second volume on page 29 in the entry for 104 Squadron and the loss of DH.9 D2878.

LG 19 February 1924, issue 32909, page 1460 - Seniority 11th February and 31st January 1924 respectively

FLYING OFFICER

18193 TAYLOR Howard William F/Lt 11.02.38 Relinquished

18194 PALLIN George Roland Alexander F/O 31.01.33 Relinquished

George Roland Alexander Pallin was appointed to the rank of 2nd Lieutenant, temporary, in the Army Service Corps on 26th September 1914 [LG 25th September 1914, issue 28914, page 7595]. In the Second World War he returned to duty with the army and was appointed Captain in the Royal Army Service Corps on 2nd April 1940 [LGG 10 May 1940, supplement 34846, page 2794], his service number being 118657. Sadly, after serving his country through two world wars he faced a Court Martial in the autumn of 1946, was found guilty and cashiered on 22nd October 1946 [LG 24th December 1946, supplement 37826, page 6238].

LG 4 March 1924, issue 32915, page 1931 - Seniority 20th February 1924

FLYING OFFICER

18195 LEE Herbert Cyril F/Lt 18.01.40 Relinquished
On account of ill-health [LG 28 May 1940, issue 34859, page 3191].

LG 11 March 1924, issue 32917, page 2136 - Seniority 26th February 1924

FLYING OFFICER

18196 TREMELLEN Arthur Cleverton F/O + 06.02.26 RAF Heliopolis
Flying Officer Arthur Cleverton Tremellen was killed and Flight Lieutenant Sturley Philip Simpson injured when their unidentified Bristol F.2b crashed at Heliopolis.

LG 25 March 1924, issue 32921, page 2535 - Seniority 15th March 1925; the terms of engagement on the Active list were for seven and five years respectively

FLYING OFFICERS
5

18197 CARTER Richard Fenner F/Lt + 13.05.27 RAF Gosport
Honorary Flight Lieutenant Richard Fenner Carter was killed when his Fairey IIID lost power whilst banking, spun and crashed at Bedenham NNW of the airfield a d roughly midway between Fareham and Gosport. His death, along with other service pilots, was reported in *The Times* in their edition of Saturday, May 14, 1927, the extract regarding Flight Lieutenant Carter reads: *"A reconnaissance plane piloted by Flight-Lieutenant Richard Fenner Carter crashed yesterday at Gosport, Hants. Flight-Lieutenant Carter was so seriously injured that he died shortly after being admitted to Haslar Hospital."*
18198 DUKE Allen Lingard Rae W/Cdr 10.02.54 Relinquished
18199 HUMPHERY William Frederic F/Lt 29.05.29
Born I France on 20th February 1900 William Frederic Humphery was formerly of the Royal Navy and I strongly suspect he returned to the service for he was promoted lieutenant-commander on 15th September 1928 [LG 18 September 1928, issue 33422, page 6094] and he continued to serve throughout the Second World War and by 8th May 1946 held the rank of Commander. The promotion noted above was Honorary.
18200 STORRIE Max Edward Baden Powell F/Lt 15.05.31 Relinquished
Returned to service and granted a commission in class CC of the Reserve of Air Force Officers, General Duties Branch, 9th June 1939 as an Honorary Flight Lieutenant. However, his service was brief and he relinquished his rank on termination of his service on 01.04.40 Terminated
18201 STRINGER George Norman Patrick F/Lt 15.03.31 Relinquished

Block 18202 - 18231

18202 BABB Brian Osborne P/O 26.11.24 Resigned
18232 BENNETT Robert Ruston F/O 15.09.34 Retired list
At own request [LG 18 September 1934, issue 34088, page 5907].
18203 BINGHAM-HALL MC Vincent Bingham F/O + 18.10.26 208 Squadron
18204 BURTON Henry Engelschion North F/O 14.09.27 Resigned
18205 COHU John Messurier AV-M 10.05.57 Retirement
Air Vice-Marshal John Messurier Cohu CBE, died on Thursday, 1st August 2002.
18206 DAVID Frederick Hector Stewart F/O 21.11.28 Relinquished
On account of ill-health [LG 20 November 1928, issue 33440, page 7556].
18207 FEATHER Cecil F/Lt 10.02.54 Relinquished
Unusually with no retention of rank.
18208 FISHER Erskine Arthur Hamilton F/O 15.03.37 Resigned
18209 FORD Ronald Arthur G/Capt 10.02.54 Relinquished
18210 FRANCOMBE Aubrey Noel F/O 15.05.33 Relinquished
Returned to service in the General Duties Branch and was promoted squadron leader 3rd September 1941 [LG 30 September 1941, issue 35292, page 5662]. W/Cdr 10.02.54 Relinquished
18211 GEE Verity Gofton Hutton W/Cdr 10.02.54 Relinquished
18212 GOLDIE Maurice Wyndham F/O + 18.05.28 CFS Wittering
Paul McMillan reports that Flying Officer Maurice Wyndham Goldie was admitted to hospital for what was thought to be a relatively minor operation to remove some fluid that had built up near his heart. Sadly, the surgeons discovered that his heart had become enlarged and was extensively diseased and his death was unavoidable. According to a report in the *Dundee Evening Telegraph* which published an account of the inquest held at Marylebone in London, Flying Officer Goldie asked that he be cremated and his ashes scattered from an aeroplane.
18213 HILLIER Christopher Ernest P/0 + 12.08.24 5 FTS Sealand
Pilot Officer Christopher Ernest Hillier and his fellow trainee Pilot Officer Hampden Charlton Mason Shaw died at around 1005 when their Bristol F.2b C806 spun and crashed near the airfield. Pilot Officer Hillier had been briefed to carry out an instrument flying test, Pilot Officer Mason to accompany him as the safety pilot. The Court of Inquiry members reported as follows: *"The cause of the accident was in our opinion due to the Pilot losing control of the machine probably when on its back and diving with the engine full on. As the machine gathered speed he was unable to regain control."*
18214 JOHNSTON Leslie Milnes P/O 01.08.24 Terminated
18215 LEWIS William James P/O 06.08.24 Terminated
18216 LOWRY Herbert Richard F/Lt 19.06.41 Cashiered
By sentence of General Court Martial [LG 4 July 1941, issue 35208, page 3838].
18217 LUXMOORE Henry Frederick F/O + 20.09.26 56 Squadron
18218 MACMILLAN Angus Lancelot F/O 15.03.39 Relinquished
On 26th February 1940, Angus Lancelot Macmillan was granted an honorary commission in the rank of squadron leader within the Administrative and Special Duties Branch [LG 5 March 1940, issue 34805, page 1319]. Subsequently and with effect from 27th May 1941 and still within the Administrative and Special Duties Branch he was commissioned as a pilot officer for the duration of hostilities [LG 20 June 1941, issue 35916, page 3525] his service number now being 67235 though his original number was later restored. P/O 01.09.45 Relinquished
18221 MARTIN Aubrey William Graham F/O 31.12.32 Relinquished
Returned to service and commissioned within the Administrative and Special Duties Branch, 1st September 1939 [LG 28 November 1939, issue 34742, page 7966]. W/Cdr 10.02.54 Relinquished
18222 MARTIN Hector Stuart F/O 15.03.34 Relinquished
On account of ill-health [LG 20 March 1934, issue 34034, page 1867].
18219 McDONALD Arthur William Baynes AM 20.04.62 Retirement
Air Marshal Sir Arthur McDonald KCB AFC four times mentioned in despatches, died on Friday, 26th July 1996.
18220 McDOWELL Angus David

18223 NICHOLL William Von Rahn F/O 15.03.33 Relinquished
18224 PARKER Hugh Marcus Geoffrey G/Capt 29.04.58 Retirement
18225 POWER David Keith P/O 20.11.24 Dismissed
By sentence of General Court Martial [LG 2 December 1924, issue 32998, page 8783].
18226 RHIND George Bruce Milligan A/Cmdr 30.04.57 Retirement
Air Commodore George Bruce Milligan Rhind died on Tuesday, 29th May 1962.
18227 SHEARING Charles Durban P/O 22.08.25 Terminated
18228 SHEPHERD Ernest Leonard P/O 01.08.24 Terminated
18229 STANILAND Christopher Stainbank F/Lt 15.05.37 Relinquished
18230 STEWART Hugh William Patrick P/O 23.12.29 Relinquished
18231 WEST Norman Alfred W/Cdr 10.02.54 Relinquished

LG 1 April 1924, issue 32923, page 2719 - Seniority 18th and 25th March respectively

FLYING OFFICERS
2

18233 BATEMAN Reginald Lee
Granted a commission in the Royal Air Force, Reserve of Air Force Officers, General Duties Branch, class CC in the rank of flight lieutenant on 19th September 1938 [LG 13 December 1938, issue 34579, page 7921]. His Class CC commission was relinquished on 23rd September 1939 [LG 5th March 1940, issue 34805, page 1318]. On 24th September 1947, still ranked Flight Lieutenant, he was granted a commission in the Secretarial Branch, class CC [LG 21 October 1947, supplement 38102, page 4963] his service number being amended to 192461. He continued to serve until relinquishing his commission under the terms of the Reserve of Navy, Army and Air Force Reserves Act 1954, by which time his service number was noted as 18233. S/Ldr 10.02.54 Relinquished
18234 MADDOX MC Ernest Reynolds F/Lt 25.03.33 Relinquished
Formerly of the 1st Battalion, Hampshire Regiment, Ernest Reynolds Maddox was born on 30th October 1898 and transferred to the RFC on 24th October 1917. He served with 3 Squadron [F.1 Camel] from 25th November 1917 until 13th June 1918 on which date he was posted to Home Establishment. As 2nd Lieutenant Maddox, his MC was *Gazetted* on 22nd June 1918, supplement 30761, page 7417: *"For conspicuous gallantry and devotion to duty. During an enemy attack he repeatedly dived to a very low altitude and engaged the enemy troops with bombs and machine gun fire. The enemy were in massed formations, and sustained very heavy casualties. On numerous occasions during the recent operations he has inflicted very heavy casualties, and caused the greatest panic among enemy troops and transport by the daring manner in which he has employed his bombs. His gallantry and skill have been most praiseworthy."* The recommendation for the award of the MC was made on, or by 12th April 1918, and I am in no doubt it was the result his actions during the German Spring offensive launched on 21st March 1918.

LG 8 April 1924, issue 32925, page 2924 - Seniority 27th March and 1st April respectively

FLYING OFFICERS
2

18235 GEARING Harold James S/Ldr 10.02.54 Relinquished
Formerly of the Highland Light Infantry, 2nd Lieutenant Gearing was attached to 9 Squadron [BE.2] from 19th October 1916 to 11th January 1917 when by orders of a Medical Board he was struck off the strength of the RFC while on leave, an extension being promulgated which authorised his absence until 9th January 1917.

The London Gazette 6th May 1938, issue 34508, page 2993 and 22nd November 1938, issue 34573, page 7418 are in respect of bankruptcy hearings in respect of Flying Officer Harold James Gearing described as being late of HQ Fighter Command, Royal Air Force, Stanmore, Middlesex. The latter entry a hearing in regard to an application for discharge. An earlier entry, 31st May 1932, issue 33830, page 503, promulgated the transfer from class C of Reserve of Air Force Officers to Class A on 17th April 1932, his rank being recorded ass Flight Lieutenant. During the Second World War he remained in the General Duties Branch and was promoted squadron leader on 3rd September 1941 [LG 30 September 1941, issue 35292, page 5662]
18236 HAINES Alfred F/O 16.03.32 Relinquished
On account of ill-health. At the time Flying Officer Alfred Haines was in class C of the Reserve of Army Officers [27.03.29]. Born on 5th July 1898 and commissioned to the RFC on 15th October 1917, 2nd Lieutenant Alfred Haines was posted to 104 Squadron [DH.9] at Azelot on 21st June 1918. He was wounded [a gun shot injury to his left leg] on operations of 1st August 1918 [see page 103 of my second volume for details] and and following initial attention in 8 General Hospital was returned to the UK aboard HMHS *Gloucester Castle* on 8th August 1918.

LG 15 April 1924, issue 32927, page 3102 - Seniority 7th April 1924

FLYING OFFICER

18237 ROSE Geoffrey S/Ldr 10.02.54 Relinquished
I am not one hundred percent certain, but it is a possibly that Geoffrey Rose is the Lieutenant Rose who was made a prisoner of war following bombing operations with 207 Squadron on 18th-19th July 1918 - see page 64 of my second volume. If I am correct, then he was born 27th December 1897 and was first commissioned to the RNAS.

LG 22 April 1924, issue 32929, page 3302 - Seniority 15th and 14th April respectively

FLYING OFFICERS
2

18238 ECCLES Reginald Yarrow G/Capt 27.11.46 Retirement
18239 WILSON Cyril F/O 03.02.26 Relinquished
On account of ill-health [LG 2 Febrary 1926, issue 33129, page 794].

LG 13 May 1924, issue 32935, page 3846 - Seniority 1st May 1924

FLYING OFFICER

18241 BARBOUR Reginald Stanley F/Lt + 17.06.50
Paul McMillan has sifted through the many *Gazette* references to this officer whom, he suspects, died while still in the service. From 1st May 1935 through to the eve of the Second World War he was in various classes of the Reserve; then, on 1st September 1939 he was transferred from the General Duties Branch to the Administrative and Special Duties Branch. In the Air Force List for 1945 he is shown as a squadron leader at around which time he was granted a commission in class CC on transfer to the Secretarial Branch. He then seems to have dropped a rank to that of flight lieutenant and for reasons known only to those in the Manning and Record offices his service number was amended to 192769. AIR 76/21/175, held at TNA Kew, shows he was born in Galway, Ireland on 19th March 1897 and died in Fetcham, Surrey on 17th June 1950, a Saturday.

LG 3 June, issue 32942, page 4440 - Seniority 23rd May 1924

FLYING OFFICER

18242 BENNETT Gordon Herbert P/O + 30.04.40 17 Squadron
Pilot Officer Gordon Herbert Bennett, 45 years of age, is buried in Gulval [St. Gulval] Churchyard and Cemetery, Cornwall, his being one of four service graves located here from the Second World War. The Royal Air Force Commands website shows his death as heart failure whilst on leave.

LG 1 July 1924, issue 32952, page 5089 - Seniority 19th June 1924

FLYING OFFICERS
2

18243 LOCK Charles Vine F/Lt 19.06.37 Relinquished
Returned to service and granted a commission in the Administrative and Special Duties Branch on 1st September 1939 in his rank [LG 12th December 1939, issue 34752, page 8256]. S/Ldr + 18.02.50
Although my co-author cannot be certain, it is very likely that Squadron Leader Charles Vine Lock was still serving at the time of his death and was on the Isle of Wight where he was undergoing treatment at a hospital in Shanklin.

As an interesting aside Paul McMillan has also discovered that Squadron Leader Lock's wife's sister, a Miss Emily Fender, a registered nurse, had an affair with Sir Anthony St. John Mildmay MC, eighth Baronet and was so named in Sir Mildmay'd divorce. However, despite his promise of marriage this was not forthcoming, the outcome being that Miss Fender, supported by Mildmay's now ex-wife, took the baronet to court where his lawyer accused Miss Fender of lying. Such an accusation could not be allowed to go unchallenged and the following appeared in *The Daily Mirror* on October 31st, 1935: *"A slander action based on alleged statements made in evidence during the breach of promise action by Miss Emily Fender against Sir Anthony St. John Mildmay, Bart., was settled in the King's Bench Division yesterday.*

"The plaintiffs were Mr. Charles Vine Lock and his wife, Mrs. Lillian Alice Davis Lock, of Goldthorn, Church-lane, Corley, Warwickshire. Mrs. Lock is a sister of Miss Fender.

"Damages were claimed from Mr. Dudley Dyster Chaffey Giddins and his wife, Mrs. Norah Giddins, of Belmont Grove, Lewisham. Mr. J P Eddy, for Mr.and Mrs. Lock, said the parties in the case had come to terms.

"He said that during Miss Fender's action against Sir Anthony Mildmay, Mrs. Lock gave evidence on behalf of her sister and council cross-examined her and suggested on his instructions, that she and her husband were endeavouring to blackmail Sir Anthony. This Mr. Lock denied.

"The cross-examination," he added, "received considerable publicity and Mrs. Lock, who was not a witness in that action, felt that he had no alternative but to bring this action to vindicate the good name of himself and of his wife."

"Mr. And Mrs. Goddins had expressed their unqualified regret for the publication of the words complained of and had unreservedly withdrawn all imputations upon Mr. And Mrs. Lock.

"They had also agreed to pay a suitable sum by way of damages and indemnity against costs."

18244 WALLINGFORD Sidney F/Lt 21.06.29 Relinquished
On appointment to a commission in the New Zealand Permanent Air Force [LG 16 July 1929, issue 33517, page 4706]. Rising to the rank of Air Commodore [Acting] the following appeared in the Fifth Supplement to *The London Gazette* of Friday the 18th of February 1944 supplement 36392, page 907: *"The KING has been graciously pleased, on the advice of His Majesty's New Zealand Ministers, to give orders for the following appointments to the Most Excellent Order of the British Empire in recognition of conspicuous service in operations against the Japanese:-*

To be an Additional Commander of the Military Division of the said Most Excellent Order:-

Acting Air Commodore Sidney WALLINGFORD, Royal New Zealand Air Force.

Born on 12th July 1898 Air Commodore Sidney Wallingford OBE, died on Tuesday, 25th July 1978. His biography can be read on the website Hobsonville Point which I have much pleasure in recommending. Here, it is noted, he saw some action in the Salonika campaign before transferring to the RFC in March 1918 and undergoing flying instruction in Egypt where before the end of the *Great War* he saw active service, and in Palestine.

LG 8 July 1924, issue 32954, page 5255 - Seniority 30th June 1924

Block 18245 to 18257

18245	CLARKSON	Christopher	G/Capt	10.02.54	Relinquished
18246	CUBITT	Cyril Ralph	S/Ldr	13.06.53	Relinquished
18247	GAPE	Roy Nugent Treherne	F/O	18.08.26	19 Squadron
18248	JOLLEFF	Henry Charles Vincent	S/Ldr	10.02.54	Relinquished
18249	LIMBERT	Richard Charles Louis	P/O	23.07.25	Resigned

Paul McMillan has unearthed a fascinating amount of information in respect of Richard Charles Louis Limbert who in the Second World War operated alongside Italian partisans in their war against the German occupiers, much of their activity being in support of the US Fifth Army . It seems Captain Limbert worked mainly in organising camps for the hundreds of refugees. Numerous localities are mentioned including Florence where under his direct supervision a camp housing some 16,000 refugees was established. An account of his time in Italy is contained within six large folders which chronicles his activities between 1943 and 1945. This archive was auctioned under the brochure title *"Resistenza in Italia - Limbert, Charles Louis Captain Limbert."* [See the website Ars value.com]. There are six administrative entries for Captain R C L Limbert in *The London Gazette* ranging between supplement 368886, page 331 of 9th January 1945 and supplement 40127, page 1667 of 16th March 1954.

18250 McLAREN Walter Lawrence S/Ldr 10.02.54 Relinquished
Commissioned to the Royal Air Force Volunteer Reserve, Training Branch. F/O 04.03.55 Resigned
18251 OTTWAY Albert Leslie F/O 30.06.33 Relinquished
On 2nd May 1939 Albert Leslie Ottway was commissioned as 2nd Lieutenant to Royal Corps of Signals [LG 21 July 1939, issue 34647, page 5028]. He served throughout the Second World War, retiring with the honorary rank of Major [having exceeded the age limit] on 18th June 1958, as *Gazetted* 17th June 1958, supplement 41421, page 3857.

18252	SAYER	Philip Edward Gerald	F/O	02.03.37	Relinquished
18253	SENDER	John Harry	F/Lt	18.02.39	Relinquished

On appointment to the Air Branch of the Royal Navy [LG 25 April 1939, issue 34619, page 2757]. On 9th May 1939 he was made Lieutenant-Commander [Air] with seniority from 1st January 1939 [LG 12 May 1939, issue 34625, page 3188]. Attached to the aircraft carrier HMS *Eagle* Lieutenant Commander John Harry Sender was a passenger aboard the SS *Baltistan* which was sunk by a torpedo from the Italian submarine *Michele Bianchi* roughly 400 miles west of Valentia Island off the Iveragh Peninsular in County Kerry, Ireland. From a complement of sixty-nine crew and passengers under the command of Master John Hobson Hedley fifty-one, including Captain Hedley, perished. Lieutenant Commander Sender is commemorated on the Lee-on-Solent Memorial bay 1 panel 7; Master Hobson is commemorated on panel 13 at the Tower Hill Memorial in London.

18254	SKELLON	Joseph Thomas Cleverdon	P/O		17.11.26	Resigned
18255	SMITH	Cecil William Montague	P/O	+	20.11.25	29 Squadron
18256	WILLIAMS	Cyril Vivian	F/O		19.10.27	Resigned
18257	WOOLLETT	Walter	F/O		05.05.33	Relinquished

On leaving the service, Flying Officer Walter Woollett emigrated to Canada. For a description of his career in Canada's aviation, please refer to the entry in Appendix D and the entry for Flying Officer Charles Roy Troup whose short service commission was *Gazetted* on 24th July 1923.

LG 15 July 1924, issue 32956, pages 5405 and 5406 - Seniority 8th July, 30th June, 5th July and 8th July 1924 respectively, the four Flying Officers terms of service being for seven years on the Active list and for the probationary Pilots Officers five years.

FLYING OFFICER
4

19010 BETT Patrick John S/Ldr 28.04.45 Resigned

19020 GOODWIN* Noel Thomas F/Lt 08.07.31 Relinquished

Granted a commission in class C, retaining his rank [LG 7 January 1936, issue 34240, page 138]. G/Capt 18.02.47 Resigned

MACDONALD-LAWSON Denis Hugh F/O 13.08.25 Dismissed

By sentence of General Court Martial. Paul McMillan reports that his Court Martial was for repeated offences of being drunk. Subsequently, he received a commission as a Lieutenant in the Auxiliary Military Pioneer Corps but, as noted on an ancestry website, he relinquished his commission on 9th September 1940. His death from chronic bronchitis and emphysema occurred on the 1st of March 1943 in Birmingham.

PHELAN* Patrick Joseph F/O 07.04.25 Relinquished

On account of ill-health [LG 21 April 1925, issue 33040, page 2686].

* Ex-Indian Army attached. Note. The reason for the probationary Pilot Officers being entered in the manner below is that they were *Gazetted* on various dates and this had a bearing on the issue of their service numbers.

19023 HOLMES Reginald Henry W/Cdr 28.11.55 Terminated

19030 MACKENZIE Ian Wilfred Campbell W/Cdr 12.06.54 Relinquished

19034 PARKINSON William Fairbank F/O + 12.08.40 2 Training Flight Kenya

Flying Officer William Fairbank Parkinson was granted a commission in Class A of the Reserve of Air Force Officers. General Duties Branch, retaining his rank and with effect from 10th August 1937 [LG 20 August 1937, issue 34228, page 5330]. Posted to Kenya he lost his life on active service and is buried in Nairobi [ForestRoad] Cemetery. He was the pilot of a DH Gypsy Moth belonging to No. 2 Training Flight Kenya.

CRUCIKSHANK George Alexander P/O 22.06.25 Dismissed

By sentence of General Court Martial [LG 14 July 1925, issue 33066, page 4704].

19026 LEADER Eustace Lionel F/O 05.07.33 Relinquished

Returned to service and granted a commission in class CC of the Reserve of Air Force Officers, General Duties Branch, in the rank of Flight Lieutenant 10th October 1938 [LG 21 February 1939, issue 34600, page 1215]. W/Cdr 16.05.59 Relinquished

BARRETT Henry Baillie F/O + 16.06.29

Flying Officer Henry Baillie Barrett died in RAF Hospital Uxbridge while undergoing treatment for injuries sustained in a motorcycle accident.

BELL Sydney Fleetwood F/O + 16.06.27 CFS Wittering

CARPENTER Alfred Edward P/O 20.02.25 Terminated

CLAYTON Daniel Preece P/O 09.02.25 Resigned

COOKE William Arthur F/O 08.07.33 Relinquished

DAVIES John Edward F/O 08.07.33 Relinquished

DOWLING Brian Broadbent F/O 08.07.29 Relinquished

[Lieutenant RARO Manchester Regiment] On account of ill-health [LG 9 July 1929, issue 33515, page 4544]. He had been commissioned as a temporary 2nd Lieutenant to the Manchester Regiment, the 17th Battalion [2nd City] on 11th January 1915 [LG 10 February 1915, supplement 29064, page 1411]. His health improved, he was granted a commission in the Reserve of Air Force Officers, General Duties Branch, on 1st June 1937 [his rank being noted as Lieutenant] [LG 6 July 1937, issue 34415, page 4349]. He was transferred from class C to class CC on 7th May 1938, by which time he was ranked Flight Lieutenant [LG 15 November 1938, issue 34570, page 7197]; then, on 1st July 1939, and again noted as a Lieutenant, he was accepted in the Administrative and Special Duties Branch with the service number 75184 [LG 27 October 1939, supplement 34718, page 7182]. W/Cdr 10.02.54 Relinquished

19017 EGGLESFIELD Laurence Alfred W/Cdr 30.04.45 Resigned

19018 EVANS-EVANS Anthony Caron G/Capt + 21.02.45 83 Squadron

[2nd Lieutenant Northants Regiment] Group Captain Antony Caron Evans-Evans DFC was the captain of Lancaster III NE165 OL-Y and tasked to mark the Mitteland Canal near Gravenhorst. Whilst over a liberated area of Holland the bomber was intercepted by a night fighter and shot down, falling at Gertruda Farm at Rips in the province of Noord-Brabant some 12km NE of Helmond. For details of the crew, please refer to page 87 of my RAFBCL 1945. Those who perished are buried in Mierlo War Cemetery where Group Captain Evans-Evans headstone is inscribed *"Constantly Faithful To Each Of His Responsibilities."* His DFC, without citation, had been *Gazetted* on 16th February 1945, supplement 36942, page 932.

GILLESPIE Herbert Ross P/O 11.11.25 Removed

GRAY William Edward F/O 09.12.31 Removed

No reason being given [LG 8 December 1931, issue 33778, page 7910].

HENDY Ronald Cary Baker P/O 09.02.25 Resigned

HUNTER James Harold P/O 09.02.25 Resigned

[Lieutenant RARO Worcestershire Regiment] Graduating as a Gentleman Cadet from the Royal Military College he was commissioned to the Worcester Regiment as a 2nd Lieutenant on 7th April 1916 [LG 6 April 1916, supplement 29537, page 3684].

JENKS Maurice Harold W/Cdr 25.01.48 Retirement

[Captain RARO Gloucestershire Regiment] Commissioned to the General List, Infantry, as a temporary 2nd Lieutenant on 26th August 1914 [LG 31 August 1914, supplement 28885, page 6890]. On 30th May 1927 he transferred from the General Duties Branch to the Stores Branch as a probationary Flying Officer [LG 14 June 1927, issue 33284, page 3840] and on successful completion of his probationary period was appointed to a permanent commission with seniority backdated to 30th May 1927 [LG 1 May 1928, issue 33380, page 3054], his service number being amended to 21104. The entry on 14th June 1927 made reference to his previous army service.

19028 LITTLE Norman Seymour F/O 26.02.38 Relinquished

Returned to service and granted a commission in the Administrative and Special Duties Branch, retaining his rank, and for the duration of hostilities, 16th January 1940 [LG 11 June 1940, issue 34870, page 3522]. F/O 25.03.41 Relinquished

On account of ill-health [LG 28 March 1941, issue 35119, page 1818].

LLOYD David John P/O + 04.04.26 60 Squadron

MARTIN Clifton William F/O 27.03.29 Relinquished

On account of ill-health [LG 5 April 1929, issue 33483, page 2284].

MILLER Horace F/O 30.05.27 CFS Wittering

Flying Officer Horace Miller's biography is published in Sherborne School's 'Book of Remembrance' which the authors dutifully acknowledge. Born in Sherborne, Dorset, on 4th August 1897 he was a day pupil at the school from January 1911 to July 1913. His untimely death, which is copied to his biography, appeared in the *Dundee Courier* on 1st June 1927: *"What happened in the air prior to the accident which resulted in the death of Flying-Officer Horace Miller while practising forced-landings near Wittering Aerodrome, Northants, was described at the Inquest at Peterborough yesterday by Flying-Officer Horden, who accompanied him on the flight. They were both going through a course of training at the Central Flying School, Wittering, said the witness, prior to becoming instructors. Miller had done about 350 hours flying and was flying a two-seater Avro with dual controls at the time of the accident. When at a height of about 1,500 feet Miller shut off the engine and approached the landing field in a series of turns. When 200 feet up Miller found he was too high to land straight ahead. He made a turn to the left, but lost flying speed, and the machine stalled. He endeavoured to bring the nose of the machine up but pulling back the control column, but this had no effect. He then opened up the engine twenty feet from the ground, but it nose-dived to earth. The machine turned over, and the witness was able to scramble out uninjured. The fuselage of the machine broke in half, and the tail end fell over the front portion. The witness found the controls alright when he flew the machine. He attributed the accident to an error of judgement. Loss of flying speed involved loss of control. The medical evidence showed that Miller died two hours after admission to Peterborough Infirmary from concussion and shock. A verdict of accidental death was returned."*

	MORGAN	Cecil Horatio	F/O		08.07.33	Relinquished
	STEELE	Robert Walter	F/O		08.07.35	Relinquished

Paul McMillan reports that Flying Officer Robert Walter Steele born on 10th March 1902 died in July 1943. After leaving the service, and by the time of the Second World War he was Assistant to Departmental Manager of the Rubber Footwear Company.

19037	SYMONDS	William Ewart	S/Ldr		10.02.54	Relinquished
19038	THOMPSON	Arthur John	F/O		08.07.33	Relinquished
19039	TRUSK	Claude William Leighton	S/Ldr		05.11.37	Cashiered

By sentence of General Court Martial [LG 16 November 1937, issue 34455, page 7189]. As Flying Officer Claude William Leighton Trusk he was one of five officers awarded the AFC *"... in recognition of valuable services rendered by them during the recent evacuations from Kabul."*

Promulgated in the Edinburgh edition of the *Gazette* April 9th, 1929, issue 14537, page 372. Leading Aircraftman George Donaldson received the AFM for his part in the evacuation.

19040	WALKER	Harold	W/Cdr		19.10.60	Relinquished
	WILSON	Daniel Geoffrey	P/O	+	26.06.25	4 FTS Abu Sueir

Pilot Officer Daniel Geoffrey Wilson and Leading Aircraftman Wilby Gammage were practicing aerobatics in DH.9A ER8649 when at the top of a loop structural failure occurred.

LG 29 July 1924, issue 32960, page 5723 - Seniority 15th, 16th and 21st July respectively

Block 19043 - 19069

19043	BALLANTYNE	John Alexander	P/O	+	16.10.25	SAC Old Sarum

Along with Pilot Officer John Stroyan Branch, John Alexander Ballantyne perished when their Bristol F.2b came down in poor visibility at Wilton some 3 miles SW of the airfield. Both officers had recently gained their 'Wings'; both were just 20 years of age. For an account of the accident, please refer to the entry for Pilot Officer Branch, named with those officers short service commissioned on 25th September 1923.

19044	BIRT	Lascelles Spence	F/O		01.01.29	Class A

Gaining a flying appointment with Imperial Airways, Flying Officer [Captain] Lascelles Spence Birt lost his life on Saturday 26th October 1929, when the Short Calcutta G-AADN *City of Rome* of which he was captain descended into the sea in bad weather some 10 miles SW of La Spezia, a port city roughly midway between Genoa and Pisa on Italy's west coast. There were no survivors, the crew and passengers being named as Terence Francis Pembroke the aircraft's flight engineer, wireless operator Sidney Jarvis Stone and passengers Miss Marjorie Ruth Bomford and Messrs Charles Ritchie, Henry King Robinson and Bertie Ernest Turney. According to the Aviation Safety Network website, which the authors acknowledge, the Calcutta had departed Naples and was bound for Genoa-Cristoforo Colombo Airport. It seems an attempt was made to tow the seaplane to the shore but it sank in the process.

19045	BLOCKEY	Paul Sandland	AV-M		12.04.60	Retirement

Air Vice-Marshal Paul Sandland Blockey CB CBE, died on Thursday, 10th October 1963. His death at the relatively early age of 58 was, I suspect, connected to his retirement on the grounds that he was medically unfit for Air Force service.

19046	BREALEY	Charles Victor	P/O	+	15.08.24	2 FTS Digby

Pilot Officer Charles Victor Brearley died while being instructed by Flying Officer George Searle Lomax Hayward MC when their Avro 504K H9863 dived into the ground in the wake of engine failure, crashing circa 1130 near Metheringham Heath, 8 miles SE of Lincoln. Despite the serious damage that must have been caused to the airframe, H9863 was repaired and by October 1929, was in the hands of No. 23 Group Headquarters. Flying Officer Hayward was an observer on Bristol F.2bs with 22 Squadron and was credited with 22 combat victories between November 1917 and April 1918. Formerly of the Royal West Kent Regiment, his MC was *Gazetted* on 26th July 1918, supplement 30813, page 8807: *"For conspicuous gallantry and devotion to duty. On three separate occasions when engaged with large hostile formations, he has attacked and sent crashing to earth two hostile machines on each occasion. He has displayed consistent skill, courage and determination in dealing with hostile aircraft."*

The Court of Inquiry into the accident reported: *"The cause of the accident was in our opinion due to an error of judgement on the part of the pilot in stalling the aeroplane at a height of about 150 feet."*

19047	COLLINS	William Thomas	P/O		10.10.25	Resigned
19048	CROKER-WALSH	Frank Edward John	P/O		11.02.25	Terminated
19049	CROWDEN	Clarence Graham	F/O	+	30.11.26	CFS Wittering

Flying Officer Clarence Graham Crowden was killed and his pupil Pilot Officer Edward Blakeway Steedman injured when their Avro 504N went out of control in a spin and crashed at Easton-on-the-Hill some 3 miles NW of the airfield. Pilot Officer Steedman had recently graduated from the Cadet College at Cranwell and, subsequently, would lose his life after being captured by the Japanese in the Second World War - see Appendix E and the entry to the College in February 1924.

19050	FARROW	Francis Hastings	P/O		01.07.25	Resigned
19051	FRANCIS	Reginald Frederick	F/O	+	05.06.30	202 Squadron
19052	HAES	Arthur Ernest				

Flying Officer Arthur Ernest Haes transferred from the General Duties Branch to the Stores Branch on 10th January 1929 [LG 25 January 1929, issue 33460, page 619]. His service number was amended to 21139. W/Cdr 23.04.49 Retirement

19053	HOLMES	William Tatham	W/Cdr	+	08.02.41	759 Squadron FAA

Wing Commander William Tatham Holmes died when his Gloster Sea Gladiator I N5545 crashed at Lour House Farm some 3 miles to the south of Forfar; he is buried in Arbroath Western Cemetery.

19054	JAMES	Kenneth Woodyatt	P/O		21.01.25	Terminated
19055	KELLY	Leslie Anthony Gerrard Dundas	P/O		13.05.25	Terminated
19056	KREGOR	Charles Albert Edward Stuart	P/O		26.09.25	Removed

Removed from the service [LG 25 September 1925, issue 33087, page 6206].

19057	MIDDLETON	Geoffrey Denis	W/Cdr		10.02.54	Relinquished
19058	MILWARD BASON	Harold	P/O		24.06.25	Terminated
19059	NEWMAN	Evelyn Henry	F/O		15.07.33	Relinquished
19060	NICHOLLS	Philip Hedgeland	F/O		01.10.26	20 Squadron
19161	NICHOLLS	William Erle	P/O		24.02.26	Resigned
19062	NOBLE	Cecil Hyatt	G/Capt		14.05.46	Resigned

In a supplement to *The London Gazette* 26th February 1948, supplement 38216, page 1415, showing Appendix C to the Report on RAF Operations in Malaya and NEI 1941-2 and the RAF Order of Battle as at 22nd November 1941, Wing Commander Noble is shown as the Station Commander at Kota Bahru on the Mainland of Malaya.

19063 PICKERING Ardley George F/Lt 15.07.38 Relinquished

As Flying Officer Arley George Pickering he was *Gazetted* with the AFC on 3rd June 1927 [LG 3 June 1927, supplement 33280, page 3620].

19064 POLLARD VC MC DCM Alfred Oliver F/O 15.12.26 Resigned

As a 2nd Lieutenant serving with the Honourable Artillery Company, Alfred Oliver Pollard was *Gazetted* with the MC in supplement 30001, page 2985, of the paper published on 26th March 1917: *"For conspicuous gallantry and devotion to duty. He led a patrol and carried out a dangerous reconnaissance. Later, he assumed command of a company and repulsed two strong enemy counter-attacks."* Three months later and the *Gazette* of 8th June 1917, supplement 30122, pages 5703 and 5704 carried the citation for his Victoria Cross: *"For most conspicuous bravery and determination. The troops on the left of this Officer's battalion had become disorganised owing to the heavy casualties from shell fire; and a subsequent determined enemy attack with very strong forces caused further confusion and retirement, closely pressed by hostile force. 2nd Lt. Pollard at one realised the seriousness of the situation, and dashed up to stop the retirement. With only four men he started a counter-attack with bombs, and pressed it home till he had broken the enemy attack, regained all that had been lost and much ground in addition. The enemy retired in disorder, sustaining many casualties. By his force of will, dash and splendid example, coupled with an utter contempt of danger, this Officer, who has already won the DCM and MC, infused courage into every man who saw him."* Born on 4th May 1893, at Wallington in Surrey, his entry on *Wikipedia* places the date and action where he won his VC as 29th April 1917, at Gavrelle. Following his Royal Air Force service, Alfred became a professional writer and published more than sixty books, both fiction and non-fiction. His Victoria Cross is held by the Honourable Artillery Company in London with a copy on display in the Medal Room. Captain Alfred Oliver Pollard VC MC* DCM died at the comparatively early age of 67 in Bournemouth on 6th December 1960.

19063 ROSLING Edward Geoffrey P/O 02.01.26 Relinquished

On account of ill-health.

19066 SHARP Alfred Charles Henry AV-M 01.02.53 Retirement

At his own request. Air Vice-Marshal Alfred Charles Henry Sharp CBE DSO AFC, died from a heart attack on Wednesday, 1st February 1956. At the time of his death he was Director of Sales for the Glenn Martin Corporation; he was only 51 years of age. His DSO was *Gazetted* on 10th November 1944, supplement 36788, page 5149, when as Acting Air Commodore he was commanding 54 Base Coningsby : *"This officer has participated in many sorties during which he has attacked such targets as Hamburg, Bremen and heavily defended centres in the Ruhr area. Throughout these operations he has displayed the highest qualities of skill and leadership, and his example has proved most inspiring. In addition to his work in the air, Air Commodore Sharp has shown great organising ability and his excellent work has contributed in a large way to the successes of the squadrons he commands. This officer has rendered outstanding service."*

54 Base Coningsby formed on 1st January 1944 within 5 Group and was responsible for the Bomber Command stations of Coningsby, Metheringham and Woodall Spa which housed the following squadrons; 61, 619, 83 and 97 at Coningsby, 106 at Metheringham and 617 and 627 Squadrons at Woodhall Spa. Apart from 627 Squadron which was equipped with Mosquitoes, all were Lancaster units. Air Commodore Sharp commanded the Base from 5th February to 19th October 1944. However, his operational sorties are believed to have been flown in a P-38J Lightning which was on loan from the USAAF [originally, he had been 'gifted' with a P-47 Thunderbolt but this was not to his liking, hence the acquisition of the Lightning]. On leaving 54 Base to become Air Officer Administration 'Tiger Force' he took the Lightning with him.

19067 STUDDERT Alfred Theodore Stanley F/O 13.09.29 Relinquished

On transfer to the Indian Army [LG 3 December 1929, issue 33557, page 7869].

19068 TYRINGHAM Douglas Mackworth P/O 23.09.25 Relinquished

On account of ill-health [LG 25 September 1925, issue 33087, page 6206]

19069 YOUNGER Geoffrey Adrian P/O 01.09.25 Terminated

FLYING OFFICER

BERESFORD Rodney F/O 22.02.39 Relinquished

On account of ill-health [LG 21 February 1929, issue 34600, page 1215]. On Thursday, 13th October 1927, Flying Officer Rodney Beresford was on approach to land at Worthy Down in Hampshire when one of the wheels of his Bristol F.2b struck and killed four year old Alice M Dennet.

LG 5 August 1924, issue 32962, page 5892 - Seniority 29th July 1924

GAPLIN Charles Edson F/O + 08.01.30 4 FTS Abu Sueir

New Zealand During the course of routine flying training a tragic midair collision occurred in the vicinity of the aerodrome between Avro 504N J8981 and Avro 504N J8716. Flying Officer Charles Edson Gaplin of Wanganui, New Zealand, was the instructor in J8981 and Flight Lieutenant Richard Samuel Greenslade in J8716, their pupils being Corporal W M Chilman and Leading Aircraftman L V Green, though as to which pupil was being instructed by Gaplin and Greenslade is not clear. There were no survivors.

LG 30 September 1924, issue 32978, pages 7117 and 7118 - Seniority 15th and 16th September 1924 for the three Flying Officers and 15th September for the probationary Pilot Officers

FLYING OFFICERS

3

19071 BERTRAM* Ian Anstruther G/Capt 02.11.46 Retirement

At his own request [LG 19 November 1946, supplement 37791, page 5674].

PEACOCKE Gerald Ivan Crozier F/O 02.04.28 Resigned

ROWBOTHAM Alfred William F/Lt 10.09.30 Resigned

* Formerly Lieutenant RN retired followed by two Lieutenants retired from the Indian Army. Their terms of service were for seven years on the active list. The terms for the Pilot Officers named below were for five years on the active list.

19074 BADCOCK Edgar Clifford Graham F/Lt 20.09.33 Relinquished

Flight Lieutenant Edgar Clifford Graham Badcock was granted a commission in class C of the Reserve of Air Force Officers, General Duties Branch, on 20th September 1938 [LG 20 September 1938, issue 34553, page 5955]. G/Capt 13.08.56 Retirement

19075 BOSWELL Clive Noel P/O 18.02.25 Terminated

19076 COLLET Gerald Bourke F/O 15.09.29 Relinquished

[Lieutenant in the Hampshire Regiment] On account of ill-health [LG 17 September 1929, issue 33535, page 5971].

19077 CONNOLLY Leopold P/O 11.02.25 Terminated

19078 DALTON-MORRIS* Leslie AV-M 02.07.63 Retirement

Air Vice-Marshal Sir Leslie Dalton Morris KBE CBE mentioned in despatches, died onThursday, 28th October 1976. A signals specialist Air Vice-Marshal Leslie Dalton Morris [he was knighted on 13th June 1959] assumed the twin duties of Assistant Chief of the Air Staff [Signals] and Air Officer Commanding No. 90 [Signals] Group on 1st March 1956, Medmenham, the latter being upgraded to Command status on 3rd November 1958. Sir Leslie's final appointment was as Air Officer Commanding-in-Chief Maintenance Command commencing 1st March 1961.

* On 28th September 1958, Corporal William Richard Chorley reported to RAF Medmenham where I was attached to the Traffic Analysis section of No. 90 [Signals] Group. This was my final posting before being granted early release on 11th October 1960 to take up communication duties with the Ministry of Defence [Army].

19079 FLORENCE James Andrew Charles F/O 15.09.33 Relinquished

19080 FROST Arthur Henry P/O 25.10.26 Dismissed

By sentence of General Court Martial.

19081 GEORGESON John Sclater F/O 08.06.29 Relinquished

On account of ill-health [LG 21 June 1929, issue 33508, page 4123]. Subsequently, he returned to the service and was granted a commission in the General Duties Branch of the Royal Air Force Volunteer Reserve as a pilot officer on 18th September 1939 and allotted 74717 as his new service number [LG 10 October 1939, issue 34705, page 6800]. Served throughout the war and beyond.. S/Ldr 10.05.54 Relinquished

19082 GRONER Ernest Bernard Charles F/O 28.12.28 Relinquished

On account of ill-health [LG 18 January 1929, issue 33458, page 466].

19083 HARVEY George David AV-M 29.10.58 Retirement

Air Vice-Marshall Sir George Harvey KBE CB DFC mentioned in despatches, died on Monday, 24th February 1969. His niche in Royal Air Force history is that while attached to 7 Squadron at Worthy Down in 1928 he piloted the Virginia in which his Commanding Officer, Wing Commander Charles Portal [later Sir Charles Portal and Chief of the Air Staff], was the bomb aimer and winning the Laurence Minot Bombing Competition; his DFC was one of only two awarded for operations in North Kurdistan and was *Gazetted* 6th October 1933.

19084 HILL Reginald George May F/O 13.08.27 Cashiered

[2nd Lieutenant, London Regiment] By sentence of General Court Martial [LG 11 October 1927, issue 33319, page 6402].

19085 KERANS Robert Drury P/O 25.03.25 Resigned

Pilot Officer Robert Drury Kerans died in the UK on Tuesday, 5th April 1938.

19086 KIRBY Alfred Reginald Claude P/O 27.05.25 Terminated

19087 MIZEN Leslie Rodway F/O 20.09.29 Relinquished

On appointment to a commission in the Indian Army [LG 15 October 1929, issue 33543, page 6551]. In recognition of his *"gallant and distinguished services in Burma"* he was appointed MBE on 17th January 1946 as promulgated in supplement 37433, page 493, his rank being recorded Brigadier [temporary] of the 12th Frontier Force Regiment, Indian Army.

19088 NOLAN John Joseph F/Lt + 02.09.39 23 ERFTS Rochester

While in Class A of the Reserve Flight Lieutenant John Joseph Nolan was employed as a flying instructor with 23 Elementary & Reserve Flying Training School at Rochester in Kent. On the last day of peace he took off from Rochester in Miles Magister I N3981 with Leonard William Bartlett and headed for RAF Brize Norton where they landed safely. Departing for home both perished when their trainer plunged to the ground near the Oxfordshire village of Cassngton some 5 miles NW from the centre of Oxford.

19089 RIMMER William Fleming S/Ldr 10.02.54 Relinquished

19090 ROWLAND Frederick Cecil W/Cdr 13.11.49 Retirement

19091 STEVENS Ronald John F/O 22.10.29 Relinquished

On transfer to the Indian Army [LG 3 December 1929, issue 33557, page 7869].

19092 SWITZER Christopher Wilfrid F/O 15.09.33 Relinquished

19093 TROTTER David William P/O 16.12.25 Resigned

During the Second World War he returned to the Royal Air Force, retaining his service number, and commissioned as a pilot officer in the Administrative and Special Duties Branch, his appointment being confirmed on 6th July 1941 [LG 15 August 1941, issue 35247, page 4735]. He served throughout the period of hostilities and beyond. F/Lt 10.02.54 Relinquished

19094 VANDERBEECK John Wyatt F/O 18.01.28 Relinquished

On account of ill-health [LG 17 January 1928, issue 33348, page 371].

19095 WALKER Alfred James F/O 31.08.32 Resigned

19096 WHITEHEAD Gervase Albert P/O 10.12.25 Dismissed

By sentence of General Court Martial [LG 22 December 1925, issue 33116, page 8482].

LG 3 October 1924, issue 32979, page 7188 - Seniority 22nd September 1924

19097 MACPHAIL Hugh Charles S/Ldr 13.06.46 Resigned

A file for Squadron Leader Hugh Charles Macphail is held by TNA Kew under AIR 76/329/14. He was awarded the DFC, citation not appended, on 17th January 1941 [LG 17 January 1941, issue 35045, page 346].

LG 2 December 1924, issue 32998, page 8783 - Seniority 24th November 1924

FLYING OFFICER

19098 WHITE Gilbert Standbridge F/Lt + 05.09.39 RAE Farnborough

Flight Lieutenant Gilbert Stanbridge White died from his injuries following the crash of the Supermarine Spitfire prototype K5054 which stalled on landing at Farnborough on 4th September 1939, turning over on striking the ground. It had been on Farnborough's establishment since 7th November 1938 where it was undergoing a series of engine tests. First flown by Joseph 'Mutt' Summers on 6th May 1936, K5054 was mainly used by the Aeroplane & Armament Experimental Establishment at Martlesham Heath from as early as 26th May 1936 it had 'survived' three accidents, the first occurring on 22nd March 1937 when it forced-landed with a misfiring engine at Sutton in Suffolk followed by two 'incidents' at Martlesham Heath on 15th and 23rd March 1938 respectively.

Flight Lieutenant White had been placed on class C of the Reserve on 24th November 1938. My co-author, Paul McMillan, has corresponded with CWGC requesting that Flight Lieutenant White's details be added to their database; at the time of publication he has been unsuccessful, the Commission's response being that he was not on 'Active Service.'

ROLL OF HONOUR
FOR
1924 SHORT SERVICE COMMISSION
OFFICERS

P/O	BALLANTYNE	John Alexander	16 October 1925	SAC Old Sarum
F/Lt	BARBOUR	Reginald Stanley	17 June 1950	
F/O	BARRETT	Henry Baillie	16 June 1929	
F/O	BELL	Sydney Fleetwood	16 June 1929	CFS Wittering
P/O	BENNETT	Gordon Herbert	30 April 1940	17 Squadron
F/O	BINGHAM-HALL MC	Vincent Bingham	18 October 1926	208 Squadron
P/O	BREALEY	Charles Victor	15 August 1924	2 FTS Digby
F/O	BRETHERTON	Norris Carden	21 June 1925	60 Squadron
F/Lt	BRETT	William James	30 March 1940	
F/Lt	CARTER	Richard Fenner	13 May 1927	RAF Gosport
F/Lt	COUPLAND	Robert Knyvett	21 February 1942	Flying Control Staff Hurn
F/O	CRANSWICK MC	Philip	5 June 1928	3 Squadron
F/O	CROWDEN	Clarence Graham	30 November 1926	CFS Wittering
G/Capt	EVANS-EVANS DFC	Anthony Caron	21 February 1945	83 Squadron
P/O	FitzGERALD	John Jellett	12 August 1925	84 Squadron
F/O	FRANCIS	Reginald Frederick	5 June 1930	202 Squadron
F/O	GAPLIN New Zealand	Charles Edson	8 January 1930	4 FTS Abu Sueir
F/O	GOLDIE	Maurice Wyndham	18 May 1928	CFS Wittering
P/O	HALL	Geoffrey Shewell	6 August 1924	2 FTS Duxford
P/O	HALL	Stanley Edward	22 September 1924	4 FTS Abu Sueir
P/O	HILLIER	Christopher Ernest	12 August 1924	5 FTS Sealand
W/Cdr	HOLMES	William Tatham	8 February 1941	759 Squadron FAA
F/Lt	HOWLETT Australia	Alexander Harold James	25 November 1930	100 Squadron
P/O	LLOYD	David John	4 April 1926	60 Squadron
S/Ldr	LOCK	Charles Vine	18 February 1950	
F/O	LUXMOORE	Henry Frederick	20 September 1926	56 Squadron
F/O	MILLER	Horace	30 May 1927	CFS Wittering
F/Lt	NOLAN	John Joseph	2 September 1939	23 ERFTS Rochester
F/O	PARKINSON	William Fairbank	12 August 1940	2 Training Flight Kenya
F/O	PECKOVER	Richard Gurney	17 October 1924	4 FTS Abu Sueir
P/O	PELLEW	Edward Humphrey Longford	27 March 1924	2 FTS Duxford
P/O	SMITH	Cecil William Montague	20 November 1925	29 Squadron
F/O	SLATER	Herbert Gerald	10 August 1926	47 Squadron
F/O	TREMELLEN	Arthur Cleverton	6 February 1926	RAF Heliopolis\
F/Lt	WHITE	Gilbert Stanbridge	5 September 1939	RAE Farnborough
P/O	WILSON	Daniel Geoffrey	26 June 1925	4 FTS Abu Sueir

Appendix D - RAF [Cadet] College, Cranwell

COMMANDANT
Air Commodore Amyas Eden Borton CB CMG DSO AFC mentioned in despatches

Throughout 1924, the Commandant of the Cadet College remained in the capable hands of Air Commodore Borton whose brief biography I report in the heading to the 1923 appendix.

February 1924 entry : 24

16191 BETT* Alan Profeit A/Cmdr 29.12.53 Retirement
Air Commodore Alan Profiet Bett mentioned in despatches, died on Thursday, 12th January 1978. He had not been long at the College when he fell off his motorcycle while riding in Leadenham, requiring medical treatment for his injuries. I believe he was was the younger brother of Flight Lieutenant David Lindsey Gordon Bett who was a Flight Cadet in the September 1920 entry to the College and whose details are shown on page 272 of my third volume. Both were educated at Berkhampstead.

16192 CHARNOCK* Harry Walpole F/O 12.12.30 Cashiered
By sentence of General Court Marshal [LG 23 December 1930, issue 33672, page 8259]. Flying Officer Harry Walpole Charnock had graduated from the College on 16th December 1925, and with his fellow graduates was appointed to a permanent commission [LG 12 January 1926, issue 33123, page 300]. Despite his fall from grace he was accepted by the Royal Air Force Volunteer Reserve for flying duties within days of the outbreak of the Second World War and as 901005 and as a Sergeant Pilot flying Spitfires with 19 Squadron he was awarded the DFM, *Gazetted* 7th April 1942: *"This airman has displayed great skill and courage in air combat and has destroyed at least 4 enemy aircraft. He has, on occasions, led his flight, and his high standard of morale has set an inspiring example."* Promoted warrant officer and joining 72 Squadron [Spitfires] he gain a DFC [LG 26th February 1943, supplement 35919, page 977] and following being commissioned, and now a flight lieutenant, he was conferred, with a host of other officers, by His Royal Highness the Prince Regent of Belgium with the Order of Leopold II with Palme and Croix de Guerre 1940 with Palme [LG 27th June 1947, supplement 37998, page 2938]. Turning to Derek Wood and Derek Dempster\s classic *The Narrow Margin* the compilation prepared by Flight Lieutenant J H Holloway MBE for the Battle of Britain Fighter Association shows Sergeant Charnock as being attached to 64 Squadron [Spitfires] ahead 19 Squadron. F/Lt 31.01.55 Relinquished

16193 EYRE* Vickers Osbourne F/O + 27.06.29 56 Squadron

16194 FESTING-SMITH* Patrick De Courcy F/Lt 11.01.37 Retired list
At his own request [LG 19 January 1937, issue 34361, page 413]. When war broke out in Europe for a second time, Flight Lieutenant Patrick De Courcy Festing-Smith returned to the service and according to his obituary published in *The Cheltonian* he returned to Cranwell but was in France at the time of the *Blitzkrieg* returning to the UK by way of Dunkirk. He next served in Northern Ireland and then in September 1940, sailed for duties in Khartoum where he died from wounds on Wednesday, 1st November 1940, and was laid to rest in Khartoum War Cemetery.

16195 HALE* Alfred William Beverly F/O + 03.04.28 440 Flight HMS *Hermes*
Operating from HMS *Hermes* off Hong Kong and flying in Fairey IIIF S1216, Flying Officer Alfred William Beverly Hale and his RN crew, Lieutenant John Henry Patrick Graham and Telegraphist Stanley Jackson perished when the engine of their aircraft exploded.

16196 HEARD* Cyril Montague A/Cmdr 01.05.56 Retirement
Air Commodore Cyril Montague Heard CBE mentioned in despatches, died on Wednesday, 30th September 1987. Awarded a cadetship to Cranwell from Halton, on graduating he was awarded the Humanities. Cranwell's photographic archive contains his graduation photograph where he is with four fellow cadets. The cadet seated centre is Eric Bingham Webb, recipient of the Sword of Honour which he is holding on his lap.

16197 HOLDEN* Arthur Leslie P/O + 16.05.27 32 Squadron

16198 LESLIE-MELVILLE* Alexander Ronald F/O 31.01.30 Retired list
On account of ill-health [LG 4 February 1930, issue 33576, page 729]. His death occurred on Friday, 12th June 1942, notice of which was reported in *The London Gazette* 5th January 1943, issue 35852, page 194.

16199 LOWE-HOLMES* Patrick William G/Capt 19.03.53 Retirement
Group Captain Patrick William Lowe-Holmes died on Wednesday, 9th June 1976. During his time at Cranwell he suffered a serious injury on 18th May 1924, when his arm went through a pane of glass.

16200 MERTON* Walter Hugh ACM 29.08.63 Retirement
Air Chief Marshal Sir Walter Merton GBE KCB three times mentioned in despatches, died on Sunday, 23rd March 1986. In addition to his United Kingdom honours, he had been conferred with the Royal Order of George III {Greece].

16201 PEARSON-ROGERS* Henry William G/Capt 03.04.48 Retirement
Group Captain Henry William Pearson-Rogers CBE twice mentioned in despatches, died on Monday, 17th August 1992. Educated at Marlborough, his younger brother, Peter John Pearson-Rogers entered Cranwell with the January 1931 entry and was tragically killed in a flying accident on 12th February 1935.

16202 PIKE*Thomas Geoffrey MRAF 01.03.67 Retirement
Marshal of the Royal Air Force Sir Thomas Pike GCB CBE DFC* four times mentioned in despatches and Officer of Legion of Merit USA, died on Wednesday,1st June 1983. Including members of the Royal Family, Sir Thomas was the 16th appointee to this five-star rank. Apart from nearly four years attached to 56 Squadron [16th December 1925 to 2nd October 1928], his sole squadron command did not come until 4th February 1941, when he took over 219 Squadron [Beaufighter I] at Tangmere and in the ten months of his command gained a DFC and First Bar, the citations being *Gazetted* on the 13th and 30th May 1941, respectively: *"This officer, who recently assumed command of the squadron, has shown great skill in intercepting enemy aircraft at night. During his first night patrol, he intercepted and, it is believed, destroyed a raiding aircraft. He has since destroyed 3 enemy aircraft, of which 2 were destroyed during one night. His keenness and example have had a splendid effect on other members of his squadron."* That for his First Bar reads: *This officer has displayed outstanding skill and keenness in his efforts to seek and destroy enemy aircraft at night. One night recently while his aerodrome* [Tangmere] *was being bombed, he took off to engage the attackers when the aerodrome was illuminated by the glare from a large number of incendiary bombs."* Following his death at RAF Hospital Halton, he was buried in North Weald Bassett [St. Andrew's] Churchyard. In 2004, Pen & Sword published *Beaufighter Ace* written by his son, Richard Pike, copies of which are available from Amazon in both hardcover and as a Kindle edition.

16203 PILCHER* Geoffrey Norman F/O + 26.07.30 8 Squadron

16204 RYLEY* Douglas William Robert AV-M 02.01.62 Retirement
Air Vice-Marshal Douglas William Robert Ryley CB CBE, died on Sunday, 29th December 1985.

16205 SHENTON* Richard Francis G/Ca[t 28.09.53 Retirement
Group Captain Richard Francis Shenton died on Tuesday, 22nd August 1995. He had been conferred with the Norwegian War Cross.

16206 SOUTHEY* Harold Frederick George A/Cmdr 11.08.57 Retirement
Air Commodore Harold Frederick George Southey CB twice mentioned in despatches, died on Friday, 16th February 1979.

16207 SPRECKLEY* Herbert Dorman AM 01.03.62 Retirement
Air Marshal Sir Herbert Spreckley KBE CB Commander of Legion of Merit USA, died on Thursday, 29th August 1963.

16208 STAPLETON* Patrick Joseph F/O 01.04.32 Retired list

16209 STEEDMAN* Edward Blakeway W/Cdr + 17.05.42

Wing Commander Edward Blakeway Steedman twice mentioned in despatches, was executed by the Japanese for refusing to order the pilots under his command to fill out a questionnaire in respect of their flying experience. He is buried in Jakarta War Cemetery, Indonesia, where his headstone has been inscribed: *"Here Lies A Gallant English Officer."* He is mentioned in Brian Cull's superbly researched *Hurricanes over Singapore* with Paul Sortenhaug. On the last day of November 1926, while undergoing instruction at CFS Wittering in an Avro 504N captained by Flying Officer Clarence Graham Crowden, the Avro entered a spin from which it was not recovered before crashing at Easton-on-the-Hill, 3 miles NW of the airfield. Pilot Officer Steedman was seriously injured but, sadly, his instructor did not survive the impact.

16210 WALLIS* John Beresford Martin A/Cmdr 29.06.57 Retirement

Air Commodore John Beresford Martin Wallis OBE four times mentioned in despatches, died onFriday, 19th April 1974.

16211 WARD* Ellacott Lyne Stephens A/Cmdr 30.07.57 Retirement

Air Commodore Ellacott Lyme Stephen Ward CB DFC, died on Tuesday, 1st October 1991. In addition to his British decorations, he had been conferred with Cloud and Banner Decoration with Special Badge and Knot, and Decoration Chien Yuan. The former was *Gazetted* 15 March 1946, supplement 37501, page 1379. His DFC was published on 25 October 1940, supplement 34977, page 6177: *"... in recognition of gallant and distinguished service during operations in Waziristan 1st January 1939, to 31st December 1939."*

16212 WEBB* Eric Bingham G/Capt + 02.04.42 OC RAF Snaith

Group Captain Eric Bingham Webb mentioned in despatches, was Station Commander at Snaith when on 1st-2nd April 1942, he joined the crew of Wellington Ic X9814 JN-O of 150 Squadron for an operational sortie to Poissy. Captained by Pilot Officer Ralph Hubert Powell their aircraft was shot down by Flak in the Vélizy-Villacoublay in the southwestern suburbs of Paris. Braving the flames, Monseur Albert Guerbet rescued the Wellington's rear gunner, Sergeant Christopher W Maltby who was to spend the rest of the war in Stalag-Luft III Sagan and Belaria. A Sword of Honour winner, Group Captain Webb rests with the rest of the crew who died in Les Gonards Communal Cemetery at Versailles.

16213 WISHER* Herbert George G/Capt 25.03.50 Retirement

Group Captain Herbert George Wisher mentioned in despatches died at San Isidro, Peru, on Sunday, 4th February 1968.

16214 YONGE* John Vaughan W/Cdr 22.01.52 Retirement

Wing Commander John Vaughan Yonge died on Friday, 27th April 1973.

* My co-author reports that Flight Lieutenant Charnock was born in Saltijkovo, Russia, on 20th June 1905, and in addition to his Christian names of Harry Walpole, a third was added 'Schelinsky', though this appears to have been 'dropped'. His dismissal from the Royal Air Force in 1930, resulted from a charge of unauthorised low-flying, which, I daresay, many of his compatriots of the time thought *"there for the grace of God go I."* Harry died in Buckinghamshire on Friday, 24th May 1974. Back-classed from the September 1923 entry, Flight Cadet Lionel Hubert Anness graduated on 16th December 1925, along with the cadets whose surnames have an asterisk appended [LG 12 January 1926, issue 33123, page 300].

SWORD OF HONOUR
Flight Cadet Eric Bingham Webb

ROLL OF HONOUR
FEBRUARY 1924 ENTRY

F/O	EYRE	Vickers Osbourne	27 June 1929	56 Squadron
F/O	HALE	Alfred William Beverly	3 April 1928	440 Flight HMS *Hermes*
P/O	HOLDEN	Arthur Leslie	16 May 1927	32 Squadron
F/Cdt	PICKFORD*	Henry Francis Morrell	15 July 1926	
F/O	PILCHER	Geoffrey Norman	26 July 1930	8 Squadron
W/Cdr	STEEDMAN	Edward Blakeway	17 May 1942	
G/Capt	WEBB	Eric Bingham	2 April 1942	OC RAF Snaith

* Possibly from the September 1924 entry.

September 1924 entry : 27

16215 ABRAMS* William George G/Capt 24.09.56 Retirement

Paul McMillan has unearthed by way of Sean Feast's *The Last of the 39ers'* [Grub Street, 2013] some interesting material in respect of Group Captain William George Abrams whom, it seems, spent the majority of his service associated with flying boats serving with 201 Squadron and 205 Squadron, with the latter as a flight commander during which he was often tasked for duties on the most challenging routes of the time. Between April and December 1941, he returned to 201 Squadron as their Commanding Officer. Approaching the end of his service he commanded RAF Felixstowe, a station that he was familiar with in that he was posted to MAEE Felixstowe in the spring of 1927. His death occurred circa January 1989, in the Kensington and Chelsea district of London.

16234 ARBUTHNOT Terence John G/Capt 09.10.54 Retirement

Group Captain Terence John Arbuthnot twice mentioned in despatches and conferred with the Order of Leopold with Palme, died in London on Sunday, 31st December 1995.

16216 BENNETT* Leslie Clive W/Cdr + 09.07.40 21 Squadron

New Zealand Detached from Watton to Lossiemouth, Wing Commander Leslie Clive Bennett led his squadron on a daylight raid on the airfield at Stavangar-Sola. Intercepted off the coast by the Luftwaffe five of the Blenheim IVs were shot down, including R3732 YH-L flown by Wing Commander Bennett whose body was eventually washed ashore; he is buried in Denmark in Lonstrup Churchyard. For details on all the crews lost from this operation please refer to my RAFBCL 1939-1940, page 86 and 165 of the revision.

BERTHON Peter Loraine Ashton P/O 02.11.27 Retired list

On account of ill-health [LG 1 November 1927, issue 33325, page 6899].

16217 BRAKE* Kenneth Stanley G/Capt + 29.12.50 OC RAF Hawarden

Group Captain Kenneth Stanley Brake died while undergoing treatment in RAF Hospital West Kirby. As Flying Officer Brake he had a very narrow escape from death on 11th April 1930 when he was testing the sole Hawker Hornet J9682 which was being trialed by 1 Squadron. My summary for this date describes what happened.

16239 CARY Basil Malins W/Cdr 11.12.50 Retirement

Wing Commander Basil Malines Cary died in Inverness-shire in 1981.

16218 CHILTON* Charles Edward AM 07.09.62 Retirement

Air Marshal Sir Edward Chilton KBE CB, died on Tuesday, 4th August 1992. Specialising almost from the start of his service in navigation [following graduation he was posted to RAF Base Calshot where he underwent conversion from land planes to seaplanes] and apart from duties between February 1934 and 1943, when he was appointed Navigation Officer at CFS, Bomber Command and Flying Training Command, his postings leaned towards coastal matters, subsequently finishing his distinguished service as Air Officer Commanding in Chief Coastal Command and Air Commanding in Chief Channel Command.

16219 CUNNINGHAM* James Charles W/Cdr + 29.09.39 144 Squadron

Wing Commander James Charles Cunningham IGSM died when leading a flight of Hampden bombers on an armed reconnaissance of Sylt and Heligoland when they were intercepted by a strong force of Me109s from I./ZG28 out from Jever. The entire flight of five aircraft [a sixth had turned back with failing engines] were shot down. Sixteen aircrew died with four recovered from the sea to become prisoners of war one of which was Aircraftman H Liggett from the wing commander's aircraft. Wing Commander Cunningham has no known grave and is commemorated on panel at the Runnymede Memorial. Pages 80 and 81

16220 DARBISHIRE* Roy Severs W/Cdr 02.02.56 Retirement

Wing Commander Roy Severs Darbishire mentioned in despatches, died during July 1975.

16221 FINCH* Eric Stanley G/Capt 28.05.55 Retirement

Group Captain Eric Stanley Finch three times mentioned in despatches, died on Saturday, 20th August 1960.

16222 FREEBODY* Wilfred Leslie AV-M 26.04.60 Retirement

Air Vice-Marshal Wilfred Leslie Freebody CB CBE AFC 4 times mentioned in despatches, died on Wednesday, 8th May 1991. He was also a recipient of Poland's Polonia Restituta 3rd Class. The Air of Authority website has a photograph Flight Cadet Sergeant Peabody taken at the College where he was awarded the Abby Gerrard Fellows Memorial Prize and Humanistics Prize.

16223 HAMBLIN* Richard Kaye A/Cmdr 25.05.56 Retirement

Air Commodore Richard Kaye Hamblin CBE four times mentioned in despatches, died on Tuesday, 30th August 1988.

16246 JACKSON Valentine Brice Jephson G/Capt 12.12.49 Retirement

Wing Commander Valentine Brice Jephson Jackson died on Wednesday, 7th July 1976.

16260 LINDLEY Walter John Hugh W/Cdr 26.03.53 Retirement

Wing Commander Walter John 'Jack' Hugh Lindley died on Monday, 19th May 1975.

16250 MARETT Philip Lee Prangley W/Cdr 13.02.48 Retirement

Wing Commander Philip Lee Prangley Marett twice mentioned in despatches, died on Sunday, 7th February 1982.

16251 MARSON John AV-M 24.08.61 Retirement

Air Vice-Marshal John Marson CB CBE, died on Sunday, 1st May 1988.

16225 MARTIN* Harold Harland W/Cdr 05.11.45

Re-instated on the active list and relinquishing, at his own request, the temporary rank of group captain [LG 23 April 1946, supplement 37541, page 2011]. G/Capt 18.07.47 Retirement

Group Captain Harold Harland Martin died on Thursday, 13th July 1961.

MAUGHAM Harold Benjamin F/O 36.03.31 Retired list

On account of ill-health [LG 24 March 1931, issue 33701, page 1991].

MOON* Francis Jack F/O 29.03.29

Flying Officer Francis Jack Moon was admitted to RAF Hospital Aden stricken with Typhoid and died during treatment. He was buried in Maala Cemetery on 29th March 1929.

26002 MUTCH James Richard A/Cmdr 15.06.59 Retirement

Air Commodore James Richard 'Jock' Mutch CB, died on Sunday, 12th August 1973. Born on the 21st of July 1905, James Mutch arrived at Cranwell as a youth accepted for the 4th entry of apprentices. He was appointed to his permanent commission, ranked as a pilot officer on probation, on 11th March 1927 [LG 12 April 1927, issue 33265, page 2411] and was attached that same day to 4 Squadron [Bristol F.2b] Farnborough.

16227 PART* Rodney Frank F/Lt 01.01.34 Retired list

On account of ill-health [LG 2 January 1934, issue 34011, page 57]. On 1st September 1939, he relinquished his honorary commission in class C on appointment to a commission in the Royal Air Force Volunteer Reserve [General Duties Branch] but was transferred to the Administrative and Special Duties Branch with effect the same date [LG 31 October 1939, issue 34721, pages 7275 and 7276]. S/Ldr 10.02.54 Relinquished

16228 PURVIS* Harry Alexander G/Capt 28.11.46 Retirement

Group Captain Harry Alexander Purvis DFC AFC* mentioned in despatches, died on Friday, 23rd December 1966. His DFC, less citation, was *Gazetted* 20th February 1940, supplement 34795, page 1055.

16229 ROBERTS* David Neal A/Cmdr 29.05.58 Retirement

Air Commodore David Neal Roberts CBE AFC, died during October 2000. Initially, David Roberts had elected for a life at sea and prior to his resignation from the Royal Navy had seen service as a Midshipman on the carrier HMS *Glorious* and the battleship HMS *King George V*

16230 STEVINSON* Guy P/O + 17.01.28 17 Squadron

16231 UTLEY* Richard Peter Hugh F/O 01.09.28 Resigned

16232 WARING* Horace A/Cmdr 29.08.55 Retirement

Air Commodore Horace Waring mentioned in despatches, died on Monday, 26th July 1999.

16233 YARDE* Brian Courtenay AV-M 12.03.57 Retirement

Air Vice-Marshal Brian Courtenay Yarde CVO CBE three times mentioned in despatches, died on Wednesday, 29th October 1986. Over four decades previously he was aboard HMT *Lancastria* when she was bombed and sunk off St. Nazaire with horrendous loss of life. Despite the machine-gunning of survivors in the water Wing Commander Yarde was instrumental in saving many lives.

The Flight Cadets with an asterisk appended to their surnames graduated on 30th July 1926 [LG 17 August 1926, issue 33192, page 5446].

SWORD OF HONOUR
Flight Cadet Brian Courtenay Tarde

ROLL OF HONOUR
SEPTEMBER 1924 ENTRY

W/Cdr	BENNETT	Leslie Clive	9 July 1940	21 Squadron
G/Capt	BRAKE	Kenneth Stanley	29 December 1950	OC RAF Hawarden
W/Cdr	CUNNINGHAM	James Charles	29 September 1939	144 Squadron
P/O	STEVINSON	Guy	17 January 1928	17 Squadron

FLYING ACCIDENTS

Tuesday 29 July 1924
Bristol F.2b F4552 F/Cdr H H Aspinall +
T/o Cranwel and spun out of control at Cold Harbour, a hamlet roughly 3 miles SSE from Grantham, Lincolnshire. The findings of the Court of Inquiry into this accident read:

"The cause of the accident was in our opinion - [1] The aeroplane spun into the ground from a height of approximately 500ft accidentally.

"[2] It is possible the pilot lost his sense of balance during the first spin which was prolonged causing him to lose control of the aeroplane which spun into the ground.

"[3] The first spin was carried out contrary to instructions received by him from his flight commander for this flight.

"[4] The accident was not caused through any defect in the aeroplane or engine."

On 17th January 1923, Flight Cadet Harry Howarth Aspinall was injured during the course of a rugby football match at Bury St. Edmunds.

Monday 13 October 1924 Avro 504K E3725 F/Cdt G W Hayes While stationary on the airfield was struck by the Avro summarised below; possibly damaged beyond repair.

Avro 504K E4197 F/O J B Allen Safe
F/Cdt D Neil Safe
T/o Cranwell and wrecked in the following manner: *"In taking off* [as stated by Flying J B Allen] *in Avro F4197, I failed to see Avro E3725 owing to the peculiar contour of the aerodrome at this spot. This aircraft was stationary and very slightly to the right of me. I had not sufficient speed to "jump" so at once shut off my engine and applied full rudder with the hope of swinging clear. In this I was unsuccessful, hitting Avro E3725."*

Flight Cadet Guy Wingfield Hayes was a September 1923 entrant [his details are reported in Appendix E for 1923]; it is assumed Flight Cadet D Neil failed to graduate as he is not listed in *The List of Graduates.* Flying Officer Allen was credited with 845 flying hours experience, 340 of these on Avro 504s.

Appendix E - Roll of Honour

ROYAL AIR FORCE

AC2	ADAMS	Arthur Lee	11 April 1924	84 Squadron
F/O	ANDERSON	Ian Patrick	28 April 1924	28 Squadron
P/O	BAILLIE	Arthur Douglas	15 September 1924	17 Squadron
F/O	BELL	Edward	28 July 1924	28 Squadron
F/O	BOUSFIELD	Colin	2 October 1924	14 Squadron
Sgt	BREWER	William Henry	5 June 1924	39 Squadron
F/O	BYRNE	Cyril William Anthony	28 November 1924	29 Squadron
AC1	CARPENTER	Charles	26 August 1924	13 Squadron
AC1	COPPLESTON	Leslie	5 June 1924	39 Squadron
F/O	CREAMER DFC	Reginald Cyril	26 June 1924	14 Squadron
F/O	DALY DSC DFC mentioned in despatches	Rowan Heywood	5 June 1924	39 Squadron
F/Lt	DAY MC	William Conway	24 July 1924	84 Squadron
Sgt	DICKS	Charles Albert	22 July 1924	55 Squadron
F/O	FRANKLIN	John Hayward Godfrey	11 October 1924	84 Squadron
Cpl	HALL	Thomas Henry	11 February 1924	27 Squadron
F/O	HARCOURT-VERNON	John William Carl	26 August 1924	13 Squadron
F/O	HARRISON	Robert Cuthbert	4 January 1924	84 Squadron
F/O	HUGH-JONES	David Jasper	29 January 1924	27 Squadron
F/Lt	KEMP AFC	Walter Horace Ernest	11 April 1924	84 Squadron
LAC	KEY	Harold Walter	4 January 1924	84 Squadron
F/O	LUCAS	Leslie Gordon	5 June 1924	39 Squadron
LAC	MASKELL	George William	31 July 1924	11 Squadron
F/O	MASON	Stanley James	28 August 1924	19 Squadron
F/O	McALERY	John Mecredy	4 January 1924	1 Squadron
Sgt	MORFETT	Frederick George	10 November 1924	11 Squadron
F/O	MORPHY	Douglas McGillycuddy	4 August 1924	28 Squadron
F/O	PECK	Jasper Godfrey	3 March 1924	111 Squadron
LAC	PERRIN	Frank Charles	26 June 1924	14 Squadron
F/Lt	QUINLAN	Arthur Francis	1 November 1924	5 Squadron
F/O	REID	Ellis	12 November 1924	1 Squadron
P/O	RYDER	Walter Harry	17 March 1924	45 Squadron
P/O	SAVORY	John Charles	15 February 1924	56 Squadron
F/Lt	SCUTT MC	George Howard Homer	15 February 1924	25 Squadron
AC1	SLACK	Percy	30 July 1924	28 Squadron
LAC	STEVENS	Albert Victor	25 January 1924	20 Squadron
F/O	STEWART	Donald Ramsay	24 July 1924	84 Squadron
F/O	STIRLING	Archibald Hay	2 October 1924	13 Squadron
P/O	ST. GEORGE-TAYLOR	Harold St. George	9 October 1924	41 Squadron
Sgt	TAYLOR	George	10 November 1924	11 Squadron
LAC	TAYLOR	Kenneth Robert	28 April 1924	28 Squadron
LAC	TURNER	Kenneth	17 March 1924	45 Squadron
AC1	TURTON	William James Arthur	2 October 1924	13 Squadron
F/Lt	USHER MC AFC	Robert Howard Craster	5 June 1924	41 Squadron
F/O	USHER-SOMERS	Edmund Cronin	16 May 1924	20 Squadron
F/O	WATSON	Myles Birket Foster	21 July 1924	1 Squadron
LAC	WORDSWORTH	Harry Charles	23 July 1924	20 Squadron

His service number 158559 signals entry as a boy airman between October 1917 and December 1918.

ARMY

Lt	MACKENZIE	Edward Charrington	16 May 1924

CIVILIAN

Mohamed Agra Crag — 22 July 1924
Deputy of Lacchi

SQUADRON LOSSES
1925

JANUARY

Tuesday 6 January 1925
25 Squadron *Not reported*
Grebe II J7410
T/o Hawkinge and crash-landed near the airfield after developing 'wing flutter'. Please refer to my summary for 27th October 1924 and the loss from the squadron of J7411 for an explanation as to how this fault was overcome.

Wednesday 14 January 1925
84 Squadron *Not reported*
DH.9A J7026
T/o Shaibah and in flight a sparking plug blew out setting light to gases that had built up under the engine cowling. The crew landed safely, but there are no further movement reports leading me to suspect the DH was left to languish, despite an observation on the accident report noting *"No damage to aircraft."* Frustratingly, the identity of the crew has been omitted;

Saturday 17 January 1925
14 Squadron F/O R R H Bruce Injured
Bristol F.2b F4502 LAC A Sutton Injured
T/o Ramleh where it is reported flying Officer Ronald Reid Hardcastle Bruce crashed. His short service commission, effective from 2nd September 1921 was *Gazetted* 27th September 1921, issue 32468, page 7569.
On 3rd October 1923, he had 'walked away' from a crash that wrecked his aircraft; for information, please refer to my summary for the date in question.

208 Squadron F/O J A McLaren MC +
Bristol F.2b HR1636
T/o Ismailia and believed to have been totally destroyed in a crash on or near the airfield. Flying Officer James Alexander McLaren's details, including the citation for his MC, are recorded on page 231 of my third volume.
This, and the fatal accident summarised for 14 Squadron, were reported in *The Daily News* on Tuesday, January 20th, 1925, under the headline *'Flying Tragedies - Two British Officers Killed in the East'*
"Two fatal RAF flying accidents are officially reported by the Air Ministry. As the result of an accident at Ismailia to a Bristol Fighter of No. 208 [Army Co-operation] Squadron, Moascar, Ismailia, Flying Officer James Alexander McLaren MC, the pilot of the aircraft was killed.
"At Ramleh, Transjordan, a Bristol Fighter of No. 14 [Army Co-operation] Squadron, Amman, met with an accident on the same date, when Flying Officer Ronald Reid Hardcastle Bruce, the pilot of the aircraft, and 326113 LAC Alexander Sutton were seriously injured.
"Flying Officer Bruce died at Palestine General Hospital the same day. Major McLaren joined the 6th Liverpool Rifles as a rifleman on the outbreak of the war, and went to France and was in severe fighting. He received the Military Cross.
"He leaves a wife and little boy. He was home on leave three weeks ago."
A brief account appeared in Monday's issue of *The Halifax Courier and Guardian.*

Thursday 22 January 1925
60 Squadron Sgt D Munro Safe See 24 September 1925
DH.9A E8717/12
T/o Risalpur and wrecked following a forced-landing at Renala Khura near Lahore.

FEBRUARY

Monday 2 February 1925
1 Squadron P/O F G Jennings Safe
7F.1 Snipe E7639
T/o Hinaidi and in making a landing across the wind collided with a stationary DH.9A; the later's airframe serial is not known, but the Snipe was damaged sufficiently for it to be written off charge. For details regarding Pilot Officer Frederick Godfrey Jennings, please refer to Appendix C for 1923 and the list of officers granted short service commissions on 24th July 1923. It is further noted that he gained his 'Flying Badge' on the 14th of June 1924.

Friday 27 February 1925
99 Squadron P/O C S M Woode +
Avro 504K H3083 AC1 E Forrester Injured
T/o Bircham Newton where in spun in following a stall turn. Pilot Officer Cecil Stanley Marshal Woode entered the Cadet College at Cranwell with the September 1922 entry, graduating on 31st July 1924 [LG 26 August 1924, issue 32968, page 6424]. At Cranwell he had been assigned to B Squadron.

The accident report reads: *"Shortly after leaving the ground and when at a height of 600-800ft the aeroplane went into a spin from which the pilot failed to make a complete recovery, the aeroplane striking the ground nose first. The pilot was in the front cockpit and was killed instantly and the passenger sustained some injury. The cause of the accident cannot be determined but the evidence of the majority of the eyewitnesses suggest that the pilot stalled the aircraft in an attempt to make a rapid recovery from a spin at a low altitude."*

The coverage provided by the reporter [who waxed lyrical in an appreciation of the character of Pilot Officer Woode] from *The Diss Express and Norfolk and Suffolk Journal* as reported in the paper's edition of Friday, March 6th, 1925, provided its readers with not only a comprehensive account of the inquest, but also a lengthy account of Pilot Officer Woode's funeral service.

'Fersfield'

'Tragic Death of Mr. C S M Woode'

It is our very painful duty to record a terrible fatality involving the death of Pilot Officer Cecil Stanley Marshal Woode, eldest son of the Rev C E Woode, Recor of Fersfield. Mr. Woode, who was 20 years of age, and connected with 99 Bombing Squadron, was the victim of a fatal air crash, which occurred at Bircham Newton, on Friday. Another officer, first class AC Ernest Forrester was seriously injured and is now lying in the West Norfolk and Lynn Hospital. The mishap occurred only about a quarter of a mile from Bircham NewtonAerodrome, the machine, a 2-seater Avro, crashing from a height of 2,000 feet. The flight was for training purposes.

"Pilot-Officer Cecil Stanley Marshal Woode was educated at Norwich Grammar School, passing from there to Cranwell, and at the entrance examination was awarded the "Wakefield" Scholarship by the Air Ministry. He was a good all-round athlete and represented the Royal Air Force Cadet College in their Athletic Team for their "two and three miles." He was captain of the Cadet Association Team and was the Cadet-Whip to the College Beagles, and during his time at Bircham Newton was Captain of the Association Team there.

"Endowed with a very genial temperament the deceased was immensely popular among his fellow officers and the men who served under him. He also most ably discharged his very perilous duties. His connection with the Air Force was not, as is frequently the case, of a temporary character, but of life-engagement and he could always be depended upon for courage, tact and presence of mind. These qualifications did not forsake him when engaged on his last and fatal flight and when face to face with a terrible death. As an illustration of his popularity and good nature it may be mentioned that very recently one of his air mechanics died in hospital from double pneumonia. It came to his knowledge that the airman's widow was very badly off and when she came over in connection with the obsequies Mr. Woode not only paid her railway fare back to her home, but at the officers' mess made a collection on her behalf which raised no less than £18. Kindly acts and sympathy for others were inbred in his nature and his bright sunny disposition and generosity secured him hosts of friends. Those who shard his duties are lavish in their praise of his kindness and speak without any qualification of his cheerfulness, integrity and good fellowship. He was a thorough sportsman in the true sense of the term, for "he played the game," and when visiting his home at Fersfield he delighted to take part in the local football and cricket matches on the Roydon Road ground and other fields and could always be depended upon to add credit to his side.

"Unbounded sympathy is felt for the parents and members of the family in their terrible bereavement. Every post has brought letters and messages of condolences and on Tuesday morning about 100 were received from sympathisers from all parts of the country. A pathetic note is struck in a letter written last week to his parents, in which the deceased referred to the pleasant anticipation of paying a visit to his home on Monday, but alas! before that day arrived his name had been added to the long list of those whose lives have been sacrificed in the conquest of the air.

'The Inquest'

"An inquest of the late Me. Woode was held at the Bircham Newton Aerodrome on Saturday, before Mr. Coroner Barton.

"Oswald Bartle Swain, FlyingOfficer, adjutant 99th Squadron, RAF, identified the body. Deceased had been stationed at the aerodrome. He was 20 years of age last August.

"William Charles Ward, Pilot-Officer, stated that at 10.15 a.m. on Friday he saw Pilot-Officer Woode take off with an Avro 2-seater machine. Aircraftman Ernest Forrester was also in the machine. After deceased had been up about five minutes he came over the aerodrome at a height of about 800 feet. He went into a stall turn, and did not seem to recover, but skidded across the sky with the nose out. The machine then commenced to spin, and after one spin it stopped, but continued in the nose dive, and almost immediately started spinning again. From the spin it nose-dived to the ground. Witness was about a quarter of a mile from the accident, and the machine fell into a field next to the aerodrome grounds. Help was sent as soon as the accident was seen.

"Arthur Francis Riggs, flying-officer, stated that at 10.5 a.m. on Friday he took up the machine, which was an Avro No. 3083. He did a circuit of the aerodrome and landed. He took off again and did a second circuit and second landing. The machine, in his opinion, was in perfect flying condition. An Avro machine was one on which everyone learned to fly, and was easy under controls. On landing the second time he taxied up to the tarmac and Pilot Officer Woode got into the machine in the front seat. Aircraftman Ernest Forrester got into the rear cockpit. Woode then took off and witness walked to the flight office. Five minutes later Pilot-Officer Ward rushed in and said that Woode had spun onto the ground. Witness went out to the wrecked machine, and when about ten yards from it he saw Forrester half standing up and bent forward a bit. His face was frightfully injured. Witness lifted Forrester by the shoulders and he was carried over the plane. Witness then lifted away the seat, which was on top of Woode, and raised him by the shoulders. He was dead. The machine was badly smashed up.

"Pilot Sergeant Charles William Wood stated that he saw the machine 800 feet from the ground. At this height it did a stall turn, and appeared to get out of control, going into a right hand spin. After one spin the machine ceased spinning,

but continued to nose dive, and almost immediately she began spinning again and hit the ground, The machine began to spin when about 400 feet up.

"Dr. Alexander Muirhead described the injuries. [In view of this being a very local report, and to spare the family, this part of the inquest was not reported].

"An accident expert stated that no definite opinion had yet been formed as to the cause of the accident. Investigations were being made and would probably last a fortnight. Even then the cause of the accident might remain obscure. The evidence showed that the machine got into a spin and failed to get out of it.

"George Reynold Read, Officer-Commanding 99th Squadron, said deceased joined the Air Force in February 1923. He was a Cranwell Cadet. He had done a great deal of flying. He had been at the Bircham aerodrome since last September.

"A verdict of "Accidental death" was recorded.

'The Funeral'

"The body was conveyed from Bircham Newton to Fersfield on Tuesday afternoon, and the coffin covered by the British Ensignwas placed in the Church, where it remained until the time of the funeral at 2.30 on Wednesday. The remains were received at the Church by the Rev. C J Eastwood, Rector of North and South Lopham, who recited suitable sentences as they were borne to the Chancel. A large number of the Royal Air Force attended, one officer, 39 non-commissioned officers and men being present from Martlesham, and several of deceased's brother officers from Bircham Newton. A miltary guard of honour was stationed in the churchyard as the mourners passed through, other members of the Air Force acted as bearers, pall bearers and a firing party, while some took places in the choir and were joined there by the regular choristers. The Church was thronged, and many could not obtain admission. Miss Woodcock, who was at the organ, played suitable music as the congregation assembled. The service which was a very simple character and deeply impressive commenced with the singing of the hymn "Nearer my God to Thee;" this was followed by the reading of Psalm xxiii, and the usual lesson was read by the Rev. H C Frere, Rector of Roydon, the prayers being said by the Rev. Leonard Holt Wilson, Rector of East Harling; another hymn, "How bright those glorious spirits shine," was sung, and the coffin was being borne from the Church to the grave the organist played as a voluntary the tones set to the hymns "On the resurrection morning" and "Onward Christian Soldiers." The Rev. L H Wilson officiated at the graveside, and at the close the firing party discharged three volleys and the "Last Post" brought a very reverent but extremely sad service to a close.

"The principle mourners were Rev. C E and Mrs Woode [father and mother], Cadet D M Woode [brother], Miss Mollie Gladden [fiancée], Mr. W Bronger [cousin], Miss Bronger, Mr. and Mrs. Gladden [Bressingham], Mr. Ronald Gladden, Miss B Gladden, Midshipman F M Woode [brother] was unable to be present owing to being on his ship in the Pacific."

Then followed in the paper the extensive list of close friends, lists of floral tributes, and in conclusion tributes in the form of wreaths from the Royal Air Force and Navy: *"Air Officer Commanding and Officers at head quarters Inland Area, RAF; the Officer Commanding and Officers, Bircham Newton Station, RAF; the Officer Commanding and Officers 99 Squadron, RAF; Officer Commanding and Officers 7 Squadron, RAF; the Warrant Officers, NCOs and Airmen No. 99 Squadron, RAF; the Warrant Officers, NCOs and Airmen No.7 Squadron, RAF; the Corporals RAF Bircham Newton; the Captain, Officers, Staff and Cadets HMS "Worcester"; the Mechanical Transport Section RAF Bircham Newton; Officers and Men, A and AEE Martlesham Heath; Brother Officers, No. 3 Group head quarters."*

Incorrectly quoted in the *J File* as *29 February 1925* 45 Squadron wrote off Vernon II J7142 in a forced-landing between Landing Grounds 'O' and 'P' [Iraq].

February 1925 witnessed the first flight of the prototype Gloster Gamecock J7497.

MARCH

Wednesday 4 March 1925

32 Squadron P/O A H Montgomery Injured
Grebe II J7364

T/o Kenley and while east of Southampton Water and to the NE Warsash crashed circa 1015 into a hut at Locks Heath School. A full account of the accident in which a 12-year old student at the school was killed appeared in the *Portsmouth Evening News* on Wednesday, 18th March 1925, and is repeated in ASN Wikibase Occurrence 162483, which the authors acknowledge: *"The inquest on Dora Ball, the little twelve year old victim of the Locksheath plane crash was resumed at the Guildhall, Southampton, today, and was conducted by the Borough Coroner, Mr H K Pope. The fatality occurred during the morning of Wednesday, 4th March. Seven girls, including Dora Ball, were receiving instruction in bread making at the cookery hut at Locksheath Council School when an aeroplane crashed into the building.*

"Miss Lena Booker, the cookery mistress, and several of the scholars received severe injuries, and the deceased child was conveyed to The Royal South Hants and Portsmouth Hospital in an unconscious condition, suffering from a compound fracture of the skull and lacerations of the brain. She died the same evening without regaining consciousness.

"At the previous enquiry the only evidence taken was that of identification, given by the deceased child's step father, William Ball, a gunner's mate in the Royal Navy, and the medical testimony, it being stated by Dr. Seagar Thomas, Honorary Pathologist at the hospital, that death was due to injury of the brain and haemorrhage resulting from fracture of the skull. Pilot Officer A H Montgomery, who was flying the machine at the time of the crash, and Miss Booker, were unable to attend owing to the injuries they received.

"Mr Arthur Emmanuel attended the inquest of behalf of the parents of the deceased child; Mr C Eustace Fulton [instructed by Messrs Swayne, Havers and Hartfield] represented Pilot Officer Montgomery; and Mr A L Roberts [County Architect] attended on behalf of The County Council. Others present included Mr Campbell representing the Air Ministry; and Mr R F Casey RAF of The Royal Aero Club.

In the absence of Miss Booker, the first witness called was the Headmaster, Mr Edward George Loader who under questioning from the Coroner and Mr Emmanuel, indicated he heard the sound of an aeroplane and then saw if fly past the windows of the school and a height that he judged to be about seven or eight feet and on going outside he saw the wreckage of the plane in the playground and the pilot walking nearby. He then went into the cookery hut where he saw Dora Ball lying on the floor. He was then asked if he know a tree had been damaged to which he replied that he saw a piece had been broken off and the pilot told him one of the wing's of his aircraft had struck a tree. It was then revealed that relatives of Pilot Officer Montgomery lived close by in Jesmond House. Although earlier in the report it was indicated that Pilot Officer Montgomery was unable to attend owing to his injuries, this seems not to have been the case as under the heading *Pilots Story* the article continued: *"After further evidence had been given by eye witnesses Pilot Officer Montgomery went into the witness box and having been warned by The Coroner he said he was stationed at Kenley Aerodrome, Surrey. He said that on 4th March he was instructed to make a practice flight, which involved him being up a number of hours and flying where he pleased. He started his Flight Commander's machine at 9.20 a.m. and found himself over Warsash village at about 10.10 a.m. Until he received orders that morning he had no idea he would fly that day."*

When asked by Mr Fulton if his relatives knew he would be flying in their area, Pilot Officer Montgomery replied *"No"* and then went on to say *'he was flying at a height of between 500 and 800 feet and as he turned the nose of the machine went downwards, and decreased the altitude rapidly. His speed was then 110 m.p.h. and he failed to pull up quickly enough to avoid the trees. The witness added that the result of striking the trees was that he broke the wing, which drooped downwards, and for all practical purposes the machine was quite out of control. He saw an open space beyond the school and made up his mind rapidly to try and land there. He was unable to effect a landing and approached the hut with a drooping wing. He managed to clear the hut with his undercarriage, but the damaged wing struck the centre of the hut and swung the aeroplane around. He then crashed."*

Additional to the report above, the accident was reported the following day by the *Aberdeen Journal* while the *Portsmouth Evening News* in their edition of 5th March, named Florence Humby as being injured along with her friend Dorothy Malins, Dorothy losing some of her teeth, while Alexander Montgomery sustained a cut above one of his eyes.

One additional casualty has been identified by co-author Paul McMillan as Miss Lean Booker. Meanwhile, Dora Ball was laid to rest in Southampton Old Cemetery, though the location of her grave is not known.

In summing up the conclusion was that the accident was an error of judgement and a verdict of 'Accidental Death' was returned and that there was no evidence to suggest culpable negligence on the part of the pilot who continued to be attached to 32 Squadron. Alexander had recently graduated from the RAF [Cadet] College at Cranwell and, subsequently, would rise to the rank of Air Commodore before retiring on the 16th of February 1946.

Saturday 21 March 1925

27 Squadron F/O E J Dashwood +
DH.9A E8792 F/O N C Hayter-Hames +

T/o Risalpur for bombing operations over the North West Frontier region of Waziristan. On reaching the target area at Torra Tukka, Flying Officer Edward John Dashwood dived to carry out his attack but came under sustained and accurate fire from the ground. Most likely incapacitated, he crashed, with his bomb load intact, and on impact the DH exploded in a ball of fire. His was granted a short service commission on 12th July 1921, his details appearing in issue 32387 page 5561. His observer entered the Cadet College at Cranwell with the Schools entry of February 1920 [see pages 270 and 271 of my third volume].

On the 2nd of June 1924, while being flown by Flying Officer Horace William Westaway [see summary for 4th June 1921] it was badly damaged at Rawalpindi where on landing the undercarriage collapsed.

Wednesday 25 March 1925

32 Squadron P/O I M Scott + Whyteleafe [St. Luke's] Churchyard
7F.1 Snipe E6792

T/o Kenley and crashed in a field adjoining allotments on Tilling Down, Caterham, Surrey. The Kenley Revival website carries the report published in the *Surrey Mirror,* Friday 3rd April 1925, which the authors gratefully acknowledge: *"There were particularly sad features about the death of Pilot-Officer Ian Malcolm Scott, of the Royal Air Force, Kenley Aerodrome, the victim of the aeroplane disaster at Tilling Down, Caterham, last week. The Coroner [Mr. P J Nightingale] held the inquest in the Medical Officer's Room at the Aerodrome Hospital on Friday afternoon last week, and by a singular coincidence that day would have been the young officer's twenty-first birthday. He was to have gone on leave on the Thursday, so that he could have spent his coming-of-age birthday with relatives. He was an orphan, and belonged to a family well-known at Stockport, and also had relatives in London and Horley. He had been at the Kenley Aerodrome only about two months, going there direct from the Aviation School.*

"Mr Bruce Aitken, solicitor[of London and Salfords, Horley], cousin of the deceased, watched the proceedings on behalf of the relatives. P.C. Newball acted as Coroner's officer. Charles Gerald Leslie Scott, of Leinster Square, Bayswater, London, gave evidence of identification, and said the deceased, who was his brother, would have been 21 on that day, March 27th.

"Anthony Ayton, an ex-Police-sergeant, of 97 Beechwood-road, Caterham Valley, deposed that on Wednesday morning, March 25th, he was working on his allotment at Tilling Down when he heard a loud roaring noise. He had

frequently heard the noises of aeroplanes, but this was an unusual noise. He looked up and saw the machine coming overhead. It just got over the hedge of the adjoining field, and then something went "bang, bang." He thought it was going to land in the field, but the engine re-started, and it went up again slightly, but when it got across the other side of the field there were two more bangs, and it just went over the hedge and then down between two trees, tearing right through them. The machine then went into the next field and pitched upon its nose and turned completely over. Witness ran to the spot and saw that the pilot was dead. Witness cut the straps that held the body in the seat, and pulled it clear of the wreckage, and then sent somebody down to the nearest telephone to send a message to the Aerodrome. Witness remained till the doctor and the police arrived.

"William Henry Scrivener, a carpenter, of 44 Beechwood-road, Caterham Valley, and employed by Sir Bernard Greenwell, said on Wednesday morning about half-past ten, he was near Tilling Down Farm, when he notices the aeroplane. It was making a tremendous roaring noise and also reports, and was only about thirty feet above the ground as it came over the field. Witness thought that the pilot had got trouble with the engine. The machine was going up and down until it got over Tilling Down, and then he lost sight of it. Soon afterwards he heard the engine restart, and there was more banging and then he heard the crash. He went directly to the spot to render assistance.

"Flight-Lieut. Francis John Vincent of the RAF at Kenley Aerodrome, deposed that he saw the machine before he gave orders to the deceased to fly about 10 o'clock. For about a quarter of an hour before taking to the air the deceased practised four runs and landing, and as far as witness could tell the machine was perfectly all right. Undoubtedly, if the machine had not been all right the deceased would not have carried on with it. Witness saw him go up, and also saw him make the practice runs, which were in accordance with his instructions. Witness took to the air later and did not see the crash. In reply to the Coroner, witness said the deceased probably had some slight engine trouble, but the noises mentioned by the witnesses were quite usual and normal, with the engine of the rotary type, which was on the machine. It was quite usual to make a bang. It was very difficult to tell the cause of the actual crash, but witness thought the deceased never saw the trees at all.

"Answering Mr. Bruce Aitken, witness said that in this immediate neighbourhood, airmen did not experience air pockets owing to the valleys, but he did not think it could have happened in this case. It would have been possible if he had been down in the valley. There was no cowl on the aeroplane that would obstruct the pilot's vision.

"Squadron-Leader E Brown the medical officer at the Kenley Aerodrome, gave evidence that he was called to the scene of the accident. Having described the injuries the doctor stated that death must have been absolutely instantaneous.

"The Coroner, in summing up, said he thought it was very possible, as the Flight-Lieutenant had said, that the deceased did not see the trees. He would certify a verdict of "Accidental Death."

At the time of his death, officially attributed to his failing to keep a close look out on what was in front of him whilst practicing high-speed flying at very low altitude, he had logged eleven and a half hours on type and in total had flown for ninety hours. This, I suspect, was combined duel and solo flying.

Monday 30 March 1925

28 Squadron F/O T D Berridge +
Bristol F.2b AC2 A Bidmead Injured

T/o Quetta and believed to have crashed in the vicinity of the aerodrome. Flying Officer Thomas Donald Berridge entered Cranwell as a Flight Cadet in February 1921, and was placed in B Squadron. He graduated and was appointed to a permanent commission on 22nd December 1922 [LG 23 January 1923, issue 32789, page 533].

APRIL

Saturday 4 April 1925

60 Squadron S/Ldr T F Hazell Safe
DH.9A H52 DSO DFC* MC

T/o Risalpur and crashed on arrival at Sorarogha in the NWF. First issued to 27 Squadron H52 had been damaged twice, the first occasion being a landing accident at Risalpur on the 7th of June 1920, followed by a similar mishap in that same year on 14th December. On both occasions its pilot had been Flight Lieutenant John Lyne Vachell MC who had won his award whilst a temporary captain attached to the Royal Field Artillery, the citation being published in supplement 30651, page 5017, of the *Gazette* of 25th April 1918: *"For conspicuous gallantry and devotion to duty. He did excellent work on many occasions, continually locating and engaging successfully enemy heavy batteries."* Appointed to a permanent commission [see page 193 of my third volume], he rose to the rank of air commodore ahead of retiring on 21st May 1943, owing to ill-health contracted while fulfilling the post of Senior Air Staff Officer at Headquarters Air Forces in India. His death [possibly while undergoing treatment in RAF Hospital Halton] was announced on 11th July 1947.

The Air of Authority website shows that as early as 29th August 1914, he was with B Battery of the 2nd Monmouthshire Royal Field Artillery, and that he trained as a pilot during 1916, whilst in Egypt.

Squadron Leader Thomas Falcon Hazell's biography is reported on *Wikipedia* which shows he was born on 7th August 1892, at Rondstone in Co. Galway and died at Newport in Co. Mayo at the comparatively early age of 54 on 4th September 1946. The citation for his MC was *Gazetted* on 26th July 1917, supplement 30204, page 7630: *"For conspicuous gallantry and devotion to duty. On several occasions he displayed marked courage and determination in attacking and destroying enemy aircraft."*

Citations for his DFC and First Bar were published in supplement 30989, pages 12966 and 12960 respectively in the paper's issue of 2nd November 1918: *"This officer is conspicuous for his bravery and skill, having destroyed twenty enemy machines and four kite balloons. On one occasion, while attacking troops on the ground, he observed seven enemy scouts above him; he at once engaged them, shooting down one out of control. Some days later he, with another pilot, attacked a kite balloon, driving it down in flames; they then attacked a second balloon, driving it down in a deflated condition."*

The citation for the First Bar reads: *"This officer has accounted for twenty-seven enemy machines and four kite balloons. On the 8th of August* [the opening day of the *Battle of Amiens* - squadron losses on this day are covered in my second volume, pages 113 to 126] *he shot down two machines out of control, and destroyed a third in the air. In these combats he was so heavily engaged that all his instruments were wrecked, and only one strand of his elevator control cable was intact. Relentless in attack, Capt. Hazell displays disregard of personal danger in a marked degree."*

His *Wikipedia* entry carries the citation for his DSO, awarded on 8th February 1919: *"A brilliant fighter, distinguished for his bold determination and rare courage, he has accounted for twenty-nine enemy machines, twenty being destroyed and nine driven down out of control; he has also destroyed ten balloons. On 4th September he rendered exceptionally valuable service in leading his flight to attack hostile balloons that were making a certain road impassable. Within an hour three of these balloons were destroyed, Major Hazell accounting for two."*

One of 294 captains granted a permanent commission on 1st August 1919, his name and details are in my third volume, page 192. For a table of his combat successes, please refer to the Aerodrome website which shows he gained twenty with 1 Squadron [Nieuport 17] between 4th March 1917 and 16th August 1917, and twenty-three flying SE.5a with 24 Squadron.

Tuesday 14 April 1925

84 Squadron *Not reported*
DH.9A E8669 *Not reported*

T/o from a desert strip, lost power and in the crash-landing that followed the DH caught fire and was burnt out.

Friday 17 April 1925

84 Squadron F/Lt C J Truran AFC Injured
DH.9A F/O T Thomson +

T/o Shaibah and reported as crashed near the airfield. Flight Lieutenant Cyril Jameson Truran was granted a short service commission on 16th September 1919, *Gazetted* the same date, issue 31554, page 11588. Page 225 of my third volume records details pertaining to his dismissal from the service, plus additional notes.

Saturday 18 April 1925

6 Squadron F/O R W Pontifex +
Bristol F.2J F4961 AC2 E Barber +

T/o Mosul for an offensive patrol which included bombing during which the crew came under intensive and accurate rifle fire; crashed and burnt out at Mirkhan near Sinjar, Iraq. Flying Officer Rupert William Pontifex was among the School entry flight cadets that reported to Cranwell in February 1920. He graduated on 20th December 1921 [LG 24th January 1922, issue 32586, page 643]. While at the College he excelled at cricket and rugby football.

When attached to 14 Squadron at Ramleh he had been injured when his Bristol F.2b F4459 crashed on 3rd September 1923, my summary for that date refers.

His observer Aircraftman Edward Barber joined the service from civilian life at sometime after September 1919, his service number 344579 being in a block of numbers set aside for civilians which ran from 340001 - 360000 the last of which being issued in June 1925.

Thursday 30 April 1925

207 Squadron F/O B G Pool Injured
DH.9A J7112 AC1 W J Spare Injured

T/o Eastchurch for practice in flying in formation and it was during a turn at 1,200 feet that control was lost and the DH spun to the ground in a semi-control crash-landing which left both airmen seriously injured. According to the squadron's history, these formation practices were in preparation for the forthcoming Hendon pageant during which a display of aircraft landing as a formation would be included in the programme. A photograph of the smashed DH has been reproduced on page 30 of *Always Prepared.*

I strongly suspect Flying Officer Pool to be Bernard George Pool who received a short service commission on 19th June 1923 [see Appendix D in this volume for the year 1923] and who subsequently transferred to the Stores Branch. Notes regarding his *Great War* service with 49 Squadron have been appended to his entry in Appendix D.

MAY

Monday 4 May 1925

6 Squadron F/Lt W A B Savile Injured
Bristol F.2b Lt J E Griffith +

T/o Mosul and reported to have crashed at Kani Uthman in the As Sulaymānīyah district some 191 miles north of Baghdad. Flight Lieutenant Walter Arthur Bouchier Savile of the Royal Regiment of Artillery is reported in *the London Gazette* published on 5th January 1925, issue 33009, page 139, as resigning his army commission on being appointed to a permanent commission in the Royal Air Force on 24th December 1924. He had been seconded for air force service on 23rd March 1921 [LG 27 April 1921, supplement 32305, page 3360]. Lieutenant John Ellerthorpe Griffith was attached to the Iraqi Levies.

Tuesday 5 May 1925
5 Squadron *Not reported*
Bristol F.2b J6637
T/o Dardoni and damaged beyond repair here when on forced-landing with a failing engine the starboard wheel dropped into a ditch.

Thursday 9 May 1925
31 Squadron F/O R R S Waller Injured
Bristol F.2b
T/o Ambala to practice night flying; crashed and succumbed to his injuries the following day. A graduate from the Cadet College at Cranwell, Flying Offi er Robert Richard Studdert Waller was appointed to a permanent commission on 16th August 1922 [LG 29 September 1922, issue 32751, page 6910]. Robert, educated at Harrow, reported to Cranwell with the September 1920 entry and was placed with B Squadron.

Wednesday 20 May 1925
31 Squadron F/O A Findley +
Bristol F.2b Capt G Rich +
T/o Ambala and crashed into one of the streets in the winter city of Sailkot in the State of Kashmir some 78 miles NW of Lahore. Flying Officer Arthur Findley was granted a short service commission, having been on the unemployed list, on 29th March 1921 [LG 29 March 1921, issue 32271, page 2472]. Captain Gregory Rich was attached to the Indian Army.

Friday 22 May 1925
32 Squadron F/O A R Woodyatt +
7F.1 Snipe E6794/G
T/o 2110 Northolt bound for Wembley but while climbing out stalled and dived into the ground. The accident was reported in Monday 25th's edition of the *Western Daily Press*: *"The announcement was made on Saturday night by the Air Ministry that as the result of an accident on Friday at Northolt Aerodrome to the Snipe machine of No. 32 Squadron Kenley, Pilot Officer* [sic] *Arthur Reinagle Woodyatt, of Thames Ditton, the pilot of the machine, was killed. The aeroplane was on its way to Wembley to take part in "Spectacle of London Defended" at the Stadium. Its place in the squadron was taken by a spare machine which was in reserve, and none of the officers in the other machines knew of the fatality until they returned to the aerodrome."*

Flying Officer Arthur Woodyatt had been granted a short service commission [LG 26th December 1922, issue 32780, page 9120] and had escaped unhurt from a crash that wrote off his aircraft on 7th February 1924 [see my summary for details]. His promotion to flying officer was promulgated on 9th August 1924 [LG 12th August 1924, issue 32964, page 6054].

Monday 25 May 1925

100 Squadron	P/O J T Eve	+	Grantham Cemetery
Fawn II J7226	AC1 G E Bruce	Injured	Grantham Cemetery
	AC2 P T Sharpe	Injured	

T/o Spittlegate and following a stall while banking at around 100 feet came down at Ropsley, a little over 4 miles ESE from Grantham, Lincolnshire. Pilot Officer Jack Terence Eve arrived at the Cadet College, Cranwell, with the September 1922 entry of Flight Cadets and had graduated as recently as 31st July 1924 [LG 26 August 1924, issue 32968, page 6424]. Aircraftman George Edward Bruce and Percival Thomas Sharpe were very severely injured and the former died within hours of being admitted to hospital. The former's service number was 341626.

Press reports of the tragedy appeared in two newspapers, *The Grantham Journal* and *The Daily News*. First, the account presented to its readers by *The Grantham Journal*

'Flying Fatality at Grantham'
'Officer and Mechanic Killed'
'Result of a Spin'

"A considerable period of immunity from fatal accidents in connection with the RAF Spittlegate, was broken on Monday evening, when a 'plane developed a spin which the pilot was unable to correct, and crashed to earth. Pilot-Officer Jack Terrence Eve, aged 21, of South Nutfield, Surrey, was killed instantly. AC1 George Edward Bruce, aged 25, married, of Erewash-street, Long Eaton, died two hours later, and a third occupant of the machine, AC1 Percival Thom. Sharpe, of Swineshead, Boston, was seriously injured. They were all attached to the 100th Squadron. The machine was a three-seater Fairey Fawn. The sad event aroused great sympathy in the town and district.

"On Wednesday, Dr. C H D Robbs, the Deputy Coroner for the Grantham district, held an inquest at the Aerodrome.

"Flight-Lieut. J A Perdrau, M.D., RAFMS, Medical Officer in charge of the RAF Station at Spittlegate, said that after being informed of the accident, the ambulance was sent to Ropsley, and they first brought back the two men then living. Bruce was unconscious, suffering from a fracture at the base of the skull, and he died two hours later without regaining consciousness. Sharpe was injured, and was at present under treatment at the Hospital. He was expected to recover, but he was not in a fit state to give evidence, as he was suffering from shock. Proceeding, witness said he had had a conversation with Sharpe, who told him that Pilot-Officer Eve warned him that he was going to do:

'A Stalling Turn'

" and in doing that turn the machine went into a spin, which he was unable to correct, and he struck the ground. At the time they were between 1,000 and 1,500 feet up. Pilot-Officer Eve, continued witness, was an ex-Cranwell cadet, and a capable pilot. - By the Deputy Coroner: A stalling turn was frequently done, and evidently on that occasion something happened that was not expected - Witness added that Pilot-Eve's skull was fractured, and his death was instantaneous.

"Squadron-Leader H F A Gordon, of the 100th Squadron, said on Monday evening his attention was drawn to the machine which was spinning. He did not see the actual start of the spin, but saw it whilst it was spinning and watched it until it disappeared behind some trees. Pilot-Officer Eve was a very capable pilot. - By the Deputy Coroner: The probabilities were that he got into

'An Accidental Spin'

"and the version given to Dr. Perdrau by Sharpe was probably correct. Witness agreed that Pilot-Officer Eve went into a spin which he was unable to correct. There was every reason to believe that the aeroplane was in perfect order.

"Aircraftman E J Fuller, a rigger, said that on Monday he twice ascended in that particular machine with Pilot-Officer Eve in rehearsals for the Aerial Pageant. The machine behave quite satisfactorily, He had examined it and everything was in order. - Inspector Haywood. Did anything go wrong with it on Saturday? Has it fired at anytime? - Witness: There was nothing wrong. The machine had not fired.

"John Edward James, labourer, Red House, Ropsley, said about 6.15 he was having tea when he heard a little bump followed a second later by a big crash. He ran out and found an aeroplane had crashed in the paddock close to his house. He, with Wm. Moore, and other assistance, removed three men from the machine.

"The Deputy Coroner returned a verdict of "Death by Misadventure."

"Dr. Perdrau said he would like to thank the people of Ropsley for the prompt assistance they gave to the ambulance Staff. Without their ready help they could not have got the injured men under treatment at the Hospital fifteen minutes after the accident had happened.

'The Funeral'

"The funeral of Pilot-Officer Eve and Aircraftman Bruce took place on Thursday in Grantham Cemetery, in the presence of a very large number of people, the ceremony being most impressive. The graves of the deceased were side by side, and both were accorded full military honours. The bodies were enclosed in oak coffins, which were covered with Union Jacks, and placed on trailers, drawn by tenders, whilst on the top were deceaseds' caps, and wreathes. There was an escort of one officer and thirty men, a firing party, comprising a sergeant, a corporal and ten men bearers, a supporting party of eight officers, and relatives. The Band from Cranwell headed the mournful procession, playing Chopin's "Funeral March" en route and into the cemetery. The Rev. C N Gardner officiated, and at the end of the service the firing party gave three volleys, and trumpeters sounded the "Last Post." The beautiful wreaths included one for each man from both the 100 Squadron and 39 Squadron Officers' Messes, Sergeants' Messes, Airmen, Officers of Digby, and Inland Area Headquarters."

The Daily News began its coverage beneath:

'2,000 Feet Drop From Plane'
'Parachute Fails to Open'
'3 RAF Deaths in a Day'

"Two air accidents, resulting in three deaths, were officially reported by the Ministry of Air yesterday.

"At Andover, on Monday evening, while engaged in a practice parachute jump, Corporal Sydney Ronald Wilson [241627], of No. 12 Squadron, was killed.

"According to a correspondent, Wilson leapt from the plane when it was at a height of 2,000 feet, and the parachute failed to spread.

'The jump was made in the sight of a large crowd. Wilson fell like a stone into the RAF aerodrome.

"Wilson, a single man, aged 23, is said to be a native of Beverley.

The paper then gave a brief account on the accident affecting 100 Squadron, before continuing: *"At the inquest yesterday the jury returned a verdict that Wilson's death was due to "Misadventure." Witnesses stated that he failed to pull the "rip cord" which opened the parachute. An expert said the "rip cord" had not been pulled.*

'Rip Cord Not Pulled'

"At the inquest at Andover yesterday, Flying Officer Horace John White, pilot of the machine, said that he saw Wilson's hand on the "rip cord"which would open the parachute, but did not see him actually pul the cord. Wilson got down the ladder all right to make the jump, but seemed a little tremulous.

"Another witness, Reginald Charles Read, also said that Wilson appeared nervous when he got out on to the ladder. As he was leaving the steps, he had hand on the rip cord ring, but afterwards took it away, and when he left the aeroplane his hands came out as if he wanted to clutch back at the machine.

'Taken Unaware'

"Flying Officer Frank Soden, an inspector in parachutes, said Wilson had been instructed in the use of the parachute, and the harness was properly fitted before he left the ground. The rip cord had never been pulled, of that he was certain.

"His theory was that:when the pilot opened out the engineWilson was taken unawares just as he had one hand on the ladder and one on the rip cord, and, feeling himself going off, he released the hold of the cord and clutched at the ladder. He was too panic-stricken to find the rip cord afterwards."

Tuesday 26 May 1925

An unusual, and tragic, accident occurred during the day - again, it featured a Fair Fawn II [J7221 on 12 Squadron establishment] - when an electrical fault in the aircraft's wireless equipment took the life of Flight Sergeant Frank Lowry, a non-commissioned officer of considerable promise for his service number 334286 indicates he had only been in the service for around six years.

The Fawn was being Flown by a seconded army officer, Flying Officer John Kenneth Smith, who resumed his army duties with the Lancashire Fusiliers in September 1925.

JUNE

Sunday 21 June 1925

60 Squadron F/O N C Bretherton +
DH.9A Sgt H E Blanche +

T/o Risalpur and crashed at Peshawar. Having left the service, Flying Officer Norris Carden Bretherton was granted a short service commission, *Gazetted* 8th January 1924, issue 32896, page 269. Previously, he was one of fifty-seven officers *Gazetted* to the Unattached List for the Indian Army [LG 3 August 1920, supplement 32005, page 8141].

His observer, Sergeant Henry Eustace Blanche, served with RNAS [he was a 1917 entrant] until the merger of 1st April 1918. His service number 240535 comes within the block 22506 - 244710.

Monday 29 June 1925

99 Squadron P/O W G Wainwright-Fahy Injured
Avro 504K E3760

T/o Bircham Newton and was lost just off Hunstanton's shoreline. Pilot Officer William George Wainwright-Fahy had been *Gazetted* with a short service commission as recently as 24th April 1925, issue 33040, page 2686, and was attached to 99 Squadron for flying instruction. His experience to date amounted to just over sixteen flying hours and this accident came close to ending his life; he was, indeed, very fortunate to be rescued with little more than superficial injuries: *"Following an intentional spin over the sea the pilot failed to recover normal flight before the aeroplane struck the water three quarters of a mile from the foreshore and was wrecked. The pilot sustained slight injuries to the head. The accident was due to the atmospheric conditions over the sea causing the pilot to lose all perception of the height and attitude of his machine on recovering from a spin."*

Owing to ill-health, he left the service on 26th June 1929, and was permitted to retain his rank of flying officer.

JULY

Thursday 2 July 1925

19 Squadron F/O H V Kerckhove MC + Whittlesford [St. Mary and St. Andrew's] Churchyard
Avro 504K H3098

T/o Duxford and while in the landing phase stalled off a steep turn and crashed out of control. Flying Officer Herbert Vincent Kerckhove was granted a short service commission on 15th March 1923 [LG 30 March 1923, issue 32810, page 2420]. As a 2nd Lieutenant attached to the 9th Battalion, East Surrey Regiment, he was *Gazetted* with the MC on 30th July 1919, supplement 31480, page 9746: *"For gallantry and resourceful leading on October 16th, 1918, during the attack on Haussy. After several attempts had failed to rescue a wounded man who was lying in front of our posts, he crept out under heavy machine-gun fire and got the man in. Later, he organised a party of 10 men and surrounded an enemy post in a sunken road, which was inflicting great damage and casualties upon the attacking force, and succeeded in capturing the whole garrison of 60, with two trench mortars and two anti-tank rifles. His courage and coolness were admirable."*

Note. Haussy is a commune in the Nord department some 15km south of Valenciennes. At the time 2nd Lieutenant Kerckhove won his MC the days of trench warfare on the Western Front were over. In August 1918, the *Battle of Amiens* heralded what historians refer to as the 'last hundred days' and the advance on Haussy was the precursor for the attack by the Canadian Corp on Valenciennes where the Germans had stubbornly resisted the British assaults during the last days of October. The taking of the town is vividly described on pages 242 and 243 of Nick Lloyd's *Hundred Days* [Penguin Books, 2014].

Wednesday 8 July 1925

30 Squadron F/O M G Penny +
DH.9A Lt G D E Heather +

T/o Kirkuk and crashed near Chamchamal which according to *Wikipedia* is about a thirty minute drive east of Kirkuk. It is in a region now controlled by Kurdistan. Of the Royal Artillery, Lieutenant Marcus Glanfield Penny was granted a temporary commission as a flying officer for years service commencing 20th January 1922 [LG 7 February 1922, issue 32602, page 1089]. His passenger, Lieutenant George Donald Edward Heather was attached to the Iraqi Levies.

Thursday 9 July 1925

100 Squadron *Not reported*
Fawn II J7209/3

T/o Spittlegate though Weston Zoyland practice camp cannot be ruled out as it was here that the Fawn crashed.

Monday 20 July 1925
60 Squadron P/O N W P Mason Safe
DH.9A E8729
T/o Peshawar and as in so many cases its flying days ended when engine failure was followed by a forced-landing, in this instance at Baston in Baluchistan. Pilot Officer Neville Walter Frederick Mason entered Cranwell as a flight cadet with the February 1922 entry and went on to serve throughout the Second World War before retiring as a group captain on the 5th of September 1950. Prior to the mishap here recorded, on 22nd October 1924, he crash-landed on the perimeter of Risalpur aerodrome in DH.9A E9683 which was repaired and continued in service.

It is believed Grebe II J7380 on 29 Squadron establishment may have been damaged beyond repair after turning over on landing during the month.

AUGUST

Wednesday 5 August 1925
55 Squadron Sgt J R Gaze +
DH.9A J7042 LAC F Young +
T/o Hinaidi and reported to have been consumed by fire following a crash. Sergeant John Reginald Gaze and Leading Aircraftman Francis Young were the first all non-commissioned officer crew to be killed in squadron service in 1925. Both had joined the Royal Air Force from civilian occupation and probably within weeks of each other ass their service numbers were 355635 and 353435 respectively, these numbers coming within the block 340001 - 360000 which was extant between September 1919 and June 1925.

Wednesday 12 August 1925
84 Squadron P/O J J FitzGerald +
DH.9A AC1 F E Leatherdale Injured
T/o Shaibah and crashed near Ur in Iraq after losing control in a sandstorm. In ancients times Ur was a coastal city near the mouth of the Euphrates on the Persian Gulf, since when the coastline has shifted leaving Ur on the river's south bank some 10 miles from Nasiriyah. Pilot Officer John Jellett FitzGerald's short service commission was *Gazetted* on 8th January 1924, issue 32896, page 269.

Monday 17 August 1925
11 Squadron P/O R Matheson Safe
Fawn II J7220 AC2 Wells Safe
T/o Netheravon in squadron formation; collided with Westland Limousine G-EAFO both machines being wrecked. A description of the Westland Limousine may be read on Wikipedia where it is described as light transport biplane with provision for three passengers and a pilot in an enclosed cabin, the pilot being seated behind the passengers but with his controls at a higher level and with provision for his seat to be raised so that his head protruded through the roof of the cabin.

Pilot Officer Robert Matheson's short service commission had been *Gazetted* as recently as 21st April 1925, issue 33040, page 2686, with seniority from the last day of March 1925. Promotion followed in the usual way, but in 1929, he 'blotted his copybook' and found himself facing a General Court Martial. Although escaping dismissal from the service, the consequences were serious and his rank [now flying officer] was reduced in seniority by no less than thirty three months.

His release from the Royal Air Force is reported in the list of officers granted short service commissions in 1925 [Appendix C].

It has come to our attention that in September 1992, the aviation magazine *Wingspan* carried an article regarding the Fairey Fawn which in turn prompted a letter from a reader who enclosed three photographs and indicated that the pilot of the Fawn was *"Pilot Officer Mattason [needs verification] and the observer was AC2 Wells."* The writer also gave the names of the two persons sitting in the Limousine, subsequently amended, as Major Laurence Pratt Openshaw, Westland's Chief Test Pilot and a Mr Robert Arthur Bruce. Neither were injured, though quite shaken by the sudden impact. The three photographs referred too were supplied by P Halliday of High Wycombe and the amendments to names comes from Col Bruggy whom the authors acknowledge.

Friday 28 August 1925
111 Squadron P/O H Peck +
Siskin IIIDC J7181
T/o Duxford for continuation training during which pilot Officer Hugh Peck came into collision a few miles ESE of the airfield with the Siskin summarised below, the tragedy occurring at around 1150 over Hinxton Grange.

111 Squadron F/O H Butlin +
Siskin IIIDC J7553 P/O D De Robeck +
T/o Duxford for a training sortie and destroyed in the manner described above. Harry Butlin received a short service commission on 11th August 1922, *Gazetted* on the 22nd August in issue 32740, page 6163. The two pupil pilots, Hugh Peck and Robert De Robeck were both aged 18, had been granted their short service commissions earlier in the year on the last day of March 1925, their names appearing in the paper's edition of 21st April 1925, issue 33040, page 2686.

An account of the accident was published the next day in *The Glasgow Herald* an extract reading: *"A special representative of the Press Association telephoning last night from Hinxton Grange says the accident occurred yesterday just before noon, when two biplanes from Duxford Military Aerodrome collided when on thousand feet up in the sky near Hinxton Grange, a well known estate, and crashed down into a cut cornfield close to the Cambridge-Newmarket Road and a mile or so from the aerodrome. There are no house in the vicinity.*

"The machines were seen to fall by some harvesters, who ran to the spot only to find three aviators dead in the wreckage of the 'planes. One of the machines in falling flattened out and was smashed to match-wood. The other dived and buried its nose in the ground, with its tail sticking up. The conditions were apparently ideal for flying, and the land thereabout is very flat. Assistance was sent from the aerodrome, and the bodies were taken to the hospital in the aerodrome. The machines came down at a distance of over a quarter of a mile apart. The cause of the accident is at present unknown. Both machines were making ordinary service flights.

"Flying Officer Harry Butlin, who is an instructor, and Flying Officer [sic] *Dermot de Robeck were in one machine, and Pilot Officer Hugh Peck was alone in the other.*

"The remains of one machine which was smashed up were soon cleared away by a squad of mechanics from the aerodrome, but it took some hours to dig up the other machine and clear it away. An earlier report which stated that another officer was injured was incorrect. Flying Officer Butlin had seen service in France at the end of the war."

Prior to this fatal accident, Flying Officer Butlin had been involved in a ground collision at Duxford on 12th December 1924 while at the controls of Siskin III J7153, his aircraft being struck by Siskin III J7158. A Court of Inquiry was held and the findings were duly noted as: *"The cause of the accident was in our opinion that [I] the pilot continued to taxi his attention on the tarmac instead of on what he was doing & [II] the mechanics on Siskin No. 153 were employed in the hangar and did not meet it as it was taxied in [III] the Court are of opinion that the primary responsibility for the accident rests with the pilot, vide reason [I]. A.O.C. concurs."*

Earlier still, and he had been injured in a motorcycle accident in Lincoln on 18th September 1923 during which he fractured his right clavicle, the injury being deemed not serious. He was on duty at the time and was attached to 2 FTS Digby.

SEPTEMBER

Monday 14 September 1925
60 Squadron F/O C J Pooley Safe
DH.9A E728
T/o Peshawar but swung violently and ran into E8646 which although damaged was repaired and continued in service. Flying Officer Cecil James Pooley had been granted a short service commission on 19th September 1922, *Gazetted* in issue 32744, page 6715.

Monday 21 September 1925
502 Squadron SR F/O H C Evans Injured
Avro 504K E9410 AC2 V E Giles Safe
T/o Aldergrove and in attempting to avoid flying into a tree at Tirgracey in Co. Antrim stalled and crashed. Flying Officer Henry Collins Evans was a permanent officer appointed on 20th December 1923, with seniority of rank backdated precisely one year [LG 8 January 1924, issue 32896, page 269].

The first of the Special Reserve squadrons, '502' formed at Aldergrove in Northern Ireland on 15th May 1925, and assigned as a 'heavy bomber' squadron. Vickers Vimy commenced arriving in June along with secondary types such as Avro 504s to assist with pilot training. The loss of E9410 was the squadron's first serious accident.

Extensive coverage was given to the crash, the following being reported by the *Belfast News-Letter* on the Wednesday following the crash.

'Fatal Aeroplane Crash'
'How Flying-Officer Evans was Killed'
'Inquest at Antrim'

"The circumstances surrounding the death of Flying Officer Henry Collins Evans, aged 24 years, who was fatally injured on Monday evening through the crashing of an aeroplane, of which he was the pilot, at Tirgracay, near Antrim, were investigated yesterday by Dr. J J Adams, JP, Coroner for Antrim district, and a jury, of which Mr. James Abernethy was the foreman. The proceedings took place in the boardroom of the Massereene Hospital. Flight Lieutenant Ralph Chevalier Preston was present on behalf of the Royal Air Force, and Head Constable Magowan watched proceedings on behalf of the police authorities.

"The first witness called was Flight-Commander Charles Francis Toogood, officer in charge of Aldergrove, who gave evidence of identification. He last saw deceased at the aerodrome the previous day at 1-40 p.m., when he gave him instructions to take out an Avro machine, E9410. The machine had been tested previously that morning. It was in perfect condition, and passed as airworthy. He did not see deceased again until after he had received the injuries. He was alive then. Witness heard of the accident at about half-past two, and came to where the machine was lying on the ground at Tigracay, but when he got there, the injured man had been removed to hospital. The machine was then lying as it had crashed, and badly damaged. The machine went up about seven o'clock, and landed about 12-15 p.m., being sent up again at about a quarter to two.

"Flying Officer Victor John Hatton, RAF Aldergrove, said he tested the machine at eleven o'clock in the morning, and was up for a flight, remaining in the air for an hour and a quarter. He found the machine in perfect order, and the engine all right. There were three machines the air together in formation, but he tested the machine before joining the formation.

"To the Foreman - The deceased was not with him when he test the machine.

"Answering the Coroner, witness said when he landed he signed the inspection book "O.K."

"Second-Class Air Craftsman Victor Edward Giles. RAF Aldergrove, No. 502 Bombing Squadron, who accompanied the ill-fated officer on the flight, said the machine was ground-tested for the engine at a quarter to two, and went up at ten minutes to two, with Flying-Officer Evans in charge of the 'plane. After they started they went up 3,000 feet, the machine going all right. They went in the direction of Belfast, and after flying for fifteen or twenty minutes they turned in the direction of Antrim, still keeping at the same altitude. They circled Antrim two or three times, and the officer then pointed to the field and did a series of stalling turns to lose height. To do that he had to stop the engine for a few seconds and start it again. The officer intended to land on that field. Witness thought the officer intended to land and take off there, as it was a fairly large field to practice on. It was usual to have such a field for a forced-landing place close to an aerodrome.

"Coroner - What was the approximate height when the officer pointed to the field?

"Witness - About 2,000 feet

'What occurred then? - He then side-slipped towards the field.

"What height was the machine then? - He came down to about 40 or 50 feet from the ground, and turned the machine round to take the full length of the field.

'The Fatal Tree'

"Head-Constable Magowan - What impression then did you get? - I noticed a tree in front.

"And what did the pilot do then? - He pulled up the nose of the machine to clear the tree. The pilot then stood up in the cockpit, and the machine struck the ground.

"Head-Constable Magowan - Did you jump out before the machine crashed? - No, it was took sudden.I waited in the cockpit until the machine struck the ground, then I go out and assisted Flying-Officer Evans.

"Replying to the Coroner, the witness said he was strapped in, and the flying officer was strapped in the front cockpit. Some civilians assisted him to get the injured officer out.

Coroner - Did the machine travel any distance after striking the ground? - It nose-dived and twisted.

"When he came right over the tree was he not able to go farther on? No, the machine stalled.

"Flight-Lieutenant Preston said that when the machine lost speed it stalled and came down, nose first. It had to do a certain speed to keep in the air.

"Craftsman Giles, further examined, said his officer did not speak to him after the machine struck, as he was unconscious. Witness sent for a doctor, and the officer was conveyed to the Massereene Hospital. He did not know of any other machine which attempted to land in a field outside the aerodrome.

"The Coroner - In your opinion the machine went right the whole way round until it came down about fifty feet from the ground, and you were going to alight in this particular field and there was a tree in front of you and he put the nose of the machine up to get over the tree, but as soon as he got over the tree the machine stalled and came down nose first.

"The witness said that was what happened. The engine stopped.

"Head-Constable Magowan - Would starting the engine have brought it up again? - There was no attempt made to start it again.

"Did the machine clear the tree without the engine going, but with the speed on? - Yes.

"The Coroner - From the start of the flight until you went over the tree you saw nothing wrong with the engine? - That is so.

"Flight-Lieutenant Preston said that if a machine always landed at the aerodrome the flying officers got used to it. In flying it might happen that some day the engine would cease working and they would have to make a forced-landing, so it was a good thing for an officer to practice landing in a field which, he thought, would be large enough for that purpose. In this case the flying officer perhaps thought that this field was a suitable one to land in and saw the tree too late. It was scarcely correct to say that they had a field for forced-landing near their aerodrome. Officers practised forced-landing, but they had no authority to land in anyone's field. An officer could, however, come low down and rise again.

"The Coroner - Would he do this without any authority being given?

"Flight-Lieutenant Preston - Yes; on his own initiative.

"The Coroner - If he had started his engine could he have gone on and been all right?

"Craftsman Giles - Yes, if he had started it again.

"The Coroner - The machine was all right? - Yes.

"Flight-Lieutenant Preston said it was difficult to say if he could have got his engine going again. It was what was known as a rotary engine, and the machine might have been going so slowly that it would have been difficult to pick up again. Mr. Evans might have made efforts to get it going again and failed. Arrangements were made for machines to be watched all the time they were in the air, and in the case of a crash the doctor was notified.

"Dr. T B H Scott, Antrim, said that on receiving a message that the aeroplane had crashed he went at once to the scene of the accident. The injured officer was taken to Massereene Hospital, where he died about half an hour after admission. The deceased had received severe lacerations of the right side, the right leg, and the knee, while his right forearm was also broken, and badly lacerated, but the cause of death was compression and laceration of the brain, due to severe cerebral injury. When witness saw him deceased was quite unconscious.

"Dr. Hunter, Crumlin, Medical Officer to the Air Force at Aldergrove, said he saw the injured officer in hospital before he died, but he was unconscious. He corroborated Dr. Scott as to the cause of death, and said the body was extensively injured from head to feet.

'Practicing Forced Landings;

"This concluded the evidence, and the Coroner, addressing the jury, said it was perfectly clear from the evidenceas to what had happened. Flying-Officer Evans was sent out on this particular machine, on which he had previously made a complete flight. He made his flight all right, and was back very close to the aerodrome when he wanted to practice a

forced-landing on a field near Freemount. So far as they know he did this off his own initiative. No orders were given to him to do so as far as they know, and as far as the witnesses examined were concerned. Perhaps, therefore, he landed on his own initiative, and it seemed that that was done occasionally - as one of the officers had stated - for if they always landed on the same place they got quite accustomed to it, and in the event of something happening when they were flying - say for fog or something else - and they wished to land in some other place, they practised it occasionally when out. Probably this poor officer thought he saw a very suitable field to alight in, and brought down his machine, but when he came pretty near the ground he found there was a tree in the way, and to avoid it he let his machine rise up, the result being that when he went over the tree the machine stalled- the force was not sufficient to carry it on- and nose-dived into the ground, the officer being so badly injured that he died soon afterwards.

"Continuing, the Coroner said that he was glad that Craftsman Giles was able to be present, for he had given them a clear account of what had happened, and he himself had had a marvellous escape. He might mention that since the aerodrome was opened at Aldergrove this was the first case of fatal injury in connection with flying there, and it spoke very well both for officers and machines. Another matter had been cleared up there, and that was that the machine was perfectly worthy and satisfactory in every way, so Mr. Evans' death was not due to any defect in the aeroplane, but to an error of judgement. There was no blame attachable, as far as he could see, to either the officers or the aerodrome authorities.

"The jury returned a verdict in accordance with the medical evidence, and added that no blame was attachable to anyone as they were satisfied that the machine was in perfect order.

"It was decided, on the motion of the Coroner, seconded by Mr. Abernethy, to send a letter of sympathy to the relatives of the deceased. Head-Constable Magowan, on behalf of the Royal Ulster Constabulary, associated himself with the expression of sympathy."

Thursday 24 September 1925

17 Squadron F/Lt A W Cuddon-Davis + Shorncliffe Military Cemetery
7F.1 Snipe E6490

T/o Hawkinge and totally destroyed in a crash on Castle Hill on the outskirts of Folkestone. Flight Lieutenant Arthur Wilfred Cuddon-Davis, previously described as Arthur Bottoms, was granted a short service commission on 30th January 1920 [see page 274 of my third volume]. This was cancelled on 12th December 1922, on which date he was appointed to a permanent commission [LG 12 December 1922, issue 32776, page 8799]. The crash was attributed to failure of the wings.

The Sussex History Forum website, which the authors have pleasure in acknowledging, carries three extracts pertaining to this accident, the first being an extract from the *Western Daily Press* published on the following Monday: *"The important announcement that the Air Ministry had decided to equip all RAF machines with parachutes was made by a flying officer at the inquest near Folkestone, on Saturday, on Flight-Lieut. A W Cuddon Davies* [sic] *whose machine crashed fatally on Thursday. It was said that Lieut. Cuddon Davies had been acting as a target for a camera-gun test by another officer when his machine suddenly nose-dived. The finding of the Court of Inquiry was that the accident was due to the breaking of the starboard wing, owing to overstrain resulting from performing evolutions in the air. The verdict at the inquest was one of "Death from Misadventure.""*

A related source suggests it was the left wing that failed, while the *Folkestone, Hythe, Sandgate & Cheriton Herald* in their issue of Saturday, 3rd October 1925, reports an account of Flight Lieutenant Cuddon-Davis's funeral: "..... *took place with full military honours at Shorncliffe Military Cemetery on Monday. On Sunday night the remains were conveyed from Hawkinge to the Garrison Church and a requiem mass was conducted on Monday morning. In the afternoon the cortege proceeded to the Cemetery, where the last rites were conducted by Father Parisotti, Catholic Chaplin to the Forces. The coffin, which was draped with the Union Jack, was carried on a trailer drawn by a tender, and was accompanied by a firing party with arms reversed. Eight of the deceased's brother officers acted as pall-bearers. After the committal service three volleys were fired over the grave and the "Last Post" was sounded by a trumpeter of the Royal Air Force."*

60 Squadron Sgt D Munro Safe See 27 August 1926
DH.9A J599

T/o Kohat and wrecked in a crash at Whad. Please refer to 22nd January 1925, for details concerning Sergeant Munro's previous accident.

Friday 25 September 1925

29 Squadron F/Lt B R Carter AFC +
Grebe II J7385

T/o Duxford in the company of the Grebe summarised below and when at 1,500 feet over Elmdon, a village in Essex some 7 miles ESE of Royston, Cambridgeshire, came into a midair collision, both fighters falling out of control. Flight Lieutenant Basil Royston Carter had been appointed to a permanent commission as recently as 1st July 1925 [LG 30th June 1925, issue 33062, page 4370]. According to Air-Britain's *J File* J7385 was repaired and following service with 56 and 25 Squadrons was taken to RAE Farnborough where it was one of two Grebes modified for trials suspended beneath the R33 airship, one such trial using J7385 taking place on 21st October 1926. The second Grebe was J7400 which was later converted to a dual control trainer and sold to New Zealand as NZ503. A third Grebe II J7408 is also said to be have been modified for the R33 trials while J7587 is also mentioned in connection with the trials.

29 Squadron Sgt T J McGrath +
Grebe II J7395
T/o Duxford and lost in the circumstances described above. A report on this accident appeared in *The Guardian from London* in its edition of 28th September 1925 [which also gave an account of the Folkestone crash 24-hours previously] *"No definite explanation as to the cause of the collision in the air by Flight Lieutenant Basil Royston Carter and Pilot Sergeant Thomas James McGrath of the 29th Fighter Squadron attached to the Duxford Aerodrome, who met their death at Elmdon on Friday morning, was given at the inquest on Saturday. The accident occurred while three machines were carrying out practice attacks on two other machines. Evidence having been given that the machines were tested in the morning of the flight, Flying Officer William Alfred Pattershall said he was flying in one machine, while there were two other machines flown by Carter and McGrath. They were all practising and attack on two target machines. They had made one attack, and manoeuvred for position for a second. Flight Lieutenant Carter gave the signal and the attack was proceeded with, and on coming out of his dive witness saw a machine falling to earth. He tried to catch sight of the other aeroplane, but failed, and he then flew back to the aerodrome to report. Three machines were in one formation, and there were also two target machines. He could give no explanation as to how the collision occurred. A farmer of Elmdon said he saw one machine hit another. One fell immediately, pieces flying in all directions. The other flew for a short distance further and then made a spiral dive and crashed to earth. The Coroner found that the men had accidentally crashed to the ground, receiving injuries from which they died whilst flying in the execution of their duty."*

Similar reports appeared in a number of papers, one stating that the fighters fell on land owned by a local Justice of the Peace, Mr. J F Wilkes of Lofthall Estate, who gave evidence that he and his groom went to the scene of both crashes and together extricated the bodies of the pilots. From the evidence given at the inquest that one machine flew for a minute or two after the collision before falling out of control suggests this might have been J7385. These were the first fatalities involving the Gloster Grebe.

Sergeant Thomas James McGrath had undoubtedly seen active service in the *Great War* though in what capacity it is difficult to say for his number 402111 comes in the block 400000 - 410432 allocated in September 1918 to unspecified transferees.

OCTOBER

Friday 2 October 1925
20 Squadron F/O E T O'N Hogben Injured
Bristol F.2b
T/o Kohat and believed to have crashed on the airfield, or close by. Flying Officer Edgar Thomas O'Neil Hogben died from his injuries on the 5th of October. He had been seconded from the Royal Artillery.
Officer

Monday 5 October 1925 On this day at Henlow where 43 Squadron was stationed, Flying Rose introduced a young Leading Aircraftman by the name of Arthur John 'Bill' Pegg to the exciting world of becoming a Royal Air Force pilot. The young Pegg already have five years of service life under his belt; three years as a Cranwell apprentice and two as a fitter with 9 Squadron at Manston. His first flight was in an Avro 504K H3105 and lasted for thirty-five minutes during which a height of 3,000 feet was attained. So began the flying carrier of Bill Pegg who would become Bristol Aeroplane Company's Chief Test Pilot who is probably now best remembered for putting one of the Britannia prototypes G-ALRX into the mud of the River Severn following an inflight engine fire on Thursday, 4th February 1954.

Tuesday 13 October 1925
8 Squadron Sgt T A Graham Injured
DH.9A J7102 AC1 R Stanton Injured
T/o Hinaidi and while in flight a con rod fractured severing a pipe which in turn led to a fire breaking out. Sergeant Thomas Alexander Graham effected a forced-landing at the junction of the Lesser Dab and Tigris rivers. Very Sadly, he sustained multiple burns and passed away five days later. His service number 327517 identifies him as an ex-**b**oy airman who joined the Royal Air Force between December 1918 and March 1919.

Aircraftman Ridley Stanton also suffered burns, but of a lesser nature and he recovered. His service number 352796 identifies him as joining after September 1919.

58 Squadron Avro 504K H2305 Collied on the ground at Worthy Down with one of the squadron's Virginia Vs J7427, which was little damaged, but it is belied the Avro was *"hors d'Combat."*

NOVEMBER

Friday 20 November 1925
29 Squadron P/O C W M Smith +
Grebe II
T/o Eastchurch for armament practice and misjudged his recovery when diving on a target anchored off Leysdown-on-Sea on the Isle of Sheppey. Pilot Officer Cecil William Montague Smith was one of thirteen Pilot Officers granted a short service commission as reported in *The London Gazette* of 8th July 1924, issue 32954, page 5255.

The following press report, under the headline *'Pilot Officer Killed at Leysdown - Tragic Ending to a Good Dive'*
'Jury's Verdict of "Accidental Death"'
appeared in Thursday, November 26th's, 1925 edition of *Sheerness Times*. The paper's reporter wrote down a very full description of events:

"Mr. E Cecil Harris, County Coroner, held an inquiry at the Air Station, Eastchurch, on Monday afternoon, with regard to the death of a young pilot officer attached to the Royal Air Force Station, who met his death while carrying out target practice over the flats at Leysdown on Friday, Nov. 20th. The Coroner sat with a jury comprised of Messrs. George Y Dickson [foreman], Charles H Byrne, Charles Godden, Arthur H Newman, William J Barter, Charles Graveley and Henry W Tomlin.

"PC Mummery, stationed at Eastchurch, acted as Coroner's officer, and Sergt. G Collins was also in attendance.

"The first witnessed called was father of the deceased, Albert John Smith, of Ilford, who identified the body as that of his son, Pilot Officer Cecil William Montague Smith, bachelor, aged 27 years.

"Flying Officer John Leslie Wingate, stationed at Eastchurch, stated that on Friday last he witnessed the accident as he was flying round his target off Leysdown, at a height of 2,000 feet, to mark the pupil's shooting as they came over. The machine in which the deceased was flying had dived four times on the target, and the officer was shooting extremely well. After each dive deceased pulled out in a left-hand turn, which appeared to witness to be rather close to the water. His last dive was the best one of the lot, and he fired three "bursts" and pulled out of his dive, performing a steep turn to the left, turning through an angle of approximately 160 degrees. Witness saw the left wing of the machine tip and strike the water, the machine breaking up at once. Deceased was diving off the left, and when he crashed he had turned and was heading for land, when the machine struck the water. The machine he was flying was a single-seater Grebe.

"At what height does the firing commence? - About a thousand feet. He had fired two 200 rounds previously, and was firing the third 200 rounds.

"Witness, continuing, said that the rule was that they should not go below three hundred feet, because water was deceptive. He had warned the deceased on this point. It was a good day for that kind of practice, because there were some "white horses" on the sea, which made the judging of distance much easier.

"Had he any instrument which would give him some idea that he was 300 feet from the water? - The altimeter is not a reliable guide during a dive, and the officers have been advised not to rely on it.

"Does it come to a question of using one's own judgment, pure and simple? - Yes, that is what it means, really.

"Had you known the deceased long? - I have only met him since he has been doing a course the last two months.

"This was not his first course on the flats? - Oh, no; he had completed his ground target course, and was doing exceptionally well on the last one.

"What, in your opinion, was the cause of the accident? - In my opinion the accident was due to deceased losing height on a steep near the water, there being a tendency to do this when flying over water.

"There was nothing wrong with the machine? - The machine was going alright, and he seemed to be flying perfectly well. The last dive was an exceptionally good one.

"Answering Mr. Smith, father of the deceased, witness said pilot officers were strapped in their machines. They had a strap over each shoulder and round the body. The deceased broke through his in the crash, and that accounted for the body being in the water.

"LAC Stanley Richard Brown stated that he recovered the body from the water just before three o'clock on Friday last, when out in a motor-boat that was in attendance during firing practice. The machine struck the water, as stated by the previous witness. Those in the motor-boat proceeded to the spot, and on arriving there found the deceased lying on his back among the wreckage. The motor-boat got as near as it could, and witness sent two men in a dinghy to pick the body up. After recovering the body they returned to shore. The officer was dead.

"Flight-Lieut. H H R Bayley, Medical Officer at Eastchurch Air Force Station, stated that he examined the bodywhen it was brought ashore, and found a punctured wound behind the left ear, causing a probable fractured skull, flesh wounds about the face and scalp, a fractured left femur, fractured left ankle, and both bones of the left forearm were fractured. There would be a great impact at the time of the accident, through the machine striking the water, and in his opinion death was probably instantaneous, and the deceased would know nothing about his injuries.

"After a question put by the foreman of the jury had been satisfactorily answered, the Coroner said he thought they had got all the material evidence that was necessary. In summing up, he pointed out that the deceased was going through a certain course at Eastchurch, and a witness had told them how he was keeping observance on the machines at a height of 2,000 feet. The deceased was doing extra good work, the last dive being the best one. In completing the dive it appeared that the deceased pulled out of it in a steep turn, and was heading for land when the machine struck the water. He had been warned that water was deceptive as regards judging distance. It was a similar accident to the last case upon which an inquiry was held. The deceased apparently lost height in doing a steep turn. The motor-boat was in attendance, and all that could be done was done by the authorities. Probably the deceased was killed immediately the machine struck the water and nothing could have saved his life.

"The jury briefly considered the facts, and through the Foreman returned a verdict of "Accidental Death," expressing sympathy with the relatives and the Air Force at the loss of such a promising officer.

"The deceased's home was at Ilford, and the coffin was conveyed to his home on Tuesday for internment in that district. During the war he served in the Manchester Regiment, and was wounded at St. Quentin. Prior to joining the Royal Air Force he also served in the King's African Rifles out in East Africa.

"The funeral arrangements were carried out by Mr. E T Kemp, of Sheerness and Queenborough."

Monday 23 November 1925
30 Squadron F/O J A Moore +
DH.9A H120 AC1 A A Rickaby +
T/o Kirkuk and was totally destroyed in a crash, followed by an all consuming fire. Flying Officer Joseph Albert Moore's short service commission had been granted as recently as 25th May 1925 [LG 5 June 1925, issue 33054, page 3793].

Aircraftman Arthur Algernon Rickaby's service number 354707 indicates he was one of many featured in this volume as joining the service at sometime between September 1919 and June 1925.

Thursday 26 November 1925
3 Squadron F/Lt J A Slater MC* DFC + Upavon [St. Mary the Virgin] Churchyard
7F.1 Snipe DC P/O W J R Early + Upavon [St. Mary the Virgin] Churchyard
T/o Upavon and within minutes of take off nose-dived and crashed at Pewsey near the airfield. Flight Lieutenant James Anderson Slater's military service started as a private in the Royal Sussex Regiment before being granted a temporary commission and training as an observer with the RFC. As such he was attached to 18 Squadron[Vickers FB.5], serving from 11th Nov- ember 1915, to 18th March 1916. On returning to England he re-mustered for pilot training and returned to the Western Front on 2nd August 1916, and joined 60 Squadron at St. André-aux-Bois [the squadron arrived here on the 3rd]; how-ever, on 18th August he was cross-posted to 1 Squadron at Bailleul, at the time both squadrons being equipped with Nieuport 17s.

On completion of his second tour of operations he returned to the UK for flying instructor duties, but on 27th July 1917, he reported to 64 Squadron [DH.5] at Sedgeford in Norfolk to command a flight, the squadron working up in preparation for deployment to France, and it was during his third operational tour that he excelled in aerial combat, finishing with a total of twenty-four combat victories [two with 1 Squadron and the rest with 64 Squadron]. The citations for his awards are reproduced in my summary for 11th July 1924, when he was attached to 1 Squadron at Hinaidi.

Postwar, and now a permanent officer, he served two tours as a flying instructor, the latter in Egypt at Abu Sueir. On 1st April 1925, and now back in the UK, he took up a post at Upavon attached to 3 Squadron. Born on 29th November 1896, James was just three days short of his 29th birthday. His pupil, Pilot Officer William John Reginald Early had been granted a short service commission as recently as April, details of this appearing in issue 33040, page 2686 of the *Gazette* published on 21st April 1925.

Friday 27 November 1925
56 Squadron *Not reported*
Grebe II J7289
T/o Biggin Hill and forced down after flying into a snowstorm near the tiny hamlet of Arpinge between Paddlesworth and Newington villages to the WNW and west of Folkesstone. From the first production batch of twelve aircraft [J7283-J7294] the Grebe had first been issued to 25 Squadron.

DECEMBER

Monday 14 December 1925
23 Squadron 7F.1 Snipe F2419 Wrecked in the manner summarised below.

43 Squadron P/O J R Addams Safe See 11 January 1927
7F.1 Snipe E6836
T/o Duxford for an aerobatic display and on landing collided with the Snipe featured above, both aircraft being damaged beyond repair. A Cranwell graduate, Pilot Officer James Ramage Addams received his flying badge on 11th December 1924, joining 43 Squadron for his first tour of squadron duties.

In a statement he said he thought he had landed clear of a line of parked aircraft. His flying hours are shown as 216 in total of which 112 were solo flights.

Wednesday 16 December 1925
9 Squadron LAC E E Dunn +
Avro 504K E2914
T/o Manston in company with other trainee pilots and during the course of the sortie Leading Aircraftman Edward Emmanuel Dunn entered a spin and collided with the Avro summarised below. At the time 9 Squadron, as with other operational squadrons, had the additional commitment of assisting with the air force's flying training programme and Leading Aircraftman Dunn was one of the first to lose his life while undergoing tuition at a front-line unit. His service number 345286 falls within the now familiar block of numbers allocated to civilian entrants between September 1919 and June 1925.

9 Squadron LAC W E Parrish Injured See 23 July 1926
Avro 504K E3798
T/o Manston briefed for a solo training sortie during which he was involved in a midair collision with the Avro flown by Leading Aircraftman Dunn. William Edward Parrish managed to land, though seriously injured, but an inspection of the damage to his aircraft deemed it to be beyond economical repair and it was struck off charge. He was taken to Ramsgate Hospital for treatment to injuries to his head and right ankle.

The inquest into the accident was published by *Blyth News, Ashington Post* on Monday, December 21st, 1925, under the headline *'Bound to Take Risks - Coroner's Comments at Air Crash Inquest'*

"The Royal Air Force is bound to take risks," said the East Kent Coroner at Friday night's inquest on Leading Aircraftman Edward Emmanuel Dunn [25], of Maidstone, who was killed on Wednesday through an air collision at Manston Aerodrome. In attempting a spiral dive from a height of 700 feethe crashed 200 feet below on to a machine flown by Leading Aircraftman Parrish, who is recovering in hospital.

"Returning a verdict of "Misadventure," the Coroner said that no amount of regulations would make flying safe, but it was necessary for the protection of the country that these young men should learn to fly, and all appreciated their courage."

This was followed by an equally dramatic report concerning a midair collision at Andover: *"Four men stationed at Andover Aerodrome had a remarkable escape in a collision between two aeroplanes in mid-air on Thursday. One 'plane crashed, and the other was brought safely to the ground.*

"The machines concerned were a Bristol Fighter flown by Flying Officer Lee and an Avro piloted by Flying Officer O'Brien Taint. In the collision the Avro'd tail was partly cut away, and the machine dropped in a field. The pilot was pinned under a portion of the machine, which was smashed, and received cuts to the face. His passenger, Aircraftman Bennett, was more seriously hurt about the head."

Sunday 20 December 1925
55 Squadron *Not reported*
DH.9A J7113
T/o Hinaidi and merely reported as *"crashed."* During its relatively brief service this DH had passed through the hands of 8 Squadron and 30 Squadron before acceptance by 55 Squadron.

APPENDICES
1925

Appendix A - Squadron Losses Table and Losses by Aircraft Type

Column 1 - Squadron

Column 2 - Aircraft type

Column 3 - Written off

Column 4 - Fatalities

1 Squadron	Sopwith 7F.1 Snipe	1	
3 Squadron	Sopwith 7F.1 Snipe DC	1	2
5 Squadron	Bristol F.2b	1	
6 Squadron	Bristol F.2b	2	3
8 Squadron	Airco DH.9A	1	1
9 Squadron	Avro 504K	2	1
11 Squadron	Fairey Fawn II	1	
14 Squadron	Bristol F.2b	1	
17 Squadron	Sopwith 7F.1 Snipe	1	1
19 Squadron	Avro 504K	1	1
20 Squadron	Bristol F.2b	1	1
23 Squadron	Sopwith 7F.1 Snipe	1	
25 Squadron	Gloster Grebe II	1	
27 Squadron	Airco DH.9A	1	2
28 Squadron	Bristol F.2b	1	1
29 Squadron	Gloster Grebe II	3	3
30 Squadron	Airco DH.9A	2	4
31 Squadron	Bristol F.2b	2	2
32 Squadron	Sopwith 7F.1 Snipe	2	2
	Gloster Grebe II	1	
43 Squadron	Sopwith 7F.1 Snipe	1	
55 Squadron	Airco DH.9A	2	2
56 Squadron	Gloster Grebe II	1	
58 Squadron	Avro 504K	1	
60 Squadron	Airco DH.9A	6	2
84 Squadron	Airco DH.9A	4	2
99 Squadron	Avro 504K	2	1
100 Squadron	Fairey Fawn II	2	2
111 Squadron	Armstrong Whitworth Siskin III DC	2	3
207 Squadron	Airco DH.9A	1	
208 Squadron	Bristol F.2b	1	1
502 Squadron SR	Avro 504K	1	1
Totals		51	38
	Airco DH.9A	17	13
	Armstrong Whitworth Siskin III DC	2	3
	Avro 504K	7	4
	Bristol F.2b	9	8
	Fairey Fawn II	3	2
	Gloster Grebe II	6	3
	Sopwith 7F.1 Snipe	6	3
	Sopwith 7F.1 Snipe DC	1	2
Totals		51	38

The authors cannot be certain that every 'write off' for the year has been identified, but the table shows quite a reduction in losses when compared with 1924.

Appendix B - Squadron Locations and Commanding Officers

Apart from a series of 'musical chairs' moves by the India based squadrons the year 1925 may be regarded as very much like 'treading water' though the defence of the realm was increased by the reforming of 23 Squadron at Henlow which along with 43 Squadron, also Henlow based, and 17 Squadron at Hawkinge were by the end of the year the sole UK based squadrons operating Tommy Sopwith's 7F.1 Snipe.

In addition to carrying out the duties of their primary roles, as will be seen from the summaries, a handful of squadrons continued to accept officers and airmen for primary flying instruction.

Worthy of note was the formation of a single squadron [more would follow] in what was termed the 'Special Reserve' and the establishment of the Auxiliary Air Force. Subsequently, squadron in the 'Special Reserve' would be absorbed in the Auxiliary Air Force.

1 Squadron	7F.1 Snipe	Hinaidi	01.01.25-31.12.25	
2 Squadron	Bristol F.2b	Manston	01.01.25-31.12.25	
3 Squadron	7F.1 Snipe/Woodcock II	Upavon	01.01.25-31.12.25	7F.1 Snipe withdrawn in October
4 Squadron	Bristol F.2b	Farnborough	01.01.25-31.12.25	
5 Squadron	Bristol F.2b	Dardoni	01.01.25-22.01.25	
		Kohat	22.01.25-15.10.25	
		Risalpur	15.10.25-31.12.25	
6 Squadron	Bristol F.2b	Mosul	01.01.25-31.12.25	
7 Squadron	Vimy	Bircham Newton	01.01.25-31.12.25	
8 Squadron	DH.9A	Hinaidi	01.01.25-31.12.25	
9 Squadron	Vimy/Virginia	Manston	01.01.25-31.12.25	Vimy withdrawn during June
11 Squadron	Fawn III	Netheravon	01.01.25-31.12.25	
12 Squadron	Fawn III	Andover	01.01.25-31.12.25	
13 Squadron	Bristol F.2b	Andover	01.01.25-31.12.25	
14 Squadron	Bristol F.2b	Ramleh & Amman	01.01.25-31.12.25	
XV Squadron	*Various*	Martlesham Heath	01.01.25-31.12.25	
16 Squadron	Bristol F.2b	Old Sarum	01.01.25-31.12.25	
17 Squadron	7F.1 Snipe	Hawkinge	01.01.25-31.12.25	
19 Squadron	Grebe II	Duxford	01.01.25-31.12.25	
20 Squadron	Bristol F.2b	Quetta	01.01.25-05.01.25	
		Peshawar	05.01.25-22.05.25	
		Kohat	22.05.25-12.10.25	
		Peshawar	12.10.25-31.12.25	
22 Squadron	*Various*	Martlesham Heath	01.01.25-31.12.25	
23 Squadron	7F.1 Snipe	Henlow	01.07.25-31.12.25	Reformed Home Defence squadron
24 Squadron	*Various*	Kenley	01.01.25-31.12.25	
25 Squadron	Grebe II	Hawkinge	01.01.25-31.12.25	
27 Squadron	DH.9A	Risalpur	01.01.25-26.05.25	
		Peshawar	26.05.25-12.10.25	
		Risalpur	12.10.25-31.12.25	
28 Squadron	Bristol F.2b	Peshawar	01.01.25-05.01.25	
		Quetta	05.01.25-31.12.25	
29 Squadron	Grebe II	Duxford	01.01.25-31.12.25	
30 Squadron	DH.9A	Kirkuk	01.01.25-31.12.25	
31 Squadron	Bristol F.2b	Ambala	01.01.25-31.12.25	
32 Squadron	Grebe II	Kenley	01.01.25-31.12.25	
39 Squadron	DH.9A	Spittlegate	01.01.25-31.12.25	
41 Squadron	Siskin III	Northolt	01.01.25-31.12.25	
43 Squadron	7F.1 Snipe	Henlow	01.01.25-31.12.25	
45 Squadron	Vernon	Hinaidi	01.01.25-31.12.25	
47 Squadron	DH.9A	Helwan	01.01.25-31.12.25	
55 Squadron	DH.9A	Hinaidi	01.01.25-31.12.25	
56 Squadron	Grebe II	Biggin Hill	01.01.25-31.12.25	
58 Squadron	Vimy/Virginia	Worthy Down	01.01.25-31.12.25	Vimy withdrawn during March
60 Squadron	DH.9A	Risalpur	01.01.25-28.05.25	
		Peshawar	28.05.25-15.10.25	
		Kohat	15.10.25-31.12.25	
70 Squadron	Vernon	Hinaidi	01.01.25-31.12.25	
84 Squadron	DH.9A	Shaibah	01.01.25-31.12.25	
99 Squadron	Aldershot/Hyderabad	Bircham Newton	01.01.25-31.12.25	Aldershot withdrawn in December
100 Squadron	Fawn II	Spittlegate	01.01.25-31.12.25	
111 Squadron	Grebe II/7F.1 Snipe/Siskin III	Duxford	01.01.25-31.12.25	Grebe II & 7F.1 Snipe withdrawn in January
207 Squadron	DH.9A	Eastchurch	01.01.25-31.12.25	
208 Squadron	Bristol F.2b	Ismailia	01.01.25-31.12.25	
216 Squadron	Vimy	Heliopolis	01.01.25-31.12.25	

Special Reserve Squadron

502 Squadron SR	Vimy	Aldergrove	15.05.25-31.12.25	Heavy bomber squadron

Auxiliary Air Force

600 Squadron AAF	DH.9A	Northolt	14.10.25-31.12.25	Day bomber duties
601 Squadron AAF		Northolt	14.10.25-31.12.25	Day bomber duties; awaiting aircraft
602 Squadron AAF	DH.9A	Renfrew	12.09.25-31.12.25	Day bomber duties
603 Squadron AAF	DH.9A	Turnhouse	14.10.25-31.12.25	Day bomber duties
1 Squadron	Squadron Leader E D Atkinson DFC AFC		In situ	See Appendix B 1924

2 Squadron	Squadron Leader L F Forbes	In situ	See Appendix B 1922
	Squadron Leader R E Saul DFC	2 March 1925	AV-M retirement 29 June 1944
3 Squadron	Squadron Leader J C Russell DSO mid *Croix de Guerre* [Belgium]	In situ	See Appendix B 1924
4 Squadron	Squadron Leader C H B Blount	In situ	See Appendix B 1921
	Squadron Leader J C Slessor MC mid	4 April 1925	MRAF retirement 31 December 1952
5 Squadron	Squadron Leader A J Capel	In situ	See Appendix B 1923
6 Squadron	Squadron Leader D S K Crosbie OBE	In situ	See Appendix B 1923
	Squadron Leader D F Stevenson OBE DSO MC* twice mid	13 November 1925	AV-M retirement 10 February 1948
7 Squadron	Squadron Leader E O Grenfell MC DFC AFC mid	In situ	See 1 Squadron 1923
	Squadron Leader J S T Bradley OBE	19 November 1925	AM retirement 27 October 1945
8 Squadron	Squadron Leader W A McClaughry DSO MC DFC three time mid Australia	In situ	See Appendix B 1924
9 Squadron	Squadron Leader A P V Daly	In situ	See Appendix B 1924
	Squadron Leader W J M Guilfoyle OBE MC six times mid Australia	19 January 1925	A/Cmdr retirement 21 September 1941
11 Squadron	Squadron Leader E A B Rice MC	In situ	See 6 Squadron 1921
12 Squadron	Squadron Leader A Gray MC	In situ	See Appendix B 1923
13 Squadron	Squadron Leader C C Durston	In situ	See Appendix B 1924
14 Squadron	Squadron Leader A N Gallehawk AFC	In situ	See Appendix B 1924
XV Squadron	Squadron Leader P C Sherren MC	In situ	See 60 Squadron 1921
16 Squadron	Squadron Leader J O Archer CBE	In situ	See Appendix B 1924
	Squadron Leader W A Coryton MVO DFC	30 September 1925	ACM retirement 5 May 1951
17 Squadron	Squadron Leader J Leacroft MC*	In situ	See Appendix B 1924
19 Squadron	Squadron Leader P Babington MC AFC	In situ	See 56 Squadron 1921
	Squadron Leader H W G Jones MC	23 July 1925	G/Capt killed 14 May 1943
20 Squadron	Squadron Leader C B Cooke mid	In situ	See Appendix B 1924
	Squadron Leader J B Cole-Hamilton twice mid	14 October 1925	AV-M died 22 August 1945
22 Squadron	Squadron Leader T H England DSC	2 March 1925	G/Capt retirement 14 June 1944
23 Squadron	Squadron Leader R Collishaw DSO* OBE DSC DFC three times mid	1 July 1925	See 30 Squadron 1921
24 Squadron	Squadron Leader R S Maxwell MC DFC* AFC	In situ	See Appendix B 1923
	Squadron Leader W H L O'Neill MC	27 August 1925	S/Ldr killed 5 October 1931
25 Squadron	Squadron Leader A H Peck DSO MC*	In situ	See Appendix B 1923
27 Squadron	Squadron Leader L M Bailey AFC	In situ	See Appendix B 1924
28 Squadron	Squadron Leader C S Wynne-Eyton DSO	In situ	See Appendix B 1924
29 Squadron	Squadron Leader M L Taylor AFC	In situ	See Appendix B 1924
30 Squadron	Squadron Leader J M Robb DFC	In situ	See Appendix B 1924
	Squadron Leader F H Coleman	5 June 1925	A/Cmdr retirement 29 October 1945
31 Squadron	Squadron Leader H S Powell MC	In situ	See Appendix B 1923
	Squadron Leader /Wing Commander J O Archer CBE	18 November 1925	See 16 Squadron 1924
32 Squadron	Squadron Leader H P Lale DFC mid	In situ	See Appendix B 1924
39 Squadron	Squadron Leader T Whittaker MC	In situ	See 28 Squadron 1922
	Squadron Leader H V Champion de Crepigny MC DFC	26 January 1925	See 60 Squadron 1922
41 Squadron	Squadron Leader G W Murlis-Green DSO* MC* three times mid *Croix de Guerre* [France[*Croix de Chevalier Croix de Guerre* [Belgium]	In situ	See Appendix B 1924
43 Squadron	Squadron Leader A F Brooks	1 July 1925	S/Ldr retired list 12 October 1932
45 Squadron	Squadron Leader R M Hill MC AFC mid	In situ	See Appendix B 1924
47 Squadron	Squadron Leader M Henderson DSO	In situ	See 216 Squadron 1921
	Squadron Leader R S Maxwell MC DFC* AFC	22 September 1925	See 24 Squadron 1923
55 Squadron	Squadron Leader E R L Corballis DSO	In situ	See Appendix B 1924
	Squadron Leader E D Johnson AFC mid	27 October 1925	A/Cmdr retirement 21 April 1944
56 Squadron	Squadron Leader Sir C J Q Brand KBE DSO MC DFC South Africa	In situ	See Appendix B 1923
	Squadron Leader F J Vincent DFC	22 September 1925	A/Cmdr retirement 8 February 1946
58 Squadron	Squadron Leader W H Longton DFC AFC	In situ	See Appendix B 1924
	Squadron Leader A T Harris AFC	25 May 1925	See 31 Squadron 1921
60 Squadron	Squadron Leader A W H James MC	In situ	See Appendix B 1924
	Squadron Leader T F Hazell DSO MC DFC	27 February 1925	See 55 Squadron 1923
70 Squadron	Squadron Leader T Q Studd DFC	In situ	See Appendix B 1924
	Wing Commander E W Norton DSC *Croix de Guerre* [Belgium]	1 December 1925	A/Cmdr retirement 24 February 1944
84 Squadron	Squadron Leader D E Stodart DSO DFC mid Australia	In situ	See Appendix B 1924
	Squadron Leader W B Farrington	2 June 1925	G/Capt retirement 9 February 1946
	Squadron Leader D E Stodart DSO DFC mid Australia	15 December 1925	See above
99 Squadron	Squadron Leader G R M Reid DSO MC*	In situ	See Appendix B 1924
	Squadron Leader L T N Gould MC	4 September 1925	G/Capt retired list 17 May 1943
	Squadron Leader W J Ryan MBE	1 October 1925	W/Cdr retired list 16 March 1931
100 Squadron	Squadron Leader H F A Gordon	In situ	See Appendix B 1923
	Squadron Leader L T N Gould MC DFC	10 October 1925	See 99 Squadron above
111 Squadron	Squadron Leader T F Hazell DSO MC DFC	In situ	See 55 Squadron 1923
	Flight Lieutenant H W Woollett DSO MC* *Chevalier Legion d'Honneur Croix de Guerre ave Palme* [France]	6 February 1925	S/Ldr resigned 3 February 1932
	Squadron Leader G W Robarts DFC	2 March 1925	W/Cdr retired list 23 May 1936
207 Squadron	Squadron Leader V Gaskell-Blackburn DSO AFC	In situ	See 55 Squadron 1923
208 Squadron	Squadron Leader H M Probyn DSO mid	In situ	See Appendix B 1924
	Squadron Leader A S C Stuart-MacLaren OBE MC DFC AFC	December 1925	S/Ldr retired list 1 June 1930
216 Squadron	Wing Commander L D D McKean OBE mid	In situ	See Appendix B 1924
502 Squadron SR	Flight Lieutenant E F Turner	15 May 1925	G/Capt retirement 9 November 1945
	Squadron Leader R D Oxland	3 June 1925	AV-M retirement 10 May 1946

600 Squadron AAF	Flight Lieutenant The Hon. H B Rodney MC	14 October 1925	
	Wing Commander A W H James MC	17 November 1925	See 60 Squadron 1924
601 Squadron AAF	Squadron Leader Lord E Grosvenor	1 August 1925	Died 26 August 1929
602 Squadron AAF	Squadron Leader C N Lowe MC DFC	14 September 1925	G/Capt retirement 7 October 1944
603 Squadron AAF	Squadron Leader J A McKelvie AFC	1 August 1925	

Annex

Squadron Leader Richard Ernest Saul was commissioned to the Army Service Corps four years to the date prior to Armistice Day. In early June 1916, he was accepted by the RFC for training as an observer, serving as such with 16 Squadron [BE.2 variants] from the August of that year, and prior to taking command of 2 Squadron had held similar responsibilities with 4 Squadron, 93 Squadron - both during the *Great War* - and post-armistice with 7 and 12 Squadrons in the Rhineland. His DFC, less citation, was published in the New Year's Honours list for 1919 [LG 1 January 1919, supplement 31098, page 96].

As a child John Cotesworth Slessor was struck down by the terrible affliction of polio which left him lame in both legs. Nevertheless, he overcame this disability and was accepted for training as a pilot, gaining RAeC Certificate No. 1447 on the 6th of July 1915. His operational service during the *Great War* was varied between attachment to home based squadrons, to service in Egypt and Sudan with 17 Squadron which was equipped with a mix of BE.2 types, Bristol Scouts and DH.2s. Back in the UK he was attached to 58 Squadron [various] for flight commander duties before going out to the Western Front for similar duties with 5 Squadron [RE.8] before returning home and, eventually, seeing out hostilities at the Central Flying School.

His MC was *Gazetted* on the 1st of January 1917, supplement 29886, page 41, without citation. On 1st January 1956, Cassell's published his major work as an author titled *The Central Blue - The Autobiography of Sir John Slessor, Marshal of the RAF* copies of which may be purchased on the secondhand books market.

The military service of Squadron Leader Donald Fasken Stevenson began as an officer commissioned to the Nottingham [Sherwood Foresters] Yeomanry but twelve months on, and in December 1916, he transferred to the RFC and won the MC as a flight commander flying BE.2 variants with 12 Squadron. *Gazetted* on 17th September 1917, the citation reads: *"For conspicuous gallantry and devotion to duty in carrying out three contact patrols in one day in bad weather, and at low altitudes. Although attacked by enemy machines in superior numbers, he drove them off, and by his fine reconnaissance work brought back valuable information.. He has at all times displayed indomitable pluck and initiative."*

Later, a First Bar was promulgated in *The London Gazette* on 26th July 1918: *"For conspicuous gallantry and devotion to duty while carrying out low-flying reconnaissances and contact patrols, under very heavy machine-gun, rifle, and anti-aircraft fire. In his patrols, often lasting many hours, and in bad weather conditions, he attacked enemy infantry, transport and batteries from a low level, using his machine gun and dropping bombs, frequently returning with his machine riddled with bullets, and the information he obtained was quite invaluable. His cheerful spirit, consistent dash, and fearlessness, and his magnificent work have set a splendid example to all in his squadron, and greatly encouraged them at a time when the casualties in it were extremely heavy "*

Interspersed between these two citations was that for his DSO awarded on 7th March 1918: *"For conspicuous gallantry and devotion to duty in obtaining photographs of a raid carried out by our troops which necessitated his flying through a barrage at a height of less than 1,000 feet. On another occasion he brought down a hostile machine. He was under heavy fire from the ground the whole time, and was eventually forced to land behind our lines owing to his petrol tank being shot through."*

During the Second World War he was appointed Air Officer Commanding No. 2 Group, Bomber Command, a Group from the very outset of hostilities had sustained horrendous casualties in both men and material [summaries showing these losses are reported in my Royal Air Force Bomber Command losses series up to the time that the Group became part of 2nd Tactical Air Force] and, it has to be said, that Air Vice-Marshal Stevenson did not endear himself to the squadrons under his command in insisting that low level operations by day should continue. It is noted that his tenure in command lasted for less than a year [17th February 1941-2nd January 1942] after he relinquished the temporary rank of air vice-marshal.

Although conjecture on my part, I suggest his seemingly indifference to the attritions being reported from the squadrons harks back to his time on the Western Front where he witnessed severe losses from the reconnaissance squadrons who flew countless sorties at low level, often in the face of hostile fire from the ground.

Oddly, his name is omitted from the list of Air Officers Commanding the Group as recorded in Appendix 30 of Philip Moyes' *Bomber Squadrons of the RAF and their Aircraft.*

Squadron Leader William James Yule Guilfoyle served as a flight commander with 1 Squadron AFC and 2 Squadron AFC, his MC being *Gazetted* on 3rd March 1917: *"For conspicuous gallantry in action. He carried out a daring bombing raid and made valuable reconnaissance under heavy fire during the same flight. He has at all times set a fine example."*

Bon in Llandello, Carmarthenshire, on 7th October 1890, Hubert Wilson Godfrey Jones was first commissioned to the 4th Battalion, The Welsh Regiment on 17th April 1913 [LG 13 May 1913, issue 28718, page 3441], subsequently transferring to the Royal Flying Corps and following pilot training joined 32 Squadron [DH.2] for operational service over the Western Front.

The citation for his MC, *Gazetted* 26th March 1917, supplement 300001, page 2984 reads: *"For conspicuous gallantry in action. With a patrol of three scouts he attacked a hostile formation of ten enemy machines. Although wounded, he continued the combat and drove down an enemy machine. Later, although again wounded, he remained with his patrol until the enemy retired."*

Appointed in August 1919, to a permanent commission the 1920s was spent mainly in flying duties, both military and civil for he was a keen competitor in the King's Cup air races of the time. Also in the '20s he assumed the surname 'Penderel' and saw service in the Middle East attached to 216 Squadron leading a flight of three Vickers Victoria on a flight from Heliopolis to CapeTown and return. For this achievement he was awarded the Air Force Cross which was personally conferred on him by HM the King at Buckingham Palace.

Attaining group captain rank on 1st January 1938, his service continued with various staff appointments before on 14th May 1943, he took off from Middle Wallop in Hurricane IIB HV895 and flew to Martlesham Heath where his aircraft took on a bomb for a low level test drop over the ranges at Orford Ness. Tragically, something went terribly wrong for the weapon exploded prematurely and he crashed into Sudbourne Marshes and he was killed instantaneously. Group Captain Hubert Wilson Godfrey Jones Penderel MC AFC is buried in Llanguicke [St. Ciwg] Churchyard.

Attached to the Indian Army, Captain William Hickley Lovell O'Neill, seconded RFC, was *Gazetted* with the MC on 8th March 1918, supplement 30563, page 2974. The citation was not reported. On 5th October 1931, he was a passenger aboard the Air Ministry's airship R101 G-FAAW which came down in bad weather with heavy loss of life at Beauvais in France. There are a number of websites devoted to this disaster.

Squadron Leader Francis John Vincent was one of three officers *Gazetted* with the DFC on 6th June 1924, issue 32943, page 4529, *"... for distinguished service rendered during operations in Iraq, 1922."* I suspect he was attached to 1 Squadron at Hinaidi.

Squadron Leader Lionel Thomas Nutcombe Gould was *Gazetted* with the MC on July 10th, 1917, in the Edinburgh edition, issue 13116, page 1401: *"For conspicuous gallantry and devotion to duty. He has done good and consistent valuable work while co-operating with the artillery, often under most difficult conditions. He has always set a splendid example to his squadron throughout."*

His death at the age of 54 was most tragic. Visiting his brother, a commander in the Royal Navy, he was found the morning after his arrival in a gas-filled room, the pipe to the fire having become disconnected. It is thought Group Captain Gould was trying to light the fire and was overcome by fumes. He is buried Fulbeck Churchyard in Lincolnshire. His son, Flying Officer Auriol Stephen Nutcombe Gould rests in South Queensferry Cemetery; he lost his life in a 197 Squadron Typhoon crash; he was just 20 years of age.

Like so many of his RFC contemporaries, service life started in the army; in Henry Winslow Woolletts' case with a commission in the Infantry [LG 19 November 1914, supplement 28980, page 9519] subsequently being attached to the 6th Battalion , Lincolnshire Regiment with which he served in the disastrous Gallipoli campaign, after which he decided he had enough soldering and put in a request to join the Royal Flying Corps.

Accepted, and by November 1916, he was on the Western Front flying DH.2s with 24 Squadron, later converting to the DH.5. As a fighter pilot he excelled, not only in forcing down hostile aircraft but also in the dangerous pursuit of destroying enemy observation balloons. Rested from operations in August 1917, he returned home to pass on his fighting knowledge as an instructor before returning to France and continuing his successful career as a scout pilot, this time with 43 Squadron [F.1 Camel].

The London Gazette 9th January 1918, supplement 30466, page 654, recorded his award of the MC: *"For conspicuous gallantry and devotion to duty in engaging three enemy aircraft and following them down to a low altitude behind the enemy's lines, destroying one driving down another out of control during the operations. He has done excellent work as a patrol leader, and has always displayed great gallantry in aerial combats, having brought down three other enemy machines in addition to those already mentioned."*

A First Bar was published in supplement 30761, page 7401, of the *Gazette* 22nd June 1918: *"For conspicuous gallantry and devotion to duty. On one occasion, when on offensive patrol, he dived on to an enemy plane, and fired 100 rounds in to it at 100 yards range, causing it to burst into flames and crash to the ground. He then dived on to another hostile machine, which went down in a spin and finally crashed to earth. On a latter occasion he attacked and brought down in flames two enemy observations balloons. The gallantry and skill exhibited by this officer have been most inspiring to his flight."*

On 16th September 1918, he was *Gazetted* with the DSO, supplement 30901, page 10875: *"For conspicuous gallantry and devotion to duty during recent operations. In two days during three patrols he destroyed eight enemy machines, making his total twenty-two. His leadership, dash and courage were of the highest order."*

He served very briefly [February 1941 to February 1942] in the Second World War as an acting pilot officer in the Training Branch of the Royal Air Force Volunteer Reserve. His death at the age of 74, was announced on the last day of October 1969.

To conclude, his impressive list of combat successes may be read on the Aerodrome website, which the authors acknowledge, which shows the destruction of five hostile aircraft achieved when flying with 24 Squadron, and nineteen aircraft and eleven balloons with 43 Squadron, the eleven balloons confirmed making him the highest scoring 'balloon buster' of the *Great War.*

Geoffrey Ward Robarts won the MC while ranked temporary lieutenant, the citation being published in *The Edinburgh Gazette* November 16th, 1916, issue 13012, page 2089: *"For conspicuous skill and gallantry when attacking hostile machines. On one occasion, when on offensive patrol, he brought down two machines."*

Oddly, considering his decorations for gallantry, the citations for these in respect of Squadron Leader Archibald Stuart Charles Stuart-MacLaren have, as yet, not come to light. What is readily available, and particularly on the History Net website [which the authors acknowledge] is an excellent account, written by Derek O'Connor, describing in detail Squadron Leader Stuart-MacLaren's attempt to fly around the world in a Vulture amphibian with Flying Officer William Noble Plenderleith*and Sergeant W H Andrews.

It has to be said the Air Ministry were not enthusiastic and although the attempt was made, Squadron Leader Stuart-Maclarn, a permanent officer, was reduced to half-pay. Taking off from Calshot in G-EBHO on 25th March 1924, the flight was dogged with trouble almost from the start and eventually the crew had to change to the reserve Vulture G-EBGO in order to continue. This, too, ended in failure when G-EBGO ditched just off the western Aleutians and was damaged beyond repair; the date - 4th August 1924. Their valiant attempt was over at 13,100 miles.

Obliged to leave the service owing to ill-health, Squadron Leader Stuart-Maclaren died on the island of Madeira on 18th June 1943, his heart finally giving out as a consequence of the rheumatic fever contracted during his service in Egypt.

* Flying Officer Plenderleith had been mentioned in despatches for distinguished service in the Hinterland of Aden during February 1922, *Gazetted* 10th October 1922, issue 32754, page 7134.

Appendix C - Officers Granted Short Service Commissions

The majority of officers granted short service commissions during the year had no previous military experience. Service numbers for the year commenced with 19099 and ran in sequence to 19250 when a new block commencing 22001 was introduced. Initially, the sequence followed a logical pattern until commissions notified in *The London Gazette* published on 25th September 1925. Despite the illogical sequences of numbers I am confident that all short service commissioned officers for the year have been identified, the block running to 22099. The authors suspect that 22100 was unused and 22101 was the first issue for officers short service commissioned in 1926.

LG 2 January 1925, issue 33008, page 56 - Seniority 18th December 1924

FLYING OFFICER

19099 PARRY John Howard S/Ldr 01.05.45 Resigned
Appointed to a commission in the Administrative and Special Duties Branch class CC and in the rank of flight lieutenant 11th September 1946 [LG 29th October 1946, supplement 37770, page 5304].

LG 13 January 1925, issue 33011, pages 301 and 302 - Seniority 6th and 7th January and terms of engagement seven and five years respectively

FLYING OFFICER
3

19100 GANDY Gerard Leslie F/Lt 06.01.32 Relinquished
Formerly served with the Royal Navy. Returned to service and still in the General Duties Branch promoted to squadron leader [temporary] on 1st June 1940 [LG 7 June 1940, issue 34866, page 3438]. W/Cdr 10.02.54 Relinquished
19101 HILL Percy F/Lt 06.01.32 Relinquished
Lieutenant Indian Army retired.
19102 WOLEDGE Cecil George Charles F/O 06.01.32 Relinquished
Lieutenant Indian Army retired. Returned to service and received a commission in the Administrative and Special Duties Branch in the rank of pilot officer employed for the duration of hostilities with effect from 19th July 1940 [LG 13 August 1940, issue 34920, page 4947]. Served throughout the remainder of the war and beyond until: S/Ldr 10.02.54 Relinquished

Block 19103 - 19126

19103 BAKER Kenelm Courtenay F/Lt 10.02.54 Relinquished
19104 BOWMAN George Samuel John P/O 05.02.26 Terminated
19105 BRYANTON William Francis F/O 06.01.34 Relinquished
I am of the opinion that Flying Officer William Francis Bryanton was either Rhodesian by birth or that he went out to Rhodesia after relinquishing his commission. Whatever the case *The London Gazette* for 3 January 1941, issue 35032, page 65 beneath the heading Royal Air Force Volunteer Reserve General Duties Branch names a William Francis Bryanton receiving a commission for the duration of hostilities in the rank of pilot officer with effect from 1st April 1940, his service number being 80057 which is in line with numbers allocated to Rhodesian airmen. During the course of the war he transferred from the General Duties Branch to the Administrative and Special Duties Branch, relinquishing his commission in the rank of squadron leader [temporary wing commander] OBE on reversion to Southern Rhodesian forces, 13th April 1946 [LG 16 July 1946, supplement 37651, page 3663. He was mentioned in despatches in the King's Birthday Honours list for 8th June 1944 [LG 8 June 1944, supplement 36544, page 2613].
19106 CHUBB Philip Bernard F/O 06.01.35 Relinquished
Granted a commission in Class A of the Reserve of Air Force Officers, General Duties Branch, 23rd November 1937 [LG 30 November 1937, issue 34459, page 7520]. F/O 22.01.39 Resigned
19107 COPPERTHWAITE Percy Kenyon P/O 25.11.25 Resigned
Percy Kenyon Copperthwaite was granted a commission as a 2nd Lieutenant in Regular Army, Emergency Commissions, and attached to the Royal Armoured Corps, Royal Tank Regiment, on 29th August 1940 [LG 3 October 1940, supplement 34959, page 5820]. Paul McMillan reports that postwar he emigrated to Australia where he died on Wednesday, 4th March 1964 in the State of South Australia.
19108 CRIPPS Geoffrey Walter P/O + 21.10.25 4 FTS Abu Sueir
Pilot Officer Geoffrey Walter Cripps died when his unidentified DH.9A dived into the ground on, or near, the airfield.
19109 ELLIS Edwin John W/Cdr 10.02.54 Relinquished
19110 EVANS-EVANS* Howard Arthur G/Capt 01.07.56 Retirement
19111 FAGAN Thomas Philip Feltrim Patrick A/Cmdr 07.01.51 Retirement
Air Commodore Thomas Philip Feltrim Patrick Fagan died on Monday, 22nd April 1985.
19112 GUNTON Herbert Desmond F/O 01.05.29 Relinquished
On account of ill-health [LG 21 May 1929, issue 33497, page 3405].
19113 HAMILTON Alan Edward P/O 08.07.26 Resigned
19114 HOMERSHAM DCM Francis Stanhope W/Cdr 10.02.54 Relinquished
19115 INKSTER John Andrew Edward F/O 13.08.29 Relinquished
On account of ill-health [LG 13 August 1929, issue 33525, page 5278]. On 26th April 1940, he was granted a commission as a pilot officer for the duration of hostilities in the Administrative and Special Duties Branch [LG 14 May 1940, issue 34849, page 2899] and was issued with a new service number 78806. However, by 2nd December 1940, when he was transferred to the General Duties Branch, he had reverted to his original service number of 19115 [LG 18 July 1941, issue 35222, page 4136]. W/Cdr 10.02.54 Relinquished
While attached to 30 Squadron in Iraq, Flying Officer John Andrew Edward Inkster had a 'brush with death' when his DH.9A came into collision at 6,000 feet with a similar machine on 25th April 1927. See my summary for this incident and additional information.
19116 McGOVERNE Lionel Beaumont F/O 04.06.29 Resigned
19117 MEE George Percy F/O 23.11.27 Relinquished
On account of ill-health [LG 22 November 1927, issue 33331, page 7424]. This may have resulted from the crash that he was involved in on 26th July 1926, when he was a passenger aboard a 45 Squadron Vernon that lost power on take off from Hinaidi and came down on the roof of a hangar - please refer to my summary for details.
19118 MOODY Brian Elgar S/Ldr 10.02.54 Relinquished
19119 SHAW Geoffrey Maynard Edward F/Lt + 12.01.31 2 FTS Digby
Flight Lieutenant Geoffrey Maynard Edgar Shaw was the pilot of Vickers Vimy F9178 which departed Brooklands on a delivery flight to Digby where it would be taken over by No. 2 Flying Training School. Aboard the Vimy was Pilot Officer John Edward Furlong Chapman, aged 29, Flight Sergeant Alfred George Rogers, aged 34, and Aircraftman Cecil Alfred James Jones. During the flight north the crew strayed well to the west of their intended track and in making a precautionary landing overshot the selected field and struck the bank of a dyke between Westwoodside and Haxey some 7 miles NNW of Gainsborough in Lincolnshire. Three died in the impact but Aircraftman Jones was thrown clear and apart from shock and bruises was relatively unharmed. A report of the inquest was published in *The Aeroplane* on 21st January 1931: *"... Aircraftman Cecil Jones, who was*

the only survivor of the accident, said they were flying low in the bad light to try and read the name of the railway station. They ascended again and prepared to land on what appeared to be a green field. The aeroplane overshot this field and landed in a ploughed field. It struck a bank only about a foot high and turned up on its nose, crushing the three men who were in the front. A verdict of misadventure was returned."

19120 SHERMAN Dick Culverwell P/O + 14.09.26 31 Squadron

19121 SHORTEN William Alfred F/O 06.01.30 Relinquished

On account of ill-health [LG 7 January 1930, issue 33568, page 137].

19122 SOFIANO Vincent John F/O 26.05.30 Relinquished

On appointment to a short service commission on the Supplementary List RAF [LG 3 June 1930, issue 33612, pages 343494 and 3495] and retaining his rank. G/Capt 09.01.47 Relinquished

On account of medical unfitness for Air Force service [LG 21 January 1947, supplement 37857, page 398].

19123 STEWART MC Eric George Duncan F/O + 21.07.37 Plane Advertising Limited

On 21st January 1937 Flying Officer Eric George Duncan Stewart MC accompanied by Mechanic Cyril Poole took off from Aldergrove in Northern Ireland in Avro 504N G-AEIJ registered to Plane Advertising Limited, setting a course that would take them to Speke Airport, Liverpool. Over the Irish Sea the weather deteriorated and Captain Stewart [as he is described on the Aviation Safety Network website] had, it seems, little choice but to ditch, this being accomplished within sight of the Steamer *Corrib* which launched a boat and recovered Cyril Poole, shocked but otherwise unhurt. Sadly, Captain Stewart either died when he ditched or drowned when the Avro sank. The location is given as being 25 miles off the Mersey Bar Lightship. At the time of his death he had been transferred from Class A of the Reserve of Air Force Officers to class C on 5th March 1934. The Avro was formerly J8507 and flew with the digit '3' at RAFC Cranwell between July 1930 and November 1932 when after a period of storage it was sold as G-AEIJ with a Certificate of Air Worthiness to Air Travel Limited who passed it to Plane Advertising Limited circa September 1936.

Flying Officer Stewart was transferred from class A to class C of the Reserve on 5th March 1934 [LG 20 March 1934, issue 34034, page 1868].

19124 WATKINS Arthur Charles W/Cdr 10.02.54 Relinquished

19125 WILTSHIRE Edward Thomas P/O 07.02.26 Resigned

19126 WOODBYRNE Cecil William P/O + 23.12.25 4 FTS Abu Sueir

Pilot Officer Cecil William Woodbyrne was flying over the Suez Canal near Nefisha when his DH.9A E8751 clipped the mast of a boat, sending the trainer crashing out of control. Aircraftman Arthur Thomas Groom was pulled from the wreckage critically injured and he died on Christmas Eve.

LG 27 January 1925, issue 33015, page 595 - Seniority 17th January 1925

Black 19127 - 19150

19127 ADAMS Richard Dingle F/O 07.03.30 Relinquished

On appointment to a commission in the Indian Army [LG 8 April 1930, issue 33595, page 2256]. Returned to the Royal Air Force and granted a commission as a flying officer in Class A of the Royal Air Force Reserve [LG 2 March 1937, issue 34376, page 1418].

19128 ADDIS Edward F/O 17.01.30 Relinquished

On account of ill-health [LG 21 January 1930, issue 33572, page 430].

19129 BELL Cedric Arnold A/Cmdr 29.11.58 Retirement

Air Commodore Cedric Arnold Bell died on Thursday, 1st August 1996.

19130 BURNETT Robert Leslie W/Cdr 10.02.54 Relinquished

Paul McMillan advises that Wing Commander Robert Leslie Duncan Stewart died in Salisbury on New Year's Day 1990.

19131 CHAMBERLAIN Joseph Geoffrey P/O 05.01.27 Relinquished

On account of ill-health [LG 7 January 1927, issue 33237, page 121].

19132 DREW Ernest Lewis F/Lt 30.11.33 Relinquished

19133 EGAN Thomas Desmond P/O 22.08.25 Terminated

19134 EVANS Sidney Arthur Vernon P/O + 04.02.27 56 Squadron

19135 FLEMING William Ernest P/O 27.05.25 Terminated

19136 GREEN Donald Salisbury W/Cdr 27.11.53 Retirement

19137 HOLMES Albert John G/Capt 24.08.45 Relinquished

On account of medical unfitness for Air Force Service.

19138 HOWARD Nigel Kenneth F/Lt + 06.09.50 18 RFS Fairoaks

Gazetted with the AFC [LG 31 August 1943, supplement 36152, page 3870]. Flight Lieutenant Nigel Kenneth Howard relinquished the rank of squadron leader [temporary] on 1st November 1947 following transfer to the reserve Class A and granting of an extension of service for five years [LG 30 August 1949, supplement 38700, page 4177. On Wednesday, 6th September 1950 he took off from Fairoaks Airport near Chobham, Surrey with a pupil in Chipmunk T.10 WB644 and during the flight began a roll at low altitude and while inverted lost height and flew into the ground. The pupil was extricated from the wreckage with serious injuries but 47 year old Flight Lieutenant Howard was killed; he is buried in Brookwood Military Cemetery. The Chipmunk had been issued to the unit as recently as 31st May 1950.

19139 INGLIS Carl Melville P/O 24.06.25 Terminated

19140 KELLAWAY Frederick Martin P/O + 16.09.25 2 FTS Digby

Pilot Officer Frederick Martin Kellaway was receiving instruction from Flying Officer William Cay Williams when their Bristol F.2b F4485 crashed at Branston, some 9 miles NNW of Digby. On Thursday, September 17th, 1925, *The Times* reported: *"A Bristol Fighter aeroplane, belonging to No. 2 Flying Training School at Digby, Lincolnshire, crashed near Digby yesterday morning. Pilot-Officer F M Kellway, RAF, of London, who was in charge of the machine was killed, and Flying Officer W G Williams, RAF, of South Shields, died soon after from his injuries, It is stated that when the aeroplane was over Branston, about four miles from Digby, it got into a spin, and crashed to the ground."*

19141 MILLER Herbert William P/O 03.02.26 Relinquished

On account of ill-health [LG 2 February 1926, issue 33129, page 794].

19142 MUMMERY William Lance P/O 15.07.25 Relinquished

On account 0f ill-health [LG 14 July 1925, issue 33066, page 4704].

19143 NOEL John Cecil F/O 17.01.34 Relinquished

Returned to service and granted a commission in the rank of 2nd Lieutenant in the Land Forces, Emergency Commissions, Royal Artillery, with effect from 6th September 1939 [LG 17 October 1939, supplement 34712, page 7024].

19144 PRICE Leslie Frederick Talbot F/O 06.04.27 Resigned

Returned to service and granted a commission in the Administration and Special Duties Branch on 24th June 1940, initially with the service number 81185 [LG 16 July 1940, issue 34898, page 4369] but later reverted to his original number. Now referred to as Leslie Frederick Talbot-Price he was was commissioned to the Equipment Branch on 8th October 1949, ranked Flying Officer [LG 15 November 1949, supplement 38760, page 5417].

19145 PURVIS John Harry Campbell F/O + 09.12.26 25 Squadron

19146 SATCHWELL Allen Francis P/O 24.06.25 Terminated

19147 SHAW Donald Campbell F/O 19.06.29 Resigned

Midshipman in the Royal Navy Reserve.

19148 STANIER Edward P/O 29.07.25 Terminated

19149 VINES Charles Pakenham F/O 17.01.34 Relinquished

19150 WAY Douglas Raymond P/O 22.08.25 Terminated

LG 3 February 1925, issue 33017, page 782 - Seniority 17 January 1925

WALSH Leonard Arthur F/O 16.05.28 Resigned
During his service, and while attached to 25 Squadron at Hawkinge, Flying Officer Leonard Arthur Walsh had a close brush with death when his Grebe fighter collided in the air with a similar machine. For details, please refer to my summary of 17th February 1928.
LG 27 March 1925, issue 33033, page 2117 - Seniority 14th March 1925

Block 19153 - 19177

19153 BARRINGER John Howard S/Ldr 11.05.54 Relinquished
19154 BLOMFIELD James Stanley F/Lt + 15.10.30 3 FTS Grantham
Flight Lieutenant James Stanley Blomfield was killed when his Avro 504N K1059 in which he was giving instruction to Aircraftman Cyril Williamson spun out of control and crashed at Spittlegate Heath Farm near the airfield. His pupil also died. Their death were reported on Wednesday, October 15th, 1930, in the *Nottingham Evening Post* under the heading *'Grantham Air Crash - Pilot and Aircraftman Killed - Fatal Test Flight'*
"Machine Comes to Grief on Spittlegate Heath"

"A terrible aeroplane crash by which two flying men lost their lives occurred just outside the Grantham borough boundary this morning. Flying Officer [sic] *James Stanley Blomfield, of Southampton, accompanied by Aircraftman Cyril Williams, of Norwich, both of whom are attached to the 3rd Flying School at Grantham Aerodrome, took out a machine for test purposes. Flying Officer Blomfield was the pilot.*

"It had only proceeded a very short distance when the machine developed a spin, and crashed into a field on the Heath Farm, Spittlegate. The pilot was killed outright, and Williams died from terrible injuries a quarter of an hour later."

Beneath was a report on a fatal crash in Malta: *"The RAF, Aircraft No. 461, OHMS Glorious crashed this morning at Halfar, says a Reuter Malta message. The Pilot, Lieutenant Maurice Thomas Cowan and L C A* [sic] *Edward George Barker being killed. The cause of the accident is obscure. The machine in question belongs to the Fleet Torpedo Bomber Flight No. 401.*

"This makes 55 deaths in RAF aeroplane accidents since the beginning of the year, compared with 42 last year."

19155 FALLICK Eric Edward
The following was published in *The Edinburgh Gazette* on Friday, January 19th, 1945 issue 16196, page 29: *"I ERIC EDWARD FALLICK residing at Rosemount, Goose Green, Gullane, East Lothian, but presently serving in the Royal Air Force, India, being a British subject, hereby give notice that, after the expiration of twenty-one days from the publication of this Notice, I intend to assume the name ERIC EDWARD SUTTON FALLOCH for all purposes in lieu of my present name. Dated this 27th day of December 1944. Alex Lyall & Son, Enrolled Law Agents, Montrose, Agents for Eric E Fallick."* W/Cdr 30.06.54 Retirement
At own request [LG 27 July 1954, supplement 40240, page 4385].

19156 FEATHER Alfred Rodney F/O + 17.08.28 2 FTS Digby
During the course of an instructional flight with Pilot Officer Bertrand Guy d'Olier, their DH.9A J7795 came into a midair collision with one of the School's Avro 504N J9016, both machines falling out of control with fatal consequences for the three officers involved. A detailed report of the accident was published in *The Times* on Monday, August 20th, 1928:-

"Royal Air Force authorities at Digby, Lincolnshire, pointed out that the air crash on Friday, in which three officers were killed at Digby Flying School, was not in anyway connected with the air manoeuvres over London. All three officers were young men in training. The record of the manoeuvres has therefore been kept clear of any fatal accident, although hundreds of machines were in use.

"The victims of the crash were:- Pilot Officer Adrian Gordon Cole, Pilot Officer Bertrand Guy D'Olier and Flying Officer Alfred Rodney Feather. Cole, who had been training at the school only a few months, was flying an Avro machine, and the other two officers in a DH.9a, came into collision with it. The tail of the Avro was severed and both aeroplanes crashed to the ground. Cole and D'Olier were killed instantly, and Feather died in hospital at Cranwell some hours afterwards. The inquest on the bodies of Cole and D'Olier were opened at Digby on Saturday.

"The Coroner, opening the inquest, said that both machines had been flown by other pilots just before the accident, and they were found to be in good condition. He thought it would be clear that there had been no negligence in preparing the aeroplanes for flight.

"Cyril Thomas Perry, a rigger of the RAF, said he taxied the DH.9 used by Feather and D'Olier, across tge aerodrome just before the flight. The machine was then in good order.

"Walter Arnold, a RAF fitter, said the engine was quite sound when he examined it before the flight. Pilot-Sergeant Osborn made a successful test flight before the aeroplane was used by D'Olier and Feather.

"Pilot Officer W Cullum said that everything was quite alright with the other machine, the Avro, in which Cole was killed. The officer explained he flew it earlier in the day, before Cole used it.

"Dr. Frederick J Murphy, Air Force Medical Service, said the D'Olier was 26 years of age and Cole 22. Their skulls were fractured by the crash and both died instantaneously.

"Albert Edward Baldwin, aircraft hand, said that when the crash occurred he was working on a football field and saw the Avro coming from the direction of Cranwell. The DH.9 was approaching it at a right angle and overtook the Avro. "The Avro was coming down to land on the aerodrome, and when the pilot saw the DH.9 he apparently straightened out to avoid it," he said. "The right wing of the DH.9 caught the tail of the Avro when they were about 500ft up.. Both machines got into a spin and crashed. I ran to the spot where they fell in the next field and found Flying Officer Feather unconscious. I got him out with the assistance of Aircraftman Lumley, and I was the overcome by fumes from the machine, which did not catch fire, however."

"Aircraftman Frederick Lumley said the DH.9 banked to make a landing just before the crash.

"The Coroner, summing up said: "Apparently both machines wanted to land, and it seems from the evidence that, owing to a possible error of judgement, one of the machines failed to clear the other. I do not believe that you can impute any blame to anybody, but simply say it was an error of judgement attended with unfortunate results,"

"The jury returned a verdict of "Death by misadventure while on duty," and found that there was no negligence.

"The inquest on the body of Flying Officer Feather was held at Cranwell. Flight Lieutenant Thompson, Medical Officer at Cranwell Hospital, said that Feather, who was 26, was unconscious after the accident, and was taken to Cranwell RAF Hospital suffering from a fractured skull.

"Recording a verdict of "Accidentally killed while flying," the Coroner said, "It is a technical matter which neither a jury or a Coroner understands. Knowing that the Air Ministry investigates the technical side of such accidents, I consider that the coroner's inquiry is a mere formality."

"Pilot Officer D'Olier came from Windysfield, Ireland, Pilot Officer Cole from The Hill, Sandbanks, Dorset, and Flying Officer Feather lived at Rowston near Cranwell."

19157 GIBB James Clifford McEwen F/O 24.08.31 Transferred
From Class A in the Reserve of Air Force Officers to the Special Reserve [LG 15 September 1931, issue 33753, page 5969]. Transferred from the Special Reserve to Class A of the Reserve of Air Force Officers 5th February 1932 [LG 29 March 1932, issue 33812, page 2111]. Promoted squadron leader [war substantive] [wing commander temporary] [LG 21 August 1942. Supplement 35675, page 3653]. W/Cdr 10.02.54 Relinquished

19158 GIBBON Douglas Wells F/Lt + 30.11.30 HAD Henlow
While attached to the Home Aircraft Depot, Henlow, Flight Lieutenant Douglas Wells Gibbon lost his life when he stalled his Avro 504N K1041 and dived into a field at Parrier Park, Bedfordshire.. He had taken off earlier from RAF Worthy Down with the intention of returning to Henlow. He is buried in Pinner [Paines Lane] Cemetery. *The Times* reported the accident in their edition on Monday, December 1st, 1930:-

"A Royal Air Force aeroplane crashed in a field at Pinner Park Farm, Moss-lane, Pinner, yesterday. The pilot, Flight-Lieutenant Douglas Wells Gibbon, who was the only occupant, was killed instantly. The machine was wrecked.

"Mrs. Noel Ustricke, of Pinner, who was walking in the field at the time, said that the machine was flying low, and circling round as though the pilot was looking for a landing-place. After flying through a belt of mist, during which it was lost to view for a few seconds, the aeroplane came towards

her, swerved, and turned completely upside down. In this position it continued for some yards, and then nose-dived to the ground, bumped several times, and came to rest with its nose buried in a water-logged part of the field."

19159 GIVEEN Francis Waldron P/O 21.10.25 Resigned
19160 HEARD-WHITE Colin W/Cdr 10.02.54 Relinquished
19161 HOAR George Nelson P/O 16.04.28 Relinquished
On account of ill-health [LG 17 April 1928, issue 33376, page 2744].
19162 NANCARROW James William Milne F/O 14.03.30 Relinquished
On account of ill-health [LG 18 March 1930, issue 33589, page 1731].
19163 NORWOOD Verney Tenison P/O 02.02.27 Resigned
19164 PAGE Alfred Lionel René P/O 31.08.26 16 Squadron

19165 PANKHURST Leonard Thomas AV-M 18.04.57 Retirement
Air Vice-Marshal Leonard Thomas Pankhurst CB CBE mentioned in despatched, died on Sunday, 1st December 1996.
19166 PARKER Stanley Charles F/O 14.03.34 Relinquished
Returned to service and commissioned in the Administrative and Special Duties Branch, 11th June 1940, as a pilot officer, initially as 79837 [LG 25th June 1940, issue 34881, page 3870] but later reverted to his original number. S/Ldr 10.02.54 Relinquished
19167 ROBERTS Cyril Hubert F/O 09.05.29 Relinquished
On account of ill-health [LG 14 May 1929, issue 33495, page 3242]. Formerly Lieutenant with the Argyll and Sutherland Highlanders
19168 RUMFITT William Harvey Osborne F/O + 20.10.27 Training Base Leuchars
South Africa Flying Officer William Harvey Osborne Rumfitt along with Aircraftman Francis William Tomlinson died when their Fairey IIID lost engine power and spun in on approach to Leuchars. A third member of the crew, Aircraftman Herbert William Furness was lifted from the wreckage in an injured state and is believed to have recovered. As reported in *The Times* on Friday, October 21st, 1927, the crew *"... was engaged on wireless experiments* [when] *it crashed in a field adjoining the aerodrome at Leuchars, Fife, yesterday. The pilot, Flying Officer William Harvey Osborne Rumfitt, 23, of South Africa, was killed, and Aircraftman Francis William Tomlinson and Herbert William Furness, of the wireless section, were seriously injured. The machine, a Fairey 3D, had been about two hours in the airwhen from a height of about 2,000ft it nose-dived and crashed.*

"Some parts of the aeroplane had to be cut before the pilot could be got out, and he was then found to be dead. Tomlinson was unconscious, with bad cuts about the face and both thighs fractured, while Furness had his right wrist fractured and his face cut. Both were taken to Dundee Infirmary, where Tomlinson died last night."

19169 RUSSELL-STACEY Edward George Honeywood F/Lt 13.11.37 Class C
19170 SISSON Frank P/O 01.11.25 Terminated
19171 SMYTH Reginald Carrington Wallace P/O 01.09.25 Terminated
19172 SPITTLE Walter Richard John F/O 25.02.30 Relinquished
On transfer to the Indian Army [LG 18 March 1930, issue 33589, page 1731].
19173 SPURWAY William Langdon P/O + 14.09.25 5 FTS Sealand
Pilot Officer William Langdon Spurway died when his Bristol F.2b C799 crashed and burst into flames near the airfield. The inquest into his death was reported in *The Times* as a follow on to its report on Thursday, September 17th, 1925, regarding the deaths of Flying Officer Williams and Pilot Officer Kellaway [see the short service commission entry for 27th January 1925]: *"At an inquest at Chester yesterday on the body of Pilot Officer William Langdon Spurway, who was fatally injured in an aeroplane crash on Monday afternoon, Flying Officer Delaney said that Spurway was a pupil pilot, and immediately before he went for his flight he [the witness] took the same machine for an experimental flight. All was correct, and he could offer no explanation as to the cause of the aeroplane catching fire.*

"The Government inspector of accidents informed the coroner that he was carrying out investigations for the Government, but could not express any opinion ass to the cause of the accident until they were completed, which would be in a fortnight's time.

"A verdict of "Accidental death" was returned."

19174 TAITE Clifford P/O 27.01.28 Relinquished
On account of ill-health [LG 26 January 1926, issue 33127, page 622]. His health improved, Pilot Officer Clifford Taite return to service and was commissioned to the Equipment Branch, [LG 14 January 1941, issue 35042, page 291], initially as 89241, on 20th December 1940. Reverting to his original number he served until: S/Ldr 10.02.54 Relinquished
19174 TOMKINS Frederick Basil W/Cdr 08.11.45 Resigned
On Monday 27the August 1928, whilst attached to 84 Squadron at Shaibah, Flying Officer Frederick Basil Tomkins was involved in a night flying accident, the details of which are reported in the summaries for that year. Transferred to Class A of the Reserve on 23rd December 1929 [LG 31st December 1929, issue 33565, page 8507], he was *Gazetted* with the AFC on 31sst March 1942, promulgated in the *Gazette* of the same date, supplement 35507, page 1450. On 24th September 1943, and now ranked Wing Commander, he was conferred by the President of the Republic of Poland with the Order of Polonia Restituta [Officer] [LG 24 September 1943, supplement 36183, page 4248].
19175 VEEVERS Charles James F/O 25.02.30 Relinquished
On transfer to the Indian Army [LGG 18 March 1930, issue 33589, page 1731].
19176 VINES Duncan Stratford Eyre W/Cdr 10.02.54 Relinquished
19177 WILLIAMS Patrick Vaughan S/Ldr 10.02.54 Relinquished

LG 21 April 1925. issue 33040, page 2686 - Seniority 31st March 1925

Block 19178 - 19198

19178 BARDON Harold Rice W/Cdr 14.10.47 Relinquished
On account of medical unfitness for Air Force service [LG 21 October 1947, supplement 38102, page 4960].
19179 BRUNTON Maurice F/O 31.03.38 Relinquished
19180 CLAVELL-BLOUNT Patrick P/O 14.10.25 Terminated
19181 COWAN Edward Lionel P/O 02.03.27 Relinquished
On Account of ill-health. With a general improvement in his health he returned to service and received a commission in the Equipment Branch on 20th January 1940 [LG 20 February 1940, issue 34794, page 1006]. S/Ldr 21.11.58 Retirement
19182 DALE Ivor Gordon Easton
Commanding 21 Squadron [Mosquito VI] he was *Gazetted* with the DFC, less citation, on 11th August 1944 supplement 36649, page 3715. Still at the helm Wing Commander Ivor Gordon Easton Dale DFC was killed on 2nd February 1945. He is buried in the Netherlands at Sittard War Cemetery where his headstone is inscribed: *"Life To Them Is Not Given To Be Safeguarded But Lived."* According to the Royal Air Force Commands database, which the authors acknowledge, and from research by the late Dutch historian Henk Welting, Wing Commander Dale and his navigator Flying Officer Kenneth Arthur Hackett died after abandoning their Mosquito VI PZ314 during a night intruder sortie.
19183 DE ROBECK Dermot P/O + 28.08.25 111 Squadron
18184 DUNLOP Alexander Ronald P/O 31.10.25 Resigned
19185 EARLY William John Reginald P/O + 26.11.25 3 Squadron
19186 FIELD Francis Walter F/O 31.03.34 Relinquished
19187 HARRIES Seymour Arthur Bellairs P/O 30.09.25 Relinquished
On account of ill-health [LG 29 September 1925, issue 33088, page 6280].

19188 HANNAFORD Francis Henry F/O 31.03.38 Relinquished
19189 KELLY William James F/O + 19.04.27 9 Squadron
19190 MAHONEY Geoffrey John Comyn F/O 31.03.34 Relinquished
19191 MATHESON Robert F/O 22.04.34 Relinquished
19192 PECK Hugh P/O + 28.08.25 111 Squadron
19193 PERRY-KEENE Thomas Henry F/Lt + 21.07.34 Station Flight Hal Far
Flight Lieutenant Thomas Henry Perry-Keene was in command of Fairey IIIF S1860 of the Station Flight Half Far when he made a heavy landing, probably at night on 19th July 1934, ran onto a flare whereupon the machine burst into flames. Critically burned, he died two days later. A photograph of his grave in Capuccini Naval Cemetery on the Island of Malta has been reproduced on the website Military Images, which the authorss dutifully acknowledge. The inscription reads *"He Hath Awakened From The Dream Of Life."* His age is shown as 32. His observer on that fateful flight was Leading Air-craftman Leslie Charles Tite who, although injured, recovered.
19194 ROWLANDS Thomas Horace P/O 25.11.25 Terminated
19195 TAYLOR Vincent Corbett F/O 31.03.34 Terminated
19196 TURNER Richard Rudyard P/O 04.05.26 Dismissed
By sentence of General Court Martial [LG 25 May 1925, issue 33165, page 12]. Following his dismissal [at the time he was attached to 99 Squadron], Paul McMillan has discovered that Richard Rudyard Turner emigrated to Canada, arriving in Quebec on 8th May 1927. Pursuing his piloting skills he was killed the following year on 24th June 1928 when his Swallow Plane G-CANG in which he was instructing Edgar Atkinson Broadway crashed following an induced spin. Richard Turner died from a fractured skull and haemorrhage inside the brain, his pupil escaped with injuries. According to a contemporary newspaper report, Edgar Broadway of Berkeley, California, was taking his first lesson; he sustained *"a broken nose, his jaw broken in two places and a broken arm."* The authors also extend their gratitude to John Davis of Air-Britain [Historians] who consulted *The Canadian Civil Register* compiled by John R Ellis and published in the '70s by the Canadian Aircraft Historical Society.
19197 WAINWRIGHT-FAHY William George F/O 26.06.29 Relinquished
On account of ill-health [LG 25 June 1929, issue 33509, page 4195].
19198 WEIR Henry Alexander Mitchell F/O 15.11.32 Relinquished

LG 28 April 1925, issue 33042, page 2843 - Seniority 7th April 1925

FLYING OFFICER

19199 POTTER Leslie Stephen S/Ldr 14.11.45 Resigned
TNA Kew has a file for Squadron Leader Leslie Stephen Potter in the AIR 76 series.

LG 5 June 1925, issue 33054, page 3793 - Seniority 25th May 1925

FLYING OFFICER

19200 MOORE Joseph Albert F/O + 23.11.25 30 Squadron

LG 14 July 1925, issue 33066, page 4704 - Seniority 1st July 1925

FLYING OFFICER

19232 WALTER Cyril G/Capt 08.03.46 Retirement
TNA Kew has a file for Cyril Walter under AIR 76/528/5. Paul McMillan reports that Cyril was born in the Streatham district of London in January 1900 and died in Chelmsford, Essex, in January 1967. On 15th January 1951 he was granted a Class J commission in the rank of flight lieutenant, this being relinquished on 15th January 1963; he had been appointed OBE.

LG 17 July 1925, issue 33067, page 4785 - Seniority 7th July and 18th July 1925 in regard to Pilot Officer Arthur John Lloyd Hughes. Terms of engagement seven and five years respectively on the Active List.

FLYING OFFICERS
4

19201 BURBURY William Hawkesley W/Cdr 10.02.54 Relinquished
Lieutenant Indian Army retired. Acting Wing Commander William Hawkesley Burbury AFC, commanding 31 Squadron [Dakota]. Was *Gazetted* with the DFC on 22nd September 1942, issue 35712, page 4111" *"In the operations in Burma and Assam this officer carried out a large number of hours flying in the face of great difficulties. Throughout, he set an inspiring example to all under his command."*
19202 DRAKE Henry Leonard F/Lt + 06.06.30 RAFC Cranwell
Lieutenant Indian Army retired. Please refer to the RAF C Cranwell Flight Cadet entries for January 1930, for the circumstances of his death.
19203 PASCOE Maurice Clive S/Ldr 15.04.39 Relinquished
Lieutenant RN retired.
19204 PLATTS Maurice Arthur F/O 07.07.32 Relinquished
Lieutenant Indian Army retired.

Block 19205 5o 19228

19205 BARNICOTT William Stuart P/O 01.07.26 Terminated
19206 BERRYMAN Patrick Edwin G/Capt 20.03.57 Retirement
19207 BUSTEED John William F/O 07.07.30 Relinquished
On account of ill-health [LG 8 July 1930, issue 33623, page 4274].
19208 BUTCHER George Patrick S/Ldr 10.02.54 Relinquished
19209 BYRNE Henry Alfonso Sprague F/O 07.07.34 Relinquished
Henry Alfonso Sprague Byrne was granted a commission in the Reserve of Officers, class C, within the General Duties Branch on 6th April 1938 with the rank of flight lieutenant [LG 9 August 1938, issue 34540, page 5121]. His service number was now 75218. On 1st September 1939, retaining his rank, he transferred from the General Duties Branch to the Administrative and Special Duties Branch [LG 27 October 1939, supplement 34718, page 7183]. S/Ldr 10.02.54 Relinquished
19210 CAMPBELL-HORSFALL Archibald Hume P/O 14.08.26 Terminated
19211 COLLINSON MC Edward Howe F/O 31.10.27 Resigned
Edward Howe Collisnon received a commission in the Special Reserve of Officers on 1st July 1915 and as a 2nd Lieutenant was attached to the 4th Battalion, East Surrey Regiment [LG 1 July 1915, supplement 29213, page 6416]. He rose to the rank of Major and was on the Reserve of Regular Army Officers when appointed to a short service commission.
19212 CROWDER Harold Vivian S/Ldr 10.02.54 Relinquished

19213 EWENS Frederick George Hicks A/Cmdr 20.07.48 Retirement

Air Commodore Frederick George Hicks Ewens twice mentioned in despatches, died on Wednesday, 16th December 1959. A signals specialist his final appointment was as Senior Air Staff Officer at Headquarters 90 [Signals] Group. From February 1942 until April 1945 he was Chief Signals Officer at Headquarters Air Forces in India.

19214 FLOOD Samuel Bailey P/O 05.05.26 Terminated

19215 FRAME Maxwell Harvey P/O 04.10.26 Resigned

Maxwell Harvey Frame returned to the service and was granted a commission as a probationary Pilot Officer in the Administrative and Special Duties Branch on 10th October 1939 [LG ISSUE 34713, PAGE 7046], his service number now being 75041. He served throughout the war and beyond and was honoured with the MBE. F/Lt 10.02.54 Relinquished

19216 GOODWYN Julius Norton P/O 03.02.26 Terminated

19217 HAWKINGS John Alfred A/Cmdr 12.06.56 Retirement

Air Commodore John Alfred Hawkings CBE twice mention in despatches, died quite suddenly while undergoing treatment in RAF Halton Hospital on Thursday, 15th January 1976. His passing was notified in the deaths column in *The Daily Telegraph,* Tuesday, January 20th, 1976.

19218 KNIGHT Laurence Maxwell Stanley P/O 26.01.27 Relinquished

On account of ill-health [LG 28 January 1927, issue 33243, page 584].

19219 PATTON Charles Alfred Carnsew W/Cdr 10.02.54 Relinquished

19220 RICHARDSON Edward Cload Lindsey F/O 07.07.36 Relinquished

19221 ROBERTSON William Lewis F/O 07.07.34 Relinquished

19222 SPAIGHT William James Molony F/O 16.09.30 Relinquished

On appointment to a commission on the Unattached List for the Indian Army [LG 30 September 1930, issue 33648, page 5955].

19223 SQUIRE Noel Edgar Cyril

19224 SWEETING Ivan Randolph P/O + 26.03.26 4 FTS Abu Sueir

Along with his instructor, Sergeant Rupert Horrocks, Pilot Officer Ivan Randolph Sweeting died when the their DH.9A stalled while recovering from a spin, crashing on or in the vicinity of the aerodrome.

19225 TOWNEND Walter Simeon

19226 TWEEDIE Patrick Graeme F/Lt 01.04.38 Relinquished

On 3rd October 1939 he was granted an honorary commission in the rank of wing commander in the Administrative and Special Duties Branch [LG 27th October 1939, supplement 34718, page 7184]. In the New Year's Honours List for 1960 he was appointed CBE [Civil Division] for his services as Chief Inspector of Accidents [Civil Aviation], Ministry of Aviation [LG 1 January 1960, supplement 41909, page 12].

19227 WATHEN Edward John Hulbert P/O + 27.12.25 4 FTS Abu Sueir

Pilot Officer Edward John Hulbert Wathen died in an accident at Port Said; possibly unconnected with flying.

19228 WHITLE Robert Cecil F/Lt 28.06.62 Relinquished

On cessation of duty [LG 2 October 1962, supplement 42797, page 7692] at which time he serving in the Secretarial Branch and his service number had been amended to 192858.

19229 HUGHES Arthur John Lloyd F/Lt 14.11.35 Relinquished

On appointment to a commission on the Unattached List for the Indian Army [LG 3 December 1935, issue 34226, page 7675].

LG 21 July 1925, issue 33068, page 4869 - Seniority 9th and 14th July 1925 respectively

FLYING OFFICERS
2

19230 FENWICK Thomas Burrough S/Ldr 10.02.54 Relinquished

MEYRICK-JONES Aylmer Stewart Meyrick F/O 12.01.26 Relinquished

On account of ill-health [LG 12 January 1926, issue 33123, page 301].

LG 28 July 1925, issue 33070, page 5051 - Seniority 18th July 1925

Block 19233 to 19250 and 22001 to 22008

19233 BARTON Horace Bertram Massey P/O 09.12.25 Terminated

19234 CONNOR Rowland P/O 30.06.26 Resigned

19235 FOREMAN Andrea Clifford P/O 20.01.26 Terminated

19236 GEORGE Edward John G/Capt 23.07.55 Retirement

19237 GILBERT Stanley James F/O 07.03.28 Relinquished

On account of ill-health [LG 6 March 1928, issue 33363, page 1583]. However, his health improved and he was granted a class C commission in the Reserve of Air Force Officers, General Duties Branch, with the rank of flight lieutenant with effect from 9th April 1938 [LG 15 November 1938, issue 34570, page 7196]. His service number was now 76487 and an entry in the *Gazette* 30th April 1940, issue 34840, page 2560 indicates transfer to the Administrative and Special Duties Branch, noting he was a Major in the Territorial Army Reserve of Officers. Regarding the latter, Paul McMillan reports that prior to his return to Royal Air Force service Stanley James Gilbert was granted a commission in the Territorial Army Reserve of Officers when he was appointed 2nd Lieutenant on 18th July 1930 attached to the Royal Army Service Corps, 47th [2nd London] Divisional Train. During his eight years of Territorial Army service he rose to the rank of Major [9th September 1938]. On 8th January 1946, and now a squadron leader, his commission was amended to class CC and his identity became 1992254. This commission was relinquished on cessation of duty on 24th August 1948 and finally under the terms of the Navy, Army and Air Force Reserves Act 1954 his commission was relinquished on 10th February 1954 retaining the rank of squadron leader, by which time his service number had been altered to 70915.

19238 GREAVES John Dawson G/Capt 31.07.56 Retirement

The following was promulgated in *The London Gazette* 22nd September 1933, issue 33980, page 6149: *Whitehall, September 20, 1933*

"The KING has been pleased to give and grant unto the undermentioned gentlemen His Majesty's Royal licence and authority to wear Decorations conferred upon them by His Majesty the King of Iraq, in recognition of valuable services rendered by them:-

ORDER OF AL RAFIDAIN

Insignia of the Fifth Class [Military Division]

FlightLieutenant John Dawson Greaves, RAF

19239 GRENFELL Pascoe Ernest F/O 18.07.34 Relinquished

On 15th August 1939 Flying Officer Pascoe Ernest Grenfell was granted a Class A commission in the Reserve of Air Force Officers, General Duties Branch, with seniority backdated to 18th March 1932 [LG 29 August 1939, issue 34660, page 5930]. His service number was now 70938. He continued in service until: S/Ldr 10.02.54 Relinquished

19240 HALL Frederick Walter Hick G/Capt 28.12.50 Retirement

At his own request.

19241 HARVEY Arthur Vere F/O 01.06.37 Relinquished

On 1st June 1937 Arthur Vere Harvey was granted a commission in the Auxiliary Air Force and in the rank of squadron leader was appointed to command No. 615 [County of Surrey] [Army Co-operation] Squadron [LG 3 August 1937, issue 34423, page 4957]. His introduction to the Auxiliary Air Force can be traced back to his final year as a short service commissioned officer when he was attached to No. 602 [City of Glasgow] Squadron on 13th September 1929 as Assistant Adjutant and Qualified Flying Instructor. Postwar he resumed his business activities and later became the Member of Parliament for Macclesfield. Elevated to the House of Lords, Air Commodore Lord Arthur Harvey of Prestbury Kt CBE twice mentioned in despatches, died on Tuesday, 5th April 1994.

19242 HILL Allen Edward W/Cdr 10.02.54 Relinquished

19243 HODDER Francis Samuel G/Capt + 06.09.43 OC RAF Syerston

Group Captain Francis Samuel Hodder elected to fly with Pilot Officer Angus Alan Robertson on a Main Force attack on the German city of Mannheim on 5th-6th September 1943. At 1950 their 106 Squadron Lancaster III DV182 ZN- took off from Syerston and either on the outward flight, or returning, their aircrafdt was intercepted by a night fighter whose opening burst of cannon fire killed Angus Robertson and mortally wounded the flight engineer. From the crew only the bomb aimer, Flying Officer G Willatt, survived; for additional information, please refer to my RAFBCL 1943 and page 314. Group Captain Hodder is buried in Rheinberg War Cemetery where his headstone is inscribed with the immortal phrase *"Greater Love Hath No Man Than This."*

19244 INGLE Geoffrey Hugh Conningsby F/O + 30.01.29 A&GS Eastchurch

Flying Officer Geoffrey Hugh Conningsby Ingle, along with Leading Aircraftman Frank Nelson Howick and Aircraftman George Henry Johnson, died when their Fairey IIID N9759 of the Armament and Gunnery School, Eastchurch, spun in near the airfield following a steep turn. *The Times* reported twice on the crash; the first on Thursday, January 31st, 1929 and the second two days later.

"Three members of the Royal Air Fprce - a pilot and two mechanics - were killed in a crash at Eastchurch Aerodrome, Isle of Sheppey, yesterday. Flying Officer Geoffrey Hugh Conningsby Ingle, the pilot, was found dead beneath the engine, the front part of which was buried in the ground. No. 359819 Aircraftman George Henry Johnson died soon after the arrival of a party from the aerodrome, and No. 357373 Leading Aircraftman Frank Nelson Howick died in hospital. Howick had been married only a month.

"The machine, a Fairey 3 D, belonging to the Armament and Gunnery School, Eastchurch, got into a spin when banking steeply at a height of 500ft., and nose-dived to earth. The men, who were attached to the Coast Defence Force, had made a flight to Leysdown, a few miles east of Eastchurch, and, after completing a wireless reconnaissance, were about to come down when the crash took place at 11.30 a.m."

The inquest into their deaths was held on the Friday: *"An inquest was held yesterday by Mr. E C Harris, Coroner for the Sittingbourne Division of Kent, on the bodies of the three RAF men who lost their lives when their machine crashed on Wednesday at Eastchurch. The victimes were Flying Officer Geoffrey Hugh Conningsby Ingle, 22, single; Leading Aircraft Frank N.Howick, 25, married; and Aircraftman George H Johnson, 22, single.*

"Flying Officer G. Landsdowne said that he ordered Flying Officer Ingle to take the machine, a Fairey 3D, into the air for a practice flight at the conclusion of a flight to be undertaken by Flying Officer Donkin. The machine was refuelled and examined when Donkin came down and was then taken into the air by Flying Officer Ingle. The machine was twice examined that morning. Ingle had flown that type of machine [for] *80 hours, and most of the time had been spent on that particular plane. He was regarded as a good average pilot. The machine was on an ordinary practice flight with its normal crew of pilot, observer, and wireless operator.*

"Flying Officer R H Donkin said that earlier in the morning he had taken up the machine which crashed. She was in perfect order then, and was examined again when he came down before Flying Officer Ingle took her up.

"Flight-Lieutenant E L Ardley said he was flying at about a height of 2,000ft when he saw a machine spinning down about a mile away and slightly lower than himself. The spin appeared to be a normal one. He lost sight of the machine for a few seconds, and when he saw it again it was dangerously low and still spinning. The spin this time did not appear to be normal. The aeroplane appeared to be out of control. Then she hit the ground, There were patches of cloud at about 900ft., which partly obscured the aerodrome as he was coming down.

"The Coroner:- Do you think that had anything to do with it? - It might have made it more difficult that usual to judge his height off the ground.

"Summing up, the Coroner said that the pilot was experienced in the sense that he had flown that type of machine for 80 hours. It would appear that unless some defect had suddenly developed in the second flight the aeroplane was in perfect working order. Probably the pilot realised he had got too low and was attempting to regain height in order to land safely, It seemed to him it was an error of judgement in nose-diving so low before flattening out. A verdict of "Accidental Death" was returned."

19245 JONES Wilfrid Tom P/O 10.11.26 Resigned

19246 KEAY Gerard Harold Carruthers P/O 31.03.26 Resigned

19247 KEMPTHORNE Hugh James Fitzgerald P/O + 23.08.26 58 Squadron

19248 LEWIS John Charles F/O 16.09.30 Relinquished

On appointment to a commission on the Unattached List for the Indian Army [LG 30 September 1930, issue 33648, page 5955].

19249 MERRETT Thomas Kilminster F/O 18.04.30 Relinquished

On transfer to the Indian Army [LG 22 April 1930, issue 33599, page 2564].

19250 PRINCE Stanley Frank F/O + 17.07.29 207 Squadron

22001 STOKES Frederick Owen Watkins P/O 11.11.25 Terminated

22002 STOKES John Westley

Flying Officer John Westley Stokes was transferred to the Stores Branch, on probation, 15th October 1927 [LG 18 October 1927, issue 33321, page 6555]. Completing his probationary period satisfactorily, he was appointed to a permanent commission [effective from 15th October 1927], promulgated in the *Gazette* 26th February 1929, issue 33470, page 1349. W/Cdr 16.08.56 Retirement

22003 THOMAS Denys Stanley F/O 01.08.29 Cashiered

By sentence of General Court Martial [LG 13 August 1929, issue 33525, page 5278]. See Appendix G and notes appended against Flight Lieutenant Cecil George Hancock, Volume 3, page 270.

22004 WALKER Geoffrey Horton W/Cdr 17.09.46 Resigned

22005 WHITTA Adolphus William S/Ldr 10.02.54 Relinquished

22006 WILLS Ronald Arthur W/Cdr 10.02.54 Relinquished

22007 WILSON Frederick George Shaw F/O 19.05.32 Removed

Removed from the service [LG 24 May 1932, issue 33828, page 3350].

22008 YOUNG John Ninnem W/Cdr 12.11.54 Retirement

LG 4 August 1925, issue 33072, page 5218 - Seniority 27th July 1925

FLYING OFFICER

22009 THOMSON George Valentine Thorpe F/Lt 23.12.37 Class CC

The notification of his class CC commission was promulgated in the *Gazette* on 15th November 1938, issue 34570, page 7196. It seems, however, that he returned to Naval duty and rose to Lieutenant-Commander[A] rank: Lt-Cdr 29.04.48 Retired list

TNA Kew has a file for George Valentine Thorpe Thomson, born 14th February 1899, under ADM 273/18/278 [these files are for Royal Naval personnel].

LG 11 August 1925, issue 33074, page 5365 - Seniority 5th August 1925

22010 WAYTE Alline Patrick F/O 05.08.34 Relinquished

Subsequently cancelled by the *Gazette* issue for 19th Februuary 1935, issue 34134, page 1175. On 29th June 1943 and now ranked Squadron Leader he was transferred from the General Duties Branch to the Administrative and Special Duties Branch [LG 13 July 1943, supplement 36089, page

3159]. By 1st April 1952 it appears he was holding a class CC commission in the Secretarial Branch as a flying officer but now promoted flight lieutenant [LG 15 July 1952, supplement 39596, page 3812]. F/Lt 16.03.61 Relinquished
On cessation of duty [LG 4 July 1962, supplement 42403, page 4936].

LG 18 September 1925, issue 33085, page 6089 - Seniority 2nd September 1925

FLYING OFFICER

22011 SEATON Robert Alexander F/Lt 10.02.32 Relinquished
On account of ill health [LG 9 February 1932, issue 33797, page 880].

LG 25 September 1925, issue 33087, page 6205 - Seniority 14th September 1925; the probationary Pilot Officers seniority from 12th September 1925 and engaged for five years on the Active List

FLYING OFFICERS
2

22035 HAWKER Herbert Nelson F/Lt 18.01.36 Relinquished
On appointment to a commission in the South African Air Force Special Reserve of flying officers [LG 31 March 1936, issue 34269, page 2081].
MASON Cyril Rutherford F/Lt + 12.12.32 55 Squadron

FLYING OFFICER

22059 ARBUTHNOTT John St. Clair F/Lt 05.08.35 Class A
Formerly Lieutenant attached to the Indian Army; terms of service - seven years on the Active List with seniority 12th September 1925. Paul, my co-author, has discovered that John St. Clair Arbuthnot faced a General Court Martial which resulted in a reduction in rank to Flying Officer [12th September 1927]. However, he was restored as Flight Lieutenant and subsequently relinquished his commission under the terms of the Navy, Army and Air Force Reserves Act of 1954: S/Ldr 10.02.54 Relinquished

ALLEN Alec William Lawrence Chard P/O 27.06.27 Resigned
22018 ANDREWS Hugh Thornley
Transferred to the Reserve class A on 1st March 1930 [LG 11 March 1930, issue 33587, page 1579], Flying Officer Hugh Thornley Andrews was granted a commission in class CC with the rank of flight lieutenant on 3rd January 1939 [LG 28 February 1939, issue 34603, page 395] and continuing in the Reserve of Air Force Officers, General Duties Branch, his service identity now 75193. However, it appears he was transferred from the General Duties Branch to the Administrative and Special Duties Branch with effect the same date. He continued in service throughout the Second World War and beyond until: W/Cdr 10.02.54 Relinquished
22014 BARLING Leslie Clement G/Capt 10.02.54 Relinquished
Transferred to the Reserve Class A in the rank of flight lieutenant on 1st May 1935 [LG 7 May 1935, issue 34158, page 2986] he was promoted squadron leader on 30th June 1939 [LG 15 August 1939, issue 34654, page 5610].
BAYES John Walden F/O + 16.05.29 19 Squadron
BRADBURY Geoffrey F/O + 20.05.28 41 Squadron
22026 DAVID Arthur Meuric Nairne G/Capt 25.09.48 Retirement
On account of medical unfitness for Air Force service [LG 5 October 1948, supplement 38420, page 5282].
DU BÉDAT William George P/O 01.06.26 Terminated
22022 EAST Terence O'Neill S/Ldr 29.09.43 Relinquished
On account of ill-health.
FIELD Douglas Cookson P/O 17.02.26 Terminated
HORNE Cedric Spencer F/O 12.02.30 Relinquished
On account of ill-health [LG 11 February 1930, issue 33578, page 896].
22024 HOWES Harold Albert S/Ldr 13.02.54 Relinquished
On account of medical unfitness for Air Force service [LG 9 March 1954, supplement 40120, page 1461].
22029 LOVERING William Frank S/Ldr + 01.03.47
During his service Squadron Leader William Frank Lovering had at least two 'brushes' with the law when he fined for obstructing Greyfriars Lane with his car, this being reported by the *Coventry Evening Telegraph* on Tuesday, 8th November 1938. He was described as being being attached to Air Service Training Depot, Ansty [numerous young volunteers wishing to become service pilots passed through Ansty before those who successfully passed the grading tests proceeded to the flying training schools]. A second misdemeanour was reported in the *Westminster & Pimlico News* on Friday, 23rd June 1939, in which he is described as a test pilot residing at 'Redroofs', Moat Drive, Ruislip, when he was fined for being under the influence of drink while in charge of a motor car.

His death at the age of 47 occurred while being treated in Scio House Hospital for Officers, Portsmouth Road, Wandsworth; he is buried in Gillingham [Woodlands] Cemetery in Kent.
McEVOY Clarence Reginald F/O + 03.07.28 31 Squadron
Australia
22023 MONK Ronald Cecil Howe W/Cdr 10.02.54 Relinquished
MOSSMAN Cyril Vernon P/O + 09.11.26 4 Squadron
RUSSELL Edward George Lambert F/O 12.09.38 Relinquished
On leaving the service Edward George Lambert Russell joined the Civil Service and employed by the Air Ministry was appointed *Assistant Inspector II, Aeronautical Inspection Directorate.*
22019 SHAW Arthur Wright S/Ldr 11.07.40 Relinquished rank
At his own request, and is transferred to the General Duties Branch in the rank of flight lieutenant [LG 31 December 1940, issue 35028, page 7302].
Served until: W/Cdr 10.02.54 Relinquished
SHORTER William Horace P/O + 18.07.27 13 Squadron
SMART Archibald Allan P/O 10.02.26 Terminated
22012 SWISS Eric Arthur F/O 10.02.54 Relinquished
My co-author reports that Flying Officer Eric Arthur Swift died in the Dorset seaside resort of Weymouth on during March 1973.
22030 TAYLOR Alexander Edward G/Capt + 20.12.45 OC RAF Waddington
On 7th May 1927, Pilot Officer Alexander Edward Taylor was involved in a road traffic accident when his car hit a motorcyclist, Mr. Ernest Arthur Strechs, with fatal consequences and for which Pilot Officer Taylor was duly charged with manslaughter. A report of his trial was published in *The Bedfordshire Times and Independent* on Friday, 3rd June 1927, under the heading 'The Manslaughter Charge - The Result of an Accident near Luton':
"The jury also returned a true bill against Alexander Edward Taylor [22], Upavon, an RAF officer, for the manslaughter of Ernest Strechs on the road at Razor Hill, south of Luton. The prosecution, which was the out-come of a motor collision, was in the hands of Mr. J F Eales. Mr. Cassels, KC, and Mr. C L Henderson [briefed by Mr. Guest] were for the defence.

"In outlining the case for the prosecution Mr. Eales said the scene of the alleged negligent driving was a rise on the road from Harpenden to Luton, where the road, in approaching Luton Hoo Park, divided into two - one branching to the left going to Stockwood and Caddington, the other going towards Luton. About 9.15 p.m. on 7th May a man named Strechs was riding on a motor-bicycle from Luton down the hill with his headlights on, and

was on his proper side of the road, which was 23 feet wide. It is alleged he was run into by the accused, who was driving a motor-car, and that Taylor had swung out to his wrong side of the road in a desire to pass another vehicle that was going in front of him up the hill, thus finding himself in front of the motor-bicycle, and colliding with it with such force that the motor-cyclist died within a short time.

"On Monday Mr. Stanley Ward, assistant surveyor in the County Surveyor's Office, Bedford, produced and proved plans of the locus in quo; Leslie Gye, Luton, proved photographs of a motor-bicycle and Morris-Cowley 2-seater motor car; and P.c. A H Bridges described what he saw when he arrived on the spot at 10 p.m. A Morris-Cowley car was on the near side of the road, facing Luton; and on the opposite side of the road and on the grass verge, 111 feet away from the motor-car, was a damaged motor-cycle facing Harpenden. Near the Morris-Cowley, but 14 feet nearer Luton, was a Trojan car facing Luton. He found the body of the deceased on the left hand side of the road [facing Harpenden] 45 feet from the motor-cycle.

"Dr. Herbert O'Meara, medical practitioner of Luton, described the nature of the injuries. Both legs were badly broken, and the cause of death, in his opinion, was shock due to the injuries." The Court then adjourned until Tuesday and on commencement the first witness called was Thomas Gledhill of Letchworth, who said: *"he was driving a motor car from St. Albans to Luton on the 7th May. Approaching the Stockwood turn he saw a Morris-Cowley car which was being driven in a reckless manner. When he came round a bend he could see two red lights, and one small white light, about 200 or 300 yards ahead. The car with the red light cut out the white light, and he heard a crash. He went on to where the deceased lay near to the fence on the left-hand side of the road going towards Harpenden. He got out of his car and saw two girls. He saw the wrecked motor cycle by the side of the road, on its correct side, about 12 to 18 inches from the grass. He also saw a Morris-Cowley and a Trojan car. It was 111 feet from the motor cycle to the Morris-Cowley, which was its correct side where it stopped, and about 10 feet from the Trojan car, which was also on its correct side, facing Luton. The distance from the motor cycle to the deceased was 45 feet. He had seen the Morris-Cowley before at the top of Holywell Hill, St. Albans, when it cut in front of him in a reckless manner, and went ahead. He passed it on the common outside St. Albans, where it was stationary while of the riders went to get his hat which had blown off. Nearer Harpenden the car passed him again at a terrific speed, and he called out to the driver "Hi! Hi! Have you gone mad?" There was no verbal reply, but one of the people waved to him.*

"By Mr. Cassels: The width of the grass verge where the body was lying was 17 feet from the edge to the fence, including ditch and footpath. The body was at an angle of about 40 degrees with the fence, and his head was about 6 inches from the fence. The body had gone through the air at least that width, and had cleared the ditch. If he had come off his motor cycle at some spot on the road he had gone in a sloping direction to the spot where he was lying. The motor cycle was about 18 inches from the edge of the road, but he could not say that that was where the collision took place.

At St. Albans there was a policeman at the top of Holywell Hill, and another at the Victoria Street turning. Policemen were capable of dealing with reckless or dangerous driving. Cyril Harris, Luton, said he was driving a Trojan car up Razor Hill, when he saw two young ladies walking, and behind them a motor cycle, which had a light. Behind him was a beam of light, and he heard the roar of a car accelerating up the hill. Glancing sideways he practically saw the motor cycle and car come into contact. The motor cycle was on its proper side. When the crash occurred the motor cycle had hardly passed him, and the car was almost level with his back. He did not stop immediately, as he did not think it was safe to do so, and the next thing he heard was a bump into the back of his car, and then he pulled up, got out, and found that the car behind him had buckled his near-side wing underneath the wheel. There was also a dent in the tool box at the rear of his car. The Morris-Cowley car was just behind. He assisted P.c. Fisher and Mr. Glehill in taking the measurements.

"Stanley M Fraser, of West Hampstead, said he was a friend of the deceased, and they were both riding motor cycles on the night in question from Luton towards London, but witness was some distance in front. His friend had a light on his machine when coming out of Luton. As his friend did not overtake him, witness turned back, and found an accident had happened.

"By Mr. Cassels: The deceased was riding a "Cotton", which was a fast motor cycle, and they were making for London. His friend was wearing glasses.

"Evidence was given by Miss Doris L Henton and Miss Margery Vincent as to their observations of the accident. P.s. Tillman spoke to interviewing the defendant at a house in Waterloo Road, Luton, on the 8th May, and taking down a statement which the defendant signed. It was to the effect that he was driving a Morris-Cowley car and about 1 ½ miles out of Luton was travelling roughly 20 to 25 m.p.h. and accelerated up the hill to about 35 m.p.h. When about to overtake another car he suddenly heard and saw a motor cycle coming in the opposite direction without lights. He put on all his brakes and drew as near to the other side of the road as possible, but he failed to do so before he was hit by the motor cycle. He stopped in 10 to 15 feet, jumped out of his car, and saw that the driver of the cycle was injured. He at once sent for a doctor. Being badly injured, the motor cyclist was taken to Bute Hospital." At this juncture Mr. Cassels for the defence began his address pointing out: *"that the defendant was charged with being responsible to the criminal law for the death of another person. The task of the jury was to decide whether was such reckless driving as would amount to manslaughter, and an error of judgement on the part of the defendant would not justify them in coming to that conclusion. Negligence amounting to manslaughter was different from that which justified damages in a civil action. Laying stress on the suddenness of the accident, Mr. Cassels said the circumstances suggested that it was done in a flash. The distance which separated the motor cycle from the spot where the body was found was indicative of the speed at which the cycle was going when the head on collision occurred, and the angle at which the body was found showed that the motor cyclist must have been coming from the middle of the road to the side when the accident occurred. He submitted that the Morris-Cowley was about on the crown of the road when the motor cycle suddenly appeared before him. So far as the driver and his passenger saw there was no light on it, and this pointed to the conclusion that the very moment when they saw the motor cycle was the moment of the collision which put the light out, and so suddenly that the motor cycle came out of the darkness. The defendant profoundly regretted this unfortunate collision, but learned council submitted that Mr. Taylor was not responsible to the criminal law.*

"The defendant gave evidence, and said he and a brother officer were coming from Gerrard's Cross to Bedford. As they were approaching the hill he slowed down from 30 to 25 miles per hour, and accelerated on starting to climb the hill. Going in the same direction was a motor car, and he pulled out to see if the road was clear, and saw it was, but he pulled in again. When he was about 20 yards behind the Trojan he sounded his hooter and proceeded to overtake the car. When his front wheels drew level with the back wheels of the Trojan he suddenly saw in front a motor cycle without any lights. He applied the front brake and tried to pull to the left behind the motor car, but failed to do so. After the collision he continued for about 10 to 15 feet, and came to rest on the left-hand side of the road. When he got out of his car the motor cycle was about ten yards away, and nearly on the crown of the road. He was a bit dazed, and made no measurements. He did not see the motor cycle until it was about 3 or 4 yards away. He should think the pace he was going was 25 to 30 m.p.h., and he was on the crown of the road.

"Richard Kellett, officer in the RAF [September 1923, entrant to the RAF [Cadet] College, Cranwell], *said he was riding with the accused in the Morris-Cowley car, and confirmed generally the evidence of the last witness. He should say they were on the crown of the road when the collision occurred, and that the motor cycle was about 5 yards ahead when he first saw it.*

"H W Bamber, consulting engineer, said the damage to the car was on the front off-side. The force that threw the man to the spot where he was found could only have been the stored momentum of his own machine. The other vehicle could not in any way have affected the distance. An optician was called, and stated that the glasses produced were worn by a person who was very short-sighted. After retiring for about 20 minutes, the jury found the accused "guilty."

"Called as to character, Mr. W N Moncis, of Surrey, said accused's father had been abroad for many years, and during that absence accused had spent his holidays with him, being a friend of his children. He was of athletic proclivities, and clean-living. Witness had a crippled boy, and accused gave up a considerable part of his time to give him a little pleasure. Accused's Commanding Officer V S Brown, said he had found accused a very decent young fellow, who always behaved in a circumspect manner.

"Mr. Cassel's added that accused's motor character was also perfectly good and clean, and he appealed to His Lordship to exercise his well-known leniency. For all time it must be a terrific thing upon this man's mind that he had been responsible for the death of a fellow man. He must also lose his position as an officer in the RAF, and it passed a line across his career.

"The Judge said he entirely agreed with the verdict, and he thought it was a bad case, and one for which he must give a substantial sentence, as an example to others. It was high time some example was made. The conditions of the highway from reckless drivers got worse from day to day. The sentence would be 12 months' imprisonment. Mr. Cassels: Can you make it second division? His Lordship: No, certainly not."

Continuing to serve Alexander Edward TAYLOR rose to the rank of group captain and was commanding RAF Waddington when he was taken serious ill and died following admission to hospital. He is buried in Gunnersbury Cemetery, Middlesex.

THOMPSON Eric Morilleau F/O 12.09.30 Relinquished

On account of ill-health [LG 16 September 1930, issue 33644, page 5690].

WALKER Frederick Benjamin Goddard F/O + 11.03.30 RAF Depot Uxbridge

While fulfilling the role of acting mess secretary, Flying Officer Frederick Benjamin Goddard Walker was struck down with pleurisy and was taken into RAF Hospital Uxbridge where he developed double pneumonia and died. The Sussex History Forum website, which the authors acknowledge, carries the following extract from the *Thanet Advertiser & Echo*: *"The funeral was a military one, the deceased officer being escorted by officers and men of the Manston Depot from his home to St. Peter's Church* [Broadstairs] *and the coffin was placed on an aeroplane carrier, draped with the Union Jack, and bearing the officer's cap, surrounded by many beautiful wreaths. Handel's Funeral March was played by the RAF band as the cortege left the house. At the church the procession was met by the RAF Chaplin [Capt. Still] who conducted the service. Three volleys were fired, and the "Last Post" sounded. Flying Officer Walker had many friends in Broadstairs. Educated at St. Lawrence College, he entered the RAF and was well known as an athlete. He was a member of the Ski Club of Great Britain, and had won many trophies at Golf."*

LG 29 September 1925, issue 33088, page 6280 - Seniority 21st and 26th September 1925

KAVANAGH Denis Leo P/O 10.02.26 Terminated

LEACH Joseph Harold F/O 07.09.39 Relinquished

Flying Officer Joseph Harold Leach was granted a class CC commission on 23rd March 1939 [LG 18 July 1939, issue 34646, page 4932]. Prior to this he held a class C commission in the rank of flight lieutenant with effect from 21st January 1937 [LG 12 March 1937, issue 34379, page 1646]. It seems he served with the RNVR during the Second World War, transferring to the Army and a commission as Lieutenant and Paymaster in the Royal Army Pay Corps with effect from 16th June 1952 [LG 5 August 1952, supplement 39614, page 4181]. His service number was now 423486. Captain and Paymaster Joseph Harold Leach served until: Capt 16.06.60 Relinquished

THORN Sydney Albert F/O 04.11.37 Relinquished

22058 WALKER Donald George Keith F/O 21.09.34 Relinquished

Returned to service and commissioned to the Administrative and Special Duties Branch as a pilot officer for the duration of hostilities, 8th November 1940 with the service number 60592 [LG 28 February 1941, issue 35090, page 1213]. Served throughout the Second World War and beyond and reverted during this time to his original service number. F/Lt 10.02.58 Relinquished

ANDREWS William Arthur F/O 31.05.29 Resigned

22038 BARNES Wilfrid Edward F/Lt + 04.04.34

Promoted flight lieutenant on 4th February 1931 William Edward Barnes was taken seriously ill and following a long struggle to recover died on 4th April 1934 at the age of 34. His death was reported in the Uxbridge & West Drayton Gazette on Friday 13th April, 1934, reporting his residence as Broxtun, Richings-way, Richings Park. It is possible he had been medically discharged from the service.

BLACKMORE Jack F/O 25.01.28 Resigned

Returned to service and commissioned for the duration of hostilities as a pilot officer in the Administrative and Special Duties Branch with the service number 74428 [LG 3 October 1939, issue 34700, page 6662]. S/Ldr 10.02.54 Relinquished

22040 CAMPEBLL William Gardner G/Capt 19.07.55 Retirement

CRACKANTHORPE George Christopher P/O 10.03.26 Resigned

DAUNCEY Harold Campbell Gambier F/O + 23.01.28 A&AEE Martlesham Heath

Flying Officer Harold Campbell Gambier Dauncey, attached to the Aeroplane & Armament Experimental Establishment at Martlesham Heath lost his life while test flying the Blackburn F.1 Turcock which had been registered G-EBVP. First flown at the Company's airfield at Brough on 14th November 1927, it was sent to Martlesham Heath in the New Year for service evaluation and it was during the course of a test flight that a wing struck the ground while turning at low altitude over the airfield. G-EBVP was the sole example of the type, two photographs of which, prior to having its registration applied, are published on pages 237 and 239 of A J Jackson's *Blackburn Aircraft since 1909*.

HUNTER John Matthew P/O 17.05.27 Resigned

22045 LAWN John Frederick F/O + 04.08.35 Phillips & Powis Reading

Flying Officer John Frederick Lawn went into Class A of the Reserve on 31st October 1932 [LG 27 December 1932, issue 33896, page 8294] and was killed, along with his passenger, Emil Martin Jacoby Boysen, age 23, from Denmark when their Miles M.2F Hawk G-ACOP registered to Phillips & Powis Flying School, Reading, crashed onto Woodley airfield whilst performing aerobatics. *The Courier and Advertiser* reported the crash on Thursday, August 8th, 1935 under the heading 'Loose Joystick may have Caused Crash - Inquest on Air Pilot and Pupil.'

"The possibility that the joystick of an aeroplane, which was looping the loop, became disconnected, so that the pilot lost control, was advanced by an Air Ministry investigator yesterday at an inquest at Sonning, near Reading, on the two victims of the crash at Woodley Aerodrome on Sunday.

"The men were John Frederick Lawn, aged 37, of Wargrave, Berkshire, a pilot inspector at Woodley Aerodrome, and Emil Martin Jacoby Boysen, aged 23, of Genloftegarde, Genlofte, Denmark.

"Mr. W Boysen, father of the Dane, said his son was staying at Woodley, as he was anxious to obtain a pilot licence in Britain. Evidence was given that the machine looped three times, but during the fourth nose-dived to the ground and burst into flames. Two employees at the aerodrome estimated the height at the commencement at 1,500 feet.

"Miss Florence Watts, who said her employer was an airwoman, put it at no more than 600 feet. The third loop was lower than the previous two. In the fourth, when on top, it seemed to hang for an appreciable time, and then it dived to earth. There did not seem to be any attempt to correct it.

"Major S F V Fill, Investigating Officer, Accidents Branch, Air Ministry, said it was found that the controls of the machine were intact with the exception that the control column in the front cockpit was completely detached from its socket and was found five yards from the wreckage.

"This strongly suggested that at the time the machine struck the ground the control column was disconnected.Flying Officer Lawn being seated in the first cockpit, it was possible that he lost control through the joystick coming out of his hand.

"The jury returned a verdict of accidental death. They said they could not arrive at any conclusion as to the real cause of the accident."

LOCH Hugh Granville F/Lt + 30.12.33 Imperial Airways

Flight Lieutenant Hugh Granville Loch transferred to the Reserve Class A on 29th April 1932 [LG 19 July 1932, issue 33847, page 4705], joining Imperial Airways in whose serve he was killed along with Flying Officer John Moore Gittins and their eight civilian passengers, named as Alfred Dennis Druitt Brown, Miss Maude Desmond, Louis John Herman Grein [Dutch], Samuel Halperin [Polish], Gerard Mes [Dutch], Thomas Robert Sydenham Perry, Victor Hugh John Schroeder and Charles Alfred Young, when Avro 618 Ten G-ABLU *Apollo* collided with a radio mast and crashed at Ruiseled [West Vlaanderen] near Bruges in Belgium on 30th December 1933. The Avro had departed Brussels on a scheduled passenger service to Croydon. Soon after take off the crew encountered fog and low cloud and a decision was made to reduce height in order to maintain visual contact with the ground. By this time the airliner had drifted at least 15km from its prescribed route and in the poor visibility it collided with the aforesaid radio mast. One wing was sheared off and moments later it crashed out of control into a field. A photograph taken in 1932 of the high-wing tri-motor Fokker F.VII licence built by Avro as an Avro 618 Ten at Ramleh may be viewed on the Air History website.

John Moore Gittins had been granted a Class AA commission in the Reserve of Air Force Officers on 23rd April 1928 [LG 8 May 1928, issue 33382, page 3252].

The New Year's Day 1934 issue of *The Times* reported the disaster in full having received a report filed by their Brussels correspondent the previous evening: *"Ten lives were lost in an accident to the Apollo, one of the smaller air liners of Imperial Airways, near Ruysselede, Belgium, yesterday afternoon. The machine collided with an aerial at the big wireless station there, and, after striking a strut of one of the masts and losing one wing, fell to earth. Shortly afterwards the wreckage caught fire and attempts at rescue were impossible.*

"The aeroplane, an Avro Ten, had come from Cologne and had left Brussels some 40 minutes before the accident. It was on its way to London with a full load of eight passengers [the names match those reported above, plus their home address, adding the following regarding the two pilots:- Mr. J M Gittins, of 26 St. John's Grove, Croydon and Mr. H G Loch, of 35 Castlebar Park, Ealing].

"The aeroplane left Haren Aerodrome, near Brussels, at 20 minutes past noon and was carried off its normal route to the north, probably because of fog. At 1.15 it was flying over Ruysselede, between Ghent and Bruges, at a fairly low altitude. Suddenly it struck and aerial and then the strut of the mast. The mast, which is about 870ft high, was cut in two and the aeroplane crashed. Workmen from the wireless station went to the spot to give help. They heard groans, but immediately afterwards there was an explosion, and the aeroplane caught fire. Four rescue workers were burnt, and the machine was reduced to ashes. One wing of the aeroplane fell in a road hard by, and a wheel was hurled 90 yards from the scene of the crash.

"As soon ass the noise of the engine had stopped a dozen inhabitants of Ruysselede ran towards the aeroplane and one of them succeeded in making a hole in the bottom, and saw a heap of bodies. Only one passenger - an old man with with white hair - seemed sstill alive; his face was covered with blood. An attempt was made to get him out, but it was too late, as the aeroplane suddenly flamed up like a torch. The pilot had a piece of iron embedded in his thigh. The rescue workers brought fire extinguishers, but the flames were so strong that all their efforts were in vain. The greater part of the mail was lost and all the luggage destroyed except one suitcase.

"Another witness said the pilot attempted to rise again after striking the mast, but that the machine crashed after having touched the roof of a building. On account of the fog all the masts of the station had been lit since 9 o'clock in the morning.

"There is little doubt the accident was due to fog. The pilot, who left Haren Aerodrome 20 minutes late, had been warned that there was thick fog in the country he had to cross.

"Work on clearing the wreckage was begun to-day, but had been rendered difficult by a heavy fall of snow. A number of representatives of Imperial Airways, the Belgian Director-General of Civil Aviation, and directors of the Sabena Company have arrived, and the judicial authorities from Bruges are making an inquiry into the crash.

"As soon as he heard about the accident King Albert telephoned to the aerodrome for news of the victims, and during the evening he was kept informed of what had happened. M. Forthomme, the Minister of Transport, has sent a message of sympathy to the British Secretary of State for air.

"The following message has been sent by the King from Sandringham to Sir Eric Geddes, chairman of Imperial Airways:-

"The Queen and I are much distressed at the accident to the air liner Apollo, in which 10 lives have been lost, and we offer to the bereaved relatives and to you, as chairman of Imperial Airways, our deep sympathy in this disaster. - George R.I.

"The following reply was sent by Sir Eric Geddes:- "I beg with my humble duty to your Majesty and Her Majesty the Queen to acknowledge your Majesties' message of condolence to those so unfortunately bereaved by the accident to Imperial aircraft Apollo. Your Majesties' condolences will be conveyed appropriately to the bereaved. Your Majesties' sympathy is also deeply appreciated by myself and my colleagues and our staff. Safety has been our prime aim and object, and your Majesties' gracious sympathy will serve as nothing else could to encourage us to uphold the high standard hitherto attained."

Over the next few days *The Times* continued to report on the accident; on the 2nd January 1934 it noted that Flight Lieutenant P H Davey travelled on New Year's Day to Belgium as the Air Ministry's Accident Branch representative, while from Bruges came news that Major Brackley, Air Superintendent of Imperial Airways opined that the pilot was flying low after encountering *"a new "weather" front."*

Meanwhile, the bodies would be taken to Ostend on Wednesday 3rd for onward despatch by sea to Dover. Before departure from Ostend it was expected the Belgian Minister of Transport would make a brief speech. Finally, on Friday, 5th January 1934, *The Times* reported:

"The enquiry at Ruysselede into the cause of the accident to the Imperial Airways machine in which 10 persons were killed last week-end has so far established that the aeroplane touched the strut by which the wireless mast was secured and not the mast itself.

"M. Lippens, the Minister of Transport, and the Burgomaster of Bruges have visited the hospital at Bruges and sseen M. Van Hove, who was seriously burned during the efforts to rescue the victims of the accident. The King of the Belgians has conferred upon M. Van Hove, whose condition has much improved, the Croix Civique of the First Class."

Immediately below this article was a brief report, filed by the paper's Berlin correspondent on the 4th, that two persons died when an aeroplane of the commercial school at Brunswick flew into a wireless mast while landing in fog.

22048 McNEIL William Cecil W/Cdr 10.02.54 Relinquished

22049 MASON Leslie Herbert S/Ldr 10.02.54 Relinquished

22050 MOLONEY Thomas Francis G/Capt 01.08.56 Retirement

22051 PEABODY Cyril Martin P/O 10.03.27 Dismissed

By sentence of General Court Martial [LG 22 March 1927, issue 33259, page 1883].

22052 READ Robert Thomas F/O 11.08.30 Relinquished

On account of ill-health [LG 26 August 1930, issue 33638, page 5298]. With a marked improvement in his general well being he was granted a commission in the Auxiliary Air Force and as a pilot officer was attached to No. 924 [East Lancashire] [Balloon] Squadron on 30th August 1939, his service number now being 91083 [LG 12 September 1939, issue 34679, page 6197]. W/Cdr 10.02.54 Relinquished

22053 RICHMOND Gordon Lennox George S/Ldr 02.02.42 Relinquished

On account of ill-health [LG 10 February 1942, supplement 35451, page 666].

22954 RIGGS John Trevor F/Lt 26.11.36 Cashiered

By sentence of General Court Martial [LG 5 January 1937, issue 34357, page 84]. At the time he was attached to the Equipment Branch.

22055 RUMSEY Leonard George S/Ldr 10.02.54 Relinquished

On 5th March 1956 Flight Lieutenant Leonard George Rumsey was granted a class CC commission in the Secretarial Branch [LG 6 April 1956, supplement 40746, page 1998].

SMALLEY Edward Terence Michael F/O 05.12.28 Resigned

LG 6 October 1925, issue 33090, page 6421 - Seniority 28th and 30th September respectively

22062 BARWELL Philip Reginald G/Capt + 01.07.42 OC RAF Biggin Hill

Squadron Leader Philip Reginald Barwell when commanding 46 Squadron won one of the earliest DFCs of the Second World War. *Gazetted* 28th November 1939, issue 34742, page 7961, the citation reads: *"During October 1939, this officer led a flight of six aircraft over the North Sea to intercept enemy bomber aircraft which were approaching a British convoy about 30 miles from the mainland. After shooting down the first enemy aircraft he renewed the attack and, in collaboration with two other pilots of the flight, succeeded in destroying a second aeroplane. The engagement ultimately resulted in at least six, and possibly seven, of the nine raiding aircraft being brought down into the sea and its success was very largely due to the high standard of gallantry and leadership displayed by Squadron Leader Barwell."*

Born at Knowle in Warwickshire on 2nd July 1907 Philip Reginald Barwell received his flying instruction at Duxford, attached to 19 Squadron, and prior to the outbreak of the Second World War saw service in Iraq before returning to the UK and qualifying as a flying instructor under the tutelage of the Central Flying School. Subsequently, he took command of 46 Squadron at Digby on 4th January 1937 and during his tenure he oversaw the squadron's conversion from Gauntlet II biplanes to the then potent Hawker Hurricane and it was in the latter stages of his command that he won the DFC recorded above.

In June 1941, and now Group Captain he assumed the duties of Commanding Officer at Biggin Hill and immediately made himself available tor operational sorties, flying as No. 2 to the legendary 'Sailor' Malan on fighter sweeps. During these sweeps he shared a probable '109 with 'Sailor' followed by a claim in his own right in mid-July 1941. A year later on 1st July 1942 he took off in the company of Squadron Leader Robert Wardlow Oxspring for a sunset patrol between Dungeness and Beachy Head during which the controller at Biggin Hill put out a call for the two pilots to be wary of two Spitfires out from Tangmere with pilots still inexperienced in operations. In one of those many tragic outcomes of war Group Captain Barwell failed to hear the warning and as a result was shot down by what 'we' now refer to as 'friendly fire', his 72 Squadron Spitfire Vb AB806 going down over the Channel. On his return to base Squadron Leader Oxspring*reported that he saw the Group Captain attempting to open the

canopy of his aircraft but he never the left the cockpit; despite an extensive search nothing was found. Eventually, his body was washed onto a beach in France and he now rests in Calais Canadian War Cemetery.
A photograph of Group Captain Philip Reginald Barwell DFC is published on page 44 of Norman L R Franks *Royal Air Force Fighter Command Losses of the Second World War - Volume 2.*

* Robert Wardlow Oxspring was granted a short service commission on 7th May 1938, issue 34513, page 3357. His details will be reported in the fifth volume.

	BOLT	James Edward	F/O		02.04.28	Resigned
	CAYLEY	Edward Gordon	F/O	+	20.01.29	19 Squadron

On Monday 10th December 1928, Flying Officer Edward Gordon Cayley saved his life by parachuting following a midair collision over Whittlesford between his 19 Squadron Siskin IIIA J8851 and Siskin IIIA J8872 from Duxford's Meteorological Flight [see my summary for details]. A month later and he was killed, not in a service machine, but whilst flying DH.60 Moth G-EBPS registered to Philip Aubrey Wills who had accompanied him on a flight at Duxford. Later to become a noted glider pilot, Philip Wills survived the crash and in 1933 he joined the London Gliding Club, pursuing a career in gliding in which in the 1930s through to the '50s he was to hold a number of records in the sport and becoming a prominent member with the British Gliding Team until 1958. The accident that took the life of Flying Officer Cayley was attributed to loss of speed while making a turn near Duxford airfield.

	DOWNING	Frederick George	F/O		28.09.34	Relinquished
22066	GARDINER	Percy Geoffrey Spear	W/Cdr		10.02.54	Relinquished
	GARSTON-JONES	Kenneth	F/O		01.02.34	Resigned
22069	HALL	Raymond Eglington	S/Ldr		16.10.44	Relinquished

Granted a commission in class CC of the Reserve of Air Force Officers, General Duties Branch, with the rank of flight lieutenant on 6th October 1937 [LG 15 November 1938, issue 34570, page 7196], but this was relinquished on 20th September 1939. On 16th May 1942 he transferred from the General Duties Branch to the Administrative and Special Duties Branch. Paul McMillan reports Squadron Leader Raymond Eglington Hall's death as occurring on 9th June 1969.

	JONES	Charles Henry	F/O	+	14.08.29	23 Squadron
	KELLY	Harold Cyprian	P/O	+	26.08.27	3 Squadron
22074	TUTTLE	Geoffrey William	AM		13.12.59	Retirement

Air Marshal Sir Geoffrey Tuttle KBE CB DFC three times mentioned in despatches, died on Wednesday, 11th January 1989.

22075	WHITE	Sidney Harry	F/O		16.08.34	Relinquished

Returned to service and was granted a commission in the Administrative and Special Duties Branch in the rank of pilot officer on 30th December 1939 [LG 23 January 1940, supplement 34778, page 466] with the service number 77063 but reverted to his original number and served until 13th June 1946 when on account of medical unfitness for Air Force service he relinquished his commission while holding the rank of flight lieutenant [LG 25 June 1946, supplement 37625, page 3221].

	WHITLOCK	William Lawson	F/O		26.09.34	Relinquished

On 18th March 1938 William Lawson Whitlock was granted a class C commission in the Reserve of Air Force Officers, General Duties Branch in the rank of flight lieutenant [LG 19 April 1938, issue 34503, page 2600]. His service now became 74855. He served throughout the Second World War, eventually relinquishing his commission in the rank of wing commander on 10th February 1954 under the terms of the Navy, Army and Air Force Reserves Act of 1954.

	ANDERSON	Ian Andrew	F/O	+	25.07.27	17 Squadron
22061	BARRETT	Frederick Fox	F/O		29.04.31	Relinquished

On account of ill-health [LG 28 April 1931, issue 33711, page 2739]. On 1st February 1940 he was granted a commission in the Administrative and Special Duties Branch as a pilot officer on probation for the duration of hostilities, retaining his service number [LG 23 February 1940, issue 34799, page 1104]. W/Cdr 10.02.54 Relinquished

	GARTHWAITE	Frank Norman	P/O		03.11.26	Relinquished

On account of ill-health [LG 2 November 1926, issue 33217, page 7050].

22070	HARRISON	Douglas John	S/Ldr		27.04.60	Relinquished

On 27th April 1954 he was appointed to a commission in the Fighter Control Branch for four years active service followed by two years on the reserve, retaining the rank of wing commander [LG 17 August 1954, supplement 40255, page 4746];

22073	MURRAY	Evan Aitken Thurston	F/Lt		10.02.54	Relinquished

No retention of rank [LG 25 October 1955, supplement 40614, page 5986]
He had been granted a class C commission in the Administrative and Special Duties in the rank of flight lieutenant on 6th December 1943 [LG 21st December 1943, supplement 36294, page 5532].

LG 13 October 1925, issue 33092, page 6617 -Seniority 28th and 30th September respectively

	CHADWICK	James Leslie	P/O		08.12.26	Relinquished

On account of ill-health.

	GOWER	Hugh Forbes	F/O		10.10.28	Dismissed

New Zealand By sentence of General Court Martial [LG 23 October 1928, issue 33432, page 6780]. Following his dismissal from the service it seems Hugh Forbes Gower's life drifted downwards, though in the year prior to his dismissal the *Acton Gazette,* Friday, 30th September 1927, reported that he had been fined ten shillings for driving a car without a licence. Then, two months after leaving the Air Force the *Yorkshire Evening Post* picked up on another of Gower's motoring offences in its issue of Wednesday, 12th December 1928, until finally *The Herald* carried a piece on 19th January 1929, reporting that Gower was sent to prison for two months following a string of motoring offences culminating in being found guilty for drunkenness while in charge of a car. In total he had fines totalling £65 against his name. In addition to the prison sentence, the Andover court imposed a fine of £20, Paul McMillan also reports that Hugh Forbes Gower, described as a travelling engineer, died on the 7th of June 1969. His place of birth on 20th December 1902 was at New Plymouth, Taranaki on New Zealand's North Island.
Furthermore, my co-author suggests that both were serving officers at the time their short service commissions were granted, both being attached to 19 Squadron at Duxford where they underwent their flying instruction.
LG 27 October 1926, issue 33096, page 6923 - Seniority 26th October 1925

FLYING OFFICERS
2

22080	JENKINS	Harold Francis	W/Cdr	10.02.54	Relinquished
22079	STEMP	Geoffrey Charles	G/Capt	10.06.48	Retirement

Formerly a Lieutenant in The Buffs and attached to the Reserve of Army Officers

LG 1 December 1925, issue 33110, pages 7954 and 7955 - Seniority 29th November 1925

ANDERSON Colin Arthur F/O 28.11.34 Relinquished
Returned to service. F/O 03.02.39 Resigned
ADAMS John Leslie F/O 17.12.28 Dismissed
By sentence of General Court Martial [LG 1 January 1929, issue 33453, page 72].
22083 BENHAM Robert S/Ldr 10.02.54 Relinquished
BYRNE Thomas Brian F/O 28.11.34 Relinquished
DOWDESWELL John Frederick P/O + 19.04.27 9 Squadron
ECCLESTON Albert Eric Gerald P/O 27.10.26 Terminated
In the Second World War Albert Eric Gerald Eccleston was commissioned to the Leicestershire Regiment [LG 23 August 1940, supplement 34928, page 5143].
22099 GRAY Lionel George F/Lt 02.03.40 Relinquished
Captain Indian Army retired. On account of ill-health [LG 5 March 1940, issue 34805, page 1318].
22086 IVINS Donald Vernon W/Cdr + 18.05.43 151 Squadron
On Tuesday, 3rd December 1929, Flying Officer Donald Vernon Ivins accompanied Flying Officer Harold Vernon Forbes in Bristol F.2b J8454 which had been converted as a dual control trainer, attached to the Home Aircraft Depot at Henlow. In poor visibility they became lost and whilst trying rto pinpoint their position lost control and dived into the ground, inverted, at Clifton just to the NW of Henlow. Flying Officer Forbes was killed, but Flying Officer Ivins survived. Rising to the rank of wing commander he was killed on operations during the night of 17th-18th May 1943, while commanding 151 Squadron. As recorded by Norman L R Franks in his second volume devoted to the losses of Fighter Command, he took off from Colerne [near Bath in Somerset] in Mosquito in Mosquito II DZ712 with his navigator Flight Sergeant William Patrick Daly for an evening *Ranger* to the *Luftwaffe* airfield at Laval. Wing Commander Ivins's headstone in Dinard English Cemetery is inscribed: *"Worthy Is The Lamb That Was Slain To Receive ... Honour, And Glory, And Blessing."* His navigator, promoted warrant officer, rests alongside, his epitaph being *"In Proud And Everlasting Memory, R.I.P."*
MUMFORD-MATTHEWS Horace James Joseph F/O + 14.03.28 2 Squadron
PARKER Frank Jason F/O 28.11.34 Relinquished
22089 PARKIN John Graham S/Ldr 10.02.54 Relinquished
PHILLIPS Leslie Clifford F/O 28.11.34 Relinquished
SMITH Lionel Hedley P/O 14.12.28 Relinquished
On account of ill-health [LG 18 December 1928, issue 33448, page 8330]. Returned to service and was granted a commission in the Ballon Branch with effect from 18th July 1940 and with 82113 as his service number [LG 6 August 1940, issue 34915, page 4816]. Relinquished on 10th February 1954 in the rank of squadron leader under the terms of the Navy, Army and Air Force Reserves Act, 1954.
22091 STOKES Edgar George Cleave G/Capt 02.02.45 Retirement
On account of medical unfitness for Air Force service [LG 27 February 1945, supplement 36957, page 1121].
22097 STONE Reginald Jack F/O 10.02.31 Resigned
2nd Lieutenant Norfolk Regiment TA. Returned to service and granted a Class A commission in the General Duties Branch [LG 13 September 1938, issue 34551, page 5835]. On 10th March 1940 he was transferred from the General Duties Branch to the Administrative and Special Duties Branch [LG 7 May 1940, issue 34844, page 2726]. S/Ldr 15.04.54 Relinquished
22092 TAYLOR Rex Oliver Oxley S/Ldr + 07.10.40 38 Squadron
Squadron Leader Rex Oliver Oxley Taylor, age 35, was a flight commander attached to 38 Squadron at Marham when on the night of 7th-8th October 1940 he took off, with his crew, in Wellington IC P9287 HD- and headed for Berlin. His aircraft crashed in the general vicinity of the German capital for he is buried, with his crew of five sergeants [see page 218 of my revised RAFBCL 1939-1940], in the Berlin 1939-1945 War Cemetery. His was the penultimate loss from the squadron which departed for operations in the Middle East on 12th November 1940, the ground crew departing on that date followed by the aircrews on the 22nd November.
22093 WILSON Ernest Leonard F/O + 10.04.30 A&GS Eastchurch
While performing an aerobatic loop with Telegraphist James Ronald Armison in Grebe IIIDC J7530, Flying Officer Ernest Leonard Wilson lost control and spun in on, or near, the airfield.
22094 WINN Richard Horry F/O 10.08.31 Relinquished
Residing at West Tisted Manor, near Winchester, Hampshire, Flying Officer [Retd.] Richard Horry Winn was notified that a bankruptcy petition was presented to him by the Court [Southampton] by Herbert Joseph Moreton of 3 Swithun Street, Winchester described as a builder and decorator [LG 16th September 1938, issue 34552, page 5932]. Subsequently, he moved to Widworthy Barton, Widworthy near Honiton, Devon, his name in connection with his bankruptcy being *Gazetted* on 21st January 1941, issue 35049, pages 451 and 452, where he is described as having no occupation.

But, as Paul McMillan reports, he was employed as Air Auxiliary Transport pilot and lost his life on 28th January 1942 while ferrying Master I T8614. The following is an extract from the Yorkshire Aircraft website, which I have pleasure in acknowledging: *"In all probability this aircraft had been collected from Kinloss the day before this incident and had been flown to Prestwick where it had remained overnight. It had just been allotted to No. 12 Group HQ [Fighter Command] at RAF Watnall, Nottinghamshire but this was not a flying unit and had no airfield so if this was the end user the intention must have been to operate the aircraft out of nearby Hucknall airfield as part of No. 12 Group Communications Flight. The following morning at 1024hrs on 28th January 1942 the ATA pilot set out from Prestwick to ferry the aircraft to the airfield in England where it had been assigned. After leaving Prestwick the pilot had also probably landed at Dumfries to refueland when the accident occurred he was flying a leg between Dumfries and Catterick when he flew into bad weather over the Pennines.*

"Weather reports for January 1942 state that it was colder than average this month and in the week before the incident there had been snow and rain falling with cold and unsettled weather with frequent precipitation in the last few days of the month.

"The RAFs record card for this incident do not give any proper reason for the eventual crash but using the Met Office's archived weather report it is high likely snow was on the ground on Stainmore and the hills may well have been covered in low cloud with rain or snow falling, this must have effected the pilot's visibility as he flew the common ATA route across the Pennines using the Stainmore railway line and the A66 road as navigation aids. The aircraft flew into high ground in the Stainmore area of Beldoo Hill and disintegrated with the pilot sadly been killed in the crash. Because of the time of year and the crash site being well out of sight of the road and railway line nothing was seen of the missing aircraft until 4th April 1942.

"The RAF compiled two AM Form 1180s; one on 28th January 1942 when it was simply as having an unknown fate and the second when it was found on 4th April 1942 but neither give any proper explanation as to what might have happened. The pilot's body was recovered from the crash site and the site was cleared. The incident occurred just outside the North Riding of Yorkshire boundary."

Second Officer Richard Horry Winn is buried in Maidenhead Cemetery without reference to his next of kin or other details.
22095 WOOLLIAMS Walter George S/Ldr 09.03.40 Retired list
On account of ill-health [LG 19 March 1940, issue 34814, page 1638] but with effect from the 9th of March 1940 was granted a commission in the Administrative and Special Duties Branch with the rank of flight lieutenant and service number 81289 [LG 16 July 1940, issue 34898, page 4370]. He later reverted to his original service number and served until: W/Cdr 10.02.54 Relinquished

ROLL OF HONOUr
FOR
1925 SHORT SERVICE COMMISSION
OFFICERS

F/O	ANDERSON	Ian Andrew	25 July 1927	17 Squadron
F/Lt	BARNES	Wilfrid Edward	4 April 1934	
G/Capt	BARWELL DFC	Philip Reginald	1 July 1942	OC RAF Biggin Hill
F/O	BAYES	John Walden	16 May 1929	19 Squadron
F/Lt	BLOMFIELD	James Stanley	15 October 1930	3 FTS Grantham
F/O	BRADLEY	Geoffrey	20 May 1928	41 Squadron
F/O	CAYLEY	Edward Gordon	20 JNUry 1929	19 Squadron
P/O	CRIPPS	Geoffrey Walter	21 October 1925	4 FTS Abu Sueir
F/O	DAUNCEY	Harold Campbell Gambier	23 January 1928	A&AEE Martlesham Heath
P/O	DE ROBECK	Dermott	28 August 1925	111 Squadron
P/O	DOWDESWELL	John Frederick	19 April 1927	9 Squadron
F/Lt	DRAKE	Henry Leonard	6 June 1930	RAF Cranwell
P/O	EARLY	William John Reginald	26 November 1925	3 Squadron
P/O	EVANS	Sidney Arthur Vernon	4 February 1927	56 Squadron
F/O	FEATHER	Alfred Rodney	17 August 1928	2 FTS Digby
F/Lt	GIBBON	Douglas Wells	31 November 1930	HAD Henlow
G/Capt	HODDER	Francis Samuel	6 September 1943	OC RAF Syerston
F/Lt	HOWARD	Nigel Kenneth	6 September 1950	18 RFS Fairoaks
F/O	INGLE	George Hugh Coningsby	30 January 1929	A&GS Eastchurch
W/Cdr	IVINS	Donald Vernon	18 May 1943	151 Squadron
P/O	JONES	Charles Henry	14 August 1929	23 Squadron
P/O	KELLAWAY	Frederick Martin	16 September 1925	2 FTS Digby
P/O	KELLY	Harold Ciprian	26 August 1927	3 Squadron
F/O	KELLY	William James	19 April 1927	9 Squadron
[/O	KEMPTHORNE	Hugh James Fitzgerald	23 August 1926	58 Squadron
F/O	LAWN	John Frederick	4 August 1935	Phillips & Powis
F/Lt	LOCH	Hugh Granville	30 December 1933	Imperial Airways
S/Ldr	LOVERING	William Frank	1 March 1947	
F/Lt	MASON	Cyril Rutherford	12 December 1932	55 Squadron
F/O	McEVOY	Clarence Reginald	3 July 1928	31 Squadron
F/O	MOORE	Joseph Albert	23 November 1925	30 Squadron
P/O	MOSSMAN	Cyril Vernon	9 November 1926	4 Squadron
F/O	MUMFORD-MATTHEWS	Horace James Joseph	14 March 1928	2 Squadron
P/O	PECK	Hugh	28 August 1925	111 Squadron
F/Lt	PERRY-KEENE	Thomas Henry	21 July 1934	Station Flight Hal Far
F/O	PRINCE	Stanley Frank	17 July 1929	207 Squadron
F/O	PURVIS	John Harry Campbell	9 December 1926	25 Squadron
F/O	RUMFITT South Africa	William Harvey Osborne	20 October 1927	Training Base Leuchars
F/Lt	SHAW	Geoffrey Maynard Edward	12 January 1931	2 FTS Digby
P/O	SHERMAN	Dick Culverwell	14 September 1926	31 Squadron
P/O	SHORTER	William Horace	18 July 1927	13 Squadron
P/O	SPURWAY	William Langdon	14 September 1925	5 FTS Sealand
F/O	STEWART	Eric George Duncan	21 July 1937	Plane Advertising Ltd.
P/O	SWEETING	Ivan Randolph	26 March 1926	4 FTS Abu Sueir
G/Capt	TAYLOR	Alexander Edward	20 December 1945	OC RAF Waddington
S/Ldr	TAYLOR	Rex Oliver Oxley	7 October 1940	38 Squadron
F/O	WALKER	Frederick Benjamin Goddard	11 March 1930	RAF Depot Uxbridge
P/O	WATHEN	Edward John Hulbert	27 December 1925	4 FTS Abu Sueir
F/O	WILSON	Ernest Leonard	10 April 1930	A&GS Eastchurch
P/O	WOODBYRNE	Cecil William	23 December 1925	4 FTS Abu Sueir
2nd Officer	WINN	Richard Horry	28 January 1942	Air Transport Auxiliary

Appendix D - RAF [Cadet] College Cranwell

COMMANDANT
Air Commodore Amyas Eden Borton CB CMG DSO AFC mentioned in despatches

No change in Command, but the first entry was now brought forward from February to January while leaving the autumn term unchanged. Note, too, commencement of the service numbering block 26001.

January 1925 entry : 24

26001 BIGGS Frank Dennis W/Cdr 25.03.48 Resigned
Wing Commander Frank Dennis Biggs died on Saturday, 18th February 1967.

16236 BLACKDEN* Vyvian Quentery W/Cdr + 10.04.41 12 Squadron
Wing Commander Vyvian Quentery Blackden had commanded 12 Squadron since the summer of 1940, and oversaw the squadron's conversion from Fairey Battles to Vickers Wellingtons. On 15th August 1940, he landed at Martlesham Heath in Battle L5093 and while on the ground the airfield came under attack from the Luftwaffe during the afternoon, *"Considerable damage was caused to buildings but casualties were light."* So wrote Michael J F Bowyer on page 152 of *Action Stations - 1. Military Airfields of East Anglia.* Among those minor casualties was Wing Commander Blackden who was wounded in his right foot and L5903 destroyed. Eight months later and with the conversion programme completed, 12 Squadron, now based at Binbrook, resumed operations - the target being harbour facilities at Emden. At 2230, Vyvian Blackden took off at the head of his squadron and at around 0059, his Wellington II W5375 PH-D was intercepted by *Oberleutnant* Egmont Prinz zur Lippe Weissenfeld of 4./NJG1 and shot down over the IJsselmeer. Wing Commander Blackden, the son of Brigadier-General Shadwell Blackden CBE and Mary Helen Blackden MBE, is buried in Lemsterland [Lemmer] General Cemetery where his headstone is inscribed: *"I Thank My God On Every Remembrance Of You."* For his parents this was the second time that they had experienced the loss of a son on active service for on 28th September 1916, 18 year old 2nd Lieutenant Arthur Worsley Blackden serving with the 189th Brigade, Royal Field Artillery fell during the fighting on the Somme; Arthur is commemorated on the Thiepval Memorial. Then, in the last winter of the Second World War tragedy struck for a third time when Flight Lieutenant Walter Anthony Seton Blackden's 224 Squadron Liberator failed to return to its base at Milltown in Morayshire. Walter is commemorated on the Runnymede Memorial.

16237 BLAIN* William Neal S/Ldr + 01.07.38
Squadron Leader William Neal Blain died while undergoing treatment in the Citadel Military Hospital, Cairo.

BROWN* Richard F/Lt + 23.04.34 1 Squadron
Flight Lieutenant Richard Brown's accident will be reported up in the next volume.

CLARKE* John F/O + 11.10.29 29 Squadron

16241 COOPER* William Charles A/Cmdr 01.10.46 Retirement
Air Commodore William Charles Cooper CBE, died during October 1984. It is noted that prior to being accepted as a Flight Cadet, he was an aircraft apprentice at Cranwell [5th entry] and on graduating he was awarded the Hyde Thompson and Humanities trophies.

16242 DICKEN* Charles Worwood A/Cmdr 02.12.55 Retirement
Air Commodore Charles Worwood Dicken CBE four times mentioned in despatches and conferred with the Order of Leopold with Palme and Croix de Guerre, died on Monday, 6th July 1970. Prior to his gaining a cadetship at Cranwell, he had entered the service as an Aircraft Apprentice at No. 1 School of Technical Training, Halton.

DICKENS* Thomas Charles A/Cmdr 06.12.56 Retirement
Air Commodore Thomas Charles Dickens CB CBE twice mentioned in despatches, died on Tuesday, 11th January 1972.

DRUMMOND Reginald John F/Lt

16244 ELDERTON* Patrick Charles Ibbetson F/O 11.02.31 Retired list
On account of ill-health [LG 10 February 1931, issue 33688, page 932]. Returned to the service and received a commission as a pilot officer on probation in the Administrative and Special Duties Branch with effect from 31st January 1940 [LG 5 March 1940, issue 34805, page 1319]. On 1st January 1947, he was transferred to the Aircraft Control Branch. W/Cdr 29.09.57 Retirement
At his own request [LG 20 May 1958, supplement 41390, page 3181]. Wing Commander Patrick Charles Ibbetson Elderton died on Tuesday, 15th June 1993.

FRANCIS* Geoffrey G/Capt 18.09.51 Retirement
Group Captain Geoffrey Francis DSO DFC twice mentioned in despatched and conferred with the DFC Greece, died on

16247 JOHNSON John Charles Ashley A/Cmdr 12.04.54 Retirement
Air Commodore John Charles Ashley Johnson died on Wednesday, 10th August 1966. Although undecorated, the Air of Authority website, which the authors dutifully acknowledge, contains an extensive note regarding his expertise in Urdu and Pushtu and Arabic languages to the extent that he became a first class Interpreter, this knowledge being gained during his time in India where he spent eighteen months on the NWF and later in Iraq where in 1941, he was briefly held prisoner of war during the rebellion mounted by Rashid-Ali. His final appointment was as Air Attaché in Moscow and following retirement he emigrated to New Zealand, becoming President of the Mercury Bay Aero Club.

16248 LEWIS* Evan Christopher G/Capt 01.01.47 Retirement
Group Captain Evan Christopher Lewis who had been conferred with Polonia Restituta [Poland] and the AFC [Greece], died while being treated in the Princess Alice Hospital, Eastbourne, on Friday, 22nd January 1960.

LEWIS* Gomer Flower P/O + 02.02.27 3 Squadron

16253 NORWOOD* John G/Capt 15.07.52 Retirement
Group Captain John Norwood mentioned in despatches, died in December 1978, while residing in the New Forest area of Hampshire. His father, also named John, so Paul McMillan reports, won a Victoria Cross during the Boer War, the citation for his award being *Gazetted* on the 20th of July 1900, issue 27212, page 4509.

16254 SAREL* Alistair Ross S/Ldr 01.05.40 Retired list

16255 SAYE* Geoffrey Ivor Lawrence AV-M + 06.03.59 AOC No. 19 Group
Air Vice-Marshal Geoffrey Ivor Lawrence CB OBE AFC mentioned in despatches collapsed and died shortly after taking the salute at the disbandment of 228 Squadron [Shackleton MR.2] at St. Eval, Cornwall, on Friday, 6th March 1959. At the time of death he was Air Officer Commanding No. 19 [Reconnaissance] Group. His address was reported in *Flight* in their issue of 13th March 1959: *"I am particularly sorry to say "au revoir" to your squadron because I fear it also marks the beginning of the last chapter of St. Eval RAF station itself. But I cannot think of any squadron in this group which has done more than yours to boost my morale." Flight* also mentions that the eldest of his four sons had graduated the previous December from Cranwell. Jeremy Geoffrey Saye entered the College with the 74th entry. Jeremy was promoted group captain in the General Duties Branch on 1st January 1982 [LG 12 January 1982, supplement 48858, page 488]. His late father was correct in forecasting the end of St. Eval on the north Cornwall coast as an operational RAF station for on the day of 228 Squadron's disbandment all remaining units moved down the coast to St. Mawgan. However it is still a Ministry of Defence site for communications and as such it is operated by Babcock International Group.

26019 STOWELL Robert Arthur Terence G/Capt 01.03.56 Retirement
Group Captain Robert Arthur Terence Stowell OBE DFC mentioned in despatches and conferred with the Bronze Star Medal [USA], died in Guilford on Saturday, 27th December 1969.

TEALE* Robert Pridgin F/O + 08.04.30 19 Squadron

WATSON Eric James P/O + 17.02.28 25 Squadron

16257 WATT* Percy McGregor S/Ldr + 23.11.39 49 Squadron
Squadron Leader Percy McGregor Watt died along with his crew when his Hampden L4034 on a training flight from Scampton crashed into a hangar at Waddington, one of the bomber's engines falling through the roof and crushing several airmen at work in the hangar. For details, please refer to my RAFBCL 1939-1940, page 23.
16258 WATTS-READ* Archibald Martin S/Ldr + 13.03.41 102 Squadron
Squadron Leader Archibald Martin Watts-Read died when the Whitley V T4326 DY-K captained by Flight Lieutenant Frank Hugh Long DFC, a New Zealander by birth, was shot down by Flak over Holland during a raid to Berlin on 12th-13th March 1941. For additional details please refer to my RAFBCL 1941, page 30.
26004 WHEELER Harry George G/Capt + 21.09.43
Group Captain Harry George Wheeler mentioned in despatches is buried in Rhodes War Cemetery, Greece. His headstone is inscribed with the words: *"But The Souls Of The Righteous Are In The Hands Of God."* The Royal Air Force Commands website, which the authors acknowledge, reports Group Captain Wheeler died from injuries sustained in a road traffic accident.
16259 WHISTONDALE* George Frederick G/Capt + 01.03.42
Group Captain George Frederick Whistondale was one of thousands of Allied servicemen who fell into the hands of the Japanese following the surrender of our forces in Singapore. He has no known grave and is therefore, commemorated on the Singapore Memorial, Column 411. The Imperial War Museum holds a collection of five photograph albums and two flying log books in respect of Group Captain Whistondale.

Those names with an asterisk appended graduated as Flight Cadets appointed to permanent commissions on 11th December 1926, along with the following that had been back-classed from the September 1924 intake: Basil Malins Cary, Valentine Bryce Jephson Jackson, Peter Lorraine Ashton Berthron, Harold Benjamin Maugham, John Marson, Philip Leigh Prangley Marett and Terence John Arbuthnot [LG 7 January 1927, issue 33237, page 121].

SWORD OF HONOUR
Flight Cadet John Clarke

ROLL OF HONOUR
JANUARY 1925 ENTRY

W/Cdr	BLACKDEN	Vyvian Quentery	10 April 1941	12 Squadron
S/Ldr	BLAIN	William Neal	1 July 1938	
F/Lt	BROWN	Richard	23 April 1934	1 Squadron
F/O	CLARKE	John	11 October 1929	29 Squadron
P/O	LEWIS	Gomer Flower	2 February 1927	3 Squadron
AV-M	SAYE CB OBE AFC mid	Geoffrey Ivor Lawrence	6 March 1959	AOC No. 19 Group
F/O	TEALE	Robert Pridgin	8 April 1930	19 Squadron
P/O	WATSON	Eric James	17 February 1928	25 Squadron
S/Ldr	WATT	Percy McGregor	23 November 1939	49 Squadron
S/Ldr	WATTS-READ	Archibald Martin	13 March 1941	102 Squadron
G/Capt	WHISTONDALE	George Frederick	1 March 1942	

September 1925 entry : 17

BARTLETT* James Oliphant F/Lt + 07.10.36 RAFC Cranwell
Posted to the College on 5th August 1936, for flying instructor duties, Flight Lieutenant James Oliphant Bartlett was killed following a midair collision that occurred during camera-gun practice while over Navenby, 8 miles SS of Lincoln. Flight Lieutenant Bartlett was flying in Fury I K5682 and the pupil under instruction, Flight Cadet Harold Frizelle Burton was flying Fury I K5681. He managed to bale out, but is reported to have been injured. Subsequently, he graduated and was awarded the Sword of Honour, rose to the rank of wing commander and was killed on active service on 3rd June 1943, when, as a passenger, he was flying out to the Middle East in a Hudson *en route* from Portreath to Gibraltar. Additional information as to his loss will appear in a future volume.
26006 BERKELEY* Arthur Pakenham Fitzhardinge Murray S/Ldr 18.01.40 Retired list
On account of ill-health. However, as my co-author has discovered, Squadron Leader 'Boy' Berkeley joined Gloster Aircraft at Brockworth that same year and a year later on the 4th of August 1941, was killed when the Hurricane he was testing collied in the air with another aircraft. The location of the crash is reported as Kings Field near Park Lane, Woodchester, just a few miles to the south of Stroud. Earlier in the year he had been fined 30 shillings for leaving his car displaying a light.
26007 BOYCE* Clayton Descon Clement AV-M 12.09.59 Retirement
Air Vice-Marshal Clayton Descon Clement Boyce CB CBE three times mentioned in despatches, died on Saturday, 19th December 1987. He also held the Order of Rafidian, an Iraqi honour.
26008 BUTLER* Walter Donald G/Capt + 18.09.43 OC 285 Wing
Group Captain Walter Donald Burton mentioned in despatches, is buried in Italy at Salerno War Cemetery. His headstone carries the words: *"Beloved Father Of Jennifer And Michael. We Walk In Memory's Garden Every Day."* A reconnaissance wing, '285' was constantly on the move and at the time of Group Captain Butler's death was operating fro, Isola II. In addition to his commemoration on the CWGC website, he is also remembered on Dauntsey's School, West Lavington, Roll of Honour.
26009 COOKE* De Lancy S/Ldr + 08.07.40 65 Squadron
Squadron Leader De Lancy Cooke mentioned in despatches, but identified on the CWGC website as Desmond Cooke, had commanded 65 Squadron since October 1937. On 8th July 1940, he took off from Hornchurch in Spitfire I K9907 for an afternoon patrol and was shot down off Dover by a Me109. His body was never recovered and he is commemorated on panel 3 of the Runnymede Memorial. Unmarried, his parents lived in Cyprus. Command of 65 Squadron was taken over by a fellow Cranwellian, Squadron Leader Henry Cecil Sawyer who, sadly, survived less than a month for he was killed during the *Battle of Britain* on 1st-2nd August 1940, when he crashed taking off for a night patrol from Rochford in Spitfire I R6799.
26010 GILLAN* John Woodburn G/Capt + 29.08.41 Wing Leader North Weald
Wing Commander John Woodburn Gillan DFC* AFC was killed in action while flying a 111 Squadron Spitfire Vb W3715 and leading a Wing Sweep in the early afternoon towards Dunkirk where he is buried in the town cemetery, his headstone inscribed with the words: *"His Dauntless Spirit Is Alive For Evermore."* In the New Year's Honours List for 1939, published in *The London Gazette* supplement 34585, page 21, Squadron Leader Gillan was one of thirteen officers awarded the AFC, while issue 34910, page 4675, of the paper recorded his award of the DFC, but without the citation appended. The RAF Commands website records the citation for his First Bar, which was *Gazetted* on the 9th of September 1941: *"This officer has led the Wing on nineteen occasions since July 1941, and his fine leadership and cool courage has been an inspiration to his fellow pilots throughout all operations. On three recent escort missions Wing Commander Gillan has displayed especial skill and determination. He has destroyed one and damaged another enemy aircraft."* Meanwhile, the Aviation Safety Network website records details of a crash on 17th June 1937, when as a squadron leader he was attached to 601 Squadron AAF. This will be summarised in a future volume.

26011 GRANNUM* Clifton Winnington S/Ldr + 28.10.40 105 Squadron
Squadron Leader Clifton Winnington Grannum and his crew failed to return from operations to Homberg in the Ruhr on 28th-29th October 1940, their Blenheim IV T1891 being lost without trace. For additional details, please refer to my RAFBCL 1939-1940, page123 and 230 in the revised edition.
26012 GRIERSON* Colin McKay A/Cmdr 31.08.50 Retirement
Air Commodore Colin McKay Grierson CBE mentioned in despatches, died in May 1991. Colin Grierson was awarded a cadetship from No. 1 School of Technical Training, Halton. At Cranwell he was an outstanding hockey player and winner of the Humanities Prize.
26034 HILL Edward Joseph F/O 25.02.31 Resigned
On 21st March 1936, Flying Officer Edward Joseph Hill was granted a commission in Class A of The Royal Air Force Reserve, General Duties Branch [LG 21 April 1936, issue 34276, page 2561], becoming active on 3rd September 1939 [LG 26 April 1940, issue 34838, page 2477]. Attaining Squadron Leader rank he served throughout the period hostilities. S/Ldr 19.04.46 Retired list
26013 LOUDEN* James Arnold Hamilton P/O 17.10.28 Resigned
But re-instated on 17th October 1929 [LG 29 October 1929, issue 33547, page 6856]. G/Capt + 13.12.58
Group Captain James Arnold Hamilton Louden twice mentioned in despatches, died in Bridgwater, Somerset on Saturday, 13th December 1958.
26014 MOORE* Lawrence Patrick A/Cmdr 27.08.61 Retirement
Air Commodore Lawrence Patrick Moore CBE mentioned in despatches, died on Thursday, 15th January 1976.
26015 MOORE* William Melland F/O 29.07.30 Retired list
On account of ill-health [LG 29 July 1930, issue 33629, page 4740]. On 27th July 1936, he returned to the service and was granted a commission in the rank of flight lieutenant within the Stores Branch [LG 22 September 1936, issue 34325, page 6080]. Heserved throughout the Second World War. Wing Commander William Melland Moore died on Friday, 7th September 1956. W/Cdr 10.02.54 Relinquished
26016 O'GRADY* Claude Cecil G/Capt 01.02.55 Retirement
Group Captain Claude Cecil O'Grady died on Tuesday, 18th January 1994, in the southern resort of Bournemouth; his birth was in Egypt on 12th June 1907, at Al Qahirah.
26017 PHILPOT* Montague George G/Capt 28.05.56 Retirement
Group Captain Montague George Philpott mentioned in despatches, died in Brighton during the month of April 1988.
26018 SANDEMAN* Austin Wollaston F/Lt 01.09.35 Resigned
Returned to the service and active until: F/Lt 10.02.54 Relinquished
Flight Lieutenant Austin Wollaston Sandeman died on Monday, 30th June 1975. My co-author reports that Austin Sandeman entered Holy Orders and was granted a commission in Class A of the Reserve of Air Force Officers, effective 30th May 1939, with an honorary rank o Squadron Leader. Apparently, he relinquished his second Christian name 'Wollaston' in favour of 'Michael' and having become a Monk was known as 'Father Michael.'
26020 TURNER* Claude Henry G/Capt 23.02.50 Retirement
Group Captain Claude Henry Turner mentioned in despatches, died at Witney in Oxfordshire in January 1979. Again, my co-author has unearthed an interesting episode of his life after leaving the services which in late 1950, to the expulsion from Poland of five diplomats declared *persona non grata* and the closure of the British Information Centre in Warsaw This, it seems, stemmed from Group Captain Turner, now an assistant purser sailing with the 2,592-ton freight *Baltavia,* attempting with others to smuggle a 29 year old Polish girl, Barbara Bobrowska out of the country. This enterprise met with failure and the Group Captain along with two other men, named as Henry Upperton of Richmond, Surrey and Gordon Elmes of London, went on trial in Warsaw. For aiding and abetting Group Captain Turner, Upperton and Elmes were sentenced to seven months imprisonment with the Group Captain being sent down for eighteen months; all had pleased guilty to the charges. The background was a love-affair between Group Captain Turner and Miss Bobrowska. Much of what is here reported was published in the *Birmingham Daily Gazette* on Wednesday, 13th December 1950.
26022 WORTHINGTON* Francis Richard G/Capt + 05.09.53 OC RAF Jurby
Group Captain Francis Richard Worthington, Station Commander at RAF Jurby on the Isle of Man had flown the station's Communicationss Flight Anson T.20 VM418 over to RAF Millom in the morning in order to collection Group Captain George Arthur Richmond who was to succeed him as Station Commander on 10th September. At 1240, the Anson took off to return to Jurby and in addition to the two Group Captains, Wing Commander Francis James Fenton and Squadron Leader Roy Patrick Charter BEM boarded the aircraft as passengers. The weather was described as misty with the high ground on the island shrouded with cloud. When sometime had elapsed after 1315, at which time the Anson was due to land, the alarm was raised and search parties found wreckage on the slopes of Clagh Ouyr, 1,800 feet, above the Black Hut on Snaefell. All four airmen had died on impact with the mountain. A Court of Inquiry could find no evidence of mechanical failure and that the crash was owing to an error in navigation, a conclusion that was agreed at the subsequent inquest held at Ramsay. Additional observations pertaining to the tragedy can be read on the Aviation Safety Network, occurrence report 28711. As a Flight Cadet, Francis Richard Worthington had won the Sword of Honour and the Abdy Gerrard Fellows Memorial Prize. He was laid to rest in Jurby Cemetery.

* Graduated as Flight Cadets and appointed to permanent commissions, along with Eric James Watson and Robert Arthur Terence Stowell from the January 1925 entry [LG 30 August 1927, issue 33307, page 5608].

SWORD OF HONOUR
Flight Cadet Francis Richard Worthington

ROLL OF HONOUR
SEPTEMBER 1925 ENTRY

F/Lt	BARTLETT	James Oliphant	7 October 1936	RAFC Cranwell
G/Capt	BUTLER mid	Walter Donald	18 September 1943	OC 285 Wing Isola II
S/Ldr	COOKE mid	de Lancy 'Desmond'	8 July 1940	65 Squadron
G/Capt	GILLAN DFC* AFC	John Woodburn	29 August 1941	Wing Leader North Weald
S/Ldr	GRANNUM	Clifton Winnington	28 October 1940	105 Squadron
G/Capt	LOUDEN twice mid	James Arnold Hamilton	13 December 1958	
G/Capt	WORTHINGTON	Francis Richard	5 September 1953	OC RAF Jurby
F/Cadet	BENTLEY	Alfred Cyril	13 May 1927	

FLYING ACCIDENTS

Monday 30 March 1925
Bristol F.2b F4692 F/Cdt A V Hammond Safe
T/o Cranwell and collided with Avro 504K D4432 which was parked. Flight Cadet Alfred Vavasour Hammond was of the September 1923 entry and at the time of the accident he had a total of 33 hours of flying logged, eleven of these being solo. He was judged not to have complied with the orders laid down for pilots taking off. Following his graduation he was attached to 2 Squadron [Bristol F.2b] at Manston.

Subsequently attaining the rank of group captain he retired from the Royal Air Force on 31st July 1955, and died on 25th September 1992. During his lifetime he was an accomplished artist, his subjects mainly having a connection with the Norfolk Broads and Cornwall, often with sailing vessels incorporated.

Appendix E - Roll of Honour

ROYAL AIR FORCE

LAC	BACCHUS	William Richard John	6 June 1925	56 Squadron

Leading Aircraftman William Richard John Bacchus was killed at Biggin Hill when he was struck by the propeller of a Grebe fighter. His service number 281918 comes within the block 275001 - 307973 allocated to civilian entrants and transferees from other arms of the military between July and October 1918.

AC2	BARBER	Edward	18 April 1925	6 Squadron
F/O	BERRIDGE	Thomas Donald	30 March 1925	28 Squadron
Sgt	BLANCHE	Henry Eustace	21 June 1925	60 Squadron
F/O	BRETHERTON	Norris Carden	21 June 1925	60 Squadron
AC1	BRUCE	John Edward	25 May 1925	100 Squadron
F/O	BRUCE	Ronald Reid Hardcastle	17 January 1925	14 Squadron
F/O	BUTLIN	Harry	28 August 1925	111 Squadron
F/Lt	CARTER AFC	Basil Royston	25 September 1925	29 Squadron
F/Lt	CUDDON-DAVIS	Arthur Wilfred	24 September 1925	17 Squadron
F/O	DASHWOOD	Edward John	21 March 1925	27 Squadron
P/O	DE ROBECK	Dermot	28 August 1925	111 Squadron
LAC	DUNN	Edward Emmanuel	16 December 1925	9 Squadron
P/O	EARLY	William John Reginald	26 November 1925	3 Squadron
P/O	EVE	Jack Terence	25 May 1925	100 Squadron
F/O	FINDLEY	Arthur	20 May 1925	31 Squadron
P/O	FITZGERLAND	John Jellett	12 August 1925	84 Squadron
Sgt	GAZE	John Reginald	5 August 1925	55 Squadron
Sgt	GRAHAM	Thomas Alexander	18 October 1925	8 Squadron
F/O	HAYTER-HAMES	Noel Cecil	21 March 1925	27 Squadron
F/O	HOGBEN	Edgar Thomas O'Neil	5 October 1925	20 Squadron

Flying Officer Edgar Thomas O'Neil had been seconded from the Royal Artillery.

F/O	KERCKHOVE MC	Herbert Vincent	2 July 1925	19 Squadron
F/Sgt	LOWRY	Frank	26 May 1925	12 Squadron
F/O	McLAREN MC	James Alexander	17 January 1925	208 Squadron
Sgt	McGRATH	Thomas James	25 September 1925	29 Squadron
AC1	MILLS	Ernest Edward	7 April 1925	9 Squadron

Aircraftman Mills was a member of crew flying in Vickers Virginia J7439 captained by Pilot Officer Eric Alfred Claude Bushell who encountered a thick fog while flying on the Kent coast. Alighting in the Channel off Birchington-on-Sea he was slightly injured. Sadly, two of his crew, including Aircraftman Mills were presumed drowned, while Aircraftman Horace Eustace Grellis was rescued with very serious injuries. The Virginia was salved and following repairs and by March 1937, was showing in returns from 215 Squadron.

Aircraft Mills's service number 335778 identifies him as joining as a boy between August 1919 and January 1921.

F/O	MOORE	Joseph Albert	23 November 1925	30 Squadron
P/O	PECK	Hugh	28 August 1925	111 Squadron
F/O	PENNY	Marcus Glanfield	8 July 1925	30 Squadron

Flying Officer Marcus Glanfield Penny was on attachment from the Royal Artillery.

F/O	PONTIFEX	Rupert William	18 April 1925	6 Squadron
AC1	RICKABY	Arthur Algernon	23 November 1925	30 Squadron
F/Lt	SLATER MC* DFC	James Anderson	26 November 1925	3 Squadron
P/O	SMITH	Cecil William Montague	20 November 1925	29 Squadron
Sgt	STANTON	Thomas Alexander	13 October 1925	8 Squadron
F/O	THOMSON	Thomas	17 April 1925	84 Squadron
P/O	WALKER	Neil Coull	7 April 1925	9 Squadron

See Aircraft Mills, above, for details.

F/O	WALLER	Robert Richard Studdert	10 May 1925	31 Squadron
Cpl	WILSON	Sidney Ronald	25 May 1925	12 Squadron
P/O	WOODE	Cecil Stanley Marshal	27 February 1925	99 Squadron
F/O	WOODYATT	Arthur Reinagle	22 May 1925	32 Squadron
LAC	YOUNG	Francis	5 August 1925	55 Squadron

ROYAL AIR FORCE SPECIAL RESERVE

F/O	EVANS	Henry Collins	21 September 1925	502 Squadron SR

ARMY

Lt	GRIFFITH	John Ellerthorpe	4 May 1925	Iraqi Levies
Lt	HEATHER	George Donald Edward	8 July 1925	Iraqi Levies

Captain	RICH	Gregory	20 May 1925	Indian Army
CIVILIAN				
Miss	BALL	Dora E [12]	4 April 1925	

SQUADRON LOSSES
1926

A paucity of accurate records results in an unknown date, or the circumstances, for the loss of 45 Squadron Vernon II J7138 *Morpheus* which was taken on service charge on 11th December 1923, despatched to Ascot for packing and shipment to Hinaidi from where it was issued to 45 Squadron by December 1924. It is merely recorded as *"crashed"* and written off during 1926.

Similarly, a handful of crashes are summarised without the names of the pilot; again, a lack of records being the reason for their omission.

JANUARY

To the best of the authors knowledge, there were no fatal accidents involving squadron aircraft in January 1926. This benign start to the year would not last and by New Year's Eve 1926, both accidents and fatalities were up on the previous year.

FEBRUARY

Monday 8 February 1926
29 Squadron *Not reported*
Grebe II J7785
T/o Duxford where it was damaged beyond repair after running through a fence.

Tuesday 9 February 1926
43 Squadron 7F.1 Snipe E7565 F/O J A T Ryde While taxying at Henlow ran into the Snipe featured below having failed to see that the path ahead of him was clear. Flying Officer John Alexander Thompson Ryde reported to the Cadet College at Cranwell along with fellow flight cadets accepted for September 1922 entry. Placed with A Squadron, he excelled at cricket. Rising to group captain rank, he retired on 17th November 1945.

At the time of his mishap, he had logged at least 234 flying hours of which it is believed 101 were at the controls of Snipe fighters.

43 Squadron 7F.1 Snipe F2435 While taxying at Henlow struck by the Snipe reported above.

MARCH

Wednesday 10 March 1926
55 Squadron *Not reported*
DH.9A J7330
T/o Hinaidi and on reaching Wasta Khedir crashed whilst landing. Shipped from the Packing Depot at Ascot, on arrival at Basra its packing case was found to be damaged and, consequently, the airframe on being brought to Hinaidi went into the repair shop.

Friday 26 March 1926
47 Squadron F/O C K J Coggle Safe
DH.9A E8760
T/o Helwan for formation flying and on landing was struck by H3519 flown by Sergeant F Walker. At first it was thought both aircraft were damaged beyond repair but, it seems, H3519 was salvaged for it appears on returns sent from 14 Squadron in 1927 and 1928.

Flying Officer Cyril Kenneth Joseph Coggle graduated from the Cadet College, Cranwell, on 15th August 1923 [LG 18 September 1923, issue 32863, page 6279]. During the Second World War he was captured by the Japanese. Surviving his incarceration he retired with the rank of group captain on 12th July 1953, but, sadly, died seven years later on 16th January 1960.

Wednesday 31 March 1926
28 Squadron F/O R J Willson +
Bristol F.2b LAC A J Burgess +
T/o Quetta tasked to carry out an exercise involving wireless communications during which the Bristol crashed. Flying Officer Reginald John Willson qualified as an observer and was appointed 2nd Lieutenant on 21st September 1918 [LG 24th September 1918, issue 30918, page 11350]. Remaining in the service after the war he re-mustered to pilot. It seems his accident was the first involving fatalities from a squadron since the start of the year.

Leading Aircraftman Arthur John Burgess's service number 344845 identifies him as one of the many civilians who came to the service between September 1919 and June 1925.

APRIL

Thursday 1 April 1926
1 Squadron F/O J G Jennings Safe
7F.1 Snipe E6960
T/o Hinaidi for formation flying practice and on return, and landing, collided with 7F.1 Snipe E7715 which was parked. The Court of Inquiry came to the conclusions that the accident was owing to an error of judgement on both the part of

the formation leader, and Flying Officer Jennings. Although his aircraft was beyond repair, damage to E7715 was not to severe and it was repaired.

Sunday 4 April 1926
60 Squadron P/O D J Lloyd +
DH.9A E8648 Lt W J Vezey RE +
T/o Arawali in the NWF and destroyed here. Pilot Officer David John Lloyd received a short service commission in the summer of 1924, *Gazetted* 15th July 1924, issue 32956, page 5406. The Air History website, which the authors acknowledge, states the following in respect of Arawali: *"... an RAF airfield in the Kurram Valley of what was then the North-West Frontier of British India. RAF bases in this part of the country were essentially forts, with high walls to protect airmen and ground crew from snipers and raids."* Lieutenant Walter John Vezey was commissioned to the Royal Engineers. At the time of the accident, 60 Squadron's main base was at Kohat.

Thursday 15 April 1926
84 Squadron F/O J E Tomes +
DH.9A LAC F E Leatherdale +
T/o Shaibah and crashed near Jaliba some 100 miles N of Basra, the DH being brought down by a violent sandstorm. Flying Officer James Eric Tomes was a short service commissioned officer [LG 30 March 1923, issue 32810, page 2420].

His passenger, Leading Aircraftman Frank Edward Leatherdale's service number 348244 falls into the block issued between September 1919 and June 1925 to civilian entrants.

Friday 16th April 1926
47 Squadron S/Ldr R S Maxwell MC DFC* Safe
DH.9A J7094
T/o Helwan to go to the aid of a Spanish Breguet whosse crew had forced-landed during a flight from Amman to Baghdad, coming down in the desert between landing grounds L and K. Locating the Breguet, Squadron Leader Maxwell landed, but on very rough ground, damaging his DH beyond worthwhile repair, though it was salvaged, a Vickers Victoria being despatched to bring the wreck back to Helwan. For information concerning Squadron Leader Maxwell, please refer to my summary for a 55 Squadron incident on 5th May 1921, at which time his rank was Flight Lieutenant.

Saturday 17 April 1926
14 Squadron S/Ldr H A Tweedie OBE AFC +
DH.9A J7108 F/Lt S H Wallage MC +
T/o Amman and wrecked, totally, after losing control and spinning in from a height estimated at 800 feet. Squadron Leader Harley Alec Tweedie served throughout the *Great War* being appointed as a temporary 2nd Lieutenant in the Cavalry with effect from 29th September 1914 [LG 2 October 1914, issue 28922, issue 7811]. His AFC for services in India was *Gazetted* in the New Year's Honours list for 1919 [LG 1 January 1919, supplement 31098, page 98], and this was followed by the announcement of his OBE in the paper's supplement 31974, page 7422 of 12th July 1920.

Flight Lieutenant Stanley Harry Wallage, born on 24th July 1895, initially served with the Suffolk Regiment, transferring to the RFC on 9th March 1917, and joining 22 Squadron [Bristol F.2b] at Boisdinghem on 9th September of that year. Barely had he unpacked his kit when he was the move 24-hours later to Estrée Blanche. His early weeks with the squadron were plagued with illness; on 2nd October he was hospitalised with tonsillitis and within weeks of his discharge he was taken to 7 General Hospital suffering from a septic throat. Discharged to duty on 13th December, after which he applied himself to the serious business of aerial fighting scoring ten combat victories between February 18th and November 4th, 1918. His fighting spirit was recognised with the award of the MC, *Gazetted* 16th September 1918, supplement 30901, page 11030: *"For conspicuous gallantry and devotion to duty during recent operations. He personally destroyed seven enemy machines. He showed a fine spirit of dash and tenacity, and his skill and success as a fighting pilot was a fine example to others in his squadron."*

As with hundred of his fellow officers, he was transferred to the unemployed list on 18th May 1919, but returned to the service in January 1921, with the granting of a short service commission, *Gazetted* on the 28th in issue 32209, page 781.

Monday 19 April 1926
8 Squadron Sgt J Gaillie Safe
DH.9A E8496
T/o Hinaidi but accelerated to quickly and collided with the DH ahead of him. Both aircraft were wrecked with Sergeant Gaillie's machine going up in flames.

8 Squadron P/O B W Knox Safe
DH.9A H3529
T/o Hinaidi but was struck from behind by the DH summarised above. Pilot Officer Brian Wright Knox graduated from Cranwell on 31st July 1925 [LG 1 September 1925, issue 33080, page 5770]. Taking part in athletics on Saturday, 24th February 1923, Flight Cadet Knox received a painful injury to one of his feet when a fellow runner accidentally clipped

him with his spiked running shoes. His service continued until retiring at his own request on 13th August 1946. At the time he was ranked squadron leader. Squadron Leader Knox died on Tuesday, 20th August 1968.

Tuesday 27 April 1926
100 Squadron *Not reported*
Fawn II J7208
T/o Spittlegate and believed damaged beyond repair in a landing mishap.

MAY

During the month the first issues of the Gloster Gamecock Mk.1 were made, 23 Squadron at Henlow having the honour of being the first squadron to receive the new fighter. At least seven Gamecocks arrived J7892 to J7898.

Thursday 6 May 1926
41 Squadron *Not reported*
Siskin III J7155
T/o Northolt and crashed owing to engine failure. First flown on 5th June 1924, J7155 went to 111 Squadron at Duxford before being transferred to 41 Squadron.

Thursday 13 May 1926
1 Squadron P/O S A Young +
7F.1 Snipe E8384
T/o Hinaidi for night flying practice in the course of which the Holt Flare ignited setting fire to the petrol tank. Surviving the crash, Pilot Officer Stuart Adolphus Young died 24-hours later. His short service commission was reported in *The London Gazette* on 30th March 1923, issue 32810, page 2420.

Friday 14 May 1926
32 Squadron F/O B D J Broadway + Whyteleafe [St. Luke's] Churchyard
Grebe II
T/o Kenley and totally destroyed when it nose dived and crashed on nearby Caterham Hill. Flying Officer Basil Douglas John Broadway arrived at the Cadet College, Cranwell, with the September 1921, entry of flight cadets. Marlborough educated, he graduated on 15th August 1923 [LG 18 September 1923, issue 32863, page 6279], with the Robert Marsland Groves Memorial Prize having achieved the best all-round performance as a pupil-pilot. He was also noted for his fencing and skill at arms along with prowess on the hockey and rugby football fields.

The Kenley Revival website, which the authors acknowledge, carries the following report: *"Broadway had only taken off from Kenley minutes earlier and was flying over Caterham at around 300ft, when a witness, Mr. S Daniels of 16 Oak Road, noticed the unusual sound of the engine, which stopped shortly afterwards. The aircraft nose-dived into a field.*

"Rescuers found the pilot's body amongst the remains of the Grebe. Alongside him was his half opened parachute - evidence of his desperate attempt to save himself.

"The aircraft was brand new and had been test flown for fifteen minutes, earlier that day, by F/Lt Augustine Boret, who reported that everything appeared to be in working order. The Coroner concluded that there had been a mechanical failure while the Grebe was airborne and delivered a verdict of accidental death.

"Flying Basil Broadway was born in Murree, Punjab, India on 26th September 1903. His parents, Sir Alan Brice Knight Broadway [a Barrister]and Lady Agnes Mabel Broadway [nee Bennell] were still living in India when their son died, so his Uncle, Theodore Broadway, from Dorchester, represented the family at his funeral."

Additional information regarding the crash appears on the Sussex History Forum website, again acknowledged, which suggests that structural failure may have occurred as parts of the Grebe were reported by witnesses [unnamed] to have fallen ahead of the aircraft hitting the ground; furthermore, their evidence suggests that Flying Officer Broadway got into difficulties while flying above cloud, and that he had descended to 300 feet when the engine 'cut' out. The death of Flying Officer Broadway was the first from a home based squadron in 1926.

He must have been reaching the end of his tour of duty with the squadron for he features three times in the 1924, in crashes that wrote off his machine, though without injury to himself - see 25th July 1924 for the first of these mishaps.

Monday 17 May 1926
12 Squadron Sgt R E Hawkins +
Fawn II J7221 LAC S M Cox +
T/o Andover and on return and approaching from the SW lost flying speed and spun-in at Abbott Ann, a village on the western side of the A343 Salisbury to Andover main road. A year ago, on Tuesday 26th May, J7221 was being flown by Flying Officer John Kenneth Smith when an electrical fault killed his observer/wireless operator, Flight Sergeant Frank Lowry who is commemorated in the 1925 Roll of Honour appendix.

A report of the inquest held into the deaths of the two airmen was reported on May 22nd, 1926, in *The Hampshire Advertiser and Independent:*

"The inquest on Sergeant Ralph England Hawkins, of Blackpool, the pilot, and Sydney Marsh Cox, of Bristol, the observer, both single men, killed in the aeroplane crash at Abbott's Ann, near Andover, on Monday, was held at the Andover Aerodrome on Wednesday, by the Deputy Coroner [Mr. W R Graham].

"Flight-Lieut. Harold Alan Hamersley said he was leading the flight in which the deceased men were taking part. He saw both men before the commencement of the flight and they were in their usual health. Sergt. Hawkins machine was a Fairey Fawn, and with eight others was taking part in formation practice. The machine was serviceable and had been flown three times previously that day, and on the last occasion before they started at 3 p.m. on Monday it was flown by Hawkins.At the conclusion of the exercise witness gave the signal for landing, which was the last time he saw Hawkins's machine. Their position would then be over Abbott's Ann. The machine appeared to be flying perfectly normally and was in the right place in the formation. When he noticed one machine was missing he took off again and went back to look for it. He saw the wreckage on the ground at Abbott's Ann.

"Flight-Lieut. Aneurin, Medical Officer at the Andover Aerodrome, stated that he took the ambulance, and from the wrecked machine the bodies of the deceased were removed to the aerodrome. He found that Hawkins' skull was fractured and the brain lacerated. Death must have been instantaneous. Cox had received multiple fractures including the skull and neck, and death must have been instantaneous in his case also.

"Charles Dear, living at Little Ann, said he heard a report like the back-firing of the engine of a car, and then the plane dropped.

"The Coroner returned a verdict of "Accidental death by an aeroplane falling while in the exercise of duty.""

Note. A reminder that when the Air Ministry released the names of non-commissioned officers killed in flying accidents, the individual's service number was quoted and in respect of the above, Paul McMillan advises that Sergeant Ralph England Hawkins, aged 25, was 84631 and Leading Aircraftman Sydney Marsh Cox, aged 21, was 335934. Armed with this information it is possible to arrive at a rough date for their enlistment; thus, Sergeant Hawkins number falls within the block 75001-99700 allocated to the RFC for civilian enlistments and transfers from other services between April and October 1917. Leading Aircraftman Cox came to the service as a boy entrant - his block being 335001-336000 spanning August 1919 through to January 1921.

Wednesday 26 May 1926

19 Squadron F/Lt T J West MC Injured
Grebe II J7378 Australia

T/o Duxford and crashed here, Flight lieutenant Theodore James West being taken to hospital with life threatening injuries. Thankfully, he recovered but such were the after effects that owing to ill-health he relinquished his short service commission, retaining his rank, on on 19th April 1927 [LG 2 August 1927, issue 33299, page 5001]. His fighter had been on 19 Squadron establishment since September 1924.

On the 1st of June 1924, he had taken temporary command of the squadron, pending the arrival of Squadron Leader Philip Babington. Although restored to squadron status on the 1st of April 1923, for the next fourteen months 19 Squadron was an integral part of the resident flying school, namely No. 2 Flying Training School.

As a 2nd Lieutenant he was awarded the MC, *Gazetted* 25th November 1916, supplement 29837, page 11546: *"For conspicuous gallantry in action. He attacked an enemy machine and brought it down, displaying great courage and ability."*

Returning to serve his country on the outbreak of the Second World War he was granted a commission in the Administrative and Special Duties Branch, effective 1st September 1939 [LG 7 November 1939, issue 34727, page 7503], retaining his rank and prior to being taken seriously ill was promoted to the rank of temporary squadron leader.

Flight Lieutenant Theodore James West MC died on the 19th of September 1942, while undergoing treatment at the Royal Military Hospital Edinburgh; he is buried in St. Olave Churchyard, Fritwell in the Cherwill District of Oxfordshire. His death certificate, Paul McMillan advises, was issued by the Stirling Royal Infirmary on which it is stated that he died from papilloma of the kidney and bladder.

JUNE

Wednesday 16 June 1926

41 Squadron F/O A C Addams +
Siskin III

T/o Northolt but climbed too steeply and while turning stalled and spun back to the ground. Flying Officer Anthony Clifford Addams had been granted a short service commission [LG 24 July 1923, issue 32847, page 5074]. From 'threads' on the RAF Commands website, which I have pleasure in acknowledging, Anthony completed his flying training at Duxford under the tutelage of 2 FTS and was posted to 41 Squadron on 14th July 1924. In the September, he went out to Iraq where he was attached to 1 Squadron, returning to the UK in December 1925, and back to 41 Squadron.

In their Bristol paper, published on Saturday, June 19th, 1926, *The Wester Daily Press* headed its account:

'To Keen Airman'

'Coroner on Rough Luck of Flying Officer'

""It was rough luck," commented the West Middlesex Coroner, when at Northolt Aerodrome, an inquest was held on Flying Officer Anthony Clifford Addams, aged 22, who was killed in a flying accident. A verdict of "Accidental Death" was recorded.

"The circumstances of the tragedy were related by a brother officer, Flight Lieutenant Chas. Spackman, Chief Instructor, No. 41 Fighter Squadron, Northolt.

"The deceassed, he said, had been stationed at the Aerodrome since September, and had many hours flying experience. On Wednesday, added witness, he took off in a Siskin machine and he pulled up into a very steep climbing turn. He was going to steeply, however, and lost flying speed, and, at a height of 200 feet, spun to the ground. The cause was an error of judgement.

"The Coroner - "He was over keen, was he?"

"Witness - "Yes."
"Witness added that the machine was completely wrecked.
"Medical evidence showed that deceased died a minute after admission to hospital owing to a fractured skull."

JULY

Friday 2 July 1926
100 Squadron F/O H V Alder Safe
Fawn II J7191/1 LAC F W Miller +
T/o Weston Zoyland*but swung out of control struck a car in which a Miss Fanny Vera Clare, aged 19, was travelling, and turned over. Leading Aircraft Frederick William Miller was killed, as was Miss Clare.

Flying Officer Herbert Victor Alder's short service commission was *Gazetted* on 13th January 1922, issue 32576, page 375. As a consequence of the accident he was dismissed the service by sentence of General Court Martial [LG 26 October 1926, issue 33215, page 6824].

Leading Aircraftman Miller whose service number was 349176 was one of the many airmen who joined from a civilian occupation between September 1919 and June 1925.

An extract of the tragedy appeared in the *Western Morning News* on Wednesday 7th July: *"The pilot stated he swerved in order to avoid a night flare on the ground, and doing so must have gone a little too far to starboard. He did not realise the road was near and did not know the car was in the road. A girl who was sitting in the car reading a book was Miss Fanny Vera Clare [aged 19] who was also killed."*

* RAF Weston Zoyland opened in 1925 to provide squadrons with a summer camp [May through to September] and was extensively used by units carrying out their annual armament practice over the Bristol Channel ranges off the port of Watchet. Sighted some four miles ESE of Bridgwater, Somerset, the airfield closed in 1947, but was kept in good order and with postwar tensions increasing, and in particular with the war in Korea, Weston Zoyland re-opened in 1952, to become base for No. 209 Advanced Flying Training School equipped with Meteor T.7 twin-seat tandem jet trainers.

On 10th November 1955, 76 Squadron arrived with their Canberras to work-up for their departure to Australia. Further reading on this part of the squadron's history is reported in my 1981, publication *To See The Dawn Breaking - 76 Squadron Operations.* By 1958, Weston Zoyland had ceased flying operations. However, parts of the airfield remain active for Microlights while a second strip, now named Middlezoy Aerodrome, opened s recently as 2018.

Tuesday 6 July 1926
5 Squadron F/O C C Harris +
Bristol F.2b LAC C R Avery +
T/o Razmak and wrecked here after stalling on the approach. Lieutenant Clement Conrad Harris of the Royal Artillery had been seconded for four years duty with the Royal Air Force with effect from 1st August 1924 [LG 12 August 1924, issue 32964, page 6053] with the temporary rank of flying officer.

Leading Aircraftman Cecil Robert Avery came to the service between the months of March and August 1919, his service number being 330954.

56 Squadron P/O S A V Evans Safe See 4 July 1927
Grebe II
T/o Biggin Hill and came to grief in a forced-landing near Lord Avebury's estate at High Elms, Farnborough, Kent. The Grebe skilled through a fence and was wrecked, leaving Pilot Officer Sidney Arthur Vernon Evans shaken, but otherwise unharmed.

Friday 23 July 1926
9 Squadron LAC W E Parrish Safe
Avro 504K F2332
T/o Manston in continuance of his flying instruction which had been interrupted by a serious crash on December 16th last, when he was involved in a midair collision followed by a crash-landing which left him with head and leg injuries. Recovering well, he had resumed instruction on 19th May, and now he had been briefed for a solo flight during which he was to practice aerobatics and it was during a loop in full view of people on the beach at Margate that the controls locked. By good fortune, Leading Aircraftman Parrish was wearing a parachute and with his machine falling into a field his 'audience' were treated to what was then the unusual spectacle of watching an airman coming down safely beneath the canopy of a parachute. It seems William Edward Parrish was only the second RAF pilot to escape a crashing aeroplane by this method and he later visited the Air Ministry to relate his experience.

Meanwhile, the Court of Inquiry reported that the cause of the crash was owing to the instructor's safety strap snagging on the control column, hence the sudden locking of the controls.

Thursday 29 July 1926
12 Squadron F/Sgt H C Steanes Safe
Fox I J7944
T/o Andover for formation flying practice and while at 1,000 feet near the airfield came into collision with Fox I J7942. Flight Sergeant Harry Cheshire Steaness parachuted as did Flight Sergeant Walter James Frost. An account of the midair collision was published the following day in the *Western Morning News:*

'Saved by Parachutes'
'RAF Pilots Escape after Collision'

"Two sergeants of the Air Force, stationed at Andover, had a remarkable escape from death as the result of a collision in mid-air which occurred at Weyhill, near Andover, yesterday. The two men concerned in the accident were Sergt. H C Steanes of the 12th Bomber Squadron, whose home is in Birmingham, and Sergt. W J Frost of the same squadron, who resides in London. It appears that the men were engaged in ordinary flying practice when the pilots, who were both flying Fairey Fox machines, found they were unable to right the machines after the impact and they both jumped out, using their parachutes, and neither man was seriously injured. Steanes was unhurt, but Frost received injuries to the arm and cheek. Both 'planes were wrecked.

"There were other airmen in the vicinity at the time when they collided at a height of one thousand feet. The pilots apparently had a good view of each others machines, and they both turned to avoid one another. The wing of one of the machines, however, touched the other, and one came down in a nose dive in a field 100 yards from the Andover - Cheltenham branch line of the Great Western Railway - Sergeant Steane's machine came down in a nose dive in a field near the Andover station. The pilot of this machine landed in his parachute in the station yard within a few feet of the line.

"The other machine dropped into a cornfield about 200 yards away on the other side of the road, and Frost landed near-by. The first to Steane's aid was the wife of the station master, who found him standing laughing with his parachute."

Note. Air-Britain's *J File* reports the date as 26th July 1926, but the authors lean towards the 29th as suggested by the paper.; and, according to the *J File* J7942 was sent to Fairey's for rebuilding and in August 1928, it returned to Andover where it was reassigned to 12 Squadron. Apparently, the station master's house is still in situ. Timothy Mason's history of 12 Squadron [see sources and private publications] mentions the above, confirming Flight Sergeant Steane was flying J7944 and Flight Sergeant Frost J7942. Their service numbers were 81644 and 244430 respectively which places Flight Sergeant Steane joining the RFC either on transfer from another of the armed services, or from civilian life, between April and October 1917, while his colleague was formerly of the 1917 entry into the Royal Naval Air Service.

A replacement for the disappointing Fairey Fawn, the Fox proved to be a very successful light bomber for its age and with 12 Squadron it continued in use until 1931, when it was replaced by Hawker's Hart. Licence built in Belgium, the type saw limited service in the Second World War until overwhelmed in the *Blitzkrieg* of May 1940.

The type was also used by the Peruvian air force and navy and Switzerland bought two for evaluation. The loss of J7944 was the first in Royal Air Force service.

45 Squadron	F/O O K Stirling Webb	+
Vernon III JR7143	S/Ldr E M Pollard	+
	F/Lt R C B Brading DFC*	+
	P/O G P Mee	Injured
	Sgt E Kennedy	+
	AC1 H L Davis	+
	AC1 J D Henderson	Injured

T/o Hinaidi for a mail-run to Kirkuk but on becoming airborne and engine 'cut' which resulted in the Vernon crashing onto the roof of a hangar used by No. 1 Squadron. Apart from the crew, Aircraftman Edgar Whittle who was working inside the hangar was fatally injured and the death is also reported of a civilian, Mr. Francis Crawford Inglis.

Flying Officer Oswald Kempson Stirling Webb was *Gazetted* with a short service commission on 29th May 1923, issue 32828, page 3753. Of the remaining officers who perished, Squadron Leader Eric Miller Pollard had been granted a permanent commission, in his rank, on 19th March 1924 [LG 18 March 1924, issue 32919, page 2329]. Flight Lieutenant Reginald Carey Brenton Brading, born in Croydon of 14th May 1899, served initially with the RNAS. Following the merger of the two air arms, he flew SE.5as with 1 Squadron, eventually being credited with thirteen confirmed combat victories. He was among the many officers appointed to a permanent commission on August 1st, 1919, by which time he had been awarded a DFC and First Bar, as *Gazetted* 2nd November and 3rd December 1918, supplement 30989, page 12962 and supplement 31046, page 14316: *"This officer has accounted for seven enemy machines - two shot down in flames and five out of control. In addition he has displayed marked skill and bravery in attacking enemy troops and transport. Four times in one day he engaged troops, etc, on the roads with machine-gun fire, inflicting casualties and causing great confusion."* The citation for the First Bar reads: *"An exceptionally keen and daring patrol leader who has accounted for five enemy machines during the last month. On 2 September, while leading his flight, he observed twelve Fokker biplanes, which he at once engaged, driving one down out of control. Later, on the same day, he engaged a formation of Fokkers that were harassing our Corps machines, causing one to crash. This officer's skill and bravery have proved a great incentive to the other pilots of his squadron."*

Pilot Officer George Percy Mee who was injured received a short service commission, *Gazetted* 13th January 1925, issue 33011, page 302, but was obliged to leave the Air Force the following year owing to ill-health [LG 22 November 1927, issue 33331, page 7424].

A photograph of the Vernon lying where it fell appears on page 89 of *The Flying Camels*. The rear fuselage and tailplane look little damaged but the centre section and wings appear to be totally smashed.

The three non-commissioned officers who lost their lives, Sergeant Edgar Kennedy, Aircraftman Horace Leslie Davis and Aircraftman Edgar Whittle received service numbers 155685, 345662 and 354222 respectively. Of the trio, Sergeant Kennedy joined as a boy airman at sometime after October 1917, while Aircraftman Davis and Whittle enlisted postwar from civilian life.

AUGUST

Sunday 1 August 1926
31 Squadron F/O J C Marcy Injured
Bristol F.2b J6640/K LAC P W E Crunden +
T/o Multan in the Punjab and crashed out of control. Flying Officer Jack Courtney Marcy was *Gazetted* with a short service commission on 29th January 1924, issue 32902, page 875.
Leading Aircraftman Percy William Edward Crunden had around a decade of active service to his credit having enlisted either in late 1916, or early in 1917, his service identity being 62441 which is within the block 17401 - 68950.

Tuesday 10 August 1926
47 Squadron F/O H G Slater +
DH.9A ER928 AC1 T R Harvey +
T/o Helwan and crashed near the pyramids after flying into dense fog. Its service with squadron can be traced back to May 1923, followed by a rebuild [hence its airframe serial becoming ER928] at Aboukir. Between April 1924 and January 1925, it appears on returns submitted by 4 FTS before returning on an undisclosed date to the squadron and surviving a crash-landing, during which it turned over, this being recorded as 'circa 1924'.
Details of Flying Officer Herbert Gerald Slater's short service commission were promulgated in *The London Gazette* on 8th January 1924, issue 32896, page 269.
Aircraftman Thomas Reginald Harvey was another young airmen who would not be returning to a civilian life, one that he left behind in the 1920s as his service number was 342173.

Sunday 15 August 1926
20 Squadron W/Cdr J O Archer CBE Injured
Bristol F.2b LAC W S Bolam +
T/o Dalbandin in Baluchistan and reported as 'crashed'. Wing Commander John Oliver Archer recovered from his injuries and served for a further nine years before being placed on the retired list [LG 24 September 1935, issue 34201, page 6008]. Come the Second World War and he returned to the service and rose to Group Captain rank before relinquishing his commission on 1st May 1946 [LG 21 May 1946, supplement 37571, page 2396].
Joining as a boy airman twixt December 1918 and March 1919, Leading Aircraftman William Slater Bolam received 326349 as his service number.

Monday 16 August 1926
13 Squadron F/O T H J Wright +
Bristol F.2b Lt W L Roberts MC Injured
T/o Odiham*presumably to return to the squadron's base at Andover but while flying in the vicinity of Frimley, Surrey, stalled and crashed on Old Dean Common. Flying Officer Theodore Harold James Wright passed out of Sandhurst on 15th September 1915, and was *Gazetted* as a 2nd Lieutenant to the Seaforth Highlanders [Roos-shire Buffs, The Duke of Albany's] [LG 14th September 1915, issue 29295, page 9096]. He was granted a temporary commission as a flying officer for four years on 15th March 1924 [LG 18 March 1924, issue 32919, page 2329].
Early in his flying training, overseen by instructors at 5 FTS Shotwick, and with 14.30 flying hours logged, he was involved in a flying accident on Tuesday, 8th July 1924. Flying solo in Avro 504K H2540 when on approach to land "... *aeroplane was in a straight glide towards the aerodrome when at a height of 200-300 feet it fell in a nosedive from which the pilot failed to recover completely before the machine struck the ground."*
A Court of Inquiry was held; the Avro was a total wreck, and in the Court's opinion Flying Officer Wright mishandled the flying controls.
His passenger, Lieutenant William Lewis Roberts of the Middlesex Regiment, attached to the Monmouth Regiment, won his MC in 1917, *Gazetted* 16th August 1917, supplement 30234, page 8381: *"For conspicuous gallantry and devotion to duty when in charge of digging operations. In spite of heavy artillery fire he kept his men in hand, and by his fine personal example successfully completed the work under very trying conditions. His work on all occasions during the past two years has been marked by great courage and ability."*

'Air Fatality Near Aldershot'
'Flight Officer Killed and Observer Seriously Injured'

So the *Cheltenham Chronicle and Gloucestershire Graphic'* headed their piece on Saturday, August 21st, 1926, continuing: *"While on manoeuvres on Monday, Flight Officer Wright, of No. 13 Squadron, RAF Odiham, crashed from a great height on Old Dean Common, Trimley, and was killed instantaneously. His observer, Lieut. Roberts, of the Middlesex Regiment, was seriously injured and removed to the Cambridge Hospital, Aldershot.*
"It was stated that the accident occurred after the machine had dropped a message. For which purpose it had descended to a rather low altitude. There seemed to be a failure in the reascent, and the aeroplane suddenly stalled and nose-dived, crashing into a batch of fir trees.'';

* RAF Odiham's association with flying began in 1925, but it would be another twelve years before it was established as a permanent airfield, since when apart from brief spells as a prisoner of war camp [post-the Allied invasion of Normandy] and being placed under 'care and maintenance' on ceasing fighter operations in 1959, Odiham has been in continuous occupation by the Royal Air Force.

Wednesday 18 August 1926
19 Squadron F/O R N T Gape + St. Albans [Hatfield Road] Cemetery
Grebe II J7576
T/o Duxford and crashed out of control while attempting to forced-land on Gog Magog Golf Course at Shelford Bottom some 4 miles south of Cambridge. Flying Officer Roy Nugent Treherne Gape's short service commission was *Gazetted* 8th July 1924, issue 32954, page 5255. The Find a Grave website, which the authors acknowledge, shows Roy Gape being born in 1904, in Co. Limerick, Ireland.

The *Evening Telegraph and Post* advertised as the most circulated evening paper in Scotland, and costing one penny, in its Dundee edition that same evening carried the following:

'Fatal 'Plane Crash on Golf Course'
'Pilot Officer Killed'

"An aeroplane crashed in a forced landing, and burst into flames near Cambridge today, and a pilot officer, Roy Nugent Treherne Gape, 19th [Fighter] Squadron of the Royal Air Force, was killed.

"It was some time before the body could be taken from the pilot's seat owing to the heat of the flames.

"The Gloucester-Grebe single-seater which he was flying, was carrying two machine guns and a quantity of ammunition, and the cartridges burst in the fire owing to the heat.

"Spectators who were waiting for an opportunity to recover the pilot's body, said the bullets flew in all directions.

"The machine by the misfiring of its engine was observed to be in difficulties over the Gog Magog Golf Course, and after circling round several times the officer tried to land by number one tee. The machine crashed on the side of the road, and dashed into the hedge, which is by the golf course, and burst into flames.

"The body was recovered from the wreckage by Police-Sergeant Payne of the County Constabulary, who said that it was in a crouching position in the pilot's seat.

"The inquest is to be held this evening."

Monday 23 August 1926
58 Squadron P/O H J F Kempthorne +
Virginia
T/o Worthy Down and crashed near the airfield following a spin. Pilot Officer Hugh James Fitzgerald Kempthorne was thirteen months into his short service commission which was reported in *The London Gazette* on 28th July 1925, issue 33070, page 5051.

Friday 27 August 1926
60 Squadron Sgt D Munro Safe
DH.9A J7341/W
T/o Kohat where on landing it sustained damage of a magnitude that repairs were unlikely to proceed. For details of Sergeant Munro's previous mishaps, please refer to my summaries of 22nd January and 24th September 1925.

Tuesday 31 August 1926
16 Squadron P/O A L R Page +
Bristol F.2b LAC E A L Lowe Injured
T/o Old Sarum and headed for an exercise over the New Forest where 19 year old Pilot Officer Alfred Lionel René Page flew into a tree and crashed at Decoy Pond Farm near Beaulieu Road Station. He had served for close on a year-and-a-half having been *Gazetted* with a short service commission on 27th March 1925, issue 33033, page 2117. Leading Aircraftman Eric Arthur Lister Lowe died from his injuries the following day. He entered the service as a Boy, his service number 328941 indicating he volunteered between December 1918 and March 1919, and I suspect it was either late February or March that he joined.

Press coverage extended to the Irish papers, *The Londonderry Sentinel* in its Thursday edition under the heading *'Aeroplane Pilot Killed - Mechanic Seriously Injured'* reported: *"During military manoeuvres in New Forest on Tuesday and aeroplane which was co-operating with infantry crashed after striking a tree. The pilot officer, Alfred Lionel René Page, was killed, and his mechanic, Aircraftman Eric Arthur Lister Lowe, was seriously injured. The pilot seemed to be about to land, but struck the tree unexpectedly, and the machine nose-dived. Page belongs to Cagkeel, near Saltash, and Lowe to Hill."*

A more descriptive account was published in the *Westminster Gazette* filed on Tuesday by their own correspondent from Southampton, where the headlines read:

'Pilot Killed in Nose Dive'
'Fatal Low Flight at Manoeuvres'

"Pilot Officer Alfred Lionel Rene Page, aged 19, of Carkeel, near Saltash, met with instantaneous death in the New Forest to-day during the Army Manoeuvres.

"His observer, Air-Craftsman Eric Arthur Lister Lowe, who was terribly injured, lies in a critical condition in Netley Hospital with a fractured thigh and laceration of the brain.

"The aeroplane was engaged in dropping messages to the troops not far from Beaulieu station, and was flying low.

"When above a belt of trees it planed down towards a large field at Decoy Pond Farm, as if to land.

"There was, however, a tree in the path of the 'plane, and the pilot, now down to about 20ft., tried to rise and clear it, but the 'plane collided with the upper branches.

"It went on someway towards the farmhouse, and then suddenly nose-dived, and became a complete wreck.

"The pilot and observer were at once taken from the wreckage, but the pilot was already dead.

"Eleven RAF pilots have lost their lives in the past month. Since the beginning of the year there have been 55 fatal accidents to airmen.

"Mr. Percy George Allen, of Makepeace-avenue, Highgate, who was in the neighbourhood at the time, described at the inquest held in the evening, how he ran to the aeroplane and found Lowe, the mechanic, in the back seat with a large splinter sticking in his mouth.

"He lifted Lowe from the machine, after cutting away his helmet.

"A verdict of "Accidental Death" was returned."

SEPTEMBER

Wednesday 1 September 1926

55 Squadron F/O W O Du Port +
DH.9A LAC W A Pearse Injured

T/o Hinaidi and reported to have crashed either on the airfield or, possibly, close by. Flying Officer William Osmond Du Port reported to the Cadet College at Cranwell with the September 1922, entry of flight cadets and graduated on 31st July 1924 [LG 26 August 1924, issue 32968, page 6426].

Leading Aircraftman William Arthur Pearse died the following day; his service number 335313 indicates boy airmen service, the number block 335001 - 336000 being used between August 1919 and January 1921.

Friday 10 September 1926

2 Squadron F/O R R Reedman +
Bristol F.2b Major O Birkbeck Injured

T/o either from Manston or West Down Camp at Tilshead where the accident occurred. Flying Officer Reginald Richard Reedman, educated at Stamford Grammar School, arrived at Cranwell with the February 1922, intake of flight cadets and was assigned to A Squadron. He graduated and was appointed to a permanent commission [LG 22 January 1924, issue 32900, page 688]. His passenger, Major Oliver Birkbeck was serving with the Royal Artillery, Territorial Forces.

Monday's edition of *The Daily Mirror* carried a brief report:

'RAF Pilot Killed'

'Major Severely Injured in Machine's Second Attempt to Land'

"In an accident at Tilshead [Wilts.] to a Bristol Fighter, Flying Officer Reginald Richard Reedman, the pilot, was killed.

""Major Oliver Birkbeck, 108th [Suffolk and Norfolk Yeomanry], Field Brigade, Royal Artillery, was seriously injured.

"The pilot apparently tried to land, but ascended again without touching the ground. While making a second attempt the machine crashed.

"This is the thirty-eighth accident to a Service machine this year, and brings the total number of deaths to fifty-nine."

On the same page, *The Mirror* reported on a recent interview with London's Lord Mayor regarding unauthorised parachute jumps in Britain and Northern Ireland from civilian aeroplanes which, apparently, the participants were unaware that these jumps were strictly forbidden and a 'Notice to Airmen' had been issued by the Air Ministry reminding pilots to the effect. The Lord Mayor added; *"Not only are they dangerous to individuals making them, but also a danger to the public at large."*

Tuesday 14 September 1926

31 Squadron P/O D C Sherman +
Bristol F.2b

T/o Ambala and destroyed in a crash near Lahore. Pilot Officer Dick Culverwell Sherman's short service commission was *Gazetted* on 13th January 1925, issue 33011, page 302.

Monday 20 September 1926

39 Squadron *Not reported*
DH.9A J7812/12

T/o Spittlegate and crashed at Manor House, Gosberton, 5 miles NNW from Spalding in Lincolnshire.

56 Squadron F/O H F Luxmoore +
Grebe II J7584

T/o Biggin Hill and while indulging in aerobatics at a low altitude stalled and crashed on or near the airfield. Flying Officer Henry Frederick Luxmoore was a short service commission officer, *Gazetted* on 25th March 1924, issue 32921, page 2535. He underwent flying training at Shotwick with 5 FTS and his first squadron attachment was at Northolt where between 16th February 1925 and 19th July 1926, when he reported to Biggin Hill, he flew Siskin IIIs with 41 Squadron.

According to the Aviation Safety Network website, Flying Officer Luxmoore stalled off a manoeuvre at under 500 feet.

An account of his death appeared for days later in *The Courier*

'Young *Airman's Fatal Crash'*

'Entangled in Blazing Wreckage'

"The Greenwich Coroner [Mr. Sewell] held an inquest at the Lecture Hall, Biggin Hill Aerodrome, on Tuesday, on Flying Officer Henry Frederick Luxmoore, aged 24, son of Mr. C F C Luxmoore, of Stafford Barton, and attached to the

56th Flying Squadron, who met his death on the previous day as the result of a machine, in which he was flying, crashing. Mr. Blundell was chosen foreman of the jury.

"Pilot Officer T E G Pike said he had flown in the machine in question, on the day of the accident and found it satisfactory. While in the air he fancied there was some engine trouble, and came down, but found he had made a mistake, so took it up again without even stopping the engine. He could afterwards find no fault with it at all. He had intended going up again in the machine after deceased had finished film practice. Deceased went up about 2.15 p.m., and had finished his second film when witness's attention was drawn to the machine, which was about 150feet up, and in what was obviously the result of a "stall." The plane never recovered from the stall, and the engine was full on when it crashed on the other side of the hedge on the boundary of the aerodrome and burst into flames. Witness went to the spot on the fire engine, but it was at least two or three minutes before they could get deceased, who was lying on the ground, just out of the cockpit and entangled in the wreckage. He was of opinion that deceased had been attempting some "stunt," such as a "roll" or "half roll" when too close to the ground. It was a common practice for pilots to do stunts after their practice was finished, as they had little other opportunity of doing them.

"Flying Officer Armstrong said he saw the plane flying perfectly straight and rather slowly towards the corner of the aerodrome, but did not pay very much attention to it until he saw that the pilot was in difficulties. The aeroplane stalled with the left wing down and commenced a spin. It was still "stalled" when it hit the ground. Witness was first to reach the machine, and the heat was intense. He did not think deceased was a man to have taken an unnecessary risk, but he thought that in making the steep turn he went over the vertical. So far as witness knew, the machine was absolutely all right.

"Coroborative evidence was given by Flight-Lieut. J G Skeet, medical officer, who witnessed the accident. The primary cause of death was a fractured base of the skull.

"The jury returned a verdict of "accidental death," and the Coroner expressed sympathy with the young airman's father."

Wednesday 22 September 1926
5 Squadron F/O D Robinson Injured
Bristol F.2b AC1 P Jones +

T/o Risalpur and came down in the River Indus near Attock in the northern region of the Punjab. Tragically, before he was able to reach the river bank, Aircraftman Percy Jones [who may well have been injured] drowned. Flying Officer Dennis Robinson's short service commission and his release from the service, owing to ill-health, may be found in the *Gazettes* of 29th January 1924 and 11th September 1928, issues 32902 page 875 and 33420, page 5977, respectively.

Aircraftman Percy Jones was among the many civilians joining between September 1919 and June 1925, his service number being recorded as 344719.

OCTOBER

Friday 1 October 1926
20 Squadron F/O P H Nicholls Injured
Bristol F.2b J6631 LAC G Cairns Injured

T/o Peshawar where it crashed and caught fire. Both airmen were pulled from their cockpits, Flying Officer Philip Hedgeland Nicholls in a critical condition. For nearly a week he lingered in terrible pain before passing away on the 5th. Leading Aircraftman George Cairns is believed to have recovered.

Flying Officer Nicholls was one of 27 probationary pilot officers granted a short service commission, *Gazetted* 29th July 1924, issue 32960, page 5723.

The Bristol had followed the familiar pattern of being delivered to the Ascot packing depot ex-works, and on arrival in India passed through the depots at Dright Road and Lahore before being flown to Dardoni where it was taken on charge by 5 Squadron, the letter 'P' being noted by August 1924. It was first recorded in use with 20 Squadron in March 1926.

Friday 8 October 1926
56 Squadron WO1 E G Haug + Keston Churchyard
Grebe II

T/o Kenley but lost control and crashed with fatal consequences. Erik Gutzeit Haug's death was reported in the press, the following extract being published in the *Belfast Telegraph* on 12th October 1926, and repeated on the Kenley Revival website: *"An inquest was held at Kenley Aerodrome on Monday on First-Class Warrant Officer Erik Gauzeit* [sic] *Haug [28] a Norwegian subject, who belonged to the RAF, and was attached to the Biggin Hill aerodrome, Kent. Evidence was given that deceased joined the RAF in 1918, and was an experienced pilot, having flown over 900 miles. Last Friday, he flew from Biggin Hill to Kenley Aerodrome on a single-seater Gloucester Grebe.*

"When he started on the return journey two officers at Kenley Aerodrome said the machine swerved to the right after travelling 100 yards along the ground. It then turned round in a circle. The left wing touched the ground, and one of the wheels of the undercarriage buckled. The machine turned over on its nose. They expressed the opinion that the machine had got out of control, and that the accident was caused by deceased taking off "slightly out of the wind."

"Medical evidenced showed that death was due to a fracture of the base of the skull and a verdict of accidental death was returned."

The website notes that Warrant Officer Haug was born on 30th December 1896, in Bragenes, Buskerud, Norway, and learnt to fly in 1918, gaining certificate No. 69. Prior to arriving in the UK, he served with the Norwegian military. Although the paper indicates Erik Haug as joining the Royal Air Force, I suggest he was attached as the rank of Warrant Officer 1st Class is a Norwegian Army Air Service rank. Furthermore, the press report that he had flown *"over 900 miles"* is an error for over 900 hours. The website has three photographs, one showing Erik Haug, copyright *Norsk Luftfartsmuseum* and two showing his grave in Keston Churchyard in Greater London.

Monday 18 October 1926
208 Squadron F/O V B Bingham-Hall MC +
Bristol F.2J C802 P/O W Higgins +
T/o Ismailia and wrecked in a crash at Moascar*near the town of Ismailia. Flying OfficerVincent Bingham Bingham-Hall was granted a short service in his rank and with a term of engagement for seven years on the active list, as *Gazetted* 25th March 1924, issue 32921, page 2535. His military service began with a commission as a temporary 2nd Lieutenant with the Gloucestershire Regiment on 23rd October 1915 [LG 4 November 1915, supplement 29352, page 10903]. Rising to the rank of Acting Captain, he won his MC late on in the war while attached to the 1/5th Battalion from his parent battalion, the 8th Gloucestershires: *"For conspicuous gallantry near Bazuel on 19th October 1918. He led his company on to the attack, though the unit on his right was held up and his flank was exposed. He also led his company 250 yards beyond the objective to outflank the enemy on his right, who were subjecting him to heavy fire. His fine conduct helped the advance of the flanking unit, so the whole objective was taken."* [EG 11 December 1919, issue 13536, page 3947].

Pilot Officer William Higgins had been attached from the Royal Marines.

* The site of a large CWGC War Cemetery which is situated just off the main Ismailia to Cairo road. It contains close on 900 graves of which 475 are the resting places of Commonwealth servicemen, while 495 are non-war graves with a further 19 being burials of other nationalities.

Wednesday 20 October 1926
100 Squadron *Not reported*
Fawn II J7223
T/o Spittlegate and damaged beyond economical repair after forced-landing and turning turtle on soft ground near Bulby, 4 miles NW of Bourne, Lincolnshire.

Monday 25 October 1926
3 Squadron F/O A T K Shipwright DFC Safe
Woodcock II J7973
Wrecked following the collision reported below. Commanded by Squadron Leader James Milne Robb*DFC, the squadron had been detached to Eastchurch from Upavon for armament training. Flying Officer Alan Thomas Kingston Shipwright was short service commissioned, his details being *Gazetted* on 12th July 1921, issue 32387, page 5561. He had, however, served as a fighter pilot in the *Great War* flying Spad VIIs with 19 Squadron and it was on the 16th of August 1917 during the *Battle of Ypres* that he was shot down in A6634. Taking off from Poperinghe shortly before midday it is believed he fell victim to Johannes Klein of Jasta 18. An Officers Casualty Card exists which shows he was posted to the squadron, then at Lièttres, on 24th July 1917 and notes he was *"Officially reported Prisoner of War."*

The 16th of August 1917 was a costly day for the RFC squadrons fighting on the Western Front with Trevor Henshaw recording the loss of at least thirty-two aircraft with five Spad VIIs missing from 19 Squadron, a casualty count only surpassed by 9 Squadron which filed returns for six of their RE.8s as either being wrecked or damaged in action.

Flying Officer Shipwright's DFC was promulgated in the Edinburgh edition of the *Gazette* June 13th, 1924, issue 14031, page 812: *"His Majesty the King has been graciously pleased to approve of the undermentioned awards for distinguished service rendered during the operations in Kurdistan between 15th February and 19th June 1923."*

It is further reported that he was involved in a crash while taking off from a landing ground near Jerusalem on 10th September 1929, his DH.9 failing to become airborne and colliding with a building which ripped away a wing and the undercarriage. Coming to a stop the crew [his passenger is named as Sergeant Fred Keats] jumped out and seconds later the petrol tank exploded. However, as yet I have not been able to find a record of this in *The DH.4/DH.9 File.* For additional information concerning Flying Officer Shipwright, please refer to his entry in Appendix D for 1921.

The 'write off' of J7973 was the first in squadron service. The Woodcock, produced by Hawker Engineering, successor to Sopwith Aviation, was introduced to front-line service by 3 Squadron in May 1925.

* Subsequently Air Chief Marshal Sir James Milne Robb GCB KBE DSO DFC AFC three times mentioned in despatches.

207 Squadron *Not reported*
DH.9A J7859
T/o Eastchurch where on landing the DH ran into a 3 Squadron Woodcock which was taxying. Both machines were damaged beyond repair.

Note. Some reports suggest the Woodcock had just become airborne when it came into collision with the DH, both machines falling to the ground, damaged beyond repair, but, thankfully, without the pilots being injured.

NOVEMBER

Tuesday 9 November 1926

4 Squadron P/O C V Mossman +
Bristol F.2b AC2 C H Hayward +

T/o Farnborough and spun in on approach to South Farnborough. Pilot Officer Cyril Vernon Mossman was granted a short service commission a little over a year ago on 12th September 1925 [LG 25 September 1925, issue 33087, page 6205]. His passenger, Aircraftman Cecil Herbert Hayward was a former boy who enlisted between July 1922 and January 1924, probably at some time in 1923, as his service number 364117 comes more or less midpoint between the block 361601-37000.

Thursday 11 November 1926 - Armistice Day

207 Squadron Sgt G F Taylor +
DH.9A J7610 AC2 P C Hinton +

T/o Eastchurch and destroyed following a spinning nose dive. On impact the DH burst into flames. Aircraftman Percy Charles Hinton at 18 years of age was amongst the youngest airmen to lose their life in a flying accident.

The service numbers of the two airmen are 315176 and 364039 respectively, thereby identifying Sergeant Taylor as a transferee from the Royal Naval Air Service in April 1918, and Aircraftman Hinton as a former boy - see my summary above and the remarks attributed to Aircraftman Hayward.

A press report covering both accidents appeared in Friday's edition of *The Daily News* beneath a photographs of thousands gathered in front of the Mansion House and adjacent buildings including The Bank of England standing in respectful silence for two minutes in remembrance of the *Great War* dead. In order of reporting the two articles were headed:

'Airmen Killed'

'Burned to Death in Crash'

"At 3.45 p.m. yesterday, at the Eastchurch Aerodrome, Sheppey, Pilot Sergeant George Frederick Taylor, accompanied by a passenger, Aircraftman Percy Charles Hinton, was flying when the machine crashed.

"It burst into flames and the two men were burned to death.

"The boundary of the aerodrome is a 6ft. wide ditch, and neither ambulance nor fire brigade was able to reach the spot.

"The wife of Pilot Sergeant Taylor is at present in hospital.

"There have now been 72 fatal casualties in the Royal Air Force this year, including two at Farnborough [Hampshire] on Tuesday."

'Farnborough Inquest'

"At the inquest at Aldershot yesterday on Pilot Officer Cyril Vernon Mossman and Aircraftman Cecil Herbert Hayward, who were killed at Farnborough last Tuesday, the only theory of the cause of the accident was offered by Pilot Officer Halliwell, who suggested that the pilot, who was training to observe artillery fire, must have been looking back to see a puff trailer [a machine which counterfeits artillery fire] and so have dropped into an angle of glide too steep for safety."

Monday 22 November 1926

24 Squadron F/Lt F St. J Woollard AFC + Whyteleafe [St. Luke's] Churchyard
DH.9A J7310 F/O F L Collison Injured

T/o Kenley but while making a climbing turn stalled and fell onto the roof of a hangar and caught fire. Flying Officer Frederic Laing Collison was pulled from burning wreck alive but died soon after. Formerly of the 4th Battalion, Essex Regiment, he had been granted a short service commission ass recently as 6th September 1926 [LG 5 October 1926, issue 33208, page 6374].

Flight Lieutenant Felix St. John Woollard, formerly of the Easst Kent Regiment, was one of many officers awarded the AFC, *Gazetted* 3rd June 1919, supplement 31378, page 7035. He was appointed to a permanent commission, effective 1st August 1919, and *Gazetted* on 28th October 1919, issue 31620, page 13139. An account of the tragedy appeared the next day in the *Western Morning News* and recently repeated on the Kenley Revival website, which I dutifully acknowledge: *"The pilot and passenger of a Royal Air Force 'plane were killed in a crash at Kenley Aerodrome to-day. The machine, which was a DH.9A of No. 24 Communications Squadron, stationed at Kenley, burst into flames, and when the pilot, Flight-Lieut. Feliz* [sic] *St. John Woollard was extricated, he was dead. His passenger, Flying Officer Frederic Laing Collison, was injured, and he died five minutes after admission to Purley Cottage Hospital.*

"The pilot had started an ordinary practice flight, and at a height of about 200 feet he "stalled", and the 'plane nose-dived to the ground. A young Flying Officer who was at the aerodrome at the time of the crash gave me a graphic account of what happened.

"I was not on duty at the time," he said, "but happened to be at the aerodrome at the time watching the flying. Flight-Lieut. Woollard's 'plane had only just taken off, and the machine had attained a height of only about 200ft. I was watching closely from the time it left the ground, and I saw the machine get into a nasty stall. I knew at one there was no time for the pilot to right himself, and the 'plane nose-dived straight down, the engine burying itself in the ground just behind the sheds. There was an explosion as the petrol tank burst, and the flames quickly enveloped the whole machine. I could see at once that all hope of rescuing Flight-Lieut. Woollard was gone. We broke the fuselage of the 'plane and got out Flying-Officer Collison, whose face was badly cut about."

The remainder of the report records Felix Woollard as being born in Paris in June 1892, but at the time of the outbreak of the *Great War* he was living in Bournemouth on the South Coast and employed as an Estate Agent's clerk; however, on enlisting in 1914, he gave his profession as a 'lorry driver.' He married in 1915, by which time he had fathered two daughters, Eileen and Marie. Two photographs accompany are 'posted' on the website, courtesy of Andy Long and Linda Duffield, the former being a photograph of Flight Lieutenant Woollard and latter an image of his grave.

A Memorial Plaque to Flying Officer Collison may be seen in Epping Old Church which shows he was serving with the Artists Rifles in 1916, transferring to the RFC in 1917, and service in France from 1918 to 1919. Postwar, he joined the 4th Battalion, Essex Regiment, Territorial Force before returning to the Royal Air Force shortly before his death.

DECEMBER

Tuesday 7 December 1926

22 Squadron F/O G V Wheatley +
Gamecock I J7891

T/o Martlesham Heath for continuation test flying during which major structural failure occurred with the wings becoming detached. Moments later the remains of the fighter fell into nearby Martlesham village. The first Gamecock in squadron service had been destroyed.

The Aviation Safety Network website [which the authors acknowledge] reports the Gamecock as undergoing a test following re-balancing of the ailerons which had been subject to 'flutter,' and it was within ten minutes or so of the test that disaster overtook Flying Officer Gilbert Vernon Wheatley, aged 27. His details are recorded in Appendix D and the entry for 5th July 1921, and is mentioned in my summaries for 4 Squadron on 26th July 1921, and 5 Squadron on 29th January 1924.

Kesgrave Wood is mentioned as the location where at least some of the debris fell. Gamecock I J7891 was the first aircraft in a batch of thirty [J7891-J7920 all fitted with 425hp Jupiter VI nine-cylinder single-row radial engine produced by the Bristol Aeroplane Company].

A report in the *Aberdeen Press and Journal* headlined *'Plane Falls Apart - Flying Officer Killed in Test Flight'* reads:

"Flying Officer Gilbert Vernon Wheatley, No. 22 Bombing Squadron, was killed in a remarkable aeroplane accident near Martlesham Aerodrome yesterday.

"The officer was making test flights with a Gloucester Gamecock single-seater machine, when suddenly the lower wings seemed to become unconnected, and the machine crashed to earth from a height of about 400 feet.

"Men from the aerodrome rushed to the spot, but the pilot had been killed instantly. He had evidently attempted to get out of the cockpit as the machine was falling, and his body was found 30 yards from the wreckage, which had almost completely buried itself.

"An eye-witness, who was motoring in the district, said that he saw the machine flying over the main Ipswich road apparently in perfect order. Suddenly both wings appeared to come apart from the fuselage, and the undercarriage fell to the ground, leaving the wings floating for a short time in the air.

"Another message says that apparently the machine had been looping the loop and accident occurred as it came out of a loop.

"When assistance arrived at the spot it was found that the parachute attached to the officer was open. A wing of the machine was found half a mile away.

"Mr. Gilbert Vernon Wheatley was 27 years of age. He became attached to the Martlesham Experimental Station, Suffolk, about a year ago, having previously served in India. He was an experienced pilot with war service, and was popular among his brother officers.

"The number of Royal Air Force fatalities since January 1, 1926, now totals 77."

Referring to Army Form B.103c, it shows Flying Officer Wheatley, born 17th March 1899, joined the RFC of 13th August 1917, and, coincidentally, was attached to 22 Squadron [Bristol F.2b] at Serny on 24th April 1918. On completion of his tour of duty he was posted back to the UK on 26th October 1918.

Thursday 9 December 1926

25 Squadron F/O J H C Purvis +
Grebe II

T/o Hawkinge and while making a low turn nose-dived and crashed. On impact the fighter went up in flames. Flying Officer John Harry Campbell Purvis's short service commission was *Gazetted* on 27th January 1925, issue 33015, page 595. He was twenty years of age.

A full report of the accident and the inquest that followed was published in the *Folkestone, Hythe, Sandgate & Cheriton Herald* on Saturday, 11th December 1926, under the headline *"Fatal Aeroplane Crash - Flying Officer Killed at Hawkinge - Farmer Burnt in Rescue Attempt."*

"Flying Officer John Harry Campbell Purvis, of the 25th Squadron, RAF, stationed at Hawkinge, was killed instantly in an aeroplane crash on Thursday morning. His machine, a single seater Gloster Grebe fighting 'plane nose dived from a low altitude on the edge of the aerodrome and after striking the ground with great force burst into flames. The deceased was the son of Major R W Purvis, a well known landowner, of Gilmerton, St. Andrews, Fife, and a nephew of Sir John Gilmour, Secretary for Scotland, and was twenty-one years of age. After the machine had crashed and caught fire Mr. Albert Daniels of Terlingham Farm, and a young man named Thomas Carman, of Alkham, who was helping him, rushed to the wreckage and succeeded in extricating the pilot. Unfortunately this plucky effort was of no avail as the officer had been killed instantly by the crash. Mr. Daniels was burnt about the face and right hand, and subsequently received surgical treatment by members of the aerodrome staff. A fire picket from the aerodrome was rushed to the scene, but in spite of their efforts, the machine was reduced to a charred and tangled mass.

"Mr. Daniels subsequently stated that the machine at one time appeared to be coming straight towards him, and he thought it would hit him. The heat given off by the burning mass was terrific. The accident occurred just after engaged on camera gun practice. Flying Officer Purvis, who was a very popular officer, was married about a year ago. This makes the eighty-third death in the RAF this year through flying accidents, but there has not been a fatal accident at Hawkinge since September 1925.

"The East Kent Coroner [Mr. Rutley Mowll] held an inquest on Flying Officer Purvis at Hawkinge Aerodrome yesterday [Friday]afternoon. The Coroner, in outlining the facts to the jury, referred to Mr. Daniel's gallant effort to extricate the pilot from the machine, and said he was only sorry he could not have brought the pilot out.

"Flt-Lieut. J E Cox, Medical Officer at Hawkinge Aerodrome, identified the body. He said deceased had only been at Hawkinge a few months. Witness got to the scene of the crash two or three minutes after it had happened, just after 10 a.m. the previous day. The machine was about 200 yards away from the Aerodrome. The body had been extricated. He found deceased was quite dead. Death was due to a fracture of the base of the skull. From the nature of the injuries witness thought the pilot must have been killed instantaneously.

"Pilot Sergt. F C Stanford, of the 25th Squadron, said before the accident he had been working with the deceased in camera gun practice. Witness completed his film, and signalled to that effect. They were then both going to land. They both began to descend, and as he [witness] was gliding in to land he saw deceased in front of him. Witness thought he was going to land there and then, but he apparently changed his mind and turned to the left. This turn took him off the aerodrome over some trees. That was the last he saw of deceased's machine, as he [witness] then landed. As he was taxing towards the sheds he looked round and saw a cloud of smoke going up. When deceased turned he seemed to be about 50ft up. He thought deceased believed he had sufficient height to do a complete turn, but he was too near the ground to do so. Deceased might have deflected his machine off the aerodrome to give witness an opportunity of landing. He broke away from deceased at a height of 2,000ft., and they came down independently.

"Mr. Albert Daniels, of Terlingham Farm, Hawkinge, whose head and right hand were swathed in bandages, said he was cutting wood down in a copse adjoining the aerodrome, with a lad named Carman, when he saw an aeroplane coming right over his head at a very low altitude. The machine was climbing, and when it got about a hundred yards away the pilot made a sharp turn to the right, and then nose dived to the ground from a hight of about 75 feet. The 'plane struck the ground about fifteen yards from where he was standing. It turned over on its back and immediately burst into flames. Witness rushed to the machine, and with the assistance of Carman tried to get the pilot who was strapped in, out. After removing some of the wreckage he was able to cut the strap. He sustained burns to the face and right hand. When deceased made the turn the engine was full on. When he first saw deceased's machine it was very low.

"The Coroner said they all very much appreciated Mr. Daniel's gallant efforts, and trusted he would get over his burns all right. Thos. Carman, aged 19, of Upper Standing, Alkham, also gave evidence.

"Sergt. J S A Bance said he saw the machine nose dive after making one turn.

"Flight Sergt. A Springate said he examined the engine of the machine before deceased took off, and it was the OK. There was no failure on the part of the engine.

"Flying Officer L A Walsh said deceased had flown one hundred and forty hours with this particular machine. He was an experienced and very good pilot, but very erratic. He thought deceased must have stalled the machine, By that he meant that in the turn deceased lost complete flying speed. The machine was being examined by the Air Inspection Dept.

"The Coroner:- "Is there any way of preventing these fires when a crash takes place?" Witness:- "This is only the second machine of this kind which has caught fire since it has been adopted by the RAF." Coroner:- "You mean to say it is unusual for a Grebe to catch fire?" Witness:- "Yes."

"The jury returned a verdict of "Accidental Death." The Foreman [Mr. H Kettle] said the jury desired to express sympathy with the deceased's relatives and the members of the Squadron. They hoped the Air Ministry would officially the plucky efforts of Mr. Daniels to extricate the pilot."

Wednesday 29 December 1926

28 Squadron F/O A N MacNeal +
Bristol F.2b LAC C A Overy +

T/o Ambala and wrecked here in a fatal crash. Flying Officer Alastair Neil MacNeal, formerly of the Royal Navy, was granted a short service commission, *Gazetted* 17th April 1923, issue 32815, page 2816.

Leading Aircraftman Cyril Arthur Overy's service had been relatively brief. Joining as a boy between July 1922 and January 1924, his service number 362102 is within the allotted block 361601 to 370000.

Although the precise date has not been recorded 47 Squadron DH.9A J7119 BIV was totally wrecked during a landing at the Baharia Oasis in Egypt.

Similarly, Grebe IIIDC J7535 reported with 56 Squadron between February and August 1926, is noted in the *J File* as *"Overturned on landing."* Presumably during the year, and possibly in August.

APPENDICES
1926

Appendix A - Squadron Losses Table and Losses by Aircraft Type

Column 1 - Squadron

Column 2 - Aircraft type

Column 3 - Written off

Column 4 - Fatalities

1 Squadron	Sopwith 7F.1 Snipe	2	1
2 Squadron	Bristol F.2b	1	1
3 Squadron	Hawker Woodcock II	1	
4 Squadron	Bristol F.2b	1	2
5 Squadron	Bristol F.2b	2	3
8 Squadron	Airco DH.9A	2	
9 Squadron	Avro 504K	1	
12 Squadron	Fairey Fawn II	1	2
	Fairey Fox I	1	
13 Squadron	Bristol F.2b	1	1
14 Squadron	Airco DH.9A	1	2
16 Squadron	Bristol F.2b	1	2
19 Squadron	Gloster Grebe II	2	1
20 Squadron	Bristol F.2b	2	2
22 Squadron	Gloster Gamecock I	1	1
24 Squadron	Airco DH.9A	1	2
25 Squadron	Gloster Grebe II	1	1
28 Squadron	Bristol F.2b	2	4
29 Squadron	Gloster Grebe II	1	
31 Squadron	Bristol F.2b	2	2
32 Squadron	Gloster Grebe II	1	1
39 Squadron	Airco DH.9A	1	
41 Squadron	Armstrong Whitworth Siskin III	2	1
43 Squadron	Sopwith 7F.1 Snipe	2	
45 Squadron	Vickers Vernon	2	5
47 Squadron	Airco DH.9A	4	2
55 Squadron	Airco DH.9A	2	2
56 Squadron	Gloster Grebe II	3	2
	Gloster Grebe II DC	1	
58 Squadron	Vickers Virginia	1	1
60 Squadron	Airco DH.9A	2	2
84 Squadron	Airco DH.9A	1	2
100 Squadron	Fairey Fawn II	3	1
207 Squadron	Airco DH.9A	2	2
208 Squadron	Bristol F.2b	1	2
Totals		55	50

	Airco DH.9A	16	14
	Armstrong Whitworth Siskin III	2	1
	Avro 504K	1	
	Bristol F.2b	13	19
	Fairey Fawn II	4	3
	Fairey Fox I	1	
	Gloster Gamecock I	1	1
	Gloster Grebe II	8	5
	Gloster Grebe II DC	1	
	Hawker Woodcock II	1	
	Sopwith 7F.1 Snipe	4	1
	Vickers Vernon	2	5
	Vickers Virginia	1	1
Totals		55	50

Appendix B - Squadron Locations and Commanding Officers

Very much a year 'steady as she goes' with the gradual introduction of new types and the withdrawal from front-line service of the 7F.1 Snipe which made its debut with 43 Squadron as a fighter in the closing months of the *Great War*. Appropriately it fell to the 'Fighting Cocks' to be among the last to fly this versatile fighter, though it continued in use with 1 Squadron in Iraq until the November.

The autumn of the year also saw the formation of a second Special Reserve squadron, Fairey Fawn Iis, now being discarded by the front-line units, being taken on as initial equipment.

1 Squadron	7F.1 Snipe	Hinaidi	01.01.26-01.11.26	Disbanded
2 Squadron	Bristol F.2b	Manston	01.01.26-31.12.26	
3 Squadron	Woodcock II	Upavon	01.01.26-31.12.26	
4 Squadron	Bristol F.2b	Farnborough	01.01.26-31.12.26	
5 Squadron	Bristol F.2b	Risalpur	01.01.26-31.12.26	
6 Squadron	Bristol F.2b	Mosul	01.01.26-20.10.26	
		Hinaidi	20.10.26-31.12.26	
7 Squadron	Vimy	Bircham Newton	01.01.26-31.12.26	
8 Squadron	DH.9A	Hinaidi	01.01.26-31.12.26	
9 Squadron	Vimy/Virginia	Manston	01.01.26-31.12.26	Vimy withdrawn during June
11 Squadron	Fawn III/Horsley	Netheravon	01.01.26-31.12.26	Fawn III withdrawn in December
12 Squadron	Fawn III/Fox	Andover	01.01.26-31.12.26	Fawn III withdrawn in December
13 Squadron	Bristol F.2b	Andover	01.01.26-31.12.26	
14 Squadron	DH.9A	Ramel & Amman	01.01.26-31.12.26	
XV Squadron	*Various*	Martlesham Heath	01.01.26-31.12.26	
16 Squadron	Bristol F.2b	Old Sarum	01.01.26-31.12.26	
17 Squadron	7F.1 Snipe/Woodcock II	Hawkinge	01.01.26-14.10.26	7F.1 Snipe withdrawn during March
		Upavon	14.10.26-31.12.26	
19 Squadron	Grebe II	Duxford	01.01.26-31.12.26	
20 Squadron	Bristol F.2b	Peshawar	01.01.26-31.12.26	
22 Squadron	*Various*	Martlesham Heath	01.01.26-31.12.26	
23 Squadron	7F.1 Snipe/Gamecock	Henlow	01.01.26-31.12.26	7F.1 Snipe withdrawn during May
24 Squadron	*Various*	Kenley	01.01.26-31.12.26	
25 Squadron	Grebe II	Hawkinge	01.01.26-31.12.26	
27 Squadron	DH.9A	Risalpur	01.01.26-31.12.26	
28 Squadron	Bristol F.2b	Quetta	01.01.26-15.12.26	
		Ambala	15.12.26-31.12.26	
29 Squadron	Grebe II	Duxford	01.01.26-31.12.26	
30 Squadron	DH.9A	Kirkuk	01.01.26-31.12.26	
31 Squadron	Bristol F.2b	Ambala	01.01.26-15.12.26	
		Quetta	15.12.26-31.12.26	
32 Squadron	Grebe II/Gamecock II	Kenley	01.01.26-31.12.26	
39 Squadron	DH.9A	Spittlegate	01.01.26-31.12.26	
41 Squadron	Siskin III	Northolt	01.01.2631.12.26	
43 Squadron	7F.1 Snipe/Gamecock I	Henlow	01.01.26-12.12.26	7F.1 Snipe withdrawn during May
		Tangmere	12.12.26-31.12.26	Ground party arrived 07.12.26
45 Squadron	Vernon	Hinaidi	01.01.26-31.12.26	
47 Squadron	DH.9A	Helwan	01.01.26-31.12.26	
55 Squadron	DH.9A	Hinaidi	01.01.26-31.12.26	
56 Squadron	Grebe II	Biggin Hill	01.01.26-31.12.26	
58 Squadron	Virginia	Worthy Down	01.01.26-31.12.26	
60 Squadron	DH.9A	Kohat	01.01.26-31.12.26	
70 Squadron	Vernon/Victoria	Hinaidi	01.01.26-31.12.26	Vernon withdrawn in December
84 Squadron	DH.9A	Shaibah	01.01.26-31.12.26	
99 Squadron	Hyderabad	Bircham Newton	01.01.26-31.12.26	
100 Squadron	Fawn II/Horsley II	Spittlegate	01.01.26-31.12.26	Fawn II withdrawn in December
111 Squadron	Siskin III/IIIA	Duxford	01.01.26-31.12.26	Siskin III withdrawn in November
207 Squadron	DH.9A	Eastchurch	01.01.26-31.12.26	
208 Squadron	Bristol F.2b	Ismailia	01.01.26-31.12.26	
216 Squadron	Vimy/Victoria	Heliopolis	01.01.26-31.12.26	Vimy withdrawn in January
502 Squadron SR	Vimy	Aldergrove	01.01.26-31.12.26	
503 Squadron SR	Fawn II	Waddington	05.10.26-31.12.26	
600 Squadron AAF	DH.9A	Northolt	01.01.26-31.12.26	
601 Squadron AAF	Avro 504K/504N	Northolt	01.01.26-31.12.26	Avro 504K/504N withdrawn in June
	DH.9A			DH.9A issued during June
602 Squadron AAF	DH.9A	Renfrew	01.01.26.-31.12.26	
603 Squadron AAF	DH.9A	Turnhouse	01.01.26-31.12.26	
605 Squadron AAF	DH.9A	Castle Bromwich	05.10.26-31.12.26	Day bomber duties

Squadron	Commanding Officer	Date	Notes
1 Squadron	Squadron Leader E D Atkinson DFC AFC	In situ	See Appendix B 1924
2 Squadron	Squadron Leader R E Saul DFC	In situ	See Appendix B 1925
3 Squadron	Squadron Leader J C Russell DSO mid *Croix de Guerre* [Belgium]	In situ	See Appendix B 1924
	Squadron Leader J M Robb DFC	23 April 1926	See 30 Squadron 1924
4 Squadron	Squadron Leader J C Slessor MC mid	In situ	See Appendix B 1925
5 Squadron	Squadron Leader A J Capel	In situ	See Appendix B 1923
6 Squadron	Squadron Leader D F Stevenson OBE DSO MC* twice mid	In situ	See Appendix B 1925
	Squadron Leader C N Lowe MC DFC	24 November 1926	See 602 Squadron AAF 1925
7 Squadron	Squadron Leader J S T Bradley OBE	In situ	See Appendix B 1925
	Wing Commander C H B Blount OBE MC	1 May 1926	See 4 Squadron 1921
8 Squadron	Squadron Leader W A McClaughry DSO MC DFC three times mid Australia	In situ	See Appendix B 1924
9 Squadron	Squadron Leader W J M Guilfoyle OBE MC six times mid Australia	In situ	See Appendix B 1925
	Wing Commander V Gaskell-Blackburn DSC AFC	March 1926	See 55 Squadron 1921
	Wing Commander C C Durston	29 December 1926	See 13 Squadron 1924
11 Squadron	Squadron Leader E A B Rice MC	In situ	See 6 Squadron 1921
12 Squadron	Squadron Leader A Gray MC	In situ	See Appendix B 1923
	Squadron Leader T E Salt AFC	19 May 1926	S/Ldr killed 14 October 1931
13 Squadron	Squadron Leader C C Durston	In situ	See 13 Squadron 1924
	Squadron Leader H I Hanmer DFC	16 November 1926	G/Capt retired list 21 September 1941
14 Squadron	Squadron Leader A N Gallehawk AFC	In situ	See Appendix B 1924
	Squadron Leader J Everidge MC	26 June 1926	S/Ldr retired list 5 August 1929
	Squadron Leader A N Gallehawk AFC	2 December 1926	See 14 Squadron 1924
XV Squadron	Squadron Leader P C Sherren MC	In situ	See 60 Squadron 1921
16 Squadron	Squadron Leader W A Coryton MVO DFC	In situ	See Appendix B 1925
17 Squadron	Squadron Leader J Leacroft MC*	In situ	See Appendix B 1924
19 Squadron	Squadron Leader H W G Jones MC	In situ	See Appendix B 1925
20 Squadron	Squadron Leader J B Cole-Hamilton twice mid	In situ	See Appendix B 1925
	Squadron Leader J V Steel OBE	23 July 1926	See 100 Squadron 1921
22 Squadron	Squadron Leader T H England DSC	In situ	See Appendix B 1925
23 Squadron	Squadron Leader R Collishaw DSO* OBE DSC DFC three times mid	In situ	See 30 Squadron 1921
24 Squadron	Squadron Leader W H L O'Neill MC	In situ	See Appendix B 1925
25 Squadron	Squadron Leader A H Peck DSO MC*	In situ	See Appendix B 1923
	Squadron Leader E D Atkinson DFC AFC	12 September 1926	See 84 Squadron 1924
27 Squadron	Squadron Leader L M Bailey AFC	In situ	See Appendix B 1924
28 Squadron	Squadron Leader C S Wynne-Eyton DSO	In situ	See Appendix B 1924
	Squadron Leader A W Mylne	15 February 1926	A/Cmdr retirement 21 May 1945
29 Squadron	Squadron Leader M L Taylor AFC	In situ	See Appendix B 1924
30 Squadron	Squadron Leader F H Coleman	In situ	See Appendix B 1925
31 Squadron	Wing Commander J O Archer CBE	In situ	See Appendix B 1925
	Squadron Leader J F Gordon DFC	1 April 1926	S/Ldr retired list 25 November 1936
32 Squadron	Squadron Leader H P Lale DFC mid	In situ	See Appendix B 1924
	Squadron Leader R B Mansell OBE	3 August 1926	AV-M died 2 January 1945
39 Squadron	Squadron Leader H V Champion de Crepigny MC DFC	In situ	See 60 Squadron 1922
41 Squadron	Squadron Leader G W Murlie-Green DSO* MC* three times mid *Croix de Guerre* [France] *Croix de Chevalier Croix de Guerre* [Belgium]	In situ	See Appendix B 1924
	Squadron Leader F Sowrey DSO MC AFC	2 February 1926	See 8 Squadron 1924
43 Squadron	Squadron Leader A F Brooks	In situ	See Appendix B 1925
45 Squadron	Squadron Leader R M Hill MC AFC mid	In situ	See Appendix B 1924
47 Squadron	Squadron Leader R S Maxwell MC DFC* AFC	In situ	See 24 Squadron 1923
55 Squadron	Squadron Leader E D Johnson AFC mid	In situ	See Appendix B 1925
56 Squadron	Squadron Leader F J Vincent DFC	In situ	See Appendix B 1925
	Squadron Leader C H Elliott-Smith AFC	9 September 1926	A/Cmdr retirement 12 June 1944
58 Squadron	Squadron Leader A T Harris AFC	In situ	See 31 Squadron 1931
60 Squadron	Squadron Leader T F Hazell DSO MC DFC	In situ	See Appendix B 1925
70 Squadron	Wing Commander E W Norton DSC *Croix de Guerre* [Belgium]	In situ	See Appendix B 1925
	Wing Commander H R Nicholl OBE	3 September 1926	AV-M retirement 15 March 1942
84 Squadron	Squadron Leader D E Stodart DSO DFC mid Australia	In situ	See Appendix B 1924
99 Squadron	Squadron Leader W J Ryan MBE	In situ	See Appendix B 1925
100 Squadron	Squadron Leader L T N Gould MC DFC	In situ	See Appendix B 1925
111 Squadron	Squadron Leader G W Robarts DFC	In situ	See Appendix B 1925
207 Squadron	Squadron Leader V Gaskell-Blackburn DSO AFC	In situ	See 55 Squadron 1923
	Squadron Leader J B Graham MC AFC	20 January 1926	See 1 Squadron 1921
208 Squadron	Squadron Leaders A S C Stuart-MacLaren OBE MC DFC AFC	In situ	See Appendix B 1925
	Flight Lieutenant J H Green	November 1926	S/Ldr retired list 20 July 1935
216 Squadron	Wing Commander L D D McKean OBE mid	In situ	See Appendix B 1924
502 Squadron SR	Squadron Leader R D Oxland	In situ	See Appendix B 1925
	Wing Commander A C Wright AFC	1 May 1926	A/Cmdr retirement 9 March 1942
503 Squadron SR	Squadron Leader R D Oxland	November 1926	See 502 Squadron SR 1925
600 Squadron AAF	Wing Commander A W H James MC	In situ	See 60 Squadron 1924
	Squadron Leader The Hon. F E Guest PC DSO mid MP	19 November 1926	
601 Squadron AAF	Squadron Leader Lord E Grosvenor	In situ	See Appendix B 1925
602 Squadron AAF	Squadron Leader C N Lowe MC DFC	In situ	See 602 Squadron AAF 1925
	Squadron Leader J D Latta MC	1 February 1926	
603 Squadron AAF	Squadron Leader J A McKelvie AFC	In situ	See Appendix B 1925
605 Squadron AAF	Squadron Leader J A C Wright AFC TD	6 July 1926	

Annex

Army Form B.103c for Squadron Leader Cyril Nelson Lowe reads:

		Embarked 2.10.16	
7.10.16	*Posted to No 11 Squadron*	*02.10.16*	*B.213 11 Sqdn*
09.12.16	*To No. 2 AD on Temp. Duty 4.12.16 to 9.12.16*		*- " -*
06.01.17	*Leave 5.1.17 to 19.1.17*		*- " -*
17.02.17	*Appt. Acting Flt. Commdr.*	*11.02.17*	*- " -*
23.02.17	*To be Flight Commdr.*	*11.02.17*	*L G*
24.03.17	*Wounded*	*24.03.17*	*Summ. 934 GOC RFC*
03.04.17	*Admitted [GS on Shldr. R]*	*03.04.17*	*W.3034 6 Stat.*
17.04.17	*To England per H S Grantully Castle*	*19.04.17*	*W.3084 3 Gen.*
		Re-embarked 18.04.19	*N Q List N Q 20.04.18*

Hiss gallantry awards were published in 1918, that for his MC in supplement 39001, page 10980 of the paper issued on 16th September 1918: *"For conspicuous gallantry and devotion to duty. This officer and another pilot were escorting a formation of machines engaged in a bombing raid when seven enemy scouts attacked the bombers. They both attacked these scouts, but at the outset this officer's machine was set on fire, and the other pilot's right hand top wing broke. During the fight that ensued each came to the rescue of the other. The other pilot first caused Capt. Lowe's pursuer to break off his attack, and then Capt. Lowe shot down the scout attacking his comrade. The action of both these officers, in practically un-manoeuvrable machines, in coming to the rescue of each other in turn, showed courage and self-sacrifice of a very high order."*

The citation for his DFC appeared in supplement 30827, page 9201, of 3rd August 1918: *"this officer has destroyed five enemy machines and driven down two others out of control. On one occasion he attacked two enemy triplanes, although at the time only one of his guns was serviceable; he shot down one of the machines in flames. On another occasion, while leading a formation of eight scouts he engaged a hostile formation of twenty-six machines. Having shot down a Fokker biplane he went to the assistance of one of our scouts and drove the enemy machine down to 500 feet; at this low altitude half of a blade of his propeller was shot off by fire from the ground."*

Wikipedia, meanwhile, notes that Squadron Leader Lowe, known to all his friends as 'Kit,' was an international rugby football player who for over sixty years held the record for the number of tries scored in international matches. Undoubtedly, but for the war, he would have ran in far more [his England career having started pre-1914]; as it was, he 'hung up his boots' in 1923, with 25 caps to his credit. In eighteen Five Nations matches matches twixt February 1914 and his final match, against Ireland at Leicester's ground, he was only once on the losing side [Wales at Cardiff Arms Park on 21st January 1922].

Referring to his *Great War* service, his wounds were inflicted by Reinold Jörke; having recovered, and returned to the Western Front, he flew SE.5as with 24 Squadron and at the time of the armistice he had been credited with a total of nine combat victories, two with 11 Squadron and seven with 24 Squadron.

Group Captain Cyril Nelson Lowe MC DFC died at the age of 91 during 1983.

On 14th October 1931, the service career of Squadron Leader Trevor Edward Salt AFC, now attached to the Aircraft Depot, Karachi, came to an end when a Wapiti that he was testing crashed onto the bed of the Hubb River, Marud Khan, near Karachi. Squadron Leader Salt was killed, but his passenger, Leading Aircraftman Albert Emsley Parker was pulled from the wreckage, alive but badly injured.

Squadron Leader James Everidge was awarded the MC for his work in Mesopotamia. Formerly of the Surrey Regiment, the citation appeared in *The Edinburgh Gazette,* January 13, 1919, issue 13385, page 263: *"For conspicuous gallantry and devotion to duty. He performed bold and darng workon reconnaissance, artillery co-operation and contact patrol, and also carried out many successful bombing raids by day and night. He rendered excellent service."*

"An exceptional leader, who has carried out thirty-one bombing raid and twenty photographic reconnaissances, many of these flights were of great distance and carried out at a very high altitude, calling for great courage and stanima. This officer possesses these qualities in a marked degree, and his example has been of the greatest service to his squadron," so the read the citation for Squadron Leader John Farquhar Gordon's DFC *Gazetted* on 2nd November 1918, supplement 30989, pages 12965 and 12966.

Born on 23rd March 1893, he joined the RFC [formerly he was an officer in the Gordon Highlanders] on 22nd November 1915, his Army Form B.103c showing:

		Embarked 5.07.16	*F.. 1982*
08.07.16	*Posted to No. 6 Sqdn*	*07.07.16*	*B.213 6 Sqdn*
28.10.16	*Leave 24.10.16 to 31.10.16*		*- " -*
17.02.17	*Posted to No. 5 Sqdn*	*14.02.17*	*- " -*
17.02.17	*To be A/Flt. Commander*	*14.02.17*	*- " -*
24.02.17	*To be F/Commdr. & Tempy. Capt.*	*14.02.17*	*L G*
03.03.17	*Leave 24.02.17 to 10.02.17*		*B.213 5 Sqdn*
05.05.17	*To Home Establishment*	*24.04.17*	*- " -*
		Re-embarked & Disembarked 08.02.18	*L R 25 Sqdn*
16.02.18	*Posted to No. 25 Sqdn*	*08.02.18*	*B. 213 25 Sqdn*

Squadron Leader Reginald Baynes Mansell's military service may be said to have started as a cadet with Bristol Grammar School Officer Training Corps in which he attained lance corporal rank, and from where he was commissioned on 15th May 1914, to the 4th Battalion, The Gloucestershire Regiment.

By early 1916, he was attached to the RFC and in that year went to the Western Front to fly Sopwith one and half Strutters with 70 Squadron, possibly becoming a flight commander with the squadron, though this is not confirmed.

Come the Second World War he was appointed as Director of Operation Requirement, followed by a year as Commandant at Boscombe Down before crossing the Atlantic in 1943, to take the post of Controller of Technical Services, attached to the RAF Delegation in Washington DC and it was while performing these duties that he was struck down with a heart attack and died on 2nd January 1945.

Air Vice-Marshal Reginald Baynes Mansell CB CBE mid is commemorated on panel 4, column 1, of the Ottawa Memorial which commemorates service personnel who died in North America and the British West Indies who have no known grave. This seems odd when considering his was office work in Washington.

Appendix C - Officers Granted Short Service Commissions

The hiatus apparent in service numbers during 1925 appears to have been resolved. During the year in the region of one hundred and eighty seven short service commissions were approved, though for a variety of reasons not all would see out their terms of service which for the majority was five years on the Active List before being placed on the Reserve. Observant readers will notice that '24036' is missing from the year's allocations; it is a possibility that it was overlooked as it would have been a single allocation, as were '24035' and '24037.'

The vast majority of entrants in 1926 were fresh to service life with only a handful of officers with previous service in their background.

LG 15 January 1926, issue 33124, pages 373 and 374 - Seniority 6th and 7th January 1926

Block 22101 to 22130

22101 ANDERSON Noel Jardin P/O + 29.06.26 4 FTS Abu Sueir
Pilot Officer Noel Jardin Anderson died when his DH.9A J7843 came down near Station No.6 Suez Canal while landing in fog. Leading Aircraftman Edward Ernest Gregg also was killed.
22102 BEATTIE Gilbert Melville F/O 06.01.39 Relinquished
22103 BINNIE James Eric Arbuckle F/O 06.01.31 Relinquished
On account of ill-health [LG 6 January 1931, issue 33677, page 148].
22104 BRADLEY Timothy Joseph Leo P/O 23.07.26 Terminated
22105 BROWN Lowman Sidney Tice S/Ldr 10.02.54 Relinquished
22106 BUCKLE Nevile Raby A/Cmdr 02.12.47 Retirement
At own request [LG 16 December 1947, supplement 38147, page 5920]. Air Commodore Nevile Raby Buckle MVO, died on Saturday, 14th February 1981. With Flight Sergeant Scott he restored Sopwith Triplane N5912 for display at the 1936 Hendon Pageant and following further refurbishment this historic aircraft was placed in RAFM Hendon during 1972. In 1938 he purchased Bristol F.2b G-AFHJ formerly F4587 which, very unfortunately fell victim to enemy action.
22107 CAUSER Walter Brettell P/O 11.04.28 Relinquished
On account of ill-health [LG 13 April 1928, issue 33375, page 2676].
22108 CLARKE George Robert Thomas P/O 14.07.28 Resigned
22109 COWAN Malcolm Angus F/O 05.01.35 Relinquished
22110 DANGER Percy Hugh P/O 22.12.26 Terminated
22111 DE WOULFE DE WYTT Athal Patrick F/O + 19.09.28 A&GS Eastchurch
Flying Officer Athal Patrick De Woulfe De Wytt died when on taking off from the Armament & Gunnery School at Eastchurch in Siskin IIIA J8871 he stalled and crashed out of control.
22112 ECKERSLEY-MASLIN Charles Edward S/Ldr 09.05.39 To Royal Navy
Squadron Leader Charles Edward Eckersley-Maslin of the Reserve of Air Force Officers to be Lieutenant-Commander[A] with seniority backdated to 1st January 1939 [LG 12 May 1939, issue 34625, page 3188].
22113 EDWARDS Charles Leon P/O 30.06.26 Relinquished
On account of ill health [LG 29 June 1926, issue 33177, page 4237].
22114 GODWIN Geoffrey Herbert F/O 29.08.31 Class C
South Africa Flying Officer Geoffrey Herbert Godwin was transferred to class C of the Reserve of Air Force Officers on 29th August 1931 [LG 8 September 1931, issue 33751, page 5831], subsequently receiving a commission in the Royal Air Force Volunteer Reserve on 25th January 1943 as a pilot officer on probation [emergency] [LG 2 March 1943, supplement 35923, page 1027] his service number now becoming 139015. He served until. S/Ldr 26.02.47 Resigned
Paul McMillan reports Geoffrey Herbert Godwin was born on 15th November 1904 at Boksbury a city in the East Rand of Gauteng province of South Africa and died in Swindon, Wiltshire in June 1978.
22115 GRIEVE William Eric Warr G/Capt 10.02.54 Relinquished
22116 HAWKER Hector Beginald P/O + 23.11.26
Pilot Officer Hector Beginald Hawker died during treatment at the Military Hospital, Moascar, Egypt.
22117 HENDERSON James Ewart McConnell S/Ldr 10.02.54 Relinquished
Transferred from the General Duties Branch to the Administrative and Special Duties Branch, with the Reserve of Air Force Officers, in the rank of flying officer [LG 12 December 1939, issue 34752, page 8254].
22118 HYLTON Donald Joseph Raymond F/O 16.02.33 Removed
Flying Officer Donald Joseph Raymond Hylton was removed from the service; *Gazetted* 21st February 1933, supplement 33913, page 1180.
22119 MILTON Harry Eugene F/O 22.12.27 Relinquished
On account of ill-health [LG 10 January 1928, issue 33346, page 227].
22120 MORITZ Philip Arnold F/O 04.06.34 Resigned
22121 NELSON Antony William Hamilton F/O 01.10.30 Relinquished
On account of ill-health [LG 7 October 1930, issue 33650, page 6097].
22122 OLSON Edward George F/O 04.09.33 Relinquished
New Zealand Edward George Olson was born in New Plymouth on New Zealand's North Island on 27th February 1906. While serving his time in the Reserve, he returned to New Zealand and issued with a pilot's licence he enrolled in the Air Force Territorial Reserve and at various times carried out the duties of a flying instructor at Wigram and Otago.

In 1935 he was accepted in the RNZAF, ranked Squadron Leader, and returned to the UK in 1941 as the RNZAF Liaison Officer at the Air Ministry. Subsequently, he commanded 75[New Zealand] Squadron from 6th April to 30th July 1942. He was *Gazetted* with the DSO, less citation, on 20th April 1943, supplement 35983, page 1798.

Promoted air commodore he was appointed Air Officer Commanding RNZAF; sadly, his health failed and he returned to New Zealand in March 1945 where he died on 15th May 1945 at the comparatively early age of 39; he is buried in New Plymouth [Te Henui] Cemetery.

In presenting this brief biography the authors are pleased to acknowledge the Puke Ariki and 75NZ Squadron websites, the latter showing a photograph of squadron personnel standing in front of a Wellington, the officer standing with his arms folded being Wing Commander Olson.
22123 POOL Joseph Harbit G/Capt 01.06.54 Retired
22124 RADCLYFFE Arnold Ayscough F/Lt + 24.12.41
On 10th July 1939 he was granted a commission in the Royal Air Force Volunteer Reserve, Administrative and Special Duties Branch [LG 27 October 193, supplement 34718, page 7183] with 75207 as his service number. Flight Lieutenant Arnold Ayscough Radclyffe is buried in Kensal Green [St. Mary's] Roman Catholic Cemetery.
22125 SILCOX Henry Thomas Alexander S/Ldr 24.11.44 Relinquished
22126 TIMMINS Lloyd Miller F/O 19.01.36 Relinquished

Returned to service and granted a commission in the Administrative and Special Duties Branch, retaining his rank, with effect from 23rd February 1940 [LG 26 March 1940, issue 34817, page 1781]. S/Ldr + 21.03.44
Squadron Leader Lloyd Miller Timmins is buried in Rayne [All Saints] Churchyard, Essex.
22127 TINDALL Lewis Stanley F/Lt + 28.07.41 25 EFTS Belvedere
Flight Lieutenant Lewis Stanley Tindall lost his life in Southern Rhodesia and is buried in Harare [Pioneer] Cemetery where his headstone bears the inscription *"They Shall Mount Up As With Wings As Eagles - Isaiah XL.31."* He had been admitted three days previously to the War Emergency Hospital Salisbury where he was diagnosed ass suffering from Arsenical Encephalitis.
22128 WARSOW Claude F/O 15.10.32 Removed
Flying Officer Claude Warsow was removed from the service [LG 25 October 1932, issue 33876, page 6705].
22129 WELCH Charles Donald Graham F/O 06.01.35 Relinquished
Formerly a Lieutenant commissioned to the Honourable Artillery Company, Territorial Force. Returned to service and granted a commission in the Administrative and Special Duties Branch as a probationary Pilot Officer on 14th February 1939 [LG 21 February 1939, issue 34600, page 1217] his service number now 72733. W/Cdr 10.02.54 Relinquished

22130 BAILEY Francis Heading F/O 19.10.28 Resigned

LG 26 January 1926, issue 33127, page 621 - Seniority 16th January 1926; terms of engagement seven and five years respectively.

FLYING OFFICER

22140 HORN Reginald Ettrick Havelock F/O 08.12.26 Relinquished
Lieutenant Indian Army retired.

Block 22131 to 22139 and 22141 to 22154

22131 ASHTON-JINKS Clement Philip F/Lt + 20.06.32 RAF Henlow
Flight Lieutenant Clement Philip Ashton-Jinks died in quite tragic circumstances, as reported by the *Bucks Herald* in their issue of June 24th, 1932: *"A severe attack of pleurisy brought to a tragic and untimely close to the promising career of a young Royal Air Force officer, Clement Philip Ashton-Jinks who had been brought to the Princess Mary RAF hospital from the RAF station at Henlow, Beds., the previous Friday with a severe attack of pleurisy. On Monday evening, whilst the nurse attending him was at the door of his private ward of a period of less than half a minute, a bump was heard and investigation proved that the patient was no longer in the ward. The window at the foot of his bed had an opening that could be reached by climbing on to a radiator, and the deceased was found in the hospital grounds beneath. He died the same night."*
22132 BATESMAN William Lemeul W/Cdr 10.02.54 Relinquished
22133 COOK Philip Samuel F/O 06.01.42 Resigned
22134 EVANS Charles Henry Lee F/O + 21.01.30 6 Squadron
22135 GODFREY Cecil Vivian P/O 21.04.26 Terminated
22136 GOWER-JONES Frank F/Lt + 24.12.39 Station Flight Turnhouse
Flight Lieutenant Frank Gower-Jones died when the Miles Magister I N3806 of Station Flight Turnhouse that he was piloting dived and crashed some 3 miles to the southwest of the airfield; he is buried in Edinburgh [Corstorphine Hill] Cemetery.
22137 GRIEVES John Alan P/O 01.06.26 Terminated
22138 HATCHER Victor George Aidan A/Cmdr 22.06.58 Retirement
Flight Lieutenant Victor George Aidan Hatcher was honoured with the AFC on 1st February 1937 [EG February 5, 1937, issue 15359, page 114]. Subsequently specialising in signals, Air Commodore Victor George Aidan HATCHER OBE AFC mentioned in despatched, died on Wednesday, 16th February 1983. Paul McMillan reports that he was born In the United States of America.
22139 HILLS Wallace Adrian P/O 21.04.26 Terminated
22141 HUGGETT Vivian Watkin P/O 07.07.26 Terminated
22142 JOHN Conrad Southey F/Lt presumed 10.02.54 Relinquished
Paul McMillan has traced his birth to Surbiton in Surrey on the last day of April 1905 and his death on Sunday, 10th March 1974 at Beckford in Gloucestershire.
22143 JOHNSON Hugh Coleman F/Lt 02.07.40 Relinquished
Canada On appointment to a commission in the Royal Canadian Air Force Special Reserve LG 4 October 1940, issue 34960, page 5835
22144 LUCAS Carlton George P/O 27.01.29 Relinquished
On account of ill-health [LG 1 February 1929, issue 33462, page 775]. Returned to service and granted a commission in the Administrative and Special Duties Branch as a probationary Pilot Officer, effective 1st October 1940 [LG 28 January 1941, issue 35057, page 565] his service number now being 89640. With a general improvement in his well being he transferred from the Administrative and Special Duties Branch to the General Duties Branch on 19th June 1943, his service number now reverted to 22144; his rank being Flying Officer [LG 16 July 1943, supplement 36100, page 3284. F/Lt 21.02.46 Resigned
22145 MACKENZIE Donald F/O + 21.01.30 207 Squadron
22146 MERRITT Arthur Frederick W/Cdr 06.01.60 Retirement
22147 PATTON-BETHUNE Douglas Howard Aubrey Claude Debonair P/O 10.08.27 Resigned
22148 PHILLIPS William Miles F/O 10.06.29 Relinquished
On account of ill-health [LG 11 June 1929, issue 33505, page 3864].
22149 PICKARD Walter John G/Capt 15.09.52 Relinquished
22150 SEARSON* Edward Greville P/O 01.02.28 Relinquished
2nd Lieutenant commissioned to the Royal Artillery, Territorial Force. On account of ill-health [LG 31 January 1928, issue 33352, page 688].
22151 TUNES Leslie Sam Seymour P/O 17.11.26 Resigned
22152 UNDERDOWN Gerald Arthur F/O + 11.05.28 16 Squadron
22153 WALKER Henry John G/Capt 03.02.58 Retirement
22154 WARD William Francis P/O 22.09.26 Terminated

LG 2 February 1926, issue 33129, page 794 - Seniority 22nd and 23rd January respectively

22155 DONKIN Reginald Hawtrey W/Cdr 29.11.52 Retirement
22156 GRAY Selwyn Harmar Cecil A/Cmdr 01.01.57 Retirement
Air Commodore Selwyn Harmer Cecil Gray OBE mentioned in despatches, died on Monday, 28th April 1969. On graduating from 2 FTS Digby Pilot Officer Gray was posted to 13 Squadron [Bristol F.2b} at Andover. Two years later he went out to India where he remained until early 1933. Back in the UK he was posted to 26 Squadron [Atlas/Audax] at Catterick and following a year as a QFI with 10 FTS Ternhill he returned to 13 Squadron, now at Odiham and equipped with Hawker Hector, to command and thence to Andover as Station Commander. His wheel had turned a full circle.

LG 26 March 1926, issue 33145, page 2182 - Seniority 13th March 1926

Block 22157 to 22179

22157 BARNETT Richard Adrian F/O 13.03.35 Relinquished

Returned to service with a commission in the Royal Air Force Volunteer Reserve, Administrative and Special Duties Branch, with effect from 23rd September 1940 as 85861 [LG 22 October 1940, issue 34976, page 6146]. However, his original service number was restored and he remained in the service until: W/Cdr 10.02.54 Relinquished

22158 BUSHE-CARYESFORD Bernard Joseph P/O 13.04.27 Resigned

22159 CARLETON Guy P/O 25.12.26 Resigned

22160 CONSTABLE-ROBERT John F/O 03.03.30 Relinquished

Flying Officer John Constable-Roberts while in the Reserve of Air Force Officers relinquished his commission on 3rd March 1930 on being granted a short service commission [LG 18 March 1930, issue 33589, page 1732]. A/Cmdr 25.01.58 Retirement

Air Commodore John Constable-Roberts CBE mentioned in despatches, died on Saturday, 18th May 1991. For much of his service he was employed on operations with a nautical flavour having attended a course of instruction at the Flying Boat training school at Calshot after gaining his flying badge with 5 FTS Sealand. In early 1934, after a spell with 823 Squadron [Fairey IIIF]. He underwent training for flying instructor duties but in May 1939 he returned to coastal work and in June 1940 took over command of 206 Squadron [Hudson I].

Postwar he served two spells as an Air Attaché - the first in Brazil and for his final appointment he enjoyed the delights of Athens.

22161 DUGGAN John William W/Cdr 10.02.54 Relinquished

22162 FITCH Isaac John A/Cmdr + 26.07.44 AOC Tarawa

Air Commodore Isaac John Fitch is buried in Bourail New Zealand War Cemetery on the western coast of New Caledonia. Instead of the customary CWGC headstone the markers take the form of a white square slab upon which is raised white stone, sloped, with a slate grey inscription slab attached - the inscription for Air Commodore Isaac John Fitch reads: *"Be Thous Faithful Unto Death, And I Will Give Thee A Crown Of Life."* According to the Air of Authority website, Air Commodore Fitch had been appointed circa November 1943 Air Officer Commanding the British Protectorate of Tarawa. He died on 25th July 1944 whilst flying as a passenger in a Consolidated C-87 Liberator Express 41-11706 operated by Consairways under contract to Air Transport Command. During transit from Tarawa to Guadalcanal and on finals to Carney Field the Liberator flew into the side of a hilltop [reported as 750ft in height] on Florida Island. Initially, Air Commodore Fitch was buried in the US Army-Navy-Marine Cemetery at Lunga. During his Royal Air Force service he specialised in signals and prior to his final appointment served as Deputy Director of Intelligence [4].

The website Pacific Wrecks, which the authors are happy to acknowledge, has a detailed account of the loss of 41-11706 which was captained by Captain Hugh W Prince of Harnett County, North Carolina. On 26th July 1944, it departed Tarawa Airfield at 1100 hours local time bound for Henderson Field on Guadalcanal with Captain Prince and five civilian flight crew, plus twenty-one passengers [nineteen American and two British military personnel]. The weather was clear and the C-87 was identified by radar over Malaita Island at 1035 p.m. after which it disappeared and now reported overdue a search by three RNZAF PBY-5 Catalina flying boats from 6 Squadron at Halavo Bay Seaplane Base commenced searching on the 27th.

The PBY-5 Catalinas searched San Cristobal, Santa Isabel and Malaita Island without success but returning to base a burnt area of jungle on Florida Island was sighted and the next day a search party was flown in a Catalina to Florida Island where some 200ft from the hilltop the remains of the C-87 were found, having been guided to the crash site by local inhabitants. Here, Dick Wood, Consairways station manager, found a briefcase marked 'Top Secret' which he subsequently handed in to military officials on Guadalcanal [apparently the briefcase contained war plans from the US President, Franklyn D Roosevelt for General Douglas MacArthur and such was the sensitivity of the plans that Wood was twice interrogated to determine whether or not he had opened the briefcase, which he had not].

On the same day, the remains of the crew and passengers were recovered and taken to the American Cemetery on Guadalcanal. The official date for their deaths has been recorded as 26th July 1944 though, erroneously, Air Commodore Fitch, Captain John S Ingraham USAAF and Jack 'Arthur' Strumph, the C-87's radio operator were reported as having died on the 25th.

Accompanying Air Commodore Fitch was Major Ronald Barton-Tales of the Royal Corps of Signals; he is buried on Honolulu National Memorial Cemetery of the Pacific. CWGC records his date of death as occurring on the 26th July 1944.

22163 FLEMING Robert Sutherland P/O 24.08.27 Terminated

22164 HARRIS Jack Harris F/O 14.10.30 Relinquished

On transfer to the Indian Army [LG 24 October 1930, issue 33655, page 6479].

22165 HUDSON Harold Perisone W/Cdr 22.08.47 Resigned

22166 LEGG Richard James A/Cmdr 04.11.53 Retirement

Air Commodore Richard James Legg mentioned in despatches, died on Saturday, 6th February 1960, following a road accident near Pretoria in South Africa where, I suspect, he had settled for his final service appointment had been as Head of RAF, UK Services Liaison Staff, South Africa.

22167 LESLIE Andrew Arthur S/Ldr 10.02.54 Relinquished

22168 McLEOD Norman W/Cdr 10.02.54 Relinquished

22169 NASH Richard Rupert G/Capt 08.02.54 Retirement

At his own request [LG 2 March 1954, supplement 40114, page 1307]. Richard Rupert Nash also became a member of the Caterpillar Club when he abandoned Fairey Flycatcher N9907 on 11th April 1933 whilst serving at the Leuchars Training Base.

22170 PACE Richard Griffith P/O + 20.07.27 32 Squadron

22171 PENTLAND Eric John P/O 28.07.26 Resigned

Paul McMillan reports that Pilot Officer Eric John Pentland was the first Royal Air Force officer to save his life by parachute; on 16th June 1926 whilst under instruction at 5 FTS Sealand he took off for a solo flight in Avro 504K H5144 during which he got into an inverted spin. Taking to his parachute, which deployed at around 500ft, he landed safely, thereby becoming the first British holder of a 'Caterpillar' badge. The accident is referred to AIR 10/1441 Report on Flying Accidents between January and June 1926. Although he was unhurt, it is noted that a little over a month later he resigned his commission.

His 'adventure' is also recorded in John Neal's 2005 book *Bless You, Brother Irvin - The Caterpillar Club Story* where the author writes *"...he was practicing half-rolls in an Avro over Heswell Golf Course when the aileron controls went wrong. He was thrown out head first as the aircraft spun at 500 feet."It was a matter of seconds before I landed, hitting the ground rather hard, but otherwise unhurt,: he wrote in a letter to Leslie Irwin. "I certainly owe my life to the prompt way in which the parachute opened.""*

22172 PLEASANCE Norman Charles G/Capt + 23.03.44 OC RAF Bardney

Group Captain Norman Charles Pleasance elected to accompany Flying Officer Albert Edward Manning and crew for a Main Force raid on the well defended German city of Frankfurt. Their Lancaster III LM430 WS-B was shot down over Belgium, falling at Lembeek [Brabent], 2km S of Halle. Flying Officer Manning was an experienced bomber captain and was engaged on his twentieth operational sortie [see my RAFBCL 1944 and page 122 for additional information].

22173 ROSS-ROBERTS Norman Cecil F/O 13.03.35 Relinquished

22174 SHAW Grenville Hammerton W/Cdr + 27.09.40 2 SFTS

Wing Commander Grenville Hammerton Shaw is buried in Montreal [Mount Royal] Cemetery. A document for 2 Service Flying Training School, which came under the aegis of the British Commonwealth Air Training Plan, is held by TNA Kew under AIR 81/3479.

22175 SHERMAN Stephen Ronald W/Cdr 10.02.54 Relinquished

22176 SMYTH Marcus Athelstan F/O 23.11.27 Relinquished
On account of ill-health [LG 22 November 1927, issue 33331, page 7424].

22177 STOKES Leonard Rendell G/Capt 17.05.44 Retirement
Wing Commander Leonard Rendell Stokes was *Gazetted* with the DFC, less citation. on 22nd October 1940 [LG 22 October 1940, issue 34976, page 6136]. He was appointed to a permanent commission on 1st October 1930 [LG 24 October 1930, issue 33655, page 6479].

22178 TYSON Geoffrey Arthur Virley F/Lt 10.02.54 Relinquished

22179 WAIN Edward Frederick G/Capt 29.03.62 Retirement
Born on 22nd October 1906 Edward Frederick Wain died in Gloucester during January 1978.

LG 6 April 1926, issue 33148, page 2436 - Seniority 13th March 1926

22180 FOREMAN Edward Charles W/Cdr 10.02.54 Relinquished

LG 1 June 1926, issue 33168, page 3570 -Seniority 8th, 9th and 10th May respectively

22182 ALLCROFT John Derby P/O 28.03.28 Terminated

22183 ALLEN Aubrey G/Capt 12.09.56 Retirement

ASHTON Charles Frederick P/O 20.07.27 Resigned

BAVERSTOCK Edwin Sewell P/O 13.02.29 Resigned

BELL Stanley Charles P/O 02.02.27 Terminated

BURSLEM Eric Lane F/O 23.12.29 Resigned
On Christmas Day 1941 he was granted a commission in the Administrative and Special Duties Branch with the rank of Honorary Wing Commander [LG 13 January 1942, issue 35416, page 237].

22187 BUTT Acton Maclean W/Cdr 10.02.54 Relinquished
2nd Lieutenant Devonshire Regiment, Territorial Army. On 3rd August 1937 Flying Officer Acton Maclean Butt, now in the Reserve of Air Force Officers, was granted the honorary rank of flight lieutenant on 3rd August 1937 [LG 21 September 1937, issue 34437, page 5904]. Then, on 7th May 1938 he relinquished his honorary rank on being commissioned to class CC as a flying officer, Acting Flight Lieutenant [LG 12 September 1939, issue 34679, page 6195].

COLEMAN John Froude O'Reilly P/O 04.05.27 Terminated

22190 EDMONDES Morgan Rice F/Lt 08.05.39 Relinquished
2nd Lieutenant, Royal Artillery, Territorial Army. On 1st August 1940 Flight Lieutenant Morgan Rice Edmondes was granted a commission in the Administrative and Special Duties Branch, his service number amended to 61520 [LG 28 March 1941, issue 35119, page 1815]. By 1st July 1943 he had reverted to his original service number and was now attached to the Technical Branch and promoted wing commander [temporary] [LG 14 July 1943, supplement 36092, page 3207]. With effect 1st January 1948 his substantive rank was Flight Lieutenant [LG 17 February 1948, supplement 38209, page 1125]. W/Cdr 10.02.54 Relinquished

FISHER MC Lionel Edward Ruggles P/O + 09.01.28 6 Squadron
Lieutenant in the Reserve of Regular Army Officers. As a 2nd Lieutenant commissioned to the Hampshire Regiment he was *Gazetted* with the MC, less citation, on 25th August 1917, supplement 30252, page 8855.

HAWKESWORTH Philip Anthony P/O 15.06.27 Terminated

HOCKLY Cedric Haffenden F/O 08.05.35 Relinquished

22194 HOWES Arthur Milner Dickeson W/Cdr 24.03.46 Resigned

JENKINS Gilbert Hanmer George Stratford F/O 26.08.32 Class A
Under the heading for Territorial Army units, *The London Gazette* 10th February 1933, issue 33910, page 918 published: *"1st Bn. Mon. R.-2nd Lt. G H G S Jenkins [Flying Offr. Res. of Air Force Offrs.] resigns his commission 7th Dec. 1932."*

JOHNSON William Evelyn Patrick F/Lt 08.05.36 Relinquished
Gazetted with the Air Force Cross on 1st January 1932 [EG January 5, 1932, issue 14823, page 23] as a flight lieutenant. Returned to service and served with the service number 70927 until. F/Lt 10.02.54 Relinquished

22197 KEENS Leonard Thomas G/Capt 02.01.57 Retirement

LAWRENCE Frederick Leslie F/O 25.07.28 Dismissed
By sentence of General Court Martial [LG 31 July 1928, issue 33408, page 5137].

22199 LUCAS Philip Gadesden F/Lt 10.02.54 Relinquished
Promoted flying officer on 8th November 1927 [LG 29 November 1927, issue 33333, page 7668], Philip Gadesden Lucas by 1941 was a test pilot in the employment of Hawker Aircraft and was *Gazetted* with the George Medal on 9th May 1941, supplement 35156, page 2643: *"Test Pilot Lucas displayed great courage and presence of mind during a test flight and, by his skill and coolness, saved an aircraft from destruction."*

Philip Gadesden Lucas joined Hawker Aircraft Limited as a test pilot in 1931 and foreign sales representative. Between 1937 and 1945 he was joint Chief Test Pilot and from 1946 to 1947 when he joined De Havillands as Technical Sales Manager he was Hawker's Director and General Manager.

He is mentioned on numerous occasions in Francis K Mason's excellent history of Hawker aircraft, a posed photograph of Lucas about to climb into the cockpit of a Hurricane being published on page 9.

Concerning his Reserve service, as Flying Officer Philip Gadesden Lucas his transfer to the Reserve Class A is dated 8th May 1931. On 10th February 1932 he was promoted flight lieutenant and was granted a four year extension in Class A. On 8th May 1939 he transferred from Class A to C , subsequently, as shown above, he relinquished his commission under the terms of the Navy, Army and Air Force Reserves Act, 1954.

22200 MARTIN Lionel George W/Cdr 10.02.54 Relinquished

22201 MORTIMER Alister Lodge W/Cdr 09.05.45 Relinquished
2nd Lieutenant Royal Artillery, Territorial Army attached to Hampshire Heavy Brigade. He resigned his commission on appointment to the RAF on 11th February 1928 [LG 10 February 1928, issue 33355, page 954]. On account of medical unfitness for Air Force servce.

NETHERTON Kenneth Charles F/O 28.08.31 Relinquished
On appointment to a commission in the Regular Army [LG 22 September 1931, issue 33755, page 6109].

PRITCHARD-BARRETT Stanley F/O 27.05.29 Relinquished
On account of ill health [LG 4 June 1929, issue 33503, page 3694].

22204 PROUD Harold John Granville Ellis A/Cmdr 24.09.56 Retirement
Air Commodore Harold John Granville Ellis Proud CBE, died on Sunday, 19th March 1995. His final service appointment was ass Provost Marshal and Chief of RAF Police.

SMITH Bernard Frederick Owers F/O 08.05.31 Relinquished
On account of ill-health [LG 12 May 1931, issue 33715, page 3072].

22206 TAYLOR Robert Henry Cunninghame S/Ldr 10.02.54 Relinquished

22207 TURNER Elpinstone Docura F/Lt 17.06.55 Relinquished
During his service Flight Lieutenant Elphinston Docura Turner survived a serious crash on 11th June 1929 while attached to 17 Squadron, For details please see my summary for the date in question.

LG 8 June 1926, issue 33170, page 3755 - Seniority 29th and 30th May 1926 respectively

22208 BAIRD William Roy S/Ldr 09.01.43 Retired list

22209 MACKAY Ulrich Sinclair F/Lt 21.10.41 Relinquished
On account of ill-health [LG issue 35326, page 6255].

LG 29 June 1926, issue 33177, page 4237 - Seniority 14th June 1926

FLYING OFFICER

22210 POPE DFC mid Ralph Phillip Patrick G/Capt 06.12.45 Relinquished
On account of medical unfitness for Air Force service [LG 18 December 1945, supplement 37393, page 6150]. His mentioned in despatches was promulgated in *The London Gazette* on 12th July 1920, supplement 31975, page 7423 where it is noted he was attached to 63 Squadron, Afghanistan, and formerly of the East Surrey Regiment. On 21st August 1921 he relinquished his commission in the Royal Air Force on return to Army duty [LG 27th September 1921, issue 32468, page 7569].

LG 20 July 1926, issue 33184, page 4801 - Seniority 30th June and 14th July 1926 respectively. The probationary Pilot Officers were engaged for five years on the active list.

FLYING OFFICER

22211 HOWES Ernest James F/Lt 11.09.36 Resigned
Lieutenant on the Reserve of Regular Army Officers and now short service commissioned for a period three years on the active list. Paul McMillan reports TNA Kew hold a file for Flight Lieutenant Ernest James Howe, born 27th August 1895, under AIR 76/241/20.

Block 22212 to 22233

22212 ASHTON Bertram Henry G/Capt 18.11.54 Retirement
22213 BARTON Bernard William F/O 17.02.34 Resigned
22214 BARTON John F/O + 19.01.31 7 Squadron
22215 COLLINS Henry Bernard
Gazetted with the DFC on 14th June 1940, issue 34873, page 3621: *"In May 1940, this officer undertook a mission involving an exceedingly hazardous flight. Flying a very large and comparatively slow aircraft, which was unarmed and unprotected, he delivered much needed anti-tank ammunition to the army in France. Showing great coolness, determination and tenacity he succeeded in his mission although faced with hostile action on both the outward and return flight."*

As Acting Wing Commander, he was *Gazetted* on 2nd July 1943, supplement 36077, page 2995 as follows under the heading Central Chancery of The Orders of Knighthood. St Jame's Palace, SW.1, 2nd July 1943: *"The KING has been graciously pleased, on the occasion of His Majesty's recent visit to North Africa and Malta, to make the the following promotion in, and appointments to, the Royal Victorian Order:-*

"To be Members of the Fourth Class:-
Ten names were tabled, including that of Henry Bernard Collins. W/Cdr 28.11.44 Resigned
22216 CONEYBEER Ronald William P/O + 10.08.26 4 FTS Abu Sueir
Sent out to Egypt for instruction at 4 Flying Training School at Abu Sueir, Pilot Officer Coneybeer was killed in a propeller accident involving DH.9A J6967 at Bilbeis. He is buried in Ismailia War Memorial Cemetery. Apparently, as discovered by my co-author, he was standing near Sergeant Newton William Baker [342070] who was unhurt.
22217 CRUMMY Bertram Arnold James G/Capt 24.01.55 Retirement
Paul McMillan reports that Bertram Arnold James Crummy was born in 1905 at Amritsar in the Punjab, India and died in Worthing, Norfolk at some time in 1995.
22218 EDWARDS Robert Conrad S/Ldr 10.02.54 Relinquished
Paul McMillan reports Robert Conard Edwards was born on 23rd January 1905 and died on Saturday, 16th December 1989.
22219 FORBES Harold Vernon F/O + 03.12.29 HAD Henlow
While attached to the Home Aircraft Depot at Henlow, Flying Officer Harold Vernon Forbes was killed after becoming uncertain of his position while flying Bristol F.2b J8454 which had been converted as a dual control trainer. Inverted, the trainer hit the ground at Clifton on the NW side of the airfield. Amazingly, his passenger, Flying Officer Donald Vernon Ivins was extricated from the wreckage and taken to hospital for treatment to his injuries. Following is the report as published in *The Times* in their edition of Wednesday, December 4th, 1929:

"A Bristol fighter aeroplane piloted by Flying Officer H V Forbes, with Flying Officer D V Ivins as passenger, crashed at Clifton, near Henlow, yesterday morning. The pilot was severely injured, and died two hours later at Henlow Aerodrome Hospital. Flying Officer Ivins was also badly injured.

"The following official statement was issued:- "The Air Ministry regrets to announce that as the result of an accident near Henlow, to a Bristol Fighter machine of the Home Aircraft Depot, Henlow Camp, Bedfordshire, to-day, Flying Officer Harold Vernon Forbes, the pilot of the aircraft, was dangerously injured and died after admission to sick quarters. Flying Officer Donald Vernon Ivins, the other other occupant of the aircraft, was seriously injured.""

The same edition also reported that the Prince of Wales was taken for a test flight at Northolt in what the paper described as *"the big Fairey monoplane"* piloted by Squadron Leader A G Jones-Williams and navigated by Flight Lieutenant Jenkins, this being the machine which will attempt a non-stop flight from the UK to South Africa. His Royal Highness was particularly impressed by the provision of comforts for the crrew and wished them both every success; after the flight the machine was flown to Cranwell.
22220 GREENHALGH Robert Crook F/O 20.03.34 Removed
Removed from the service [LG 27 March 1934, issue 34036, page 2041]. At the time of his removal Flying Officer Robert Crook Greenhalgh was in Class A of the Reserve of Air Force Officers, his transfer being promulgated on 14th July 1931 [LG 14 July 1931, issue 33735, page 4633].

Paul McMillan suggests the following, published in the *Eastbourne Courier* the previous November might be the reason:-

"A flying officer's worthless cheque, rendered in payment of accommodation for himself and a man fried at the Grand Hotel, was the subject of two charges at the Police Court on Monday against Robert Crook Greenhalgh, of Watford. They were: obtaining £10 by false pretence, and incurring a debt to pay the hotel £4 7s 3d., obtaining credit by fraud other than false pretences. Mr. L A Nidermayer appeared for the accused who admitted both offences.

"The Chief Constable said that on the night of August 9, the prisoner called at the Grand Hotel, in company with another man, and engaged two rooms for the night. On the afternoon of the following day prisoner was presented with an account of £4 7s 3d. He said he was short of cash. He was supplied with a temporary cheque, which he made out for £14 7s 3d, and was given £10 change. The cheque was later returned marked "No Account."

"About September 4, prisoner wrote to the hotel enclosing £14 in cash, and stating that it was cover the cheque, which he understood was wrongly endorsed. No address was given.

"A warrant had been applied for and granted before the money was received by the hotel. The warrant was dated August 19. When it was read over to the prisoner, he said "I have sent the money."

"He came of respectable parents at Watford. He had been out of work for the past two years and had caused his parents a good deal of trouble. His father had told him he would have to leave home, as he [the father] could not afford to keep him in idleness and pay his debts.

"Mr. Niedermayer said he was instructed that the defendant came to Eastbourne with a friend, who undertook to pay all hotel expenses. They stayed at the Grand Hotel and apparently engaged in a very heavy drinking bout. The next morning the friend that he had no cash, and the defendant then drew a cheque on Barclays Bank, Lombard-street, where once he had an account, which was closed.

"The warrant was issued on August 19, but before it came to the knowledge of the defendant he was able to get £14 together, which he sent to the hotel.

"Mr. F J Gill, assistant manager at the Grand Hotel, said, in reply to the Chairman [Colonel Gwynne], that it was not the custom of the hotel to accept payment by cheque from a stranger. In this case defendant had referred them to an army officer in Eastbourne. They communicated with that officer before cashing the cheque, and they understood it would be all right. The officer said he had known Greenhalgh for about two years, having met him on a boat.

"Mr. Niedermayer stated that the defendant had received a commission in the Royal Air Force in 1926 and saw service in Egypt, Irak [sic] *and Afghanistan. He had a medal for service in Irak and was mentioned in despatches from Afghanistan. He was transferred to the reserve of officers in 1931and was still on it. He was a consulting engineer and carried on business in London. He had never been in trouble before. In this case he made amends after leaving the hotel. Greenhalgh gave evidence bearing out his solicitor's statement.*

"The Chairman said the charges were very serious and could not lightly be overlooked. Defendant would be fined £10for false pretence and £15 for obtaining credit by fraud, the alternative being two months' imprisonment on each charge, the sentences to run together."

22221 HENNESSY DSO MC Richard George F/O 14.07.35 Relinquished

Formerly a Major commissioned to the Border Regiment. His MC, less citation, was *Gazetted* on New Year's Day 1918, supplement 30450, page 38, while his DSO, won on the Italian front as an Acting Captain with the 2nd Battalion, Border Regiment, was *Gazetted* on 10th December 1919, supplement 31680, page 15287: *"For conspicuous gallantry and initiative. On the 27th October 1918, he was sent forward to ascertain the situation in front of the battalion on the eastern bank of the Piave, and found a proportion of the brigade front held up by machine-gun nests. He quickly had the situation in hand, organising parties, and led them forward to the final objective. His quick appreciation of the situation and fine display of leadership inspired all ranks. Again, on the 28th October, when the battalion was ordered to advance from the "Red dotted line" to the "Blue dotted line" his grip of the situation on the left and the speed with which he got the two left companies going, cleared several machine-gun nests, enabling the advance to the "Blue dotted line" to be carried out."*

22222 HEWISON Douglas Kendall F/O 16.07.29 Relinquished

On account of ill health [LG 16 July 1929, issue 33517, page 4705].

22223 KAY Cyril Eyton F/O 08.07.35 Relinquished

New Zealand On appointment to a commission in the Royal New Zealand Air Force [LG 11 February 1936, issue 34254, page 913].

22224 MARETT Harold Claude F/Lt + 12.10.32 3 FTS Grantham

New Zealand Flight Lieutenant Harold Claude Marett and his pupil Pilot Officer Adrian Kinross White, a fellow New Zealander, were killed when their Avro Tutor I K2509 crashed at Great Ponton Heath near the airfield. The following account was published on Thursday, October 13th, in *The Daily Telegraph* under the heading 'Two Officers Killed - Low-Flying 'Plane Crashes' *"Flight-Lt. Harold Claude Marett and Acting Pilot Officer Adrian Kinross White were killed yesterday in a flying accident at Great Ponton near Grantham.*

"The Air Ministry communique states that they were pilot and passenger respectively of a Tutor aircraft of No. 3 Flying Training School, Grantham. Major R W Newton, of Grantham, on whose land the 'plane crashed, said that the machine, which was flying low, seemed to go into a spin and dive straight to earth.

"The passenger attempted to escape by parachute, but the 'plane was too near the ground and he crashed before the parachute had a chance to open. Both he and the pilot were killed instantly.

"Farm labourers working in the fields went to the rescue. The man with the parachute was lying dead some distance from the machine, and when they had dragged the pilot from the twisted fuselage he also was found to be dead. The total death roll in RAF accidents during the present year is now forty-five."

22225 MOORES Arthur Owen F/O 01.04.31 Resigned

TNA Kew has a file for this officer under AIR 76/ 354/18 and the Air Force List 555 1565 published in 1926 names him as being at No. 4 Flying Training School at Abu Sueir. He reported to the RAF Depot at Uxbridge on on 185h January 1931.

Paul McMillan reports Arthur Owen Moores died in Hastings in 1985 and, it is believed, faced a General Court Martial in the early 1930s.

22226 MUNDY Leslie Kenward P/O 09.11.27 Relinquished

On account of ill-health [LG 8 November 1927, issue 33327, page 7119]. Early in the Second World War he was commissioned as a 2nd Lieutenant in the Auxiliary Military Pioneer Corps, effective 12th August 1940 [LG 15 October 1940, supplement 34969, page 6012]. By 1949 he was serving as part of the Territorial Army based in Somerset [LG 11 September 1951, supplement 39329, page 4761].

22227 PITT-HARDACRE Cecil P/O 05.01.27 Relinquished

On account of ill-health [LG 7 January 1927, issue 33237, page 121].

22228 RESTELL-LITTLE Murray Meyrick F/Lt + 19.05.33 5 FTS Sealand

Flight Lieutenant Murray Meyrick Restell-Little died in a midair collision between his Avro 504N J8533 and J8676, both Avros being on approach to the airfield. Flight Lieutenant Restell-Little had been promoted to his rank on 1st February 1932 [LG 2 February 1932, issue 33795, page 709]. His death was reported in *The Times* in their edition of Saturday, 20th May 1933 beneath the heading 'Collision in the Air - Three RAF Officers Killed'

"Three Royal Air Forces were killed and one was injured in a flying accident yesterday. Flight Lieutenant Murray Meyrick Restell-Little and Acting Pilot Officer John Frederick Napier Fairbanks, the pilots of two Avro aircraft of No. 5 Flying Training School, Sealand, Cheshire, lost their lives as the result of a collision in the air at Sealand. An Air Ministry announcement states that Acting Pilot Officer Patrick Hunter Dunn, the second occupant of one aeroplane, was uninjured, and that Acting Pilot Officer Fairbanks was the sole occupant of the other aircraft.

"A second accident occurred at the Aeroplane and Armament Experimental Establishment at Martlesham Heath, Suffolk. Here two Bristol Bulldog fighters crashed. One of the pilots, Flight Lieutenant George Edwin Campbell, suffered injuries from which he died late last night, the other, Flight Lieutenant James Francis Moir, escaped with slight bruises.

"Eye-witnesses of the accident at Sealand reported that one machine was seen to touch the rudder and tail of the other. After the collision one of the occupants, believed to be Flight Lieutenant Restell-Little, attempted unsuccessfully to reach the ground by parachute.

"This was the third fatal accident in three consecutive days to officers of the RAF in England. Flight Lieutenant Restell-Little was born in 1900 at Acton, and joined the Royal Air Force in 1926. Until lately he was a flying instructor at No. 2 Flying Training School, Digby, Lincolnshire.

"Acting Pilot Officers Fairbanks and Dunn entered the service on probation on March 18 this year, and were posted to No. 5 Flying Training School for instruction."

22229 SEARL Francis Henry Louis F/O 13.04.29 Relinquished

On account of ill-health [LG 26 April 1929, issue 33489, page 2766]. His health improved and on 10th November 1936 he was granted a class C commission in the General Duties Branch of the Reserve of Air Force Officers [LG 10 November 1936, issue 34339, page 7233]. He served throughout the Second World War and beyond. G/Capt 23.08.56 Resigned

22230 SMYTHE Francis Sydney P/O 27.04.27 Relinquished

On account of ill-health [LG 26 April 1927, issue 33269, page 2694]. On 15th December 1941 he was granted an emergency commission in the rank of flying officer in the Administrative and Special Duties Branch [LG 17 March 1942, issue 35491, page 1221]. However, Flying Officer Smythe changed his allegiance to the army and was granted a commission as a 2nd Lieutenant in the General List on 31st January 1944 [LG 18 February 1944, supplement 36384, page 841].

22231 VAUGHAN Arthur James P/O 02.08.27 Terminated

22232 WALTON William Thomas W/Cdr 10.02.54 Relinquished

22233 WARD Albert Ross F/O + 29.10.29 442 Flight HMS *Hermes*
Flying Officer Albert Ross Ward took off from the carrier in Fairey IIID S1018 but banked too steeply, stalled and plunged into Hong Kong harbour. By a miracle, his crew, Telegraphist Walter Francis Sidney Aplin and Leading Aircraftman G T Cant were picked up and apart from a bad fright and a soaking were unhurt.

LG 27 July 1926, issue 33186, page 4963 - Seniority 17th July 1926

Block 22235 to 22250 and 2401 to 2403

22235 ABRAHAM Thomas Maxfield
As a flight lieutenant he was *Gazetted* with the DFC for his services in Waziristan during the period 17th January to 15th September 1937 [LG 21st December 1937, issue 34465, page 8001].
22236 ANSON Philip Vernon P/O 09.11.27 Relinquished
On account of ill-health [LG 8 November 1927, issue 33327, page 7119].
22237 BUXTON Geoffrey Mungo G/Capt 24.06.57 Retirement
Joining the Training Branch of the Royal Air Force Volunteer Reserve and ranked Flying Officer, he resigned his commission on 1st November 1965 [LG 21 December 1965, supplement 43844, page 11990]. During his long and distinguished service he had been made an OBE, achieved a Master of Arts degree and made a Fellow of the Royal Aeronautical Society.
22238 CARVELL Ronald Joseph G/Capt 22.04.56 Retirement
22239 ELLISON Henry Havelock S/Ldr 10.02.54 Relinquished
22240 FARROW Bernard George G/Capt 01.05.57 Retirement
As Wing Commander Bernard George Farrow he was appointed OBE in the New Year's Honours List 1941 [LG 1 January 1941, supplement 35029, page 11].
22241 GRENFELL Charles Granville P/O 27.10.26 Terminated
22242 HILL Leslie Stuart F/O 07.12.38 Relinquished
On account of ill-health [LG 6 December 1938, issue 34577, page 7696].
22243 MARTIN Ernest Joseph P/O 11.11.27 Terminated
22244 PARKER Kenneth Evelyn W/Cdr 04.07.44 Relinquished
On account of ill-health [LG 18 July 1944, supplement 36612, page 3336].
22245 PEASE John Walter F/O 23.09.31 Relinquished
On appointment to a commission in the Indian Army [LG 6 October 1931, issue 33759, page 6396].
22246 RUMSEY Arnold Arthur F/O 15.09.37 Relinquished
On appointment to a commission in the South African Air Force Special Reserve of flying officers [LG 2 November 1937, issue 34450, page 6824].
22247 SCOTT MOORE Alan Edward P/O 17.11.26 Terminated
22248 SEEMAN Norman Walter Keith F/O 06.06.32 Resigned
22249 SHINE Ernest Frederick P/O 23.05.28 Resigned
22250 SOWARD Kenneth Roxburgh P/O 12.01.27 Resigned
New Zealand

My co-author, Paul McMillan, reports Kenneth Roxburgh Soward was born in New Zealand's North Island at Rawhiti, Auckland, on 25th November 1907 and died in Wellington, the capital, on 7th August 1980. He is suspected, as having made a false statement on his application for he had, while in Australia, committed a civil offence which earned him an entry in *The South Australia Police Gazette* published on April 9th, 1924: *"Re J R DePury's larceny. Kenneth Roxburgh Soward, 16, has been arrested for this offence. A portion of the stolen property has been recovered."*

Following his resignation from Royal Air Force service he was reported to have been in Australia by December 1927 where in New South Wales he fell foul of law, the following being extracted from page 736 of the *New South Wales Police Gazette* dated 21 December 1927:

"Kenneth Roxburgh Soward, charged with attempting to obtain goods, value £6, by false pretences, has been arrested by Detective-sergeant Sadler and Constable Shepherd, Sydney Police. Sentenced to six months' hard labour. Further charged with obtaining goods, value £3 10s., £2 7s 6d., £4 2s., and £1 13s 6d. [recovered], the property of Farmer and Company Limited, by similar means. Sentenced to six months' hard labour on each charge [five], concurrent."

The Sun an afternoon newspaper published in Sydney picked up on the case and under the heading 'He Smiled - Young Swindler Jailed' reported:

"A chance meeting on the Transcontinental train from Perth brought Kenneth Roxburgh Soward, a smartly-dressed youth of 19, into contact with John Bryden Brown, company director, of Torquay Flats, Darling Point.

"On arriving in Sydney Soward went to various departments and Farmer's and represented himself as a son of Brown, obtaining boots, slippers, shirts, underwear, white trousers, and other goods, of a total value of £17 13s., asking that they be charged to Brown's account.

"To-day at the Central Police Court he was before Mr. Gates, C S M, on five charges of false pretences, to which he pleaded guilty. The Police Prosecutor. Sergeant Cummings, read out a list of convictions in South Australia, and said that the police in that State had been looking for him. He was sentenced to six months' on each of the charges, the sentences to be concurrent. Soward left the dock smiling."

In the spring of the following year Kenneth Soward was re-acquainted with Detective-sergeant Sadler and Constable J R Shepherd, plus Constable Campbell, of the Sydney Police, this time in connection with a forged cheque: *"... charged on provisional warrant with forging a cheque for £60 purporting to be signed by Mabel L Hudd, and uttering the same in the State of South Australia." "... remanded to South Australia."*

In 1930, a full face and profile photograph of Kenneth Roxburgh Soward, alias Kenneth Robert Soward, featured on page 67 of the *New Zealand Police Gazette* this time the 26 year old Soward being charged with theft, and reported in the *Pahiatu Herald* on 7th May 1930:

"Kenneth Soward, aged 26, charged with theft of £3 18s, the property of his employers, and the theft of jewellery, valued at £10, the property of Mrs E M Brooker, of Waverley, appeared before Mr. J H Salmon S.M. in the Wanganui Police Court this morning.

"The report from the probation officer," said Mr. Salmon, "is not favourable." He sentenced Soward to three months' imprisonment for the theft of jewellery. On the other charge he was convicted and discharged."

In conclusion, further investigation by my co-author reveals that in the 1930s he underwent a seed-change and obtained employment as a civil servant. In the Second World War he served in the Royal New Zealand Air Force where his service number was NZ4310741, subsequently becoming treasurer to a tennis club as well as serving his community as a local politician. To this information 'we' can add through the input of researchers in New Zealand, namely Errol Martyn and David Duxbury, that Kenneth Roxburgh Soward served between 20th August 1943 and 8th February 1946 in a clerical position.
24001 TAYLOR Denis P/O 01.06.27 Resigned
24002 WHITLEY John René AM 29.05.62 Retirement
Air Marshal Sir John Whitley KBE CB DSO AFC* three times mentioned in despatches, died on Boxing Day 1997 at the age of 92. He was the last surviving Bomber Command Group Commander having in the war years commanded No. 4 Group and No. 8[PFF] Group, albeit briefly on each occasion, and postwar from April 1953 through to November 1956 No. 1 Group.

Returning to the war years, on 23rd May 1941 he was appointed Station Commander at Linton-on-Ouse where some two years later he elected to accompany Flight Lieutenant Horace Arthur Hull and crew on a Main Force attack on Frankfurt. Taking off at 2311 in Halifax II JB871 MP-V the Halifax was intercepted while outbound and shot down by a night fighter over France. Details of the crew are recorded on page 101 of my RAFBCL 1943. Here, it suffice to say that of the survivors, four evaded capture including Group Captain Whitley who, mindful of the risks of being shot down during bomber operations, had with him an escape kit of his own design and with the assistance from the Comet escape line he made excellent progress through France and into Spain, sometimes on foot and when possible by bicycle.

He is mentioned in the text [pages 217 and 218] of Oliver Clutton-Brock's richly researched history of Royal Air Force evaders and in the appendices where he Oliver identifies his Comet escape line number as 98. Such was the pace of his evasion that he arrived back at Hendon by air from Gibraltar on 25th May 1943 and, subsequently, was *Gazetted* with the DSO.

During his time as Air Officer Commanding No. 1 Group Air-Vice Marshal Whitley became a more than proficient jet pilot and on the last day of February 1955 set an unofficial flight record from Scampton to Nicosia in Cyprus by a Canberra in a time of 4 hours and 13 minutes. Also, he was nearing the end of his tenure of command at the time of Vulcan crash [see the entry for Air Chief Marshal Sir Harry Broadhurst towards the end of this appendix] at London Heathrow, 230 Operational Conversion Unit from which the Vulcan was tasked coming under the aegis of No. 1 Group.

24003 WILLIAMS Cyril Charles Douglas W/Cdr 15.03.58 Retirement

LG 3 August 1926, issue 33188, page 5131

FLYING OFFICER

24004 POWER Henry Eustace S/Ldr + 29.05.37 2 FTS Digby

Formerly of the East Surrey Regiment. On the 21st of October 1929 Flying Officer Henry Eustace Power was instructing Pilot Officer Sidney Noel Wiltshire [see my Short Service Commissioned officers appendix for 9th July 1929] when their aircraft crashed whilst landing. The actions of Pilot Officer Wiltshire that followed gained him an MBE in the Military Division of the Honour *For Gallantry* as *Gazetted* on 31st January 1930, issue 33575, page 645: *"For conspicuous gallantry displayed at Temple Bruer Landing Ground, Sleaford, on 21st October 1929.*

"This officer, who is a pilot under instruction, was flying with his instructor, Flying Officer H E Power, in an aeroplane that crashed on landing and at once caught fire.Having extricated himself from the wrecked machine, he found that his companion's foot was caught in the wreckage and that he could not get out.

"Although fully realising the risk he was running, Pilot Officer Wiltshire re-entered the flames and helped Flying Officer Power to get clear, during which process he sustained burns on his neck and face. Power's clothing was by this time well alight and he would undoubtedly have lost his life but for the prompt and courageous action taken by his pupil. As it was, he was badly burnt.

"Both officers were shortly afterwards taken by air to Cranwell Hospital. The aeroplane was completely burnt out."

The Lincolnshire Aviation website, which the authors acknowledge, identifies the aircraft as Avro 504N J9014 belonging to 2 FTS Digby, the accident occurring as Pilot Officer Wiltshire was practising forced-landings.

Meanwhile, Flight Lieutenant Power recovered from his burns and, subsequently, was promoted to squadron leader rank. On Empire Air Day 1937 and while still attached to 2 FTS Digby he flew over to Waddington where he was briefed to perform a display in Hawker Fury II K8228 and it was while performing a slow roll that he lost control and crashed with fatal consequences. The following is an extract from *Hansard,* the written record of Parliamentary debates:

"A Squadron Leader from No.2 Flying Training School, Digby, was lent to Waddington to give a display of individual aerobatics in a Fury single-seater aircraft, a type not in normal use at Waddington. Several rehearsals were carried out successfully at a minimum height of some 2,500feet.

"On the 29th May, the officer in the course of his display began a slow roll at a height of some 500 feet. This was contrary to King's Regulations from which no deviation had been authorised. When in an inverted position the aircraft commenced the second half of a loop and dived into the ground. It is a matter of conjecture whether the pilot misjudged his height or lost control of his aircraft.

"Although this officer had only completed six or seven hours flying on Fury aircraft he was a highly experienced pilot with well over 3,000 hours flying to his credit."

Paul McMillan adds that Henry Eustace Power was born in London on 23rd February 1938.

24005 CHESHIRE Walter Graemes ACM 06.04.65 Retirement

Air Chief Marshal Sir Walter Cheshire GBE KCB twice mentioned in despatches, died on Sunday, 10th December 1978. During his long service he served at a variety of overseas posts commencing with Egypt with 45 Squadron, Sudan attached to 47 Squadron and in the Second World War as Air Attaché in Moscow, thence to India as Chief Air Intelligence Officer at Headquarters Air Command South East Asia. Postwar he was appointed Air Officer Commanding Indo China followed by a similar position in Gibraltar and later to senior posts in Germany and Malta.

24006 FULLER James William Okes P/O 27.10.26 Terminated

LG 10 September 1926, issue 33200, page 5912 - Seniority 1st September 1926

Block 24007 to 24017

24007 CARRUTHERS Leonard Turnell F/Lt 05.04.34 Dismissed

By sentence of General Court Martial [LG 10 April 1934, issue 34040, page 2319].

24008 DOWNES Thomas Harold F/Lt 28.01.38 Relinquished

On appointment to a commission on the Unattached List for the Indian Army [LG 22 March 1938, issue 34495, page 1941].

24009 ELTON John Goodenough AV-M 29.03.59 Retirement

Air Vice-Marshal John Goodenough Elton CB CBE DFC AFC twice mentioned in despatches, died on Saturday, 16th April 1994.

24010 MACLEAN Douglas Lachlan F/O 06.02.35 Removed

Flying Officer Douglas Lachlan Maclean was transferred to class C of the Reserve of Air Force Officers on 1st September 1931 [LG 1 September 1931, issue 33749, page 5695] and thence from class C to class A on 1st February 1932 [LG 29 March 1932, issue 33812, page 2111]. Notification of his removal from the service was promulgated on 19th February 1935, issue 34134, page 1175.

Although, at present, the cause for his removal from the service has not been established, it is suspected that financial difficulties may have played a part. Paul McMillan reports that TNA Kew has a document under AIR 76324/177 for Flying Officer Douglas Lachlan Maclean who was born on 12th August 1907 and died relatively early on 14th April 1960. My co-author adds that by 1939, and now married, he was residing at Biggleswade in Bedfordshire where his occupation was given as a Travelling Engineer Sales Manager.

24011 MOIR James Francis W/Cdr 10.02.54 Relinquished

24012 MUNDAY Ralph Silvanus F/Lt 10.02.54 Relinquished

Paul McMillan reports that Ralph Silvanus briefly served in the *Great War* as a cadet attached to the Royal Flying Corps.

24013 NEWCOMBE Leslie F/Lt 01.09.35 Relinquished

24014 POWELL Griffith James A/Cmdr 15.08.45 Relinquished

On 25th March 1943 Griffith James Powell was appointed to a class CC commission as air commodore in the Administrative and Special Duties Branch [LG 11 May 1943, supplement 36009, page 2100]. At some point he served with the Royal Canadian Air Force with the service number C1227. Born in Cardiff on 11th August 1907 Air Commodore Griffith 'Taffy' James Powell died on Monday, 8th March 1999.

24015 ROBINSON Geoffrey Arnold P/O 18.05.27 Terminated

24016 VIGORS Alan Doyne P/O 19.01.27 Resigned

Alan Doyne Vigors born on the 11th of March 1908 at Laverstock in Wilshire gained the reputation as an 'habitual criminal' as the following extracts from the *UK Registers of Habitual Criminals and Police Gazettes, 1834-1934'* reveals. In chronological order of date, Paul McMillan has unearthed the following from *The Police Gazette*:-

Thursday, February 19, 1931

"Re-Convictions - 34. - Alan Doyne Mercer Vigors CRO No. 16205-28 was sentenced at Windsor [Co.] P. Sess. 7.2.31, to 3 mos. impt. See Case No. 14, 5.2.31."

Saturday, July 3, 1931

"Re-Convictions - 29. - Alan Doyne Mercer Vigors CRO No. 16205-28 was sentenced at Margate Pol. Ct. 15.7.31, to 3 mos. impt. Six cases of fraud were taken into consideration when sentence was passed. See Case No. 11. 9.7.31."

Wednesday, December 16, 1931

"Re-Convictions - 61 - Alan Doyne Mercer Vigors CRO No. 16205-28 was sentenced at Wimbledon P. Sess. [L.] 8.12.31. to 3, 3 and 3 moss. impt. [cons.] for being a suspected person [loitering] annd obtaining money by false pretences [2 cases]. Three other cases of false pretence were taken into consideration when sentence was passed. See Casse No. 13, 2.12.31."

The above are just three examples of his petty crimes for in addition my co-author has traced various newspaper reports concerning his activities which resulted in terms of imprisonment in 1930, 1934 and 1939, the latter for obtaining the sum of £4 15s from a lady in Clifton by false pretences and for which he appeared at the Bristol Police Court. On this occasion he was sent down for six months hard labour.

His penchant for defrauding people that he met continued postwar as my co-author's discovery of a report in *The North Devon Journal - Herald* published on September 22nd, 1949: *"Alan Doyne Vigors of no fix abode, was remanded in custody until to-day by the borough bench on Saturday, charged with having obtained 33 by false pretences from Miss Daisy Barham - Det. Inspector J G Vickery said that on September 13th accused ..... accommodation at Miss Barham's house, 49 Rolle Street* [Barnstaple]. *He stated that he had been in a motoring accident with his friend who was in hospital. The next day he told Miss Barham he had no money but he would be able to borrow from his friend who had £15. Believing his story she let the accused have £3. On the Friday, Vigors left Barnstable, but was later apprehended at Lynton. Det. Con. B A T Lee said, that with Inspector Vickery he saw Vigors at Lynton police station. Accused had subsequently made a statement and when charged he made no reply. On the application of Inspector Vickery accused was remanded in custody."*

Alan Doyne Mercer Vigors died on Sunday, 17th December 1989 at Richmond-on-Thames.

24017	WILLIAMS	Hugh Noël Crawford	P/O		16.10.27	Terminated

LG 1 October 1926, issue 33207, page 6296 and 6297 - Seniority 18th September 1926

24018	BAINBRIDGE	Geoffrey Charles	P/O		26.01.27	Terminated
24019	BARTHOLOMEW	Gilbert	A/Cmdr	+	14.08.49	Air Attaché Ankara

On Sunday 14th August 1949 Acting Air Commodore Gilbert Bartholomew was one of four passengers aboard a Turkish Air Force C-47A-25-DK which crashed shortly after departing Ankara-Etimesgut Airport bound for Izmir Airport in Turkey. In addition to the four passengers who perished, the crew of three also perished. The cause of the crash was suspected to have been failure of one of the engines. An Air Ministry release named the four passengers as:-

Air Commodore Gilbert Bartholomew, his assistant Wing Commander Simon Napier Leslie Maude OBE DFC*, Wing Commander Lewis George Burnand OBE DFC who was to replace Wing Commander Maude and Sergeant Sydney Whitworth. Air Commodore Gilbert Bartholomeww CBD had served previously as Air Attaché Chunking [Chongqing] the provisional wartime capital of the Republic of China. He is buried in Wimbledon [Sacred Heart] Cemetery.

The crew of the C-47 were identified as Schit Hv Plt Yzb Irfan Dogan, Schit Hv Mkns Bcvs Ahmet Kavurmaci and Schit Hv Plt Kur Bnb Semih Yurukaslan.

24020	CALWELL	Alexander Kirk Kennedy	F/O	+	27.09.30	RAFC Cranwell

The following was published in *The Belfast Gazette* on February 20th, 1931, under the heading 'Notice of Charitable Bequests'

"In the goods of Flying Officer Alexander Kennedy Kirk Calwell, late of 56 Wellington Park, Belfast, and of Cranwell, Lincolnshire, deceased, NOTICE is hereby given that the above-named Alexander Kennedy Kirk Calwell, late of 56 Wellington Park, Belfast, Belfast and Cranwel, Lincolnshire, by his last Will, dated 26th September, 1928, directed that One-fifth Share in his residuary Estate should be held by his Trustees in trust for the Minister of Air for the time being, to devote the same in his uncontrolled discretion for the benefit of the Survivors and children of Royal Air Force Officers who had been or may be killed in flying accidents, and Testator directed that the Minister of Air should be absolutely unfettered as to the way in which he should distribute the said share.

"The said Testator died on the 27th September, 1930, and Probate of said Will was on the 16th day of February, 1931, granted forth of the Principal Registry, King's Bench Division of the High Court of Justice in Northern Ireland to Robert Norman McNeill, 56 Wellington Park, Belfast, and Patrick Brooke Webb, Randalstown, Executors named in the said Will.

"Dated this 16th day of February, 1931, E & R D Bates, Solicitors, 2 Arthur Street, Belfast, To the Ministry of Finance in Northern Ireland, and all others to whom it may concern."

His death as the result of a motorcar accident was given full coverage in *The Bedfordshire Chronicle And Bedfordshire Gazette* on Friday, October 3rd, 1930 under the heading 'Motor Tragedy at Seddington - Young Flying Officer's Error of Judgement at Night - Crashed into Tarred Barn at Roadside in Rainstorm - Remarkable Escape of Two Passengers'

"Three Flying Officers on week-end leave from Cranwell RAF Depot [Lincs.] were involved in a remarkable motor accident in the early hours of Saturday morning when the car in which they were driving to London skidded, crashed into a tarred brick-built barn and broke apart [body from chassis] at the Seddington bend on the Great North Road. It was a dark night and the rain was falling in torrents when the accident occurred at about 3.30 a.m.

"As a result of the accident Flying Officer Alexander Kirk Kennedy Calwell, aged 23, of 56 Wellington Park, Belfast [the owner and driver of the car], received such severe head injuries that he died in the County Hospital at 6.30 a.m. on the same day.

"His companions, Flying Officer Alliston Temple Clough Hazeldine of 46 Clapham Road, Bedford, and Flying Officer Richard Penry Garson-Williams of Aberelydach, Talybont-on-Usk, Wales, received concussion and minor injuries.

"The inquest was held at the Bedford County Hospital on Tuesday afternoon when the Coroner, Mr. H G Rose, sat with a jury, and a verdict of accidental death was returned.

"Those present at the inquiry included Sir Richard Dawson Bates Minister for Foreign Affairs to the Parliament of Northern Ireland, and deceased's uncle, Dr. W Calwell of Belfast [formerly guardians of the deceased up to the time of his majority]. Flying Officer Calwell was an orphan and had been a Ward in Chancery. His career in the RAF had been a brilliant one and he was looked upon as one of the most promising junior officers in the Force.

"Dr. Dennis Godfrey Hamilton, House Physician at the Hospital, stated that the deceased was admitted to the hospital at 5.45 a.m. on Saturday. Examination revealed that he was unconscious and had a deep wound in the scalp. He was bleeding from the left ear. Some damage was apparent to the cartilages of the neck. Witness stitched the wounds and had the patient removed to the ward where counter measures were taken against shock, and injection of morphia was given. His condition became rapidly worse and he died at 6.30 a.m. The cause of death was lacerations of the brain. There was practically no hope from the beginning.

"In reply to Mr. Dawson Bates [representing the family], witness said there was no sign of intoxication. Sir Richard Dawson Bates, Hollywood, Co. Down, Ireland, Minister for Foreign Affairs in N. Ireland, said that he had been the legal guardian of the deceased up to the time that he attained full age. His uncle [Dr. William Calwell] was joint guardian. Deceased was an orphan and Ward in Chancery, being discharged a few months ago. With permission of the Court he joined the RAF, a few years ago. He was an exceptionally healthy boy and his sight and hearing were good. At the last interview between them deceased told witness that he passed for a permanent commission in the Force. In habits he was temperate, practically a total abstainer. Witness last saw him alive at the end of July when he had just been engaged. He had owned a car for some years.

"Flying Officer Alliston Temple Clough Hazeldine, 46 Clapham Road, Bedford, stationed at the Electrical and Wireless School, Cranwell, said that he was in the car with Flying Officer Garnons-Williams and Flying Officer Calwell who was driving. Witness sat beside the driver and F/O Garnons-Williams was in the rear. They left Cranwell shortly after midnight. They were on leave, going to London for a day and returning to Bedford next day. The car was a Riley 9 Monaco Saloon. It was a fairly fast car and they were coming along fairly fast, but at the time of the crash they were going slower than usual owing to the rain. The car had no windscreen wiper. When the rain came down heavily, visibility was poor. The headlights were

good. They past through Sandy between 2.30 and 3 a.m. At Seddington it appeared to witness that Calwell took the right hand bend a little too sharp and his impression was that he touched the right hand bank which threw him into a skid to the left and that was all he could remember until he picked himself up. He then saw Flying Officer Garnons-Williams standing in the middle of the road holding his head and after he had found out that he was alright they both looked for F/L Calwell. They found him at the front of the car with his head under the front axle, They lifted the car which witness held up with his back while F/O Garnons-Williams pulled the deceased out. F/O Garnons-Williams summoned help from some cottages nearby and after some time a woman came along and went away again. Eventually someone brought a door on which they carried deceased back to the cottage with the assistance of two lorry drivers who pulled up. Mr A G Jeeves JP telephoned from the house next door for the police, who arrived after some minutes, and a doctor. Inspector G H Goodwin brought first aid dressings and then the doctor arrived and the ambulance, and after first aid had been applied they all went off to Bedford. Deceased was alive but unconscious. The people at the cottage named Undwrwood were exceedingly kind and helpful.

"In reply to the Coroner, witness added that they had all been in Lincoln between 9 p.m. and 10 p.m. where they had one round of drinks: that would be three each. Then they had two in the Mess between 10.45 and 12.5 a.m. Deceased was driving remarkably well. Witness had never driven with him before but he struck him as a particularly good driver.

"Questioned as to the speed at the time of the crash, witness said it would be between 30 and 35 m.p.h. They had been going faster. He had no recollection whether they turned round or turned over. They might have done anything. He was not surprised to heart that they grazed a wall for some distance. There was no traffic in the road at the time. The first vehicle passed at least half an hour afterwards.

"F/O Richard Penry Garston-Williams, Electrical and Wireless School, Cranwell, said that he had nothing to add to what F/O Hazeldine had said.He was partly asleep at the time, but he felt the car hit something and skid violently. The he felt it going over to the right. He found himself in the middle of the road. The car had the body stripped off it, leaving just the bare chassis which was on its wheels afterwards.

"Insp. G H Goodwin, Sandy, stated that about 3.15 a.m. on Saturday morning he received a telephone message and called Dr. T Campbell. He then hurried to the scene of the accident and found Calwell lying on the floor of a cottage owned by Mr. Underwood at Seddington, and being tended by F/O Hazeldine. Witness had some first aid dressing, but there was very little that could be done except to hold a pad near the head wound which was a very severe one. He sent for the ambulance at once and shortly afterwards Dr. Campbell arrived and dressed deceased's wounds and they all went to the County Hospital. Witness had treated F/Os Hazeldine and Garston-Williams in the meantime. Returning to the scene of the accident, he found the wrecked car on the east side of the road. The body was completely detached and torn away from the chassis. It had crumpled up and lay close to the chassis. He did not think he had ever seen such a complete smash. According to the marks the car must have crashed slantwise along the brick wall of a barn on the east side of the road. This brought it to a standstill on the footpath, which runs parallel with the wall of the barn. None of the wheels were damaged and the steering gear was in order. This seemed to show that the body struck the wall and not the chassis. At the scene of the accident there is a sharp bend to the right and the line of vision when leaving the straight is about 35 yards. Marks upon the road and grass appeared to indicate that deceased failed to take the right hand bend and keep straight on. This would cause him to mount the gravel footpath on the east and run into the brick wall. The length of graze along the wall was 13 feet. The point of impact to where the car came to a standstill [where there is another graze on the wall] was 34 feet. The length of the barn was 46 feet. It had been raining very hard during the night, and the whole of the buildings except the houses and low wall are tarred. With bad visibility the driver might not have seen the barn at all. Marks on the body seemed to indicate that it struck the wall first with the nearside and then turned round and struck it with the offside.

"The Coroner summed up briefly in favour a verdict of "Accidental death." The jury concurred and expressed sympathy with the deceased's relatives. Sir Dawson Bates and Mr. McNeil MP of Belfast expressed thanks on behalf of the deceased's relatives to the Hospital's authorities, the police and everybody concerned for their kindness."

24021	DUFF	John Frederick	P/O		21.09.27	Terminated
24022	FAIRHEAD	Frank George	F/O		24.12.32	Removed

Flying Officer Frank George Fairhead's removal from the service was promulgated on 3rd January 1933, issue 33899, page 54. It is believed he obtained a commission as a Lieutenant in the East Surrey Regiment on 7th September 1940 [LG 6 September 1940, supplement 34939, page 5393].

24023	GIBBONS	Gerald Preston Telford	P/O		16.02.27	Terminated
24024	GRIFFITHS	Morgan	W/Cdr		10.02.54	Relinquished
24025	HAYTER	Herbert Cecil Douglas	W/Cdr		16.12.47	Resigned
24026	KING	Douglas Stanley	F/O	+	21.04.40	Air Transport Auxiliary

Douglas Stanley King joined the Air Transport Auxiliary in whose service he lost his life on 21st April 1940. He is buried in Heston [St. Leonard] Churchyard in the County of Middlesex. His headstone bears the inscription *"Always Brave, Devoted To Duty, Glad To Serve, He Gave Himself To His Country."* His widow's address is shown as Washington, DC, USA. At the time of the outbreak of war he was in Class A of the Reserve of Air Force Officers having been transferred to Class A from class C on 11th May 1934 [LG 24 July 1934, issue 34072, page 4744].

My co-author has forwarded a copy of the Aviation Safety Network report on the accident which involved a Lockheed 14-WF62 Super Electra registered to British Overseas Airways Corporation as G-AFKD. Captain King had departed Perth Airport with the intention of transiting to Heston but flew off course and crashed at Beinn Uird near Loch Lomond, all three members of crew being killed. Commander King's co-pilot was First Officer Derek Ernest Eveleigh and the radio operator was John William Elliot.

24027	LIDDELL REYNOLDS	Frank Eric	P/O		05.01.27	Terminated
24028	MORSHEAD	Vernon Dillon	A/Cmdr		05.07.60	Retirement

New Zealand Air Commodore Vernon Dillon 'Alan' Morshead died on Friday, 18th August 1978. Transferring from the General Duties Branch to the Technical Branch in April 1940, his final appointment was as Air Officer Commanding RAF St. Athan and No. 4 School of Technical Training. Prior to this he had served as Senior Technical Staff Officer in Transport Command and with the 2nd Tactical Air Force.

24029	ROGERS	Joseph Alfred	F/Lt		10.06.45	Relinquished

On account of medical unfitness for Air Force service [LG 26 June 1945, supplement 37146, page 3318].

24030	ROWE	Ernest Leslie Jack	G/Capt		15.05.59	Retirement
24031	SCHLEAN	Hilton Henry Roy	P/O		12.01.27	Terminated
24032	TURNER HUGHES	Charles Keir	F/Lt		30.03.39	Resigned
24033	WEIGHILL	Reginald George	S/Ldr	+	16.07.41	40 Squadron

Squadron Leader Reginald George Weighill died with his crew when their Wellington Ic X3220 BL-H crashed shortly before midnight and soon after taking off from Alconbury for bombing operations over Hamburg. For details of the tragedy, please refer to page 93 of my RAFBCL 1941. Squadron Leader Weighill is buried in Scottow Cemetery, Norfolk.

LG 5 October 1926, issue 33208, page 6374 - Seniority 6th September 1926

FLYING OFFICER

24034	COLLISON	Frederic Laing	F/O	+	22.11.26	24 Squadron

Lieutenant 4th Essex Regiment

LG 12 October 1926, issue 33210, page 6547 - Seniority 1st October 1926

24035	BROADHURST	Harry	ACM		01.03.61	Retirement

Air Chief Marshal Sir Harry Broadhurst GCB KBE DSO* DFC* AFC three times mentioned in despatches, died on Tuesday, 29th August 1995.

Without a shadow of doubt Harry 'Broady' Broadhurst was one of the legendary Air Force officers of the Second World War, his numerous exploits being on a par with such luminaries as Basil Embry, Victor Beamish, 'Cats Eyes' Cunningham, Douglas Bader, Leonard Cheshire VC and Guy Gibson VC and the like, all of whom stamped an indelible mark of outstanding bravery in the face of great adversity.

Formerly of the Hampshire Heavy Brigade, Royal Artillery, TA he 'persuaded' his Commanding Officer to sign his application to be seconded to the Royal Air Force, the service that his father, a retired army officer, was opposed. Thus, with this degree of subterfuge the young Broadhurst joined the service of his dreams and by the time of the Second World War he was a permanent commissioned officer and had risen in rank to Squadron Leader, commanding 111 Squadron, the first squadron to be equipped with the Hawker Hurricane.and it was whilst based at Acklington in November 1939 that he was awarded the Distinguished Flying Cross, the citation being published in *The London Gazette* 2nd January 1940, issue 34765, page 23:-

"This officer was in command of the duty Squadron at an East coast aerodrome during November 1939, when he was informed of an approaching enemy aircraft. He stated that the weather conditions were unfit for formation flying and yet, despite the rain and clouds at ground-level, he took off alone, flying blind by means of instruments. Emerging above the cloud and endeavouring to clear an iced-up windscreen, he sighted the enemy aircraft. Squadron Leader Broadhurst attacked and caused it to turn on its side and dive vertically into cloud close to sea level. In following it down he narrowly escaped from crashing into the sea. On his return weather conditions had not improved, and it was only at the third attempt that he was able to regain his aerodrome."

A plethora of postings followed in the wake of his handing over command of 111 Squadron to Squadron Leader J M Thompson but in December 1940 he settled in as Station Commander at RAF Hornchurch and it was here on 4th July 1941 that his life came close to being ended. Throughout the *Battle of Britain* he had participated in operations and it was more of the same during his tenure at Hornchurch. Thus it was that he 'borrowed' one of 54 Squadron's Spitfire Vbs ['W3244'] in order to take part in *Circus 32,* and leading the Hornchurch Wing. Tangling with a bunch of '109s he was to claim two before he to was hit and wounded, his Spitfire going into a spin which he managed to recover at 1,000 feet. Rather than abandon 'W3244' over Cap Griz Nez he headed back across the Channel but not before some alert *Flak* gunners caused additional damage to his aircraft.

Dredging up his reserves of skill and determination he made it home where he executed a wheels up landing. Here it should be noted that according to Air-Britain's W1000 to W9999 listings, W3244 was never on 54 Squadron's establishment.

On the same day as this 'adventure' he was *Gazetted* with the DSO, issue 35208, page 3824: *"This officer has been almost continuously employed on active operations since the war began. He distinguished himself during the intensive air operations over this country in August 1940, by his determined efforst to intercept and destroy enemy bombers at night. In December 1940, Group Captain Broadhurst assumed command of his present unit and throughout has performed outstanding operational work. He has destroyed at least four enemy aircraft besides damaging several others. One day in June 1941, he took off in an endeavour to locate a pilot whom he believed had been forced down in the sea. In his efforts to direct a rescue boat he flew some 8 miles off Cap Griz Nez but had to return owing to lack of petrol. His ability, keenness and outstanding powers of leadership have been an inspiration to all and have contributed materially to the successes obtained by the squadrons under his command."*

His wounds must have been relatively light for he was soon back in action and on 19 December 1941 in the Third Supplement to *The London Gazette* of 16th December 1941, supplement 35386, page 7173, a First Bar was added to his DSO: *"This officer has organised and led his Wing with conspicuous gallantry and success. During a heavy engagement over Bethune, in June 1941, Group Captain Broadhurst's aircraft was hit by a cannon shell which, besides making a large hole in the port wing, put the port wing guns out of action and damaged the aileron thus making control difficult. A second shell hit the side of the fuselage, causing havoc in the cockpit. Group Captain Broadhurst received many small wounds in the arm and legs and only recovered from the effects of the shell-fire at 1,000 feet over the target area. Nevertheless, he flew the aircraft back to England. Within a few days, Group Captain Broadhurst was again leading the Wing in action over Northern France. On the return journey he was attacked by a force of 6 Messerschmitt 109s but, by brilliant tactics, Group Captain Broadhurst fought them off and, it is believed, destroyed two of them before the engagement was terminated some 15 miles north of Gravelines. Although his aircraft was damaged by the enemy's fire, Group Captain Broadhurst flew it safely back to this country. Since being awarded the Distinguished Service Order in June, he has destroyed 8 and probably destroyed a further 4 enemy aircraft. He has set an example worthy of the highest traditions of the service."*

A First Bar to his DFC was promulgated on 29th September 1942 in the Second Supplement to *The London Gazette* of 25th September 1942, supplement 35721, page 4215: *"In the combined operations against Dieppe on 19th August 1942, this officer flew with great distinction. He completed several sorties during which he constantly flew amongst enemy bomber and fighter patrols. Although he was several times engaged by hostile aircraft, 1 of which he destroyed, Group Captain Broadhurst displayed great skill and furnished much valuable information regarding the trend of air operations. In the course of his duties he flew alone for some 8 hours in the area where hostile patrols were operating in great strength. His skill and gallantry were of the highest order."*

At the time of the costly [particularly to Canadian forces] Dieppe operation, Group Captain Broadhurst was Deputy Senior Air Staff Officer at No. 11 Group headquarters, having departed Hornchurch the previous December. For a brief appreciation of some of the tactics employed by the air force in support of the Dieppe landings, I recommend a reading of chapter 14, titled 'Summer Escapade' of Michael J F Bowyer's excellent book *2 Group RAF - A Complete History 1936-1945,* and for a table of Fighter Command losses during this historic day, please refer to pages 56 through to 62 of Norman L R Franks second volume of Fighter Command losses.

Two months after his participation in the Dieppe saga, Group Captain Broadhurst was on his way to the Middle East where from July 1943 to March 1944 he was Air Officer Commanding Desert Air Force. Fast-forward ten years and with various Staff duties behind him, and perhaps to his surprise when considering his background of mainly fighter operations, Air Marshal Sir Harry Broadhurst found himself arriving at High Wycombe to take over from Air Marshal Sir George Mills the key position of Air Officer Commanding-in-Chief Bomber Command, a post that he would hold from January 1956 to May 1959 and it was still relatively early in his tenure that he was involved in the highly publicised accident involving the loss of Avro Vulcan I XA897 which had been chosen for a tour of the world to show off one of the three V-force bombers.

Selected from the establishment of Vulcans based at 230 Operational Conversion Unit at Waddington, XA897 was commanded by Squadron Leader D R Howard with Air Marshal Sir Harry Broadhurst as his co-pilot and a four-man crew comprising of Squadron Leader J G W Stroud, a qualified Vulcan pilot, Squadron Leader E J Eames, navigator, Squadron Leader A E Gamble, Air Electronics Operator and a civilian, Mr. F Bassett from Avro's. Departing from Waddington the tour ran smoothly and was regarded as highly successful, covering a 26,000 mile round trip to New Zealand and Australia where the sight of this huge delta-wing bomber left an lasting impression on all who witnessed its sheer power and flying capabilities.

To crown the success of the tour, it was planned for the Vulcan to land at London Heathrow where a welcoming home party had gathered. The outcome was a tragedy of the first order and the description reported by *Flight* in its issue of 5th October 1956 captures the final moments of the XA897's flight: *"The Vulcan was due to land at 1108 hr. Weather was poor, with visibility of 1,500 to 2,000 yd in mist and rain. Civil airline flights were operating at a reduced rate, using runway No. 1 [100 deg]. The G C A caravans were in position beside runway 10 Left.*

"First sign of the Vulcan's arrival was the sound of a brief burst of full power out in the mist at the touchdown end of 10 Left. Flight's representative standing on the roof of the Queen's building in the airport central area, then saw the Vulcan climbing very steeply up from the runway with under-carriage down. At an angle of about 40 deg it climbed quietly to about 800 ft when the cabin roof blew off and both pilots ejected in quick succession. The automatic devices of the Martin-Baker Mk 3 seats functioned immediately and both men were in a stable descent before losing any height. The Vulcan then turned gently to starboard and dived at an angle of 20 to 30 deg onto the starboard edge of runway No. 4 where it exploded on impact, leaving a 300 yd swath of wreckage which burnt for nearly an hour.

"Sir Harry Broadhurst landed on runway 10 Left and injured both his feet; S/L Howard touched down on the grass and had a bruised forehead and slightly hurt back.

"A Hawker Siddeley Group statement issued later in the day said that S/L Howard was making a normal G C A approach and that nothing appeared to be wrong with the aircraft. Some 600 yd short of the runway the aircraft touched down in a field and lost 15 of its 16 main wheels and parts of the undercarriage legs. Power was immediately applied, but seconds later it was clear that the machine was out of control and the order was given to abandon ship. Only the two pilots have ejector seats; the rest of the crew have to escape through a hatch in the cabin floor, and none of them succeeded in doing this in the seconds available. An RAF court of enquiry was opened on Tuesday headed by Air Chief Marshal Sir Donald Hardman, Air Member for Supply and Organisation.

"When the accident occurred that Vulcan was concluding a most successful to Australia and New Zealand where its outstanding performance and impressive appearance had created great interest, official and unofficial. It had made the flight from Australia in four stages, landing at Singapore, Negombo and Aden. Though seeking no records it had averaged well over 500 mph on many of its flights overseas."

The magnitude of this terrible accident in full view of the waiting dignitaries and press reporters resulted in a far reaching enquiry, the findings leading to acrimonious exchanges between the various parties involved. Again I quote extracts from *Flight's* editorial leader published on 4th January 1957 in which a number of pertinent observations are made concerning the statement made in the House of Commons on December 20th, last [summarised on page 27 of the magazine], the first of which set the tone for the entire editorial: *"But careful consideration of its contents - and of other statements, noted in our news pages overleaf - leaves us with the unhappy conclusion that the accident has not in fact been explained at all."*

Much hinged on those crucial last minutes of the flight when Squadron Leader Howard was following the instructions from the GCA controller and until now had not made a full GCA approach and landing in a Vulcan. Evidence was given that a number of corrections were given during the approach and, it is alleged, the controller was still in conversation with the pilot when the Vulcan undershot, lost most of its undercarriage before commencing its final climb to a height where ejection was the only option as it was no longer responding to the controls.

The editorial ends: *"Not to seek a scapegoat, but for the peace of mind of all concerned, a detailed record of the occurrences during the few critical seconds should be made public."*

To conclude, Sir Harry's mini-biography on the Air Authority - A History of RAF Organisation website notes that a year later he accompanied Wing Commander F L Dodd, Officer Commanding 230 OCU, in another Vulcan demonstration flight, this time Waddington to Naples during which it covered the 1,121 miles in one hour and fifty minutes at an average speed of 615 mph. It is further noted that it was during his time at High Wycombe that the Quick Reaction Alert [QRA] was established in which the V-force bombers were held in readiness and capable of being in the air within four minutes of the order to "scramble" had been given.

Air Chief Marshal Sir Harry Broadhurst's final appointment was at Fontainebleau, southeast of Paris, as Commander, Allied Air Forces Central Europe.

LG 14 December 1926, issue 33229, page 8187 - Seniority 3rd December 1926

24037 GRIFFITHS John Francis G/Capt + 09.05.45

Canada As Wing Commander John Francis Griffiths he was an early recipient in the Second World War of the DFC and the first Canadian to be so honoured, his award been promulgated in the same issue and on the same page as that for Squadron Leader Harry Broadhurst who had been short service commissioned two months previously:-

"During December 1939, in spite of adverse weather and strong enemy opposition by anti-aircraft guns and enemy fighters, this officer led his squadron of 12 aircraft, and carried out a successful reconnaissance over strong naval enemy forces. The determination with which he pressed home this reconnaissance enabled him to bring back information of vital importance. In the course of this operation his formation accounted for no less than 5 enemy aircraft. By his personal example and thoroughness, he has been largely instrumental in maintaining his unit's high standard of efficiency."

Group Captain John Francis Griffiths DFC Czechoslovakian Military Cross and mentioned in despatches is buried in Hotton War Cemetery, Belgium. He is also commemorated on The Canadian Virtual War Memorial.

ROLL OF HONOUR
FOR
1926 SHORT SERVICE COMMISSION
OFFICERS

P/O	ANDERSON	Noel Jordan	29 June 1926	4 FTS Abu Sueir
F/Lt	ASHTON-JINKS	Clement Philip	20 June 1932	HAD Henlow
A/Cmdr	BARTHOLOMEW CBE	Gilbert	14 August 1949	Air Attaché Ankara
F/O	BARTON	John	19 January 1931	7 Squadron
F/O	CALWELL	Alexander Kirk Kennedy	27 September 1930	RAFC Cranwell
F/O	COLLISON	Frederic Laing	22 November 1926	24 Squadron
P/O	CONEYBEER	Ronald Williams	10 August 1926	4 FTS Abu Sueir
F/O	DE WOULFE DE WYTT	Athal Patrick	19 September 1928	A&GS Eastchurch
P/O	FISHER MC	Lionel Edward Ruggles	9 January 1928	6 Squadron
A/Cmdr	FITCH	Issac John	25 July 1944	AOC Tarawa
F/O	FORBES	Harold Vernon	3 December 1929	HAD Henlow
F/Lt	GOWER-JONES	Frank	24 December 1939	Station Flight Turnhouse
G/Capt	GRIFFITHS DFC Czechoslovakian Military Cross	John Francis	9 May 1945	
P/O	HAWKER	Hector Reginald	23 November 1926	
F/O	KING	Douglas Stanley	21 April 1940	Air Transport Auxiliary
F/O	MACKENZIE	David	21 January 1930	207 Squadron
F/O	MARETT New Zealand	Harold Claude	12 October 1932	3 FTS Grantham
A/Cmdr	OLSON New Zealand	Edward George	15 May 1945	
P/O	PACE	Richard Griffith	20 July 1927	32 Squadron
G/Capt	PLEASANCE	Norman Charles	23 March 1944	OC RAF Bardney
S/Ldr	POWER	Henry Eustace	29 May 1937	2 FTS Digby
F/Lt	RADCLYFFE	Arnold Ayscough	24 December 1941	
F/Lt	RESTELL-LITTLE	Murray Meyrick	19 March 1933	5 FTS Sealand
S/Ldr	TIMMINS	Lloyd Miller	21 March 1944	
F/Lt	TINDALL	Lewis Stanley	28 July 1941	25 EFTS Belvedere
W/Cdr	SHAW	Grenville Hammerton	27 September 1940	2 SFTS
F/O	UNDERWOOD	Gerald Arthur	11 May 1928	16 Squadron
F/O	WARD	Albert Ross	29 October 1929	442 Flight HMS *Hermes*
S/Ldr	WEIGHILL	Reginald George	16 July 1941	40 Squadron

Appendix D - RAF [Cadet] College Cranwell

COMMANDANT
Air Commodore Amyas Eden Borton CB CMG DSO AFC mentioned in despatches
Air Commodore Frederick Crosby Halahan CMG CBE DSO MVO mentioned in despatches

On the 1st of November 1926, Air Commodore Frederick Crosby Halahan succeeded Air Commodore Amyas Eden Borton as Commandant of the Cadet College.

His military service had commenced in 1894 as a naval cadet at the Britannia Naval College from where he graduated as a Midshipman in 1896. Prior to the outbreak of the *Great War* he had served seagoing commissions aboard HMS *Immortalite, Dreadnought* and *Cochrane*. Postwar, he was one of seventeen Colonels appointed to a permanent commission in the Royal Air Force on 1st August 1919 [see page 180 of Appendix D of the third volume].

January 1926 entry : 25

26023 ALLEN John Edward G/Capt 11.02.48 Retirement
Group Captain John Edward Allen gained a Cranwell cadetship as an aircraft apprentice at No. 1 School of Technical Training, Halton. Paul McMillan, my co-author, adds that from the outbreak of the Second World War until 1943, he was on service in the Mediterranean and Middle East theatres after which he was on special duties with the Ministry of Aircraft Production and, subsequently, was appointed Deputy Chief of the Air Training Corps. He died in Chelsea on Monday, 11th October 1971.

26024 BEAMISH Charles Eric St. John G/Capt 18.09.48 Retirement
The youngest of the three Beamish boys to be accepted as a Flight Cadet at Cranwell, Group Captain Charles Eric St. John Beamish emulated his older brothers, particularly on the sports field where he represented the College at Hockey, Rugby Football and cricket. On graduating he was a recipient of the Robert Marsland Groves Memorial Prize and in his air force career he was awarded a DFC, mentioned in despatches and conferred with two American honours, Officer of Legion of Merit and the Silver Star. Group Captain Charles Eric St. John Beamish died at Templemore in Co. Tipperary on Friday, 18th May 1984

26025 BEISIEGEL Walter Carl A/Cmdr 10.04.56 Retirement
Air Commodore Walter Carl Beisiegal OBE mentioned in despatches, died on Monday, 8th January 1973. The Air of Authority website shows his second Christian name as 'Karl.'

26026 BLUNT Samuel Leslie G/Capt 01.08.56 Retirement
Group Captain Samuel Leslie Blunt mentioned in despatches, died in South Africa on Thursday, 25th October 1979.

26027 CHALMERS Peter John Basil P/O + 08.02.28 43 Squadron

26028 CONSTANTINE Hugh Alex ACM 30.05.64 Retirement
Air Chief Marshal Sir Hugh Constantine KBE CB DSO five times mentioned in despatches, died on Thursday, 16th April 1992. In addition to his Royal Air Force honours, he was conferred with Poland's Order of Polonia restituta [3rd Classs]. As a young Pilot Officer stationed at North Weald and attached to 56 Squadron [Siskin IIIA] he crashed off Leysdown on the Isle of Sheppey on 10th December 1928. His plight was noticed by Flying Officer Walter Anderson and Corporal Thomas McTeague who effected his rescue and in doing so were awarded the British Empire Medal.

26029 DEWAR John Scatliff W/Cdr + 11.09.40 213 Squadron
Wing Commander John Scatliff Dewar DSO DFC mentioned in despatches, attached to 213 Squadron, was shot down over the Channel while flying between Exeter and Tangmere in Hurricane I V7306. His body was washed ashore on 30th September 1940, and he is buried in North Baddesley [St. John The Baptist] Churchyard, Hampshire. His headstone bears the inscription: *"In Loving Memory He Has Fond The Freedom For Which He Fought The Glory Of Which He Dreamed."* It is noted 213 Squadron had been based at Exeter until 7th September on which date he transferred to Tangmere.

26030 DILLON-TRENCHARD John Harry Luke F/O 21.01.31 Resigned
Returned to the service and was granted a commission as a pilot officer under probation, effective from 20th January 1940, in the Administrative and Special Duties Branch [LG 13 February 1940, issue 34790, page 856]. S/Ldr 10.02.54 Relinquished
Squadron Leader John Harry Luke Dillon-Trenchard died on Sunday, 23rd September 1962.

26158 FIELD Denys Brian Douglass S/Ldr + 06.06.40 83 Squadron
Squadron Leader Denys Brian Douglas Field failed to return from operations to Hamburg on 5th-6th June 1940* his Hampden I P1348 being shot down by Flak to crash at Barnkrug [Niedersachsen] on the west bak of the Elbe, 9km north of Stade. There were no survivors and all now rest in Becklingen War Cemetery. Squadron Leader Field's headstone is inscribed: *"To The Beloved And Everlasting Memory Of My Husband Denys."* He is mentioned on page 60 of Guy Gibson's Enemy Coast Ahead where Gibson refers to him as being *"... golf champion of the Air Force."* By cruel co-incidence, another Cranwell graduate, Squadron Leader George Ernest Peacock DFC [September 1931 entry], lost his life that same night when his Wellington IA P9232 WS-M failed to return to Honington following a raid on Duisburg. Hit by Flak on crossing the Dutch coast, the bomber came down in Zuid Holland at Simonshaven, 16km SW of Rotterdam. Along with his observer, Sergeant Ronald Charles Hargrave DFM, Squadron Leader Peacock is buried in Geervliet [Smonshaven] Protestant Cemetery. The rest of his crew survived to become prisoners of war.

26032 GROOM Samuel Robert W/Cdr + 21.11.40 102 Squadron
Commanding 102 Squadron, Wing Commander Samuel Robert Groom had accompanied Flying Officer Anthony Marmaduke Langdale Shelby and crew in Whitley V P5072 DY-P for a raid on Duisburg. Taking off from Topcliffe their aircraft came down in the North Sea at 0634; there were no survivors and all are commemorated on the Runnymede Memorial.

26033 HALAHAN Patrick John Handy W/Cdr 04.11.43 Retirement
Wing Commander Patrick John Handy Halahan DFC, died on Friday, 12th November 1982.

26055 HEWITT Francis Peter F/O 17.08.32 Retired list
At his own request [LG 16 August 1932, issue 33855, page 5303]. He returned to the service and was active within the General Duties Branch from 2nd September 1939. S/Ldr 20.04.46 Retired list
Squadron Leader Francis Peter Hewitt OBE, died on Sunday, 30th October 1994.

26035 HUNT Alfred William G/Capt 15.06.48 Retirement
On account of medical unfitness for Air Force service [LG 22 June 1948, supplement 38328, page 3638]. Group Captain Alfred William Hunt CBE mentioned in despatches, died . On graduation he was awarded the Sword of Honour.

26036 HUTTON Walter Howard A/Cmdr 10.03.58 Retirement
Air Commodore Walter Howard Hutton CBE twice mentioned in despatches and conferred with the Belgian Order of Leopold with Palme and Croix de Guerre, died on Friday, 28th August 1981.

26037 JONES Edgar Albert G/Capt 08.08.55 Retirement
Group Captain Edgar Albert Jones mentioned in despatches, died on Tuesday, 28th November 1978.

26038 LEECH Haliburton Hume F/Lt 17.09.38 Retired list
On account of ill-health [LG 20 September 1938, issue 34553, page 5954]. An extremely sick gentleman, Flight Lieutenant Haliburton Hume Leech died while undergoing treatment in St. Bartholomew's Hospital, London, on Friday, 5th May 1939.

26039 MacCALLUM John Evelyn Matier G/Capt + 16.10.43

Group Captain John Evelyn Matier MacCallum, aged 37, died during the morning of Saturday, 16th October 1943, in St. Hugh's Hospital, Oxford, where he had been admitted with multiple injures received in a motor vehicle accident; he is buried in Bangor Cemetery in Co. Down. For a brief biography of his service, I recommend the website Bangor Cemetery Project which has a photograph of his grave. The attached notes indicates that he entered the service in 1923 [possibly at Cranwell] and his early years following graduation he was employed on army co-operation squadrons. At the outbreak of the Second World War he was serving in Singapore.

26040 NORRIS Nigel Blanford W/Cdr 01.01.56 Retirement

Wing Commander Nigel Blanford Norris died on Saturday, 19th September 1992.

26041 PARKER Hewson Christopher G/Capt 10.02.54 Retirement

Group Captain Hewson Christopher Parker died on Tuesday, 2nd June 1970.

26042 PICKLES Kenneth Frederick Travis G/Capt 01.05.55 Retirement

Group Captain Kenneth Frederick Travis Pickles OBE four times mentioned in despatches and conferred with the Polish honour, Polonia Restituta 3rd Class, died in Scotland at some time during 1983.

26043 POTT John Robert Hallings AV-M 13.07.57 Retirement

Air Vice-Marshal John Robert Hallings-Pott CBE DSO AFC three times mentioned in despatches, died on Monday, 26th January 1976. Early in the Second World War he commanded 25 Squadron [Blenheims] and for his leadership of a dusk raid on the German seaplane base on Borkum he was awarded the DSO [LG 20 February 1940, supplement 34795, page 1055].

26044 PROCTER George Henry Herbert G/Capt 12.06.58 Retirement

Group Captain George Henry Herbert Procter CBE mentioned in despatches, died in New Zealand on Sunday, 22nd April 2001. He is buried in Awa Tapu Cemetery, Paraparaumu, Wellington.

26045 TAIT Norman Alexander A/Cmdr 20.06.59 Retirement

Air Commodore Norman Alexander Tait OBE, died in January 1988.

26046 WAGHORN David John A/Cmdr + 01.04.45 106 PR Group Benson

Air Commodore David John Waghorn CBE AFC died in a flying accident at Boscombe Down when his Spitfire XIX PS831 of 541 Squadron based at Benson crashed. Spitfire XIX PS831 was the first aircraft in a batch of 70 airframes delivered between November 1944 and May 1945, the majority of which going to storage units from where they were sold in 1949 to the Swedish Air Force. Air Commodore Waghorn was Air Officer Commanding No. 106 [Photographic Reconnaissance] Group which had formed from No. 106 [Photographic Reconnaissance] Wing on 14th April 1944, its head-quarters being at Fifield House, Benson, and coming under the aegis of Coastal Command. It will be recalled that his elder brother, Henry, had preceded him to Cranwell [September 1922 entry] and died from injuries received in a flying accident at Farnborough on Nay 5th, 1931.

26047 WHITE Ernest Richard F/O + 24.03.30 58 Squadron

SWORD OF HONOUR
Flight Cadet Alfred William Hunt

ROLL OF HONOUR
JANUARY 1926 ENTRY

P/O	CHALMERS	Peter John Basil	8 February 1928	43 Squadron
W/Cdr	DEWAR	John Scatliff	11 September 1940	213 Squadron
S/Ldr	FIELD	Denys Brian Douglas	6 June 1940	83 Squadron
W/Cdr	GROOM	Samuel Robert	21 November 1940	102 Squadron
G/Capt	MacCALLUM	John Evelyn Matier	16 October 1943	
A/Cmdr	WAGHORN	David John	1 AprIL 1945	AOC 1[PR] Group
F/O	WHITE	Ernest Richard	24 March 1930	58 Squadron

September 1926 entry : 32

26077 BAYNE David Walter G/Capt 29.08.55 Retirement

Australia Group captain David Walter Bayne died on Wednesday, 11th June 1986.

26048 COOPER* Reginald John G/Capt 15.12.42 Dismissed

By sentence of General Court Martial. Although conjecture on the part of my co-author, the dismissal of Group Captain Reginald John Cooper may be linked with that of Pilot Officer Norman de Mattos Bentwich OBE MC who was found guilty of losing documents [subsequently found by a member of the public and handed in to the authorities] linked with *Operation Torch*, the Allied landings in French North Africa of 8th-16th November 1942. Both officers were attached to No. 1 Depot RAF Uxbridge. A considerable amount of additional information may be gleaned on the RAF Commands website, mainly in respect of the unfortunate Pilot Officer Norman de Mattos Bentwich. Group Captain Reginald John Cooper died in Welwyn, Hert-fordshire on Tuesday, 29th April 1986.

26049 COUNCELL* Richard Basil G/Capt 07.09.55 Retirement

Group Captain Richard Basil Councell OBE, died at Mortimer [Caldwell County] in northwestern North Carolina, America, on Wednesday, 25th January 1984. This is interesting for according to *Wikipedia,* Mortimer, a mill town with a population of around 800, flooded in 1940, since when it has been a 'ghost town' with only the odd remnants of machinery to remind visitors of its existence.

26050 DALE* Herbert Reginald W/Cdr + 11.05.41 XV Squadron

Wing Commander Herbert Reginald Dale and crew took off from Wyton in Stirling I N3654 LS-B for operations to Berlin in the course of which they were intercepted over Holland by *Oberleutnant* Egmond Prinz zur Lippe Wiessenfeldof 4./NJG1 and shot down between Hoodwoud and Opmeer in Noord Holland. Their Stirling, the first to be lost from the squadron since converting from Wellingtons, fell into soft ground from which only the body of Wing Commander Dale was recovered; he is buried in Bergen General Cemetery while his crew are commemorated on the Runnymede Memorial.

26051 DARK* Albert Edward F/Lt 17.02.59 Retired list

Granted a commission in class CC which was relinquished on his return to active service 18th December 1939 [LG 23 February 1940, issue 34799, page 1102]. G/Capt 01.01.56 Retirement

Group Captain Albert Edward Dark CBE, died on Sunday, 27th April 1997, whilst undergoing treatment in Dr. Gray's Hospital, Elgin, Morayshire. My co-author has come across a letter written by Group Captain Dark and published in November 1994 in the aviation magazine *Aeroplane* in which he challenged the validity of a report stating that the Fairey Fox that crashed at Hendon on 11th October 1928, bore the airframe serial J7946, and that the Fox that crashed was probably J8423. My summary for the date in question will explain Group Captain Dark's reasoning. It is further noted that at one stage in his service, and now ranked Group Captain, he was the Station Commander at Kinloss and though it is conjecture on my part, it would appear that he so loved the Moray area that he retired here instead of his birth county of Kent. Group Captain Albert Edward Dark was cremated in Inverness.

26052 DUDGEON* Peter William Archdale F/O 18.07.33 Resigned

Granted a commission in class C of the Reserve of Air Force Officers following his resignation of a permanent commission [LG 8 August 1933, issue 33967, page 5302]., his service number now being 70934. On 24th July 1939, his commission was amended from class C to class A [LG 1 August 1939, issue 34650, page 5325]. On 23rd July 1940, and now Acting Flight Lieutenant, he was *Gazetted* with the DFC [LG 23 July 1940, issue 34903, page 4530]. W/Cdr 10.02.54 Relinquished

Wing Commander Peter William Archdale Dudgeon DFC, died on Wednesday, 15th February 1967.

26098 EASTON James Alfred A/Cmdr 12.02.49 Retirement

Air Commodore Sir James Easton KCMG CB CBE, died on Friday, 19th October 1990. Although he had specialised as an armaments officer, shortly after the outbreak of the Second World War he was posted to the Directorate of Intelligence and such was the expertise that he gained in thiss specialist field that on retiring from the service he joined MI.6 and within two years he was appointed Deputy Director of the Service, a position that he held until retiring in 1958. He then accepted the position of Her Majesty's Consul-General in Detroit, a post that he held for the next ten years.

26053 FRANKS* Alexander Lumsden S/Ldr + 29.05.40 610 Squadron AAF

Squadron Leader Alexander Lumsden Franks AFC is buried in Sage War Cemetery, his headstone bearing the inscription: *"Among The Very Brave, The Very True."* Commanding 610 Squadron AAF, Squadron Leader Lumsden was flying Spitfire I N3177 DW-T when his squadron was 'bounced' by Me109s off the coast of Holland. Four of his patrol were shot down without a single survivor. His body was later washed onto a beach on Zeeland. In addition to his AFC, he had been conferred with the Insignia of the Order of Al Rafidian Class IV, an Iraqi decoration.

26054 GRUNDY* Edouard Michael Fitzfrederick AV-M 07.01.66 Retirement

Air Vice-Marshal Sir Edouard Grundy KBE CB twice mentioned in despatches, died on Monday, 15th June 1987.

26056 HOMER* John Wood G/Capt + 18.07.44 353 Squadron

Group Captain John Wood Homer was a passenger aboard Hudson III V9106 which suffered a double-engine failure shortly after taking off from Mauripur, crashing and bursting into flame; he is buried in Karachi War Cemetery. His younger brother, Michael Giles Homer arrived at Cranwell with the January 1937 intake; tragically, he was killed during the *Battle of Britain* when his 242 Squadron Hurricane I P2967 was shot down near Sittingbourne. Michael is buried in Swanage [Godlingston] Cemetery.

26057 HUGHES* George Barnes W/Cdr 14.07.45 Retirement

Wing Commander George Barnes Hughes is believed to have died circa March 1978, in the Chichester area of West Sussex. My co-author has discovered that he came to Cranwell by way of an aircraft apprenticeship at Flowerdown having enlisted on 11th September 1923. It comes as no surprise to learn that much of his service concerned signals duties. Subsequently, his medals [for service on the NWF] and his flying log book were advertised by Medals Military with a guide price of £950.00.

26058 JORGENSEN* James Ernest P/O + 17.06.29 3 Squadron

26059 LAINÉ* Edward James G/Capt 01.06.55 Retirement

Group Captain Edward James Lainé CBE DFC mentioned in despatches, born in Uttar Pradesh, India died on the Channel Island of Guernsey on Thursday, 26th April 2001.

26060 LLEWELYN* John Griffith W/Cdr + 23.05.40 40 Squadron

The death of Wing Commander John Griffith Llewelyn is described in some detail by David Gunby, author of 40 Squadron's history, where on page 134 of *Sweeping the Skies* he writes: *"On 23 May, however, it was a different story. Two sections led by the newly arrived CO were detailed to attack German columns near Arras, in company with two from XV Squadron* [both squadrons were operating from Wyton]. *Low cloud prevented this, so motorized columns near Boulogne were bombed. Two 40 Squadron aircraft and one from XV were lost, neither John Llewelyn nor F/O Ralph Jacoby returning. The latter survived, though the other crew members were killed. From Llewelyn's aircraft only the observer [Sgt Beattie] escaped, returning to the Squadron several days later. A story circulating amongst ground crew, and recalled by Joe Raybould, is that Llewelyn's aircraft caught fire, and he was seen trying to open the sliding hatch above his head. Joe gives credence to this, since the CO's aircraft had a hatch which was notoriously difficult to open."* A photograph of Wing Commander Llewelyn accompanies the author's account. Meanwhile, my RAFBCL 1939-1940 identifies Wing Commander Llewelyn's Blenheim IV as P4909 and Flying Officer Jacoby flying L8834. Both had taken off at 1010, with the CO coming down between Beuvry and Sailly-Labourse in the Pas-de-Calais. Wing Commander John Griffith Llewelyn is buried in Beuvry Communal Cemetery where his headstone is inscribed with the words: *"The Eternal God Is Thy Refuge, And Underneath Are The Everlasting Arms."*

LOCKWOOD Frank Day F/O 05.05.32 Retired list

On account of ill-health [LG 10 May 1932, issue 33824, page 3055]. Flying Officer Frank Day Lockwood was born in West Bengal, India, and died in Australia at Carnagie Caulfeld in the State of Victoria on Tuesday, 9th August 1979.

26089 MANNING-FOX Joseph Henry F/O 07.07.34 Retired list

At his own request [LG 17 July 1934, issue 34070, page 4593]. Flying Officer Joseph Henry Manning-Fox died circa June 1988, in the Havering district of Greater London. My co-author also reports that in 1939, he was serving as a ground instructor at the Reserve Flying School at Woodley.

26061 MUTCH* John A/Cmdr 01.10.58 Retirement

Air Commodore John Mutch CB CBE commenced his Royal Air Force service at Cranwell in September 1923, as an Aircraft Apprentice, 8th Entry in No. 4[Boys] Wing and in August 1926, passed out as a qualified Fitter/Rigger.

26062 OWEN* John Jervis W/Cdr + 06.07.43 466 Squadron RAAF

Wing Commander John Jervis Owen mentioned in despatches, failed to return from a mine laying operation in French coastal waters on 5th-65h July 1943. Attached to 466 Squadron RAAF, he took off from Leconfield at 2211 hours in Wellington X HF601, his crew being all commissioned officers. Four, including Wing Commander Owen, are buried in Le Conquet Communal Cemetery [Finistère], while the fifth member, Flying Officer Frank Darbyshire is commemorated on the Runnymede Memorial.

26063 PRATT* Charles Valancy John W/Cdr + 14-15.12.42 38 Squadron

Wing Commander Charles Valancy John Pratt DSO failed to return from operations and is commemorated on the Alamein Memorial, Column 247.

26064 PRINGLE* Herbert John G/Capt 28.09.51 Retirement

Group Captain Herbert John Pringle AFC, died on Friday, 23rd November 2001.

16204 RYLEY* Douglas William Robert AV-M 02.01.62 Retirement

Air Vice-Marshal Douglas William Robert Ryley CB CBE, died on Sunday, 29th December 1985.

26066 SINCLAIR* Laurence Frank AV-M 29.07.60 Retirement

Air Vice-Marshal Sir Laurence Sinclair GC KCB CBE DSO* twice mentioned in despatches, died on Monday, 14th May 2001. The citation for his George Cross was published in *The London Gazette* supplement 35048, page 403: *"During a night in September 1940, an aircraft burst into flames while taking off. Wing Commander Sinclair immediately went to the scene to render assistance, but two 250 lb bombs exploded before he reached it. Undeterred, and knowing that two more bombs were in the aircraft, he pressed on and dashing into the fire he succeeded in dragging the air gunner to a safe distance. In this act this officer displayed complete disregard for his own safety. Unfortunately the injured air gunner has since died of his injuries."* Searching through my RAFBCL 1939-1940, I have traced the aircraft to a Blenheim IV belonging to 107 Squadron based at Wattisham which crashed taking off on 30th September 1940, to bomb one of the ports where German barges were gathering for the planned invasion of the UK. The pilot, Sergeant Jack Edwin Merrett was killed [he is buried in Reading [Henley Road] Cemetery, while the observer, Sergeant A G Byron was pulled clear and was about to be put into the ambulance when the remaining bombs exploded. The blast caused the stretcher bearers to be thrown to the ground, adding further suffering to Sergeant Byron who eventually was admitted to Ipswich Hospital where one of his legs was amputated. The air gunner, Sergeant Sidney Walters who was rescued by Wing Commander Sinclair died within hours of the crash; he is buried in Probus [SS Probus and Grace] Churchyard, Cornwall.

26067 SPRAGUE* Richard Alphonso W/Cdr + 18.11.42 47 Squadron

Wing Commander Richard Alphonso Sprague DFC was killed when his Beaufort I DE118 crashed some 50 miles SSW of Sidi Haneish airfield in the Western Desert; he is buried in El Alamein War Cemetery, his headstone bearing the Latin inscription: *"Requiescat In Pace."* The airfield was in German occupation in the summer of 1942, and on the night of 26th-27th July 1942, was targeted by a British Special Air Services unit commanded by Major David Stirling. In a lightning strike carried out by a force of eighteen heavily armed jeeps a number of enemy transport aircraft were destroyed and others damaged. Caught by surprise, German infantry quickly rallied but Major Stirling successfully withdrew his force for the loss of one of his men killed by machine-gun fire.

26068 STEPHENSON* John Noel Tracey AV-M 29.05.59 Retirement

Air Vice-Marshal John Noel Tracey Stephenson CB CBE mentioned in despatches and conferred with the Legion of Merit [USA], died on Friday, 2nd August 1985.

26079 STRATTON* John Arthur Charles G/Capt 24.08.57 Retirement
Group Captain John Arthur Charles Stratton CBE mentioned in despatches, and conferred with the Czechoslovakian honour Medal of Merit 1st Class, died on Thursday, 18th September 1980.
26070 TINDAL-CARILL-WORLSLEY* Geoffrey Nicholas Ernest A/Cmdr 29.08.60 Retirement
Air Commodore Geoffrey Nicholas Ernest Tindal-Carill-Worsley CB CBE twice mentioned in despatches, died on Sunday, 28th April 1996.
26071 WALL* Arnold G/Capt 24.02.51 Retirement
New Zealand Group Captain Arnold Wall OBE mentioned in despatches, died 1998 . The Wings Over New Zealand Aviation Forum, which the authors are delighted to acknowledge, reports that while attached to 60 Squadron he lost the sight of his right eye when goat herdsman aimed his *Shanghai* at Arnold's aircraft, the stone hitting him in the face with devastating results. Shocked, he managed to land safely, but his days as a pilot were over. Returning to New Zealand his post-service career involved with broadcastings and the book world of A W & A H Reed Publishing, where by retirement in 1973, he was senior editor.
26072 WEAIT* Arthur Lewin F/O + 02.01.33
Flying Officer Arthur Lewin Weait died in a road traffic accident.
26073 WHITE* Nicholas Erskine F/O + 06.05.32 CFS Wittering
Flying Officer Nicholas Erskine White flying Avro 504N K1050 collided during a change in formation with Avro 504N K1042, piloted by Flying Officer Duncan Shimwell McDougall, the formation being in the vicinity of Stamford at the time. An outstanding sportsman whilst in training at Cranwell, Flight Cadet Nicholas Erskine White was the entry's Sword of Honour winner.

Their deaths were reported in the *Sheffield Daily Telegraph* on Monday, 9th May 1932, beneath the headline 'Pilots Did Not See Each Other'

"A verdict of "Accidental Death" was returned at Wittering Aerodrome, on Saturday, on Flying Officer Duncan Shimwell McDougall, [28], of 'Hackenham' Bucks, and Flying Officer Nicholas Erskine White, [25], of Fairy Cross, Devon.

"The officers were attached to the Central Flying School at Wittering, and were taking part in formation manoeuvres in preparation for the Hendon Air Pageant, when their machines collided.

"Squadron Leader Harrison, senior flying officer at the Central Flying School, said he was watching the manoeuvres of a formation of five machines in which McDougall and White were taking part, when, as they were changing, he saw two of the collide in the air. They locked together and immediately descended, falling at a moderate speed, and disappeared from view behind a ridge about three-quarters of a mile away. Almost immediately he saw a volume of smoke arise.

"In reply to the Coroner Squadron Leader Harrison said when changing positions machines had to fly with a span space between them.The Coroner: That's not much, is it? - It is the width of a machine.

"Witness added that both officers were experienced and skilful pilots. One machine appeared to come down from above and hit the one below, and it was his opinion that the pilots did not see each other. The altitude at which the collision occurred was about 1,000 feet."

26074 WHITTLE* Frank A/Cmdr 26.08.48 Retirement
Air Commodore Sir Frank Whittle OM KBE CB Order of Legion of Merit USA, died at the age of 89 in Columbia in Howard County, Maryland, on Friday, 9th August 1996. Without any shadow of doubt, Sir Frank Whittle rates among the outstanding aviation innovators of his age with his outstanding work on developing the turbojet engine being the pinnacle. Success, however, came with serious detrimental consequences on his health and in the space of four years he was to suffer nervous breakdowns, the first occurring in 1940, at which time he was on the board of Power Jets Limited which with two former Royal Air Force servicemen he formed to build, with the aid of British Thomson-Houston, the prototype turbojet which after many set backs eventually emerged as the W.1X fitted to Gloster's E.28/39 which following a series of ground tests at Gloster's factory was taken [rather appropriately] to Cranwell where it flew for the first time during the evening of Thursday, 15th May 1941. For a full appreciation of Sir Frank Whittle's life I recommend his biography published by Frederick Muller in 1953, under the title *Jet: The Story of a Pioneer* while his *Wikipedia* entry gives an excellent flavour of this remarkable aviation pioneer. New and used copies of his book are still available on Amazon with prices ranging [as at 2021] between £18.45 and for second-hand copies from £15.03.
26075 WILLIAMS* Rolf Dudley F/O 01.11.34 Retired list
On account of ill-health [LG 6 November 1934, issue 34102, page 7087]. Flying Officer Rolf Dudley Williams died in Yeovil, Somerset, on Thursday, 8th October 1987. As my co-author reports, soon after leaving the service [he was invalided out following a serious flying accident whilst serving at the Central Flying School] he joined with James Collingwood Tinling in setting up Sir Frank Whittle's Power Jets Limited in 1936, and in 1941, he was appointed Managing Director. Subsequently, he went into politics and in the 1951, General Election won Exeter for the Conservatives which he held until 1966, by which time he had changed his surname, by Deed Poll, to Dudley-Williams and had been created baronet of the City and County of the City of Exeter on 2nd July 1964. Further notes on Sir Rolf Dudley Dudley-Williams, 1st Baronet, can be read on *Wikipedia.*
26076 WORSTALL* William Robert A/Cmdr 15.02.57 Retirement
Air Commodore William Robert Worstall OBE, died on Thursday, 3rd August 1978.

Flight Cadets whose surnames have an asterisk appended graduated from the College with a permanent commission on 28th July 1928 [LG 21st August 1928, issue 33414, page 5575]. Also graduating was Flight Cadet Francis Peter Hewitt from the January 1926 entry.

Flight Cadet Robert Spencer Beddall who arrived at the College during the year died when his DH.9A spun in near Leadenham Hill Top, just to the north of the A27 and a shade over 6 miles WNW from the airfield on Friday, 9th September 1927. Critically injured, Flight Cadet Beddall died the next day; he was 19 years of age. With 1926 drawing to a close, David Gam Harcourt Wood lost control of DH.9A J7354 and crashed and caught fire between Ailsworth and Castor, villages some 4 miles or so WSW from the centre of Peterborough on Friday, 12th November. His name has not been included in the Roll of Honour of Flight Cadets killed before graduating, thus I have not been able to establish the year of his arrival.

SWORD OF HONOUR
Flight Cadet Nicholas Erskine White

ROLL OF HONOUR
SEPTEMBER 1926 ENTRY

W/Cdr	DALE	Herbert Reginald	11 May 1941	XV Squadron
S/Ldr	FRANKS	Alexander Lumsden	29 May 1940	610 Squadron AAF
G/Capt	HOMER	John Wood	18 July 1944	353 Squadron
P/O	JORGENSEN	James Ernest	17 June 1929	3 Squadron
W/Cdr	LLEWELYN	John Griffith	23 May 1940	40 Squadron
W/Cdr	OWEN	John Jervis	6 July 1943	466 Squadron RAAF
W/Cdr	SPRAGUE	Richard Alphonso	18 November 1942	47 Squadron
F/O	WEAIT	Arthur Lewin	2 January 1933	
F/O	WHITE	Nicholas Erskine	6 May 1932	CFS Wittering
F/Cdt	MEAKIN	Peter Anthony	26 April 1928	RAF [C] Cranwell

FLYING ACCIDENTS

Tuesday 8 June 1926
7F.1 Snipe E6310 F/Cdt R J D Brown Safe
T/o Cranwell but collided with DH.9A J7318. Damage to the DH was repairable but the Snipe was beyond redemption. Prior to E6310 arriving at Cranwell it had been involved in two propeller accidents, the first at CFS Upavon on 18th June 1922 and the second at Eastchurch on 25th July 1923 when it was on charge with the Armament and Gunnery School.

Thursday 15 July 1926
7F.1 Snipe E6530 Flight Cadet Henry Francis Morrell Pickford failed to arrest a spin and crashed in the vicinity of the College.

Appendix E - Roll of Honour

ROYAL AIR FORCE

F/O	ADDAMS	Anthony Clifford	16 June 1926	41 Squadron
LAC	AVERY	Cecil Robert	6 July 1926	5 Squadron
F/O	BINGHAM-HALL	Vincent Bingham	18 October 1926	208 Squadron
LAC	BOLAM	William Slater	15 August 1926	20 Squadron
F/Lt	BRADING DFC*	Reginald Carey Brenton	26 July 1926	45 Squadron
F/O	BROADWAY	Basil Douglas John	14 May 1926	32 Squadron
LAC	BURGESS	Arthur John	31 March 1926	28 Squadron
LAC	COX	Sydney Marsh	17 May 1926	12 Squadron
LAC	CRUNDEN	Percy William Edward	1 August 1926	31 Squadron
AC1	DAVIS	Horace Leslie	26 July 1926	45 Squadron
F/O	DU PORT	William Osmond	1 September 1926	55 Squadron
F/O	GAPE	Roy Nugent Treherne	18 August 1926	19 Squadron
AC1	HARVEY	Thomas Reginald	10 August 1926	47 Squadron
Sgt	HAWKINS	Ralph England	17 May 1926	12 Squadron
LAC	HAYWARD	Cecil Herbert	9 November 1926	4 Squadron
AC2	HINTON	Percy Charles	11 November 1926	207 Squadron
AC1	JONES	Percy	22 September 1926	5 Squadron
P/O	KEMPTHORNE	Hugh James Fitzgerald	23 August 1926	58 Squadron
Sgt	KENNEDY	Edgar	26 July 1926	45 Squadron
LAC	LEATHERDALE	Frank Edward	15 April 1926	84 Squadron
LAC	LOWE	Eric Arthur Lister	1 September 1926	16 Squadron
P/O	LLOYD	David John	4 April 1926	60 Squadron
F/O	LUXMOORE	Henry Frederick	20 September 1926	56 Squadron
F/Lt	MacNEAL	Alastair Neil	29 December 1926	28 Squadron
LAC	MILLER	Frederick William	2 July 1926	100 Squadron
P/O	MOSSMAN	Cyril Vernon	9 November 1926	4 Squadron
F/O	NICHOLLS	Philip Hedgeland	5 October 1926	20 Squadron
LAC	OVERY	Cyril Arthur	29 December 1926	28 Squadron
P/O	PAGE	Alfred Lionel René	31 August 1926	16 Squadron
LAC	PEARSE	William Arthur	2 September 1926	55 Squadron
S/Ldr	POLLARD	Eric Miller	26 July 1926	45 Squadron
F/O	PURVIS	John Harry Campbell	9 December 1926	25 Squadron
F/O	REEDMAN	Reginald Richard	10 September 1926	2 Squadron
P/O	SHERMAN	Dick Culverwell	14 September 1926	31 Squadron
F/O	SLATER	Herbert Gerald	10 August 1926	47 Squadron
F/O	STIRLING WEBB	Oswald Kempson	26 July 1926	45 Squadron
Sgt	TAYLOR	George Frederick	11 November 1926	207 Squadron
F/O	TOMES	James Eric	15 April 1926	84 Squadron
F/O	WHEATLEY	Gilbert Vernon	8 December 1926	22 Squadron
AC2	WHITTLE	Edgar	26 July 1926	1 Squadron
F/Lt	WILLSON	Reginald John	31 March 1926	28 Squadron
F/Lt	WOOLLARD AFC	Felix St. John	22 November 1926	24 Squadron
P/O	YOUNG	Stuart Adolphus	14 May 1926	1 Squadron

RESERVE OF AIR FORCE OFFICERS

F/O	BIGG-WITHER	Arthur Orde	2 May 1926	G-EAGP
F/O	PACKMAN	Stanley Arthur	24 June 1926	Gull No. 2

ROYAL MARINES

P/O	HIGGINS	William	18 October 1926	208 Squadron

ARMY

F/O	COLLISON	Frederic Laing	22 November 1926	24 Squadron
Of the 4th Battalion, Essex Regiment				
F/O	HARRIS	Clement Conrad	6 July 1926	5 Squadron
Of the Royal Artillery				
Lt	VEZEY	Walter John	4 April 1926	60 Squadron
Of the Royal Engineers				

F/O	WRIGHT	Theodore Harold James	16 August 1926	13 Squadron

Of the Seaforth Highlanders.

Norwegian Army Air Service

WO1	HAUG	Erik Gutzeit	8 October 1926	56 Squadron

CIVILIANS

Miss	CLARE	Fanny Vera	2 July 1926
Mr.	INGLIS	Francis Crawford	26 July 1926

SQUADRON LOSSES
1927

JANUARY

Tuesday 11 January 1927
43 Squadron F/O J R Addams Injured See 18 October 1927
Gamecock I J8418
T/o Upavon and set a course for Tangmere and home but on reaching the Goodwood Downs near Chichester, Flying Officer James Ramage Addams encountered a thick mist and with ground features fast becoming obscured he elected to the forced-land on Goodwood's golf links. However, on touchdown his fighter turned a complete somersault and finished up wedged between two trees on nearby Trundle Hill.

His predicament was seen by some golfers out on the links and, as reported two days later by *The Scotsman, "Crowds of men and caddies from the links, going to the airman's assistance, found he escaped with cuts on his face, but was unable to get out of the aeroplane, parts of which were sawn away before he could extricated."*

Flying Officer Addams reported to the Cadet College at Cranwell with the February 1923, entry of flight cadets. Placed with A Squadron, he represented the College at cricket, hockey and rugby football and following over twenty years of service retired with the rank of group captain on on 3rd July 1946. His death in September 1990 occurred in America [see Appendix E for 1923 for details].

Please refer to my summary of 14th December 1925, for his first serious flying mishap.

55 Squadron F/O B N Murgatroyd Safe
DH.9A J7017
T/o Hinaidi where, on return, a tyre burst on touch down sending the DH careering into the aircraft summarised below. Flying Officer Benjamin Norman Murgatroyd received a short service commission, his details being *Gazetted* on 19th September 1922, issue 32748, page 6715.

55 Squadron DH.9A J7344 Wrecked in the circumstances described above.

Thursday 21 January 1927
84 Squadron *Not reported*
DH.9A J7121
T/o Shaibah and damaged beyond repair in a landing mishap.

Friday 28 January 1927
41 Squadron F/Lt W G Meggitt MC +
Siskin III J7171
T/o Northolt and in squally weather conditions Flight Lieutenant William Geoffrey Meggitt lost control and crashed into the garden of a house in Beatrice Avenue, Norbury in SW London. His military service began in March 1915, when he was commissioned as probationary 2nd Lieutenant in the 3rd Battalion, Welsh Regiment, but by the summer of 1916, he had transferred to the RFC for duties as an observer.

On completion of his training he embarked for France, reporting on 26th August 1916 to 25 Squadron [FE.2b] at Auchel. Serving a full tour of operations, he returned to the UK on 26th February 1917, with the recommendation that he be awarded the MC. This was *Gazetted* on 17th April 1917, supplement 30023, page 3684: *"For conspicuous gallantry and devotion to duty whilst one of a patrol engaging five hostile machines. He drove down one enemy machine and then attacked another, which was seen to go down vertically. He has previously brought down three hostile machines."*

On 6th September 1917, now re-mustered to pilot, William returned to the Western Front and 22 Squadron [Bristol F.2b] at Boisdinghem [but soon to move to Estrée Blanche]. On 10th and 11th October 1917, he added to his score of victories but on 8th November of that year he was shot down and taken prisoner, the circumstances of this being recorded on page 130 of Trevor Henshaw's excellent *The Sky Their Battlefield.* It was a day of heavy losses for the RFC, 22 Squadron sustaining two losses and one damage to their Bristols. William's aircraft, B1123, came down in the vicinity of Moorslede where he was picked up in a wounded condition; sadly, his observer, Captain F A Durrad who had been wounded twice in the combat was thrown out on impact and died; he has no known grave and is, therefore, commemorated on the Arras Flying Services Memorial.

William Meggitt was repatriated on 2nd June 1918, and in 1919, was one the large number of appointees to a permanent commission on the 1st of August, details of which appear in my third volume.

'Plane Crashes in Back Garden'
'MC Pilot Killed - Machine Wrecked on Fence'
'Battle With Gale'
'Women's Story of 500ft - Nose Dive - Men's Rescue Dash'

So read the headlines on page 3 of Saturday's *The Daily Mirror* which the went on to describe to its readers the unfolding tragedy that took the life of Flight Lieutenant Meggitt; *"Flight-Lieutenant W G Meggitt, MC, RAF, was killed in a remarkable accident at Norbury yesterday.*

"From a height of 500ft, the 'plane he was piloting - a Siskin fighter - crashed on to a fence separating the back gardens of two houses.

"The officer, who is married, his home being at Clapton, was alive when extricated, but died in hospital. Just before crashing Flight-Lieutenant Meggitt had been battling with a gale of wind.

"Like a Thunderbolt"

'Men Rush Into Garden and Try to Drag Pilot from Wreckage'

"Flight-Lieutenant Meggitt's machine was attached to No. 41 Squadron, Northolt Aerodrome. It was battling against a gale of wind when flying at a height of about 500ft., over Norbury, and was suddenly seen to fall.

"It crashed like a stone on to the wooden fence separating the back gardens of two houses in Beatrice-avenue, Norbury.

"The pilot, who was terribly mutilated, was extricated alive from the wreckage and taken to Croydon General Hospital, where he died.

"Flight-Lieutenant Meggitt was a Nottingham man, and before the war served in the Territorial Force of the Hertford shire Regiment.

'Pilot's Presence of Mind'

"He was with the Air Force in France, and was gazetted MC for bringing down two enemy machines during a patrol, having previously accounted for three enemy aeroplanes. He was married, and lived at Clapton.

"Mrs. Platt, of 11 Beatrice-avenue, in a graphic account of the accident said; "I heard the 'plane and went outside. It was some distance away, and as it approached nearer I detected a change in the steady whir. The machine seemed to wobble for a moment, and then it came down like a thunderbolt."

"It shivered for a moment with its nose in the ground, and then seemed to collapse and topple over on its left side."

"Two passers by rushed into the garden and attempted to drag the pilot from the wreckage." "There were no flames," Mrs. Platt added. 'The pilot seems to have had the presence of mind to shut off his engine when he found something was wrong."

Photographs of the wrecked Siskin were published in *The Evening Standard* including a shot of a policeman, wearing a cape, and several spectators viewing the remains of the rear fuselage and tail on which J7171 is clearly visible.

FEBRUARY

Wednesday 2 February 1927

3 Squadron P/O G F Lewis +

Woodcock II J7736

T/o Upavon and crashed near the airfield when control was lost at 400 feet on the approach to land. Pilot Officer Gomer Flower Lewis entered the Cadet College at Cranwell with the January 1925 intake of flight cadets and was assigned to B Squadron. He graduated on 11th December 1926 [LG 7 January 1927, issue 33237, page 121] and reported to Upavon for attachment to 3 Squadron a few days later. He was 19 years of age and had survived for only a month as a fighter pilot. The Aviation Safety Network website indicates Woodcock II J7783 was ordered as its replacement.

'Upavon Flying Fatality'

'Death of Youngest Officer in Royal Air Force'

This was the headline in Thursday's *Daily Mail* which continued: *"Upavon, Wilts. Thursday, - Pilot Officer George Flower Lewis, second son of Sir Herbert D W Lewis and Lady Lewis, of Cathedral-road, Cardiff, who was killed in a flying accident at Upavon, Wilts., yesterday, was educated at Cheltenham College, qualifying as a first-class pilot at Cranwell as recently as December last.*

"He was the youngest officer in the Royal Air Force being only nineteen. Pilot Officer Lewis was a keen Rowing enthusiast and good Rugby player. Among his colleagues he was highly popular and those who knew his work regarded him as a most promising officer with a brilliant career in front of him.

"Sir Herbert Lewis has rendered work of inestimable value to the Order of St. John of Jerusalem and Wales."

Friday 4 February 1927

56 Squadron P/O S A V Evans +

Grebe II J7582

T/o Biggin Hill having been briefed for a map reading exercise and while flying in the vicinity of Rottingdean, 5 miles ESE from the centre of Brighton encountered fog and crashed on the Downs near Woodingdean. Pilot Officer Sidney Arthur Vernon Evans was granted a short service commission on 17th January 1925 [LG 27 January 1925, issue 33015, page 595].

As recounted on the Aviation Safety Network, Pilot Officer Evans had married as recently as the 10th of October 1926, and, subsequently, his widow would become a television personality in her own right as 'Fanny Cradock'*a forerunner in bringing before the public the appeal of cookery programmes in which she 'starred' on the BBC between 1955 and 1976. In addition to her cooking, and literary, skills she married four times - twice, the report states, bigamously! 'Fanny Cradock' died on 27th December 1994.

The Daily Mirror on its page 3 the next day gave an account of the crash; however, readers were treated to a page width headline, in capitals, *'£10,000 STOLEN FROM TRAIN ON JOURNEY TO LONDON'* with the demise of Pilot Officer Evans reported below:

'Air Pilot Killed on South Downs'
'Machine Somersaults and Bursts Into Flames'
'Tragedy of the Mist'

"Pilot Officer S A V Evans, twenty-five, of Weybridge, Surrey, was killed in a flying accident on the South Downs yesterday.

"He was flying from Biggin Hill Aerodrome, Kent, when his Gloster Grebe aeroplane, of No. 56 Squadron, crashed on the Downs between Brighton and Rottingdean and afterwards caught fire and was destroyed.

"The pilot, who was instantly killed, was seen to be flying from the direction of Brighton, and ran into a dense mist.It is believed he lost his bearings in consequence, and tried to make a forced-landing, but without success. He had also released his parachute.

"He was seen to nearly strike the Brighton gas works, situated in the extreme east of the town, and he also narrowly missed a hayrick.

"In crashing, the machine turned a double somersault over a rising bank. Within a few minutes of the tragedy the mist lifted and there was brilliant sunshine."

Returning, very briefly, to the 'Great Train Robbery' of 1927, it is though the thieves made off with their haul at one of three places - Newport [Mon.], Swindon or Reading, stopping places on the Cardiff to London service.

* Paul McMillan has forwarded the following which was written by Clive Ellis, whom the authors have pleasure in acknowledging. And which he titled *'Fabulous Fanny Craddoc: TV's Outrageous Queen of Cuisine'*

"Fanny's guiding light of a grandmother died at the end of September 1926and a fortnight later she was circumventing parental permission [which would not have been granted] to marry Sidney, by then stationed with 56 Squadron at Biggin Hill in Kent. He was twenty-two, she was seventeen, though she claimed on the marriage certificate that she was twenty-one. Two of Sidney's fellow pilots were the sole witnesses to the wedding, which the couple celebrated by going sailing off Goodwin Sands."

The write of the above then quoted extracts from a local Brighton paper, *The Evening Argus,* which more or less parallels *The Daily Mirror* but adds the rising bank was on land belonging to a Mr. Filkins' and that Sidney attempted to jump in the last seconds of flight.

In one final comment to this very sad tale of young love and death, later in life Fanny is alleged to have remarked to friends of her late husband *"I married on Wednesday, settled his debts on Friday, and he died on Sunday,'* to which I suggest the Miss Craddock was thinking of James Orchard Halliwell-Phillips 1842 children's nursery rhyme *Solomon Grundy'* who indeed married on Wednesday took ill on Thursday got worse on Friday, died on Saturday and was buried on Sunday.

Thursday 24 February 1927
23 Squadron F/Lt D D'A A Greig Safe See 22 April 1927 - 24 Squadron
Gamecock I J8039
T/o Kenley for an air test fully equipped with 1,000 rounds of ammunition. What happened during the test is described in detail by Flight Lieutenant [subsequently Air Commodore] David D'Arcy Alexander Greig in his book *My Golden Flying Years.* Here I will restrict my summary to the salient facts. Having climbed to around 10,000 feet the Gamecock was deliberately spun which to the concern of the pilot became a flat-spin from which he was unable to recover. It took a considerable effort to pull himself out of the cockpit which was suddenly aided by the Gamecock turning onto its back and ejecting him out at around 3,000 feet. With a perfect view of the last seconds of the machine's plunge to earth he was momentarily concerned that it might fall into a built up area and it was with considerable relief that he saw it fall into a ploughed field near Warlingham and explode in a ball of flames. Meanwhile, a brisk wind took him in the direction of the village of Chelsham [between Warlingham and Biggin Hill] where he came safely to earth. Please refer to my summary for 17th December 1921, and 216 Squadron for a previous crash involving Flight Lieutenant Greig.

MARCH

Saturday 12 March 1927
60 Squadron F/Lt R O Rigg +
Fairey IIIF S1139 LAC W J Meaden +
LAC P J Sexton +
T/o Kohat and crashed at Peshawar. Honorary Flight Lieutenant Robert Owen Rigg, formerly of the Royal Navy, was granted a short service commission for a term of seven years commencing on 10th April 1923 [LG 24 April 1923, issue 32817, page 2970], which leads me to suggest he may have been on attachment, with his crew, to 60 Squadron.

The service numbers for Leading Aircraftman William James Meaden and Leading Aircraftman Patrick John Sexton were 327848 and 362688 respectively. Thus, that for the former shows he joined as a boy between December 1918 and March 1919, while the latter shows he, too, joined as a boy but between July 1922 and January 1924.

Friday 18 March 1927
11 Squadron P/O F Priestman +
Horsley II J8012 LAC J W Pickering +
T/o Netheravon tasked for a cross-country flight to Hawkinge and while over the Kent countryside lost flying speed and dived into a meadow at Water Farm near Elham, roughly 3 miles NW from Hawkinge airfield. Pilot Officer Frederick Priestman entered the RAF College at Cranwell with the February 1923, entry of flight Ccadets and was placed with A

Squadron. As well as progressing satisfactorily with his flying training, Frederick demonstrated his prowess on the river as an oarsman.

His passenger, Leading Aircraftman John William Pickering joined the service from civilian occupation at sometime between September 1919 and June 1925, and was issued with the service number 341348.

The loss of J8012 was first Horsley to be written off in squadron service. Referring to Francis K Mason's *Hawker Aircraft Since 1920* the Horsley was the last wooden aircraft to emerge from the factory with 11 Squadron, commanded at the time by Wing Commander J H A Landon DSO OBE, being the first squadron to equip with examples arriving in January 1927, to replace the squadron's Fawns.

An extensive report on the tragedy appeared in the *Folkestone, Hythe, Sandgate& Cheriton Herald* the paper describing in graphic detail the extracting of the two airmen once the fire had been subdued by firemen despatched from RAF Hawkinge. The paper's reporter interviewed three witnesses to the crash, one being Mr. Ben Wylie of the Rose and Crown, Elham: *"I was in my garden at the time when I saw the machine flying very low. As it flew over the village the engine did not seem to be going properly. The pilot just missed colliding with two trees adjoining the field in which the crash took place, and then rose again. He seemed to be in trouble, and after side-slipping a short distance the machine nose dived from a very low height into the ground. Just before the accident I saw sparks coming from the engine, but I do not think the machine was then on fire. As soon as the crash occurred people from the village rushed to the field. Everyone was anxious to do something, but we could not get near the wreckage for the fire. The flames at times were forty feet high, and to make matters worse, blazing petrol ran down the field towards the railway."*

Another witness, a Mr. T Goatman of Elham described seeing the Horsley running into a bank of fog which was shrouding the railway station, and this was a factor mentioned by Colonel Day when questioning the Secretary of State for Air [Sir Samuel Hoare] regarding the circumstances of the accident were debated in the House of Commons [*Hansard* 6th April 1927]. The debate, which is reported in detail, can be read of the Aviation Safety Network website, ASN Wikibase Occurrence 212114, which the authors duly acknowledge.

99 Squadron *Not reported*
Hyderabad J7741
T/o Bircham Newton where, on return, the pilot realised he was likely to land on a Virginia which was in the process of taxying. Side-slipping in order to avoid a collision, control was lost and the Hyderabad was damaged beyond repair in the ensuing crash-landing.

Monday 21 March 1927
9 Squadron F/O R H Barlow Safe
Virginia VIII J7425
T/o Manston for night flying during which a double-engine failure occurred which led to the Virginia being ditched shortly after 2100 in the Thames Estuary. Believing they were down fairly close to the shore, the crew tried to alert their plight by firing off Verey lights and shouting, but to no avail and six hours passed before the skipper of the trawler SS *Pickmere* came alongside the now waterlogged bomber and took four cold and by now near exhausted airmen from their precarious position on the top mainplane aboard.

Then, with the Virginia secured by the aid of a tow-line, the trawler, which had no radio facilities, headed for Sheerness from where at around noon on the 22nd the squadron received news of their rescue. An examination of the bomber discovered that inadvertently two of the main fuel cocks had been turned off. Totally wrecked, it was replaced by Virginia VII J7132 which was damaged a month later when it was run in to by a taxying Avro 504K H2623 of the locally based No. 1 School of Technical Training.

Repaired in works, and modified at the same time to Mk.IX standards, the Virginia was returned to the squadron. Subsequently, it underwent another rebuild and returned to 9 Squadron as a Mk.X; it was last noted in June 1936 in the hands of 58 Squadron at Upper Heyford.

Flying Officer Sir Richard Hugh Barlow entered the Cadet College at Cranwell with the September 1922 entry; please refer to Appendix E for that year where his service details, and death in an airliner accident in the Andes on December 3rd, 1946, are reported.

APRIL

Saturday 9 April 1927
605 Squadron AAF *Not reported*
Avro 504N J738
T/o Castle Bromwich and wrecked moments later after flying into a line of telegraph wires. This was the first serious accident reported from the squadron which had formed the previous autumn at Castle Bromwich in the Midlands on 5th October 1926; also, it is believed to have been the first loss of an aircraft since the establishment of the Auxiliary Air Force in 1925.

Tuesday 19 April 1927
9 Squadron F/O W J Kelly +
Virginia J7714 VI P/O J F Dowdeswell +
F/Sgt A G Alderton +
AC2 E Daniels +
T/o Eastchurch only to collide with a parked DH.9A. Flying Officer William James Kelly was granted a short service commission on 29th January 1924, issue 32902, page 875, page 2686]. Pilot Officer John Frederick Dowdeswell's probation was completed on 4th October 1926, at which date he was confirmed in his rank [LG 26 October 1926, issue

33215, page 6823]. According to ASN Wikibase Occurrence report 212115, which the authors have pleasure in acknowledging, the Virginia clipped one of the DH's wings but continued with the take off, rising to around 100 feet before diving headlong into the ground where it burst into flames. The report also indicates that J7714 was the last Virginia issued to the squadron [July 1926], and, subsequently, questions regarding the crash were raised in the House of Commons, the extract from *Hansard* being repeated on the website. Although brief, I get the feeling that the exchanges between Colonel Day and Sir Samuel Hoare, Secretary of State for Air, were, to put it politely, slightly acrimonious.

For readers of *The Daily Mirror* the full impact of the tragedy was summed up on page 3 with a banner headline taking up the full width of the page *'FOUR DEAD IN RAF DISASTER - FLAMES 40 FT. HIGH* followed by headers outlining the report that will follow *'Bomber Crashed from 250ft. After Collision With a Stationary Plane' 'Bodies Dragged From Burning Debris'* and poignantly *"I am too stunned even to cry," says Wife of a Victim - News While on Holiday'*

"Four airmen were killed yesterday when a RAF bombing 'plane crashed at Eastchurch, Kent, and burst into flames. The victims were two officers, a sergeant and an aircraftsman. The machine, it is stated, was rising from the aerodrome when it collided with a stationary 'plane. Although the bomber rose to a height of 250ft., it crashed and burst into flames. Flames shot 40ft., or more into the air, but despite this would be rescuers dragged the bodies from the still burning debris. The wife of one of the victims received the tragic news while on holiday, "I am too stunned, even to cry," she said.

'Explosion Heard A Mile Away'

'Sheds Narrowly Missed in Crash to the Ground'

'Noise Like A Gun'

"The bomber had flown from Manston to Eastchurch, and it was when she was taxi-ing along the ground to commence the return journey that she hit the wings of another machine.

"Although its balance was disturbed, the 'plane took the air properly and rose to a height of 250ft.

"The pilot then appeared to lose control and the machine, narrowly missing some sheds, and, with the engines still running, hit the ground nose first, the petrol tank exploding.

"The aeroplane turned completely over and the flames rose high in the air. The sound of the explosion was heard at Eastchurch village, more than a mile away.

"Many persons rushed to the scene, and though the flames were very fierce, rising to a height of 40ft., or more, they managed to get the bodies out of the wreckage.

"The machine - a Vickers-Virginia of No. 9 Squadron, Manston - was left a tangled wreck of burnt and blackened debris.

"The four occupants, all of whom were burnt to death were:-

"Flying-Officer William James Kelly [the pilot[, Pilot-Officer Frederick John Dowdeswell, Flight-Sergeant Albert George Alderson and Aircraftsman Everett Daniels. Flying-Officer Kelly belonged to Weston-super-Mare, Pilot-Officer Dowdeswell to London, Sergeant Alderson to Sheerness and Aircraftsman Daniels to Ramsgate.

'Damaged Controls?'

'Pilot Whose Machine was Struck Believes Bomber's Cables Were Broken'

"Sergeant-Pilot Ward, who had three machines out on the aerodrome in readiness to fly to Somerset, and who saw the accident, said:-

"I saw the Virginia strike my 'plane, which was one of three DH.9A machines which I had got out on the aerodrome. The two main struts of the left wing of my machine were broken.

"I saw her climb up in order to clear the obstacle in her path, and than noticed as she went over my head at a height if abut 80ft., to 100ft., that she was banking steeply to the right.

"I think this was due to the cables controlling the ailerons having being damaged through contact with my machine. The pilot appeared to be able to control the rising and turning of his machine, but the heavy banking to the right compelled him to fly in a circle and it seemed to me that, realising this, he tried to bring her down on the aerodrome.

'Seemed to Stall'

"He seemed to stall her once or twice, and lost height until he was about 50ft., above ground level, and in another 200 or 300 yards of flight would have landed safely on the aerodrome.

"I am convinced that the pilot intended to bring her down near the hangars, which were the last obstacle in his way, and knew that a nose dive was inevitable. It was really the only thing he could do.

"When the machine crashed I immediately rounded up all the flying personnel in my section and forbade them to go near the scene of the accident.

"I never allow my flying men to approach the wreckage of an accident of this kind for fear that they should lose their nerves."

Of the two non-commissioned airmen on board the ill-fated aircraft, Flight Sergeant Albert George Alderton either enlisted or was transferred from another arm of the military between January and February 1918, his service number being 134932, which comes within the block 129001 - 137000.

Aircraftman Everett Daniels also saw service in the *Great War*, probably having being accepted as for boy service at sometime between October 1917 and December 1918, his service number being 157294.

Friday 22 April 1927
24 Squadron F/Lt D D'A A Greig DFC Safe
Gamecock I
T/o Kenley to carry out spinning tests. An explanation as to what happened during the test is recorded on the Kenley Revival website, which the authors acknowledge: *"Intentional right-hand spins were forbidden in the Gamecock, as high engine torque made them practically impossible to recover from, using conventional methods. After twenty-seven turns and a height loss of 6,000 feet, Greig's aircraft became uncontrollable and he had no option but to take to his parachute. He was flung clear as the wind caught him and fell for several hundred feet before regaining his wits enough to pull the ripcord. The wind caused him to drift for about two miles before landing safely. The Gamecock, on the other hand, was loaded with more than fifty gallons of fuel. Greig saw it erupt in a sheet of flame at Riddlesdown* [a mile east from the centre of Purley], *as he descended on his 'chute.*

"Miraculously, Greig was uninjured, picked up his parachute and set off to try and find a telephone. The first person he encountered was a little girl called Betty Knight., whose mother ran the Hare and Hounds pub in Chelsham. She was quite taken aback by the appearance of this strange man who she later described as "wearing women's clothes, carrying sheets." He asked her where he could use a telephone and she directed him towards Fairchild, the home of Colonel Arthur Stewart Daniell. He was back at Kenley within the hour."

The website also gives a brief resume of Flight Lieutenant David D'Arcy Alexander Greig's early life, mentioning that during the *Great War* while flying FE.2b with 83 Squadron he was shot down behind enemy lines on 13th September 1918 [sic] - actually, it was Saturday, 21st September 1918 - and a summary of what happened is described in my second volume on page 240. Subsequently, he rose to air rank and retired as an air commodore with the DFC and AFC on 23rd November 1946; his death was announced in July 1986.

In conclusion, his name first appears in this volume on 17th December 1921, and my summary for 216 Squadron and as recently as 24th February 1927 regarding 23 Squadron.

Monday 25 April 1927
30 Squadron F/Lt Collins Safe
DH.9A H3633
T/o Kirkuk and while flying at 6,000 feet over Sulaimaniyah collied with the DH summarised below. For 2,000 feet both machines were in a spiral dive before control was re-established and safe forced-landings accomplished. However, such was the damage both aircraft were consigned to the scrap yard. A photograph of one very 'second-hand' looking H3633 is shown on page 88 of the squadron's history, written by John Hamblin under the title *Flat Out.*

30 Squadron F/O J A E Inkster Safe
DH.9A J7114
T/o Kirkuk and damaged beyond worthwhile repair following the incident reported above. Flying Officer John Andrew Edward Inkster was granted a short service commission [LG 13 January 1925, issue 33011, page 302].

MAY

Wednesday 11 May 1927
3 Squadron *Not reported*
Woodcock I J6987
T/o Upavon and believed damaged beyond reasonable repair in a forced-landing near *Tilstock* [sic], Berkshire. One of three prototypes, J6987 first flew with F P Raynham at the controls in March 1923, and was reported at Martlesham Heath on or by 14th August of that year. By November 1924, it was at Farnborough in the hands of the Royal Aircraft Establishment and following a rebuild to Mk. I standards went to Upavon and 3 Squadron on 1st March 1927.

On 21st March, three weeks after acceptance, it was damaged in a forced-landing at Maidenhead, Berkshire, but was repaired and continued in use until the incident mentioned above.

Saturday 14 May 1927
99 Squadron F/O F H Hannaford Safe
Hyderabad J7751 P/O H C Johnson Safe
Canada
Sgt Mitchell Safe
Sgt Price Safe
T/o Bircham Newton and when over the North Sea and roughly 6 miles off the Lincolnshire resort of Skegness forced-landed on the Dogo Sands. The bomber was later salvaged by an unnamed German ship and brought to the Norfolk port of King's Lynn.

Both Flying Officer Francis Henry Hannaford and Pilot Officer Hugh Coleman Johnson were shot service commission officers whose details are reported in Appendix C for officers *Gazetted* on 21st April 1925 and 26th January 1926 respectively.

Monday 16 May 1927
32 Squadron P/O R G Pace Safe
Gamecock I J8042
T/o Kenley tasked for formation flying and collided with the Gamecock summarised below. Pilot Officer Richard Griffith Pace was killed on 20th July 1927, when his Gamecock II J7907 crashed on the Holbeach ranges during the

squadron's attachment to Sutton Bridge for armament training. He had survived sixteen months of active service, his short service commission being *Gazetted* on 26th March 1926, issue 33145, page 2182. The Kenley Revival website, which the authors have pleasure in acknowledging, records his birth as 7th May 1905, at Leyton in Essex, and that he was first pilot to lose his life over the ranges which had opened the previous September. He is buried in Waltham Forest [St. Mary The Virgin] Churchyard, just to the NNW of Leyton.

Despite the seriousness of the accident his aircraft was repaired and was still in service with the squadron until its transfer to 23 Squadron circa November 1930. A photograph of J7907 can be viewed on the Revival's website.

32 Squadron P/O A L Holden + Whyteleaf [St. Luke's] Churchyard
Gamecock I J8043
T/o Kenley in the company of two squadron pilots and leading them for tight formation flying practice. The first exercise was carried out but on landing Pilot Officer Arthur Leslie Holden insisted that his two colleagues had not closed in tight enough, even though one had already 'touched' Arthur's aircraft. Thus, shortly after midday the trio took to the air again and what happened next is best described by Pilot Officer Richard Pace who was flying J8042: *"We closed in to about half a span. The weather was very bumpy when Holden's machine appeared to swing towards me. Then a gust of wind threw my aircraft towards his. I felt no actual impact, but on looking round saw Holden's machine diving towards the ground."* It seems the pilot managed to regain control, but only temporarily for it stalled and nose-dived to the ground, narrowly missing an airman who, literally, had to throw himself from his bicycle as the Gamecock crashed onto its left lower wing. On impact Pilot Officer Holden was ejected from the cockpit, landing on his head and fracturing his skull. Rushed to hospital he died without regaining consciousness.

As recorded on the Kenley Remembered website, to which the authors are indebted, Pilot Officer Holden was one of the squadron's most colourful characters and describes an incident that took place on Christmas Day 1926, when Holden took a fellow officer on an aerial 'joy-ride' during which he flew under London's Tower Bridge in weather that is described as *"appalling."* This in part is expanded upon by Group Captain N W F Mason which, I suggest, was read at Arthur's funeral: *"Holden was a remarkable fellow, and a delightful personality; quite fearless, possessor of a good brain, and excellent all round sportsman, giving a good account of himself on the rugger field. While he was under arrest, he would play to you on his violin, read to you in French, or any language in which you might be interested, or paint pictures for you, in fact, make your brief stay with him more enjoyable than that offered by the carefree Mess of the 1926 Kenley. My last remembrances of him were when he received a reprimand from the A.O.C. for flying in tight formation with a civilian airliner from Croydon and his voluntary delayed parachute jump at Biggin Hill where his delayed action was mercifully assisted by a drop in the level of the airfield."*

Reading the above it is worth emphasising that Pilot Officer Holden was an exceedingly fortunate young officer not to have been cashiered for such a series of undisciplined displays, a fate that was to befall a fellow officer from his entry, Flying Officer Harry Walpole Charnock who was dismissed the service on 12th December 1930, having been found guilty on the charge of low-flying [see my remarks in Appendix E for the January 1924 entry].

The website goes on to record that at the funeral for Pilot Officer Holden, attended by full military honours, at St. Luke's, Whyteleaf, no less a personage than Air-Vice Marshal Henry Robert Moore Brooke-Popham, Air Officer Commanding, Fighting Area, Air Defence Great Britain, was in attendance, while among the wreaths were one from Air Marshal Sir John Salmond, Air Officer Commanding in Chief, Air Defence of Great Britain.

A separate entry expands on the Tower Bridge episode; *"Attired in their Mess kit, they flew between two spans of Tower Bridge before rolling off a loop and heading towards Piccadilly, where they beat up a crane that was situated on the roof of the Swan and Edgar Department Store. The they got lost on the way home in the poor weather and had to land to ask directions to Kenley! On their return, they were placed under open arrest, pending court martial. At the hearing, a policeman who had witnessed the stunt said that the cloud level was down at the height of the bridge!"*

Reading the above one cannot but help to draw parallels with the exploits of a young Pilot Officer Douglas Bader and fellow Cranwellian who crashed and was critically injured in a crash while visiting Woodley Airfield near Reading from Kenley on 14th December 1931.

Tuesday 24 May 1927
19 Squadron *Not reported*
Grebe II J7578
T/o Brockworth for delivery to Duxford and 19 Squadron to which squadron the Grebe had been assigned; however, at some point in the flight the controls became locked and the Grebe was abandoned.

Wednesday 25 May 1927
14 Squadron F/O R D V Howard +
DH.9A J7831 Mr. A E Turvey +
T/o Ramleh and crashed at Gaza, Palestine. Both airmen were employees of Imperial Airways, Flying Officer Robert Douglas Vernon Howard having being granted a short service commission [LG 18th October §1921, issue 32490, page 8205. Robert had been transferred to the Reserve Class A as recently as 5th October 1926 [LG 5 October 1926, issue 33208, page 6374]. At TNA Kew a document for this officer is held under WO 339/123150.

JUNE

Saturday 11 June 1927
84 Squadron *Not reported*
DH.9A H143
T/o Shaibah and came off second best following a collision with H142. It is not clear if the accident occurred in the air or on the ground. However, neither pilot is named and H142 was repaired and was later taken over by 55 Squadron. By September 1931, it had returned to '84' by which time it had been converted to a dual control aircraft.

Friday 24 June 1927
31 Squadron F/O R E Slacke +
Bristol F.2b LAC A C Hart +
T/o Quetta tasked for an exercise in "shadow fighting" and crashed at Old Chaman on the NWF, and on the border between present day Pakistan and Kandahar Province, Afghanistan. Randal Earl Slacke was granted a short service commission in the late summer of 1923 [LG 25 September 1923, issue 32865, page 6279].

Leading Aircraftman Alfred Claudius Hart's service number was 349473 indicating he joined from a civilian occupation twixt September 1919 and June 1925.

Tuesday 28 June 1927
111 Squadron *Not reported*
Siskin IIIA J8397
T/o Duxford and on arrival at Farnborough landed only to tip forward onto its nose; believed damaged beyond repair.

JULY

Tuesday 5 July 1927
17 Squadron Sgt F T Pennicott + Portfield [All Saints] Churchyard
Woodcock II J8300
T/o Upavon where, it is reported, Frederick Thomas Pennicott crashed, his fighter going up in flames. His death, and a long account of his funeral, was published by *The Observer and West Sussex Recorder* in their Wednesday, 13th July 1927, edition:

'Chichester Pilot Killed'
'Crash and Flames at Upavon'
'Prominent City Footballer'
'Funeral Scenes at Portfield'

"The news of the death in a flying accident at Upavon [Wiltshire] on July 5th, briefly reported in last week's "Observer," of Sergeant Frederick Thomas Pennicott, aged 25, eldest son of Mr. amd Mrs. F Pennicott, of Oving Road, Chichester, has created a keen sense of grief and sympathy in the city and district.

"Popularly known as 'Derick,' the young pilot was well known to a large number of C........ as a clever forward in the Chichester Football Club's first eleven, and generally as a bright, companionable fellow, as keen on his job as he was on sport. Whenever he could get down from his air station, he would willingly place his services at the disposal of the Football Club, and he played in many important matches, including the final of the Summer Senior Cup, won by Chichester two seasons ago.

"Derek was a popular member of the Chichester End Triangle Club, and will be greatly missed by his friends there. He received his early education at the Chichester Central Boys' School, and from there gained a scholarship to the Midhurst Grammar School, where his brother Ralph Pennicott, who is now a schoolmaster in Australia, also attended. In May of 1920, Derick joined the Air Force at Uxbridge, and became a wireless operator, He was drafted to Egypt in the following month, and in November of 1923, returned to England. He gained his pilot's certificate in December 1925, and had been flying continuously since. He was typical of the fearless, enthusiastic young flying men of to-day, and was never happier than when up in the clouds. He had just taken his final examination before qualifying for a commission, the result of which is not yet announced.

"Details of the accident are rather sparse, but it appears Derick was piloting a new 'plane when the crash came.He had only been up a few minutes when the machine was observed to swoop towards the earth. It fell near some aero-drome buildings, and the petrol tank exploded, enveloping the wreckage in flames. Troops hurried to the scene, but it was impossible to get near the pilot, who most have been killed instantaneously. News of the tragedy caused much grief at the station, where Derick was popular with all ranks."

"There were impressive scenes at the funeral, which took place in brilliant sunshine on Monday afternoon at Portfield Church. Full service honours were accorded the young airman. A firing party attended from Tangmere Aerodrome, and six sergeants from Upavon acted as pall bearers. Officers present from Upavon were Squadron Leader Leacroft, Flight Lieutenant Don and Flying Officer Engenhagen. The church was filled for the choral service which preceded the internment. The hymns sung were "Thy Way, Not Mine, Oh Lord" and "Jesus Lives, No Longer Now." Assisting the Vicar, the Rev. F B Foster Palmer, was the Rector of Tangmere, the Rev. W D J C Mears, who is also Chaplin at Tangmere Aerodrome. As the cortege left the church, the organist, Mr. T M Faulkner, played the Dead March a Soul. After three volleys had been fired over the grave the Last Post was wounded.

"There was a wealth of flowers, and an RAF lorry and trailer was loaned by the Tangmere authorities to convey them to the churchyard.

"The principal mourners were the father and mother, the Misses Marjorie and Doris Pennicott [sisters], Mr. Sidney Pennicott [brother], Mr. and Mrs. D Howard [brother-in-law and sister]." Followed by a long list of relations, friends and concluding *"Members Sergeants Mess No 3 Fighter Squadron RAF Biggin Hill."*

The first sergeant-pilot to lose his life while in squadron service in 1927, Sergeant Frederick Thomas Pennicott's service number was 341348.

Monday 18 July 1927

13 Squadron P/O W H Shorter +
Bristol F.2b J7671 AC1 L Rogers +

T/o Andover and crashed, on fire, at Camberley in Surrey. Pilot Officer William Horace Shorter had been granted a short service commission on 25th September 1925, issue 33085, page 6089.

Aircraftman Leslie Rogers was one of many young youths attracted to a service life and in his case choosing the Royal Air Force, which he entered as a boy airman, between July 1922 and January 1924. His service number is reported as 362994.

The following day, page 3 of *The Daily Mirror* carried a full report of the tragedy, its banner headline reading:

'RAF Bomber Crashes in Flames on Main Road'

'Two Airmen Killed - Pilot Buried in Wreck and Mechanic Falls on Fire from Machine'

'Many People Narrowly Escape Being Struck by Falling 'Plane at Camberley'

"While flying an RAF bomber, which burst into flames in the air and crashed on to the main London road at Camberley last night, two airmen lost their lives. With his clothes ablaze, one occupant, the mechanic, jumped or fell from the machine as it neared the ground. The pilot's body was terribly burned and buried in the wreckage. When the burning 'plane, which was engaged on night operations, swept over Camberley Recreation Ground on to the road many narrowly escaped being struck by it, and several women felt the fierce heat as it passed them.

"Last night, the victims of the crash were identified as Pilot Officer W H Shorter and First Class Airman L Rogers.

'Children's Escape as 'Plane Crashed'

Machine Just Misses Falling on Cricket Pitch'

'Cyclist's Run for Life'

"When the aeroplane, a Bristol Fighter from No. 13 Squadron, Andover, crashed it was engaged with an infantry brigade and a squadron of cavalry from Aldershot on night operations.

"The work in connection with these operations had just commenced when a few minutes before 7 o'clock the aeroplane was observed coming across Camberley Recreation Ground enveloped in a mass of dense smoke. Half-way across the ground the machine burst into flames and continued its course to the north boundary of the ground. Here it turned over and crashed on to the main London-Southampton road and blazed fiercely.

"When the aeroplane was nearing the ground, one occupant was seen to fall through the air in flames as though he had tried to jump.

'Women's Escape'

"All that was left of the aeroplane was a heap of charred and twisted wreckage. Traffic on the main road was held up for a considerable time by the accident.

"Several people on the recreation ground and on the main road had narrow escapes from being hit by the burning 'plane, and several women stated that they felt the fierce heat from the machine as it passed on to its destruction.

"Several witnesses noticed explosions from the machine, and said it emitted a number of red and blue lights which, it is understood, were being carried on the machine for use in the night operations.

'Pilot Trapped in Seat'

'Plane Strikes Road Just After Stream of Traffic had Passed'

"The position where the machine crashed was just opposite a children's playground, and it was a miracle that it did not crash at the spot where a number of children were playing cricket.

"The pilot just managed to clear a belt of trees and crash nose first into the main thoroughfare. The machine was seen just over the recreation ground, flying very low and apparently in trouble. When near the road it burst into flames and nose-dived, just missing a cyclist. Fortunately a stream of vehicles had just passed, for at this time in the evening the road is usually thronged with traffic.

"The cyclist, Mr. J S Rush, looked up just in time to see the machine and jumped off his cycle and ran. The wing just missed his shoulder. The mechanic when picked up was dead, and had one of his legs missing.

"The pilot was trapped in his seat, and was not found until the flames had been extinguished by the Frimley Fire Brigade.

"Sergeant E Smith, of the King's Dragoon Guards, was close by, and with the help of bystanders dragged the body of the dead mechanic clear of the wreckage. The victims were identified as Pilot Officer William H Shorter and First Class Aircraft L Rogers.

"Mr. Rush said; "I just saw the flames and ran. I then helped to get the observer from the flames, but he was dead."

"Mr. Claude Comper, who was working in a garden adjoining the recreation ground, said, "I thought the aeroplane would crash among the children, but the pilot seemed to right the machine and just clear the trees."

On its front page appears a photograph of all that remained of the Bristol, a completely unrecognisable heap of metal, barely covering a part width of the main road. The scene is being viewed by the obligatory policeman, three men, while the pavement is thronged with curious spectators. The building in the background is titled 'The Corner House - London ....' While parked is an open topped car, registration, I believe, PF 3565.

Then, in its issue of the 22nd July, the *Mirror* published a brief report on the inquest which seemed to have reached some rather strange conclusions as indicated by the headline *'Air Stunts Danger'* followed by *'Jury's Rider on Unnecessary Tricks Over Populated Areas'*

"Unnecessary stunts in the vicinity of populated districts" were objected to by the jury at yesterday's inquest on the two victims of the RAF crash at Camberley.

"The inquest was on Pilot Officer W H Shorter and First-Class Aircraftman L Rogers, and a verdict of Accidental death was returned.

"In the rider to the verdict the jury also thought there should be individual supervision of all machines regarding equipment of oil, fuel and water by a responsible person before leaving the aerodrome."

Tuesday 19 July 1927
45 Squadron *Not reported*
DH.9A J7841
T/o Heliopolis where it crashed and caught fire. During the months of August and September 1926, the DH was reported at Amman and Ramleh with 14 Squadron.

Wednesday 20 July 1927
19 Squadron F/O W A Andrews Safe
Grebe II J7580
T/o Sutton Bridge and came down on the Holbeach Marsh Range. Initially used by 25 Squadron at Hawkinge followed by a spell at Farnborough with the RAE before returning to 25 Squadron; thence on an unrecorded date to Duxford and 19 Squadron.

Flying Officer William Arthur Andrews had been granted a short service commission, *Gazetted* 29th September 1925, on page 6280 of issue 33088. He resigned his commission on the last day of May 1929.

39 Squadron F/O J C McE Gibb Safe
DH.9A J7074/4 LAC Hutchings Safe
T/o Spittlegate and came to grief in a crash at Wykeham, described on Wikipedia as *"a deserted medieval village in the civil parish of Weston in the South Holland district of Lincolnshire."*

A brief account was published by the *Sheffield Daily Telegraph* whose sub-editor elected to head the report:

'Aeroplane Wrecked'

'Airmen's Miraculous Escape in Wykeham Crash'

"An aeroplane from the Spittlegate Aerodrome, belonging to the 39th Bombing Squadron was completely smashed while making a forced landing at Wykeham, Lincolnshire, yesterday morning on account of engine trouble.

"The pilot was Flying Officer Gibb and the observer Leading Aircraftman Hutchings, both of Grantham.

"The airmen had a remarkable escape from serious injury, and beyond a few scratches were none the worse for their alarming experience.

"In landing the wheels of the 'plane struck an irrigation ditch, and turning upside down was completely wrecked. The airmen were pressed down by the wreckage, but managed to crawl out.

Friday 22 July 1927
2 Squadron *Not reported*
Bristol F.2b J7664
T/o Shanghai race course and crashed on return; wrecked.

47 Squadron F/O F S Homersham DCM MM Safe
DH.9A AC1 H K Bacon +
T/o Helwan and crashed at El Tabbin on the River Nile. Aircraftman Harold Kauntze Bacon was reported missing, but Flying Officer Francis Stanhope Homersham DCM MM escaped unharmed. A short service commission officer, his details appear in Appendix C for 1925 and officers named in *The London Gazette* of 13th January 1925.

Aircraftman Bacon's service number, 355883, shows him as one of many joining the service between September 1919 and June 1925, from civilian life.

Monday 25 July 1927
17 Squadron F/O I A Anderson +
Woodcock II J7967
T/o Northolt for an Air Defence Great Britain exercise and while landing in formation was struck from behind by the aircraft summarised below. On hitting the ground Flying Officer Ian Andrew Anderson's fighter caught fire; his short service commission was promulgated in *The London Gazette* issue 33090, page 6421, published on 6th October 1925.

Being in the capital the *Evening Standard* that same evening made the crash their front page headline news:

'London "Raid" Airman Killed'

'Machines Collide in the Air'

Flying Officer Burned to Death Outside Northolt Officers' Mess'

'Scores see the Tragedy'

'Five "Raids" by "Enemy" During the Big London Manoeuvres'

"Flying Officer Ian A Anderson, of 17th [Fighter] Squadron, stationed at Upavon, this afternoon crashed and was burned to death at Northolt Aerodrome, whence his squadron was returning after having taken part in the mock war over London.

"The Air Ministry states that the machine was of the Woodcock type. Officers were sitting outside their mess quarters at the aerodrome, watching the 'planes, when two machines met and a wing of one cracked.

"Anderson'a machine crashed down in flames in front of the mess verandah. Efforts at rescue were defeated by the intensity of the flames, and the officer was burned beyond recognition.

"Five air "raids" were made on London during the operation. In one the "enemy" obtained a "direct hit" on the Duke of York's School at Chelsea in bad visibility.

'Comrade's Distress'

"The squadron with which Flying Officer Anderson was engaged consisted of nine flying planes, and was returning to Northolt Aerodrome, flying in close formation.

"At a height of about 200 feet one of the machines was seen to go ahead and turn inwards. Then the tips of the two 'planes touched and pieces of wreckage fell from one of them.

"Above the roar of the engines a sharp crack of an impact could be heard and two machines were seen to grip one another.

'Tail Broken Off'

"The tail of Anderson's machine was broken off and came hurtling down in the presence of scores of people.

"The machine was at this time immediately over the officers' mess, but continued its flight for about 300 yards.

"It was completely out of control, and came spinning down among the long grass of the landing ground.

"All round the aerodrome at the time were men engaged on their ordinary duties. A group of officers, who had just finished lunch, were sitting in deck chairs on the mess verandah immediately in front of which Anderson crashed.

'Burst Into Flames'

"There was an instant Cry and a rush for help in all directions.

"Men came running through the long grass towards the aeroplane, which on crashing had burst into flames.

"Tongues of fire shot up into the air with a terrific roar, and the heat could be felt 200 yards away.

"The machine was a wreck in less than a minute.

"The airman's charred body was eventually recovered from the debris.

'"Greatest Pal's" Distress'

"A Press representative who approached an officer with a view to obtaining some information of the accident saw tears come into his eyes as he replied: "He was my greatest pal."

"The aeroplane with which Anderson collided landed safely. As soon as it was seen that no more could be done, the order "back to work"went out, and within a quarter of an hour the aerodrome was continuing its ordinary business.

'The Alsatian wolfhound, the officer's pet at the aerodrome was one of the first to reach the burning machine, and appeared as if it was anxious to save the pilot, but was prevented from jumping into the flames."

17 Squadron Sgt E Smith-Marriott Safe
Woodcock II J7976

T/o Northolt similarly tasked and crash-landed on the airfield after striking the tailplane of the aircraft reported above. *The Courier and Advertiser* also covered the crash, thus enabling the authors to identify the pilot of the other machine involved who, at the inquest, gave the following account to the Coroner;

"I was flying the right hand machine of the left hand formation in the patrol. My machine, when we got to Northolt, got into a slop stream, that is, disturbed air from the propeller of the flight leader's machine. It caused by left wing to fall. I then lost complete control of the machine, which caused me to slip across the tail of the leader's machine, and my propeller hit the tail of Flying Officer Anderson's machine, who was at the outside left of the formation. I never saw his machine from the time my propeller hit him. I was occupied with my own machine.

"The Coroner - "In the circumstances I suppose the collision was unavoidable?" - "Absolutely."

"Recording a verdict of accidental death the Coroner said it seemed to have been a pure accident."

AUGUST

Monday 1 August 1927

13 Squadron F/O A G Boon +
Bristol F.2b LAC S N Vincent +

T/o Andover and crashed during its approach to Farnborough. Flying Officer Alexander Goodison Boon had been attached for temporary duty with the Royal Air Force from the Royal Scots.

Leading Aircraftman Stanley Noel Vincent, a former boy entrant, whose service number was 363269 joined shortly after Aircraftman Rogers, summarised on 18th July 1927.

This, and a crash at Leuchars, appeared in *The Manchester Guardian* on Tuesday, August 2nd, 1927:

'2 RAF Men Killed: 4 Injured'

'Crashes at Farnborough and Leuchars'

'Buildings Struck'

"Two Royal Air Force men were killed yesterday and four injured in flying accidents. One machine crashed at Farnborough [Hants.] in a forced-landing, the two occupants being killed. The second accident was at Leuchars Aerorome [Scotland], where a two-seater bombing 'plane crashed into a building. The two occupants and two other officers were injured.

"The Hampshire crash brings the total of fatal flying accidents in the RAF to 38. The machine was a Bristol Fighter aeroplane belonging to No. 13 Army Co-operation Squadron, and was flying in company with five others from the squadron's old aerodrome at Andover to new quarters at Manston, near Ramsgate.

"The pilot, Flying Officer A G Boon, of Brossley, Salop., and the passenger, Leading Aircraftman S N Vincent, of Worthing, were killed instantly. The six machines were compelled to land at Farnborough owing to heavy rain, and after the break-up of the squadron formation Flying Officer Boon's machine was seen to spin from a height of about 400 feet. He succeeded in getting the machine under control when very close to the ground and made a desperate attempt to get clear, but it struck a hillock on a golf course while travelling at full speed.

"At Leuchars a two-seater bombing 'plane crashed into the offices of the aerodrome. Flight Lieutenant Murray, an accountant officer, was hurled against a wall and seriously injured in the head and legs, and Lieutenant Brownless, Medical Officer, was injured to the legs. Flight Lieutenant Winkler and Pilot Officer Jack, who were in the machine were cut about the face. The machine was wrecked. "

The Daily Mirror in its coverage remarked that Flying Officer Boon was Pilot Officer Shorter's flight commander, the latter having been killed at Camberley on the 18th of July 1927.

The paper also published an account of Ladies' Purse air race held on Sunday at Hucknall where Mrs. Elliott-Lyne pipped Lady Bailey over the finishing line by the narrowest of margins - three yards!

Friday 19 August 1927
55 Squadron *Not reported*
DH.9A E8796/C1 *Not reported*
T/o Hinaidi and crashed at Hilah; possibly on squadron charge for a mere 24-hours.

Wednesday 24 August 1927
45 Squadron Sgt G B Gillie Injured
DH.9A F/Sgt G Smith Injured
T/o Helwan and wrecked in an accident at Heliopolis. Flight Sergeant Gilbert Smith was critically injured and died two days later. He had served with either the Royal Navy, or its air arm, prior to April 1918, his service number 314826 coming within the block 313001 - 316000 issued to such transferees.

Friday 26 August 1927
3 Squadron P/O H C Kelly +
Woodcock II J7734
T/o Upavon and crashed in the vicinity of the airfield after losing control whilst making a turn at low altitude. Pilot Officer Harry Cyprian Kelly received a short commission in the autumn of 1925, *Gazetted* 6th October 1925, issue 33090, page 6421.

An illustration as to how quickly detailed reporting by the press could be in the 1920s comes to light in this instance for *The Citizen* in its Friday issue headed the crash *'Crash at Upavon Aerodrome - Pilot Officer Dies From Injuries - Machine Completely' 'Upavon, Friday.'*

"Upavon Aerodrome, Wiltshire, was the scene of an aeroplane crash this morning in which Pilot Officer Harold C Kelly of No. 3 Squadron, Upavon, received terrible injuries. He was badly crushed and broken and died shortly after reaching hospital.

"An ambulance and an RAF Medical Officer reached the spot within a few minutes of the crash. The first person to rush to the assistance of the pilot were three Fleet Street journalists. They were motoring to Upavon in connection with the forthcoming Atlantic flight of Colonel Minchin and Captain Hamilton, and were only a short distance away when the crash happened.

'Penned in by Wreckage'

"Kelly was flying at a height of about 400 feet when the machine suddenly tilted, and after three or four spins struck the ground with terrific force. The front of the machine, a Woodcock fighter, was completely smashed, and the pilot was hurled forward. He was completely pinned in by the wreckage and it was necessary to use axes and wire cutters before he could be extricated.

"While this was being proceeded with strychaine was administered. When he was lifted from the cockpit and placed on a stretcher it was found his injuries were even more serious than at first been thought.

'Deceased's Second Mishap'

"Kelly met with a similar accident about two years ago, on which occasion he broke both arms and a leg. Undismayed, however, he continued flying exercises with a view to passing an examination for flying officers.

'Fifth Fatal Accident in Six weeks'

"This is the fifth fatal accident associated with Upavon Aerodrome within six weeks, three being flying crashes and two being the result of motor accidents."

At an unrecorded date in the month Horsley I J7992/2 of 100 Squadron collided with a hay-cart while making a night landing at Weston Zoyland.

SEPTEMBER

Thursday 15 September 1927
30 Squadron W/Cdr A B Gaskell DSC +
Bristol F.2b H1632 LAC W R Kittow-Roberts +
T/o Hinadi and destroyed here in a flying accident at around 7 o'clock in the morning. Wing Commander Arthur Bruce Gaskell DSC is commemorated on the Lancing College War Memorial, the College's website recording a very detailed biography of his life. Born at Guestling, Hastings on 11th September 1888, Arthur was in Olds House from September 1902 until April 1903, and on leaving entered the Britannia Royal Naval College the following month.

His pre *Great War* service was extensive, his final sea-going commission being with the cruiser HMS *Gloucester* from October 1910 to the end of January 1913, after which he gained his Aero Club Aviator's Certificate at the Central Flying School, Upavon. Extensive operational service followed, much of which took place in the Dardanelles and the Aegean. With the merger of the two air arms in April 1918, he became a Major in the fledgling Royal Air Force and was one of the many officers appointed on August 1st, 1919 to a permanent commission.

At the time of his death he was attached to the staff of Air Vice-Marshal Sir Edward Ellington's Iraq Command. I strongly suspect the purpose of the flight was to maintain currency on flying.

For details pertaining to Leading Aircraftman William Ronald Kittow-Roberts boy service, during which he received 361810 as his service number, please refer to Leading Aircraftman Vincent's summary of August 1st, 1927.

Note. There is some dispute as to the ownership of Bristol F.2b H1632; both Air-Britain's *J File* and its publication recording the history of the Bristol Fighter shows it belonged to Air Headquarters Iraq Command Training Flight, but the file reporting fatal accidents to overseas Royal Air Force aircraft indicates 30 Squadron; meanwhile, the *J File* shows Bristol F.2b J7622 written off on 19th December 1927, as being on 30 Squadron's establishment.

Saturday 24 September 1927
111 Squadron Sgt J Kelly +
Siskin IIIA J8057
T/o Duxford and while over the airfield, or in its close proximity, came into collision with Avro 504K J8361 flown by Sergeant Osmond Cecil Tostevin who was instructing Leading Aircraftman Locke, both of locally based 19 Squadron. Sergeant Tostevin retained control and landed safely, and following repair the Avro continued in service and by June 1929, was on the strength of 32 Squadron at Kenley.

The loss of this aircraft was reported in Sunday's edition of *The Observer:*

'Collision in the Air'
'Sergeant-Pilot Killed at Duxford'
'Two machines Fall'

"The following communication was issued yesterday:- "The Air Ministry regrets to announce that as the result of a collision in the air at Duxford Aerodrome at 10.30 a.m., between an Avro 504K machine of No. 19 [F] Squadron and a Siskin 3A machine, No. 111 [F] Squadron, No. 346825 Sergeant James Kelly, pilot and sole occupant of the Siskin, was killed. The pilot and a passenger of the Avro machine were uninjured.

"An eye-witness of the accident told a Press representative that the Avro had just taken off and was turning as the Siskin was coming in to land. Suddenly the Siskin hit the tail of the Avro, knocking it clean off, and then fell. Its nose was buried some distance in the ground.

"The Avro pilot accomplished a fine feat of flying by landing in the neighbouring field without injury to himself or his passenger. At the time of the accident the morning was fine, with a cold, strong, and gusty wind.

"flight-Sergeant O C Tostevin, of No. 19 Fighter Squadron, pilot of the Avro, said he had just taken off, and when at a height of about 1,000ft., he heard a loud explosion, and then found his controls would not act. He tried to get his machine into wind, but was unable to do so. He was, however, able to glide to earth down wind. He saw nothing of the other machine, but on landing found his starboard plane, rudder and elevators damaged, and concluded he had been struck.

"At the inquest held last evening at the aerodrome the Coroner returned a verdict that Kelly met his death from injuries received from crashing whilst flying in the execution of his duty."

Sergeant James Kelly, 346825, was a civilian entrant between September 1919 and June 1925.

OCTOBER

Sunday 2 October 1927
216 Squadron *Not reported*
Victoria IIIA J8064
T/o Heliopolis and believed to have been damaged beyond repair following an undercarriage collapse when forced-landing at Rutbah Wells in Iraq.

Monday 3 October 1927
47 Squadron *Not reported*
DH.9A H138
T/o Helwan and reported as a total write off following a crash.

Wednesday 5 October 1927
47 Squadron DH.9A H174 F/O C G H Gee Safe While on the ground, presumably at Helwan, struck by an unidentified aircraft and damaged beyond repair.

Sunday 16 October 1927
55 Squadron *Not reported*
DH.9A F1093 *Not reported*
T/o Nasiriyah and came to grief soon after.

Tuesday 18 October 1927
43 Squadron F/O J R Addams Injured See 11 January 1927
Gamecock I
T/o Tangmere and, as reported by the *Aberdeen Journal* the following day: *"Known as 'The Lucky Pilot,' Flying Officer J Addams, Tangmere Aerodrome, West Sussex, had a remarkable escape yesterday when his machine crashed from a height of 1,000 feet into a field near Chichester. He was badly shaken and received a slight cut on the face, but was able to return to the aerodrome calmly smoking a cigarette, apparently little the worse,Flying-Officer Addams has been in several crashes, and has always come out of them without serious injury. His machine yesterday was completely wrecked."*

Please refer to my summary for 11th January 1927, for details of his service and 14th December 1925 for his first accident.

NOVEMBER

Saturday 19 November 1927
84 Squadron Sgt A A Cole +
DH.9A LAC P Conlon +
T/o Shaibah where, it is reported, the DH stalled, spun and on impact burst into flames. Both Sergeant Arthur Alfred Cole and his observer Leading Aircraftman Patrick Conlon joined the Royal Air Force from civilian life, probably within a few months of each other as their respective service numbers were 345692 and 342720.

Wednesday 23 November 1927
99 Squadron *Not reported*
Vimy IV J7238
T/o Bircham Newton and on landing at Upper Heyford tipped onto its nose; possibly damaged beyond repair.

DECEMBER

Saturday 3 December 1927
12 Squadron F/O R D Whelan +
Fox I J7941 AC2 A H Lacy +
T/o Andover and set a course for Northolt. On nearing their destination the crew encountered thickening fog and while attempting to make a precautionary landing flew into trees at The Chantry, The Ridgeway at Enfield in Middlesex.

Flying Officer Robert Darley Whelan arrived at the Cadet College, Cranwell, with the Schools Entry in February 1920 [see page 271 of the third volume]. Aircraftman Arthur Henry Lacy, 357736, enlisted between September 1919 and June 1925.

This was the first fatal accident involving a Fairey Fox since its introduction to service in June of the previous year:

'Two Dead in RAF Crash'
'Aeroplane Hits an Apple Tree'

Was the introduction to its readers by *The Daily Herald* in its Monday paper, the report sandwiched between two other dramatic headlines, one referring to a spy case and the other how a brave news vendor in Fulham saved shoppers from a runaway horse.

"Two members of the RAF were killed when their aeroplane crashed in a garden at The Ridgeway, Enfield, on Saturday. They were:- Flying-Officer R D Whelan and Aircraftman A H Lacy. The machine was from Andover, where both men were stationed.

"Just before the accident the machine was flying low over the shoppers at Enfield. It apparently got into difficulties through engine trouble, and owing to the slight fog which hung over the district the pilot was unable to find a good landing place.

"An eye-witness said that the machine seemed suddenly to lose power and then "dropped like a stone."

"It just missed a wireless aerial and some outhouses and collided with an apple tree, narrowly escaping as it crashed to the ground, a man who had just put a horse into a stable.

"The two men were killed instantaneously. Their injuries were so severe that they were barely recognisable, and their was some difficulty in extricating them from the wreckage."

A photograph showing the scene of the accident appeared in *The Daily Mirror.*

Monday 19 December 1927
30 Squadron Bristol F.2b J7622 Whilst parked at Hinaidi it was struck by DH.9A E8513 which was in the process of taking off with Flying Officer Kenneth Clephan Garvie at the controls. The Bristol, which seems to have been a 'one off' allotment to the squadron was damaged beyond repair but the DH was lodged with the local aircraft

deport and repaired. Flying Officer Garvie was a short service commissioned officer whose details appear in Appendix D, 24th July 1923.

Neither Air-Britain's *J File* or the very detailed *DH.4/DH.9 File* has a date for probable destruction of 84 Squadron DH.9A J7881/A which turned onto its back while landing in a gale force wind.

A report, undated apart from the year, from 55 Squadron suggests DH.9A J8147/CI was damaged by Arabs following a crash-landing.

APPENDICES
1927

Appendix A - Squadron Losses Table and Losses by Aircraft Type

Column 1 - Squadron

Column 2 - Aircraft type

Column 3 - Written off

Column 4 - Fatalities

2 Squadron	Bristol F.2b	1	
3 Squadron	Hawker Woodcock I	1	
	Hawker Woodcock II	2	2
9 Squadron	Vickers Virginia	2	4
11 Squadron	Hawker Horsley II	1	2
12 Squadron	Fairey Fox I	1	2
13 Squadron	Bristol F.2b	2	4
14 Squadron	Airco DH.9A	1	2
17 Squadron	Hawker Woodcock II	3	2
19 Squadron	Gloster Grebe II	2	
23 Squadron	Gloster Gamecock I	1	
24 Squadron	Gloster Gamecock I	1	
30 Squadron	Airco DH.9A	2	
	Bristol F.2b	2	2
31 Squadron	Bristol F.2b	1	2
32 Squadron	Gloster Gamecock I	2	1
39 Squadron	DH.9A	1	
41 Squadron	Armstrong Whitworth Siskin III	1	
43 Squadron	Gloster Gamecock I	2	
45 Squadron	Airco DH.9A	2	1
47 Squadron	Airco DH.9A	3	1
55 Squadron	Airco DH.9A	4	
56 Squadron	Gloster Grebe II	1	1
60 Squadron	Fairey Fairey IIIF	1	3
84 Squadron	Airco DH.9A	3	2
99 Squadron	Vickers Vimy	1	
	Handley Page Hyderabad	2	
111 Squadron	Armstrong Whitworth Siskin IIIA	2	1
216 Squadron	Vickers Victoria	1	
605 Squadron AAF	Avro 504N	1	
Totals		50	32

	Airco DH.9A	16	6
	Armstrong Whitworth Siskin III	1	
	Armstrong Whitworth Siskin IIIA	2	1
	Avro 504N	1	
	Bristol F.2b	6	8
	Fairey Fox I	1	2
	Fairey IIIF	1	3
	Gloster Gamecock I	6	1
	Gloster Grebe II	3	1
	Handley Page Hyderabad	2	
	Hawker Horsley II	1	2
	Hawker Woodcock I	1	
	Hawker Woodcock II	5	4
	Vickers Victoria	1	
	Vickers Vimy	1	
	Vickers Virginia	2	4
Totals		50	32

Appendix B - Squadron Locations and Commanding Officers

Following two months where its 'number plate' lay in abeyance 1 Squadron reformed at Tangmere as a Home Defence fighter squadron on the 1st of February 1927. Overall, the strength of the Royal Air Force in terms of squadrons increased by one with 26 Squadron reforming at Catterick for army co-operations duties and in doing so becoming the second squadron to receive the Atlas - 13 Squadron at Andover having been issued with the first examples during the August. Developed as a private venture by Armstrong Whitworth it was destined to remain in squadron service until the mid-1930s.

The detachment of 2 Squadron to China in the spring of 1927 was as a precaution for the simmering unrest within the Shanghai International Settlement. In the event good order was restored and the squadron was home well in time for Christmas.

1 Squadron	Siskin IIIA	Tangmere	01.02.27-31.12.27	Reformed Home Defence squadron
2 Squadron	Bristol F.2b	Manston	01.01.27-20.04.27	Left for China
		Shanghai Racecourse	1.05.27-13.09.27	Left for UK
		Manston	27.10.27-31.12.27	
3 Squadron	Woodcock II	Upavon	01.01.27-31.12.27	
4 Squadron	Bristol F.2b	Farnborough	01.01.27-31.12.27	
5 Squadron	Bristol F.2b	Risalpur	01.01.27-31.12.27	
6 Squadron	Bristol F.2b	Ismailia	01.01.27-31.12.27	
7 Squadron	Virginia	Bircham Newton	01.01.27-07.04.27	
		Worthy Down	07.04.27-31.12.27	
8 Squadron	DH.9A	Hinaidi	01.01.27-27.02.27	
		Khormaksar	27.02.27-31.12.27	
9 Squadron	Virginia	Manston	01.01.27-31.12.27	
11 Squadron	Horsley	Netheravon	01.01.27-31.12.27	
12 Squadron	Fox I	Andover	01.01.27-31.12.27	
13 Squadron	Bristol F.2b/Atlas	Andover	01.01.27-31.12.27	
14 Squadron	DH.9A	Ramel & Amman	01.01.27-31.12.27	
XV Squadron	*Various*	Martlesham Heath	01.01.27-31.12.27	
16 Squadron	Bristol F.2b	Old Sarum	01.01.27-31.12.27	
17 Squadron	Woodcock II	Upavon	01.01.27-31.12.27	
19 Squadron	Grebe II	Duuxford	01.01.27-31.12.27	
20 Squadron	Bristol F.2b	Peshawar	01.01.27-31.12.27	
22 Squadron	*Various*	Martlesham Heath	01.01.27-31.12.27	
23 Squadron	Gamecock	Henlow	01.01.27-06.02.27	
		Kenley	06.02.27-31.12.27	
24 Squadron	*Various*	Kenley	01.01.27-31.12.27	
25 Squadron	Grebe II	Hawkinge	01.01.27-31.12.27	
26 Squadron	Atlas	Catterick	11.10.27-31.12.27	Reformed Army Co-operation duties
27 Squadron	DH.9A	Risalpur	01.01.27-31.12.27	
28 Squadron	Bristol F.2b	Ambala	01.01.27-31.12.27	
29 Squadron	Grebe II	Duxford	01.01.27-31.12.27	
30 Squadron	DH.9A	Kirkuk	01.01.27-27.10.27	
		Hinaidi	27.10.27-31.12.27	
31 Squadron	Bristol F.2b	Quetta	01.01.27-31.12.27	
32 Squadron	Gamecock II	Kenley	01.01.27-31.12.27	
39 Squadron	DH.9A	Spittlegate	01.01.27-31.12.27	
41 Squadron	Siskin III/IIIA	Northolt	01.01.27-31.12.27	
43 Squadron	Gamecock I	Tangmere	01.01.27-31.12.27	
45 Squadron	Vernon	Hinaidi	01.01.27-17.01.27	Absorbed by 47 Squadron
	DH.9A	Heliopolis	25.04.27-21.10.27	Patrol duties Egypt & Palestine
		Helwan	27.10.27-31.12.27	
47 Squadron	DH.9A	Helwan	01.01.27-21.10.27	
		Khartoum	21.10.27-31.12.27	
55 Squadron	DH.9A	Hinaidi	01.01.27-31.12.27	
56 Squadron	Grebe II/Siskin IIIA	Biggin Hill	01.01.27-12.10.27	Grebe II withdrawn
		North Weald	12.01.27-31.12.27	
58 Squadron	Virginia	Worthy Down	01.01.27-31.12.27	
60 Squadron	DH.9A	Kohat	01.01.27-31.12.27	
70 Squadron	Victoria	Hinaidi	01.01.27-31.12.27	
84 Squadron	DH.9A	Shaibah	01.01.27-31.12.27	
99 Squadron	Hyderabad	Bircham Newton	01.01.27-31.12.27	
100 Squadron	Horsley II/III	Spittlegate	01.01.27-31.12.27	
111 Squadron	Siskin III/IIIA	Duxford	01.01.27-31.12.27	
207 Squadron	DH.9A/Fairey IIIF	Eastchurch	01.01.27-31.12.27	DH.9A withdrawn in December
208 Squadron	Bristol F.2b	Ismailia	01.01.27-27.10.27	
		Heliopolis	27.01.27-31.12.27	
216 Squadron	Victoria	Heliopolis	01.01.27-31.12.27	
502 Squadron SR	Vimy	Aldergrove	1.01.27-31.12.27	
503 Squadron SR	Fawn II	Waddington	01.01.27-31.12.27	
600 Squadron AAF	DH.9A	Northolt	01.01.27-18.01.27	
		Hendon	28.01.27-31.12.27	
601 Squadron AAF	DH.9A	Northolt	01.01.27-15.01.27	
		Hendon	15.01.27-31.12.27	
602 Squadron AAF	DH.9A/Fawn II	Renfrew	01.01.27-31.12.27	Fawn II supplied during September

603 Squadron AAF	DH.9A	Turnhouse	01.01.27-31.12.27
605 Squadron AAF	DH.9A	Castle Bromwich	01.01.27-31.12.27

1 Squadron	Flight Lieutenant F L Luxmoore DFC	21 March 1927	F/Lt Retired list 3 August 1929
	Squadron Leader E D Atkinson MC DFC AFC	11 April 1927	See 84 Squadron 1924
2 Squadron	Squadron Leader R E Saul DFC	In situ	See Appendix B 1925
	Squadron Leader W Sowrey DFC AFC mid	9 January 1927	A/Cmdr retirement 21 September 1942
3 Squadron	Squadron Leader J M Robb DFC	In situ	See 30 Squadron 1924
	Squadron Leader E D Johnson AFC	15 September 1927	See 55 Squadron 1925
4 Squadron	Squadron Leader J C Slessor MC mid	In situ	See Appendix B 1925
5 Squadron	Squadron Leader A J Capel	In situ	See Appendix B 1923
6 Squadron	Squadron Leader C N Lowe MC DFC	In situ	See 602 Squadron AAF 1925
7 Squadron	Wing Commander C H B Blount OBE MC	In situ	See 4 Squadron 1921
	Wing Commander C F A Portal DSO* MC three times mid	11 March 1927	MRAF retirement 31 December 1945
8 Squadron	Squadron Leader W A McClaughry DSO MC DFC three times mid Australia	In situ	See Appendix B 1924
9 Squadron	Wing Commander C C Dustron	In situ	See 13 Squadron 1924
11 Squadron	Squadron Leader E A B Rice	In situ	See 6 Squadron 1921
12 Squadron	Squadron Leader T E Salt AFC	In situ	See Appendix B 1926
13 Squadron	Squadron Leader H I Hanmer DFC	In situ	See Appendix B 1926
	Squadron Leader G R A Deacon	13 April 1927	W/Cdr retired list 16 November 1935
	Squadron Leader H H MacL Fraser	4 October 1927	AV-M retirement 20 December 1945
14 Squadron	Squadron Leader A N Gallehawk AFC	In situ	See 14 Squadron 1924
	Squadron Leader E G Hopcraft DSC	26 September 1927	G/Capt retired list 17 December 1941
XV Squadron	Squadron Leader P C Sherren MC	In situ	See 60 Squadron 1921
	Squadron Leader C E H James MC	2 December 1927	G/Capt retirement 1 October 1944
16 Squadron	Squadron Leader W A Coryton MVO DFC	In situ	See Appendix B 1925
17 Squadron	Squadron Leader J Leacroft MC*	In situ	See Appendix B 1924
19 Squadron	Squadron Leader H W G Joness MC	In situ	See Appendix B 1925
20 Squadron	Squadron Leader J V Steel OBE	In situ	See 100 Squadron 1921
22 Squadron	Squadron Leader T H England DSC	In situ	See Appendix B 1925
	Squadron Leader E R L Corballis	3 May 1927	W/Cdr retired list 8 February 1932
	Squadron Leader J Noakes AFC MM	15 July 1927	G/Capt retirement 27 March 1945
23 Squadron	Squadron Leader R Collishaw DSO* OBE DSC DFC three times mid	In situ	See 30 Squadron 1921
	Flight Lieutenant J MacG Fairweather DFC mid South Africa	18 November 1927	W/Cdr perished 28 May 1940
24 Squadron	Squadron Leader W H L O'Neill MC	In situ	See Appendix B 1925
	Flight Lieutenant H W Woollett DSO MC* *Chevalier Legion d'Honneur Croix de Guerre avec Palme* [France]	25 July 1927	See 111 Squadron 1925
	Squadron Leader S N Cole	28 August 1927	S/Ldr retired list 26 July 1929
25 Squadron	Squadron Leader E D Atkinson MC DFC AFC	In situ	See 84 Squadron 1924
	Squadron Leader W H Park MC DFC New Zealand	11 April 1927	S/Ldr died 19 October 1928
26 Squadron	Squadron Leader R L Stevenson	11 October 1927	W/Cdr died 21 November 1937
27 Squadron	Squadron Leader L M Bailey AFC	In situ	See Appendix B 1924
28 Squadron	Squadron Leader A W Mylne	In situ	See Appendix B 1926
	Squadron Leader J T Whittaker MC	16 September 1927	See 28 Squadron 1922
29 Squadron	Squadron Leader M L Taylor AFC	In situ	See Appendix B 1924
30 Squadron	Squadron Leader F H Coleman	In situ	See Appendix B 1925
	Flight Lieutenant R Harrison DFC *Croix de Guerre* [France]	23 July 1927	AV-M retirement 24 April 1946
	Squadron Leader F H Coleman	23 October 1927	See Appendix B 1925
31 Squadron	Squadron Leader J F Gordon DFC	In situ	See Appendix B 1926
32 Squadron	Squadron Leader R B Mansell OBE	In situ	See Appendix B 1926
39 Squadron	Squadron Leader H V Champion de Crepigny MC DFC	In situ	See 60 Squadron 1922
41 Squadron	Squadron Leader F Sowrey DSO MC AFC	In situ	See 8 Squadron 1924
43 Squadron	Squadron Leader A F Brooks	In situ	See Appendix B 1925
45 Squadron	Squadron Leader R M Hill MC AFC mid	In situ	See Appendix B 1924
	Squadron Leader J K Summers MC mid	25 April 1927	G/Capt 1retirement 1 March 1943
47 Squadron	Squadron Leader R S Maxwell MC DFC* AFC	In situ	See 24 Squadron 1923
	Squadron Leader C R Cox AFC	12 October 1927	A/Cmdr retirement 14 July 1946
55 Squadron	Squadron Leader E D Johnson AFC mid	In situ	See Appendix B 1925
	Squadron Leader H A Whistler DSO DFC*	19 July 1927	G/Capt killed 1 March 1940
56 Squadron	Squadron Leader C H Elliott-Smith AFC	In situ	See Appendix B 1926
58 Squadron	Squadron Leader A T Harris AFC	In situ	See 31 Squadron 1931
	Squadron Leader E W Norton DSC	28 July 1927	See 70 Squadron 1925
60 Squadron	Squadron Leader T F Hazell DSO MC DFC	In situ	See Appendix B 1925
	Squadron Leader R H G Neville MC	2 September 1927	G/Capt retirement 15 March 1946
70 Squadron	Wing Commander H R Nicholl OBE	In situ	See Appendix B 1926
84 Squadron	Squadron Leader D E Stodart DSO DFC mid Australia	In situ	See Appendix B 1924
	Squadron Leader F J Vincent DFC	11 February 1927	See 56 Squadron 1925
99 Squadron	Squadron Leader W J Ryan MBE	In situ	See Appendix B 1925
	Wing Commander B E Smythies DFC	30 April 1927	See 41 Squadron 1923
100 Squadron	Squadron Leader L T N Gould MC DFC	In situ	See Appendix B 1925
111 Squadron	Squadron Leader G W Robarts DFC	In situ	See Appendix B 1925
	Flight Lieutenant A C Collier mid	14 October 1927	AV-M retirement 2 July 1946
	Squadron Leader K R Park MC* DFC New Zealand	18 November 1927	ACM retirement 20 December 1946
207 Squadron	Squadron Leader J B Graham MC AFC	In situ	See 1 Squadron 1921

208 Squadron	Flight Lieutenant J H Green	In situ	See Appendix B 1926
	Squadron Leader V E Lindop	14 March 1927	S/Ldr retired list 25 February 1935
216 Squadron	Wing Commander L D D McKeen OBE mid	In situ	See Appendix B 1924
502 Squadron SR	Wing Commander A C Wright AFC	In situ	See Appendix B 1926
503 Squadron SR	Squadron Leader R D Oxland	In situ	See 502 Squadron SR 1925
	Wing Commander The Hon. L J E Twistleton-Wykeham-Fiennes	21 February 1927	See 29 Squadron 1923
600 Squadron AAF	Squadron Leader The Hon. F E Guest PC CBE DSO MP	In situ	See Appendix B 1926
601 Squadron AAF	Squadron Leader Lord E Grosvenor	In situ	See Appendix B 1925
602 Squadron AAF	Squadron Leader J D Latta MC	In situ	See Appendix b 1926
	Squadron Leader J Fullerton	6 May 1927	S/Ldr resigned 6 May 1931
603 Squadron AAF	Squadron Leader J A McKelvie AFC	In situ	See Appendix B 1925
605 Squadron AAF	Squadron Leader J A C Wright AFC TD	In situ	See Appendix B 1925

Annex

Assuming temporary command on the reformation at Tangmere in Sussex of No. 1 Squadron, Flight Lieutenant Francis Logan Luxmoore gained the DFC whilst serving in Iraq [LG 23 December 1924, issue 33004, page 9337]. Although his unit details have not been appended, I suspect it was won whilst attached to 1 Squadron, but this may be a false assumption.

Fortunately, his Army Form B.103c has survived, and although the entries do not cover his postwar service, there are sufficient entries to provide some background on his *Great War* service.

		Embarked 20.10.16	
03.02.17	*Leave 3.2.7 to 16.2.17*		*B.213 46 Sqd*
16.06.17	*Leave 14.6.17 to 28.6.17*		*- " -*
24.6.17	*To Home Est.*	*18.06.17*	*- " -*
		Re-embarked 12.02.18	
11.01.18	*To be Flight Commander & Temp. Captain*	*01.01.18*	*L G*
16.02.18	*Post to No. 54 Squadron*	*13.02.19*	*B.213 54 Sqd*
19.03.18	*MISSING*	*18.03.18*	*Summ 1292 GOC RFC*
12.05.18	*Believed Prisoner of War*		*RAF 153[A] GOC RAF*
15.06.18	*Officially Reported as Prisoner of War*		*DAAG C 822/2*
			WO List .M.429 a/7 6 18

Turning to Trevor Henshaw's revised *The Sky Their Battlefield,* which the authors are always pleased to acknowledge, Captain Francis Logan Luxmoore was shot down during a fierce day of aerial engagements over the Western Front on 18th March 1918, just days before the opening of the German spring offensive. No less than eighteen fighters, or to use the parlance of the time "scouts," were either shot down or rendered *hors de combat.* Around eight airmen of those involved in these actions were later reported prisoners of war, while of the remainder the majority were either dead or unaccounted for. In Captain Luxmoore's case, his F.1 Camel C6720 went down while struggling to return to his airfield with his guns out of action having led his flight to the enemy airfield at Busigny, a costly 'show' for 54 Squadron with five Camels failing to return.

Squadron Leader William Sowrey received his DFC, promulgated in *The London Gazette,* on 10th October 1922, issue 32754, page 7134, *"... for distinguished services rendered during active service operations in Iraq during 1920-21."* The list of recipients for awards was quite lengthy with two officers receiving First Bar's to their DFC, four, including Squadron Leader Sowrey, receiving a DFC, five airmen *Gazetted* with a Distinguished Flying Medal, eight non-commissioned officers gaining the Meritorious Service Medal and twenty-six officers and airmen named as having been mentioned in despatches.

Charles Frederick Algernon Portal, born 21st May 1918, was one of the most outstanding officers to serve with the Royal Flying Corps and the Royal Air Force and following a brief spell in the Second World War as Air Officer Commanding in Chief, Bomber Command, was promoted ahead of more senior officers to the post of Chief of the Air Staff, a post that he held from 25th October 1940 through to the cessation of hostilities in 1945.

For an appreciation of this outstanding officer's life, Denis Richards book *Portal of Hungerford* published by William Heineman in 1978, is required reading. Copies at £40 are still available from Amazon.

The citation for his MC, published in the *Edinburgh Gazette* January 12th, 1917, issue 13038, page 126, reads: *"For conspicuous gallantry in action. He has done excellent artillery work in the air, often in bad weather and at low altitudes; he has always set his flight the best example. On one occasion he shot down a hostile machine."*

The *Edinburgh Gazette,* July 20th, 1917, issue 13116, page 1385, promulgated his DSO: *"For conspicuous gallantry and devotion to duty. For many months he has done magnificent work in co-operation with the artillery. During an attack he succeeded in silencing nine active hostile batteries, ranging our artillery. His splendid example has been of the greatest value."*

A First Bar to his DSO also appeared in the *Edinburgh* edition, that published on July 29th, 1918, issue 13296, page 2611: *"For conspicuous gallantry and devotion to duty. During a period of four months, chiefly under adverse weather conditions, he repeatedly carried out successful raids by day and night, his ingenuity and daring enabled him to drop many tons of bombs on important enemy posts. One night he crossed the lines five times, only landing between each flight to replenish with bombs. Another day he took on single-handed five enemy machines, and drove down three of them - a most gallant and splendid feat. On another day, despite thick mist, he registered one of our batteries on an enemy battery, causing the destruction of one pit and obtaining one fire and two explosions; and another day, flying for 5 1/4 hours, he carried out two very successful counter-battery shoots, observing 350 rounds. He has always set a most magnificent example to the squadron under his command."*

This last citation refers to his time as Commanding Officer No. 16 Squadron which was equipped with RE.8s, while the two earlier citations reflect his time with 3 Squadron - various types of BE.2 machines.

South African born Flight Lieutenant James MacGregor Fairweather lost his life when the SS *Aboukir* was torpedoed in the North Sea by the E-boat S-34 on the 28th of May 1940. At the time he was 42 years of age and held the rank was wing commander. Prior to his sad demise, and returning to his *Great War* service, he was *Gazetted* with a mention in despatches for his work in the Baltic [LG 22 December 1919, supplement 31703, page 15841], this being followed by the DFC for service in the same area [LG 12 July 1920, supplement 31974, page 7422]. No citation was appended to the entry for his DFC.

"For conspicuous gallantry and devotion to duty. He undertook a long-distance reconnaissance under the most adverse conditions, and though several other machines were compelled to abandon the attempt he by his persistence completed his task and returned with valuable information. He is a patrol leader of the highest order, and his consistent gallantry and valuable services cannot be too highly praised," so read the citation for the MC won by temporary captain William Henry Park.

Subsequently, he gained a DFC which was *Gazetted* 18th November 1919, supplement 31647, page 14001: *"An exceptionally good Pilot who has displayed marked ability and courage during the operations with the "Syren" Force in North Russia. His service flights have been specially praised on six occasions by the Commander of the Force during a period of three months, and his determination in pressing home the attacks on the enemy contributed in a large measure to the success which attended the work of the Air Force."*

At the time of his death, reported from Shorncliffe Hospital following an operation, he was commanding RAF Hawkinge. An obituary published in *The Post* [New Zealand] filed by the paper's London correspondent reads: *"Squadron-Leader Walter Henry Park, MC DFC, commanding the Royal Air Force station at Hawkinge, died at the Shorncliffe Military Hospital on Friday, 19th October, after an operation, in his 39th year.*

"At the beginning of the war Squadron-Leader Park enlisted in the New Zealand Forces, and served with them in Egypt and in the Dardanelles, where he was wounded. He was then given a commission in the Royal Irish Rifles, and joined the 6th Battalion in Salonika. In 1916 he transferred to the Royal Flying Corps and after training at Ismailia and Dover he fought with No. 11 Squadron in France, receiving the Military Cross for bringing down enemy machines. At the end of the war he was sent to North Russia, and took command of a seaplane unitat Murmansk. After a further period of service at Gormanstown, in Ireland, he went out to Egypt and Iraq. He had charge of the evacuation by air of Sulaimani, in Kurdistan, and for this operation was awarded the Distinguished Flying Cross. After serving for three years in Iraq he was posted to the headquarters of the Air Defence of Great Britain, and remained on Sir John Salmond's staff until his promotion to the rank of squadron-leader at the beginning of 1927, when given command of the Hawkinge station. He leaves a widow."

Promoted wing commander, Robert Little Stevenson who oversaw the re-formation of 26 Squadron [Atlas] at Catterick collapsed and died while playing golf at the Faversham Club in Kent on Sunday afternoon, 21st November 1937.. At the time he was commanding the Air Armament School at Eastchurch and had been appointed MBE.

Appointed as a temporary commanding officer, Flight Lieutenant Richard Harrison served with 52 Squadron [RE.8] during the last year of the *Great War.* His DFC was *Gazetted* on 8th February 1919: *"Owing to his skill and initiative this officer has been able to obtain most valuable information which has proved of the greatest assistance to our advance, notably on 29th October, when he carried out a reconnaissance to clear up the situation in a certain area. This information was urgently required. Flying at an extremely low altitude, Captain Harrison not only succeeded in locating our troops and those of the enemy, but he also obtained an accurate estimate of their respective strength. He further observed and reported the position of six enemy batteries in action, which were in consequence successfully engaged by our artillery."*

At the outbreak of the Second World War he was commanding 78 Squadron, a Group Pool formation in No. 4 Group, Bomber Command. Later, he served at Headquarters Bomber Command at High Wycombe as Deputy Senior Air Staff Officer and was thought highly of by the Air Officer Commanding in Chief, Sir Arthur Harris who in in February 1943, was fully supportive of Air Vice-Marshal Harrison's appointment as Air Officer Commanding No. 3 Group, Bomber Command.

Squadron Leader John Keith Summers, formerly of 13th Battalion, Royal Warwickshire Regiment, gained his MC for his work with 3 Squadron: *"For conspicuous gallantry and devotion to duty. He has continuously performed valuable work in co-operating with artillery. He has on many occasions flown at a very low altitude in order to give information to the infantry, which has proved on the utmost value."* [LG 17 July 1917, supplement 30188, page 7246].

Prior to being awarded the MC, his name was mentioned by Field Marshal Sir Douglas Haig in his despatches from his headquarters on the Western Front, while post his attachment to 3 Squadron he went on to fly F.1 Camels with 208 Squadron and between 23rd June and 11th August 1918, he destroyed four enemy scouts - one going down, burning - drove three down out of control and along with Lieutenant Kenneth Walker on 10th August 1918, drove down a Fokker D.VII which fell into allied hands and classed as 'captured.'

His final years of service were spent in Southern Rhodesia which in the Second World was a key location for training of aircrew under the British Commonwealth Air Training Plan.

Squadron Leader Harold Alfred Whistler gained his DFC [LG 3 August 1918, supplement 30827, page 9204] where for reasons unknown he was being referred to as 'Alfred Harold' Whistler: *"A very courageous and enterprising patrol leader, who has rendered valuable services. He has done exceptionally good work in attacking ground targets, which he engages at very low altitudes. During the past month his patrol attacked eight enemy scouts who were flying above him. He attacked a triplane and brought it down in a crash, and whilst thus himself engaged another of his pilots destroyed a second enemy machine. The remainder of the enemy formation were then driven off."*

Three months later on 2nd November 1918, supplement 30989, page 12960, published the citation for his DSO: *"During recent operations this officer* [formerly of the Dorset Regiment] *has rendered exceptionally brilliant service in attacking enemy aircraft and troops on the ground. On August 9th* [Second day of the successful *Battle of Amiens* which heralded the final collapse of the German armies in France] *he dropped four bombs on a hostile battery, engaged and three into conclusion a body of troops, and drove down a hostile balloon, returning to his aerodrome after a patrol of one and a half hours duration with a most valuable report. He has in all destroyed ten aircraft and driven down five others out of control."*

One final accolade was to follow, namely a First Bar to his DFC, this being promulgated on 8th February 1919, supplement 31170, page 2034: *"This officer has twenty-two enemy machines and one balloon to his credit. He distinguished himself greatly on 29th September* [Opening day for a ferocious allied assault on the enemy's Hindenburg Line], *when he destroyed two machines in one combat, and on 15th September, when following two balloons to within twenty feet of the ground, he destroyed one and caused the observer of the second to jump out and crash. He has, in addition, done arduous and valuable service in bombing enemy objectives and obtaining information. Captain Whistler is a gallant officer of fine judgement and power of leadership."*

Referring to his Army Form B.103c, this shows 'Alfred Harold' scored through and 'Harold Alfred' inserted; it also shows he was born on 30th December 1896, and joining the RFC on 9th July 1916. Although his record of service is incomplete, the following entries are certainly of interest.

		Embarked 25.10.16	*T S 2329*
04.11.16	*Posted to No. 3 Squadron*	*01.11.16*	*B.213 1 AD*
30.01.17	*Wounded*	*29.01.17*	*Summ. 881 GOC RFC*
29.01.17	*Admitted [GSW] Chin & knee abras.*	*29.01.17*	*GD 9275 45 FA*
04.02.17	*To England per H S St. Patrick*	*04.02.17*	*W.3082 8 Gen.*
		Re-embarked 24.01.18	
		Disembarked 25.01.18	*LR No. 80 Squadron*
20.04.18	*Admitted [Concussion of brain] [NW]*	*16.04.18*	*ESB23 45 CCS*
24.04.18	*Discharged to Duty [80 Sqdn]*	*24.04.18*	*N3034 24 GH*
04.05.18	*Leave 30.04.18 to 14.05.18*		*B.213 80 Sqdn*

The wound referred to on 29th January 1917, Trevor Henshaw, author of the revised edition of his excellent *The Sky Their Battlefield,* reports occurred near Mametz Woods when his Morane P A239 was shot about. His observer, Corporal E J Hare was unscathed by the gunfire buut was injured in the ensuing forced-landing.

Referring to the Aerodrome website, gratefully acknowledged by the authors, this shows Captain Whistler obtained his total of twenty-three aerial successes with 80 Squadron [F.1 Camel] between 17th March and 2nd October 1918.

Tragically, early in the Second World War, and while acting air commodore Chief of Staff of RAF India he disappeared without trace while returning to England as a passenger aboard BOAC's Handley Page HP.42E G-AAGX *Hannibal* [Captain Noel Townsend] which went missing over the Gulf of Oman on March 1sr, 1940. Group Captain Harold Alfred Whistler DSO DFC** is commemorated on column 409 of the Singapore Memorial.

Prior to his distinguished service with the RFC and from April 1918, the RAF, Squadron Leader Keith Rodney Park saw active service as a gunner attached to the New Zealand Field Artillery, participating in the Gallipoli campaign before going to the Western Front where he was wounded so seriously during fighting on the Somme that he was invalided from the service. Regaining his fitness, he joined the RFC and following training as a pilot he returned to France, attached to 48 Squadron [Bristol F.2b] in July 1917, becoming their commanding officer in April 1918, and by war's end had achieved at least twenty combat victories.

The citation for his MC was published in *The London Gazette* on 9th January 1918, supplement 30466, page 634: *"For conspicuous gallantry and devotion to duty. During an engagement with several large hostile formations, the two machines with which he was patrolling were put out of action. In spite, however, of being left alone, he continued to attack, and engaged the enemy machines in so determined a manner that he and his observer between them destroyed one and drove three others down completely out of control. He has performed several other fine feats, and has at all times set a most inspiring example by his dash and tenacity."*

The above must be reflecting his early days with 48 Squadron as his rank is described as *'2nd Lt.'* And he was still ranked as such when the citation for a First Bar was written, this being promulgated on 18th March 1918, supplement 30583, page 3418: *"For conspicuous gallantry and devotion to duty in accounting for nine enemy aircraft, three of which were completely destroyed and six driven down out of control."*

The announcement that he had been awarded the DFC appeared in the *Edinburgh* paper, less citation, on June 5th, 1918, issue 13458, page 2048. His appointment to a permanent commission, in the rank of captain, is noted in the third volume on page 194.

Appendix C - Officers Granted Short Service Commissions

LG 14 January 1927, issue 33239, page 289 - Seniority 4th January 1927 [11 entrants]

Block 24038 to 24048

24038 DAVIES Arthur Reginald Sinclair F/Lt 13.10.40 Released

Whilst in the Reserve of Air Force Officers transferred from the General Duties Branch to the Administrative and Special Duties Branch on 24th April 1940 [LG 11 June 1940, issue 34870, page 3521], his rank at the time being Flying Officer. Five days after his release from the Royal Air Force, Flight Lieutenant Arthur Reginald Sinclair died in a road accident, his death being reported in *The Advertiser and Gazette* [a local London-based paper] on Friday, October 25th, 1940, under the heading 'RAF Officer Who Flew Over Germany - Killed By Bus At Uxbridge'

"Had your husband done any flying in the war? "Yes, The top of his lungs were frozen during a flight over Germany in the early part of the war." This was the question and answer at the inquest on Monday at the Rockingham Arms, Uxbridge, on Archibald Reginald Sinclair Davies, aged 36, a flight lieutenant, formerly in the RAF, who was knocked down and killed by a bus on Friday - five days after he had been demobilised.

"The accident occurred near the car park of the Swan and Bottle, High-street, Uxbridge, during the black-out and an air-raid alert. The night was described as very dark. The driver of the bus involved has this remarkably fine record: Driven for a total period of 38 years - seven years horse-drawn vehicles and 31 motor vehicles. Possesses a clean licence. No accident of any sort. Holds six Safety First certificates and silver medal for meritorious driving, with four bars.

"When the driver, Mr. Henry Robert Brown, who lives at 87 Brixham-crescent, Ruislip, confirmed this record which was read out by his solicitor, he was deeply affected.

"In returning a verdict of "Accidental Death," Mr. Harold Broadbridge, Deputy Coroner, said he was going to depart from his usual custom in traffic cases and exonerate the driver from blame. The evidence showed that there was no negligence, and he thought it a case in which the driver, who had such an extraordinary record, should be exonerated.

"Giving evidence of identification, Mrs Davies, of 15 Palace-court, Bayswater, said her husband was on the reserve of officers before war broke out, and rejoined the RAF. She last saw him alive on the morning of the accident.

"She knew he was going to be demobilised, but did not know he had actually left. The Coroner: I am informed he was demobilised on October 13, so, for the purpose of this inquiry, I shall describe him as a flight lieutenant, formerly in the RAF.

"Dr. Hotson said that he saw Mr. Davies at the scene of the accident. He was dead. The post-mortem examination showed the cause of death was fracture of the skull and shock from multiple injuries,

"Mr. Frank Gearing, of 6 Dickens-avenue, Hillingdon, the bus conductor, said they were proceeding from the garage along Denham-road to Pinner. He was standing at the front entrance, and as they were passing the Swan and Bottle he saw a shadowy form move from the car park into the road in front of the bus. The bus swerved, there was a bump, and the bus pulled up quickly,

"PC Lane said he found Mr. Davies lying in front of the wing of the near-side hind wheels under the lifeguard, with his head towards the kerb. The bus was about seven feet from the near-side kerb and brake marks showed it had pulled up within six feet. The driver said: "I was approaching the canal bridge when I saw a shadow walk from the pavement about two feet in front of me. I braked and swerved to my off-side, felt a bump and stopped."

"Mr. Brown confirmed this statement. Ass he was passing the car park, he said, a dark object loomed up about two feet in front of the bus, coming from the near-side. He did not know what it was. He swerved and pulled up at once. An air-raid alert was in progress and the bus was carrying the regulation wing lights and tail lights. His vision was about six feet.

"After the Coroner had recorded his verdict Mr. Angelo Thompson, on behalf of the driver, and London Transport Board, expressed sympathy with the widow in a most unfortunate accident.

"The funeral of Flt-Lieutenant Davies took place in Hillingdon Cemetery on Tuesday, the arrangements being carried out by Messrs. H C Grimstead of Ruislip."

24039 GANDY Robert Frank A/Cmdr 31.03.52 Retirement

Air Commodore Robert Frank Gandy died on Friday, 31 August 1979. Senior in years when he was commissioned, Robert Frank Gandy spent a large part of his service in training appointments which began in the early autumn of 1931 when he attended the Central Flying School at Wittering for training as a flying instructor. Subsequently, he held Qualified Flying Instructor posts at Cranwell, Grantham, Digby and Abu Sueir where he had been instructed twixt January 1927 and February 1928. From May 1940 to April 1945 when he left for service in South East Asia, he was on the administrative staff at Flying Training Command headquarters at Shinfield Park, near Reading.

His final service appointment was as Senior Air Staff Officer at No. 1 Group headquarters, Bawtry Hall in Yorkshire.

24040 HONEYBALL Lawrence Ley-Kempthorne P/O 09.06.27 Terminated

For an appreciation of Lawrence Ley-Kempthorne Honeyball's life, I recommend readers access the website Teynham - The Sons of Colonel James Frederick Honeyball. One of the many aspects of Lawrence's life is contained in the paragraph *"...registered an early patent for pre-war radar and radio technology* [and] *came up with the idea for reusing air raid sirens after the war, and then gambled away the family fortune as a London socialite."* His brother's life is no less fascinating.

24041 KNAPP John Bruce F/Lt 15.07.41 Relinquished

On account of ill-health [LG 18 July 1941, issue 35222, page 4128].

24042 McKEE Andrew AM 13.06.59 Retirement

New Zealand Air Marshal Sir Andrew McKee KCB CBE DSO DFC AFC three times mentioned in despatches, died on Thursday, 8th December 1988. As Squadron Leader Andrew McKee AFC, Commanding 9 Squadron, he was *Gazetted* with the DFC, less citation, on 20th February 1940, supplement 34795, page 1055. His final appointment was Air Officer Commanding-in-Chief Transport Command during which, in 1957, he was in the Command's official tour of South America. In all, fourteen countries were visited, seventy two hours were flown and some 32,000 miles travelled.

24043 MAUND John Henry Lorraine P/O + 26.06.28 14 Squadron

24044 MILLER Percy Clive P/O 22.02.28 Relinquished

On account of Ill-health. On 29th March 1946 he obtained a commission in the Training Branch of the Royal Air Force Volunteer Reserve from which he resigned, as a flying officer, on 26th October 1952. Paul McMillan reports that Percy Clive Miller died on Monday, 9th November 1964.

24045 SURÉN Hermann Felix W/Cdr 10.02.54 Relinquished

Flight Lieutenant Hermann Felix Surén was transferred, whilst in the Reserve of Air Force Officers, from the General Duties Branch to the Administrative and Special Duties Branch [LG 12 December 1939, issue 34752, page 8254].

24046 TAYLOR Frederick John G/Capt 25.01.59 Retirement

24047 TURNER Charles Kenneth S/Ldr + 20.08.46 1 PHU Innsworth

Squadron Leader Charles Kenneth Turner died whilst undergoing treatment in the Brompton Hospital, London. He was cremated in Golders Green Crematorium and is commemorated on panel 3.

24048 WOOD Jack Whitworth F/O + 02.04.28 30 Squadron

LG 28 January 1927, issue 33243, page 584 - Seniority 15th January 1927 [9 entrants]

Block 24049 to 24057

24049 BLATCHFORD Keith Conway P/O + 03.05.27 2 FTS Digby
Pilot Officer Keith Conway Blatchford crashed at Temple Bruer which is the vicinity of RAF Digby's Operations Room after losing control of an Avro 504N. The accident happened 24-hours before his death; he was eighteen years of age. A brief report was published in *The Daily Telegraph* on Wednesday, 4th May, 1927: *"Pilot Officer Keith Conway Blatchford, who was attached to No. 2 Flying Training School at Digby, Lincolnshire aerodrome, died from injuries received yesterday by his aeroplane crashing at Templebruer, near Sleaford, on Monday. The dead officer's home was at Knolls Hill, Newton Abbot."*

Although omitted from the report, Pilot Officer Blatchford died in Cranwell Aerodrome Hospital where, it is reported, his last words were *"Oh, Mother."*

24050 BRUCE James Douglas Ferrier G/Capt 01.11.60 Retirement
24051 COMERFORD Harry Alfred George F/Lt 10.04.43 Resigned
24052 EWING William George Hamilton A/Cmdr 15.08.50 Retirement
At own request [LG 5 September 1950, supplement 39010, page 4480]. Air Commodore William George Hamilton Ewing OBE, died in June 1992.
24053 FRANCIS Hugh F/Lt 10.02.54 Relinquished
24054 JOHNSTON Geoffrey Augustus Graydon G/Capt 29.12.57 Retirement
24055 MORRIS Robert James Pilgrim A/Cmdr 21.09.57 Retirement
On account of medical unfitness for air force service [LG 1 October 1957, supplement 41189, page 5706]. Air Commodore Robert James Pilgrim Morris CBE mentioned in despatches, died on Tuesday, 30th May 1989.
24056 PAWLEY Christopher P/O 20.10.27 Resigned
Formerly 2nd Lieutenant 23rd Battalion, London Regiment, Territorial Forces.
24057 TURTON Cecil Ernest Noble P/O 13.05.27 Terminated

LG 1 February 1927, issue 33244, page 654 - Seniority 24th and 17th January respectively. Terms of engagement for the probationary Pilot Officers granted their commissions with seniority of 17th January 1927, four years on the Active List [8 entrants in total]

GRIFFITH Ronald Harold P/O 28.07.27 Terminated

COLMAN Cyril Henry Arthur F/O 17.01.31 Relinquished
FOREMAN John Godsell P/O 10.10.27 Relinquished
On transfer to the Royal Australian Air Force Reserve [LG 18 October 1927, issue 33321, page 6555].
IRVING Edward Heron F/O 17.01.31 Relinquished
On transfer to the Royal Australian Air Force Reserve [LG 20 January 1931, issue 33682, page 464].
KOCH Albert Aubrey F/O 17.01.31 Relinquished
On transfer to the Royal Australian Air Force Reserve [LG 20 January 1931, issue 33682, page 464].
MURRAY Lee Cameron Lathrop F/O 29.05.29 Relinquished
On transfer to the Royal Australian Air Force Reserve [LG 28 May 1929, issue 33499, page 3520].
SELK Grosvenor F/O 17.01.31 Relinquished
On transfer to the Royal Australian Air Force Reserve [LG 20 January 1931, issue 33682, page 464].
TOWNSEND Frederick F/O 17.01.31 Relinquished
On account of ill-health [LG 20 January 1931, issue 33682, page 464]. During his service, and while attached to 6 Squadron, he had the misfortune to write off Bristol F.2b J7638 on 7th June 1929. See summary for details.

LG 5 April 1927, issue 33263, page 2215 - Seniority 2 April 1927

24066 FOUNTAIN-BARBER Martin F/O 10.02.54 Relinquished

LG 12 April 1927, issue 33265, page 2411 - Seniority 19th March 1927 [10 entrants]

Block 24067 to 24076

24067 BRADLEY Percy Frederick George G/Capt + 18.07.46 Gloster Aircraft
A non-digitised record held by TNA Kew states that Meteor F.4 EE538 crashed near Langbourn [sic] - Report W2355. The RAF Commands website amends the location to Greendown Farm, Childrey. Childrey is an Oxfordshire village just to the west of Wantage and north of the Lambourn Downs. According to Air-Britain's EA100-EZ999 register EE538, one of forty airframes built at Gloster's Hucclecote works, crashed before delivery to the Royal Air Force. Group Captain Percy Frederick George Bradley is buried in Oxford [Botley] Cemetery.
24068 CRACROFT Peter Dicken AV-M 29.12.58 Retirement
Air Vice Marshal Peter Dicken Cracroft CB AFC mentioned in despatches, died on Sunday, 27th July 2003. Practically all of his service was spent with coastal related units, his final appointment being Air Officer Commanding No. 18 [Reconnaissance] Group, which was linked with the duties of Senior Royal Air Force Officer Scotland.
24069 DAVID Reginald S/Ldr 11.01.50 Resigned
24070 HANCOCK Richard Claude W/Cdr + 10.06.41
Wing Commander Richard Claude Hancock is buried in Lustleigh Church Cemetery, Devon.
24071 HATTON Samuel F/O + 06.09.28 422 Flight HMS *Argus*
Flying Blackburn R.1 N9834 from HMS *Argus* in the Cromarty Firth, Flying Officer Samuel Hatton failed to return to the carrier and is thought to have descended into the North Sea. Also lost was Lieutenant Charles Sheldon Booth RN and Telegraphist Edmund George Burke Grigson RN.

The Times in their edition of Monday, September 10th, 1928, reported: *"The following notice was issued by the Air Ministry on Saturday:- The Air Ministry regrets to announce that as the result of a presumed descent in the North Sea on September 6th, 1928, of a Blackburn aircraft of No. 422 Flight of HMS Argus, the following personnel are reported missing:- Pilot Officer Samuel Hatton [pilot], Lieutenant Charles Sheldon Booth, Royal Navy, and J77.760 Telegraphist Edmund George Burke Grigson.*

"The missing men started on a reconnaissance flight from the Aircraft Carrier Argus on September 6, and when they did not return a wireless message asking ships in the locality to keep a look-out for the aeroplane was at once transmitted.

"A wide area of the North Sea has been searched by seaplanes from Felixstowe, and shipping has been warned. So far no trace of the airmen has been found, but is is possible that they may have been picked up by a fishing vessel not equipped with wireless apparatus."

24072 LANE Gerald Nassau Stuart F/O 19.03.32 Relinquished
On account of ill-health [LG 22 March 1932, issue 33810, page 1962].
24073 MACE Arthur George P/O + 16.05.27 5 FTS Sealand
A mere four weeks after his commissioning, and possibly while attempting his first, or an early solo flight, Pilot Officer Arthur George Mace died

when his Avro 504N H255 spun out of control near the airfield. He was 21 years of age. According to the report published in *The Times* on Tuesday, May 17th, 1927, the Avro came down between two hangars on the outskirts of the airfield, Pilot Officer mace sustaining a broken neck.

24074 MONK Geoffrey William W/Cdr 10.02.54 Relinquished

Flying Officer Geoffrey William Monk was *Gazetted* with the DFC *"... jn recognition of gallant and distinguished service in connection with operations over the North-West frontier of India between 23rd April and 12th September 1930."* [EG June 30, 1932, issue 14769, page 735].

24075 SOMERHOUGH Anthony George Carl W/Cdr 17.02.49 Relinquished

Wing Commander Anthony George Carl Somerhough OBE at some point in his service transferred from the General Duties Branch to the Legal Branch and relinquished his commission at his own request [LG 18 January 1949, supplement 38514, page 299]. Subsequently, the following notices were promulgated in *The London Gazette*, the earliest on 12th February 1954, issue 40099, page 920:

The Colonial Office, The Church House, SW.1,
5th February, 1954

"The QUEEN has been pleased to give directions for the appointment of Eric Newton Griffith-Jones, Esq., Solicitor General, Anthony George Carl Somerhough, Esq., Deputy Public Prosector, Lazarus Kaplan, Esq., Nahar Singh Mangat, Esq., and Clive Wilfred Salter, Esq., to be Her Majesty's Counsel for the Colony of Kenya."

This was followed by his appointment *"... to be a Pruisne Judge of Her Majesty's High Court of Northern Rhodesia."* [LG 24 September 1954, issue 40285, page 5438] and in *The London Gazette* published 9th July 1957, issue 41122, page 4097 his appointment, with others, *"As Commander [Brother] ... to the Most Venerable Order of the Hospital of St. John of Jerusalem."*

24076 STUART-LYON James Edward F/O 12.01.29 Relinquished

On account of ill-health [LG 18 January 1929, issue 33458, page 466].

24077 FORBES Robert Good

LG 24 May 1927, issue 33277, page 3371 - Seniority 9th May 1927

FLYING OFFICER

24078 MACDONALD George Peter G/Capt 26.02.48 Retirement

Formerly of the Reserve of Air Force Officers he resigned his Class A commission on 9th May 1927 [LG 24 May 1927, issue 33277, page 3372].

LG 19 July 1927, supplement 33295, pages 4648 and 4649 - Seniority 1st July 1927 [31 entrants]

Block 24079 to 24109

24079 BARKER Charles Philip F/O 03.02.36 Relinquished
24080 BARRY Alexander Sherlock P/O 01.11.27 Terminated
24081 BATEMAN Edward Sutherland P/O 20.12.28 Resigned
24082 BIRCHAM Michael Guy F/O 08.05.35 Relinquished

On account of ill-health [LG 7 May 1935, issue 34158, page 2986]. Subsequently, he was granted a class C commission in the Reserve of Air Force Officers, General Duties Branch on 19th May 1937 [LG 29 June 1927, issue 34413, page 4181]. On 21st April 1941, he was granted a commission as a probationary Pilot Officer in the Training Branch with his service number amended to 64694 [LG 16 May 1941, issue 35165, page 2823]. He was promoted flying officer on 1st April 1947 [LG 16 December 1947, supplement 38147, page 5927]. F/O 16.11.49 Resigned

24083 COLLINGS Raymond William Pennington G/Capt 28.08.56 Retirement
24084 DAVIDSON Thomas Jerrard F/Lt 28.11.41 Relinquished

On account of ill-health [LG 9 December 1941, issue 35375, page 6994].

24085 DICKSON Denis S/Ldr 22.06.41 Resigned
24086 DUFFEY Hubert Wentworth F/O 01.07.32 Relinquished

New Zealand On account of ill-health. Born at Christchurch in the South Island, Hubert Wentworth Duffey died in the North Island at Auckland on on Thursday, 29th January 1959.

24087 DUNNE Francis Joseph P/O 25.04.28 Terminated
24088 DYAS Mortimer Vivian P/O 23.06.28 Terminated
24089 FERRIER Frederic Guy W/Cdr 10.02.54 Relinquished
24090 FITZPATRICK Douglas Graham Percy F/O 12.08.35 Resigned
24091 FRESSON Noel Holroyde A/Cmdr 15.11.56 Retirement

During his tenure of commanding 97 Squadron, then attached to No. 8 [PFF] Group, Group Captain Noel Holroyde Fresson gained an immediate DFC, as *Gazetted* 22nd October 1943, supplement 36219, page 4673: *"One night in October 1943, this officer captained an aircraft detailed for an operation against Hagen. Before reaching the target, the aircraft was hit by fire from ground defences. Two engines were damaged, one of them becoming completely unserviceable, the rear turret was damaged, while the lighting system failed. In spite of this, Group Captain Fresson continued to the target and bombed it. This officer has completed many sorties and has displayed inspiring leadership, great skill and determination."*

The target, Hagen, as Martin Middlebrook writes on page 434 of the *Bomber Command War Diaries* was bombed on the night of 1st-2nd October 1943 by a force comprising of 243 Lancaster and 8 Mosquitoes drawn from 1, 5 and * Groups and was a complete success. Apparently, Hagen was covered by cloud but the *Oboe* equipped Mosquitoes marked with such precision that Albert Speer, Nazi Germany's 'Minister of Armaments and War Production' stated that one of industrial facilities destroyed was a manufacturer of accumulator batteries for U-boats and the loss of the factory *"... slowed down the output of U-boats considerably."*

Air Commodore Noel Holroyde Fresson DFC twice mentioned in despatches, died on Saturday, 17th April 1993. His final appointment was Air Officer Commanding the Rocket testing range at Woomera in Australia. In retirement he assisted in the establishment of RAFM Hendon.

24092 HARRIS Maurice George Robert W/Cdr 10.02.54 Relinquished
24093 HARRISON Thomas Lewen F/Lt 27.02.62 Relinquished
24094 HAZLEDINE Alliston Temple Clough F/O 10.02.32 Relinquished

On account of ill-health.

24095 JONES Archibald Douglas P/O 27.02.28 Terminated
24096 KELLY Miles Roy F/O 27.07.37 Resigned
24097 MANNING Patrick Barry P/O 12.10.27 Terminated
24098 MODLEY Leonard William Waldron W/Cdr 15.10.63 Relinquished

As a flight lieutenant Leonard William Waldron Modley faced a General Court Martial circa 1941, the following being promulgated in *The London Gazette* 4th November 1941, issue 35335, page 6375: *"... to take rank and precedence as if his appt. as Flt. Lt. bore date 3rd Dec. 1940. Reduction to take effect from 23rd Aug. 1941."*

24099 MONRO Hector Alexander Urquhart P/O 12.10.27 Terminated
24100 MONRO Higgs Walter Roy F/Lt 28.03.38 Relinquished

To be 2nd Lieutenant Unattached List for the Indian Army. My co-author states Higgs Walter Roy Monro was born at Wimbledon, Surrey on 5th June 1906 and died in Norfolk at Worthing on Tuesday, 7th October 1986.

24101 NAISH Alan Lennox Thomson W/Cdr 20.03.50 Removed
At the time of his removal, Wing Commander Alan Lennox Thomson Naish was in the Reserve of Air Force Officers. His fall from grace is described in the *Burnley Express and Burnley News,* forwarded by my co-author, in their edition published on Wednesday, March 22nd, 1950, under the heading 'Two Gaoled For £20,485 Fraud' *"A former RAF group captain* [sic] *three times mentioned in dispatches, who was personally commended by Lord Mountbatten and received the OBE for his work at the siege of Imphal, denied at Manchester Assizes on Monday any dishonesty in his dealings with a Burnley firm of which he was a director.*

"He was Alan Lennox Thomson Naish, [40], Forest-row, Sussex. With Clarence Henry Witcomb, [36], formerly of Knaresborough-place, Kensington, he pleaded not guilty to charges of conspiracy, fraudulent conversion and the fraudulent application of £20,485 belonging to George Keighley Ltd., textile machinery manufacturers of Burnley.

"After a trial which had lasted a week, the jury took only 20 minutes to find them guilty on 16 charges arising out of fraudulent misapplication and conversion.

"They heard Mr. Justice Cassels say there was not the slightest doubt that they had entered into a scheme to obtain very large sums of money, and had succeeded in getting more than £20,000. Witcomb was sentenced to five years imprisonment, and Naish was sent to prison for three years.

"It was alleged that Witcomb and Naish, after buying shares in the firm of George Keighley Ltd., fraudulently applied to their own use a total of £20,541 belonging to the firm. Witcomb asked for five other offenses, invovling the theft of £700 by means of a trick, to be taken into consideration.

"The judge said he could not help feeling that Witcomb's was the brain behind the scheme, and that he made use of Naish, though he did not regard Naish as the simple tool and fool that had been suggested. Such conduct, he said, ate into the very heart of commerce.

"On Monday, Naish said he was a partner with Witcomb in the firm of Witcomb, Naish and Company Ltd., and Philamore Sakes Ltd., which dealt in steel. They purchased shares in George Keighley Ltd., and Witcomb, Naish and Co. Lyd., were given authority to buy steel on behalf of the company and its subsidiary, Sheflex Lyd.

"When financial difficulties ensued they raised £20,000 on the security of the shares. Questioned about the signing of cheques drawn on the account of George Keighley Ltd., Nais said he understood they were for purchase of steel. Asked about a cheque alleged to have been cashed by Witcomb, he added, "I was signing dozens of cheques all day and I didn't ask specifically of what some of them were for."

"A cheque for £224 he had presented was for an advance of benefits. He had never asked an employee to prepare invoices in respect of cheques which were queried but had told him to send receipts. We had the money, and George Keighley Ltd., were entitled to receipts to keep their books straight. Naish added he lost everything and became a bankrupt.

"In cross-examination, he said that a cheque for 5,662 from George Keighley to Witcomb, Nash and Co. Ltd., was in connection with purchase of steel. He agreed that a cheque for £5,000 in settlement of a loan raised by Witcomb, Naish and Co. Ltd., had been paid out.

"Mr. B S Wingate Saul [Prosecuting]: "Is it fair to say that the money of George Keighley Ltd., was being used to repay money loaned to Witcomb, Naish and Co. Ltd." - "Yes."

"You did not regard that as dishonest?" "At the time I did not look at it in the light in which you are looking at it now."

"Inspector Joseph Kennedy of Scotland Yard, said Witcomb has lived most extravagantly in London clubs drinking and gambling heavily. Many thousands of pounds passed through his hands, most of it wasted. He mixed in London with men and women known to have convictions for serious crimes. Inspector Kennedy said the two companies, Witcomb, Naish and Co. Ltd., Philamore Sales Ltd., which were controlled by the defendants, were now in compulsory liquidation and deficiencies were in the region of £60,000.

"Naish, said the inspector, was a former RAF group captain, three times mentioned in dispatches, personally recommended by Lord Mountbatten and awarded the OBE. He had been Witcomb's "fool and tool." It was stated that as joint managing directors both the accused had £1,500 a year.

"What Mr. Juustice Cassel described as their "ingenious, skilful and subtle transactions" took from George Keighley's more than £20,000. Witcomb had £2,400 put into his personal account. Naish £224 12s 6d. The rest was transferred to their companies accounts."

For Wing Commander Naish [there are no references to him being a group captain] the ultimate disgrace was published in *The London Gazette*, 15th August 1950, supplement 38994, page 4151: *"The KING has directed that the appointment of Alan Lennox Thomson Naish, late Wing Commander [24101], Reserve of Air Force Officers, to be an Additional Officer of the Military Division of the Most Excellent Order of the British Empire, dated 1st January 1946, shall be cancelled and annulled, and his name erased from the Register, in consequence of his having been convicted by the Civil Power, and dismissed from His Majesty's Service."*

24102 NICHOLAS Bryan David A/Cmdr 09.06.62 Retirement
Air Commodore Bryan David Nicholas CBE mentioned in despatches, died on Monday, 28th December 1992. Specialising in signals from the early days of his service [he was appointed Signals Officer at 502 Squadron on 18th June 1928, his first posting following graduation from 2 FTS Digby] and after transferring from the General Duties Branch to the Technical Branch in April 1940 he served as a Chief Signals Officer for the remainder of the Second World Wr. His final appointment was Director of Radio Engineering.

24103 ROLLINGS Leslie Stuart

24104 STEVENS Arthur Montague W/Cdr 11.12.57 Retirement

24105 STEVENS James William P/O 12.12.28 Relinquished
On account of ill-health [LG 11 December 1928, issue 33446, page 8174].

24106 STEWART Douglas Ian F/O 18.02.30 Relinquished
On account of ill-health [LG 18 February 1930, issue 33580, page 1054].

24107 STROUD Richard William Alexander F/O + 17.05.30 11 Squadron

24108 THOMSON Wilfred Peter John G/Capt 16.11.56 Retirement

24109 WHALLEY Noel Ernest P/O 03.04.29 Terminated

LG 26 July 1927, issue 33297, pages 4840 and 4841 - Seniority 18th July 1940 [27 entrants]

24110 ATKINSON Patrick George Joseph W/Cdr 10.02.54 Relinquished

24111 BEESLEY Ivo Blyton F/O 12.11.30 Relinquished
On account of ill-health [LG 11 November 1930, issue 33660, page 7178]. On 11th October 1937 he was granted a class C commission in the Reserve of Air Force with the rank of flight lieutenant in the General Duties Branch [LG 9 November 1937, issue 34452, page 6970]. On 7th May 1938 he was transferred from a class C commission to a class CC commission, retaining his ran. [LG 15 November 1938, issue 34570, page 7198]. By 26th June 1939, his service number now being 75206, he was attached to the Administrative and Special Duties Branch [LG 27 October 1939, supplement 34718, page 7183]; subsequently, it seems, his service number was amended to 173093 [by 28th March 1944], and then on appointment to a class CC commission in the Secretarial Branch with the rank of flying officer, 1st February 1949, it was amended to 192847 [LG 29 March 1949, supplement 38573, page 590]. F/O 19.06.63 Relinquished

24112 BOX Harold P/O 07.02.29 Relinquished
On account of ill-health [LG 26 February 1929, issue 33470, page 1349].

24113 BULLMORE Francis Tresillian King W/Cdr 10.02.54 Relinquished
2nd Lieutenant Royal Artillery, Territorial Army

24114 CLARK Ronald William Macdonald G/Capt 15.07.55 Retirement
As Flight Lieutenant Ronald William Macdonald Clark he was *Gazetted* with the DFC for *"... distinguished services rendered in connection with the emergency operations in Palestine, during the period 15th April to 14th September 1936."* [LG 6 November 1936, issue 34338, page 7127].

24115 COMBE Arthur Ronald G/Capt 04.07.48 Retirement
At his own request [LG 6 July 1948, supplement 38344, page 3899].

24116 CROSS Harry John F/O 18.07.32 Relinquished
On account of ill-health [LG 19 July 1932, issue 33847, page 4705].

24117 DAWSON Frank Donald P/O 28.06.28 Resigned
24118 FACHIRI George F/O 10.12.30 Resigned
24119 FEASEY Colin Edward Victor L'Estrange F/O 28.06.33 Relinquished
On account of ill-health [LG 27 June 1933, issue 33954, page 4302]. On Wednesday 2nd January 1929, whilst attached to 55 Squadron at Hinaidi, Pilot Officer Colin Edward Victor L'Estrange, accompanied by Pilot Officer Raymond Russell Carroll, was air testing DH.9A J7838 when an engine failed and in the ensuing forced-landing the DH turned over.
24120 GRENFELL Alexis René P/O 03.10.28 Relinquished
On account of ill-health. Alexis René Grenfell was granted an honorary commission in the rank of flight lieutenant, no service number quoted, on 5th February 1943 in the Administrative and Special Duties Branch [LG 23 February 1943, supplement 35914, page 933]. Subsequently, his service number was 71685 and he relinquished his commission on cessation of duty on 1st February 1946 [LG 5 March 1946, supplement 37489, page 1236].
24121 HORNER George Kenneth S/Ldr 07.01.70 Relinquished
24122 HUGHES-MORGAN David James F/Lt 26.05.41 Relinquished
On account of ill-health [LG 6 June 1941, issue 35183, page 3238].
24123 JACKSON George Russell F/Lt 10.02.54 Relinquished
24124 JONES Keith Francis F/O 18.07.36 Relinquished
Returned to service and received a hostilities only commission in the rank of pilot officer attached to the Administrative and Special Duties Branch on 23rd September 1940 and with a new identity of 85864 [LG 22 October 1940, issue 34976, page 6146]. Served throughout the Second World War and beyond until: S/Ldr 10.02.54 Relinquished
24125 MATHEWS John Robert F/O 18.07.36 Relinquished
24126 MIGNON Ulric Hanbury P/O 30.07.28 Resigned
24127 MILLER Alexander Purves S/Ldr 10.02.54 Relinquished
24128 MURISON Frederick William S/Ldr 10.02.54 Relinquished
24129 SARSFIELD-SAMPSON Francis John P/O 29.06.28 Resigned
Granted a commission in the Royal Air Force Volunteer Reserve and within the Administrative and Special Duties Branch on 15th September 1939 in the rank of flight lieutenant. His service number now 75501. [LG 14 November 1939, issue 34733, page 7645] He served throughout the Second World War and beyond until: S/Ldr 10.02.54 Relinquished
24130 SEDORSKI Mayre Glen F/O 10.10.38 Relinquished
On appointment to the Air Branch of the Royal Navy [LG 25 October 1938, issue 34564, page 6638]. At the time he was in Class A of the Reserve of Air Force Officers [from 18th July 1932].
24131 SINGLETON George Edwin Eugene S/Ldr 10.02.54 Relinquished
Flying Officer George Edwin Eugene Singleton was transferred to Class A of the Reserve on 18th July 1932 [LG 19 July 1932, issue 33847, page 4705], subsequently granted a commission in Ccass CC of the Reserve of Air Force Officers with the rank of flight lieutenant with effect from 19th September 1938 and retained in the General Duties Branch [LG 13 December 1938, issue 34579, page 7921]. His class C commission was relinquished on 3rd September 1939 [LG 5 March 1940, issue 34805, page 1318]. Postwar, he was granted a commission in class CC of the Reserve of Air Force Officers, transferring to the Administrative and Special Duties on 5th March 1946, retaining flight lieutenant rank [LG 2 April 1946, supplement 37518, page 1627].
24132 SMYTH Vere Stainer Wallace W/Cdr 10.02.54 Relinquished
24133 THOMPSON Benjamin Glossop P/O 13.01.28 Terminated
24134 WILLIAMS Oswald Gerald F/O 18.07.36 Relinquished
Returned to service and was granted a commission in the Administrative and Special Duties Branch; he was confirmed in his appointment on 20th February 1941 [LG 21 March 1941, issue 35114, page 1666]. F/O 26.12.44 Resigned
24135 WOOLVERIDGE Leslie Maurice F/Lt 19.07.33 Relinquished
On account of ill-health. Returned to service and granted a commission in the Administrative and Special Duties Branch of the Royal Air Force Volunteer Reserve as a probationary pilot officer on 9th September 1939 [LG 19 September 1939, issue 34687, page 6356]. Allotted service number 73927. Served throughout the Second World War and beyond until: W/Cdr 10.02.54 Relinquished
24136 WRIGHT Peter William Mellor G/Capt 04.03.48 Retirement
At his own request

Most unusually, it is believed none of the twenty-seven entrants died whilst on active service.

LG 9 August 1927, issue 33301, page 5180 - Seniority 9th August 1927 [2 entrants]

FLIGHT LIEUTENANT

MUMFORD Philip Stearn F/Lt 29.11.33 Relinquished
Of the Regular Army Reserve of Officers, Captain Philip Stearn Mumford was granted a short service commission for three years on the Active List. First commissioned 29th August 1914 as a 2nd Lieutenant to the 2nd County of London [Westminster Dragoons], Territorial Forces [LG 28 August 1914, issue 28881, page 6811] he returned to the Army and the General List on 20th June 1940 [LG 30 July 1940, supplement 34909, page 4666]. His Royal Air Force commission was relinquished on account of ill-health.

24138 PEARSON Alexander Cuninghame W/Cdr + 29.11.44 107 OTU Melton Mowbray
As Acting Wing Commander Alexander Cuninghame Pearson he was *Gazetted* with the DFC, less citation, for his leadership with 202 Squadron [Catalina], on 2nd June 1944, supplement 36542, page 2535. On the day of his death, a Wednesday, he had flown down in the morning to Biggin Hill in Dakota III KG527 to visit his brother Aircraftman Herbert Pearson. After lunch he took off but the elevator locks had not been removed and after gaining some height he managed to make two circuits of the airfield and then came in to make a landing with the wheels retracted. On touch down a propellor came off [probably from the port engine, and sliced into the cockpit with fatal results. The Dakota was subsequently salvaged and used as a ground training aid with the maintenance airframe serial 4989M applied.. Wing Commander Alexander Cuninghame Pearson DFC is buried in Kent at Cudham [SS Peter and Paul] Churchyard, Orpington.

LG 27 September 1927, issue 33315, pages 6127 and 6128 - Seniority 18th July [Charles Raymond Shillingford] and 2nd September 1927 respectively. [entrants 21, 1, 2 and 3 respectively0

Block 24139 to 24160

24139 APPLETON Charles Henry G/Capt + 12.08.44 124 Wing Coulombs
Wing Commander Charles Henry Appleton was *Gazetted* with the DFC on 9th July 1940, issue 34892, page 4177.Although less a citation and unit identification, as Squadron Leader Appleton he took over B Flight, 77 Squadron [Whitley III] at Driffield in November 1938 [he may have been with the squadron at Honington in July 1938 when it was equipped with Welesley I]. On 30th January 1939 he took over command of 77 Squadron on the departure to Eastchurch of Wing Commander C R Strudwick and was 'in the chair' until the arrival on 20th February 1939 of Wing Commander J Bradbury DFC. On 1st November 1939 Wing Commander Bradbury was posted to the Air Ministry, Wing Commander Appleton now taking command. As far as I can tell, he flew his first operational sortie on 16th December 1939 when he captained Whitley V N1367 for a North Sea patrol.

The principal tasks assigned to the Whitley squadrons of No. 4 Group were leaflet [Nickel] dropping over Germany and the Occupied Countries of Poland and Czechoslovakia and Reconnaissance operations. In such work Wing Commander Appleton is known to have flown the following sorties:

09-10.01.40	Whitley V N1365	Reconnaissance	Despite no moon 'gin clear' perfect visibility; ground covered in snow.
23-24.02.40	Whitley V N1351	Nickel	Prague-Plzen no opposition.
17-18.04.40	Whitley V N1367	Stjørdal-Vaernes	Aerodrome - duty not carried out owing to weather. Operated from Kinloss.
01-02.05.40	Whitley V N1371	Oslo-Fornebu	Aerodrome - returned early with engine trouble.
09-10.05.40	Whitley V N1366	Stavanger	Aerodrome - received recall signal; weather unsuitable in target area.
10-11.05.40	Whitley V N1388	Kleve	Bombed railways in M/Gladbach region.
21-22.05.40	Whitley V N1508	Euskirchen	Returned early with wireless unserviceable.
23-24.05.40	Whitley V N1508	Avesnes and Bavay	Bombed cross-roads at Bavey from 3,000 feet.

A year later and he was *Gazetted* with the DSO on 5th August 1941, issue 35238, page 4515: *"This officer has commanded the squadron* [604 Squadron AAF equipped with Beaufighter I] *since February 1941, and by his sound organisation, drive, energy and high skill in flying has enabled it to attain a splendid record in night fighting. Whilst under his inspiring leadership, the squadron has destroyed at least 45 enemy aircraft at night and damaged many others. He has personally destroyed two and damaged two enemy aircraft."*

His death is reported in detail by Christopher Shores and Chris Thomas in their Second Volume of 2nd Tactical Air Forces losses, page 255: *"124 Wing's Commanding Officer, was also killed when shot down in a 247 Squadron aircraft* [Typhoon Ib MN928 ZY-G] *near Flers. As Commanding Officer of the Wing there was no requirement for him to fly on operations, but when a Typhoon went unserviceable as the rest of the formation was about to depart, he had stepped in to fill the gap, borrowing Sqn Ldr McNair's aircraft."*

Group Captain Charles Henry Appleton OBE DSO DFC twice mentioned in despatches and Czechoslovak Military Cross is buried in Bannelville-la-Campagne War Cemetery, his headstone inscribed *"Death Is Only An Horizon" 77 Squadron, 604 Squadron, Tangmere, 322 Wing, 124 Wing."* He was 38 years of age. The address of his widow, Yvonne Marjarie Appleton given as Marandellas in Southern Rhodesia.

24140	BENNETT	Arthur Donald	W/Cdr		10.02.54	Relinquished

As Squadron Leader Arthur Donald Bennett was *Gazetted* with the AFC on 30th September 1941, issue 35291, page 5650.

24141	BROWN	Basil Ellman	P/O		25.04.28	Terminated
24142	COLLINS	Montague Cecil	G/Capt		19.07.54	Retirement
24143	HETHERINGTON	Thomas Aidan Deane	P/O		21.12.27	Terminated
24144	HICKS	Herbert George	F/O	+	15.02.32	Training Base Leuchars

Flying Officer Herbert George Hicks and Aircraftman Richard Beattie died in a midair collision when their Fairey IIIF S1332 came into collision with Avro 504N J8509 piloted by Sub-Lieutenant Arthur Allison Fitzroy Talbot [subsequently Vice-Admiral Sir Arthur Talbot KBE CB DSO* DL who for the last two years of his service [1965-1967] was Commander-in-Chief, Plymouth]. The tragedy was reported in *The Shepton Mallet Journal* on Friday, February 19th, 1932: *"Nearly the whole of the staff at Leuchars Aerodrome in Fifeshire were witness of a terrible accident, Monday, when two RAF machines crashed together at a height of about 1,000 feet.*

"Both machines dived to the ground, and, when the horrified spectators had reached the scene, they found that Flying Officer George Hicks and Aircraftman Beattie were dead, and Sub-Lieutenant Arthur Allison Fitzroy Talbot RN [attached to the RAF] was seriously injured. The aeroplanes were descending when the accident occurred.

"Flying Officer Hicks, with Aircraftman Beattie, was flying a Fairey 3F machine over the mouth of the River Eden at the time of the collision, Sub-Lieutenant Talbot was in an Avro machine.

"RAF men had to break down a fence to enable an ambulance to reach the spot where they crashed. Sub-Lieutenant Talbot had both legs broken and was otherwise seriously injured."

24145	HOWARD	Leonard William	G/Capt		12.02.54	Relinquished

As Squadron Leader Leonard William Howard he was *Gazetted* with the DFC on 23rd May 1941, issue 35171, pages 2943 and 2944, for his time flying Whitley bombers with 77 Squadron: *"This officer has commanded an operational flight since July 1940. During this period he has taken part in numerous attacks on important targets in Germany, and also on the enemy-occupied port of Bordeaux. He has at all times displayed a fine spirit in the execution of these flights, and set and maintained a high standard of operational efficiency throughout his command."*

24146	KIERNANDER	Charles Robert Maurice	P/O		24.11.27	Resigned
24147	LUXTON	Philip Francis	F/O		10.02.32	Relinquished

On account of ill-health [LG 9 February 1932, issue 33791, page 880]. He had been injured on Monday 26th May 1930 [though this may not have had a bearing on discharge], when Avro 504N J8728 of CFS Wittering flown by Flying Officer Vincent Humphries Nicolay crashed off a sideslip at Barholm, 5 miles NE of Stamford, Lincolnshire. Flying Officer Nicolay was killed in the accident.

24148	MARKBY	Jack Eugene	F/O	+	30.10.31	3 FTS Grantham

New Zealand Flying Officer Jack Eugene Markby and a fellow-countryman, Flying Officer Louis McHardy, died when their Avro Tutor K2498 crashed whilst performing aerobatics, the trainer falling onto Bulwell Hall golf links near Nottingham. A full report of the accident was published by *The Nottingham Evening Post* on Tuesday, November 3rd, 1931 under the heading 'Air Crash - Did Pilot Have Cramp.'

"Graphic stories of the air crash on Bulwell Golf Links on Friday, when two-officers of the RAF from Hucknall Aerodrome were killed, were related to Col. H Bradwell, the Nottingham District Coroner, at the inquest at the aerodrome this afternoon.

"The two officers, both of whom came from New Zealand, were Flying-officer Lewis [sic] *McHardy, aged 27, and Flying-officer Jack Eugene Markby, aged 25. They were attached to the 504th County of Nottingham Bomber Squadron, and were stationed at the Grantham Flying Training School.*

"When they were a quarter of a mile from the aerodrome, after looping the loop, suddenly plunged to earth, and was wrecked on the 14th tee, within a few yards of a party of women golfers who were playing on the course. Both occupants of the plane were instantly killed.

"The inquest was held in one of the Army huts in the aerodrome. The Coroner sat with a jury, and Squadron-Leader C T Anderson, the Commanding Officer at the aerodrome, represented the RAF.

" The coroner mentioned that the accident actually took place with the city boundary, but he had decided to hold the enquiry. It appears the plane had only arrived from Grantham a few minutes before it was taken up by the two officers. They were both fully qualified pilots, but for some reason the machine crashed, and the duty of the jury was to determine whether in their opinion, the officer in charge at the time was qualified to carry out what particular flying they were doing.

"The coroner submitted three photographs of the wrecked plane taken at different angles and which he said gave an extraordinery good idea of the damage that was done.

"The first witness was Squadron-Leader Anderson, who said both officers were on the strength of the unit. Markby had been two months at Hucknall, and he was a certified A1 Flying Instructor, which was a higher grade than the ordinary pilot. He had completed over 1,000 hours in the air. The machine was a training machine, and had dual controls, so at the time of the accident either officer might have been in charge.

"Markby was a flying-officer pilot with over 700 [sic] *hours flying experience, and the machine was an Avro Onyx Jupiter and was used for training purposes. It had a new airframe, but the engine had been in service since 1926. It was brought over from Grantham on Friday morning, and it was the intention of the pilot to take in back either that day or the next. It reached Hucknal at about 1145, and about 10 minutes afterwards the two officers went up for the purpose of an ordinary service flight.*

"The Coroner: But the plane had only been at the aerodrome ten minutes? - Yes, and the engine was still running. I don't understand for what purpose they had it up? - It was an ordinary service training flight. Had the machine been on the ground longer than 10 minutes they would have had to stop the engine.

"Here is a machine coming from Grantham and with ten minutes of its landing two of your officers get into it and go up. Is that normal? - Yes, quite normal. Then, are their people waiting about for the planes to arrive? - Not exactly, but had they waited longer, they would have to stop and start the engine again.

"The witness went on to say it was a different type of plane from which they had at Hucknall. Flying Officer Markby had had considerable experience of that type of aircraft, and he might have been anxious to show the other officers the use of it for instruction purposes.

"The Coroner: Does it mean that these officers were anxious to try something new, and went up for a "flip?" - No, I don't think it was that, because Markby had done over 100 hours flying in similar machines at Grantham. Is there anybody to tell these men to take the machines up? - No. Markby was in authority, as he was the flying commander. But why do these two boys take the machine up when it had only landed for ten minutes? - I can only Sur ise it was a different type of machine from which we had here, and they were anxious to try it out.

"Squadron-Leader Anderson added: - Markby was quite justified in taking it up. It was all above board, and I don't see what you are getting at. He added that, so far as he knew, all the regulations of the RAF were complied with when the machine left the ground, He added that the Air Ministry expert came down the same night and examined the machine, but it would be some time before a decision could be arrived at as to the actual cause of the accident.

"Flying-Officer W G Stevenson, attached to No. 3 Flying Training School, Grantham, who flew the machine from Grantham to Hucknall on Friday, said it was his intention to stay a short time and than fly back again. He had a pupil with him. The machine had been used for service flights at Granham for some time, and had been in use all that morning, and was in perfect order.

"The Coroner: Did you know these two officers were going to use it? - No, I did not. When did you first know it had been taken up? - during the flight. He added that he was the pilot responsible for the machine while it was in his charge. The Coroner: Can anybody take the machine and use it without letting you know? - I have no authority to give permission for flying. It amounts to this; that they had no authority to take it up? - Well, it was an Air Force plane. The Coroner: It seems to me to be rather unsatisfactory. When you saw the machine in the air what was it doing? - It went into a slow roll, and when it was on its back the pilot took the machine into a spiral dive. He added that he did not see the actual crash. The machine was about 2,000 feet up. The Coroner; Does that mean they were "stunting?" - They were doing aerobatics.

"Mrs Margaret Beatrice Smith, of 56, Edward's-lane, Sherwood, said she was playing golf on the Bulwell Hall course with Dr, Stretch when she realised the plane was flying low overhead. It was much lower than they usually flew. It seemed to come out of a loop and then "flutter" to the ground, the left wing striking the ground first. It crashed about 500 yards away from where they were playing, and she and Dr. Stretch rushed to the scene, and her companion helped to get the two out of the plane.

"Captain Frank Stafford Wilkinson, of the Accident Investigation Branch of the Air Ministry, said he made an examination of the wreckage on Saturday morning. It was completely wrecked, and all he could say was that the left wing touched the ground first. He found a shoe in the front cockpit and it was later identified as belonging to Flying Officer Markby. Captain Wilkinson added that he did not think the shoe jammed in the controls while they were flying. He knew the machine had done only 7 hours flying, but he believed it was in perfect order.

"The Coroner: You will probably never will be able to form an opinion as to the cause? - We have not got as far as that yet, but there is a chance we may do so. The Coroner: I think you will have difficulty proving anything, judging from the wreckage.

"Leading Aircraftman Herbert Jones said he helped to strap the two officers in ... ... neither of them told him what they intended to do. As far as he could judge the machine was in good order. He saw the whole flight from the time of its start to the crash. After taxying across the aerodrome it took off and climbed to about 1,000 feet. They then completed a circle and then put the machine into a slow roll. The pilot then flew inverted for several seconds, before rolling back into a normal position.

Owing to the curve of the paper, the rest of Leading Aircraftman Jones's testimony is difficult to read, but before completing his version as to the final moments of the flight, Squadron Leader Atkinson intervened to the effect that Jones was not qualified to to say what had happened as he was a rigger on the aerodrome and only a pilot could say what was taking place. A section of print in bold reads: *"We are all convinced that the aeroplane went into a "spiral" at 1,500 feet from which it never recovered, but whether the pilot was attacked by cramp or whether he died, we cannot say at present, added Squadron-Leader Anderson."*

The final paragraphs dwelt, it seems, on the subject of aerobatics which Squadron Leader Anderson went at some length to explain that in part were necessary in teaching pilots how to recover from difficult situations. At the close of the inquest a verdict of "Accidental Death" was returned.

Consulting Errol Martyn's first volume dedicated to the memory of New Zealand's airmen who lost their lives in the service of their country, Errol describes the Tutor as falling just 40 yards from a party of golfers and though the trainer was on the strength of 3 FTS Grantham both deceased were attached to 500 Squadron of the Special Reserve. Regarding Avro Tutor I K2498, Air-Britain's *K Register* shows it was the third aircraft from a production batch of eighteen aircraft, all delivered between October and December 1931, K2498 being delivered to Grantham just eleven days before it was destroyed in the crash, here described..

In conclusion, A P and R M Glover's well researched *Nottinghamshire Aviation Diary* reports on page 11 *"The coffins were taken to Hucknall Parish Church on 2nd November, an hour before the service, which was attended by a large number of personnel from various RAF stations. After the service, the two coffins were carried to Hucknall Cemetery for burial.*

"F/O McHardy was a single man, F/O Markby had only been married for two months and lived on the aerodrome with his wife and both were the first fatal accidents to 504 Squadron personnel."

24149	MARSHALL	Kenneth Charles Tecklenborough	F/O		15.07.35	Relinquished
24150	MICHIE	William Donald James	A/Cmdr		02.05.60	Retirement

Air Commodore William Donald James Michie CB twice mentioned in despatches, died in Okehampton, Devon, on Wednesday, 7th February 2001. During his service he attended courses in photograph and engineering and prior to his final appointment as Senior Technical Staff Officer at Headquarters Transport Command he served for three years [from December 1954] on secondment to the Royal Pakistan Air Force.

24151	MYERS	Charles Liburn	P/O	+	06.11.28	26 Squadron
24152	PEARSON New Zealand	Charles Alfred	F/O	+	01.01.30	32 Squadron

Flying Officer Pearson died from an undisclosed illness whilst being treated in the Officers Hospital, Uxbridge, He is buried in Putney Vale Cemetery.

24153	PIPER	Harold Lord	F/Lt		10.02.54	Relinquished
24154	ROGERS	John Cecil Kelly	F/Lt		08.05.34	Promotion

Formerly Sub-Lieutenant RNR This promotion, promulgated in the *Gazette* on 8th May 1934, issue 34048, page 2941, came after his transfer as a flying officer to Class A of the Reserve on 13th June 1932 [LG 14 June 1932, issue 33835, page 3876]. However, accodring to his reasonably extensive biography published on *Wikipedia* and where his surname is referred to as Kelly-Rogers, he left the service in 1937 to pursue a career in civil aviation, joining Imperial Airways which later became British Overseas Airway Corporation. Becoming a very proficient captain of flying boats he achieved a number of 'firsts' before his main contribution to aviation history by flying the Prime Minister, Winston Churchill and most of his entourage back from Churchill's historic meeting with the American President, Franklin D Roosevelt early in 1942. The account of their flight in the Boeing 314 Clipper *Berwick* is well known and needs no re-telling here.

Captain Kelly-Rogers, born in Ireland on 8th February 1905 died in the country of his birth at the age of 75 on 29th January 1981.

24155	SMITH	James William	S/Ldr		02.09.45	Relinquished

On account of medical unfitness for Air Force service [LG 25 September 1945, supplement 37280, page 4744]. After his first departure from the service, prewar, James William Smith qualified in dentistry and his re-entry to the service was in the Dental Service.

24156	SMITH	Philip Holroyd	G/Capt		10.02.54	Relinquished
24157	STEVENS	Reginald William Kennedy	G/Capt		02.09.50	Retirement

At his own request [LG 26 September 1950, supplement 39025, page 4799].

24158	TINLING	James Collingwood Burdett	F/O		02.09.32	Relinquished

On account of ill-health [LG 4 October 1932, issue 33870, page 6252].

24159	UPTON	Alaister Le Roi Sabine	F/O		10.02.54	Relinquished

The following was promulgated in *The London Gazette* on 3rd January 1945, supplement 36869, page 138: *"The KING has been graciously pleased to give orders for the publication of the names of the undermentioned in the London Gazette as having been Commended for valuable services in the air:- Captain Alystair Le Roi Sabine Upton, British Overseas Airways Corporation."* [Note amended spelling of first Christian name]. He had been placed in Class A of the Reserve of Air Force Officers, as a flying officer, on 2nd September 1932 [LG 9 September 1932, issue 33862, page 5765].

24160	VEAL	John Bartholomew	G/Capt	28.09.54	Relinquished
	SHILLINGFORD	Charles Raymond	P/O	15.09.28	Terminated
24161	BENNETT	Leslie Vincent	F/Lt	06.07.39	Relinquished

As Flight Lieutenant Leslie Vincent Bennett he was *Gazetted* with the MC on 6th November 1936, issue 34338, page 7123, *"... for gallant and distinguished services rendered in connection with the emergency operations in Palestine during the period 15th April to 14th September 1936."*

On 8th September 1938 he was transferred to class C of the Reserve of Air Force Officers [LG 13 September 1938, issue 34551, page 5834]. On 8th September 1938 he was granted a commission in class CC of the Reserve, remaining in the General Duties Branch [LG 13 December 1938, issue 34579, page 7920], this class CC commission being relinquished on 6th July 1939 on completion of service [LG 8 August 1939, issue 34652, page 5486]. Returned to service and served until: W/Cdr 10.02.54 Relinquished

	WELLS	Frank	P/O	09.01.29	Resigned
24162	GREENSHIELDS	James Archibald	W/Cdr	29.01.45	Resigned

Whilst on the Reserve of Air Force Officers Flying Officer James Archibald Greenshields was transferred from class C to class A on 19th March 1934 [LG 19 June 1934, issue 34061, page 3908]. Come the Second World War and he was granted a commission, in the rank of flight lieutenant, in the Royal Air Force Volunteer Reserve, General Duties Branch and allocated 83206 as his service number.

24163 HARRISON Dennis Murland F/O 03.03.37 Resigned

Formerly of the Royal Artillery, TA. He was commissioned as a 2nd Lieutenant [late Cadet, King's School [Canterbury] Contingent, Junior Division OTC] on 2nd December 1924 and attached to 92nd [5th London] Field Brigade [LG 9 December 1924, issue 33000, page 8979]. On 5th October 1939 he reverted to being a 2nd Lieutenant attached to the Royal Artillery [LG 3 November 1939, issue 34725, page 7475].

24164 HENKEL Noel Francis Victor F/Lt 10.02.54 Relinquished

LG 18 October 1927, issue 33321, page 6555 - Seniority 3rd October 1927 [2 entrants]

24167 CLARE Maurice Howard F/O 03.10.32 Relinquished

On account of ill-health [LG 4 October 1932, issue 33870, page 6252].

24168 LESTER Anthony George F/O 05.07.35 Relinquished

New Zealand On appointment to a commission in the Royal New Zealand Air Force [LG 11 February 1926, issue 34254, page 913].

LG 20 December 1927, issue 33339, page 8143 - Seniority 9th December 1927 [13 entrants]

Block 24170 to 24182

24170	CARROLL	Raymond Russell	P/O	+	02.01.29	55 Squadron
24171	CHIGNELL mid	Robert Alexander	W/Cdr	+	14.02.42	

Wing Commander Robert Alexander Chignell is commemorated on the Singapore Memorial, column 411. His biography appears on The Battle of Britain London Monument website, which I have pleasure in acknowledging. This shows he trained at 2 FTS Digby and on gaining his Flying Badge he was posted to Andover where he was attached to 12 Squadron [Fairey Fox]. Between January 1930 and March 1937 when he was sent out to Ceylon he was concerned with air operations with a nautical flavour. His service at Trincomalee was brief and by the end of July 1938 he was at Biggin Hill where, subsequently, he commanded 32 Squadron [Hurricane].

It seems he qualified for the *Battle of Britain* clasp when he flew at least one sortie with 145 Squadron [Hurricane] before being posted to the Far East where he met his death, the circumstances being reported thus: *"He was aboard High Speed Launch 105 which was escaping from Singapore, it was attacked constantly by Japanese aircraft and he was killed by a shell splinter. His body had to be buried at sea."*

On 1st October 1946 in supplement 37744, page 4904, *The London Gazette* published: *"The KING has been graciously pleased to give orders for the publication of the names of the following personnel who have been mentioned in despatches, in recognition of gallant and distinguished services in Malaya, Hong Kong and the Netherlands East Indies during the operations terminating in March 1942:- Wing Commanders:- R A Chignell [24171], RAF, [deceased].*

24172	COLLINS	Dudley Stradling	P/O		03.10.28	Terminated
24173	DOWNEY	Frederick Benson Shearn	F/O	+	27.02.30	

Formerly 2nd Lieutenant Durham Light Infantry, TA. Flying Officer Frederick Benson Shearn Downey died whilst serving at Hinaidi, Iraq.

24174 HAMILTON Hector Gollan F/Lt 22.11.39 Relinquished

On account of ill-health [LG 21 November 1939, issue 34738, page 7804].

24175 McCANN James Eckford P/O 13.06.28 Terminated

Probably, as my co-author has discovered, on account of being declared a bankrupt.

24176 MACDONALD John Fraser P/O 09.11.28 Terminated

Formerly 2nd Lieutenant Highland Light Infantry, TA

24177 MENZIES Duncan F/Lt 24.08.35 Class A

Flying Officer Duncan Menzies became a test pilot for Fairey's and in respect of the Fulmar he is mentioned on page 307 of H A Taylor's history of Fairey aircraft as being at the controls for the first flight of the first production Fulmar N1854 at Ringway on 4th January 1940. What is not mentioned is the loss of a Fulmer, flown by Duncan Menzies, which broke up during a terminal velocity dive test, and which is reported in Matthew Willis in his book *Flying To The Edge - The Groundbreaking Career Of Test Pilot Duncan Menzies.*

24178 OVERBURY Geoffrey Fox W/Cdr 10.02.54 Relinquished

Conferred by Her Majesty The Queen of thw Netherlands, Wing Commander Geoffrey Fox Overbury was an Officer in the Order of Orange Nassau with Swords [LG 2 December 1947, supplement 38137, page 5703].

24179	RICHARDSON	John Dodd	W/Cdr	08.11.58	Retirement
24180	SMALLWOOD	James Lloyd	P/O	16.11.28	Terminated
24181	TRUMAN	Frederick Lionel	F/O	10.02.36	Relinquished

On appointment to a commission in the Royal New Zealand Air Force [LG 23 June 1936, issue 34297, page 4020].

24182 UBEE Sydney Richard AV-M 26.11.58 Retirement

Air Vice-Marshal Sydney Richard Ubee CB AFC, died onTuesday, 7th July 1998. Born on 5th March, 1903, in the South London district of Camberwell, the son of a meat porter, Sydney's life was full of adventure from working as a plate layer on the Canadian Pacific Railway to an RAF career which took him to many parts of the Middle East, British India where was engaged on operations over the North West Frontier, to command of China Bay airfield in Ceylon at a time when the island was savagely attacked by Japanese carrier-borne aircraft, Staff Duties and test pilot flying both prior to and post-Second World War. And it was while testing a Hudson at RAE Farnborough shortly after the outbreak of war that he crashed and lost the sight of his right eye. This disability did not deter him from continuing to fly, or prevent him from playing squash at a very high level.

His obituary was published in *The Daily Telegraph* on Friday, July 24th, 1998, which the authors are pleased to acknowledge.

ROLL OF HONOUR
FOR
1927 SHORT SERVICE COMMISSION
OFFICERS

G/Capt	APPLETON	Charles Henry	12 August 1944	124 Wing Coulombs
	OBE DSO DFC twice mentioned in despatches Czechoslovak Military Cross			
P/O	BLATCHFORD	Keith Conway	3 May 1927	2 FTS Digby
G/Capt	BRADLEY	Percy Frederick George	18 July 1946	Gloster Aircraft
P/O	CARROLL	Raymond Russell	2 January 1929	55 Squadron
W/Cdr	CHIGWELL mid	Robert Alexander	14 February 1942	Singapore
F/Lt	DAVIES*	Arthur Reginald Sinclair	18 October 1940	
F/O	DOWNEY	Frederick Benson Shearn	27 February 1930	RAF Hinaidi
W/Cdr	HANCOCK	Richard Claude	10 June 1941	
F/O	HATTON	Samuel	6 September 1928	422 Flight HMS *Argus*
F/O	HICKS	Herbert George	15 February 1932	Training Base Leuchars
P/O	MACE	Arthur George	16 May 1927	5 FTS Sealand
F/O	MARKBY New Zealand	Jack Eugene	30 October 1931	3 FTS Grantham
P/O	MAUND	John Henry Lorraine	26 June 1928	14 Squadron
P/O	MYERS	Charles Liburn	6 November 1928	26 Squadron
W/Cdr	PEARSON DFC	Alexander Cuninghame	29 November 1944	107 OTU Melton Mowbray
F/O	PEARSON New Zealand	Charles Alfred	1 January 1930	32 Squadron
F/O	STROUD	Richard William Alexander	17 May 1930	11 Squadron
S/Ldr	TURNER	Charles Kenneth	20 August 1946	1 PHU Innsworth
F/O	WOOD	Jack Whitworth	2 April 1928	30 Squadron

* Flight Lieutenant Arthur Reginald Sinclair Davies had been released from the service a mere five days before his death in a road traffic accident, in London and at the time of the 'Blitz.' As he would have been on his release leave, I have included him in the Roll of Honour.

Appendix D - RAF [Cadet] College Cranwell

COMMANDANT
Air Commodore Frederick Crosby Halahan CMG CBE DSO MVO mentioned in despatches

The September entry to the College being noteworthy with the arrival from Iraq of five Flight Cadets.

January 1927 entry : 19

26078 *BEAMAN* William Richard G/Capt 13.06.55 Retirement
Group Captain William Richard Beaman OBE, died on Tuesday, 20th March 1973.
26079 CHARLES* Guy Pendrill W/Cdr + 13.01.42 208 Squadron
Wing Commander Guy Pendrill Charles OBE is buried in Benghazi War Cemetery where the inscription on his headstone reads: *"He Wants No Recompense Who Goes To Join The Men Of Agincourt."* From notes on the squadron's history, it would seem he was attached to the squadron which at the time was commanded by Squadron Leader L G Burnand DFC.
26080 COATES Kenneth Ronald G/Capt 13.06.57 Retirement
Group Captain Kenneth Ronald Coates mentioned in despatches, died circa February 1991 in the Scunthorpe and Barton-upon-Humber district.
26081 EAYRS* Douglas Joyce G/Capt 15.08.56 Retirement
Group Captain Douglas Joyce Eayrs CB CBE DFC, died on Friday, 25th September 1992. His DFC was *Gazetted* in the Fourth Supplement to *The London Gazette* published on Friday, 5th May 1944, pages 2065 and 2066: *"This officer has completed numerous sorties, including 4 attacks on the capital of the German Reich. On the last of these, engine trouble developed on the outward flight and soon the port engines were overheating to a dangerous degree. Never- theless, this officer flew on to Berlin and made a successful attack. His determination on this occasion was typical of that he has shown throughout his tour."* This tour was as Commanding Officer No. 640 Squadron which had formed from C Flight No. 158 Squadron, Lissett, on 7th January 1944, moving almost immediately to Leconfield where it disbanded on 7th May 1945. From formation to March 1945, it was equipped with Halifax III and then for the last few months of the war it was issued with Halifax VI.
26082 GIBBS* Hugh Washbourne P/O + 12.04.29 16 Squadron
His death in a road traffic accident was published in the *Western Daily Press* in their edition on Monday, 15th April 1929: *"Pilot Officer Hugh Washbourne Gibbs, aged 20, of the 16th Squadron, stationed at Old Sarum, was the son of Mr. Herbert Washbourn* [sic] *Gibbs, of Pulteney Street, Bath, one of Bath's senior magistrates. With other officers, he left Uxbridge on Friday in a Talbot touring car owned and driven by Flight Lieutenant W A D Brook* [sse page 270 of my third volume], *also of Old Sarum. Other passengers were Squadron-Leader A J Capel and Pilot Officer R Carter Jones. According to the evidence of the driver, the passengers, and William Crouch, R.A.C. scout, the car reached St. Thomas' Bridge, about 2 miles from Salisbury at 6.40 p.m., having covered a distance of approximately 80 miles. The driver slowed down on approaching the bridge, and then accelerated to 25 miles per hour. Rain and snow had fallen and the road was in a greasy condition. Just beyond the bridge the car skidded twice, and the driver was able to correct both skids. A third skid resulted in the car striking the bank, and completely overturning in a ditch at the road side. The deceased had the full weight of the overturned car upon his head, and was extricated in an unconscious condition. Other occupants of the car were less seriously injured. Pilot Officer Gibbs died at Salisbury Infirmary on Friday night from compression and lacerations of the brain. The jury added to their verdict of 'Accidental death' that less speed and more care."* Two years after his tragic death the *Somerset Guardian and Radstock Observer* reported that a brass plaque had been erected in Bruton parish church in memory of Pilot Officer Hugh Washbourne Gibbs of Bath and King's School Bruton. Pilot Officer Arthur John Capel was destined to rise to air rank, retiring as an Air Vice-Marshal honoured with the CB DSO DFC. His biography may be read on *Wikipedia* and on the Air of Authority website.
26083 HENZELL* Frank Louis Peregrine F/Lt 01.09.38 Retired list
On account of ill-health [LG 18 October 1938, issue 34562, page 6505]. Flight Lieutenant Frank Louis Peregrine Henzell who was born in Antigua on 2nd August 1908 later emigrated to Canada where his death occurred St. John in New Brunswick on Tuesday, 26th October 1965.
26084 HUDLESTON* Edmund Cuthbert ACM 05.06.67 Retirement
Australia Air Chief Marshal Sir Edmund Hudleston GCB CBE five times mentioned in despatches and conferred with the foreign decorations of Commander of Legion of Merit from the President of the United States of America and from the King of the Belgians the *Croix de Guerre avec Palme,* died on Wednesday, 14th December 1994.
26085 JONAS* Robert Carter A/Cmdr 29.11.57 Retirement
Air Commodore Robert Carter Jonas OBE mentioned in a despatch, died in September 1987. When Italy declared war on the Allies on 10th June 1940, Squadron Leader Jonas was commanding 80 Squadron [Gladiator] at Amriya in Egypt, but on promotion to Wing Commander was posted to command RAF Luqa on Malta, just at the time of the first air raids on the island by the *Aeronautica Militaire.*
26086 LASCELLES* David Pellow W/Cdr + 17.01.41
Awarded the Grover Memorial Prize on his graduation, Wing Commander David Pellow Lascelles has no known grave and is, therefore, commemorated on the Runnymede Memorial, panel 28. Along with his wife, he was a passenger aboard the Motor Merchant *Zealandic* which was torpedoed by U-106 [*Leutnant* Jürgen Oesten] some 230 miles NNW of Rockall while in unescorted passage Liverpool-Panama-Brisbane. The website Uboat Net, which the authors wish to acknowledge, indicates the first torpedo struck underneath the forward mast at 0045 hours and was observed by U-106 to stop. Distress signals were intercepted and then the vessel got underway. Shadowed, two more torpedoes were fired and shortly after the second struck at 0127, the crew were seen to abandon ship in three life boats. Sadly, Master, Frederick James Ogilvie, his crew and passengers, 73 in total, were never seen again. The oldest was merchant seaman John Joseph Allibone, aged 64, described as a greaser and the youngest, boy merchant seamen John Grove and Andrew Clements aged 15, the latter described as a steward.
LETCHWORTH* Robert Wilfred F/O 17.06.31 Resigned
26090 PEARSON* Herbert MacDonald A/Cmdr 31.07.55 Retirement
Air Commodore Herbert MacDonald Pearson CBE twice mentioned in despatches, died in November 1992.
POLLOCK-GORE Francis Andrew Joseph S/Ldr 31.08.55 Retirement
Squadron Leader Francis Andrew Joseph Pollock-Gore died on Saturday, 4th April 1981.
RICHARDS* Henry Gordon F/Lt 20.09.38 Retired list
On account of ill-health [LG 20 September 1938, issue 34553, page 5954]. During the Second World War he joined the RCAF rising to the rank of group captain and for his service at 5 SFTS Brantford he was appointed OBE. He died on Friday, 17th November 2000 in Louisville, Kentucky.
26092 RUTHERFORD* James Derrick G/Capt 10.01.59 Retirement
Group Captain James Derrick Rutherford emigrated to South Africa where he died in 1972.
26093 SCARLETT-STREATFIELD* James Roland AV-M + 10.05.45 AOC 38 Group
Air Vice-Marshal James Roland Scarlett-Streatfield CBE mentioned in despatches had been tasked with overseeing the surrender of German forces in Norway. Thus, on 10th May 1945 he was one of 24 crew and passengers aboard 190 Squadron Stirling IV LK297/G which departed Great Dunmow in Essex for the ironically named Operation *Doomsday* and disappeared without trace. The captain of the ill-fated flight was Squadron Leader Douglas Raymond Robertson DFC *Croix de Guerre* of the RCAF and it is mooted that on crossing into Norway he lost control in the atrocious weather conditions, crashing into mountainous terrain north of Oslo. On 21st June 1945 the burnt out wreckage was located but it was impossible to positively identify any of those on board and all now lie in a collective grave in Oslo Western Civil Cemetery. From Kamloops in British Columbia Squadron Leader Robertson's grave carries the inscription *"Sleep Gently, You Who Rest For Evermore Beyond Our Mortal Reach, Beloved Son."*

26094 SHELLEY* Bryant Thomas F/Lt + 27.05.36
Flight Lieutenant Bryant Thomas Shelley died soon after arriving in Iraq from complications arising from appendicitis and sand fever.
26095 STURGISS* Francis Claude G/Capt 21.08.54 Retirement
Group Captain Francis Claude Sturgiss OBE three times mentioned in despatches, died circa July 1985 in Exeter, the County town of Devonshire.
26096 WALKER* Edgar Richard Merton W/Cdr 03.04.57 Retirement
Wing Commander Edgar Richard Merton Walker died on the Isle of Wight on Friday, 16th March 1973.
26097 WESTON* John Gerard Willsley AV-M 11.04.64 Retirement
Air Vice-Marshal Sir John Weston KBE CB, died on Wednesday, 13th June 1979. A signals specialist he preceded Air Vice-Marshal Sir Leslie Dalton Morris as Air Officer Commanding No. 90 [Signals] Group. As a Flight Cadet he was outstanding as a sportsman and on graduating was awarded the Humanities Prize. After leaving the service he joined MI.6, eventually becoming its Deputy Head.

Flight Cadets with an asterisk appended to their surnames, graduated on 15h December 1928. Also, graduating were Flight Cadets David Walter Bayne and Frank Day Lockwood from the September 1926 entry [LG 18 January 1929, issue 33458, page 466]. An asterisk preceding the surname identifies the cadet as a former Halton apprentice.

SWORD OF HONOUR
Flight Cadet Guy Pendrill Charles

ROLL OF HONOUR
JANUARY 1927 ENTRY

W/Cdr	CHARLES OBE	Guy Pendrill	13 October 1942	208 Squadron
P/O	GIBBS	Hugh Wasbourne	12 April 1929	16 Squadron
W/Cdr	LASCELLES	David Pellow	17 January 1941	
AV-M	SCARLETT-STREATFIELD CBE mid	James Roland	10 May 1945	AOC 38 Group
F/Lt	SHELLEY	Bryant Thomas	27 May 1936	

September 1927 entry : 35

26099 BARRETT* Gareth Guilbert A/Cmdr 02.08.57 Retirement
Air Commodore Gareth Guilbert Barrett CBE, died on Saturday, 12th March 1966.
26100 BURKE* William Ivanhoe Harris S/Ldr + 08.06.40 XV Squadron
Squadron Leader William Ivanhoe Harris Burke and his crew were killed when their Blenheim IV R3746 was shot down over France during operations to Poix, the Blenheim coming down near Guerville [Seine-Maritime], 3km SSW from Gamaches. All are buried in Guerville Communal Cemetery. For an appreciation of Squadron Leader Burke's service please refer to page 146 of my revised edition of RAFBCL 1939-1940.
26101 COLE* Francis Charles W/Cdr + 08.04.41 102 Squadron
Wing Commander Francis Charles Cole took off from Topcliffe at 2027 on 7th April 1941, in Whitley V Z6468 leading his squadron on operations to Kiel. The crew were last heard on wireless telegraphy at0152 on the 8th, a direction finding fix plotting the bomber at 5005N 0348E, after which nothing further was received. All are commemorated on the Runnymede Memorial. Details of the Wing Commander's crew are recorded on page 38 of my RAFBCL 1941, and in my 9th volume, the Roll of Honour to Bomber Command.
26102 CORBALLY* Edward John AV-M 29.04.59 Retirement
Air Vice-Marshal Edward John Corbally CBE mentioned in. Despatches and conferred with Officer of Legion of Merit [USA], died on Tuesday, 19th November 1981. Between New Year's Day 1942, and 18th May 1942, Wing Commander Corbally commanded 78 Squadron based at Croft and flying Whitley Vs in No. 4 Group of Bomber Command. During his tenure of command, he oversaw the squadron's conversion from the Whitley to the more potent four-engined Halifax. Promoted acting group captain, he left Croft to command RAF Pocklington, then home for 102 Squadron which had received its first issues of Halifaxes in December 1941, and it was in Halifax II DT512 DY-0 that he had the narrowest of escapes from being killed. The occasion was the 23rd-24th October 1942, when the squadron raided the Italian port of Genoa. On return Group Captain Corbally's aircraft, captained by the squadron's Commanding Officer, Wing Commander S B Bentley DSO DFC landed safely but before it could clear the runway a tyre burst and before aid arrived to drag the bomber clear it was struck by Halifax II W1181 DY-D piloted by Flight Sergeant J L Berry. The impact killed Wing Commander Bentley and his mid-upper gunner, Flying Officer A J Graham RCAF and injured the flight engineer, Sergeant K White and the navigator Flight Sergeant J A T Simpson RCAF. By a miracle no one in Flight Sergeant Berry's aircraft appears to have been badly hurt and Group Captain Corbally escaped injury completely. Pages 247 and 248 of my RAFBCL 1941 identifies the names of both crews.
26103 *CROCKER* Leslie G/Capt 01.04.60 Retirement
Group Captain Leslie Crocker CBE mentioned in despatches, died circa April 1996.
26104 DOUGLAS-HAMILTON*Lord Malcolm Avondale F/O 20.04.32 Retired list
During his attachment 3 Squadron at Upavon, Pilot Officer Lord Malcolm Avondale Douglas-Hamilton was involved in a mist unfortunate incident when on Thursday, 12th June 1930, flying a Bristol Bulldog in the company of other squadron pilots a mock attack on a Horsley bomber was initiated during which Douglas-Hamilton's machine hit the bomber's rear fuselage, both machines then going down out of control. Pilot Officer Douglas-Hamilton parachuted, as did the observer/air gunner in the Horsley, its pilot being killed. A full account of this accident will be summarised in the 1930 section for air accidents. Subsequently, Lord Douglas-Hamilton returned to the service in the Second World War. G/Capt 29.11.46 Retired list
Group Captain Lord Malcolm Avondale Douglas-Hamilton OBE DFC AFC [Greece], died on Tuesday, 21st July 1964, in an air crash in Cameroon. An appreciation of his life will be reported in my 1930 summary.
26105 DOUTHWAITE* Dennis John F/O + 01.05.34 RAFC Cranwell
Flying Officer Dennis John Douthwaite and his pupil, Flight Cadet John Askell-Rutherford, were killed when their Hawker Hart [T] K3152 collided in the air with one of the College's Bristol Bulldog [DC] trainers K3928 which was also on a training exercise with Flying Officer William Erskine Snell Tanner [see September 1930 entry to the College] and his pupil, New Zealand born Flight Cadet John Aickin Plugge, both cadets having arrived at Cranwell in 1932. A contemporary report of the crash, which is copied on the Aviation Safety Network website, appeared in *The Sydney Morning Herald* published on Thursday, 3rd May 1934: *"A "Bulldog" fighting 'plane piloted by Flight Lieutenant Joseph Seymour* [sic] *Tanner, with Flight Cadet John Aickin Plugge, of Taupiri, New Zealand, as a passenger, collided in mid-air at Cranwell with a Hart Day bombing 'plane pilot by Flying Officer Dennis John Douthwaite, with Flight Cadet John Askell Rutherford as passenger. All four airmen were killed. The 'planes were engaged in flying training. Occupants of a lonely farmhouse and a few labourers saw one machine flying south and the west. They heard a crash like a thunder-clap. All the victims were found dead in their 'planes. They had no time to use their parachutes.*Labourers had to dodge falling fragments of the 'planes, which made huge holes in the ground. It took four hours to excavate the engines. This is the first accident involving four deaths since February 1933. It is the sixth fatal accident in the Royal Air Force in 1934, involving in all eleven deaths."* * According to the ASN Wikibase Occurrence report 186583, none of the four airmen were wearing parachutes.
26106 DREW* Frederick Robert G/Capt 01.06.57 Retirement
Group Captain Frederick Robert Drew CBE twice mentioned in despatches and conferred with the Order of Orange Nassau, died circa January 1983.
26107 FAIRTLOUGH* Geoffrey Kinglake G/Capt 30.01.50 Retirement
Group Captain Geoffrey Kinglake Fairtlough died in Ireland on Saturday, 18th January 1992.
26108 HEATH* Maurice Lionel AM 17.07.65 Retirement

Air Marshal Sir Maurice Heath KBE CB CVO mentioned in despatches, died on Thursday, 9th July 1998.
26109 HEBDEN* William Sacheverell A/Cmdr 03.10.58 Retirement
Air Commodore William Sacheverell Hebden mentioned in despatches, died during the month of April 2003. He was the first commanding officer of No. 109 Squadron which reformed at Boscombe Down from the Wireless Intelligence Development unit on 10th December 1940.
HOFTHI BIN AZIZ
Iraq
26110 HOOD* Hilary Richard Lionel S/Ldr + 05.09.40 41 Squadron
Squadron Leader Hilary Richard Lionel Hood DFC, commanding 41 Squadron since April 1940, died as the *Battle of Britain was* approaching its peak. Flying in Spitfire I P9428, he was shot down over the Channel during the afternoon's air battles. He has no known grave and is commemorated on the Runnymede Memorial, panel 4. His DFC, effective from 11th August 1940, was *Gazetted* on 27th May 1941, issue 35173, page 3024.
26111 KEARY* Richard Cosby S/Ldr 02.06.39 Retired list
On account of ill-health [LG 4 July 1939, issue 34642, page 4581]. Returned to service. G/Capt 11.11.64 Retired list
Group Captain Richard Cosby Keary died circa September 1989.
26112 *LANE* David William A/Cmdr 24.05.58 Retirement
Air Commodore David William Lane CBE mentioned in despatches, died on Friday, 2nd June 1978.
26113 *LEWIS* Kenneth Purdon G/Capt 18.03.58 Retirement
Group Captain Kenneth Purdon Lewis twice mentioned in despatched and conferred with the Polish Polonia Restituta 3rd Class, died in Somerset circa June 1999.
26114 LUCAS* Lawrence Errington Jeff P/O + 10.09.29 17 Squadron
26115 MEAD* Roger Clutton A/Cmdr 20.04.58 Retirement
Air Commodore Roger Clutton Mead CBE DFC AFC mentioned in despatches, died on Friday, 20th July 1973. The Air of Authority website, which I have pleasure in acknowledging, remarks that shortly after assuming command of RAF Holmsley South [a Coastal Command airfield on the southern fringes of the New Forest in Hampshire] Group Captain Mead joined the crew of one of the resident squadrons that had been briefed for an anti-submarine patrol. Frequently, such patrols passed without any sightings but on this occasion an enemy U-boat was sighted and attack carried out in the face of accurate defensive fire which damaged the aircraft so severely that ditching became inevitable. Everyone managed to evacuate the sinking bomber successfully and for the next eleven days the crew drifted; then, with all hope fading their plight was sighted by two naval destroyers and all were picked up by HMS *Mahratta.* Although the website gives no date for this operation, it does identify the U-boat as U-221 which according to *Wikipedia was* sunk by a straddle of eight depth charges from a 58 Squadron Halifax on 27th September 1943, southwest of Ireland. The report goes on to say that the Halifax ditched three miles distance from the sinking, along with two of the bomber's air gunners. U-221, which was on its fifth patrol, was lost with all hands - fifty in all. The Uboat Net website identifies the Halifax as Halifax II HR982 BY-B captained by Flying Officer E L Hartley and the commander of U-221 as *Kapitan* Hans-Hartwig Trojer a holder of the Knights Cross.
26116 MOLESWORTH* Anthony Oliver G/Capt + 15.08.44
Group Captain Anthony Oliver Molesworth was killed when the Oxford I L4635 of the Metropolitan Communications Squadron, Hendon, in which he was a passenger, caught fire in the air. The pilot attempted to reach RAF Newmarket but control was lost on approach when the Oxford suddenly rolled and dived into the ground. Group Captain Molesworth is buried in Cambridge City Cemetery. His commemorative inscription reads: *"I Can Do All Things Through Christ Which Strengtheneth Me."* A Facebook link, which the authors acknowledge, posted on 12th December 2019, adds that the Oxford came down at Warbrabham Farm, Heath Road, Burwell [which is just inside the Cambridge/Suffolk border and roughly 3 to 4 miles NW of New-market] and that the Group Captain was the sole occupant. However, the researcher who put up the post to The Glorious Dead in the UK delved further and suggests that two other persons were on board the aircraft, namely Squadron Leader George Albert Wilkins DFC of MCS Hendon and a civilian from the Ministry of Aircraft Production, Mr. Frederick William Thomas Griffin Connell.
MUHAMMAD ALI
BIN JEWAD Iraq
26117 MURRAY* Sydney Stuart G/Capt 09.04.57 Retirement
As Squadron Leader Sydney Stuart Murray, he became a prisoner of war along with his entire crew [see my RAFBCL 1939-1940 page 15] on 8th-9th September 1939, when his 102 Squadron Whitley III K8950 DY-M of 102 Squadron came down near Kassel [Hessen], Germany during a 'Nickel' operation.*Held at Stalag-Luft III Sagan his prisoner of war number was 60. Erroneously, the caption for the photograph appearing on page 77 of Chaz Bowyer's *The Wellington Bomber* states he was shot down on the Wilhelmshaven raid of 18th December 1939. Group Captain Sydney Stuart Murray OBE, died on
MUSA BIN AL
IraqI
NASIR HUSSAIN
JANABI Iraq
NATIQ BIN MUHAMMAD
TAIE Iraq
26118 NEWBIGGING* Ian Balmford G/Capt 01.08.57 Retirement
Group Captain Ian Balmford Newbigging DFC mentioned in despatches, died on Friday, 14th January 1994.
26119 NIBLETT* Kenneth William G/Capt 04.04.60 Retirement
Group Captain Kenneth William Niblett DFC, died circa July 1980; his DFC, less citation, was *Gazetted* on 8th March 1940, issue 34807, page 1394.
26120 PHILLIPS* Ronald Lancelot A/Cmdr + 22.11.56 AOC 27 Group
Air Commodore Ronald Lancelot Phillips won a cadetship to Cranwell having been an apprentice, 6th entry, at the Electrical and Wireless School at Flowerdown near Winchester. On graduating from Cranwell he was awarded the Hyde-Thompson Memorial Prize later adding the Abdy Gerrard Fellows Prize for aeronautical scince. It is also reported that he was very much involved with the development and operation of the navigation aid GEE. At the time of his death he had been honoured with the CB CBE and three times mentioned in despatches. His death occurred while undergoing treatment in RAF Wroughton Hospital; he is buried in Yatesbury [All Saints] Churchyard. His obituary was published in *The Times* on Saturday, November 24th, 1956.
26122 POWELL* John Alexander G/Capt + 18.08.44 OC 254 Wing Biferno
Group Captain John Alexander Powell DSO OBE mentioned in despatches and conferred with the American DFC failed to return to Biferno while flying on an operational sortie with 19 Squadron SAAF his aircraft being Beaufighter VIF X7891; he is buried in Belgrade War Cemetery. In 1941 he was commanding 149 Squadron at Mildenhall gaining the DSO, *Gazetted* 4th February 1941, issue 35065, page 692: *"One night in January 1941 this officer was detailed to carry out an attack on the oil storage plant and refinery at Porto Marghera. Flying over his target, at a height of 700 feet, he scored a direct hit on the refinery. He then made a second run over the target in the face of considerable anti-aircraft opposition, and dropped two more bombs on the now fiercely burning building. Wing Commander Powell then flew to Padua, where the aerodrome was machine-gunned from an exceedingly low altitude. He has displayed outstanding leadership, skill and courage in all his operational missions, and by his untiring efforts has raised the morale of his squadron to a high level."* I believe this operation was flown on 12th-13th January 1941, Martin Middlebrook recording nine Wellingtons were engaged on operations *"to Italy."* No. 254 Wing was a light bomber Wing uunder the aegis of the Balkan Air Force. Prior to itss arrival in the Middle East Beaufighter IVF X7891 had seen operational service with 96 Squadron and 406, 409 and back to 406 Squadron of the Royal Canadian Air Force.
26123 SELWAY* Anthony Dunkerton AM 20.02.65 Retirement
Air Marshal Sir Anthony Selway KCB DFC mentioned in despatches, died on Tuesday, 19th June 1984.

26124 SIMONDS* Eric Rolfe F/Lt + 28.07.37 A&AEE Martlesham Heath
Flight Lieutenant Eric Rolfe Simonds died in tragic circumstances after bailing out over the sea off Felixstowe following an irrecoverable spin Miles Magister I L5912. Two rescue boats were despatched but owing to confusion each thought the other had picked up Flight Lieutenant Simonds. His body was never recovered.
26125 SPENDLOVE* William Vernon Lewis G/Capt + 22.06.43 Station Commander Methwold
Group Captain William Vernon Lewis Spendlove DSO twice mentioned in despatches accompanied the Commanding Officer of 21 Squadron Wing Commander Robert Henry Swan King and crew in 21 Squadron Ventura I AE910 YH-Y for an attack on the *Luftwaffe* airfield at Abbeville-Drucat. Running into a hail of intense and accurate flak the Ventura was shot down roughly 5km north of the target. Group Captain Spendlover is buried along with the rest of the crew in Abbeville Communal Cemetery extension. At the time 21 Squadron was based at Oulton, though it is possible the operation was mounted from Methwold. They were amongst the earliest casualties from the newly formed 2nd Tactical Air Force.
26126 STANNARD* Frank William G/Capt 25.05.58 Retirement
Group Captain Frank William Stannard mentioned in despatches and conferred with the Polonia Restituuta [3rd Class], died in the South Devonshire resort of Torbay circa February 1988.
26127 VINTRAS* Roland Eugène de Trevières A/Cmdr 01.08.49 Retirement
Air Commodore Roland Eugène de Trevières CBE and Commander of the Legion of Merit [USA], died on Sunday, 15th January 1984. Fluent in French he played an important role in organising air services between Hendon and France for the Allied Military Committee and following the fall of France he became closely involved in protracted negotiations with Portuguese authorities which, eventually resulted in Portugal allowing the Azores to be used as a base for the 'Very Long Range' Fortresses and Liberators which now were able to close the Atlantic Gap in the ongoing *Battle of the Atlantic*.
26128 WATT* Charles Alpine G/Capt 05.02.58 Retirement
Group Captain Charles Aline Watt twice mentioned in despatches, died on Thursday, 27th October 1994.
26129 WIGHTMAN* William Taylor Froest G/Capt 18.01.61 Retirement
Group Captain William Taylor Froest Wightman DFC AFC mentioned in despatches and honoured by the Netherlands with the Order of Orange Nassau, died circa February 1990.

Flight Cadets with an asterisk appended after their surname graduated with a permanent commission on 27th July 1929 [LG 27 August 1929, issue 33529, page 5569]; also graduating Flight Cadet Francis Andrew Joseph Pollick-Gore from the January 1927, entry. Those surnames preceded with an asterisk arrived at the College following a Halton aircraft apprentices.

* On page 1 of Oliver Clutton-Brock's indispensable *Footsteps On The Sands Of Time* the author writes in respect of Squadron Leader Murray and his co-pilot Pilot Officer Thompson: *"... soon found themselves in a Berlin hotel shaking hands with Reichmarschall Hermann Göring, Commander-in-Chief of the Luftwaffe, who jokingly 'complained that they had disturbed his sleep and had obliged him to take shelter. He assured them, however, that he appreciated the chivalrous way the Royal Flying Corps had fought in the last war said he intended to see that Royal Air Force prisoners were treated accordingly."*

SWORD OF HONOUR
Flight Cadet Kenneth William Niblett

ROLL OF HONOUR
SEPTEMBER 1927 ENTRY

S/Ldr	BURKE	William Ivanhoe Harris	8 June 1940	XV Squadron
W/Cdr	COLE	Francis Charles	8 April 1941	102 Squadron
F/O	DOUTHWAITE	Dennis John	1 May 1934	RAFC Cranwell
S/Ldr	HOOD	Hilary Richard Lionel	5 September 1940	41 Squadron
P/O	LUCAS	Lawrence Errington Jeff	10 September 1929	17 Squadron
G/Capt	MOLESORTH	Anthony Oliver	15 August 1944	
A/Cmdr	PHILLIPS CB CBE Three times mid	Ronald Lancelot	22 November 1956	AOC 27 Group
G/Capt	POWELL DSO OBE mid	John Alexander	18 August 1944	OC 254 Wing Biferno
F/Lt	SIMONDS	Eric Rolfe	28 July 1937	A&AEE Martlesham Heath
G/Capt	SPENDLOVE DSO twice mid	William Vernon Lewis	22 June 1943	Station Commander Methwold

FLYING ACCIDENTS

Monday 11 April 1927
Avro 504K F9721 *Not known*
T/o Cranwell and became lost; forced-landed, not doubt to ascertain his location. Taking off, he stalled and crashed, possibly damaging the trainer beyond repair.

Friday 13 May 1927
Bristol F.2J F4940 F/Cdt A C Bentley +
T/o Cranwell tasked for a cross country exercise. Approaching RAF Henlow and whilst downwind of the landing area Flight Cadet Alfred Cyril stalled and dived into the ground. His death, along with the names of other service pilots killed, appeared the next day in *The Times*: *"The Air Ministry announces that as the result of an air accident at Henlow Aerodrome, Bedfordshire, to a Bristol fighter of the RAF College, Cranwell, yesterday, Flight-Cadet Alfred Cyril Bentley, the pilot and sole occupant of the aircraft, was killed.*
"Flight-Cadet Bentley was about to land at Henlow when the machine crashed in a field adjoining the aerodrome, near the spot where five Henlow station men were killed recently. The cause of the crash is unknown at present."

Wednesday 30 November 1927
Avro 504N J8576 Struck, while parked, by DH.9A DC J8476 which at the time was taking off. The Avro was deemed beyond repair, but not so the DH which by January 1931 was reported to be with the Communications Flight at Hinaidi.

Appendix E - Roll of Honour

ROYAL AIR FORCE

F/Sgt	ALDERTON	Albert George	19 April 1927	9 Squadron
F/O	ANDERSON	Ian Andrew	25 July 1927	17 Squadron
AC1	BACON	Harold Kauntze	22 July 1927	47 Squadron
F/O	COCKS	John James Crofts	26 May 1927	60 Squadron
Sgt	COLE	Arthur Alfred	19 November 1927	84 Squadron
LAC	CONLON	Patrick	19 November 1927	84 Squadron
AC2	DANIELS	Everett	19 April 1927	9 Squadron
P/O	DOWDESWELL	John Frederick	19 April 1927	9 Squadron
P/O	EVANS	Sidney Arthur Vernon	4 February 1927	56 Squadron
W/Cdr	GASKELL DSC	Arthur Bruce	15 September 1927	30 Squadron
LAC	HART	Alfred Claudius	24 June 1927	31 Squadron
P/O	HOLDEN	Arthur Leslie	16 May 1927	32 Squadron
P/O	KELLY	Harold Cyprian	26 August 1927	3 Squadron
Sgt	KELLY	James	24 September 1927	111 Squadron
F/O	KELLY	William James	19 April 1927	9 Squadron
LAC	KITTOW-ROBERTS	William Ronald	15 September 1927	30 Squadron
AC2	LACY	Arthur Henry	3 December 1927	12 Squadron
P/O	LEWIS	Gomer Flower	2 February 1927	3 Squadron
LAC	MEADEN	William James	12 March 1927	60 Squadron
F/Lt	MEGGITT MC	William Geoffrey	28 January 1927	41 Squadron
P/O	PACE	Richard Griffith	20 July 1927	32 Squadron
Sgt	PENNICOTT	Frederick Thomas	5 July 1927	17 Squadron
LAC	PICKERING	John William	18 March 1927	11 Squadron
P/O	PRIESTMAN	Frederick	18 March 1927	11 Squadron
F/Lt	RIGG	Robert Owen	12 March 1927	60 Squadron
AC1	ROGERS	Leslie	18 July 1927	13 Squadron
LAC	ROWSTON	Jack	26 May 1927	60 Squadron

See Appendix C for 1923, and officers granted a short service commission on 30th March 1923, and the entry for Flying Officer John James Crofts Cox. Leading Aircraftman Rowston's service number 349739 indicates joining from civilian employment between September 1919 and June 1925.

LAC	SEXTON	Patrick John	12 March 1927	60 Squadron
P/O	SHORTER	William Horace	18 July 1927	13 Squadron
F/O	SLACKE	Randal Earl	24 June 1927	31 Squadron
F/Sgt	SMITH	Gilbert	26 August 1927	45 Squadron
LAC	VINCENT	Stanley Noel	1 August 1927	13 Squadron
F/O	WHELAN	Robert Darley	3 December 1927	12 Squadron

RESERVE OF AIR FORCE OFFICERS

F/O	HOWARD and Imperial Airways	Robert Douglas Vernon	25 May 1927	14 Squadron

ARMY

F/O Royal Scots	BOON	Alexander Goodison	1 August 1927	13 Squadron

CIVILIAN

Mr.	TURVEY and Imperial Airways	Albert Edward	25 May 1927	14 Squadron

SQUADRON LOSSESS
1928

JANUARY

Monday 9 January 1928
6 Squadron P/O L E R Fisher MC +
Bristol F.2b Lt S G Haserick Injured
T/o Hinaidi laden with mail destined for Mosul and crashed almost immediately. Pilot Officer Lionel Edward Ruggles Fisher was killed outright, his passenger, Lieutenant Sidney Gordon Haserick of the King's Own Yorkshire Light Infantry, attached to the Iraqi Levies, was taken to hospital suffering from head injuries; he died from a fracture of the skull later in the day.

A very detailed biography of Pilot Officer Fisher may be read on the Lancing College website which shows Lionel as being born at Falkland House, Long Melford, Suffolk on 29th January 1897, and was a pupil at Lancing from September 1911 to July 1913, during which time he was in Heads House and was a member of the College's Officer Training Corps. This was an era when hundreds of young public school educated young men looked to the Empire for their future, Lionel emigrating to Canada where in Alberta he set up as a rancher near Calgary. However, within a year of his arrival war was declared and without hesitation he travelled to Halifax in Nova Scotia and enlisted as a private soldier with the 63rd Regiment [Halifax Rifles]. Prior to arriving in England he transferred to the 2nd Canadian Divisional Cycle Company. It would seem, however, that soon after disembarking he left the Canadians and was commissioned to the 3rd/4th Battalion, Hampshire Regiment [I have yet to trace the relevant *Gazette* entry].

His active *Great War* service was spent in Mesopotamia where he transferred to the 1st/4th Battalion, Royal Hampshire Regiment and it was during an attack on Turkish positions at Shumran Bend on the Tigris river on 24th February 1917, that Lionel was slightly wounded by shrapnel which cut his face. Admitted to 21st Field Ambulance for treatment, he rejoined the battalion later in the day. His MC was *Gazetted,* less citation, on 25th August 1917, supplement 30252, page 8855].

Deciding he would like to pursue a career in the army, he applied for a regular commission; granted, he was commissioned to 3rd [King's Own] Hussars. However, another change of heart resulted in his resigning his commission and he returned to his ranch in Canada. But less than six years later his restless spirit found him applying to join the Royal Air Force and on 8th May 1926, he was granted a short service commission [LG 1 June 1926, issue 33168, page 3570].

Friday 27 January 1928
84 Squadron *Not reported*
DH.9A J7797
T/o Shaibah and wrecked whilst landing at Nugrat Salman,*Iraq.

* Nugrat Salman during the years of Saddam Hussein's rule of terror was the site of a desert prison to which thousands of political prisoners were sent, the vast majority never to be seen again.

Monday 30 January 1928
45 Squadron Sgt F E O'Meara Injured See 12 June 1930
DH.9A J8118/2 LAC H E Fisher +
T/o Helwan and reported to have crashed at an undisclosed location. Leading Aircraftman Harold Edwin Fisher began his Royal Air Force service as a boy airman, his service number 361890 coming within the lock 361601 - 370000 which was in use between July 1922 and January 1924.

FEBRUARY

Friday 3 February 1928
55 Squadron *Not reported*
DH.9A F2850/A2 *Not reported*
T/o Hinaidi and encountering a sandstorm forced-landed near Guchan which according to information pertaining to the railway systems of Iraq lies south of Baghdad between Hillah and Diwaniyah. As the DH trundled to a stop the undercarriage dropped into a ditch and moments later the crew found themselves looking at the desert floor.

Wednesday 8 February 1928
43 Squadron P/O P J B Chalmers +
Gamecock I J7919
T/o Tangmere and crashed between the Hampshire village of Emsworth and Stoughton, 6 miles NW of Chichester, Sussex. Weather conditions at the time of the accident are described as misty. Pilot Officer Peter John Basil Chalmers, 20 years of age, was a graduate from the January 1926, entry to the RAF [Cadet] College, Cranwell.

A press report outlining the circumstances of the accident was presented to the readers of *The Observer and West Sussex Recorder* beneath the headline *'Tangmere Pilot's Death - 'Plane's Crash into Hills at Stoughton - Half Open Parachute'*

"Despite the proximity of Tangmere Aerodrome, flying accidents - especially those ending fatally - are very rare in the Chichester district, and therefore the whole neighbourhood was shocked to hear of the terrible fate of the 20-year-old

Tangmere Pilot Officer, Peter John Basil Chambers, of Richmond, who, while flying in thick mist over the hills at Stoughton, near Chichester, on Wednesday morning of last week, crashed and was killed instantly.

"The inquest was held at Liphook Game Farm, Stoughton, on Friday of last week, Mr. J W Loader-Cooper, Coroner for the Chichester District presiding.

"The first witness was Flying Officer C G Lumsden, Officer Commanding "A" Flight 43 Squadron, stationed at Tangmere. Deceased was a pilot officer in witnesses' flight, having come to Tangmere only a fortnight ago from Cranwell, where he received his training. Chalmers went for his first flight - a dual one - at Tangmere on January 28th, but he went for a solo flight the following day, and had since been in the air ten hours by himself, proving a keen and competent officer. He had always flown the same type of machine while at the Aerodrome.

"On February 6th witness put Chalmers down for a flight on the 8th, and he inspected the machine deceased was to use - a Gloucester Gamecock single seater fighter - finding it quite alright except for one rudder control and two skid controls being frayed, but as there were four such controls on the machine, this did not make any difference.

"Chalmers had orders to be back at 10.45a.m., but as he did not return witness reported the fact to the Commanding Officer, and at 12 they received a telephone message about the accident.

"By the Coroner: Can you give any explanation as to how the accident was caused?

"Witness: I think probably he was a little over confident, went too far and lost his way. Possibly, when he got out of the clouds he got too low and stalled.

"Witness, continuing, said when he visited the scene of the accident a portion of the propellor and the engine were in the ground, and the machine was completely smashed.

"Dr. Ralph Martin Soames, of Emsworth, said that when he arrived on the scene he found Chalmers was dead, his injuries including a fracture of the base of the skull.

"Evidence as to the examination of the machine in the usual way on the Monday before the accident, was given by First-class Aircraftsman William Malcolm Adam and second-class Aircraftsman Frederick Nettlefold, both of 43 Squadron, based at Tangmere.

"Percy Hounsome, a gamekeeper, in the employ of Mr. H S Horne, of East Marden, said that he was working on the Downs, at Stoughton at about 11.5 a.m. on Wednesday, when he saw an aeroplane coming from a northerly direction, flying low, but seemed all right. It went to the top of the hill south of witness, disappeared, and the came back, falling out of witnesses' sight into a valley.

"Witness ran to the spot, which was about 300 yards away and found the pilot lying almost out of the machine, face downwards. The 'plane had nosedived into the ground and turned over close to a thick hedge. The pilot had a half-opened parachute on his back. Witness turned him over and pulled him out of his seat. There was a little blood coming from his earsand his face was much bruised, witness concluded that he was dead.

"By the Coroner: What were the weather conditions like that morning?

"Witness: There was a very thick atmosphere, with a thick mist over the hills.

"Robert A Frances, a gamekeeper employed at Liphook Game Farm, said he saw the 'plane falling out of the mist, and it was turning as it did so. He did not hear the engine. Witness was a quarter of a mile away, but he ran to the spot, and later went to the Farm and telephoned for a doctor.

"P.C. Morris also gave evidence.

"A verdict of "Accidental Death" was returned, the Coroner expressing his sympathy with the relatives and friends of deceased."

Tuesday 14 February 1928
27 Squadron F/Lt S Graham Safe
DH.9A E828
T/o Risalpur and while circling Miramshah at 100 feet lost control and crashed heavily.

Friday 17 February 1928
25 Squadron P/O E J Watson Injured
Grebe II J7372
T/o Hawkinge having been briefed to practice dogfighting with Flying Officer Leonard Arthur Walsh and it was in the vicinity of Chapel-le-Ferne*on the Kent cliffs ENE of Folkestone that a collision occurred at around 1424, when the two fighters were flying at between 2,000 and 1,000 feet. Both machines were abandoned and left to crash near Cauldham Farm.

Pilot Officer Eric James Watson arrived at the RAF [Cadet] College, Cranwell in January 1925, graduating on 30th July 1927 [LG 30 August 1927, issue 33307, page 5608] and reported to 25 Squadron soon after. A pupil at Lancing College, his biography is reported on the College website which shows he was born in Siam on the 7th of November 1906, his father, C L Watson, being a Legal Advisor to the Civil Court at the Ministry of Justice, Siam.

Eric joined Sandersons House at the College in September 1920, remaining until December 1923. His tragic death is best described in the summary concerning Flying Officer Walsh.

* Chapel-le-Ferne is close to the present day Memorial commemorating those who lost their lives in the *Battle of Britain.*

25 Squadron F/O L A Walsh Safe
Grebe II J7392
T/o Hawkinge and lost in the manner described above, Flying Officer Leonard Arthur Walsh escaping by parachute, opening his 'chute immediately and he drifted for nearly half a mile before his decent was arrested by telegraph wires from where he was helped to the ground by some labourers who happened to be working nearby. Badly shocked, he was taken to the Royal Oak public house [where, I suspect, a medicinal tot of alcohol helped to restore his equilibrium].

At the inquest held at RAF Hawkinge on the following Monday, Flying Officer Walsh stated: *"On Friday afternoon I told Pilot Officer Watson to do individual combat with me. I was his senior. We both went up and practised getting into position. When we were just over 2,000 ft up he attacked me three times. After that he broke away, and I saw him about a mile away from me. To enable him to catch me I throttled my engine back to 1,000 revolutions and flew straight and level towards Dover. The next thing, I looked round and saw a pair of planes in a vertical bank turning into me on the starboard side. Then I felt the impact and my machine went out of control. My wings were not damaged but the tail of my plane was cut off. When I realised the positionI did my best to get out of the seat in my machine. I succeeded. When I got out of the machine I counted eight and then pulled my ripcord. My parachute immediately opened and acted well. Owing to the strong north wind I was blown towards the sea. By "spilling" air, however, I managed to come down on some telegraph wires some 20 yards from the edge of the cliff on the main Dover - Folkestone road. A civilian helped me down to the road."* A verdict of misadventure was returned.

Pilot Officer Watson was still alive when found alongside his partially open parachute and was rushed to Shorncliffe Hospital where he died within an hour of being admitted; his funeral was held on Wednesday, 22nd February 1928.

I strongly suspect the collision undermined his confidence in flying for Flying Officer Walsh, who had been granted a short service commission on 3rd February 1925 [issue 33017, page 782], resigned his commission on 16th May 1928 [LG 15 May 1928, issue 33384, page 3427].

Both aircraft were from the second production batch of forty-six airframes with J7272 first being issued to Duxford where it was taken in hand by 19 Squadron. It arrived at Hawkinge for 25 Squadron circa September 1927.

25 Squadron F/O L E Maynard Safe
Grebe II J7412
T/o Hawkinge and abandoned after colliding in the air with an unidentified aircraft. Flying Officer Leslie Edward Maynard was *Gazetted* with a short service commission on 19th September 1922, issue 32748, page 6715. He went on to fulfil his terms of engagement, relinquishing his commission on 2nd September 1931.

On 17th November 1924, this aircraft had clipped the roof of a house near Hawkinge after its pilot misjudging recovery from a dive while engaged in camera gun training.

Monday 20 February 1928
55 Squadron F/O R B H Jackson + See 29 June 1924 - 32 Squadron
DH.9A
T/o Hinaidi for operations against Wahabi rebels operating near Busaiyah and running into accurate ground fire the DH was shot down and the unnamed observer/air gunner captured, though an entry on the RAF Commands website indicates the aircraft was operating with Flying Officer Rolf Booth Hilton Jackson as the sole occupant.

Whatever the case, Flying Officer Jackson, Tonbridge educated, was one of fifteen flight cadets that reported in February 1922, to the RAF [Cadet] College at Cranwell where he was placed with A Squadron. The Edinburgh edition of the *Gazette* in its issue of March 19th, 1929, page 298, carried the following announcement from the Air Ministry: *"The names of the under- mentioned have been brought to notice by Air Vice-Marshal Sir Edward L Ellington KCB CMG CBE, Air Officer Commanding British Forces in Iraq, for distinguished services rendered in connection with the operations against the Akhwan in the Southern Desert, Iraq, during the period November 1927 - May 1928."* Then follows the names of ten officers, with the annotation 'killed' appended to Flying Officer Jackson's name, and four non-commissioned officers.

Wednesday 22 February 1928
12 Squadron *Not reported*
Fox I J8426
T/o Andover and may have been damaged beyond economical repair following a forced-landing at *Old Chalford* [sic] near Reading, Berkshire, with a fractured oil pipe. This Fox had been on squadron charge since 17th October 1927.

MARCH

Thursday 1 March 1928
29 Squadron Sgt H Trickett +
Grebe II J7293
T/o Duxford and reported to have come down in a nearby field after failing to recover from a stall as it approached to land. Sergeant Herbert Trickett's service number is quoted as 256240 which comes within the block 244711 - 260000 indicating RNAS service prior to April 1918. As Herbert was only 24 years of age when he was killed, this suggests his service may have started as a boy sailor. The Grebe in which he was killed was the eleventh aircraft in the first production batch of twelve machines.

"A verdict of accidental death was returned at an inquest at Duxford aerodrome on Friday evening on Pilot-Sergeant Herbert Trickett, aged 25, of No. 29 Squadron, Royal Air Force, who was killed through a machine, of which he was the sole occupant, crashing on Thursday.

"The deceased had been engaged flying in formation, and the crash is believed to be due to loss of flying speed when landing.

"Flying-Officer Hale-Monro, who was in the lead of the formation said the flight was broken up to land, He was bringing three 'planes, and seeing an obstruction on the aerodrome signalled the other two to land separately. The deceased turned away.

"When the witness landed he saw the deceased's machine doing a vertical dive from which it did not recover.

"Sergeant Charles Edwards said the machine was in a left bank above a clump of trees, then seemed to right itself, stalled and dived to earth.

"The pilot was terribly mutilated."

So reported the *Belfast Telegraph* in its Saturday, March 3rd, 1928, edition. On the same page, and in its advertising for forthcoming pictures, The Classic was promising its patrons all the romance, beauty and thrills of two new film stars, Janet Gaynor and Charles Farrell in *"7th Heaven"* a plot outline being available on *Wikipedia.*

Friday 2 March 1928

207 Squadron	Sgt W B Maltman	+
Fairey IIIF S1168	LAC S C Mason	+
	AC1 W G Lowman	+

T/o Eastchurch in the company of Flying Officer Lionel H Weedon to practice formation flying and while banking steeply near the Isle of Grain it dived out of control and crashed. As recorded by John Hamlin in his history of the squadron, '207' was the first UK based squadron to equip with the Fairey IIIF, two being received from the Home Aircraft Depot at Henlow the previous December, though Sergeant William Bean Maltman's machine probably came from the Fleet Air Arm store at Gosport.

This was the first occasion where a squadron aircraft was the subject of a fatal crash that it was crewed by three non-commissioned officers, all of whom had begun their service as boy airmen. Sergeant Maltman's service number 327050 places him as joining between December 1918 and March 1919, while Leading Aircraftman Sydney Cresswell Mason and Aircraftman William George Lowman started their service between July 1922 and January 1924, their numbers being 363670 and 361877 respectively.

The crash was witnessed by dockyard workers at nearby Sheerness who were of the opinion that the aircraft spun through around fifteen revolutions before coming down on the beach near the sea wall. At the inquest into their deaths, the Station Medical Officer said Sergeant Maltman was found hanging over the side of his cockpit with his parachute partially opened and his death, and those of his crew, must have been instantaneous.

Included in the myriad of headlines published in Saturday's edition of *The Western Morning News and Mercury* was reference to the crash 24-hours previously:

'Three Killed in 'Plane Crash'
'Machine Falls Like a Dead Leaf'

[From our own correspondent, Sheerness, Friday]

"Fifteen minutes after leaving Eastchurch Aerodrome, Kent, to-day, a large Fairey 3F bombing aeroplane crashed on the beach at the Isle of Grain in the Thames estuary, and the three occupants were killed. They were:-

Sergt. William Bean Maltman, the pilot,
Leading Aircraftsman Sidney Cresswell Mason,
Aircraftsman William George Lowman

"Three eye-witnesses gave the graphic stories of the crash to-night. Two of them, Jack Smith and Charles Barber, were at work on the sea wall when the machine fell 300 yards away.

"Mr. Smith, who lives at 10 Beatty-cottages, Stoke, Kent, Said:- "We heard the aeroplane before we saw it. It was a very hazy morning, and suddenly the machine seemed to shoot out of nowhere. My mate suggested they were doing stunts, but I said, "No. It is in a spin and can't get out," and true enough it was.

"A moment later they hit the ground with a fearful crash. When Barber and I reached them we noticed the sergeant hanging out of the cockpit. He was dead. Lowman, his name I saw on his glove, was bleeding and could not speak, and before we could get him out of the machine he was dead. The other man also died immediately.

"Mr. Barber said, "To get the bodies out of the wreckage we had to tear away the cordage and frame of the machine before we could move them. The engine did not stop running until it hit the ground, but obviously the machine was out of control. The sergeant had evidently tried to get out as the machine fell, as he had got his parachute out, the cord of which was tangled about him. The other two apparently had not tried to use their parachutes."

'Dipped and Wavered'

"Mr. S Wright, who lives at Grain, told me that about ten minutes past eleven this morning he saw an aeroplane about 2,000ft up, travelling from the direction of Eastchurch to London. Suddenly, something seemed to go wrong. The aeroplane dipped and wavered, and then started to fall, spinning like a dead leaf. "I ran towards the sea, and found the machine had crashed on the beach, about a quarter of a mile south of Grain, and 50 yards from the sea wall. The plane, which was a large one, was a mass of wreckage.

"To-night the aeroplane was still lying within a few feet of the sea wall, with the engine embedded in the ground. It was a complete wreck. The accident was seen from Grain Fort half a mile away, and the news was telephoned to the aerodrome. The other machines of the squadron were sent out, and they circled over the wreckage, but on receiving a

signal from the ground that the occupants were dead, returned to the aerodrome. The bodies were removed from Grain to Eastchurch Aerodrome.

"Today's accident brings the number of RAF crashes this year to nine, involving eleven deaths."

Note. On the same page announcing the crash at Grain, the paper also reported from Rome on the forthcoming 1928 challenge for The Schneider Trophy, headlining ;*Speeds of 350 Miles an Hour Expected in Next Race'* while from home an Air Ministry release headed *'New RAF Scheme - Early Promotion for the Ambitious Officers'* the article outlining the various specialist disciplines that will attract early promotion for junior officers pursuing skills in engineering, navigation and languages.

Tuesday 13 March 1928
84 Squadron *Not reported*
DH.9A J7882
T/o Shaibah and on arrival at Nugrat Salman flew into a ridge, smashing the undercarriage and damaging the airframe beyond repair.

Wednesday 14 March 1928
2 Squadron F/O H J J Mumford- +
Bristol F.2b J7666 Mathews
Lt D F C Scott +
T/o Manston and destroyed following a midair collision with a Virginia J8239 belonging to 9 Squadron, which appears to have landed safely. Flying Officer Horace James Joseph Mumford-Mathews was granted a short service commission on 28th November 1925 [LG 1 December 1925, issue 33110, page 7955].

A partial report on the inquest into the deaths of the two airmen were published in the *Belfast Telegraph* on the following Saturday, immediately below a long report of the disappearance of Captain Walter Hinchcliffe and the Honourable Elsie Mackay, both of whom were preparing to set off from Cranwell on a crossing of the North Atlantic in a single-engined Stinson Detroiter, the outcome of which ended with both aviators disappearing without trace. Lady Mackay had recently converted to the Catholic faith and prior to departure attended Grantham's Roman Catholic Church, dressed in her flying clothing, and took Holy Communion - an event described by the priest, Father Arensen, as most moving and with great piety.

The article on the inquest read: *"An inquest was opened at Manston on Friday on Flying-Officer Horace James Joseph Mumford-Mathews, RAF, and Lieutenant David Francis Cumin Scott, of the 1st Battalion Essex Regiment, attached to the Army Co-operation Squadron for instruction, who were killed in the flying accident at Manston on Wednesday. Mr. Rutley Mowll, the coroner for East Kent, conducted the inquest with a jury.*

"It was stated that Flying-Officer Mumford-Mathews had been flying for three years. He left the flying training school with a certificate above the average. He was accustomed to the type of machine he was flying when he was killed - a Bristol fighter.

"The Coroner said it might be necessary to adjourn the inquest owing to the absence on important business for the RAF of the pilot who landed safely.

"Evidence was given that Flying-Officer Mumford-Mathews was 22 years of age. Lieut. Scott was 27 years old, and was on a course of a week's flying instruction at the time of the accident. He was flying as a passenger.

"An RAF officer said he was watching the manoeuvres of five Vickers Virginia machines of the bombing squadron. The Bristol Fighter was near the bombers, and apparently the pilot was going to execute a stall turn. He got about halfway through the turn when he hit a wing of the bomber under which he was flying. The Bristol Fighter went above the Virginia, turned over, and dropped down behind some buildings. The accident might have been due to mis-calculation of the distance between the machines, or by the disturbance of air by the heavier machine.

"Flying-Officer Love said that the pilot of the Vickers Virginia shut off his engine and glided straight on. He appeared to have the machine under control, and made a safe landing, although the machine was damaged. Flight-Lieutenant [sic] *Love though that the pilot of the Bristol Fighter might have gone near the formation to show the Army officer the formation.*

"The Coroner - "Is it up to anyone to join the formation?"

"Flight-Lieutenant Love - "No, not usual."

"Army officers who came down for a week's course were so keen on flying that it was very difficult to keep them on the ground. They even sought permission to go up at night. The observer in this machine might have asked his pilot to join the formation. Medical evidence was given that the cause of death in each case was fracture of the skull.

"The inquest was adjourned until Friday."

Tuesday 27 March 1928
2 Squadron *Not reported*
Bristol F.2J F4836
T/o Manston and wrecked at Stamford, Lincolnshire. This particular Bristol had accompanied the squadron on its Shanghai deployment. Although I have shown the departure airfield as Manston it may be the case that the squadron was exercising in the Stamford area.

2 Squadron *Not reported*
Bristol F.2b J6775
T/o Manston and in inclement weather dived from 1,000 feet and crashed neard Woldingham, 2 miles ENE from Caterham, Surrey. First reported during May 1924, when it was on the strength of the RAF Staff College Flight Andover, J6775 travelled as far as Shanghai during 2 Squadron's detachment to the Far East in the spring and summer of 1927.

Wednesday 28 March 1928
14 Squadron F/Lt G McCormack +
DH.9A LAC J Kimberley +
T/o Amman and crashed in the vicinity of the airfield. Flight Lieutenant George McCormack, formerly of the 10th Battalion, Royal Irish Rifles, was born on 11th February 1896, and was accepted ass a probationary observer circa August 1917, only to be 'wounded' within a few days of starting his training.

Recovered, he was formally accepted in the RFC on 11th February 1918, and on the last day of August 1918, he joined 22 Squadron [Bristol F.2b] at Maisoncelle. On 24th September, as allied ground forces commenced preparing for an assault on the Hindenburg Line, air operations over the front intensified [see my second volume and pages 244 to 247 for squadron casualties for this day] and in one of the many encounters with enemy scouts Captain George McCormack was wounded [the identity of his Bristol is not known] and taken to 13 Casualty Clearing Station for attention to gun shot wounds to his arms and legs.

Leading Aircraftman James Kimberley joined between September 1919 and January 1925, from civilian occupation and was attested as 349781.

APRIL

Monday 2 April 1928
2 Squadron F/O J Hadden +
Bristol F.2b J7651 AC1 G H Towers +
T/o Manston and while flying at low-altitude near Old Heath on the SSE fringes of Colchester, collided with a tree and crashed out of control. Flying Officer Jack Hadden, a Lieutenant in the Black Watch, was granted a temporary commission in the rank of flying officer, attached for flying duties for a term of four years, as *Gazetted* 28 July 1925, issue 33070, page 5051.

Aircraftman George Henry Towers enlisted in June 1925, his service number 370079 being in a relatively small block of numbers issued between June and September 1925, 370001 - 370986:

'Air Crash Near a Town'
'Comment by the Jury'

"At the inquest at Colchester last night on Flying Officer Jack Hadden and Aircraftsman George Henry Towers, who were killed when their machine crashed just outside Colchester on Monday, it was stated that in swooping to attack troops engaged in manoeuvres the 'plane hit a tree and nose-dived.

"A jury asked Captain H P Sparkes, a witness, if it was necessary to carry out operations so near the town. Captain Sparkes replied that the attack was not intended to be anywhere near the town.

"Another officer thought Hadden started to attack five minutes too soon, and stated that Towers volunteered to go up in the 'plane vico [sic] *another man, who was wanted elsewhere.*

"Returning a verdict of "Accidental death," the jury advocated representation to the military authorities to prevent aircraft manoeuvring so low near the town."

So read the report in *The Scotsman* newspaper, published on Thursday, April 5th, 1928.

30 Squadron F/O J W Wood +
DH.9A J7854 AC1 W Waugh +
T/o Hinaidi and destroyed in a crash near Hillah while attempting to land near an aeroplane that had forced-landed. Making a flat turn at 100 feet, Flying Officer Jack Whitworth Wood lost control and spun to the ground, the two 20-lb bombs that he was carrying exploding as the DH went up in flames.

Born on 25th September 1901, he had been granted a short service commission, published in *The London Gazette* of 4th January 1927, issue 33239, page 289, upon which he was sent out to Egypt for training with No. 4 Flying Training School at Abu Sueir.

Aircraftman William Waugh's service number 358180 identifies him as coming to the air force from civilian life between September 1919 and June 1925.

39 Squadron *Not reported*
DH.9A J8181
T/o Bircham Newton and while flying in the Thetford area of Norfolk lost power. Forced-landing, the DH collided with a tree and was wrecked.

56 Squadron F/O V O Eyre Safe See 27 June 1929
Siskin IIIA
T/o North Weald for an authorised practice flight, the outcome of which is vividly described in Friday's edition of the *Chelmsford Chronicle - Saved by parachute; a pilot of the Royal Air Force, Flying Officer V O Eyre, of 56 [Fighter] Squadron, North Weald, met with an unusual accident on Monday, when he was thrown out of his machine at Little Laver, but with the use of his parachute he came to the ground unhurt.*

"The officer was flying a Siskin single-seater fighter, when, at a height of 2,000ft., a map which he was using slipped from its place into a corner of the cockpit. It was impossible to recover it without undoing the safety straps, and leaning down he must have unconsciously pushed the control stick forward. This action turned the level flight into a dive, which rapidly grew steeper until, before the pilot realised it, the machine was beginning to fly on its back.

'He was flung out of the machine, with the parachute in cushion attached to his body. Luckily, he was able to pull the ring of the parachute release, and he then floated safely to the ground.

"The machine crashed a mile from where the pilot landed and was wrecked."

Thursday 12 April 1928
502 Squadron SR F/O S Davidson Injured
Avro 504N E9352
T/o Aldergrove and crashed, owing to engine failure during aerobatics, onto the roof of a house at Dunmurry near Lisburn. Tragically, Miss Winifred Daphne Fox, aged 8, was struck by the Avro and was killed.

With air accidents given plenty of coverage by newspapers, it is no surprise to find an account of the sad outcome of Flying Officer Stewart Davidson's accident reported in a Somerset paper, namely *The Shepton Mallet Journal.*

"A little girl playing in the main street at Dunmurry, a village five miles from Belfast, was killed Thursday afternoon under dramatic circumstances.

"An aeroplane belonging to the Ulster Bombing Squadron, RAF Reserve, crashed while the pilot, Flying Officer Stewart Davidson, was attempting to make a forced landing. While the seriously injured officer was being lifted from the cockpit it was found that the eight-year-old daughter of Mr. and Mrs. W Fox, was pinned beneath the wreckage.

"She had been struck by the engine as the machine crashed, and killed instantly.

"The plane was completely wrecked. The pilot was removed to hospital in Belfast, where it was found he was suffering from a broken leg and serious head wounds.

*"A verdict of accidental death was returned on Friday afternoon at the inquest. The jury added a rider condemning evolutions by aeroplanes over villages, and Wing Commander Wright,*RAF, commanding the squadron to which the machine belonged, said the Air Ministry would hold an inquiry."*

A similar report appeared in Saturday's edition of *The Portadown News* but is worth copying for the additional information: *"When the inquest was held at Dunmurry on Friday on Winifred Daphne Fox, aged 7* [sic], *Neville Terrace, Dunmurry, who was killed on Thursday when an aeroplane crashed there, the jury returned a verdict that the deceased died from shock and injuries accidentally received through being struck by an aeroplane. They added a rider strongly disapproving of aeroplanes carrying out evolutions over inhabited areas, and calling upon the Air Ministry to take drastic steps to prevent the recurrence of similar action.*

"Wing Commander Wright, who is in command of Aldergrove Aerodrome, stated during the proceedings that an official inquiry would be held into the cause of the accident.

"The main features of the inquest, which was conducted by Dr. Robert Reid JP, the Deputy Coroner, were the narratives of the eye-witnesses and the jury's questions regarding the carrying out of evolutions of aeroplanes over the village."

* See Appendix B 1926.

Monday 21 April 1928
70 Squadron Victoria III JJ8229 Caught fire and burnt out on the ground at Ur, Iraq; please refer to my summary on 7th June 1928, for a description of Ur.

Tuesday 24 April 1928
55 Squadron *Not reported*
DH.9A E865 *Not reported*
T/o Kirkuk and while banking stalled and crashed.

Wednesday 25 April 1928
6 Squadron Bristol F.2b J7647 While in the process of taxying at Hinaidi swung and crashed out of control. Taken on Royal Air Force charge on 16th June 1925, it was first issued to 13 Squadron at Andover before being despatched to Ascot for packing and despatch to Iraq. The date of its acceptance by 6 Squadron is not known. It was deleted from records on 11th May 1928.

During the month Vernon III J7139 belonging to 70 Squadron was destroyed in a heavy storm that swept across Hinaidi.

Also in the month of April, 70 Squadron signalled that Victoria II J7922 forced-landed at Busaiya, Iraq, with a broken con-rod. There are no further entries, leading to a suggestion its location, or damage, may have ended its service life.

MAY

Sunday 6 May 1928
600 Squadron AAF P/O H O Young Injured
DH.9A J7083/7
T/o Hendon for formation flying practice during which Pilot Officer Harold Oswald Young lost control during a formation turn, spun and crashed at Mill Hill, London, the DH being burnt out.

A detailed account of the crash was reported by *The Hendon, Finchley, Edgware and Mill Hill Times and Golders Green Guardian* in their edition of Friday, May 11th, 1928: *"A Hendon RAF pilot had a marvellous escape from instant death when his 'plane crashed in the grounds of St. Joseph's Foreign Missionary College, Mill Hill. But for the bravery of four of the Brother-students, , however, he would have been burned to death when the machine, after burying itself in the ground, burst into flames, and was reduced to scrap iron in a few moments.*

"Pilot Officer H O Young was flying over Mill Hill, when, for some unknown reason, the 'plane got out of control. He just skimmed over St. Joseph's College, missed some trees, and the crashed to earth with a terrific report.

"A German Brother was looking out of his window in the College, when he saw an accident was about to happen. Without a moment's hesitation he dashed through the building, across the fields in his cassock and red girdle.

"The 'plane was in flames, but he saw the pilot lying half out of it, unconscious. He pluckily best through to the scene and tried to pull the officer clear, but the heat was so intense he was driven back. The accident had been witnessed by three other students, however, two Dutch and one Irish, Brothers McGough, Van Vlugt and Vercauteren, who made a combined rush at the man, and succeeded in getting him clear in the nick of time.

"A man and a women, who had been first on the scene, stood by helpless, and shouted constantly, "Oh, Pull him out, pull him out."

"In a few moments a crowd of students and residents were on the spot. Father L Oosterlaan rushed out with first aid and requisites, and had the police, the ambulance and the Hendon Fire Brigade summoned.

"Dr, A H Morley and Dr. E B Morley, happened to be passing along the Ridgeway in a car, saw the inevitable crash, and rushed to the spot.

"Men from the Hendon Aerodrome were rushed up to the scene by car, and played fire extinguishers on the burning wreckage. When the Hendon Brigade arrived, more than a mile of hosepipes were laid across the grounds from Lawrence-street.

"Brother Stoiber said to a representative of this journal the same evening, "I did not look round or mind anyone. I just rushed straight and with the idea of saving the man. But the heat was so intense, although I did pull him a little way. I was driven back by the flames and the fumes. Then some more came, I did not know who they were, except that they were students, and we managed to get him clear:. I saw the accident happening when I was looking out of my window."

"Another priest said he was walking in the grounds talking to a companion when the aeroplane came over. "I was just pointing out ..... to my friend," he went on, "when the aeroplane passed. I looked up and saw smoke from behind the College. I thought a chimney was on fire. Then I thought the College was on fire, and then I thought it might be St. Mary's Abbey School. I never connected it with aeroplane, and I did not hear the report, although it was heard nearly a mile away by a student."

"Father Oosterlaan remarked the pilot was rather a fortunate man, and 'actually' owed his life to the four students. The summer like weather had attracted excursionists to Mill Hill and within an hour of the crash the fields of the College, knee deep in hay earlier in the day, had been worn down in hard tracks by the throng of sight-seers.

"The injured man was conveyed to Hendon Cottage Hospital by an RAF ambulance and was found to be suffering from head wounds and injuries to his legs.

"Pilot Officer Young, when in civilian life is a member of the staff at Lloyds Bank, is attached to No. 600 City of London Bombing Squadron Auxiliary Air Force of which ... the Hon. F E Guest is leader. The machine is officially stated to have fallen from a height of 1,200 feet."

A late footnote, published in the same edition, reported that although not yet off the danger list, his overall condition was very much improved.

The Illustrated London News published on May 12th, 1928, shows a photograph of the burnt out wreck of the DH along with the caption *"A Gallant Rescue By Theological Students At Mill Hill After An Aeroplane Crash : The Four Students Beside The Burnt Wreckage."*The four ran to the scene in the grounds of St. Joseph's Foreign Missionary College and succeeded in pulling Pilot Officer Young clear, thus saving him from a certain death.

In conclusion, AIR 76/566/150 held by TNA Kew records his full name as Harold Oswald Young, born 6th December 1900, and residing at 42 Falconer Road, Bushy, Hertfordshire. There is little doubt that his injuries were severe for Paul McMillan notes that Pilot Officer Young relinquished his commission, owing to ill-health, on 29th October 1930.

Tuesday 8 May 1928
41 Squadron F/O G Bradbury Injured
Siskin IIIA J8402
T/o Sutton Bridge for armament practice over the Holbeach ranges and reported to have crashed on the ranges after failing to recover from a dive. Owing to the isolated spot on the ranges where the accident occurred, Flying Officer Geoffrey Bradley, aged 23, lay beneath wreckage for nearly an hour before help arrived. Critically injured, he died in King's Lynn Hospital on Sunday, 20th May 1928. His short service commission was *Gazetted* on 25th September 1925, issue 33087, page 6205.

His initial flying training was carried out at Shotwick with No. 5 Flying Training School where on Wednesday, 30th June 1926, he very nearly drowned when the Sopwith 7F.1 Snipe which he was piloting crashed in the sea off Rhos-on-Sea, an event that was reported *The Evening News;*

'Flying Thrills'
'Airman Escapes Under the Sea'
'Strapped to Machine'

"A young flying officer of the RAF, named Geoffrey Bradbury, had a thrilling experience and a narrow escape from drowning at Rhos-on-Sea yesterday.

"He was flying a Snipe machine over the bay when something went wrong with the engine and he came down in the sea about a quarter of a mile from shore in view of people on the pier.

""When the machine touched the water," said an eye witness, "it turned a somersault and the sank."

"Bradbury was strapped in his seat and went down with his machine. There were hundreds of people on the promenade, and they held their breath in an agony of suspense until the head of the aviator suddenly appeared above the water and he struck out for land.

"While under the water he had managed to unstrap himself.

"Bradbury was met by a boat half way and taken to a hotel. His foot was slightly hurt, but otherwise he was unharmed."

For an excellent account of how Flying Officer Bradley was fatally injured on the ranges, the authors recommend Alastair Goodrum's excellent book *School of Aces - The RAF Training School That Won The Battle of Britain* published by Amberley in June 2019, and available both in Kindle and Hardcover from Amazon, prices vary.

Friday 11 May 1928

16 Squadron F/O G A Underdown +
Bristol F.2b LAC D M Thomas +

T/o Old Sarum and on return banked too steeply and dived into the ground short of the airfield. Flying Officer Gerald Arthur Underdown's short service commission was *Gazetted* 26th January 1926, issue 33127, page 621.

His observer, Leading Aircraftman Donald Martin Thomas's service number 370390 comes within the block 370001 - 370986 issued to former civilians enlisting between June and September 1925.

This accident, and comments on other crashes, appeared the following day in *The Northern Whig and Belfast Post*

"Flying-Officer Gerald Arthur Underdown, the pilot, and Leading-Aircraftsman Donald Martin Thomas, were killed instantly when their plane, a Bristol Fighter, crashed yesterday at Old Sarum [Wiltshire].

"The machine was engaged in a short practice flight over the aerodrome. It was flying at a height of 300ft when it suddenly dipped and crashed.

"Members of the staff aerodrome rushed to the scene and found the machine wrecked. This makes a tragic total of five British airmen killed and two injured in seven days.

"Corporal Bradford was killed and an officer injured in an accident on Thursday at Invergordon [Northern Scotland] to a Southampton flying boat.

"Two members of the Bristol and Wessex Air Club were killed at Filton Aerodrome, near Bristol, last Sunday, and on the same dayPilot-Officer Young crashed into a field at Mill Hill, and was seriously injured."

Saturday 19 May 1928

39 Squadron Captain Piascolni Safe
DH.9A H3432 Poland

T/o Bircham Newton and reported as *"crashed."*

Monday 21 May 1928

602 Squadron AAF F/O J P Drew +
Avro 504N

T/o Renfrew and while attempting to perform an aerobatic loop near Paisley, lost control and spun in at Gleniffer Braes. Flying Officer James Pearson Drew was, to the best of my knowledge, the squadron's first fatality [and also the first Auxiliary Air Force fatality] since formation on 12th September 1925, as a day bomber squadron, equipping with DH.9A, though at the time of this accident '602' had re-equipped with Fairey Fawn, the first examples having been delivered to Renfrew in September 1927, with the last of the DH.9As being disposed of during January 1928.

Flying Officer Drew, commissioned within 602 Squadron [LG 20 July 1926, issue 33184, page 4802], had been promoted to his rank 48-hours before his death [LG 12 June 1928, issue 33393, page 4023]:

'Scottish Air Crash'

'Paisley Man Killed'

So read the headline in *The Scotsman* which also carried articles on events which ultimately would lead the world in war; Japan's military 'adventures' in Manchuria and closer to home a detailed report on recent elections held in Germany and contested by nine major contestants, plus a host of fringe parties. No names are mentioned but it shows the Nationalists [Herr Hitler] losing ground but still winning the most seats:

"By the crashing of a light aeroplane in a field at Gleniffer Braes, near Paisley, last night, a young Paisley man, James Pearson Drew, was killed.

"The airman had been observed flying for some time during the evening in the vicinity of the Braes and had been seen by many people to be engaged in a graceful flying exhibition. After looping the loop several times, he was observed to get into a tail spin, and suddenly dived to earth. Spectators at a junior football match at Newton Park, Elderslie, and golfers on Elderslie course, who had been watching the flyer, rushed to the spot where the 'plane had come down in a ploughed field.

"From the position of the aeroplane, it would appear that the pilot had almost succeeded in righting his machine, which was almost in a horizontal position, and to all appearances not badly smashed, but with the landing wheels embedded in the soil. One of the first to arrive was a Paisley doctor, who was of the opinion that the pilot was still alive. Efforts were made to remove the unfortunate young man from the 'plane, but to enable this to be done part of the machine had to be smashed away. When he was removed from the cockpit the pilot was found to have sustained a fractured skull and many injuries to his body and legs. He died within a few minutes of being taken from the cockpit.

"Mr. Drew, who was 21 years of age, was a member of the Auxiliary Air Force at Renfrew Aerodrome, and officials from the aerodrome flew over to the spot when the tragedy was reported. Mr. Drew was also a member of the Scottish Flying Club and took his "A" licence some time ago, but did not have his "wings." He was one of the first men in the district to own his own aeroplane. He was an enthusiastic aeronaut, an all round sportsman, and a member of the Lanarkshire and Renfrewshire Hunt. He was associated with the firm of M Drew & Sons [Ltd.], Paisley."

Friday 25 May 1928
603 Squadron AAF P/O C Musgrave Safe
DH.9A J8129
T/o Turnhouse and crashed whilst overshooting, hitting another aircraft, in his attempt to avoid a hangar.

Wednesday 30 May 1928
2 Squadron *Not reported*
Bristol F.2J F4965
T/o Sutton Bridge and wrecked in a landing mishap. This aircraft had accompanied the squadron to Shanghai.

Thursday 31 May 1928
13 Squadron *Not reported*
Atlas I J8793
T/o Sutton Bridge and crashed almost immediately. The squadron was on detachment from Andover.

During the month at Upper Heyford, 99 Squadron wrote off Hyderabad J7744/O in a landing mishap during which the undercarriage collapsed.

JUNE

Tuesday 5 June 1928
3 Squadron F/O P Cranswick MC +
Woodcock II J7728
T/o Upavon briefed to carry out practice attacks with a squadron colleague on an 11 Squadron Horsley and whilst doing so a collision occurred and both machines crashed on Chisenbury Down on the SSE side of the airfield. Flying Officer Philip Cranswick had seen extensive service in the *Great War,* first as a private soldier before being commissioned 2nd Lieutenant to the East Riding [Fortress] Engineers [LG 6 September 1915, supplement 29285, page 8835]. He was *Gazetted* with his award [less citation] on 3rd June 1918, supplement 30716, page 6464. His short service commission was promulgated on 29th January 1924, issue 32902, page 875.

Air-Britain's *J File* notes the two fighters and the Horsley were rehearsing for the forthcoming Hendon pageant.

3 Squadron F/O D J F McMillan +
Woodcock II J8316
T/o Upavon similarly briefed and lost in the manner outlined above. Flying Officer Douglas James Frederick McMillan was *Gazetted* with his short service commission on 25th September 1923, issue 32865, page 6429.

The deaths of the two officers were reported were reported in the *Aberdeen Press and Journal* beneath the headline:

'Jumped Too Late'
'Two Airmen Killed in 'Plane Collision'

"An airman's unsuccessful last minute effort to save himself from death by making a parachute jump from his falling machine was described at the inquest at Upavon Aerodrome yesterday on the two victims of a mid-air collision which took place earlier in the day. They were - Flying Officer Philip Cranswick [36] and Flying Officer Douglas James Frederick McMillan.

"Wing Command William Robert Reed, Officer Commanding RAF Upavon, said he ordered up certain machines for practising formation attack. The two officers were piloting single-seater Woodcock machines.

"In the third phase of the operation, in which four Woodcocks were matched, the machines carried out a dive in pairs, and the pair piloted by Flying Officer Cranswick and McMillan came into contact by the wing tips, about 1,500 feet up. Both machines immediately collapsed.

"The pilots were equipped with regulation parachutes, and McMillan jumped out of his machine when about 500 feet from the ground. This did not give the parachute time to open, and it had just started to open as he touched the ground. The machines fell 300 yards apart. Cranswick was unable to get clear, and fell with his machine.

"The Coroner recorded a verdict of "Accidental death.""

Thursday 7 June 1928
70 Squadron Victoria II J7923 Totally destroyed at Hinaidi in a hangar fire.
70 Squadron Victoria II J7927 Totally destroyed at Hinaidi in a hangar fire.
70 Squadron Victoria III J8226 Totally destroyed in a hangar fire at Hinaidi.
70 Squadron Victoria III J8227 Totally destroyed in a hangar fire at Hinaidi; earlier in the year this aircraft had forced-landed on 5th March 1928, some 45 miles SWW from Ur, described by Wikipedia as the site of an important Sumerian city-state in ancient Mesopotamia. At one time a coastal city, the shifting sands of time now finds the site well inland and on the south bank of the Euphrates river, 16km from Nasiriyah in modern-day Iraq.

Friday 8 June 1928

6 Squadron Sgt A J Garner +
Bristol F.2b Sgt W F Futcher +
T/o Mosul and crashed from an unrecovered spin near the airfield. The crew were aged 23 and 26 respectively. It is known that Sergeant Alexander Joseph Garner began his service as a boy entrant and the same may be the case for his companion Sergeant William Frank Futcher for both have service numbers that relate to such status - 335654 and 158714, the later indicating service in the *Great War* and coming within the block 155001 - 160000 which was issued between October 1917 and December 1918, encompassing Royal Flying Corps, Royal Air Force and boy servicemen.

Tuesday 12 June 1928

84 Squadron Sgt F G Bamford +
DH.9A LAC A S Frost +
T/o Shaibah where it spun in off a low turn. The second all non-commissioned officer crew to lose their lives in less than a week Sergeant Francis George Bamford's service number was 359131 while Leading Aircraftman Arthur Sidney Frost attested as 359418, both joining from civilian occupation.

Saturday 16 June 1928

602 Squadron AAF *Not reported*
Fawn II J7188
T/o Renfrew where it was written off in unexplained circumstances. A remarkably fine movements record has survived for this Fawn: first flown 20th February 1924; delivered to HAD Henlow and thence to RAE Farnborough on 11th August 1924. Returned to HAD Henlow and issued on 8th May 1925, to 100 Squadron; HAD Henlow between May and July 1926, and returned during July to 100 Squadron. Returned to HAD Henlow, noted here during April and May 1928, and then to 602 Squadron AAF either in May or early June.

Wednesday 26 June 1928

14 Squadron P/O J H L Maund +
DH.9A AC1 J J H Middleton +
T/o Amman and destroyed in the general area of the aerodrome. John Henry Lorraine Maund was eighteen months into his short service commission which was *Gazetted* on 4th January 1927, issue 33239, page 289, while his observer Aircraftman Jack James Heatherstone Middleton had enlisted as a boy airman between July 1922 and January 1924, his service number being 363194.

JULY

Sunday 1 July 1928

23 Squadron F/Lt H C Calvey + Henlow [St. Mary's] Churchyard
Avro 504N H2534 F/Sgt W C Hollier +
T/o Kenley to transit to Sutton Bridge where the squadron had been detached for armament practice and *en route* crashed at Clifton, a mile or so NW of RAF Henlow. A report of the accident was carried by *The Bedfordshire Time and Independent* in their edition of Friday, 6th July, 1928, and reproduced on the Kenley Revival website, which the authors are pleased to acknowledge: *"The fatal accident at Clifton on Sunday evening caused deep concern in the village, for the pilot, Flight-Lieutenant H C Calvey, was very well known there and at Henlow Camp. Before being transferred to Kenley about 18 months ago he was stationed at Henlow and lived at Clifton Lodge, a residential hotel only a short distance from where he met his death. He had paid frequent visits here since his departure, and would announce his arrival to brother-officers at the hotel by circling three times overhead, sometimes flying upside-down, and doing other "stunts" before going off to land at Henlow, where his companions would meet him. It is thought that Flight-Lieutenant Calvey was about to follow his usual practice when the accident happened, but as Clifton is on the direct line from London to Sutton Bridge, where he was proceeding for ground firing practice, it may be merely coincidence that the accident occurred at this spot. At all events, the cause of the disaster remains a matter of conjecture. All that is known is that the machine was seen flying at about 1,000 feet and approaching the lodge from over the church when without warning it went into a spiral nose-dive and crashed to the ground. It fell near a corner of Church Close, an open hay field, and the crash was heard several miles away. When the first people from the village reached the spot they found the dead bodies of the pilot and his passenger, Flight-Sergeant W C Hollier, in the middle of the wreckage. The Henlow Aerodrome fire brigade and an ambulance were sent for, and P.C. Jackson, assisted by members of the RAF and other helpers, extracted the bodies. The machine was an Avro-Lynx two-seater.*

"Mr F Humphreys, the proprietor of Clifton Lodge Hotel, told our representative on Sunday night that he was in the house when about 6.45, he heard a terrific noise. "I ran out with several officers who were staying at the house," he said, "and I saw the smashed aeroplane just across the field. At first it was impossible to recognise the occupants, so badly were they injured, and when it was discovered that one of them was Lieut. Calvey we had an awful shock, as he often stayed with us and was a personal friend. Mrs Humphreys stated that all he husband and two officers were able to do was to send for the ambulance and assist in removing the bodies.

"The accident was actually seen by Mr G W Secker, who said that the machine fell at something over a hundred miles an hour with the engines [sic] *still running apparently full out until it hit the ground. There was nothing to indicate that anything was wrong until the nose-dive began. Another witness, Mrs Rodwell, who saw the smash from her house about 400 yards away, said that as the machine fell one of the airmen appeared to be waving. She added, "The whole village will mourn for Lieut. Calvey, for everyone here knew him, and there has never been a more popular officer in the*

village. It is like losing one of our community, and his death happening at a spot that was so familiar to him makes this tragedy seem all the worse."

"People in the church heard the roar of the Avro's engine during the reading of the Lesson, but no one seems to have attached any undue importance to the noise of the crash that happened a few minutes later, and the service proceeded without interruption. However, the Rector's wife, Mrs La Porte Payne, who was not at the service, called Mr C Revitt, the pay reader, from the church and informed him of the occurrence and the Rector later announced the sad news to the congregation and offered special prayers on behalf of the bereaved relatives.

"Flight-Lieutenant Calvey was about 30 years of age, and leaves a widow and a little boy aged four. On Saturday he took part in the Air Pageant at Hendon, afterwards dining with friends in London. Flight-Sergeant Hollier was also married."

Other contributions are reported on the website, including a contribution from Georgina Calvey sent on 23rd February 2021, which corrects the age of flight lieutenant's son, who, subsequently became a wing commander*serving as a test pilot and assisted in setting up the Air Wing of the Abu Dhabi Defence Force.

A veteran of the *Great War,* Flight Sergeant William Charles Hollier commenced his service with the Royal Flying Corps in 1915.

Additional to that reported on the Kenley Revival website, *The Biggleswade Chronicle and Bedfordshire Gazette* carried a very detailed account of the tragedy along with a photograph showing the smashed remains of the Avro. Unfortunately, the quality of the image makes it unsuitable for reproduction.

* John Michael Calvey commissioned from Sergeant rank on 20th July 1944 [LG 19 September 1944, supplement 36705, page 4314], who retired from the service at his own request on 31st January 1970, retaining the rank of wing commander [LG 16 June 1970, supplement 45126, page 6670].

Tuesday 3 July 1928

31 Squadron F/O C R McEvoy +
Bristol F.2b Australia
LAC J L Mason +

T/o Quetta and crashed, possibly in the general area of Quetta aerodrome. Flying Officer Clarence Reginald McEvoy was granted a short service commission on 25th September 1925, *Gazetted* in issue 33087, page 6205. Clarence had served as a private soldier in the *Great War* with the 13th Light Horse Regiment. The Australian War Memorial website, which the authors dutifully acknowledge, shows he embarked aboard HMAT *Borda A30* at Melbourne on 20th October 1916, as part of the 12th Reinforcement heading for Europe. His civilian occupation, shown on the Reinforcement Roll, was 'Public Servant' with his father, John McEvoy, recorded as his next of kin at Strangeway P.O. via Newstead, Victoria. For a brief outline of the history of the 13th Light Horse Regiment, please refer to *Wikipedia.*

Leading Aircraftman James Leslie Mason, 363249, began his military service as a boy entrant twixt July 1922 and January 1924.

Wednesday 4 July 1928

6 Squadron F/O A B Kay +
Bristol F.2b LAC A H Bolton Injured

T/o Mosul and following a collision with telegraph wires plunged into the Tigris near Mosul. Flying Officer Alexander Bruce Kay entered the Cadet College at Cranwell in September 1922, having being educated at Imperial Service College. Leading Aircraftman Alfred Henry Bolton was rescued in an injured state, but is thought to have recovered.

Saturday 7 July 1928

603 Squadron AAF P/O J T L Shiells +
Avro 504N

T/o Turnhouse and dived into the ground at Sighthill Farm at Hermiston on the WSW fringes of Edinburgh. Pilot Officer John Temple Lyall Shiells received a commission in the Auxiliary Air Force on 22nd July 1927, on being accepted by No. 601 City of Edinburgh [Bombing] Squadron. Similar to 602 Squadron AAF [see my summary for 21 May 1928], '603' received DH.9As along with Avro 504s for training, when it formed at Turnhouse on 14th October 1925. The death of Pilot Officer Shiells marked the squadron's first fatality.

The following account was presented to the readers of *The Scotsman* in their Monday edition, headlined:

'Air Accident'
'Crash Near Edinburgh'
'Turnhouse Pilot Killed'

"A fatal aeroplane accident occurred on Saturday afternoon on the outskirts of Edinburgh, a Royal Air Force aeroplane crashing into a field at Saughton, and the pilot-officer, Mr. J T L Shiells, son of Mr. Shiells, C A, of Messrs. Scott-Moncrieff, Thomson, & Shiells, 17 Melville Street, being killed.

"Tuurnhouse is an important east coast base, and seaplanes from the centre are seen over Edinburgh daily. The accident mars a long record of flying without mishap, which has been a considerable factor in creating an impression amongst the public of the safety of flying under modern conditions.

"So far as is known, the accident was witnessed only by two persons - a woman who was walking near the point at which the aeroplane came down, and a boy, twelve years of age, James Drummond, Broomhouse Cottage, who was about a quarter of a mile away. The woman states that she saw two aeroplanes, one of which was flying at a very low altitude. She noticed that the engine of the latter suddenly ceased, and she saw the aeroplane nose-diving into a field at

Sighthill Farm, Hermiston. The point at which the aeroplane crashed is about a quarter of a mile off the main road from Edinburgh to Mid-Calder, a little beyond Old Saughton, and to the south of Cordorphne. The machine was a two-seater Avro Lynx; but Mr. Shiells was the only occupant. The boy, James Drummond, was about a quarter of a mile away. He states that he saw the aeroplane go down after it had circled about as if something had gone wrong. It reached the earth with an alarming crash. Intimation of the accident was telephoned to Turnhouse by a signaller.

"Mr. Shiells was one of the pilots of the 603rd City of Edinburgh Bombing Squadron, who, with half a dozen machines left Turnhouse on Saturday in order to carry out practice flights. Mr. Shiells was the last to go up. Some of the other aeroplanes went off in couples. Mr. Shiells took his own course, flying north, and then turning west, and thereafter heading south. He had been up only about a quarter of an hour when the accident took place. It is, of course, impossible to state what was the cause, although the circumstances point to engine trouble.

"A friend of Mr. Shiells who had come out from Edinburgh saw him start, and conversed with him previous to the flight. Mr. Shiells conducted him round the aerodrome, and arranged that his friend should wait on and motor him into Edinburgh after the flight.

"The wings of the machine crumpled up with the force of the landing, and the cockpit had turned completely over, the pilot's seat being only a matter of a foot from the ground. The 'plane was virtually flattened to the ground, the only part of the machine visible in the long grass from a distance being the exhaust pipe, which stuck out of the ground for about four feet. The engine was buried nearly two feet in the ground, and control wires were strewn all about.

"On information as to the accident having occurred being received at Turnhouse an ambulance was sent from the aerodrome and the body of the pilot-officer was removed to Edinburgh.

"The deceased pilot was 26 years of age, and was regarded as a thoroughly experienced and skilful airman. He was a member of the same firm as his father, and was popular amongst a wide circle of friends. One of his interests was fencing, and he took part in recent competitions in Edinburgh."

Sunday 8 July 1928

17 Squadron Woodcock II J8292 Believed damaged beyond repair at Upavon when it was struck, while parked, by Siskin IIIA J8639. Damage to the latter was repairable and following attention in works, it returned to service and was on the books of 41 Squadron at Northolt in January 1931, having being involved in another contretemps on 17th July 1930, when it flew into the tail of Siskin IIIA J8936, both machines returning to *terra firma* safely.

Tuesday 31 July 1928

8 Squadron Sgt C N Morris +
Fairey IIIF Sgt G Williams Injured

T/o Khormaksar and wrecked in a crash near the port of Aden. Sergeant Cecil Norman Morris was a 1918 entrant to the RNAS, his service number 248736 falling within the block 244711 - 260000.

AUGUST

Thursday 2 August 1928

3 Squadron F/Lt L H Browning MC DFC +
Woodcock II

T/o Sutton Bridge where the squadron was engaged in its annual armament training, and crashed on the Holbeach ranges following failure of one of the aircraft's wings. Flight Lieutenant Lance Harold Browning's DFC was awarded for his work with 63 Squadron during operations in Kurdistan and was *Gazetted* 12th July 1920, supplement 31974, page 7422.

There are three Army Form B.103s for this officer, held by RAFM Hendon, the first showing his embarkation at Devonport on 11th September 1917, and disembarking over two months later on 20th November at Basrah. In those now long distant times, keeping healthy in these Middle Eastern countries was not easy under hostile conditions and less than a month later he was undergoing treatment in a Field Hospital for dysentery. Although I have not be able to find the *Gazette* entry for his MC, the citation for the award has been hand-written onto the Form: *"For conspicuous gallantry and daring whilst carrying out independent bombing behind the enemy's lines. He was attacked by a fast enemy scout machine which by skilful piloting and accurate shooting he drove down to its aerodrome. As soon as the enemy aeroplane landed then Lt Browning dropped a bomb completely obliterating the pilot who had started to run away and damaging his machine. He then continued bombing and whilst doing so was attacked by two more enemy scouts, both of which he drove down."*

This report is dated 31st May 1918, Order of the Day 106, dated 22nd May 1918. The second Form B.103 opens with Embarked Bombay HT *Franz Joseph* and disembarking Suez 12th August 1918. Qualified as a pilot on both land and sea aeroplanes, Lieutenant Browning was posted to 58 Training Squadron [Suez] on 17th August, and thence to 111 Squadron on 2nd September and coming under the aegis of Palestine Brigade.

On 4th April 1919, he underwent another spell in hospital, this time at 26 Static Hospital at Ismailia, and on release went to 113 Squadron [RE.8] at Ismailia.

The third and final B.103 shows he embarked at Suez on 29th May 1919, sailing to Basrah on HT *Covejana.* Arriving on 19th June, and was attached to 63 Squadron [RE.8] at Baghdad effective the same day. A third spell in hospital lasting for ten days 30 Casualty Clearing Station [20th to 30th August 1919] , during which he was informed he had been awarded a permanent commission on the 1st August, thus giving up his acting rank of Captain for Lieutenant.

His medal card is held by TNA Kew under WO 372/3/136930 which covers his service, initially with the Royal Field Artillery 1914, through to 1920.

Please refer to the summary on 8th May 1928, and Flying Officer Geoffrey Bradbury for details of a publication in which Flight Lieutenant Browning's death is recorded.

Friday 3 August 1928
84 Squadron Sgt H P Murray Safe
DH.9A E963
T/o Shaibah only to clip the wing of a parked DH, J7872. Damage to J7872 was fairly minimal but Sergeant Murray crashed out of control and his DH was damaged beyond repair. See my summary for 14th October 1930, and the probable end of J7872.

Tuesday 14 August 1928
8 Squadron F/Lt E N T Edwardes +
Fairey IIIF LAC A W Jones Injured
T/o Khormakser and crashed following an encounter with a sudden and violent sandstorm near Sheik Othman, Aden. Flight Lieutenant Edward Norman Tickner Edwardes was a permanent officer whose commission was promulgated in *The London Gazette* on 27th April 1926, issue 33155, page 2863. Leading Aircraftman Albert Wyndham Jones survived and is believed to have made a good recovery from his injuries.

Thursday 16 August 1928
1 Squadron Siskin IIIA J8640 Caught fire on the ground, possibly at Northolt where the squadron arrived on the 7th of the month from Tangmere. Twenty-four hours after the incident, 1 Squadron headed back to Tangmere. The destruction by fire of J8640 was the first Siskin to be written off by the squadron since giving up its Sopwith Snipes and re-equipping with Siskins in February 1927.

12 Squadron *Not reported*
Fox I J7954
T/o Andover and to the concern of the crew a fire broke out while flying contentedly at 2,000 feet. A successful forced-landing was achieved, the Fox coming down in a field of standing crops. Soon after being evacuated, the flames reached the petrol tank and in the explosion that followed the bomber was totally destroyed.

605 Squadron AAF *Not reported*
DH.9A J7814
T/o Manston and wrecked in a forced-landing on a river bank close to the airfield. At the time 605 Squadron AAF was on its summer camp from Castle Bromwich.

Monday 27 August 1928
84 Squadron *Not reported*
DH.9A J7876
T/o Shaibah for night flying practice during which it burst a tyre. Taxied clear of the landing area, which was lit by flares, to await assistance it was struck a few minutes later by E8694 which had landed safely only for the pilot, Flying Officer Frederick Basil Tomkins to taxi into J7876, damaging it beyond repair. As for his own aircraft, it is believed it was repaired though its subsequent service has not been recorded. Flying Officer Tomkins short service commission was *Gazetted* 27th March 1925, issue 33033, page 2117. Additional information regarding his service is shown under his name in Appendix D for the 27th of March 1925.

Friday 31 August 1928
14 Squadron Sgt V R Saunders +
DH.9A J7833 LAC F W Fletcher +
T/o Amman and while making a turn downwind stalled and fell to the ground, bursting into flames as it impacted. There's was the seventh all non-commissioned officer crew where one or more had died in the year to date.

Both Sergeant Victor Robert Saunders, 335369, and Leading Aircraftman Frederick William Fletcher, 335898, had joined as boys between August 1919 and January 1921.

SEPTEMBER

Sunday 2 September 1928
605 Squadron AAF P/O G H Aldridge + Newton Harcourt [St. Luke's] Churchyard.
DH.9A J8107
T/o Castle Bromwich and it was while making a very sharp turn over the village of Great Glen [east of the present day A.6] and on the SE side of Leicester, that Pilot Officer George Herbert Aldridge lost control and crashed, his DH bursting into flames. So died the first of the squadron's Auxiliary Air Force establishment of pilots.

His father, the late Major John Barttelot Aldridge of the Royal Horse Artillery held the DSO. It seems his son, George, had been appointed to his commission as recently as 17th July [LG 7 August 1928, issue 33410, page 5313]. I strongly suspect George was making an aerial visit to his home for Newton Harcourt, where he is buried, is within a mile or two WSW from the crash site. His headstone carries the inscription: *"I Bear You On Eagles' Wings And Brought You Unto Myself."* The authors have pleasure in acknowledging the Geni ancestry website.

On Monday, September 3rd, 1928, the *Leicester Mail* presented its readers with a full account of the tragedy, which in banner headlined;

'Gt. Glen Disaster : Pictures on Page 9'
'YoungLeicester RAF Pilot's Terrible Death'
'A Side Slip and Dive'
'Plane Bursts into Flames and is Unapproachable Owing to Heat'

"A terrible flying tragedy occurred at Great Glen last night, when a young Leicester RAF pilot met with his death following a nose-dive. The machine was rising again after an unsuccessful attempt to land when the accident occurred. Hitting the ground with a sickening thud, the 'plane burst into flames, and so intense was the heat that it was impossible to approach the wreckage. The pilot, however, must have met an instantaneous death.

"A young Leicester pilot met with a terrible death at Great Glen at 5 o'clock last evening, his aeroplane crashing in a field near the Station, just after hundreds of people had seen him flying fairly low over Leicester.

"Until early this morning the body had not been definitely identified, but it has now been established that it is that of Mr. George Herbert Aldridge, aged 27, of Craven House, Princes Road, Leicester.Mr. Aldridge was an articled pupil with the firm of Messrs. Rolleston and Co, land agent and surveyors, etc, of Grey Friars, Leicester.

"He was a member of the Auxiliary Air Force, or "Air Territorials," and was a pilot officer of the 605th County of Warwick Bombing Squadron. He had been flying for some time, it is understood, though he had not yet got his "wings," and he generally spent his week-ends flying from Castle Bromwich Aerodrome, Birmingham, where the Flight is stationed.

"According to eye-witnesses, the 'plane was being flown up again after an unsuccessful attempt to land in a field off the main road, near the Station. It nose-dived after a side slip, and crashed with a terrific force, the pilot being probably killed instantaneously. The machine burst into flames, and it was some time before the terribly mutilated and charred body could be recovered from the blazing wreckage.

'Hovering Low'

"A graphic description of the crash was given to a "Leicester Mail" representative last night by an eye-witness, Mr. Edward Fox, of 9 Carrington Street, Leicester, who was fishing in the canal at Great Glen at the time.

"Mr. Fox, seeing the machine overhead, and flying low, realised that he was in difficulties, and hurriedly mounted his bicycle, he rushed to the field over which the 'plane was hovering.

""The aeroplane had come from the direction of Leicester," he said, "and it was flying very low. He circled right round over the village at a good speed, and then turned round again towards the canal, describing a figure eight. Then he turned again, banked low, and made as if to land in the small field near the station. At the other end there was a hedge and a row of trees. The machine skimmed the surface of the field, but did not actually touch the ground, and then the pilot evidently realised that he did not have sufficient room to taxi along without hitting the hedge and the trees.

"He could not possibly turn, so he opened his engine out full again, and with a roar the 'plane rose in the air almost in a straight line. It took some branches off one of the trees as it climbed, but it seemed to be going up all right."

'A Terrific Crash'

"He had only risen about four times the height of the trees, however, when the machine seemed to turn right overon its side. It nose-dived, and before it could be righted it hit the ground with a terrific crash, with such a force that it bounced seven or eight yards. There was an explosion, probably as the petrol tank blew up, and then the aeroplane burst into flames."

"A number of people saw the crash, and Mr. Fox and four or five others rushed to the spot to try to get the pilot out. So intense was the heat from the burning aeroplane, however, that they could not get within a dozen yards of it for some time, and it was not until the flames had almost exhausted themselves that they could approach near the wreckage.

"In the meantime several motor-cars had been pulled up on the road nearby, and an attempt was made to secure extinguishers from them to subdue the blaze, but this was not successful.

"The 'plane had landed in the field upside, and its occupant was thrown right out of the cockpit. Through the flames it could be seen that a Vickers gun was mounted in the forepart.

'Rescue Efforts'

"Eventually, while the debris was still burning, Mr. Fox managed to secure a strut from the wreckage, and with this he was able to assist in pulling the body of the pilot clear.

"He was, of course, already dead, and his body was terribly maimed and broken. The knees were drawn up, both feet were severed, the left wrist and arm were fractured, the bone being exposed, and the head was fearfully injured. All the clothes were burned away, and all that remained were a few charred ashes, whilst it was impossible to recognise the face.

"The unfortunate man's watch was found among the debris, and it had stopped at exactly 5.10- the time of the crash. His purse and a charred portion of his flying licence were also found, the name "Aldridge" just being discernible on the latter.

"Mr. E F Gunning, of 34 Laurel Road, Leicester, who was motoring past the spot, also saw the crash. "It seemed to me that it was due to inexperience on the part of the pilot," he told a "Mail" representative to-day. "He was flying too low, and seemed to be looking for a landing. He could have come down in a big field some distance away, and he circled it half a dozen times, but then flew off. He was only about 100 feet up, and all the time flying dangerously low. When he came down he just missed the church, and then grazed the trees at the side of the field. I think the tail of the machine must have struck the tops of them. It made one spiral, and then crashed. It was enveloped in smoke, then the fuselage burst into flames, and the tank exploded. I and several others tried hard to get the man out, but it was impossible.

"The engine seemed to be running splendidly all the time, and I think the whole trouble was due to a bad landing."

"It is stated that a man and his family, with a motor cycle combination, were picknicking in the field at the time, and that the plane swooped right over their heads. They ran for their lives, thinking they would be struck, but a moment later it crashed on the other side.

"Mr. R W Kaye, the High Sheriff, who lives at Great Glen, placed a motor vehicle at the disposal of the police, and in this the body was removed to the skittle alley of a neighbouring public house.

'Villagers Tribute'

"A touching feature of the tragedy was that a memorial service was held at the Great Glen Church, quite near the scene of the accident, within a short time afterwards. The crash had taken place only an hour or so before the usual Sunday evening service, and many of the worshippers who attended the service, so appropriately and thoughtfully held to the memory of the young victim, had seen him lose his life.

"Several police officers were on the spot, in charge of Supt. Hall, who had motored over from Leicester, and during the night a police guard was kept on the wrecked and charred aeroplane. Little remained to be seen, but large and curious crowds of sightseers remained in the vicinity to nightfall.

'Parachute Detached'

"Another eye-witness suggested that Aldridge probably made an attempt to use his parachute, as this was detached from the 'plane when it fell, he stated.

"The field in which the machine crashed is owned by Mr. Ellis C Johnson, of "The Yews," Great Glen, and Mr. Aldridge was a great friend of the Johnson family. Several times recently he has been over the district doing "stunt" flying, and it is also stated he endeavoured, though unsuccessfully, to drop a letter from the 'plane to Miss Johnson on one occasion.

"He was a native of the South of England, but for some time he resided at the "White House," Great Glen, where he had many friends. Within the last year, however, he came to live in Princess Road, and for the last four years he has been with the firm of Messrs. Rolleston, to whom he was articled."

Although it has to be conjecture, it would seem that Pilot Officer Aldridge, having committed himself to landing in the field near the station, at the last moment saw the family, unnamed, who were reported by the paper to be having a picnic. In attempting to overshoot, the DH clipped the tree tops, probably damaging the flying controls. This would account for witnesses statements of hearing a roar from the engine [Mr. Edward Fox] and from Mr. Gunning who thought the tail might have come into contact with the trees.

A very brief account was published on Tuesday, September 4th, 1928, by the *Belfast News-Letter* which gave the Greyhound Hotel as the venue for the inquest and a statement made by Mr. Gerald Victor Briggs of Leicester who told the Coroner that he had a conversation with the deceased on Saturday during which Pilot Officer Aldridge told him he would be flying over Leicester the following day.

Adjourned until Wednesday, the conclusion on the inquest was reported by *The Londonderry Sentinel* on Thursday, September 6th, 1928: *"Dr. Phillips of Kibworth, said Aldridge's head was charred on the right side, but his opinion was that the airman died before any part of the body was burned.*

"A verdict of accidental death was returned."

Tuesday 4 September 1928

24 Squadron *Not reported*
DH.60 Moth J9104

T/o Northolt and on return landed with some force, ballooned back into the air on its second arrival turned over and caught fire.

Wednesday 16 September 1928

84 Squadron F/O F E Nuttall Safe
DH.9A J6961

T/o Shaibah and damaged beyond repair when the bomb load it was carrying fell off moments after becoming airborne. Flying Officer Frank Edward Nuttall reported to the Cadet College at Cranwell with the February 1921, entry of Flight Cadets. He was appointed to a permanent commission on graduating on 20th December 1922 [LG 23 January 1923, issue 32789, page 533]. For details concerning his eventual retirement, please refer to his entry in Appendix E 1921.

Friday 21 September 1928

5 Squadron *Not reported*
Bristol F.2J H1428

T/o Risalpur for night flying practice; undershot, crashed and damaged beyond repair.

27 Squadron F/Lt A R Prendergast Safe
DH.9A H3450/K LAC J A Dwyer Safe

T/o Risalpur with mail destined for units operating on the NWF. Having located the drop zone in the Lowari Pass, Flight Lieutenant Archer Robert Prendergast dived in readiness to make the drop only to be caught in a downdraft and crash-land. Shaken, but otherwise unhurt, the crew awaited recovery but their DH was now beyond repair. Earlier in the year while being flown by Sergeant David Irving it had descended into the River Indus near Attock; Sergeant Irving escaped injury but his observer/air gunner, Leading Aircraftman Ernest Arthur Turner was drowned.

Flight Lieutenant Prendergast was a short service commission officer [LG 30 March 1923, issue 32810, page 2420] who relinquished his commission on completion of his service on 30th March 1930 [LG 18 March 1930, issue 33589, page 1731]. On 24th October 1930, he was granted a commission in Class A of the Reserve of Air Force Officers [LG 4th November 1930, issue 33658, page 6959].

Prior to its service with 27 Squadron, H3450 was shipped from the UK to India and the Aircraft Park at Lahore where it was noted on 12th April 1924. By 18th November of that year it was with 60 Squadron at Risalpur wearing the code number '2' before being transferred to '27' in the summer of 1925.

Tuesday 25 September 1928

70 Squadron Victoria IIIA J8915 Burnt out on the ground at Mosul while being refuelled.

OCTOBER

Thursday 11 October 1928

12 Squadron F/Lt W E Somervell AFC +
Fox I J7946* Cpl C J Loud +

T/o Hendon for a demonstration flight in front of the Sultan of Oman that Flight Lieutenant William Edmund made an extremely fast dive and in doing so exceeded the structural limitations of the airframe, resulting in the tail assembly parting company with the fuselage. Out of control, the Fox crashed in the vicinity of the airfield.

Corporal Christopher John Loud, 243592, began his service in 1917 with the Royal Naval Air Service, his number coming in the block 225061 - 244710.

Flight Lieutenant Somervell was *Gazetted* with the AFC on June 5th, 1925, as promulgated in the Edinburgh edition, issue 14133, page 640, and it was the Edinburgh's *Evening Post* that carried the following report of the crash:

'200-Mile-An-Hour Death Dive'
'The Hendon Air Crash Inquest'
'Coroner Complains of Want of Detail'

"The verdict the accident was due to some structural defect in the machine, death being caused instantly, was returned by a jury at Hendon yesterday on Flight-Lieut. William Edmund Somervell, [36], and Corporal Fitter Christopher John Loud, [26], of the RAF.

"Both men, who were stationed at Andover with No. 12 Day Bombing Squadron, were killed on Thursday last, when their aeroplane, a Fairey Fox, crashed at a display at Hendon Aerodrome given in honour of the Sultan of Oman and Muscat.

'Going Over 200 Miles and Hour'

"The tail was stated to have broken from the machine when it was flying at a speed of over 20 miles an hour.

"Evidence of identification was given by Robert Somervell, a schoolmaster, and Squadron Leader Trevor E Salt of the RAF stationed at Andover, who identified Corporal Loud.

"Squadron Leader Salt said the machine in which the men were killed was a Fairey Fox bomber and had flown 52 hours.

"The Coroner observed that the log-book in reference to the machine was not provided, which, he said, was a very unusual thing.

''No Aid for Coroner'

"The Coroner, addressing the jury, said his officer could get no information from the aerodrome. They would give him no assistance in this case, therefore, if the evidence was not sufficient, he might to adjourn the case.

"Squadron Leader Salt said he had never heard of anything being wrong with the 'plane, and he understood it was tested before the display. He said the could be damaged and come off through an aeroplane going to fast, but this machine had travelled at over 250 miles an hour in a dive. Generally, a broken tail was due to some defect in the machine or to bad handling.

'A Good Pilot'

"Lieut. Somervell was an exceptionally good pilot, and there would have apparently been some hidden defect in the machine.

"Wing Commander Edward Rice of Andover, said he had inspected the log-book, and there was nothing abnormal relating to the aeroplane. The machine was inspected thoroughly on September 27and was reported in perfect order. The machine had done an hour and a half's flying since that inspection and it was tested on the morning of the accident.

"It was apparently in perfect order, and witness could only suggest that the defect was caused by a strain while landing at Hendon. This would not be found out except by a minute inspection, which would not be carried out unless the pilot thought he had done some damage. If any part of the fuselage was damaged it would be liable to cause the accident. Once the tail came off no skill could stop the aeroplane dropping."

* According to the late Group Captain Albert Edward Dark, a Cranwell graduate of the September 1926 entry, and at the time of the accident a young pilot officer attached to 12 Squadron at Andover, the serial should read 'J8423' for in his letter to the aviation magazine *Aeroplane* [November 1994] he stated that he had a photograph taken the following year showing J7946 flying in company with J9028 and J7943 which were received at Andover on 14th February and 1st March 1929, respectively. In support of his claim, J8423, flown for the first time on 23rd June 1927, and taken on charge by the squadron a month later, is that it is not mentioned after October 1928.

Thursday 17 October 1929
13 Squadron *Not reported*
Atlas I J9045
T/o Netheravon and on landing collided with Avro 504N J9434 from the resident No. 1 Flying Training School, which was also approaching to land. Both machines were written off. Although Air-Britain's *J File* shows the previous unit for the Atlas as *"1 FTS"*, I suspect this to be an error and the Atlas was on transfer from 26 Squadron at Catterick.

NOVEMBER

Tuesday 6 November 1928
26 Squadron P/O C L Myers +
Atlas I J9043 AC2 H Chadwick +
T/o Catterick and while flying in marginal visibility crashed on Grinton Moor above the village of Grinton. Situated on the NE edge of the North Yorkshire Moors, the Atlas came down roughly a dozen miles WNW from Catterick. Pilot Officer Charles Lilburn Myers was granted a short service commission on 2nd September 1927, *Gazetted* on the 27th of the month in issue 33315, page 6127. This was his first posting after gaining his 'Wings'; he was just 20 years of age, a year younger than Aircraftman Henry Chadwick whose sservice number 359460 suggests he enlisted circa late May or early June 1925.

The loss of J9043 was the first fatal crash involving an Atlas army co-operation aircraft and the first reported from Catterick based 26 Squadron which had reformed with a single flight on 11th October 1927.

Headlined *'Airmen's Fate On Moor - No One to Blame for Double Tragedy'* the *Aberdeen Press and Journal* reported:

"A verdict of accidental death was returned yesterday at the inquest at Redmire, Yorkshire, on Pilot Officer Charles Lillburn Myers and Aircraftsman Henry Chadwick, who left Catterick Aerodrome of Tuesday for a short flight, and on Wednesday night were found lying among the wreckage of the machine on a lonely stretch of moorland between Wensleydale and Swaledale in North Yorkshire.

"The Coroner said he did not think anyone was to blame, and it was possible the machine had got into a spin.

"Flight-Lieut. Herbert said: It was a quite good morning for flying. The object of the flight was to train pilot to pick out certain points, and take pin-point photographs.

"Coroner - It has struck me as possible that, in the fog, he came down to see where he was and descended lower than he thought. What is your theory? - It is difficult to say. It looks as though they got into a spin."

Immediately below the piece reported above, was a report of a second air accident fatality with claimed the life of Pilot Officer Richard Harold Coupe - see Appendix C for 1928, and the continuation of the press coverage, while in the paper's Late News item, the death of Sergeant Lockwood [see below] was noted.

On the same page, and dominating the news items in the left and far right columns were reports on the volcanic eruption of Mount Etna and Germany's success in 'persuading' its citizens to eat more fish, for which the paper opined was good news for the British Fishing industry.

Thursday 8 November 1928
100 Squadron Sgt H E Lockwood +
Horsley AC2 C R Thane Injured
T/o Bicester for night flying practice and forced-landing caught fire and was burnt out near Gawcott, 2 miles SSW of Buckingham. The circumstances of Sergeant Herbert Edward Lockwood's death appeared in the Scottish paper, *The Courier and Advertiser* on Wednesday, December 12th, 1928, attached to its report regarding the midair collision over Duxford on 10th December 1928 between a 19 Squadron Siskin and a similar machine from the Meteorological Flight [which has been summarised]:

"A verdict of accident death was returned at the inquest at Bicester Aerodrome yesterday on Sergt. Pilot Lockwood, who was killed near Gawcott, Bucks., on November 6 [sic] *through his machine striking a tree.*

"Flying-Officer Buckley said three aeroplanes were returning to the aerodrome from Northolt in the late afternoon, and the pilots lost their way from Bletchley to Castllethorpe. Lockwood's machine, a day bomber, was leading.

"They lost sight of the third machine which landed at Wolverton.

"The other two machines landed in a field to discover their position, and both ran through a strong barbed wire fence parallel with a hedge, Buckle's [sic] *machine getting clear.*

'Lockwood, however, either lost his head or thought he could get clear by taking off.

"On reaching the boundary hedge, 100 yards distant, the starboard wing the top of one of three trees, and broke into flames before reaching the ground, Lockwood being pinned under the tail of the fuselage, which had swung round and turned over. His skull was fractured, and he was burned to death."

A much fuller report was presented on Friday, 9th November 1928, to the readers of the *Northern Daily Mail* its four line headline outlining the awfulness of the crash:

'Another Crash'
'RAF Pilot Pinned Under Burning 'Plane'
'Passenger in Flames'
'Terrible Accident Near Buckingham'

"An RAF aeroplane crashed near Buckingham yesterday evening and burst into flames. The pilot, Sergeant Lockwood, was killed and the passenger severely injured and burned.

"The accident happened at 5.30 p.m. at Gawcutt Field Farm, about half a mile from Buckingham. The injured passenger, Aircraftsman Charles Robert Thane, managed to crawl from the burning machine. Police and other helpers arrived and took him to hospital.

"He was stated this morning to be severely burned and in a dangerous condition. Thane's home is at Altingham, Cheshire.

'Porter's Graphic Story'

"Mr. T H Williams, a railway porter at Buckingham Station, gave the following graphic account of the accident to the press association reporter to-day;

"I was working on my allotment on the railway embankment between Gawcutt and Buckinghamwhen I saw two aeroplanes circling very low, apparently looking for a landing place.

"They were fairly close together when suddenly one swerved away and landed in a field. The other machine continued circling round, and, as it was nearly dark at the time, I thought the pilot was trying to see where his friend had come down. Apparently he saw the other 'plane at last and attempted to land.

"The first 'plane had alighted close to two elm trees. The second machine, in its descent, struck a small ash tree, which ripped away about a yard of one of the wings and caused the 'plane to turn a complete somersault.

'A Burst of Flame'

"The engine was running at full speed, and, immediately the 'plane touched the ground, there was a loud report and a burst of flame.

"I dashed across the field and found a man lying on the ground about 20 yards from the fallen 'plane. His clothes was on fire and he was groaning. I guess he must have scrambled from the 'plane and started to run before collapsing.

"The pilot of the first 'plane was there. We attended to Thane and then went over to the machine to look for the pilot. We could see no sign of him until the flames had died down. Then we found him pinned under one of the wings, burned beyond recognition.

'Where's Lockwood'

"Thane kept crying out, "Where's Lockwood." "We told him not to worry, as Lockwood was all right. This was simply to comfort him because we knew the pilot was dead.

"The pilot of the other 'plane himself had a very narrow escape. In descending his machine struck a wire fence and was damaged. He was not hurt, however.

"The nearest farm was about four fields away. I hurried there and telephoned to the police. Then Dr. A M Lawrence arrived at the scene and attended to Thane, who afterwards was taken in ambulance to the Buckingham Cottage Hospital."

"Another account of the accident states that Sergt. Lockwood attempted a landing, but saw a hedge looming up in front of him. He was trying to ascend when the 'plane struck the ash tree.

"The remains of the dead airman were removed to Bicester, and members of the RAF mounted guard over the wrecked 'plane through the night.

"The two pilots and the passengers were stationed at Bicester, and it is understood that all were unmarried."

Sergeant Lockwood joined the Royal Air Force from civilian life and was issued with 351106 as his service number. His death, and the serious injury to Aircraftman Thane, was the eighth in which an all non-commissioned officer crew had been involved in a flying accident where the outcome proved fatal to one or all members of crew in 1928.

Monday 28 November 1928
31 Squadron *Not reported*
Bristol F.2b J6647
T/o Quetta and wrecked during landing at Hyderabad. At Dright Road by March 1923, the Bristol went to 31 Squadron as 'K' by the July of that year and was damaged at Dardoni on 11th January 1924, when the starboard wheel went into a ditch. Repaired, it was next used by 20 Squadron as 'F' and later 'D' before returning to 31 Squadron on an unrecorded date.

DECEMBER

Friday 7 December 1928
503 Squadron SR *Not reported*
Avro 504N J8516
T/o Waddington and merely reported as *"crashed."*

Monday 10 December 1928
19 Squadron F/O E G Cayley Safe
Siskin IIIA J8851
T/o Duxford and abandoned following a midair collision with Siskin IIIA J8872 attached to Duxford's Meteorological Flight flown by Flight Sergeant Osmond Cecil Tostevin who, sadly, was killed. The collision occurred near Whittlesford on the NNW side of the airfield. Flying Officer Edward Gordon Cayley received a short service commission in the autumn of 1925, as promulgated in the *Gazette* of 6th October, issue 33090, page 6421.

His escape was witnessed by a shepherd and his description of the collision was reported by the Scottish edition of *The Courier and Advertiser* its sub-editor headlining the drama:

'Airman's Escape By Parachute'
Shepherd Describes Mid-Air Collision

"The collision of two aeroplanes at a height of 3,500 feet was described by George Unwin, a shepherd, at the inquest last night on Flight-Sergeant Pilot Osmond Cecil Tostevin, who was killed at Duxford Aerodrome, Cambridgeshire, on Monday.

"Unwin said he saw two aeroplanes circling round, and they collided. One that had the wing broken dived straight down to earth, the other glided down, and he saw the pilot jump from his machine with his parachute.

"Flying-Officer Edward Gordon Cayley, who escaped by means of his parachute, said that he did not see Sergeant Tostevin's machine u til the collision. His machine came down vertically out of control, and he got out as quickly as he could.

"The Coroner returned a verdict that Sergeant Tostevin was "accidentally killed while flying in the execution of his duty."

Wednesday Boxing Day 1928

47 Squadron F/O A W A Ricks +
Fairey IIIF S1206 Capt J C Doyle +
Sgt C L Long +

T/o Khartoum and while flying at a low altitude stalled and crashed at El Obeid, capital city of North Kurdufan, Sudan. Flying Officer Arnold William Alexander Ricks on leaving Portsmouth Grammar School obtained a flight cadetship to Cranwell, entering the Cadet College in September 1923, and was placed with A Squadron.

Captain James Charles Doyle had served for many years in the army and was commissioned with the honorary rank of Lieutenant on his appointment to Quarter Master on 9th October 1912 [LG 8 October 1912, issue 28651, page 7371].

Sergeant Charles Leonard Long was in his fourteenth year of military service having joined the Royal Flying Corps in 1915; his service number was 82899.

60 Squadron S/Ldr R H G Neville Safe
DH.9A E8660/V

T/o Kohat and crashed at an undisclosed location in the NWF.

During the year, and on an unspecified date, 84 Squadron at Shaibah probably wrote off DH.9A J7852/P in a crash at Samawa, Iraq, the DH turning over onto its back.

Another unspecified date concerns 55 Squadron DH.9A J8151/B2 reported as *"Wrecked after 28 days in desert.*

APPENDICES
1928

Appendix A - Squadron Losses Table and Losses by Aircraft Type

Column 1 - Squadron

Column 2 - Aircraft type

Column 3 - Written off

Column 4 - Fatalities

1 Squadron	Armstrong Whitworth Siskin IIIA	1	
2 Squadron	Bristol F.2b	5	4
3 Squadron	Hawker Woodcock II	3	3
5 Squadron	Bristol F.2b	1	
6 Squadron	Bristol F.2b	4	5
8 Squadron	Fairey IIIF	2	2
12 Squadron	Fairey Fox I	3	2
13 Squadron	Armstrong Whitworth Atlas	2	
14 Squadron	Airco DH.9A	3	6
16 Squadron	Bristol F.2b	1	2
17 Squadron	Hawker Woodcock II	1	
19 Squadron	Armstrong Whitworth Siskin IIIA	1	
23 Squadron	Avro 504N	1	2
	Gloster Gamecock I	1	
24 Squadron	DH.60 Moth	1	
25 Squadron	Gloster Grebe II	3	
26 Squadron	Armstrong Whitworth Atlas	1	2
27 Squadron	Airco DH.9A	2	
29 Squadron	Gloster Grebe II	1	1
30 Squadron	Airco DH.9A	1	2
31 Squadron	Bristol F.2b	2	1
39 Squadron	Airco DH.9A	2	
41 Squadron	Armstrong Whitworth Siskin IIIA	1	1
43 Squadron	Gloster Gamecock I	1	1
45 Squadron	Airco DH.9A	1	1
47 Squadron	Fairey IIIF	1	3
55 Squadron	Airco DH.9A	4	1
56 Squadron	Armstrong Whitworth Siskin IIIA	1	
60 Squadron	Airco DH.9A	1	
70 Squadron	Vickers Victoria	6	
84 Squadron	Airco DH.9A	7	2
99 Squadron	Handley Page Hyderabad	1	
100 Squadron	Hawker Horsley II	1	1
207 Squadron	Fairey IIIF	1	3
502 Squadron SR	Avro 504N	1	
503 Squadron SR	Avro 504N	1	
600 Squadron AAF	Airco DH.9A	1	
602 Squadron AAF	Avro 504N	1	1
	Fairey Fawn II	1	
603 Squadron AAF	Avro 504N	1	1
	Airco DH.9A	1	
605 Squadron AAF	Airco DH.9A	1	1
Totals		76	48

Airco DH.9A	24	13
Armstrong Whitworth Atlas	3	2
Armstrong Whitworth Siskin IIIA	4	1
Avro 504N	5	4
Bristol F.2b	13	12
DH.60 Moth	1	
Fairey Fawn II	1	
Fairey Fox I	3	2
Fairey IIIF	4	8
Gloster Gamecock I	2	1
Gloster Grebe II	4	1
Handley Page Hyderabad	1	
Hawker Horsley II	1	1
Hawker Woodcock II	4	3
Vickers Victoria	6	
Totals	76	48

Appendix B - Squadron Locations and Commanding Officers

The United Kingdom strength of the Royal Air Force was increased by three squadron, two being reformed with a view to bombing duties.

1 Squadron	Siskin IIIA	Tangmere	01.01.28-07.08.28	
		Northolt	07.08.28-17.08.28	
		Tangmere	17.08.28-31.12.28	
2 Squadron	Bristol F.2b	Manston	01.01.28-31.12.28	
3 Squadron	Woodcock II	Upavon	01.01.28-31.12.28	Woodcock II withdrawn during September
	Gamecock I			Gamecock issued during August
4 Squadron	Bristol F.2b	Farnborough	01.01.28-31.12.28	
5 Squadron	Bristol F.2b	Risalpur	01.01.28-15.12.28	
		Quetta	15.12.28-31.12.28	
6 Squadron	Bristol F.2b	Hinaidi	01.01.28-31.12.28	
7 Squadron	Virginia	Worthy Down	01.01.28-31.12.28	Various Mks on establishment
8 Squadron	DH.9A	Khomakser	01.01.28-31.12.28	DH.9A withdrawn during January
	Fairey IIIF			Fairey IIIF issued during January
9 Squadron	Virginia IX	Manston	01.01.28-31.12.28	
10 Squadron	Hyderabad	Upper Heyford	03.01.28-31.12.28	Reformed for bombing duties
11 Squadron	Horsley	Netheravon	01.01.28-29.12.28	Horsley withdrawn during November
	Wapiti I			Two received for training
12 Squadron	Fox I	Andover	01.01.28-31.12.28	
13 Squadron	Bristol F.2b/Atlas	Andover	01.01.28-31.12.28	Bristol F.2b withdrawn during January
14 Squadron	DH.9A	Ramleh and Amman	01.01.28-31.12.28	
XV Squadron	*Various*	Martlesham Heath	01.01.28-31.12.28	
16 Squadron	Bristol F.2b	Old Sarum	01.01.28-31.12.28	
17 Squadron	Woodcock II	Upavon	01.02.28-31.12.28	Woodcock II withdrawn during January
	Gamecock I			Gamecock I issued January to September
	Siskin IIIA			Siskin IIIA issued during September
19 Squadron	Grebe II	Duxford	01.01.28-31.12.28	Grebe II withdrawn during March
	Siskin IIIA			Siskin IIIA issued during March
20 Squadron	Bristol F.2b	Peshawar	01.01.28-31.12.28	
22 Squadron	*Various*	Martlesham Heath	01.01.28-31.12.28	
23 Squadron	Gamecock I	Kenley	01.01.28-31.12.28	
24 Squadron	*Various*	Northolt	01.01.28-31.12.28	
25 Squadron	Grebe II	Hawkinge	01.01.28-31.12.38	
26 Squadron	Atlas	Catterick	01.01.28-31.12.28	
27 Squadron	DH.9A	Risalpur	01.01.28-17.12.28	
		Kohat	17.12.28-31.12.28	
28 Squadron	Bristol F.2b	Ambala	01.01.28-31.12.28	
29 Squadron	Grebe II	Duxford	01.01.28-01.04.28	Grebe II withdrawn during March
	Siskin IIIA	North Weald	01.04.28-31.12.28	Siskin IIIA issued during March
30 Squadron	DH.9A	Hinaidi	01.01.28-31.12.28	
31 Squadron	Bristol F.2b	Hinaidi	01.01.28-31.12.28	
32 Squadron	Gamecock II	Kenley	01.01.28-31.12.28	Gamecock II withdrawn during April
	Siskin IIIA			Siskin IIIA issued during April
36 Squadron	Horsley I	Donibristle	01.10.28-31.12.28	Reformed as Torpedo Bomber Squadron
39 Squadron	DH.9A	Spittlegate	01.01.28-21.01.28	DH.9A withdrawn during December
		Bircham Newton	21.01.28-31.12.28	Departed for India 29 December
41 Squadron	Siskin IIIA	Northolt	01.01.28-31.12.28	
43 Squadron	Gamecock I	Tangmere	01.01.28-31.12.28	Gamecock I withdrawn during June
	Siskin IIIA			Siskin IIIA issued during June
45 Squadron	DH.9A	Helwan	01.01.28-31.12.28	
47 Squadron	DH.9A/Fairey IIIF	Khartoum	01.01.28-31.12.28	DH.9A withdrawn during April
55 Squadron	DH.9A	Hinaidi	01.01.28-31.12.28	
56 Squadron	Siskin IIIA	North Weald	01.01.28-31.12.28	
58 Squadron	Virginia	Worthy Down	01.01.28-31.12.28	Various Mks on establishment
60 Squadron	DH.9A	Kohat	01.01.28-31.12.28	
70 Squadron	Victoria I/III	Hinaidi	01.01.28-31.12.28	
84 Squadron	DH.9A	Shaibah	01.01.28-31.12.28	DH.9A withdrawn during October
	Wapiti IiA			Wapiti IIA issued during July
99 Squadron	Hyderabad	Bircham Newton	01.01.28-05.01.28	
		Upper Heyford	05.01.28-31.12.28	
100 Squadron	Horsley II/III	Spittlegate	01.01.28-10.01.28	
		Bicester	10.01.28-14.04.28	
		Weston Zoyland	14.04.28-19.05.28	
		Bicester	19.05.28-31.12.28	
101 Squadron	Sidestrand III	Bircham Newton	21.03.28-31.12.28	Reformed for day bombing duties
111 Squadron	Siskin IIIA	Duxford	01.01.28-01.04.28	
		Hornchurch	01.04.28-31.12.28	
207 Squadron	Fairey IIIF	Eastchurch	01.01.28-31.12.28	
208 Squadron	Bristol F.2b	Heliopolis	01.01.28-31.12.28	
216 Squadron	Victoria II/V	Heliopolis	01.01.28-31.12.28	
502 Squadron SR	Vimy	Aldergrove	01.01.28-31.12.28	Vimy withdrawn during June
	Hyderabad			Hyderabad issued during June
503 Squadron SR	Fawn II	Waddington	01.01.28-31.12.28	
594 Squadron SR	*Not known*	Hucknall	26.03.28-31.12.28	Formed
600 Squadron AAF	Hendon	DH.9A	01.01.28-31.12.28	

601 Squadron AAF	Hendon	DH.9A	01.01.28-31.12.28	
602 Squadron AAF	Renfrew	DH.9A	01.01.28-31.12.28	Withdrawn during January 1928
		Fairey Fawn II		
603 Squadron AAF	Turnhouse	DH.9A	01.01.28-31.12.28	
605 Squadron AAF	Castle Bromwich	DH.9A	01.01.28-31.12.28	

1 Squadron	Squadron Leader E D Atkinson MC DFC AFC	In situ	See 84 Squadron 1924
	Flight Lieutenant F L Luxmore DFC	5 January 1928	See Appendix B 1927
	Flight Lieutenant S F Vincent AFC	3 February 1928	AV-M retirement 6 February 1950
	Squadron Leader E O Grenfell MC DFC AFC	19 March 1928	See 1 Squadron 1923
2 Squadron	Squadron Leader W Sowrey DFC AFC mid	In situ	See Appendix B 1927
	Squadron Leader H M Probyn DSO mid	1 April 1928	See 208 Squadron 1924
3 Squadron	Squadron Leader E D Johnson AFC	In situ	See Appendix B 1927
4 Squadron	Squadron Leader J C Slessor MC mid	In situ	See Appendix B 1925
	Squadron Leader N H Bottomley AFC	15 October 1928	ACM retirement 1 January 1948
5 Squadron	Squadron Leader A J Capel	In situ	See Appendix B 1923
	Flight Lieutenant A C Sanderson DFC	2 November 1928	AM retirement 14 February 1955
	Squadron Leader O C Bryson MC DFC AM	November 1928	G/Capt retired list 15 August 1943
6 Squadron	Squadron Leader C N Lowe MC DFC	In situ	See 602 Squadron AAF 1925
	Squadron Leader C H Keith	10 January 1928	G/Capt retired list 29 April 1943
7 Squadron	Wing Commander C F A Portal DSO* MC three times mid	In situ	See Appendix B 1927
	Wing Commander E R Manning DSO MC	30 November 1928	See 6 Squadron 1922
	Australia		
8 Squadron	Squadron Leader W A McClaughry DSO MC DFC three time mid	In situ	See Appendix B 1924
	Australia		
	Squadron Leader G H Bowman DSO MC DFC	1 February 1928	See 8 Squadron 1922
9 Squadron	Wing Commander C C Durston	In situ	See 13 Squadron 1924
	Wing Commander W V Strugnell MC*	28 November 1928	G/Capt retirement 7 June 1945
10 Squadron	Wing Commander H R Busteed OBE AFC *Croix de Guerre* [France]	3 January 1928.	A/Cmdr retirement 14 November 1932
	Australia		
	Wing Commander F L Robinson DSO MC DFC	4 October 1928	G/Capt retirement 1 May 1939
11 Squadron	Squadron Leader E A B Rice MC	In situ	See 6 Squadron 1921
	Squadron Leader P H Cummings	26 January 1928	G/Capt retirement 11 July 1944
12 Squadron	Squadron Leader T E Salt AFC	In situ	See Appendix B 1926
13 Squadron	Squadron Leader H H MacL Fraser	In situ	See Appendix B 1927
14 Squadron	Squadron Leader E G Hopcraft DSC	In situ	See Appendix B 1927
XV Squadron	Squadron Leader C E H James MC	In situ	See Appendix B 1927
16 Squadron	Squadron Leader W A Coryton MVO DFC	In situ	See Appendix B 1925
	Squadron Leader D O Mulholland AFC	25 September 1928	G/Capt retirement 23 July 1946
17 Squadron	Squadron Leader J Leacroft MC*	In situ	See Appendix B 1924
	Squadron Leader A R Arnold DSC DFC	1 April 1928	G/Capt retirement 22 May 1945
19 Squadron	Squadron Leader H W G Jones MC	In situ	See Appendix B 1925
	Flight Lieutenant M H Coote	1 May 1928	F/Lt retired list 12 December 1928
	Squadron Leader E C Emmett MC DFC	10 August 1928	G/Capt retired list 28 March 1945
	South Africa		
	Flight Lieutenant G A F Bucknall	12 December 1928	F/Lt killed 28 February 1929
20 Squadron	Squadron Leader J V Steel OBE	In situ	See 100 Squadron 1921
	Squadron Leader C H Nicholas DFC AFC mid	2 May 1928.	A/Cmdr retirement 12 November 1944
22 Squadron	Squadron Leader J Noakes AFC MM	In situ	See Appendix B 1927
23 Squadron	Flight Lieutenant J MacG Fairweather DFC mid	In situ	See Appendix B 1927
	South Africa		
	Squadron Leader A G Jones-Williams MC* *Croix de Guerre avec Palme*	21 January 1928	S/Ldr killed 17 December 1929
24 Squadron	Squadron Leander S N Cole	In situ	See Appendix B 1927
25 Squadron	Squadron Leader W H Park MC DFC	In situ	See Appendix B 1927
	New Zealand		
	Flight Lieutenant W E Swann	6 September 1928	W/Cdr retired list 28 January 1942.
26 Squadron	Squadron Leader R L Stevenson	In situ	See Appendix B 1927
27 Squadron	Squadron Leader L M Bailey AFC	In situ	See Appendix B 1924
28 Squadron	Squadron Leader J T Whittaker MC	In situ	See 28 Squadron 1922
	Squadron Leader A F Brooks	23 February 1928	See 43 Squadron 1925
29 Squadron	Squadron Leader M L Taylor AFC	In situ	See Appendix B 1924
30 Squadron	Squadron Leader F H Coleman	In situ	See Appendix B 1925
	Squadron Leader H P Lale DFC mid	7 January 19278	See 32 Squadron 1924
31 Squadron	Squadron Leader J F Gordon DFC	In situ	See Appendix B 1926
32 Squadron	Squadron Leader R B Mansell OBE	In situ	See Appendix B 1926
36 Squadron	Squadron Leader A W Mylne	2 July 1928	See 28 Squadron 1926
39 Squadron	Squadron Leader H V Champion de Crepigny MC DFC	In situ	See 60 Squadron 1922
41 Squadron	Squadron Leader F Sowrey DSO MC AFC	In situ	See 8 Squadron 1924
	Squadron Leader R S Aitken MC AFC	1 September 1928	AV-M retirement 20 July 1946
43 Squadron	Squadron Leader A F Brooks	In situ	See Appendix B 1925
	Squadron Leader C N Lowe MC DFC	10 January 1928	See 602 Squadron AAF 1925
45 Squadron	Squadron Leader J K Summers MC mid	In situ	See Appendix B 1927
	Squadron Leader F J Vincent DFC	15 November 1928	See 56 Squadron 1925
47 Squadron	Squadron Leader C R Cox AFC	In situ	See Appendix B 1927
55 Squadron	Squadron Leader H A Whistler DSO DFC*	In situ	See Appendix B 1927
	Squadron Leader A H Peck DSO MC*	25 April 1928	See 25 Squadron 1923
56 Squadron	Squadron Leader C H Elliott-Smith AFC	In situ	See Appendix B 1926
	Squadron Leader A Lees	7 February 1928	AM retirement 26 November 1949
58 Squadron	Squadron Leader E W Norton DSC	In situ	See 70 Squadron 1925
60 Squadron	Squadron Leader R H G Neville MC	In situ	See Appendix B 1927

70 Squadron	Wing Commander H R Nicholl OBE	In situ	See Appendix B 1926
	Wing Commander J A G De Courcey	26 November 1928	G/Capt died 30 December 1940
84 Squadron	Squadron Leader F J Vincent DFC	In situ	See 56 Squadron 1925
	Squadron Leader J J Breen three times mid	22 October 1928	AM retirement 2 May 1946
99 Squadron	Squadron Leader B E Smythies DFC	In situ	See 41 Squadron 1923
100 Squadron	Squadron Leader L T N Gould MC DFC	In situ	See Appendix B 1925
101 Squadron	Squadron Leader J C P Wood	28 March 1928	W/Cdr cashiered 6 January 1940
111 Squadron	Squadron Leader K R Park MC* DFC New Zealand	In situ	See Appendix B 1927
207 Squadron	Squadron J B Graham MC AFC	In situ	See 1 Squadron 1921
	Squadron Leader E A Beaulah	December 1928	G/Capt relinquished 10 October 1948
208 Squadron	Squadron Leader V E Lindop	In situ	See Appendix B 1927
216 Squadron	Wing Commander L D D McKeen OBE mid	In situ	See Appendix B 1924
502 Squadron SR	Wing Commander A C Wright AFC	In situ	See Appendix B 1926
503 Squadron SR	Wing Command The Hon. L J E Twistleton-Wykeham-Fiennes	In situ	See 29 Squadron 1923
504 Squadron SR	Squadron Leader C H Elliott-Smith	23 April 1928	See 56 Squadron 1926
600 Squadron AAF	Squadron Leader The Hon. F E Guest PC CBE DSO MP	In situ	See Appendix B 1926
601 Squadron AAF	Squadron Leader Lord E Grosvenor	In situ	See Appendix B 1925
602 Squadron AAF	Squadron Leader J Fullerton	In situ	See Appendix B 1927
603 Squadron AAF	Squadron Leader J A McKelvie AFC	In situ	See Appendix B 1925
605 Squadron AAF	Squadron Leader J A C Wright AFC TD	In situ	See Appendix B 1925

Annex

An exceptionally detailed service biography for Flight Lieutenant Stanley Flamank Vincent can be accessed on the Air of Authority website, which the authors constantly refer too - and gratefully acknowledge. A highlight concerns his narrow escape from death when following a tour of operations on the Western Front he was performing the duties of a flying instructor on 29th April 1917, his aircraft broke up in the air. Unconscious when extricated from the wreckage he remained so for four days and it was a full seven months before he was deemed fit to once more take to the skies. His AFC, one of the first to be awarded, was in recognition of his work as a flying instructor.

Flight Lieutenant Alfred Clifford Sanderson whose command of 5 Squadron was of a temporary nature, pending the arrival of Squadron Leader Oliver Campbell Bryson [see below] gained his DFC in the closing days of the *Great War* when as the citation reads: *"On 5th November this officer set a fine example of determination and devotion to duty. In pouring rain and at a height seldom over 200 feet, he carried out a reconnaissance of the Army front, locating the enemy forces by drawing their rifle fire and machine-gun fire. The information thus obtained proved of great value."* [LG 8 February 1919, supplement 31170, page 2045]. At the time he was attached to 46 Squadron [F.1 Camel] at Busigny; the entries on his Army Form B.103 showing:

			Embarked 25.03.17	
07.04.17	*16 Sqdn*	*Posted to 16 Sqdn*	*27.03.17*	*B.213*
03.04.17	*London Gazette*	*To be Flying Officer*	*15.03.17*	*L G*
07.05.17	*GOC RFC*	*Wounded*	*06.05.17**	*Summary RFC*
13.05.17	*42 CCS*	*Admitted [GSW Hand* [unreadable] *Chest]*	*06.05.17*	*G D 4629*
09.05.17	*5 Gen*	*Admitted [GSW R Hand/Slt*	*09.05.17*	*W.3034*
	- " -	*To England per HS "Panama"*	*13.05.17*	*W.3093*
22.04.18	*London Gazette*	*To be Tempy Lieut.*	*05.02.18*	*Lon. Gaz.*
			Re-embarked 28.09.18	*L R 46 Sqdn*
05.10.18		*Posted to No. 46 Sqdn*	*29.09.18*	*B.213 - " -*
30.11.18		*Appt A/Captain [Flying]*	*11.11.18*	*- " - - " -*
01.12.18	*5 Bde*	*Awarded the DFC*		*r o 286*
15.12.18	*46 Sqdn*	*Leave 13.12.18to 27.12.18*		

* Trevor Henshaw on page 87 of *The Sky Their Battlefield* shows that with his observer, Lieutenant P A B Lytton, they were engaged in a photographic sortie when their RE.8 A4596 was attacked by a number of enemy aircraft at 1,000 feet and forced down at Farbus. Lieutenant Lytton was unscathed, their RE then attracted enemy artillery fire.

Air Marshal Sir Clifford Sanderson's final appointment was Command in Chief Far East Forces; he retired at his own request in order to facilitate promotion for younger officers.

Squadron Leader Oliver Campbell Bryson's MC was promulgated in *The London Gazette* on 5th July 1918, supplement 30780, page 7899; *"For conspicuous gallantry and devotion to duty. He made several difficult flights in unfavourable weather, and destroyed several hostile machines. He proved himself a determined and undaunted leader, and set a splendid example of courage on all occasions."*

Participating in operations over North Russia he was awarded the DFC [EG November 21,1919, issue 13528, page 3628]: *"He commanded a squadron of heavy bombing machines in North Russia during the whole of the summer of 1919, during which period he carried out a large number of successful raids on the enemy's territory. During the operations on the Dwina in August, and on the Pinega in September 1919, he flew a Snipe machine with exceptional skill and daring. A very gallant officer he has proved himself during these exceptionally difficulty aerial operations."*

In the meanwhile, he had been awarded the Albert Medal: *Whitehall, January 10, 1918.*

"The KING was pleased, at Buckingham Palace, on Wednesday, the 9th instant, to present to Captain Oliver Campbell Bryson, Flight Commander, Royal Flying Corps, the Albert Medal, which was awarded by His Majesty in recognition of his gallantry in endeavouring to save life in March last. The circumstances are as follows:-

'On the 15th March 1917, Captain [then Lieutenant Bryson, with Second Lieutenant Hillebrandtas passenger, was piloting an aeroplane at Wye Aerodrome when, owing to a sideslip, the machine crashed to the ground and burst into flames. On disentangling himself from the burning wreckage Captain Bryson at once went back into the flames, dragged lieutenant Hillebrandt from the machine, and, notwithstanding his own injuries, which were undoubtedly aggravated by his gallant efforts to rescue his brother officer from the fire, endeavoured to extinguish the fire on Lieutenant Hillebrandt's clothing.

"Lieutenant Hillebrandt succumbed to his injuries a few days later."

Born on 18th August 1897, and formerly of the Dorset Yeomanry, he joined the RFC on Christmas Day 1916. His MC was won whilst attached to 19 Squadron[Spad S.13]. Unfortunately, his service as per Army Form B.103c ends with notification of being awarded the MC.
It is reported on the Air of Authority website that Squadron Leader Henry Richard Busteed was the first Australian to hold a pilot's flying licence. Prior to the outbreak of war in August 1914, he was Chief Test Pilot for Bristol and Colonial Aircraft Company. He returned, briefly, to the service in the Second World War and was Air Officer Commanding No. 33 [Balloon Barrage] Group followed by No. 34 [Balloon Barrage} Group before reverting to the retired list in August 1941.

A Record of Service exists for William Victor Strugnell, entries showing he was treated between 16th and 27th April 1916, in 7 Stationary hospital, followed by a note dated 3rd June 1916, that he had been awarded the Military Cross; but as to the identity of his unit, this is absent. It was duly *Gazetted,* less citation, on 3rd June 1916, supplement 29608, page 5577, and followed a year later on 26th July 1917, supplement 30204 and page 7621 of *The London Gazette* by a First Bar: *"For conspicuous gallantry and devotion to duty. While leading an offensive patrol he attacked and brought down a hostile machine. In all he has accounted for five machines and a kite balloon."*

An Olypian Hockey Player, Irishman, Wing Commander Franks Lubbock Robinson won the MC with the Royal Marine Artillery while serving in the Ypres sector: *"For conspicuous gallantry and devotion to duty ass Artillery Observing Officer between 30th July and 10th August 915, when posted on a high building in the neighbourhood of Ypres. The building was continually shelled by the enemy with heavy guns, but he maintained his position, a most precarious and dangerous one, even when the building was in imminent danger of falling, and supplied valuable information throughout."* [EG September 10, 1915, issue 12849, page 1380].

Now long since transferred to the Royal Air Force and for his services as a squadron commander in Mesopotamia, he was *Gazetted* with the DSO [EG April 11, 1919, issue 13431, page 1442]: *"A very gallant and able Squadron Commander who, by his fine leadership and personal example, has raised high the morale of his command. By his untiring energy he has rendered most valuable service on reconnaissance duty and bombing raids."*

And in *The London Gazette* of 28th October 1921, issue 32501, page 8496, his DFC was promulgated as follows: *"For continuous good work, gallantry and devotion to duty. This officer has flown over 100 hours during operations, and has shown at all times an untiring example throughout. He has had three machines put out of action by hostile fire from the ground."* It is noted his substantive rank was now flight lieutenant.

As a squadron commander with the RNAS, Anthony Rex Arnold received the DSC, less citation appended, in *The London Gazette* supplement 30654, page 5059. So far, details for his DFC remain untraced.

Serving with the South Africa Forces, Temporary Captain Edwin Cheere Emmett received the MC in 1917 [EG February 6, 1917, issue 13048, page 292]. Serving in Egypt, he received the DFC [LG 8 February 1919, issue 31170, page 2038]: *"During the late operations this officer has been distinguished for gallantry and devotion to duty. Before an attack he took a series of oblique photographs of the enemy's lines - a service that entailed considerable personal risk, as he was compelled to fly at a very low altitude in the face of heavy machine-gun fire."*

Commanding 20 Squadron for the better part of two years on India's Northwest Frontier, Squadron Leader Charles Henry Nicholas was *Gazetted* with the DFC *"For consistent good work, and gallantry and devotion to duty. This officer has not only led his squadron in nearly every raid, but by his energy and devotion to duty has kept the squadron in a high state of efficiency. He was mainly responsible for bringing his squadron from Baghdad 14 days after landing at Basra, which is in itself a remarkable achievement."* [EG November 1, 1921, issue 13756, page 1847].

The sad demise in December 1929 of Squadron Leader Arthur Gordon Jones-Williams during his tenure of commanding No. 23 Squadron has been recorded on the Kenley Revival website, acknowledged by the authors. Born in British Columbia at Coldstream Ranch on 6th October 1898, his nationality according to the 1911 Census was "Welsh." Commissioned to the Welsh Regiment it seems he was immediately transferred to the RFC and by the spring of 1917, he was flying Nieuport scouts with 29 Squadron and winning the MC and First Bar, the citations for which read: *"For conspicuous gallantry and devotion to duty. He has continuously shown the utmost dash and gallantry in attacking superior numbers of hostile machines. On one occasion he attacked twelve hostile scouts and succeeded in destroying one and driving down another."* [LG 18 July 1917, supplement 30188, page 7234} and; *"For conspicuous gallantry and devotion to duty when engaged in combat with hostile aircraft. On several occasions he attacked enemy formations although they were in superior numbers, fighting them in more than one instance single-handed, and showing the finest offensive spirit. He drove several machines down out of control, fighting until his ammunition was expended."* [LG 17 September 1917, supplement 30287, page 9559] respectively.

His *Croix de Guerre avec Palme* was conferred by the President of the French Republic and *Gazetted* on 5th April 1919, supplement 31273, page 4512.

In this abridged account, the concluding paragraphs reporting his untimely death show: *"In December, Arthur Jones Williams was attached to the Long Distance Flight at RAF Cranwell.*

"Immediately prior to Jones-Williams arriving at Cranwell, the RAF had taken delivery of a Fairey Long-range Monoplane [J9479]. Preparations for a record attempt [Cranwell to Cape Town] *began and Jones-Williams teamed up with First Lieutenant* [sic] *N H Jenkins OBE DFC DFM. A 24-hour test flight was carried out on 22-23 March 1929 before the decision was made to attempt a flight to Banglore in India, a distance of around 5,000 miles. After taking off from Cranwell on 24 April 1929, when the attempt was hampered by headwinds, jones-Williams and Jenkins landed at Karachi after being airborne for 50 hours and 48 minutes. Although they had failed in their distance record attempt, this was the first non-stop flight between Britain and India.*

"Undeterred by this disappointment, a decision was made to mount another attempt later in the year, this time on the Britain to South Africa route. Flying J9479 again, Jones-Williams and Jenkins left Cranwell on 16 December 1929. However, disaster struck the following day when the aircraft crashed at Djebel Lit, Zaghouan, a mountainous region south of Tunis, killing both men. Locals from Sainte Marie Du Zit saw the aircraft come down, found the bodies beneath the wreckage and reported their discovery to the authorities. Troops were rushed to the scene and by nightfall on Wednesday 18th, it was established that it was indeed the missing Fairey Monoplane, at which point the President General in Tunis was alerted and he sent condolences to the British Consul General, Mr. J McLeod. The sad news reached The House of Lords as they rose that night and was announced by Lord Thomson "with great emotion." The following day the bodies of the two airmen were taken to Tunis with full military honours.

"As part of the investigation into the crash, the navigational log was recovered revealing differences between their recorded and actual height, the crew had believed they were flying at 5,000 feet but had impacted the ground at 2,300 feet. The crash was the result of either an altimeter failure or differences in the barometric pressure between Britain and Tunisia giving a false reading."

Squadron Leader Arthur Gordon Jones Williams MC* and *Croix de Guerre avec Palme* was laid to rest on New Year's Day 1930, at St. John the Evangelist Church, Newtimber in West Sussex.

Squadron Leader Robert Stanley Aitken's appointment as Commanding Officer, No. 41 Squadron, was, undoubtedly, a very pleasant occasion for during the *Great War* he was attached to the squadron from October 1916 to July 1917, when he was posted to 52 Squadron [RE.8] for flight commander duties, during which he would gain the Military Cross [LG 26 July 1917, supplement 30204, page 7621]: *"For conspicuous gallantry and devotion to duty. On several occasions he made most valuable reconnaissances of the enemy's lines, and on two successive days he engaged and severely damaged hostile batteries, working under most adverse weather conditions."*

Prior to his appointment as commanding officer, he had attended the Electrical and Wireless School at Flowerdown and, subsequently, he served as Signals Officer at HQ Iraq Command and in the Mediterranean [1922 and 1924]. With advancement to air rank he fulfilled the duties of Chief Signals Officer with various commands and in 1940 was Fighter Command's chief signals officer during which time he transferred from the General Duties Branch to the Technical Branch

For the last two years of his service, Air Vice-Marshal Aitken CB CBE MC AFC was Chief Signals Officer, Headquarters Mediterranean Allied Air Forces.

Like so many of his generation, military service began in the army and in his case as a lowly private on the 2nd of December 1914, on which date his service record shows he was in 'A' Company, 2/15th London Regiment [PWO Civil Service Rifles] at Bishop's Stortford, while a year on he was commissioned to 1st/1st East Anglian [Essex] Royal Garrison Artillery, Cavenham, Mildenhall.

As a 2nd Lieutenant he joined the Royal Flying Corps in August 1916.

Appendix C - Officers Granted Short Service Commissions

A total of 269*names have been traced for officers granted short service commissions in 1928, from which at least forty-one lost their lives, either during their terms of active service, or whilst in the Reserve of Air Force Officers and in the case of Captain Noel William Aubrey Cullum after he had been commissioned to the Unattached List of Indian Officers.

Also of note is the inclusion in the Roll of Honour, Warrant Officer Denis Lascelles Iremonger whose life was taken on New Year's Eve 1942, while attached to 104 Squadron. Denis, whose short service commission was *Gazetted* on 10th July 1928, 'blotted his copybook' and it was only through the intervention of his father petitioning His Majesty King George V that his entry reads 'Resigned' and not 'Dismissed,' as the verdict of his General Court Martial found him guilty and recommended his dismissal from the service.

However, as noted in his entry, he returned to the Air Force on the outbreak of the Second World War and had he not been killed it is likely he would have received a wartime commission.

* Practically doubling the number commissioned in 1927.

LG 3 January 1928, issue 33344, page 47 - From 14th, 15th and 16th December 1927 and all with seniority 9th December 1927 [11 entrants]

24190 CARTER Edgar Ernest P/O 16.07.28 Terminated
24191 MURRAY William Farquhar W/Cdr 10.02.54 Relinquished
24192 OUTHWAITE John Arthur Stephen A/Cmdr 29.08.55 Retirement
Air Commodore John Arthur Stephen Outhwaite OBE twice mentioned in despatches, died on Wednesday, 19th June 1968. A technical officer, his final service appointment was Senior Technical Staff Officer at Bomber Command headquarters.

FREEMAN Malcolm Morris P/O 27.06.28 Terminated
24188 HALES George Francis W/Cdr + 09.05.51 RAF Sutton-on-Hull
Wing Commander George Francis Hales was Station Commander at RAF Sutton-on-Hull when, as reported in the *Bradford Observer* in their edition of Saturday, 10th March 1951: *"While attending morning parade at the RAF firefighting school at Sutton Hull yesterday, the station's commanding officer, Wing-Cmdr. George F. Hales [45], of Bournemouth, collapsed in front of nearly 200 men and died within five minutes. He was posted to the school only a month ago. His parents live in London."* His body was taken back to London and cremated at St. Marylebone Crematorium.

A book, titled *RAF Sutton on Hull* was written by Len Bacon who, sadly, died in August 2007 and though no longer in print it can be read online via the Sutton and Wawne Museum website.
LITTLE Charles Hugh Rudgard F/O + 01.04.31 A&GS Eastchurch
Flying Officer Charles Hugh Rudgard Little died when his Gloster Gamecock I J8073 crashed as he approached to land at Rochford Aerodrome. A report in *Aeroplane* magazine published on 15th April 1931, reported: *"An inquest was held at Rochford on April 13, on Flying Officer C H R Little, who was killed at Rochford on April 1st. Evidence was given that Mr. Little had not made sufficient allowance for a gusty wind which caught the tail of his machine as he was about to land. A verdict of "Accidental Death" was returned."*
24193 STEPHENSON Clifton G/Capt 01.08.55 Retirement
Paul McMillan reports, Group Captain Clifton Stephenson died at the age of 87 in Ambilly [Haute-Savoie] France on Tuesday, 29th December 1992.

ACKERLEY Harold Reginald Ravenhill P/O 06.06.28 Terminated
Paul McMillan has come across a piece of interesting information concerning Harold Reginald Ravenhill Ackerley who was born in Llandrindod Wells in the County of Radnorshire, Wales in July 1908: Under the heading 'Fascist Movement in Reading': *"Sir Oswald Moseley's mother visits local branch ... Saturday, from the mother of their leader, Sir Oswald Moseley - Maud, Lady Moseley. She was met at Reading Station by H R R Ackerley, who escorted her to the Headquarters, 68 London Street, where a guard of honour consisting of 20 menand 12 women in orthodox Fascist manner."* Published by the *Reading Standard* on Friday, 12th October 1934. My co-author also adds that in 1939, Harold Ackersely was living in the Hendon area of London and was employed as a Aircraft Progress Clerk.
24184 BUFTON Sydney Osborne AV-M 17.10.61 Retirement
Air Vice-Marshal Sydney Osborne Bufton CB DFC, died Monday, on 29th March 1993. Strikingly handsome in appearance, Sydney Osborne Bufton was a 'Bomber Baron' through-and-through though from November 1941 his services in Bomber Command were concerned with Staff work [he was Deputy Director of Bomber Operations from November 1941 and Director from March 1943] and his views on the conduct of the 'Bombing Campaign' often brought him into conflict with the Air Officer Commanding, Sir Arthur Harris who regarded Bufton and his ilk as interfering bureaucrats. Perhaps there best known 'spat' came in 1942 when Bufton 'floated' proposals for the establishment of a specialised target marking force. This raised the hackles within Sir Arthur but, eventually, he had to concede and 'Pathfinder Force' came into existence on 15th August 1942, gaining Group status as No. 8 [PFF] Group on 8th January 1943 with Air-Vice Marshal D C T Bennett appointed to command.

Prior to these senior officer differences of opinion, as Wing Commander Bufton he had taken over command of 10 Squadron on 21st July 1940 from the dynamic Wing Commander William Ernest 'Bull' Staton, a larger that life character who during his leadership of 'Shiny 10' formulated the ideas of marking a target by the use of flares. In the spring of 1941, Wing Commander Bufton was briefly in command of 76 Squadron, the second bomber squadron to be equipped with the four-engined Halifax.
24187 GRISEWOOD Peter Henry Edmund P/O 09.05.28 Terminated
Returned to service and commissioned in the Administrative and Special Duties Branch with the rank of pilot officer for the duration of hostilities, effective from 12th March 1940 [LG 9 April 1940, issue 34826, page 2075]. P/O 11.02.41 Relinquished
On account of ill-health [LG 14 February 1941, issue 35076, page 911].
24190 McGILL Duncan Bassett S/Ldr 10.02.54 Relinquished
24194 WOOD Geoffrey F/Lt 10.02.54 Relinquished

Note. Although published in groups of three, four and five respectively, their service numbers appear to have been issued in alphabetical order of surnames.

LG 17 January 1928, issue 33348, page 371 - Seniority 30th December 1927 [27 entrants]

Block 24195 to 24221

24195 BAILEY Henry F/O 30.12.32 Class A
Flying Officer Henry Bailey was employed by Blackburn Aircraft as a test pilot and it while testing Blackburn B20 V8914 that he and his crew perished in a crash on 7th April 1940. The following extract has been taken from the Aviation Safety Network, ASN Wikibase Occurrence Report 204426 which I have pleasure in acknowledging: *"On 7 April 1940, the B.20 [now bearing RAF serial V8941] took to the air from Dumbarton for its*

first attempt at a high speed run. The pilot was Blackburn test pilot Flt Lt Harry Bailey, with him were Ivan Waller, a Rolls-Royce flight test engineer, Fred Weeks, a Blackburn flight test engineer, and Duncan Roberts and Sam McMillan, both Blackburn aircraft riggers along to monitor instruments during the flight. The flight that day was over the Forth of Clyde and Sound of Bute on Scotland west coast. A high speed run took place at which a speed of 345 mph was reached, but shortly afterwards severe vibration set in. Reducing speed did not help and Flt Lt Bailey ordered the crew to take to their parachutes. Up in the cockpit Fred Weeks was able to get out of one of the escape hatches in the roof, but Ivan Waller deployed his chute too early and it got caught in the radio mast with him only half way out of the escape hatch. Then the vibration stopped and Ivan was able to climb along the top of the fuselage, untangle his parachute and drop free. Flt Lt Bailey stayed with the aircraft until the last possible moment to give the other two crew members a chance to escape, his parachute did not open fully and he was drowned. The aircraft crashed into the sea off Gourock Head, Isle of Bute. No trace was ever found of Duncan Roberts and Sam McMillan. The two surviving crew members were rescued by the improbable sounding HMS Transylvania [a Merchant Ship converted into an auxiliary cruiser]. The crew of the Transylvania reported seeing a large rectangular unit come down out of the thick cloud cover, probably an aileron. The most likely explanation for the crash is that the initial vibration was aileron flutter, this ceased when the aileron broke free [gving Ivan Waller the chance to free his parachute]. But with the loss of an aileron the aircraft would have been uncontrollable, leading to its crash. With the loss of the one and only example of the B20 the project ended."

Flight Lieutenant Bailey's body was recovered; he was cremated at Hull Crematorium where he is commemorated on the Screen Wall, Panel 1. Four excellent photographs of the ill-fated Blackburn B-20 are reproduced on pages 394, 395, 396 and 397, along with a very detailed report on the B-20s design and construction, of A J Jackson's superb history of Blackburn Aircraft.

24197 BOWLING Victor Swanton AV-M 01.08.61 Retirement

Air Vice-Marshal Victor Swanton Bowling CB CBE mentioned in despatches, died on Saturday, 27th December 1971. Hiss service career was unusual in that following graduation from 2 FTS Digby his flying up to the end of January 1930, when he was posted to Wittering for training as a flying instructor, was confined to service with squadrons of the Special Reserve, during which he was attached to 503 Squadron County of Lincoln and 501 Squadron County of Gloucester.

As a QFI he instructed at Digby, where he trained, and later with 5 FTS Sealand. From April to October §935, he was attached to 41 Squadron [Demon] for flight commander duties, after which he returned to flying instruction at home and in Egypt.

His final appointment was as Director of Air Defence combined with Assistant Chief of Staff - Air Defence at SHAPE.

24198 BUTLER George Cyril G/Capt 10.02.54 Relinquished

Group Captain George Cyril Butler was Conferred by Her Majesty the Queen of the Netherlands as a Commander of the Order of Orange Nassau [LG 28 August 1945, supplement 37242, page 4342].

24199 CARTER Cyril Walter Francis S/Ldr 05.09.48 Relinquished

On account of medical unfitness for Air Force service [LG 14 September 1948, issue 38401, page 4948].

24200 CLARKE Thomas Joyce P/O 29.08.28 Relinquished

On account of ill-health [LG 4 September 1928, issue 33418, page 58359]. On 19th December 1935, he received a class C commission in the Reserve of Air Force Officers, General Duties Branch, with the rank of flight lieutenant [LG 4 February 1936, issue 34252, page 738] and served until completion of service on 1st May 1938 [LG 12 July 1938, issue 34531, page 4540]. Subsequently transferred to the Administrative and Special Duties Branch he was granted a class CC commission on 28th November 1946 [LG 31 December 1946, supplement 37833, page 6324].

24201 CREASY Noah Wilmot F/Lt 07.12.42 Resigned

24202 DASHWOOD-TANDY Reginald Napper P/O 19.06.29 Relinquished

On account of ill-health [LG 21 June 1929, issue 33508, page 4123].

24203 DE COURCY-WHEELER Wigstrom Hercules Beresford P/O 06.06.28 Terminated

Subsequently he was commissioned as a 2nd Lieutenant to the Irish Guards on 8th January 1940 [LG 26 January 1940, supplement 34779, page 520].

24204 D'OLIER Bertrand Guy P/O + 17.08.28 2 FTS Digby

Please refer to Appendix D and LG 27th March 1925, issue 33033, page 2117, and for the entry appended to Flying Officer Alfred Rodney Feather.

24205 ELLIOTT Eric Douglas G/Capt 01.12.55 Retirement

As Squadron Leader Eric Douglas Elliott he was appointed to command 253 Squadron on its re-formation at Manston on 20th October 1939. Initially equipped with Miles Magisters and Fairey Battles, Hurricanes began to arrive in January 1940 and shortly after '253' moved to Northolt before lodging at Kenley on 8th May 1940, A Flight detaching to Hawkinge on 21st May 1940, to participate in proving additional fighter cover for the *Battle of France.* Leading a patrol to Lens in Hurricane I P3552 Squadron Leader Elliott was shot down by ground fire, parachuting near Douai and taken into captivity. Held at Stalag-Luft III his identity was 3592.

24207 FORBES Donald Abercrombie P/O 27.06.28 Terminated

24209 HARTWRIGHT William Richard W/Cdr 12.03.50 Retirement

On account of medical unfitness for Air Force service [LG 14 March 1950, supplement 38861, page 1274].

24210 HUGGETT John Osborne Courtenay P/O 16.07.28 Resigned

24211 MACKENZIE John Burslem F/O + 28.11.31 RAF Gosport

Flying Officer John Burslem Mackenzie's death was reported in the *Belfast News-Letter* of Wednesday, December 2nd, 1931, under the heading 'Did Pilot Faint - Officer's Opinion at Inquest on Air Crash Victims':

"A verdict of accidental death was returned at the inquest at Fort Grange, Gosport, yesterday on Flying Officer John Burslem Mackenzie and Flying Officer Arthur George Teidman, who were killed on Saturday when the aeroplane in which they were flying crashed into a garden at Hill Road, near Lee-on-Solent.

"Flight-Lieutenant John Harrison, Commanding Officer RAF Fort Grange, said that in his opinion the pilot fainted, and there was not time for the second pilot to take charge as it was only 500 feet from the ground.

"John Stuart Shea, an RAF rigger, a passenger in another service 'plane, said the machine that crashed was stunting. It went into a slow "roll' and flew upside down for several seconds, and in that position it disappeared into the clouds at a height of 900 feet.

"Mr. F S Wilkins, an expert from the Air Ministry, said in his opinion fit men did not faint, Full service honours were rendered at the funeral at Gosport yesterday. Three volleys were fired."

The twwo officers were airborne in DH 60M Moth K1203 attached to the Base Training Flight, Gosport.

24212 NORMAN-WRIGHT Kenneth Ivor Frank Chartres P/O 09.05.28 Terminated

24213 ODBERT Norman Cyril W/Cdr 01.01.69 Relinquished

Appointed to a Class J commission in the Reserve of Air Force Officers [LG 23 April 1957, supplement 41052, page 2473].

24214 ROWLAND Patrick Basil Trevor P/O 26.09.28 Terminated

24215 SILK Boyce Pomeroy P/O 07.07.28 Terminated

24216 SIMPSON John Herbert Thomas A/Cmdr 01.06.59 Retirement

Air Commodore John Herbert Thomas Simpson DSO AFC twice mentioned in despatches, died on Saturday, 26th August 1967. As recorded in David Gunby and Pelem Temple's first volume devoted to bomber losses in the Middle East and Mediterranean theatres, Wing Commander Simpson was the captain of 70 Squadron Wellington IC Z1045 which was destroyed in unknown circumstances on 26th April 1942, details of the crew being reported on page 140 of the aforementioned volume.

During his tenure as Commanding Officer of the Bomber Development Wing, Central Bomber Establishment at Marham, he executed a perfect wheels-up landing on the airfield when the undercarriage of Spitfire XVI SL563 jammed. As noted in Air-Britain's SA100-VZ999 serial register, SL563 was not repaired.

24217 TANNER Joseph Seymour P/O 18.12.28 Resigned

Please refer to Appendix D for 1929 and the entry for 11th October 1929.

24218 TOPE William Richard F/O 30.12.36 Relinquished
Returned to service and commissioned in the Administrative and Special Duties Branch with effect from 26th November 1939 [LG 27 February 1940, issue 34801, page 1175]. S/Ldr 27.07.54 Relinquished
24219 WARNER Richard Cecil W/Cdr + 29.11.56
Service extended for five years in the Aircraft Control Branch, 1st January 1955 [LG 4 January 1955, supplement 40375, page 87]. Wing Commander Richard Cecil Warner died in the National Hospital for Nervous Diseases, Queen Square, London, retitled 'National Hospital for Neurology and Neurosurgery' in 1990 and is part of the University College London Hospitals NHS Foundation Trust.

On 7th May 1933, Richard Cecil Warner, then in the employment of Hillman Airways Ltd., took off from Maylands Aerodrome, Romford, in DH.80 Puss Moth G-ABSB on a non-scheduled flight to Clacton-on-Sea, Essex, where it was damaged beyond repair whilst landing wet and slippery ground. Before coming to a stop in crashed through a hedge, injuring the pilot and his two passengers.
24220 WILKINS William Raymond Cary F/O 30.12.36 Relinquished
During the Second World War, William Raymond Cary Wilkins worked as a ferry pilot with the Air Transport Auxiliary, resigning on 15th April 1943 following his sixth flying accident for which he was deemed responsible.
24221 WRIGHT Leslie Ernest Arnold F/O 30.12.36 Relinquished

24208 FYFE John Bernard S/Ldr + 11.08.40 107 Squadron
Flying Officert John Bernard Fyfe was *Gazetted* with the DFC on 8th September 1933, issue 33976, page 5866: *"... in recognition of gallant and distinguished services rendered in connection with the operations on the North-West Frontier of India during the periods 28th January 1932, to 6th February 1932, and 6th March 1932, to 18th March 1932."*

Squadron Leader John Bernard Fyfe DFC* IGSM and his crew were lost without trace whilst attacking an aerodrome near Dinard. Details of the operation, which were flown in Blenheim IV T1850, and notes on his prewar service are reported on page 181 of my revised RAFBCL 1939-1940.

24196 BIRCH Ronald Antony Edward P/O 19.05.28 Resigned
Returned to service and promoted flying officer 8th September 1940 [LG 27 September 1940, issue 34954, page 5721] but was obliged to relinquish his commission on account of ill-health on 7th July 1942 [LG 10 July 1942, issue 35628, page 3051]. At the time he was ranked Flight Lieutenant.

24206 FIGGINS Bernard Wilkinson F/Lt 10.02.54 Relinquished

LG 31 January 1928, issue 33352, page 688 - Seniority 13th, 13th and 21 January 1928 respectively [3 entrants]

Block 24222 to 24224

24223 EVERETT Ernest Norman Victor F/O + 25.08.35 Madras Flying Club
Flying Officer Ernest Victor Everett was placed on class C of the Reserve of Air Force Officers on 6th October 1933 [LG 4 June 1935, issue 34167, page 3625], subsequently going out to India where he gained employment as a flying instructor with the Madras Flying Club [still extant].

On the day of his death he had taken off from Juhu Aerodrome, Madras, in DH.80 Puss Moth VT-ABU intending to fly to Hyderabad, but in the vicinity of Chowtapalem near Ponnalur, some 13 miles south of Kandukur, Nellore, a wing detached and the machine crashed out of control killing Flying Officer Everett, the aircraft's owner, Rajan IV Krishna Rao and Mr. H J Carter, an employee of Imperial Tobacco Company.

The Times of India reported the tragedy in their issue of August 26th, 1935, in which it was stated that Flying Officer Everett had flown to Gopal-puram to collect Raja Krishna Rao who wished to attend the annual meeting of the Madras Flying Club and it was during the return flight that the accident occurred. The report went on the say that Flying Officer Everett had married the previous year and during his RAF service had been posted to India where he was involved in operations in the North-West Frontier.

Recently, he had established records in cross-country flights, two being a flight from Karachi to Madras in 10 hours and 20 minutes and from Colombo to Madras, non-stop, in four hours. Raj Krishna Rao was *"a well known zamindar and Indian flier. He organised the Madras air taxi service between Madras and Calcutta."*

A report of their funerals was published in *The Times of India* on August 30th, 1935: *"The funeral of Flying-Officer E N V Everett and Mr. H J Carter, the victims of the air crash Chowtapalem, near Ponnalore, took place at Ponnalore, their remains being interred in the local police station grounds.*

"No clergyman being available in the locality, Mr. H D Latham, District Superintendent of Police, read portions of the burial service. Dr. Dyson and Mr. H F Prynne, representing the Madras Flying Club, and Mr. C A S Foulkes, representing the Imperial Tobacco Company, Madras, were present at the funeral. They expressed appreciation of the help rendered by the district police and other officers, particularly Mr. Latham, District Superintendent of Police.

"The body of Raja Krishna Rao was taken to Kollapuram, the Raja's native place, for cremation. The three ill-fated airmen were keen flyers, the Raja and Mr. Everett being, in addition, experienced and able pilots. Dr. Dyson added that they had lost their only pilot-instructor and that it would not be easy to find an officer to take his place.

"The Secretary of the Madras Flying Club has received condolence messages from the RAF Quetta, and the Delhi, Bombay, Karachi, Calcutta and Lucknow Flying Clubs.

"Government have received a report from the District Magistrate, Nellore, regarding the crash, giving particulars of the plane, the names of the occupants and the injuries sustained by them. It also refers to the arrangements made for the burial of the remains of Flying-Officer Everett and Mr. Carter and the handing over of the body of Raja Krishna Rao to relatives.

"The Madras Flying Club, it is understood, will be making arrangements to raise suitable memorials to the dead aviators."
24224 MORETON Esmond John Hugh Fulford S/Ldr 05.06.54 Relinquished
Please refer to my summary for 24th October 1929, for details of his accident in which his observer/air gunner was killed.
24222 BRITTON Alan Francis G/Capt 28.10.55 Retirement
My co-author reports Alan Francis Britton was born at Stony Stratford in Buckinghamshire on 17th August 1908, and died in London's Westminster district in January 1996.

LG 28 February 1928, issue 33361, page 1413 - Seniority 14th February 1928 [6 entrants]

Block 24225 to 24230

24225 CAMERON Ivan McLeod W/dr + 28.09.39 110 Squadron
Australia Wing Commander Ivan McLeod Cameron and his crew died when their Blenheim IV N6212 was shot down during a morning reconnaissance of the Münster area. The details pertaining to his final flight, and notes on his service between commissioning and death, are reported in my RAFBCL 1939-1940 revised edition, page 80. From Bealiba in the State of Victoria, and buried in the Reichswald Forest War Cemetery, he is believed to have been the first Australian pilot to lose his life on operations in the Second World War. He had been granted a permanent commission on 1st September 1932 [LG 9 September 1932, issue 33862, page 5765].

24226 CLARKE Cecil Ralph F/O 14.02.32 Relinquished
Australia On transfer to the Royal Australian Air Force [LG 16 February 1932, issue 33799, page 1053].
24227 KLEIN Garth Edmunds F/O 14.02.32 Relinquished

24228 LINDELL John Henry F/O 14.02.32 Relinquished
Australia On transfer to the Royal Australian Air Force [LG 16 February 1932, issue 33799, page 1053].
24229 McKENNA John Fergus F/O 14.02.32 Relinquished
Australia On transfer to the Royal Australian Air Force [LG 16 February 1932, issue 33799, page 1053].
24230 SAVILLE Donald Teale F/O 14.03.32 Relinquished
Australia On transfer to the Royal Australian Air Force [LG 16 February 1932, issue 33799, page 1053].

LG 13 March 1928, issue 33366, page 1861 - Seniority 2nd March 1928 [8 entrants]

Block 24231 to 24238

24231 BOOTES Ronald Yule P/O + 02.07.29 1 FTS Netheravon
Pilot Officer Ronal Yule Bootes death was reported in *The Dover Express and East Kent News* on Friday, 5th July 1929, under the heading 'Dover Air Officer Killed': *"On Tuesday, Pilot-Officer Ronald Yule Bootes, was killed at Netheravon while flying an Atlas machine of No. 1 Flying Training School. Mr. Bootes resided for some time with his parents first at Crabble and later at 5 Maison Dieu Road. His father was in the Pruudential Assurance Co., offices at Dover and has recently taken over the Deal office, and the family have just removed there. Mr. R Y Bootes was only 23 years of age. After leaving college he took up farming and about a year ago joined the Air Force, and was just passing his final examination when the fatal accident occurred. The body was taken to Deal on Wednesday, and the funeral takes place this afternoon at 2."*
24232 COWELL Ambrose Murray F/O 17.04.35 Removed
Flying Officer Ambrose Murray Cowell's removal from the service was promulgated in *The London Gazette* on 30th April 1935, issue 34155, page 2827 and TNA Kew AIR 76/109. He had been placed on Class A of the Reserve of Air Force Officers on 2nd March 1933 [LG 7 March 1933, issue 33918, page 1516] and it while serving his time in the Reserve that he committed the following offence, as communicated by Richard Cawsey to Paul McMillan, both reports having been published in the *Hampshire Telegraph* on Friday, 4th January and Saturday, 19th January 1935 respectively:
"Alleged robberies on Christmas Day at the Air Service Training Ltd., Hamble, and the Air Service Training Club, had a sequel at Eastleigh Petty Sessions on Monday, when Ambrose Malcombe Murray Cowell a smartly-dressed man of 25, giving his home address as St. Andrews, Bognor, was charged with breaking and entering an office, and stealing two bottles of whisky, and £1 1s 3d in money. There was a further charge of breaking and entering the A.S.T. Club, and stealing £1. 19s 6d in money.
"Cowell was represented by Mr. T W Cutts [Bognor]. The accused is an air student at Air Service Training Ltd. The evidence showed that memorandums found on the prisoner had come from the office of the assistance secretary of the A.S.T. Ltd. When detained by the police he showed signs of having been drinking. He had visited the bar of the club on several occasions during the previous twenty days. Accused said [in a statement to the police]. "I did not break in. I came in to telephone. Someone must have come in before me."
"At the Police Station he said. "If I did it, I don't remember it. It sounds as though there is a lot of circumstantial evidence against me." The casse for the prosecution being closed, Mr. Cutts pleaded guilty on behalf of the accused, and reserved the right to address the court in extenuation.
"Accused was committed for trial at the Hampshire Quarter Sessions on January 15. He was admitted to bail."
The heading reporting Ambrose Cowell's appearance at the Petty Sessions was headed 'Frolice at Hamble.'
"A Christmas Day incident at the Air Service Training Ltd. Aerodrome at Hamble was recalled at the Hampshire Quarters Sessions at Winchester, on Tuesday, when Ambrose Malcombe Murray Cowell, aged 25, pleaded guilty on a charge of breaking and entering the office of the A.S.T. Ltd., and also the club house and stealing £2 7s 11d in money, two bottles of whisky, a memorandum, and a rate of exchange note. Mr Blake Odgers [prosecuting] said at the time of the offences, Cowell was undergoing a course in flying at the A.S.T. school. "He seems to have spent a very curious Christmas Day," said Counsel, "because just after dinner he broke into these two buildings. I understand the outer doors of the premises were opened by the application of a shoulder and not by any instrument. It was all done in an open manner, as there were on the premises employees of A.S.T. Ltd., who saw him there and knew he was a student." Council added that there was some evidence that accused had been drinking.
"Superintendent Pragnell said accused had served in the R.A.F. and was now on the reserve. He bore a good character in the service.
"Mr. Seymour Collins for the defence, said "It was all a drunken frolic, and he has only the vaguest recollection of what happened."
"I hope you will take this chance and not play the fool again, particularly with drink," said the Chairman [Judge Barnard Lailey, K.C.] in announcing that Cowell would be bound over for two years."
Just over a year later Ambrose Malcombe Murray Cowell was dead, killed when the Aircraft Constructions Ltd., Lympne, Mignet HM.14 Pou du Ceil [Flying Flee] G-AEEW crashed in the cousse of a test flight at Penshurt Airfield, some 5 miles SW from Tonbridge, Kent. The Aviation Safety Network website gives a detailed account of the crash in ASN Wikibase Occurrence Report 204952, which the authors dutifully acknowledge:-
"The second fatal accident involving a Pou de Ciel in this country occurred at Penshurt last Monday, when Flt Lt A M Cowell lost his life. He had reached a height of 300-400feet, when his machine went into a dive from which, apparently, that pilot was unable to extract it.
"Flt Lt Cowell was formerly a Short Service Officer in the R.A.F. After leaving the service he was in Sir Alan Cobham's displays, and last autumn he joined the Air League of the British Empire as the League's official test pilot for the Pou du Ciel. Cowell had accumulated considerable experience piloting the Pou, and was always very careful over checking rigging and centre of gravity position before taking the machines up. On this occasion, it is understood, he tested the machine in straight flight and found it satisfactory. Air Commodore Chamier, of the Air League, has applied to the Air Ministry for the grounding of all Pou du Ciel pending an enquiry."
Referred to throughout the above report as 'Flt Lt' Cowell, it would seem that Ambrose had taken it upon himself to promote himself to a rank that he was not entitled to following his removal from the service. This, in my opinion, in no way detracts from his undoubted flying experience.
24233 GROOM Arthur John Pelham F/O 09.03.32 Relinquished
On account of ill-health [LG 8 March 1932, issue 33806, page 1607]. With effect 6th January 1936, in the rank of flight lieutenant, he was granted a commission in class C of the Royal Air Force Reserve, General Duties Branch [LGG 10 March 1936, issue 34263, page 1563]. Transferred to the Administrative and Special Duties Branch by 1st November 1936, he was granted a commission, retaining his rank, and with his service number now 74847 [LG 20 October 1939, issue 34713, page 7043]. W/Cdr 27.03.45 Relinquished
On account of medical unfitness for Air Force service [LG 17 April 1945, supplement 37034, page 2018].
24234 HAYWOOD Alfred W/Cdr 29.10.57 Retirement
Granted a Class J commission on 25th April 1960. S/Ldr 01.12.71 Relinquished
My co-author reports that Alfred Hayward died in October 1992, in the Hillingdon district of Greater London.
24235 JAFFÉ Alred Daniel S/Ldr 20.11.45 Relinquished
On account of medical unfitness for Air Force service [LG 4 December 1945, supplement 37373, page 5893].
24236 REDPATH Robert Victor F/O 02.03.37 Relinquished
2nd Lieutenant Royal Artillery TA received a commission in the Royal Air Force Volunteer Reserve, Training Branch, with effect from 18th April 1941 [LG 16 May 1941, issue 35165, page 2823] with service number 64620. P/O 12.01.44 Resigned
24237 VINNING Raymond Edgard Sydney Malmenayde P/O 27.06.28 Terminated
24238 WESTWOOD Arthur Hamil P/O 20.02.29 Relinquished
On account of ill-health [LG 19 February 1929, issue 33468, page 1198].

LG 27 March 1928, issue 33370, page 2243 - Seniority 16th March 1928 [40 entrants]

Block 24239 to 24256 and 27001 to 27022

24239 BAKER John Allan Gerald P/O 29.05.29 Terminated

24240 BARNARD Harold Melville Southard P/O 25.07.28 Terminated

24241 BARNETT Max Ian F/O + 04.11.30 56 Squadron

24242 BEAUMONT John W/Cdr 10.02.54 Relinquished

And very unusually the remark: *"No retention of rank,"* considering he had been appointed OBE and held an AFC.

24243 BISHOP Frank Anthony Russell F/O 03.06.31 Resigned

24244 BRAMBLE Bernard Sidney P/O 09.10.29 Cashiered

By sentence of General Court Martial [LG 5 November 1929, supplement 33549, page 7074].

24245 CATLING William Ernest P/O 20.08.28 Terminated

24246 CHADWICK Reginald S/Ldr 14.05.44 Retirement

24247 COTTON Ralph Douglas P/O 28.06.30 Terminated

24248 CRISHAM William Joseph AV-M 02.06.61 Retirement

Air Vice-Marshal William Joseph Crisham CB CBE twice mentioned in despatches, died on Friday, 24th July 1987. On 29th August 1942, when he was Station Commander RAF Kirton-in-Lindsey, he was very seriously injured when his Magister I L8226 'borrowed' from 253 Squadron, crashed 3 miles NE of the airfield. Group Captain Crisham had flown over to Church Fenton and was on the return flight when the accident occurred. Weather conditions in the area were described as extremely poor with visibility lowering with each passing minute, thus leading to the Group Captain to attempt a forced-landing. His unnamed passenger escaped unhurt. On recovering from his injuries, Group Captain Crisham was posted on 30th April 1943 to take command of the Tangmere Sector.

Postwar, and while Air Officer Commanding Levant, he attended the ceremony, along with King Hussein of Jordan, for the formal handing over RAF Masfriq, the last RAF Station in Jordan, to the Royal Jordanian Air Force. Thus, on this historic day, 31st May 1957, Royal Air Force presence in Jordan ended after forty years. Just over a year later he was appointed Air Officer Commanding Germany, his final service appointment.

24249 DARBYSHIRE Rupert Stanley W/Cdr + 05.11.41 608 Squadron AAF

Acting Sub-Lieutenant RNR Commanding 608 Squadron AAF Wing Commander Rupert Stanley Darbyshire took off, with his crew, in Hudson V AM657 UL-D to lead his squadron on an anti-shipping strike off the Frisian Islands. Airborne from Thornaby at 2001 they were lost without trace, as were Flight Sergeant Gordon Richardson Yeates and crew in Hudson V AM642 UL-R. All are commemorated on the panels at the Runnymede Memorial.

24250 DONOVAN Francis Patrick F/Lt 16.03.37 Class C

Appointed MBE of on 3rd June 1933, Paul McMillan states Flight Lieutenant Francis Patrick Donovan became a test pilot at Westlands Aircraft, Yeovil. He was slightly injured whilst making a practice parachute jump from Vickers Virginia X K2327 at RAF Henlow on 16th September 1933, this being documented on AIR 76/137 which is held by TNA Kew. This document shows his date of birth as 8th March 1899, my co-author adding 'Fleet, Hampshire.' His death occurred in Aldershot on 21st January 1949; it is believed he many have died whilst still in the Reserve.

24251 FORSTER Harold James S/Ldr 10.02.54 Relinquished

24252 FREEMAN Frederick Charles Gordon S/Ldr + 11.07.42 101 Squadron

Squadron Leader Frederick Charles Gordon Freeman and his crew were lost without trace whilst on a sea-mining operation in Wellington IIIZ1751 on 11th-12th July 1942. Details of the crew, all of whom are commemorated on the Runnymede Memorial, are recorded on page 149 of my third volume of RAFBCL.

24253 GARRATT Oswald Vernon P/O 01.08.28 Terminated

24254 GILSON Oliver Ingham G/Capt 10.05.56 Retirement

24255 GREENWOOD Eric Stanley F/O 10.02.54 Relinquished

There are numerous websites mentioning Eric Stanley Greenwood who, after leaving the service, became a test pilot for Gloster Aircraft. Quoting from the website 'History of Manston Airfield,' which I have pleasure in acknowledging, Eric Greenwood, by then the Company's Chief Test Pilot, flying Meteor IV EE455 'Yellow Peril' [also known as 'Forever Amber'] flew at over 600 m.p.h. over the Thames Estuary on a course running from Herne Bay Pier to Reculver Point. The date was 7th November 1945, and it was Group Captain Hugh Joseph Wilson CBE AFC, Commandant of the RAF Test Pilot's School at Cranfield in Bedfordshire who set the first world speed record in a jet aircraft when flying Meteor IV EE454 'Britannia' he achieved 606.36 m.p.h. at an altitude of 250 feet. Both pilots used Manston as their base. Both Meteors came from an order for 250 F.3 airframes which were delivered from Gloster's Hucclecote factory between November 1944 and December 1946, though EE454 and EE455 were delivered to F.4 configuration. EE454 became 6735M in November 1949, while EE455 went to RAE Farnborough before being struck off charge on New Year's Day 1954. Photographs of EE454 in its high gloss standard RAF camouflage scheme and EE455, displaying a Union Jack on its nose, are reproduced on pages 123 and 124 respectively of Edward Shacklady's excellent *The* Gloster *Meteor* published in 1962, by Macdonald.

Eric Stanley 'Terry' Greenwood died on the last day of February 1979.

24256 HALL Aubrey Noel Edmund F/O 01.03.38 Relinquished

2nd Lieutenant 17th London Regiment TA Returned to service and transferred from the General Duties Branch to the Administrative and Special Duties Branch on 29th August 1939 [LG 20 February 1940, issue 34794, page 1004]. F/Lt 10.02.54 Relinquished

27001 HANLON Charles Peter F/O + 25.12.30 30 Squadron

27002 HARRIS Joseph Ashley W/Cdr 10.02.54 Relinquished

27003 HARTWELL Brodwick William Charles Elwin P/O 15.08.28 Relinquished

On account of ill-health. Paul McMillan has found the following on *Wikipedia*: *"Sir Brodrick William Charles Elwin Hartwell, 5th Baronet .... Born on 7th August 1909, the son of Sir Brodrick Cecil Denham Arkwright Hartwell, 4th Baronet [1876-1948], Sir Brodrick Hartwell, 5th Baronet, was educated at Bedford School. He was the fifth of the Hartwell baronets of Dale Hall in the County of Essex, created on 26 October 1805for Admiral Francis Hartwell, succeeding to the title on the death of his father, the 4th Baronet, on 24 November 1948. During the Second World War he served as a captain with the Leicestershire Regiment. He was dismissed from the army on 30 April 1949."*

A report of his dismissal was published in Australia in *The Argus* [Melbourne] under the heading 'Army Officer Dismissed' London [AA[]:-

"Defending Council told a Court Martial which dismissed Captain Sir Broderick W C E Hartwell, bart, from the service that Hartwell's mind had given way under the strain of money demands from "an overbearing wife."

"Hartwell was found guilty of fraudulent misapplication of £234 from Army depot funds, Council said that when he told his wife of their financial position, she threatened that if he did not comply with her demands she would report him."

Sir Brodrick Hartwell, 5th Baronet, died on 14 December 1993; he was succeeded by his son, Sir Francis Anthony Charles Peter Hartwell.

27004 HITCHINGS Ernest George F/O 16.05.37 Relinquished

On 29th May 1928, issue 33388, page 3769, the following notice was promulgated:-

"Notice is hereby given, that ERNEST GEORGE BANHAM, of 12 St. Jame's-terrace, Plymouth, in the County of Devon, an Officer in the Royal Air Force, lately called Ernest George Hitchings, a natural-born British subject, has assumed, and intends henceforth on all occasions and at all times to sign and use to be called and to be known by the name of Ernest George Banham, in lieu of and substitution for his former name of Ernest George Hitchings, and that such intended change of name is formerly declared and evidenced by deed poll under his hand and seal dated the 5th day of May, 1928, duly executed and attested and enrolled in the Central Office of the Supreme Court of Judicature on the 23rd day of May, 1928.-Dated the 24th day of May, 1928.

LEES SMITH and CRABBE, Oakley House, 14, 16 and 18, Bloomsbury-street, W.C.1., Solicitors for the said Ernest George [022] Banham."

27005 HOPE Thomas Robertson W/Cdr 10.02.54 Relinquished

Wing Commander Thomas Robertson Hope was *Gazetted* with the DFC, less citation, on 9th July 1943, supplement 36084, page 3094. At the time of the award, he was Commanding 158 Squadron [Halifax II] at Lissett. He features in my history of the squadron, revised edition, published privately in February 1990 under the title *In Brave Company - 158 Squadron Operations.* On 10th-115h August 1943 he failed to return from a Main Force attack on the city of Nürnberg, his Halifax II HR938 NP-L being shot down by a night-fighter over Belgium. Wing Commander Hope and two other members of crew survived, the remainder, sadly, perished. Please refer to page 264 of my RAFBCL 1943 for their details.

Taking over the squadron from Wing Commander C G S R Robinson DFC on 10th March 1943, Wing Commander Hope flew the following operations sorties:-

12-13.03.43	Essen	Halifax II DT700 NP-S	High concentration of fires
29-30.03.43	Berlin	Halifax II HR715 NP-A	Hit by Flak and port outer engine 'knocked out,' bombs jettisoned
03-04.04.43	Essen	Halifax II W1217 NP-L	A confused attack
16-17.04.43	Plzen	Halifax II HR720 NP-B	Took Group Captain Seymour Lucas as 2nd pilot
12-13.05.43	Duisburg	Halifax II HR738 NP-Z	Bombed primary at 0215 from 21,000 feet
27-28.05.43	Essen	Halifax II HR776 NP-O	Bombed primary at 0111 from 18,000 feet
11-12.06.43	Düsseldorf	Halifax II JD789 NP-V	Orbited target area for 10 minutes waiting to markers
19-20.06.43	Le Creusot	Halifax II JD789 NP-V	Bombed primary at 0153 from 6,000 feet - landed Chipping Warden
13-14.07.43	Aachen	Halifax II HR938 NP-L	Bombed primary 0147 from 17,500 feet
10-11.08.43	Nürnberg	Halifax II HR938 NP-L	Failed to return

Wing Commander Hope was held in Stalag 9C Muhlhausen, his prisoner of war number being 1767.

27006 LINES Harold Thomas S/Ldr 20.10.45 Relinquished
On account of medical unfitness for Air Force service [LG 6 November 1945, supplement 37336, page 5388].

27007 LINTOTT Victor Burke P/O 01.07.28 Terminated
Returned to service in the Royal Air Force Volunteer Reserve, General Duties Branch, and granted a commission as an Acting Pilot Officer on 18th May 1940 [LG 18 June 1940, issue 34876, page 3708] as 79581. F/Lt 15.10.54 Relinquished

27008 LOCK John Henry F/Lt 10.02.54 Relinquished
2nd Lieutenant Royal Signals TA

27009 MILLS Eric David F/O 09.04.32 Relinquished
On account of ill-health.

27010 MOUNTAIN Ralph F/O 07.09.34 Class A
Subsequently became a senior Captain with British Overseas Airways Corporation + 05.11.43 BOAC

Ralph Mountain's biography may be read on the website Poole Flying Boats Celebration, to which I am indebted. Born in Battersea on 5th July 1906, Ralph was a pupil at Westminster School, later becoming a graduate at London University where he studied at the College of Estate Management before being accepted for a short service commission.

From October 1930 until November 1932 he was attached to HMS *Courageous* while his final service posting was at Martlesham Heath. On leaving the service he found employment in Africa before returning to the UK and joining the Power Petroleum Company, becoming their area representative for Cheshire. Then, in March 1936, he was accepted by Imperial Airlines and following a good deal of study and application to flying seaplanes he joined the Company's Empire Flying Boat division in September 1937. Two months into his appointment as a flying boat pilot he was to come to the notice of Royal Humane Society for his bravery in respect of the loss of the Short S.23 Flying boat G-ADUZ *Cygnet* on 5th December 1937.

Taking off from Brindisi Harbour, Italy, Ralph, then a First Officer, was sitting behind two very experienced pilots, namely Captain R P Mollard and Acting Captain F U Hollins. Initially, the take off run across the harbour proceeded normally but with the airspeed hovering at around 50 knots *Cygnet* began to porpoise violently and before corrective action could be taken the boat nosed over, staving in the front section, and propelling Ralph and a colleague through what remained of the windscreen.

Considerably dazed and shocked, Ralph swam back to the sinking aircraft, ignoring a rescue launch which was quickly on the scene, and managed to find three passsengers in the rear cabin area. With some difficulty he managed to get them to the main hatchway from where they were lifted to safety. For his outstanding courage he was awarded the Society's 'Stanhope Gold Medal' thereby acknowledging his was the bravest act by a British subject for the year. Ralph, accompanied by his wife, received his award in March 1939 at a ceremony presided over by His Royal Highness the Duke of Gloucester.

Salvaged, the cause of the crash was traced to incorrect setting of the flaps. A report of the crash can be accessed via the Aviation Safety Network, which indicates two fatalities from the crew of six and seven passengers, the latter including Marshal of the Royal Air Force, Sir John Salmond who required hospital treatment for his injuries.

During the Second World War, and with Imperial Airways and British Airways merged into British Overseas Airways Corporation, Ralph was very much involved in flying boat work which took him into the war zones of the Middle East. Sadly, he was destined to lose his life when Sunderland III G-AGIA *Haslemere* [built as ML728] in which he was a supernumerary to Captain Shakespeare, crashed whilst *en route* to the UK, some 130 miles south of Tobruk at El Taurub Taawale, near Sollum, in the Western Desert following a fire in one of the wings, which broke away. There were no survivors; Captain Ralph Mountain is buried in Egypt in Halfaya Sollum War Cemetery.

27011 NICOLAY Vincent Humphries F/O + 26.05.30 CFS Wittering
Flying Avro 504N J8728 with fellow officer, Flying Officer Philip Francis Luxton, Flying Offcer Vincent Humphries Nicolay failed to recover from a sideslip and crashed at Barholm, 5 miles NE from Stamford, Lincolnshire. His passenger survived, though was badly injured. The Aviation Safety network website in Wikibase Occurrence 209354 states the Avro's starboard wing hit the ground; also, the report shows Flying Officer Nicolay was on attachment to CFS from 4 Squadron.

27012 POLE John Sheldon F/O 30.11.32 Relinquished
On account of ill-health [LG 29 November 1932, issue 33887, page 7591].

27013 PROCTOR Gerald Edwin Frederick W/Cdr 10.02.54 Relinquished

27014 PUGH John Bernard Walter F/Lt 16.07.40 Relinquished
On appointment to a commission in the Royal Navy Volunteer Reserve [LG 28 March 1941, issue 35119, page 1813]. The Edinburgh Gazette, June 3rd, 1932, promulgated the award of the Air Force Cross to Flying Officer John Bernard Walter Pugh, and the following was published in *The London Gazette,* 9th June 1955, supplement 40497, page 3292: *"The QUEEN has been graciously pleased, on the occasion of the Celebration of Her Majesty's Birthday, to give orders for the publication of the names of the undermentioned in the London Gazette:- Queen's Commendations for Valuable Services in the Air - Overseas Territories : Captain John Bernard Walter Pugh OBE AFC Chief Pilot, Cyprus Airways."*

27015 ROBBINS Cyril Howard P/O 29.06.29 Dismissed
By sentence of General Court Martial [LG 9 July 1929, issue 33515, page 4544].

27016 SHELDRICK Norman Xavier S/Ldr 10.02.54 Relinquished

27017 SNELLING Leonard Howard G/Capt 16.02.47 Resigned
Appointed to a permanent commission in the rank of squadron leader 11th August 1947 and transferred from the General Duties Branch to the Secretarial Branch. A/Cmdr 14.07.65 Retirement
Air Commodore Leonard Howard Snelling AFC, died onTuesday, 26th March 1985. His final service appointment was as Air Officer Commanding the RAF Record Office at Innsworth.

27018 TAYLOR Frederick Barry F/Lt 19.09.64 Relinquished

27019 TIMMS David P/O 14.07.28 Terminated

27020 WALLING José Greet P/O 23.06.28 Relinquished
On account of ill-health [LG 26 June 1928, issue 33397, page 4347].

27021 WILLIAMS Ronald Frank F/O 16.03.33 Relinquished
On account of ill-health [LG 21 March 1933, issue 33923, page 1967].

27022 WILLIAMS Ronald Frederick Anderson Whittaker F/Lt 16.03.37 Relinquished

LG 24 April 1928, issue 33378, page 2904 - Seniority 2nd and 13th April 1928 respectively [14 entrants]

Block 27023 to 27036

27036 WILSON Hugh Patrick F/Lt 16.04.41 Dismissed
By sentence of General Court Martial [LG 2 May 1941, issue 35151, page 2514]. [14 entrants]

27023 ADDISON John
27024 CAMPBELL Donald Archibald Lang F/O 29.10.36 Relinquished
Returned to service and served until: F/Lt 07.05.56 Relinquished
27025 CHAPMAN Hubert Huntlea AV-M 28.03.63 Retirement
In the Third Supplement to *The London Gazette* published 3rd May 1946, supplement 37553, page 2127, Group Captain Hubert Huntlea Chapman was Conferred by the President of the United States [Harry S Truman] with the Bronze Star Medal. Air Vice-Marshal Hubert Huntlea Chapman CB CBE, died on Monday, 10th April 1972. A signals specialist for most of his service career, he retired from the Royal Air Force on account of medical unfitness.
27026 DEACON Paul Le Mesurier Carodyce F/O + 20.12.39 Bristol Aeroplane Company
Flying Officer Paul Le Mesurier Carodyce Deacon was transferred to the Reserve Class A on 13th April 1933 [LG 18 April 1933, issue 33931, page 2632]. Joining the Bristol Aeroplane Company he lost his life on 30th December 1939, whilst testing Bristol Beaufort I L4468, the 23rd aircraft from the fist production batch L4446-4548 [73 airframes]. Taking off from Filton for a routine test L4468 crashed into the Severn river, the *Western Daily Press* publishing the following on Thursday, 25th January 1940: *"The adjourned inquest of Paul Le Mesurier Caradyce Deacon, aged 30, of 10 Beaufort Road, Clifton, who died when an aeroplane in which he was conducted a flight test crashed into the water off Avonmouth docks on December 20, was resumed yesterday by the Bristol City Coroner, Mr. A E Barker. A verdict of "Accidental death" was recorded.*

"Dr. A D Fraser, the pathologist at Bristol infirmary, said that death was due to concussion following fracture of the skull accelerated by multiple injuries. In answer to a question the doctor said he had examined Deacon's heart three months before and he would have pronounced it fit. Some unexpected shock mid-air might have affected his heart, although he would have been fit for normal purposes of flying.

"Arthur John Pegg [subsequently the Company's Chief Test Pilot] *of Hazlecote, Rudgeway, who described himself as an assistant test pilot, said the machine was found airworthy. He described Deacon as a highly competent pilot, and he was looking perfectly fit just before he made the flight.*

"Ronald Alfred Kennett said that he saw the 'plane come suddenly straight out of the clouds in an almost perpendicular dive and dive into the water.

"Frederick Francis White of 148 Cotswold road, whose boat put out to sea after the accident, described how the pilot's body was recovered from the water. "His parachute was open, spread out in the tide, It was attached to him."

Very unusually, bearing in mind wartime censorship rules, the pilot's name was reported. He is buried in Papworth Everard [St. Peter] Churchyard.
27027 HAWKE John William F/O + 05.05.30 20 Squadron
27028 JONES Frank Richard G/Capt 19.06.65 Retirement
At his own request [LG 20 July 1965, supplement 43716, page 6937].
27029 JONES Walter Henry W/Cdr 20.10.43 Retirement
On account of ill-health [LG 2 November 1943, supplement 36230, page 4816].
27030 KERR Hamish W/Cdr 10.02.54 Relinquished
27031 McGREGOR Hector Douglas AM 27.09.64 Retirement
New Zealand Air Marshal Sir Hector McGregor KBE CBE DSO seven time mentioned in despatches, died on Wednesday, 11th April 1973. His final service appointment, commencing on the last day of May 1962, was as Commander in Chief Far East Air Force.
27032 MACPHERSON George Francis G/Capt 02.10.50 Retirement
At his own request [LG 31 October 1950, supplement 39055, page 5427].
27033 WHALLEY Richard Goodhart P/O 12.12.28 Resigned
From the UK Calendar of Prisoners 1868-1929, Paul McMillan found:-
"Name: Richard Goodhart Whalley - Trial Age: 22 - Birth Date: abt 1906 - Trial Date: 21 March 1928 - Trial Place: Newington, London, England Occupation: Flying Officer - Charge: Drunk in charge of a motor car - Sentence: Not guilty - Discharged

In the Second World War Richard Goodhart Whalley served in the Army.
27034 WHITAKER Eric Stuart P/O 29.08.28 Resigned
Returned to service and granted a commission for the duration of hostilities as a probationary Pilot Officer in the Equipment Branch, effective 1st June 1940 [LG 25 June 1940, issue 34881, page 3871], his service number, initially, being 80510, but subsequently reverted to 27034. He was transferred to the Reserve [Flight Lieutenant] on 1st May 1953, but was immediately called up for air force service [LG 19 May 1953, supplement 39856, page 2776]. S/Ldr 01.05.57 Relinquished
27035 WILLIAMS Hubert John Aldridge W/Cdr 24.10.60 Retirement

LG 1 May 1928, issue 33380, page 3054 - Seniority 18th, 19th and 20th April 1928 respectively [4 entrants]

Block 27037 to 27040

27037 BALFOUR Frank Ruddach F/O 13.04.33 Class A
Promoted flight lieutenant 1st April 1937, whilst in the Reserve of Air Force Officers, General Duties Branch [LG 26 October 1937, issue 34447, page 6617], and now with a class CC commission, which was relinquished on 20th November 1939 [LG 5 March 1940, issue 34805, page 1318]. Transferred from the General Duties Branch to the Administrative and Special Duties Branch 17th June 1942 [LG 30 June 1942, issue 35615, page 2879] retaining his rank. F/O 01.01.60 Relinquished
27038 DAVIES Cyril Gordon S/Ldr 10.02.54 Relinquished
27039 JOHNSTONE Edward Leo P/O + 31.08.28 3 FTS Grantham
Pilot Officer Edward Leo Johnstone died during a solo flight in an Avro 504N when he stalled off a flat turn and dived into the ground near the airfield.
27040 OXFORD Maxwell Norman S/Ldr 10.02.54 Relinquished
My co-author, Paul McMillan, reports that Maxwell Norman Oxford was born in Parkstone in the Poole district of Dorset on 3rd May 1905. In 1932, he was *Aide de Camp* to the Governor of Nyasaland and was transferred to the Reserve Class A [8th October 1932] on his return to the UK. Mobilised on 28th August 1939, and ranked Flight Lieutenant, he found himself in Hong Kong at the time Japan entered the war on the side of the Axis in December 1941 [Flight Lieutenant Oxford had been Air Attaché at the Chungking Embassy in southwest China]

The website Hong Kong Escape, which we acknowledge, reports that on Christmas Day Squadron Leader 'Max' Oxford was invited by Mike Kendall, a Canadian born mining engineer who had lived in Hong Kong since his childhood days, to join his escape party.

The account of the escape is extremely lengthy and features numerous personalities; in brief, Squadron Leader Oxford, along with others, arrived in Chunking in mid-January 1942 and following debriefing he went to India. Postwar, he returned to Hong Kong charged with the task of restoring civil flight at Kai Tak airport.

Squadron Leader Maxwell Norman Oxford OBE died on Friday, 1st August 1980, in Topsham, Devon.

LG 15 May 1928, issue 33384, page 3427 - Seniority 1st May 1928 - Terms of service, three years on the active list

FLIGHT LIEUTENANT

27041 MONTAGU-DOUGLAS-SCOTT Walter George Leon F/Lt 28.09.28 Resigned

LG 12 June 1928, issue 33393, page 4022 - Seniority 25th and 27th May respectively [30 entrants]

Block 27042 to 27071

27042 ALLAN John Crawford F/O 29.10.30 Resigned
27043 BLACK Charles William F/O 03.09.32 Relinquished
On account of ill-health [LG 9 September 1932, issue 33862, page 5765]. On 8th October 1938, granted a commission in class CC and in the rank of flight lieutenant in the Reserve of Air Force Officers, General Duties Branch [LG 24 January 1939, issue 34592, page 547]. Granted a commission in the Administrative and Special Duties Branch with effect from 17th July 1939 [LG 20 October 1939, issue 34713, page 7044] with service number 74897. W/Cdr 06.06.47 Resigned
27044 BLOICE Reginald Alfred P/O 03.10.28 Terminated
27045 CHAMEROY Gasrton Rupert P/O 25.09.28 Terminated
27046 CONNOLLY Patrick Joseph F/Lt 30.05.38 Relinquished
On appointment to the Air Branch of the Royal Navy [LG 12 July 1938, issue 34531, page 4540].
27047 COOK Horace P/O 16.11.28 Resigned
27048 COVERDALE John
27049 COX Joseph
27050 CULLINAN Patrick John Joseph F/O 13.07.32 Relinquished
On account of ill-health [LG 12 July 1932, issue 33845, page 4561].
27051 DORAN WEBB Richard Francis Joseph P/O 01.12.28 Terminated
27052 EADY Thomas William George G/Capt 01.06.53 Retirement
At own request [LG 10 July 1953, supplement 39910, page 3861].
27053 FLOWER John Keane F/O 04.06.37 Relinquished
Returned to service and within the General Duties Branch of the Reserve of Air Force Officers was granted a commission, in the rank of flying officer, in class A with effect from 4th August 1939 [LG 15 August 1939, issue 34654, page 5610]. S/Ldr 06.02.45 Relinquished
On account of medical unfitness for Air Force service [LG 20 February 1945, supplement 36945, page 984].
27054 FRIDAY Harry Clifford F/O 22.01.33 Resigned
27055 GAHAN Brian Herbert P/O 23.03.39 Terminated
27056 HARCOMBE John Cozens S/Ldr 10.02.54 Relinquished
27057 HARKNESS George Augustus Erskine W/Cdr 01.02.56 Retirement
27058 HOWES Charles Victor
Commanding 102 Squadron [Whitley V], Wing Commander Charles Victor Howes was *Gazetted* with the DFC, less citation, on 22nd August 1941, issue 35254, page 4864. G/Capt 09.03.49 Retirement
27059 LOUIS Ronald G/Capt 10.02.54 Relinquished
27060 McCULLOCH Martin Lindsay P/O 23.03.29 Terminated
27061 MITCHELL Alan Cunningham W/Cdr + 18.09.40 HQ RAF Aden
New Zealand Wing Commander Alan Cunningham Mitchell, age 35, is buried in Yemen in Maala Cemetery. His biography is recorded on page 350 of Errol Martyn's third volume of *For Your Tomorrow.* Thus shows he trained at 4 FTS Abu Sueir and on gaining his 'Wings' he was posted to 55 Squadron [DH.9A/Wapiti]. Following his return to the UK he served as a flying instructor at RAFC Cranwell before training for seaplane duties and service with 201 Squadron [Southampton].

Subsequently, he flew Singapore's with 209 Squadron, underwent a flying instructor course at the Central Flying School and as an instructor was attached to 9 FTS Thornaby and later with 7 FTS at Peterborough. He was posted to the Middle East on 25th October 1938 for Staff Duties at HQ RAF Aden.

27062 PASSMORE Eric Charles G/Capt 09.03.64 Retirement
Retiring to the Seychelles, Group Captain Eric Charles Passmore CBE, died Wednesday, on 18th February 1981. His obituary was published in *The Times* on Wednesday, March 4th, 1981:-

"*Group Captain Eric Charles Passmore CBE, who died in Seychelles on February 18, aged 71, had a distinguished record of service, latterly in communications. He joined the Royal Air Force in 1929* [sic] *with a short service commission, learnt to fly in Egypt, and subsequently served in Iraq.*

"*After a long signals course at Cranwell, he gained a permanent commission in the Signals Branch. He served with the Fleet Air Arm for four years in HMS Furious until 1938. In the Second World War he served first in Fighter Command Groups and later in the Middle East and Italy. After the war he served in England and then from 1950 to 1954 was lent to the Indian Air Force as Director of Signals.*

"*He was made an OBE in 1942 and a CBE in 1952.*

"*On his retirement from the Royal Air Force after a Nato tour at HQ AAFCE* [Allied Air Forces Central Europe] *Fontainebleau, he settled in Seychelles and was soon asked to help in establishing a radio station and broadcasting service there. He was the designer and founder of what was to become Radio Seychelles, and stayed with organisation ass Manger and Chief Engineer until 1976. He leaves a widow, a son, and two daughters.*"

27063 PEARSE Richard Courtenay Ilbert S/Ldr 10.02.54 Relinquished
27064 ROBERTSON Paul Kendall F/O 25.05.33 Relinquished
On account of ill-health [LG 24 October 1933, issue 33989, page 6843]. Returned to service and granted a commission in the Administrative and Special Duties Branch as a probationary Pilot Officer, 15th April 1940 [LG 14 May 1940, issue 34849, page 2899] and with 78784 as his service number, subsequently amended to his original number of 27064. On 3rd November 1947 he was transferred to the Aircraft Control Branch and served until: F/Lt 25.07.59 Relinquished
27065 ROBINS John Rumney F/Lt 30.05.38 Relinquished
On appointment to the Air Branch of the Royal Navy [LG 12 July 1938, issue 34531, page 4540]. As Lieutenant [A] serving on the aircraft carrier HMS *Ark Royal* John Rumney Robins died on 1st August 1940. He is buried in Tunisia at Medjez-el-Bab War Cemetery. His headstone is inscribed "*Dearly Loved Son Of John N And Muriel W Robins.*"
27066 ROTHERAM Edward F/O 10.02.54 Relinquished
27067 SMITH William P/O 03.10.28 Terminated
27068 THOMAS Henry Vaughan P/O 03.10.28 Terminated
27070 WILKIN Peter Corbett P/O 14.12.28 Terminated
27071 WILSON John P/O + 24.08.29 216 Squadron

27069 WATTS Ronald Edwin W/Cdr 14.08.50 Resigned
The London Gazette published on Tuesday 2 December 1947, supplement 38137, page 5703, promulgated the conferring by the Queen of the Netherlands that Acting Wing Commander Ronald Edwin Watts was an Officer in the Order of Nassau with Swords.

LG 10 July 1928, issue 33402, page 4662 - Seniority 29 June 1928 [27 entrants]

Block 27072 to 27098

27072 AYLING James Reginald F/Lt 09.07.62 Relinquished
27073 BALFOUR Thomas Frank F/O 29.06.33 Class A
27074 BENNET Robert Logie W/Cdr 26.04.45 Resigned
As Flight Lieutenant Robert Logie Bennet he was granted a class CC commission in the Administrative and Special Duties Branch [LG 4 September 1945, supplement 37249, page 4428].
27075 BINLEY Alan Keith Hilton F/O 29.06.33 Class A
New Zealand TNA Kew holds a document in AIR 76/39/56 in respect of Alan Keith Hilton Binley which shows his date of birth as 25th April 1907. While in the Reserve he died on 18th November 1934, when DH.60M Moth VT-ABB of the Bombay Flying Club crashed during an approach to Juhu aerodrome, Bombay. His passenger, C W Ring was injured.
27076 BROWN John Howat W/Cdr 10.02.54 Relinquished
27077 CLARE HUNT Reginald John G/Capt 28.01.59 Retirement
27078 CLAXTON John Cecil Lauga F/O + 18,06.30 School of Photography
Flying Officer John Cecil Lauga Claxton died when his Bristol F.2b spun and crashed at Farnborough. He was 21 years of age.
27079 COLE Adrian Gordon P/O + 17.08.28 2 FTS Digby
Pilot Officer Adrian Gordon Cole, late of the 7th Middlesex Regiment TA, died less than six weeks since his appointment to a commission; for details of the crash that ended his life and that of Pilot Officer Bertrand Guy d'Olier, please refer to the entry for Flying Officer Alfred Rodney Feather, a flying instructor at 2 FTS Digby, whose short service commission is reported under LG 27th March 1925, issue 33033, page 2117.
27080 COUPE Richard Harold P/O + 07.11.28 2 FTS Digby
Pilot Officer Richard Harold Coupe died when he stalled his Avro 504K E3150 off a turn near the village of Boothy Graffoe, 8 miles south of Lincoln and a similar distance WNW from Digby.
Reported in the *Aberdeen Press and Journal* beneath the by-line *'Nose-Dive to Death - RAF Officer Killed While at Landing Practice'*
"Evidence given at the inquest at Cranwell, Lincolnshire, yesterday of Pilot Officer Richard Harold Coupe, [23], stationed at Digby, who was killed on Wednesday as the result of a crash at Boothby, showed that the machine was in perfect order. Coupe was practising advanced forced landings.
"An eye-witness stated that he saw the machine gliding down, but took no notice. Hearing the engine start, as though the machine were lifting, he looked up and saw it turn on one wing and nose-dive.
"An officer of the RAF Medical Services described the injuries, and said that death was instantaneous. Coupe's head struck the instrument board.
"A verdict of "Accidental death while flying" was returned."
27081 DAVIS Sidney Alexander F/O + 17.02.31 36 Squadron
27082 EDNEY HAYTER Frederick Charles F/O 14.03.35 Resigned
27083 ELLISON Richard Charles William F/Lt 10.02.54 Relinquished
27084 GARRETT-PETTS William Christopher P/O 05.11.28 Terminated
Returned to service and granted a commission in the Administrative and Special Duties Branch as a pilot officer with effect from 26th February 1940 [LG 19 March 1940, issue 34814, page 1639] with service number 77731 [subsequently amended to his original number 27084]. Served throughout the Second World War until: F/Lt 10.02.54 Relinquished
27085 IREMONGER Denis Lascelles F/O 06.01.33 Resigned
Paul McMillan reports *"In 1930 Denis* [Iremonger] *was posted to India. It was while in India that Denis ran into some trouble. It appears he may have misappropriated some money from the Mineral Water Fund in which he as in charge of. He was found guilty by a General Court Martial at Lahore in 1932. He was sentenced to be dismissed; but an appeal by his father to King George V resulted in the sentence being commuted to a severe reprimand, a loss of one year's seniority and he called upon to resign, which he did on 6th January 1933."*
Circa 1940, Denis Lascelles Iremonger joined the Royal Air Force as an airman, underwent refresher flying, and by December 1942, had been promoted warrant officer and was attached to 104 Squadron based in Malta. On New Year's Eve 1942, he took off from Luqa with his crew in Wellington IC HD955 for operations against a target at Stax and failed to return. All are commemorated on the Malta Memorial. For details of the crew, please refer to David Gunby and Pelem Temple's first volume of bomber losses in the Middle East and Mediterranean, page 211.
27086 ISRAEL Jack Morris F/O 16.07.40 Relinquished
On appointment to a commission in the Royal Naval Volunteer Reserve. Prior to switching his allegiance from the Royal Air Force to the Royal Navy, and whilst in the Reserve of Air Force Officers, Paul McMillan has discovered that Jack Morris Israel joined Jersey Airways as a pilot in 1934 and was in their service until the Channel Islands were occupied by German forces.
At some point he gave up the surname 'Israel' in favour of 'Keene-Miller' and in December 1944, was appointed OBE. Postwar, he left the Royal Navy in 1945, and took up the post of General Manager of Channel Island Airways. He retained thus position when Channel Airways became a division of British European Airways. Jack Morris Keene-Miller retired in 1970.
Paul has also discovered that on 7th June 1944, as Commander Flying [A] at RNAS Lee-on-Solent he 'borrowed' Seafire NF486 from 808 Squadron and was shot over the Allied beachheads and made a prisoner of war.
Reaching for my copy of *The Seafire* by David Brown, I was delighted to find an account of this on pages 64 and 65: *"The Commander [Flying] of Lee-on-Solent, Commander J H Keene-Miller RNVR, and his No.2, Lieutenant Commander C P Campbell-Horsfall RN, flying Spitfire LVBs of 808 Squadron, were bounced by six Bf. 109Gs, about ten miles inland. Commander Keene-Miller was shot down and made a prisoner of war, but his weaver held off three very determined Germans, jinking violently and turning every pass into a head-on approach until he reached the coast and the protection of the naval AA barrage at very low level."*
27087 JAMES Edward George P/O 29.05.29 Relinquished
On account of ill-health.
27088 JARRETT Geoffrey William Jones S/Ldr + 03.04.43 9 Squadron
Squadron Leader Geoffrey William Jones Jarrett and his crew died when their Lancaster III ED479 WS-Z was shot down oveR Germany during operations to Essen on 3rd-45h April 1943. All are buried in the Recihswald Forest War Cemetery. Their names are recorded on page 89 of my RAFBCL 1943. Squadron Leader Jarrett took over B Flight from Squadron Leader Denis Clyde-Smith; his operational sorties commenced:-

13-14.01.43	Essen	W4133 WS-Z	Bombed at 1934 from 22,000 feet through cloud
16-17.01.43	Berlin	W4144 WS-Z	Bombed at 2031 from 18,000 feet - scattered attack
17-18.01.43	Berlin	W4133 WS-Z	Bombed at 2056 from 16,000 feet - concentrated in SE area of city
30-31.01.43	Hamburg	ED479 WS-Z	DNCO rear gunner's electrically heated suit failed
02-03.02.43	Cologne	ED479 WS-Z	Bombed at 2147 from 18,00 feet - landed with 4,000HC still in bay
04-05.02.43	Turin	ED479 WS-Z	Bombed at 2149 from 12,000 feet - excellent visibility
13-14.02.43	Lorient	ED480 WS-U	Bombed at 2126 from 12,000 feet - layer of smoke in target area
16-17.02.43	Lorient	ED480 WS-U	Bombed at 2050 - target indicators slightly off aiming point
18-19.02.43	Wilhelmshaven	ED480 WS-U	Bombed at 2035 from 20,000 feet - good fires burning
26-27.02.43	Cologne	ED479 WS-Z	Bombed at 2134 from 18,000 feet - red target indicators
01-02/03.43	Berlin	ED479 WS-Z	Bombed at 2225 from 18,000 feet - bombed north of aiming point
03-04.03.43	Hamburg	ED479 WS-Z	Bombed at 2136 from 14,000 feet - smoke obscuring target
05-06.03.43	Essen	ED479 WS-Z	Bombed at 2118 from 20,000 feet - concentrated fires
22-23.03.43	St. Nazaire	ED479 WS-Z	Bombed at 2143 from 12,000 feet - landed Portreath

26.27.03.43 Duisburg ED479 WS-Z Bombed at 2152 from 20,000 feet - target indicators scattered
27-28.03.43 Berlin ED479 WS-Z Bombed at 2320 from 20,000 feet - good fires
03-04.04.43 Essen ED479 WS-Z Failed to return
27089 LEMPRIERE George Rollo O'Connell P/O 13.09.29 Terminated
27090 McLOUGHLIN Charles Norman F/O 14.01.30
Granted a Ccass C commission in the Reserve of Air Force Officers, General Duties Branch, retaining his rank [LG 2 August 1938, issue 34537, page 4973]. Subsequently transferred to the Administrative and Special Duties Branch service number now 74887; postwar granted a permanent commission, attached to the Secretarial Branch and served until: W/Cdr + 06.05.61 Retirement
27091 RIESS James Graydon P/O + 31.08.28 2 FTS Digby
Probationary Pilot Officer James Graydon Riess, formerly of the 20th London Regiment TA, was critically injured during a solo flight on 30th August in Avro 504N H2201 when he stalled during a turn at Nocton Heath a village roughly 6 miles NNW from the airfield.
27092 ROBERTSON John Douglas P/O 26.10.29 Dismissed
By sentence of General Court Martial [LG 5 November 1929, supplement 33549, page 7074].
27093 SALES Horatio Edward S/Ldr 10.06.45 Relinquished
On account of medical unfitness for Air Force service [LG 26 June 1945, supplement 37146, page 3315].
27094 SMITH Ian Maxwell P/O 04.01.30 Dismissed
By sentence of General Court Martial [LG 17 January 1930, issue 33571, page 348].
27095 SPURRIER Ronald Humphry P/O 15.12.28 Terminated
27096 STEVENSON William Graham S/Ldr 10.02.54 Relinquished
27097 VANDYCK Kenneth Gordon F/O 01.07.31 Relinquished
On account of ill-health. Returned to service as a temporary Lieutenant in the Royal Navy on 13th December 1940. Born on 14th April 1907, Paul McMillan has traced Kenneth Gordon Vandyck's death in October 1972, whilst residing in the Chelsea district of London.
27098 WOOD Frederick Kingsley F/O + 04.02.31 209 Squadron

LG 17 July 1928, issue 33404, page 4822 - Seniority 29th June 1928

27099 CULLUM Noel William Aubrey S/Ldr 05.08.38 Relinquished
On appointment to a commission on the Unattached List for the Indian Army [LG 29 November 1938, issue 34575, page 7534]. At the time he was in Class A of the Reserve of Officers to which he had been placed on 6th July 1938 [LG 3 July 1938, issue 34528, page 4334]. Attached to the Royal Indian Army Service Corps, Captain Noel William Aubrey Cullum, age 34, died on 6th June 1941; he was cremated in Brighton [Woodvale] Borough Crematorium, his name being commemorated on panel 1.

LG 7 September 1928 - Seniority 24th August 1928 [13 entrants]

Block 27100 to 27112

27100 ADAMS Wilfrid Sydney Charles F/O + 13.05.40 3 Squadron
Flying Officer Wilfrid Sydney Charles Adams was killed three days after the German's launched their *Blitzkrieg* against the West. Flying Hurricane I N2654 QO-W he was returning to the squadron's base at Merville [the squadron had been sent here from Croydon on the 10th of May 1940] when he collided with Hurricane I N2653 flown by fellow squadron colleague, Flying Officer Raymond Bryce Lines Roberts. According to the Aviation Safety Network website, which the authors acknowledge, the two Hurricanes exploded on impact, both falling near Nieppe [Nord] in the vicinity of Armentieres.

Both pilots are buried in Cite Bonjean Military Cemetery, Armentieres where Flying Officer Adams's headstone bears the Latin inscription *"Lux Et Tenebrae Sed Amor Semper"* and that for his colleague *"To The Glory Of God And Every Loving Memory Of My Dearly Beloved Husband."*

Peter D Cornwell in his closely researched book *The Battle of France - Then and Now* times the crash at 1600 hours as taking place five miles from Merville Airfield.
27101 BEYNON Richard Arnold W/Cdr 10.02.54 Relinquished
27102 BRIGHTON Eric James F/O 19.11.33 Relinquished
27103 CRAIK David Archibald W/Cdr 10.02.54 Relinquished
Wing Commander David Archibald Craik died on Saturday, the 15th of February 1997.
27104 GRACE Eric Basil W/Cdr 10.02.54 Relinquished
27105 HOYLAND George Donald F/O 01.02.37 Relinquished
27106 JONES Roderick F/O 11.06.33 Relinquished
On account of ill-health [LG 20 June 1933, supplement 33951, page 4128]. Returned to service and granted a commission in the Administrative and Special Duties Branch, retaining his rank, effective from 1st September 1939 [LG 20 October 1939, issue 34713, page 7043], his service number now 74841. Subsequently reverting to 27106 and by 1st January 1950 attached to the Provost Branch, and promoted group captain. He served for another thirteen years: G/Capt 19.08.63 Retirement
27107 KING George Stephen S/Ldr + 13.05.41 82 Squadron
Squadron Leader George Stephen King, age 33, flying Blenheim IV V6430 from the squadron's advanced base at Portreath for operations to the French port of St-Nazaire is believed to have gone down into the sea, his body being washed ashore and buried in Escoublac-la-Baule War Cemetery, his headstone inscribed *"In Loving Memory Of George Stephen."* For additional information, please refer to page 57 of my RAFBCL 1941.
27108 LEWIS John P/O 28.07.29 Terminated
Paul McMillan reports, Pilot Officer John Lewis was posted to 1 FTS Netheravon on 8th September 1928; it is assumed he was one of many who failed to meet the demands of the Royal Air Force flying training syllabus.
27109 MACKAY Stewart Sinclair F/O + 02.05.31 2 FTS Digby
During a spell as a flying instructor, Flying Officer Stewart Sinclair Mackay was killed when his Avro 504K F8813 stalled off of a low flat turn and crashed at Ashby-de-la-Launde just a few miles WNW of the airfield. His passenger/pupil Aircraftman Josiah Swain was injured.
27110 MONTGOMERY George Rodgers G/Capt 02.01.58 Retirement
27111 PARKER Maurice Gordon W/Cdr 10.02.54 Relinquished
27112 RICHARDS Singleton Powell W/Cdr 20.12.49 Relinquished
On appointment to a commission in the Royal Air Force [LG 21 February 1950, supplement 38845, page 919]. Appointed to a permanent commission he served until: W/Cdr 20.10.63 Retirement

LG 25 September 1928, issue 33424, page 6219 - Seniority 14th September 1928 [40 entrants]

Block 27113 to 27152

27113 ADNAMS Alfred Guy A/Cmdr 25.08.57 Retirement
Air Commodore Alfred Guy Adnams mentioned in despatches, died on Friday, 12th September 1969. His final appointment was a 'plum' posting out to Australia as Air Officer Commanding RAAF Land-Air Warfare School. Williamstown in New South Wales.

27114 ANNING Antony Frederick Paul F/O + 13.02.31 RAFC Cranwell

Whilst instructing Flight Cadet Arthur Moreland Acton-Adams in the procedures for making a forced-landing, their Armstrong Whitworth Atlas Trainer K1187 lost speed while making a gliding turn and crashed out of control onto the airfield with fatal consequences for both airmen.

Lieutenant 69th Brigade RA TA

27115 ARMSTONG Alexander Robert P/O 21.09.29 Terminated

Returned to service and granted a commission in the Administrative and Special Duties Branch, effective 16th August 1940 [LG 3 September 1940, issue 34937, page 5438] with the service number 83478. F/Lt 10.02.54 Relinquished

27116 BALLIN Julian Frederick P/O 19.12.28 Terminated

27117 BABER Alfred Colborne P/O 17.09.29 Resigned

27118 BEYNON John Ennis S/Ldr 10.02.54 Relinquished

Lieutenant Essex Regiment TA

27119 BLYTHE Basil Adair F/O 14.09.37 Relinquished

27120 BRAIN Arthur Laurence W/Cdr 10.02.54 Relinquished

27121 CHAMBERS Charles Michael Dalby S/Ldr 10.02.54 Relinquished

27122 CHAMPION de CRESPIGNY Claude Montgomery G/Capt 15.09.58 Retirement

His older brother, Hugh Vivian Champion de Crespigny, born 8th April 1897, served in the *Great War* and was granted a permanent commission on 1st August 1919 - see page 188 of our third volume.

27123 CLARKE George Hallam F/O 21.10.31 Resigned

27124 COLLINS Herbert Rowdon W/Cdr 20.03.59 Retirement

At his own request [LG 16 June 1949, supplement 41739, page 3907]. The following announcements were published in *The Edinburgh Gazette* and *The London Gazette* on 9th December 1952 and 5th December 1952 respectively. The entries appearing beneath the heading 'Order Annulling, Revoking, or Rescinding Orders' *Herbert Rowdon Collins, described in the Receiving Order as H R Collins, Wing Commander, Orchard Cottage, West Drive, Wentworth, in the county of Surrey, gentleman of means."*

27125 CRUIKSHANK Robert Grant P/O 10.04.29 Terminated

After leaving the service, Paul McMillan reports, Robert Grant Cruikshank joined the police, the Police Files and Ledgers 1850-1950, recording the following: *"Robert Grant Cruikshank : [R G Cruikshank] : Joined Age 20 : Birth Date 15 Aug 1902 : Birth Place Chatorque, America : Joined Date 25 Jul 23 : Leaving Date 23 Sep 23 : Employment Place West Midlands, England : Force Birmingham City Police : Division or Department 'B' : Cause of Leaving Own request : Warrant Number 9934."* My co-author adds, Robert was born at Lakewood, Chatorque, New York.

27126 DOWNING Eric William F/O 22.02.33 Relinquished

On account of ill-health [LG 21 February 1933, supplement 33913, page 1180].

27127 FENTON Harold Arthur A/Cmdr Retirement

Wing Commander Harold Arthur Fenton was *Gazetted* with the DFC on 28th July 1942, supplement 35646, page 3302: *"This officer has led his Wing successfully on many sorties. One day in May 1942, he encountered 15 enemy bombers escorted by an equal number of fighters. Wing Commander Fenton, with two other pilots, immediately attacked the bombers and delivered four attacks before his own aircraft was hit by fire from an enemy fightrr. Wing Commander Fenton's windscreen became covered in oil but he was able to return to base where he made a safe landing. This officer is a fine leader who inspires much confidence in others."*

The above award recognised his inspiration leadership of No. 243 Wing which formed at El Adem on 1st March 1942, moving to Landing Ground 013 at Sidi Haneish South on 20th April 1942 from where the above action took place.

The award of the DSO was promulgated in *The London Gazette* 16th February 1943, supplement 35904, page 815, in recognition of his leadership of No. 212 Group in the Middle East.

On 8th January 1952 Harold Arthur Fenton was granted a commission in the Reserve of Air Force Officers for a period of five years which he relinquished on 8th January 1957, his rank at the time being recorded as Squadron Leader. Air Commodore Harold Arthur Fenton CBE DSO DFC twice mentioned in despatches, died on Monday, 11th December 1995.

27128 GARLE Kennard Robin P/O 17.09.29 Terminated

27129 GIBSON Leslie Irving P/O 17.07.29 Terminated

27130 GUEST Ivor Cecil P/O 29.06.29 Resigned

27131 HEMPHILL Francis Neville P/O 28.05.30 Relinquished

On account of ill-health [LG 27 May 1930, issue 33609, page 3330].

27132 HUGHES-HALLETT Humphrey Raymond S/Ldr 20.06.41 Relinquished

On account of ill-health [LG 4 July 1941, issue 35208, page 3830].

27133 IONS Eustace P/O + 17.04.29 RAF Sealand

Pilot Officer Eustace Ions died in Cornelia Hospital, Poole, Dorset, following an operation.

27134 LOUKS Arthur Edward W/Cdr 30.12.49 Retirement

27135 McDOUGALL Duncan Shimwell F/O + 06.05.32 CFS Wittering

Flying Officer Duncan Shimwell McDougall and Flying Officer Nicholas Erskine White perished when their Avro 504Ns K1042 and K1050 collided in the air while changing formation, both machines falling locked together near Stamford, Lincolnshire.

The report of the inquest, published in the *Sheffield Daily Telegraph,* has been appended against the entry for Flying Officer Nicholas Erskine White, a Cranwell graduate, in Appendix E for 1926.

27136 McNEILL Frederick Alexander W/Cdr 10.02.54 Relinquished

27137 MANSON Colin Campbell Charles F/O 14.03.35 Relinquished

New Zealand On appointment to a commission in the Royal New Zealand Air Force [LG 11 February 1936, issue 34254, page 913].

27138 MORRIS George Oswald St. John F/Lt 19.01.52 Relinquished

On appointment to a commission in the Territorial Army [LG 7 October 1952, supplement 39663, page 5273].

27139 O'REILLY Michael Patrick F/O + 03.09.40 20 SFTS Cranborne

Flying Officer Michael Patrick O'Reilly and Sergeant George Herbert Loomes died when their Oxford II P6856 crashed at Nelson Farm, Fedza, Southern Rhodesia. Both airmen are buried in Harare [Pioneer] Cemetery.

27140 PELL Kenneth Wright S/Ldr 12.01.63 Relinquished

2nd Lieutenant Royal West Kent Regiment TA

27141 POWELL Alexander Frank W/Cdr 28.11.57 Retirement

27142 RAY Cyril F/O 29.07.47 Relinquished

27143 READ Frank F/O 16.12.30 Dismissed

By sentence of General Court Martial [LG 23 December 1930, issue 33672, page 8259].

27144 ROBINSON Robert Algernon Rokeby F/O 23.07.30 Relinquished

On account of ill-health [LG 25 July 1930, issue 33628, page 4645].

27145 RODEN John Desmond P/O 08.01.30 Relinquished

On account of ill-health [LG 7 January 1930, issue 33568, page 137]

27146 ROWLEY Louis Percy F/Lt + 14.10.40 233 Squadron

Flight Lieutenant Louis Percy Rowley and crew were lost during operations with 233 Squadron, their Hudson I T9343 ZS-Z failing to return to Leuchars from a reconnaissance off the Norwegian coast. Please refer to Ross McNeill's Coastal Command losses, page 70 for additional details.

27147 RUSSELL Frederick William Henry P/O 29.01.29 Resigned

27148 SATCHWELL Denis Frank S/Ldr 23.07.46 Relinquished
As a Captain flying with British Overseas Airways Corporation, Denis Frank Satchwell was appointed OBE in the 1943 New Year's Honours List [LG 4 January 1943, supplement 35843, page 65].
27149 SHAKESPEARE Joseph Stuart F/O + 05.11.43 BOAC
Captain Joseph Stuart Shakespeare was the captain of Sunderland III G-AGIA *Haslemere* [ML728] which crashed in the Western Desert while *en route* to England. Please refer to the entry for 27010 Flying Officer/Captain Ralph Mountain for details. Captain Shakespeare is buried in Halfaya Sollum War Cemetery.
27150 SHIRTCLIFFE Geoffrey Charles P/O 05.01.29 Terminated
27151 STREATFEILD Victor Charles Frederick S/Ldr 09.06.50 Dismissed
By sentence of General Court Martial [LG 30 June 1950, supplement 38955, page 3361]. He had been appointed OBE.
27152 THOMAS Leslie Picton P/O 17.11.28 Terminated

LG 16 October 1928, issue 33430, page 6636 - Seniority 12th October 1928 [18 entrants]

Block 27153 to 27170

27153 BALLANTYNE Maurice Hutcheson P/O 30.04.30 Terminated
27154 BARRETT Roderick John Torrington F/Lt 30.05.38 Relinquished
On appointment to the Air Branch of the Royal Navy [LG 12 July 1938, issue 34531, page 4540].
27155 CHERRILL John G/Capt 01.10.58 Retirement
27156 CRAIG Douglas Henry Vincent G/Capt 23.01;54 Relinquished
27157 FINNEGAN Eric James S/Ldr 27.01.46 Relinquished
27158 GADD Thomas S/Ldr 10.02.54 Relinquished
27159 GARNONS-WILLIAMS Richard Penry W/Cdr 21.10.54 Relinquished
27160 HAWKINS Charles Richard John G/Capt 19.10.59 Retirement
27161 HYLAND Michael Thomas Mary S/Ldr 10.02.54 Relinquished
He was *Gazetted* with the Air Force Cross on 10th June 1948.
27162 LOBLEY John Oliver Hargreaves S/Ldr 10.02.54 Relinquished
27163 MILNER Lionel Treadway P/O + 02.05.29 3 FTS Grantham
2nd Lieutenant King's Own Yorkshire Light Infantry TA Pilot Officer Lionel Treadway Milner and his instructor, Sergeant Geoffrey Leslie Williams died ass the result of their Armstrong Whitworth Atlas ™ J9470 stalling soon after take off and spinning out of control near the airfield. Alive when pulled from the wreckage, Pilot Officer Milner was mortally injured and succumbed later in the day.
27164 OAKLEY Brian Arthur W/Cdr 10.02.54 Relinquished
27165 ROGERS Peter Bagwell F/O + 15.07.30 23 Squadron
27166 SLADE John Duncan Harcourt W/Cdr 20.04.59 Relinquished
27167 STEBBING John Reynolds S/Ldr 19.05.55 Relinquished
27168 WILSON Anthony Thomas P/O 28.01.31 Resigned
27169 WOOLFE Denis Allen P/O 19.10.28 Resigned
27170 WORGER-SLADE Arthur Neville Innes S/Ldr 10.06.43 Resigned

LG 23 October 1928, issue 33432, page 6780 - Seniority 29th September 1928

27171 STRANGE Royle Frederick John
Paul McMillan advises that Flight Lieutenant Royle Frederick John Strange, although short service commissioned to the General Duties Branch was an Intelligence Officer. On 1st September 1937, now on the Supplementary List, he was transferred to the Reserve of Air Force Officers, class C [LG 17th September 1937, issue 34436, page 5837] in the rank of flight lieutenant.

Further research by my co-author confirms that Royle Strange, who was born in Egypt, presumably to a British service family, was certainly involved in gathering intelligence in Palestine in the 1930s, as recorded by Yitzhak Gil-Har in his work titled *British Intelligence and the Role of Jewish Informers in Palestine* [which as co-authors of this volume, we are pleased to acknowledge] and published on the Taylor & Francis Group website. Sourced from the *Middle Eastern Studies* the author's work is extremely detailed and there are numerous references to Allied service personnel, particularly those working in the Air Staff Intelligence Bureau which came under the aegis of the Air Officer Commanding, General Headquarters and which had been established by the Air Ministry's Intelligence Service Branch and it is within this section that Flight Lieutenant Strange is identified as being responsible for gathering intelligence from the Haifa area.

Three fellow flight lieutenants are named, along with their areas of responsibility, all being referred to as Special Service Officers and all were active, in the field, by the beginning of 1931 and working closely with other service agencies.

The author's work makes for fascinating reading as he records a period of Middle Eastern history, largely overlooked. As for Flight Lieutenant Strange, he was still on the Supplementary List of Royal Air Force officers in July 1945, and though his out of service date is not known, it is reasonably safe to assume that he relinquished his commission under the Navy, Army and Air Force Reserves Act of 1954.

LG 6 November 1928, issue 33436, page 7215 - Seniority 2nd November 1928 [18 entrants]

Block 27172 to 27189

27172 ABBOTT Arthur Henry W/Cdr 15.08.62 Relinquished
27173 BARRON Francis Slade P/O + 23.04.30 47 Squadron
27174 CARY Alwyn Geoffrey Morgan F/O + 04.11.38 Jersey Airways
Flying Officer Alwyn Geoffrey Morgan Cary was the captain of Jersey Airways DH.86 G-ACZN *St. Catherine's Bay* which came down at Rue es Minquiers shortly after departing Jersey Airport on a scheduled flight to Southampton. In total thirteen aboard the DH.86 perished and a farm worker by the name of Edmund le Cornu died after being crushed by debris from the airliner. According to *Wikipedia* the crash occurred at 1050 a mere 500 yards east of the airport in the parish of Saint Brélade. The sky was overcast and the base of the cloud was down to as low as 120 to 150 feet. On becoming airborne, Flying Officer Cary, who was still serving his time in the Reserve of Air Force Officers, made a climbing turn into cloud and, *it is assumed* [my italics], inadvertently allowed the DH to sideslip. On impact their was an explosion and a number of passengers were thrown from the aircraft.

The aircraft's wireless operator was Reginald John Syner Lyons and the eleven passengers were names as Captain William Dermot Swan, his wife Mrs Rozel Clifton Swan and their one year daughter, Bridget Jennifer Swan; Major Gerald Hazzard Voisin and his wife, Mrs Eleanor Ruby Courtney Voisin, Mrs Lucy Helena Wall, Sister Janet Hansford four men named Harold Kersley, Thomas Olaf Cox, Stuart Spring and Frank Berry.

A report of the tragedy was published the next day in Saturday's edition of *The Times* which records the addresses and professions of the deceased, adding: *"Mr. Louis Morris, cinema proprietor, of Shaftesbury Avenue, London, and Mr. Opie, of Guernsey, arrived at the airport too late to claim the seats they had booked.*

"When the aeroplane, the St. Catherine's Bay, took offa companion machine was already in the air with a full load of passengers for Southampton. The weather was not very good. The cloud base was only 150ft above the surface of the aerodrome, but the conditions at Southampton were good, and, with the assistance of directional wireless, flying in these circumstances was quite normal. The first machine had got clear away when the SSt. Catherine's Bay took off and made the usual circuit round the aerodrome.

"One onlooker said flames and smoke was belching from one of the engine exhaust and the aeroplane wwas soon seen to turn towards the aerodrome. The liner quickly lost height and passed out of view behind trees. The noise of its crash was heard and this was followed by the sound of an explosion, caused no doubt by petrol from the burst tanks. The airport fire engine and ambulance were at once sent to the scene, but the wreck was already enveloped in flames and little could be done.

"What remained of the wreck of this wooden aeroplane was carefully guarded last night so that it might be examined this morning, when Captain F S Wilkins, Assistant Inspector of Accidents at the Air Ministry, will arrive to make the official investigation. Up to the present there is no conclusive evidence as to what was the immediate cause of the accident.

"In the field in which the liner fell a farm had was working, and the aeroplane fell on him and killed him immediately. By the force of the crash or through the explosion which followed some of the occupants of the machine were flung out, but the whole of the aeroplane's complement, whether they were thrown clear or were still in the machine when it took fire, died in the crash. This particular aeroplane had been in service for more than three years and, like the four sister cradt which belong to Jersey Airways, had never before met with serious mishap. The company, during the five years of its existence, has operated services regularly between Jersey and mainland, and although it has carried about 130,000 passengers, had never until yesterday had an accident in which a passenger was killed or injured."

27175 FIELD Charles Brian F/O 02.04.31 Resigned
27176 GRANVILLE Edward Gerard W/Cdr 02.08.52 Retirement
27177 HUNTER Norman Ross Gordon P/O 01.03.31 Terminated
27178 INGRAM-JOHNSON Robert S/Ldr 10.02.54 Relinquished

2nd Lieutenant 67th Field Brigade RA TA On 17th April 1952, Flying Officer Robert Ingram-Johnson was granted a commission in the Training Branch of the Royal Air Force Volunteer Reserve [LG 15 July 1952, supplement 39596, page 3814]. F/O 04.03.58 Resigned

27179 LAWSON John Allison Cancelled [LG 20 November 1928, issue 33440, page 7556]
27180 McCULLCH Hugh Lindsay F/Lt 01.06.39 Relinquished

On 3rd September 1930, whilst attached to 30 Squadron at Mosul, Flying Officer Hugh Lindsay McCulloch survived a midair collision, the circumstances being described in my summary for that date. On 1st June 1939, he was granted a short service commission in the Air Branch of the Royal Navy. Rising to the rank fo Commander, and surviving the Second World War, he was created MBE in the Queen's Birthday Honours list of June 1966, in recognition of his work as Vice Chairman, Ayr Sea Cadet Unit [LG 11 June 1966, supplement 44004, page 6546]..

27181 MESSITER Richard Moulton SS/Ldr 10.0154 Relinquished
27182 O'FARRELL Gershom Frederic Partington W/Cdr 10.02.54 Relinquished
27183 O'HARA Owen John P/O 23.04.29 Terminated
27184 PELLY Charles Edmund William Nigel Cavendish G/Capt 03.07.46 Relinquished
27185 SARSFIELD-SAMPSON Cecil W/Cdr 10.02.54 Relinqusihed
TEW Walter Henry Edward Cancelled [LG 20 November 1928, issue 33440, page 7556]

See *The London Gazette* 11th December 1928, issue 33446, page 8173

27187 WALLACE Ralph William G/Capt 06.02.56 Retirement
27188 WHEELER Errol Charles Archer Cancelled [LG 20 November 1928, issue 33440, page 7556]
27189 WHITTOME Thomas Eustace P/O + 23.10.30 NFS Hanworth

Pilot Officer Thomas Eustace Whittome and Mr. Arthur Raymond Ellis were killed when their DH.60 Moth G-EBPR spun out of control and crashed on Boddington Hill near Wendover in Buckinghamshire. As reported on the Aviation Safety Network, Pilot Officer Whittmore had taken off from RAF Halton with the intention of returning to Hanworth Aerodrome in Middlesex. A copy of the accident report is held at TNA Kew under AVIA 5/12/C177. It has not been digitised but a copy may be obtained from Kew by quoting this reference.

LG 20 November 1928, issue 33440, page 7555 - Seniority 2 November 1928 [2 entrants]

MACKENZIE Archibald Charles Romanes P/O 23.03.29 Terminated
RIDLER Eric Charles P/O 23.03.29 Terminated

LG 11 December 1928, issue 33446, page 8173 - Seniority 19th, 19th and 25th November 1928 respectively [3 entrants]

LAWSON John Allison P/O 20.04.29 Resigned
Lieutenant A I R O
WHEELER Errol Charles Arthur P/O 23.03.29 Terminated

Obtained a commission as 2nd Lieutenant in 8th Battalion, Middlesex Regiment, TA [LG 28 February 1930, issue 33584, page 1313\.

27186 TEW Walter Henry Edward F/O 15.11.37 Class C

Whilst in the Reserve of Air Force Officers granted the honorary rank of flight lieutenant whilst serving with the Royal Air Force as a civilian assistant employed on "P" Staff duties, 20th December 1935 [LG 18 February 1936, issue 34256, page 1061]. Subsequently served in the Royal Air Force Volunteer Reserve: S/Ldr 10.02.54 Relinquished

Attached to the Secretarial Branch and issued with the service number 192441. S/Ldr 24.08.51 Relinquished

ROLL OF HONOUR
FOR
1928 SHORT SERVICE COMMISSION
OFFICERS

F/O	ADAMS	Wilfrid Sydney Charles	13 May 1940	3 Squadron
F/O	ANNING	Antony Frederick Paul	13 February 1931	RAFC Cranwell
F/Lt	BAILEY	Henry	7 April 1940	Blackburn Aircraft
F/O	BARNETT	Max Ian	4 January 1930	56 Squadron
P/O	BARRON	Francis Slade	23 April 1930	47 Squadron
F/O	BINLEY New Zealand	Alan Keith Hilton	30 November 1934	Bombay Flying Club
P/O	BOOTES	Ronald Yule	2 July 1929	1 FTS Netheravon
W/Cdr	CAMERON Australia	Ivan McLeod	28 September 1939	110 Squadron
F/O	CARY	Alwyn Geoffrey Morgan	4 November 1938	Jersey Airways
F/O	CLAXTON	John Cecil Lauga	18 June 1930	School of Photography
P/O	COUPE	Richard Harold	7 November 1928	2 FTS Digby
Captain	CULLUM	Noel William Aubrey	6 June 1941	Royal Indian Army Service Corps
W/Cdr	DARBYSHIRE	Rupert Stanley	5 November 1941	608 Squadron AAF
F/O	DAVIS	Sidney Alexander	17 February 1931	36 Squadron
F/O	DEACON	Paul Le Mesurier	30 December 1939	Bristol Aeroplane Company
P/O	D'OLIER	Bertrand Guy	17 August 1928	2 FTS Digby
F/O	EVERETT	Ernest Norman Victor	25 August 1935	Madras Flying Club
S/Ldr	FREEMAN	Frederick Charles Gordon	11 July 1942	101 Squadron
S/Ldr	FYFE DFC IGSM	Bernard	11 August 1940	107 Squadron
W/Cdr	HALES	George Francis	9 May 1951	RAF Sutton-on-Hull
F/O	HANLON	Charles Peter	25 December 1930	30 Squadron
F.O	HAWKE	John William	5 May 1930	20 Squadron
P/O	IONS	Eustace	17 April 1929	RAF Sealand
W/O	IREMONGER	Denis Lascelles	31 December 1942	104 Squadron
S/Ldr	JARRETT	Geoffrey William Jones	3 April 1943	9 Squadron
P/O	JOHNSTONE	Edward Leo	31 August 1928	3 FTS Grantham
S/Ldr	KING	George Stephen	13 May 1941	82 Squadron
F/O	LITTLE	Charles Hugh Rudgard	1 April 1932	A&GS Eastchurch
F/O	MACKAY	Stewart Sinclair	2 May 1931	2 FTS Digby
F/O	MACKENZIE	John Burslem	28 November 1931	Base Training Flight Gosport
F/O	McDOUGALL	Duncan Shimwell	6 May 1932	CFS Wittering
P/O	MILNER	Lionel Treadway	2 May 1929	3 FTS Grantham
W/Cdr	MITCHELL New Zealand	Alan Cunningham	18 September 1940	HQ RAF Aden
Captain	MOUNTAIN	Ralph	5 November 1943	BOAC
F/O	NICOLAY	Vincent Humphries	26 May 1930	CFS Wittering
F/O	O'REILLY	Michael Patrick	3 September 1940	20 SFTS Cranborne
P/O	RIESS	James Graydon	31 August 1928	2 FTS Digby
F/Lt	ROWLEY	Louis Percy	14 October 1940	233 Squadron
Captain	SHAKESPEARE	Joseph Stuart	5 November 1943	BOAC
W/Cdr	WARNER	Richard Cecil	29 November 1956	
P/O	WHITTOME	Thomas Eustace	23 October 1930	NFS Hanworth
P/O	WILSON	John	24 August 1929	216 Squadron

Appendix D - RAF [Cadet] College Cranwell

COMMANDANT

Air Commodore Frederick Crosby Halahan CMG CBE DSO MVO mentioned in despatches

1928 was the final year that the Cadet was included in the title of the College for on 1st February 1929, its title would change to Royal Air Force College Cranwell, maintaining its Command status.

January 1928 entry : 21

26130 BOWER* Leslie William Clement AM 30.03.65 Retirement

The citation for his DFC appeared in thee Fifth Supplement [36392, page 907] to *The London Gazette* on Tuesday, 22nd February 1944: *This officer has completed numerous sorties and has invariably displayed leadership and skill of a high order. His determination to complete his tasks successfully has always been evident and was well illustrated during a recent sortie. Before reaching the target his aircraft was hit by anti-aircraft fire but he went on to complete his attack. On the return flight the aircraft was again hit by fire from ground defences. Much damage was sustained, including one engine which was put out of action. Group Captain Bower displayed great skill in his endeavour to reach home but, just before the English coast was reached the damaged engine burst into flames. Group Captain Bower crossed the coast, however, but was compelled to make a landing in difficult circumstances. As the aircraft touched down it became enveloped in flames and a petrol tank burst. Group Captain Bower was rendered unconscious but was dragged clear by a comrade. This officer displayed great courage and resolution throughout."*

Still ranked Group Captain he was awarded the DSO [LG 22 June 1945, supplement 37142, page 3271: *"This officer has set a magnificent example of courage and devotion to duty in operations against the enemy. He has commanded the squadrons at his station for a considerable time and much of the success achieved during the period can be attributed to Group Captain Bower's high powers of leadership, unsurpassed skill and iron determination. His services have been of immense value."*

Both awards were gained during his tenure of Officer Commanding 138 [Bomber] Wing, Lasham, which came under the Aegis of No. 2 Group and 2nd Tactical Air Force.

His name appears twice in *Mosquito* [C Martin Sharp and Michael J F Bowyer] where on page 252 he is reported as taking part in a raid led by Air Vice-Marshal Basil Embry against a school that was believed to house S.S. troops operating against the Maquis, while his second mention comments *"By 17 August, seventy-two days after D-Day, one Mosquito Wing, commanded by Grp. Capt. L W C Bower DFC, with Wg. Cdr. H J W Meakin DFC, as Wing Leader, had made 2,319 sorties, averaging thirty-two sorties daily irrespective of weather condition."*

Air Marshal Sir William Bower KCB DSO DFC twice mentioned in despatches, died on Monday, 17th February 1991.

CLARKSON Rodney Thomas Playford F/O + 10.02.34 RAF Base Gosport

Flying Officer Rodney Thomas Playford Clarkson died in Haslar Hospital from injuries received when the car in which he was travelling collided with a tree near the airfield. An extremely detailed report of the accident was reported by *The Gosport Journal* in their edition of Friday, February 23rd, 1934, under the headline 'Car's Crash in Gomer Lane - RAF Officer's Death - Tremedous Blow says Coroner.'

"The adjourned inquiry into the Alexsstoke motor fatality in which Flying Officer Rodney Thomas Palyford Clarkson, 24, of the Royal Air Force, Gosport, was the victim, was re-opened at Gosport Police Court yesterday morning by the Coroner for South Hants, Mr. Leonard Warner.

"Flying Officer Clarkson, with Flying Officer Charles Milson Rees, were passengers in a Bentley car driven by Flying Officer Benjamin Heywood Jones, also of the Gosport Base, which on the night of February 5 crashed into a tree in Gomer Lane.

"At the previous hearing on February 11, Surgeon Commander A C Shaw said that Flying Officer Clarkson, who died on February 10, had a fractured fight thigh and dislocated right ankle, and death was due to paralysis of the intestines, following shock.

"Mr. Warner sat this morning with a jury, and Mr. Fearnley Whittingstall [instructed by Mr. G H Syrett] appeared for Flying Officer Jones, while Flight Lieut. F Woolley, of the Royal Air Force, Gosport Base, also watched the proceedings.

"Charles Collins, an omnibus driver said, he was driving an omnibus towards Lee-on-Solent, and had reached the bend in Gomer Lane at about 1030 on the night of February 5, when he saw a car huddled under the trees with the bonnet projecting into the road. Witness pulled up and went to the car, and as far as he could make out there were three people in the car, as he heard three voices. Witness, with two others wrenched open the offside door, and one of the occupants got out. Hearing some scrambling in the rushes witness went round the car and found another man lying between the car and the wall surrounding Bay House. With assistance, witness lifted the man, who complained of his ankle, into an omnibus which was proceeding towards Gosport and the other two occupants of the car also went on the omnibus and were taken to the War Memorial Hospital.

"In answer to the Coroner, Collins said the car was badly damaged. The road at this point was very misleading to a stranger because the wall was very much the colour of the road. The surface of the road was alright, but the camber was bad.

"Flying Officer Jones, who appeared in Court supporting himself on crutches said he was driving [with Flying Officers Clarkson and Rees] a 16 h.p. Bentley car towards Lee-on-Solent. They were all sitting side-by-side. He knew the road very well.

"Witness said he had come from Farnham, and his intention was to take Flying Officer Clarkson back to the mess at Lee-on-Solent. He knew of the bend in the road and started to slow down. At the bend the car skidded, and as to what happened afterwards he had little recollection. He remembered having some difficulty in getting our of the car, and remembered being put to bed at Haslar Hospital.

"By Mr. Fearnley Whittingstall: He had driven along this road several times in daylight, but only once or twice at night. Flying Officer Rees said he was sitting in between the other two. The car was slowed up by the driver as they neared the corner, and then it started to swing. He remembered nothing more until he found himself sitting half undressed before a fire at Haslar Hospital.

"Police Sergeant J O Elliott said the car was firmly fixed between two trees. It was completely wrecked. There was a skid marked in the road 14 yards from the point of impact. The skid had ploughed through the soft ground. The road was 20ft wide, and the camber at that sport was slightly to the disadvantage of a driver.

"The Coroner summing up said there was no doubt that the car was going very fast. The driver probably did not realise he had reached the bend, and then tried to check the car. What the pace was could only be surmised from the results. He had seen the car, and it was dreadfully smashed - telescoped almost. The blow which caused such destruction must have been tremendous. It was not a case approaching manslaughter, but it justified them in saying the accident was caused by too great a pace round the bend.

"The jury returned a verdict of "Accidental death," and added that the accident was due to an error of judgement on the part of the driver when taking the bend, and owing to the speed of the car. They added a rider that a light should be placed at this particular spot."

Flying Officer Clarkson was cremated at Golders Green Crematorium and his ashes, reports my co-author, at St. Paul's Walden, Whitwell in Hertfordshire.

26131 DRURY* Edward Stephe Dru G/Capt + 17.09.48 RAF Manby

Group Captain Edward Stephen Dru Drury AFC mentioned in despatches died while at RAF Manby in Lincolnshire. A plaque to his memory may be viewed in St. Edward the Martyr Church at Corfe Castle, Dorset, the inscription reading *"Remember Before God Edward Stephen Dru Drury AFC Group Captain Royal Air Force Born 24 March 1910 Died 17 September 1948."*

26132 EARLE* Alfred AM 06.06.66 Retirement

Air Marshal Sir Alfred Earle GBE CB, died on Tuesday, 27th March 1990. Prior to his arrival at Cranwell, Alfred Earle had been an Aircraft Apprentice at Halton where he was awarded a scholarship to Cranwell. During the Second World War he was appointed to the Staff of the War Cabinet and during his two years fulfilling this key post he accompanied, along with other senior officers, Winston Churchill to conferences in Cairo and Yalta [held in February 1945, in the resort city of Yalta on the Black Sea coast, this was the last of the 'Big Three' conferences of the Second

World War between Churchill, Roosevelt [who died two months laterr] and Stalin]. His final service appointment was as Vice Chief of the Defence Staff and on retirement remained closely associated with the Defence Staff as Director-General of Intelligence.

26133 ELSMIE* George Reginald Alexander W/Cdr + 18.04.41 114 Squadron

Wing Commander George Reginald Alexander Elsmie AFC and his crew perished when their Blenheim IV R3837 RT-T was shot down in flames in the course of an attack on enemy shipping off the coast of Norway. All are commemorated on the Runnymede Memorial. This was a costly operation for Wing Commander Elsmie's squadron, based at Thornaby, the details of which are reported by Ross McNeill on pages 113 and 114 of his *Royal Air Force Coastal Command Losses of the Second World War - Volume 1 Aircraft and Crew Losses 1939-1941.*

As Flight Cadet George Reginald Alexander Elsmie, he was awarded 'The Sword of Honour' on graduating from the College , 19th December 1929 [LG 17 January 1930, issue 33571, page 347].

26134 FRASER* Blair Alexander G/Capt 07.12.56 Retirement

26221 GILES Cyril James W/Cdr 23.06.60 Retirement

Wing Commander Cyril James Giles OBE won a scholarship to Cranwell as a Halton apprentice. He was appointed OBE in his Majesty's [George VI] Birthday Honours list of June 1949 [LG 9 June 1949, supplement 38628, page 2801] - See the entry for William Neal McKechnie of the same entry.

26135 GRIERSON* John F/Lt 30.01.46 Resigned

26136 HEATH* Peter G/Capt 04.12.54 Retirement

Group Captain Peter Heath was twice mentioned in despatches.

26137 HEBER-PERCY John G/Capt 09.07.54 Retirement

Group Captain John Heber-Percy was mentioned in despatches. On 1st June 1936, he was seconded for service as *Aide de Camp* to the UK's High Commissioner for Egypt [LG 16 June 1936, issue 34294, page 3840] during which time he was promoted squadron leader. He relinquished the post on 12th October 1938 [LG 15 November 1938, issue 34570, page 7196].

26138 HEYCOCK* George Francis Wheaton A/Cmdr 01.05.64 Retirement

Air Commodore George Francis Wheaton Heycock CBE DFC mentioned in despatches, died on Monday, 27th June 1983. During his cadetship he was a notable sportsman, representing Cranwell at cricket, tennis, soccer, rugby and athletics. He won his DFC while commanding 141 Squadron [Defiant/Beaufighter 1f] [LG 29 September 1942, supplement 35721, page 4215] *"By his thorough knowledge, skill and untiring efforts, this officer has built up the squadron he commands into a most efficient unit, thereby contributing materially to the success obtained. In August 1942, his squadron shot down at least 4 enemy aircraft at night. Wing Commander Heycock has always displayed the greatest devotion to duty.:*

Taking command in July 1941 from Squadron Leader Edward Chatham Wolfe DFC, 141 squadron gave up its Defiants the following month. His final appointment was Air Attaché Paris and in retirement he became a Justice of the Peace in the County of Northamptonshire.

26139 HUMPHREYS* Joseph York F/Lt 17.06.39 Retired

26140 JONES* Benjamin Heywood W/Cdr + 03.07.43 1680 Flight

Old Etonian, Wing Commander Benjamin Heywood Jones is buried in Scotland at Campbeltown [Kilkerran] Cemetery. He lost his life when Fokker F.XXII HM159 [formerly G-AFXR] caught fire in flight and plunged into Loch Talbert. No. 1680 [Western Isles Communications] Flight based at Abbotsinch was responsible for ferrying Very Important Persons to service establishments on the Hebrides, Orkneys and Shetlands and was equipped with a variety of aircraft types. The Fokker F.XXII was a four-engined high-wing airliner built Schipol in 1934 for the Dutch Airline K.L.M. HM159's original identity was PH-AJR *Roerdomp.* In 1939, it was purchased, along with two similar machines, by Scottish Aviation for use as navigation trainers and for two years operated with its civilian registration G-AFXR before being impressed late in 1941.

Early in February 1942, it was issued to 24 Squadron at Hendon, the name *Brontosaurus* being applied; in October 1942, HM159 was transferred to 1680 Flight and was re-named *Sylvia Scarlet.* Its loss on 3rd July 1943, was pinpointed on the west side of Kintyre and roughly 40 miles west of Abbotsinch; there were no survivors from twenty persons on board. Page 111 of Peter W Moss's *Impressment Log - Volume III* provides further information, along with a photograph of a Fokker F.XXII.

26141 KYLE* Wallace Hart ACM 09.11.68 Retirement

Australia Air Chief Marshal Sir Wallace Kyle GCB KCVO CBE DSO DFC four times mentioned in despatches, died on Sunday, 31st January 1988. As Wing Commander Wallace Kyle he took over command of No. 139 Squadron [Blenheim IV] at Horsham St. Faith on the 1st of December 1940, and it was towards the end of his tenure that he won his DFC when leading his squadron on a low-level daylight attack on the Dutch steelworks at Ijmuiden, the citation reading: *"In April 1941, this officer led an attack against Ijmuiden Iron and Steel Works. In spite of intense anti-aircraft fire and interference from a patrol of Messerschmitt 109's, he dropped his bombs on the target from a height of 50 feet. The enemy fighters followed Wing Commander Kyle out to sea, but, by skilful flying, he forced them to break off the attack. The operation was an outstanding success. He has now completed a number of operational missions and his resolute determination and leadership have been largely responsible for the high standard of efficiency in his squadron."*

The pinnacle of his service came with his appointment as Air Officer Commanding in Chief, Bomber Command, on 19th February 1965, which was re-titled Strike Command on 30th April 1968.

26142 L'ESTRANGE* Edgar Francis John F/O 04.01.34 Resigned

Educated at Cheltenham, Flying Officer Edgar Francis John L'Estrange had been mentioned in despatches for his service in Kurdistan. His service ended under some sort of a cloud for the following was promulgated in *The London Gazette* on 27th March 1934, issue 34036, page 2041: -

"Flying Officer Edgar Francis John L'Estrange takes rank and precedence as if his appointment as Flying Officer bore date 16th Oct, 1932. Reduction takes effect from 17th Nov. 1933. [This officer resigned his permanent commission on 4th Jan. 1934, vide London Gazette on 16th Jan. 1934]. As a Flight Cadet he represented the College at rowing.

26143 McINTYRE* Richard Valentine G/Capt 03.12.57 Retirement

26144 McKECHNIE* William Neal G/Capt 30.08.44 106 Squadron

While in traing at Cranwell, Flight Cadet William `Neal McKechnie saved the life of a fellow Cadet from the same entry, the details of his heroism being *Gazetted* on 18th October 1929, issue 33544, page 6615: *"The KING has been graciously pleased to approve of the Award of the Medal of the Military Division of the Most Excellent Order of the British Empire to the under mentioned:- For Gallantry - Flight Cadet William Neal McKechnie, Royal Air Force. On the 20th June 1929, an aeroplane piloted by Flight Cadet C J Giless crashed on landing at Cranwell Aerodrome and burst into flames. The pilot was stunned but managed to release his safety belt and fall out of the machine in a dazed condition. Flight Cadet McKechnie, who had landed in another aeroplane about the same time some two hundred yards away,, left his machine and ran at full speed towards the scene of the accident. The petrol had spread over an area of about ten yards diameter in full blaze, with Giles lying in it, semi-conscious. McKechnie, without hesitation, ran into the flames and pulled out Giles, who was badly burnt about the legs and face, with his Sidcot suit and clothes actually burning. After dragging him clear of the flames, during the process of which he was scorched and superficially burned, McKechnie proceeded to extinguished the flames of Giles' burning clothing.*

"By this time, the machine was in full blaze, with the petrol spreading along the ground so that without McKechnie's assistance Giles would have been burned to death, as he was quite incapable of moving himself.

"Ultimately the machine was entirely destroyed by fire and the ground for some distance around was completely burned up by the spread of the ignited petrol."

On 29th-30th August 1944, Group Captain William Neal McKechnie put his name on the *Battle Order* at RAF Metheringham for a No. 5 Group raid on Königsberg which the historian and author, Martin Middlebrook, records on page 575 of *The Bomber Command War Diaries* was for the force of 189 Lancasters *"... target at extreme range. Only 480 tons of bombs could be carried because of the range of the target but severe damage was caused around the 4 separate aiming points ..."* Opposition from the enemy defences was heavy and fifteen bombers failed to return, including that of Group Captain McKechnie [Lancaster III JB593 ZN-T]. The Group Captain and his crew are commemorated on the Runnymede Memorial. For details of the Command's losses that night please refer to pages 401 to 407 of my RAFBCL 1944.

By co-incidence, William Neal McKechnie, too, had won a scholarship for Cranwell as an Halton aircraft apprentice.

26145	SAWYER*	Wilfred	P/O	+	06.08.30	41 Squadron
26146	TEIDMAN*	Arthur George	F/O	+	28.11.31	RAF Base Gosport

See Flying Officer John Burslem Mackenzie's entry in Appendix D for short service commission officers 1928 for details.

26147	WALLACE*	Richard Lindsay	G/Capt		28.04.53	Retirement

As a wing commander he was *Gazetted* with the Air Force Cross on 30th September 1941 [LG 30 September 1941, issue 35291, page 5650] and he was also honoured with a CBE and mentioned in despatches before retirement.

26148	WICKS*	Frederick Francis	G/Capt		04.11.58	Retirement

Group Captain Frederick Francis Wicks CBE DFC won a scholarship to attend Cranwell whilst an apprentice at Flowerdown. His DFC, *Gazetted* 6th May 1932, issue 33823, page 2961] was awarded *"... in recognition of gallant and distinguished services rendered in connection with the operations on the North West Frontier of India during the period October 1930 - March 1931."*

* Graduated with permanent commissions and seniority 14th December 1929 [LG 17 January 1930, issue 33571, page 347]

SWORD OF HONOUR
Flight Cadet George Reginald Alexander Elsmie

ROLL OF HONOUR
JANUARY 1928 ENTRY

F/O	CLARKSON	Rodney Thomas Playford	10 February 1934	RAF Base Gosport
G/Capt	DRURY	Edward Stephen Dru	17 September 1948	RAF Manby
W/Cdr	ELSMIE AFC	George Reginald Alexander	18 April 1941	114 Squadron
W/Cdr	JONES	Benjamin Heywood	3 July 1943	1680 Flight
G/Capt	McKECHNIE GC OBE	William Neal	30 August 1944	106 Squadron
P/O	SAWYER	Wilfred	6 August 1930	41 Squadron
F/O	TEIDMAN	Arthur George	28 November 1931	RAF Base Gosport

September 1928 entry : 23

26150	ANGELL*	David Victor	P/O	+	19.03.31	29 Squadron
26151	BADER*	Douglas Robert Steuart	G/Capt		30.04.33	Retired

On Monday, 5th December 1931, Pilot Officer Douglas Robert Steuart Bader piloting Bulldog IIA K1676 of 23 Squadron took off from Kenley and when clear of the airfield immediately indulged in his favourite passion, namely aerobatics. As fate would have it, while so engaged he caught sight of two squadron colleagues taking off and bringing to mind that they had planned to fly over to Woodley airfield near Reading, the young Bader decided to tag along.

The events that followed are related in Paul Brickhill's biography of Douglas Bader, *Reach For The Sky* and the aftermath that in the years to come would elevate Douglas Robert Steuart Bader into becoming a legend in his lifetime.

Despite the loss of both legs in that terrible crash at Woodley and his departure from the prewar air force, come the Second World War and his return to the service, his exploits as a fighter pilot would gain him a DSO and First Bar, DFC and First Bar and twice mentioned in despatches.

His first experience of meeting the enemy came over the Dunkirk beaches, followed by the *Battle of Britain* and then, and now promoted wing commander, he led the Tangmere Wing from March 1941 until the 9th of August 1941, when during a high cover sweep over Northern France his Spitfire VA W3185 D B fell victim to what is now believed to have been *"friendly fire"* [though Brickhill's account, written in 1954, follows the assumption by Bader that his aircraft was struck by a Messerschmitt 109].

Whatever the cause, Wing Commander Bader, with great difficulty, managed to bale out and become a prisoner of war, eventually ending up in Kolditz Castle; his prisoner of war identity in AIR 20/2336 Royal Air Force and Commonwealth Air Forces Prisoner of War File is shown as 3797.

Postwar, and now ranked Group Captain, he reverted to the Retired List on 21st July 1946, and obtained a position with Royal Dutch Shell. As the postwar years past, Douglas's boundless energy played havoc with his health and following a dinner honouring another wartime legend, Marshal of the Royal Air Force, Sir Arthur Harris, Douglas died from a heart attack while being driven home. The date was 5th September 1982.

Numerous accounts have been written of his life and I have little doubt his name will feature in many more pages of print in the future. Here, I will conclude with the citations for his awards:

The London Gazette 1st October 1940, issue 34958, page 5789, DSO: *"This officer has displayed gallantry and leadership of the highest order. During three recent engagements he has led his squadron* [242 Squadron] *with such skill and ability that thirty-three enemy aircraft have been destroyed. In the course of these engagements Squadron Leader Bader has added to his previous successes by destroying six enemy aircraft."*

The London Gazette 7th January 1941, issue 350357, page 151, DFC in recognition of his leadership of 242 Squadron [Hurricane]: *"Squadron Leader Bader has continued to lead his squadron and wing with the utmost gallantly on all occasions. He has now destroyed a total of ten hostile aircraft and damaged several more."*

The London Gazette 15th July 1941, issue 35219, page 4063, First Bar to his DSO: *"This officer has led his wing on a series of consistently successful sorties over enemy territory during the past three months. His high qualities of leadership and courage have been an inspiration to all. Wing Commander Bader has destroyed 15 hostile aircraft."*

The London Gazette 9th September 1941, issue 35270, page 5217, First Bar to his DFC: *"This fearless pilot has recently added a further four enemy aircraft to his previous successes; in addition he has probably destroyed another four and damaged five hostile aircraft. By his fine leadership and high courage Wing Commander Bader has inspired the wing on every occasion."*

Postwar, and having left the Royal Air Force, he was appointed CBE in the New Year's Honours List for 1956, and KB in the Queen's Birthday Honours List, 1976, in recognition of his services to disabled people.

26152	BAINES*	Cyril Edgar Joseph	G/Capt		01.03.58	Retirement

Group Captain Cyril Edgar Joseph Baines CBE was mentioned six time in despatches.

26172	BELCHAM	Lawrence George	S/Ldr	+	14.07.42	119 Squadron

Squadron Leader Lawrence George Belchem failed to return from an operational sortie 14th-15th July 1942, in Catalina I AH545 whilst on an Atlantic patrol out from Loch Erne in Northern Ireland. He is commemorated on panel 65 at the Runnymede Memorial.

26153	CHANCE*	John Anthony	P/O	+	19.11.30	26 Squadron
26154	CLELAND*	Albert Gwilliam	F/O	+	22.12.32	47 Squadron
26155	COOTE	Patrick Bernard	W/Cdr	+	13.04.41	211 Squadron

On 13th April 1941, 211 Squadron {Blenheim I] at Paramythia in Greece was tasked for a low-level attack on German units operating in the Florina district. Intercepted short of the target area by a strong force of Me109s, the formation of six Blemheims were shot from the sky with only two pilots surviving and, as recorded by David Gunby and Pelham Temple on pages 52 and 53 in their first volume of bomber losses in the Middle East and Mediterranean, both were shot up when their Lysander taking them to Athens was intercepted on take off by a Me109 - one survived, though losing two fingers, his companion, Flight Sergeant Arthur Graham James was killed.

Wing Commander Patrick Bernard Coote, described as the Royal Air Force Area Commander, was flying as an observer in Blenheim I L4819; he now rests in Phaleron War Cemetery. He was formerly an Halton aircraft apprentice who gained a scholarship to Cranwell.

26156 DASHPER* Robert Bruce W/Cdr + 06.05.46 Air Ministry
Wing Commander Robert Bruce Dashper twice mentioned in despatches, died in tragic circumstances having been arrested 24-hours previously in Richmond and charged with two serious offences. Bailed to appear at Richmond Police Court he committed suicide with a gunshot wound to the head which proved fatal.

At the time of his death he was in lodgings in Richmond,as reported in *The Daily Mirror in its issue of May 11th, 1946: "When Mrs. Gertrude Lobley, of Richmond, Surrey, took his breakfast up to the wing-commander who was living at her home, she saw that his face was under the bedclothes.*

"In the evening her son insisted on seeing him and found he had been beaten up. Early next morning the wing-commander shot himself outside Richmond police station.

"At the inquest yesterday on the shot man - Wing Commander Robert Bruce Dashper- Mrs. Lobley said he was temperamental at first when he began to stay at her home a year ago, but always "a perfect gentleman."

"Police-Sergeant Sims said the wing commander had been treated for a cut on the nose and a bruised eye at the police station, and then bailed out, after being charged with soliciting and indecent assault on a man. At 4.20 a.m. next day a shot was heard and Dashper was found in the yard, with a bullet in the head. A Service revolver was near by. He died in hospital. Verdict: Suicide while balance of mind disturbed."

Wing Commander Dashper was attached to the staff of the Director of Air Tactics at the Air Ministry; he is buried in Brookwood Military Cemetery.

26157 EDWARDS* Morgan Brownson G/Capt 15.12.56 Retirement
Group Captain Morgan Brownson was appointed OBE for his gallant actions as described in *The London Gazette* 24th December 1943, supplement 36299, page 5585: *"One morning in September 1943, a Beaufighter aircraft crashed on an airfield and immediately burst into flames. Group Captain Edwards, the station commander, proceeded to the scene of the accident and, ignoring the danger from exploding ammunition and air bottles, entered the aircraft to rescue the trapped pilot. He released the pilot's harness and then helped him out of the aircraft, at the same time giving directions and inspiration to others who had come to assist. Thirty seconds after the pilot had been dragged clear of the wreckage the oil tanks exploded. Group Captain Edwards showed courage of a high order and set a fine example to all personnel at the station. His action was all the more commendable as, during the night, two other aircraft had crashed and Group Captain Edwards had had a disturbed and trying time as a result."*

26158 FIELD* Denys Brian Douglas S/Ldr + 06.06.40 83 Squadron
Squadron Leader Denys Brian Douglas Field was killed in the early stages of what would become known as the 'Bombing Campaign' when on the night of 5th-6th June 1940, his Hampden I P1348 failed to return to Scampton from a raid on Hamburg. There were no survivors from the crew and all are buried in Becklingen War Cemetery. For additional information, please refer to page 144 of my RAFBCL 1949-1940 revised edition. Whilst at Cranwell, Flight Cadet Field excelled at athletics, hockey, tennis and cricket.

26159 LITTLER* Charles Eric W/Cdr + 30.03.41 103 Squadron
Wing Commander Charles Eric Littler was cremated in Liverpool [Anfield] Crematorium and is commemorated here on panel 2. On 30th-31st March 1941, commanding 103 Squadron, he put himself on the *Battle Order* for Brest and with his crew he took off from Newton in Wellington IC R1043 . Possibly during the outbound flight technical problems overtook the bomber and in making an emergency landing the Wellington crashed into a tree whilst avoiding a building at Manor Frm, Mudford, some 2 miles NE of Yeovil, Somerset. Please refer to page 35 of my RAFBCL 1941 for details of the crew.

26160 MASSEY* John Peter P/O 19.10.33 Resigned
It is suspected he had committed an offence for *The London Gazette* published on 5th January 1932, issue 33787, page 125, carried the following: *"Pilot Officer John Peter Massey takes rank and precedence as if his appointment as Pilot Officer bore date 26th Jan. 1931. Reduction takes effect from 15th Dec. 1931."*

Although shown in *List of Graduates* as being active in the Royal Air Force Volunteer Reserve between 11th November 1939 and 17th February 1946, Paul McMillan suspects he was a non-commissioned airman throughout. John Peter Massey was born in Canada at Kelowna in British Colombia on 29th September 1910, and died in Scotland at Edinburgh on 9th August 1973. My co-author also notes that Massey obtained a Royal Aero Club Aviators' Certificate, 18945, on 1st July 1939, his test taken under the aegis Air Service Training in a Avro Cadet, Genet Major, 150.

26161 MORE* James Winter Carmichael G/Capt + 12.09.44 224 Group Burma
There are a number of websites where Group Captain James Winter Carmichael More is mentioned. One of the best, which the authors acknowledge, is Traces of War which shows he commanded 73 Squadron [Hurricane] during the *Battle of France* claiming two enemy aircraft [one a probable] ahead of the *Blitzkrieg* and six between the 10th and 17th May 1940 [John Rawlings *Fighter Squadrons of the RAF* shows his tenure of command as being April to August 1940, thus qualifying him for inclusion in the *Battle of Britain* register]. His DFC, less citation, was *Gazetted* 30th July 1940, issue 34910, page 4675.

Following Staff appointments in 1940 and '41, he was posted to the Far East where, according to the RAF Commands website and a 'post' sent by John Larder in January 2003, Group Captain More OBE [New Year's Honours List 1942], DFC, *"... went to Maungdaw to brief crews for an attack on Prome. On impulse took a 615 Sqn Hurricane on the raid. Hit by ground fire and captured. Shipped to Japan but ship [SS Rakuyo Maru] sunk 12/9/44 lost, last seen on a raft."* To this, Errol Martyn adds that the *Rakyo Maru* was sunk by a torpedo from the American submarine *Sealion I I* some 100 miles NE of the Paracel Islands in the South China Sea.

Group Captain James Winter Carmichael More OBE DF is commemorated on Column 431 at the Singapore Memorial.

26162 NEWCOMBE* Jack Stewart P/O + 26.02.31 12 Squadron
Pilot Officer Jack Stewart Newcombe was a member of the British Bobsleigh team, made up entirely of former Cranwell graduates, participating in the 1931 World Championships at St.Moritz from where the following report appeared on Monday, February 9th, 1931, in *The Scotsman* beneath the headline 'Tobogganing - English Successes in Italian Cup.'

"St. Moritz - February 7 - The Italia Cup, one of the chief events decided on the Cresta Run, was won today by an Englishman, I M Bageley, whose net time for the three courses was 2 mins. 56 9-10 secs. Englishmen were also second and third, K Myer being less than 2 seconds behind Bageley, and Captin Coats being third, 1-10th of a second behind Myer.

"Great Britain finished third in the Bobsleigh Derby; by which they were represented by the Royal Air Force team - Pilots Officers D B D Field [steersman], P B Coote, R L Wallace and J S Newcombe [brakeman]. Switzerland won in an aggregate time of 5 mins. 35 ... secs. for four course. Germany was second in 5 mins. 36 1.5 secs, and Britain's time was 5 mins. 36 3-16 secs.

"Another Englishman: Henry Martineau, won the Calreroya Speed Cup for the fastest course, his time being 82 1-5 secs. - Press Association."

Continuing coverage, as reported in *The Times* in their edition of Thursday, February 12th, 1931, concerning the final runs [which was won by Germany], confirms Pilot Officer Newcombe was struck down by the illness that claimed his life later in the month, the salient part of the article reading *"... were without the services of Pilot Officer J Newcombe, their brakeman, who is indisposed."*

For his parents, tragedy would strike again in the final months of peace when his brother, Lieutenant Gordon Clifford Newton RN died in a midair collision between two Swordfish torpedo-bombers [K5933 and K5976] from 825 Squadron. The accident occurred at night off Alexandria when the the two aircraft were approaching HMS *Glorious,* all six crew dying as a result.

26163 PRETTY* Walter Philip George AM 03.10.66 Retirement
Air Marshal Sir Walter Pretty KBE CB twice mentioned in despatches, died on Friday, 17th January 1975. A signals specialist he was much involved with the development of 'Radar' and at Biggin Hill he was in the team headed by Sir Henry Tizard and Dr. Watson-Watt. Throughout the Second World War he was involved with technical matters ranging from commanding the 'Chain Home Low' station at Clacton, the establishment of No. 1 Radio School at Cranwell, Command Signals Officer at Fighter Command to name but three of his appointments,. From 1st March 1964 until his retirement, he served as Deputy Chief of the Defence Staff [Personnel & Logistics].

26164 SHIRLEY* Thomas Ulric Curzon AV-M 09.08.66 Retirement
Air Vice-Marshal Sir Thomas Shirley KBE CB mentioned in despatches, died on Saturday, 16th January 1982. Prior to Cranwell he was in the 8th entry of aircraft apprentices at the Electrical and Wireless School, Flowerdown from where he gained a scholarship to the College. It is no surprise that with his background in wireless technology his flying duties were enhanced by duties as the squadron's signals officer and as he rose to senior

rank, so his natural progression was to transfer from the General Duties Branch to the Technical Branch. His final appointment was Air Officer Commanding in Chief at Signals Command, retiring from the post and the Royal Air Force owing to medical unfitness. His retirement years were dogged by illness and prior to his death at Aylesbury in Buckinghamshire he was seriously incapacitated for many months.

It is noted on the Air of Authority website that he won the Hyde Thompson and Humanistics Trophy at Cranwell and was the first ex-aircraft apprentice [and sole Flowerdown apprentice] to serve as *Aide de Camp* to the Monarch, serving both George V in his final years and Elizabeth II in her initial years.

26191	SMITH	Roger Furnell	W/Cdr		05.01.51	Resigned

Paul McMillan has identified the following concerning Wing Commander Roger Furnell Smith. Which appeared in *The London Gazette* 9th January 1951, supplement 39118, page 187: *"Forfeiture of Seniority - Wing Commander R F Smith [26191] takes rank and precedence [with effect from 8th Nov. 1950] as if his appointment as Wing Commander bore date 8th Nov. 1950."*

On 27th April 1959, Roger Furnell Smith died from injuries received in a road traffic accident, the circumstances being reported in *The Chester Observer* published on Saturday, 16th May 1959: *"A verdict of accidental death was returned by the jury at St. Albans on Tuesday on Mr. Roger Furnell-Smith, aged 56, a retired RAF Wing Commander of Upper Drive Flats, Broughton Hall, Broughton, who died in St. Albans City Hall Hospital on 27th April, a week after a motoring accident near Markyate.*

"When the inquest opened on 28th April, Mrs Ellen Furnell-Smith, who was a passenger in the car at the time of the accident, said she and her husband were driving from Chester to Canterbury. She was checking a map when the crash occurred and she remembered nothing until she woke in hospital.

"On Tuesday, Mr. Eric Edward Dix, of Milton-road, Harpenden, said he was driving north along the A.5 road on 19th April, and he was passing an RAF lorry coming south when a black saloon car dived across the road from behind the lorry, apparently in an uncontrolled skid, and collided with his car.

"The driver of the lorry, Mr. David Henry Williams, of Wellington, Shropshire, said there was room in the middle traffic lane for Mr. Furnell-Smith to pass.

"Addressing the jury, the Coroner, Mr. J C Ottoway, it appeared for some reason the car got out of control as Mr. Furnell-Smith was about to overtake the lorry."

26165	STEPHENSON*	Geoffrey Dalton	A/Cmdr	+	08.11.54	CFE West Raynham

Air Commodore Geoffrey Dalton Stephenson's service was interrupted when as Squadron Leader Stephenson and commanding 19 Squadron his Spitfire I N3200 was shot down on 26th May 1940 over the Dunkirk beaches [from where it was recovered in 1986 and in time restored to flying conditions by March 2014] during a top fighter cover sortie during operation *Dynamo*. As a prisoner of war he was a 'thorn in the side' of his captors and, subsequently, he was 'despatched' to Kolditz Castle where in Paul Brickhill's biography of Douglas Bader, of the same entry, they were re-united, page 338 records their meeting *"... Douglas! There you are. He* [Bader] *swung round. Geoffrey Stephenson in an old sweater and army trousers was grinning by the steps."*

Remaining in the postwar air force and promoted to air rank, he was appointed Commandant of the Central Fight Establishment at West Raynham during which he went to America as head of a team of Royal Air Force officers. At Elgin Air Force Base on 8th November 1954, he was briefed for a test flight in a North American F-100A Super Sabre [first flight 25th May 1953] during which he got into difficulties and crashed before being able to eject. His death was reported in *Flight and Aircraft Engineer* in its issue on 19th November 1954, under the heading 'Venom and F-100 Restrictions.'

"Temporary restrictions were imposed last week on the flying of all de Havilland and Sea Venom aircraft in the British Services. They forbid the use of wing-tip tanks and ban certain types of aerobatics and manoeuvres. A D.H. spokesman has stated that the defect is not of a structural nature [at the time a searching enquiry was still in progress in connect with the DH Comet airline crashes that had grounded the fleet]. *In America, an order has been issued grounding all North American F-100 Sabres following three recent crashes, in one of which A.Cmdr. D G Stephenson, Commandant of the Central Fighter Establishment, West Raynham, was killed. A/ Cmdr. Stephenson was heading a team of RAF officers which was engaged in studying defence problems and operational procedures. In another recent F-100 crash Mr. George Welch, North American's chief test pilot, met his death in California. From a third machine of the same type the pilot parachuted to safety, sustaining minor injuries."*

His body was recovered from the pine forest where the F-100 fell and, following a Memorial Service held on 10th November 1954, at the Elgin Base chapel, it was flown, with a contingent of RAF and USAF officers to Maxwell Air Force Base, Montgomery, Alabama, where he was laid to rest in the Royal Air Force plot.

As an aside, the 1950s was still a time of air forces transitioning from tried and tested piston-engined types to jet propelled aircraft, and though the Royal Air Force was familiar with the Meteor/Vampire types, more advanced jets were still in the prototype stage with many snags yet to identified and ironed out - the Swift/Hunter being an example, though early production aircraft of both types were in squadron service.

26166	VAUGHAN-FOWLER*	Dennis George	P/O	+	07.08.31	41 Squadron
26167	WALKER*	Nigel Charles	G/Capt		12.09.59	Retirement

Group Captain Nigel Charles Walker received a mention in despatches during his service.

26168	WHITEHEAD*	John	G/Capt		17.01.58	Retirement

A Halton aircraft apprentice who won a scholarship to attend Cranwell, Group Captain John Whitehead received a mention in despatches during his service.

26169	WILLS-SANDFORD*	William Robert	G/Capt		03.02.56	Retirement

Group Captain William Robert Wills-Sandford received a mention in despatches during his service.

26170	WRIGLEY*	Henry Bertram	AV-M		11.07.64	Retirement

Air Vice-Marshal Henry Bertram Wrigley CB CBE, died in December 1999. An 8th entry aircraft apprentice at the Electrical and Wireless School, Flowerdown, he won a scholarship to the College. His final service appointment was as Senior Technical Staff Officer at Fight Command Head-quarters. In retirement he joined Hawker Siddeley Dynamics as a sales manager in their air weapons division, retiring in 1976.

The September 1928 entry is noteworthy in that just over fifty percent died before completing their service.

* Graduated with permanent commissions and seniority of 26th July 1930 [LG 26 August 1930, issue 33638, page 5298]

SWORD OF HONOUR
Flight Cadet Patrick Bernard Coote

ROLL OF HONOUR
SEPTEMBER 1928 ENTRY

P/O	ANGELL	David Victor	19 March 1931	29 Squadron
S/Ldr	BELCHAM	Lawrence George	14 July 1942	119 Squadron
P/O	CHANCE	John Anthony	19 November 1930	26 Squadron
F/O	CLELAND	Albert Gwilliam	23 December 1932	47 Squadron
W/Cdr	COOTE	Patrick Bernard	13 April 1941	211 Squadron
W/Cdr	DASHPER	Robert Bruce	6 May 1946	Air Ministry
S/Ldr	FIELD	Denys Brian Douglas	6 June 1940	83 Squadron
W/Cdr	LITTLER	Charles Eric	30 March 1941	103 Squadron

G/Capt	MORE	James Winter Carmichael	12 September 1944	224 Group Burma
P/O	NEWCOMBE	Jack Stewart	26 February 1931	12 Squadron
A/Cmdr	STEPHENSON CBE	Geoffrey Dalton	8 November 1954	CFE West Raynham
P/O	VAUGHAN-FOWLE	Dennis George	7 August 1931	41 Squadron

FLYING ACCIDENTS

Thursday 26 April 1928
Siskin IIIA J8956 F/Cdt P A Meakin* Injured
T/o Cranwell and fatally injured when his Siskin dived, crashed, and caught fire. Flight Cadet Peter Anthony Meakin died 24-hours later from his injuries.

Friday 14 September 1928 Avro 504N J8536 Struck, while parked, by DH.9A J8214 which was in the process of taxying. The Avro was a write off, the DH was repaired.

Wednesday 3 October 1928 DH.9A J8216 Damaged beyond repair while parked when Avro 504N J8575 collided with the DH. The Avro was repaired and, subsequently, went out to Egypt where it was issued to 4 Flying Training School. Still in use, September 1933.

* His death in *The List of Graduates* appears on page 127, the Roll of Honour which commemorates those flight cadets who lost their lives ahead of graduating. From information published, it appears he arrived at the College during 1926, but in which entry I am unable to say. At the time of his death he had been promoted to the rank of flight cadet corporal.

Appendix E - Roll of Honour

ROYAL AIR FORCE

Sgt	BAMFORD	Francis George	12 June 1928	84 Squadron
F/Lt	BROWNING MC DFC	Lance Harold	2 August 1928	3 Squadron
F/Lt	CALVEY	Harold Charles	1 July 1928	23 Squadron
AC2	CHADWICK	Henry	6 November 1926	26 Squadron
F/O	CRANSWICK MC	Philip	5 June 1928	3 Squadron
F/Lt	EDWARDES	Edward Norman Tickner	14 August 1928	8 Squadron
LAC	FISHER	Harold Edwin	30 January 1928	45 Squadron
P/O	FISHER MC	Lionel Edward Ruggles	9 January 1928	6 Squadron
LAC	FLETCHER	Frederick William	31 August 1928	14 Squadron
LAC	FROST	Arthur Sidney	12 June 1928	84 Squadron
Sgt	FUTCHER	William Frank	8 June 1928	6 Squadron
Sgt	GARNER	Alexander Joseph	8 June 1928	6 Squadron
F/Sgt	HORRIER	William Charles	1 July 1928	23 Squadron
F/O	JACKSON Mentioned in Despatches	Rolf Booth Hilton	20 February 1928	55 Squadron
F/O	KAY	Alexander Bruce	4 July 1928	6 Squadron
LAC	KIMBERLEY	James	28 March 1928	14 Squadron
Sgt	LOCKWOOD	Herbert Edward	8 November 1926	100 Squadron
Sgt	LONG	Charles Leonard	26 December 1928	47 Squadron
Cpl	LOUD	Christopher John	11 October 1928	12 Squadron
AC1	LOWMAN	William George	2 March 1928	207 Squadron
Sgt	MALTMAN	William Bean	2 March 1928	207 Squadron
LAC	MASON	James Leslie	3 July 1928	31 Squadron
LAC	MASON	Sydney Cresswell	2 March 1928	207 Squadron
P/O	MAUND	John Henry Lorraine	26 June 1928	14 Squadron
F/Lt	McCORMACK	George	28 March 1928	14 Squadron
F/O	McEVOY Australia	Clarence Reginald	3 July 1928	31 Squadron
F/O	McMILLAN	Douglas James Frederick	5 June 1928	3 Squadron
AC1	MIDDLETON	Jack James Heatherstone	26 June 1928	14 Squadron
Sgt	MORRIS	Cecil Norman	31 July 1928	8 Squadron
F/O	MUMFORD-MATHEWS	Horace James Joseph	14 March 1928	2 Squadron
P/O	MYERS	Charles Lilburn	6 November 1928	26 Squadron
F/O	RICKS	Arnold William Alexander	26 December 1928	47 Squadron
Sgt	SAUNDERS	Victor Robert	31 August 1928	14 Squadron
F/Lt	SOMERVELL AFC	William Edmund	11 October 1928	12 Squadron
LAC	THOMAS	Donald Martin	11 May 1928	16 Squadron
AC1	TOWERS	George Henry	2 April 1928	2 Squadron
Sgt	TRICKETT	Herbert	1 March 1928	29 Squadron
LAC	TURNER*	Ernest Arthur	25 April 1928	27 Squadron
F/O	UNDERDOWN	Gerald Arthur	11 May 1928	16 Squadron
P/O	WATSON	Eric James	17 February 1928	25 Squadron
AC1	WAUGH	William	2 April 1928	30 Squadron
F/O	WOOD	Jack Whitworth	2 April 1928	30 Squadron

* Leading Aircraftman Ernest Arthur Turner, 362706, was drowned following the crash of DH.9A H3450, flown by Sergeant David Irving who was unhurt, which came down in the River Indus after flying beneath a bridge near Attock. Salvaged, the DH was repaired only to come to grief later in the year - see my summary for 21st September 1928.

AUXILIARY AIR FORCE

P/O	ALDRIDGE	George Herbert	2 September 1928	605 Squadron AAF
F/O	DREW	James Pearson	21 May 1928	602 Squadron AAF
P/O	SHIELLS	John Temple Lyall	7 July 1928	603 Squadron AAF

Of the forty-five fatalities regarding officers and airmen who lost their lives during 1928, in accidents whilst attached to squadrons, twenty four were non-commissioned officers.

ARMY

Capt	DOYLE	James Charles	28 December 1928	
F/O	HADDEN	Jack	2 April 1928	2 Squadron
	Lieutenant in the Black Watch			
Lt	HASERICK	Sidney Gordon	9 January 1928	
	Lieutenant in the King's Own Yorkshire Light Infantry, attached Iraqi Levies			
Lt	SCOTT	David Francis Cumin	14 March 1928	2 Squadron

CIVILIAN

Miss	FOX	Winifred Daphne	5 April 1928

SQUADRON LOSSES
1929

Another year where lack of information concerning the names of pilots in non-fatal air accidents prevails. As the appendices will show, the phasing out of familiar types, for example the venerable DH.9A, commenced, though their replacements were still of the biplane age with only marginally improved performance.

Also of note was the elevating of various coastal Flights to squadron status four such examples being recorded early in the year while 204 Squadron's 'number plate' was restored. All five squadrons employed in seaplane operations and the influence of Royal Air Force air cover was now extended to the Far East with the Southampton boats of No. 205 Squadron [previous known as the Far East Flight, the Southamptons completed their passage between October 1927 and February 1928].

First flown on 10th March 1925, Supermarine's Southampton was one of the success stories of the inter-war years, deliveries to No. 480 [Coastal Reconnaissance] Flight at Calshot commenced in August of the same year. Although its maximum speed was less than 100 miles per hour, it had an impressive endurance of over six hours, thereby setting the bench mark for future seaplanes which reached their pinnacle with Short's magnificent Sunderland. In operational service in time for the Second World War it would remain 'on duty' throughout the conflict and beyond.

JANUARY

Wednesday 2 January 1929
55 Squadron P/O C E V L'E Feasey Injured
DH.9A J7838 P/O R R Carroll +
T/o Hinaidi for an air test during which the engine failed. Forced-landed, but overturned in the process. Pilot Officer Edward Victor L'Estrange Feasey was granted a short service commission on 18th July 1927 [LG 26 July 1927, issue 33297, page 4840].

His observer, Pilot Officer Raymond Russell Carroll was just into his second year of service, his short service commission having been *Gazetted* on 20th December 1927 [see Appendix C for 1927].

Thursday 10 January 1929
43 Squadron *Not reported*
Siskin IIIA J8875
T/o Tangmere and reported to have crashed at Eastchurch, home of the Armament and Gunnery School.

Friday 18 January 1929
45 Squadron *Not reported*
DH.9A J7860
T/o Helwan for night flying practice. Undershot an approach and smashed the undercarriage; possibly damaged beyond repair.

Saturday 19 January 1929
601 Squadron AAF F/O N H Jones AAF Safe
DH.9A J8130
T/o Hendon and on return the winter sun was setting and a mist was forming across the airfield. In these somewhat marginal conditions Flying Officer Jones failed to see the DH summarised below. Although considered for repair, I suspect J8130 had made its final landing.

601 Squadron AAF P/O D B H Coates AAF Safe
DH.9A J8165
While awaiting clearance to take off, struck and damaged beyond repair by the DH summarised above.

Tuesday 29 January 1929
70 Squadron *Not reported*
Victoria II J7926
T/o Hinaidi [though Kabul is a possibility] and forced-landed on a plateau some 2 miles from *Sarobi* [sic], Afghanistan and abandoned to its fate. This was at the time of the Kabul Airlift evacuation.

Note. The location may well be Surobi, capital of the Sarubi District, and some 60km east of Kabul.

FEBRUARY

Monday 4 February 1929
6 Squadron *Not reported*
Bristol F.2J J6742
T/o Aboukir for delivery to the squadron at Hinaidi but crashed at *Zangai* [sic].

Friday 15 February 1929
At Hinaidi, Leading Aircraftman John Prunty 505489 is believed to have sustained injury during the starting of DH.9A J8192. This has been recorded in Air-Britain's *J File* and with no further entries reported. The *DH.4/DH.9 File* shows similar information, adding that Leading Aircraftman Prunty, a wireless operator by trade, died from his injuries. He joined the service as a civilian, circa late 1925, his number coming in the block 505001 - 549999; he was the first with a 505001 block number to be fatally injured while serving with a squadron.

Monday 18 February 1929
25 Squadron F/Sgt J W Pearce +
Siskin IIIA J9319
T/o Filton and set course for Hawkinge only to crash at Langham Manor, South Godstone in Surrey, 6 miles or so ESE from Redhill. An inquest into the death of 28 year old Flight Sergeant John William Pearce, 244149, found that he had been overcome by carbon monoxide fumes. He saw service with the Royal Naval Air Service in 1917.

Although of Armstrong Whitworth design, Siskin IIIA J9319 was one of twenty-seven airframes built by the Bristol Aeroplane Company with J9319 completed and awaiting collection on 30th November 1928.

The death of Flight Sergeant Pearse and general remarks on accidents so far in the year were published by the *Aberdeen Press and Journal* beneath the headline *'Burned to Death - Aeroplane Crashes in Garden'*

"The pilot of a single-seater RAF aeroplane was killed last night when the machine crashed and burst into flames in a garden at South Godstone, Surrey. His name was Sergt. John William Pearce, stationed at Hawkinge.

"The machine, which appeared to be out of control at a high altitude, dropped like a stone, and burst into flames when it struck the ground. The fire was so fierce that the horrified onlookers were unable to approach the blazing machine, and were powerless to assist the pilot, who was burned to death in his seat.

"The machine crashed into the garden of Langham Manor, narrowly missing the Gardner, who was at work.

'Noise Like Explosion'

"The machine was flying fairly high, when the pilot appeared to lose control, the eye-witness told a press representative.

"It zig-zagged for a few minutes, and the dropped like a stone. I realised there was little hope of the pilot regaining control, for it fell faster and faster as it neared the ground. There was a nise like an explosion when the impact occurred, and immediately flames burst out.

"People rushed to the spot from neighbouring houses and tried vainly to assist the pilot, who could be seen clearly amid the flames. The heat, however, was too intense, and we could do nothing until the fire practically burned itself out. When the body of the pilot was at last dragged from the wreckage it was burned beyond recognition.

*"The accident brings the total of deaths in RAF crashes in Britain this year to four. Three men were killed in the crash at Eastchurch on January 30.*On January 2 one fatality occurred in Iraq. Last year's total was seventy-six.*

'Pilot Injured'

"Corporal Kenneth Muara of the RAF Training School at Digby, Lincolnshire, struck a tree while making a forced-landing yesterday, and received concussion and severe injuries to his face. He lives at Zing House, Zing Road, Plymouth. The machine was badly damaged."

Five weeks later, the *Birmingham Gazette* on Saturday, 23rd March, 1929, picked up on the notion that the root of the accident was Flight Sergeant Pearce being overcome by carbon monoxide fumes: *'Poisoned In The Air - Pilot's Death from Inhaling Exhaust Before Crash'*

"The theory that Flight Sergeant John William Pearce, aged 26, of the RAF, was dead before his aeroplane crashed near Godstone, Surrey, on 18 February, was put forward by experts at the resumed inquest at Kenley aerodrome yesterday.

"Sergeant Pearce was in a single-seater new machine and was flying from Bristol to Hawkinge aerodrome, near Folk-stone when the accident happened.

"Dr. Bronte said that carbon monoxide could easily come from the exhaust of the engine and could be inhaled gradually.

"There was no smell at all. The recipient gradually became slightly drowsy and fell asleep then became unconscious and death followed.

"Major P J Carre-Cooper, Government Inspector of Accidents, said that for some reason now being investigated an exhaust pipe had burst.

"A verdict of "Death by misadventure from the inhaling of fumes, and the crash which caused the injuries," was returned."

* Fairey IIID N9759 belonging to the Armament & Gunnery School, the deceased crew being named as Flying Officer Geoffrey Hugh Conningsby Ingle [22], Leading Aircraftman Frank Nelson Howick [25] and Aircraftman George Henry Johnson aged 22.

Monday 25 February 1929
208 Squadron Bristol F.2b J6596 Caught fire during refuelling and destroyed.

Thursday 28 February 1929
19 Squadron F/Lt G A F Bucknall +
Siskin IIIA
T/o Duxford and destroyed here following a dive from which Flight Lieutenant George Anthony Fielding Bucknall failed to recover. His permanent commission was *Gazetted* on 6th January 1922, issue 32569, page 173.

The following appeared in Saturday's *Daily Mirror:*

'Stunting Complaint'

'Jury and the Dangers if Trick Flying Near the Ground'

"Complaints of low stunt flying were made at the Cambridge inquest yesterday on Flight Lieutenant Bucknall. An Accidental death verdict was returned.

"Flying Officer J E Jones said Bucknall put the machine into a spin at about 1,600ft., and came out of it at about 500ft.

"A member of the jury complained of low flying in the district, and the jury added a rider to their verdict that stunts at low altitude over civilians working on the ground should be avoided as far as possible."

MARCH

Friday 1 March 1929
23 Squadron F/O P N Sealy-Allin + Whyteleafe [St. Luke's] Churchyard
Gamecock I J8094
T/o Kenley and destroyed in a midair collision with the Gamecock summarised below. A permanent officer, his commission was promulgated on 27th September 1927, issue 33315, page 6127. Born on 11th November 1905 and baptised 4th January 1906, at Vizianagaram, Andhra Pradesh, India, the inscription on his headstone reads: *"I bore you on eagle's wings and brought you unto myself,"* Exodus chapter 19, verse 4.

23 Squadron F/Sgt J G Freeman Safe
Gamecock I J8415
T/o Kenley and lost in the circumstances outlined above. Although this tragedy most likely made the local press, the following appears on the Kenley Revival website, which the authors acknowledge, from the Australian journal, the *Western Mail* [Perth]: *"Flying Officer Patrick N. Sealy-Allin, of 23 [Fighter] Squadron RAF, was killed and Sergeant Pilot J G Freeman had a wonderful escape, when the aeroplanes they were piloting were in collision above Kenley aerodrome, England. The two machines went out of control after the collision at 1,000ft. Sergeant Freeman threw himself out with his parachute and landed safely on the roof of a hangar. Mr Sealy-Allin was apparently unable to free himself, and was found dead, jammed in the cockpit of his wrecked machine. Sergeant Freeman was blown by the wind towards the hangars, and could be seen tugging at his parachute ropes in a desperate effort to steer himself clear of the obstruction. He was unsuccessful and only by desperate kicking was he able to throw himself clear of a glass roof, into which he nearly crashed. He landed on the sloping roof of a hangar and was stranded their until a number of men took a ladder across and helped him down. "I heard a crash as the two machines came together in mid-air," said a spectator "then both machines twisted and turned as they crashed earthwards. I saw Freeman throw himself out and, for a minute or two I thought his parachute was not going to open. It did, however, and he came down safely.""*

"At the inquest into the accident, on 5th March, Sgt. Freeman described how he had been aloft about 35 minutes, practising aerobatics and had just completed a roll when he saw the other Gamecock, flown by Sealy-Allin, disappear under his starboard wing, hitting his aircraft from underneath. The impact caused him to flip over, so he undid his harness and baled out. Freeman could offer no explanation of how two aircraft got so close together, but Flight Commander Croome explained to the coroner that the upper and lower wings obstructed the pilot's view, causing blind spots. The jury returned a verdict of accidental death."

"Both aircraft crashed 150-200 yards apart on the airfield. One of them had begun to break up in the impact and large pieces of the wing together with the petrol tank rained down on the fields near the aerodrome - several workmen had narrow escapes from falling wreckage."

Saturday 2 March 1929
A serious starting accident at Hinaidi involving Victoria IV J8916 seriously injured Corporal P J Griffon. This particular aircraft had been taken on service charge on 13th December 1927, as a Mk.IIIA but was converted to Mk.IV standards ahead of despatch to the Middle East which was by way of London's West India Docks and the SS *Nigaristan.*

Throughout its service it was attached to 70 Squadron, during which it was modified to Mk. VI standards, and eventually as a Valentia until damaged beyond repair on 8th November 1937, details of this will appear in Volume 5.

Monday 11 March 1929
70 Squadron *Not reported*
Victoria IIIA J8929
T/o Hinaidi and believed to have been damaged beyond repair following engine failure and a forced-landing at *Rapih* [sic] in the Persian Gulf.

Monday 18 March 1929
47 Squadron F/O Y W Burnett +
Fairey IIIF SR1191 Sgt T C Turner +
T/o Gwelo in Southern Rhodesia, presumably to return to Khartoum, and crashed out of control. Flying Officer Yvon William Burnett was a short service commission officer whose details were published in *The London Gazette* on 24th July 1923, issue 32847, page 5074. The serial of his aircraft, which had been diverted from FAA stock, indicates it had undergone a major repair.

Sergeant Thomas Condy Turner joined as a boy airman between July 1922 and January 1924, his service number being 362709.

During the month, the date not being specified, 503 Squadron SR reported one of their Fairey Fawn's J6991 as having crashed at Metheringham, 8 miles SE of Lincoln.

APRIL

Monday 22 April 1929
3 Squadron *Not reported*
Gamecock I J8417
T/o Upavon and wrecked here in a landing accident.

Friday 26 April 1929
13 Squadron *Not reported*
Atlas I J8782
T/o Old Sarum and believed to have been damaged beyond repair while in the course of landing back on the airfield. It first served with the squadron between August and October 1927, before a brief spell with the School of Army Co-operation.

208 Squadron Bristol F2.J F4883 Landed safely at Heliopolis and the crew had vacated the aircraft when static electricity started a fire in the front cockpit and the Bristol was burnt out.

Monday 29 April 1929
12 Squadron *Not reported*
Fox I J8425 *Not reported*
T/o Andover and after forming up in formations set off for Lincolnshire and the armament practice camp at North Coates Fittes and it was on arrival here that crew crashed while attempting to land. First flown on 28th Jun 1927, the Fix was accepted by the squadron on 7th July 1927.

MAY

Thursday 16 May 1929
19 Squadron F/O J W Bayes +
Siskin IIIA
T/o Duxford and crashed at Northolt when Flying Officer John Walden Bayes was attempting a slow roll. His short service commission was published in issue 33087, page 6205 of *The London Gazette,* 25th September 1925.

'Flying Officers Error of Judgement'

So read the heading in the *Warwick & Warwickshire Advertiser & Leamington Gazette* of Saturday, May 25th, 1929:

"An inquest was held at Northolt Aerodrome, Middlesex, on Flying Officer John Walden Bayes [24], of No. 19 Fighting Squadron, RAF, stationed at Duxford, who was killed during a flying display. He had completed a "roll," and was flying low when the aeroplane crashed and burst into flames.

"Rigger Alan Bond, who was responsible for preparing the machine, said it was in good order when he inspected it.

"Squadron Leader Robert Stanley Aitken, commanding the Northolt Station, said Bayes had not sufficient speed to complete the evolution nor sufficient height to recover himself by diving. Witness thought the accident was caused by the officer attempting an evolution at too slow a speed for the height at which he was flying.

"The Coroner [Dr. Cross] recorded a verdict of "Accidental death."

Note. Little changes over the years and on the same page reporting the inquest into Flying Officer Bayes's death was an article lamenting the disappearance of wild flowers which according to the Council of the Society for the Promotion of Nature Reserves was *"... a matter of grave concern for some years ..."*

JUNE

Friday 7 June 1929
6 Squadron F/O F Townsend Safe
Bristol F.2b J7638 Sgt Gunn Safe
T/o Hinaidi only to lose engine power. Flying Officer Frederick Townsend attempted to regain the airfield but stalled and in the ensuing crash-landing the Bristol was damaged beyond repair. A short service commissioned officer, his details are recorded in Appendix D under the entries for 1st February 1927, issue 33244, page 654.

Saturday 8 June 1929
601 Squadron AAF *Not reported*
DH.9A J8108
T/o Hendon and damaged beyond repair when forced-landing with engine failure at Greenford in Middlesex.

Tuesday 11 June 1929
17 Squadron F/O E D Turner Injured
Siskin IIIA J8880
T/o Sutton Bridge and crashed into a field near the hamlet of Arpinge which is practically bordered by Paddlesworth which is about a mile to the SW of Hawkinge, the intended destination for Elphinstone Docwra Turner. The Saturday edition of the *Folkestone, Hythe, Sandgate & Cheriton Herald* published an account of the crash: *"A single-seater fighter aeroplane of No. 17 [Fighter] Squadron, Upavon, Wilts., piloted by Flying Officer E D Turner, burst in flames while flying over the Downs north of Cheriton, in the vicinity of Paddlesworth, on Tuesday afternoon. The pilot was seen to jump from the machine and his parachute opened after he fallen a short distance. He appeared to make a good descent. The 'plane dived towards the ground and crashed in an oat field on Mr. C Davson's land, at Arpinge, close to the reservoir at Paddlesworth.*

As the machine struck the ground a great burst of smoke and flames shot up, and in a few moments only debris remained. An ambulance dashed to the scene shortly afterwards, and it was found that the pilot, who had landed safely some distance away, had sustained a broken arm. A number of farm works and others ran to the spot where the 'plane had crashed. They rendered such assistance as they could. The 'plane was flying at a fair height when it was first seen in flames.

"I saw the pilot leave the 'plane," said one eye-witness to an "Herald" representative. "His parachute seemed to have opened perfectly and he came down very steadily. The 'plane hit the ground with terrific force and parts of it were scattered. There was a burst of flame when it hit the ground."

Not only was the crash reported by the local press, but as late as 24th July 1929 *The Singapore Free Press and Mercantile Advertiser* considered it was worth a mention, adding that a farm worker spoke to the pilot to ask whether he was hurt to which he replied *"No, only a broken arm thanks very much"* and continued to walk unaided to Hawkinge aerodrome from where he was taken to the military hospital at Shorncliffe for treatment. The *Advertiser* also reported that the fire started in the port side of the engine.

Monday 17 June 1929
3 Squadron P/O J E Jorgensen +
Siskin IIIDC J9196 Sgt C B Groom +
T/o Upavon and while performing aerobatics in the vicinity of Netheravon airfield structural failure of the wings occurred and the fighter plummeted to the ground. Pilot Officer James Ernest Jorgensen, Marlborough College educated, arrived at the Cadet College, Cranwell with flight cadets joining the September 1926. He graduated with a permanent commission on 28th July 1928 [LG 21 August 1928, issue 33414 page 5575].

Sergeant Charles Benjamin Groom was a *Creat War* survivor, his service having started either towards the end of 1917, or early in 1918. Furthermore, it is possible it may have begun as a boy airman.

'Air Crash'
'Two Victims: one From Portsmouth'
'Plane Nose Dives From 1,000 Feet'

Read the headline in the *Hampshire Telegraph and Post* on Friday, June 21st, 1929, continuing: *"As tbe result of an accident near Netheravon to a Siskin machine of No. 3 Fighter Squadron, Upavon, on Monday, Pilot Officer James Ernest Jorgensen, the pilot of the aircraft, and 157686 Sergeant Charles Benjamin Groom were killed.*

"A farmer living near the scene of the crash described it to the "Daily Sketch."

''I should say the machine was travelling at about 1,000feet," he said, "when suddenly it nose-dived with terrific speed to earth."

""I rushed to the scene and found that it had fallen in a heap in the corner of a field. There were no flames. The bodies of the airmen were in the midst of the wreckage. I think there is no doubt they were killed outright by the impact. They were quickly recovered and taken back, I understand to Upavon."

"Sergeant Groom was a Portsmouth man, whose parents live at 34 Lucknow Street, Fratton. A relation of the deceased sergeant told a "Hampshire Telegraph and Post" representative on Tuesday morning that Groom, who wss 26 years of age, was to have been married early in September.

"Educated at Beasant Road School under Mr. Suter, Groom entered the Air Force as an apprentice in 1916, and was promoted to the rank of sergeant three years later.

"The inquest took place on Tuesday. It is expected the remains will be interred in Kingston Cemetery on Saturday."

Note. On the same day a major air accident occurred over the English Channel when a Handley Page W.12 airliner operated by Imperial Airways registration G-EBMT *City of Ottawa* and piloted by Captain Bralli was obliged to ditch owing to a connecting rod in the starboard engine failing. From the crew of two and eleven passengers, six injured survivors, including both members of crew, were rescued by the Belgian trawler *Gaby.* At the time of the tragedy, the airliner was *en route* from Croydon to Paris Le Bourget and thence to its final destination at Zurich in Switzerland.

Thursday 27 June 1929
56 Squadron F/O V O Eyre + See 2 April 1928
Siskin IIIA J8949
T/o Hendon for a rehearsal for the forthcoming Hendon Pageant and while over the airfield failed to recover from a spin. The squadron had moved from Biggin Hill to North Weald on 12th October 1927, and the death of Flying Officer Vickers Osborne Eyre who graduated from Cranwell with a permanent commission on 16th December 1925 [LG 12 January 1926, issue 33123, page 300] appears to have been the first fatality. *Aeroplane* in its issue of 3rd July 1929, reported: *"At the inquest on Mr. Eyre which was held at Hendon on July 1st, Flt Lt L T Jones said that the machines were flying in 'V' formation at 11,000 feet. Eyre had to pretend he was shot down and go into a spinning nose dive. He went down to 300 feet and tried to write the machine but he left it a little too late and just as the machine was beginning to write itself it struck the ground."*

Please refer to my summary of Monday, 2nd April 1928, for an account of his very lucky escape from death when he fell from a similar machine whilst over Little Laver in Essex.

The account, as published by the *Evening Sentinel* beneath the sub-editor's heading *'The Hendon Air Crash - Fatal Nose-Dive During Rehearsal - Coroner on Pilot's Error of Judgement'* 'mirrors's that of the *Aeroplane,* reading as follows: *"How a few yards made all the difference between an escape and fatal injury was described at Hendon to-day, at the inquest on Flying Officer Vickers Osborne Eyre, of the RAF, stationed at Northweald* [sic], *ho was killed last Thursday during a rehearsal for the Air Force display at Hendon on July 13th.*

"Flight-Lieut. Jones of Hendon, stated that the machine was flying in "V" formation, Eyre flying a single-seater Siskin on the tail of the left rank.

""Eyre had to pretend he was shot down and go into a spinning nose-dive," he said. "The machine was supposed to be under control the whole time. The 'planes were flying at about eleven thousand feet, and Eyre's machine went into a spin down to a height of three hundred feet, he tried to right it, but had left it a little too late, and just as the machine was beginning to right itself it struck the ground."

"He thought the accident was due to an error of judgement on the part of the pilot, who did not commence to pull the machine up to an even keel until it was just too late."

"Flight-Lieut. Plenderleith said that Flying Officer Eyre was a very experienced pilot, he had put in 731 actual flying hours, which was a considerable number. He had several times rehearsed the spinning nose-dive. In fact, he was doing it almost every day.

"Frederick Parker, and RAF fitter, said that the engine was in perfect order, and John Coles, a rigger, said that the fabric was perfect when the machine set out.

"The Coroner [Dr. George Cohen], in recording a verdict of "Accidental death," said that it was plain the tragedy was due to a most unfortunate error of judgement on the part of an exceptionally experienced officer. It was a sad case."

JULY

Sunday 7 July 1929
605 Squadron AAF *Not reported*
DH.9A J8125
T/o Castle Bromwich and wrecked here in a landing accident.

Wednesday 17 July 1929
23 Squadron *Not reported*
Gamecock I J8080
T/o Kenley to practice flying at night and in the course of making one landing misjudged his height and on touch down smashed the undercarriage. Damage to the airframe was extensive and the Gamecock was written off.

207 Squadron F/O S F Prince +
Fairey IIIF K1758 LAC E W Buttenshaw +
T/o Catfoss for rear-gun firing practice during which Flying Officer Stanley Frank Prince collided with the drogue and crashed into the sea within sight of the beach at Skipsea some 7 miles or so south of Bridlington, Yorkshire.

Leading Aircraftman Edward William Buttenshaw, 363348, began his service as a boy between July 1922 and January 1924. In addition to being an air gunner, I suspect he may well qualified as a wireless operator.

The squadron's personnel had detached to Catfoss on the 10th, the aircraft following over the next few days. Flying Officer Prince's short service commission was promulgated in the *Gazette* on 28th July 1925, issue 33070, page 5051.

'The Skipsea Air Crash'
'Error of Judgement'
'Pilot's Manoeuvre When Too Low'

Was a very accurate description for the above tragedy, which continued in the *Northern Daily Mail* [see below and the paper's report on the 7 Squadron night flying accident] *"A verdict of "Accidental death" was returned at the inquest to-day on Flying Officer Stanley Frank Prince [22] and Leading Aircraftman Edward William Buttenshaw, of the RAF, who were killed in the 'plane accident at Skipsea, on the East Yorkshire coast, which occurred about noon yesterday.*

"It was stated that there were two 'planes flying at altitude of 4,000ft., another at 500ft., and the machine piloted by Flying Officer Princewas at a still lower altitude.

"After going through manoeuvres and looping the loop, the machine in which Prince and Buttenshaw were flying swooped down and crashed into the water.

"Flying Officer Combe expressed the opinion that the accident was due to an error of judgement. He thought that Prince essayed a roll too low down, and losing flying speed, he was unable to bring the nose of the machine up again.

"He added that after the accident he swam out to the machine, but could find no trace of the airmen.

"Medical evidence was given that Prince died from drowning, and that Buttenshaw received a fractured neck.

"The Coroner recorded a verdict of "Accidental death," and complimented Flying Officer Combe on his pluck."

Note. The month of July 1929, was marred by fatal accidents involving five officers attached to the Reserve of Air Force Officers, four of these accidents being summarised against their names in the appendices. The fifth officer, Flying Officer [Honorary Flight Lieutenant] Arthur Statham White, aged 37, and the Chief Demonstration Pilot employed by de Havilland Aircraft was killed when his DH.60G Moth G-AAKL in which he was giving a demonstration to a Mr. Frederick Lincoln Knight, was struck from below by DH.60G Moth G-AAJU piloted by Captain George Frederick Boyle who had taken off from nearby Heston Aerodrome. The collision occurred over Valley Farm, near Kingsbury in Middlesex, both Moths falling out of control and crashing with fatal consequences to all three airmen. From remarks on the Aviation Safety Network website, it is believed G-AAKL was on its maiden flight having been registered just three days previously. A report of the accident can be obtained from TNA Kew by quoting AVIA 5/11/C144.

Thursday-Friday 18-19 July 1929

7 Squadron	F/O J H Lindell	Injured
Virginia	Australia	
	P/O A Wall	Injured
	Lt J V C Moberley RE	Injured
	LAC Bagshaw	Injured
	AC1 Mould	Safe

T/o Worthy Down for a local night flying exercise during which it came to grief in the manner described by the *Northern Daily Mail* whose sub-editor headed the article: *'Big Bomber Crashes - Hit Top of Hill - Four Members of Crew Injured' "Four men were injured when a Vickers Virginia aeroplane, attached to No. 7 Bomber Squadron, crashed near Lasham [Hants.] early this morning.*

"The names of the injured are Flying Officer John Henry Lindell [See Appendix D 1928 and officers granted a short service commission on 28th February 1928], *Pilot Officer Arnold Wall, Lieut. J V C Moberley, and Aircraftsman Bagshaw. Aircraftsman Mould escaped unhurt.*

"Leading Aircraftsman Bagshaw is suffering from a dislocated right ankle; Flying Officer J H Lindell had both ankles dislocated and a fractured jaw and left arm; Lieut. Moberley, whois understood to be an officer of the Royal Engineers, was unconscious when admitted to hospital and is suffering from cuts, abrasions and concussion.

"The machine was flying from Worthy Down Aerodrome, near Winchester. Apparently it flew into fog or a low cloud 300 feet up, and later hit the top of a hill. The undercarriage caught in a hedge, and the machine dived into a ploughed field."

Friday 19 July 1929

2 Squadron *Not reported*
Bristol F.2b J6794
T/o Manston and deployed to Salisbury Plain where it crashed near Tilshead, an isolated village on the A360 major road and roughly midway between Shrewton in the south and West Lavington in the north.

Monday 29 July 1929

55 Squadron *Not reported*
DH.9A J7348
T/o Hinaidi but while climbing away another aircraft passed in front and in order to avoid a collision the DH was pulled up into a steep turn which resulted in a stall from which it failed to recover before falling to the ground; wrecked. During its service with 5 FTS Shotwick it was damaged on 1st July 1925 when Flight Lieutenant E J A Burke collided with Pilot Officer D L Evans who had landed his DH.9A J7077 at the opposite end of the landing area.

AUGUST

Sunday 4 August 1929

605 Squadron AAF *Not reported*
DH.9A E8711 *Not reported*
T/o Manston but swung badly, crashed and caught fire.

Wednesday 14 August 1929

23 Squadron F/O C H Jones +
Gamecock I J7914
T/o Sutton Bridge and stalled off a steep turn with seconds of becoming airborne. Flying Officer harles Henry Jones was a short service commissioned officer whose details were promulgated in the *Gazette* on 6th October 1925, issue 33090 page 6421. A photograph of his Gamecock can be viewed on the Kenley Revival website which adds that J7914 had been armed with 200 rounds of ammunition and on impact it burst into flames.

Reported by the *Sheffield Daily Telegraph* on Thursday, August 15th, 1929:

'RAF Pilot's Crash'
'Sergeant's Theory as to Cause of Fatality'

"A verdict of "Misadventure" was returned at an inquest at Sutton Bridge, Royal Air Force practice camp yesterday, on Flying Officer Charles Henry Jones, [21], 23 Squadron RAF, who was killed yesterday morning as the result of a 'plane crash. Deceased was a native of Scotland.

"Pilot Sergeant James Hickling said he saw deceased's machine take off quite normally. He was seen after passing the boundary of the aerodrome to turn swiftly to the right, and when at a heigh of from 30 to 40 feet, the nose of the 'plane went down and the machine crashed and burst into flames. Witness thought the accident was due to deceased turning too soon after leaving the ground.

"Medical evidence showed that deceased was killed outright.

"It was stated that the machine was tested before deceased went up and it was found satisfactory."

601 Squadron AAF. *Not reported*
DH.9A J7835
T/o Lympne and wrecked following a collision with a landing light. At the time the squadron was on its annual summer camp from Hendon.

Thursday 22 August 1929
503 Squadron SR *Not reported*
Avro 504N J9258
T/o Waddington and recorded as burnt out in a crash at an undisclosed location.

Saturday 24 August 1929

216 Squadron	Sgt J Melville	+
Victoria	P/O J Wilson	+
	Sgt S Deacon	Injured
	LAC M H Creed	Injured
	LAC C E Langan	+
	AC1 F W Mabbett	Injured

T/o Heliopolis and reported as *"crashed"*, Leading Aircraftman Mervyn Henry Creed dying from his injuries 24-hours following the crash. Pilot Officer John Wilson, short service commissioned - *Gazetted* 12th June 1928, issue 33393, page 4022 - had recently qualified for his Flying Badge. The accident was reported in *The Citizen* on August 26th, 1929

"A Vickers Victorian troop carrying type plane with a crew of seven crashed after leaving the ground at Heliopolis on Saturday afternoon, states a Reuters message. Three men were killed, including the pilot and four [sic] *injured.*

"The Air Ministry stated yesterday that the names of the three airmen who were killed are Sergeant John Melville [No. 360011], first pilot; Pilot Officer Wilson, second pilot, and Leading Aircraftman Charles Ernest Langan [No. 335956] a member of the crew.

"The names of the three crew who were injured are, Leading Aircraftman Mervyn Henry Creed [No. 354179], dangerously injured, First-class Airman Frank Wilfred Mabbett [No. 363187], dangerously injured, and Sergeant Sydney Deacon [No. 335284], slightly injured. These three men have been admitted to the bomber station station sick quarters at Heliopolis.

"The causes of the accident are obscure at the moment. It is stated there was no fire when the machine crashed."

Sergeant Deacon, Paul McMillan notes, made a good recovery and was commissioned in the Second World War on 19th May 1940.

The service numbers for the non-commissioned officers who perished indicate in the case of Sergeant Melville *Great War* service from 1915, Leading Aircraftman Langan joining as a boy between August 1919 and January 1921, while Leading Aircraftman Creed may have either been a civilian volunteer, or having been conscripted - I suspect the former.

Tuesday 27 August 1929
1 Squadron *Not reported*
Siskin IIIA J8943/F
T/o Tangmere for night flying practice during which the Siskin caught fire after running onto a Monkey Flare, thus becoming the squadron's second loss of a Siskin owing to fire.

SEPETEMBER

Tuesday 10 September 1929
17 Squadron P/O L E J Lucas +
Siskin IIIA
T/o Upavon and believed to have crashed either on the airfield, or close by. Pilot Officer Lawrence Errington Jeff Lucas was twenty years of age and had graduated from Cranwell with a permanent commission as recently as 27th July [LG 27 August 1929, issue 33529, page 5569].

His death was briefly mentioned in *The Cornishman and Cornish Telegraph* on Thursday, September 12th, 1929, noting that Pilot Officer Lucas came from Falmouth.

Wednesday 11 September 1929
During the day at Hawkinge, Aircraftman H Holland, 363440, was injured when the propeller of Siskin IIIDC J9218 struck him during starting. Holland's service number indicates he joined the service as a boy entrant at sometime between January 1922 and July 1924, while J9218 arrived, according to Air-Britain's *J File* during the month of September 1929 and was retained until 1932 when it was passed to RAFC Cranwell. Its fate has not been recorded.

Wednesday 18 September 1929
39 Squadron *Not reported*
Wapiti IIA J9394
T/o Risalpur in formation and having climbed to 3,000 feet came into collision with Wapiti I J9083. Out of control, J9394 spun in near the airfield, but although damaged, the crew of J9083 managed to land safely and their aircraft was repaired at Drigh Road. It was last recorded at Lahore during July 1932.

Saturday 21 September 1929
14 Squadron *Not reported*
DH.9A J8141
T/o Ramleh and following a crash on the Kolundia landing ground caught fire and was burnt out.

Sunday 29 September 1929
84 Squadron *Not reported*
DH.9A J7054
T/o Shaibah and reported as *"crashed"*; no further details. First reported at Netheravon during September 1924, and in use by No. 1 Flying Training School, it was soon earmarked for overseas and by August 1927, it was reported at Shaibah where it was on establishment with 84 Squadron.

On 25th September 1927, it was damaged in an accident at Alum Rahal, Iraq, and following repairs was taken in hand by 30 Squadron before being returned to 84 Squadron.

OCTOBER

Friday 11 October 1929
29 Squadron F/O J Clarke +
Siskin IIIA
T/o Brough [though the squadron's base was North Weald in Essex] and while making a very low pass over Blackburn\s airfield at Brough collided with the roof of the factory. Flying Officer John Clarke, a graduate from the January 1925, entry to the Cadet College at Cranwell, his permanent commission being appointed on 11th December 1926 [LG 7th January 1927, issue 33237, page 121], was the Sword of Honour Flight Cadet from his entry.

The *Belfast Telegraph* describing the accident in its late edition of the same day remarked how Flying Officer Clarke on the day previous to his death *"had thrilled a great crowd at the opening of Hull municipal aerodrome at Hedon, where he gave a remarkable performance of "stunt flying."*

Although his take off was witnessed by a number of airfield workers, many of whom rushed to the scene of the crash, none were able to reach the cockpit, so fierce were the flames.

Monday 14 October 1929
43 Squadron *Not reported*
Siskin IIIA J9362
T/o Tangmere and on return landed heavily which resulted in the fighter ballooning into the air and on its second arrival the lower starboard wing struck first sending the Siskin on to its nose; believed damaged beyond repair.

Thursday 24 October 1929
55 Squadron F/O E J H F Moreton Injured
DH.9A J8176 Cpl W Walmsley +
T/o Hinaidi and wrecked in a bizarre accident near Diyala after flying into a signpost. Flying Officer Esmond John Hugh Fulford Moreton was granted a short service commission on 18th January 1928 [LG 31 January 1928, issue 33352, page 688].

Corporal William Walmsley, 336670, enlisted between August and September 1919, his service number coming within the block 336001 - 338000.

Air-Britain's *J File* shows J8176 as awaiting collection on 8th November 1926 [presumably from the Parnall facility], thence to Ascot where it was packed and despatched by sea to Aboukir where it remained crated for eighteen months before being re-erected and test flown on 13th April 1928.

Ferried a few days later to Hinaidi it underwent an extensive maintenance check which was completed on 16th October 1928 [at the time it had 33 hours and 45 minutes flying time recorded], and was taken on charge by 55 Squadron under whose supervision on 9th June 1929, automatic slots were fitted.

Monday 28 October 1929
36 Squadron F/Lt A H J Howlett Injured See 25 November 1930
Horsley TB II S1245 AC2 R H Wilson +

T/o Donibristle and crashed into the Firth of Forth off Queensferry while exercising with the carrier HMS *Argus*. For *Flight Lieutenant* Alexander Harold James Howlett this was his second very serious accident, the first is described in Appendix C [1924] against the entry for Flying Officer [Lieutenant RN] John Yarnton Mills.

Aircraftman Robert Henry Wilson's service number 370380 had served a little over four years.

Reformed at Donibristle on 1st October 1928, from the Coastal Defence Torpedo Flight, this was the squadron's first serious accident in which a member of crew perished.

The Falkirk Herald provided its readers with a report on Saturday, November 2nd, 1929, heading the article *'Flying Tragedy - Airman's Death in the Firth of Forth - Pilot Injured'* - the quality of reproduction is poor, but it begins: *"An official announcement issued on Tuesday the Air Ministry reported a fatal flying accident which occurred in the Firth of Forth on Monday. The announcement stated:- As the result of an accident in the Firth of Forth to a Hawker Horsley machine of No. 36 [Torpedo Bomber] Squadron, Donibristle, on October, 28th, 1929. No. 37038 Aircraftsman Robert Henry Wilson, 24, occupant of the aircraft, was killed. The pilot, Lieutenant Alexander Howard James Howlett, was slightly injured.*

"On Tuesday a newspaper representative obtained an eye-witnesses's account of the accident from an officer of the ferry-boat, who saw the whole occurrence from start to finish. At the time of the crash the ferry itself was making its passage from South to North Queensferry. The captain was just about to give the order to go to the rescue when it was seen that boats were making for the scene.

"For some time another aeroplane which was involved was engaged in executing some manoeuvres over the Atlantic Fleet, lying at anchor below the Forth Bridge. According to the observer on the ferry-boat, the machine went through a series of banks and dives and half-rolls, never rising far above the water and for most of the time within 200or 100 feet of the surface.

"There was a wind of about twenty miles an hour blowing from the west at the time. A few moments before the crash the aeroplane, two miles or more below the bridge, was flying westward between Argus and Repulse, but nearer to the Argus. The machine was flying low, and began to make a right-hand turn into the wind.

"As far as could be judged from the ferry-boat, what happened at this moment was that the machine made its turn, but losing flying speed as it came into wind, swooped down to the water. The aeroplane was still in its bank and the right wing struck first, with such force that a great splash was seen, and the machine began to sink slowly, tail up.

"In a moment drifters from Repulse, Tiger and the aircraft carrier Argus, and a packet boat from HMS Emperor of India, were speeding to the sinking aeroplane. It was calculated that they reached the scene three minutes from the time of the accident. They found Second Aircraftsman Wilson dead and Lieutenant Howlett suffering from facial injuries. Both were taken from the cockpit of the machine, and conveyed to the aircraft carrier, where it was found that Second Aircraftsman Wilson's skull had been fractured by the impact. Lieut. Howlett was conveyed to a nursing home in Dunfermline.

"Wilson, who was in his twenties, belonged to Redcar, Yorkshire, and arrived at Donibristle about a year ago.

"The splash made by the machine as it hit the water was seen by several observers at South Queensferry, and various witnesses on shore and on board warships near the scene had been struck by the low height which the pilot was executing by his banks and other evolutions.

"It was learned on inquiry at the nursing home in Dunfermline that Lieut. Howlett was not in a position to see anyone to make a statement. He is understood to be suffering severely from shock as well as other injuries."

The subsequent inquiry into the accident considered that although Flight Lieutenant Howlett had been authorised for flying over water his manoeuvres constituted dangerous flying. A wartime pilot, he had accumulated 1,688 flying hours of which 212 were at the controls of Horsley machines.

NOVEMBER

Thursday 7 November 1929
23 Squadron F/O R S Collins Safe
Gamecock I J7903

T/o Kenley to practice 'battle tactics' during which a midair collision occurred with the Gamecock reported below. Flying Officer Reginald Stradling Collins was appointed to a permanent commission, in the rank of pilot officer, on 10th September 1928, his seniority backdated for precisely one year [LG 18 September 1928, issue 33422, page 6097]. He was destined to lose his life in another midair collision, this time while attached to 401 Flight operating from HMS *Courageous*. Flying Fairey Flycatcher S1273 off Grand Harbour, Malta he struck Flycatcher N9679 flown by Lieutenant-Commander Hugh Ditton who also died; the fateful date being 25th of February 1932.

23 Squadron Sgt F L White Safe
Gamecock I J8409

T/o Kenley similarly tasked, the Gamecock being totally destroyed in the collision at 3,000 feet in the vicinity of Wallington, Surrey. A press cutting 'posted' on the Airport of Croydon website and reproduced by the Kenley Revival society reads: *"Two RAF aeroplanes collided over Wallington this afternoon. The pilots made safe descents by parachute, but one the wrecked 'planes crashed on the roof of a house at Ross Road, Wallington. The machines were bombing 'planes engaged in fighting practice. An eye-witness stated that the tips of the wings of the machines touched while manoeuvring. The two machines commenced a whirligig spin to earth. Suddenly two men leaped out. There were parachutes attached to them and they came down safely.*

One 'plane burst into flames in the air. Another eye-witness said he heard an aeroplane making an awful noise. It seemed to be misfiring badly, and looking up he saw the machine falling. He also saw two men gliding to earth with parachutes."

In addition to the press clipping, three photographs published in the paper are appended plus a photograph of J8409 taken the previous May at RAF Northolt where it was participating in the Sassoon Cup competition. The press photographs show damage to houses in Ross Road and Tharp Road. The photograph taken at Tharp Road carries the following description: *"After the aeroplane collision in mid-air: wreckage of one of the 'planes in Tharp Road, minus its 40 gallon petrol tank, which smashed through the roof of a house into a bed-room."* It also notes that one pilot landed a mile away and the other came down in Bandon Hill Cemetery. The 'Revival' website notes that the property in Ross Road was No. 68, the ensuing fire spreading to the neighbouring house. The other Gamecock fell into a shed belonging to Mr. Honeyfield's grocery shop on the corner of Tharp Road and Demense Road and it was the petrol tank from this machine that set fire to the house in Ross Road, the flames setting off some of the ammunition that was mixed in with the debris. Croydon Airport fire services were quickly on the scene and tackled the fires.

Francis Lawrence White was an ex-apprentice and who, subsequently, would be granted a permanent commission. Throughout the '30s he served tours at Martlesham Heath, Leuchars in Scotland and Hal Far on the Island of Malta before returning to the UK and posting to RAF Cranwell before 'flying a desk' 21 Group headquarters. Then on 25th February 1940 he proceeded to Hornchurch to take command of 74 Squadron [Spitfire]. On 23rd May 1940 he shared in the destruction of a Henschal Hs126 reconnaissance aircraft but his Spitfire I N3243 was damaged by return fire and he forced-landed on Calais-Marck airfield. His dramatic rescue by squadron colleagues is vividly related between pages 48 and 52 of Group Captain Alan C Deere's biography *Nine Lives* published by Hodder & Stoughton in 1959, and which I purchased that same year for the cover price of fifteen shillings. It still has a treasured place in my library.

Following his safe return in the squadron's Master, piloted by Flight Lieutenant Leathart, he continued to command '74' until posted to Fighter Command headquarters; his operational flying days were over. He retired in the rank of group captain on 9th September 1952 [LG 3 October 1952, supplement 39658, page 5192].

Friday 8 November 1929
56 Squadron *Not reported*
Siskin IIIA J8832
T/o North Weald and merely reported as *"crashed."* This particular Siskin was accepted by the squadron as recently as the 9th of August 1929.

Monday 11 November 1929
56 Squadron *Not reported*
Siskin IIIA J8835
T/o North Weald for night flying only to become uncertain of his position and attempting to forced-land crash-landed near the airfield.

Friday 15 November 1929
60 Squadron Sgt W C Henley Safe
DH.9A E878/Z
T/o Kohat and crashed whilst making a night landing at Risalpur. This particular DH had been on 60 Squadron's establishment since June 1924, and at various times carried the codes 8, 7, T and O. On two occasions it was repaired at Drigh Road following accidents of a minor nature.

Saturday 30 November 1929
11 Squadron Wapiti IIA 9402 While taxying at Kohat ran into a 60 Squadron DH.9A H89. It is believed the damage to the Wapiti was significant as there are no further entries regarding movements; however, the DH was repaired and was certainly extant during April 1930. The report from 11 Squadron was the first indicating one of their establishment had sustained very serious damage was the first since arriving in India earlier in the year.

DECEMBER

Tuesday 10 December 1929
29 Squadron *Not reported*
Siskin IIIA J8668
T/o North Weald for night flying practice, a detail that ended with the fighter down, and on its back, following a misjudged landing.

During the month a 14 Squadron Bristol F.2b J6633 broke its 'V' strut while landing at Ramleh. There are no further movement reports; therefore, it is possible in was deleted from charge.

During palisade trials aboard HMS *Eagle* 35 Squadron DH.9A J8143/4 crashed. Although no precise date is reported, the month of June is a possibility.

APPENDICES
1929

Appendix A - Squadron Losses Table and Losses by Aircraft Type

Column 1 - Squadron

Column 2 - Aircraft type

Column 3 - Written off

Column 4 - Fatalities

1 Squadron	Armstrong Whitworth Siskin IIIA	1	
2 Squadron	Bristol F.2b	1	
3 Squadron	Gloster Gamecock I	1	
	Armstrong Whitworth Siskin IIIDC	1	2
6 Squadron	Bristol F.2b	2	
7 Squadron	Vickers Virginia	1	
11 Squadron	Westland Wapiti IIA	1	
12 Squadron	Fairey Fox I	1	
13 Squadron	Armstrong Whitworth Atlas	1	
14 Squadron	Airco DH.9A	2	
17 Squadron	Armstrong Whitworth Siskin IIIA	2	1
19 Squadron	Armstrong Whitworth Siskin IIIA	2	2
23 Squadron	Gloster Gamecock I	6	2
25 Squadron	Armstrong Whitworth Siskin IIIA	1	1
29 Squadron	Armstrong Whitworth Siskin IIIA	2	1
36 Squadron	Hawker Horsley II	1	1
39 Squadron	Westland Wapiti IIA	1	
43 Squadron	Armstrong Whitworth Siskin IIIA	2	
45 Squadron	Airco DH.9A	1	
47 Squadron	Fairey IIIF	1	2
55 Squadron	Airco DH.9A	3	2
56 Squadron	Armstrong Whitworth Siskin IIIA	3	1
60 Squadron	Airco DH.9A	1	
70 Squadron	Vickers Victoria	2	
84 Squadron	Airco DH.9A	1	
207 Squadron	Fairey IIIF	1	2
208 Squadron	Bristol F.2b	2	
216 Squadron	Vickers Victoria	1	3
502 Squadron SR	Avro 504N	1	
	Fairey Fawn II	1	
601 Squadron AAF	DH.9A	4	
605 Squadron AAF	DH.9A	2	
Totals		53	20

	Airco DH.9A	14	2
	Armstrong Whitworth Atlas	1	
	Armstrong Whitworth Siskin IIIA	13	6
	Armstrong Whitworth Siskin IIIDC	1	2
	Avro 504N	1	
	Bristol F.2b	5	
	Fairey Fawn II	1	
	Fairey Fox I	1	
	Fairey IIIF	2	4
	Gloster Gamecock I	7	2
	Hawker Horsley II	1	1
	Vickers Victoria	3	3
	Vickers Virginia	1	
	Westland Wapiti IIA	2	
Totals		53	20

Appendix B - Squadron Locations and Commanding Officers

1 Squadron	Siskin IIIA	Tangmere	01.01.29-31.12.29	
2 Squadron	Bristol F.2b	Manston	01.01.29-31.12.29	
	Atlas			Atlas introduced during December
3 Squadron	Gamecock I	Upavon	01.01.29-31.12.29	Gamecock I phased out July
	Bulldog II			Bulldog II introduced during May
4 Squadron	Bristol F.2b	Farnborough	01.01.29-31.12.29	Bristol F.2b phased out October
	Atlas			Atlas introduced during October
5 Squadron	Bristol F.2b	Quuetta	01.01.29-31.12.29	
6 Squadron	Bristol F.2b	Hinaidi	01.01.29-28.10.29	
		Ismailia	28.10.29-31.12.29	Detachment at Ramleh
7 Squadron	Virgina *various*	Worthy Down	01.01.29-31.12.29	
8 Squadron	Fairey IIIF	Khormakser	01.01.29-31.12.29	
9 Squadron	Virginia IX	Manston	01.01.29-31.12.29	
10 Squadron	Hyderabad	Upper Heyford	01.01.29-31.12.29	
11 Squadron	Wapiti IIA	Risalpur	22.01.29-31.12.29	
12 Squadron	Fox I/IA	Andover	01.01.29-31.12.29	
13 Squadron	Atlas	Andover	01.01.29-23.09.29	
		Netheravon	23.09.29-31.12.29	
14 Squadron	DH.9A	Ramleh & Amman	01.01.29-31.12.29	DH.9A phased out in December
	Fairey IIIF			Fairey IIIF introduced during December
XV Squadron	*Various*	Martlesham Heath	01.01.29-31.12.29	
16 Squadron	Atlas	Old Sarum	01.01.29-31.12.29	
17 Squadron	Siskin IIIA	Upavon	01.01.29-31.12.29	Siskin IIIA phased out during October
	Bulldog II			Bulldog Ii introduced during October
19 Squadron	Siskin IIIA	Duxford	01.01.29-31.12.29	
20 Squadron	Bristol F.2b	Peshawar	01.01.29-31.12.29	
22 Squadron	*Various*	Martlesham Heath	01.01.29-31.12.29	
23 Squadron	Gamecock I	Kenley	01.01.29-31.12.29	
24 Squadron	*Various*	Northolt	01.01.29-31.12.29	
25 Squadron	Grebe Ii	Hawkinge	01.01.29-31.12.29	Grebe II phased out in June
	Siskin IIIA			Siskin IIA introduced in May
26 Squadron	Atlas	Catterick	01.01.29-31.12.29	
27 Squadron	DH.9A	Kohat	01.01.29-31.12.29	
28 Squadron	Bristol F.2b	Ambala	01.01.29-31.12.29	
29 Squadron	Siskin IIIA	North Weald	01.01.29-31.12.29	
30 Squadron	DH.9A	Hinaidi	01.01.29-25.10.29	DH.9A phased out in September
	Wapiti IIA	Mosul	25.10.29-31.12.29	
31 Squadron	Bristol F.2b	Quetta	01.01.29-31.12.29	
32 Squadron	Siskin IIIA	Kenley	01.01.29-31.12.29	
33 Squadron	Horsley II	Netheravon	01.03.29-14.09.29	Reformed for day bombing duties
		Eastchurch	14.09.29-31.12.29	
35 Squadron	DH.9A/Fairey IIIF	Bircham Newton	01.03.29-31.12.29	Reformed for day bombing duties
36 Squadron	Horsley I	Donibristle	01.01.29-31.12.29	
39 Squadron	Wapiti IIA	Risalpur	22.01.29-31.12.29	Arrived from the UK
41 Squadron	Siskin IIIA	Northolt	01.01.29-31.12.29	
43 Squadron	Siskin IIIA	Tangmere	01.01.29-31.12.29	
45 Squadron	DH.9A	Helwan	01.01.29-31.12.29	DH.9A Phased out during September
	Fairey IIIF			Fairey IIIF introduced in September
47 Squadron	Fairey IIIF	Khartoum	01.01.29-31.12.29	
55 Squadron	DH.9A	Hinaidi	01.01.29-31.12.29	
56 Squadron	Siskin IIIA	North Weald	01.01.29-31.12.29	
58 Squadron	Virginia *various*	Worthy Down	01.01.29-31.12.29	
60 Squadron	DH.9A	Kohat	01.01.29-31.12.29	
70 Squadron	Victoria I/III	Hinaidi	01.01.29-31.12.29	
84 Squadron	Wapiti IIA	Shaibah	01.01.29-31.12.29	
99 Squadron	Hyderabad	Upper Heyford	01.01.29-31.12.29	
100 Squadron	Horsley II/III	Bicester	01.01.29-31.12.29	
101 Squadron	DH.9A	Bircham Newton	01.01.29-10.10.29	DH.9A phased out in June 1929
	Sidestrand III	Andover	10.10.29-31.12.29	Sidestrand III introduced in March 1929
111 Squadron	Siskin IIIA	Hornchurch	01.01.29-31.12.29	
201 Squadron	Southampton II	Calshot	01.01.29-31.12.29	Reformed from No. 408 Flight
202 Squadron	Fairey IIID	Kalafrana	01.01.29-31.12.29	Reformed from No. 481 Flight
203 Squadron	Southampton II	Mount Batten	01.0129-31.12.29	Reformed from No. 482 Flight
	Fairey IIIF	Basra	14.03.29-31.12.29	Fairey IIIF added during March
204 Squadron	Southampton II	Mount Batten	01.02.29-31.12.29	Reformed for seaplane duties
205 Squadron	Southampton iI/III	Seletar	08.01.29-31.12.29	Reformed from Far East Flight
207 Squadron	Fairey IIIF	Eastchurch	01.01.29-07.11.29	
		Bircham Newton	07.11.29-31.12.29	
208 Squadron	Bristol F.2b	Heliopolis	01.01.29-31.12.29	
216 Squadron	Victoria II/V	Heliopolis	01.01.29-31.12.29	
501 Squadron SR	Avro 504N	Filton	14.06.29-31.12.29	Formed
502 Squadron SR	Hyderabad	Aldergrove	01.01.29-31.12.29	
503 Squadron SR	Fawn II	Waddington	01.01.29-31.12.29	Fawn II phased out during February
	Hyderabad			Hyderabad Introduced in February
504 Squadron SR	Horsley	Hucknall	01.01.29-31.12.29	
600 Squadron AAF	DH.9A	Hendon	01.01.29-31.12.29	DH.9A phased out during August

	Wapiti IIA			Wapiti IIA introduced during August
601 Squadron AAF	DH.9A/Wapiti IIA	Hendon	01.01.29-31.12.29	Wapiti IIA deliveries during November
602 Squadron AAF	Fawn II	Renfrew	01.01.20-31.12.29	Fawn II phased out in September
	Wapiti IIA			Wapiti IIA introduced during July
603 Squadron AAF	DH.9A	Turnhouse	01.01.29-31.12.29	
605 Squadron AAF	DH.9A	Castle Bromwich	01.01.29-31.12.29	

1 Squadron	Squadron Leader E O Grenfell MC DFC AFC	In situ	See 1 Squadron 1923
2 Squadron	Squadron Leader H M Probyn DSO mid	In situ	See 208 Squadron 1924
3 Squadron	Squadron Leader E D Johnson AFC	In situ	See Appendix B 1927
4 Squadron	Squadron Leader N H Bottomley AFC	In situ	See Appendix B 1928
5 Squadron	Squadron Leader O C Bryson MC DFC AM	In situ	See Appendix B 1928
6 Squadron	Squadron Leader C H Keith	In situ	See Appendix B 1928
7 Squadron	Wing Commander E R Manning DSO MC Australia	In situ	See Appendix B 1928
	Squadron Leader C E H C MacPherson	2 November 1929	W/Cdr died 18 July 1944
8 Squadron	Squadron Leader G H Bowman DSO MC DFC	In situ	See 8 Squadron 1922
	Squadron Leader The Hon. R A Cochrane AFC twice mid	1 February 1929	ACM retirement 29 November 1952
	Squadron Leader J L Vachell MC	14 November 1929	A/Cmdr retirement 21 May 1943
9 Squadron	Wing Commander W V Strugnall MC*	In situ	See Appendix B 1928
10 Squadron	Wing Commander F L Robinson DSO MC DFC	In situ	See Appendix B 1928
	Squadron Leader A S G Lee MC	5 February 1929	AV-M retirement 21 January 1946
	Wing Commander A T Whitelock	4 April 1929	W/Cdr retired list 25 March 1938
11 Squadron	Squadron Leader P H Cummings	In situ	See Appendix B 1928
12 Squadron	Squadron Leader T E Salt AFC	In situ	See Appendix B 1926
	Squadron Leader F H M Maynard AFC	1 September 1929	AV-M retirement 12 November 1945
13 Squadron	Squadron Leader H H MacL Fraser	In situ	See Appendix B 1927
	Squadron Leader J B Cole-Hamilton twice mid	18 November 1929	See 20 Squadron 1925
14 Squadron	Squadron Leader E G Hopcraft DSC	In situ	See Appendix B 1927
	Squadron Leader F O Soden DFC	3 December 1929	See 111 Squadron 1929
XV Squadron	Squadron Leader C E H James MC	In situ	See Appendix B 1927
	Wing Commander J K Wells AFC	2 September 1929	G/Capt retired list 11 June 1945
16 Squadron	Squadron Leader D O Mulholland AFC	In situ	See Appendix B 1928
17 Squadron	Squadron Leader A R Arnold DSC DFC	In situ	See Appendix B 1928
19 Squadron	Flight Lieutenant G A F Bucknall	In situ	See Appendix B 1928
	Squadron Leader E C Emmett MC DFC South Africa	11 February 1929	See Appendix B 1928
	Flight Lieutenant E R Openshaw	12 June 1929	G/Capt retirement 12 March 1946
	Squadron Leader L H Slatter OBE DSC DFC	31 July 1929	See 203 Squadron 1921
	Flight Lieutenant E R Openshaw	23 October 1929	See 19 Squadron 1929
	Squadron Leader C R Keary	9 December 1929	G/Capt retirement 12 December 1924
20 Squadron	Squadron Leader C H Nicholas DFC AFC mid	In situ	See Appendix B 1928
22 Squadron	Squadron Leader J Noakes AFC MM	In situ	See Appendix B 1927
	Squadron Leader E S Goodwin AFC twice mid	8 January 1929	AV-M retirement 9 March 1948
23 Squadron	Squadron Leader A G Jones-Williams MC* *Croix de Guerre avec Palme*	In situ	See Appendix B 1928
24 Squadron	Squadron Leader S N Cole	In situ	See Appendix B 1927
	Squadron Leader F H Coleman DSO	14 February 1929	See 30 Squadron 1925
	Squadron Leader D S Don MVO	4 April 1929	S/Ldr retired list 23 September 1931
25 Squadron	Flight Lieutenant W E Swann	In situ	See Appendix B 1928
	Squadron Leader L G S Payne MC AFC	1 January 1929	A/Cmdr retirement 22 June 1938
26 Squadron	Squadron Leader R L Stevenson	In situ	See Appendix B 1927
27 Squadron	Squadron Leader L M Bailey AFC	In situ	See Appendix B 1924
28 Squadron	Squadron Leader A F Brooks	In situ	See 43 Squadron 1925
29 Squadron	Squadron Leader M L Taylor AFC	In situ	See Appendix B 1924
	Flight Lieutenant J V Kelly	26 February 1929	F/Lt retired list 4 May 1932
	Flight Lieutenant E Brewerton	5 March 1929	S/Ldr retired list 14 May 1946
	Squadron Leader M L Taylor AFC	3 May 1929	See Appendix B 1924
	Squadron Leader P G Scott	6 December 1929	W/Cdr retired list 2 April 1945
30 Squadron	Squadron Leader H P Lale DFC mid	In situ	See 32 Squadron 1924
31 Squadron	Squadron Leader J F Gordon DFC	In situ	See Appendix B 1926
32 Squadron	Squadron Leader R B Mansell OBE	In situ	See Appendix B 1926
	Squadron Leader B E Baker DSO MC AFC mid *Croix de Guerre* [France]	30 November 1929	AM retirement 10 May 1950
33 Squadron	Squadron Leader F P Don	10 April 1929	AV-M retirement 2 February 1943
	Squadron Leader J J Breen three times mid	2 November 1929	See 84 Squadron 1928
35 Squadron	Flight Lieutenant L M Elworthy	1 March 1929	S/Ldr killed 8 June 1932
	Squadron Leader G S M Insall VC MC	11 March 1929	G/Capt retirement 30 July 1945
	Squadron Leader B E Harrison AFC	10 July 1929	S/Ldr retired list 27 May 1937
36 Squadron	Squadron Leader A W Mylne	In situ	See 28 Squadron 1926
39 Squadron	Squadron Leader H V Champion de Crepigny MC DFC	In situ	See 60 Squadron 1922
41 Squadron	Squadron Leader R S Aitken MC AFC	In situ	See Appendix B 1928
43 Squadron	Squadron Leader C N Lowe MC DFC	In situ	See 602 Squadron AAF 1925
45 Squadron	Squadron Leader F J Vincent DFC	In situ	See Appendix B 1928
47 Squadron	Squadron Leader C R Cox AFC	In situ	See Appendix B 1927
	Flight Lieutenant O R Gayford DFC* mid	19 January 1929	A/Cmdr retirement August 1944
	Squadron Leader C R Cox AFC	1 April 1929	See Appendix B 1927
55 Squadron	Squadron Leader A H Peck DSO MC*	In situ	See 25 Squadron 1923
	Squadron Leader J W B Grigson DSO DFC** mid	21 March 1929	A/Cmdr died 3 July 1943
	Squadron Leader C H Elliott-Smith AFC	13 November 1929	See 56 Squadron 1926

56 Squadron	Squadron Leader A Lees	In situ	See Appendix B 1928
58 Squadron	Squadron Leader E W Norton DSC	In situ	See 70 Squadron 1925
60 Squadron	Squadron Leader R H G Neville MC	In situ	See Appendix B 1927
70 Squadron	Wing Commander J A G De Courcey	In situ	See Appendix B 1928
	Wing Commander R S Maxwell MC DFC* AFC	February 1929	See 32/24 Squadrons 1923
84 Squadron	Squadron Leader J J Breen three times mid	In situ	See Appendix B 1928
	Squadron Leader H Stewart	7 November 1929	S/Ldr killed 5 January 1931
99 Squadron	Squadron Leader B E Smythies DFC	In situ	See 41 Squadron 1923
	Squadron Leader W B Hargreaves OBE	26 July 1929	G/Capt retirement 17 April 1946
	Squadron Leader G H Cock	19 November 1929	G/Capt retired list 1 February 1943
100 Squadron	Squadron Leader L T N Gould MC DFC	In situ	See Appendix B 1925
	Squadron Leader W B Farrington	16 January 1929	See 84 Squadron 1925
101 Squadron	Squadron Leader J C P Wood	In situ	See Appendix B 1928
	Squadron Leader R S Lucy AFC	17 July 1929	S/Ldr retired list 1 April 1935
111 Squadron	Squadron Leader K R Park MC* DFC New Zealand	In situ	See Appendix B 1927
	Squadron Leader F O Soden DFC	8 March 1929	G/Capt retirement 21 May 1945
	Squadron Leader L H Slatter OBE DSC DFC	25 October 1929	See 203 Squadron 1921
201 Squadron	Squadron Leader D G Donald DFC AFC	1 January 1929	See 3 Squadron 1921
	Flight Lieutenant A C Stevens	3 November 1929	A/Cmdr retirement 14 December 1953
202 Squadron	Squadron Leader C Boumphrey DFC mid	1 January 1929	S/Ldr retired list 8 July 1939
203 Squadron	Group Captain H R Busteed OBE AFC *Croix de Guerre* [France] Australia	1 January 1929	See 10 Squadron 1928
	Flight Lieutenant A P Revington	6 February 1929	A/Cmdr retirement 4 January 1954
	Wing Commander T E B Howe AFC	14 March 1929	See 32 Squadron 1923
204 Squadron	Squadron Leader F H Laurence MC	1 February 1929	G/Capt retirement 31 December 1945
205 Squadron	Group Captain H M Cave-Brown-Cave DSO DFC	8 January 1929	AV-M retirement 18 September 1940
	Squadron Leader G E Livock DFC AFC	10 January 1929	G/Capt retirement 24 June 1945
	Group Captain H M Cave-Brown-Cave DSO DFC	29 September 1929	See 205 Squadron 1929
207 Squadron	Squadron Leader E A Beaulah	In situ	See Appendix B 1928
208 Squadron	Squadron Leader V E Lindop	In situ	See Appendix B 1927
216 Squadron	Wing Commander L D D McKeen	In situ	See Appendix B 1924
	Wing Commander E A B Rice MC	9 November 1929	See 6 Squadron 1921
501 Squadron SR	Flight Lieutenant L P Winters	14 June 1929	
	Squadron Leader R S Sugden AFC	26 August 1929	
502 Squadron SR	Wing Commander A C Wright AFC	In situ	See Appendix B 1926
	Squadron Leader C L King MC DFC mid Canada	10 September 1929	G/Capt retirement 17 February 1944
	Wing Commander F P Don	2 November 1929	See 33 Squadron 1929
503 Squadron SR	Wing Commander The Hon. L J E Twistleton-Wykham-Fiennes	In situ	See 29 Squadron 1923
504 Squadron SR	Squadron Leader C H Elliott-Smith	In situ	See 56 Squadron 1926
600 Squadron AAF	Squadron Leader The Hon. F E Guest PC CBE DSO MP	In situ	See Appendix B 1926
601 Squadron AAF	Squadron Leader Lord E Grosvenor	In situ	See Appendix B 1925
	Squadron Leader The Rt. Hon. Sir P Sassoon MP	23 September 1929	S/Ldr Resigned 3 September 1931
602 Squadron AAF	Squadron Leader J Fullerton	In situ	See Appendix B 1927
603 Squadron AAF	Squadron Leader J A McKelvie AFC	In situ	See Appendix B 1925
605 Squadron AAF	Squadron Leader J A C Wright AFC TD	In situ	See Appendix B 1925

Annex

Squadron Leader Ralph Alexander Cochrane had, by comparison, with his contemporaries, fairly minimal minimal flying experience in aeroplanes for throughout the *Great War* and beyond he was principally engaged with airship operations and it was not a meeting with Sir Hugh Trenchard in 1921, that he underwent flying instruction. It is reputed that Trenchard told Cochrane he was wasting his time with airships and that he should go off an learn to fly an aeroplane. Thus it was that prior to taking command of 8 Squadron, his squadron experience appears to have been limited to just over a year flying Vickers Vernon's with 45 Squadron.

From this point on his duties were mainly Staff orientated, including over two years in New Zealand assisting the government in establishing an independent Royal New Zealand Air Force of which for his final year he was the Air Force's Chief of Staff.

In the Second World War he came to the fore when he was appointed Air Officer Commanding No. 5 Group on 28th February 1943, and was immediately intrinsically linked with the formation of No. 617 Squadron [commanded by the much decorated Wing Commander Guy Penrose Gibson] and bringing to fruition the raid on the Ruhr dams in May 1943.

The remaining years of the "'Bombing Campaign" in which No. 5 Group developed its own method of target marking often caused their Air Officer Commanding to be at odds with his counterpart in No. 8 [Pathfinder} Group, Air Vice-Marshal Donald Clifford Tyndll Bennett, at the time of his appointment the youngest air vice-marshal in the service.

Postwar, Air Marshal Cochrane took the reigns at Transport Command, followed by Flying Training Command, serving both His Majesty The King and on his death, The Queen, as their *Aide de Camp* until his final duty as Vice Chief of the Air Staff

Squadron Leader John Lyne Vachell, successor to Squadron Leader Cochrane at 8 Squadron, was *Gazette* with the MC on 25th April 1918, supplement 30651, page 5017; *"For conspicuous gallantry and devotion to duty. He did excellent work on many occasions, continually locating and engaging successfully enemy heavy batteries."*

At least two Record of Service cards must have been raised in respect of this officer, who was born on 12th June 1892, but, it seems, the all important one which would have recorded the squadron in which he gained his MC has not survived.

			Ew-embarked 2.10.18	*1 ASD*
05.10.18	*1 AD*	*Attached to No. 1 ASD*	*05.10.18*	*B.213*
12.101.18	*1 AD*	*Posted to No. 12 Squadron*	*11.10.18*	*- " -*
02.11.18		*Admitted [Influenza]*	*31.1018*	*A36*
11.11.18	*1 ASD*	*Discharged to duty [1 ASD 12.11.18]*	*11.11.18*	*W.3034*
21.12.18	*1 ASSD*	*Posted to No. 15 Squadron*	*14.12.18*	*B.213*
04.01.19	*53 Sqd*	*Posted to No. 53 Squadron*	*29.12.18*	*- " -*
08.02.18	*53 Sqd*	*Leave 1/2/19 to 15/2/19*		*- " -*

28.03.19	*To Home Establishment*	*16.03.19*	*NR 29 53 Sq*

An excellent biography of Squadron Leader Arthur Stanley Gould Lee can be accessed on the Air of Authority website, constantly referred to by the authors, while for an insight into his time with 46 Squadron, then next to the squadron's operations diary, none can be better than the numerous entries concerning his eye-witness accounts of tank action at the *Battle of Cambrai* in November 1917, these being superbly interlinked in the narrative of the battle by historian and author, Bryn Hammond in his epic *Cambrai 1917 - The Myth of the First Great Tank Battle.*

Turning to The Aerodrome website, this shows Temporary Captain Lee was credited with seven aerial successes between 4th September and 30th November 1917, the citation for his MC [LG 5 July 1918, supplement 30780, page 7913] reading: *"For conspicuous gallantry and devotion to duty. He bombed an enemy battery and fired on the gunners with his machine gun, and then attacked and drove off three enemy machines.While flying in very low clouds he lost his way, and could not steady his compass, and after flying for some distance, in what he believed to be the direction of our lines, he landed in open country, and was at once attacked and fired on by enemy cavalry. He had kept his engine running and succeeded in getting off, and, having fired on the enemy, found his position and returned to our lines. On another occasion he made a flight in very thick mist, and drove down an enemy machine, bombed an enemy position, and assisted the infantry to repel an enemy attack. He showed splendid courage and initiative."*

Omitted from the citation is the fact that during the Cambrai offensive, he was shot down three times.

Retiring on the 22nd of June 1938, as an acting air Commodore, Lionel Guy Stanhope Payne returned for service during the Second World War and held two appointments - Personal Staff Officer to the Air Member for Development and Production and from March 1941, Director of Intelligence [Operations] - reverting to the retired list on 10th December 1945.

Formerly of the Suffolk Regiment, he won his MC as a flight commander with 101 Squadron [LG 18 July 1918, supplement 30801, page 8469} *"For conspicuous gallantry and devotion to duty. On four occasions he bombed important enemy railway stations, obtaining direct hits on each occasion. He also carried out a long distance raid on an enemy aerodrome, which he bombed from 1,100 feet, making the return journey at 800* [feet] *with his machine damaged. He has also taken part in many night bombing raids, always at a low altitude, and has set a fine example of determination to all ranks of his squadron."*

Issue 13134, page 1796, provided the readers of *The Edinburgh Gazette* August 27th, 1917, with the citation for Temporary Captain Brian Edmund Baker's MC: *"For conspicuous gallantry and devotion to duty. He led his patrol with great skill against a hostile formation, which he attacked, accounting for five enemy machines out of six. Later, he drove down a hostile machine in flames, and attacked and destroyed another one by diving 7,000 feet on to it and firing at such close range as to nearly collide with it. His gallantry has been at all times of great value to his squadron."*

It was *The London Gazette* of 4th March 1918, supplement 30555, page 2727, that promulgated his DSO, but without a citation attached. However, the Air of Authority obliges: *"For conspicuous gallantry and devotion to duty. Whilst on patrol he engaged nine Albatross scouts, five of these being driven down, two of which he accounted for. On another occasion, whilst leading his flight on an offensive patrol, he dived alone on a formation of six enemy scouts, driving one down out of control. During the course of his patrol work he has brought down ten enemy machines, and his work on all occasions has been magnificent. He is a dashing patrol leader, and inspires all with greatest keenness."*

The tragic circumstances of Flight Lieutenant Leonard Maurice Elworthy's death in a parachuting accident on 8th June 1932, will be reported in Volume 5. Meanwhile, appended here is a copy of Army Form B.103c covering his service from 9th July to 15th September 1917:

15.07.16	*Attached to No. 18 Sqdn*	*09.07.16*	*B.213 18 Sqdn*
12.08.16	*Posted to No. 2 Sqdn*	*05.08.16*	- " - -"-
21.10.16	*Qualified Observer*	*14.10.16*	- " - *2 Sqdn*
25.11.16	*Leave 20.11.16 to 30.11.16*		- " 1. - " -
10.03.17	*Leave 3.3.17 to 17.3.17*		- " - - " -
17.03.17	*To be Flying Officer [Obs] with sen. from 9.7.16 & to be seconded*	*15.11.16*	*L G*
21.04.18 [sic]	*To Home Est*	*15.09.17*	*B.213 2 Sqdn*
29.09.17	*To be Flying Officer with sen. from 9.7.16*	*05.09.17*	*L G*

Gazetted in the Edinburgh paper, December 28th, 1915, issue 12887, page 1945, was one of those rare occasions where the recipient of the Victoria Cross was unable to be present at the time of the KING's pleasure as he was a prisoner of war, thus was the case for Second Lieutenant Gilbert Stuart Martin Insall, No. 11 Squadron, Royal Flying Corps: *"For most conspicuous bravery, skill and determination, on 7th November 1915, in France.*

"He was patrolling in a Vickers Fighting Machine, with First Class Air Mechanic T H Donald as Gunner, when a German machine was sighted, pursued, and attacked near Achiet.

"The German pilot led the Vickers machine over a rocket battery, but with great skill Lieutenant Insall dived and got to close range, when Donald fired a drum of cartridges into the German machine, stopping its engine. The German pilot then dived through a cloud, followed by Lieutenant Insall. Fire was again opened, and the German machine was brought down heavily in a ploughed field 4 miles south-east of Arras.

"On seeing the Germans scramble out of their machine and prepare to fire, Lieutenant Insall dived to 500 feet, thus enabling Donald to open heavy fire on them. The Germans then fled, one helping the other, who was apparently wounded. Other Germans then commenced heavy fire, but in spite of this, Lieutenant Insall turned again, and an incendiary bomb was dropped on the German machine, which was last seen wreathed in smoke.

"Lieutenant Insall then headed west in order to get back over the German trenches, but as he was only at 2,000 feet altitude he dived across them for greater speed, Donald firing into the trenches as he passed over. The German fire, however, damaged the petrol tank, and, with great coolness, Lieutenant Insall landed under cover of a wood 500 yards inside out lines.

"The Germans fired some 150 shells at our machine on the ground, but without causing material damage. Much damage had, however, been caused by rifle fire, but during the night it was repaired behind screened lights, and at dawn Lieutenant Insall flew his machine home with First Class Air Mechanic T H Donald as passenger."

A month later and Gilbert Insall and his resourceful air mechanic Donald wer a prisoners of war, and wounded to boot, when their Vickers FB.5 5074 was shot forced down near Bapaume following combat with a Fokker whose fire shot through the FB.5s petrol tank and damaged its flying controls. In *The Sky Their Battlefield,* page 26, Trevor Henshaw summaries the action, mentioning that enemy anti-aircraft fire joined the fight.

In captivity Lieutenant Insall made two unsuccessful attempts at escape, succeeding on the third, this being mentioned on page 214 of John Lewis-Stempel's excellent *The War Behind The Wire* where the author writes; *"Three made it to Holland, crossing over at Sustrum on 6 September* [1917]. *They were Michael Harrison, Second Lieutenant G S M Insall VC [his third attempt] - and Claude Francis Lethbridge Templer, thirteenth time lucky."*

And it was the Edinburgh edition of the *Gazette* December 19th, 1919, 13541, page 4107, that published the award of his MC: *"His Majesty The KING has been pleased to approve of the undermentioned rewards being conferred on Officers and other ranks of the Royal Air Force in recognition of gallantry in escaping from captivity whilst Prisoners of War."*

Born on 14th May 1894, in the French capital, Group Captain Gilbert Stuart Martin Insall VC MC mid died at Scrooby in Nottinghamshire at the age of 77 on 17th February 1972. Headstones to his memory may be seen at Rose Hill Crematorium, Doncaster and at Nocton Churchyard, Lincolnshire.

In conclusion, Air Mechanic First Class T H Donald was awarded the Distinguished Conduct Medal for his part in the action on 7th November 1915.

Awarded a DFC and First Bar, Squadron Leader Oswald Robert Gayford is, perhaps, best remembered for his part in the establishing a new world long-distance record between 6th to 8th February 1933, when the Fairey Long Range Monoplane flew from Cranwell to Walvis Bay in South Africa, a distance of 5,340 miles.. Formerly of the RNAS, his DFC was *Gazetted* on 21st September 1918, supplement 30913, page 11256, jointly with Captain

John William Boldero Grigson: *"These two officers have flown together for a period of twelve months, during which time they participated in a number of bombing raids, carried out a large number of valuable reconnaissance patrols and escort flights in all weathers, by day and night, during the performance of which duties they have brought down hostile aircraft on several occasions. No task is too difficult for these officers."*

The First Bar was headed: *'His Majesty the KING has been graciously pleased to approve of the undermentioned rewards to Officers and other ranks of the Royal Air Force in recognition of distinguished services rendered during the War and since the close of hostilities."* For Flying Officer Gayford, this was for his services in South Russia.

By coincidence, two months after Squadron Leader Gayford took 'the chair' at 47 Squadron, his wartime colleague, Captain John William Boldero Grigson reported to Hinaidi to take command of 55 Squadron. Thus, the citation for his DFC is the same as that for Squadron Leader Gayford, and is also mirrored in the First Bar and the DSO for his services in South Russia. The citation for a Second Bar to his DFC reads: *"For gallant conduct and devotion to duty. This officer has always set a fine example to his flight y his courage and devotion to duty and by constant keenness and hard work."* [EG November 1, 1921, issue 13756, page 1847].

By the summer of 1943, he was performing the duties of Senior Air Staff Officer to the Rhodesian Air Training Group , part of the British Commonweakth Air Transport Plan, and it was while keeping up to date with training procedures with No. 20 Service Flying Training School that he was killed when Harvard IIa EX163 on 3rd January 1943. Although omitted from Air-Britain's EA100-EZ999 aircraft serial register, Air Commodore Grigson's entry on *Wikipedia* [which the authors acknowledge] indicate his Harvard came down at Antelope Mine near Bulawayo. He is buried in Harare [Pioneer] Cemetery, with further remembrance on the Wherwell War Memorial in Hampshire and at his old school, St. John's, Leatherhead.

A biography of Squadron Leader Frank Ormond Soden may be read on *Wikipedia* which shows he was born on 3rd November 1895 in Canada at Petitcodiac in the province of New Brunswick but in childhood came with his parents to England. Somewhere along the way in his life he acquired the nickname 'Mongoose,' whether, as I suspect, in the services or as a schoolboy, I cannot be certain.Initially commissioned to the South Staffordshire Regiment he was officially transferred to the RFC on 27th April 1917, and as qualified pilot he went to the Western Front where he was attached to 60 Squadron where he quickly established himself as a first class fighter pilot, scoring two combat successes in Nieuport 17s on 25th June and 3rd July 1917, before converting to SE.5a scouts and notching up fourteen more victories, the last being on 5th February 1918.

Turning to his Record of Service - two Army Form B.103s have survived and are held by RAFM Hendon - these chart his operational service thus:

			Embarked 02.06.17	*W.O. List 2/6/17*
			Dis-embarked 02.06.17	*L R*
09.06.17		*Attached to No. 1 AD*	*03.06.17*	*B.213 1 AD*
09.06.17		*Posted to No. 60 Sqdn*	*07.06.17*	*- " - 60 Sqdn*
31.07.17		*Appointed Flying Officer & Trans to Gen List [Substituted for notification in L R 17.05.17]*	*27.07.17*	*l R*
18.08.17		*Leave 19.08.17 to 2.09.17*		*B.213 60 Sqdn*
10.11.17		*To Aerial Range on temporary duty*	*09.11.17*	*B.213 60 Sqdn*
17.11.17		*Leave 17.11.17 to 1.12.17*		*B.213 60 Sqdn*
o8.12.17		*To be Flt Commander & Temp Captain*	*03.12.17*	*- " - - " 1*

His return to Home Establishment date has not survived the passage of time, the second Army Form B.103 showing his return to France:

			Dis-embarked 13.07.18	*L R 41 Sqdn*
20.07.18		*Posted to No 41 Sqdn*	*13.07.18*	*B.213 41 Sqdn*
16.08.18	*HQ RAF*	*Injured accidentally*	*30.07.18*	*AF W.3428*
03.08.18		*Admitted [lae wd head]*	*30.07.18*	*A36 49 CCS*
03.08.18		*Discharged to duty*	*03.08.18*	*- " - - " -*
21.09.18		*Leave 19.08.18 to 03.10.18*		*B.213 41 Sqdn*
12.01.19		*Leave 7-21.01.19*		*- " - - " -*
01.03.19	*2 ASD*	*Attached to 1 AR*	*21.02.19*	*- " - - " -*
15.03.19	*- " -*	*Posted to 18 Sq*	*11.03.19*	*- " - - " -*
21.03.19	*18 Sq*	*Posted 29*	*12.03.19 [?]*	*- " - - " -*

Attached to 41 Squadron and flying SE.5a he added eleven more combat successes to bring his total to twenty-seven. The citation for his DFC [LH 8th February 1919, issue 31170, page 2047] is one of the shortest on record: *"A bold and skilful officer who has accounted for three enemy aeroplanes and two balloons during recent operations."* In retirement he emigrated to Kenya where in 1953, he fought off an attempt by a band of Mau Mau bandits which attempted to take his house at Timau; Group Captain Frank Ormond Soden DFC died in Westminster at the relatively early age of 65 on 12th February 1961.

The awards of the DFC and a mentioned in despatches awarded to Squadron Leader Colin Boumphrey were in recognition of his postwar services in the Baltic. A mention in despatches was promulgated in supplement 31703, page 15841 of *The London Gazette* published on 22nd December 1919, followed on 12th July 1920, reporting his DFC - supplement 31974, page 7422. Numerous officers and other ranks were listed in both editions, less citations. At the time he was ranked flight lieutenant.

Squadron Leader Frederic Hope Laurence was *Gazetted* with the MC, less citation, on 26th November 1917, supplement 30399, page 12319.

Similarly, Wing Commander Henry Meyrick Cave-Brown-Cave's DSO was promulgated without a citation [LG 26 April 1918, supplement 30654, page 5059].

Squadron Leader Gerald Edward Livock received a DFC for his work on sea patrols: *"Has rendered valuable services on numerous occasions on reconnaissance patrols in enemy waters, in attacks on hostile seaplanes, and in connection with anti-submarine patrol work."*

"For conspicuous gallantry and devotion to duty when working with artillery in carrying out thirteen successful shoots, by which numerous enemy gun pits were destroyed and fires and explosions caused. He also carried out two very good long reconnaissances, taking excellent photographs and obtaining valuable information." So read the citation for temporary lieutenant Charles Ley King's MC as published by *The London Gazette* on 16th September 1918, supplement 30901, page 10975. Less than two months later the Edinburgh edition on November 4th, 1918, issue 13346, page 4058, reported his DFC: *"This officer has done excellent work both on reconnaissance duty and in co-operation with our artillery. In the latter service he shows remarkable skill and keen observation. In carrying out a shoot on the 31st of August 848 rounds were fired in five and a half hours, and four pits were destroyed - a fine performance, reflecting great credit on this officer's capability."*

Prior to taking command of 502 Squadron, Special Reserve, he served with distinction in Iraq: *"The names of the undermentioned have been brought to notice by Air Vice-Marshal Sir Edward L Ellington KCB CMG CBE Air Officer Commanding, British Force in Iraq, for distinguished services rendered in connection with operations against the Akhwan in the Southern Desert, Iraq, during the period, November 1927 - May 1928."*

A gap in his service records makes identification of his squadron in Iraq difficult to establish, though it may have been 70 Squadron as he was posted to Hinaidi in mid-December 1925. His MC and DFC were gained whilst attached to 34 Squadron.

Appendix C - Officers Granted Short Service Commissions

LG 1 January 1929, issue 33453, page 72 - Seniority 28th December 1928 [21 entrants]

Block 27192 to 27212

27192	ABBOTT	Frederick Ernest	F/O	+	01.10.31	208 Squadron
27193	BEVAN	Francis Richard	P/O		13.09.29	Terminated
27194	BROWN	Justin Arrowsmith	F/O	+	20.03.33	5 Squadron

Claims against the estate of Flying Officer Justin Arrowsmith Brown was notified in *The London Gazette* 21st July 1933, supplement 33962, page 4915 as inserted by Devonshire, Wrenford, Brown of 38 Old Jewry, London EC.2.

27195	CROW	Cedric Rex	F/O	+	26.10.35	Railway Air Services

Flying Officer Cedric Rex Crow had been transferred to the Reserve Class A on 28th December 1933 [LG 2 January 1934, issue 34011, page 57]. Employed for flying duties with Railway Air Services, he was killed, along with Mr. Ronald Swales, when their DH.84 Dragon 2 G-ADEE crashed after encountering fog, impacting on Fairsnape Fell, Forest of Bowland, near Garstang in Lancashire. Quoting from the Aviation Safety Network, ASN Wikibase Occurrence Report 24961, which is gratefully acknowledged, the events leading up to the crash were as follows:

"On Saturday October 26th, 1935, G-ADEE was flying a regular route from Manchester to the Isle of Man and took off from Manchester [Barton] at 11:00 for the first leg of the journey to Liverpool [Speke]. The aircraft was flown by Capt. Cedric Rex Crow, aged 25, who had graduated as a pilot whilst in the RAF in 1929 and had been granted a Class 'A' civil pilot's licence on leaving the service in 1933. Overall he had over 1,300 hours solo flying experience, 640 of which were with the RAF and including 114 on the Dragon.

"He had transferred to the Manchester/Isle of Man route at the beginning of October 1935, and had completed the journey in both directions a dozen or more times, but not in bad weather conditions, when it was normal for pilots to follow the coastline rather than an inland route. Weather conditions that day were described as bad, but not so much as to disrupt normal schedules, yet only 15 minutes after leaving Barton, Capt. Crow returned to the airfield and landed. He requested the latest weather report from Speke, even though he had already been briefed on the conditions before take off and the report was obtained for him. He took off again at 11:25 and landed at Speke at 11:35, where he picked up a passenger, Mr. Ronald Swales, aged 24, from Port Erin on the Isle of Man and took off for Blackpool [Squire's Gate] at 11:44.

"Two radio contacts were received from the aircraft, firstly the pilot reported he was flying in and out of clouds at 1,000 feet and he was advised that another aircraft was flying the same route in the opposite direction at 800 feet. The second message was at 11:55 when he reported he was flying at 500 feet in poor visibility.

"A number of witnesses saw or heard the aircraft along its route and it was noted that at the last radio contact, it was some 8 miles inland and it was seen flying over the River Ribble at a few hundred feet near the western outskirts of Preston. G-ADEE was last seen as it just cleared a 780 feet peak, probably Beacon Fell, flying in thick mist and the steady roar of the engines was heard to continue right up to impact. At approximately 12:08 the aircraft struck the steep slope of Fairsnape Fell, some 200 feet below its 1,700 foot summit, in a very "steeply climbing altitude," no doubt the pilot saw the obstacle at the last moment and tried to avoid it.

"Both occupants were killed instantly on impact and the wrecked aircraft burst into flames, being almost completely destroyed by the time the first locals, who had heard the crash, made their way up the fell and located the burning plane."

27196	DOUGLAS	James Sholto	F/O		28.12.33	Class A
27197	EASTON	George Melhuish	P/O		12.08.30	Relinquished

On account of ill-health [LG 15 August 1930, issue 33634, page 5094].

27198	ESMONDE	Eugene	F/O		28.12.33	Relinquished

Of Irish lineage, Eugene Esmonde was born on 1st March 1909, and during his short service commission service flew Siskin [and possibly Fury fighters] with 43 Squadron, plus a brief spell attached to the Fleet Air Arm. On his release, and committed to four years on the Reserve, he joined Imperial Airways gaining experience in multi-engine types in both land and seaplane operations. However, in 1939, at the invitation of the Admiralty, he re-joined the services in the rank of Lieutenant-Commander FAA and following a spell of refresher flying on service aircraft was appointed to command 754 Squadron FAA at Lee-on-Solent on 8th May 1939, followed within weeks command of 825 Squadron FAA [Swordfish] based at HMS *Kestrel* [Worthy Down, near Winchester]. Over the next twelve months Esmonde worked up the squadron to peak efficiency and on 11th July 1940, '825' embarked on HMS *Furious* subsequently transferring to the Fleet Carrier, HMS *Victorious* and it was aboard *Victorious* that Lieutenant-Commander Esmonde led his Swordfish crews in a successful attack on the German battleship *Bismarck* that was being hunted down in the Atlantic following the sinking of HMS *Hood.* The operation, flown in atrocious weather on 23rd May 1941, damaged the Atlantic raider and in a subsequent strike by Swordfish from HMS Ark Royal in which one torpedo exploded aft and close to the port rudder shaft sealing the Bismarck's fate for with the rudder jammed the mighty battleship was reducing to sailing in a wide circle. The end was nigh and pummelled by more torpedoes fired from Allied destroyers the latest pride of the German navy was scuttled four days later. For his leadership in the first Swordfish strike, Eugene Esmonde was *Gazetted* with the DSO [LG 16 September 1941, supplement 35275, page 5357].

Following the successful actions against the *Bismarck,* 825 Squadron transferred to HMS *Ark Royal* which was torpedoed off Gibraltar on 13th November 1941, and though eventually sinking loss of life among her crew of 1,488 officers and sailors, only one lost his life. Without a carrier, 825 Squadron was re-formed at Lee-on-Solent and it was while in the process of working up that the German battleships that had been under numerous attacks from Bomber Command at their French ports in Brittany were recalled to Germany and thus begun what historians have referred to as the *"Channel Dash"*, an audacious operation that commenced on the 11th of February 1942, with *Scharnhorst, Gneisenau* and *Prinz Eugen* heavily escorted by destroyers and with overhead cover provided by the *Luftwaffe* sailing at high-speed toward the Dover Strait and the North Sea.

The outcome has been well reported countless times, but the actions of Lieutenant-Commander Eugene Esmonde whose flying career began as a probationary Pilot Officer in the RAF are worthy of reporting in this appendix. With his squadron still below operational strength, he led a flight of six Swordfish to RAF Manston and it was shortly after noon on the 11th that he led his crews into what can only be regarded as a near suicidal attack on the German battleships. The promise of a fighter escort comprising of five squadrons failed to materialise, though over Ramsgate the Swordfish were joined by ten Spitfires. The winter weather over the Channel can only be described as bad with a mass of black cumulus cloud forming. As described by Chaz Bowyer in his book on the air VCs, Esmonde sighted the enemy fleet shortly before 1 o'clock and his flight immediately came under fire from both the ships and their escort of fighters. With *Scharnhorst* selected as his target Esmode dropped his torpedo by which time his Swordfish had taken a direct hit from a shell which carried away most of the port lower wing, while fighters were pouring round after round into the stricken aircraft which, on fire, crashed headlong into the water. This was witnessed by Sub-Lieutenant Edgar Lee, the observer in Sub-Lieutenant B W Rose's aircraft which itself was coming under sustained attack and with Rose, wounded in the spine by shrapnel from a shell and their telegraphist/air gunner, Leading Airman A L Johnson dead at his post, they ditched, their torpedo launched more in hope than expectation.

The third Swordfish in Esmonde' Flight managed, miraculously, to penetrate the destroyer screen and with his aircraft burning furiously Sub-Lieutenant C M Kingsmill and his crew, all now wounded, dropped his torpedo from a range of 1,500 yards before turning away and ditching close to a naval launch which soon had them safely aboard. Of the second flight comprising of Lieutenant J C Thompson, Sub-Lieutenant C R Wood and Acting Sub-Lieutenant P Bligh, their fate can only be a matter of conjecture. Edgar Lee, the only unwounded airman from the five that survived, caught just a brief glimpse of the Flight heading through a myriad of shell bursts, spray and pursuing fighters. It was one of the most glorious but tragic actions in the rich history of the Fleet Air Arm. For the five survivors, the officers received DSOs and the non-commissioned officers a Conspicuous Gallantry Medal, and on the recommendation of Group Captain Tom Gleave, Manston's Station Commander, a VC for Lieutenant-Commander Eugene Esmonde DSO and mentioned in despatches. Subsequently, his body was washed ashore in the April and he was buried with full military honours in Gillingham [Woodlands] Cemetery. In the meantime, his mother accompanied by two of his navy-serving brothers attended Buckingham Palace on St. Patrick's Day, 17th March 1942, to receive from His Majesty, George VI a richly deserved posthumous Victoria Cross.

Returning briefly to that February day in 1942, it is reported by some sources that as the Swordfish took off, Group Captain Gleave stood at attention out on the airfield, saluting until the last of the aircraft had departed.

27199 GLEN James William Craven S/Ldr 30.09.48 Relinquished

27200 KNAPP Denis Bruce F/O 14.11.35 Relinquished

On appointment to a commission on the Unattached List for the Indian Army [LG 3 December 1935, issue 34226, page 7675].

27201 L'AMY Henry Vernon S/Ldr + 28.08.44

Squadron Leader Henry Vernon L'Amy was a passenger in Dakota III FL568 operated by BOAC as G-AGIR which crashed at Telmest in the base of the Atlas Mountains, SSW of Casablanca, with the loss of seven lives; he is buried in Morocco in Ben M'Sik European Cemetery which is located approximately 6km from the centre of Casablanca.

27202 MATHIAS Arthur Edward Vincent W/Cdr 01.04.45 Relinquished

New Zealand On appointment to the RNZAF [LG 17 July 1945, supplement 37179, page 3666].

27203 MONROE Walter Sydney F/O + 19.01.31 7 Squadron

27204 MUSSON George Bertram F/O + 14.09.42 BOAC

Southern Rhodesia Transferred to the Reserve class C [I believe a misprint for A] on 28th April 1933 [LG 9 May 1933, issue 33938, page 3101], and thence from class A to class C on 28th April 1934 [LG 19 June 1934, issue 34061, page 3908]. According to the RAF Commands website, Flying Officer George Bertram MUSSON was seconded for duties with BOAC and on the day of his death he was the first pilot on the Short S.30 Empire Flying Boat G-AFCZ *Clare* transiting from Bathurst, Gambia to the UK by way of Lisbon. On board were aircrew from 37 Squadron, the most senior being Wing Commander Ronald Ogilvie Maurice Graham, the squadron's commanding officer.

Forced to alight in the sea, owing to engine trouble, at 14.20N 17.32W [42km southwest of M'bour, Senegal] G-AFCZ broke up with the loss of all nineteen passengers and crew, Flying Officer Musson being commemorated on column 3, panel 1, of the Malta Memorial. He was 35 yards of age.

27205 ORCHARD Arthur Thomas F/O 10.02.54 Relinquished

27206 PAYNE Geoffrey Mannington P/O 21.05.29 Terminated

27207 REES Thomas John W/Cdr 10.02.54 Relinquished

27208 ROBERTSON Gerald Herbert P/O 21.05.29 Terminated

27209 SHARP Eric Granville F/Lt + 14.06.41 Bristol Aeroplane Company

Attached to the Bristol Aeroplane Company for aircraft production testing, Flight Lieutenant Eric Granville Sharp died when the Beaufort [AW215] that he was testing, pre-delivery to service, crashed. Details may be obtained from TNA Kew by accessing AIR 81/6914. Flight Lieutenant Sharp is buried in Minster-in-Sheppey [SS Mary and Sexburga] New Churchyard; he was age 31.

27210 SIMPSON James Archibald

2nd Lieutenant 19th London Regiment TA On 6th January 1936, James Archibald Simpson was granted the honorary rank of flight lieutenant while, as a civilian, he was performing the duties of Station Adjutant [LG 18 February 1936, issue 34256, page 1062]. On 2nd September 1936, his honorary rank was withdrawn on termination of the aforementioned duties [LG 6 October 1936, issue 34329, page 6368]. In the Second World War he returned to service and was retained until: W/Cdr 10.02.54 Relinquished

27211 WARNER George Robert P/O 14.01.31 Dismissed

By sentence of General Court Martial [LG 20 January 1931, issue 33682, page 464].

27212 WHEELER Ernest Fitzpatrick P/O 01.05.29 Terminated

LG 1 February 1929, issue 33462, page 775 - Seniority 16th January 1929

FLYING OFFICER

27213 PAIN John Fisher Fosbroke G/Capt 10.02.54 Relinquished

Lieutenant 1st King's Dragoon Guards [on retirement from the Army].

LG 19 February 1929, issue 33468, page 1197 - Seniority 7th February 1929

27214 BARROW Leonard Valentine Grantham F/O 24.10.32 Relinquished

On account of ill-health [LG 25 October 1932, issue 33876, page 6705]. Returned to service and granted a commission in the Administrative and Special Duties Branch as a probationary Pilot Officer, and with 76981 as his service number [LG 19 January 1940, supplement 34776, page 381] but subsequently reverted to 27214. S/Ldr 10.02.54 Relinquished

AIR 76/25/8 held by TNA Kew shows his date of birth as 6th February 1902 at Southwell. He was first commissioned to the Special Reserve, effective 17th November 1927, and was posted to No. 503 Squadron as at that date. He was authorised to wear the Pilot's Flying Badge on 26th September 1928.

LG 1 March 1929, issue 33473, page 1468 - Seniority 22nd February 1929 [27 entrants] Terms of engagement 5 years on the active list.

Block 27215 to 27241

27215 AXTEN Russell Jeffrey P/O 03.04.29 Relinquished

On account of ill-health [LG 5 April 1929, issue 33483, page 2284].

27216 BEATON Reginald Ernest Hardy F/O + 18.10.33 101 Squadron

The circumstances of Flying Officer Reginald Ernest Hardy Beaton's tragic death, found by Paul McMillan, and as reported in *The Times* on Saturday, October 21st, 1933, under the headline 'Flying Officer's Death - Worried over Eyesight' reads as follows:-

"A verdict of "Suicide, while of unsound mind" was returned at the inquest yesterday on the body of Flying Officer Reginald Ernest Hardy Beaton, RAF, who was killed by a tube train at Piccadilly Circus on Wednesday. Mr. Beaton was 28 years old.

"Mr. Ernest Walter Hardy Beaton, of Sussex Gardens, identified the as that of his son, who had been staying with him. He had been on leave about two weeks, and had two or three more weeks' leave to come.

"The Coroner [Mr. Ingleby Oddie] - Did he like his life? - He, loved it."

"Mr. Beaton added that his son was particularly healthy, but his eyesight was not too good. He had no other troubles whatever.

"Dennis Anthony Bradley, of Kingston Vale, SW, said that he was a fried of Mr. Beaton and saw him last on Wednesday evening some time after 7 o'clock in his [Mr. Bradley's] office in Old Bond Street, where about 120 people of both sexes met at a cocktail party. When Mr. Beaton left he said good-bye, and seemed quite sober.

"George James Penton, of Alperton, said he was driving a train into Piccadilly Circus Station, and when he emerged from the tunnell he saww Mr. Beaton 75ft away on the platform, and was a yard from the edge. "He was looking straight ahead across the line," added Mr. Penton. "When I was a few feet from him he put his hands in front of him and dived in front of the train."

"The Coroner - "Was there any question of his falling?" - "No, I think it was a dive." "Deliberate?' - "Yes."

"Mrs. Margery Eva O'Brien, of St. Alban's Court, Nonington, Dover, said Mr. Beaton, an intimate friend of hers, told her he had conjunctivitis and had been to see a specialist, who told him he had a germ in one eye. That germ was to be tested, and the specialist was to give him the result on Thursday. He also told her that once while flying he went blind for a few moments and that he had a similar experience in her drawing-room that night. That worried him, because when flying he said it might cause an accident. She knew of no reason why he shoud jump under the train.

"Captain Roland Spencer said that he met Mr. Beaton at lunch time at the RAF Club on the day of his death. He asked how he was feeling, and Mr. Beaton said, "A bit shook up."He said he had a sort of black-out and had fallen flat on his face, adding, "It was only a matter of a second, but I came an awful purler on my face."

"Miss Jean Stourton, of Fulham Road, said that she saw Mr. Beaton at 7.55 on the night he died at Old Bond Street. He complained that he was having trouble with his eyes. He said he would come and see her at tea-time the next day, and seemed in very good spirits.

"Flight Lieutenant Alfred D Rogers, stationed at Andover, said that Flying Officer Beaton was a popular and capable officer and pilot. He had conjunctivitis about six or nine months ago, but he had passed a medical board three months ago, and since then had done a good deal of flying.

"The Coroner said he had a pretty shrewd idea that Mr. Beaton was worried about his sight and he gave way to sudden impulse to get rid of anxiety and trouble and to end his life.

"A memorial service for Flying Officer Beaton will be held at 10.40 today at St. James Sussex Gardens, and the funeral will take place at Hampstead at 11.30."

27217 BISHOP Eric Douglas F/O + 05.12.32 7 Squadron

Flying Officer Eric Douglas Bishop was a member of the Hampshire Aeroplane Club and with his friend and fellow Club member, Pilot Officer Richard James Berens, took off from Hamble in DH.60X Moth G-AAYS for a pleasure flight on 4th December 1932. Some twenty minutes later, and now over Southampton Water, off Netley, the Moth suddenly dived and failed to recover before striking the water. The impact was severe and when aid arrived at the scene [at this stage the Moth was still afloat] young Berens - he was 21 - was dead and Flying Officer dreadfully injured. The crash was reported in the *Western Morning Ness* on 5th December 1932, and the *Western Daily Press* 24-hours later:

"Pilot Officer Richard J Berens, RAF, was killed, and Flying Officer Eric D Bishop, RAF, was seriously injured, when an aeroplane belonging to the Hampshire Aeroplane Club, fell into Southampton Water today. The two officers, members of the club, were on a pleasure flight, and had been in the air about 20 minutes when the accident occurred.

"The crew of a Hythe speed-boat saw the 'plane strike the water, and rushed to the rescue. The 'plane was badly damaged and was sinking, but they succeeded in extricating both men. The condition of Flying Officer Bishop was so critical that he was immediately operated on. Late to-night it was stated that he had a chance of recovery."

Sadly, these hopes were not realised and the *Western Daily Press* reported: *"Flying Officer Eric D Bishop of Nether Street, Finchley, who was injured when a light aeroplane in which he was a passenger crashed in Southampton Water on Sunday, died in the Royal South Hants and Southampton Hospital, yesterday. His friend, Flying Officer R J Berens, 22,* [sic] *of Kevington, St. Mary Cray, Kent, who was piloting the machine, was killed. The two men were stationed at Worthy Down, near Winchester, and were flying a DH Moth belonging to Hampshire Aeroplane Club, of which they were members. Two speed boats raced to the scene of the crash, and the two airmen were dragged from the sinking machine."*

27218 BLACKWOOD Guy Hamilton Ava W/Cdr 11.10.54 Relinquished

27219 BOOTH Arthur Frank Calvert W/Cdr 12.07.41 107 Squadron

Wing Commander Arthur Frank Calvert Booth and his crew, flying Blenheim IV Z7487 OM- went into the sea of IJmuiden during anti-shipping operations on 'Beat 9', the observer, Sergeant T Scott surviving to become a prisoner of war [my RAFBCL 1941 page 90 refers]. Wing Commander Booth, he had commanded 107 Squadron for about a week, now rests in Kiel War Cemetery where his headstone is inscribed *"Greater Love Hath No Man."* The Blenheim's air gunner, Flight Sergeant Colin Gordon Goodfellow, is commemorated on panel 36 at the Runnymede Memorial.

27220 BROOKE-BEER Ronald Christian Antrobus F/O 20.10.31 Resigned

Returned to service and was granted a class CC commission in the Reserve of Air Force Officers, General Duties Branch [LG 27 October 1939, supplement 34718, page 7181] in the rank of flight lieutenant and as 75209. Subsequently granted a class CC commission, retaining his rank, in the Administrative and Special Duties Branch [LG 26 November 1946, supplement 37797, page 5778], effective 26th October 1946. Continued to serve postwar until: F/Lt 01.06.60 Relinquished

27221 COOKE Edward Annesley F/O 21.04.33 Resigned

27222 DAVIES Robert Ardwick S/Ldr 25.12.54 Relinquished

27223 GILL Charles Sydney F/O + 17.08.36 British Airways Limited

Flying Officer Charles Sydney Gill transferred to Class A of the Reserve on 22nd February 1934 [LG 27 February 1934, issue 34028, page 1348]. Employed for flying duties with British Airways Limited, he lost his life, along with his wireless operator Kenneth John Bayliss, when their DH.86 Express G-ADEB crashed whilst carrying mail on the night run from Hannover - Cologne - London, coming down on high ground near Altenkirchen [Rheinland-Pfaltz] well to the southeast of Köln-Bützweilerhof which the Aviation Safety Network report of the crash indicates was its destination. Co-author, Paul McMillan, has located a newspaper report of the accident, published in a Dutch journal at Leeuwarden, which indicates it was carrying mail that originated in Scandinavia and when people reached the scene both members of crew were alive but badly injured.

27224 GOAD Frederick Robert Walter F/O + 04.11.30 9 Squadron

2nd Lieutenant 52nd [Kent] Medium Brigade RA TA

27225 HOYLE Trevor William F/Lt 14.08.46 Relinquished

27226 JACKSON Malcolm Menzies P/O + 10.05.29 1 FTS Netheravon

Pilot Officer Malcolm Menzies Jackson died when he forced-landed his Avro 504N J8727 near Beaches Barn, Fittleton a village on the northern side of Netheravon airfield and was unable to free himself from the cockpit before the trainer caught fire and was burnt out.

27227 JARMAN Lancelot Elworthy A/Cmdr 05.08.58 Retirement

New Zealand Air Commodore Lancelot 'Michael' Elworthy Jarman DFC three time mentioned in despatches, died on Thursday, 30th October 1986. Following an introduction to the Wellington bomber while attached to 214 Squadron, on 20th December 1939, he arrived at Honington to command a flight in 9 Squadron, a position he held until 15th May 1940, during which time he flew the following sorties:

20.01.40	Wellington IA N3017 WS-	D	Special Sweep North Sea Base - HTAA - YXAA - Base
24.01.40	Wellington IA N3014 WS-	D	Special Sweep Base - Lowestoft - HTAA 0000 - YXAA 0000 - Base
11.02.40	Wellington IA N3014 WS-	D	Special Sweep Base - 53N 2.30E - 55N 2.30E - Wells - Base
13.02.40	Wellington IA N3014 WS-	D	Routine Sweep Base 53N 2E - 55N 2E - 53N 2E - Base
22.02.40	Wellington IA N3014 WS-	D	Special Sweep Base - 53N 2E - 55.20 N 1E - Wells - Base
06.03.40	Wellington IA P9231 WS-A	N	'Nickel' Hannover 14,000 feet - slight AA fire
15.03.40	Wellington IA P9231 WS-A	D	Special Sweep searching for enemy minelayer
19.03.40	Wellington IA N2981 WS-F	D	Special Sweep Base - 53.00N 02.30E - 54.00N 02.05E - Base
25.03.40	Wellington IC P9239 WS-H	N	'Nickel' NW German ports
04.04.40	Wellington IC P9239 WS-H	D	18 Group exercise NW of the Orkney Islands
09.04.40	Wellington IC P9239 WS-H	D	Reconnaissance Bergen - Kristiansand - Stavanger area
11.04.40	Wellington IC P9239 WS-H	D	Shipping Strike Troopship N of Bergen - target not found
20.04.40	Wellington IC P9239 WS-H	N	Bombing Stavanger Aerodrome - DNCO

Handed over command of flight to Squadron Leader J B S Monypenny [see Appendix D LG 8 July 1930].

27228 JENNINGS Eric Henry P/O 27.03.30 Terminated

27229 LONGFIELD Geoffrey Phelps W/Cdr + 26.02.43 105 Squadron

Wing Commander Geoffrey Phelps Longfield and his observer, Flight Lieutenant Ralph Frederick Millns, took Off at 1646 from Great Massingham in Norfolk to attack a naval stores depot at Rennes and it was in the target area that their Mosquito IV DZ365 GB-V collided with Mosquito IV DZ413 GB-K crewed by Flying Officer Spencer Griffith Kimmel RCAF and Flying Officer Harry Nettleton Kirkland RCAF. There were no survivors from eith crew. Wing Commander Longfield is buried in Rennes Eastern Communal Cemetery; for additional information pertaining to the two crews, please consult page 50 of my RAFBCL 1943.

Wing Commander Longfield he is mentioned in Appendix C in the Report of RAF Operations in Malaya and Netherland East Indies 1941-2 as reported in *The London Gazette* 26th February 1948, supplement 38216, page 1415. During the period of the Report, he commanded 34 Squadron which was equipped with seventeen Blenheim IV bombers.

27230 MARVIN Gerald Price W/Cdr 27.07.69 Relinquished

As Squadron Leader Gerald Price Marvin he was attached, as a flight commander, to 51 Squadron [Whitley IV/Whitley V]. His operational flying is recorded as:-

27-28.10.39 Whitley IV 8981 MH-A 1740-2010 'Nickel' - DNCO weather

02-03.03.40 Whitley V N1418 MH- 1735-0320 'Nickel' and Reconnaissance Berlin - Landed Manston

11-12.04.40 Whitley V N1418 MH- 1945-0550 Shipping in the Kattegat - Flares dropped, no ships seen

02-03.05.40 Whitley V N1406 MH- 1855-0505 Oslo-Fornebu Aerodrome - Flew to target at 10,000 feet and bombs dropped in a single stick. Descended to 8,000 feet and on crossing the coast advised by Dishforth that the cloud base over the airfield was 700 feet. Unable to raise Linton-on-Ouse or Driffield; circled the area for an hour and with fuel almost exhausted ordered the crew to bale out. A detailed report on their fate may be accessed on the Yorkshire Aircraft Website and on page 119 of my RAFBCL 1939-1940 revised edition. Squadron Leader Marvin was admitted to Fulford Military Hospital, York, with leg and back injuries.

27231 MOON Vivian Reginald G/Capt 05.06.62 Relinquished

27232 MUSTARD Geoffrey Evelyn F/Lt 06.10.55 Relinquished

27233 PRATT Percy James P/O + 24.03.30 58 Squadron

27234 PRIMROSE Hugh Dunsmuir F/O 07.07.37 Relinquished

On account of ill-health [LG 6 July 1937, issue 34415, page 4349]. While undergoing instruction at 1 FTS Netheravon, Pilot Officer Hugh Dunsmuir Primrose was injured when his Atlas TM J9437 came into collision with Atlas TM J9440 at Netheravon. The latter caught fire and its pilot, Leading Aircraftman Thomas White Caird who was serving as Thomas White Kelly was killed.

27235 RANKIN William Muirhead F/O 20.01.33 Cashiered

By sentence of General Court Martial [LG 24 January 1933, issue 33905, 526].

27236 ROBERTS Geoffrey Newland F/O 22.03.34 Class A

New Zealand Transferred to the RNZAF and rose to the rank of Air Commodore. The following was promulgated in *The London Gazette* on 22nd March 1946, supplement 37508, page 1483: *"The KING has been graciously pleased, on the advice of His Majesty's New Zealand Ministers, to give orders for the following appointments to the Most Excellent Order of the British Empire in recognition of conspicuous service in operations against the Japanese:- To be an Additional Commander of the Military Division of the said Most Excellent Order:- Acting Air CommodoreGeoffrey Newland Roberts AFC [NZ1087]."*

This was followed by a Knighthood, published in the *Gazette* on 15th June 1973, issue 46005, page 7341: *"Under the authority of a Royal Warrant, the Governor-General of New Zealand of Government House, Wellington, on 11th May 1973, conferred the honour of Knighthood upon:- Sir Geoffrey Newland Roberts, CBE, AFC. Her Majesty's approval of the Knighthood was signified on 1st January 1973."*

27237 SMITH Herbert Legh W/Cdr 27.05.59 Relinquished

At which time he had adopted the surname LEGH-SMITH.

27238 SMYTHE Dennis William G/Capt 29.05.59 Retirement

27239 SWAINE Reginald Montague P/O + 11.07.29 1 FTS Netheravon

Pilot Officer Reginald Montague Swaine, 19 years of age, died when trying to forced-land in his Avro 504N J9006 at Upper Studley on the SE fringes of Trowbridge, Wiltshire.

27240 WATSON Arthur Courtenay G/Capt 01.10.56 Retirement

Paul McMillan reports that Group Captain Arthur Courtenay Watson died on 6th March 1974, at Wycombe Marsh in Buckinghamshire.

27241 WILSON Thomas Herbert S/Ldr 19.10.55 Relinquished

LG 26 March 1929, issue 33480, page 2087 - Seniority 15th March 1929 [30 entrants] Terms of engagement 5 years on the active list.

Block 27243 to 27261 and 28001 to 28011

27243 ASHWORTH John Edwin P/O 11.09.29 Terminated

27244 BAKER-CARR John Darcy AM 01.02.64 Retirement

Air Marshal Sir John Baker-Carr KBE CB AFC, died on Thursday, 9th July 1998. On 28th February 1934, Flying Officer John Darcy Baker-Carr was posted to the Air Armament School at Eastchurch as a student on No. 12 Specialist Armament Course and a year later, now promoted flight lieutenant, he was appointed Armament Officer at RAF Andover and for the remainder of his service career he was mostly concerned with technical matters, transferring from the General Duties Branch to the Technical Branch on 24th April 1940. His final appointment was as Acting Air Member for Supply and Organisation.

27245 BINKS Louis William Albert P/O 24.07.29 Terminated

27246 BINNS Gerald Harrison P/O 24.07.29 Terminated

27247 CORBETT Paul Felvus P/O 07.09.29 Terminated

27251 DAWKINS Robert Cecil G/Capt 15.03.55 Retirement

27248 de SARGINY Derek Richard Charles Barrois S/Ldr 18.08.57 Relinquished

Paul McMillan advises TNA Kew hold a document in respect of Squadron Leader Derek Richard Charles Barrois de Sarginy under AIR 76/132/10.

27249 FLETCHER Ronald Francis G/Capt 30.09.58 Retirement

Group Captain Ronald Francis Fletcher, born on 7th September 1906, died in Uckfield, East Sussex, during June 1995.

27250 GOWING Derek Arthur P/O 08.10.39 Terminated

27252 HODGSON Thomas Winton W/Cdr 21.05.57 Retirement

27253 HOLMES Richard Robert Ralph Joseph P/O 04.02.30 Terminated

27254 HUCKER Ernest George P/O 06.07.29 Terminated

27255 HURREN Bernard John F/O 26.02.38 Relinquished

27256 KEILY Gerald Barnard A/Cmdr 18.03.55 Retirement

Gazetted with the DFC on 20th August 1940, supplement 34927, page 5091: *"On 28th July 1940, Squadron Leader Keily was the pilot of an aircraft detailed to carry out a special reconnaissance over Libya. The reconnaissance had to be carried out at a low altitude owing to clouds. He was attacked by five enemy aircraft but, displaying great skill, he destroyed one of them. During the engagement the observer was hit by a bullet. Notwithstanding the handicap of having the observer's body leaning against him, Squadron Leader Keily continued with the reconnaissance, returning with information of great value. He has invariably displayed exceptional leadership, courage, and devotion to duty."*

At the time Squadron Leader Keily was attached to 113 Squadron [Blenheim IV]. Two months later, and piloting Blenheim IV T2048 and operating from LG 14 [Maaten Bagush] he was shot down during an attack on Tmimi and taken prisoner of war, his two crew being killed. For further information, please refer to page 26 and 18th September 1940, of David Gunby and Pelham Temple's Bomber Losses in the Middle East and Mediterranean. Initially held in camps on the Italian mainland, following Italy's exit from the war in September 1943, he was taken to Germany and incarcerated in Stalag Luft III, his prisoner of war number being 228356.

Air Commodore Gerald Barnard Keily DFC AFC twice mentioned in despatches, died on Friday, 14th September 1962, four days short of the 22nd anniversary of being taken prisoner of war.

27257 LEMON Frank F/O + 12.01.31 29 Squadron

27258 LOUSADA Charles Rochford A/Cmdr 17.08.59 Retirement

Air Commodore Charles Rochford Lousada mentioned in despatches, died on Wednesday, 5th October 1988.

27258 MACKEWN Allen Raymond P/O 18.10.29 Terminated

27259 MAYES Harry Edward F/Lt 15.03.38 Relinquished

27260 McLAREN Arthur Alexander P/O 11.09.29 Terminated

28001 MESSITER Herbert Lindsell A/Cmdr 11.05.59 Retirement

Air Commodore Herbert Lindsell Messiter CB twice mentioned in despatches, died in Andover, Hampshire, on Friday, 15th April 1994. Transferring from the General Duties Branch to the Technical Branch on 14th April 1940, Air Commodore Messiter's final appointment was as Senior Technical Staff Officer, HQ Middle East Air Force, an area that was familiar to him as prewar he had been appointed Engineering Officer, HQ RAF Middle East.

28002 MILES John Stuart Dixon F/Lt + 17.01.41 1 PRU Benson

Flight Lieutenant John Stuart Dixon Miles, attached to Coastal Command, failed to return from a reconnaissance sortie in Spitfire I [PR] Type C R6906, details of his flight being recorded on pages 90 and 91 or Ross McNeill's Coastal Command losses; he is buried in the Pas-de-Calais at Marquise Communal Cemetery.

28003 OGDEN Cecil Victor W/Cdr 10.02.54 Relinquished

28004 PAWSON Geoffrey John S/Ldr 10.02.54 Relinquished

On 30th September 1930, Pilot Officer Geoffrey John Pawson was slightly injured when his 17 Squadron Bulldog IIA J9587 crashed in Arundel Park, West Sussex during air exercises from nearby Tangmere. Two companions in his flight died in the incident.

28005 REES Charles Milsom S/Ldr 28.02.46 Resigned

28006 SHOTTER Hamilton Alec F/O 27.09.35 Resigned

28007 STAVELEY John Charles William F/O 05.08.38 Relinquished

On appointment to a commission on the Unattached List of the Indian Army [LG 29 November 1938, issue 34575, page 7534].

28008 TANNER Eric Arthur Henry F/O 09.02.38 Relinquished

28009 TUNNARD Anthony John F/O + 13.04.37 Edinburgh Flying Club

Transferred to the Reserve Class A on 15th March 1934 [LG 20 March 1934, issue 34034, page 1867], Flying Officer Anthony John Tunnard was an instructor with the Edinburgh Flying Club died following a long illness, his obituary appearing in *The Scotsman* on Wednesday, April 14th, 1937, beneath the headline 'Edinburgh Flying Club's Loss.'

"By the death of Mr. A J Tunnard, instructor to the Edinburgh Flying Club, which took place in an Edinburgh nursing home yesterday, civil aviation has lost an accomplished airman.

"Mr. Tunnard, whose death has followed an illness extending over ten weeks, came to the Edinburgh Flying Club at Macmerry last year, and soon established himself in the regard of members as a highly popular and efficient teacher of flying. He did much to promote the interests of the Edinburgh Club which, under his skilled guidance, steadily increased in membership. During the winter Mr. Tunnard acted as lecturer in aeronautics at Leith Technical College.

"He was known in aviation circles in the country and abroad as a pilot of exceptional ability. Before coming to Scotland, and after leaving the Royal Air Force, in the Reserve of which he held the rank of flying officer, he was instructor to the Bombay Flying Club.

"Mr. Tunnard, who was 33, was the son of Mr. Ambrose Tunnard, of Newport, Berkeley, Gloucestershire, and was educated at Christ Church, Oxford. He is survived by his wife."

28010 WESTHORPE Arthur Charles Philip W/Cdr 30.08.46 Resigned

28011 WHITTLESEA Donald Ernest Tom P/O 18.02.30 Terminated

LG 23 April 1929, issue 33488, page 2697 - Seniority 2nd and 4th April 1929 respectively [20 entrants] Terms of engagement 5 years on the active list. Block 28012 to 28031

28012 ALEXANDER George Frederick G/Capt 30.09.58 Retirement

28013 BANKS William Noel Hamilton F/Lt + 07.04.38 233 Squadron

28014 CARR Sidney Joseph Horace W/Cdr 2801.59 Retirement

The Edinburgh Gazette June 26th, 1931, issue 14768, page 718, promulgated the following: *"The KING has been graciously pleased to approve of the undermentioned awards in recognition of gallant and distinguished service in Iraq:- Awarded the Distinguished Flying Cross:- Flying Officer Sidney Joseph Horace Carr."*

28015 CAUTHERY Ronald Peart G/Capt 08.01.58 Retirement

28016 CAVE PENNEY Roy Humphrey F/O 17.05.33 Relinquished

On Account of ill-health [LG 16 May 1933, issue 33940, page 3285].

28017 COLLINS Herbert Michael Bouneviall e W/Cdr 10.02.54 Relinquished

28018 DURBIN Egbert Charles F/Lt 04.01.65 Relinquished

Wing Commander Egbert Charles Durbin was appointed MBE in the 1945 New Year's Honours List [LG 29 December 1944, supplement 36866, page 22]. His 'Wing Commander' rank was temporary, and he relinquished the rank on 1st November 1947, subsequently being granted a class CC commission in the rank of flight lieutenant, effective 2nd May 1962. Prewar he held the honorary rank of flight lieutenant while carrying out the duties of statin adjutant in a civilian capacity.

28019 HARTLEY Christopher Edgar A/Cmdr 26.11.58 Retirement

Air Commodore Christopher Edgar Hartley CBE, died on Sunday, 18th February 1962 at the comparatively early age of 56. His final appointment was as Director of Aeronautical Inspection Services.

28020 HEARNE James Frederick Martyn P/O 24.07.29 Terminated

28021 HESSION Patrick Stephen P/O 13.08.29 Terminated

28022 HOFFMAN Origen William P/O 13.08.29 Terminated

28023 LARMUTH Alfred Churchill F/O + 03.07.38 Railway Air Services

Captain Alfred Churchill Larmuth along with his engineer, Reginald H Vaughan, died when their DH.89 Dragon Rapide G-AEBX *Star of Scotia* spun out of control and crashed at Belfast Harbour Airport, Sydenham. The accident occurred as the crew were on approach to land, which is at odds with the brief report published in *The Times* on Monday, July 4th, 1938: *"A Railway Air Services aeroplane crashed near the airport, Belfast, this evening, and the pilot and engineer, the only occupants, were killed.*

"Engine trouble apparently was experienced when at a height of about 300ft, and the machine got into a spin and crashed, afterwards bursting into flames. The pilot was Captain A C Larmuth, and the engineer was named Vaughan.

"The body of the pilot was pulled from the aeroplane quickly, but it was nearly an hour before the remains of the engineer were recovered. The aircraft had flown from Renfrew, and was leaving Belfast for Glasgow when it crashed."

On the same page was a report on the 'Open Day' held at the aircraft apprentices school at Halton where according to paper's special correspondent, 5,000 aircraft apprentices are undergoing training. Although the 'Open Day' was relatively brief in duration, parents and friends were able to see for themselves the conditions in which the apprentices were being taught [courses ran for three years and concentrated on instruction for engine fitters and riggers, with the opportunity to advance to a commission]. The article ends: *"The living quarters here compare very favourably with the usual barracks, and the boy's social life is full and healthy."*

28024 LUSK Percy Butler F/O 02.04.34 Relinquished

On account of ill-health [LG 3 April 1934, issue 34038, page 2190].

28025 MAXWELL-CHANNELL Reginald Robert P/O 29.10.29 Relinquished
On account of ill-health [LG 5 November 1929, supplement 33549, page 7074].
28026 MILLAR Charles Skipper F/O 03.05.32 Resigned
28027 MURTAGH Michael Aiden P/O 31.12.29 Terminated
28028 ROBERTSON Harold Bertie F/O + 25.03.39 34 E&RFTS Rochford
Flying Officer Harold Bertie Robertson was transferred to the Reserve of Air Force Officers, Class A, on 2nd April 1934 [LG 3 April 1934, issue 34038, page 2190]. He was killed, along with his pupil Sergeant Edward George Dyas when their DH.82 Tiger Moth I N6454 came into collision at 2,000 feet over North Benfleet, Essex. The other aircraft, Hawker Audax I K8329 of the same unit, piloted by Sergeant Lawrence Thomas Wilton-Jones, landed safely with only minor damage and was repaired on site. Subsequently, according to Air Britain's K Register it went to 9 FTS Hullavington where it was badly damaged on 5th August 1940, in a forced-landing near Sopworth, 6 miles WSW from Malmesbury, Wiltshire, and was eventually struck off charge on 14th August 1940, after 873.15 hours of flying.
28029 TURNER Stanley Howard P/O 07.05.30 Terminated
28030 WARDELL Frederick Augustus S/Ldr ....07.45 AFL
Prior to his short service commission, Pilot Officer Frederick Augustus Wardell had been commissioned to the Special Reserve, 1st June 1928 [LG 5th June 1928, issue 33391, page 3874]. He was *Gazetted* with the AFC on 31st March 1942 [LG 31 March 1942, supplement 35507, page 1450]. It was awarded for his services at No. 7 Elementary Flying Training School, Desford.

Interestingly, Paul McMillan has received the 'chain of command' sequence of recommendations that led to this award, the first originating [I assume] from the Station Commander at Desford on 10th January 1942: *"As Chief Flying Instructor, this officer has done excellent work and continues to carry out all his duties in a most conscientious and zealous manner. He has recently shown initiative and energy inputting into effect an intensive Night Flying Programme, and has been unsparing in his personal efforts to make it a success. He thoroughly deserves recognition for his excellent services."*

Within 24-hours this recommendation was actioned by the Air Officer Commanding, No. 51 [Training] Group, Air Commodore B E Baker,*who added: *"Squadron Leader Wardell has performed the duties of Chief Flying Instructor at No. 7 Elementary Flying Training School in a most efficient manner. He has completed 2,686 hours as a flying instructor, 186 of which have been flown in the last six months testing pupils and instructors. Principally through his enthusiasm, elementary night flying at his station is far in advance of any other station in the group. I strongly recommend that his sservices to flying training be rewarded by the award of the Air Force Cross."*

Appended to the RAF Commands website is the following, submitted by Hugh A Halliday, on 3rd December 2021: *"Commissioned 1 June 1928. Commenced instructional duty, 12 June 1933. Commenced duty at No. 7 EFTS, 10 October 1938, as a civilian until 2 August 1939; starting again as a service pilot, 3 September 1939. Public Record Office AIR 2/9621, courtesy Steve Brew, has citation drafted when he had flown 2,686hours 25 minutes on instructional duties, 173 hours 40 minutes in last six months [169 instructional]. Also had flown 3,998 hours 45 minutes in his career [plus 32 hours as passenger], 814 hours 15 minutes since outbreak of war. Document gives full name as Frederick William Augustus Wardell."*

* Air Marshal Sir Brian Baker KBE CB DSO MC AFC mentioned in despatches and *Croix de Guerre* [France]. Following his command of No. 51 [Training] Group he was appointed Air Officer Commanding Iceland.

28031 KAT FERREIRA Ignatius Marthinus Lambertus P/O 29.06.29 Terminated

LG 26 April 1929, issue 33489, pages 2765 and 2766 - Seniority 13th April 1929 [35 entrants] Terms of engagement 5 years on the active list.

Block 28032 to 28065

28032 BELLAIRS Edmund Hamon W/Cdr 13.09.48 Retirement
Between 1st April 1930 and 24th March 1931, Flying Officer Edmund Hamon Bellairs was attached to 41 Squadron [Siskin IIIA].
28033 BLACK Hugh Robertson W/Cdr 07.01.56 Relinquished
As Acting Squadron Leader Hugh Robertson Black he was *Gazetted* with the AFC on 1st January 1941 [LG 1 January 1941, supplement 35029, page 33].
28034 BRACKENBURY Edward Lugard W/Cdr 19.11.60 Retirement
28035 BRETT Walter Kingsley F/O 13.04.38 Relinquished
Paul McMillan reports that during the Second World War he was *Gazetted* as a 2nd Lieutenant in the Egypt Section, relinquishing his commission on 11th December 1941 [LG 29 March 1946, supplement 37514, page 1573].
28036 COLEMAN Eric Harold W/Cdr 10.02.54 Relinquished
Squadron Leader Eric Harold Coleman was *Gazetted* with the AFC on 31st March 1942 [LG 31 March 1942, supplement 35507, page 1450].
28037 ELLISON Edward Everard S/Ldr 01.01.65 Relinquished
Granted a class CC commission in the Reserve of Air Force Officers [LG 12 September 1939, issue 34679, page 6196].
28038 ELLISON Ronald F/O 13.04.34 Class A
The website The Tartan Terror which as authors we have delight in acknowledging has an excellent biography regarding Flying Officer Ronald Ellison [the initials C W have been added] along with his photograph posing with a Royal Air Force pilot and Hugh Statham [I suspect a flight test engineer] in front of Beaufighter: *"Few test pilots anywhere can have equalled the total of over 7,000 hours of flying for one firm. Such is the record of Ronald Ellison, when he retired from test flying for the Bristol Aeroplane Co. His Bristol experience embraced at least 36 different types of aircraft and development flying on nine engines - Pegasus, Mercury, Perseus, Aquila, Taurus, Hercules, Centaurus, Theseus and Proteus. He was the first man to take the Proteus into the air [in a Lincoln*testbed] and has flown in all some 8,000 hours, on 80 different types of aircraft. Born in 1908 and educated at Bedford School and in HMS Conway, Mr. Ellison spent three years in the Merchant Service before taking a short-service commission in the RAF in April 1929. In 1930 he was posted to No. 17 [Fighter] Sqn, at Upavon, where he flew his first Bristol aircraft, the Bulldog. After a course at the CFS, he was posted as an instructor at Cranwell. During the last year of service he flew Wallaces and Wapitis with No. 501 Reserve Squadron at Filton, where he became well known to staff of the Bristol Flying School. As a result, he was offered a post as instructor when, with some 1,000 hours in his log, he left the RAF in 1934. In addition to acting as instructor at the school [then equipped with Tiger Moths], Mr. Ellison was employed on the development flight testing of a variety of Bristol engines. When war broke out, he joined the test pilot staff and on January 1st, 1941, became chief production test pilot at the Company's Weston-super-Mare shadow factory. Of the total of over 3,300 Beaufighters built at Weston during the next five years, he flew precisely 1,800, including the 1,000th, 2,000th and 3,000th and last aircraft. In 1945 he returned to Filton, where he was engaged on the flight testing of the Buckingham, Buckmaster, Brigand and Freighter and the development testing of Hercules, Centaurus, Theseus and Proteus engines. In 1949 he was made assistant chief test pilot* ['Bill' Pegg], *a position which he relinquished at the end of 1952. Since the war's end, Ronald Ellison had flown many thousands of miles as the pilot of Bristol Freighters. While demonstrating the aeroplane or instructing new pilots, he visited Pakistan [three times], Brazil, Argentina, Canada, Australia, New Zealand, Burma and Iraq. Early this year he flew to Johannesburg a Freighter loaded with supplies and equipment for the Britannia tropical trials. He made the flight of over 6,000 miles with four night stops in a total flying time of 43 hours."*

* Lincoln B.2 SX972 allocated to Bristol Aeroplane Company and fitted with two Proteus engines, replacing the outboard Rolls-Royce Merlins. Struck off Charge 21st July 1953.

28039 FARNHILL Geoffrey W/Cdr + 05.04.41 Aircraft Depot Far East
Wing Commander Geoffrey Farnhill was transferred from the General Duties Branch to the Technical Branch on 24th April 1940 [LG 28 February 1941, issue 35090, page 1209]. Posted to the Far East, he lost his life when during the course of salvage operations south of Siglap Obelisk where a Blenheim had gone into the sea, HMS *Buffalo,* described as a Mooring Vessel, struck an enemy mine and sank with heavy loss of life. Wing Commander Farnhill is commemorated on the Singapore Memorial, panel 409.
28040 FLEMING Guy Desmond W/Cdr 15.03.46 Relinquished
Squadron Leader Guy Desmond Fleming was *Gazetted* with the AFC in the New Year's Honours List 1943 [LG 1 January 1943, issue 35841, page 34]. His commission was relinquished on account of medical unfitness for Air Force service [LG 26 March 1946, supplement 37511, page 1534].
28041 GILLAN George Michael F/O 14.11.35 Relinquished
On appointment to a commission on the Unattached List for the Indian Army [LG 3 December 1935, issue 34226, page 7675].
28042 HALL Samuel Robert P/O 24.12.29 Resigned
28043 KNOCKER Kenneth Duke W/Cdr + 03.07.42 214 Squadron
Wing Commander Kenneth Duke Knocker and his entire crew perished when their Stirling I BF313 BU-T was shot down by a night fighter during operations to Bremen on 2nd-3rd July 1942. All are buried in Holland at Westerieland General Cemetery, De Marne. For full details of the crew and additional notes, please refer to page 145 of my RAFBCL 1942. According to Air-Britains *The Stirling File - Revised Edition* compiled by Bryce B Gomersall, 1987, BF313 was lost on its first operational sortie. In conclusion, CWGC shows Wing Commander Knocker's headstone as being inscribed with the words *"Always In My Heart, Mother."*
28044 LOVERSEED John Eric F/O 23.12.37 Removed
Flying Officer John Eric Loverseed was removed from the service, promulgated in *The London Gazette* 4th January 1938, issue 34470, page 38. He was permitted to rejoin the service on the outbreak of the Second World War and as a Warrant Officer was awarded the Air Force Cross, *Gazetted* in the New Year's Honours List for 1943 [LG 1 January 1943, issue 35841, page 34].
28045 MacDONALD William Mary Laurence ACM 11.08.66 Retirement
Air Chief Marshal Sir William MacDonald GCB CBE DFC twice mentioned in despatches, died on Friday, 9th November 1984. When the Second World War broke out, Squadron Leader William Mary Laurence MacDonald was attached to 150 Squadron which was deployed to France on the eve of hostilities as part of the Advanced Air Striking Force and was based at Ecury-sur-Coole. During an operational reconnaissance on 30th September 1939, the formation of six, almost immediately reduced to five when one crew was obliged to return with a failing engine, was intercepted by Me109s and four Battles were shot down. Chased at tree top height, Squadron Leader MacDonald crash-landed, two of his crew being injured. For a detailed account, please refer to pages 264 and 265 of my RAFBCL 1939-1940 revised edition.
Air Chief Marshal Sir William MacDonald's final appointment was *Aide de Camp* to Her Majesty, Queen Elizabeth II.
28046 McHARDY Louis F/O + 30.10.31 3 FTS Grantham
See Appendix D Short Service Commission Officers 1927 and the entry for 24148 Flying Officer Jack Eugene Markby for details.
28047 MARSH Gerald Lewis Score P/O 31.12.29 Terminated
28065 MATHESON William Robert Abercrombie W/Cdr 10.02.54 Relinquished
28048 MAY Peter Rodriguez W/Cdr + 13.07.43 296 Squadron
Wing Commander Peter Rodriguez May is commemorated on panel 6, column 1 of the Malta Memorial. He was a holder of the Distinguished Flying Cross [USA] and had served previously in the Chinese Air Force.
28049 MEGAW Eric Jack Kennedy S/Ldr + 26.02.41 8 AACU Old Sarum
Squadron Leader Eric Jack Kennedy Megaw lost his life during a *Luftwaffe* air raid; he is buried in Somerset at Middlezoy [Holy Cross] Churchyard.
28050 MESSITER Denis Arthur F/Lt 03.07.45 Dismissed
By sentence of General Court Martial [LG 17 July 1945, supplement 37179, page 3666].
28051 MYERS Vivian Bryce F/O 24.10.35 Relinquished
28052 ORR Lionel Frank Hastings F/O + 10.08.36 Imperial Airways Limited
Captain Lionel Frank Hastings Orr, aged 26, died along with his second pilot, Captain Stanley Miles Ferguson, aged 32, and two wireless operators, namely Robert Arbuckle and Jeffrey Denis Dear, aged 22 and 21 respectively, when their Vickers Vellox G-ABKY crashed at 0200, just minutes after departing Croydon Airport on a night scheduled mail flight to Paris Le Bourget.

The Times reported the crash that same day under the heading 'Night Crash At Croydon - Four Killed - Experimental Freight Service'

"The Imperial Airways machine Vellox crashed about 2.15 this morning while taking off at Croydon Aerodrome for Paris on an experimental night air-freight service. There were four occupants, all of whom were killed. The machine, which burst into flames, crashed into the side of a house in Hillside Gardens, off Sandy Lane, Wallington. The Vellox was a twin-engined biplane."

The report then gives the names of the four persons on board, continuing, *"The flames involved two houses in a semi-detached block, but the fire was soon under control, One wing was within 10ft of a house.*

"Captain Orr had spent the last two months operating the service, but it was Captain Ferguson's first trip on the experimental service. Both lived in Fairfield Road, Croydon. Captain Orr was Irish and Captain Ferguson Australia. The latter was one of six Imperial Airways pilots who recently gained their first class air navigator's certificate."

The Times provided a more detailed account in their edition of 11th August 1936, of which the following is an extract, *"People who heard the roar of engines overhead had the impression that the machine was turning back to Croydon. Then came a crash, as the machine struck a house in South View Gardens, followed by a second as it hit a house in Hillside Gardens, and then hurtled into a garden and burst into flames. There was apparently no explosion either before or after the first impact. As soon as the machine struck the ground a sheet of flames burst from it and set fire to the two nearest houses.*

"People hurried out , and telephone calls were put into the Wallington and Carshalton fire brigades and to a nearby hospital. The brigades were quickly at work, and it was not long before they had mastered the fire. The occupant of one of the houses said, "Nothing could be done for the four unfortunate men in the aeroplane. Even had they survived the force of the crash, the fury of the blaze was so sudden that they had no chance of escape, and so intense the heat that no one could approach to attempt a rescue."

A contemporary newspaper report [one of many] covering the inquest which was opened on 13th August, but adjourned until 8th October 1936, appeared in the *Birmingham Daily Gazette* in their edition of Friday, 9th October 1936:

"A scene occurred at the inquest yesterday on the four victims of the Imperial Airways plane that crashed in flames at Wallington, Surrey, when Councillor H A Heath [of the Wallington Ratepayer's Association] asked if the plane was "air vicious."

"Mr. R A Patterson [representing Imperial Airways], protesting, said that he did not wish to fight on such an occasion, but he objected to the question and allegations that had been made. There were loud cries of "Hear, hear" in court.

"Accidental death" was the verdict returned, the jury stating that no blame attached to anyone. Frank Sanders, an Imperial Airways ground engineer, who was on duty at Croydon on the night of the crash, said that the plane's Certificate of Airworthiness was in the machine at the time and was burnt. He denied that the flight was a test one, as had been suggested. It was an ordinary freight one, but there was no freight on as there was none available.

"The Coroner: "Was there any low flying over adjacent property?" - "No, sir, definitely none at all."

Describing the crash, Sanders said, "We saw the tail-light dip. The machine fell straight to earth. The next thing I saw was the tail-light going down and disappearing behind the houses and then there were flames instantaneously."

"The machines, he said, were given a routine overhaul every night of the week, going into "dock" about one a year. This particular machine went in about six months ago. The defect of unequal distribution of petrol, he added, was remedied before the machine left.

"Flight-Lieut. Geoffrey William Monk, aerodrome officer, said it was obvious from the plane's movements that it was turning to get back to the aerodrome, and he switched on the lights on the side to enable to come down,

"Squadron-Ldr. Hellyer said that a ten day's examination and investigation of the machine had been made. "There was no reasonable evidence," he said, "to suggest that any part of the plane's structure or control was defective before the machine crashed."

"As a result of the examination of the engines no evidence whatever was found of a mechanical breakdown. "I think it is possible," he added, "that there was some moveable obstruction in the petrol system that I could not find because of the fire. If that is so it is possible that the trouble did not manifest itself in the previous running-up of the engines." Further questioned, he said, "It was apparently not in an airworthy condition, or it would not have crashed in the short time it did unless by some error on the part of the pilot, but I have no proof that it was un-airworthy. It was apparently adequately inspected."

"Replying to a juror, Squadron-Leader Hellyer said it would be a very rash person to say that the machine was airworthy because of the state it was in when examined after the crash.On the other hand he could not find any proof that it was not airworthy. He admitted that the engines had been flown without complaint for many hundreds of hours."

On 17th December 1936, *Flight* published the following [having in an earlier editions identified the crash site as thr back gardens of Nos. 10, 12, 14 and 16 Hillside Gardens, Croydon}:-

"It may be remembered that on August 10, Imperial Airways' Vickers Vellox crashed three minutes after taking off from Croydon on a night flight to Paris, and the Accident Department of the Air Ministry has now - four months later published the findings of the inspector.

"The machine, carrying only its crew, their personal belongings and some sand ballast, took off normally, flew straight in a south-westerly direction until it was well outside the aerodrome boundary and had climbed to a height estimated by officials on duty in the control tower to be in the neighbourhood of 500 feet, when it began to turn to the left - in the direction of the regular aerodrome circuit and towards its course for Paris.

"Shortly afterwards the turn was changed to the right, throughout about 180 degrees, the machine losing height as it did so, and ultimately crashed among houses about a quarter of a mile outside the western boundary. An outbreak of fire occurred and the four occupants lost their lives. The machine was completely destroyed.

"As a result of his investigation, the inspector of accidents came to the following conclusions:

" [a] That the accident was due to a sudden loss of engine power occurring in circumstances that were unfavourable for and may even have rendered impossible - the carrying out of a successful forced-landing.

" [b] That the cause of the sudden loss of engine power cannot be determined, but the evidence is suggestive of the starboard engine having been either the first or the only engine to fail, and

" [c] That the most likely cause was either some obstruction of the fuel system or incorrect setting of the fuel controls. A new type of engine was, incidentally, being used."

28053 PERKINS Maxwell Edmund Massy AV-M 11.04.64 Retirement

Air Vice-Marshal Maxwell Edmund Massy Perkins CB CBE mentioned in despatches, died on Friday, 9th August 1985. A technical officer, his final appointment was Director General of Engineering.

28054 PHILLIPS George Walter F/Lt 06.02.40 Relinquished

On account of ill health [LG 27 February 1940, issue 34801, page 1174]. With his health sufficiently of a standard for ground duties, George Walter Phillips was granted a commission in the Administrative and Special Duties Branch with effect from 19th June 1940 [LG 9 July 1940, issue 34892, page 4184] in the rank of pilot officer and service number 80938, though subsequently reverting to 28034. Served throughout the remainder of hostilities. S/Ldr 10.02.54 Relinquished

28055 RIDGEWAY Moray Vibart G/Capt 14.04.49 Retirement

On account of medical unfitness for Air Force service [LG 19 April 1949, supplement 38588, page 1936].

28056 SCALLY Francis Noel Desmond P/O 23.07.29 Terminated

28057 SINGER Noel Christie A/Cmdr 26.09.49 Retirement

Granted a permanent commission on 13th April 1934 [LG 17 April 1934, issue 34042, page 2471, Flying Officer Noel Christie Singer, now promoted squadron leader, was *Gazetted* with the DSO *"... for gallant and distinguished service rendered in Palestine."* [LG 28 February 1939, issue 34603, page 1393]. Subsequently commanding 101 Squadron [Blenheim IV], he was *Gazetted* with the DFC, less citation, on 17th January 1941, issue 35045, page 346]. Retirement notice, promulgated in *The London Gazette* 27th September 1949, supplement 38723, page 4610, was at his own request. Air Commodore Noel Christie Singer CBE DSO DFC twice mentioned in despatches, died on Monday, 25th March 1974. His final appointment was Deputy Director of Accident Prevention. The Air of Authority website includes two excellent photographs, one, in colour, showing his medals and a second, in black and white, identifying the types of 'Aircraft Flown' [from his flying log book showing fifty-nine in total ranging from Avro 504 to Liberator [58th] and last the DH Chipmunk.

28058 SINGLETON Henry Charles F/O + 26.10.31 13 Squadron

28064 SMITH Albert Edmund S/Ldr 10.02.54 Relinquished

28059 SMITH Robert S/Ldr 14.02.45 Resigned

28060 TODD Robert F/Lt + 14.06.36 4 Aircraft Park Atbara

While taking a repair party to the scene of a forced-landing in the desert, some 25 miles SE from Adarama, Sudan, their Vincent K4669 sides-slipped and before correction could be made it struck the ground with a force sufficient to killed everyone on board. They were named as Squadron Leader William Catchpole AFC, aged 42, Flight Lieutenant Robert Todd, aged 25, Sergeant Ernest Alfred Whetter, aged 31 and 21 year old Aircraftman William Marlow. K4669 was the 145h aircraft in a batch of 95 airframes delivered to the service between September 1935 and February 1926. Shipped to the Middle East on 23rd October 1935, it was held at 4 Aircraft Park, earmarked for issue to 45 Squadron at Helwan. Squadron Leader William Catchpole's promotion had been *Gazetted* on 1st December 1935 [LG 3 December 1935, issue 34226, page 7674].

28061 WATSON Michael A/Cmdr 01.06.54 Retirement

Air Commodore Michael Watson CB CBE twice mentioned in despatches, died in California on Friday, 22nd March 1991. A signals specialist who transferred from the General Duties Branch to the Technical Branch on 24th April 1942, his final service appointment was Director of Signals. Interestingly, prior to this appointment he had reverted to the General Duties Branch. His retirement from the Royal Air Force was at his own request, leaving the UK for America soon after and where in 1956 he was Rolls-Royce's representative to North American Aviation Inc. At his retirement in 1971, he was in the Sales Division of North American Rockwell.

28062 WHITTINGHAM Frank F/Lt 30.05.38 Relinquished

On appointment to the Air Branch of the Royal Navy [LG 12 July 1938, issue 34531, page 4540]. While serving aboard the aircraft carrier HMS *Furious* Lieutenant [A] Frank Whittingham lost his life on 18th April 1940. He is commemorated on bay 1, panel 12 at the Lee-on-Solent Memorial.

28063 WOOD David Harry Gadsdon F/O + 24.04.31 20 Squadron

28066 SLOCOCK Walter Edmund Merrick P/O 18.02.30 Terminated

Returned to service and granted a commission as a probationary Pilot Officer in the Administrative and Special Duties Branch, 16th October 1940, as 87511 [LG 26 November 1940, issue 35001, page 6761], reverting to 28066. F/Lt 10.02.54 Relinquished

14 May 1929, issue 33495, page 3242 - Seniority 1st May 1929

28067 HUMPRIES George Frederick G/Capt 10.02.54 Relinquished

First commissioned as a pilot officer in the Special Reserve on 14th November 1927 [LG 6 December 1927, issue 33335, page 7824] and relinquished on granting of a short service commission, as shown above.

LG 22 May 1929, issue 33503, pages 3693 and 3694 [6 entrants] Terms of engagement 4 years on the active list.

Block 28068 to 28073

28068 FRITH Reginald Richmond F/O 22.05.33 Relinquished
Australia On transfer to the Royal Australian Air Force Reserve [LG 23 May 1933, issue 33942, page 3457].
28069 WELLS James Murray F/O 22.05.33 Relinquished
On account of ill-health [LG 20 June 1933, supplement 33951, page 4128]. Returned to service and granted a class CC commission in the General Duties Branch, retaining his rank, with effect from 9th May 1938 [LG 13 December 1938, issue 34759, page 7921], his service number now being 74889. Transferring to the Secretarial Branch, he was appointed to a permanent commission on 6th March 1947, in the rank of squadron leader [LG 22nd July 1947, supplement 38020, page 3423]. W/Cdr 02.09.57 Retirement
28070 SAMPSON George Edward G/Capt 26.08.54 Retirement
On account of medical unfitness for Air Force service [LG 31 August 1954, supplement 40266, page 5010].
28071 GRIFFIN Robert Vernon F/O + 04.07.31 101 Squadron
Flying Officer Robert Vernon Griffin, born in Bristol during July 1905, was victim of a road traffic accident whilst attending the squadron's armament practice camp at RAF Catfoss. His death was reported in the *Leeds Mercury* on Monday, 6th July 193, under the heading 'RAF Officer Killed - Fond Dead Beside Damaged Car.'

"Flying Officer Robert Vernon Griffin, attached at the Royal Air Force Camp at Catfoss, on the East Yorkshire coast, was found lying dead on the grass verge beside a damaged car between Beeford and Brandesburton yesterday morning.

"He left Bridlington in a sports car, and it is surmised that he was thrown out and killed by the bursting of the near side front tyre Flying Officer Griffien had been at the Catfoss Camp only three days.".

28072 JORDAN Reginald Charles G/Capt + 23.06.43 126 Squadron
Australia Group Captain Reginald Charles Jordan is commemorated on panel 5 of the Malta Memorial and on the Australian War Memorial. At the time of his death, 126 Squadron was based at Safi and equipped with Spitfire VC.
28073 TULLOCH George Keith G/Capt 19.09.49 Retirement
At his own request [LG 18 October 1949, supplement 38738, page 4954].

LG 9 July 1929, issue 33515, pages 4543 and 544 - Seniority 28th June 1929 [30 entrants] Terms of engagement 5 years on the active list.

Block 28074 to 28103

28074 AGARD-BUTLER George Edward F/O 28.06.34 Class A
Thence to the Unattached List for the Indian Army from the Reserve of Air Force Officers as Lieutenant, 5th November 1938 [LG 9 December 1938, issue 34578, page 7786].
28075 ALEXANDER Norman W/Cdr 10.02.54 Relinquished
28076 ALLEN Francis Cecil F/Lt 10.02.54 Relinquished
28077 BALL Charles Abbott W/Cdr 26.06.47 Resigned
Acting Wing Commander Charles Abbott Ball was *Gazetted* with the AFC on 7th September 1945, supplement 37256, page 4485.
28078 BEARNE Guy AV-M 05.11.61 Retirement
Air Vice-Marshal Guy Bearne CB twice mentioned in despatches, died on Tuesday, 1st November 2005.
28079 CALVERT George F/O 13.05.32 Dismissed
By sentence of General Court Martial [LG 17 May 1932, issue 33826, page 3223]. The unfortunate Flying Officer George Calvert's dismissal was the subject of a report in the *Portsmouth Evening News* in its edition of Wednesday, May 18th, 1932, under the heading 'Low Flying Penalty - RAF Officer Dismissed The Service.'

"The following announcement by the Air Ministry appeared in last night's issue of the "London Gazette." Flying Officer George Calvert is dismissed the Service by sentence of General Court Martial, May 13, 1932.

Omitted from the *Gazette* it appears, *"Mr. George Calvert appeared before a court martial at Upper Heyford RAF Station, Oxford, on April 1st, last, on a charge of flying unnecessarily low over Bicester in such as was likely to cause a nuisance to the residents."*

Although conjecture on my part, I suspect that a resident [or several] of Bicester noted the low-flying aircraft's seria,l for this was a time when the aircraft's identify was emblazoned with an easily readable serial, and duly reported it to the authorities.
28080 CAPPER Noel John W/Cdr 21.04.44 Relinquished
On account of ill-health [LG 9 May 1944, supplement 36503, page 2112]. As Squadron Leader Noel John Capper was *Gazetted* with the AFC on 1st January 1941, supplement 35029, page 33.
28081 CARLYLE David Ivan P/O 18.12.29 Relinquished
On account of ill-health [LG 17 December 1929, issue 33561, page 8210].
28082 CRITCHLEY Ivor Arthur G/Capt 02.09.55 Transferred to the Reserve
28083 GLOVER Christopher Hugh F/O 28.06.34 Class A
Christopher Hugh Glover was granted the honorary rank of flight lieutenant on 7th May 1937, whilst in the General Duties Branch of the Reserve of Air Force Officers [LG 13 July 1937, issue 34417, page 4520] and, subsequently, promoted flight lieutenant on 1st April 1937 [LG 26 October 1937, issue 34447, page 6617]. His commission was amended to class CC on 7th May 1937 [LG 15 November 1938, issue 34570, page 7196]. This was relinquished on 1st September 1939 [LG 5 March 1940, issue 34805, page 1318]. At some point in his service he was appointed OBE and his service number is noted as 192470 when in the rank of flight lieutenant he was granted a class CC in the Secretarial Branch on 10th November 1947 [LG 2nd December 1947, supplement 38137, page 5709].
28084 GOLEGE-STEEL Donald Henry Alfred F/O 24.09.32 Dismissed
By sentence of General Court Martial [LG 3 January 1933, issue 33899, page 54]. HE had previous been disciplined as per the entry in *The London Gazette* 1st December 1931, issue 33776, page 7742: *"Flying Officer Donald Henry Alfred Golege-Steel takes rank and precedence as if his appointment as Flying Officer bore date 28th Mar. 1931. Reduction takes effect from 19th Oct. 1931."*
28085 GRANT William Edward F/O + 02.02.32 502 Squadron SR
Whilst attached to 502 Squadron SR at Aldergrove, Flying Officer William Edward Grant was taken seriously ill. Flown to the RAF Hospital at Halton, he died whilst undergoing treatment.
28086 HARRISON Douglas Charles F/O 28.12.55 Relinquished
With, unusually, no retention of rank.
28087 HODGE William John P/O 01.10.29 Terminated
28088 HOUGHTON Archibald Harold F/Lt + 08.10.37 14 Squadron
28089 IEVERS George Maurice F/O + 25.02.32
Flying Officer George Maurice Ievers lost his life in a road traffic accident, the details of which were reported in *The Northern Wing and Belfast Post.*

"A verdict of accidental death was returned at an inquest at Windsor on Saturday on Flying Officer George Maurice Ievers, the well-known Service Rugby footballer, who was killed in a motoring accident early on Thursday.

"Flying Officer Ievers who formerly attended Campbell College, Belfast, was return ing from London to Worthy Down, Hampshire, where he was stationed, when his car ran into the back of a stationary lorry.

"Lady Agnes Georgina Warren, of Beaufort Gardens, SW, identified the body as that of her nephew. She last saw him during the week-end. He was a teetotaller and non-smoker.

"On Wednesday afternoon, Flying Officer Ievers travelled to London to see his fiancé and they went to the theatre.

"The driver of the lorry said that he had left it at the side of the road while he went to a coffee stall. He heard a crash and found the car wedged under the back of the lorry. Flying Officer Ievers was trapped to his seat by the steering wheel. Although the brakes of the lorry were on it had been pushed several feet by the impact.

"A road patrol scout said that the rear light of the lorry, although lifted out of position, was still alight when he arrived.

"A fellow officer stated that the width of the road was .... Feet, and the lorry was right up against the kerb."

Flying Officer George Maurice Ievers is buried in Magdelen Hill Cemetery, Winchester.

28090 KEAST Francis John Baptist S/Ldr 28.04.46 Resigned

28091 LYDALL Douglas Wykeham W/Cdr 10.02.54 Relinquished

28092 McNICOL Ian Ludwig Steel F/O 10.02.54 Relinquished

New Zealand Paul McMillan report, Ian Ludwig Steel McNicol was born in Wanganui on 30th June 1907. It appears he settled in the UK for his death occurred in Grantham, Lincolnshire, on Sunday, 6th September 1992.

28092 MARRIOTT Charles Weatherley P/O 09.10.29 Resigned

28094 MELLOR Thomas Graham P/O 07.09.29 Resigned

Literally within days of his acceptance of a short service commission!

28095 MORSE Cyril Ernest G/Capt 29.07.51 Retirement

At his own request [LG 4 September 1951, supplement 39325, page 4666].

28096 MYNORS John Towers G/Capt 29.11.57 Retirement

28097 PADDON Brian G/Capt 20.02.50 Retirement

Squadron Leader Brian Paddon was *Gazetted* with the DSO on 6th October 1942, supplement 35731, page 4342, no citation appended, but it was for gallant and distinguished service with 40 Squadron with which he served in the time of the *Blitzkrieg* until 6th June 1940 when his Blenheim IV L8827 was shot down by '109s during an early morning raid on enemy forces in the St. Valéry-sur-Somme area, his crew surviving as prisoners of war. For details of his loss, please refer to page 144 of my RAFBCL 1939-1940 revised edition, and the many entries in David Gunby's superb history of 40 Squadron.

28098 PURCELL Herbert Gerard Joseph F/O 14.11.35 Relinquished

On appointment to a commission on the Unattached List for the Indian Army [LG 3 December 1935, issue 34226, page 7675].

28099 STRATTON Noel F/O 19.07.33 Resigned

28100 WADDELL John Main F/Lt 16.07.40 Relinquished

On appointment to a commission in the Royal Naval Volunteer Reserve [LG 28 March 1941, issue 35119, page 1813].

28101 WARRINGTON George Ninian G/Capt + 08.09.45 HQ RAF Northern Ireland

Group Captain George Ninian Warrington is commemorated on the Runnymede Memorial, panel 264.

28102 WILLIAMS George Elyton Sloan F/O + 24.05.34 Station Flight Andover

New Zealand Flying Officer George Elyton Sloan Williams and Corporal Robert Foley Brown died when their Armstrong Whitworth Atlas TM K2533, which was taking part in the station's 'Empire Air Day' display, spun and crashed into a wheat field at Monxton some 3 miles west of the airfield. On impact the machine burst into flames. A report on the accident was published in *Aeroplane* on 30th May 1934: *"An inquest was held at Andover on May 25. Flight Lieutenant R Hart, who was in another machine, said that he saw the Atlas go into a spin from which it did not recover. The witness said that he tried to land three times but he failed. He saw a man try to rescue the crew, but he was driven back by the flames.*

"A shepherd described how he tried to get the men out of the wreck, but failed because of the fire. The jury returned a verdict of "Accidental Death on Duty" and expressed appreciation of the efforts of the shepherd and of Flight Lieutenant Hart to effect a rescue."

Historian and author, Errol Martyn, covers the accident in his first and third volumes of his epic *For Your Tomorrow* noting in the biography for Flying Officer Williams [third volume, page 508] was born at Wairau, Marlborough on 21st September 1907, and was educated at Wellington College. On arrival in the UK he was processed through the RAF Depot at Uxbridge ahead flying training at 2 FTS Digby. Subsequently he flew Vickers Virginia bombers with 58 Squadron and was posted to Andover for duties with the Station Flight on 10th January 1934. Like many of his kins folk sport played an important part in his life, rugby and boxing [heavy weight class] being mentioned. Flying Officer Williams is buried in Penton Mewsey [Holy Trinity] Churchyard, Hampshire.

28103 WILTSHIRE Sidney Noel F/Lt 12.12.54 Relinquished

The following was promulgated in *The London Gazette* 31st January 1930, issue 33575, page 645, beneath the heading 'CENTRAL CHANCERY OF THE ORDERS OF KNIGHTHOOD' *St Jame's Palace SW.1, 31st January 1930:-*

"The KING has been graciously pleased to approve the Award of the Medal of the Military Division of the Most Excellent Order of the British Empire to the under-mentioned:- For Gallantry:- Pilot Officer Sidney Noel Wiltshire, Royal Air Force.

"For conspicuous gallantry displayed at Temple Bruer Landing Ground, Sleaford, on 21st October 1929.

"This officer, who is a pilot under instruction, was flying with his instructor, Flying Officer H E Power, in an aeroplane that crashed on landing and at one caught fire. Having extricated himself from the wrecked machine, he found that his companion's foot was caught in the wreckage and could not get out.

"Although fully realising the risk he was running, Pilot Officer Wiltshire re-entered the flames and helped Flying Officer Power to get clear, during which process he sustained burns on his neck and face. Power's clothing was by this time well alight and he would undoubtedly have lost his life but for the prompt and courageous action taken by his pupil. As it was, he was badly burnt.

"Both officers were shortly afterwards taken by air to Cranwell Hospital. The aeroplane was completely burnt out."

Flying Officer Wilshire EGM made a good recovery from his injuries, and duly qualified for his Flying Badge. For an appreciation of Flying Officer Henry Eustace Power's service, please refer to Appendix D and his entry for 3rd August 1926 [the above citation has also been appended against his entry]. In due course of time Flying Officer Wiltshire's EGM was replaced with the George Cross.

LG 27 August 1929, issue 33529, page 5569 - Seniority 6th and 15th August respectively [23 entrants] Terms of engagement for the probationary Pilot Officers 5 years on the active list.

Block 28104 to 28125

FLYING OFFICER

28126 CAREY Gordon Valentine G/Capt 10.02.54 Relinquished

28104 ABRAHAM Ralph Bagshaw G/Capt 07.01.58 Retirement

At the time of his retirement he had adopted the surname "Ward" as is explained herewith by co-author Paul McMillan: *"NOTICE is hereby given that by deeds poll each dated the 9th day of February, 1949, and duly enrolled in the Supreme Court of Judicature on the 21st day of February, 1949, THOMAS MAXFIELD WARD of West End House, Bridlington, Yorkshire, CBE DFC, a Group Captain in the Royal Air Force RALPH BAGSHAW WARD of 26 Upper West Street, Reigate, Surrey, a Wing Commander in the Royal Air Force and MOLLIE ELIZABETH WARD of 306 Grenville House, Dolphin Square, London, Spinster natural born British subjects and children of the late Albert and Florence Abraham have adopted their mother's maiden name of Ward and have renounced and abandoned their former names of Thomas Maxfield Abraham, Ralph Bagshaw Abrahm and Mollie Elizabeth Abraham respectively and have assumed in lieu thereof the names of Thomas Maxwwell Ward, Ralph Bagshaw Ward and Mollie Elizabeth Ward. - Dated this 21st day of February, 1949. LEE and PEMBERTON, 46 Lincoln's Inn Fields, London, WC.2, Solicitors for the said Thomas Maxfield Ward, Ralph Bagshaw [369] Ward and Mollie Elizabeth Ward. "*

Additional to the above, the authors are pleased to acknowledge the website hosted by the Royal School of Needlework for a 'post' dated 23rd July 2020, headed 'Back to the 1960s' and the following extract:-

"The Hastings Embroidery was the idea of Group Captain Ralph Bagshaw Ward to commemorate the 900th anniversary of the Battle of Hastings, the last time the British Isles were successfully invaded by a foreign force, but instead of focusing just on the town's history, it took a wider view of British History. It comprises 27 panels each of which featured two or three scenes which told of key events over the 900 year period. Overall more than 80 events were featured. While many of the scenes selected were famous events, one of the challenges was what should be commemorated for 1966 itself - alas, the Football World Cup ccurred too late to be considered."

Returning to his service, by early 1942, he was a flight commander attached to 12 Squadron and it was during a raid on the port of Kiel on 25th-26th February 1942, that his Wellington II Z8410 forced-landed in Denmark with failing engines and the entire crew taken prisoners of war [see my RAFBCL 1942 and page 36 for details]. Omitted, however, is the following extract from the Kings College London website, unearthed by Paul McMillan, and the deposit of a box containing material relating to Group Captain Ralph Bagshaw Ward 1911-1992: *"Born 1911; commissioned into RAF, [1929], served with 11 Sqn, RAF, North West Frontier, India, 1920-1933; Flying Officer, 1931; Flight Lt. 1936; Instructor; RAF Flying Training Command, UK, 1939; served in World War Two, 1939-1945; service with RAF Bomber Command, 1939-1942; shot down on raid on Kiel, Germany, and captured by German forces, 25 Feb 1942; POW, East Compound, Stalag Luft III, Germany, 1942-1945; member of escape committee and helped to plan 'wooden horse'POW escape [29 Oct1943; worked for Imperial Airways, 1946-1950; changed name by deed poll, from Abraham to mother's maiden name, Ward, Feb 1949; acted in and Technical Advisor for the film The Wooden Horse, released in 1950; served as Wg Cdr Administration, RAF Bletchley, Buckinghamshire, and the Air Ministry, 1952-1955; served at RAF Hullavigton, Wiltshire, 1956-1957; retired 1958; died 1992."*

Held by the Liddell Hart Archives, a much larger extract pertaining to the collection, and his service life, is also recorded on the website. Mention is made of a photograph album containing 201 mostly captioned photographs relating to his service in India.

In conclusion, his prisoner of war identity was 1446.

28105 ADAM Maurice James S/Ldr + 12.09.38 RAE Farnborough

Posted to RAE Farnborough where he commanded the Wireless and Electrical Flight, Squadron Leader Maurice James Adam AFC was killed when the aircraft, a Whitley I K7207, in which he was a member of crew as opposed to being the pilot crashed in the circumstances reported by the *Dundee Courier* and appended to the Aviation Safety Network website [ASN Wikibase Occurrence 207638] which the authors are pleased to acknowledge:

"Accidental death was the verdict at the inquest at Aldershot yesterday on the three occupants of a large RAF bomber which crashed at Farnborough, Hants., on Monday. The victims were Squadron Leader Maurice James Adam[29], of St. Andrews, holder of the world's altitude record; Flight-Lieutenant Reginald Monks [27], and Benjamin Thomas Bond [36].

"Adam commanded the Wireless and Electrical Flight of the experimental squadron at the Royal Aircraft Establishment, Farnborough, to which Monks was also attached, and Bond was a civilian technical assistant.

"Charles Wm. Brawn, a labourer, who was working near the aerodrome, said the machine took off and appeared to be flying normally when it passed. It then banked to the left over some trees and crashed behind them, bursting into flames. He managed to pull two of the occupants clear.

"Captain Percival Victor Hoare said the machine, a Whitley Bomber, reached a height of about 100 feet, flying normally until it banked very heavily and disappeared behind some trees.

"Another witness said Monks, who was piloting, had 937 hours flying experience and flown the same machine on a previous occasion. Evidence was given that the aircraft was thoroughly inspected on the morning of the accident. Everything was in perfect order.

"The Coroner, Mr. H M Foster, told the jury there appeared to be no question of neglect on anybody's part, and the would have to leave it to someone else to thrash out the cause of the accident."

As Flight Lieutenant Adam, he had in June 1937, established a new altitude record of 53,937 feet while flying a Bristol 138 [K4879] at Farnborough, for which he was *Gazetted* with the Air Force Cross on 9th June 1938, supplement 34518, page 3708.

For details regarding Flight Lieutenant Reginald Monks, a Cranwell graduate, please refer to Appendix E and the January 1930 entry.

28106 BAILEY Adam Carter W/Cdr 27.01.58 Retirement

Flight Lieutenant Adam Carter Bailey was *Gazetted* with the AFC on 1st July 1941, supplement 35204, page 3752.

28107 BANKS John Langton Cortenay F/Lt 10.02.54 Relinquished
28108 BARCLAY David F/O 04.01.55 Relinquished
28109 CARR David F/O 08.02.32 Resigned
28110 COHEN Ronald Joseph F/O 29.06.35 Relinquished
New Zealand On appointment to a commission in the Royal New Zealand Air Force [LG 11 February 1936, issue 34254, page 913].
28111 KIRKHAM Norris S/Ldr 26.08.46 Resigned
28112 LUXMOORE Arthur Noble W/Cdr + 12.05.40 144 Squadron

Wing Commander Arthur Noble Luuxmoore died during operations to Mönchengladbach on 11th-12th May 1940, when his Hampden I P1326 was crippled by *Flak* in the target area. With great skill he managed to maintain control and, subsequently, crossed the battle lines, ordering his crew to bale out; all successfully doing so. Sadly, he was unable to get clear and he died when his aircraft crashed Finnevaux [Namur] some 11km SSE of Dinant in Belgium. For additional information, please refer to page 122 of my RAFBCL 1939-1940 revised edition.

Wing Commander Arthur Noble Luxmoore is buried in Belgium at Finnevaux Communal Cemetery, his headstone inscribed with the words *"Mark The Perfect Man, And Behold The Upright; For The End Of That Man Is Peace."* Psalm 37, verse 37, from the King James Bible.

28113 McCLURE John Evelyn Crosland F/O 08.09.33 Resigned
28114 NOBLSTON Reuben Michael F/Lt + 02.03.40 6 AONS Staverton

Flight Lieutenant Reuben Michael Noblston was piloting Anson I N9879 when in crashed into a cloud shrouded ridge near Hay Bluff, a prominent hill at the northern tip of the Black Mountains overlooking the middle of the Wye Valley and the town of Hay-on-Wye. The two trainee observers and their civilian instructor survived, their names being reported as Leading Aircraftman Walter Noel Blau and J N Nightingale and Mr. R M Knight.

Flight Lieutenant Noblston is buried in Boddington [St. Mary Magdalene] Churchyard, Gloucestershire.

28115 PAGE Arthur Wilfrid Brian F/O + 07.10.32 58 Squadron
28116 PICKFORD Maurice Edward W/Cdr 06.05.56 Relinquished

As Acting Wing Commander Maurice Edward Pickford, he was *Gazetted* with the DFC, less citation, 13th October 1944, supplement 36745, page 4691, for his service with 149 Squadron [Stirling/Lancaster].

28117 SCOTT William Joseph W/Cdr 10.02.54 Relinquished

As Acting Wing Commander William Joseph Scott attached to the Central Flying School, Upavon, he was *Gazetted* with the AFC 31st March 1942, supplement 35507, page 1450. A First Bar to the award was *Gazetted* 8th June 1944, supplement 36544, page 2647. For his service with 107 Squadron [Mosquito] he was *Gazetted* with the DSO, less citation, 29th June 1945, Supplement 37154, page 3406.

28118 SHARP William Bernard John F/O 26.08.31 Dismissed

By sentence of General Court Martial [LG 8 September 1931, issue 33751, page 5831].

28119 STONEY George Edward Bowes F/Lt + 18.08.40 501 Squadron AAF

Flight Lieutenant Edward George Bowes Stoney died when his Hurricane I P2549 was shot down by Me.110s during an evening patrol over the Thames Estuary. His body was recovered and laid to rest in Sefton [St. Helen] Churchyard, Lancashire. His headstone bears the simple inscription *"Dearly Loved Husband Of Aileen H B Bowes Stoney."*

His death came during the daily air battles associated with the *Battle of Britain* and for 501 Squadron AAF operating out of Gravesend, the 18th was a particular hard day with six of their Hurricanes shot down. Four pilots, some wounded, managed to bale out but two were killed, Flight Lieutenant Stoney being one and Pilot Officer John Wellburn Bland [Hurricane I P3208 SD-T] the other.

28120 STROUD Graham Robertson W/Cdr 20.09.55 Relinquished
28121 WATSON Leslie F/O 15.08.38 Relinquished

28122 WEST Ralph Leonard F/Lt 07.06.38 Relinquished
On appointment to the Air Branch of the Royal Navy [LG 12 July 1938, issue 34531, page 4540].
28123 WOOD Allan Morton P/O 05.01.30 Terminated

28124 ATKINS John Croft S/Ldr + 12.09.41 40 Squadron
Squadron Leader John Croft Atkins failed to return from operations to Frankfurt on 12th-13th September 1941, his Wellington IC R1328 BL-T being last heard on wireless at 2206 indicating the port engine had failed. Squadron Leader Atkins is buried in Rheinberg War Cemetery; for further information, please refer to page 145 of my RAFBCL 1941.
28125 POOLE Edward F/Lt 10.02.54 Relinquished

LG 10 September 1929, issue 33533, page 5855 - Seniority 30th August 1929 [12 entrants] Terms of engagement 5 years on the active list.

Block 28127 to 28138

28127 CASS Kenneth Maxwell F/O 30.08.34 Class A
Flying Officer Kenneth Maxwell Cass, whilst in the Reserve of Air Force Officers, was promoted flight lieutenant 1st April 1937 [LG 26 October 1937, issue 34447, page 6617]. During the Second World War he was attached to BOAC and in the New Year's Honours list for 1947, received the King's Commendation for Valuable Services in the Air [LG 1 January 1947, supplement 37835, page 27].
28128 CLAY Herbert Robert F/Lt 10.02.54 Relinquished
28129 CUBITT Leonard Alexander S/Ldr 08.10.39 Relinquished
On appointment to to the Royal Navy [LG 1 July 1954, supplement 40229, page 4094]. Postwar received a commission in the Royal Air Force Volunteer Reserve [Training Branch]. W/Cdr 17.10.57 Relinquished
28130 DIXON Geoffrey Good F/Lt 10.02.54 Relinquished
28131 FRAYLING Gerard Dunstan Warren P/O 19.04.30 Relinquished
On account of ill-health [LG 6 May 1930, issue 33603, page 2800].
28132 HEATH Douglas Walter Harman F/Lt 10.02.54 Relinquished
28133 HITCHEN-KEMP Robert John Brooks P/O 21.01.30 Terminated
28134 MIDDLETON Hugh de Montmorency S/Ldr + 06.02.43 RAF Ashbourne
Flying Officer Hugh de Montmorency was granted a commission in class CC and granted the acting rank of flight lieutenant with effect from 1st October 1938 [LG 13 December 1938, issue 34579, page 7921]. This class CC commission was relinquished on appointment to a commission in the Royal Air Force Volunteer Reserve on 1st September 1939, continuing in the General Duties Branch [LG 5 December 1939, issue 34747, page 8107]. His death in SSQ Ashbourne was owing to very high blood pressure which led to a haemorrhage of the brain and heart failure. Squadron Leader Hugh de Montmorency was buried with full military honours in Ashbourne Cemetery. A simple *"R.I.P."* adorns his headstone.
28135 PARKHOUSE Reginald John F/O 19.05.36 Removed
Flying Officer Reginald John Parkhouse's removal from the Service was promulgated in *The London Gazette* 2nd June 1936, issue 34290, page 3527.
28136 RICHARDSON Alfred Clayton S/Ldr 07.12.43 Resigned
28137 TATNALL James Benjamin W/Cdr + 15.02.44 7 Squadron
Wing Commander James Benjamin Tatnall OBE lost his life on 15th-16th February 1944, on the penultimate raid by Bomber Command in what is historically referred to as the *Battle of Berlin.* Accompanying Squadron Leader John Alfred Hegman DSO DFC RNZAF, their Lancaster III JB414 MG-Y was shot down in the vicinity of Berlin where both officers are buried in Berlin 1939-1945 War Cemetery.
Additional information regarding the loss of this Path Finder Force crew can be found on page 74 of my RAFBCL 1944. As Acting Group Captain James Benjamin Tatnall was appointed OBE in the 1944 New Year's Honours List [LG 1 January 1944, supplement 36309, page 17].
28138 TRAVIS Heber P/O 21.01.30 Terminated

LG 17 September 1929, issue 33535, page 5970 - Seniority 30th August 1929

29139 NOBLE Roger Cholmley P/O 30.01.31 Resigned
Obtained a commission as 2nd Lieutenant in the Supplementary Reserve of Officers attached to the Inniskilling Fusiliers [LG 12 May 1931, issue 33715, page 3071].

LG 24 September 1929, issue 33527, page 6103 - Seniority 13th September 1929 [31 entrants]

Block 28140 to 28170

28140 ADAMS Harold George F/lt + 08.10.37 144 Squadron
28141 BELL Sidney Horace S/Ldr 15.05.60 Relinquished
Born in Liss, Hampshire on 3rd March 1903, Paul McMillan reports Squadron Leader Sidney Horace bell died during the month of May 1998 in the West Sussex town of Chichester.
Promoted flight lieutenant whilst in the Reserve of Air Force Officers with effect from 1st April 1937 [LG 26 October 1937, issue 34447, page 6617]. Granted a class CC commission as Flying Officer [honorary Flight Lieutenant] 10th October 1938 [LG 13 December 1938, issue 34579, page 7921]; relinquished 3rd September 1939 [LG 5 March 1940, issue 34805, page 1318].
28142 BOITEL-GILL Derek Pierre Aumale W/Cdr + 18.09.41 59 OTU Crosby-on-Eden
Promoted flight lieutenant whilst in the Reserve of Air Force Officers with effect from 1st April 1937 [LG 26 October 1937, issue 34447, page 6617]. Wing Commander Derek Pierre Aumale Boitel-Gill DFC died after failing to recover from a dive at Crosby-on-Eden, his Hurricane I V6998 smashing into the station's fuel dump; he was cremated at West Norwood Crematorium where his name is commemorated on the crematorium's screen wall. As Flight Lieutenant Boitel-Gill he participated in the *Battle of Britain* attached to 152 Squadron [Spitfire].
28143 BRUCE John Charles Langlois P/O 10.10.30 Terminated
28144 CHAPMAN Richmond Rougier P/O 01.01.30 Terminated
28145 CHISWELL Lawrence Edward S/Ldr 19.12.58 Relinquished
28146 COLEMAN George Byrne Stanislaus S/Ldr 30.09.45 Resigned
28147 DAVIES Cecil Rhys S/Ldr + 24.12.41 224 Squadron
According to Ross McNeill's Coast Command losses Squadron Leader Cecil Rhys Davies and his crew died when their Hudson V AM669 QX-F failed to return to St. Eval from a 'Stepper Patrol.' It is highly likely that the Hudson came down in the Channel for he, along with Sergeant Tom Ford Houldsworth, are buried in Bayeux War Cemetery, while the remainder of the crew are commemorated on the Runnymede Memorial. For further information, please refer to page 172 of *Royal Air Force Coastal Command Losses of the Second World War.*
28148 DAVYS John Llewellyn Mapletoft F/O 13.09.34 Class A
Promoted flight lieutenant whilst in the Reserve of Air Force Officers with effect from 1st April 1937 [LG 26 October 1937, issue 34447, page 6618], John Llewellyn Mapletoft Davys joined BOAC and was commended for his valuable services in the air, the announcement being *Gazetted* in the New Year's Honours List for 1944, supplement 36312, page 75.

28149 EGAN Stephen William Huntley S/Ldr 15.02.54 Relinquished
Paul McMillan adds, Stephen William Huntley Egan was during July 1904 in Hendon, Middlesex and died in the same county, but in Westminster, on Friday, 16th March 1962.
28150 EGERTON-HINE Greville P/O 10.09.30 Terminated
28151 FRASER Thomas Naylor P/O 15.10.30 Terminated
28152 HAMILTON John Stewart F/O 30.07.38 Relinquished
28153 HANSFORD Clifford James F/O 12.06.40 Relinquished
On account of ill-health [LG 25 June 1940, issue 34881, page 3867].
28154 HEPWORTH John Nigel P/O 02.09.30 Terminated
28155 HOOPER Laurence Mayleston W/Cdr 05.02.53 Retirement
28156 HOSKEN Raymond George P/O 18.02.30 Terminated
28157 HYDE Noel Challis A/Cmdr 20.11.62 Retirement
Air Commodore Noel Challis Hyde CBE mentioned in despatches, died on Saturday, 12th December 1987. Whilst commanding 207 Squadron, Wing Commander Noel Challis Hyde was shot down during operations to Kiel on 8th-9th April 1941, his Manchester I L7302 EM-R being successfully abandoned [see my RAFBCL 1941 page 38]. For the remainder of the war he was incarcerated in Stalag-Luft III where his prisoner of war identity was 628. For additional reading, I recommend Robert Kirby's *Avro Manchester - The Legend behind the Lancaster* [Midland Publishing Limited, 1995] where his operational record is shown as:

24-25.02.41	Brest	Machester I L7300	
12-13.03.41	Hamburg	Manchester I L7303 EM-P	
08-09.04.41	Brest	Manchester I L7302 EM-R	Failed to return

Air Commodore Hyde's final appointment was Commandant of the RAF Staff College at Andover.
28158 MATSON Bernard Nelson G/Capt + 04.05.44
Group Captain Bernard Nelson Matson is buried in Delhi War Cemetery where his headstone is inscribed *"To The Glorious Memory Of My Beloved Husband. Until The Day Break, My Love."*
28159 MOUATT Laurence Rayson S/Ldr 21.06.54 Relinquishe
As Squadron Leander Laurence Rayson Mouatt Mentioned in despatches 14th June 1945, supplement 37119, page 2993.
28160 NODDINGS Eric Edward F/Lt + 22.04.41 9 SFTS Hullavington
While giving night flying instruction to Leading Aircraft James Arthur Baxter Day their Master I T8468 at the Babdown Farm satellite control was lost on becoming airborne, owing to incorrect trim setting, and the trainer stalled into the ground just to the south-southwest of the airfield. Flight Lieutenant Eric Edward Noddings is buried in Hartlepool [Stranton] Cemetery.
28161 PARKER Robert Clive F/O 13.09.34 Class A
Promoted flight lieutenant whilst in the Reserve of Air Force Officers with effect from 1st April 1937 [LG 26 October 1937, issue 34447, page 6618], Robert Clive Parker joined BOAC and was commended for providing valuable services in the air, *Gazetted* 9th January 1946, supplement 37412, page 338. Subsequently, in the Queen's Birthday Honours List, 5th June 1952, supplement 39555, page 3012, he was appointed to the Royal Victorian Order - To be a Member of the Fourth Class.
28162 ROOME Ian Napier S/Ldr 10.02.54 Relinquished
28163 SAYERS Keith Norman W/Cdr 02.06.56 Retirement
As Flight Lieutenant Keith Norman Sayers he was *Gazetted* with the AFC 1st April 1941, issue 35214, page 1903.
28164 SEABOURN George Douglas P/O 16.01.30 Terminated
28165 SIMONS Mervyn William P/O 18.02.30 Terminated
28166 SLOCUM Sydney Dennis F/O + 03.03.40 224 Squadron
Flying Officer Sydney Dennis Slocum rests in Micheldever [St. Mary\ Churchyard, Hampshire. His death occurred in tragic circumstances when his Hudson I N7334, attached to No. 2 Camouflage Unit Heston was shot down by a Hurricane near Gravesend. Details of the tragedy, in which at least two of his crew perished, are recorded in AIR 81/99.
28167 TEACHER John Angus MacDonald P/O 14.10.30 Terminated
28169 WARD Harold James P/O 02.06.31 Relinquished
On account of ill-health [LG 2 June 1931, issue 33721, page 3559].
28169 WASHER Charles Alan F/Lt 27.08.38 Relinquished
28170 WILSON Hugh Joseph G/Capt 20.06.48 Retirement
At his own request. As Acting Squadron Leader Hugh Joseph Wilson he was *Gazetted* with the AFC 1st January 1941, supplement 35029, page 33.

LG 11 October 1929, issue 33542, page 6478 - Seniority 23rd September 1929 [3 entrants]

Block 28171 to 28173

28171 NICHOLSON John Aristotle F/O 19.12.32 Resigned
Paul McMillan reports that in the case of Pilot Officer John Aristotle Nicholson 'survived' three General Court Martial, explained as follows:-
"Pilot Officer John Aristotle Nicholson takes rank and precedence as if his appointment as Pilot Officer bore date 23rd Mar. 1930. Reduction to take effect from 23rd Feb. 1931."
"Flying Officer [he was promoted 14th October 1931, issue 33774, page 7585] *John Aristotle Nicholson takes rank and precedence as if his appointment as Flying Officer bore date 13th Apr. 1932. Reduction takes effect from the same date."*
"Flying Officer John Aristotle Nicholson takes rank and precedence as if his appointment as Flying Officer bore date 13th Oct. 1932, immediately following Flying Officer Peter Heylin Heygate on the gradation list. Reduction takes effect from 19th Dec. 1932."

The respective entries in *The London Gazette* were 28 April 1931, issue 33711, page 2738, 14 June 1932, issue 33835, page 3876 and 14 March 1933, issue 33921, page 1781.

Leaving the Service, it seems his penchant for low-flying continued and he appeared in court in 1933, where he was fined for *"hedge-hopping*' in the vicinity of Bottisham, Cambridgeshire. His address was given as Eardley Crescent, Earl's Court. This, my co-author, located in the *Police Gazette*. Sadly, there was more to come as the following piece from the *Nottingham Journal* of Thursday, 23rd November 1939, reveals:-

"A retired colonel's daughter and three men were at the Old Bailey yesterday found guilty of conspiring to cheat and defraud such persons as might be induced to give them credit and cash in exchange for worthless cheques. They were Mrs. John Arethusa Scott[37] of Redcliffe-square, Earl's Court, London; John Aristotle Nicholson [38], air pilot; Charles Kendall Gratton-Bushe [23] air pilot; and Douglas James Gillis [34] solicitor.

"Nicholson was sentenced to twelve months' imprisonment. Sentence on the others was postponed until the next sessions."

Released, and with the Second World War in progress, John Aristotle Nicholson volunteered his services and was accepted as a non-commissioned officer in the Royal Air Force Volunteer Reserve . Undergoing [the authors suspect] refresher flying at 5 FTS Ternhill he was killed when his Master I N7894 struck a tree whilst low-flying some 6 miles north of Uttoxeter, Staffordshire, on the 2nd of May 1941, details of the accident being contained in AIR 81/6194.

Sergeant John Aristotle Nicholson, 29 years of age and married, was laid to rest in market Drayton Cemetery. His parents, who when the registers were compiled, were living in India requested the following inscription *"In Proud And Loving Memory Of Our Eldest Son."*

So, tragically, the numerous past warnings from his superiors about the dangers inherent when flying an aeroplane at very low altitude went unheeded and, eventually, led to his death. Nevertheless, his name will be included in the Roll of Honour appended to this appendix.

28172 STRANRAER-MULL Gerald Willis P/O 09.01.30 Terminated

28173 TANNER Joseph Seymour F/Lt + 01.05.34 RAFC Cranwell

Please refer to Appendix D 1928 and the entry for 17th January 1928. Flight Lieutenant Joseph Seymour Tanner and Flight Cadet John Aickin Plugge of New Zealand died when their Bulldog Trainer K3928 collided in the air, near Digby, with Hart Trainer K3152 flown by Flying Officer Dennis John Douthwaite who was instructing Flight Cadet John Askell Rutherford. There were no survivors from either aircraft.

Please refer to Appendix E and the September 1927 entry, which names Dennis John Douthwaite, and the report of the accident as published in *The Sydney Morning Herald.*

LG 15 October 1929, issue 33543, page 6551 - Seniority 30th September 1929 - terms of engagement 3 years on the active list.

HONORARY SQUADRON LEADER

KENNY-LEVECK MBE Vivian Mortimer S/Ldr 28.06.30 Relinquished

Major in the Reserve of Army Officers On account of ill-health [LG 1 July 1930, issue 33621, page 4114]. His health continued to fail and he died on the 1st of April 1942 [initially granted a short service commission in 1923; please refer to Appendix D and 18th September 1923].

LG 22 October 1929, issue 33545, page 6692 and 6693 - Seniority 11th October 1929 [30 entrants] Terms of engagement 5 years on the active list.

Block 28174 to 28203

28174 ADYE Capel Francis Goodson F/Lt + 26.05.40 17 Squadron

Flight Lieutenant Capel Francis Goodson Adye is commemorated on panel 4 of the Runnymede Memorial having lost his life during *Operation Dynamo* when his Hurricane I P3483 was shot down during a patrol over the evacuation beaches and bailing out he fell into the sea.

An excellent biography of his life can be read on the Kenley Revival website, extracts of which read [which the authors are delighted to acknowledge]: *"At the end of his five year commission in October 1934he was transferred to the Reserve as a flying officer. He immediately left for Canada and remained there for the next five years until, following the outbreak of war, he was recalled to the colours. He arrived back in Southampton, aboard the "Aquitania," on 30 September 1939."*

A lengthy resume of his reintroduction to flying follows, including his time with 213 Squadron [Hurricane] before joining 17 Squadron at Martlesham Heath on 15th May 1940, and thence following a plethora of movements, to Kenley on 24th May 1940, the report concluding: *"After landing and refuelling at Hawkinge, the squadron again took off with six Hurricanes of 79 Squadron, however, their formation only comprised fifteen aircraft, to patrol Calais and Dunkirk. The patrol was uneventful but as they headed home they were bounced by three Me.109s, they managed to bring one down. Flight Lieutenant Adye was not so lucky."*

28175 ALDERSON Christopher Perceval Forrest F/O 16.05.32 Relinquished

On account of ill-health [LG 17 May 1932, issue 33826, page 3223].

28176 BALDWIN Ivor Osborne S/Ldr 23.02.54 Relinquished

28177 BAXTER John Neville G/Capt 31.05.58 Retirement

28178 BERTRAM Neville Vezey F/O 11.10.34 Relinquished

On account of ill-health [LG 16 October 1934, issue 34096, page 6556].

28179 BONSEY Bruce William Edmund Robert W/Cdr 16.07.54 Relinquished

28180 CANDLER Maurice Quartano G/Capt 11.10.55 Retirement

28181 COKE William Otway Jacynth P/O 24.06.31 Terminated

28182 DAWSON Vincent Augustine S/Ldr 01.08.58 Retirement

Appointed to a permanent commission in Flight Lieutenant rank, 1st January 1949, and transferred from the General Duties Branch to the Secretarial Branch [LG 10 May 1949, supplement 38605, page 2285].

28183 DUNMAN Charles Cecil Morgan P/O 02.08.30 Terminated

28184 DUNVILLE Thomas Edward P/O 15.01.30 Resigned

28185 DUNWORTH Felix Patrick Raphael S/Ldr 06.08.54 Removal

Emergency list commission [LG 15 March 1955, supplement 40429, page 1534].

28186 FOSTER-PACKER Noel F/O 27.10.36 Relinquished

On appointment to a commission in the South African Air Force Special Reserve of flying officers [LG 12 January 1937, issue 34359, page 269]. Returned to Royal Air Force service and granted a Class A commission in the Reserve of Air Force Officers, General Duties Branch, retaining his rank and with effect from 17th October 1939, as 70943 [LG 27 October 1939, supplement 34718, page 7181]. My co-author states Flight Lieutenant Foster-Packer was still included in the Air Force List published in 1945. After leaving the service, the date not being established, he returned to Africa where his death occurred on 11th August 1957, in Iringa Tanganyika Territory, East Africa.

28187 GAHAN Henry Michael F/O 12.02.36 Relinquished

On appointment to a commission on the Unattached List for the Indian Army [LG 31 March 1936, issue 34269, page 2081].

28188 HAYWARD Frank Bernard Howard

28189 HILL Noel

28190 JOHNSTONE Meuric Vivian F/O + 27.07.38 Imperial Airways

Whilst in the Reserve of Air Force Officers Flying Officer Meuric Vivian Johnstone was employed by Imperial Airways in whose service he lost his life when the Armstrong Whitworth 15 Atlanta G-ABTG *Amalthea* crashed at Kisum, Kenya. Also killed were First Officer John Everitt Ray, aged 22, Maurice James Gough, aged 29 and described as a ground engineer and wireless engineer Trevor Morris. The Atlanta was a high wing four-engined airliner of which eight were ordered by Imperial Airways. A photograph of G-ABTG taken at Moshi may be obtained from Getty Images, Three sizes, small, medium and large are advertised at £150.00, £250.00 and £3750.00 respectively.

28191 LAMB Norman Daniel F/O + 09.05.33 Aircraft Park Lahore

Flying Officer Norman Daniel Lamb was critically injured when the Hawker Hart that he was air testing crashed at, or near, Lahore on the 5th of May 1933. He died from his injuries four days later.

28192 LAWSON George Walter F/O + 19.12.31 SF Boscombe Down

The circumstances of Flying Officer George Walter Lawson's death are described in the 1923 appendix for short service commissioned officers against the entry for Flight Lieutenant George Justice Southam who was *Gazetted* 25th September 1923.

28193 McGREGOR-CHEERS Duncan P/O 26.03.30 Terminated

28194 MAHON Lionel Edward Patrick F/O + 12.06.32 54 Squadron

Flying Officer Lionel Edward Patrick Mahon died while undergoing treatment in RAF Hospital Uxbridge.

28195 MILSON Denis Edwin W/Cdr 10.02.54 Relinquished

28196 MOODY William Stevenson P/O 20.02.30 Terminated

28197 MYERS Philip Edmund Leo Augustine P/O 11.08.30 Terminated

28198 RAYNEAU Robert William Henry F/O 10.06.32 Dismissed

By sentence of General Court Martial.

28199 REED Edgar George S/Ldr 10.02.54 Relinquished

28200 SMITH Philip Arthur P/O 16.03.31 Dismissed

By sentence of General Court Martial [LG 24 March 1931, issue 33701, page 1991].

28201	SUTTON	John Frederick	F/O	+	29.04.32	502 Squadron SR
28202	WILLIAMS	Charles Harry	W/Cdr		03.02.57	Retirement

Transferred from the General Duties Branch to the Administrative and Special Duties Branch Squadron Leader Charles Harry Williams was appointed to a permanent commission on 20th March 1947, and transferred to the Secretarial Branch [LG 10 June 1947, supplement 37981, page 2621].

28203	WORRALL	Stanley Myddleton	P/O	15.09.30	Terminated

LG 12 November 1929, issue 33551, page 7308 - Seniority 21st October 1929

28205	CANNING	Philip Francis	G/Capt	24.05.54	Retirement

Previously commissioned in the Special Reserve

LG 3 December 1929, issue 33557, page 7868

28206	MORRIS	Edward Michael	W/Cdr	01.01.44

Previously commissioned in the Special Reserve

ROLL OF HONOUR
FOR
1929 SHORT SERVICE COMMISSION
OFFICERS

F/O	ABBOTT	Frederick Ernest	1 October 1931	208 Squadron
F/Lt	ADAM AFC	Maurice James	12 September 1938	RAE Farnborough
F/Lt	ADAMS	Harold George	8 October 1937	14 Squadron
F/Lt	ADYE	Capel Francis Goodson	26 May 1940	17 Squadron
S/Ldr	ATKINS	John Croft	12 September 1941	40 Squadron
F/Lt	BANKS	William Noel Hamilton	7 April 1938	233 Squadron
F/O	BEATON	Reginald Ernest Hardy	18 October 1933	101 Squadron
F/O	BISHOP	Eric Douglas	5 December 1932	7 Squadron
W/Cdr	BOITEL-GILL DFC	Derek Pierre Aumale	18 September 1941	59 OTU Crosby-on-Eden
W/Cdr	BOOTH	Arthur Frank Calvert	12 July 1941	107 Squadron
F/O	BROWN	John Arrowsmith	20 March 1933	5 Squadron
F/O	CROW	Cedric Rex	26 October 1935	Railway Services Limited
S/Ldr	DAVIES	Cecil Rhys	24 December 1941	224 Squadron
Lr Cdr	ESMONDE VC	Eugene	12 February 1942	825 Squadron FAA
W/Cdr	FARNHILL	Geoffrey	5 April 1941	Aircraft Depot Far East
F/O	GILL	Charles Sydney	17 August 1936	British Airways Limited
F/O	GOAD	Frederick Robert Walter	4 November 1930	9 Squadron
F/O	GRANT	William Edward	2 February 1932	502 Squadron SR
F/O	GRIFFIN	Robert Vernon	4 July 1931	101 Squadron
F/Lt	HOUGHTON	Archibald Harold	8 October 1937	14 Squadron
F/O	IEVERS	George Maurice	25 February 1932	
P/O	JACKSON	Malcolm Menzies	10 May 1929	1 FTS Netheravon
F/O	JOHNSTONE	Meuric Vivian	27 July 1938	Imperial Airways Limited
G/Capt	JORDAN Australia	Reginald Charles	23 June 1943	126 Squadron
W/Cdr	KNOCKER	Kenneth Duke	3 July 1942	214 Squadron
F/O	LAMB	Norman Daniel	9 May 1933	Aircraft Park Lahore
F/O	LARMUTH	Alfred Churchill	3 July 1938	Railway Services Limited
F/O	LAWSON	George Walter	19 December 1931	Station Flight Boscombe Down
F/O	LEMON	Frank	12 January 1931	29 Squadron
W/Cdr	LONGFIELD	Geoffrey Phelps	26 February 1943	105 Squadron
W/Cdr	LUXMOORE	Arthur Noble	12 May 1940	144 Squadron
S/Ldr	L'AMY	Henry Vernon	28 August 1944	
F/O	MAHON	Lionel Edward Patrick	12 June 1932	54 Squadron
G/Capt	MATSON	Bernard Nelson	4 May 1944	
W/Cdr	MAY	Peter Rodriguez	13 July 1943	296 Squadron
F/O	McHARDY	Louis	30 October 1931	504 Squadron SR
S/Ldr	MEGAN	Eric Jack Kennedy	26 February 1941	8 AACU Old Sarum
S/Ldr	MIDDLETON	Hugh de Montmorency	6 February 1943	RAF Ashbourne
F/Lt	MILES	John Stuart Dixon	17 January 1941	1 PRU Benson
F/O	MONROE	Walter Sydney	19nJanuary 1931	7 Squadron
F/O	MUSSON Souther Rhodesia	George Bertram	14 September 1942	BOAC
Sgt	NICHOLSON	John Aristotle	2 May 1941	5 FTS Ternhill
F/Lt	NOBLSTON	Reuben Michael	2 March 1940	6 AONS Staverton
F/O	NODDINGS	Eric Edward	22 April 1941	9 FTS Hullavington
F/O	ORR	Lionel Frank Hasting	10 August 1936	Imperial Airways Limited
F/O	PAGE	Arthur Wilfrid Brian	7 October 1932	58 Squadron
P/O	PRATT	Percy James	24 March 1930	58 Squadron
F/O	ROBERTSON	Harold Bertie	25 March 1939	34 E&RFTS Rochford
F/Lt	SHARP	Eric Granville	14 June 1941	Bristol Aeroplane Company
F/O	SINGLETON	Henry Charles	26 October 1931	13 Squadron
F/O	SLOCUM	Sydney Dennis	3 May 1940	224 Squadron attached 2 Camouflage Unit Heston
F/Lt	STONEY	Edward George Bowes	18 August 1940	501 Squadron AAF
F/O	SUTTON	John Frederick	29 April 1932	502 Squadron SR
P/O	SWAINE	Reginald Montague	11 July 1929	1 FTS Netheravon
F/Lt	TANNER	Joseph Seymour	1 May 1934	RAFC Cranwell
W/Cdr	TATNALL OBE	James Benjamin	15 February 1944	7 Squadron
F/Lt	TODD	Robert	14 June 1936	4 Aircraft Park Atbara

G/Capt	WARRINGTON	George Ninian	8 September 1945	HQ RAF Northern Ireland
F/O	TUNNARD	Arthur John	13 April 1937	Edinburgh Flying Club
Lt[A]	WHITTINGTON	Frank	18 April 1940	HMS *Furious*
F/O	WILLIAMS New Zealand	George Elyton Sloan	24 May 1934	Station Flight Andover
F/O	WOOD	David Harry Gadston	24 April 1931	20 Squadron

Note. The entries where civilian airlines, flying clubs et al are shown, the deceased had been transferred to the Reserve of Air Force Officers.

Appendix D - RAFC Cranwell

Commandant
Air Vice-Marshal Frederick Crosby Halahan CMG CBE DSO MVO mentioned in despatches
Air Commodore Arthur Murray Longmore CB DSO mentioned in despatches

On the 1st of February 1929, the RAF [Cadet] College Cranwell was re-titled Royal Air Force College Cranwell. Air Commodore Longmore assumed command on 16th December 1929.

January 1929 intake : 22

26171 BAKER* Maurice William L'Isle La Vallette W/Cdr + 21.02.45 196 Squadron
Wing Commander Maurice William L'Isle La Vallette Baker mentioned in despatches was shot down in Stirling IV LJ894 7T-W during operations on the night 21st-22nd February 1945, his target being a bridge at Rees in Germany. Some sources suggest his aircraft fell victim to 'friendly fire.' He had commanded 196 Squadron [Stirling IV] since August 1944. Buried in Holland at Mierlo War Cemetery his headstone is in inscribed thus *"To Our Most Beloved Husband, Son And Brother "In Our Hearts He Is Living Yet.""* During his time at the College, where he was placed in B Squadron, he excelled at soccer, hockey and boxing.

Air Britain's *The Stirling File* indicated his aircraft was hit by *Flak* and crashed at Rips [De Rips] in the province of Noord Brabant, east of Helmond. It had flown a total of fourteen operational sorties as 7T-W, some of these during Operation *Market Garden.*

26173 BENNETT* Hubert Thomas G/Capt 23.06.61 Retirement
Born on 26th October 1910 in Rugby, Warwickshire, Group Captain Hubert Thomas Bennett died on Monday, 23rd June 2003.

26174 BROAD* Harold Peter G/Capt 01.09.57 Retirement
Group Captain Harold Peter Broad CBE DFC twice mentioned in despatches and Officer of Legion of Merit [USA], died on Monday, the 1st of February 1988, in Hertfordshire. His DFC was awarded for his operational tour, as a squadron leader, flying Hampdens with 44 Squadron [LG 17th January 1941, issue 35045, page 346]. He was appointed CBE in the New Year's Honours List for 1946 [LG 1 January 1946, issue 37407, page 34]. His American honour, conferred by the President of the United States, was *Gazetted* on 27th November 1945, supplement 37366, page 5756.

CAZALET* Robert Travers S/Ldr + 16.02.39 A&AEE Martlesham Heath
Squadron Leader Robert Travers Cazalet was killed, along with Mr. Richard Peter Alston, a Senior Scientific Officer at the Royal Aircraft Establishment, Farnborough, during a flight test in Harvard I N7000 which spun into the ground at Eyke, a Suffolk village a couple of miles NE of Woodbridge. Squadron Leader Cazalet is buried in Holbrook [All Saints] Churchyard.

Their deaths were reported in *The Times* in its edition of Saturday 18th February 1939: *"An anti-spin parachute, designed to assist pilots to regain control of aeroplanes in a spin, was described at the inquest , held at Martlesham, near Ipswich, yesterday, on the bodies of Squadron Leader Robert Travers Cazalet, RAF, 27, and his passenger, Richard Peter Alston, 32, of Windlesham, Surrey, a Scientific Officer attached to the RAF Establishment at Farnborough, Hants, who were killed when one of the new North American Harvard trainers crashed and took fire at Eyke, near Ipswich on Thursday. They had flown from Farnborough to test the aeroplane, which had been in use for about eight weeks.*

"Squadron Leader S W D Collis, of the RAF Station Martlesham Heath, said that before Squadron Leader Cazalet took off he showed him the controls of the anti-spin parachute. Cazalet remarked, "I shall not need that as I am not going to spin the machine." The parachute was to assist a pilot who dropped into a spin to regain control of the machine.

"Pilot Officer W J Carr said that the machine had been flown continuously while at Martlesham and had not shown any faults. The flight was specially to enable the scientific officer to give his opinion of the aeroplane.

"Describing the crash, Superintendent C F Quarn of the RAC, Ipswich, a former member of the Royal Fling Corps, said that when the aeroplane was 3,000ft up, it got into a flat spin. It did six spins and then straightened out, but it got into another spin and this time the pilot could not regain control, Medical evidence was that both men were killed instantly."

Squadron Leader Cazalet's brother, Flying Officer Alexander Brise Travers Cazalet, serving with 107 Squadron at Wattisham failed to return from operations to Ostend on 8th-9th September 1940, his Blenheim IV T1851 being lost without trace [see page 203 of my RAFBCL 1939-1940 revised edition].

26176 CECIL-WRIGHT* John Patrick G/Capt 28.01.51 Retirement
Group Captain John Patrick Cecil-Wright died in Cornwall towards the end of March 1992.

26178 COSLETT* Thomas Norman AM 20.07.66 Retirement
Air Marshal Sir Norman Coslett KCB OBE, died on Monday, 9th November 1987. Gaining a scholarship to the College post-aircraft apprentice at Halton, Flight Cadet Thomas Norman Coslett represented the College at rugby football and in the boxing ring. Attending the Officers' Engineering Course at the Home Aircraft Depot, Henlow in 1934, his service from then on was slanted towards specialising in technical matters and in April 1940, he transferred from the General Duties Branch to the Technical Branch. Twice during his service ass a senior officer he was posted to America, first, in 1942, as a liaison officer with the United States aircraft manufacturers and with the United States Army Air Force and postwar he was attached for three years [1950-1953] to Wright Field near Dayton, Ohio. After leaving the service he took up a directorship with Alan Cobham's Flight Refuelling.

26177 EELES* Henry A/Cmdr 29.01.59 Retirement
Air Commodore Henry Eeles CB CBE twice mentioned in despatches, died in Warminster, Wiltshire, on Wednesday 15th July 1992. He is buried at Sutton Veny [St. Leonard] Churchyard; a photograph of his grave appears on the Find a Grave website.

Harrow educated, he held one squadron command, that being 263 Squadron [Hurricane/Whirlwind] from June to December 1940. He was the squadron's second commanding officer, succeeding Squadron Leader John William Donaldson DSO whose life was lost when the aircraft carrier HMS *Glorious* was sunk during passage from Norway home waters. Then, having overseen the transition from the Hurricane to the Whirlwind, handing over the reigns of office to Squadron Leader Munro.

26179 GASKELL* Reginald Charles G/Capt 01.04.48 Retirement
Group Captain Reginald Charles Gaskell died in Australia at Bowral in New South Wales on Monday, 30th May 1988. Co-author Paul McMillan reports Reginald Charles Gaskell was born in Cardiff on 28t December 1910.

26180 HOBSON* William Francis Cripps G/Capt 23.05.56 Retirement
Group Captain William Francis Cripps mentioned in despatches, who was born 28th December 1910, in Hanover on the island of Jamaica, died in London at 17 Cheyne Gardens on Tuesday, 20th December 1994

26181 HOGAN* Henry Algernon Vickers AV-M 29.04.62 Retirement
Air Vice-Marshal Henry Algernon Vickers Hogan CB DFC and Officer of Legion of Merit [USA], died on Monday, 28th June 1993. As Squadron Leader Hogan he distinguished himself during the *Battle of Britain* after assuming command of 501 Squadron AAF [Hurricane] which had been heavily engaged in the *Battle of France,* returning to Croydon on 21st June 1940, by way of the Channel Islands [soon to fall into German occupation]. Leading from the front he was obliged to forced-land with a punctured glycol tank on 27th August, followed by narrow brushes with death when on 15th September and again on 18th September 1940, he abandoned his Hurricane in fierce combat. Norman Franks does not mention the episode on the 15th, but identifies his Hurricane I on the 18th as V6620, shot down shortly after midday in fighting over West Malling. With the *Battle of Britain* closing down at the end of October 1940, he was posted to Grangemouth on 11th November 1940, to form No. 58 Operational Training Unit but owing to the unsuitability of the airfield he was temporarily attached to No. 54 Operational Training Unit at Church Fenton before returning to Grangemouth early in the New Year.

His DFC was *Gazetted* on 25th October 1940, issue 34978, page 6193: *"This officer has led his squadron with distinction. Sixty-nine hostile aircraft have been destroyed and many others damaged. Three of this number were destroyed by Squadron Leader Hogan."*

26182 HORNER* Thomas Quintus G/Capt 25.04.58 Retirement

Group Captain Thomas Quintus Horner mentioned in despatches, died at Callington in Cornwall on Wednesday, 25th May 1994. He was born, Paul McMillan reports, in Northern Ireland at Limavady, Londonderry.

As a Halton aircraft apprentice he gained a scholarship to the College where he proved his worth on the football field and in the boxing ring.

26183 MacDONALD* John Charles A/Cmdr 25.12.64 Retirement

Air Commodore John Charles MacDonald CB CBE DFC* AFC mentioned in despatches, died At the outbreak of the Second World War, and ranked Squadron Leader, he was commanding B Flight of 102 Squadron at Driffield, subsequently making a sideways transfer on being promoted wing commander in June 1940, to command 77 Squadron, both squadrons being equipped with the Armstrong Whitley.

102 Squadron - Operational record

08-09.09.39	Whitley IV K8957 DY-	2359-0750	Leaflets over the Ruhr - landed Manston.
27-28.11.39	Whitley V N1380 DY-R	2100-0430	Operational Order 12 - DNCO after being struck by lightning.
14.12.39	Whitley V N1380 DY-R	1350-1735	Security Patrol Borkum and Sylt - Recalled after reaching Terschelling
18.12.39	Whitley V N1380 DY-R	....	Security Patrol Borkum and Sylt - Dropped 6 bombs in sticks of 3. 5 *Flak Ships* sighted between Borkum and mainland. Bombed a pier on SE corner of Borkum - stick of 3. Went to Nordeney and on return to Borkum saw lights in the channel so sent down another stick of 3 - 1 bomb burst 20 yards from lights. *Flak* ships opened up - aircraft unscathed.
12-13.01.40	Whitley V N1351 DY-	1430-2120	Security Patrol Borkum and Sylt
22-23.02.40	Whitley V N1378 DY-Q	2030-0530	'Nickel' and Reconnaissance to Wien and München - Operation mounted from Villeneuve-les-Vertuss. Six flares released over Wien [Vienna]; no response from local defences. Continued to München [Munich] where more flares were released. Observed aerodrome zn aerodrome 10 miles west of München with 10 aircraft on the tarmac.
19-20.03.40	Whitley V N1380 DY-R	1745-2350	Hörnum Seaplane Base - Weather was very cloudy to start with but cleared up nicely over target; visibility 15 miles, cloud 2/10 at 9,000 feet. Squadron Leader MacDonald's aircraft was the first to take off on a pre-determined bombing attack on a German land based target.
25-26.03.40	Whitley V	2048-0453	Reconnaissance of the Ruhr - Landed Villeneuve-les-Vertus
11-12.04.40	Whitley V N1420 DY-L	1905-0245	Shipping in the Kattegat - Attacked a convoy consisting of 8 merchant ships. Flares dropped from 1,500 feet and attack made at 1,000 feet. Bombs hit an 800 ton merchant ship, which later exploded - probably carrying ammunition. Slight *Flak* after bombing, no searchlights.
23-24.04.40	Whitley V N1386 DY-P	2040-0415	Åalborg Aerodrome - DNCO and returned to Kinloss.
10-11.05.40	Whitley V N1380 DY-R	2133-0355	Kleve - Communications.
16-17.05.40	Whitley V N1420 DY-L	2150-0412	Maastricht to Aachen - Bombed target at Aachen.
23-24.05.40	Whitley V N1524 DY-O	2050-0311	Aulnoye - Landed Abingdon and returned to base next day.
29-30.05.49	Whitley V N1413 DY-K	2003-0407	Givet and Guise - Troop movements. Bombed targets at Givet.

77 Squadron - Operational record

05-06.06.40	Whitley V N1501 KN-	1915-0125	Bapaume - Found a convoy and obtained at least 5 direct hits from 4,000 feet
20-21.06.40	Whitley V N1390 KN-	2115-0418	Ludwigshafen-Oppau nitrogen plant - Bombed rail lines in target area.
29-30.06.40	Whitley V N1501 KN-	2050-0350	Frankfurt - Explosive producing factories at Höchst and Sieburg.
03-04.08.40	Whitley V N1501 KN-H	2055-0445	Monheim - Oil storage tanks at the Rhenania Ossag complex - Bombed from between 8,000 and 7,000 feet.

According to his table of postings, as recorded on The Air of Authority - A History of RAF Organisation, Wing Commander MacDonald received a posting order as Chief Instructor at No. 20 Operational Training Unit, Lossiemouth [a Wellington training unit], effective from 14th August 1940, but this was cancelled and he was ordered to take command of 82 Squadron [Blenheim IV] at Watton following the almost complete destruction of the squadron [for a second time] following a morning strike on Åalborg aerodrome the previous day. His tenure of command lasted until mid-December 1940, when he took up Staff Duties at Headquarters No. 3 Group.

82 Squadron - Operational record

05.10.40	Blenheim IV T2031 UX-	0640-0843	Targets under GOO No.11 - Recalled owing to lack of cloud cover.
05.11.40	Blenheim IV T2031 UX-	1735-2104	Flushing - Night bombing.

Between January and June 1942, he commanded XV Squadron [Stirling}.

XV Squadron - Operational record

02-03.02.42	Stirling I N3699 LS-C	1902-2347	Paris-Billancourt - 7 x 1,000 10 x 500 Found target at 2115 and bombed from 2,000. Bombs fell across island. Bursts seen and blast felt. Large fires raging and many sticks seen bursting.
05-06.04.42	Stirling I N3674 LS-T	0205-0615	Cologne - 5 x 2,000 HC. Target area bombed from 14,000. Gunner put on a good show when attacked by enemy fighters. Cloud cover at 11,000. Intense light flak near coast.
01-02.06.42	Stirling I N3757 LS-G	2310-0314	Essen - 90 x 4, 12 x 8, x 30lbs Inc.Target reached. Much smoke and haze made identification impossible. Electrical failure caused bombs to be brought back.

Promoted group captain he took command of Horsham St. Faith during which he undertook a sortie to Flensburg with the resident 105 Squadron on 2nd July 1942, and his Mosquito IV DK298 which ended with a crash-landing in Germany and for Group Captain MacDonald and his navigator Flight Lieutenant A E Skelton close on three years 'behind the wire.'

During his time at Stalag-Luft I and later at Stalag-Luft III he was Senior British Officer. Following his release he fulfilled posts at home and overseas before his final appointment on the Staff at the Air Ministry.

He was *Gazetted* with the DFC, without a citation appended, on 9th July 1940, issue 34892, page 4177; a First Bar, effective from 15th June 1942, less citation was *Gazetted* 16th March 1943, issue 35940, page 1246.

MOORBY* George Richard F/O 19.06.34 Resigned

It is known that as a pilot officer he was posted to 14 Squadron at Amman where on 16th February 1933, he was engaged in formation flying near Ma'an, the formation being led by Flight Lieutenant Richard Llewelyn Roger Atcherley [see Appendix E and September 1922 entry to the College]. Perhaps owing to inattention, Pilot Officer Moorby's Gordon I K2636 began to over-take the leader's Fairey IIIF K1158 and in attempting to regain his position in the formation his Gordon was caught in the leader's slip stream and struck the tail causing it to tilt. Occupying the rear cockpit of the IIIF was Aircraftman Charles Stocks and such was his concern that he baled out. Tragically, his parachute failed to deploy and he plunged to his death. Ironically, both the IIIF and the Gordon effected a safe landing. It is pure conjecture as to whether this incident had a bearing on his decision to resign his commission.

Just over a year later, George Richard Moorby, now residing at the Norfolk Hotel in London's Kensington district, died on 20th July 1935, whilst performing aerobatics in a Simmonds Spartan Three-seater G-ABYH belonging to Air Transport and Sales Limited. Taking off from Portsmouth Aerodrome he headed for nearby Hayling Island where he began to preform aerobatics, one manoeuvre being a loop which he commenced at a very low altitude and ended in a fatal crash.

On Monday, July 22nd, 1935, *The Daily Telegraph* beneath the heading 'Pilot Killed While Looping At 300ft - Machine Too Low'

"Mr. George Richard Moorby, of the Norfolk Hotel, Kensington, was killed on Saturday when his 'plane crashed just after leaving Hayling Island Aerodrome, Hants.

"Eye witnesses state that when about 300 feet in the air the seemed to begin a loop. The machine was too low, and it crashed, the engine partly burying itself in the ground.

"Moorby's landlady and her son, whom he had promised to take up for a flight, motored to the aerodrome on Saturday and, noticing the crowd, thought the pilot was busy. They reached the 'plane and found him dead among the wreckage."

26815 MOORE* Charles Stuart AV-M 23.07.62 Retirement

Air Vice-Marshal Charles Stuart Moore CB OBE, died on Thursday, 26th May 2005. In November 1936, he was posted to Egypt and attached as a Qualified Flying Instructor to No. 4 Flying Training School at Abu Sueir, a post he held for two years before assuming Staff Duties at RAF Headquarters Middle East. With war intervening he remained in the Middle East and in July 1941, was appointed Officer Commanding Port Sudan.

In May 1943, he received orders to return by sea to Home Establishment and whilst on passage his ship was torpedoed and sunk, taking with it all his personal possessions [which I assume included his flying log books]. Back in the UK he commanded various operational training units and completed his service as Air Officer Administration, Headquarters Near East Air Force.

After leaving the service he joined Her Majesty's Diplomatic Corps, serving from October 1962 to March 1969, one of his postings being to the British Embassy in Tehran.

26186 MORRISON* Norman Eric G/Capt 02.10.57 Retirement

Group Captain Norman Eric Morrison AFC mentioned in despatches and conferred with the Order of Orange Nassau with Sword, died, as reported by Paul McMillan, in the United States in Escambia County, Florida, on Sunday, 13th April 1986. He was born in Spain at Huelva, Andalucia on 2nd October 1910, and following his death, as reported, his body was brought for burial in the British Cemetery, Lisbon, Portugal, a photograph of his headstone being published on the Find a Grave website.

26194 NICHOLS William Trefor Hugh G/Capt 06.04.65 Retirement

Group Captain William Trefor Hugh Nichols OBE, a former Flowerdown apprentice, died at Urchfont, Wiltshire on Monday, 5th May 1986.

26187 PEARCE* Fergus Alexander A/Cmder 19.05.58 Retirement

Air Commodore Fergus Alexander Pearce CBE twice mentioned in despatches, died on Sunday, 12 May 1991, a mere three days short of his 90th birthday. During his cadetship he represented the College at swimming, on the squash courts as well as being picked for cricket and soccer, along with fencing. On graduating, he was awarded the Humanities Prize.

Early in 1935, he attended a specialist course in navigation at RAF Calshotwhere five years earlier he had undergone training on seaplanes. Apart from spells as navigation instructor at 5 FTS Sealand and at the School of Air Navigation, most of his active service was associated with maritime operations and from March 1941, through to at least November of that year, and possibly beyond, he commanded 95 Squadron [Sunderland].

Unsurprisingly, his final appointment was concerned with Staff Duties at Headquarters Coastal Command.

26188 REED* William Stanley G/Capt 17.08.59 Retirement

Group Captain William Stanley Reed conferred with the Insignia of the Order Al Rafidian [Class IV] when he was a squadron leader [LG 13th May 1941, issue 35161, page 2733], the citation reading: *"The KING has been pleased to give and grant unto Squadron Leader William Stanley Reed, RAF, His Majesty's Royal Licence and authority to wear the Insignia of the Fourth Class [Military Division] of the Order of Al Rafidian, which decoration has been conferred upon him by His Majesty the King of Iraq, in recognition of valuable services rendered by him in the capacity of Technical Inspector, Iraqi Air Force,"* died in the Oxfordshire town of Banbury on Tuesday, 23rd December 1993.

26189 ROBINSON* Maurice Wilbraham Sandford A/Cmdr 01.03.58 Retirement

Air Commodore Maurice Wilbrham Sandford Robinson CBE Krzyz Waleszynch [Poland] [Cross of Valour], died on Saturday, 2nd April 1977. Posted to 73 Squadron [Hurricane] as a supernumerary on 31st July 1940, he took over the squadron from Squadron Leader James Winter Carmichael More [see Appendix E and the September 1928 entry to the College] on 5th September 1940. Ten days later he was admitted, wounded, to the Kent and Sussex Hospital after baling out in late afternoon over Tonbridge when his Hurricane I L2039 TP-F was shot down.

Referring to Norman Franks' revised edition of *Fighter Command Losses,* on page 74 it is reported that he forced-landed in Hurricane I P2815 on 5th September following a 'brush' with a Heinkel HeIII.

Air Commodore Robinson's final appointment was as Air Officer Commanding Caledonian Sector.

26190 SABINE* John Sydenham W/Cdr + 24.08.43 British Airways Repair Unit

Wing Commander John Sydenham Sabine DFC is buried in Heliopolis War Cemetery, his headstone engraved with the immortal words *"Great Love Hath No Man Than This That A Man Lay Down His Life For His Friends."* As Squadron Leader Sabine he was *Gazetted* with the DFC [less citation] on 9th July 1940, issue 34892, page 4177.

According to Henk Welting's data base, recorded on the Royal Air Force Commands website, Wing Commander Sabine had accompanied Sergeant John Tulloch and crew for, presumably, an air test of Wellington II Z8425 which Air-Britain's X1000-Z9999 registers shows was struck on the ground at Cairo West by Wellington II W5430 which was in the course of landing, Both Wellingtons had arrived at British Airways Repair Unit from operational service with 104 Squadron.

26192 WILKINSON* Rodney Levett S/Ldr + 16.08.40 266 Squadron

Squadron Leader Rodney Levett Wilkinson commanding 266 Squadron was shot down in Spitfire I R6768 by a Me109 shortly after noon near Deal in Kent, just 48-hours after brining his squadron to Hornchurch from Eastchurch. The son of Major Clement Arthur Wilkinson of The King's Shropshire Light Infantry and Ruth Violet Esther Wilkinson, he is buried in Margate Cemetery where the inscription *"Their Memory Hallowed In The Land They Loved,"* is carved on his headstone.

26193 WINDSOR* Charles Mervyn W/Cdr + 08.12.41 255 Squadron

Wing Commander Charles Mervyn Windsor was returning to Coltishall from an evening patrol in Beaufighter II R2398 YD-A when he crashed on landing; he is buried in Brookwood Military Cemetery. His radar/wireless operator, Sergeant Gordon Percival Francis Langdon, perished; his resting place is in Littleham [SS Margaret and Andrew] Churchyard, Devon. His headstone bears the beautiful words *"He Fell To Earth On Broken Wings But His Soul Still Soars Where Angels Sing."*

The flight cadets whose surnames are marked with an asterisk graduated with permanent commissions on 20th December 1930, and included Lawrence George Belchem and Roger Furnell Smith, both from the September 1928 entry [LG 20 January 1931, issue 33682, page 463]. Apart from the resignation of Flying Officer Moorby and the five who died during their service, the January 1929, entry produced one Air Marshal, two Air Vice-Marshals, four Air Commodores and nine Group Captains.

SWORD OF HONOUR
Flight Cadet Henry Algernon Vickers Hogan

ROLL OF HONOUR
JANUARY 1929 INTAKE

W/Cdr	BAKER	Maurice William L'Isle La Vallette	21 February 1945	196 Squadron
S/Ldr	CAZALET	Robert Travers	16 February 1939	A&AEE Martlesham Heath
W/Cdr	SABINE DFC	John Sydenham	24 August 1943	British Airways Repair Unit
S/Ldr	WILKINSON	Rodney Levett	16 August 1940	266 Squadron
W/Cdr	WINDSOR	Charles Mervyn	8 December 1941	255 Squadron

September 1929 intake : 30

26195 ADDENBROOKE* Derek W/Cdr + 03.04.41 101 Squadron
Wing Commander Derek Addenbrooke, commanding 101 Squadron, took off from West Raynham with his crew in Blenheim IV N3552 for a raid on the French port of Brest [3rd-4th April 1941] and was lost without trace. All are commemorated on the Runnymede Memorial where Wing Commander Addenbrooke\s name is inscribed on panel 28. Please refer to my RAFBCL 1941 and page 37 for the names of his crew.

As kindly advised by Christopher Dean via the Bomber Command Forum Group, Wing Commander Addenbrooke was appointed Commanding Officer of the squadron on 1st April 1941.

26196 ANDREWS* Lionel Vincent S/Ldr + 09.12.40 149 Squadron
Squadron Leader Lionel Vincent Andrews and crew, tasked for operations against Boulogne-sur-Mer on 8th-9th September 1940, ditched their Wellington IC P9245 OJ-W off Clacton on their return. The sole survivor was the bomber's second pilot Pilot Officer Charles Woodbine Parish who managed to swim ashore and raise the alarm. Sadly, despite an extensive search, there were no other survivors, all of whom are commemorated on the panels of the Runnymede Memorial. There names are recorded on pages 203 and 204 of my RAFBCL 1939-1940 revised edition.

Meanwhile, during the night of 20th-21st April 1943, now ranked Flight Lieutenant, Charles Woodbine Parish was captain of 7 Squadron Stirling I R9261 MG-M ordered for Pathfinder Force duties on Stettin. Shot down over Denmark by a night-fighter the sole survivor from his crew was Sergeant D V Smith who evaded capture. See my RAFBCL 1943 page 117 for additional information.

26197 BROWN* Leslie Frank G/Capt 10.11.60 Retirement
Group Captain Leslie Frank Brown died On graduating, he was awarded the Hyde Thompson Memorial Prize.

26198 CHESTERMAN* Humphrey William Albert F/Lt 15.08.36 Resigned
Flight Lieutenant Humphrey William Albert Chesterman AFC was appointed to a commission in Class A of the Reserve of Air Force Officers, effective 2nd February 1937, retaining his rank [LG 9 February 1937, issue 34369, page 896].
S/Ldr + 11.04.43 7 Squadron
Squadron Leader Humphrey Humphrey William Albert Chesterman AFC was captain of Stirling III BK760 MG-X of 7 Squadron ordered for Pathfinder Force duties on a Main Force raid on Frankfurt. Shot down by a night fighter over Belgium [see page 100 of my RAFBCL 1943] Squadron Leader Chesterman AFC is buried in Heverlee War Cemetery.

26220 DAUBNEY Frederick Claude G/Capt 01.07.46 Retirement
At his own request [LG 3 September 1944, supplement 37708, page 4390] Group Captain Frederick Claude Daubney CBE Order of Legion of Merit [USA], he died on Thursday, 9th January 1975.

26199 DREW* Peter Edward S/Ldr + 01.08.40 236 Squadron
Squadron Leader Peter Edward Drew and Flying Officer Benjamin Nokes-Cooper, the squadron's Signals Officer, took off from Thorney Island to attack an airfield near Cherbourg. Their Blenheim IV N3601 FA-K was last sighted in a dive over the target; Squadron Leader Drew rest in Biville Churchyard, Flying Officer Nokes-Cooper is buried in Bayeux War Cemetery. See RAFCCL 1939-1941 and page 53 for further details.

Both officers have inscriptions to mark their memory; they read respectively *"In Proud And Loving Memory"* and *"Went The Day Well? We Died And Never Knew, But, Well Or Ill, England, We Died For You,"* the latter taken from John Maxwell Edmonds, author of the *Four Epitaphs* published in *The Times* on 6th February 1918, with *"England"* substituted for the original *"Freedom."*

26200 HALLIDAY* Neville Anthony Roy W/Cdr + 12.08.42 461 Squadron RAAF
Wing Commander Neville Anthony Roy Halliday is commemorated on panel 64 of the Runnymede Memorial. He was lost on an operational sortie over the Bay of Biscay in Sunderland II T9090.

26201 INGHAM* Edward Cunliffe S/Ldr + 02.07.40 CGS Warmwell
Squadron Leader Edward Cunliffe Ingham and Pilot Officer T M Maggs were nearing Warmwell airfield in Defiant I L6982 when the engine 'cut' and in trying to forced-land stalled and crashed. Squadron Leader Ingham was cremated at Weymouth Crematorium; his younger brother, 2nd Lieutenant Philip Lister Ingham attached to the 1st Battalion, Oxford and Bucks Light Infantry was killed on 21st May 1940, as the British Expeditionary Force fell back towards the Dunkirk perimeter. He is buried in Belgium at Bruyelle War Cemetery.

Although seriously injured, Pilot Officer Maggs appears to have recovered well and survived the Second World War.

JACKSON* Neville Howard P/O + 26.05.32 1 Squadron

JAWAD Ibraham
Iraqi Air Force

JOHNSTONE* Archibald Campbell P/O + 26.04.32 23 Squadron

26204 LING* Christopher William Mitchell G/Capt 05.06.46 Retirement
At his own request [LG 3 September 1946, supplement 37708, page 4390]. Group Captain Christopher William Mitchell Ling DFC mentioned in despatches AFC [Greece], died in Canada at Collingwood, Simcoe, Ontario, on Saturday, 14th April 2001.

He was *Gazetted* with the Greek Air Force Cross on 29th December 1942, supplement 35837, page 5640. The citation for his DFC, in recognition of his leadership of 51 Squadron [Halifax III] appeared in supplement 36788, page 5150 of the *Gazette* published on 10th November 1944;. *"Wing Commander Ling has completed many sorties far into enemy occupied territory and his successes are an excellent testimony to his great skill and determination. He is a fine leader whose sterling qualities have contributed in good measure to the operational efficiency of the squadron which has achieved much success. Wing Commander Ling has destroyed one and has assisted in the destruction of 2 more enemy aircraft."*

The last sentence appears strange in the context of an award for Bomber Command operations and although I have no proof, it may have a connection with his award of the Greek Air Force Cross.

26206 MACNAIR* David Ivor Phorson G/Capt 22.11.57 Retirement
Group Captain David Ivor Phorson Macnair CBE mentioned in despatched and conferred with the DFC [USA], died at Buckleigh, Plymouth, on Thursday, 27th July 1989.

26205 McILWAINE* Andrew G/Capt 21.11.62 Retirement
Group Captain Andrew McIlwaine died Tuesday, on 11th January 1977, at Wycombe in Buckinghamshire.

26207 MESSENGER* Arthur Douglas A/Cmdr 22.08.60 Retirement
Air Commodore Arthur Douglas Messenger CBE mentioned in despatches and conferred with the Order of the Star of Jordan [2nd Class], died on Tuesday, 10th May 1994. Assigned to B Squadron at the College, he excelled at fencing and skill at arms, and was no mean performer on the tennis courts and at soccer and cricket. Academically, he rose to the challenge and on graduating was awarded the John Anthony Chance and Hyde Thompson Memorial Prizes.

It is further noted that he was a former Flowerdown and Cranwell apprentice and in 1935 he specialised in signals, going on to serve as a Signals Officer at both station and group level. His final service appointment was a Director of Manning.

NAQIB
Iraqi Air Force

26208 OLIVER* John Oliver William G/Capt 11.10.61 Retirement
Group Captain John Oliver William Oliver CB DSO DFC twice mentioned in despatches, died in a Portsmouth hospital on Tuesday, 4th February 1997.

The citations for his DFC and DSO appeared in the same edition of *The London Gazette* 31st May 1940, supplement 34860, pages 3252 and 3251 respectively: *"This officer commanded his squadron extremely well and has led two escort formations of 24 aircraft each to a distance of 140 miles from their base. During these escorts the formations accounted for more than a dozen enemy aircraft. In addition, in May 1940, he shot down an enemy aircraft which crashed at Hazebrouck and he has led his section magnificently on many occasions. His sangfroid and calm outlook have encouraged his squadron to a remarkable degree and the excellent spirit of the squadron and his gallant leadership is reflected in the successes attained."* The citation for his DSO reads:

"Before intensive operations started this officer injured his right shoulder in a severe flying accident. Despite this, he flew regularly and led his squadron with skill and dash, more than 60 enemy aircraft being destroyed by them. He remained in command of the squadron throughout the operations, in spite of the injured shoulder, trained his new pilots well and continued throughout to be a very efficient commander, inculcating an excellent spirit in his squadron."

Referring to Peter D Cornwell's indispensable *The Battle of France Then and Now* page 205 is headed by a photograph of Squadron Leader Oliver with four of his fellow 85 Squadron [Hurricane] pilots, identified as Flight Lieutenant Bob Boothby, Pilot Officer John Lecky, Sergeant 'Sammy' Allard and Pilot Officer Ken Blair. An official Air Ministry released photograph, it is captioned *'Five RAF pilots who got seven Germans before breakfast.'* Although undated, research by the author narrowed it down to the opening day of the *Blitzkrieg* when '85' was operating out of Lille-Seclin. Page 210 [one of nearly sixty pages devoted to this historic day], describing some of the fierce aerial fighting that took place on the 10th of May 1940, pinpoints one of the victories to a Heinkel He111P from Stab I./KG27 which was attacked circa 0500 by Squadron Leader Oliver, Pilot Officer Lecky and 'Sammy' Allard, and may well refer to the enemy aircraft downed *"at Hazebrouck"* in the citation for his DFC.

The following day he was slightly wounded in an engagement with He111s, His Hurricane P2821 being repairable and both pilot and Hurricane were back in action within forty-eight hours. However, when patrolling over Belgium he was set upon by Me109s and this time he was obliged to take to his parachute while P2821 buried itself in a field south of Diest [see page 256].

To the best of my knowledge Squadron Leader Oliver, who handed over command to Squadron Leader M Peacock during May 1940, did not fly operationally in the *Battle of Britain.*

26209 OULTON* Wilfred Ewart AV-M 01.01.61 Retirement

At own request [LG 14 February 1961, supplement 42277, page 1120[. Air Vice-Marshal Wilfred Ewart Oulton CB CBE DSO DFC three times mentioned in despatches, died on the last day of October 1997.

For much of his distinguished service he was associated with maritime operations and it was shortly after taking command of 58 Squadron [Halifax II] in April 1943, he sunk U-663 on the 7th of May, followed on the 15th by U-463 and then on the last day of May 1943, he assisted in the destruction of U-563. For these outstanding achievements, he was *Gazetted* with the DFC on 4th June 1943: *"Recently, this officer was the captain of an aircraft, which attacked a U-boat. Later in the day another submarine was observed on the surface of the water. In the face of accurate anti-aircraft fire from the vessel, Wing Commander Oulton pressed home a vigorous attack. During a patrol some days later, he executed a destructive attack on yet another U-boat. Wing Commander Oulton has displayed great keenness and efficiency."*

At the culmination of tour of duty he was awarded the DSO [LG 12 November 1943, supplement 36245, 4971]. By this time he was commanding RAF Lagens in the Azores - the *Atlantic Gap* was now firmly closed and from now on the *Battle of the Atlantic* swung in favour of the Allied anti-submarine patrols.

Postwar, and in February 1956, when the decision to appoint an Admiral to oversee the H-bomb trials, *Operation Grapple,* was overturned in favour of a senior Royal Air Force officer, Air Commodore Oulton was promoted acting air vice-marshal and filled the post. For two years he was involved with the trials before taking up his final appointment as Senior Air Staff Officer at Headquarters Coastal Command.

In conclusion, and returning to his graduation, he was awarded the Abdy Gerrard Fellows' Memorial Prize.

PAGE* Robert Humphrey F/Lt 24.10.36 Transferred

Transferring to the Reserve of Air Force Officer, Class A, Flight Lieutenant Robert Humphrey Page attained a captaincy with BOAC. On 24th-25th January 1942, Captain Page flew Liberator C.1 AM918/G-AGDR non-stop from Hurn [Bournemouth] to Cairo and it was on the return trip on 15th February 1942, and nearing Plymouth shortly after dawn that two patrolling Spitfires from 317 Squadron based at Exeter intercepted the airliner and in a tragic case of mistaken identity shot it down into the sea off the Eddystone Lighthouse. Everyone on board perished; they are named as Captain Robert Humphrey Page [first pilot], Captain John Alexander Stuart Hunter [second pilot], First Officer Richard John Williamson, Engineer Officer Horace Reginald John Spicer, Radio Officer Hubert France Parker and passengers Brigadier Frederick Morris CB MC, Lieutenant Colonel Townsend Griffiss of the USAAF [formerly Edwin Townsend Evans but took the surname Griffiss when his mother married Wilmot Griffiss], Lieutenant Oliver Charles Mansfield Vine of the Royal Naval Reserve and a Rolls-Royce representative, Howard Edward Bell.

The authors are indebted to 'posts' submitted to the Royal Air Force Forum website and entries on the RAF Davidstowe Moor web pages. During his Royal Air Force service, as Flying Officer Bell he had had a close encounter with death when his Heyford IIA K4034 of 97 Squadron based at Boscombe Down descended into the sea, at night, off the French port of Le Havre after running out of fuel. Three from the crew drowned [details will appear in the fifth volume in this series] along with a newspaper article reporting Robert Page's dramatic rescue.

PROWSE David P/O 11.10.34 Resigned

It is known that on graduating he was posted to Hornchurch and attached to 111 Squadron [Bulldog IIA].

26211 READ* George John Lacey G/Capt 08.06.59 Retirement

Group Captain George John Lacey Read AFC, died at Weymouth, Dorset, in July 1993.

26212 RUTTER* Norman Colopy Simpson AV-M 24.07.65 Retirement

Air Vice-Marshal Norman Colopy Simpson Rutter CBE, died on Friday, 9th October 1998. Formerly of the 14th entry at No. 1 School of Technical Training, Halton, he won a scholarship to Cranwell and as with many of his ilk with a technical background he transferred from the General Duties Branch to the Technical Branch in April 1940. Prewar he served for three years in India where he was attached to 39 Squadron and later 60 Squadron for flying duties, and in the Second World War he returned to the country where between 1942 and '45, he commanded 301 Maintenance Unit and later 320 Maintenance Unit, both being at Drigh Road. His final service posting was to Headquarters Bomber Command as the Command's Senior Technical Staff Officer.

26213 SHEARN* Austin Charles P/O + 20.01.32 17 Squadron

Born in January 1911, at Midsomer Norton in Somerset, Pilot Officer Austin Charles Shearn collapsed and died from heart failure shortly after playing in a rugby match at Upavon. His sudden death, including his photograph wearing a rugby shirt, was reported in *The Bath Chronicle And Herald* in its edition of Saturday, January 23rd, 1932, and captioned *'Game's Tragic Ending - Old Bath EdwardianDrops Dead - RAF Pilot Officer'*

"A well-known old Bath Edwardian dropped dead after a Rugby football match in which he had played at Upavon, near Devizes, on Wednesday. He was Pilot-Officer Austin Shearn, second son of Mr. and Mrs. Walter Shearn, Exford House, Midsomer Norton. Mr. Shearn was in the RAF stationed at Upavon.

"When the match was over and he was about to leave, he complained of violent pains, collapsing on the field and dying soon afterwards. His parents were notified by telephone and, with a brother of the dead man, Leonard, they at once motored to Upavon.

"Mr. Walter Shearn is a partner in the firm of Messers Shearn Bros., garage proprietors, Midsomer Norton.

"The young man whose career has been so untimely cut short celebrated his 21st birthday only a week ago last Monday. He was educated at King Edward School, Bath, and three years ago captained the school rugby team. As a forward he was one of the best players turned out by K E S. After spending two years at Cranwell he went to Upavon three months ago, upon receiving his commission.

"He was of fine physique and had every promise of a brilliant career in the RAF. He was well known at Bath and Midsomer Norton, and often flew over the latter town."

26214 STAINTHORPE* William Waters W/Cdr + 27.02.41 83 Squadron

Win Commander William Waters Stainthorpe AFC and his crew died when returning from Cologne, 26th-27th February 1941, when their Hampdon I X3124 OL-H strayed off course and flew into high ground near Derrington Cross, some 2 miles WSW of Stafford. Please refer to page 25 of my RAFBCL 1941 for details of his crew. Brought back to Scampton, Wing Commander Stainthorpe AFC was laid to rest with full military honours in Scampton [St. John the Baptist] Churchyard.

26215 STOKES* Donald George G/Capt 12.06.59 Retirement

Group Captain Donald George Stokes who upon graduating was awarded the Abdy Gerrard Fellowes Memorial Prize and the John Anthony Chance Memorial Prize, died on Sunday, 18th July 2004.

26216 TURNER* William Henry Nigel G/Capt 26.10.57 Retirement

Group Captain William Henry Nigel Turner DFC mentioned in despatches, died at Hewish near Yatton, Somerset, on Wednesday, 22nd June 1977.

WAHID
Iraqi Air Force

26217 WELCH* Wyndham Powis G/Capt 01.09.57 Retirement
Group Captain Wyndham Powis Welch mentioned in despatches, died on Wednesday, 1st November 1999, at Hastings, Sussex. During the Second World War he became a prisoner of the Imperial Japanese Forces and according to Ancestry, which the authors acknowledge, in October 1944 seems to have moved from Camp III to Batavia and thence to Bandoeng.

26218 WIDDOWS* Stanley Charles A/Cmdr 29.12.58 Retirement
Air Commodore Stanley Charles Widdows CB DFC twice mentioned in despatches, died on Sunday, 10th January 2010 having made a century in years. Prior to his arrival at the College, he had spent three years as an aircraft apprentice at Halton and was one of the first apprentices to gain a scholarship to Cranwell. He was an extremely active pilot and when he was attached to the Aeroplane & Armament Experimental Establishment at Martlesham Heath [where he test flew the prototype Hurricane and Spitfire] he had seen service with no less than six squadrons.

On 16th July 1940, he was appointed to command 29 Squadron at Wellingore in Lincolnshire, now fully engaged as a night fighter squadron. At the time of his arrival the squadron was equipped with Blenheim IF but from November 1940, these were gradually replaced by the more potent Beaugfighter. On 4th April 1941, he was *Gazetted* with the DFC, issue 35127, page 1959: *"This officer has commanded the squadron since July 1940, and, under difficult circumstances, has maintained a high morale among the personnel. Wing Commander Widdows has carried out a large number of difficult patrols in bade weather and has shown extreme keenness to engage the enemy. He has flown a considerable number of hours of operational flying at night, and succeeded in destroying a Junkers 88 one night in March 1941."*

His final service appointment was as Director of Air Defence Operations. In retirement he settled in the Channel Islands where from 1973 to 1979 he served a People's Deputy for the States of Guernsey.

26219 WILLIAMS* Cedric Watcyn S/Ldr + 25.08.40 17 Squadron
Formerly an aircraft apprentice at Halton, Squadron Leader Cedric Walcyn Williams took over command of 17 Squadron [Hurricane] July 1940 from Squadron Leader Ralph Ian George MacDougall on 18th July 1940. On 25th August 1940, another day of desperate aerial combat ass the *Battle of Britain* continued to hang in the balance, Squadron Leader Williams took off from Tangmere in Hurricane I R4199 and headed towards Weymouth where off Portland in the early evening he was shot down during a head-on attack against a Me110; he is commemorated on the Runnymede Memorial, panel 4. In those few weeks of his command he was credited with a Dornier Do17 destroyed on 18th August, a brace, shared, of Ju88s on the 21st, a share in Heinkel He111 on the 24th and the sole claimant of a Me110 on the 25th. Eyewitnesses to his final combat report seeing the port main plane of his Hurricane being shot away. His photograph of Squadron Leader Williams with pilots of 17 Squadron can be seen on The Battle of Britain London Monument website.

The flight cadets whose names are marked with an asterisk graduated with permanent commissions on 25th July 1931, Peter Edward Drew being noted as Pilot Officer on probation [LG 25 August 1931, issue 33747, page 5555].

SWORD OF HONOUR
Flight Cadet Christopher William Mitchell Ling

ROLL OF HONOUR
SEPTEMBER 1929 INTAKE

W/Cdr	ADDENBROOKE	Derek	3 April 1941	101 Squadron
S/Ldr	ANDREWS	Lionel Vincent	9 December 1940	149 Squadron
S/Ldr	CHESTERMAN	Humphrey William Albert	11 April 1943	7 Squadron
S/Ldr	DREW	Peter Edward	1 August 1940	236 Squadron
W/Cdr	HALLIDAY	Neville Anthony Roy	12 August 1942	461 Squadron RAAF
S/Ldr	INGHAM	Edward Cunliffe	2 July 1940	CGS Warmwell
P/O	JACKSON	Neville Howard	26 May 1932	1 Squadron
P/O	JOHNSTONE	Archibald Campbell	26 April 1932	23 Squadron
F/Lt	PAGE	Robert Humphrey	15 February 1942	BOAC
P/O	SHEARN	Austin Charles		
W/Cdr	STAINTHORPE	William Waters	27 February 1941	83 Squadron
S/Ldr	WILLIAMS	Cedric Watcyn	25 August 1940	17 Squadron

FLYING ACCIDENTS

Monday 4 February 1929
Bristol F.2b F4939/B6 *Not reported*
T/o Cranwell and wrecked here in a landing accident.

Thursday 7 March 1929
Avro 504N J8692/6 *Not reported*
T/o Cranwell and in avoiding another aircraft when about to land, lost control and crashed.

Thursday 23 May 1929
DH.9A J8210 *Not reported*
T/o Cranwell with the intention of flying to Wittering but crashed *en route* while forced-landing near Ancaster, a little over 6 miles NE of Grantham, Lincolnshire.

Thursday 20 June 1929
DH.9A J8133 *Not reported*
T/o Cranwell and on return, and while trying to avoid a collision with another aircraft, lost control and crashed. The impact was sufficient to damage the DH beyond repair.

Wednesday 10 July 1929
Avro 504N JJ013 *Not reported*
T/o Cranwell and came to grief in a field 3 miles from Digby following engine failure. The unnamed cadet forced-landed but was unable to control a swing that developed, and the trainer finished up with its nose buried in the grass.

Tuesday 22 October 1929
Siskin IIIA J9366 *Not reported*
T/o Cranwell and on landing struck a ridge, bounced, stalled, and crashed onto its starboard planes and damaged beyond repair.

Appendix E - Roll of Honour

ROYAL AIR FORCE

F/O	BAYES	John Walden	16 May 1929	19 Squadron
F/Lt	BUCKNALL	George Anthony Fielding	28 February 1929	19 Squadron
F/O	BURNETT	Yvon William	18 March 1929	47 Squadron
LAC	BUTTENSHAW	Edward William	17 July 1929	207 Squadron
P/O	CARROLL	Raymond Russell	2 January 1929	55 Squadron
F/O	CLARKE	John	11 October 1929	29 Squadron
LAC	CREED	Mervyn Henry	25 August 1929	216 Squadron
AC1	EDGLEY	George William	3 October 1929	58 Squadron

Aircraftman George William Edgley, 560604, was killed at Worthy Down while attempting to swing a propeller, at night, on Virginia X J7424. Born in 1910, he entered the Royal Air Force in, or shortly after, January 1926, as an aircraft apprentice, the first block of service numbers for apprentices being 560001 - 579999. To the best of the authors knowledge he was the first to lose his life in squadron service.

F/O	EYRE	Vickers Osbourne	27 June 1929	56 Squadron
Sgt	GROOM	Charles Benjamin	17 June 1929	3 Squadron
F/Lt	HALLIDAY	Christopher George	27 June 1929	30 Squadron

Flight Lieutenant Christopher George Halliday was killed and his observer/air gunner Aircraftman John Laverty injured when their Wapiti IIA J9408 crashed and turned over near Luqait in Iraq. Salvaged, the wreck was taken to the Aircraft Depot at Hinaidi where it was repaired and returned to service by 3rd September 1929. Subsequently, it passed through the hands of 84 Squadron, Hinaidi Communications Flight and 55 Squadron before being struck off charge on the 1st of May 1936.

F/O	JONES	Charles Henry	14 August 1929	23 Squadron
AC1	KNIGHT	James Richard	3 March 1929	84 Squadron

During operations against Wahabi raiders some 20 miles to the south of Kuwait, Aircraft James Richard Knight was mortally wounded by a gunshot. His service number 364049 shows his initial service was as a boy airman.

LAC	LANGAN	Charles Ernest	24 August 1929	216 Squadron
P/O	LUCAS	Lawrence Errington Jeff	10 September 1929	17 Squadron
Sgt	MELVILLE	John	24 August 1929	216 Squadron
F/Sgt	PEARCE	John William	18 February 1929	25 Squadron
F/O	PRINCE	Stanley Frank	17 July 1929	207 Squadron
LAC	PRUNTY	John	16 February 1929	30 Squadron

Leading Aircraftman John Prunty, a wireless operator, was critically injured at Hinaidi when he was struck by the propeller during starting of DH.9A J8192 on 14th February 1929.

F/O	SEALY-ALLIN	Patrick Nelson	1 March 1929	23 Squadron
Sgt	TURNER	Thomas Condy	18 March 1929	47 Squadron
Cpl	WALMSLEY	William	24 October 1929	55 Squadron
P/O	WILSON	John	24 August 1929	216 Squadron
AC2	WILSON	Robert Henry	28 October 1929	36 Squadron

SQUADRON LOSSES
1930

JANUARY

Thursday 2 January 1930
6 Squadron Bristol F.2b D7848 While taxying, presumably at Ismailia, the undercarriage collapsed. Reduced to produce.

Tuesday 21 January 1930
6 Squadron During the day Flying Officer Charles Henry Lee Evans died from undisclosed circumstances at Heliopolis; he is buried in Ramel War Cemetery. His short service commission was *Gazetted* on 26th January 1926, issue 33127, page 621.

207 Squadron F/O D Mackenzie +
Fairey IIIF J9637 Cpl L E Barnard +
T/o Bircham Newton to transit to the squadron's previous base at Eastchurch but nearing the Suffolk town of Sudbury the crew ran into thick fog and no doubt attempting to find a clear area in which to land flew headlong into a tree near Clifton village on the NE side of Sudbury, coming down in an orchard and with yards of the Mauldon Grey public house. A graphic description of the accident may be read on page 36 of John Hamblin's history of the squadron, taken from an eyewitness account by a Miss Chappell, owner of some nearby kennels who in a moment of clear visibility saw the machine and then, seconds later as it once again 'disappeared' into the prevailing fog heard *"... the noise of a huge hammer hitting a steel drum."* The tragedy was reported in *The Haverhill Echo* of January 25th, 1930, the final paragraph reading: *"Police say the machine came down in a pit near the 'Maldon Grey'* [sic] *at Chilton, they went to the spot and found the machine and the two dead occupants. Both men were wearing parachutes and the machine appeared to be a new one."*

Indeed, it was relatively new; it was the first aircraft in a batch of forty-five airframes and was taken on charge by the squadron on 27th October 1929 and may well have been the only aircraft from the batch to be destroyed in 1930.

Flying Officer Donald Mackenzie's short service commission was published in *The London Gazette* on 26th January 1926, issue 33127, page 621.

Corporal Edward Leonard Barnard, 361666, joined as a boy between July 1922 and January 1924.

FEBRUARY

Tuesday 11 February 1930
60 Squadron *Not reported*
DH.9A J7098
T/o Kohat and reported ass *"crashed."* For much of its time with the squadron it carried the letter 'N', at least up to late July 1928. By a quirk of coincidence, its successor as 'N' was written off here on the same day; see the summary below.

60 Squadron *Not reported*
DH.9A J7342/N
T/o Kohat but swung out of control and crashed.First issued in the summer of 1925 to 27 Squadron at Peshawar this DH had survived two crashes, both during operations in the Lowri Pass on the NWF. Following the second crash it was taken to the Aircraft Depot at Drigh Road for repair and on completion was ferried to Kohat in April 1929.

Thursday 13 February 1930
32 Squadron Sgt C A A Fell +
Siskin DC
T/o Kenley and abandoned over Coulsdon Common after the controls jammed. Tragically, Sergeant Cecil Arthur Alfred Fell, 350944, failed to pull the ripcord on his parachute pack and fell to his death. He joined from civilian life in the early 1920s.

A very detailed account of the accident is recorded on the Kenley Revival website, which is the authors pleasure to acknowledge: *"On the afternoon of his fatal accident, Sgt. Fell had flown Sgt. Arthur King, one of 32 Squadron's carpenters, over to Biggin Hill, to examine a damaged aircraft. He was going later to pick him up, so on leaving the dual-control Siskin, Sgt. King strapped his parachute into the rear cockpit, and Fell returned to Kenley without incident. It only took about ten minutes for King to complete his work at Biggin and Fell returned to collect him, but to King's surprise he didn't land, but flew past at about 15-20ft off the ground. King thought the pilot's gestures indicated that another party would pick him up later, and felt no alarm when he saw Fell make a turn to the left and head back towards Kenley, because the Siskin seemed to be flying well and under control. At Kenley, Fell flew round and round the aerodrome, and at 4.15 p.m., Flight Lieutenant Charles Frederick Le Poer Trench was instructed to go up and fly alongside Fell. The witnesses on the ground at Kenley had realised some-thing was jamming the controls of Fell's aircraft and surmised that the parachute in the back had become loose and had fallen onto the controls in the rear cockpit. Trench directed Fell to perform a loop in the hope that the parachute would fall out, but Fell was unable to comply. Finally, Trench directed the other pilot to climb and head towards Epsom, where the countryside was open and there would be less chance of civilian deaths from the crashing machine when he baled out. They climbed to 6,000ft, but Fell dived to the left, and though at first he seemed to be under control, at 2,000ft the aircraft dived again, vertically, at which point the parachute in the rear seat fell out. Just after, Fell leapt from the Siskin but failed to pull the ripcord of his parachute - a Doctor at the inquest put this down to blind panic. Pilot and aircraft plummeted into the ground next to the tennis court at Admiral Goodenough's residence in Coulsdon, where the force of the impact hammered the Siskin's engine 6ft into the ground. The spare parachute that had caused the accident was found about 50 yards away. Tragically, Fell had jumped between 1,500-1,000ft - if he had pulled the ripcord he would have survived.*

"Stanley James Bloss, a gardener, of 'The Cottage', Parson's Pightle, Coulsdon, was in the grounds when he heard the crash nearby. Running to the scene he saw the pilot lying 30 yards from the crash, and immediately sent word to the aerodrome for an ambulance and fire engine. He felt the tremor of a pulse, and sent his boy for brandy, but the dying pilot couldn't take it, so he soaked the corner of a handkerchief and moistened Fell's lips. By the time the fire engine arrived there was no sign of life. Cecil had suffered multiple injuries, including a fractured skull and broken back."

For his compassionate actions, the Coroner thanked Mr. Bloss. A verdict of accidental death was duly returned.

During the month it is believed 14 Squadron at Ramleh/Amman wrote off DH.9A J7254 though the circumstances have not been recorded.

And in the same month and the same squadron, DH.9A J8101 reported as *"crashed."*

MARCH

Monday 3 March 1930
30 Squadron *Not reported*
Wapiti IIA J9621
T/o Mosul [though Diana cannot be discounted] amd turned over while landing on the Landing Ground at Diana.

Monday 17 March 1930
23 Squadron F/Lt R L R Atcherley Injured
Grebe IIIDC J7519 Sgt J Martin Injured
T/o Kenley and on arrival at Farnborough bounced and on its second arrival the Grebe turned over, fatally injuring Sergeant John Martin though at first it was thought he might recover. It was not to be and he died in the Cambridge Military Hospital on Sunday, 6th April 1930. Sgt Martin, whose service number was 335633, was a former boy airman.

The Kenley Revival website reports from two letters written by 'Batchy' Atcherley [see my notes in Appendix E and the September 1922 entry to Cranwell] who visited John Martin in hospital: *"He is being very plucky about it all as he must be suffering agonies, mentally as well as physically. The doctors hold out hope that they may be able to put him on his feet again, but I know it is pretty long odds."*

From evidence on the website, John Martin was at the controls on arrival at Farnborough and he made two attempts to land but without success. At this point Flight Lieutenant Atcherley took over but as stated above on touch down the Grebe flipped over. An examination of the badly damaged aircraft revealed structural failure of a pin in one of the undercarriage legs. Also, Sergeant White who in formation throughout the flight observed Sergeant Martin's safety straps suddenly come loose and this no doubt had a bearing as to why he was ejected from the cockpit as it turned over.

To the best of my knowledge this was the sole DC fitted Grebe to be destroyed in Royal Air Force service. First flown on 6th July 1924, much of its service life was spent at Martlesham Heath undergoing various service trials. In July 1929, along with J7520, it was entered in the King's Cup race which was won by Flight Lieutenant Atcherley in J7520.

Tuesday 18 March 1930
20 Squadron *Not reported*
Bristol F.2J F4463/L
T/o Peshawar where on landing the Bristol taxied into Wapiti IIA J9396. The Wapiti was repaired; the Bristol was consigned to the 'bone yard.'

Monday 24 March 1930
58 Squadron S/Ldr A S Ellerton Injured
Virginia IX J7709/N F/O E R White +
P/O P J Pratt +
LAC D A Reich Injured
AC2 F B Palmer Safe
T/o Worthy Down for night flying practice. Crashed on landing and finished up inverted. Squadron Leader Alban Spencer Ellerton, a permanent officer, had been educated, privately, in Germany but on the outbreak of war in August 1914, he returned home and joined the Coldstream Guards as a private soldier, though within he a year he was commissioned.

Subsequently transferring to the RFC his war service appears to have been spent as an equipment officer and I suspect his pilot training was conducted by 99 Squadron to which he was attached in January 1928. Seriously injured in the night flying accident, he appears not to have held any further flying posts, though he rose to air rank, retiring as an Air Commodore on 14th June 1949. He died on Friday, 15th December 1978.

Flying Officer Ernest Richard White was a graduate from the January 1926, intake of Flight Cadets to Cranwell, while Pilot Officer Percy James Pratt was short service commissioned, *Gazetted* 1st March 1929, issue 33473, page 1468.

The inquest, subsequently adjourned, was reported in *The Western Morning News And Mercury* on Thursday, March 27th, 1930; *"The inquest was opened at Worthy Down Aerodrome, Hants., yesterday on Flying Officer Frederick* [sic]

Richard White and Pilot Officer Percy James Pratt, who were killed on Monday when the Vickers-Virginia machine in which they had been flying crashed at the aerodrome.

"Only formal evidence was taken, and the inquest was adjourned for three weeks in the hope that two other occupants of the machine who were injured would then be able to give evidence.

"The two injured men are Squadron Leader Ellerton, who is still seriously ill, and Aircraftsman Reich, whose condition is fairly satisfactory.

"The funeral of Flying Officer Frederick Richard White, who was a native of Cawsand, near Plymouth, will take place with Air Force honours at Rame Church at 11.30 a.m., tomorrow, under the direction of Flight-Lieut. E S Moulton-Barrett, adjutant of the Royal Air Force, Mount Batten.

"The body, on arrival by train at Plymouth this evening, will be met by an officer and a party of airmen from Mount Batten, and conveyed to St. Andrew's Church, Cawsand, where it will remain during the night. The funeral cortege will leave the church tomorrow for Rame Parish Church, where the funeral will take place."

Monday 24 March 1930
32 Squadron *Not reported*
Siskin IIIA J9376
T/o Kenley and on arrival at Duxford the undercarriage collapsed on landing. Believed damaged beyond repair.

During the month, an unnamed pilot attached to 503 Squadron SR attempted to take off from Waddington in Hyderabad J8319 with the rear control column locks in place. This resulted in the bomber coming down, nose first, near the airfield and, presumably, sustaining damage beyond economical repair as there are no further movement recordings.

Monday 31 March 1930
99 Squadron Hiniadi I JJ9036 Believed damaged beyond repair following an incident at the petrol pumps at Manston. Originally built as a Hyderabad the bomber had undergone conversion, in works, during 1929.

APRIL

Tuesday 1 April 1930
6 Squadron *Not reported*
Bristol F.2J C766
T/o Ismailia and while in the vicinity of Lake Tiberius ran out of fuel and in the ensuing forced-landing near Rosh Pina on the north side of the lake was damaged beyond repair. The Bristol was salvaged and later reduced to produce.

Tuesday 8 April 1930
19 Squadron F/O R P Teale +
Siskin IIIA J8888
T/o Duxford and stalled out of control in the process of making a gliding turn. Flying Officer Roger Pridgin Teale. A January 1925, Flight Cadet reporting to Cranwell, Roger Pridgin Teale graduated with a permanent commission on 11th December 1926 [LG 1 January 1927, issue 33237, page 121].

Wednesday 11 April 1930
1 Squadron F/O K S Brake Injured
Hawker Hornet J9682
T/o Tangmere for a trials flight and when flying at 3,000 feet collided with the Siskin featured below, both machines falling at Windmill Hill*near Chichester in West Sussex. The collision took off the top wing of the Hornet [the fore-runner of the Hawker Fury] slightly injuring flying Officer Kenneth Stanley Brake who had graduated from the Cadet College at Cranwell on 30th July 1926 [LG 17 August 1926, issue 33192, page 5446].

43 Squadron P/O J Heber Percy Safe See 19 June 1930
Siskin IIIA J9359
T/o Tangmere and destroyed in the manner described above. One report indicates the two pilots were indulging in mock dog-fighting; both pilots parachuted successfully. Pilot Officer John Heber Percy graduated from the College with a permanent commission on 14th December 1929 [LG 17 January 1930, issue 33571, page 347]. Not surprisingly the twin-crash was reported in the press, the extract that follows appearing the next day in the *Portsmouth Evening News:*
"Two aeroplanes from the RAF station at Tangmere, near Chichester, came into collision when travelling at High Speed, 3,000 feet up over the Halnaker district yesterday afternoon. The 'planes concerned were Siskin and experimental machine which were piloted by Pilot Officer H Percy [sic] *and Flying Officer Brake respectively. Both pilots made a safe landing in a ploughed field by making use of their parachutes.*

Pilot Officer Percy was unhurt, but Flying Officer Brake was not so fortunate, landing with a broken arm and several cuts to his face, his injuries being apparently received in getting clear of his machine. The aeroplanes crashed about half a mile apart. The Siskin overturned before striking the ground, and the other machine nose-dived, being almost buried in the earth."

* Probably Halnaker a hamlet in the South Downs National Park a few miles to the north of Chichester.

Saturday 12 April 1930
6 Squadron *Not reported*
Bristol F.2J FR4925
T/o Ismailia [though Ramleh is a possibility] and reduced to produce following a forced landing at Deir el Bela [probably Deir al-Balah in the Gaza Strip].

Monday 14 April 1930
6 Squadron *Not reported*
Bristol F.2J J6622
T/o Ismailia [though Ramleh cannot be discounted] and damaged beyond repair while landing at Ramleh. Broken down for spares and produce.

Tuesday 15 April 1930
84 Squadron *Not reported*
Wapiti I J9085
T/o Shaibah in what is described as *"bombing formation"* and having climbed to 6,000 feet collided with the Wapiti summarised below, both machines being written off. With no reported of fatalities, it seems most likely that both crews either abandoned their aircraft by parachute, or survived subsequent crash-landings.

84 Squadron *Not reported*
Wapiti I J8099
T/o Shaibah and lost in the manner outlined in the previous summary.

Thursday 17 April 1930
111 Squadron Lt Y Kobayashi Injured
Siskin IIIA J8861 Japan
T/o Hornchurch and destroyed near the airfield after catching fire in the air. Lieutenant Yoshito Kobayashi of the Imperial Japanese Air Service, attached to the Royal Air Force, baled out successfully though, as my co-author reports, he sustained burns to his face and wrist when the Siskin's petrol tank exploded and then sustained an injury to his left ankle when the strong winds dragged him along the ground before he could release his parachute harness. Prior to Japan's entry into the Second World War he became a Naval Test Pilot and was instrumental in the development of the Zero naval fighter. In 1941 he spent time in Nazi Germany as an observer while between 1942 and 1943 he commanded the 253rd Air Group based at Kavieng. In July 1943, and now ranked Captain, he was assigned to the Naval Air Arsenal. His final appointment in the war was as Executive Officer attached to the Yokosuka Air Group. Paul McMillan reports in RAF Commands Forum that Captain Yoshito Kobayashi died in 1950.

Wednesday 23 April 1930
47 Squadron P/O F S Barron +
Fairey IIIF S1201 AC1 C F Davis +
T/o Khartoum and crashed owing to engine failure, followed by a stall, at Heliopolis. Pilot Officer Francis Slade Barron was a short service commission officer whose details were published in *The London Gazette* on 6th November 1928, issue 33436, page 7215. He was twenty-six years of age, Aircraftman Cyril Fred Davis being twenty-two.
The latter's service number 364028 identifies him as a boy entrant, joining between July 1922 and January 1924.

Sunday 27 April 1930
31 Squadron *Not reported*
Bristol F.2b J6616/C
T/o Fort Sandeman only to fly into a line of telegraph wires; wrecked. The Bristol, which had arrived at the Aircraft Depot Drigh Road from the UK by January 1923, and was initially issued to 20 Squadron, was recovered and dumped at the Lahore aircraft park.

MAY

Monday 5 May 1930
20 Squadron F/O J W Hawke Injured
Bristol F.2b F4414/N LAC E R Charlesworth +
T/o Peshawar intending to ferry the Bristol to Lahore but on arrival at Jhelum landing ground in the Punjab collied with telegraph wires and crashed out of control. Flying Officer John William Hawke survived the crash, but died from his injuries on Thursday, 15th May, 24-hours after the squadron's second fatal accident during the month of May. His short service commission was promulgated in the *Gazette* on 24th April 1928, issue 33378, page 2904.
Probably in his fifth year of service, having joined as a civilian, Leading Aircraftman Ernest Raymond Charlesworth's service number was 359557.

101 Squadron *Not reported*
Sidestrand II J9180/B1
T/o Catfoss and on return, and with inclement weather conditions across the area, collided with a tree on approach to land. Reaching the landing area on touch down the undercarriage gave way. At the time the squadron, normally based at Andover, was engaged in armament training.

Wednesday 14 May 1930
20 Squadron F/Lt J C H Tavendale +
Bristol F.2J F4562/C LAC H J Chapell +
T/o Peshawar and crashed out of control in the wake of engine failure, coming down near the airfield at Ali Musjid. Flight Lieutenant James Charles Henry Tavendale, a permanent officer, was *Gazetted* on 13th October 1925, issue 33092, page 6617.
Leading Aircraftman Henry John Chapell joined as a boy between July 1922 and January 1925, and was allocated 363555 as his service identity.

Saturday 17 May 1930
11 Squadron F/O R W A Stroud +
Wapiti IIA AC1 C S Wiltshire +
T/o Risalpur tasked for bombing operations in the course of which Flying Officer Richard William Alexander Stroud was mortally wounded. Heroically, he had managed to regain Risalpur but crashed out of control whilst trying to land. His short service commission granted on 1st July 1927, was *Gazetted* on the 19th July 1927, issue 33295, page 4649. The loss of this aircraft and crew was the first fatal accident suffered by the squadron since arriving in India during January 1929.
Aircraftman Charles Samuel Wiltshire, like Leading Aircraftman Chapell who was killed three days previously, began his service as a boy airman, his service identity being 364367.

Thursday 29 May 1930
601 Squadron AAF *Not reported*
Wapiti IIA J9597
T/o Hendon and reported as *"crashed."*

601 Squadron AAF *Not reported*
Wapiti IIA J9599
T/o Hendon and reported to have crashed on the airfield. It is not clear if the two accidents are related..

During the month, the precise date not known, 6 Squadron Bristol F.2b F4344 was damaged beyond repair when the undercarriage collapsed taking off from Balir.

JUNE

Wednesday 4 June 1930
6 Squadron *Not reported*
Bristol F.2J F4362
T/o Ramleh and wrecked here through the combination of a tyre bursting on landing followed by one of the wheels dropping into a hole, thereby imposing a massive strain on the airframe that it was deemed beyond repair.

Thursday 5 June 1930
202 Squadron F/O R F Francis +
Fairey IIID S1078 LAC C D Harris +
T/o Kalafrana and whilst over the sea off Birzebbuga in the SE of the Island of Malta. Flying Officer Reginald Frederick Francis was short service commissioned, as promulgated in *The London Gazette* of 29th July 1924, issue 32960, page 5723.
Leading Aircraftman Charles Drewery Harris, 359622, joined soon after Leading Aircraftman Charlesworth, whose death is reported on May 5th, 1930.
This was the first fatal accident reported from the squadron since reforming at Kalafrana on New Year's Day 1929.

Thursday 12 June 1930
3 Squadron P/O Lord M A Douglas- Safe
Bulldog II J9574 Hamilton
T/o Upavon and abandoned following a collision with the aircraft summarised below. Pilot Officer Lord Malcolm Avondale Douglas-Hamilton entered the Cadet College at Cranwell as a Flight Cadet in the September 1927 term, graduating with a permanent commission on 27th July 1929 [LG 27 August 1929, issue 33529, page 5569]. His service, however, was relatively brief and he was placed on the Retired List, in the rank of flying officer, on 20th April 1932. With war between the United Kingdom and Germany breaking out in 1939, he returned to the Royal Air Force, serving until 29th November 1946, when he reverted to the Retired List, this time as a group captain OBE DFC and Greek AFC. A relatively brief *Wikipedia* biography of his life, which ended, somewhat ironically in an air accident on 21st July 1964, in the equatorial jungle in a mountainous area of Cameroon; he was 54 years of age. His son Niall, who was much involved with his father's charter flying company, also died. It will also be recalled that it was on to the family's Scottish estate that Rudolph Hess, Deputy-Führer to Adolph Hitler, parachuted in May 1941.
Bulldog J9574 is believed to have been the first of its type to be destroyed in squadron service.

100 Squadron Sgt F E O'Meara +
Horsley II J8005 LAC W Hagan Safe

T/o Upavon to return to its base at Bicester, having been at Upavon since the previous day. What happened next is described in the *Salisbury & Winchester Journal* in its issue of Friday, 20th June 1930: *"Sitting without a jury at the Aerodrome, Upavon, on Saturday* [14th] *afternoon, Mr. A L Forrester, coroner for Wiltshire, held an enquiry into the circumstances into the death of Air-Pilot Sergeant Fred O'Meara of the Royal Air Force who, as reported in our last issue* [Friday, 13th June 1930, the official announcement from the Air Ministry] *was killed whilst flying on Thursday the 12th, last. Aircraftman William Hagen of the RAF stationed at Bicester Aerodrome, said that on Wednesday the 11th inst. he left the Bicester Aerodrome in a Hawker Horsley aeroplane, piloted by Sergeant O'Meara, their destination being the aerodrome at Upavon. The next day, accompanied with O'Meara, he went up in the same machine, and when at the altitude of some 900 to 1,000 feet and between Netheravon and Upavon, three fighters were diving at the tail of their machine. Two passed safely, but the third machine struck the fuselage just ahead of the tail unit. Witness turned to Sergeant O'Meara, to see him trying to correct the machine. O'Meara turned to witness and shouted. Witness waited until he saw O'Meara make his safety valve, and commenced to climb out of the cockpit. Witness then left the aeroplane with his parachute. The parachute opened and witness landed safely. When he landed, he found the machine had crashed.*

"Lord Malcolm Douglas-Hamilton said he was a pilot officer of the Royal Air Force stationed at Upavon, and on the 12th last, at 11.15 a.m. he was engaged in an exercise consisting of air attacks on a bomber aeroplane between Upavon and Netheravon. There were three aeroplanes, and he was piloting one. The machine that he was piloting dived, and as he got on top of the Horsley machine, piloted by Sergeant O'Meara, he received what appeared to him a severe air bump. The next thing he knew he had collided with the Horsley bomber, and was falling out of control, so he fell out of the machine, and the parachute acted.

"Flight Lieutenant Charles Arthur Lindsop [sic] *of the RAF Medical Service, stationed at Upavon aerodrome, said that he was called to Chisenbury Down in the parish of Enford on the previous Thursday, where he found the deceased man lying about 20 yards from the machine, dead. His parachute was open. The deceased died from a fractured skull. The coroner returned a verdict accordingly."*

Sergeant Frederick Ernest O'Meara, 335796 [a former boy airman] it will be recalled survived a very serious crash on 30th January 1928, while attached to 45 Squadron, in which his observer, Leading Aircraftman Harold Edwin Fisher lost his life.

Friday 13 June 1930

60 Squadron Sgt E A Hindelang +
Wapiti IIA J9712 LAC W H Lansdell Injured

T/o Kohat only to stall and crash, bursting into flames on impact with the ground. Leading Aircraftman William Henry Lansdell was pulled clear, but grievously burned and, mercifully, he died the next day. Their deaths were the first involving one of the squadron's recent acquisition of Wapiti as replacement for the DH.9A.

Both had set out on their air force service as boy entrants, Leading Aircraftman William Henry Lansdell, 335828, being senior in times of service than his pilot, 363654 Sergeant Edward Albert Hindelang.

Tuesday 17 June 1930

29 Squadron W/Cdr B E Smythies DFC +
DH.60M Moth K1209 AC1 F R S Holben Injured

T/o North Weald but before becoming airborne collided with roller, crashed and caught fire. Wing Commander Bernard Edward Smythies was born on 9th December 1896, and was formerly of the Royal Engineers before transferring to the RFC. His Casualty Card shows he was attached for temporary duty with 41 Squadron [DH.5] between 28th August and 3rd September 1917, though in what capacity it is not stated, except that on completing the duty he returned to England. His DFC was published, without citation, in the Edinburgh edition of the *Gazette* on January 6th, 1919, issue 13378, page 82, noting it was for service in France. His promotion to Wing Commander was *Gazetted* on 3rd July 1923, issue 32841, page 4621.

As Squadron Leader Smythies he re-formed 41 Squadron [7F.1 Snipe] at Northolt on 1st April 1923, subsequently on 30th April 1927, taking command of 99 Squadron [Hyderabad] from Squadron Leader W J Ryan and remained 'in the chair' until 26th July 1929, when he was succeeded by Wing Commander W B Hargreaves.

Aircraftman Frederick Reginald Stanley Holben is believed to have recovered from his injuries. An account of the accident was reported the next day in the *Sheffield Daily Telegraph* beneath the headline *'Air Pilot Killed - Machine in Flames After Impact' "Two flying accidents, one of them fatal, occurred in the South of England yesterday. The fatal accident was caused through a rising aeroplane striking a grass mower at North Weald aerodrome, just outside London.The machine, a Moth, piloted by Wing Commander Bernard Edward Smythies DFC, of the 29th Fighter Squadron, was just about to take off from the aerodrome when it charged into the mower. Wing Commander Smythies was thrown from the machine, and so badly injured that he died later in hospital.*

First-class Aircraftsman F R S Holben, who was in the machine as mechanic, had a miraculous escape. He only just missed death by fire, for, immediately on impact with the grass mower, the aeroplane burst into flames, Holben jumped clear."

The non-fatal accident involved a Fairey machine attached to Lee-on-Solent which crashed while landing on Southampton Water, Flight Lieutenants Hall and Miller being picked up, uninjured, by a motor launch.

Thursday 19 June 1930
43 Squadron Sgt C G Wareham Safe
Siskin IIIA J8644
T/o Tangmere and written off following a collision in the air with the Siskin summarised below. The two Siskins were practicing flying a 'snake' formation at 2,000 feet. Sergeant Charles George Wareham was commissioned in the Technical Branch as a pilot officer for the duration of hostilities, 30th October 1940 [LG 19 November 1940, supplement 34996, page 6635]. Prior to his transfer from the General Duties Branch he was awarded the Air Force Medal for his services in Palestine [LG 8 June 1939, supplement 34633, page 3874]. On 21st October 1948, and now ranked Squadron Leader, he was appointed to a permanent commission [LG 1 February 1949, supplement 38525, page 556]. He retired, without further advancement in rank, at his own request on 29th June 1957 [LG 9 July 1957, supplement 41120, page 4087].

43 Squadron P/O J Heber Percy Safe
Siskin IIIA J9358
T/o Tangmere and destroyed in the collision referred to above. For Pilot Officer Heber Percy this was his second parachute descent in less than three months, my summary for 11th April 1930 explains what occurred on that occasion.

Tuesday 29 June 1930
602 Squadron AAF Wapiti I J9094 Damaged beyond repair at Renfrew after being struck, while parked, by the Wapiti summarised below.

602 Squadron AAF *Not reported*
Wapiti IIA J9602
T/o Renfrew but before becoming airborne collided, and damaged beyond repair, with the Wapiti reported above.

Although the exact date has not been reported, at some time in June, 207 Squadron wrote off Fairey IIIF J9168/B1 when on landing at Martlesham Heath it collided with a hangar.

JULY

Thursday 3 July 1930
70 Squadron *Not reported*
Victoria III J8235/M
T/o Hinaidi where in crashed in the course of a landing at night. Taken on service charge on 14th December 1926, its entire service life was with 70 Squadron who collected the Victoria from the Aircraft Depot at Hinaidi where it had been received from the Packing Depot at Ascot.

Wednesday 9 July 1930
55 Squadron Sgt J R Gordon +
Wapiti IIA J9625
T/o Hinaidi but before becoming airborne ran into J9636 which was in the process of taxying. The latter was repaired and continued to serve until 1st June 1935, when it was struck off charge at the Aircraft Depot Hinaidi as 'Damaged Beyond Economical Repair' following recent service with 30 Squadron. Sergeant John Ritchie Gordon's death was the first reported from the squadron in 1930, as the consequence of a flying accident.
His service number 362338 indicates he entered as a boy, just ahead of Sergeant Hindelang who crashed the previous month.

Tuesday 15 July 1930
23 Squadron F/O P B Rogers + Sevenoaks [St. Nicholas] Churchyard
Gamecock I J7894
T/o Sutton Bridge and spun into the ground at Gedney Dawsmere a Lincolnshire hamlet overlooking The Wash and the Holbeach Ranges. Flying Officer Peter Bagwell Rogers was *Gazetted* with a short service commission on 16th October 1928, issue 33430, page 6636. He had been promoted flying officer as recently as 12th April 1930 [LG 6 May 1930, issue 33603, page 2800]. The Kenley Revival website, quoting from *The Chronicle and Courier* newspaper, shows the following: *"Flying Officer Rogers was with the 23rd Squadron RAF Kenley and was down at the Sutton Bridge Training Camp with his Squadron. At about ten minutes past five on Tuesday evening he was at gun practice on the range at Holbeach Marsh, bordering the Wash, flying solo in a Gamecock aeroplane when he crashed. The only witness of the accident was his officer, Flight-Lieut. VictorCrome, who was driving a motor car from the range at Holbeach to the Sutton Bridge Camp. The officer saw Rogers' machine spin to the ground on the right hand side of him. He at once stopped his car and ran to the wrecked machine, to find deceased thrown out, and lying on the ground apparently dead. Flight-Lieut. Crome sent a message to the range, and to the camp for a doctor, who speedily arrived on the scene."*
An unacknowledged source offers: *"The accident had occurred ... while Rogers was circling, waiting for targets to be patched. He was only at about 400ft when the Gamecock went into a left-hand spin - too low to bale out. Seconds later, a civilian witness, Mr. G F Pearl, described 'a tremendous crash which seemed to shake the ground,' in George Cauldwell's beet field, followed by a cloud of smoke. The wreckage of the neat little bi-plane now, "looked just like an enormous heap of crumpled silver paper," according to Arthur Edgley, a witness from Lutton."*

Additional information remarks that he was one of five children, his father, Colonel J M Rogers DSO being a Justice of the Peace. Peter Bagwell was a keen motorist and was the proud owner of a Bugatti; his funeral was held on Friday 18th July, and was attended by his brother officers from 23 Squadron.

The Gamecock in which he lost his life was the fourth aircraft in the first production batch of thirty airframes J7891 to J7920.

111 Squadron *Not reported*
Siskin IIIA J8896
T/o Sutton Bridge and believed to have been damaged beyond repair here in a misjudged landing.

Saturday 26 July 1930
8 Squadron F/O G N Pilcher +
Fairey IIIF J9134 LAC R A Laidler +
T/o Khormaksar where it is reported it crashed. Flying Officer Geoffrey Norman Pilcher graduated with a permanent commission from Cranwell on 16th December 1925, *Gazetted* 12th January 1926, issue 33123, page 300.

Leading Aircraftman Laidler, 507565, was in his fifth year of service. The loss of this crew was only the second since acquiring the Fairey IIIF machines in January 1928; sadly, both were fatal.

Tuesday 29 July 1930
602 Squadron AAF. *Not reported*
Wapiti IIA J9602
T/o Leuchars but swung out of control and crashed.

AUGUST

Sunday 3 August 1930
603 Squadron AAF F/Lt A R H Miller +
Avro 504 F/O J E Glenny Safe
T/o Turnhouse but lost engine power, stalled and crashed. Flight Lieutenant Alexander Robertson Hunter Miller was killed on impact but, amazingly, Flying Officer James Esme Glenny was unhurt, though no doubt badly shocked by the experience.

"An unfortunate accident occurred at Turnhouse Aerodrome yesterday evening; so read the opening line of the report published by *the Scotsman* beneath the headline *'Air Crash At Turnhouse - Young Edinburgh Pilot Killed'* and continued; *"resulting in the death of Flight-Lieutenant A R H Miller, of 603 [City of Edinburgh] Bombing Squadron, Auxiliary Air Force.*

"Lieutenant Miller had gone up on a practice flight, and, after he had made a turn of the aerodrome, his engine failed. Although the engine restarted, and the pilot endeavoured to pull the nose of the machine up, the aeroplane stalled and crashed inside the aerodrome. Lieutenant Miller was killed, but his passenger accompanying him was uninjured.

"The deceased airman was an accomplished pilot and exceedingly keen on his flying duties, giving up much of his leisure time to the work of the unit. He was particularly interested in sport, and assisted in the supervision of the squadron football team. His sudden death has cast a gloom over the Turnhouse station, where he was one of the popular of the young Territorial officers.

"Flight-Lieutenant Miller was well-known to a wide circle of friends in Edinburgh. He was employed on the staff of Messrs Machlachlans [Ltd.], Castle Brewery, Craigmillar, with which firm his father is associated.

"He was 29 years of age, and lived at 32 St. Alban's Road, Edinburgh.

Beneath the above account was a report of a narrow escape from death, or serious injury, to two officers from Henlow who who were heading for Leuchars, having taken off from Henlow on Saturday morning. Over Wingates Moor, Northumberland they encountered a thunderstorm and, wisely, they elected to make a precautionary landing. All might have been well, but a wheel of their aeroplane [type not identified] dropped into a ditch causing it to somersault. Shaken, but otherwise unhurt apart from bruises to their legs, Flying Officer D L McLean and his passenger, Squadron Leader J E Crolius, scrambled out and in pouring rain walked to the nearest village where they telephoned news of their 'mishap' to the authorities. Both then continued by car to Morpeth, where they spent the night.

Wednesday 6 August 1930
41 Squadron P/O W Sawyer +
Siskin IIIA
T/o Northolt and while low-flying near the hamlet of Casthorpe to the WSW of Barrowby on the western side of Grantham, Lincolnshire, flew into a tree and crashed. Seconds later the wreckage caught fire. Pilot Officer Wilfred Sawyer, previously a Halton apprentice, had graduated the previous December from the Cadet College at Cranwell where he had been assigned to A Squadron and represented the College on the rugby football field.

The inquest into his death was reported in *The Times,* reproduced on the website World Naval Ships, which the authors have pleasure in acknowledging: *"Flight Lieutenant Leach said Sawyer, who was a fully qualified pilot, asked his permission to go up and test an engine. Witness agreed, adding that he should be down again in twenty minutes. Sawyer did not have permission to go to Casthorpe, which was outside his flying area. Evidence was given that the machine was in good order and fit for flying. Several witnesses said they saw Sawyer flying low at Casthorpe, and John Mann stated that the machine struck a large elm tree, and shortly afterwards crashed. The Coroner said it seemed that*

Sawyer was trying to give someone a friendly salute at Casthorpe House. He was flying too low and did not realise he was in a hollow. A verdict of "Accidental Death was brought about by an error of judgement" was returned."

In several ways the death of young Pilot Officer Wilfred Sawyer; he was 21, mirrors a not uncommon attitude of the time. Although it has to be conjecture on my part, I suspect Wilfred had contacted a friend - probably at Casthorpe House or nearby - that he would give them a 'buzz.' And I have little doubt he was quite prepared for a 'ticking off' when he returned to Northolt. Paul Brickhill's account of Douglas Bader's*early service flying makes several references to what today would be regarded as a very serious breach of flying discipline.

* Flight Cadet Douglas Robert Stuart Bader was in the 1928 September entry and, undoubtedly, knew Wilfred Sawyer.

Friday 8 August 1930
25 Squadron Sgt O H McNair +
Siskin IIIA J9325
T/o Hawkinge and crashed when making a slow turn near the village of Falmer some 4 miles NE of the south coast resort of Brighton in East Sussex. An inquest into Sergeant Owen Herbert McNair's death was held the next day at Falmer and was reported in *The Times*: *"Flight Lieutenant Sidney Toomer of No. 4[Army Co-operation] Squadron, said that he had come down from Hampshire to arrange a demonstration of how single-seater fighters attacked troops on the march. McNair was flying one of the aeroplanes, and the demonstration was actually over when the crash occurred. Two aeroplanes had resumed flying in formation and were waiting for McNair.*

"When I first saw him," he continued, "he was flying very slowly and at a fairly low altitude, with his engine throttled down. As soon as he passed over the troops he commenced a right-hand turn and at the same time opened his throttle, but he had lost flying speed and crashed."

"The Coroner asked whether he agreed that if McNair had not crashed he would have flown into the troops? Flight Lieutenant Toomer said that he did not. He considered it was an error in judgement. McNair was flying too slowly to make the turn. It had been said that McNair waved to the troops. I think he was flying over them to say good-bye and there is no truth in the suggestion that he was waving in order to give warning that he was about to crash.

"The Coroner, addressing the jury, said that it was apparent from the evidence that there was not question of McNair having crashed in order to avoid injuring the troops. "It was an error of judgement, and it is extraordinarily easy to make in such circumstances. The relatives may gain some measure of consolation from the fact that there are still gallant young men like McNair who hold their lives cheap in the performance of their duty. It would be a sad day for England if "Safety First" ever became the slogan of our race." A verdict of "Death by Misadventure" was returned."

The exercise which resulted in the death of former boy Sergeant McNair, service number 364199, was an army co-operation demonstration involving troops from the 167th Infantry Brigade. As I remarked in the summary for Pilot Officer Wilfred Sawyer, this inquest mirrors the acceptance by society in regard to air accidents of the time.

Monday 11 August 1930
6 Squadron *Not reported*
Bristol F.2J H1438
T/o Ismailia [though Ramleh cannot be discounted] and while landing at Imshash, Egypt struck a sharp ridge and overturned.

Thursday 28 August 1930
6 Squadron *Not reported*
Bristol F.2b JR6635
T/o Ramleh or Ismailia and forced-landed on rising ground, overturning in the process, on the Kolundia landing ground near Jerusalem. Prior to acceptance by 6 Squadron, the Bristol underwent a rebuild at Aboukir, hence the 'R' insert in the airframe serial.

Saturday 30 August 1930
13 Squadron *Not reported*
Atlas I J9525
T/o Odiham at dawn and in the gloom failed to clear some trees; crashed and damaged beyond repair. For the purpose of manoeuvres the roundels had been replaced by Maltese Crosses.

SEPTEMBER

Monday 1 September 1930
6 Squadron *Not reported*
Bristol F.2J F4349
T/o Ismailia for night flying practice and wrecked in a landing accident. At the time the squadron was maintaining a detachment at Ramleh, so the accident my have taken place at this location.

Wednesday 3 September 1930
30 Squadron F/O C P Hanlon Injured
Wapiti IIA J9489 LAC J Cooper +
T/o Mosul in the company of the crew summarised below, both being instructed to drop leaflets on tribesmen under the aegis of Sheikh Mahmoud who had only recently returned to Iraq from exile.*On completion of their assignment the

two crews heading back to Mosul, flying at 4,000 feet. Nearing the airfield, Flying Officer Charles Peter Hanlon pulled up for a wing-over, completely forgetting his companion was following and slightly above and as a consequence a collision occurred. Leading Aircraftman James Cooper was killed instantly, but Flying Officer Hanlon survived - it is assumed he took to his parachute - but was critically injured, succumbing on Christmas Day. Short Service commissioned, his details were *Gazetted* on 27th March 1928, issue 33370, page 2243.

Leading Aircraftman Cooper, 155269, probably enlisted in the late autumn of 1917.

* See page 93 of John Hamblin's history of the squadron for additional information, while on 91 two photographs show the shattered remains of the two Wapiti IIAs.

30 Squadron F/O H L McCulloch Safe
Wapiti IIA 9623 LAC T W Kent Injured
T/o Mosul and totally destroyed following the collision described above. Air-Britain's *J File* notes that J9623 had experi4nced a starting accident at Mosul on as recently as 6th August; now wrecked, it had accumulated a total off 200 and 5 minutes flying hours.

Flying Officer Hugh Lindsay McCulloch was granted a short service commission on 2nd November 1928, *Gazetted* 6th November 1928, issue 33436, page 7215. Subsequently, he became a Commander [Air] in the Royal Navy.

Wednesday 10 September 1930
25 Squadron
Siskin IIIA J8885
T/o Hawkinge*and damaged beyond repair after forced-landing on the golf links at Lampeter, Ceredigion.

* May not have been the departure airfield.

Monday 15 September 1930
11 Squadron Sgt O C Clarke +
Wapiti IIA LAC F S Valentine +
T/o Risalpur and wrecked in the Lowaria Pass in the NWF; both losses from the squadron reported to date had been fatal. Sergeant Owen Cambridge Clarke, 330150, elected to leave civilian life behind and seek adventure with the Royal Air Force and enlisted between March and August 1919. His observer, Leading Aircraftman Frank Spencer Valentine, 365072, joined the service a few later as a boy entrant.

Wednesday 24 September 1930
84 Squadron *Not reported*
Wapiti I J9097
T/o Shaibah for night flying practice and believed written off after undershooting the landing area and turning over.

Friday 26 September 1930
600 Squadron AAF *Not reported*
DH.9A DC J8469
T/o from an unidentified airfield and while over Fife-shire overtaken with engine failure. Forced-landing near Lochty Station, the DH skidded across a field, coming to an abrupt stop when it hit a stone wall and nosed over.

Normally based at Hendon in North London, the crash location suggests the squadron may have been on some form of training camp.

Tuesday 30 September 1930
17 Squadron P/O G J Pawson Injured
Bulldog IIA J9587
T/o Tangmere for a patrol in accordance with the air exercises and, as outlined below, crashed into trees in Arundel Park.

17 Squadron F/L G C A Armstrong +
Bulldog IIA K1083
T/o Tangmere leading his flight in continuation of the air exercises, his orders being to patrol an area to the north of Amberley and in the direction of Pulborough in West Sussex. What happened next is described in a report published in the Aviation Magazine *Aeroplane* and reproduced on the Aviation Safety Network website, which the authors acknowledge:

"Squadron Leader Richard Harrison, who identified the bodies, said that they were attached to the Upavon Station and temporarily stationed at Tangmere for air exercises. Armstrong was leading a flight of three Bristol Bulldog single-seaters with instructions to patrol the air immediately north of Amberley. The other machines were occupied by Sergeant Birkinshaw and Pilot Officer Pawson.

"The atmosphere was clear over the aerodrome with light clouds to the east. The airmen were experienced flyers and had been in the district the previous day. The visibility was sufficiently good for them to fly with safety. The previous patrol had reported that while flying at 3,000 feet they had noticed the ground obscured in places by cloud. They could, however, see the aerodrome.

"Pilot Officer Pawson said that they were flying at 3,000 feet. The ground became obscured with cloud. They dived through this and suddenly hit the trees.

"The Coroner asked whether the trees were obscured all the time until the machines hit them. The witness said that they were and that the mist was lying on the ground. A verdict of accidental death was returned."

The Daily Mirror newspaper. Wednesday, October 1st, outlined the above, adding: *"The sole eye-witness of the accident was an elderly employee of the Duke of Norfolk named Frank Hoare. "I was at work in the road when I heard the three 'planes approaching, obviously flying very low, though I did not see them at first owing to the thick mist," he said. "Then I was startled by a loud roaring and saw a machine diving through the trees straight at me."*

"A few moments later there was a series of crashes, and the hillside for a radius of 150 yards was littered with wreckage and branches which had been snapped off the trees.

"The machines were so badly smashed that it was with great difficulty that Flight-Lieutenant Armstrong and Sergeant Birkishaw could be extricated from the wreckage.

"The former was dead, and Birkishaw was so terribly injured that he died last night. Pilot Officer Geoffrey John Pawson, pilot of the third machine, had an amazing escape. When rescuers arrived he was limping about. He received only a few cuts, and surprised the rescuers by cooling asking for a cigarette.

"Two of the wrecked 'planes lie close together among the trees, and the other machine, which was piloted by Pawson, is in the open about one hundred yards further down the hill.

"Amid the wreckage was a parachute apparently half-opened, and part of a camera and films were also found. Some portions of the machines were discovered a considerable distance from most of the wreckage and one wheel was lying a hundred yards away."

The *Mirror* ended its report with a note regarding the inquest and a statement to the effect that the crash at Arundel Park brings the total killed in Royal Air Force accidents this year to forty-nine; the total for 1929 being forty-two.

As a flying officer, Gerald Christopher Allan Armstrong was seconded on 13th November 1926, for service as Aide de Camp to the Governor of South Australia [LG 23 November 1926, issue 33223, page 7581], an appointment that ceased on the last day of October 1927 [LG 8 November 1927, issue 33327, page 7119].

17 Squadron Sgt W Birkinshaw Injured
Bulldog IIA K1085
T/o Tangmere similarly tasked and lost in the circumstances described above. This trio of aeroplanes were the second of the Bulldog type to be written off in squadron service, 3 Squadron having reported one of their establishment being destroyed earlier in the year.

Critically injured, Sergeant Wilfred Birkinshaw, 326793, died from his injuries within hours of the accident. He was one several ex-boy entrants to lose his life in 1930.

OCTOBER

Sunday 5th October 1930
Outside of the parameters for this book, nevertheless mention has to be made of the crash near Beauvas in France of Airship R.101 G-FAAW which took the lives of forty-eight passengers and crew, including the Air Vice-Marshal Sir William Sefton Brancker KCB AFC [Retired].

Tuesday 14 October 1930
84 Squadron DH.9A J7872 Damaged during starting at Shaibah. There are no further entries thereby suggesting it may have been damaged beyond worthwhile repair. It is mentioned in my summary for 84 Squadron DH.9A E963 wrecked during take off from Shaibah on 3rd August 1928.

Sunday 19 October 1930
47 Squadron *Not reported*
Fairey IIIF IV J9815
T/o Khartoum and on forced-landing with engine failure at Assuit [believed to be Asyut] in Egypt ran up against a boulder and tipped onto its nose; believed damaged beyond repair.

During the month 207 Squadron at Bircham Newton had the misfortune to write off Fairey IIIF J9137; there are no reports of injuries.

NOVEMBER

Tuesday 4 November 1930
56 Squadron F/O M I Barnett +
Siskin IIIA J9907
T/o North Weald and suffered catastrophic failure of the wings, plummeting to the ground in Little Wood at Barnes Farm, Fryerning a mile or so NW of Ingatestone, Essex. Flying Officer Max Ian Barnett was granted a short service commission promulgated on 27th March 1928, issue 33370, page 2243.

Headed *'Plane Crash At Fryerning - RAF Officer Killed - Engine Embedded in the Earth'* Friday's edition of the *Essex Chronicle* provided its readers with a full account of the tragedy and the inquest into the death of Flying Officer Barnett: *"A tragic aeroplane crash occurred at Fryerning on Tuesday. A section of single-seater fighting machines attached to the 56th Squadron, RAF, at North Weald, was engaged in day bombing operations in the neighbourhood. One of the machines, piloted by Flying Officer Max Ian Barrett, aged 23, whose home is in Richmond Avenue, Merton Abbey, near Wimbledon, had risen to a high altitude, when, according to eye witnesses, at Ingatestone, the upper wings fell off, "looking like bits of paper in the sky." The machine made a dive to earth, falling with tremdous force in a field at Little Wood, Barns Farm, Fryerning, occupied by Mr. A Wybe. The machine was reduced to a heap of ruins, and the engine was almost embedded in the soil. Flying-Officer Barnett was dead when extricated. His injuries were so extensive death must have been instantaneous. Pieces of wing were picked up in a garden at Mountnessing, one and a half miles away. The body of the dead airman was conveyed in an ambulance to the mortary at Chelmsford to await an inquest, and a guard was place around the wreckage, which was later inspected by experts from North Weald.*

'The Inquest'

'Unconscious or a Seizure'

"The inquest was held on Wednesday at the London Road Congregational church school room, Chelmsford, by Mr. Coroner C E Lewis, who sat with a jury of which mr. Walter Dodbet was foreman.

"Flight-Lieut. Harold Ivor Chapman, North Weald, Commander of "a" Flight, 56th Fighter Squadron, RAF, said he was in charge of the squadron to which deceased belonged. On Tuesday morning he was taking his squadron on a battle flight line. There were three 'planes, deceased was on his left, and there was another machine on the right. They left North Weald Aerodrome at 10.25 a.m., and he saw the deceased get into the cockpit of his machine. Deceased was the sole occupant of that machine, and the three machines went up. Witness saw the deceased 'plane, which was slightly above witness, when they were at a height of 20,000 feet. After about twenty minutes' flight witness came down in a steady dive, and missed the deceased at about 10,000 feet.

"Witness added: I had previously detached the third aircraft at 10,000 feet, and sent it away, so when we were at 20,000 feet there were only deceased and myself there. I had previously given the deceased instructions to remain with me until we had reached 500 feet on the way down.

"The Coroner:- What did you do when you missed him? - I carried on, believing that he had met with a spot of engine trouble. I landed at the aerodrome about twenty minutes later, and expected to find him there. I was then told that the 'plane had crashed.

"Were you doing anything unusual in the way of flying? - No, everything was straightforward.

"You were not doing any stunt flying. - No, sir.

" Witness continued that deceased was accustomed to the machine in which he was flying. He was a fully proficient pilot.

"Witness produced deceased's log book, which showed he had previously carried out a similar flight to that in which he was engaged when he met his death.The machine was examined in the usual way before the flight. As a pilot he gave the greatest confidence.

"Walter J Judd, a fitter at North Weald Aerodrome, said that on the morning of the flight he made an inspection of the engine of the 'plane of which deceased was the pilot. He signed it as "serviceable for flying."

"Stanley Lang, an RAF rigger at North Weald Aerodrome, said his duties were to inspect the various parts of machines, other than the engines, before flights were started. He inspected this particular machine in the morning of the flight, and found it absolutely airworthy.

"Wm. James Sweeting, Council Houses, Fryerning, said that about 10.30 a.m. said on Tuesday he was in the garden of St. Anne's, Mountnessing, when he heard some 'planes.

"Witness continued: "Somehow I looked up. The sun shone on a 'plane which was alone. The sun caught the 'plane so that I could see it. The machine made a sudden turn to the left, and as it did so one of the wings seemed to come off. The wing, as it came to earth, looked like fragments of paper. The machine then dived straight to earth."

"In reply to Flight-Lieut. Goode [representing the RAF], witness said that when he first saw the machine, it was flying in a straight line, and continued so towards North Weald. The machine did not spin, but came down with the engine roaring.

"Flight-Lieut. Goode. That points to the possibility of the deceased being unconscious at the time; otherwise he would have shut the engine off.

"Arthur Shepherd, Green Street, Ingatestone, said he was ploughing in a field near Thoby Wood when he looked up and saw a 'plane coming straight down, and there came from it what appeared to "two fragments of paper."

"P.C. Faulkner said he was on duty at Ingatestone police Station when he heard the roar of an engine. This stopped suddenly, and he was informed that an aeroplane had crashed. He went to the scene and saw the wreck of an aeroplane. One wing was found in Wash Lane, Mountnessing, and the other wing 200 yards on the Thoby side of the main road. Deceased was in the cockpit, and witness removed him, although with difficulty. The body was the conveyed to Chelmsford Hospital.

"In reply to Flight-Lieut. Goode, witness stated that deceased's belt was fastened and the parachute was intact.

"Flight-Lieut. Goode said the reason he asked these questions was that pilots had been known to dive from a great height in order to test the strength of the wings. If the wings broke the pilot would jump out in the parachute.

"Dr. J Stirling-Hamilton said that about midday on Tuesday he saw the body of a man lying in a barn t Fryerning. The body was generally mutilated, practically every bone being fractured. Death, which was instantaneous, was due to multiple injuries.

"The Coroner observed that the possibility was that the deceased was that the deceased was either unconscious or that he had a seizure, and that as a result he was not in a position to do what he would otherwise have done to release himself. Of course that was only conjecture.

"Flight-Lieut. Goode: The RAF are conducting two inquiries regarding the cause of the crash.

'The jury returned a verdict that death was due to multiple injuries caused by the machine in which deceased was flying crashing, and that the evidence was insufficient to prove the cause of the crash.

"The coroner: - I feel sure we should like to express sympathy with the relatives and friends of the deceased officer, and also sympathy with the RAF at North Weald of the severe loss that they have sustained by the death of this officer.

"Flight-Lieut. Goode: Thank you, sir."

Friday 7 November 1930
501 Squadron SR P/O G N Warrington Injured
DH.9A DC J8491
T/o Filton for a ferry to Hawkinge where the DH was destined for storage. Approaching its destination in misty weather the pilot failed to see a haystack which lay in his path and in the resultant collision the machine caught fire, Pilot Officer George North Warrington being thrown out on impact and thereby escaping serious injury. A short service commission officer his details, including his death, are reported in Appendix D for officers granted their commissions on 9th July 1929.

I suspect the farmer felt none too happy to find his haystack and an adjacent stack a charred heap of what had been freshly mown grass.

A brief account of the crash was published in the *Dover Express* on Friday, 14th November 1930, which the authors acknowledge along with the website hosted by the Sussex History Forum.

Friday 14 November 1930
17 Squadron *Not reported*
Bulldog II J9589
T/o Upavon in formation during which it was struck by Bulldog IIA K1086, both machines being damaged beyond repair. The fact that the squadron was taking off into the sun was a factor in this accident.

17 Squadron *Not reported*
Bulldog IIA K1086
T/o Upavon and written off as described in the above summary.

Wednesday 19 November 1930
26 Squadron P/O J A Chance + Marylebone [St. Nicholas] Churchyard
Atlas Sgt A Maitland Injured
T/o Catterick and crashed into a field on the eastern side of the Great North Road near the village of Fencote and roughly 8 miles SSE from the airfield. Eyewitnesses report seeing the Atlas circling in mist with smoke coming from it; on impact it broke up, Sergeant Maitland being thrown clear of the wreckage which was now on fire. Among the first people on the scene were members of the Bedale Hunt and Miss Edith Bartram of Holtby Cottage. At great danger to themselves they managed to free John Anthony Chance from the cockpit, but it is thought, mercifully, he had perished in the crash. Additional information is reported on the Yorkshire Aircraft website.

Educated at Eton, Pilot Officer Chance was one of the Flight Cadets reporting to the Cadet College at Cranwell for the September 1928 term. Assigned to A Squadron, he graduated with a permanent commission on 26th July 1930 [LG 26th August 1930, issue 33638, page 5298]. He had survived for barely four months in active service.

A detailed report of the crash, headlined *'Local Flying Officer Burnt To Death - Fate of Mr. J A Chance in Yorkshire - "A sheet of Flame'* held the attention of readers of the *Warwick and Warwickshire Advertiser & Leamington Gazette* in its following Saturday edition: *"The member of a well-known Warwickshire family was this week burnt to death in an aeroplane accident in Yorkshire. He was Pilot Officer John Anthony Chance, aged 21, the son of Mr. Kenneth Chance, of Radford Semele. The accident occurred on Wednesday, the aeroplane in which he was accompanied bySergeant Adam Maitland - who was seriously injured- crashing in flames two miles from Catterick Aerodrome.*

"The officer was educated at Eton and received his flying training at Cranwell. He joined the 26th [Army Co-operation] Squadron of the Royal Air Force in September last.

"The aeroplane was seen circling in the mist, only a few above ground, by members of the staff of the Bedale Hunt kennels. It appeared to be in difficulties, and after wheeling several times it tilted to one side. There was a loud explosion and the machine then crashed. At first it seemed to be making a safe landing, buut when the machine touched the ground a sheet of flame rose.

"The kennel staff ran to the scene, and found Maitland lying close to the blazing aeroplane. They pulled him to safety, but they were unable to approach the machine on account of the flames.

"The scene of the tragedy was a stubble field 200 yards west of the Great North Road. There is a rift in the ground where the machine appeared to have first struck, and a charred track of at least 120 yards marks its progress along the field.

"The Air Ministry announcement is as follows:-

"As the result of an accident at Catterick to an Atlas aircraft of No. 26 [Army Co-operation] Squadron, Catterick, to-day, Pilot Officer John Anthony Chance, the pilot of the aircraft, was killed, and No. 156231 Sergeant Adam Maitland was seriously injured. This makes the forty-second RAF aeroplane crash this year and the sixty-second death.

"Miss Edith Bertram, a daughter of Mr. John Bertram, of Holtby Cottages, who was one of the first to reach the spot, said her attention was drawn to the machine owing to it flying so low.

""It circled several times above the house, and I saw smoke coming from it," she said. "One of the occupants waved to me, and I waved back. The pilot then circled above the field opposite my home, and appeared to make a normal descent, but as the aeroplane was descending I was certain it was on fire. When it touched the ground a sheet of flame shot out, and there was a terrific explosion.

"I ran across the field, and as I got there a member of the Bedale Hunt kennels staff came up. We saw Maitland in a crouching position about four yards from the blazing machine. He was very dazed, and his face and hands were badly burnt.

"We pulled him away, and he said, "There's another chap in there." It was impossible, however, to do anything."
Mr. Dan Wilkinson, an employee at the Bedale Hunt, aid: "Our kennel men and I, with bits of wood taken from the fuselage, managed to dislodge the body of the pilot. His clothes were burning all over. We put the flames out, but the man was dead."
"Mr Walter Couling, who is also employed at the Bedale kennels, said the flames rose about 40ft. high and it was a terrifying sight. "The hounds I was exercising stampeded," he added, "and some of them are still lost."

Tuesday 25 November 1930
100 Squadron F/Lt A H J Howlett + See 28 October 1929
Horsley II J8013 Australia
T/o Leuchars with the intent of returning to Donibristle but when east of the airfield collided with the Horsley summarised below. Born in the State of Victoria in 1891, Flight Lieutenant Alexander Harold James Howlett's service had been marred by at least two very serious air accidents, the first of which is reported in Appendix C 1924 and the entry against Flying Officer John Yarton Mills who was commissioned on 22nd July 1924 and the second while attached to 36 Squadron and summarised on 28th October 1929. His own short service commission had been promulgated on 22nd January 1924 in supplement 32900, page 688.

100 Squadron F/Lt G Brooks +
Horsley II J8015
T/o Leuchars and lost in the manner described above. This awful tragedy was reported in the Dundee edition of Scotland's *Evening Telegraph and Post* headlined:

'Leuchars Air Crash'
'Bodies of Victims Taken to Donibristle'
'Removal of Wreckage'

"The wreckage of the two aeroplanes that crashed on the moors near Leuchars yesterday afternoon is to-day being removed by men from the aerodrome.
"The bodies of the two officers, Lieut. H J Howlett, and Lieut. Gerald Brooks, who were killed, have been removed to Donibristle base, to which station they were attached.
"Arrangements are being made to-day for the funerals, but it is not anticipated that the bodies will be interred at Donibristle.
"Lieut. Howlett belonged to Australia and was having his second turn in training at Donibristle. Lieut. Brooks was a native of Gosport.

'The Accident'

"The machines crashed into the ground and one of them burst into flames. Both officers must have been killed outright, one of the bodies being badly burned.
"Early in the afternoon a flight of four machines arrived at the Leuchars base from Donibristle. In one machine, as a passenger, was Lieut.-Commander A E Thomson, of St. Andrews. He alighted at the aerodrome, and the machines took off again.
"The accident occurred just after the return journey had begun. Three of the 'planes were flying in "V" formation. The leading machine was in the act of turning at an altitude of about 600 feet at the time of the collision and was one of those involved.
"The machines crashed to the ground on the moors near Earlshall, about half a mile from Leuchars [as reported in the late editions of last night's "Evening Telegraph and Post."
"One of them burst into flames on reaching the ground, and the pilot was burned to death."

'Dash to Scene'

"The accident was seen from Leuchars Air Station and officers and men with ambulances and a fire tender hurried to the scene.
"Owing to the fact that the 'planes fell on what is practically marsh land considerable difficulty was experienced in reaching them. The fire tender and ambulance were "bogged."
"The machine that had taken fire burned for over two hours. It lay within a few yards of a big ditch, the water from which was of use in extinguishing the flames.
"The body of the ill-fated pilot of the burning 'plane was not recovered for some time. The other pilot's body [Flight Lieutenant Brooks] *was extricated from the wreckage of his machine by farm workers, who hurried to the scene.*
"The work of the men from Leuchars was directed by Group-Captain F E T Hewlett. The wreckage was search for a third victim, as at first it was supposed that another airman had been involved.
"The machines were Hawker-Horsley bombers."
Two photographs accompanied the article; that of Flight Lieutenant Howlett's aircraft showing a heap of wreckage, while the second photograph clearly shows J8015 on the tail section, the wings, though crumpled, more or less intact while the nose area appears totally crushed.

Thursday 27 November 1930
3 Squadron *Not reported*
Bulldog II J9579
T/o Eastchurch where it overturned, sustaining significant damage; believed written off charge.

DECEMBER

Monday 1 December 1930
43 Squadron *Not reported*
Siskin IIIA J8386
T/o Tangmere and on return landed heavily, bounced, stalled and hit the ground with a force that smashed the undercarriage. Although reported at Wittering the following April, it was probably here as a ground instructional airframe.

Tuesday 2 December 1930
19 Squadron *Not reported*
Siskin IIIA J9355
T/o Duxford and totally wrecked when, attempting to forced-land, it collided with a tree on land at Sharp's Farm, Broxted some 4 miles NE of Stanstead Mountfitchet, Essex.

Friday 5 December 1930
6 Squadron *Not reported*
Bristol F.2J JR6798
T/o Ramleh only to collide with the chimney of the station's incinerator; wrecked. First recorded with 14 Squadron during January 1924, following storage at Aboukir, J6798 was returned a year later to the UK for modification to a 'J' type Bristol. The work accomplished it was despatched to Ascot in June 1926, for packing and shipment to Egypt.

Possibly stored for two years at Aboukir, it was recorded in 1928, in the care of 208 Squadron before being sent back to Aboukir for reconditioning, during which the airframe serial was amended to JR6798. Its date of transfer to Ramleh and 6 Squadron is not known.

Monday 8 December 1930
25 Squadron *Not reported*
Siskin IIIA J9348
T/o Hawkinge for formation flying during which the pilot lost contact with his colleagues. Forced-landing [I suspect to ascertain his whereabouts] he ran onto a hay-rake while taking off and the undercarriage was ripped off; moments later the fighter overturned in the field near South Ockendon in Essex.

Tuesday 9 December 1930
13 Squadron 2nd Lt Fouad Hajjaj Safe
Atlas J8779 Egypt
T/o Netheravon and written off when forced-landing in fog. An inspection of the airframe deemed it had been damaged beyond economical repair and it was struck off charge on the 19th. Foaud Hajjaj was on attachment from the Egyptian Army.

Co-author, Paul McMillan has unearthed a report on the Aviation Safety Network website, which is acknowledged, ASN Wikibase Occurrence 221836, showing that Lieutenant Fouad Abd al-Hamid Hajjaj was killed, along with fellow Egyptian, Mechanic Sergeant Shedi Doss, in a crash on 18th November 1933, when delivering an Avro 626 to Egypt. They had taken off from Lympne in Kent on the first leg of their journey and had reached the vicinity of Monchaux-Soreng [Seine Maritime] *en route* to Paris-Le Bourget, when for the second time in his flying career Fouad Hajjaj became disorientated in fog and crashed.

Possibly during April 1930, though a precise date has not been recorded, 605 Squadron AAF DH.9A J8105 is reported to have *"crashed."*

Also shown in Air-Britain's *J File* as having crashed in 1930, Fairey IIIF IVC J9071/X attached to 8 Squadron at Khormakser.

APPENDICES
1930

Appendix A - Squadron Losses Table and Losses by Aircraft Type

Column 1 - Squadron

Column 2 - Aircraft type

Column 3 - Written off

Column 4 - Fatalities

1 Squadron	Hawker Hornet	1	
3 Squadron	Bristol Bulldog II	2	
6 Squadron	Bristol F.2b	2	
	Bristol F.2J	8	
8 Squadron	Fairey IIIF	2	2
11 Squadron	Westland Wapiti IIA	2	4
13 Squadron	Armstrong Whitworth Atlas	2	
14 Squadron	Airco DH.9A	2	
17 Squadron	Bristol Bulldog II	1	
	Bristol Bulldog IIA	3	1
19 Squadron	Armstrong Whitworth Siskin IIIA	2	1
20 Squadron	Bristol F.2b	1	2
	Bristol F.2J	2	2
23 Squadron	Gloster Gamecock I	1	1
	Gloster Grebe IIIDC	1	1
25 Squadron	Armstrong Whitworth Siskin IIIA	3	1
26 Squadron	Armstrong Whitworth Atlas	1	1
29 Squadron	de Havilland DH.60M Moth	1	1
30 Squadron	Westland Wapiti IIA	3	1
31 Squadron	Bristol F.2b	1	
32 Squadron	Armstrong Whitworth Siskin IIIA	1	
	Armstrong Whitworth Siskin IIIADC	1	1
41 Squadron	Armstrong Whitworth Siskin IIIA	1	1
43 Squadron	Armstrong Whitworth Siskin IIIA	3	
47 Squadron	Fairey IIIF	2	2
55 Squadron	Westland Wapiti IIA	1	1
56 Squadron	Armstrong Whitworth Siskin IIIA	1	1
58 Squadron	Vickers Virginia IX	1	2
60 Squadron	Airco DH.9A	1	
	Westland Wapiti IIA	1	2
70 Squadron	Victoria	1	
84 Squadron	Airco DH.9A	1	
	Westland Wapiti IIA	3	
99 Squadron	Handley Page Hinaidi	1	
100 Squadron	Hawker Horsley II	3	3
101 Squadron	Boulton Paul Sidestrand II	1	
111 Squadron	Armstrong Whitworth Siskin IIIA	2	
202 Squadron	Fairey IIID	1	2
207 Squadron	Fairey IIIF	3	2
501 Squadron SR	Airco DH.9A DC	1	
503 Squadron SR	Handley Page Hinaidi	1	
600 Squadron AAF	Airco DH.9A DC	1	
601 Squadron AAF	Westland Wapiti IIA	2	
602 Squadron AAF	Westland Wapiti IIA	3	
603 Squadron AAF	Avro 504N	1	1
605 Squadron AAF	Airco DH.9A	1	
Totals		81	36

Airco DH.9A	5	
Airco DH.9A DC	2	
Armstrong Whitworth Atlas	3	1
Armstrong Whitworth Siskin DC	1	1
Armstrong Whitworth Siskin IIIA	14	4
Avro 504N	1	1
Boulton Paul Sidestrand II	1	
Bristol F.2b	4	2
Bristol F.2J	10	2
Bristol Bulldog II	3	
Bristol Bulldog IIA	4	1
de Havilland DH.60M Moth	1	1
Fairey IIID	1	2
Fairey IIIF	7	6
Gloster Gamecock I	1	1
Gloster Grebe DC	1	1
Handley Page Hinaidi	2	
Handley Page Hyderabad	1	
Hawker Hornet	1	
Hawker Horsley II	3	3
Vickers Victoria	1	
Vickers Virginia	1	2
Westland Wapiti	15	8
Totals	81	36

Annex A - Squadron Losses January 1921 to December 1930

The table set out in this Annex is a record of losses by type and fatalities reported from squadrons during above period and the authors believe are as accurate as surviving records allow. The various types are recorded in chronological order of issue. Variants of the Avro 504 were issued to most squadrons, and particularly to those tasked to provide flying training, an example being 9 Squadron at Manston whose primary role was bomber duties.

1 Squadron	Sopwith 7F.1 Snipe	12	5
	Sopwith 7F.1 Snipe DC	1	1
	Armstrong Whitworth Siskin IIIA	2	
	Hawker Hornet	1	
2 Squadron	Bristol F.2b	18	7
	Bristol F.2J	1	
3 Squadron	Airco DH.9A	3	
	Sopwith 7F.1 Snipe DC	1	2
	Hawker Woodcock I	1	
	Hawker Woodcock II	6	5
	Gloster Gamecock I	1	
	Armstrong Whitworth Siskin III DC	1	2
	Bristol Bulldog II	2	
4 Squadron	Avro 504K	2	2
	Bristol F.2b	8	3
5 Squadron	Bristol F.2b	13	4
6 Squadron	Airco DH.10	1	
	Bristol F.2b	20	11
	Bristol F.2J	9	
7 Squadron	Vickers Virginia	1	
8 Squadron	Airco DH.9A	13	7
	Fairey IIIF	4	4
9 Squadron	Avro 504K	4	1
	Vickers Virginia	2	4
11 Squadron	Avro 504K	3	
	Fairey Fawn II	3	3
	Hawker Horsley II	1	2
	Westland Wapiti IIA	3	4
12 Squadron	Bristol F.2b	5	2
	Fairey Fawn II	3	2
	Fairey Fox I	6	4
13 Squadron	Bristol F.2b	5	9
	Armstrong Whitworth Atlas	5	
14 Squadron	Bristol F.2b	11	2
	Airco DH.9A	11	12
16 Squadron	Bristol F.2b	2	4
17 Squadron	Sopwith 7F.1 Snipe	2	2
	Hawker Woodcock II	4	2
	Armstrong Whitworth Siskin IIIA	2	1
	Bristol Bulldog II	1	
	Bristol Bulldog IIA	3	1
19 Squadron	Avro 504K	1	1
	Sopwith 7F.1 Snipe	2	1
	Gloster Grebe II	4	1
	Armstrong Whitworth Siskin IIIA	5	3
20 Squadron	Bristol F.2b	16	13
	Bristol F.2J	2	2
22 Squadron	Gloster Gamecock I	1	1
23 Squadron	Sopwith 7F.1 Snipe	1	
	Gloster Gamecock I	9	3
	Avro 504N	1	2
	Gloster Grebe III DC	1	1
24 Squadron	Airco DH.9A	6	4
	Avro 504K	2	
	Bristol F.2b	4	1
	Bristol F.2J	1	
	Gloster Gamecock I	1	
	DH.60 Moth	1	
25 Squadron	Sopwith 7F.1 Snipe	12	3

	Gloster Grebe II	6	1
	Avro 504K	1	
	Armstrong Whitworth Siskin IIIA	4	2
26 Squadron	Armstrong Whitworth Atlas	2	3
27 Squadron	Airco DH.9A	15	8
28 Squadron	Bristol F.2b	9	12
29 Squadron	Sopwith 7F.1 Snipe	1	1
	Gloster Grebe II	5	4
	Armstrong Whitworth Siskin IIIA	2	1
	de Havilland DH.60M Moth	1	1
30 Squadron	Airco DH.9A	27	7
	Bristol F.2b	2	2
	Westland Wapiti IIA	3	1
31 Squadron	Bristol F.2b	16	9
32 Squadron	Sopwith F.1 Snipe	11	2
	Gloster Grebe II	2	1
	Gloster Gamecock I	2	1
	Armstrong Whitworth Siskin IIIA	1	
	Armstrong Whitworth Siskin IIIA DC	1	1
36 Squadron	Hawker Horsley II	1	1
39 Squadron	Airco DH.9A	10	10
	Avro 504K	1	1
	Westland Wapiti IIA	1	
41 Squadron	Avro 504K	3	
	Armstrong Whitworth Siskin III	4	2
	Armstrong Whitworth Siskin IIIA	2	2
	DH.42A Dingo	1	1
43 Squadron	Sopwith 7F.1 Snipe	3	
	Gloster Gamecock I	3	1
	Armstrong Whitworth Siskin IIIA	5	
45 Squadron	Vickers Veron III	4	8
	Bristol F.2b	1	2
	Airco DH.9A	4	2
47 Squadron	Airco DH.9A	10	5
	Fairey IIIF	4	7
55 Squadron	Airco DH.9A	26	13
	Westland Wapiti IIA	1	1
56 Squadron	Sopwith 7F.1 Snipe	12	4
	Gloster Grebe II	5	3
	Gloster Grebe II DC	1	
	Armstrong Whitworth Siskin IIIA	5	2
58 Squadron	Avro 504K	1	
	Vickers Virginia	2	3
60 Squadron	Airco DH.10	4	4
	Airco DH.9A	18	4
	Fairey IIIF	1	3
	Westland Wapiti IIA	1	2
70 Squadron	Victoria	9	
84 Squadron	Airco DH.9A	30	18
	Westland Wapiti IIA	3	
99 Squadron	Avro 504K	2	1
	Airco DH.9A	1	
	Vickers Vimy	1	
	Handley Page Hyderabad	3	
	Handley Page Hinaidi	1	
100 Squadron	Avro 504K	5	1
	Bristol F.2b	6	3
	Fairey Fawn II	5	3
	Hawker Horsley II	4	4
101 Squadron	Boulton Paul Sidestrand II	1	
111 Squadron	Sopwith 7F.1 Snipe	1	1
	Armstrong Whitworth Siskin IIIA	4	1
	Armstrong Whitworth Siskin III DC	2	3
202 Squadron	Fairey IIID	1	2
205 Squadron	Parnell Panther	1	1
207 Squadron	Airco DH.9A	7	2

	Fairey IIIF	5	7
208 Squadron	Bristol F.2b	8	8
210 Squadron	Parnell Panther	1	2
216 Squadron	Airco DH.10	4	2
	Vickers Vimy	4	8
	Vickers Victoria	2	3
238 Squadron	Felixstowe F.2A	1	
501 Squadron SR	Airco HD.9A DC	1	
502 Squadron SR	Avro 504K	1	1
	Avro 504N	2	
	Fairey Fawn II	1	
503 Squadron SR	Avro 504N	1	
	Handley Page Hinaidi	1	
600 Squadron AAF	Airco DH.9A	1	
	Airco DH.9A DC	1	
601 Squadron AAF	Airco DH.9A	4	
	Westland Wapiti IIA	2	
602 Squadron AAF	Avro 504N	1	1
	Fairey Fawn II	1	
	Westland Wapiti IIA	3	
603 Squadron AAF	Avro 504N	2	2
	Airco DH.9A	1	
605 Squadron AAF	Avro 504N	1	
	Airco DH.9A	4	1
Totals		658	355

Annex B - Aircraft Losses by Type January 1921 to December 1930

The three Vickers designs, Vernon, Victoria and Virginia underwent various modifications whilst in service, this being particularly evident with the Virginia. Developed from Vimy [first flight 30th November 1917], initial issues of the Virginia were made to 9 Squadron at Boscombe Down in April 1924, followed soon after with deliveries to 7 Squadron at Worthy Down, both squadrons enjoying twelve unbroken years of Virginia operations.

Amazingly, the type remained in service until 1941, when the Henlow based Parachute Test Flight retired their last remaining Virginias in December 1941. It is also noted that as a heavy bomber it was still in frontline operational service until 1938, the year of the Munich agreement.

Thus, this Annex will show overall losses and fatalities by the type name.

Airco DH.9A	194	92
Airco DH.9A DC	2	
Airco DH.10	10	6
Armstrong Whitworth Atlas	7	3
Armstrong Whitworth Siskin III	4	2
Armstrong Whitworth Siskin IIIA	33	12
Armstrong Whitworth Siskin III DC	4	6
Avro 504K	26	8
Avro 504N	8	5
Boulton Paul Sidestrand II	1	
Bristol F.2b	144	92
Bristol F.2J	13	2
Bristol Bulldog II	3	2
Bristol Bulldog IIA	3	1
de Havilland DH.42A Dingo	1	1
de Havilland DH.60 Moth	1	
de Havilland DH.60M Moth	1	1
Fairey Fawn II	13	8
Fairey Fox I	6	4
Fairey IIID	1	2
Fairey IIIF	14	21
Felixstowe F.2A	1	
Gloster Gamecock I	17	6
Gloster Grebe II	22	10
Gloster Grebe II DC	2	1
Handley Page Hinaidi	2	

	Handley Page Hyderabad	3	
	Hawker Hornet	1	
	Hawker Horsley II	6	7
	Hawker Woodcock I	1	
	Hawker Woodcock II	10	7
	Parnell Panther	2	3
	Sopwith 7F.1 Snipe	59	19
	Sopwith 7F.1 Snipe DC	1	2
	Vickers Vernon	4	8
	Vickers Victoria	12	3
	Vickers Vimy	5	8
	Vickers Virginia	4	7
	Westland Wapiti IIA	17	8
Totals		658	355

Appendix B - Squadron Locations and Commanding Officers

Squadron	Aircraft	Location	Dates	Notes
1 Squadron	Siskin IIA	Tangmere	01.01.30-31.12.30	
2 Squadron	Atlas	Manston	01.01.30-31.12.30	
3 Squadron	Bulldog II	Upavpn	01.01.30-31.12.30	
4 Squadron	Atlas	Farnborough	01.01.30-31.12.30	
5 Squadron	Bristol F.2b	Quetta	01.01.30-16.05.30	
		Kohat	16.05.30-31.12.30	
6 Squadron	Bristol F.2b	Ismailia	01.01.30-31.12.30	With a detachment at Ramleh
7 Squadron	Virgina *various*	Worthy Down	01.01.30-31.12.30	
8 Squadron	Fairey IIIF	Khormaksar	01.01.30-31.12.30	
9 Squadron	Virgina VII/IX	Manston	01.01.30-26.11.30	Virginia VII phased out during June
	Virginia X	Boscombe Down	26.11.30-31.12.30	Virginia X introduced during May
10 Squadron	Hyderabad	Upper Heyford	01.01.30-31.12.30	
	Hinaidi			Hinaidi introduced during December
11 Squadron	Wapiti IIA	Risalpur	01.01.30-31.12.30	
12 Squadron	Fox IA	Andover	01.01.30-31.12.30	
13 Squadron	Atlas	Netheravon	01.01.30-31.12.30	
14 Squadron	Fairey IIIF	Ramleh & Amman	01.01.30-31.12.30	
XV Squadron	*Various*	Martlesham Heath	01.01.30-31.12.30	
16 Squadron	Bristol F.2b	Old Sarum	01.01.30-31.12.30	
17 Squadron	bulldog II/IIA	Upavon	01.01.30-31.12.30	
19 Squadron	Siskin IIIA	Duxford	01.01.30-31.12.30	
20 Squadron	Bristol F.2b	Peshawar	01.01.30-31.12.30	
22 Squadron	*Various*	Martlesham Heath	01.01.30-31.12.30	
23 Squadron	Gamecock I	Kenley	01.01.30-31.12.30	
24 Squadron	*Various*	Northolt	01.01.30-31.12.30	
25 Squadron	Siskin IIIA	Hawkinge	01.01.30-31.12.30	
26 Squadron	Atlas	Catterick	01.01.30-31.12.30	
27 Squadron	DH.9A	Kohat	01.01.30-31.12.30	DH.9A phased out during May
	Wapiti IIA			Wapiti IIA introduced during May
28 Squadron	Bristol F.2b	Ambala	01.01.30-31.12.30	
29 Squadron	Siskin IIIA	North Weald	01.01.30-31.12.30	
30 Squadron	Wapiti IIA	Mosul	01.01.30-31.12.30	
31 Squadron	Bristol F.2b	Quetta	01.01.30-31.12.30	
32 Squadron	Siskin IIIA	Kenley	01.01.30-31.12.30	
	Bulldog IIA			Bulldog IIA introduced during July
33 Squadron	Horsley II	Eastchurch	01.01.30-05.11.30	Horsley II phased out during May
	Hart	Bicester	05.11.30-31.12.30	Hart introduced in February
35 Squadron	Fairey IIIF	Bircham Newton	01.01.30-31.12.30	
36 Squadron	Horsley I/III	Donibristile	01.01.30-12.06.30	
		Kenley	12.06.30-28.06.30	
		Donibristle	28-06.30-14.10.30	Departed to the Far East
		Seletar	14.11.30-31.12.30	For torpedo bomber duties
39 Squadron	Wapiti IIA	Risalpur	01.01.30-31.12.30	
41 Squadron	Siskin IIIA	Northolt	01.01.30-31.12.30	
43 Squadron	Siskin IIIA	Tangmere	01.01.30-31.12.30	
45 Squadron	Fairey IIIF	Helwan	01.01.30-31.12.30	
47 Squadron	Fairey IIIF	Khartoum	01.01.30-31.12.30	
54 Squadron	Siskin IIIDC	Hornchurch	15.01.30-31.12.30	Reformed for fighter duties
	Bulldog IIA			Bulldog IIA introduced during April
55 Squadron	DH.9A/Wapiti IIA	Hinaidi	01.01.30-31.12.30	Wapiti IIA introduced during February
56 Squadron	Siskin IIIA	North Weald	01.01.30-31.12.30	
58 Squadron	Virginia	Worthy Down	01.01.30-31.12.30	
60 Squadron	DH.9A	Kohat	01.01.30-31.12.30	DH.9A withdrawn in July
	Wapiti IIA			Wapiti IIA introduced during July
70 Squadron	Victoria I/III	Hinaidi	01.01.30-31.12.30	
84 Squadron	Wapiti IIA	Shaibah	01.01.30-31.12.30	
99 Squadron	Hinaidi	Upper Heyford	01.01.30-31.12.30	
100 Squadron	Horsley II/III	Bicester	01.01.30-03.11.30	
		Donibristole	03.11.30-31.12.30	
101 Squadron	Sidestrand III	Andover	01.01.30-31.12.30	
111 Squadron	Siskin IIIA	Hornchurch	01.01.30-31.12.30	
201 Squadron	Southampton II	Calshot	01.01.30-31.12.30	
202 Squadron	Fairey IIID	Kalafrana	01.01.30-31.12.30	Fairey IIID withdrawn in September
	Fairey IIIF			Fairey IIIF introduced during July
203 Squadron	Southampton II	Basra	01.01.30-31.12.30	
204 Squadron	Southampton II	Mount Batten	01.01.30-31.12.30	
205 Squadron	Southampton II/III	Seletar	01.01.30-31.12.30	
207 Squadron	Fairey IIIF	Bircham Newton	01.01.30-31.12.30	
208 Squadron	Bristol F.2b	Heliopolis	01.01.30-31.12.30	Bristol F.2b withdrawn in May
	Atlas			Atlas introduced during May
209 Squadron	Iris III/V	Mount Batten	15.03.30-31.12.30	Reformed for long-range duties
216 Squadron	Victoria II/V	Heliopolis	01.01.30=31.12.30	
501 Squadron SR	Avro 504N	Filton	01.01.30-31.12.30	Avro 504N withdrawn in May
	DH.9A			DH.9A used March to November
	Wapiti IIA			Wapiti IIA introduced during September
502 Squadron SR	Hyderabad	Aldergrove	01.01.30-31.12.30	
503 Squadron SR	Hyderabad	Waddington	01.01.30-31.12.30	

504 Squadron SR	Horsley	Hucknall	01.01.30-31.12.30	
600 Squadron AAF	Wapiti IIA	Hendon	01.01.30-31.12.30	
601 Squadron AAF	DH.9A/Wapiti IIA	Hendon	01.01.30-31.12.30	DH.9A withdrawn in October
602 Squadron AAF	Wapiti IIA	Renfrew	01.01.30-31.12.30	
603 Squadron AAF	DH.9A/Wapiti IIA	Turnhouse	01.01.30-31.12.30	DH.9A withdrawn in May
604 Squadron AAF	DH.9A/Wapiti IIA	Hendon	17.03.30-31.12.30	Reformed for day bomber duties DH.9A withdrawn in September
605 Squadron AAF	DH.9A/Wapiti IIA	Castle Bromwich	01.01.30-31.12.30	DH.9A withdrawn in June
607 Squadron AAF	Wapiti IIA	Usworth	17.03.30-31.12.30	Reformed for day bomber duties
608 Squadron AAF	Wapiti IIA	Thornaby	17.03.30-31.12.30	Reformed for day bomber duties

Note. '606 Squadron AAF' was never formed.

1 Squadron	Squadron Leader E O Grenfell MC DFC AFC	In situ	See 1 Squadron 1923
2 Squadron	Squadron Leader H M Probyn DSO mid	In situ	See 208 Squadron 1924
	Squadron Leader S E Toomer DFC mid	29 September 1930	AV-M retirement 8 March 1948
3 Squadron	Squadron Leader E D Johnson AFC	In situ	See Appendix B 1927
	Squadron Leader C A Stevens MC* mid	6 August 1930	AV-M retirement 15 November 1954
4 Squadron	Squadron Leader N H Bottomley	In situ	See Appendix B 1928
	Squadron Leader C E H Medhurst OBE three times mid	6 January 1930	ACM retirement 19 April 1950
	Squadron Leader S P Simpson MC	29 December 1930	AV-M retirement 27 March 1947
5 Squadron	Squadron Leader O C Bryson MC DFC AM	In situ	See Appendix B 1928
6 Squadron	Squadron Leader C H Keith	In situ	See Appendix B 1928
	Squadron Leader C R Cox AFC	16 March 1930	See 47 Squadron 1927
7 Squadron	Squadron Leader C E H C MacPherson	In situ	See Appendix B 1929
	Wing Commander C W H Pulford OBE AFC *Croix de Guerre* [France]	6 January 1930	AV-M died 10th March 1942
8 Squadron	Squadron Leader J L Vachell MC	In situ	See Appendix B 1929
9 Squadron	Wing Commander W V Strugnell MC*	In situ	See Apendix B 1928
10 Squadron	Wing Commander A T Whitelook	In situ	See Appendix B 1929
	Wing Commander P C Sherren MC	15 September 1930	See 60 Squadron 1921
11 Squadron	Squadron Leader P H Cummings	In situ	See Appendix B 1928
12 Squadron	Squadron Leader F H M Maynard AFC	In situ	See Appendix B 1929
13 Squadron	Squadron Leader C B Cole-Hamilton twice mid	In situ	See 20 Squadron 1925
14 Squadron	Squadron Leader F O Soden DFC	In situ	See 111 Squadron 1929
XV Squadron	Wing Commander J K Wells AFC	In situ	See Appendix B 1929
	Flight Lieutenant T A Langford-Sainsbury DFC AFC**	8 March 1930	AV-M retirement 15 May 1949
	Squadron Leader G H Martingell AFC	22 April 1930	S/Ldr killed 20 February 1936
16 Squadron	Squadron Leader D O Mulholland AFC	In situ	See Appendix B 1928
17 Squadron	Squadron Leader A R Arnold DSC DFC	In situ	See Appendix B 1928
	Squadron Leader R Harrison DFC *Croix de Guerre* [France]	1 May 1930	See 30 Squadron 1927
19 Squadron	Squadron Leader C R Keary	In situ	See Appendix B 1929
20 Squadron	Squadron Leader C H Nicholas DFC AFC mid	In situ	See Appendix B 1928
	Flight Lieutenant W K Mercer	1930	G/Capt retirement 21 June 1944
	Squadron Leader L O Brown DSC AFC South Africa	7 April 1930	AV-M retirement 23 January 1949
22 Squadron	Squadron Leader E S Goodwin AFC twice mid	In situ	See Appendix B 1929
23 Squadron	Squadron Leader A G Jones-Williams MC* *Croix de Guerre avec Palme*	In situ	See Appendix B 1928
	Squadron Leader H W Woollett DSO MC	15 January 1930	S/Ldr resigned 3 February 1932
24 Squadron	Squadron Leader D S Don MVO	In situ	See Appendix B 1929
25 Squadron	Squadron Leader L G S Payne MC AFC	In situ	See Appendix B 1929
	Squadron Leader R S Aitken MC AFC	19 February 1930	See 41 Squadron 1928
	Wing Commander J Sowrey AFC	2 April 1930	G/Capt retired list 1 April 1939*
	Squadron Leader R S Aitken MC AFC	24 April 1930	See 41 Squadron 1928
	Squadron Leader H M Probyn DSO mid	29 September 1930	See 208 Squadron 1924
26 Squadron	Squadron Leader R L Stevenson	In situ	See Appendix B 1927
27 Squadron	Squadron Leader L M Bailey AFC	In situ	See Appendix B 1924
	Squadron Leader F W Trott OBE MC	7 March 1930	G/Capt retirement 16 April 1946
28 Squadron	Squadron Leader A F Brooks	In situ	See 43 Squadron 1925
29 Squadron	Squadron Leader P G Scott	In situ	See Appendix B 1929
	Squadron Leader E J D Routh	9 June 1930	W/Cdr retired list 10 October 1945
30 Squadron	Squadron Leader H P Lale DFC mid	In situ	See 32 Squadron 1924
	Squadron Leader R V Goddard	11 February 1930	AV-M retirement 8 April 1951
31 Squadron	Squadron Leader J F Gordon DFC	In situ	See Appendix B 1926
32 Squadron	Squadron Leader B E Baker DSO MC AFC mid *Croix de Guerre* [France]	In situ	See Appendix B 1929
33 Squadron	Squadron Leader J J Breen three times mid	In situ	See 84 Squadron 1928
35 Squadron	Squadron Leader B E Harrison AFC	In situ	See Appendix B 1929
36 Squadron	Squadron Leader A W Mylne	In situ	See 28 Squadron 1926
39 Squadron	Squadron Leader H V Champion de Crepigny MC DFC	In situ	See 60 Squadron 1922
	Squadron Leader S B Harris DFC AFC	4 April 1930	G/Capt retirement 17 April 1946
41 Squadron	Squadron Leader R S Aitken MC AFC	In situ	See Appendix B 1928
	Squadron Leader P Huskinson MC*	6 February 1930	A/Cmdr retirement 25 January 1942
43 Squadron	Squadron Leader C N Lowe MC DFC	In situ	See 602 Squadron AAF 1925
	Squadron Leader L H Slatter OBE DSC* DFC	13 November 1930	See 203 Squadron 1921
45 Squadron	Squadron Leader F J Vincent DFC	In situ	See Appendix B 1928
47 Squadron	Squadron Leader C R Cox AFC	In situ	See Appendix B 1927
	Squadron Leader E L Howard-Williams MC	8 February 1930	A/Cmdr retirement 23 November 1942
54 Squadron	Squadron Leader W E G Bryant MBE	15 January 1930	A/Cmdr died 22 August 1945**

55 Squadron	Squadron Leader C H Elliott-Smith AFC	In situ	See 56 Squadron 1926
	Squadron Leader J W Woodhouse DSO MC mid	7 February 1930	G/Capt retirement 8 April 1941
	Flight Lieutenant M M Freehill DFC	1 May 1930	S/Ldr died 3 February 1939
	Squadron Leader J W Woodhouse DSO MC	2 September 1930	See above
56 Squadron	Squadron Leader A Lees	In situ	See Appendix B 1928
58 Squadron	Squadron Leader E W Norton DSC	In situ	See 70 Squadron 1925
	Wing Commander C C Miles MC	18 August 1930	See 3 Squadron 1923
60 Squadron	Squadron Leader R H G Neville MC	In situ	See Appendix B 1927
70 Squadron	Wing Commander R S Maxwell MC DFC* AFC	In situ	See 32/24 Squadron 1923
	Wing Commander C H B Blount OBE MC	31 October 1930	See 4 Squadron 1921
84 Squadron	Squadron Leader H Stewart	In situ	See Appendix B 1929
99 Squadron	Squadron Leader G H Cock	In situ	See Appendix B 1929
	Wing Commander H G Smart OBE DFC AFC	5 February 1930	AV-M retirement 1 September 1945
100 Squadron	Squadron Leader W B Farrington	In situ	See 84 Squadron 1925
101 Squadron	Squadron Leader R S Lucy AFC	In situ	See Appendix B 1929
	Squadron Leader F H Coleman DSO	14 January 1930	See 30 Squadron 1925
111 Squadron	Squadron Leader L H Slatter OBE DSC* DFC	In situ	See 203 Squadron 1921
	Squadron Leader E R Openshaw	13 November 1930	See 19 Squadron 1929
201 Squadron	Flight Lieutenant A C Stevens	In situ	See Appendix B 1929
	Squadron Leader E F Turner	20 January 1930	See 502 Squadron SR 1925
202 Squadron	Squadron Leader C Boumphrey DFC mid	In situ	See Appendix B 1929
	Wing Commander R H Kershaw	28 January 1930	G/Capt retirement 17 May 1943
203 Squadron	Wing Commander T E B Howe AFC	In situ	See 32 Squadron 1923
	Squadron Leader G W Bentley DFC	20 November 1930	G/Capt retirement 24 March 1946
204 Squadron	Squadron Leader F H Laurence MC	In situ	See Appendix B 1929
	Squadron Leader K B Lloyd AFC	9 December 1930	AV-M retirement 28 October 1949
205 Squadron	Group Captain H M Cave-Brown-Cave DSO DFC	In situ	See Appendix B 1929
	Squadron Leader G E Livock DFC AFC	1 January 1930	See 205 Squadron 1929
207 Squadron	Squadron Leader E A Beaulah	In situ	See Appendix B 1928
208 Squadron	Squadron Leader V E Lindop	In situ	See Appendix 1927
	Squadron Leader M Moore OBE	14 April 1930	G/Capt killed 9 June 1940***
209 Squadron	Squadron Leader J H O Jones	15 January 1930	G/Capt retirement 30 April 1945
	Wing Commander C G Tucker	25 August 1930	W/Cdr killed 4 February 1931
216 Squadron	Wig Commander E A B Rice MC	In situ	See 6 Squadron 1921

* Group Captain John Sowrey AFC was recalled to the service on 28th December 1943, serving until 17th August 1947. He died in Folkestone on Monday, 9th October 1967. On his return to the service he was granted a class CC commission in the Administrative and Special Duties Branch with the rank of air commodore.

** Appointed at Air Officer Commanding, RAF Cranwell, on 8th July 1944, Air Commodore Walter Edward George Bryant MBE collapsed whilst attending a play in the station cinema. Taken to RAF Hospital Rauceby, he died that same night. He was buried with full military honours in Cranwell [St. Andrew] Churchyard where his headstone is inscribed *"A Beloved Husband And Father In Constant Memory, Sybil And Mary.;"* he was was 52 years of age.

*** Group Captain Maurice Moore OBE was aboard the aircraft carrier HMS *Glorious* on passage from Norway to Scapa Flow when on the 9th of June 1940, she was sunk in the North Sea along with her destroyer escorts by the German battleships *Scharnhorst* and *Gneisenau.* Loss of life was considerable and included pilots from 46 Squadron [Hurricane]. Group Captain Moore, aged 46, is commemorated on pane 3 at the Runnymede Memorial.

501 Squadron SR	Squadron Leader R S Sugen	In situ	See Appendix B 1929
502 Squadron SR	Wing Commander F P Don	In situ	See 33 Squadron 1929
503 Squadron SR	Wing Commander The Hon. L J E Twistleton-Wykham-Fiennes	In situ	See 29 Squadron 1923
	Squadron Leader H E P Wigglesworth DSC	7 March 1930	AM retirement 7 May 1948
	Wing Commander H P Lale DSO DFC mid	20 May 1930	See 32 Squadron 1924
504 Squadron	Squadron Leader C H Elliott-Smith	In situ	See 56 Squadron 1926
	Squadron Leader H I Hanmer DFC	10 February 1930	See 13 Squadron 1926
600 Squadron AAF	Squadron Leader The Hon. F E Guest PC CBE DSO MP	In situ	See Appendix B 1926
601 Squadron AAF	Squadron Leader The Rt. Hon. Sir P Sassoon MP	In situ	See Appendix B 1929
602 Squadron AAF	Squadron Leader J Fullerton	In situ	See Appendix B 1927
603 Squadron AAF	Squadron Leader J A McKelvie AFC	In situ	See Appendix B 1925
604 Squadron AAF	Flight Lieutenant F J Fogarty DFC mid	17 March 1930	ACM retirement 29 January 1957
	Wing Commander A S W Dore DSO TD	19 March 1930	G/Capt died 9 August 1953*
605 Squadron AAF	Squadron Leader J A C Wright AFC TD	In situ	See Appendix B 1925
607 Squadron AAF	Flight Lieutenant M Wiblin	17 March 1930	W/Cdr retirement 13 July 1948
	Squadron Leader W L Runciman	13 June 1930	G/Capt relinquished 10 February 1954**
608 Squadron AAF	Flight Lieutenant C L Falconer	17 March 1930	A/Cmdr retirement 1 April 1949
	Squadron Leader W Howard-Davies	23 April 1930	S/Ldr resigned 20 February 1953

* Wing Commander Alan Sydney Whitehore Dore DSO TD was appointed to a commission in the Auxiliary Air Force as a squadron leader, but with an honorary rank of wing commander which reflected his previous army service in which he rose to lieutenant-colonel rank. His service can be traced back to his commission as a Second Lieutenant *Gazetted* to the 1st Volunteer Battalion, The Worcestershire Regiment, on 24th March 1906 [LG 23rd March 1906, issue 27897, 2066]. His award of the DSO, less citation, was promulgated in *the Edinburgh Gazette* January 2nd, 1918, issue 13186, page 26, at which time he was attached to the Royal Flying Corps. Wing Commander Dore's name appears in *The London Gazette* 20 April 1937, issue 34390, page 2557, beneath the heading *Commissions signed by the Lord Lieutenant of the County of Middlesex.* Entries pertaining to his service continue postwar and Paul McMillan believes he was still on the Emergency List of the Royal Air Force when he died on Sunday, 9th August 1953.

** Squadron Leader Walter Leslie Runciman, born 26th August 1900, in Newcastle-upon-Tyne into what is described by *Wikipedia* [acknowledged by the authors] he was *"... a prominent member of the Runcimans, a well-known Newcastle ship-owning and political family."* His father, Walter Runciman, was created 1st Viscount Runciman, and on his death in 1949, Squadron Leader Runciman succeeded his as the 2nd Viscount of Doxford.

During his Auxiliary Air Force service he was *Gazetted* with the Air Force Cross [EG May 14, 1937, issue 15387, page 427]. His death in the Westminster district of London was announced on Friday, 1st September 1989.

Annex

Squadron Leader Sydney Edward Toomer saw action with the Royal Garrison Artillery in two theatres of war; Gallipoli and the Western Front before transferring to the RFC for training as an observer. His Record of Service shows that in his artillery days he was part of the 24th Heavy Battery; that he was born on 10th January 1895; and his acceptance by the RFC was effective from 7th April 1917.

08.02.17	*Accepted as Observer probation. AG D/3026/2/99 CR 8174/Bty 8/2/17*		
15.02.17	*Reported to Hounslow for 1 month course in Observing in acc AG D/1936 d/t 8/2/16*		*AG D/2030/3/157*
14.04.17	*Attached to No. 15 Squadron*	*07.04.17*	*B.213 15 Sqdn*
30.06.17	*Leave 24/6/17 to 8/7/17*		" "
19.06.17	*To be Flying Officer [Obs] with seniority from 13/2/17*	*30.05.17*	*London Gazette*
25.08.17	*To Home Esst.*	*22.08.17*	*B.213 15 Sqdn*
27.08.17	*To be Tempy Lieut whilst serving with RFC*	*01.08.17*	*London Gazette*

The above information has not been recorded on the Air of Authority website, but it is know whilst back in the UK he re-mustered as a pilot, returning to France and attachment to 8 Squadron [FK.8] and by the end of the *Great War* he was commanding the squadron.. His name was one of many published in the Edinburgh edition of the *Gazette* on June 5th, 1919, issue 13458, page 2048, as being a recipient of the Distinguished Flying Cross, but without an accompanying citation.

The single Record of Service for Cecil Alfred Stevens shows the following entries:-

07.04.17	*Attached to No. 1 AD*	*30.03.17*	*B.213 1 AD*
- " -	*Posted to No. 55 Sqdn*	*04.04.17*	- " - - " -
13.04.17	*Appt Flying Officer*	*14.03.17*	*L G*
30.06.17	*Leave 29 6/17 to 13 7/17*		*B.213 55 Sqdn*
15.09.17	*Appt A/ Flt Cmdr*	*11.09.17*	- " - - " -
03.10.17	*Awarded Military Cross*		*Ro 1091 HQ*
25.09.17	*To be Flt Cmdr & temp Capt*	*11.09.17*	*L G*
20.10.17	*Leave 7 10/17 to 21 10/17*		*B.213 55 Sqdn*

"For conspicuous gallantry and devotion to duty.," so the all too familiar opening sentence read in *The London Gazette* of 18th March 1918, supplement 30583, page 3432, and continuing *"He took part in over thirty successful operations over the enemy's lines, including long-distance photographic reconnaissances and bombing raids. On one occasion he was heavily attacked by enemy aeroplanes, one of which he destroyed and returned with excellent photographs and with his machine badly shot about. On another occasion, when leading a bombing raid, the formation was heavily attacked by enemy aeroplanes. He skilfully kept the formation together and led it back to the aerodrome. He consistently set a fine example by his skill and determination."*

His award was initially promulgated on 27th October 1917, a little over two weeks since the entry on his Record of Service; thus, the announcement of a First Bar preceded the above, being *Gazetted* on 18th February 1918, supplement 30530, page 2158, but no citation was attached. However, this was subsequently published in the *Gazette* on 18th July 1918: *"For conspicuous gallantry and devotion to duty as leader of numerous bombing raids. On one occasion he led ten machines a distance of 130 miles from his aerodrome, obtaining good results. During all the raids in which he has acted as leader he has lost only one machine, and he has invariably given a splendid example pf skill and courage. His skill and determination have had an admirable influence in the squadron."*

He is mentioned three times in *The DH.4/DH.9 File*; on page 19 in the entry for DH.4 A2150 reference is made to the driving down at 1145 on 4th May 1917, an Albatros D north-northwest of Douai, his observer being 2nd Lieutenant B F Sandy, and six days later, this time with Lieutenant F L Oliver occupying the rear cockpit, their DH was badly shot about during a photographic reconnaissance sortie.

On page 26 and in the movement records for DH.4 A7470, it is noted the DH was damaged during a raid on Abeelheok on 14th August 1917, 2nd Lieutenant B F Sandy*requiring medical attention for slight wounds.

Although omitted from the citations, The Air of Authority website notes that on Christmas Eve 1917, he led the first raid on Mannheim from the squadron's base at Tantonville, in terms of duration the longest raid in the war so far.

* 2nd Lieutenant Bertram Francis Sandy, born 3rd December 1887. Survived his tour of operations as an observer and returned to Home Establishment on 18th November 1917.

Squadron Leader Sturley Philip Simpson's MC was unusual in that it was not won during the *Great War,* or in postwar air operations when acts of distinguished services were recognised by the award a DFC. The announcement came on 14th May 1926, from the War Office, and promulgated in *The London Gazette* of the same date, issue 33162, page 3182: *"The KING has been graciously pleased to approve of the award of the Military Cross to Flight Lieutenant Sturley Philip Simpson, No. 6 Armoured Car Company, Royal Air Force, in recognition of valuable and distinguished services rendered in connection with operations in Kurdistan during the period July to October, 1924."*

For the greater part of the Second World War he served as Air Officer Commanding, Air Headquarters Gibraltar.

Prior too, and during the *Great War,* during which he obtained his aviator's certificate at Chingford, Conway Walter Heath Pulford served with the Royal Navy and, subsequently, with the Royal Naval Air Service. On the 9th November 1915, he was seriously injured whilst flying in the Mudros theatre and on 28th May 1916, he was hospitalised in Malta with what are described ass *"multiple injuries."*

Postwar he was one of the many officers appointed to a permanent commission on 1st August 1919, their names being published in the third volume of this series. Prior to the outbreak of hostilities in September 1939, he held various flying and staff duty posts, and I suspect one of the most enjoyable was as Officer Commanding Flying aboard the carrier HMS *Furious* [September 1926-October 1928]. This was followed by attendance at the Imperial Defence College from where he proceeded to Worthy Down and command of No. 7 Squadron.

By the early spring of 1941, he was Air Officer Commanding, RAF Far East and it was whilst in this post that he was caught up in the surrender to Imperial Japanese Forces of the Singapore Base. Along with several other senior officers, Air Vice-Marshal Pulford attempted to escape in a motor launch but their craft was sighted and attacked by Japanese fighters and the survivors managed to get ashore on an island in the Juju group. Exhausted and many now stricken with malaria, the few remaining survivors surrendered after holding out for two agonising months. Sadly, many had died, Air Vice-Marshal Pulford being one. His body was recovered and now lies in Kranji War Cemetery where his headstone is inscribed *"In Very Loving Memory "And Underneath Are The Everlasting Arms.""* His decorations are reported as CB OBE AFC *Croix de Guerre* mentioned in despatches.

Born 23rd November 1897, Thomas Audley Langford-Sainsbury, commissioned to the General List, joined the RFC on 26th September 1916, and on completion of his flying training:-

		Embarked 13.06.17 *Disembarked 13.06.17*	
15.06.17	*Posted to No. 41 Squadron*	*14.06.17*	*B.213 41 Sqdn*
01.09.17	*Leave 1 9/17 to 15 9/17*		- " - - " -
01.12.17	*To Home Est.*	*28.11.17*	- " - - " -
22.04.18	*To be Tempy Lieut.*	*26.03.18*	*L G*

So reads his surviving Record of Service form. At the time of his taking temporary command of XV Squadron he was the holder of the Air Force Cross and two Bars, the initial award bing *Gazetted* on New Year's Day, 1919, supplement 31098, page 97. The citation for his DFC [10th June 1924] has yet to be traced.

Squadron Leader Leslie Oswald Brown gained his Royal Aero Club Aviator's Certificate on 14th October 1915, and until the merger of the RNAS and RFC to form the Royal Air Force on April 1st, 1918, flew various machines with the RNAS. His DSC was *Gazetted* on 15th June 1917: *"For bravery, zeal and ability shown in many long flights over enemy territory on reconnaissance work and bomb-dropping expeditions; was repeatedly under fire."*

Francis William Trott was *Gazetted* as an infantry officer, in the rank of 2nd lieutenant, on 24th January 1915 [LG 26 January 1915, issue 29050, page 805]. His Military Cross was promulgated in the Edinburgh edition, of January 17, 1916, issue 12894, page 107, beneath the heading *New Zealand Force.* The list of names is extensive; no citations attached, his entry merely giving his rank and names and in parenthesis *"Devonshire Regiment, Service Battalion."* Also, the Edinburgh paper reports his OBE in the New Year's Honours List for 1919 [EG January 6, 1919, issue 3378, page 74].

The following announcement appeared in *The London Gazette* 30t May 1924, issue 32940, page 4313: *"His Majesty the KING has been graciously pleased to approve of the undermentioned rewards in recognition of distinguished services rendered with the Waziristan Force between January, 1922, and April, 1918:-*

Award the Distinguished Flying Cross

Flying Officer Philippe Amdré de Fontenay
Squadron Leader Eustace Osborne Grenfell, MC AFC
Flight Lt. Stafford Berkeley Harris AFC
Flight Lt. Arthur Mostyn Wray MC AFC

Formerly of the Nottinghamshire and Derby Regiment, Squadron Leader Patrick Huskinson, was accepted by the RFC on 1st September 1915. His Record of Service form showing:-

		Embarked 13.04.16	*L.3237 No. 1678*
15.04.16	*Posted to No. 2 Sqdn*	*14.04.16*	*B.213/843 2 Sqdn*
15.07.16	*Leave 12 7/16 to 19 7/16*		*B.213 2 Sqdn*
02.12.16	*Leave 28 11/16 to 12 12/16*		*- " - - " -*
23.12.16	*Posted to H Q*	*17.12.16*	*- " - HQ*
30.12.16	*Posted to No. 16 Sqdn*	*28.12.16*	*- " - 16 Sqdn*
06.01.17	*Posted to 1st Bde*	*28.12.16*	*_ " _. 1 Bde*
- " -	*Posted to No. 2 Sqdn*	*01.01.17*	*_ " _ 16 Sqdn*
11.01.17	*To be F/Cmdr & Tempy Capt.*	*19.12.16*	*L G*
19.02.17	*To Home Est.*	*07.02.17*	*B.213 2 Sqdn*

The citation for his MC [LG 27 July 1916, supplement 29684, page 7437' reads: *'For conspicuous gallantry and skill. When attacking the enemy's communications, alone and without an observer, he descended to 800 feet in order to release his bombs on a train and station. He was under continuous fire and his engine and machine were seriously damaged, but he succeeded in flying back at a low altitude and safely landing within our lines. He was again heavily fired at as he crossed the lines."*

The First Bar, awarded for his prowess as a scout pilot with 19 Squadron [Spad S VII and Sopwith 5F.1 Dolphin], was promulgated [LG 22 April 1918, supplement 30643, page 4821] and reads as follows: *"For conspicuous gallantry and devotion to duty. During a period of six months he has destroyed two hostile machines and driven down seven others out of control. He has also, during an attack, carried out a ground patrol, flying at a very low altitude, during which he engaged a company of the enemy with machine-gun fire. On a later occasion, when firing at roads from a low altitude, he received a direct hit from a shell, which carried away a portion of his machine. He, however, regained control, and, landing upside down in a shell hole full of water, was suspended in the water until nearly drowned. After his rescue, he remained all day working under shell fire until he had salved the engine. He has at all times proved himself to be a very gallant, keen and able pilot."*

An excellent biography of Air Commodore Patrick Huskinson may be read on the Sandhurst Trust website [acknowledged by the authors] which makes particular mention of his service after being totally blinded on the night of 15th April 1941, when an enemy bomb hit his Knightsbridge apartment.

At the time his expertise in weaponry prompted Winston Churchill in 1940 to appoint him to the post of Director of Armament Production with the rank of air commodore, but in the aftermath of being blinded, and invalided from the service, he was retained as President of the Air Armaments Board. His biography *Vision Ahead* written by Henry Harley Arnold was published in 1949 by Werner Laurie.

Air Commodore Patrick Huskinson CBE MC* died on Thursday, 24th November 1966.

Squadron Leader Ernest Leslie Howard-Williams first saw military service as an officer with the 11th [2nd Hull] Battalion, The East Yorkshire Regiment, subsequently transferring to the RFC for training as an observer. An award of the MC was *Gazetted* on 17th September 1917: *"For conspicuous gallantry and devotion to duty in co-operating with our artillery, often under extremely unfavourable weather conditions. On one occasion in particular, although very much hampered by mist and clouds, he ranged three of our batteries on to a hostile battery position and enabled them to demolish it. His splendid example has been of the greatest value to his squadron."*

During his time in command of 47 Squadron, he led a flight of Fairey IIIFs from Khartoum to West Africa, this exercise lasting from 19th October to 25th November 1930.

"For conspicuous gallantry and devotion to duty in carrying out special missions by night, during which he has frequently been compelled to face very bad weather. In the course of numerous bombing expeditions by night he invariably descended to a very low altitude in order to use his machine gun against hostile troops on the roads. He has consistently set a very fine example," so read the DSO citation for Lieutenant [Temporary Captain] John Whitaker Woodhouse, MC RFC, Special Reserve [EG September 19, 1917, issue 13143, page 1970]. One Army Form B.103 has survived:

			Embarked	
		Posted to No. 4 Sq	*13.08.15*	*B. 213 No. 4 Sq*
28.10.15	*No. 4 Sqdn*	*Granted leave 28 10/15 to 5 11/15*	*28.10.15*	*B.213 No. 877*
		Mentioned in Despatches		*L Gaz 1 7/16*
02.09.16	*4 Sqn*	*To Home Establishment*	*25/16*	*B.213/144*
		To be Flight Commander & Temp. Captain	*15.03.16*	*L Gaz 30 3/16*
31.03.17	*66 Sqdn*	*Embarked & Disembarked*	*24.03.17*	*B.213*
"	"	*Posted to No. 66 Sqdn*	*24.03.17*	"
07.03.17	*55 Sqdn*	*Attached to 55 Sqdn*	*06.04.17*	"
"	*9 Wg*	*Posted to 9th Wing*	*06.04.17*	"
02.06.17	*55 Sqdn*	*Attached to No. 70 Sqdn*	*30.05.17*	"
16.06.17	*70 Sqdn*	*Leave 14 6/17 to 28 6/17*		"
30.06.17	*55 Sqdn*	*Attached to 55 Sqdn*	*27.06.17*	"

Flight Lieutenant Maurice Michael Freehill who assumed command of 55 Squadron in the absence of Wing Commander Woodhouse won his DFC on the Western Front [EG February 11, 1919, issue 13400, page 797]: *"A brilliant leader who has destroyed five enemy aircraft and has displayed conspicuous bravery in attacking enemy troops on the ground. On 4th November* [1918], *observing that a machine-gun post was holding up the advance of our infantry, he attacked it from a very low altitude, inflicting heavy casualties on the crew and putting them to flight. Later on he carried out a reconnaissance of the Army front at a height of 50 feet in the face of intense machine-gun fire, bringing back most valuable information."*

Born in the Chiswick district of London on 21st January 1899, he initially served with the Hampshire Regiment. Having transferred to the RFC and successfully qualified as a pilot, he flew Sopwith F.1 Camels with 46 Squadron, claiming six aerial combat victories between 23rd March and 15th August 1918, and a single victory with 80 Squadron when on the 3rd of October 1918, and piloting F.1 Camel H773 he accounted for a Fokker D.VII near Beaurevoir.

Remaining in the postwar air force he rose to squadron leader rank and was serving as a flight commander with 58 Squadron [Whitley II] at Linton-on-Ouse when he was struck down with broncho-pneumonia and died in York Military Hospital on Friday, 3rd February 1939.

As a flight lieutenant, Harry George Smart was *Gazetted* with the DFC on 28th October 1921, issue 32501, page 8496 of *The London Gazette*: *"For energy, gallantry and leadership. This officer has shown a very fine example to his fellow officers, especially during low bombing raids, when he has frequently descended among heavy rifle fire to very low altitude to ensure accurate bombing of small targets. He has taken part in 25 day bombing raids and two night raids."*

This award was made for operations conducted in Mesopotamia at which time he was attached to 6 Squadron [Bristol F.2b]. Shortly after the outbreak of the Second World War he would find himself back in the area [now Iraq] when he was appointed Air Officer Commanding, Air Headquarters British Forces in Iraq and he was present when pre-German Iraqi forces attempted to overrun the base at Habbaniya. Evacuated on medical grounds, he served out the remainder of the war as Air Officer Commanding, No. 17 [Operational Training] Group.

Serving with No. 3 Squadron RNAS, Flight Sub-Lieutenant Horace Ernest Philip Wigglesworth gained his DSC during a raid on blast furnaces at Burbach in Germany's Saarland, the citation reading: *"For conspicuous gallantry and enterprise on 23rd January 1917, during a bomb attack by aircraft when considerable damage was done to enemy blast furnaces at Burbach. During this flight he fought five engagements with enemy aircraft in formations of three, four and five at a time."* [LG 21 April 1917].

Flight Lieutenant Francis Joseph Francis Fogarty was mentioned in despatches for his actions in Iraq between 1920 and 1921 [LG 10 October 1922, issue 32754, page 7134], and during similar operations in 1922, he received a DFC [LG 6 June 1924, issue 32943, page 4529]. At the time he was attached to 84 Squadron [DH.9A].

Appendix C - Officers Granted Short Service Commissions

LG 17 January 1930, issue 33571, page 347 - Block 28207 - 28242 - Seniority 27th December 1929 - Block 28207 to 28243

28207	ALVEN	Carl Eric	P/O		10.09.30	Terminated
28208	ALVEY	Desmond John	G/Capt		28.10.57	Retirement
28209	BAILEY	William Bernard	S/Ldr		27.02.62	Retirement
28210	BAMBER	John	S/Ldr		10.02.54	Relinquished
28211	BRAMLEY*	Eric Victor Newcomen	F/O	+	23.05.32	14 Squadron
28212	BYRNE	Robert Archie	F/O		31.08.32	Relinquished

On account of ill-health [LG 30 August 1932, issue 33859, page 5564].

28213	CHADWICK	Mervyn George Checkland	F/O		29.06.32	Resigned
28214	CHESTER	Hurll Fontayne	S/Ldr	+	02.07.40	82 Squadron

Squadron Leader Hurll Fontayne Chester and his crew died when their Blenheim IV P6895 UX-H was shot down over Holland during operations to the Dormund-Ems Canal. All are buried in Heerhugowaard {Veenhuizen] Churchyard. For additional information please consult my RAFBCL 1929-1940 Revision and page 161.

28215	CHUBB	Hubert Mackenzie	P/O		10.09.30	Terminated
28216	COKE	Anthony Richard Thomas	W/Cdr		06.09.55	Relinquished
28217	CONWAY	Clement William Walter Sydney	F/O		12.10.35	Relinquished

On appointment to a commission on the Unattached List for the Indian Army [LG 5 November 1935, issue 34216, page 6978].

28218	DALRYMPLE	Leslie Edward	S/Ldr		05.10.53	Relinquished
28219	ELGEY	Edwin	S/Ldr		10.02.54	Relinquished
28220	FARRELL	Cecil Joseph	F/Lt		27.12.38	Relinquished

In class C and granted a commission in the rank of flight lieutenant in class CC [LG 9 May 1939, issue 34624, page 3114]. With effect from 10th October 1939 he was granted a commission in the Administrative and Special Duties Branch as a pilot officer with the honorary rank of flying officer [LG 20 October 1939, issue 34713, page 7045]. F/Lt 08.07.40 Relinquished

On account of ill-health [LG 9 July 1940, issue 34892, page 4185].

28221	GURNEY	Edwin Mackenzie	F/Lt		10.02.54	Relinquished
28222	HOLLAND	George James	S/Ldr		07.11.54	Relinquished
28223	HOLT	Douglas	P/O		23.04.30	Terminated
28224	JENNENS	Lionel William Vaughan	W/Cdr		02.12.57	Retirement
28225	LAWSON	Arthur William Rupert	W/Cdr		10.02.54	Relinquished
28226	LEBORGNE	Robert Paul Joseph	F/O	+	22.11.38	British Airways

Flying Officer Robert Paul Joseph Leborgne who was transferred to Class A of the Reserve on 27th December 1934 died, ass discovered by my co-author, during an authorised test flight of a Lockheed Model 14 Super Electra G-AFGO which crashed at Walton Bay on the SW side of Portishead in North Somerset. The Electra was captained by Commander Eric Glynne Robinson with Robert Leborgne his second pilot. Commander Robinson was buried locally in Portishead [St. Peter's] Churchyard. There is some confusion as to the departure airfield; the Aviation Safety Network shows Bristol-Whitchurch, but the following report taken from the *Bristol Post,* which the authors acknowledge, indicates Heston. Beneath the headline *"Skull found on Portishead beach could be linked to plane" - "Locals say the skull could have come from a plane that crashed into Redcliff Bay just before the Second World War. The skull was discovered by the water bank at Redcliff Bay on Monday evening by a local walker. Police forensic officers have been at the scene and the skull has now been removed for tests to ascertain its age. Locals in the town say the skull, which is understood to be small in size, could have come from a plane that crashed into Redcliff Bay just before the Second World War. Commander Eric Glynne Robinson - a pilot to the then Prime Minister Neville Chamberlain - was flying the American Lockheed 14 twin engine plane on a training flight from Heston Airport on November 22, 1938, when it was seen to run into difficulty over Portishead. Eyewitnesses reported seeing the plane bank sharply along the coastline, with others claiming to have seen the aircraft somersault before careering through the sky, narrowly missing the radio station masts at Portishead Down before heading towards Redcliff Bay. Workers at the Portishead Radio Station saw smoke billowing from the pilot's cabin and jumped into their cars with fire extinguishers ready to help. However, the plane nose-dived and crashed into the rocky shoreline of Redcliff Bay near Redcliff Farm before bursting into flames. It was thought Commander Robinson had been trying to ditch the plane into the sea.*

"Commander Robinson, a senior British Airways pilot with thousands of hours of flying experience, and his co-pilot Commander Robert Paul Joseph Leborgne, were thrown from the plane and later found close together, about 20 feet away from the aircraft, on the beach. The Pair were recovered and taken to an ambulance and their bodies were handed over to the police. An inquest was opened very quickly after the incident to identify the two men and then adjourned until January 1939. The Air Ministry conducted its own inquiry and concluded the crash was due to an error of airmanship on the part of the pilot - the details of which remained a secret."

The article then continues that Commander Robinson had piloted the Lockheed [G-AFGN] that had taken the Prime Minister to Munich for his historic meeting with the German Chancellor, Adolf Hitler, returning to Heston and the now famous *"Peace in our time"* announcement to the waiting crowd.

28227	LESMERE	Norman Strangways	P/O		06.06.30	Terminated
28228	LUCKE	Douglas Webster	F/Lt		10.02.58	Relinquished

Without permission to retain his rank. Paul McMillan reports that Douglas Webster Lucke was born on 23rd June 1909 in Monterrey, Nuevo León, Mexico and died in Folkestone, Kent on Thursday, 25th May 1972.

28229	McMURTRIE*	Richard Angus	G/Capt		10.07.59	Retirement

As Squadron Leader Richard Angus McMurtrie he was *Gazetted* with the DFC, less citation, on 31st May 1940 supplement 34860, page 3256.

28230	MAKGILL*	Richard James Robert Haldane	F/O		10.02.54	Relinquished
28231	OTTEWILL	Walter Reginald	P/O		10.05.31	Resigned
28232	PITT	William Cooke	W/Cdr		23.12.47	Resigned
28233	RATCLIFFE	William Theodore	S/Ldr		24.05.56	Relinquished
28234	REYNOLDS	Basil Pelham	F/Lt		06.07.56	Relinquished

With no retention of rank [LG 16 October 1956, supplement 40902, page 5852].

28235	RILEY	Henry William				
28236	SANT	Alfred Cecil	P/O	+	25.09.30	2 FTS Digby

A report on the Aviation Safety Network website, which the authors acknowledge, states: *"On Tuesday, 23rd September 1930, an aircraft described as "an RAF bombing machine" crashed from a reported height of 40 feet into a field at Treeton, 4 miles south of Rotherham, South Yorkshire.* [The pilot had] *made a forced landing in a field and explained to the farmer that his magneto was 'missing'. He examined the engine and decided to take off again. The plane was wrecked but there was no fire. The pilot was removed from the wreckage by a passing group of miners who had witnessed the accident. Pilot Officer Alfred Cecil Sant received severe head and leg injuries from which he died two days later in Rotherham Hospital. He is buried at Scopwick Church burial ground, Scopwick, Lincolnshire."* For further reading, I recommend the website Yorkshire Aircraft which suggests Pilot Officer Sant had made a cross-country flight to Upper Heyford and had lost his way while returning to Digby. His Bristol, J8458' was the last production Bristol F.2b and was taken on charge on 27th June 1927; its sole service unit was No. 2 FTS Digby.

28237	STONHILL	Leslie Eric Bradley	S/Ldr		25.01.51	Relinquished

On account of medical unfitness for Air Force service.
28238 SUMMERS Maurice Francis F/Lt 18.10.41 Relinquished
28239 THOMPSON William Barrett S/Ldr 10.02.54 Relinquished
28240 WHITE Gordon Rutherfurd F/O 10.03.35 Relinquished
On appointment to a commission in the New Zealand Air Force [LG 11 February 1936, issue 34254, page 913].
28241 WHITTINGHAM Robert Baker F/O 06.08.39 Relinquished
28242 WILSON Allen Roy F/O + 21.10.38
Flying Officer Allen Roy Wilson was transferred to the Reserve, Class A on 27th December 1934 and Paul McMillan reports his death following a short illness in a Reading nursing home; he was cremated in Reading Crematorium.
28243 WOODWARD Frank P/O 23.04.30 Terminated

* Formerly 2nd Lieutenants with, and in descending order, Supplementary Reserve of Officers, The East Surrey Regiment; 72nd Northumbrian Field Brigade, Royal Artillery TA; 18th London Regiment.

LG 21 January 1930, issue 33572, page 429 - Seniority 4th January 1930

28244 BREW* John Kenneth S/Ldr 02.07.41 Retired list
Returned to service and granted a commission for the duration of hostilities as a pilot fficer on probation in the Administrative and Special Duties Branch [LG 15 August 1941, issue 35247, page 4734]. W/Cdr 10.02.54 Relinquished

Formerly commissioned to the Special Reserve.

LG 18 February 1930, issue 33580, page 1054 - Seniority 3rd February 1930 - Block 28245 to 28258

28245 ALEXANDER Richard Vernon G/Capt 10.02.54 Relinquished
28246 BANTOFT Norman Herbert P/O 18.06.30 Terminated
28247 BOSTON John W/Cdr 14.06.45 Resigned
28248 BOWES-LYON Hubert Malcolm F/Lt 10.02.54 Relinquished
28249 CLAYTON-DAUBENY Howard Fitzalan P/O 01.07.31 Terminated
28250 DAVY Edward Johnathan Palgrave G/Capt 01.07.56 Retirement
By way of one of the ancestry websites, my co-author reports the following: *"Edward Jonathan Palgrave Davy turned up at father's home Wombwell Hall in 1929 and eventually joined the RAF long before the war and was a squadron leader when it started. He served all through in Bomber Command doing innumerable operational flights and finally finished as a group captain after having half his left hand blown off whilst doing research work among the ruins and rubble of Cologne. He married my half-sister Mary and is now living with her in retirement at Beckley near Rye in Sussex."* Group Captain Davy died on Tuesday, 6th January 1970.
28251 EATHERLEY William Geoffrey P/O 04.02.31 Relinquished
On account of ill-health [LG 3 February 1931, issue 33686, page 750]. Returned to service and granted a commission in the Administrative and Special Duties branch as a pilot officer for the duration of hostilies, effective from 3rd May 1940 [LG 21 May 1940, issue 34854, page 3037] initially with 78947 as his service number. F/Lt 10.02.54 Relinquished
28253 MacINERNEY Thomas Joseph W/Cdr 06.03.47 Relinquished
On appointment to the reconstituted Auxiliary Air Force. At the time he was attached to the Technical Branch.
28254 MANSFIELD John Grazebrook F/O + 22.07.35 Jersey Airlines
While in the Reserve of Air Force Officers Flying Officer John Grazebrook Mansfield, now employed by Jersey Airlines, took off from Bristol with two passengers in DH.84 Dragon G-ACMP and set out for the relatively short crossing of the Bristol Channel to Cardiff Airport. On approach to land control appears to have been lost and the airliner came down in the Mouth of the Severn opposite Rumney. Eyewitnesses state the Dragon spun into the water; the two passengers, who also died, were named as Roland Cecil Edbrooke and Harold Spencer Percival.
28255 RYLAND Paul William Eyton P/O 13.10.30 Terminated
28256 SMITH Ronald Maxwell F/O + 29.09.34 Class A
Flying Officer Ronald Maxwell Smith was transferred to Class A of the Reserve on 17th February 1934. Joining London, Scottish & Provincial Airways he was killed during a scheduled Heston to Paris flight. The accident received wide coverage in the press and aviation magazines and the following has been taken from extracts posted on the Sussex History Forum website, which the authors gratefully acknowledge: *"Airspeed Courier G-ACSY had been registered to London, Scottish & Provincial Airways for little over four months when on 29th September 1934 it crashed north of Shoreham, Kent, killing all four on board. It had departed from Heston Aerodrome at about 17:00 that day on a scheduled flight to Paris Le Bourget Aerodrome that had started at Leeds earlier that day. It was flying at an altitude of over 1,200 feet when it flew into storm clouds over north-western Kent. At about 17:30 the Courier was seen to emerge from the clouds in a vertical dive, from which it did not recover, and crash into the ground at Timberden Bottom, at the bottom of Cockerhurst Road, just north of Shoreham. The pilot and the three passengers were killed instantly. Two walkers nearby were injured by debris.*

"The pilot was Ronald Maxwell Smith [26] of Ealing, and his three passengers were a mother, her daughter and a friend. Smith was an experienced pilot, who had served in the RAF, with some 1,500 hours, 150 of which were on the LSPA London to Paris service. The Courier was said to be fully airworthy on departure from Heston and its loaded weight was well below the permitted maximum. Pilot error was considered to be the cause of the crash - a conclusion which Airspeed, the manufacturer of the Courier, disputed - but the true cause was never established.

"Despite the witness who claimed that he saw the Courier come out of cloud in a dive, there is another account [that] *claims it was flying below the cloud. That account then sub-divides in that it is claimed both that the Courier stalled trying to avoid high-tension electricity cables and that it struck a ridge on one of the local hills. Flight magazine's report of the accident seems to combine all these elements. In its edition of 4th October 1934, it reports the following: "One of our newest operating companies, London, Scottish and Provincial AirwaysLtd., suffered a tragedy on Saturday afternoon, when a machine on the Leeds-Heston-Paris service crashed in Kent hills near Shoreham. Three passengers and the pilot Mr R M Smith were killed instantly. Judging from witnesses' accounts, the machine, after leaving the base of the low clouds, circled, began a spin, and hit the ground before it could be pulled out of the recovering dive. As the Airspeed "Courier" was in common with the others in the service, fitted with a turn and bank indicator, it seems possible that the pilot stalled the machine while endeavouring to pick up his position, and not while flying "blind," or that, realising the proximity of H.T. wires, he pulled up too steeply. Whatever the evidence obtainable from the wreckage, the cause is likely to remain as least as much of a mystery as that of the accident at Meopham, Kent, in 1930."*

The Sussex History Forum continues: *"The severity of the impact was such that the bodies of the pilot and passengers were so badly damaged that formal identification therefrom was not possible when the Inquest was convened at Sevenoaks the following day. Documents and personal effects were employed to identify the victims. The Courier was destroyed by the crash. While most of the wreckage was concentrated at the crash site, some parts were further away and it is reported that part of the port aileron was found nearly a mile from the crash site."*

This detailed report concludes with the disappointing news that a memorial erected at the crash site was vandalised. Removed to a barn at nearby Oxborne Farm it was later placed in the local churchyard but whether it is still extant is not known. Meanwhile, my co-author, who alerted me to the above, reports the names of the passengers as Mr. Frederick Victor Garnett-Reed [34], Mrs. Ellen Rose-Innes [66], and Dr. Picotee Elizabeth Rose-Innes [26].
28257 WHITEHEAD James Bernard Terence G/Capt 01.10.58 Retirement

28252 LOWE Brian Everard G/Capt + 18.07.43
Group Captain Brian Everard Lowe was attending a senior officers assessment course and with three fellow officers from the course took off from RAF Fulbeck in Wellington BK235 attached to 1485 Flight and captained by Warrant Officer John William Heard for a demonstration of gunnery and fighter affiliation tactics. Tragically, during the second part of the demonstration the Wellington's mainplanes failed and BK235 crashed out of control with fatal consequences for all on board, details being reported in my eighth volumes of Royal Air Force Bomber Command losses from the Second World War. Group Captain Lowe is buried in Brigg Cemetery.
28258 SHANNON Ulric Young G/Capt 16.04.56 Retirement

LG 4 March 1930, issue 33585, page 1420 - Seniority 21st February 1930 - Block 28259 to 28260 and Block 29001 to 29029

28259 BAIN Francis George Levett W/Cdr + 08.12.42 207 Squadron
Wing Commander Francis George Levett Bain arrived at Langar on 7th December 1942 to take over command of 207 Squadron from Wing Commander F R Jeffs and within 24-hours he put himself on the *Battle Order* for a raid on Turin on 8th-9th December 1942. Taking off at 1747 his Lancaster I R5570 EM-R crashed near the target killing everyone on board. All now rest in Milan War Cemetery. For details of the crew, please refer to page 273 of my RAFBCL 1942.
29001 BARRETT Gerald Spencer S/Ldr + 30.11.42 10 Squadron
Squadron Leader Gerald Spencer Barrett died when Halifax II W7871 ZA-C captained by Flight Sergeant Edward John Willmott dived out of control from 300 feet and crashed at Laytham Grange Farm, a mile to the southwest of the squadron's base at Melbourne. There ere no survivors; I suspect Squadron Leader Barrett was on a familiarisation flight; he is buried in Barmby-on-the-Moor [St. Catherine] Churchyard. For details concerning the rest of the crew, please refer to page 267 of my RAFBCL 1942.
28260 BARBER Leslie Thomas Godard G/Capt 18.01.57 Retirement
29002 BELL John Henry P/O 13.06.30 Terminated
29003 BRIGHTY William John W/Cdr 10.02.54 Relinquished
29004 BURGESS Harry George P/O 09.07.30 Terminated
29005 CLARK Henry Thomas F/O + 21.04.32 208 Squadron
29006 CROSTHWAITE Robert Charles Hastings W/Cdr 23.09.54 Dismissal
By sentence of General Court Martial [LG 19 November 1954, supplement 40328, page 6546].
29007 DABINETT Hector Ivo G/Capt 11.06.54 Retirement
29008 ENNALS Eric Selby P/O 09.07.30 Terminated
29009 FOSTER George Arthur Carey G/Capt 10.02.54 Relinquished
As Wing Commander George Arthur Carey Foster AFC of 101 Squadron [Lancaster] was *Gazetted* with the DFC, less citation, on 21st April 1944, supplement 36480, page 1836.
29010 GORDON Douglas McCaul G/Capt 23.04.54 Retirement
At own request [LG 18 May 1954, supplement 40175, page 2906].
29011 HANKINS John Annesley S/Ldr 10.02.54 Relinquished
29012 HARTON Philip Gower P/O 10.10.30 Resigned
29013 HENDRIKZ Neville Charles S/Ldr 01.03.50 Retirement
29014 KELLY Maurice Henry G/Capt 01.04.53 Retirement
At his own request [LG 12 May 1953, supplement 39850, page 2640].
29015 KIDDLE Edward Grenville Bardwell P/O 25.04.31 Resigned
29016 KIPPENBERGER Rec Laughton A/Cmdr 21.02.58 Retirement
Air Commodore Rec Laughton Kippenberger CBE mentioned in despatches, died on Friday, 21st April 1967.
29017 KYRKE-SMITH Charles Arthur Murray W/Cdr 18.10.56 Relinquished
29018 LEA SMITH The Hon. Ferdinando Dudley Henry F/O 02.08.33 Relinquished
On account of ill-health [LG 8 August 1933, issue 33967, page 5301]. On 9th June 1934 he was granted a commission in the Territorial Army as a 2nd Lieutenant attached to the 8th Battalion, Worcestershire Regiment [LG 8 June 1934, issue 34058, page 3660].
29019 LOVE Richard William Gaussen F/O 29.03.33 Cashiered
[2nd Lieutenant 1st Royal Ulster Rifles Supplementary Reserve]. By sentence of General Court Martial [LG 23 May 1933, issue 33942, page 3457]. His name is published once more in the *Gazette*. It appears he joined Messrs Frank George Utting and Clive Horace Grimwood and together established a Coupon Advertising Business with offices at Grand Buildings, Trafalgar Square, London. By mutual consent this was dissolved on 25th February 1935 [LG 5 March 1935, issue 34139, page 1590].
29020 NOLAN Joseph Gabriel P/O 06.08.30 Terminated
I suspect that following his unsuccessful attempt to become a Royal Air Force pilot, Josepj Gabriel Nolan turned his attention to the medical profession for *The London Gazette* 31st August 1943, supplement 36152, page 3875 carries an entry in the Medical Branch section for Joseph Gabriel Nolan LRCP to be a flying officer[emergency] with effect from 29th July 1943.
29021 O'LOUGHLIN Harvey Colin F/O 05.07.32 Dismissed
New Zealand By sentence of General Court Martial. Paul McMillan has discovered the following concerning Flying Officer Harvey Colin O'Loughlin, born during January 1910 in Wellington in New Zealand's North Island. *"Central Chancery of The Orders of Knighthood" "St. James's Palace, London SW.1. 31st December 1960. The Queen has been graciously pleased, on the advice of Her Majesty's New Zealand Ministers, to give orders for the following appointments to the Most Excellent Order of the British Empire: To be Ordinary Members of the Military Division of the said Most Excellent Order: Flight Lieutenant Harvey Colin O'Loughlin [1372], Air Training Corps."* His death occurred in 1964 at Palmerston North, Manawatu-Wanganui, New Zealand. Additional to the above, Errol Martyn has posted on the RAF Commands website that from 8th April 1941 to 13th January 1946 Flight Lieutenant Harvey Colin O'Loughlin was for twenty-three months operational in the Pacific theatre during which he flew fifty-two missions in Hudson aircraft with 4, 9 and 3 Squadron RNZAF respectively. He was then engaged on ferry duties before becoming personal pilot and Personal Assistant to the Air Officer Commanding No. 1 [Islands] Group, followed by Officer Commanding Utility Flight on Guuadalcanal from May 1944 to 1945. His service with the Air Training Corps spanned the period 5th June 1953 to 4th June 1963.
Whatever misdemeanour led to his dismissal from the Royal Air Force, Harvey Colin O'Loughlin certainly made up for this tenfold in the Second World War and beyond.
29022 PALMER John Ross F/Lt 21.02.37 Class A
29023 PRICE Martin Pritchard F/Lt 30.05.38 Relinquished
On appointment to the Air Branch of the Royal Navy [LG 12 July 1938, issue 34531, page 4540].
29024 RUSTON Richard P/O 18.11.30 Terminated
29025 STUCKES Robert Charles P/O 26.07.30 Terminated
29026 SUPPLE Jeffrey Hale F/O + 28.05.34 84 Squadron
Flying Officer Jeffrey Hale Supple died in Makina sick quarters while undergoing treatment for malignant malaria and is buried in Basra [Makina] RAF Cemetery.
29027 THOMPSON Malcolm Stewart P/O + 20.09.30 3 FTS Grantham
Paul McMillan has found the following report published in the *Grantham Journal* on Saturday, 4th October 1930: *"Grantham Pilot Officer killed; verdict Accidental death was returned by the jury at Molesey, Surrey, last week at an Inquest on Malcolm Stewart Thompson, aged 19, son of Dr. Francis Thompson of Epsom Downs, and a Pilot Officer in the RAF attached to the Flying School Grantham, who, as briefly reported in our last*

issue, was killed in a motorcycle accident, while his pillion-rider, Derek Hartree, of Thames Ditton, also of the RAF, was seriously injured. It was stated by a witness that the tragedy occurred about eleven o'clock on a dark, wet night while deceased was rounding a corner at West Molesey, and crashed. An operation was performed on him at Cottage Hospital, where he died the following morning. The pillion-rider was too ill to attend the inquiry. Deceased father said that from his experience as a Doctor thought pillion riding ought not to be allowed. His son was a very fine driver. The jury expressed the view that the corner was dangerous and notices should be erected to warn drivers." My co-author has not been able to trace an 'Derek Hartree' as serving in the RAF but has established he emigrated to Canada in 1931 and by 1938 was serving in the Royal Artillery.

29028 WARDMAN Reginald Bryson G/Capt 09.01.58 Retirement

29029 WATSON John Russell S/Ldr + 16.08.43 115 Squadron

[2nd Lieutenant 57th Medium [Lowland] Brigade RA]. Squadron Leader John Russell Watson was a flight commander serving with 115 Squadron at Little Snoring and was captain of Lancaster II DS684 KO-M tasked for a raid on the Italian city of Turin on 15th-16th August 1943. Either outbound or homebound his Lancaster crashed near Alencon in the Orne department of France. There were no survivors and all now rest in Le Mans West Cemetery. Please refer to my RAFBCL 1943 and page 269 for their names.

LG 18 March 1930, issue 33589, page 1731

FLYING OFFICER

CONSTABLE-ROBERTS John

LG 25 March 1930, issue 33591, page 1896 - Seniority 14th March 1930 - Block 29030 to 29054

29030 ANDERSON Leslie Harold G/Capt 02.04.58 Retirement

29031 ASHCROFT William Alfred Archibald F/O 28.08.34 Cashiered

By sentence of General Court Martial.

29032 BARTER Eric Guy P/O 31.12.30 Terminated

29033 BURDICK George W/Cdr 29.04.55 Relinquished

29034 DAUNT Neill F/Lt 14.03.39 Relinquished

29035 GLENNY Arthur Philip F/O 01.09.37 Relinquished

On account of ill-health [LG 10 September 1937, issue 34434, page 5692].

29036 HALMSHAW William F/O + 31.07.36 Jersey Airlines

Flying Officer William Halmshaw was transferred to the Reserve Class A on 14th March 1936 [LG 17 March 1936, issue 34265, page 1743] during which time he joined Jersey Airlines. On the evening of 31st July 1936 he took off from Saint Peter Port, Guernsey on a scheduled flight to Jersey in Saro A.19 Cloud G-ABXW but failed to arrive. Weather conditions were far from ideal and the Cloud went into the sea some 28km south of Jersey near the Les Minquiers Reef. Although conjecture, it was thought that on encountering turbulence a small quantity of fuel surged sufficiently to temporarily uncover the tank outlet causing one or both fuel pumps to become air-locked. On discovery of the wreckage it was apparent Captain Halmshaw had lowered the undercarriage, believing he might make land. Rescue efforts were hampered by heavy seas and because the Cloud had not been fitted with a radio, which the UK Accidents Investigation Branch reported violated established directives, establishing its position was seriously delayed. In addition to Captain Halmshaw, mechanic W Sotinet drowned along with eight passengers, there ages ranging between Claude Stewart Willis, 20, and 67 year old Charles Vuel. The remainder were named as Ernest Appleby, Miss Maud Bean, Miss Margaret Davies, Miss Alice Judd, Miss Edwina Marley and Mrs Florence Annie Simpson.

29037 KING Thomas G/Capt 07.10.64 Retirement

My co-author reports that Group Captain Thomas King's medals, less his CBE, a photograph album illustrating his time in Singapore and other ephemera was auctioned in two lots in 2010 with estimates of £300 to £400 on the first lot and £500 to £700 on the second, this lost including the aforementioned photograph album.

29038 LEWIS William Edward Lawley S/Ldr + 04.02.43 236 Squadron

Squadron Leader William Edward Lawley Lewis failed to return to North Coates from a shipping reconnaissance off the Frisian Islands whIle flying in Beaufighter VI JL450. Subsequently, his body was washed ashore and he is buried in Bergen [Mollendal] Church Cemetery, Norway.

29039 MacDERMOT Terence John W/Cdr 13.03.52 Retirement

At his own request [LG 15 April 1952, supplement 39515, page 2074].

29040 MacDONALD Donald Malcolm Thomas AV-M 15.08.61 Retirement

Air Vice-Marshal Donald Malcolm Thomas MacDonald CB three times mentioned in despatches, died on 26th October 1988.

29041 MacDOUGALL Ralph Ian George W/Cdr 09.08.66 Retirement

From June to July 1940, as Squadron Leader MacDougall he commanded 17 Squadron [Hurricane], handed over 'the reigns of office' to Squadron Leader Cedric Walcyn Williams [see Appendix E September 1929 entry]. For a biography of his service, please consult The Battle of Britain London Monument website. Wing Commander MacDougall died in the Wiltshire town of Marlborough on Friday, 22nd July 1994.

29042 McGINN Brian James W/Cdr 10.02.54 Relinquished

29043 MAXWELL Patrick Herbert G/Capt 19.05.55 Relinquished

29044 MORRIS Richard Thomas Showler F/O + 05.01.40

Flying Officer Richard Thomas Showler Morris of the Reserve of Air Force Officers and described in *The London Gazette* of 10th May 1940, issue 34847, page 2855, as a Chief Test Pilot, died during the 'blackout' in a road traffic accident at Oxford. He is buried in Farndon Cemetery.

29045 PEACOCK John Charles Francis F/O + 18.10.33 Comms. Flight Calshot

Flying Officer John Charles Francis Peacock was mortally injured when a Supermaine Southampton flying boat S1121 crashed in Southampton Water off Calshot. Although alive when picked up he died the following day. Leading Aircraftman Harry George Thomas Foley was killed in the crash but, fortunately, Wing Commander Theodore Quintus Studd DSC survived, albeit injured, while Aircraftman James Barry O'Connell escaped with no more than a bad shaking. In its issue of 23rd November 1933 *Flight* magazine reported: *"In the resumed Inquest, held at Fawley, Southampton, on F/O J F Peacock and LAC H Foley, who were killed when a wooden "Southampton" crashed at Calshot on October 17th, Captain F S Wilkins of the Accidents Branch of the Air Ministry, said that the tail actuating gear was found in a fully forward position, which would make the flying boat extremely nose heavy. He thought that it would be difficult, if not impossible, for the machine to take off from the water. In reply to the Coroner, he said that the responsibility for the position of the gear rested normally on the instructor in charge of the aircraft. The jury returned a verdict that the accident was due to an error of judgement."*

Three press reports, all generated by the *Portsmouth Evening News* on 17th, 19th and 27th October 1933 make interesting reading: *"One man was killed and two others were seriously injured when a Royal Air Force flying boat crashed into Southampton Water today. Apparently the boat was attempting to alight on the water off Calshot when she crashed into the sea. The man who was killed was Leading Aircraftman Foley and the two injured officers were the pilot, Flying Officer Peacock and Wing Commander Studd. Foley had been in the Calshot Camp about six months, having come there from the RAF training establishment at Halton. He is a native of Portsmouth, his home bing at 18 Oliver Road, Eastney. Aircraftman O'Connell, who escaped uninjured, also belongs to Portsmouth, his address being 1 Claxton Street, Fratton. The pilot was admitted to Hospital with a broken arm and a broken leg. Wing Commander Studd was suffering from cuts about the face. Aircraftman O'Connell who was in the forward cockpit was thrown clear into the water and survived uninjured.*

"Mr C Bell employed at the oil works at Fawley, near the Calshot Station, who witnessed the accident, said that he saw the flying boat in the air then "she appeared to be making a perfectly normal landing, but when only a small height off the water instead of straightening out she nose dived into the sea. Her tail remained stuck up in the air and parts of her planes were in the water.

"Another eye-witness said that the aircraft porpoised on alighting, rose into the air and then nose dived. The oil tanker "Ben Read", which was steaming up Southampton Water, lowered boats to the assistance of the flying boat, but before they could get anywhere near RAF pinnaces were on the scene The machine involved in the accident is the last of the wooden hulled Southampton type flying boats. All the Southampton boats now in usse have metal hulls.

"On enquiry at The Air Ministry, the Press Association was informed that one airman is missing. He is Leading Aircraftman Harry George Thomas Foley [562523]. The officers on board the boat were Flying Officer John Charles Francis Peacock and Wing Commander Theodore Quintus Studd DSC. Aircraftman James Barry O'Connell [561204] escaped uninjured. The machine involved was on a training flight. The injured were taken to a hospital [Netley] *attached to the Air Station. Both the injured officers are married, Squadron Leader* [sic] *Studd, who is the son of Mr and Mrs E F Studd of Starcross, Devon, was married three years ago to Miss Esther New, daughter of Mr. And Mrs. H H G of Craddock House, Collumpton, Devon. Flying Officer Peacock was married last year to Miss Doreen Shea, daughter of Major and Mrs Shea of Uppingham. He is the son of Reverend C H Peacock of Stamford, Lincs. "My son has been in the Air Force for about four years" he a reporter today. "He was sent to Calshot for a course."*

On the 19th, the paper reported: *"Flying Officer J C F Peacock, pilot of the flying boat which crashed in Southampton Water on Tuesday, died from his injuries at The Royal Victoria Hospital, Netley, yesterday. The body of Leading Aircraftman Foley, another victim of the accident, whose home was at 18 Oliver Road, Eastney, has not been found. Flying Officer Peacock's death brings the number of fatalities in RAF accidents this year to 48."*

Then on the 27th the paper carried the following: *"The body of [562523] LAC Harry George Thomas Foley, which was missing after a RAF Flying Boat crashed when taking off* [sic] *from Calshot, in Southampton Water, on October 17th, has been found. It was sighted in The Solent by the Alexandra Towing Company's tug "Romsey" which had been in attendance on the North German Lloyd liner "Bremen" in Cowes Roads. As soon as the tug returned to Southampton the police were notified, and the body was recovered by The Marine Section of the RAF."*

Sandwiched between the articles published on the 17th and 19th was a dedication to Leading Aircraftman Foley under the rather poignant headline *"A Last 'Good-Bye" At Portsmouth" "Leading Aircraftman George Thomas Foley, the victim of the fatal crash of a Royal Air Force flying-boat in Southampton Water, yesterday, was, like Aircraftman James Barry O'Connell, who escaped uninjured, a Portsmouth youth. His parents, Mr and Mrs T L Foley live at 18 Oliver Road, Eastney. He was their only son and was aged 20 years. He was educated at Chivers School and passed the examination for the Royal Air Force. He went to Halton as an apprentice at the age of 15, and has been at the Calshot Base for some time. He began flying only a month ago. Keen on rowing and sailing he was a member of the Rowing Club at Calshot and had won various races. His father, who is a boilermaker, said that his son was a quiet and reserved lad. "He was home last weekend" he added "and went to Wymering to see the motor-cycle racing. When he left home to return to Calshot, he said 'Good-Bye.' That was quite unusual. He generally said 'Toodle-oo' or something like that."*

His funeral, conducted by the Reverend Windsor Roberts, vicar of St James' Church, was held on 31st October 1933 at Milton Cemetery. Although a private ceremony a number of Royal Air Force officers and non-commissioned officers attended to pay there last respects. Reports of the inquest into the accident, as touched upon by the extract from *Flight,* appeared in *The Scotsman* as well as the *Portsmouth Evening News.* Wing Commander Studd was sufficiently recovered to attend and he was questioned as to who was responsible for checking on the position of the tail-actuating gear; particularly as it seems he had control of the flying boat. Responding, the wing commander said that following the crash he found himself in the water about twenty-five yards ahead of the wreck, adding that he was not a qualified boat captain and that responsibility for the setting of the tail-actuating gear lay with the instructor, namely Flying Officer Peacock. On this point the Coroner put it to him that in view of his flying experience did he not think some of the responsibility lay with him. On this uncomfortable point, Wing Commander Studd answered *"Quite possibly, but at the time if I had been the instructor on that machine I should have had a look at all the controls before leaving the water."* This, it seems, did not satisfy the Coroner who made the pertinent observation that Flying Officer Peacock had lost his life to which the wing commander replied *"I know he is, and that is why I do not want to say anything against him."* In returning their verdict the jury said that some proportion of the blame rested on Wing Commander Studd. Earlier, a question had been raised as to why Leading Aircraftman Foley had not been wearing a Reid life-jacket. Although not, it appears, replying directly to this point, Squadron Leader James William Hancock Steyl, Calshot's senior medical officer, thought that Foley had been rendered unconscious on the impact and his body became entangled in some of the wreckage which broke free as the Southampton was being towed to the shore. Reading all the reports, despite the evidence from two eyewitnesses that the flying-boat was landing, I am of the opinion that the crash occurred when the Southampton was taking off. This is supported by its entry in the J File which shows that it had a somewhat chequered service life; on 26th July 1927 after landing it drifted and collided with the stern of a private yacht. Then, on 29th May 1929 it struck a buoy on take off which resulted in the hull being holed and finally *"Crashed on take off, Calshot, 17.10.33 WOC."*

29046 PIERPOINT Geoffrey Blackhill P/O 06.12.30 Relinquished

On account of ill-health.

29047 RICHARDSON William Arthur G/Capt 19.07.55 Retirement

29048 SATCHELL William Arthur John G/Capt 01.07.56 Retirement

29049 SIMMONS Henry Augustus W/Cdr + 23.03.44 26 OTU

Wing Commander Henry Augustus Simmons was the captain of Wellington X LP258 of 26 OTU Wing which crashed with total loss of life during a night training flight, the details of which are recorded in my RAFBCL OTU page 283; he is buried in Oxford [Botley] Cemetery, his headstone bearing the inscription *"In Very Proud And Tender Memory."*

29050 SLOMAN Leonard P/O 17.09.30 Terminated

29051 VAN OPPEN Ernest Conrad P/O 04.02.31 Terminated

29052 VINCENT Arthur William W/Cdr 08.07.44 Dismissed

By sentence of General Court Martial [LG 9 March 1945, supplement 36978, page 1373].

29053 WILDE Reginald Geoffrey F/Lt 01.05.60 Relinquished

29054 WOODLAND John Douglas P/O + 18.08.30 5 FTS Sealand

Pilot Officer John Douglas Woodland died in a road traffic accident while returning to Sealand from Chester on his motorcycle, and with Pilot Officer Jack Satchell on the pillion, he collided with a cyclist. The impact threw everyone onto the road where moments later a second motorcyclist struck Pilot Officer Woodland.

LG 29 April 1930, issue 33601, page 2650 - Seniority 11th April 1930 - Block 29055 to 29079

29055 ARMITAGE John William Paul P/O 17.07.30 Terminated

29056 BARBER Gerald Vincent S/Ldr 24.05.57 Relinquished

29057 BARNETT Reginald James William F/Lt 10.02.54 Relinquished

29058 BIRKS Christopher Frederick F/Lt 21.12.60 Retirement

29059 BOLLAND Guy Alfred G/Capt 05.11.59 Retirement

29060 BROWN James Arthur Sheerman G/Capt 30.11.58 Retirement

29061 BULLARD Leonard Arthur F/O 10.01.33 Relinquished

On account of ill health. During the Second World War his health recovered sufficiently for his acceptance as an Air Transport Auxiliary ferry pilot. However, a copy of his service report, dated 12th November 1942, reads: *"Bullard - Unlikely to become proficient Ferry Pilot."* Various attachments show that Leonard Arthur Bullard was born on 27th April 1901 and that he had achieved approximately 800 flying hours with service in India and France noted. He had flown a number of single-engined types, his first solo being noted as June 1929. His multi-engined experience appears to have been on Vickers Virginia types. The form terminating his ATA contract is headed 'Disciplinary Action'.

29062 CATT Ronald George Edmund W/Cdr 08.07.60 Relinquished

29063 CLARKE Ronald Neville W/Cdr + 04.03.41 224 Squadron

Wing Commander Ronald Neville-Clarke DFC was captain of Hudson I N7235 QX-A which took off from Leuchars at middaywith the intention of staging to Aldergrove in Northern Ireland but crashed with fatal consequences for all on board near Loch Braden in South Ayrshire. The tragedy is reported on page 100 of Ross McNeill's Coastal Command losses where the date is shown as 3rd March 1941. Wing Commander Neville-Clarke is buried in Little Aston [St. Peter] Churchyard, Staffordshire. His brother, Lieutenant Seymour Neville-Clarke of the Royal Artillery died in captivity on 21st November 1940. He is commemorated on column 7 of the Dunkirk Memorial.

29064 CROSBIE Leonard John G/Capt + 22.06.46 353 Squadron

Australia Quoting from the website Highgate RSL, which I have pleasure in acknowledging, Group Captain Leonard John Crosbie was a passenger in an Expeditor aircraft which took off from Mergui in Burma to stage through to Germany: *"The aircraft was last seen entering cloud off the Burma coast between Tavoy and Mergui, but it failed to reach its destination. When the aircraft was reported missing search patrols interrogated a Headsman of a Burma village who informed the patrol that the aircraft had crashed into the sea about 8 miles from the shore. The Headsman produced a damaged log book [Stuart]. A later patrol between Tavoy and Mergui found a valise which had been washed ashore with the name 'Allard' marked on it. The villagers stated to this patrol that the aircraft was seen flying low, it exploded and fell into the sea." "The crew members were Flying Officer William Stanley Allard [186359] RAFVR, pilot and Flying Officer Donald Ian Paul Stuart [201103] RAFVR navigator. Group Captain Crosbie had been appointed General Duties Signals Plans in the Signals Office of Air Command South East Asia."* He is commemorated on column 459 of the Singapore Memorial. According to Air-Britain's *Squadrons of the Royal Air Force & Commonwealth 1918-1988*, 353 Squadron formed at Dum Dum on 1st June 1942 receiving Hudson IIIs for general reconnaissance duties. At the time of Group Captain Crosbie's death the squadron was based at Palam and had given up its Expeditor aircraft for Dakotas which were used for transport duties. However, I am of the opinion that the aircraft in question was an Expeditor and consulting the CWGC data base only nine Royal Air Force deaths occurred on the 22nd of June 1946, three of these, as named above, attached to 353 Squadron, which disbanded at Palam on 1st October 1946.

29065 CROSS Kenneth Brian Boyd ACM 24.02.67 Retirement

Air Chief Marshal Sir Kenneth Cross KCB CBE DSO DFC mentioned in despatches, died on Wednesday, 18th June 2003. As a squadron leader he was in command of 46 Squadron [Hurricane] detached to Norway in May 1940. With the evacuation of our forces in June, Squadron Leader Cross was successful in flying his squadron onto the aircraft HMS *Glorious,* a magnificent achievement by the pilots concerned. Tragically, while in passage to the naval base at Scapa Flow the carrier and her attendant destroyers were sunk by the German battleship *Scharnhorst.* The loss of life was heavy; from 46 Squadron only Squadron Leader Cross and his Flight Commander 'Pat' Jameson survived. For three days and two nights, along with around thirty others, they drifted on a Cayley float before being picked up by a Norwegian trawler, the *Borgund,* and taken to to the Faroes where they boarded the destroyer HMS *Veteran* and landed at Rosyth. Subsequently, Kenneth Cross was to serve with distinction in the Middle East. His final two appointments were as Air Officer Commanding-in-Chief Bomber Command from 20th May 1959 to 1st December 1963 and thence as Air Officer Commanding-in-Chief Transport Command.

29066 DAWSON Ernest F/Lt + 16.04.36 7 FTS Peterborough

While instructing Aircraftman Harold Eric Smith-Langridge, aged 19, in Hart Trainer K4986 [delivered to Peterborough for 7 FTS on 29th November 1935 and when written off had flown for a total of 96.50 hours] Flight Lieutenant Ernest Dawson performed a loop but, in pulling out struck the ground and smashed into a hangar killing him and his pupil instantly. Also killed was Leading Aircraftman Percy Cuthbert who was working in the hangar and mortally injuring his companion Leading Aircraftman Stanley Arthur Rollason who died the next day.

As was common at the time, the accident received press coverage and I am indebted to the Sussex History Forum Group for posting reports from the *Taunton Courier and Western* and the *Hastings and St. Leonards Observer.* The former, in their edition of Wednesday, 22nd April 1936, under the banner *"Warplane Loop Tragedy"* continued: *"An officer and two men of the RAF were killed in an accident at No. 7 Flying Training School, Westwood, Peterborough, on Thursday. They were Flight Lieutenant Ernest Dawson, Leading Aircraftman Percy Cuthbert, and Aircraftman [First Class] Harold Eric Smith-Langridge. It appears that the aircraft was one of three which left the aerodrome about 3 p.m. Two returned, and the leading machine, piloted by Flight Lieutenant Dawson, who had Smith-Langridge as a passenger, began to carry out formation loops.*

"According to an eye-witness, it was pulling out of a loop when it struck the ground, dashed across the tar macadam surface of the aerodrome, and struck a hangar. There was a report and the 'plane burst into flames. The hangar also caught alight and only the skeleton remained. Damage was also done to four of the five machines in the hangar. Cuthbert and Leading Aircraftman S A R King were in the hangar when the crash occurred. Both were taken to Peterborough Hospital, where Cuthbert died shortly after admittance. Flight-Lieutenant Dawson was 36 and lived at Broadway, Peterborough. His wife gave birth to a daughter two days ago. The news of his death is being kept from her. Leading Aircraftman Smith-Langridge'ss home was in Bute-road, Wallington.

"Just before the inquest was opened at Peterborough on Friday on the three victims of the RAF 'plane crash, a fourth man died in hospital. He was Leading Aircraftman Stanley Arthur Rollason King, of Ramsgate. He died, after an operation, of a fractured skull. The Peterborough Coroner, Mr. W B Buckle, returned a verdict of 'Accidental death' in the four cases, said each man died during his duty. Flying-Officer Ernest Bruce Harvey, medical officer at Westwood aerodrome, stated that Flight-Lieutenant Dawson and Smith-Langridge each had a fractured skull, and had been extensively burned. Death was instantaneous.

"Corporal Kenneth Dring said he was booking flying times when two aeroplanes came out of a loop, circled the aerodrome, and began another loop in front of the hangar at about 300 feet. He added:- "As it was flattening out, the undercarriage of the leading machine, Flight Lieutenant Dawson's - struck the ground in front of the hangar. It appeared to bounce once, and the shot inside at a terrific speed. King and Cuthbert were standing in the mouth of the hangar. They ran to get out of the way, but were not quick enough. They appear to have been struck by the starboard wing tip, and were thrown to the ground." Corporal Dring said, in reply to the Coroner, that he was not qualified to say whether 300 feet would be a reasonable height at which to loop.

"The Coroner:- Do you think there was any great margin between what would have been a safe ending to the manoeuvre and this present disastrous one?

"I think a foot would have made all the difference. It was very nearly perfect."

The report in the *Hastings and St. Leonards Observer* differs from the above in one respect in that it reports Flight Lieutenant Dawson's wife as giving birth to a son. It also notes that he was the son of a local magistrate at that the marriage took place in 1931 at Norman-r0ad, Methodist Church, St. Leonards. Since their marriage the couple had lived at Tangmere, Grantham and, finally, Peterborough. The week following this brief announcement the paper reported on the funeral: *"There were impressive scenes at the Borough Cemetery on Wednesday, when the burial of Flight-Lieutenant Ernest Dawson, who was killed when an RAF aeroplane which he was piloting crashed into a hangar at Peterborough on Thursday last week, took place in the presence of 63 officers and men. Flight-Lieutenant Dawson was buried with Air Force honours. At Christ Church, St. Leonards, the cortege was met by men from Nos. 2 and 25 Squadrons, Hawkinge [Kent] air base, under Flight-Lieutenant A C Watson, and an escort under Warrant Officer F A Ladell. The coffin, draped with the Union Jack, was borne in procession to the cemetery on an RAF trailer.*

"The funeral service was conducted by the Rev. A J Morton [minister at Norman-road Methodist Church]. A guard of honour was formed at the cemetery and the procession moved slowly from the chapel to the graveside, near where the escort stood with reversed arms. Men from No. 7 Flying Training School at Peterborough, under Flight Sergeant L M Hooper, stood in silence while the coffin was lowered into the grave. The firing party fired the last salute and the "Last Post" was sounded."

29067 DOBELL Arthur Edward F/O 11.04.39 Relinquished

29068 DONALDSON George Francis Keiller G/Capt 16.04.60 Relinquished

29069 HARRISON Rowland Baron G/Capt 01.12.58 Retirement

29070 HAUGHTON Henry Osburne P/O 29.04.31 Terminated

29071 HAYNES Philip G/Capt 23.01.59 Retirement

29072 HEAVEN Edgar Joseph Ninian F/Lt 18.04.36 Relinquished

On appointment to a commission on the Unattached List for the Indian Army [LG 26 May 1936, issue 34287, page 3375].

29073 LEFTWICH Gordon Harcourt P/O 08.08.30 Terminated

During the Second World War he obtained a commission in the Royal Regiment of Artillery, his commission from Cadet to Lieutenant being effective from 13th June 1943 [LG 26 October 1943, supplement 36222, page 4716]. My co-author reports that Lieutenant Gordon Harcourt Leftwich died in Camden, Kent on Wednesday the 1st of June 1983.

29074 McALLISTER Desmond Laurence P/O 11.08.30 Terminated
29075 MORRISH Douglas Warnes S/Ldr 01.01.44 Relinquished
On appointment to RNZAF [LG 9 January 1945, supplement 36882, page 266]. At the time his Squadron Leader rank was temporary and he had transferred from the General Duties Branch to the Equipment Branch.
29076 O'HAGAN John Gerald Brendan S/Ldr 07.04.58 Retirement
Granted a permanent commission on 5th September 1935, John Gerald Brendan O'Hagan transferred from the General Duties Branch to the Equipment Branch and in doing so his service number was amended to 29176. Paul McMillan reports that Squadron Leader O'Hagan died on Saturday, 13th October 1986 at Chichester in West Sussex.
29077 TRAPPES-LOMAX Ambrose Edmund Byrnand P/O 01.10.30 Terminated
29078 WHITE Leslie John Morris
Leslie John Morris White was appointed to a commission in class CC within the Administrative and Special Duties Branch and with Squadron Leader rank with effect from 17th June 1944 [LG 8 August 1944, supplement 36643, page 3666].
29079 WILLIAMS Gwyn Mathews F/O 20.07.32 Relinquished
On account of ill-health [LG 19 July 1932, issue 33847, page 4705].

LG 27 May 1930, issue 33609, page 3330 - Seniority 16th July 1921

FLYING OFFICER

29080 DOMVILE John Patrick G/Capt 26.09.45 Resigned
Formerly Lieutenant in the Regular Army Reserve of Officers

LG 1 July 1930, issue 33621, page 4114 - From the Supplementary List 16th June 1930 with seniority from 3rd February 1934

FLIGHT LIEUTENANT

29081 MACDONALD MC Alan David W/Cdr 10.02.54 Relinquished
TNA Kew retain a document for Wing Commander Alan David Macdonald MC under AIR 76/315/1 which shows he died on Tuesday, 28th June 1966.

LG 8 July 1930, issue 33623, pages 4273 and 4274 - Seniority 27th June 1930 - Block 29082 to 29105

29082 BALL Peter Strickland P/O + 09.09.30 2 FTS Digby
While flying solo in Avro 504N J9007 Pilot Officer Peter Strickland Ball flew into trees, crashed, whereupon the trainer caught fire, near Nocton Heath, 7 miles SE from the centre of Lincoln. He had survived a mere two months of Royal Air Force service.
29083 BATEMAN John Wilmot F/Lt 30.05.38 Relinquished
On appointment to the Air Branch of the Royal Navy [LG 12 July 1938, issue 34531, page 4540].
29084 BROWN Roger Brammer W/Cdr 08.12.48 Cashiered
By sentence of General Court Martial [LG 31 December 1948, supplement 38490, page 6728]. He had been appointed to a permanent commission of New Year's Day 1947, though notification was only *Gazetted* on 13th April 1948, supplement 38259, page 2327.
29085 CHAPMAN John Edward Furlong P/O + 12.01.31 2 FTS Digby
See Appendix E and the entry for Flight Lieutenant Geoffrey Maynard Edgar Shaw under LG 13 January 1925 for details.
29086 CHATTERTON George James Stewart F/O 09.09.36 To Class C
Flying Officer George James Stewart Chatterton was commissioned as a Lieutenant in the Territorial Army attached to the 5th Battalion, The Queen's Regiment, with effect from 24th June 1939 [LG 28 July 1939, issue 34649, page 5206].
29087 CLUBE Montagu Victor Murray F/Lt 27.06.37 To Class A
Flight Lieutenant Montagu Victor Murray Clube transferred to the Auxiliary Air Force and was promoted wing commander [temporary] on 7th June 1940 [LG 7 June 1940, issue 34866, page 3439] his service number now being 90015. G/Capt 01.04.56 Relinquished
29088 COLLINS Anthony Roland W/Cdr 22.06.55 Retirement
29089 FARLEY Walter Ronald P/O 09.07.30 Terminated
It would appear that Walter Ronald Farley had qualified for the briefest service ever recorded for an officer granted a short service commission; however, he was re-appointed with effect from 29th December 1930 [LG 13 January 1931, issue 33680, page 307] and his details will, therefore, be reported in Volume 5 [1st January 1931 to 2nd September 1939].
29090 GRACIE Edward John F/O 19.06.33 Dismissed
By sentence of General Court Martial [LG 15 August 1933, issue 33969, page 5426].

It appears, however, that he was able to return to the service and was commissioned in the Reserve of Air Force Officers, General Duties Branch, as a flying officer in Class A, with effect from 23rd March 1937 [LG 13 April 1937, issue 34388, page 2380]. His term of engagement was for five years during which war with Germany was declared on 3rd September 1939 and Flying Officer Gracie was immediately for active service, His profile on The Battle of Britain London Monument website charts a career of outstanding service. Initially he was attached to 79 Squadron [Hurricane] but in June 1940, and now ranked Flight Lieutenant, he was posted to 56 Squadron at North Weald as flight commander B Flight. With '56' he showed his excellent fighting spirit and when shot down on the 30th of August 1940 his successes in the *Battle of Britain* totalled some thirteen enemy aircraft destroyed, damaged, or shared with other pilots. It was while engaging a Heinkel He.III in Hurricane I R2689*on the 30th that he was shot down, crash-landing near Halstead in Essex. His Hurricane was burnt out but Gracie thought he had escaped unscathed; that is until the next day when it was confirmed he had fractured a bone in his neck!

Rejoining '56' on 8th October 1940 he learned he had been *Gazetted* with the DFC [LG 1 October 1940, issue 34958, page 5789]: *"This officer has destroyed seven enemy aircraft and damaged another five. By his outstanding leadership, skill and courage, he has proved an excellent example to all."* Rested in early January 1941, Flight Lieutenant Gracie was soon back on operations, this time commanding 23 Squadron [Blenheim If] at Ford and though his tenure was brief he claimed a Dornier Do.17 as a 'probable' during a night intruder over Melville in mid-March 1941. However, in April 1941 he was reunited with Hurricanes when he took over the helm of 601 Squadron AAF at Northolt and later in the year, by which time '601' was at Duxford, he oversaw the introduction of the Bell Airacobra - the sole operational squadron to receive this type and which, unfortunately, was a disappointment. Handing over the reigns to Squadron Leader E J Jones on Christmas Eve 1941, Edward Gracie was soon on his way to the beleaguered island of Malta which he reached in a Spitfire flown off with others from HMS *Eagle* to replace the Hurricanes of 126 Squadron.

Here it is suffice to say that his operational flying was a 'whirlwind' of postings until October 1943, and now back in the UK, taking over command of 169 Squadron [Mosquito] for duties in 100 Group which was supporting Main Force operations in Bomber Command. On 15th February 1944, accompanied by Flight Lieutenant W W Todd, he took off from Little Snoring in Mosquito II HJ707 VI-B to support the Command's operations to Berlin and it was while flying at 22,000 feet north of Hanover that his aircraft was intercepted by a night fighter which set the Mosquito's starboard engine on fire. Flight Lieutenant baled out and survived to become a prisoner of war but Wing Commander Edward John Gracie DFC perished; he is buried in Hanover War Cemetery [see my RAFBCL 1944 and page 81 for details]. * The identity of the Hurricane is in doubt; page 67 of Norman R Franks *Royal Air Force Fighter Command Losses of the Second World War 1939-1940* indicates R2689 but Air-Britains P1000-R9999 register shows E2689 as being Struck off Charge on 1st December 1940 following service with 249 Squadron while The Battle of Britain London Monument website has P3554 but the same register lists the units for this Hurricane as 32, 56, 213 and 607 Squadrons and damaged by '109s near Swanage and abandoned over Aldingbourne, Dorset on 5th October 1940. This is confirmed by Franks on page 91 of the aforementioned book, adding the that pilot was Pilot Officer D Evans who landed safely.

29091 GRANT George William Patrick A/Cmdr 15.02.56 Retirement

Air Commodore George William Patrick Grant CBE mentioned in despatches, died on Friday, 3rd February 1961. In March 1941 he took over command of 53 Squadron [Blenheim IV] at St. Eval during which he had a narrow escape from injury when on 26th May 1941 he was returning to base from a patrol in Blenheim IV V6301 PZ- in lowering visibility and in the gloom undershot the runway and crashed into a gun post.

29092 HARMAN Roland Gustave W/Cdr 04.12.47 Retirement

On account of medical unfitness for Air Force service [LG 23 December 1947, supplement 38153, page 6085].

29093 HILLS-SPEDDING Ian Brooke P/O 10.09.30 Terminated

29094 HOOPER William Ernest S/Ldr 04.03.47 Class A

New Zealand Paul McMillan has traced the following for Squadron Leader William Ernest Hooper who was born on 17th July 1906 at Skeet Road, Pihama, Taranaki, New Zealand. By the autumn of 1948 he was the Chief Flying Instructor at No. 8 Reserve Flying School at Woodley from where, as reported by the *Reading Standard* in its issue of Friday, 15th October 1948, Wing Commander Hooper left England for New Zealand where he was to join his brother in the horticultural business. Two years later and Wing Commander Hooper was dead. It was during the afternoon of 3rd October 1950 when he was flying DH.82A Tiger Moth ZK-AOM on a crop-spraying task near Mangahoe, Hunterville on the North Island that he executed a steep turn at low level, lost control and crashed. Alive when lifted from the wreckage he died soon afterwards from his injuries. The loss of ZK-AOM marked the 35th agricultural flying accident and the first one resulting in the death of the pilot. Formerly N9428 of the Royal Air Force it saw no active service before being sold to the RNZAF as NZ862 on 15th February 1940.

The following was published in the *Otago Daily Times* on 30th November 1950: *"Tiger Moth Aircraft - Aerial Top Dressing Work - Wanganui, November 29th. Criticism of the suitability of Tiger Moth aircraft for aerial top-dressing was given in a report by the inspector of aircraft accidents, Wing Commander R C Kean, which was brought before the inquest at Hunterville today into the death of William Ernest Hooper, aged 44, a former RAF wing commander, who was accidentally killed in aerial top-dressing operations at Mangahe, near Hunterville, last month.*

"Tiger Moths were designed as elementary trainers and, as such, fulfilled their functions wherever they were used, said the report. The machines' capability for stalling in certain manoeuvres [not encountered in normal training, but common in aerial top-dressing work] was deceptive, and even experienced pilots had been deceived, especially when turning without the benefit of a clear horizon.

"Wing Commander Kean stated that he considered the cause of the accident was the pilot's action in making a steep turn without, at the same time, maintaining adequate air speed. The coroner's finding was one of accidental death."

29095 HOYLE Ronald Leslie P/O 14.10.31 Relinquished

On account of ill-health. His health improved, Ronald Leslie Hoyle returned to the service and was granted a commission in the Royal Air Force Volunteer Reserve, General Duties Branch, as a probationary Pilot Officer [emergency] on 1st November 1941 [LG 6 January 1942, issue 35408, page 142 and with a new service number 110876. S/Ldr 28.11.55 Relinquished

29096 McDOUGALL Alan James S/Ldr 21.07.54 Relinquished

29097 MERMAGEN Herbert Waldemar A/Cmdr 14.11.60 Retirement

Air Commodore Herbert Waldemar Mermagen CB CBE AFC mentioned in despatches, died on Saturday, 10th January 1998. A most interesting biography of his service can be read on The Battle of Britain London Monument website which amongst the plethora of detail notes that he was posted from RAF Usworth to Duxford on 5th October 1939 to re-form 222 Squadron. Initially equipped with Blenheim If '222' converted to Spitfires in March 1940 and it was during *Operation Dynamo* that he shot down a Me110 over the Dunkirk beaches on 1st June 1940. Then, during the night of 19th June 1940 he intercepted and damaged a Heinkel HeIII over Hull, no mean feat in an aircraft not suited for night fighting.

During service in the Middle East he was one of a handful of pilots to fly Spitfire VB floatplanes on Lake Timsor. Postwar, and now on the Staff of SHAEF, in the first weeks of turmoil following the German surrender he assisted in the apprehension of several top-ranking Nazi officers including Wilhelm Keitel, Alfred Josef Ferdinand Jodel, both executed on 16th October 1946 after being found guilty of war crimes at the Nuremburg Trails and Karl Dönitz [received a ten year prison sentence at the same trials] and at Berchtesgaden General Karl Koller of the *Luftwaffe* fell into his hands and would briefly imprisoned in the UK..

29098 MONYPENNY John Blackwell Sinclair S/Ldr + 20.07.40 9 Squadron

Squadron Leader John Blackwell Sinclair Monypenny and his crew perished when their Wellington IC L7795 WS-G, tasked to bomb an aircraft park near Wismar [Mecklenburg-Vorpommen] on the Baltic Coast crashed into the Eckernförder Bucht to the NW of Kiel. He is commemorated on the Runnymede Memorial, panel 4. Additional details may be found in my revised edition of RAFBCL 1939-1940 pages 169 and 170.

Taking over command of A Flight from Squadron Leader Lancelot Elworthy Jarman [see Appendix D LG 1 March 1929] his record of operations are as follows:

15.05.40	Wellington IC L7795 WS-G	N	Bottrop and the Ruhr Valley
18.05.40	Wellington IC L7795 WS-G	N	Marshalling Yards in the Ruhr
20.05.40	Wellington IC L7795 WS-G	N	Enemy troop movements
24.05.40	Wellington IC L7795 WS-G	N	Enemy troop movements
27.05.40	Wellington IC L7795 WS-G	N	Road junction at Courtrai
30.05.40	Wellington IC L7795 WS-G	N	Road junction at Soex
05.06.40	Wellington IC L7795 WS-G	N	Duisburg - Very hazy and target area difficult to locate
07.06.40	Wellington IC L7795 WS-G	N	Bois de Bourlers
09.06.40	Wellington IC L7795 WS-G	N	Enemy movements in wooded areas in the border area with Belgium
13.06.40	Wellington IC L7795 WS-G	N	Foret de Nouvion
17.06.40	Wellington IC L7795 WS-G	N	Marshalling Yards Reydt, Cologne and Essen
21.06.40	Wellington IC L7795 WS-G	N	Bremen Focke Wulf factory
24.06.40	Wellington IC L7795 WS-G	N	Targets in the Ruhr - Düsseldorf, Dortmund and Kamen
01.07.40	Wellington IC L7795 WS-G	N	M61 M440
07.07.40	Wellington IC L7795 WS-G	N	Osnabrück Marshalling Yards
11.07.40	Wellington IC L7795 WS-G	N	Soest Marshalling Yards
19.07.40	Wellington IC L7795 WS-G	N	Wismar Aircraft Park - Failed to return

29099 MORRIS Douglas Griffith AM 31.03.66 Retirement

Air Marshal Sir Douglas Morris KCB CBE DSO DFC, died on Monday, 26th March 1990. Commanding 406 Squadron RCAF, the first RCAF night fighter squadron formed at Acklington in Northumberland on 10th May 1941, Wing Commander Douglas Griffith Morris was *Gazetted* with the DFC on 21st October 1941, supplement 35318, page 6104: *"One night in September 1941, this officer pursued and destroyed a Junkers 88 about 50 miles out to sea. His aircraft had been hit by the enemy's return fire and one engine put out of action. Wing Commander Morris succeeded, however, in flying back to base on the remaining engine. Two nights later, this officer destroyed a Heinkel III and a Dornier in one sortie in spite of intense evasive action by the enemy aircraft. Wing Commander Morris has set a fine example by his determination and skill."*

29100 SNAREY George Norman F/Lt 04.10.43 Resigned

Flight Lieutenant George Norman Snarey AFC held an honorary rank in the Administrative and Special Duties Branch between 12th July 1944 and 31st July 1945 when he resigned for a second time and postwar he held a commission as a flying officer in the Royal Air Force Volunteer Reserve Training Branch until 29th May 1964 when he resigned for a third time [LG 21 July 1964, supplement 43886, page 6261]. Throughout these periods of service his number was 71184.

29101 STEAD George Gatonby W/Cdr 08.09.56 Relinquished

29102 STYCHE Norman Charles Meyrick F/O + 26.09.33 40 Squadron

29103 TREWBY Maurice Robert Desmond S/Ldr 01.12.43 Relinquished

On appointment to to the RNZAF. Via the RAF Commands website a report from Errol Martyn quoting from Colin Hanson's *By Such Deeds - Honours and Awards in the Royal New Zealand Air Force 1923- 1999* [Volplane Press, 2001]: *"TREWBY, Wing Commander Maurice Robert*

Desmond AFC NZ1989; Born Otahuhu 9 Dec 1911; RAF 27 Jun 1930 to 14 Sep 1935 & Sep 1939 to 31 Nov 1943, 29103, RNZAF 1 Dec 1943 to 7 May 1945; Pilot. Citation Air Force Cross [31 Mar 1942] : [26 EFTS RAF] This officer entered the RAF in June 1930. Following nearly two years service in night bomber squadrons in this country, he was posted to Iraq, where he continued duties in a bomber transport squadron for a further two years. On his return to this county he became a flying instructor and was so employed until recently, when he became attached to his parent unit as chief flying instructor. He has proved himself to be most conscientious, reliable and exceedingly efficient. He has at all times, set a high standard in his own work and in that of the pupils under his instruction." "Wg Cdr Trewby joined the RAF in 1930 and served in England on 7 Sqn [Virginia] and then 503 Sqn [Hyderabad]. During 1933-1935 he served with 70 Sqn [Victoria] at Hinaidi, Iraq. He transferred to the RAF Reserve in Sep 1935, and until mobilised on the outbreak of war served as a flying instructor with Imperial Airways and Phillips & Powis Aircraft Ltd training pilots for the RAF. Following his services to the Directorate of Organisation and Staff duties in Air Department, Wellington, he returned to England."

29104 UPCHURCH Allan Edward P/O 14.08.30 Resigned

During the Second World War, as Paul McMilland has discovered, Allan Edward Upchurch served as an equipment officer in the RNZAF and rose to Squadron Leader rank. Postwar he faced a Court Martial at Te Rapa and was sentenced to be reduced to Flight Lieutenant rank with effect from 4th July 1956 and with seniority 4th July 1948. Soon after, however, on 14th December 1956 he retired from the service. He died at Epsom, Waitakere, Auckland on the North Island on Monday, 23rd December 1996.

29105 WARDROP Ronald P/O 24.09.30 Terminated

LG 25 July 1930, issue 33628, page 4644 - Seniority 12th July 1930 - Block 29106 to 29120

29106 HANSON Ronald W/Cdr 19.05.58 Retirement
29107 HAWKINS Horace James Leatham S/Ldr 22.08.58 Relinquished
29108 HOLE Alan Harold W/Cdr 01.07.57 Retirement
29109 JEFFERSON Thomas Anthony W/Cdr 30.07.53 Relinquished
29110 McKENNA Austin Flower G/Capt + 03.09.43 Station Commander Langar

As Station Commander at Langar, home for 207 Squadron since 20th September 1942, Group Captain Austin Flower McKenna put himself on the *Battle Order* for the squadron's participation in a Main Force raid on Berlin. Joining a very experienced crew captained by C Flight's commander, Squadron Leader Ian McAlistair Huntley-Wood DFC, a New Zealand serving with the Royal Air Force, their Lancaster III ED832 EM-X took off at 1954 and was lost without trace, one of twenty-four bombers lost that night raiding the 'Big City' 3rd-4th September 1943. Their details are recorded between pages 307 and 310 of my RAFBCL 1943. In the case of Group Captain McKenna's crew, all are commemorated on the Runnymede Memorial. Their deaths are mentioned on page 101 of John Hamlin's history of 207 Squadron.

29111 MARSACK Dudley Hardwicke G/Capt 08.02.45 Retirement

At his own request [LG 27 March 1945, supplement 37000, page 1645].

29112 MARTIN John William F/Lt 12.10.38 Relinquished

On appointment to a commission in the Royal Air Force Volunteer Reserve [LG 24 March 1939, issue 34610, page 2012]. Appointed to a permanent commission and attaining Wing Commander rank he retired on 1st December 1958. Then, within the Royal Air Force Reserve of Officers he was granted a commission, initially as a flight lieutenant and served until 1st December 1971 when he relinquished his commission as a squadron leader. His forty-one years of service rates amongst the longest for a Royal Air Force officer.

29113 MASON Francis Guy F/Lt 25.04.40 Resigned
[Lt 6th Battalion, Duke of Wellington's Regiment TA]
29114 MONCKTON Cecil Leslie F/Lt 10.02.54 Relinquished
29115 PAYN Murray Armstrong S/Ldr 28.04.54 Relinquisshed
[2nd Lt 1st Battalion, Essex Regiment SRO]
29116 RAMSBOTTOM- Henry Neville Gynes G/Capt + 24.04.50 RAF West Malling

ISHERWOOD As Wing Commander Henry Neville Gynes Ramsbottom-Isherwood AFC he is mentioned in paragraph 198 of the report 'Air Operations By Fighter Command from 25th November 1940 to 31st December 1941' as submitted to the Secretary of State for Air on 29th February 1948 by Marshal of the Royal Air Force Sir Sholto Douglas GCB MC DFC and published in *The London Gazette* Thursday 16th September 1948, supplement 38404, pages 5015 to 5036. Paragraph 198 which appears on page 5032 reads: *"From August to December two Hurricane Squadrons were detached for service on the North Russian Front in No. 151 Wing under the command of Wing Commander H N G Ramsbottom-Isherwood AFC."* On the day of his death Group Captain Ramsbottom-Isherwood took off in Meteor F.4 VT185 belonging to the Meteorological Section at West Malling. His flight commenced at Martlesham Heath and his intention was to return to West Malling but on arriving in the circuit, and now flying at 200 feet he encountered strong winds and a mid-spring snowstorm of such intensity that he was advised to divert to Manston. Moments later, at around 1045, the Meteor dived and smashed into a field at Moat Farm, Five Oak Green, 4 miles ESE of Tonbridge, Kent. He was buried with full military honours Felixstowe [St. Felix] Churchyard.

The Aviation Safety Network website, which the authors are delighted to acknowledge, notes he had accumulated a total of 3,339 flying hour of which thirteen were solo hours on Meteor types; in addition to his AFC he was one of only a handful of Royal Air Force officers to be conferred with the Order of Lenin. Interestingly, when his only daughter put up his medals for auction by Sotheby's in 2009, they were purchased by an anonymous Russian bidder for £46,000, much to the chagrin of the Group Captain's nephew who was living in New Zealand. Three years later a television documentary was aired in New Zealand titled *Operation Hurricane* which concentrated on his time in Russia.

Items from VT185 were recovered in 2003 and these are now held by the Lashenden Air Warfare Museum at Lashenden [Headcorn] Aerodrome.

29117 ROSS Ian Gibson F/O 01.05.43 Relinquished
29118 SMITH Charles Bernard P/O 22.10.30 Relinquished

On account of ill-health [LG 11 November 1930, issue 33660, page 7178]. Rejoining the service he rose to the rank of Leading Aircraftman before being commissioned as a pilot officer in the Balloon Branch on 11th June 1940 [LG 20 September 1940, issue 34949, page 5587] and with his service number amended to 84054. However, when promoted flying officer on 11th July 1941 his service number had reverted to 29118 [LG 25th July 1941, issue 35228, page 4284]. F/Lt 10.02.54 Relinquished

29119 SMITH-ROSS Edward Charles W/Cdr 16.09.53 Relinquished
29120 VILLIERS Charles Patrick W/Cdr 09.08.44 Resigned

LG 26 August 1930, issue 33638, page 5298 - Seniority 12th August 1930

29122 BATES Eric Cecil AV-M 27.01.59 Retirement
Australia Air Vice-Marshal Eric Cecil Bates CB CBE DFC mentioned in despatches, died on Sunday, 23rd March 1975.
COLEMAN George Simpson F/O 12.08.34 Relinquished
Australia On transfer to the Royal Australian Air Force Reserve [LG 14 August 1934, issue 34078, page 5195].
HARRISON Reginald William Holder F/O 23.09.33 Relinquished
On account of ill-health [LG 26 September 1933, issue 33981, page 6220].
SPENCER Cecil Eric F/O 28.12.32 Relinquished
Australia On account of ill health [LG 27 December 1932, issue 33896, page 8294]. Subsequently recovered his health sufficiently and joined the Royal Australian Air Force. Attaining the rank of flight lieutenant. On 12th June 1945 he was Conferred by the President of the United States of America with the Legion of Merit [Degree of Legionnaire] for his valuable services in connection with the war [LG 12 June 1945, supplement 37125, page 3084].

WOODHOUSE Hugh Oswald F/O 12.08.34 Relinquished
Australia On transfer to the Royal Australian Air Force Reserve [LG 14 August 1934, issue 34078, page 5195]. Subsequently granted a commission in Class A of the General Duties Branch of the Royal Air Force Reserve, Reserve of Air Force Officers in the rank of flying officer on 30th April 1935 [LG 14 May 1935, issue 34160, page 3144]. During the Second World War he joined British Overseas Airways Corporation and on 2nd June 1943 was commended [by the wishes of HM the King] for valuable services in the air [LG 4 June 1943, supplement 36025, page 2505].

LG 8 September 1930, issue 33642, page 5575

FLIGHT LIEUTENANT

29121 CUMING Alfred Charles S/Ldr 10.02.54 Relinquished

Formerly Captain and granted a short service commission on the Supplementary List as from 25th August 1930.

LG 30 September 1930, issue 33648, page 5954 - Seniority 12th September 1930 - Block 29128 to 29152

29128 AGAR John Reginald Shelton F/Lt 25.10.38 Relinquished
On appointment to a commission in the Royal New Zealand Air Force [LG 25th October 1938, issue 34564, page 6638].
29129 ANDREWS Herbert Langdale S/Ldr 01.05.45 Relinquished
On appointment to the RNZAF [LG 14 August 1945, supplement 37218, page 4114].
29130 BIGG Edward Denys Arthur F/O 20.09.33 Relinquished
Rhodesia On account of ill-health [LG 19 September 1933, issue 33979, page 6084]. With his health improved, Edward Denys Arthur Bigg was granted a commission in the Royal Air Force Volunteer Reserve, General Duties Branch, as a pilot officer [emergency] on 7th March 1940 and with his service number now being 80297 [LG 19 May 1942, issue 35566, page 2181]. F/Lt 12.10.45 Relinquished
On reversion to Southern Rhodesian Forces [LG 9 April 1946, supplement 37526, page 1796].
29131 BRICE Gordon Richard G/Capt 15.09.56 Retirement
29132 BURLEIGH Thomas Haydon F/Lt 23.04.56 Relinquished
No retention of rank [LG 3 July 1956, supplement 40820, page 3876].
29133 CRUMP Frank F/O 06.08.39 Relinquished
By which time he had changed his surname to 'Brent', the details of this being found by my co-author: *I FRANK BETT, of "Woodside", Calshot, 9 Fawley, in the county of Southampton, a British subject, heretofore called and known by the name of Frank Crump, hereby give public notice that on the 19th day of January, 1935, I formally and absolutely renounced, relinquished and abandoned the use and said surname of Crump and then assumed and adopted and determined thenceforth on all occasions whatsoever to use and subscribe the name of Brent instead of the said name of Crump; and I give further notice that by deed poll, dated the 19th day of January, 1935, duly executed and attested, and enrolled in the Central Office of the Supreme Court on the 19th day of February, 1935, I formally and absolutely renounced and abandoned the said name of Crump and declared that I had assumed and adopted and intended thenceforth upon all occasions whatsoever to use and subscribe the name of Brent instead of Crump, and so as to be at all times thereafter called, known and described by the name of Brent exclusively. - Dated the 19th day of February, 1935. [181] FRANK BRETT."*
29134 FOSS Peter Fidelis S/Ldr 24.04.55 Relinquished
29135 GARLAND Arthur Harold G/Capt 30.04.58 Retirement
29136 GIBBON Montgomery Vincent S/Ldr + 08.03.45 101 Squadron
Squadron Leader Montgomery Vincent Gibbon AFC was the captain of Lancaster I PD268 SR-O of 101 Squadron which was lost without trace from operations to Dessau on 7th-8th March 1945. All eight members of crew are commemorated on the Runnymede Memorial [see my RAFBCL 1945 page 117 for details].
29137 GLEAVE Thomas Percy G/Capt 14.11.53 Retirement
Squadron Leader Thomas Percy Gleave was commanding 253 Squadron [Hurricane] and was shot down in the *Battle of Britain* on 31st August 1940 [see Norman R Franks, Royal Air Force Fighter Command losses, page 69]. Very seriously injured with severe burns when he baled out of his burning Hurricane I P3115 he was one of the first patients to be treated by the legendary surgeon Sir Archibald McIndoe at the Queen Victoria Hospital at East Grinstead where he earned the unique distinction of being the first and only 'Chief Guinea Pig'. Although his operational flying days were over, he remained in the Royal Air Force and at the time of the 'Channel Dash' was Station Commander at RAF Manston - see my notes for Eugene Esmonde in the list of short service commissioned officers for 1st January 1929. His retirement from the service was on account of medical unfitness for further service [LG 17 November 1953, supplement 40017, page 6159]. Group Captain Thomas Percy Gleave CBE died in June 1993 at the age of 84.
29138 GLOVER Henry Lawrence Matthews F/Lt 10.02.54 Relinquished
29139 HAWKINS Percy John Walter P/O + 09.09.32 3 Squadron
29140 HEYGATE Peter Heylin F/Lt + 07.09.36 3 FTS Grantham
Flying Officer Peter Heylin Heygate took off from Grantham in Hawker Audax I K5222 to conduct a weather test during which he crashed into the sea off the Norfolk coast. No trace of the aircraft, or its pilot was ever found. According to Air-Britain's *K File* K5222 had accumulated 121.10 flying hours since its arrival at Grantham on 27th February 1936.
29141 JOHNSON Peter Warren G/Capt 10.02.54 Relinquished
Commanding 49 Squadron [Lancaster, Wing Commander Peter Warren Johnson was *Gazetted* with the DFC, less citation, on 10th September 1941, supplement 36165, page 4012. Promoted to group captain [acting] he was *Gazetted* with the DSO, again less citation, for his services with 97 Squadron on 26th October 1945, supplement 37324, page 5234. Postwar he turned to writing and was preparing his fourth book, a novel, when he died on Friday, 12th February 1999. His *Wikipedia* entry suggests that as a commander he led more bombing raids than any other similarly ranked commander, a statement that I would seriously question, but his subsequent views that the 'Bombing Campaign' against German cities was *"immoral, illegal and ineffective"* found little, if any, support with his contemporaries and certainly not by the hierarchy at the Ministry of Defence.
29142 KING Ronald Oswald Forsyth P/O 23.12.30 Terminated
29143 McAULEY James Noel F/Lt 10.02.54 Relinquished
29144 McDONALD Ronald Archibald P/O 20.05.32 Resigned
29145 NIXON George Edward Bullen F/O + 18.03.35 2 FTS Digby
Flying Officer George Edward Bullen Nixon and Acting Pilot Officer Colin Kirkley, the latter receiving instruction, died when their Avro 621 Tutor K3318 crashed during aerobatics on Martin Moor Fen, Scopwick and in the near vicinity of the airfield. A report on the tragedy was published in Australia on Thursday, 21st March 1935, by *The Sydney Morning Herald*: *"London, March 19th. At the Inquiry today into the death of Flying-Officer George Edward Bullen Nixon and Acting-Pilot Officer Colin Kirkley of New Zealand, Flight-Lieutenant John Robert gave evidence thus: "the automatic slot in the wing came off and was found half a mile distant." He had not previously heard of a slot coming off in this manner. Experts gave evidence the the plane was perfectly serviceable and had been used in the morning without mishap. The Coroner said that he hoped that the Air Ministry would inquire into the accident.*

"The airmen were killed when they crashed while looping the loop. Their plane was flying at 3,000 feet in an inverted position. Then, according to an eye-witness, a portion broke off. The plane plunged to earth disintegrating as it fell."

Air-Britain's *K File* shows K3318 as being delivered to RAF Kenley on 18th November 1933; then, on 23rd July 1934 it was reported at a Packing Depot where it seems to have been held until delivered to Digby and No. 2 Flying Training School on 3rd October 1934. It had flown for a total of 188.15 hours.

29146 POLGLASE Patrick Julyan W/Cdr + 04.04.41 106 Squadron

[2nd Lieutenant in the Royal Artillery, TA] From Perranarworthal in Cornwall, Wing Commander Patrick Julyan Polglase mid died with his crew while raiding Brest in Hampden I AD738 ZN- on 4th-5th April 1941. All rest in St-Renan Churchyard. See page 37 of my RAFBCL 1941 for their names and details of the loss.

29147 SKELTON George Felix Allin A/Cmdr 27.05.59 Retirement

Air Commodore George Felix Allin Skelton OBE, died on Friday, 18th October 1985.

29148 SKINNER Clifford George W/Cdr + 23.02.43 159 Squadron

Wing Commander Clifford George Skinner is commemorated on column 423 at the Singapore Memorial. At the time of his death 159 Squadron, a bomber squadron equipped with Liberator II, was based at Salabani in India.

29149 SLOWEY Henry Edward P/O + 23.08.32 RAF Northolt

New Zealand A mere thirteen days after the announcement of his engagement to Miss Anna Thorne of Oxford, Pilot Officer Henry Edward Slowey was critically injured when the car in which he was a passenger collided with a telegraph pole in Swakeleys Road, Ickenham, Middlesex. Taken to Hillingdon County Hospital he died within hours of being admitted. The driver, a fellow officer named as Flight Lieutenant Peter Johnson was seriously injured, but survived. Although my co-author cannot be certain, it is thought this was a mis-report for Pilot Officer Peter Warren Johnson who had been accepted for a short service commission in the same intake as Henry Slowey, and if this is correct, then his rank would have been 'Pilot Officer'

29150 TAYLOR Ambrose P/O 23.09.32 Resigned

29151 TESTER John Andrews A/Cmdr 24.04.58 Retirement

Air Commodore John Andrews Tester CB CBE twice mentioned in despatches, died on Thursday, 6th July 1972. A signals specialist, much of his service as a senior officer was spent on staff duties connected with communications.

29152 WILLIAMS Roger P/O + 26.10.31 13 Squadron

HILCHIE Wilfred Farnsworth F/O 11.04.38 Relinquished

His appointment was valid from 22nd September 1930 with seniority from 12th September 1930.

LG 23 September 1930, issue 33646, page 5814 - Seniority 31st October 1926

29154 JAQUES John Nicolson G/Capt 10.02.54 Relinquished

[Regular Army Reserve of Officers]

LG 24 October 1930, issue 33655, page 6479 - Seniority 10th October 1930 - Block 29156 to 29182

29156 ADAMS Alexander Annan AV-M 10.01.60 Retirement

Air Vice-Marshal Alexander Annan Adams CB DFC, died on Thursday, 1st March 1990. His DFC was in recognition of his service as Commanding Officer of 49 Squadron [Lancaster] and was *Gazetted* without an attached citation on 27th June 1944, supplement 36584, page 3042.

29157 BATEMAN Douglas John P/O 04.02.31 Terminated

29158 BEGG James Aldo Bartlett S/Ldr + 11.11.39 77 Squadron

Squadron Leader James Aldo Bartlett was one of Bomber Command's earliest fatalities. Operating from Villeneuve-les-Vertus forward base, he was captain of Whitley V N1364 KN- tasked for a 'Bickel' operation to Frankfurt. On return, and while trying to locate the airfield, he crashed Boux-urulles [Voges] some 6km to the SW of Charmes where the five crew are buried. For their names, pleasse consult page 88 of my revised RAFBCL 1939-1940. Squadron Leader Begg's headstone carries the inscription *"Quietly He Rests His Knightly Duties Done."*

It was his second operational sortie of the war, his first being a *Nickel* operation to the Ruhr on 5th-6th September 1939, in Whitley III K8959. His crew on that occasion comprised of Sergeants Walksh and Thomas and Aircraftman Taylor and Laybourne. Taking off from Driffield at 0055 and at 0730, in poor weather conditions and now short of fuel, he made a successful forced-landing in a field at La Motte in France where he picked up 400 litres of fuel. Taking off at around 1100, he flew on to Nevers Airfield where he refuelled, taking off for Driffield at 1500 and landing at 1840. Along with Squadron Leader Heather [K8993] and Flying Officer Boardman [K8991], 77 Squadron had accomplished the squadron's first operation of the Second World War.

29159 CANAVAN Graham Routh F/Lt 30.07.39 Relinquished

On account of ill-health [LG 4 July 1939, issue 34642, page 4581].

29160 CHRISTIAN Arnold Louis W/Cdr + 08.05.41 105 Squadron

Commanding 105 Squadron, Wing Commander Arnold Louis Christian twice mentioned in despatches, died while leading his squadron on an anti-shipping strike in the direction of Norway from their advanced base at Lossiemouth. His Blenheim IV V5828 GB-R was last sighted at the entrance to Havs Fjord with flames streaming away from its port engine. Wing Commander Christian and his crew [see page 52 of my RAFBCL 1941] are commemorated on the Runnymede Memorial.

29161 CLARKE William Ivan F/O + 17.05.33 3 Squadron

29162 CLOUSTON Arthur Edmond A/Cmdr 07.04.60 Retirement

New Zealand Air Commodore Arthur Edmond Clouston CB DSO DFC AFC*, died on New Year's Day 1984. Prior to his short service commission Arthur Edmond Clouston completed his pilot training in New Zealand; consequently, his service training on arrival in the UK was a mere couple of hours at 3 FTS Gtsntham, after which he flew Hawker Fury Is with 25 Squadron at Hawkinge before being attached to 24 Squadron at Kenley where he flew various types in carrying out the squadron's remit of communications, refresher flying and VIP transportation. On completion of his commission in 1935 he had in mind to return to New Zealand and take up a career in civil aviation [he had already declined the offer of a permanent commission] but when offered one of two newly created posts of civilian test pilot at RAE Farnborough he immediately accepted the offer, culminating in the last few months of peace by an assignment to test Westland's promising twin-engined fighter-bomber, the Whirlwind [subsequently equipping two fighter squadrons, namely 137 and 263].

Returning to Royal Air Force duties he continued with test flying, part of which was concerned with the development of the Turbonlite Boston as an aid for night fighter work. He was also involved with Leigh Light testing and to his delight was given command of 224 Squadron [Liberator V] for long-ranger anti-submarine patrols over the Atlantic. Following eleven months of operational flying he was promoted group captain and in February 1944 assumed command of RAF Langham in Norfolk.

Postwar, he accepted a permanent commission during which he returned to his native New Zealand and commanded RNZAF Ohakea for two years before returning to his 'second home' and command of RAF Leeming. His final three years of service was spent as Commandant at A&AEE Boscombe Down.

29163 DOBSON John Arnold S/Ldr 23.05.58 Relinquished

29164 DUFORT John Nesbitt

Squadron Leader John Nesbitt Dufort was *Gazetted* with the DSO for his service with 138 Squadron, a Special Duties squadron coming under the aegis of Bomber Command, on 25th November 1941, supplement 35356, page 6769: *"This officer has carried out 16 operational sorties over enemy territory, involving attacks on enemy aerodromes as well as other flights of extreme importance. His skill, determination and courage have been of the highest order."* At the time of this honour, 138 Squadron was equipped with Whitley V, Lysander IIIA [used to convey agents to and from the Occupied Countries] and from October 1941 Halifax I bombers, useful for parachuting agents and supplies. There losses are detailed in my RAFBCL series and in books by various authors, notably by Group Captain Hugh Verity DSO* DFC [principally with 138 Squadron's 'sister' squadron 161

Squadron] *We Landed By Moonlight - Secret RAF landings in France 1940-1944* [Air Data Publications, 1995], while another excellent account of the work done by '138' is Freddie Clark's *Agents by Moonlight - The Secret History of RAF Tempsford During World War II* [Tempus, 1999].

29165 FORBES John Alexander Charles F/O + 15.02.35 210 Squadron

29166 FOSTER Elliot F/Lt 12.03.38 Resigned

29167 HARGREAVES William Marshall W/Cdr 10.02.54 Relinquished

29168 HARRIS Ronald Henry G/Capt 08.05.55 Relinquished

29169 HUSBANDS William Herbert G/Capt 01.00.57 Retirement

On account of medical unfitness for Air Force service [LG 1 January 1957, supplement 40964, page 71].

29170 IRELAND Noel Arthur P/O + 30.09.31 23 Squadron

29171 LAMB Lennox Stanley S/Ldr + 30.10.39 9 Squadron

New Zealand Squadron Leader Lennox Stanley Lamb had the distinction of leading Section 1 of 9 Squadron's first operational sortie of the Second World War when six of their Wellingtons made a daylight foray to attach shipping reported in Brunsbüttel harbour on Monday, 4th September 1939. From Squadron Leader Lamb's section two bombers were shot down with total loss of life [see my RAFBCL 1939-1940 revised edition, pages 75 and 76]. The second Section of three, headed by Flight Lieutenant Peter Grant came through the *Flak* unscathed.

On Monday, 30th October 1939, Squadron Leader Lamb authorised three crews, including his own [Wellington I L4288 WS-A], to practice formation changes and it was during one such change, in site of the squadron's base at Honington in Suffolk, that a collision occurred with Squadron Leader Lamb and Flying Officer John Frank Chandler's machine [L4363 WS-] plunging into marshy ground near Sapiston Rectory. The names of both crews - there were no survivors - and their burial details are recorded on page 86 of the above mentioned publication.

29172 McGINN Lawrence Thaddeus P/O 08.07.31 Terminated

29173 MURPHY John Joseph A/Cmdr 21.08.61 Retirement

Air Commodore John Joseph Murphy OBE, died on Thursday, 10th October 2002. His OBE, *Gazetted* on 9th June 1949, supplement 38628, page 2801 for his service during the Berlin Airlift.

29174 NEALE Leonard James W/Cdr + 13.12.41 453 Squadron RAAF

Wing Commander Leonard James Neale died when his Brewster Buuffalo W8176 crashed in Sumatra; his grave is now in Jakarta War Cemetery, Indonesia, where his headstone is inscribed *"Greater Love Hath No Man Then This, That A Man Lay Down His Life For His Friends."* He is mentioned four times in *Buffaloes over Singapore*, the first occasion being on page 24 where it was recorded that he "... *was on his way from the UK to take command of the airfield at Ipoh..."* Claims against his estate were advertised by his solicitors, Fladgate and Co. of 70 Pall Mall, London, SW.1 in *The London Gazette* issue 35435, page 477 on 27th January 1942.

29175 NEWELL Frederic Rusden F/O 01.06.36 Relinquished

On appointment to a commission in the Royal New Zealand Air Force.

29176 PENDAL Herford Linton P/O 02.09.31 Terminated

29177 PHILLIPS Rodney Arnold W/Cdr 10.02.54 Relinquished

29178 PILLING Herbert S/Ldr + 30.06.40 107 Squadron

Squadron Leader Herbert Pilling of 'Mellow Thatch', Rockbourne some 4 miles NNW from Fordingbridge, was the captain of Blenheim IV 3870 one of a dozen tasked to attack Merville airfield. Hit by *Flak* he was brought down in the Pas-de-Calais close to where he is buried in Ecques Churchyard; the inscription on his headstone matches that for Wing Commander Neale [see above], and who probably trained with at 3 FTS Grantham. For further information please see page 160 of my RAFBCL 1939-1940 revised edition. Persons having a claim against his estate were advised to contact H G Beach, Solicitor, of Fordingbridge, Hampshire [LG 25 February 1941, issue 35087, page 1171].

Through the exceptional kindness of Lieutenant-Colonel Mike Richardson and Patrick Thompson, Church Warden at St. Andrew's Church at Rockbourne, an excellent biography complied by Mike Richardson enables me to present a detailed account of Squadron Leader Pilling's life.

"Herbert Pilling was born on 8 December 1907, the son of George Herbert Pilling, secretary to a salesman of a cotton spinning company, and his wife Alice. The family lived in King Street and then Drake Street in Rochdale, Lancashire. Herbert attended King William's College on the Isle of Man, leaving in 1923. It seems that he initially followed his father into the business as a raw cotton salesman, living at Stone Lea, Manchester Road in Rochdale, but a few years later he joined the Royal Air Force, being commissioned therein in 1930.

"He served in No. 1 [Fighter] Squadron flying Hawker Furies, and in September 1938, after further flying training and promotion, he was posted to 24 Squadron RAF, a 'communications' squadron based at RAF Hendon.

"At hendon, he was put in charge of 'A' Flight and flew a variety of aircraft, particularly on VIP duty. It is suggested that he carried Neville Chamberlain, Winston Churchill, Paul Reynaud and Édouard Daladier to and from London and Paris for meetings of the Supreme Allied War Council, whose purpose it was to agree on the co-ordination of British and French war production in the early months of the Second World War.

"In late 1935, Herbert married Vera, but her lineage has not been absolutely identified. Neither has the reason why the couple moved to West Hampshire. Nevertheless, they were living at Trentham Cottage, Rockbourne in 1940. Sqn Ldr Pilling was posted to the RAF Staff College at Andover in May 1940, which may explain the move. But that course ended abruptly as soon as it assembled, due to the German Blitzkrieg offensive.

"Instead, by now a squadron leader, he was sent to No. 17 Operational Training Unit at RAF Upwood in Cambridgeshire to convert to Blenheim bombers, and thereafter was posted to 107 Squadron, based at RAF Wattisham, near Ipswich, which was equipped with the Blenheim Mk.IV; a three-seat, twin-engine, light bomber."

The final two paragraphs of the biography mirrors that of my RAFBCL summary and above notes.

29179 RICE Richard Clement Joseph P/O 15.09.31 Terminated

29180 SINGLETON Denis Gordon F/O 14.12.32 Relinquished

On account of ill-health [LG 13 December 1932, issue 33891, page 7932]. In time his health recovered and by 1st September 1939 he was granted a commission in the Royal Air Force Volunteer Reserve [LG 20 October 1939, issue 34713, page 7041] and issued with a new service number 74860. However, by late 1942 he had reverted to his original identity 29180 W/Cdr 14.01.56 Relinquished

29181 SMITH Frank George Laughton W/Cdr 03.08.56 Relinquished

[2nd Lieutenant 5th Battalion, Lincolnshire Regiment, TA]

29182 YOUNGHUSAND John Geoffrey F/Lt 04.06.63 Relinquished

FAGAN Henry Patrick Feltrim F/Lt + 30.12.35 216 Squadron

[Lieutenant Somerset Light Infantry] - With effect 27th September 1930 - Seniority 15th July 1927. Sadly, possibly while in Kenya, Flight Lieutenant Henry Patrick Feltrim Fagan died by his own hand.

LG 11 November 1930, issue 33660, page 7178 - Seniority 28th October 1930

29183 WARTON Kenneth Reid W/Cdr + 14.07.48 RAF Luqa

Wing Commander Kenneth Reid Warton was a passenger in a Douglas C-47B 10-DK Dakota IV registered to BOAC which had taken off from Luqa and was due to land at Toulon-Hyères Airport in France. Approaching its destination and letting down through cloud the Dakota flew into the side of a cliff killing the crew of four and its two passengers.

Formerly held a commission in the Reserve of Air Force Officers. See Appendix G 1929.

LG 2 December 1930, issue 33666, page 7692 - Seniority 17th November 1930

FLYING OFFICER

29197 LARKING Jack Cuthbert G/Capt 17.11.55 Retirement
Formerly of the Auxiliary Air Force. As Squadron Leader Jack Cuthbert Larking he was *Gazetted* with the DFC, less citation, on 16th August 1940, issue 34923, page 5015.

LG 19 December 1930, issue 33671, page 8158 - Seniority 5th December 1930 - Block 29185 to 29196

29185 CASEY Bernard Adolf A/Cmdr 31.12.56 Retirement
Air Commodore Bernard Adolf Casey OBE twice mentioned in despatches, died on Saturday, 13th October 1979.
29186 DUNNE William P/O 24.12.31 Terminated
29187 JOHNSTON Edward Ridley Short W/Cdr 10.02.54 Relinquished
29188 LEA-COX Kenneth G/Capt 14.01.54 Relinquished
29189 MARLOW Hugh Whittall G/Capt 01.07.47
29190 MARSACK Alfred Hardwicke S/Ldr 11.11.44 Retired list
29191 PICKERSGILL William S/Ldr 21.12.44 Relinquished
[Sub-Lieutenant RNR] On account of ill-health [LG 16 January 1945, supplement 36893, page 401].
29192 SORSBIE Malin F/O 05.12.35 Class A
Subsequently Sir Malin Sorsbie Kt OBE CBE born 6th May 1906 joined Imperial Airways whilst on the Reserve. During the Second World War he opened up many new long-distance routes including the Atlantic, the Middle East and Africa. With BOAC he was appointed Overseas Operations Director while postwar he established Northolt as a base for British European Airways pending the completion of Heathrow. With his interest in Africa and helped to build up East African Airways and, in time, became Chief Game Warden in Kenya. He wrote to novels, *Dragonfly* [Hamish Hamilton Ltd, 1971] and in the year of his death on 28th October 1988, *The Pasha* [Book Guild Publishing Ltd, 1988]. In reporting this detail the authorsI acknowledge the website Aviation Brussels.
29193 TANCRED Harry Lumsden F/O 09.03.36 Relinquished
On appointment to a commission in the Royal New Zealand Air Force [LG 23 June 1936, issue 34297, page 4020].
29194 WEMYSS James Rawlinson F/O 05.12.35 Class C
Commissioned to the Unattached List of the Indian Army in the rank of Lieutenant [LG 17 March 1936, issue 34265, page 1741].
29195 WHITLEY Eric William G/Capt 09.09.52 Retirement
Squadron Leader Eric William Whitley was *Gazetted* withe DFC, less citation, on 30th July 1940, issue 34910, page 4675 followed by the DSO, less citation, *Gazetted* 18th September 1942, supplement 35709, page 4060 at which time he was an Acting Group Captain. His death was announced from New Zealand on Thursday, 25th October 1973.
29196 YATES Frederick William F/Lt 28.04.58 Relinquished
[2nd Lieutenant The Duke of Wellington's Regiment, TA]

Admittedly, a small entry of just twelve officers it is noteworthy in that none were killed in air accidents, either during training or in squadron service.

29197 LARKING Jack Cuthbert G/Capt 17.11.55 Retirement
Formerly held a commission in the Auxiliary Air Force; seniority 17th November 1930

ROLL OF HONOUR
FOR
1930 SHORT SERVICE COMMISSION
OFFICERS

W/Cdr	BAIN	Francis George Levett	8 December 1942	207 Squadron
P/O	BALL	Peter Strickland	9 September 1930	2 FTS Digby
S/Ldr	BARRETT	Gerald Spencer	30 November 1942	10 Squadron
S/Ldr	BEGG	James Aldo Bartlett	11 November 1939	77 Squadron
F/O	BRAMLEY	Eric Victor Newcomen	23 May 1932	14 Squadron
P/O	CHAPMAN	John Edward Furlong	12 January 1931	2 FTS Digby
S/Ldr	CHESTER	Hurll Fontayne	2 July 1940	82 Squadron
W/Cdr	CHRISTIAN Twice mid	Arnold Louis	8 May 1941	105 Squadron
F/O	CLARK	Henry Thomas	21 April 1932	208 Squadron
W/Cdr	CLARKE	Ronald Neville	4 March 1941	224 Squadron
F/O	CLARKE	William Ivan	17 May 1933	3 Squadron
G/Capt	CROSBIE	Leonard John	22 June 1946	353 Squadron
F/Lt	DAWSON	Ernest	16 April 1936	7 FTS Peterborough
F/Lt	FAGAN	Henry Patrick Feltrim	30 December 1935	216 Squadron
F/O	FORBES	John Alexander Charles	15 February 1935	210 Squadron
S/Ldr	GIBBON AFC	Montgomery Vincent	8 March 1945	101 Squadron
W/Cdr	GRACIE DFC	Edward John	15 February 1944	169 Squadron
F/O	HALMSHAW	William	31 July 1936	Class A
P/O	HAWKINS	Percy John Walter	9 September 1932	3 Squadron
F/Lt	HEYGATE	Peter Heylin	7 September 1936	3 FTS Grantham
S/Ldr	HOOPER Neww Zealand	William Ernest	3 October 1950	
P/O	IRELAND	Noel Arthur	30 September 1931	23 Squadron
S/Ldr	LAMB New Zealand	Lennox Stanley	30 October 1939	9 Squadron
F/O	LEBORGNE	Robert Paul Joseph	23 November 1938	Class A
S/Ldr	LEWIS	William Edward Lawley	4 February 1943	236 Squadron
G/Capt	LOWE	Brian Everard	18 July 1943	
F/O	MANSFIELD	John Grazebrook	22 August 1935	Class A
G/Capt	McKENNA	Austin Flower	3 September 1943	Station Commander Langer
S/Ldr	MONYPENNY	John Blackwell Sinclair	20 July 1940	9 Squadron
F/O	MORRIS	Richard Thomas Showler	5 January 1940	

W/Cdr	NEALE	Leonard James	13 December 1941	453 Squadron RAAF
F/O	NIXON	George Edward Bullen	18 March 1935	2 FTS Digby
S/Ldr	PILLING	Herbert	30 June 1940	107 Squadron
F/O	PEACOCK	John Charles Francis	18 October 1943	Communications Flight Calshot
W/Cdr	POLGLASE mid	Patrick Julyan	4 April 1941	106 Squadron
G/Capt	RAMSBOTTOM-ISHERWOOD AFC *Order of Lenin*	Henry Neville Gynes	24 April 1940	Station Commander West Malling
P/O	SANT	Alfred Cecil	25 September 1930	2 FTS Disgby
W/Cdr	SIMMONS	Henry Augustus	23 March 1944	26 OTU
W/Cdr	SKINNER	Clifford George	23 February 1943	159 Squadron
P/O	SLOWEY New Zealand	Henry Edward	23 August 1932	RAF Northolt
F/O	SMITH	Ronald Maxwell	29 September 1934	Class A
F/O	STYCHE	Norman Charles Meyrick	26 September 1933	40 Squadron
F/O	SUPPLE	Jeffrey Hale	28 May 1934	84 Squadron
P/O	THOMPSON	Malcolm Stewart	20 September 1930	3 FTS Grantham
W/Cdr	WARTON	Kenneth Reid	14 July 1948	RAF Luqa
S/Ldr	WATSON	John Russell	16 August 1943	115 Squadron
P/O	WILLIAMS	Roger	26 October 1931	13 Squadron
F/O	WILSON	Allen Roy	21 October 1938	
P/O	WOODLAND	John Douglas	18 August 1930	5 FTS Sealand

From the forty-nine officers who received a short service commission in 1930, twenty lost their lives during the Second World War, and four in the postwar period. Four others were killed whilst in class A of the reserve, details of their demise being reported within the appendix.

Appendix D - RAFC Cranwell

COMMANDANT
Air Commodore Arthur Murray Longmore CB DSO mentioned in despatches

January 1930 entry : 32

26222 BARNETT* Richard Edgar S/Ldr 11.08.41 Resigned
Squadron Leader Richard Edgar Barnett MBE, died on Sunday, 25th July 1971.
26253 BERESFORD-PEIRSE Francis Campbell de la Poer G/Capt 23.07.52 Retirement
On Friday 6th June 1930, Flight Cadet Francis Campbell de la Poer Beresford Peirse was undergoing instruction in Avro 504N J8709 overseen by Flight Lieutenant Henry Leonard Drake and while approaching the airfield to land their Avro came into collision with the Avro summarised below the entry for Flight Cadet George Wroughton Montagu. Flight Cadet Beresford-Peirse was injured but, sadly, his instructor was killed. The accident was reported in the aviation magazine *Aeroplane* in its issue of 11th June 1930, and is repeated on the Aviation Safety Network website, which the authors acknowledge: *"An inquest was held at Cranwell on June 7th on the body of Flight Lieutenant Drake. Flight Lieutenant D A Boyle stated that at the time of the accident Flight Lieutenant Drake was instructing Flight Cadet F P Beresford Peirse in a dual control machine. When landing, the machine crashed into another machine piloted by Flight Cadet Montagu. Flight Cadet G R Montagu said that he was flying solo in an Avro machine and as he was about to land he noticed another machine taking off on the ground where he wanted to descend. He turned on his engine and rose again and as he did so another machine seemed to come from above him. It struck his left wing putting his ailerons out of order, and then fell out of control."* Flight Cadet Beresford-Peirse's injuries were sufficiently serious for him to be back-classed and he eventually graduated with Flight Cadets from the September 1930 entry. Group Captain Francis Campbell de la Poer Beresford-Peirse died on Saturday, 11th January 1986.
BRADLEY Jack P/O + 12.06.33 14 Squadron
COLLYNS* New Zealand Eric Arthur F/O + 27.07.33 8 Squadron
DORAN* Archibald Mauritz F/O + 21.03.35
ELSNER* Leonard Nicholas F/O + 05.10.34 810 Squadron FAA
26226 EMSON* Reginald Herbert Embleton AM 01.03.69 Retirement
Air Marshal Sir Richard Emson KBE CB AFC mentioned in despatches, died on Monday, 27th March 1995. As a Flight Cadet he won the Sword of Honour and represented the College at rugby and cricket. His final service appointment was Inspector General of the Royal Air Force.
FENTON* Donald McDonald F/Lt + 15.04.37 Iraq Command
My co-author reports that Flight Lieutenant Donald McDonald Fenton is buried in Ma'asker Al Rasschid RAF Cemetery.
Flight Lieutenant Donald McDonald Fenton
FORMAN* Donald Edward P/O + 02.12.32
26229 GEOGHEGAN* Albert Woodburne G/Capt 30.06.46 Dismissed
Group Captain Albert Woodburne Geoghegan was dismissed the service by sentence of General Court Martial. ASS my co-author reports, he subsequently emigrated to Kenya where he died in Nairobi on Wednesday, 14th July 1971.
26230 GLENCROSS* Arthur Roger S/Ldr + 28.05.40 37 Squadron
Squadron Leader Arthur Roger Glencross and his crew took off from Feltwell on Saturday 25th May 1940, in Wellington IC L7793 tasked for an attack on enemy communications between Courtrai and Brussels. In the target area the crew ran into fierce ground-fire and forced-landed at Steene near Ostend from where they made their way to the evacuation beaches. All were taken aboard the SS *Aboukir* which was torpedoed and sunk off Dunkirk. For details of the crew, please refer to page 138 of my revised version of BCL1939-1940. Squadron Leader Glencross, who had been mentioned in despatches, is commemorated on panel 4 at the Runnymede Memorial.
26231 GOMEZ* Paul Slocome G/Capt 29.10.57 Retirement
Group Captain Paul Slocome Gomez CBE mentioned in despatches died during the year 1972.
26232 GOODMAN* Norman George G/Capt 02.05.59 Retirement
Group Captain Norman George Goodman CBE mentioned in despatches subsequently became a Deputy Lieutenant in the County of Middlesex. His death was announced on Sunday, 9th October 1988.
26233 HAMILTON* Matthew Barr G/Capt 02.06.48 Retirement
Group Captain Mathew Barr subsequently joined the Royal Australian Air Force, retaining his rank, and with the Service No. 297516. Paul McMillan reports that he died suddenly on Wednesday, 21st January 1981, at Karrinyup, Western Australia.
33003 HUMPHREYS Herbert York G/Capt 02.02.58 Retirement
Group Captain Herbert York DFC received his award *Gazetted* 3rd October 1944, supplement 36728, page 4536 during his tenure as Commanding Officer 57 Squadron: *"In August 1944, this officer piloted one of a formation of bombers detailed to attack a flying bomb site in Northern France. Before reaching the target heavy cloud was encountered. On flying clear, Wing Commander Humphreys had become separated from the formation but he went on to the target and executed his attack. Soon afterwards the bomber was attacked by an enemy fighter. For 45 minutes a running fight ensued. Although his aircraft was hit many times and sustained much damage, Wing Commander Humphreys manoeuvred with skill, whilst his gunners prevented the attacker from closing in.The enemy aircraft was finally driven off and Wing Commander Humphreys afterwards flew his damaged aircraft to base. This officer has completed very many sorties and invariably displayed a high degree of courage and resolution."* Group Captain Herbert York Humphreys DFC died on Saturday, 19th January 1963.
26234 JENKINS* Humphrey Petre W/Cdr 05.05.55 Retirement
Wing Commander Humphrey Petre Jenkins DFC gained his award whilst in command of 31 Squadron: *"During the operations in Burma and the Far East, this officer displayed inspiring leadership especially during the evacuation and when dropping supplies. His devotion to duty has been outstanding."* [LG 22 September 1942, issue 35712, page 4111].
26235 JOHNSON* David Victor W/Cdr + 28.04.41 45 Squadron
Wing Commander David Victor Johnson was aboard Blenheim IV Z5898 which took off from Tobruk to transport five passengers, including Wing Commander Johnson, back to Egypt. However, within seconds of becoming airborne the Blenheim [a Mk.IV Z5898] was spotted by roving ME109s and chased out to sea was attacked and shot down. The names of the seven airmen who perished [all commemorated on the Alamein Memorial] are published on pages 56 and 57 of David Gunby and Pelham Temple's first volume of Bomber Losses in the Middle East and Mediterranean theatres. The loss is also reported on page 155 continued on page 157 of *The Flying Camels* where the author hints that the victorious *Luftwaffe* pilot was Hans Joachim 'Jochen' Marseille
26236 LANGSTON* Stephen Patrick S/Ldr 05.01.41 Resigned
Squadron Leader Stephen Patrick Langston was, as reported by Paul McMillan, living in Zimbabwe in 1966.
26237 LEIGH* Rupert Henry Archibald A/Cmdr 07.12.54 Retirement

Air Commodore Rupert Henry Archibald Leigh four times mentioned in despatches, died on Friday, 1st February 1991. A Qualified Flying Instructor, he was serving at CFS Upavon at the time of Douglas Bader's request to return to the service and attachment to CFS for flying assessment. On pages 149 and 150 of *Reach For The Sky* Paul Brickhill writes of Bader's concern on clambering into a Harvard tandem-seat trainer to find it was equipped with foot-brakes which he would find it difficult, if not impossible, for him to manipulate with his artificial legs. At once Squadron Leader Leigh calmed Bader's fears: *"Forget about the brakes. I'll work them. You won't have to worry about them after today because the Harvard's the only aircraft in the Service that hasn't got a hand-brake on the stick."* At the conclusion of the test flight during which Douglas Bader performed an aerobatic loop before landing, Rupert Leigh intoned: *"Well, it's damn silly asking me if you can fly. However, I'll humour them* [the Central Medical Establishment] *and write recommending that you be re-admitted to the fold and posted here for a full refresher course."*

LONGMAN* John Tosswill P/O + 15.05.33 811 Squadron FAA

MILLS* Geoffrey Henry Owen S/Ldr + 03.02.39 Ramleh Station Flight

Squadron Leader Geoffrey Henry Owen Mills accompanied by two civilians from the Air Ministry Works Directorate, Messrs Harold Francis Charrington and Bernard Matthews Timbers, was flying in a Fairey Gordon I K2607 which went out of control after flying into cloud. Both civilians took to their parachutes and landed safely, Bernard Timbers being slightly injured. Unfortunately, Squadron Leader Mills failed to leave the Gordon which came down at Solomon's Pool near Jerusalem. The three pools are located on the south-central West Bank of the city and an explanation as to their heritage can be read on *Wikipedia.*

MONKS* Reginald F/Lt + 12.09.38 RAE Farnborough

Flight Lieutenant Reginald Monks took off from Farnborough for a test flight in Whitley I K7207 but lost height and crashed. On impact the bomber burst into flames killing Flight Lieutenant Monks and his crew of two, Squadron Leader Maurice James Adam AFC and a civilian flight test observer, 36 year old Mr. Benjamin Thomas Edwin Bond. Air-Britain's *K File* records the history of K7207 as delivered ex-works to 78 Squadron [Dishforth] on 17th October 1937 and transferred to RAE Farnborough on 2nd September 1938 for radio trials. The cause of the crash was traced to the Whitley taking off with the locks still in place on the aileron controls. K7207 flew for a total of 162 hours.

A detailed report of the accident has been appended in Appendix D against the entry for Squadron Leader Maurice James Adam who was short service commissioned on 27th August 1929.

26241 MONTAGU* George Wroughton S/Ldr + 21.12.40 236 Squadron

Flight Cadet George Wroughton Montague was slightly injured in the crash reported above under Flight Cadet Beresford-Peirse. Flight Cadet Montagu's Avro 504N J9693 although badly damaged was repaired and returned to service with the college before being given up circa March 1933 to the Central Flying School at Wittering. Upon graduating with a permanent commission, Pilot Officer Montagu was posted to 40 Squadron at Upper Heyford but by the winter of 1940, he was attached to 236 Squadron at St. Eval in Cornwall flying Blenheim IV and it was on Saturday 21st December 1940, that he took off from St. Eval at 1455 for a fighter patrol off Brest from which he failed to return. His loss in Blenheim IV R3878 FA-Z is recorded in Ross McNeill's Coastal Command losses, page 86, where the author suggests Squadron Leader George Wroughton Montagu and his crew may have been shot down by *Uffz* Schmidt of 5./JG27 at 1704 hours off Breat. The entire crew are buried in Bayeux War Cemetery.

26242 PARSELLE* Thomas Alfred Boyd AV-M 06.06.64 Retirement

Air Vice-Marshal Thomas Alfred Boyd Parselle CB CBE, died on Tuesday, 28th August 1979. On 10th December 1942, Wing Commander Parselle arrived at Langar in Nottinghamshire to take command of 207 Squadron [Lancaster], an appointment he held until the night of 25th-26th May 1943, when his Lancaster III W5001 EM-J was shot down by a night fighter over Holland during operations to Düsseldorf. Still strapped in his seat, Wing Commander Parselle was blown out of the bomber and with his bomb aimer Sergeant R E H Hood-Morris survived to become prisoners of war. Following interrogation at Dulag-Luft, Wing Commander Parselle was taken to Stalag-Luft III Sagan, his prisoner of war number being 2281. Following hiss release, he attended Staff College and on 16th April 1956, following command of the Royal Australian Air Force Staff College at Point Cook, he returned to Cranwell ass Commandant of the College. The website A History of RAF Organisation, admirably administered by Malcolm Barrass, notes he was Rhodesian by birth and in retirement lived in Spain.

26243 PORTER* Eric Frederick W/Cdr + 25.02.44 156 Squadron

Wing Commander Eric Frederick Porter and his crew failed to return from operations to Sweinfurt on 24th-25th February 1944. His Lancaster III JB479 GT-K was airborne from Warboys at 1835; he had been attached to the squadron since the previous November and had flown at least sixteen operational sorties. Details of his crew [all are buried in Dürnbach War Cemetery] are reported on page 98 in my RAFBCL 1944.

26245 PYKE* Alan A/Cmdr 05.07.61 Retirement

Air Commodore Alan Pyke CB OBE, died on Friday, 11th March 1977.

26246 RAYNHAM* Henry Digby F/O 19.01.35 Resigned

Flying Officer Henry Digby Raynham was granted a commission in the Reserve of Air Force Officers, Class A in the General Duties Branch on 19th January 1935 [LG 19 February 1935, issue 34134, page 1175]. On 3rd September 1939, he was promoted flight lieutenant [LG 26 April 1940, issue 34838, page 2477] and remained active until: S/Ldr 23.06.44 Relomquished

On account of ill-health [LG 4 July 1944, supplement 36592, page 3139]. However, on 30th April 1962, he was granted a commission in the Royal Air Force Volunteer Reserve Training Branch with the rank of pilot officer, his term of engagement being for four years [LG 24 July 1962, supplement 42739, page 5907]. This was followed by a commission in Class J of the Royal Air Force Volunteer Reserve, ranked Flight Lieutenant [LG 14 May 1963, supplement 42992, page 4146], this being promulgated after he resigned his commission in the Training Branch on 27th January 1963, page 4147 of the same *Gazette* issue. No further trace; Flight Lieutenant Raynham died on

26247 SUTCLIFFE* Walter Philip A/Cmdr 16.04.61 Retirement

Air Commodore Walter Philip Stutcliffe CB DFC mentioned in despatches and conferred with the Legion of Merit [USA], died on

26248 TYSON* Frank Hastings G/Capt 14.02.62 Retirement

Group Captain Frank Hastings Tyson MC [Czechoslovakia], died on

26249 WHITWORTH* John Nicholas Haworth A/Cmdr 25.07.64 Retirement

Air Commodore John Nicholas Haworth Whitworth CB DSO DFC* mentioned in despatches MC [Czechoslovakia], died on Wednesday, 13th November 1974. At the time of the formation of No. 617 Squadron, Group Captain Whitworth was Station Commander at RAF Scampton and in 1955, during the making of the film *The Dam Busters* he was technical advisor for the production.

26250 WILLIAMS* Mervyn Francis Douglas G/Capt 03.07.58 Retirement

Group Captain Mervyn Francis Douglas Williams CBE DSO three times mentioned in despatches, died on

26251 WORRALL* John AV-M 05.08.63 Retirement

Air Vice-Marshal John Worrall CB DFC mentioned in despatches, died on Thursday, 14th January 1988. As a squadron leader, John Worrall was appointed Operations Officer at Biggin Hill on 15th December 1939, and thence attachment to 32 Squadron as a supernumerary ahead of taking command of the squadron [Hurricane] vice Squadron Leader Robert Alexander Chignell on 6th May 1940. John Worrall led '32' in the *Battle of Britain* before assuming the duties of Fighter Controller at Biggin Hill on 16th August 1940. His DFC was *Gazetted* 6th August 1940, issue 34915, page 4809: *"This officer's splendid leadership has been reflected in the work of his squadron which has now destroyed forty-three enemy aircraft and possibly a further twenty-two. In July 1940, he led his squadron in a successful attack against a superior number of enemy aircraft, and assisted in destroying three of the enemy force. Squadron Leader Worrall has displayed great skill, courage and leadership."*

* Graduated 19th December 1931, and appointed as Pilot Officers with a permanent commission. Flight Cadet David Prowse from the September 1929, also graduated [LG 19 January 1932, issue 33791, page 423].

SWORD OF HONOUR

Flight Cadet Reginald Herbert Embleton Emson

ROLL OF HONOUR
JANUARY 1930 INTAKE

P/O	BRADLEY	Jack	12 June 1933	14 Squadron
F/O	COLLYNS New Zealand	Eric Arthur	27 July 1933	8 Squadron
F/O	DORAN	Archibald Maritz	21 March 1935	
F/O	ELSNER	Leonard Nicholas	5 October 1934	810 Squadron FAA
F/Lt	FENTON	Donald McDonald	15 April 1937	Iraq Command
P/O	FORMAN	Donald Edward	2nd December 1932	
S/Ldr	GLENCROSS	Arthur Roger	28 May 1940	37 Squadron
W/Cdr	JOHNSON	David Victor	28 April 1941	45 Squadron
P/O	LONGMAN	John Tosswill	15 May 1933	811 Squadron FAA
S/Ldr	MILLS	Geoffrey Henry Owen	3 February 1939	Ramleh Station Flight
F/Lt	MONKS	Reginald	12 September 1938	RAE Farnborough
S/Ldr	MONTAGU	George Wroughton	21 December 1940	236 Squadron
W/Cdr	PORTER	Eric Frederick	25 February 1944	156 Squadron

September 1930 entry : 29

1552 AWAN** IAF Aizad Bakhah W/Cdr 30.06.44 Resigned

26254 BERENS* Richard James P/O + 14.12.32 Worthy Down

Pilot Officer Richard James Berens, who was stationed at Worthy Down, and his friend Flying Officer Eric Douglas Bishop, took off from Hamble in a DH.60 Moth G-AAYS belonging to the Hampshire Flying Club [both were Club members] for a local pleasure flight which, tragically, ended with the Moth falling into Southampton Water, off Netley. The accident was witnessed by the crew of a Hythe speed-boat who reached the Moth, now sinking fast, and succeeded in extricating both airmen. Pilot Officer Berens, who was piloting the machine, had perished but Flying Officer Bishop was alive, though critically injured. Rushed to hospital where he underwent immediate surgery only to succumb to his injuries later in the day.

26255 BROIUGHTON* Charles AV-M 12.10.68 Retirement

New Zealand Air Vice-Marshal Sir Charles Broughton KBE CB four times mentioned in despatches, died on Sunday, 17th May 1998. As a flight cadet he represented the College at swimming and fencing. Knighted in June 1965, his final appointment from August 1966 up to his retirement two years later was as Air Member for Supply and organisation.

26256 BURWOOD* Horace Paul W/Cdr mid 29.01.58 Retirement

26257 CARTER* Robert Alfred Copsey A/Cmdr 25.04.64 Retirement

Air Commodore Robert Alfred Copsey Carter CB DSO DFC mentioned in despatches, died on Saturday, 10th November 2012. Gaining a scholarship from Halton where he had successfully trained as a fitter his service during the Second World War was almost exclusively connected with Bomber Command and ranged from being a flight commander and subsequently commanding officer with 150 Squadron [Battle/Wellington], close on a year as Chief Training Officer at Headquarters No. 1 Group, eight months as Commanding Officer 103 Squadron [Halifax/Lancaster] and thence command of Elsham Wolds for a month before moving to RAF Grimsby and later to High Wycombe as a Staff Officer in Bomber Command. He won the DSO during his time with 150 Squadron, *Gazetted* 2nd September 1941 in a joint citation with other officers and airman; *"In July 1941, large-scale attacks were made on German warships at Brest and La Pallice [including the "Gneisenau," "Scharnhorst," and "Prinz Eugen']. A smaller attack was made on Cherbourg. The operations were carried out in daylight and extremely heavy and accurate anti-aircraft fire and fighter opposition were encountered by all aircraft when approaching the targets, which at Brest was protected by a balloon barrage. The aircrews engaged succeeded, nevertheless, in securing direct hits on their objectives and inflicting very severe damage in the target area. During the combats with enemy fighters 21 hostile aircraft were destroyed and other were severely damaged. The precise timing of attack by the various formations of aircraft and their correct approach to and the accurate bombing of the objectives in the face of such powerful opposition; demanded great skill and high courage. The great success of these operations were largely due to the bravery, determination and resource displayed by the following officers and airmen, who, participated in various capacities as leaders and members of the aircraft crews."* The losses sustained in these attacks are reported in my RAFBCL 1941 between pages 97 and 102.

His DFC, less citation, was *Gazetted* on 11th June 1943, supplement 36051, page 2678.

26258 COMBE* Andrew Nicholson G/Capt 29.09.57 Retirement

Group Captain Andrew Nicholson attained the AFC and a Bronze Star Medal, the latter conferred on him by the President of the United States of America [LG 15 March 1946, supplement 37501, page 1380].

26259 de PENTHENY-O'KELLY* Raymond Howard P/O + 24.12.33 5 Squadron

26260 EVANS* Donald Randell ACM 28.02.70 Retirement

Air Chief Marshal Sir Donald Evans KBE CB DFC twice mentioned in despatches Bronze Star Medal [USA], died on Wednesday, 9th April 1975. His DFC was in recognition of his service as commanding the Fighter Interception Unit at Ford [now an 'Open Prison'] in West Sussex: *"This officer has undertaken a large number of hours flying at night and in all kinds of weather. On one occasion in January 1942, he displayed both resource and skilful airmanship when executing a safe landing at an aerodrome near the coast, after one engine of his aircraft had ceased to function. The efficiency, keenness and enthusiasm of the unit he commands reflect great credit on the efforts of Wing Commander Evans, who has himself destroyed an enemy aircraft."* [LG 14th July 1942, supplement 35630, page 3091].

His final appointment, commencing 8th January 1968, was as Commandant of the Imperial Defence College.

33001 GALE* Thomas George Lamb S/Ldr 17.11.40 Resigned

"The KING has been graciously pleased to give order for the following promotions in, and appointments to, the Most Excellent Order of the British Empire:- to be Additional Officers of the Civil Division of the said Most Excellent Order." And on page 278 of an extensive list of names published in supplement 37412, of *The London Gazette* of 9th January 1946, *""Commander Thomas George Lamb Gale, Officer Commanding, Advanced Flying Training School, Air Transport Auxiliary."*

33002 GOSNELL* Robert Jerram G/Capt 01.04.66 Retirement

Group Captain Robert Jerram Gosnell gained his DFC as a flight commander with 38 Squadron [Wellington], notification appearing in *The London Gazette* 8th April 1941, issue 35131, page 2041, no citation attached. By the winter of 1944, he was back in the UK and for his duties in commanding 571 Squadron [Mosquito XVI] he was *Gazetted* with the DSO [again, no citation attached] on 17th November 1944, supplement 36799, page 5279.

Fortunately, the website Traces of War [which the authors have much pleasure in acknowledging] the recommendations for the awards are published and in order read:-

"Squadron Leader Gosnell has commanded a flight in this Squadron since 14th August 1940, and has completed some 23 operational sorties. This officer has always shown determination, zeal, and keenness in operating against the enemy. Squadron Leader Gosnell has proved an excellent leader and has set a magnificent example to the younger pilots in his flight. On recent operations on Rhodes Island, Squadron Leader Gosnell attacked four separate targets, namely the aerodromes of Lindos, Maritza, Kattavia, and Rhodes Harbour. This attack, which was carried out with great determination, resulted in the destruction of two aircraft at Lindos and an ammuntion dump at Kattavia."

"On the night of 5th-6th October 1944, Wing Commander Gosnell was the pilot of a Mosquito aircraft detailed to lay mines from a low altitude in the Kiel Canal. The waterway is heavily defended by heavy and light anti-aircraft guns, searchlights, and balloons, demanding a high degree of skill

and determination from those detailed for the task. Undeterred by these hazards, Wing Commander Gosnell brought his aircraft down to 300 feet at the correct speed and released the mine in the allotted area while under the close range fire of three anti-aircraft guns on the banks of the canal.

"As Squadron Commander, this officer was responsible for planning the operation in 571 Squadron and the success achieved is a reflection on his courage, skill, and sense of duty. Wing Commander Gosnell has completed 34 operational sorties of which five have been on Mosquitoes."

The author adds; *"I strongly recommend the immediate award of the Distinguished Service Order."* At the time, 571 Squadron was operating from Oakington in Cambridgeshire.

GULLY* Bernard Henry P/O + 07.10.32 58 Squadron

33004 LEE* David John Pryor ACM 19.03.71 Retirement

Air Chief Marshal Sir David Lee GBE CG, died on Friday, 13th February 2004. An extensive biography of his service life may be read on the Air of Authority - A History of RAF Organisation website; one entry in particular noting that during his tenure as Air Officer Command, Middle East and Air Force Arabian Peninsular [August 1959 to an undisclosed ate in 1962] he was allotted an all-white Canberra which was named *Queen of the Arabian Skies* in which he logged over 100,000 miles visiting units under his extensive command.

33005 LEONARD-WILLIAMS* Harold Guy AV-M 02.04.68 Retirement

Air Vice-Marshal Harold Guy Leonaed-Williams CB CBE mentioned in despatches, died on Thursday, 24th November 1994. Specialising in signals following attendance at No. 17 Signals Course, Electrical and Wireless School, Cranwell, in the spring of 1936, much of service was communications orientated, though his final appointment in April 1966, was as Director-General of Manning [RAF].

33006 LLOYD* Claude Raymond Dixon Lewis G/Capt 06.09.61 Retirement

33007 MARCHBANK* Stanley Jackson A/Cmdr 07.11.59 Retirement

Air Commodore Stanley Jackson Marchbnak OBE DFC, died on Saturday, 26th November 1988. A former Halton Apprentice, his name appears on page 284 of my RAFBCL 1943 when taking off from Pocklington in Halifax II JD127 DY-U of 102 Squadron, a violent swing developed which sent the bomber off the runway and onto a direct path with the control tower. Wing Commander Marchant retracted the undercarriage and on coming to a stop, a fire broke out. Everyone scrambled clear, though two, including the wing commander, were slightly injured. His DFC was *Gazetted,* less citation, on 6th June 1944, in supplement 36550, page 2699.

33008 MICHELL* Douglas G/Capt 14.10.58 Retirement

MIDDLETON Lawrence Mark P/O 05.04.33 Retirement

33010 MORTON * Chrichton Charles A/Cmdr 26.10.66 Retirement

Air Commodore Chrichton Charles Morton CBE, died on Wednesday, 6 November 1996.For the greater part of his service he was a technical officer specialising in signals, completing his service as Command Signals Officer at Headquarters Bomber Command.

1551 MUKERJEE** IAF Subroto AM + 08.11.60

33011 PEEL* John Ralph Alexander G/Capt 20.01.48 Retirement

A flight cadet who excelled at hockey, cricket and squash, Group Captain John Ralph Alexander Peel may accurately be described as being at the sharp end of the early engagements of the *Battle of Britain.* A fighter pilot from the outset of his graduation from the College, first with 19 Squadron [Bulldog IIA] and next attached to the FAA to serve aboard HMS *Furious* with 801 Squadron, he went on to fly with 601 Squadron AAF [Demon] before 'flying a desk' at the Air Ministry from where he was appointed to command 145 Squadron [Hurricane] at Tangmere on 16th June 1940.

Credited as firing some of the first [if not the first] shots in the *Battle of Britain,* he was shot down off Selsey Bill in Hurricane P3400 in the early evening of 11th July 1940. Rescued in a semi-conscious state by the local lifeboat [he was for ever after a strong supporter of the RNLI] he returned to the fray. Then, as Kenley's Wing Leader he had a second visit to the waters of the English Channel when on 9 July 1941, and participating in *Circus 41* his 312 [Czech] Squadron Hurricane IIB Z3069 came down off the French coast. Plucked from the sea, and suffering no ill-effects, he led the Kenley Wing on a sweep the following morning.

The citation for his DFC [LG 13 August 1940, issue 34920, pages 4939 and 4940] reads: *"This officer's outstanding quality as a leader has raised the flying standard and morale of his squadron to the highest pitch. During a period of thirteen days in July, he destroyed at least two enemy aircraft. On one occasion, although his aircraft had been badly damaged in action, he followed and shot down a Dornier 17 twenty-five miles from the coast and eventually had to abandon his own aircraft over the sea. He was picked up by a lifeboat when on the verge of losing consciousness, but was again leading his squadron the next morning."*

A year later [LG 5 August 1941, issue 35238, page 4515] he was rewarded with the DSO: *"Since March 1941, this officer has led the wing over France on twenty-eight occasions and, under his leadership, it has destroyed thirty-two enemy aircraft. In April 1941, he led a formation of five aircraft on successful low flying machine-gun attack against Berck and damaged or destroyed three Messerschmitt 109's. One afternoon in July 1941, he was shot down off the French coast but, despite this experience, he led the wing the next morning. The success of the wing in escorting and destroying enemy aircraft has been duue to Wing Command Peel's training and leadership."*

After leaving the air force he turned his hand to farming, but following a move from Cambridgeshire to Devon and then to Wiltshire, he settled in Wiltshire taking up the artist's paint brush for a life of tranquil retirement until his death on Wednesday, 7th January 2004.

33012 RHYS* Mervyn Hugh G/Capt 21.07.59 Retirement

As Squadron Leader Mervyn Hugh Rhys he was *Gazetted* with the AFC on 1st April 1941 [LG 1 April 1941, issue 35124, page 1903].

33013 ROLFE* Theodore Urquhart W/Cdr + 09.02.48 MCS

Wing Commander Theodore Urquhart Rolfe OBE mid lost his life while carrying out a training flight in Anson C.19 TX168. The crash was reported in the Late Extra edition of Dundee's *Evening Telegraph and Post* beneath the headline *'Plane Crashes In Street - Wrecks Bus, Then Hits Factory'*

"The two occupants of an Anson plane were killed when their machine plunged into a trolley bus at Montrose Park, Hendon, to-day. Seven people were injured. Only one was detained in hospital.

"The occupants of the plane were Squadron Leader T U Rolfe and Flying Officer William M Meekan. The Anson demolished the front of the busand then crashed headlong into the wall of a factory. As petrol spurted in all directions men from a nearby garage dashed out and drenched the area with sprinklers. Others hacked a way through the plane and dragged out the pilot and his companion. The crash was heard a mile away.

"The plane narrowly missed Hendon's biggest civic restaurant, crowded with lunchers. It lay upside down with one wing and an engine completely smashed off and its tail embedded in the roof of a car. One factory worker told a reporter, "We heard a roar and then a tremendous crash which shook the building."

'Hit Scaffolding'

A pedestrian said, "I was standing close to the Savoy cinema when a plane came low and caught the scaffolding on L C C flats which are being built. It brought down the scaffolding.

"Then it hit a trolley bus standard. Dragged down another standard on the other side of the road, demolished the front of a trolley bus travelling towards London, and crashed headlong into the wall of the Romad factory.

"The front of the trolley bus was knocked to the other side of the road. The driver's cabin was demolished and the top part of the bus at the front was torn off. A man who had been sitting there was brought out unconscious and the conductor also had his face cut.

"Fortunately, there were few people in the street at that moment. Had it happened a quarter of an hour later the street would have been packed with factory workers breaking off for their midday meal."

"Fire began in the plane," said one of the factory employees, "but some more of the workers and men from a nearby garage made short work of that."

The local *Harrow Observer and Gazette* headlined their report *'Local Men Among The Casualties - Aircraft's Crash Into Trolley Bus'*

"Three residents in the "observer" area were among the casualties when an RAF Anson struck a chimney on a semi-completed block of L C C flats and plunged into a trolley-bus near the Savoy cinema, Burnt Oak Broadway, on Monday.

"The occupants of the plane, Wing Commander T U Rolfe and F/Lt. W McMeekan, both stationed at Hendon Aerodrome, were killed. Thirteen people were injured, ten being conveyed to Redhill Hospital, Edgware, where on was detained.

"Mr. R Nichols, aged 31, of Foxten, Evelyn-avenue, Kingsbury, was travelling on the bus, which was bound for London, when the crash occurred. He was treated at hospital for shock and injuries to the head. Also travelling on the bus was Mr. S Goodenough, aged 50, of 60 Bushey Grove-road, Bushey, who was detained at Redhill Hospital with head injuries.

'Working in a Hut'

"Mr. W Wardle, aged 45, of 49 Christchurch-gardens, Kenton, was working in a hut which was struck by the falling chimney. He sustained injuries to the back, but declined medical aid. Two of his workmates had similar injuries.

"Risking danger of fire, Mr. J O'Connor, of Crispin-road, Edgware, formerly of the RAF, climbed into the plane and released the safety belts of the pilot and passenger.

"Fire broke out in the plane almost immediately and employees from Messrs. G T Hayes Ltd., a nearby garage, tackled the flames with extinguishers. Fire appliances were called from Wembley, Kingsbury and Mill Hill. Ambulances from Wembley and Hendon were summoned, and among others which rushed to the spot was one from Harrow."

33042 SEYMOUR Paul de Gray Horatio S/Ldr + 17.11.42 158 Squadron

Squadron Leader Paul de Gray Horatio Seymour arrived at RAF Eastmoor in October 1942, where he was attached to 158 Squadron [Halifax] and took over command of A Flight from Squadron Leader A S R E Ennis DFC. During the afternoon of 17th November 1942, two of the squadron's Halifaxes and crews flew to nearby Linton-on-Ouse where they took on fuel and dozens of packets of leaflets [*Nickels*]. Squadron Leader Seymour was assigned to the Nancy and Strasbourg area while Pilot Officer Woolnough drew Vichy and Clermond-Ferrand. At 1717, Pilot Officer Woolnough was airborne in Halifax II DG223 NP-Q, followed a minute later by Squadron Leader Seymour in Halifax II W7863 NP-V, his crew comprising of Sergeant G Johnson [2nd Pilot], Sergeant R B Greensmith [Flight Engineer], P/O L J Fairbairn RNZAF [Navigator], the squadron's Bombing Leader, Flight Lieutenant R Tudor-Jones, Pilot Officer G V Slide [wireless operator] and air gunners Sergeants J D-L-W Anstruther and C J Murray.

At 0100, Pilot Officer Woolnough landed at Rufforth [158 Squadron moved here earlier in the month] to report a successful operation, noting that *"Vichy was well lit up."* Sadly, Squadron Leader Seymour, making his operational debut with the squadron, and crew failed to return; their Halifax came down near Consigny in the Haute-Marne, some 22km ENE Chaumont. There was one survivor, Pilot Officer Slide; the rest now lie in Consigny Communal Cemetery.

33014 SHAW* Richard Henry G/Capt 18.03.54 Retirement

Group Captain Richard Henry Shaw DFC was *Gazetted* with his award [in recognition of his tour of duty with 115 Squadron] on 4th December 1945, supplement 37374, page 5897. The citation was not attached.

33015 SHORE* Donald Ross G/Capt 18.09.52 Retirement

Group Captain Donald Ross Shore AFC commanded 227 Squadron [Beaufighter] winning a DFC [LG 29 September 1942, supplement 35721, page 4215] as the citation states: *"This officer has led his squadron on a number of successful attacks against enemy shipping in the Mediterranean. His squadron has also shot down numerous enemy aircraft, on of which Wing Commander Shore destroyed. Much of the success achieved can be attributed to this officer's great skill and courageous leadership."*

No. 227 Squadron was reformed at Luqa in Malta on 20th August 1942, and equipped with Beaufighters from a detachment of 235 Squadron, Wing Commander Shaw being appointed to command. His tenure was quite brief for during October 1942, he handed over the squadron to Wing Commander C A Masterman OBE.

SINGH** Amarinder P/O + 04.09.33 1 Squadron IAF

IAF Pilot Officer Amarinder Singh and Pilot Officer Bhupender Singh [see below], both aged 22, died when their Wapiti IIA J9486 spun out of control and crashed at Padidan in Sindh province. This is at odds with Air-Britain's *j File* which records the movements of J9486 as arriving at the Royal Albert Docks from the Packing Depot, Ascot, on 22nd April 1929, and shipped out to British India aboard SS *Hatimura.* It was at the Drigh Road aircraft depot by 3rd May 1929, where it was prepared for the Air Officer Commanding, India, personal aircraft. During 1933, it was reported to be on the strength of 28 Squadron [Ambala], thence to 20 Squadron but no supporting date and then, apparently taken to Iraq for use by AHQ Hinaidi before returning to British India and the Station Flight at Risalpur. The final entry reads *"Crashed 8.39."*

SINGH** Bhupindra P/O + 04.09.33 1 Squadron IAF
IAF

SIRCAR** Harish Chander F/O 11.03.35 Dismissed
IAF

Flying Officer Harish Chander Sircar was dismissed by sentence of court-martial following an avoidable flying accident when his 1 Squadron IAF Wapiti V J9738 smashed into a column of Indian soldiers a few miles north of Karachi on the banks of the Hub river. At least fifteen of the column were killed outright and eleven were injured, some very seriously after being struck by the Wapiti's propeller. Flying Officer Sircrar and his observer, Aircraftman Abdul Salaam were injured though, apparently, not too seriously. Harish Chander Sircar's death is reported to have occurred on Tuesday, 1st March 1977, at the age of 67.

Air-Britain's *J File* records the movements of J9738 as arriving at Birkenhead on on 1st March 1930, from Packing Depot, Sealand, and shipped aboard SS *City of Vienna.* Processed at Drigh Road it was delivered to 1 Squadron IAF and written off as described with the additional information reported as *"Nushkki, Baluchistan, 8.1.35."*

33016 TANNER* William Erskine Snell F/O + 23.04.34 1 Squadron
South Africa

Omitted from the *List of Graduates* Flight Cadet TANDON Jagat Narain, service number 1553. He rose to wing commander rank and was still serving when murdered during a train journey on 21st January 1944. The reason for his omission may be traced to the fact that he was considered too short of stature for pilot duties and as a consequence was assigned as an equipment officer.

The authors are delighted to acknowledge the website Bharat-Rakshak.Com.

* Flight Cadets with an asterisk appended to their surname successfully passed through the College and were granted permanent commissions as pilot officers with effect from 23rd July 1932. Also graduating Flight Cadet Herbert York Humphreys from the January 1930 intake [LG 26 August 1932, issue 33858, page 5500].

** On graduating in 1932, these five flight cadets formed the initial pilot establishment of the Indian Air Force which came into being in British India as an Auxiliary Air Force following the enactment of the Indian Air Force Act 1932 on 8th October of that year. Pilot Officer Subroto Mukerjee subsequently became the first Indian Air Force, Chief of the Air Staff with the rank of Air Marshal. Of Bengali origin, Subroto Mukerjee, born 5th March 1911, in Calcutta, his biography, accompanied by a photograph of him and fellow Indian cadet, at the College, may be accessed on *Wikipedia* [which the authors here acknowledge]. His untimely death at the age of 49, occurred during a visit to Tokyo on 8th November 1960, when during the course of a meal with a friend he choked on a morsel of food and died before help arrived. His body was flown back from Japan for cremation.

SWORD OF HONOUR
Flight Cadet Andrew Nicholson Combe

ROLL OF HONOUR
SEPTEMBER 1930 INTAKE

P/O	BERENS	Richard James	14 December 1932	Worthy Down
P/O	de PENTHENY-O'KELLY	Raymond Howard	24 December 1933	5 Squadron
P/O	GULLY	Bernard Henry	7 October 1932	58 Squadron
AM	MUKERJEE IAF	Suubroto	8 November 1960	
W/Cdr	ROLFE	Theodore Urquhart	7 February 1948	MCS Hendon
S/Ldr	SEYMOUR	Paul de Gray Horatio	17 November 1942	158 Squadron
P/O	SINGH IAF	Amarinder	4 September 1933	1 Squadron IAF
P/O	SINGH IAF	Bhupindra	4 September 1933	1 Squadron IAF
F/O	TANNER South Africa	William Erskine Snell	23 April 1934	1 Squadron

FLYING ACCIDENTS

Thursday 6 March 1930
Siskin IIIA J9364 *Not reported*
T/o Cranwell and crashed here on landing

Thursday 29 May 1930
Siskin IIIDC J7167 *Not reported*
T/o Cranwell and reported as *"crashed."*

Friday 6 June 1930
Avro 504N J8709 F/Lt H L Drake +
F/Cdt F de la P Beresford-Peirse Injured
T/o Cranwell and just before touch down collied with Avro 504N J9693. J8709 was too badly damaged to be considered for repair, but J9693 was repairable and, subsequently, went to the Central Flying School where it was sstill giving good service in March 1933. The flight cadet flying solo in J9693, George Wroughton Montagu although injured made a good recovery only to lose his life in the Second World War [see Appendix D for the current year].

Thursday 16 October 1930
Atlas ™ K1186 F/Cdt E H Fawkes +
T/o Cranwell only to stall and dive into the ground killing Flight Cadet Ernest Hamley Fawkes, aged 20.

Thursday 30 October 1930
Atlas I J9985 F/Cdet P Berry +
T/o Cranwell and totally destroyed by fire, in which Flight Cadet Peter Berry perished, when it spun and crashed on or near the airfield.

Note. It will be observed that a new block of numbers was assigned to the College with the previous block ending at 26260 and the new block commencing 33001. It is also observed that four flight cadets from the January intake lost their lives in the Second World War as opposed to a single death from the September intake. Presently, the service number allocated to Pilot Officer Bernard Henry Gully is not known; '33003' would appear to be the obvious, but this number was taken by Pilot Officer Herbert York Humphreys from the January intake.

Appendix E - Roll of Honour

ROYAL AIR FORCE

F/Lt ARMSTRONG Gerald Christopher Allan 30 September 1930 17 Squadron

LAC ARNOLD Henry Frederick 8 July 1930 202 Squadron

Leading Aircraftman Henry Frederick Arnold, 505965, in his fifth year of service, was in an RAF dinghy which 24-hours previously was struck by Fairey IIID N9730 which was taxying [the name of the pilot has been omitted], sustaining mortal injuries.

Cpl BARNARD Leonard Edward 21 January 1930 207 Squadron

F/O BARNETT Max Ian 4 November 1930 56 Squadron

P/O BARRON Francis Slade 23 April 1930 47 Squadron

Sgt BIRKINSHAW Wilfred 30 September 1930 17 Squadron

F/Lt BROOKS Gerald 25 November 1930 100 Squadron

P/O CHANCE John Anthony 19 November 1930 26 Squadron

LAC CHARLESWORTH Ernest Raymond 5 May 1930 20 Squadron

LAC CHAPELL Henry John 14 May 1930 20 Squadron

Sgt CLARKE Owen Cambridge 15 September 1930 11 Squadron

LAC COOPER James 30 September 1930 30 Squadron

AC1 DAVIS Cyril Fred 23 April 1930 47 Squadron

F/O EVANS Charless Henry Lee 21 January 1930 6 Squadron

Sgt FELL Cecil Arthur Alfred 13 February 1930 32 Squadron

F/O FRANCIS Reginald Frederick 5 June 1930 202 Squadron

F/O GOAD Frederick Robert Walter 4 November 1930 9 Squadron

Flying Officer Frederick Robert Walter Goad was captain of Vickers Virginia X J7561 when it stalled taking off from Manston, crashed and caught fire. Despite the severity of the crash and the consequences to the crew, from which Aircraftman Alan William Edwards survived, the airframe was rebuilt and reissued to the squadron, later [circa 1932] passing it to 58 Squadron. According to *The J File* it crashed and was repaired three time, once with 58 Squadron and twice with 9 Squadron. The last entry indicates it was damaged landing in a crosswind whilst on its second spell of use by 58 Squadron. Flying Officer Goad was a short service commission officer *Gazetted* 1st March 1929, issue 33473 page 1468. The accident received press coverage in *The Courier and Advertiser* on Wednesday, November 5th, 1930, in which it was reported the Virgina was at about 100 to 150 feet when it banked vertically and nosedived to the ground. Help arrived within minutes and with gas masks on braved the flames and smoke and pulled all three occupants clear. For Flying Officer Goad and Sergeant George William Roberts it was too late, but as noted above Aircraftman Edwards was not only alive, but, remarkably, little injured. Respectively, the crew hailed from Erith, New Ferry, Birkenhead and Crowthorne in Berkshire.

Sgt GORDON John Ritchie 9 July 1930 55 Squadron

F/O HANLON Charles Peter 25 December 1930 30 Squadron

LAC HARRIS Charles Drewery 5 Jun 1930 202 Squadron

F/O HAWKE John William 15 May 1930 20 Squadron

Sgt HINDELANG Edward Albert 13 June 1930 60 Squadron

F/Lt HOWLETT Alexander Howard James 25 November 1930 100 Squadron

LAC LAIDLER Robert Angus 26 July 1930 8 Squadron

LAC LANSDELL William Henry 14 June 1930 60 Squadron

F/O MACKENZIE Donald 21 January 1930 207 Squadron

Sgt MARTIN John 17 March 1930 23 Squadron

Sgt McNAIR Owen Herbert 8 August 1930 25 Squadron

AC1 MINNS William Henry Dack 9 October 1930 22 Squadron

Aircraftman William Henry Dack Minns, 508206, was killed at Martlesham Heath when the Vickers Type 150 Vanox twin-engined prototype J9131 crashed following engine failure on take off. The pilot, Flight Lieutenant Herbert Seton Broughill MC DFC was unhurt, as were Corporal Gray and Leading Aircraftman Letley. Intended as a replacement for the Vickers Virginia the Vanox - J9131 being rebuilt - proved to be a failure and only the one example was built. Reporting the accident, the Dundee edition of *The Evening Telegraph* states the aeroplane collided with a heap of cement. The engine became detached and fell on Aircraftman Minns, aged 23, of Hempstead Road, Holt, Norfolk.

Sgt O'MEARA Frederick Ernest 12 June 1930 100 Squadron

F/O PILCHER Geoffrey Norman 26 July 1930 8 Squadron

P/O PRATT Percy James 24 March 1930 58 Squadron

Sgt ROBERTS George William 4 November 1930 9 Squadron

See the above try for Flying Officer Goad. Sergeant Roberts, 356992, had joined the service from a civilian occupation in the early 1920s.

F/O ROGERS Peter Bagwell 15 July 1930 23 Squadron

P/O SAWYER Wilfred 6 August 1930 41 Squadron

W/Cdr SMYTHIES DFC Bernard Edward 17 June 1930 29 Squadron

F/O STROUD Richard William Alexander 17 M1y 1930 11 Squadron

F/Lt TAVENDALE James Charles Henry 14 May 1930 20 Squadron

F/O TEALE Roger Pridgin 8 April 1930 19 Squadron

LAC	VALENTINE	Frank Spencer	15 September 1930	11 Squadron
F/O	WHITE	Ernest Richard	24 March 1930	58 Squadron
AC1	WILTSHIRE	Charles Samuel	17 May 1930	11 Squadron

AUXILIARY AIR FORCE

F/Lt	MILLER	Alexander Robertson Hunter	3 August 1930	603 Squadron AAF

Appendix F - Fatal accidents involving seconded Royal Navy and Royal Marine Officers 1924 to 1930

When the Royal Naval Air Service and Royal Flying Corps merged to the form an independent Royal Air Force on April 1st, 1918, the onus for supplying aircrews to the postwar aircraft carriers became, in the main, the responsibility of a now much reduced air force officer corps. Six years after the merger, and with British air power in the early stages of an upward curve, the Fleet Air Arm was formed on 1st April 1924, as the naval branch of the Royal Air Force, and in order to meet the demand for an increase in trained pilots selected Royal Navy and a lesser number of Royal Marine officers were seconded, usually for terms of four years engagement, with commissions in the rank of flying officer and with flying training assigned to the care of No. 1 Flying Training School at Netheravon on Wiltshire's Salisbury Plain. On 15th February 1928, responsibility for training attached naval officers passed to RAF Base, Leuchars.

This was particularly significant for earlier in the year the first purpose built aircraft carrier, HMS *Hermes,* had been commissioned [though her construction had commenced as early as January 1918] and following a brief period working up with the Atlantic Fleet, HMS *Hermes* would soon become a familiar sight in the Mediterranean and on the China Station. Oddly, when compared to sister carriers that had been converted from existing ships, her complement of aircraft was a lowly twenty, whereas HMS *Courageous* could accommodate a very useful forty-eight.

Prior to the commissioning of the Royal Navy's first aircraft carrier, a number of ships had been converted to accommodate and operate aircraft, examples being HMS *Argus,* HMS *Courageous* and HMS *Furious,* while a fourth carrier, HMS *Eagle* was commissioned at the same time as HMS *Hermes.* Originally ordered before the *Great War* as a battleship for the Chilean Navy the vessel was incomplete when it was purchased by Britain in 1918, for conversion as an aircraft carrier. Then followed a protracted period of construction with frequent stoppages owing to labour disputes and it was not until February 1924, that HMS *Eagle* was able to embark on sea trails before assignment to the Mediterranean Fleet.

These 'floating airfields' enabled British air power to be extended to all parts of the globe, though in the main the areas that were considered of strategic importance were the Atlantic and Mediterranean and all points east of Suez. Thus, when HMS *Glorious* was commissioned in 1930, it is true to say that our global reach was significant.

Principal suppliers of aircraft for carrier operations were Blackburn and Fairey, with Avro's two-seater Bison employed as a fleet spotter and reconnaissance aircraft.

Numerous books and articles have been written about the emergence of air operations at sea, but this appendix will be confined to recording the not infrequent fatal accidents involving naval and marine officers who lost their lives whilst attached to the Royal Air Force.

Notes on Royal Air Force personnel who lost their lives during this period may be found in the appendices for Short Service Commission officers and Cranwell Graduates.

Monday 10 November 1924

1 FTS Netheravon F/O J M Chandler RN +
7F.1 Snipe E6968

T/o Netheravon and collided near the airfield with a locally based Fairy Fawn II J7202 of 11 Squadron piloted by Sergeant Frederick George Morfell. My summary for the date in question contains all relevant information, though it should be noted that Flying Officer John Maurice Chandler was in the first batch of naval lieutenants seconded for RAF service.

Friday 1 May 1925

443 Flight F/O H L Roseveare RN +
Fairey IIID N9756 Cpl T V Warwick +

T/o Leuchars and crashed circa 1000 following a midair collision near Guardbridge on the coast some 3 miles NW of St. Andrew, Fife, with Fairey IIID N9754 crewed by Flying Officer Edward Acton Alcock Gibbon RN and Aircraftman Austin Joseph Stewart. Damage in the collision to N9754 was not too serious and the crew were able to land safely, and without injury.

Flying Officer Harry Lestourgeon Roseveare and Flying Officer Gibbon had been commissioned with effect from 16th June 1924, their terms of engagement being for four years service, and *Gazetted* 22nd July 1924, issue 32958, page 5553. Corporal Tom Vincent Warwick's service number, 335838, identifies him as joining the Royal Air Force as a Boy, probably in 1920, the block of service numbers for such entrants being 335001 to 336000 which were allocated between August 1919 and January 1921.

Friday 15 May 1925

1 FTS Netheravon F/O D B Morgan RN +
DH.9A J7053

T/o Netheravon and crashed, totally out of control, following collapse and detachment of the wings as Flying Officer David Brown Morgan pulled out of a steep dive. His body was recovered from the wreckage lying near the village of Everleigh on the northern edge of Haxton Down, and 4 miles ESE from the Central Flying School at Upavon.

His commission, effective from 12th January 1925, was promulgated in *The London Gazette* of 20th January 1925, issue 33013, page 453.

Tuesday 14 July 1925
1 FTS Netheravon F/O J Ryan RN +
Avro 504K H9814
T/o Netheravon and while banking over Charlton Down on the Plain and with the airfield in sight, Flying Officer Ryan stalled and spun to the ground. His commission was published in the same *Gazette* issue as for Flying Officer Morgan who was killed at the School on15th May.

Wednesday 10 February 1926
402 Flight F/O H R Hancox RN Injured
Fairey Flycatcher N9892
T/o Hal Far with the intention of returning to HMS *Eagle,* Flying Officer Henry Roger Hancox being the last of a flight of three Flycatchers to leave. From eyewitness evidence it seems he began to close on one of the Flycatchers and then turned sharply to starboard to avoid a collision. This resulted in a high speed stall and spin which was partially recovered before entering into a left had spiral from which there was no recovery. On impact with the ground the practice bomb that was attached exploded. Critically injured he died the next day. He was one of thirty-six naval lieutenants granted temporary RAF commissions in the rank of flying officer as *Gazetted* on 22nd July 1924, issue 32958, page 5553. To the best of the authors' knowledge, he was the first to lose his life whilst on overseas service; he was 27 years of age.

Tuesday 30 March 1926
441 Flight F/O T L G Bryan RM +
Fairey IIID N9758
T/o HMS *Hermes* and on return to the carrier, sailing off Kalafrana on Malta's most southeasterly tip, landed on but swung badly and fell off the flight deck into the sea. Sadly, before rescue could be effected, Flying Officer Thomas Lawe Guy Bryan had drowned. His commission as a temporary flying officer was *Gazetted* on 20th January 1925, issue 33013, page 454.

Propeller accidents resulting in deaths were a feature between to the two wars and one such incidence occurred aboard HMS *Hermes* on Thurssday, 22nd April 1926, when Aircraftman Henry Frank Mills, aged 22, and attached to 422 Flight was struck while working on the flight deck. His skull was fractured and he died almost instantaneously; he is buried in Capuccini Naval Cemetery.

Friday 30 April 1926
406 Flight F/O N H Portal RN +
Fairey Flycatcher
T/o Donibristle and crashed near the airfield after emerging from cloud in a steep dive. Flying Officer Nigel Hugh Portal was attached from 27th April 1925, his commission being published in *The London Gazette* on 12th May 1925, issue 33046, page 3224.

A replacement for the Gloster Nightjar, the Flycatcher has been described in a number of aviation journals as being a delight to fly and the loss of this unidentified example may well have been caused by Flying Officer Portal becoming disorientated after flying into cloud. His birth is given as 24th May 1902.

Friday 21 May 1926
RAF Leuchars F/O P G Smith RN +
Fairey Flycatcher
T/o Leuchars for bombing practice and came to grief when it crashed on dunes at the Tentsmuir ranges [now administered by Scotland's National Nature Reserves]. Flying Officer Peter Granville Smith received his temporary RAF commission at the same time as Flying Portal, summarised above.

Unconfirmed reports suggest the Flycatcher's airframe serial may have been 'N9659.'

Tuesday 17 August 1926
RAF Gosport F/O J L L Rees RM +
Blackburn Dart N9799
T/o Gosport and while over the Isle of Wight encountered fog. Disorientated, Flying Officer John Leslie Llewellyn Rees crashed on Hulverstone Down near Freshwater, a large village towards the western end of the island.

He was one of six marine lieutenants *Gazetted* with temporary RAF commissions on 22nd July 1924, issue 32958, page 5553, his military service being traced back to 25th July 1917, when he was appointed as a 2nd Lieutenant in the Royal Marines [LG 11 September 1917, issue 30278, page 9372].

Thursday 21 October 1926

423 Flight F/O H N Lay RN +
Avro Bison II N9969 Lt J E S Anderson RN +
Lt R Carslake RN +
TAG R W Gibbs RN +

T/o HMS *Eagle* [though Hal Far cannot be discounted] and came down a little under 6 miles N of Malta's Valetta Harbour. Flying Hugh Nelson Lay survived the crash but drowned before help arrived. His temporary commission as a flying officer was *Gazetted* at the same time as Flying Officer Rees [see above].

The underlying cause of the crash was engine failure. At the time HMS *Eagle* and its air complement were exercising with the 3rd Cruiser Squadron.

Tuesday 18 January 1927

423 Flight F/Lt C F Brewerton DSC +
Avro Bison II N9972 F/O E Chafe RN +
Lt G Owen-Jones RN +
TAG G W Burton RN +

T/o Hal Far and fell into the Mediterranean and hitting the cliffs at Ghar Hasan on Malta's souther coastline. According to a report published in *Flight* on 27th January 1927, the Bison was flying at quite a low altitude and nearing the cliffs encountered turbulent air which blew the machine towards the cliff face where the starboard wing struck causing loss of control. Flying Officer Edwin Chafe, 27, was one of twenty naval lieutenants commissioned to the RAF for four years as *Gazetted* 12th May 1925, issue 33046, page 3224.

Friday 28 January 1927

462 Flight F/O G T Campbell RN +
Blackburn Dart N9800

T/o HMS *Furious* and while flying off Gibraltar, Flying Officer Gordon Thursby Campbell lost flying speed, stalled and crashed into the sea. He received his temporary RAF commission at the same time as Flying Chafe whose details appear in the previous summary.

Tuesday 1 February 1927

402 Flight F/O J Y Mills RN +
Fairey Flycatcher S1069

T/o HMS *Eagle* and while carrying out a mock attack on a Fairey IIID belonging to 481 Flight came into collision at 1,200 feet. Out of control, the Flycatcher fell into the sea off Benghisa Point overlooking Marsalokk Bay on the island's most southeasterly point.

Flying Officer John Yarnton Mills was granted his temporary RAF commission on 16th June 1924, *Gazetted* 22nd July 1924, issue 32958, page 5553.

Seriously damaged [reports suggest it was deemed beyond repair] the Fairey IIID landed safely, two members of the crew having sustained injuries. They were named as Wing Commander Gilbert George Herbert Cooke DFC AFC and Flight Sergeant Arthur Edmund Lawrence Worster. The aircraft's pilot, Flying Officer Alexander Howard James Howlett was unhurt, thus suggesting that perhaps the Flycatcher struck aft of the pilot's cockpit.

Tuesday 9 June 1927

402 Flight F/O H M S Forbes DSC +
Fairey Flycatcher N9887

T/o HMS *Eagle* and while engaged in low level bombing practice flew into the waters of Marsalokk Bay. Flying Officer Haydon Marriott Sutherland Forbes received his temporary RAF commission at the same time as Flying Officer Chafe whose demise is summarised on 18th January 1927.

Friday 22 July 1927

RAF Leuchars F/O R F G Salmond RN Injured Shorncliffe Military Cemetery
Fairey IIID S1094

T/o 1000 Leuchars and while climbing out on a northwesterly heading the engine burst into flames. Flying Officer Rawdon Frank Gerald Salmond made a desperate attempt to forced-land but crashed into the garden of Binn Cottage near Dundee, some 11 miles NW of the airfield. Alive when pulled from the wreckage, mercifully he died the following day from his dreadful injuries. He had received his commission for RAF service as *Gazetted* 10th September 1926, issue 33200, page 5912.

Born in Singapore on 19th October 1903, his body was conveyed south for burial in Shorncliffe on the Kent coast. His epitaph reads *"I Bare You On Eagles Wings And Brought You Unto Myself"* Exodus, chapter 19, verse 4 [God has called out to Moses from the mountain and informs him *"Ye have seen what I have done to the Egyptians, and how "I bare you on ... "*].

Saturday 12 May 1928

446 Flight	F/O E J O Ellison RM	Injured
Fairey IIIF S1260	LAC J G Bolton	+
	TAG P R Carter RN	+

T/o Gosport and set a course for Farnborough where on arrival Flying Officer Edward James Osborne Ellison came down in Alexandria Road close to the airfield on its eastern side. A marine officer, Flying Officer Edward James Osborne Ellison's RAF commission was promulgated in *The London Gazette* 22nd July 1924, issue 32958, page 5553]. He recovered from his injuries and relinquished his temporary commission on 6th December 1928, returning to duty with the Royal Marines [LG 18 December 1928, issue 33448, page 8330].

The full page width headline in the *Derby Daily Telegraph* published on the day of the accident read:

'One Man Killed And Two Injured In Aeroplane Crash'

'Big 'Plane Crash'

'On Man Killed and Two Injured'

'Stalled'

"A large aeroplane crashed at Farnborough to-day. One man was killed and two other were seriously injured. An official of the Air Ministry stated that the machine was the S1260 of the Fairey type, and was flying to Farnborough from Gosport.

"According to accounts received from the aerodrome, the aeroplane stalled and fell rapidly. The Air Ministry adds that the two passengers were a carpenter rigger and a telegraphist.

"An Aldershot correspondent telegraphs: A naval aeroplane, flown by a naval officer and carrying two passengers, met with disaster this morning at Farnborough. One of the crew was killed outright, and the other two so badly injured that their lives are dispaired of. The machine was flying from Gosport to Farnborough, and on nearing the aerodrome apparently attempted to land with the wind. Finding this impossible, the pilot took the machine up again, circled at a low altitude over the town, and in attempting a sharp turn to get over the aerodrome again lost power and crashed. The machine fell between two houses in Alexandria-road. Assistance was immediately at hand from the aerodrome, and the crew were taken out from the wreckage. First-class air mechanic Bolton was found to be dead, and the other two were rushed to Cambridge Hospital with grave injuries.

"The man killed was Aircraftman No. 1 J Bolton, RAF, base, Gosport. The other occupants of the machine were Capt. Ellison, Royal Marines, the pilot, who was badly injured, and Telegraphist Carter, RN, who is in a critical condition.

"This has been a disastrous week for air tragedies, three airman having being killed and two injured already. The number of deaths this year now total 31."

Wednesday 20 June 1928

403 Flight	F/O R A Aldridge RN	+
Fairey Flycatcher N9661		

T/o HMS *Hermes* and pulling out of a dive disintegrated and fell into the sea off Wan-Hai-Wei. Flying Officer Raymond Arthur Aldridge's details were published in *The London Gazette* on 20th January 1925, issue 33013, page 453.

According to *Wikipedia,* acknowledged by the authors, Wan-Hai-Wei was leased territory off China's northeastern coast. It covered an area of 288 square miles within which was the walled city of Port Edward, the bay of Wan-Hai-Wei, Liu-Kung Island and mainland coast strip of about 72 miles in length.

The lease was agreed in 1898 and expired in 1930. Its geographical location controlled the entrance to the Gulf of Zhili and the seaward approaches to Peking [Beijing]. There were strategic reasons for the lease as Russia had been leased Port Arthur which also controlled the entrance into the Gulf of Zhili.

Monday 25 June 1928

463 Flight	F/O J Nicholson RN	+
Blackburn Dart S1119		

T/o HMS *Courageous* but swung badly, clipped the carrier's funnel and fell into the sea off Malta. Flying Officer John Nicholson's commission for duty with the RAF was published in the same *Gazette* edition as that for Flying Officer Portal, summarised on 30th April 1926.

Wednesday 6 February 1929

441 Flight	F/O R F B Cecil RN	+
Fairey IIID S1023/S42	Lt H A J Grant RN	Injured

T/o HMS *Argus** towing a target. Having climbed to around 1,000 feet control was lost and the machine dived into Gibraltar Bay just off the South Admiralty Mole. Rescue boats found the observer, Lieutenant Heathcote Andrew John Grant, but he died within hours from his injuries. Of the pilot, Flying Officer Richard Francis Bain Cecil, there was no sign and it is assumed he went down with the aircraft which is reported to have sunk immediately on impact with the sea. He was born on the last day of January 1902.

* Some reports say HMS *Furious* was the aircraft carrier.

Monday 13 May 1929

440 Flight	F/O J E Fenton RN	Safe
Fairey IIIF S1304	AC1 F T Harding	Safe
	AC1 J A G Wallis	+

T/o HMS *Hermes* exercising off Hong Kong. On return to the carrier Flying Officer James Edmund Fenton landed but swung badly and his aircraft went overboard into Mirs Bay. Rescue was quickly on hand but too late to save Aircraftman James Arthur George Wallis who drowned.

Flying Officer James Edmund Fenton's temporary service with the RAF was *Gazetted* on 10th September 1926, issue 33200, page 5912. He returned to naval duty on 28th December 1933 [LG 9 January 1934, issue 34013, page 238] but was re-attached on 27th August 1936, in the rank of flight lieutenant [LG 8 September 1936, issue 34321, page 5793]. By 1942, he was back with the navy and ranked lieutenant-commander.

TNA Kew holds a record for this officer under ADM 196/149/281, this showing he was born on 5th November 1903, and was appointed for naval service on 15th May 1917.

Wednesday 15 October 1930

461 Flight	F/O M T Cowan RN	+
Blackburn Ripon S1365	LAC E G Baker	+

T/o HMS *Glorious* and failing to pull out of dive plunged into the sea off Malta. HMS *Glorious* which had originally been ordered as a *Courageous-class* Battle Cruiser but converted postwar for aircraft carrier service, re-commissioned on 24th February 1930, for service with the Mediterranean Fleet. Along with HMS *Courageous* she was able to embark forty-eight aircraft.

Appendix G - Additions and Amendments to Previous Volumes

Volume 1 - Page 276 : Thursday 27 June 1918
218 Squadron Lt C Briggs + Blankenberge Town Cemetery
DH.9 D5687 2Lt W H Warner + Hamburg Cemetery
T/o Petite Synthe and while diving to escape from a Fokker DVII broke up over Blankenberge. Their deaths were quickly avenged by Captain J W Pinder of 213 Squadron flying Camel F.1 C65 who shot down their attacker. It would seem that 18 year old William Henry Warner fell into the sea, hence his burial being in Germany where his headstone is inscribed *"Sleep In Jesus."*

Volume 2 - Page 102 : Wednesday 31 July 1918
98 Squadron 2Lt E W Gordon Canada + Coulommiers Communal Cemetery
DH.9 D5688 2Lt L F C Sayers + Coulommiers Communal Cemetery
T/o Chailly-en-Brie for a practice flight which ended, tragically, with the DH spinning into the ground. Erskine W Gordon had been attached to 98 Squadron from Princess Patricia's Canadian Light Infantry [Eastern Ontario Regiment]. He was 24 years old, his observer, Leslie Frederick Cecil Sayers being 18 and who had been attached to the squadron since 8th July. Their commemorations read *"Until The Day Breaks"* and *"Thy Will Be Done"* respectively.

Volume 2 - Page 167 : Monday 19 August 1918
218 Squadron Lt J E Wase + Les Baraques Military Cemetery, Sangette
DH.9 D5667 2Lt J C Cavanagh + Les Baraques Military Cemetery, Sangette
T/o Fretnum for bombing operations and on return spun in from a height estimated at 800 feet. On impact the DH burst into flames. John Edgelow Wase is commemorated with the inscription *"For His Country"* while 18 year old John Charles Cavanagh's headstone carries the words *"God Called Him To Fly Higher."*

Volume 2 - Page 178 : Sunday 25 August 1918
49 Squadron Lt E R Wallington Safe
DH.9 D7319 2Lt J D Hall Safe
T/o Beauvois and crashed out of control. Two days previous, the crew had been caught in the slipstream of another aircraft while taking off and crashed, though on that occasion the damage to their aircraft was slight and following repair continued in service. Lieutenant Wallington joined 49 Squadron on the 11th of August 1918, and served until 6th October when he was posted to 207 Squadron. It seems he injured his right leg in a minor accident on 19th November, spending eight days in hospital. Then, three days before Christmas 1918, he was hospitalised with tonsillitis. 2nd Lieutenant Hall arrived on the squadron on 10th August, serving until 9th May 1919, when he reported to St. Omer to await repatriation to the UK.

Volume 2 - Page 188 : Friday 30 August 1918
64 Squadron Lt R B Luard pow
SE.5a C6456/C
T/o 1600 Izel-le-Hameau for an offensive patrol and believed to have driven down 50 minutes later near Inchy by *Lieutnant* Otto Fruhner of *Jasta 26.* Otto Fruhner's *Wikipedia* entry credits him with 27 combat victories and that he was one of the first German pilots to save his life by parachuting. Born in Brieg, Silesia on 6th September 1893, Otto joined the *Luftwaffe* in 1935, with the rank of Major and throughout his second spell of service was employed in a flying training capacity. He died in Villach, Austria, on Saturday, 19th June 1965.

Formerly of the Royal Field Artillery, Robert Blaine Luard, born 14th June 1898, joined the RFC on 20th July 1917 and had been a fighter pilot with 64 Squadron since 20th January 1918. He must have been approaching the end of his tour of operations.

Volume 2 - Page 193 : 1 September 1918
49 Squadron 2Lt E C Moore Safe
DH.9 C6181/F6141 2Lt A Mauvy Safe
T/o Beauvois for a practice flight. On return the DH went into a flat spin and crashed. By coincidence, this DH had served previously with the squadron as C6181, and was shot about during operations on 19th May 1918, both Lieutenant C G Capel*and Private J Knight*requiring treatment for their wounds. As F6141 it had been on establishment for just over a week.

* Cecil George Capel, born 4th February 1892, and joining the RFC on 21st August 1917, arrived with the 49 Squadron at La Bellevue on 7th March 1918. His gunshot wounds were to his upper left arm and he was first treated an Australian casualty unit before being admitted to 20 General Hospital four days later. On 25th May he was sent home aboard HMHS *Brighton.* He returned to France on the 13th July 1918, and as far as I amble to ascertain he survived the war. I cannot be certain, but I believe his observer/air gunner may have been Private J Knight 223943 who enlisted on 3rd August 1917, and whose trade is described as "Aerial Gunner" for which he was paid 1 shilling and 8 pence per day.

Volume 2 - Page 212 : Friday 6 September 1918
205 Squadron Lt W E Macpherson Safe
DH.9 F1017 2Lt C F Ambler Injured

T/o Bovelles and wrecked following a crash near the airfield. 2nd Lieutenant Ambler's injuries were not serious.

Volume 2 - Page 239 : Friday-Saturday 20-21 September 1918
215 Squadron - An account of this loss has been given excellent coverage in a book written by C G and P V Hunt [see Bibliography for details] in which the authors, having accessed the squadron's war diary, state four HP O/400 bombers were tasked, the first aircraft taking off at 1943.

2nd Lieutenant Fowler was captain of the third bomber, C9732, which departed Xaffévillers at 2008. A very useful appendix [pages 45 to 59] show a detailed account of missions flown by the squadron between 6-7 August and 20-21 September 1918.

Volume 2 - Page 266 : Saturday 28 September 1918

108 Squadron	2Lt P A Haynes	Injured	Dunkirk Town Cemetery
DH.9 D7340	2Lt C Donald	+	Dunkirk Town Cemetery

T/o Capelle for bombing operations only to sideslip and crash. Although alive when pulled from the wreckage 2nd Lieutenant Haynes died soon after from a fractured skull.

Volume 2 - Page 333 : Sunday 20 October 1918

218 Squadron	Lt C S Oegger	Safe
DH.9 D2921	Sgt Paschel USA	Safe

T/o Fretnum only to spin to the ground; wrecked.

Volume 2 - Page 341 : Wednesday 23 October 1918

98 Squadron	Lt R L Lawson	Safe
DH.9 D480/F6057	Lt R H S Grundy	Safe

T/o 1405 Blangermont similarly tasked but turned back in reduced visibility and on reaching base overshot and finished up in an adjacent field with its nose buried in the earth. As D480 it had been on charge with 103 Squadron until 21st June 1918, when it was involved in a landing mishap. The crew, Lieutenant J L Roberts and 2nd Lieutenant J Y Round escaping unscathed. Rebuilt, it arrived with '98' on 24th August.

Volume 2 - Page 359 : Monday 28 October 1918

117 Squadron	2Lt F Latimer	Safe
DH.9 E699	2Lt H D H Williams	Injured

T/o Norwich and written off here in a landing accident. 2nd Lieutenant Latimer believed to be Frank Latimer who transferred, as a Corporal, from the RAMC to the RFC while serving in the Middle East. Completing his training on 10th May 1918, he embarked for the UK from Alexandria on 4th July.

Volume 2 - Page 387 : Tuesday 5 November 1918

99 Squadron	*Not reported*
DH.9 E8939	*Not reported*

T/o Azelot and crashed through a hangar, presumably on the airfield. Struck off charge two days later.

Volume 3 - Page 98 : Thursday 9 January 1919 : 100 Squadron - Andreas Metzmacher identifies the Gotha as a G.VII [Av] G.105/18 and it was *en route* to Abbeville when it came down 6 km SE of Montschau [Nordrhein-Westfalen].

Additional information has been kindly supplied by Greg Harrison who has sent for inspection a spreadsheet of data, compiled by himself, on accidents to 100 Squadron personnel. It seems 2nd Lieutenant Gardner and his observer had been tasked to fly the Gotha to England for evaluation. Quoting from entries on the spreadsheet; *"in an interview given to Patrick Wilson in the summer of 1998, World War 1 100 Squadron Navigator Roy Shillinglaw expressed a view that the aircraft had been sabotaged by Germans. He explained that the engines were "dud" and because the aircraft had been left out in the rain, the wings were full of water."*

Another view as to the feasibility of getting these Gothas to England comes from 2nd Lieutenant Basil Evans, also a pilot with 100 Squadron at the time and similarly tasked, his logbook for early January 1919, making for interesting reading; *'on the 5th of January he took off in a captured German aircraft but after attaining 1500 feet, and experiencing engine problems and difficulty in controlling the aircraft, he landed back at Bickendorf. Later the same day he took off again, in another captured German aircraft, but returned once more reporting control and engine difficulties. The following morning, the 6th, he attempted to fly a third German aircraft out of Bickendorf, and this time one of the engines failed completely, forcing his return yet again."*

Prior to military service, 2nd Lieutenant Gardner was employed in the cotton industry; he was born in New Longton in the county of Lancashire.

Volume 3 - Page 117 : Thursday 6 February 1919 : 100 Squadron - Amend the Gotha type and serial to read Gotha G.IX G.257/18 and T/o read Bickendorf. Andreas Metzmacher adds that around 30 Gotha bombers were brought to the central collection point at Bickendorf from LVG production for evaluation by the Royal Air Force. Andreas has written a book, titled *Gotha Bombers* which is in the hands of Fonthill Media for publication, possibly in 2021.

Greg Harrison's spreadsheet shows *"AEG C1V"* proceeding the serial *"No. 227"* and remarks pertaining to the crew notes the birth place of Lieutenant Hewett as Clapton in northeast London, while 2nd Lieutenant Carlton [sometimes written *"Carleton"*] was born in Chorlton, Lancashire. His widow returned to her pre-marital home as Little Brampton Farm, Clun, Shropshire, where her late husband's name has been inscribed on Clun's war memorial.

Volume 3 - Page 125 : Insert Monday 17 February 1919 : 27 Squadron DH.9 E8933 Maintenance inspection revealed fuselage twisted, mainplanes warped and tail section out of alignment owing to airframe being waterlogged. Despatched to 6 Salvage Section on 25th February for disposal.

Volume 3 - Page 157 : Insert Tuesday 27 May 1919 : 25 Squadron DH.9A E8768 Wrecked and disposed of to 6 Salvage Section.

Volume 3 - Page 213 : Insert page numbers as follows : 214, 215, 216, 217 and 218.

Volume 3 - Page 217 : Permanent commission. THOMSON William Burns in the rank of flying officer with effect 1st August 1919. Flying Officer William Burns Thomson DFC was killed in a flying accident at Abu Sueir while low-flying in Sopwith F.1 Camel F6302/G-EBER on 4th November 1922.

Volume 3 - Page 226 : Omitted: LG 10 October 1919, issue 31593, page 12554 : Short Service Commissions

Squadron Leader

LANE Robert Charlton S/Ldr 01.04.29 Relinquished

Flight Lieutenants

8

CAMPEBLL John Henry Duncan Montgomery F/Lt 10.10.19 Cancelled
COOCH Herbert F/Lt 01.08.27 Relinquished
GETHIN AFC Percy Edward Lovell F/Lt 10.10.19 Cancelled
69522 GETHIN AFC commissioned to the Administrative and Special Duties Branch with effect 5th July 1941, serving until: F/Lt 29.07.45 Relinquished
JOHNSTON AFC Ernest Livingstone F/Lt 10.04.22 Class B
Flight Lieutenant Ernest Livingstone Johnston AFC was the navigator on the ill-fated airship R.101 which crashed with heavy loss of life in France on 5th October 1930; he was one of the victims.
06103 MODIN DSC mid Charles Oscar Frithiof F/Lt 10.10.19 Cancelled
On appointment to a permanent commission; subsequently rose to air commodore rank. In April 1941, he was Air Officer Administration at HQ RAF Far East and was subsequently taken prisoner of war by the Japanese. He was held in numerous camps. Briefly remaining in the postwar air force, he retired on 26th August 1946. Air Commodore Charles Oscar Frithiof Modin CBE DSC twice mentioned in despatches, died on Sunday, 11th December 1966.
06112 OSBORN Arthur John S/Ldr 31.08.54 Relinquished
ROBARTS MC Geoffrey Ward W/Cdr 23.05.36 Retired list
At his own request. Lieutenant [temporary] Geoffrey Ward Robarts was *Gazetted* with his award on 14th November 1916, supplement 29824, page 11065: *"For conspicuous skill and gallantry in attacking hostile machines. On one occasion, when on offensive patrol, he brought down two machines."*

A partial record of his service survives at RAFM Hendon which shows that before joining the RFC he was commissioned to the Royal Field Artillery. On completion of his pilot training he was posted to Gosport where he was attached to 22 Squadron [FE.2b] and embarked with the squadron for France on 1st April 1916, spending a couple of weeks at Vert Galand before moving to their operational base at Bertangles on 16th April, remaining here for the rest of the year. His second operational tour of duty commencing 27th March 1917, was with 66 Squadron [Sopwith Pup], during which he was wounded on 8th July 1917, whilst flying Sopwith Pup B1758 [see page 101 of Trevor Henshaw's *The Sky Their Battlefield - Expanded Updated.*
WRIGLEY Noel Vincent F/Lt 27.07.35 Retired list

Flying Officers

8

GRUNDY Robert Milne F/Lt 19.12.29 Retired list
At his own request.
HOAD Henry F/O 19.09.26 Relinquished
JARVIS DFC Arthur Eyquem de Montaigne F/O 28.08.31 Relinquished
JONES Augustus Alfred F/Lt 22.08.36 Retired list
13135 LEIGH Hubert Poyntz-Gaynor G/Capt 09.03.44 Retirement
MARTYN Frederick William F/O 10.10.26 Relinquished
ROUGH DFC Herbert Leonard F/O 10.10.19 Cancelled
Permanent commission and served until: S/Ldr 01.08.39 Retired list
At his own request [LG 1 August 1939, issue 34650, page 5324]. The citation for his DFC appeared in *The London Gazette* 3 August 1918, supplement 30827, page 9203: *"A keen and gallant officer possessing great skill and judgement. He has carried out twenty-six successful bombing raids and five photographic long-distance flights. On a recent occasion, when low bombing, having obtained a direct hit on a limber, he dived to 700 feet and by skilful manoeuvring three enemy aeroplanes on the ground were set on fire, one by a direct hit from a bomb, and two by observer's fire. During the whole time his machine was subjected to heavy machine-gun fire. With the assistance of his observer, he brought his machine safely back, though he was shot through the leg."* 2nd Lieutenant Rough gained his

award with 49 Squadron; he receives three mentions in *The DH.4/DH.9 File* the first on 13th January 1918, when along with his observer, 2nd Lieutenant V Dreschfeld, flying DH.4 A7682 they drove down a Fokker Dr.I out of control in the Cambrai region. Next, on 26th February 1918, again with 2nd Lieutenant Dreschfeld, their DH.4 C4507 caught fire on landing and though sent to a repair facility it was struck off charge in March, the same month, on the 10th, that these two intrepid officers crashed whilst landing in DH.4 C4526. Again, repairs were considered but not carried out.

WEBB Edwin Robert F/Lt 10.10.26 Relinquished
On account of ill-health.

Volume 3 - Page 231 : Insert 07191 ahead KIDD Geldart. Born on 2nd November 1898 at Burntisland in Fife, he died in Richmond, Surrey on Thursday, 18th July 1963.

Volume 3 - Page 253 : Bristol F.2b H1567. Greg Harrison acknowledges that the Bristol was on 2 Squadron's establishment but Flying Officer Pithey had been attached for 100 Squadron.

Volume 3 - Page 253 : Bristol F.2b H1621. On his spreadsheet, Greg Harrison adds in respect of Flying Officer Waller: *"He had joined the RFC in November 1916, and was injured whilst at 9 Training Squadron on the 6th of July 1917, when his Fe.2b [A821] struck a hedge on take off and crashed."* At the time of his short service commission he was serving with 117 Squadron [DH.9], thence going to 105 Squadron and 2 Squadron before arriving with 100 Squadron.

Volume 3 - Page 253 : Bristol F.2b H1612 - Add to summary: *"On the 23rd of February, two days after the aircraft had last been seen, the Admiralty in London received a wireless message from the master of the 'Norfolk Range" a cargo ship operated by the Neptune Steam Navigation Company of Liverpool. The message was dated the 21st of February, and stated that the ship had seen an aircraft come down in the sea 85 miles to the southwest of the Scilly Isles at 16:35 on that date. The ship launched a lifeboat to try and save the pilot, but strong winds and heavy seas made rescue impossible."*

A note appended to the above concludes it was H1612 and that it was well off course. Flying Officer Holland was a Bournemouth man.

Volume 3 - Page 256 : Thursday 29 April 1920, correct F/L CO Modin to read F/Lt C O F Modin DSC mid.

Volume 3 - Page 258 : Greg Harrison put's forward the suggestion that the Bristol F.2b was F4526. Also, that the crash was caused by the aircraft's propeller snagging a barbed wire fence and in the ensuing crash Flight Lieutenant Norman Dimmock broke both legs; his AFC was awarded in late 1918, while attached to 141 Squadron, a particularly efficient Home Defence squadron. His passenger, Major Chads was adjutant of The Border Regiment and had been to Dublin on, according to the casualty card, on *"... urgent army business."* In fact the reason for his visit was to discuss possible legal action against the popular paper for supporters of the IRA, namely *Freeman's Journal.*

Volume 3 - Page 258 : Insert - Friday 10 September 1920 Bristol F.2b serial not known F/Lt Dement and Mech L Jones T/o Shotwick and set forth for Baldonnel. Over Dalkey Island the pilot became aware that his engine was failing. Firing a distress flare, he put the Bristol into a steep dive and ditched at the southern end of the island from where one very cold and badly shaken crew were brought to safety by a local fisherman, named as Michael Hammond. Taken to the home of a Mr. and Mrs. Cresswell, the two airmen were provided with dry clothes, warmth by the fire and some food.

Volume 3 - Page 259 : Wednesday 22 September 1920 31 Squadron *Not reported* Bristol F.2b F4424 T/o Mhow to test the radiator, climbing to 10,000 feet in the process. Either at that height or in the process of gaining altitude the radiator burst and the Bristol crashed on, or in the vicinity, of the airfield.

Volume 3 - Page 260 : Insert - Friday 17 December 1920 HP O/400 J2259 F/O J J Williamson AFC, F/O R H Haworth-Booth DFC, H Aspen [no rank indicated, LAC Burrows, LAC L Worsley and two unnamed civilians. T/o Shotwick and set a course for Baldonnel but when some fifteen miles northwest of Holyhead engine failure obliged the crew to alight in the sea. For the next two and a half hours the crew, spread between the top mainplanes and the tail section, shivered whilst awaiting rescue which came in the form of the SS *Itajahy* registered to the Edler, Dempster and Company shipping line. As remarked by Greg Harrison, their rescue was timely for fifteen minutes after being plucked to safety the bomber slipped below the waves. I will now quote from the spreadsheet, for it makes fascinating reading: *"Whilst the loss of J2259 and the subsequent rescue of the crew and civilian passengers is easy to explain, the nature of the flight is shrouded in rather more mystery. In December 1920, 100 Squadron had long-since given up there HP O/400s for the Bristol Fighters they were operating in Ireland in the anti-Shinn Fein and mail-carrying roles. So just what J2259 doing on the strength of 100 Squadron? It seems as well as the duties referred to above, 100 Squadron were also ferrying British Secret Service operatives and mails between London and Ireland. At this time the fight for Irish independence by the IRA was approaching its peak, and regular mail systems had been easily compromised by the IRA, who often knew of the mail's content long before it reached the barracks or airfield in Ireland to which it was headed. Of course, in such a climate, the need for Secret Service operatives needs no explanation. What is reasonably certain is that one of the unknown civilians was Constable John Hennigan. A young, but experienced, Royal Irish Constabulary man, he was considered to be made of the "right stuff." This he proved when he remained calm during the crash and during the sojourn on the wing of J2259, he remained tight-lipped once rescued, and managed to hold on to the dispatches he was carrying. In March 1921, he was awarded a First Class Favourable Record by the RIC, quite possibly in connection with his conduct during, and after, the crash of J2259."*

Consulting Air-Britain's *J File* J2259 had passed through the hands of No. 14 Aeroplane Acceptance Park and use by 214 Squadron before being issued to 100 Squadron; thus, it seems likely it was retained by the squadron for tasks as outlined above.

Meanwhile, Flying Officer Williamson's AFC was awarded in recognition of his work as an assistant instructor with No. 196 Squadron at the Aerial Fighting School, Heliopolis, in February 1919.

The citation for Flying Officer Robin Howard Howarth-Booth's DFC, *Gazetted* on 8th February 1919, reads: *"For gallantry and skill during a raid on Constantinople on 25 October 1918, in which he decoyed two enemy fighters into such a position that they were eventually shot down by his observer. This officer ran considerable risks in the methods he adopted, but the success attained justified his courageous action and pertinacity."*

At the time 226 Squadron was based at Mudros and flying DH.9s. In conclusion, the bomber's wireless operator, Harold Milne Aspen, was commissioned and at the time of the *Battle of Britain* he was ranked flying officer and serving as a signals officer at RAF Detling and attached to 53 Squadron [Blenheim IV]. He was killed on 13th August 1940, and laid to rest in Haddenham [St. Mary] Churchyard, Buckinghamshire; he was 45 years of age and married.

Volume 3 - Page 270 : Additional material as traced from various sources by Paul McMillan.

Volume 3 - Page 270 : 16003 COLLINGWOOD Cuthbert John : Insert OBE DFC, died circa January 1996.

Volume 3 - Page 270 : 16004 D'EATH Narborough Hugh : Add to remarks *"His death occurred in Barnstaple, Devon, on Tuesday, 21st January 1986."*

Volume 3 - Page 270 : 16007 FOOTE Henry Wells : AIR 76/165/193 Foote, Henry Wells Date of Birth: 21st April 1900. Reserve Air Force Officer. Henry Wells Foote is granted a commission in class C as a flying officer 26th July 1927. He served until relinquishing his commission under the provisions of the Navy Army and Air Force Reserves Act 1954, with effect from 10th February 1954. He was still ranked as a flying officer. My co-author then notes: *"Man drowned. Mr Henry Wells Foote [68], Church Cottage, Chichester, drowned when thrown from 28ft motor yacht Anadrina at Jersey, yesterday, 18th August 1968."*

Volume 3 - Page 270 : 16008 HANCOCK Cecil George : It appears his dismissal by sentence of General Court Martial was linked through a most unfortunate incident during which an Aircraftman Richard Frederick Mason, 19 years of age, was killed after being thrown from a Vickers Venture J7280 of the Home Aircraft Depot Henlow during low-flying, the pilot being named as Flying Officer Denys Stanley Thomas who was cashiered for being drunk and sentenced to one year's hard labour. It was disclosed that Flying Officer Thomas took Flight Lieutenant Hancock with him from Eastchurch on the Isle of Sheppey to Hendon where Flight Lieutenant Hancock entertained a women friend in the RAF Officers' Mess. It is noted that the dismissal of both officers was *Gazetted* 13th August 1929, issue 33525, page 5278.

Volume 3 - Page 270 : 16009 HARE Bertram William Trelawney : Add *"Posted to Aden Flight, Khormakser, Pilot Officer Hare crashed on 28th April 1922, sustaining injuries, when turning his Bristol F.2b H1495 into land following a ferry flight across the Red Sea. The Bristol fell into fourteen feet of water near Perim and his passenger, Leading Aircraftman Charles Francis Barnes drowned."* My co-author, meanwhile, has discovered that Flight Lieutenant Hare returned to the service and received a commission in the Administrative and Special Duties Branch, serving until his release on 10th February 1954, under the provisions of the Navy, Army and Air Force Reserves Act, 1954. He was ranked Wing Commander [LG 5 July 1955, supplement 40528, page 3878]. His death occurred on Sunday, 6th September 1959, while undergoing treatment in Greenbank Hospital, Plymouth.

Volume 3 - Page 270 : 16011 PRANCE Dennis Caldwell : Died on Sunday, 3rd May 1947, in Weston-super-Mare, Somerset, at the early age of 45 some six months before what would have been his 46th birthday on 30th October.

Volume 3 - Page 270 : 16012 SPENCER Geoffrey Roger Coe and 16013 WEEDON Colin Winterbottom : Paul McMillan notes that the former was born in Hong Kong and the latter in Durban. Both died in the United Kingdom at Aldershot and Worthing [Norfolk] respectively.

Volume 3 - Page 271 : CONNOLLY Sylvanus George : Add the following to the summary explaining his death: *"On Monday, 6th September 1926, while serving with 421 Flight aboard HMS Furious and flying Avro Bison S1113, his aircraft went over the side whilst landing-on. Flying Officer Connolly was injured, as was Leading Aircraftman George Frederick Wyborn, while, sadly, Leading Telegraphist James William Haddow drowned before help arrived. The accident happened when the carrier was off the Nab Tower near Bembridge on the Isle of Wight."*

It is believed this was the first fatal accident reported from HMS *Furious* which had underwent conversion to an aircraft carrier and commissioned circa September 1925.

Volume 3 - Page 271 : 16034 DESMOND Thomas Joseph : Group Captain Thomas Joseph Desmond died on Wednesday, 3rd August 1988.

Volume 3 - Page 271 : 11074 GORE Charles William : Delete "in June 1975" and replace with "died on Saturday, 19th April 1975, at Hindhead in Surrey."

Volume 3 - Page 271 : 16023 MANGLES Roland Arthur Ross : Group Captain Roland Arthur Ross Mangles died on Monday, 15h March 1976.

Volume 3 - Page 271 : 16026 ROWE Frank Charles Thorn : Wing Commander Frank Charles Thorn Rowe died on Sunday, 11th April 1976.

Volume 3 - Page 271 : SPRINGFIELD Cecil Montague Oakes Osbourne : Add: *"His health deteriorated over the next two years and he passed away at West Mersea, Essex, on Thursday, 4th September 1924, at the early age of 22."*

Volume 3 - Page 271 : STONE Cecil John : My co-author, Paul McMillan, has traced a most enlightening account published on Thursday, 10th March 1988, in the *Wells Journal,* though the paper's assertion that he was the last surviving member of his entry is not correct: *"The last surviving member of the first entry of trainee pilot officers to RAF College, Cranwell, Lt. Col. Cecil John Stone, of The Old Cottage, Oxford Street, Evercreech, died at the Royal United Hospital, Bath, after a fall near his home. Lt. Col. Stone, who was born in 1900, and named after another well-known adventurer, Cecil Rhodes, was educated at Lancing College, and enlisted in the forces on August 1st, 1918, a few months before the end of World War One.He was then among the elite to be selected for entry to the first training course for pilot officers at RAF College, Cranwell. His training was followed by service in the RAF in the Middle East during the difficult inter-war years. After a number of years with the RAF, Col. Stone transferred to the army and saw service in Ceylon, Burma and Kenya and became a member of Lord Mountbatten's HQ Staff. On retirement he served as an officer of SSAFA in Germany, an organisation assisting with the welfare of families of servicemen. As a young serviceman Col. Stone represented the RAF as a marathon runner and was also a well-known cricketer. During the later years of his retirement he was a keen member of the Evercreech branch of the Royal British Legion. His wife died some years ago in Wiltshire and Col. Stone later lived at Dulverton before moving to Evercreech to be near his daughter, Mrs Yvonne Coke-Wallis, of Batcombe. Following cremation at Bath, a memorial service was held at St. Peter's Church which was followed by interment at Bretton, Wiltshire."* With effect from 18th September 1950, he was appointed as a District Officer in the Nakuru District Rift Valley Province in Kenya.

Volume 3 - Page 272 : 16046 CAITHNESS James Ernest Stewart : Born in Ealing, Middlesex, my co-author has traced his date of death to Victoria in British Columbia, Canada, on Sunday, 21st January 1990.

Volume 3 - Page 272 : 16047 CHARLTON John Sills : Add: *"He died in Wandsworth, London, on Tuesday, 13th November 1973."*

Volume 3 - Page 272 : 16053 HEALEY Ernest Alton : Group Captain Ernest Alton Healey died in the Dorset village of Winfrith Newburgh, a few miles inland and NNW from the coastal village of West Lulworth, on Monday, 30th January 1978, a day after his 78th birthday.

Volume 3 - Page 272 : 16056 JOHNSON Anson Geoffrey Stewart : Add: *"He died in Birmingham on Wednesday, 29th July 1970."*

Volume 3 - Page 272 : 16059 MATURIN Charles Bagot Beaumont : Delete 'Maturin' as a Christian name. My co-author shows Wing Commander Maturin as leaving the service on 13th November 1945, and his death as Monday, 19th November 1962.

Volume 3 - Page 272 : 16062 RICCARD Cecil Stanley : Group Captain Cecil Stanley Riccard CBE died in Poole, Dorset, on Wednesday, 6th September 1995. He was born in Allahabad, Uttar Pradesh, India, on 13th August 1901.
Volume 3 - Page 272 : 16063 STEVENS Charles Herbert : Group Captain Charles Herbert Algernon Stevens OBE three times mentioned in despatches, died circa November 1986, in the South Devon resort of Torbay.

Volume 3 - Page 272 : 16064 VINTCENT Neville : My co-author adds the following: *"As the General Manager of Tata Air Lines he had been allocated a place in the crew of a Hudson III AM946 of 1 OADU which departed Portreath in Cornwall for Gibraltar on 29th January 1942, and is believed to have been shot down by enemy aircraft off the coast of Spain."* The Hudson's crew comprised of Flying Officer Derek John Randolph Gee and Flight Sergeants John Albert Bolle and Davy John Pitcher. All were attached to 59 Squadron and been detached from the squadron's base at North Coates to carry out the ferry. They are commemorated on the Runnymede Memorial, panels 67, 73 and 75 respectively. CWGC records Neville Vintcent as 'Nevill' *"Air crashes at sea."*

His DFC was *Gazetted* on 15th February 1924, issue 32908, page 1367: *"His Majesty the KING has been graciously pleased to approve of the following reward to the undermentioned officer, in recognition of gallantry and devotion to duty in Iraq:-*

"Pilot Officer Nevill Vintcent, Royal Air Force. This officer, having been forced to land owing to engine trouble, beat off an attack by hostile tribesmen with great courage and determination."

Photographs Section 1:

No. 8 Squadron in the 1920s

A selection of photographs from the 1920s featuring No. 8 Squadron aircraft and personnel. Photographs supplied by Christopher Dean and used with the kind permission of the squadron's Commanding Officer.

Although captioned 'A Flight, 8 Sqn, Mosul, Oct 1920', I suspect it was taken at Helwan where the squadron reformed on 18 October 1920, followed by transfer to Suez in December 1920, and thence to Basra in February 1921.

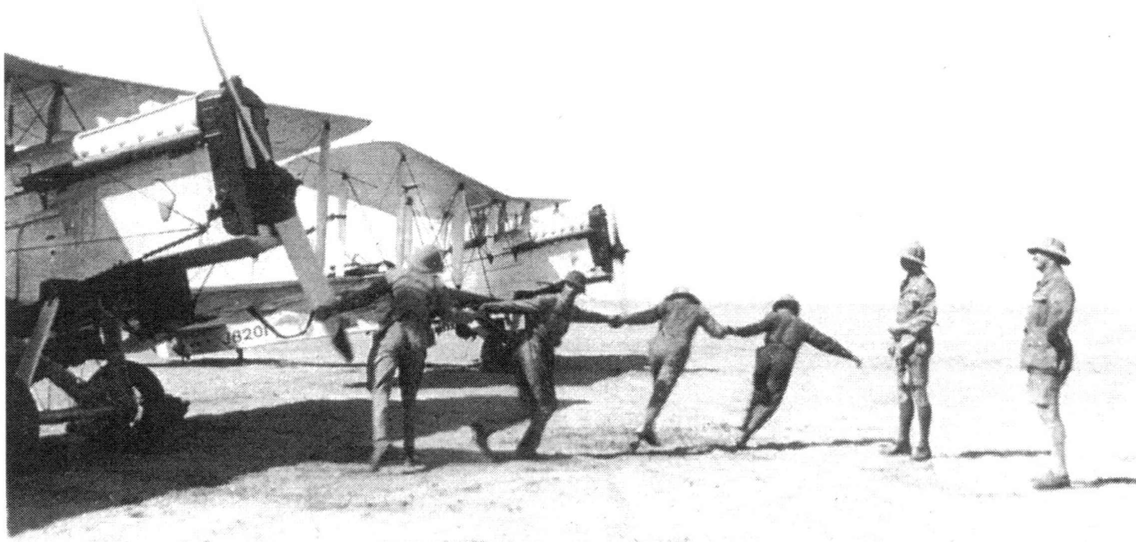

Captioned "Aden 1926" I suspect the four airmen shining the propeller of an unidentified DH.9A was taken at Khormaskar to where the squadron moved in February 1927. The DH.9A in the background J8201 is known to have been on squadron charge between August and December 1927.

Early morning raid on Sulamanya on 28 May 1924, carried out from 3,000 feet. Following the break up of the Ottoman Empire the Iraqi Kurds established the Kingdom of Kurdistan with Sulamanya as its centre [1922 - 1924] though this never received recognition.

DH.9A E954 and captioned "CO's aircraft 1926" which at the time was Squadron Leader W A McClaughry DSO DFC MC

DH.9A H-141/N captioned "Over Baghdad" but it is Hinaidi's perimeter below and the River Tigris in the background.

No. 8 Squadron, Mosul, 1922. The DH.9A at the end of the line-up of aircraft, E976, is known to have flown with the letter 'A' in the early 1920s.

Five DH.9As and a Nieuport Nighthawk at Hinaidi circa 1923. DH.9A H24 nearest the camera may have been 'L' though a year later it flew as 'E'. The Nighthawk is believed to be on establishment with No. 1 Squadron.

Captioned "Engine change" I suspect DH.9A H24 had made an emergency landing out in the desert and its replacement engine along with the maintenance crew had been brought to the site by the Vickers Victoria in the background.

Captioned "Glubb and Sheik [sic] Lagtan" undated. The British officer may be Lieutenant-General Sir John Bagot Glubb who is known to have been in Iraq in the 1920s.

Aerial view of Hinaidi, Iraq, marked with the locations of the resident squadrons. On the outskirts of Baghdad, Hinaidi was operational between 1922 and 1938. The River Tigris is in the background of the photograph.

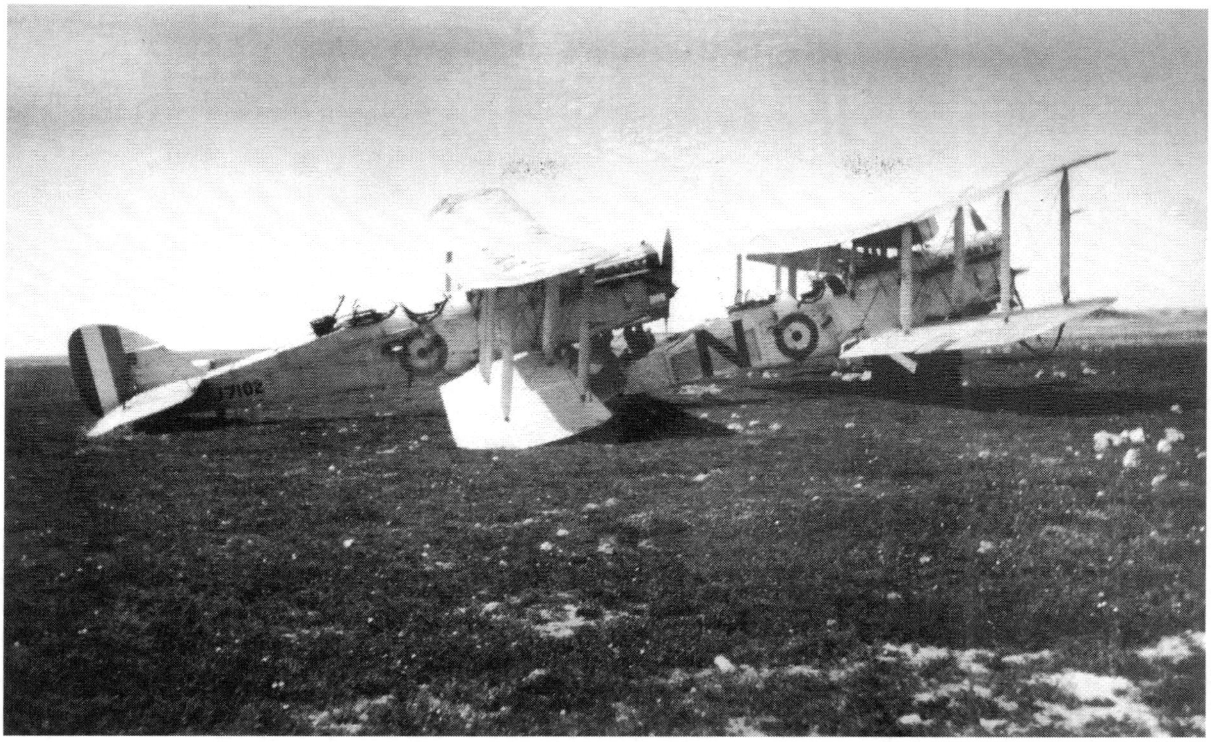

DH.9A J7102 after swinging on landing at Jamaica on 13 February 1925 and running into the tail of a DH.9A [possibly H-141]. Both aircraft were repaired, but J7102 was written off following an in-flight fire on 13 October 1925.

Captioned "Meal with Lagtan", undated.

Captioned "Aerodrome near Barbuti Bridge" taken at 0730 hours on 28 January 1925 from 1,000 feet. There are no records of this being an operational airfield; possibly one of the numerous landing grounds established in Iraq.

Operations mosaic of Sulamanya, 1924.

DH.9A H3510/L circa 1926.

. DH.9A H3523/P circa 1926.

2. Officers and airmen of No. 8 Squadron 1921, taken either at Basra, Baghdad West or Hinaidi. All appear to be wearing winter dress.

3. An informal photograph of the squadron's officers taken on the same day. Squadron Leader D L Allen AFC is seated in the centre of the front row. He commanded the squadron between October 1920 and February 1922.

Photographs Section 2:

Individual Aircraft and Types Mentioned in this Volume

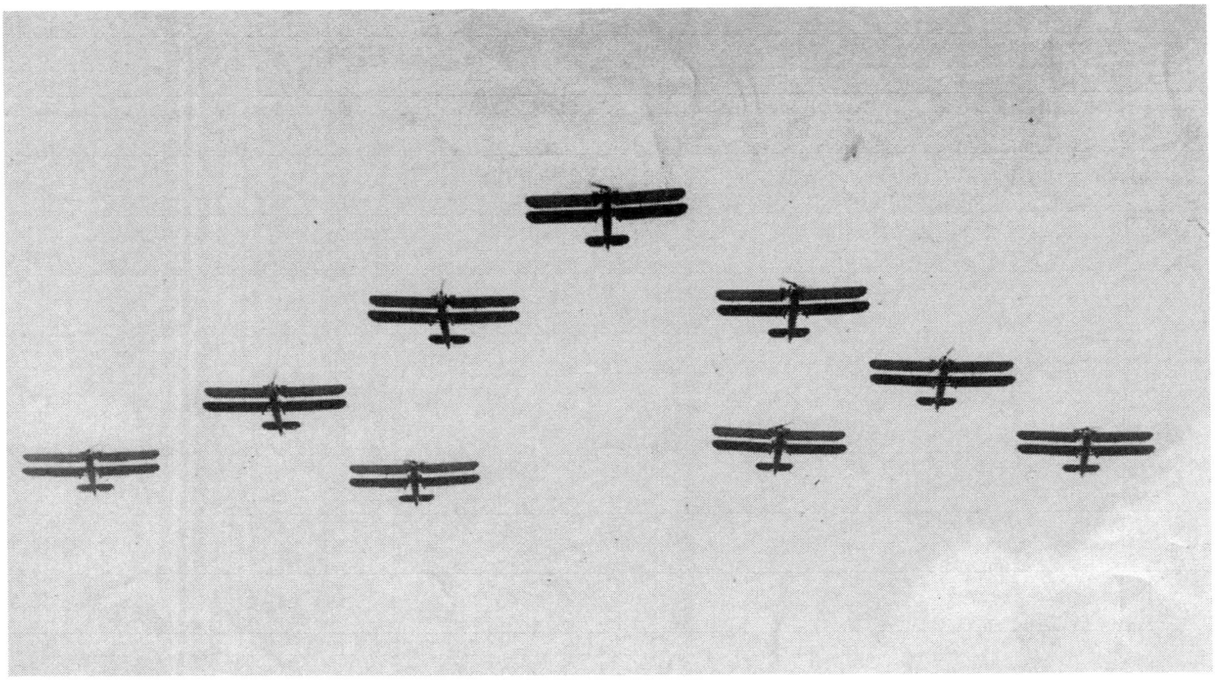

Nine Airco DH.9As of No. 100 Squadron practising formation flying (Greg Harrison).

Airco DH.9As now in line abreast; both photographs probably taken on the same day between March 1922 and May 1924. (Greg Harrison).

Unidentified Airco DH.10 Amiens. Type phased out of service during 1923 (Crown Copyright.)

Armstrong Whitworth Atlas J9537 demonstrating picking up a message. Initial service with No. 4 Squadron at Farnborough during May and June 1930 (Flightglobal).

A line of No. 29 Squadron Armstrong Whitworth Siskin IIIAs with the squadron's distinctive "XXX" markings on the fuselage. J-8950 is nearest the camera with J-8864 and J-8862 also present (Crown copyright).

Blackburn T.2 Dart N9723/75 taken at RAF Gosport circa 1929, destined for HMS Courageous. It was the last aircraft in the block N9714-NN9723 (Christopher Dean)

Blackburn Ripon II S1360/60 taken off Malta circa 1930, and belonging to either 461 Flight or 462 Flight attached to HMS Glorious (Christopher Dean).

Blackburn Ripon II S1364 believed taken at RAF Northolt. Circa 1930, it was attached to 460 Flight HMS Glorious (Christopher Dean).

Blackburn Ripon II S1267/73 down in the English Channel, either 1929 or 1930, HMS Glorious and either 460 Flight or 461 Flight. Built by Blackburn May 1928, one of a block of 7 aircraft S1265-S1271. (Christopher Dean.)

Boulton Paul Sidestrand in No. 100 Squadron markings. (Crown Copyright).

Bristol Bulldog II K-1085 issued to No. 17 Squadron and destroyed in a fatal crash in Arundel Park, Sussex on 30 September 1930 (Crown Copyright).

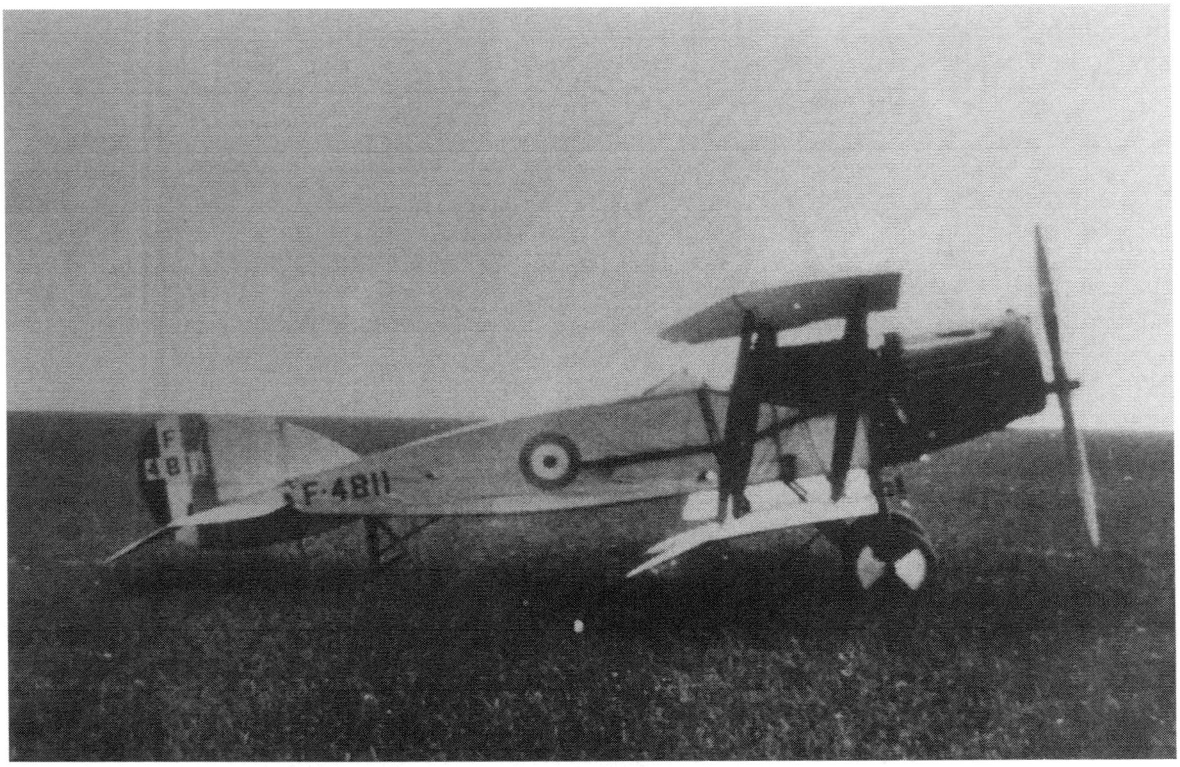

Bristol F.2b F4811 subsequently modified to a 'J' Type with dual controls and extant August 1930 (Christopher Dean).

De Havilland DH.42 Dingo J-7006 construction No. 85 and first flown 12 March 1924. Written off during service trials with No. 41 Squadron on 5 June 1924. (Crown Copyright).

An unidentified De Havilland DH.60 Moth of the Royal Canadian Air Force.

An excellent air to air photograph of four Fairey Fawns with their Hendon RAF Display numbers returning to Spittlegate on completion of the June 1925 display. The Fawn nearest the camera J7209 was written off a few weeks later (Greg Harrison).

Fairey Fawn J7205 construction No. F506 and first flown 15 March 1924. Served with No. 11 Squadron at Bircham Newton, thence to No. 100 Squadron before going to Netheravon where it was reunited with No. 11 Squadron (San Diego Air and Space Museum).

Fairey Fawn J7192 with its pilot, equipped with the obligatory officer's cane, Spittlegate circa 1924 (Christopher Dean)

Fawn J7214/2 with its fitter clad in white overalls and an airman in working dress, Spittlegate circa July 1925. By March 1926 it was painted as '1' subsequently going on to see service with No. 503 Special Reserve Squadron at Waddington (Greg Harrison).

Fairey Fox I J7943 displaying its No. 12 Squadron forward of the rudder. Ahead of the Fox is an Armstrong Whitworth Atlas J9527, Hendon 1929, probably on the occasion of the annual display. (Crown Copyright).

Fairey IIIF S1169/35 either HMS Glorious or HMS Courageous circa 1930 (Christopher Dean.).

A rather "second hand" Fairey IIIF J9053/M being lifted by crane from the water near Khormaksar following a misjudged landing by the squadron's Commanding Officer, Squadron Leader The Hon. R A Cochrane, the date quoted as "April 1928" though I suggest April 1929 as Squadron Leader Cochrane did not take command of the squadron until February 1929 (Christopher Dean).

Gloster Gamecock I J8074 on No. 32 Squadron strength March and April 1928, later with No. 23 Squadron at Kenley where the photograph was taken; thence to No. 3 Squadron and finally to the Central Flying School at Wittering. Written off near Sidcup, Kent, on 22 October 1930 (Christopher Dean).

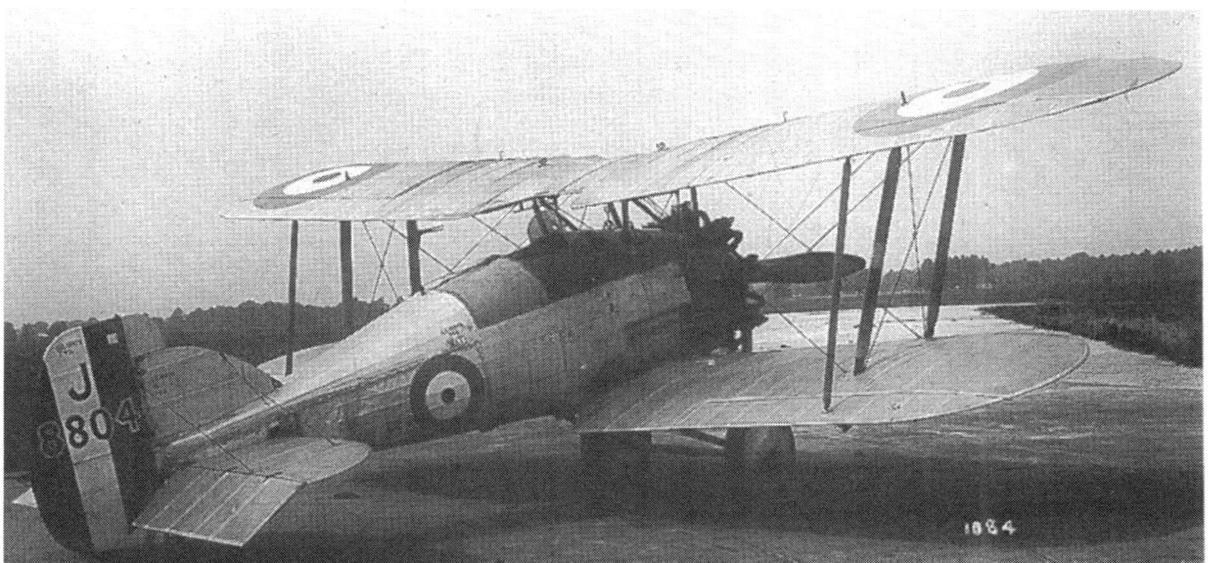

One off Gloster Grebe II J8804 tested by No. 22 Squadron at Martlesham Heath between June and August 1927, and again the from July 1928 to January 1929. In between it was back and forth between Gloster's and Farnborough (Crown Copyright).

Gloster Grebe II J-7407 served with No. 56 Squadron, No. 25 Squadron and last seen in the care of No. 19 Squadron in April 1928 (Crown Copyright.)

Handley Page Hinaidi J7745 after its conversion from a Hyderabad. Purchased by India in 1928 and broken up in 1932 (Crown Copyright).

Handley-Page HP 24 Hyderabad J8319 at RAF Waddington, date unknown. The aeroplane was probably on the strength of No. 503 Sqn SR. The pilot of this aircraft is unidentified. He did not check the rear cockpit before flight, and the control column lock straps were still in place. The aircraft failed to get airborne although the pilot escaped injury. Fortunately, he was flying solo.

The Hyderabad had two distinctions: it was the last wooden heavy bomber operated by the RAF and, despite suffering a number of accidental losses, there were no fatailites (credit for both photos Waddington Heritage Centre via Christopher Dean.)

Unidentified Handley Page Hyderabad (Crown Copyright).

Hawker Hornet J9682 prototype flown for the first time in March 1929, and destroyed 11 April 1930 while undergoing service trials with No. 1 Squadron when it collided in the air with Siskin J9359 from No. 43 Squadron (Crown Copyright).

Hawker Horsley J8009 of No. 100 Squadron. Damaged in a dusk forced-landing near Buckingham on 8 November 1928. Repaired, possibly as Henlow, and in 1929, was in the hands of No. 33 Squadron (Crown Copyright).

Tragic outcome of a midair collision on 25 November 1930 near Leuchars between two Horsley medium day bombers from No. 36 Squadron based at Donibristle. The tangle of burnt wreckage was all that remained of J8013 but J8015 was left fairly intact, though its pilot was killed (Evening Telegraph and Post, Dundee edition.)

Hawker Horsley I J8017/1 following a landing mishap. Date unknown, but it was seen at the Home Aircraft Depot, Henlow in April 1928 (Greg Harrison).

Hawker Horsley J8609/3 in flight circa 1930 (Greg Harrison).

Unidentified Hawker Woodcock (Crown Copyright).

Parnall Panther N7511 (Crown Copyright.)

Vickers Vernon JR604 the 'R' signifying it had been rebuilt. Note the pennant on the nose and the two fuel tanks fitted beneath the top mainplane. Served in Iraq with No 70 Squadron and No. 45 Squadron (Crown Copyright.)

Vickers Victoria III J7924 used throughout its service by No. 70 Squadron at Hinaidi. Written off at Ur, Iraq, in a gale on 22 May 1928. (Crown Copyright)

Unidentified Vickers Vimy with a suitably clad airman in the forward gun cockpit. (Crown Copyright)

Vickers Virginia J7421 issued initially to No. 58 Squadron at Worthy Down in 1924. Built as Mk.V during its long service life it underwent numerous modifications, eventually being rebuilt as a Mk.X. Final user was the Royal Aircraft Establishment, Farnborough, where it flew for the last time on 2 September 1936. (Crown Copyright)

An excellent air to air shot of two No. 55 Squadron Wapiti IIAs in the autumn of 1930, J9595/C and J9631/C1 (Crown Copyright).

Printed in Dunstable, United Kingdom

65439219R00264